MW01093167

Introduction to International Business Transactions

Aaron X. Fellmeth
Dennis S. Karjala Professor of Law, Science & Technology
Arizona State University

Cheltenham, UK • Northampton, MA, USA

Published by
Edward Elgar Publishing Limited
The Lypiatts
15 Lansdown Road
Cheltenham
Glos GL50 2JA
UK

Edward Elgar Publishing, Inc.
William Pratt House
9 Dewey Court
Northampton
Massachusetts 01060
USA

A catalogue record for this book
is available from the British Library

Library of Congress Control Number: 2020934077

This book is available electronically in the **Elgar**online
Law subject collection
DOI 10.4337/9781839107429

Printed on elemental chlorine free (ECF)
recycled paper containing 30% Post-Comsumer Waste

ISBN 978 1 83910 741 2 (cased)
ISBN 978 1 83910 742 9 (eBook)

Printed and bound in the USA

Summary Table of Contents

Detailed Table of Contents

Table of Cases

U.S. Cases

International and Foreign Cases

U.S. Administrative Decisions

Preface

The author owes special thanks to the Note from the Field authors, who generously contributed their time and shared their wisdom and experience:

James Altman
Dave Foster
David Hamill
Brian Hoffmann
Douglas Lanzo
Lucinda Low
John R. Magnus
Stanley Marcuss
Stephen McLaughlin
Chun Ng
Heidi L. Sachs
Michael E. Santa Maria
Marco E. Schnabl
Matthew Schultz
Michael Tyler

All errors in this book are solely attributable to the author.

The author also thanks DHL Express U.S., with special appreciation to Robert Mintz and Bob Pfautz, for allowing photography of DHL cargo loading and unloading operations.

For the sake of brevity, citations, footnotes, and dissenting opinions may be omitted from the texts of cases without notation.

Chapter 1

Introduction

1.1 What Is International Business Law?

Understanding international business law means studying multiple legal regimes, both national and international, that relate to diverse aspects of transnational business. Business firms may engage in a diverse variety of transactions that cross national boundaries. There are relatively straightforward international sales. There are longer term cross-border distribution and licensing arrangements, as well as a variety of transnational service deals. There are major international investments. And there are some regulatory dimensions of international business that allow firms to suppress harmful practices such as unfair import competition or intellectual property infringement.

All forms of international business share some common elements, and the legal regimes that govern them do as well. These tie together the field into a comprehensible subject, and this coursebook is designed to emphasize such connections and synergies. However, before we begin, it is helpful to recognize some major concepts and dimensions of international business law to put it into context.

A. Transactional Aspects

The most common kinds of international business transactions are contracts for the sale of goods, the provision of services (including employment), or the licensing of intellectual property. All of these activities and their associated agreements are common in transnational business. There are more complex contracts as well, such as those involved in the transfer of a business from an owner in one country to an owner in another, or an international project financing arrangement. Transactions, in short, represent the most direct way in which international business gets done.

Although international law may govern some aspects of such cross-border agreements, cross-border business transactions are also governed by the laws of one or more specific states.* That means French or Brazilian law can

*When the word "state" is used in this coursebook, it is always used in the sense of a sovereign "country" unless otherwise indicated. When one of the "U.S. states" is

govern most aspects of an international commercial agreement. It is even possible and indeed normal for the laws of more than one state to apply to different aspects of an international transaction, which complicates matters. Many international transactions also occur within the framework of one or more treaties affecting the rights and duties of the parties. The fact that multiple legal regimes tend to govern international transactions is one reason why international business transactions are so interesting and challenging.

Another reason is that international transactional issues usually overlap with regulatory issues. For example, a sale of goods across state borders may implicate the regulation of exports in the exporting state and will certainly require analysis of the regulation of imports in the importing state. Depending on the type of goods at issue in the contract, other regulations, such as those governing insurance or cargo carriage, may be implicated. If a sale is made under a long-term contractual relationship between the seller and buyer, then municipal laws relating to agency, professional licensing, dealer protection, or employment may apply. The same holds true for other kinds of transactions. For example, a contract for the provision of a service might implicate regulatory requirements relating to currency exchange controls or cross-border taxation.

B. Regulatory Aspects

State regulation of international business transactions takes many forms—so many, in fact, that a course such as this one can deal with only the most commonly applicable systems.

States typically promulgate and enforce detailed rules governing how goods, services, persons, money, and sometimes information may penetrate their borders, either going into its territory or coming out of it. Import regulation may serve the state government by funding its treasury through duties or taxes on imported goods; gaining a comparative advantage for local producers by discouraging competitive foreign imports; ensuring the safety and health of the state's citizens by excluding unsafe goods; preserving local cultures and languages by limiting citizen exposure to foreign ideas; and punishing other states for undesirable policies by excluding their goods. Export regulation may serve the state government by funding its treasury through export taxes; avoiding disputes with other countries that feel they are being flooded with imports; promoting world peace by limiting the transfer of dangerous technologies and materials to terrorists or hostile states; avoiding capital flight by regulating the transfer of money abroad; punishing foreign states for pursuing undesirable policies by depriving them of needed products and technology; and protecting the global environment or foreign consumers by ensuring that shipments of goods to foreign countries are safe. As these lists imply, import and export regulation can be complex, because the policy goals underlying them are often multifaceted.

---

intended, that term is used instead.

Another kind of regulation of international business transactions relates to intellectual property registration and protection. The licensing of intellectual property is primarily a contractual matter, but often a preliminary step in licensing is registration of patents or trademarks in a foreign state. Registration facilitates protection of the intellectual property and may serve the state's purpose of encouraging efficient commerce, the development and spread of creative works, and the distribution of new technologies in its territory. The international registration of intellectual property is in many ways analogous to a purely domestic registration. Nevertheless, there are some significant differences of which all lawyers—not just intellectual property lawyers—should be aware, because they may affect the rights of any client operating, or planning to operate, internationally.

Registration is of course only the first step in protecting intellectual property internationally. To adequately protect its intellectual property, an owner may have to resort to domestic or foreign litigation or administrative remedies. Litigation and administrative remedies may be separate matters. For example, in many countries, intellectual property owners may be able to register for protection with regulatory agencies such as the customs law enforcement agency so that infringing products will be automatically excluded from entry into the respective country without any litigation necessarily involved. In some cases, remedies for intellectual property infringement may include "administrative litigation"—a kind of trial before an administrative tribunal—rather than a purely administrative procedure or court litigation.

There are, of course, many more types of regulatory laws that may bear on an international business transaction. Many of these are really domestic laws more or less unique to specific countries. The important thing is not to know or even be aware of every regulation; there is no need to delve deeply into the huge diversity of regulatory laws that may brush up against an international business transaction nor to dwell on idiosyncratic regulations of one country or another. It is important, however, for international business lawyers to be aware of the possibility of such regulations, so that they may ask the relevant questions and take appropriate precautions.

C. Litigation Aspects

For a transactional or regulatory lawyer, avoiding the necessity of future litigation is a critical part of the job. This role is even more important when the transaction is international, because cross-border business creates special challenges and risks beyond those normal in the domestic context. In international litigation, issues of comity and *forum non conveniens* arise more frequently than they do in domestic cases. Conflict of laws and choice of law questions can also affect an international dispute. Another difference is the more prominent role of "alternative dispute resolution," such as arbitration. Although arbitration is increasingly popular as an alternative to domestic litigation, parties involved in international business transactions plan for and resort to arbitration almost as a matter of course.

International dispute resolution itself is properly the subject of its own course. However, in planning international business transactions, the consequences of an eventual dispute are always on a transactional lawyer's mind. For that reason, lawyers involved in international business deals need to have a basic familiarity with the options available for dispute resolution and the problems that typically arise in international disputes, especially those preventable with sufficient precautions at the negotiation stage.

D. Treaty-Based Aspects

Nations have been entering into agreements since ancient times. Most modern states are bound under international law by a large number of treaties, some of which relate to international trade and investment. The United States, for example, is currently a party to nearly 10,000 treaties.* Some treaties are bilateral, meaning that only two countries are bound. Others are plurilateral or multilateral, meaning more than two countries are parties. Treaties go by different names, such as convention, agreement, charter, protocol, or statute. Some of these correspond to a specific variety of treaty, but they all share the key characteristic of being legally binding, reciprocal commitments between two or more states.

Government officials negotiating international trade or investment treaties will sometimes seek the advice of business firms and their lawyers in negotiating terms. Although private lawyers usually cannot participate in negotiations directly, they may assist government officials by suggesting issues to be included in the negotiations, drawing the government's attention to foreign trade or investment problems faced by domestic industries, or drafting proposed language for the treaty.

With some important exceptions to be discussed in later chapters, treaty obligations undertaken by a state cannot usually be enforced by a private business firm against that state in municipal courts. This is certainly the rule in the United States. In general, private parties are powerless to obtain direct relief if a state violates a treaty obligation to the private party's detriment absent a statute creating a privately enforceable right. *Medellin v. Texas*, 552 U.S. 491, 505-06 (2008). Most treaties are enforceable only by the governments of the states that are parties to the treaty.

You will read about many different kinds of treaties in this book, and most of them follow this rule. One group of modern trade and investment treaties that you will see recurrently goes by the name of World Trade Organization (WTO) Agreements. These are the world's most comprehensive trade treaties in terms of scope and membership. They include treaties regulating trade in goods, services, intellectual property, and many specific subjects.

---

*U.S. DEPARTMENT OF STATE, TREATIES IN FORCE (2019).

How are such treaties relevant to private investors and business firms? One answer is that, insofar as a treaty binds states to adopt laws and regulations consistent with the treaty, the treaty helps an investor or business firm predict how it, or its investment, will be treated in a foreign state that is a party to the treaty.

For example, suppose the fictitious state of Freedonia is bound by a treaty with another state, Sylvania. The treaty requires each party to allow the airlines of the other party to operate out of their respective airports. The treaty commitments allow a Sylvanian airline to predict with reasonable confidence that it will be allowed to conduct air service between Sylvania and Freedonia, even though the airline itself has no power to enforce the treaty. Why? Because if Freedonia denies the Sylvanian airline access to Freedonian airports, the Sylvanian government will almost certainly complain of a breach of the treaty provisions on behalf of its airline. Although states do sometimes breach their treaty obligations, they do so relatively rarely and, when they do, they often redress the breach in response to a complaint by their treaty partners.

If a Sylvanian business firm were to be treated by Freedonia in a manner inconsistent with the Freedonian treaty obligations, the Sylvanian firm may employ an international business lawyer to lobby a Sylvanian government agency to negotiate particular treaty provisions favorable to the client, or to attempt to enforce existing treaty obligations against Freedonia. The lawyer will best assist the client by using a combination of legal arguments with political pressure to motivate the state to pursue the client's interests through international negotiation or dispute resolution.

Such private representation has become fairly common due to limitations on the staffing and fact-finding capabilities of the **U.S. Trade Representative (USTR)**, a diplomat charged with negotiating and enforcing trade and foreign investment treaties on behalf of the U.S. President. The following excerpt provides a representative example in the successful attempt by Chiquita Brands, a U.S. fruit company, to convince the USTR to oppose the banana licensing regime of the European Community (EC), the predecessor to the present European Union. The EC had given preferential import tariff rates to former colonies of the European states but not to other banana-exporting states, including those in which Chiquita had major investments:

> Carl Lindner, Chiquita's president and controlling shareholder, was among the top three contributors to the Democratic and Republic parties in 1998. He reportedly had coffee with the president and spent a night in the White House's Lincoln bedroom. * * * Lindner contributed more than $2.4 million over the 1996 and 1998 election cycles.
>
> According to one former USTR official, it certainly appeared that Lindner hoped "to buy" the WTO case from the USTR [i.e., to convince the USTR to commence a dispute before the World Trade Organization (WTO) challenging the EC's discriminatory banana tariffs]. Apparently, Lindner was present when former USTR Mickey Kantor met in a key breakfast

> meeting with U.S. Republican Senate leader Robert Dole about Congress's approval of the Uruguay Round Agreements Act, whereby the United States would join the WTO. Lindner reportedly was joined by his outside counsel, Carolyn Gleason, of the law firm McDermott Will & Emery. Senator Dole allegedly indicated to Kantor that * * * he would like the USTR to take up Chiquita's case, which Gleason could confirm was strong. Arguably, Senator Dole and Kantor reached an implicit understanding that the Clinton administration would further the chances of the act's approval were the USTR to take up Chiquita's case.
>
> With congressional and executive support, the USTR dedicated thousands of personnel hours to challenging EC barriers to Chiquita banana imports. The litigation involved four WTO panels, a total of over one thousand pages of written briefs, buttressed by thousands of pages of annexes, and an eventual settlement in Chiquita's interest. Just as the USTR fended for Chiquita's bananas, so it battled for Kodak's film, cattlemen's beef, and Pfizer's patents, bringing WTO claims on their behalf.*

Lawyers in this role typically prepare a detailed statement of facts and draft legal arguments for the USTR and members of Congress, help develop a case for political or legal action, and consult throughout the process with USTR officials.

On the European Union side, private business firms often petition the European Commission's Trade Barrier Regulation** unit to investigate alleged trade barriers in non-EU countries and to invoke WTO dispute resolution when appropriate. International trade lawyers in Europe work with the Commission to develop facts, formulate legal arguments, and settle disputes. Although the level of involvement of European private lawyers has not yet risen to that of U.S. lawyers working with the USTR due to the more active role of EU civil servants, the Commission itself sometimes employs private trade lawyers to assist in WTO matters.

Imagine that you are a partner in an international law firm with offices in both Istanbul, Turkey and Washington, D.C. Your client is a U.S. toy manufacturer with a subsidiary in Turkey. Both the United States and Turkey are parties to the WTO Agreements. Under these treaties, both states have committed to reducing import duties on toys from other treaty parties. However, because some of the materials used in making your client's toys are imported from Eritrea (not a party), Turkey treats the toys as Eritrean and subjects them to high import duties. Your client believes that the toys originate in the United States under the WTO Agreement on Rules of Origin and should benefit from reduced duties, but the treaties contain no provision allowing private firms to assert a cause of action

*GREGORY C. SHAFFER, DEFENDING INTERESTS: PUBLIC-PRIVATE PARTNERSHIPS IN WTO LITIGATION 23-24 (2003) (footnotes omitted). Reprinted with permission.

**Council Regulation 3286/94, Dec. 22, 1994, O.J. ser. L, no. 349, Dec. 31, 1994, at 71-78.

directly against a member state, so the client cannot invoke the treaties against Turkey itself.

In such a case, your firm might try to convince the U.S. government that the United States should invoke the dispute settlement provisions of the WTO Agreements against Turkey and otherwise to pressure Turkey to change its laws. The firm's effort might include both a legal component and a lobbying component. The former would consist of legal arguments, directed both at the USTR and Congress, to persuade them that Turkey has indeed failed to comply with its treaty obligations. In addition, the law firm might threaten to invoke domestic remedies, such as initiating an investigation by the USTR under Section 301 of the 1930 Tariff Act (19 U.S.C. § 1301) to convince Turkey that it will suffer from U.S. trade retaliation.

Lobbying measures might consist of making an economic case to Congress about the importance of the toy industry for U.S. jobs and possibly emphasizing the political advantages of taking up the client's case (e.g., by focusing lobbying

HOW DO LOBBYIST REGISTRATION LAWS AFFECT INTERNATIONAL BUSINESS LAWYERS?

The **Foreign Agents Registration Act** (**FARA**), 22 U.S.C. §§ 611 *et seq.*, is a federal law that requires private persons who act on behalf of foreign governments in a "political or quasi-political capacity" in the United States to declare their status publicly. Under FARA, within ten days of agreeing to represent a foreign government, lawyers must file a registration form with the U.S. Department of Justice (DoJ) describing its agreement with, income from, and expenditures made on behalf of, the client every six months. Filings are made publicly available, and the agent's records are subject to inspection by the DoJ. Failure to register is a federal crime punishable by fines and imprisonment. 18 U.S.C. § 951. FARA does not, however, limit the lobbyist's ability to influence the U.S. government or to publish information or propaganda on behalf of a foreign state.

In addition, the **Lobbying Disclosure Act** (**LDA**), 2 U.S.C. §§ 1601-14 requires registration and periodic reporting by persons who lobby the U.S. government on behalf of private foreign firms. This includes such agents as sales or purchasing representatives, lobbyists, and public relations personnel acting in the United states on behalf of foreign governments and business firms, but it also includes lawyers representing foreign clients in U.S. administrative (but not judicial) proceedings. The LDA merely requires registration with the Secretary of the Senate and the Clerk of the House of Representatives within 45 days of entering into a lobbying agreement.

efforts on senators and representatives from regions in which the toy manufacturing industry has a strong presence, because it has many employees who rely upon it for their jobs, pays local taxes, or makes campaign contributions to the congressional representatives). This effort might be buttressed by attempts to convince the U.S. International Trade Commission—a federal agency with broad trade investigatory powers—to undertake a study of foreign barriers to trade in the client's sector or industry to establish facts and to obtain political publicity for the client's arguments. The law firm might also pursue parallel efforts in other countries having similar interests in changing Turkey's customs practices. Meanwhile, your firm's Istanbul office or affiliate might undertake complementary efforts with the Turkish government to persuade it to amend the laws that govern how the country of origin for toys is determined.

While an analysis of lobbying methods does not usually fall within the scope of a course on international business law, it is useful to have a basic understanding of the treaty obligations most likely to affect international business. Only a lawyer with such knowledge can recognize discrepancies between the manner in which a state treats her client and that state's treaty obligations. A lawyer unfamiliar with such treaty obligations thus forfeits an opportunity to serve her client by mounting a challenge to a municipal law as conflicting with an international legal obligation. For this reason, the basic treaty obligations most likely to bear on international business transactions are discussed throughout this coursebook.

After the initiation of a WTO complaint by the USTR, or prior to the initiation of a WTO complaint against the United States by a foreign state, U.S. trade lawyers may assist clients who are cooperating either with the USTR or a foreign government to present a strong case before the WTO dispute resolution panel. Private trade lawyers may appear personally before a WTO panel on behalf of a *foreign* state, or they may advise and assist either the USTR or a foreign government, either directly or through a business firm or industry association. It is common for such lawyers to draft briefs to the WTO panel and to meet periodically with USTR or foreign officials to plan and develop arguments and strategies.

Finally, following a favorable WTO decision, the USTR consults with private lawyers representing U.S. companies or industry organizations to determine the amount and kind of sanctions that should be applied if the foreign state at issue fails to correct its alleged violation of WTO disciplines.

NOTE FROM THE FIELD

Being General Counsel to an International Business Firm

Michael R. Tyler, Esq.
Senior VP, General Counsel & Secretary, Jacobs Engineering Group, Inc.

Every company needs competent legal counsel, and the more successful a company becomes, the more frequently it needs international legal advice and representation. Companies doing a large volume of business typically have one or more full time in-house lawyers; the large ones, such as Jacobs, have a legal department employing many lawyers headed by a chief general counsel. The general counsel is responsible for both domestic and international legal matters affecting the company.

Unlike a private practitioner in a law firm, a general counsel has only one client: his or her employer. In large companies, the legal department may include one or more lawyers specifically in charge of international legal issues. A large multinational entity will own many U.S. and foreign subsidiary companies, and most of these subsidiaries have their own legal departments. As the parent company's international legal counsel, you would support the general counsel of these subsidiaries with international legal advice.

You might also assist business executives with the international legal aspects of their business operations. A lawyer in this position might advise on an English commercial contract in the morning, Irish regulatory matters at mid-day, and litigation in Germany in the afternoon.

As far as subject matter goes, the only constant is diversity. Moreover, this advice may not be limited to specific international legal questions, but can encompass educating employees about basic legal principles and advice about what kinds of issues should prompt them to consult company lawyers.

As may be evident, one of the most useful skills for someone in the position of international legal counsel to a company is a broad legal background in transactional law, regulatory law, and litigation. A general counsel cannot adequately represent a company in its daily operations while being highly specialized. Prior study of EU law, comparative law, and international business law are extremely useful, as is sensitivity to other cultures and the absence of ethnocentrism.

Michael R. Tyler formerly served as Executive Vice President, General Counsel & Secretary of Sanmina SCI; Chief Legal & Administrative Office of Gateway, Inc.; and international counsel for Northrop Grumman.

1.2 What Kinds of Actors Regulate International Business Transactions?

The Supremacy Clause, in Article VI of the U.S. Constitution, provides:

> This Constitution, and the Laws of the United States which shall be made in Pursuance thereof; and all Treaties made, or which shall be made, under the Authority of the United States, shall be the supreme Law of the Land; and the Judges in every State shall be bound thereby, any Thing in the Constitution or Laws of any State to the Contrary notwithstanding.

U.S. courts have consistently interpreted this language to preempt state laws that may interfere with the federal government's foreign relations power, either directly or by prejudicing the Executive or Legislative Branch's ability to adopt foreign policies with a free hand. See, e.g., *Crosby v. National Foreign Trade Council*, 530 U.S. 363 (2000); *Zschernig v. Miller*, 389 U.S. 429 (1968). U.S. federal laws, including treaties to which the United States is a party, therefore play the most prominent role in regulating the conduct of international business. U.S. state laws play a lesser, but still significant, role in most aspects of international business regulation.

The national laws of foreign countries may also apply to international business transactions. If the transaction involves direct foreign investment—a U.S. company setting up or operating a business in a foreign country, or a foreign company doing the same in the United States—international treaties and the rules of international organizations may become relevant as well. In some cases, intergovernmental organizations and even global nongovernmental organizations may play a part in regulating cross-border business transactions as well. These actors and their roles will be summarized here.

A. U.S. Federal Agencies

In the United States, many federal agencies play a role in international trade regulation. Some, such as the Department of Homeland Security's Bureau of Customs and Border Protection, or the Department of Commerce's Bureau of Industry and Security, play a general regulatory and enforcement role in international commerce. Others, such as the Patent and Trademark Office or the Securities Exchange Commision, play a primarily domestic role with some authority to promulgate or enforce regulations relating to cross-border transactions.

Other agencies, such as the Office of the USTR, develop U.S. trade policy, negotiate treaties, and represent the United States in trade disputes before the World Trade Organization. The USTR is part of the Executive Office of the President, and the USTR himself or herself is a cabinet-level ambassador. The office has about 200 employees resident in Washington D.C., Geneva, and Brussels. The USTR does not directly regulate private business firms; it interacts with them in a consultative capacity. As noted earlier, attorneys are most likely to call upon the USTR while voicing their clients' interests in a treaty negotiation or an international trade dispute.

Still other federal agencies exist to facilitate foreign trade involving U.S. business firms. The Department of Commerce, for example, through the U.S. Commercial Service and its Web site (www.export.gov) provides assistance to U.S. companies seeking to sell on foreign markets. The U.S. Small Business Administration, Overseas Private Investment Corporation, and Export-Import Bank of the United States (Ex-Im Bank) assist in financing U.S. investment in other countries and the export of U.S. goods and services to international markets. The Department of Commerce, USTR, and International Trade Commission all provide information about foreign trade opportunities and trade barriers confronting U.S. business firms.

The organization of the federal government is somewhat labyrinthine, and the agencies relevant to international business are no exception. Figure 1.1 identifies the major players in international business regulation. These will be discussed throughout the coursebook, so you may find it useful to refer back to this figure periodically.

B. Foreign Governmental Agencies

In other countries, governmental structures vary. Few states have as elaborate a system of administrative law as the United States, although many come close, especially in economically developed countries such as Australia, Canada, Japan, and most of Europe. In states lacking complex regulatory systems, trade administration may be less encumbered by bureaucracy. That also means, however, that the law may be less developed and more difficult to discern and predict, and that regulation is consequently subject to greater discretion by government officials. Every state has customs and tax agencies of some kind, however, and many are starting to develop regulatory agencies similar to those in United States, particularly in the field of trade remedies.

C. International Organizations

International organizations may become involved in an international business transaction in several ways. Sometimes these can be quite removed, as when the organizations draft an international treaty. The various organs of the **United Nations** (**UN**) are often involved in such processes. Prominent examples include the 1980 Convention on Contracts for the International Sale of Goods, which was drafted under the auspices of the UN Commission on International Trade Law, and the 1958 UN Convention on the Recognition and Enforcement of Foreign Arbitration Awards ("New York Convention"). Both of these treaties will be examined in later chapters.

The UN is an **intergovernmental organization** (**IGO**), meaning an organization of which only sovereign states are formally members. Private

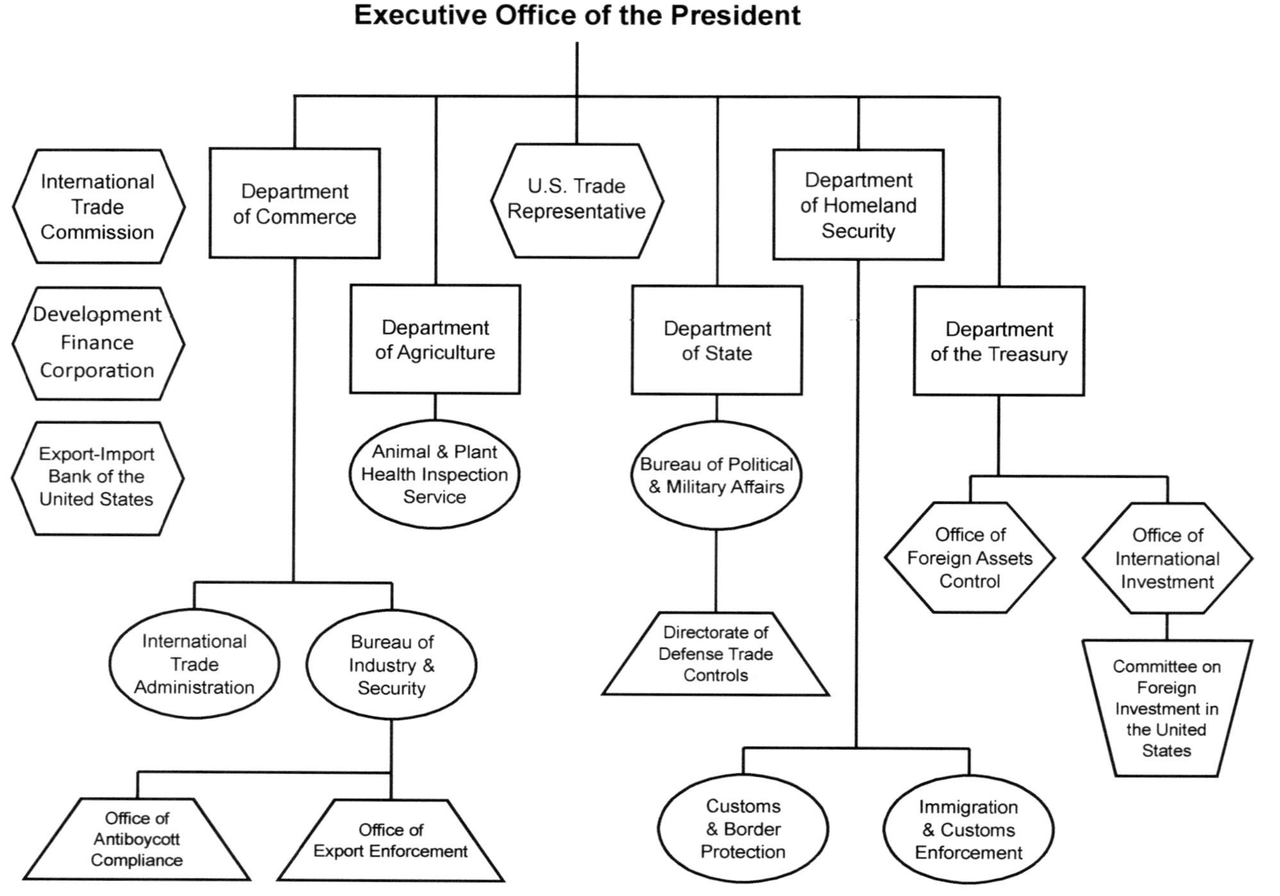

Figure 1.1. Basic organization of the major federal agencies involved in international trade regulation.

international organizations such as industry groups, nonprofit charities, or other commercial or civic organizations, classified as **nongovernmental organizations** (**NGOs**), can also become involved in the process. The uniform shipping terms used in most international transactions, known as Incoterms, are drafted by the **International Chamber of Commerce** (**ICC**), a private nonprofit organization operating out of Paris and representing firms that do business globally. The ICC plays an important role in standard-setting for international commerce.

Various kinds of international organizations administer dispute resolution specifically for international business transactions. Some of these are private organizations (like the ICC) that sponsor popular fora for voluntary international commercial arbitration and mediation. Others are IGOs, such as the World Bank's International Centre for the Settlement of Investment Disputes (ICSID). ICSID sponsors arbitration relating to certain kinds of disputes between a private business investing in a foreign country and the investment's host state.

The activities of many international organizations may sound to the layperson as if they were important to international business transactions. Some are, but many play no direct role in international business regulation. The activities of the International Monetary Fund, the World Trade Organization, or the Organization for Economic Cooperation and Development, for example, formulate state-to-state commitments on global trade, monetary policy, and financial assistance. Their relevance to private business firms may be significant, but it is usually indirect.

2 International Trading Blocs

2.1 The European Union

Of all the IGOs whose activities may be directly relevant to an international business transaction, the one most likely to affect a U.S. party is the **European Union** (**EU**). The EU is a sovereign entity encompassing almost all of Europe, except Norway, Switzerland, and some Balkan states. It is comprised of a Council of Ministers, which represents the government of each member state, a Commission that proposes and enacts legislation and directives, a Parliament having a legislative role, and a Court of Justice to resolve disputes about matters of internal EU law. Before 2010, the economic policy and lawmaking division of the EU was the EC, but the latter was absorbed into the EU with the adoption of the Treaty of Lisbon. Some documents and institutions still refer to the EC or to the "Community."

The EU began in 1951 as a cooperative coal and steel regulatory organization with only a few members. Since that time, it has expanded in both scope and membership. Eventually, the EU became a **customs union**, meaning that trade between EU members is unencumbered by legal restrictions or customs duties, and all members impose the same tariffs on imports originating outside

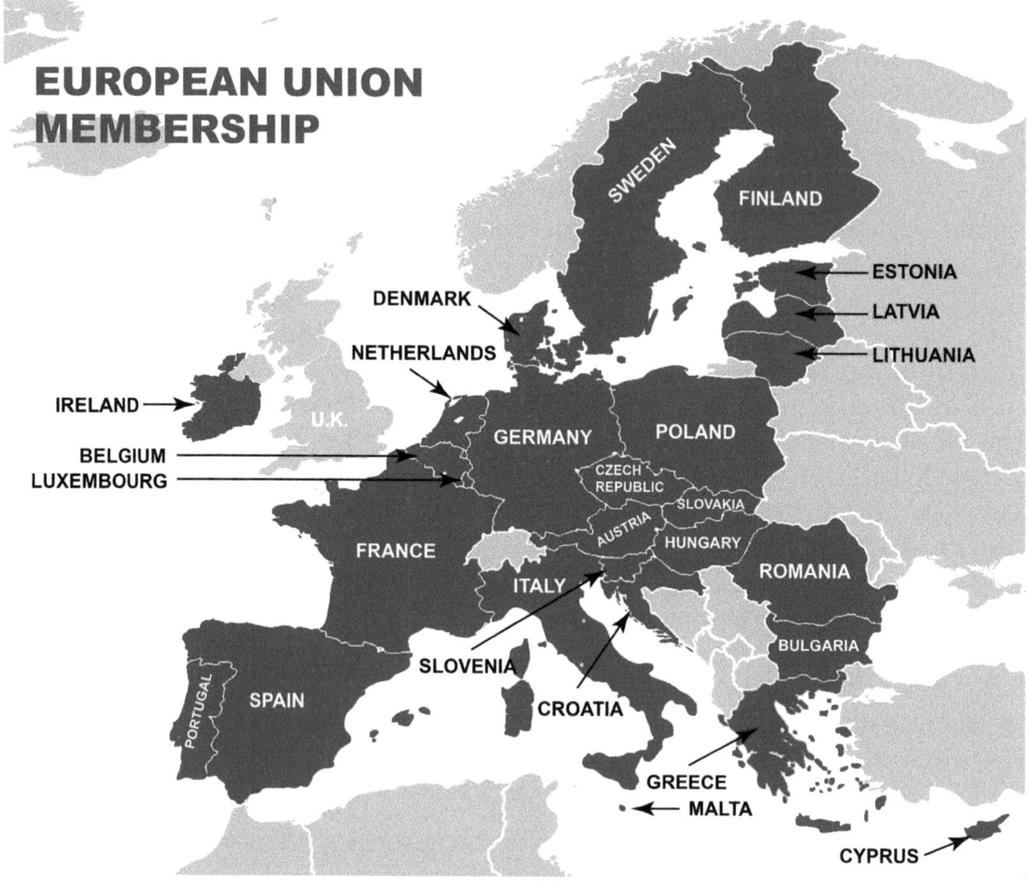

Figure 1.2. Map of the 27 EU member states as of 2020.

of the union. As of 2020, the EU includes twenty-seven member states* (see Figure 1.2) and nearly 500 million inhabitants. It has a regulatory structure that encompasses everything from common import and exports laws, trade regulation, labor and employment law, taxation, environmental protection, competition law, the movement of persons, creating a common currency for most EU member states (the **euro**, or €), and much else. Crucially, workers in one EU member state can move more or less freely to other EU member states, and

*The member states in 2020 are: Austria, Belgium, Bulgaria, Croatia, Cyprus, Czech Republic, Denmark, Estonia, Finland, France, Germany, Greece, Hungary, Ireland, Italy, Latvia, Lithuania, Luxembourg, Malta, Netherlands, Poland, Portugal, Romania, Slovakia, Slovenia, Spain, and Sweden. The United Kingdom was a founding member, but in 2016, it voted to leave the European Union. "Brexit" was accomplished in 2020. Several other countries have applied to join the EU and are under active consideration, including Macedonia, Serbia, and Turkey.

members cannot impose barriers to cross-border investment within the EU. The organization is now most accurately described as a **common market**.

The EU has a complex system of legislation and regulation that is partly determined by the separation and coordination of political power among the Council, Commission, Parliament, and Court of Justice. These powers and their limits are defined by a series of treaties establishing the EU and the other pillars of European cooperation. The **Council of Ministers**, seated in Brussels, Belgium, is both an executive and legislative branch of the EU. It is composed of ministers appointed by each EU member state, who represent the interests of their home state. The Council may exercise its executive powers directly, but it has delegated most of them to the European Commission. The most important function of the Council is legislative. In some areas of regulation, the Council exercises co-decision powers with the European Parliament to adopt legislation proposed by the Commission.

The **European Commission**, also seated in Brussels, acts in coordination with the Council as the executive branch of the EU. It is composed of commissioners delegated by the EU member states to act on behalf of the EU itself rather than their respective member states. The Commission proposes legislation for adoption by the European Parliament and the Council, implements decisions of the legislative organs, and performs the quotidian tasks necessary for the functioning of the EU. Its legislative proposal power is quite substantial, because it is exclusive; neither the Council nor the Parliament may formally introduce legislation. The Commission also enforces EU law either through its agencies or through the cooperation of member states themselves. The Commission is charged with bringing noncompliant EU member states before the judicial body, the **Court of Justice of the European Union**. The Court's organs include a **General Court** with jurisdiction to hear claims by private organizations and natural persons challenging acts of the EU and its agencies, and the **European Court of Justice** (**ECJ**), which hears all appeals. The Court decides questions of EU law, not of national laws of the EU member states.

The **European Parliament**'s primary role is legislative, and it is the only EU political organ directly elected by the population of Europe. The Parliament sits in plenary session in Strasbourg, France, but also has a seat in Brussels for smaller sessions and preparatory meetings. The Parliament's function, exercised in coordination with the Council, is to amend, reject, or adopt legislation proposed by the Commission. It can request that the Commission draft specific legislation, but the Commission need not comply.

European legislation takes several forms. The Council and Parliament may choose to adopt an **EU regulation** that is directly binding on all EU member states. The regulation will override any conflicting national law in any EU member state. Alternatively, the Council and Parliament may adopt an **EU directive**, which sets forth rules that each EU member state must adopt in its national laws within a defined time period. A directive, unlike a regulation, leaves some room for variation in implementation among EU member states. The Council and Parliament also issue nonbinding recommendations that EU members may choose to adopt, adopt with modifications, or ignore in their discretion.

Why would EU law be relevant to a U.S. lawyer? Many U.S. companies have operations in multiple European states. The Commission and Parliament propose and enforce legislation that is either applicable throughout the EU or that harmonizes national laws within the EU. Therefore, knowledge of EU law can in many cases obviate redundant requests for advice about local law to counsel in foreign countries. For example, suppose your client manufactures private commercial jet airplanes and sells them throughout Europe. If the EU has adopted a regulation that requires all jet airplanes sold or operated in the EU to have a noise reduction modification, you may be able to advise your client to install a noise reduction kit on all jet airplanes sold in any EU member state, eliminating redundant research. That advice would save your client substantial time and expense. Similarly, customs duties are uniform throughout the EU, so once you know the duty payable on the airplane in one member state, you know the duty payable in all of them.

2.2 The Eurasian Economic Union

More recently, several states in Central Asia and Eastern Europe have formed the **Eurasian Economic Union** (**EAEU**). The EAEU began as a customs union in 1996, but it soon evolved into a common market with unified customs laws and regulations, common foreign exchange controls, free movement of capital and labor, and reciprocal open foreign investment in the region. The EAEU is currently considering a common regional currency similar to the euro. As of 2020, the EAEU member states are Armenia, Belarus, Kazakhstan, Kyrgyzstan, and the Russian Federation.

2.3 Other International Trade Blocs

Although the EU is the largest common market from an economic standpoint, other countries have banded together to form customs unions as well. Among these is the Southern Common Market (**MERCOSUR**), comprised of Argentina, Brazil, Paraguay, Uruguay, and Venezuela. MERCOSUR is potentially consequential, as its treaties and shared customs code cover some 300 million persons in countries having a combined gross domestic product close to

US$ 3.5 trillion, although the group has fluctuated between greater and lesser free trade with political and economic conditions in the member states.

A smaller customs union in the region, the **Andean Community**, is comprised of Bolivia, Colombia, Ecuador, and Peru. Since 2005, the Andean Community has had a free trade agreement with MERCOSUR that removes customs duties between states in the two trading blocs. There are in addition a few other, mostly small, customs unions in the world. In any of these unions, goods properly imported may move freely between the member states without the further payment of customs duties.

Those countries not ready to band together in a customs union may nonetheless agree on a trade arrangement called a **free trade area**. A free trade area is usually created by a **free trade agreement** (**FTA**), and, like a customs union, it permits goods originating in one member state of the area to pass into other member states without the payment of customs duties. Unlike a customs union, however, a free trade area does not establish a common external tariff for imports from outside the area. In other words, an FTA eliminates customs duties within the area, but does not affect duties on imports into the area originating outside the area.

Suppose, for example, that Smalldonia and Ruritania are parties to an FTA. As in a customs union, goods originating in Smalldonia may enter Ruritania for consumption duty-free, and *vice versa*. Suppose further that Smalldonia imposes a 5% import duty on widgets from Grand Fenwick, which is not a member of the FTA. Ruritania, in contrast, imposes a 8% import duty on widgets from Grand Fenwick. (This would not be possible in a customs union, because all union members have the same external import tariffs.) If an importer in Smalldonia were to import widgets from Grand Fenwick, it would pay 5% customs duty to the Smalldonian customs authorities. However, if the importer wished to export the same widgets from Grand Fenwick into Ruritania for consumption in Ruritania, it would have to pay a 3% customs duty to the Ruritanian customs authorities. Why? Because, if the goods had been imported directly into Ruritania, an 8% customs duty would have been owed. The FTA creates benefits for the sale *within* the area of goods originating in any of the FTA member states. Importers within the area will not be allowed to take advantage of lower customs duties in any FTA member state to import goods from *outside* the area at a lower rate of duty.

Free trade areas often include only two countries. Such bilateral FTAs are extremely common, with over four hundred in force today. The United States is a party to many such treaties. A few FTAs include more than two countries. The **North American Free Trade Agreement** (**NAFTA**) created a free trade area covering Canada, the United States, and Mexico in 1994, which was replaced by a new treaty, the **United States–Mexico–Canada**

Agreement (**USMCA**), in December 2019. The **Trans-Pacific Partnership** (**TPP**) of 2016 was to create a free trade area among the NAFTA parties, as well as Australia, Brunei, Chile, Japan, Malaysia, New Zealand, Peru, Singapore, and Vietnam. After engineering the deal, however, the United States suddenly withdrew in 2017, leaving its future uncertain.

The **Association of Southeast Asian Nations** (**ASEAN**), which is an organization promoting greater political and economic unity among ten countries in the region (including Indonesia, Malaysia, Philippines, Singapore, and Thailand), also has a free trade agreement between its members. The ASEAN FTA covers over 625 million persons in countries with a combined gross domestic product of just over US$ 3 trillion.

Finally, **African Continental Free Trade Area** has formed based on an agreement signed in Kigali, Rwanda in 2018 that is ultimately intended to include all members of the African Union. It came into force in 2019 with its twenty-second ratification and is intended ultimately to cover most or all fifty-five members of the African Union.

TRADING BLOC TYPES: HOW DO THEY DIFFER?

Free trade area: A group of states that have agreed to trade among themselves duty-free (without import taxes) for all or substantially all goods originating in the area. However, each state maintains its own rates of customs duty for goods originating outside the area. If such goods are imported into one member state and subsequently reexported to another member state with a different customs duty, the importer pays (or receives a refund for) the difference.

Customs union: Like a free trade area, but the member states agree to adopt a uniform external customs duty. Goods originating outside the customs union that are imported into the union pay the same customs duties regardless of the country of importation. Notwithstanding its name, MERCOSUR is a customs union.

Common market: Like a customs union, but in addition the members seek the free movement of labor and capital (investments) among themselves. A common market may also promote broadly harmonized economic regulation among member states in such fields as competition regulation, the marking or labeling of goods, product health and safety standards, employment laws, and consumer protection. The European Union is the world's largest common market.

The Area will progressively abolish all tariffs and non-tariff barriers to trade in goods, liberal trade in services, establish customs cooperation, and ultimately harmonize policies on foreign investment, intellectual property protection, and competition law.

3 Putting It All Together

This book is organized into ten chapters, of which this is the first. The divisions are designed to help you classify the subjects covered by this course into broad conceptual categories. But you may be wondering what relation these subjects have with each other. What does protecting intellectual assets have to do with trade remedies? And what does import regulation have to do with planning for disputes? The answer, from a lawyer's point of view, is in many cases: "nothing direct." But everything changes when you adopt the perspective of the client, a business enterprise. From the business perspective, most of these subjects relate to at least one of the following four fundamental goals:

- the business firm wants to sell its products or provide its services to someone in a foreign country;
- the firm wishes to buy products or services from someone in a foreign country, or to bring in a foreign worker from his home country to provide services;
- the firm seeks to expand or move its production or service facilities to another state in order to reduce costs or taxes, to extend its global reach, or to increase its marketing opportunities;
- the firm wishes to reduce or end foreign or import competition that is harming it in some way.

Chapter 2 of this book starts off the discussion with a study of the major international treaties that structure trade and investment between states. Some of the treaties were introduced in this chapter but will be examined in greater detail, because knowing their basic provisions will help better to explain the global systems of international business regulation. Although many of these treaties do not benefit private business firms directly, some do, and all confer indirect benefits on private businesses in various ways.

Chapter 3 introduces the international systems for the protection of intellectual property and related assets, such as trademarks and trade secrets. The cross-border registration, protection, and licensing of intellectual property is an important aspect of doing business abroad for virtually all companies. You may wonder why the book starts with intellectual property. The answer is that protecting intellectual assets is frequently the first consideration in expanding trade or business operations to a foreign country for reasons of timing. Most business enterprises derive substantial revenue from, and in some cases owe their commercial success primarily to, their intellectual property. Ensuring

POLICY ISSUE

Do free trade agreements actually create free trade?

The term "free trade agreement" (FTA) both overstates and understates what an FTA typically does. Few if any FTAs actually remove all impediments to trade between the parties to the treaty. It is true that an FTA will usually provide for duty-free imports (that is, imports without customs taxes) from other states in the free trade area for a broad class of goods. However, most FTAs reserve the right of the parties to apply import duties to at least some politically, culturally, or economically sensitive imports. The FTA may also preserve a right to block some kinds of imports from the trading partner altogether, such as goods that do not meet the health and safety or labeling standards of the importing state, though they comply with the rules in the exporting state. Even for those imports that are admitted duty-free, an FTA typically includes provisions allowing for unilateral import barriers under some conditions, such as to offset certain trade or government practices deemed anticompetitive by the importing state, or to protect a domestic industry from overwhelming foreign competition.

The term also understates what many FTAs do. Although some FTAs do little more than reduce or eliminate trade barriers, others do much more. They may establish minimum standards of intellectual property protection, rules for transparency in government procurement, provisions for the protection of labor or environmental rights, harmonized customs procedures, consumer privacy and protection provisions, rules for access to telecommunications services by nationals of the other party, protections for private foreign investment, and more. All FTAs into which the United States has entered since 1993 include such varied provisions. They are still called "free trade agreements," but they regulate trade in ways that may greatly affect domestic policy.

that the host state is equipped to protect these assets properly may be a precondition to doing business in that state, and obtaining adequate intellectual property protection usually depends on getting the timing of registrations of patents and trademarks just right.

There is another reason. Some companies, regardless of whether they wish to buy or sell abroad, face competition in the United States from foreign imports that infringe their U.S. intellectual property. In other words, one of the company's *competitors*, rather than the company itself, wishes to buy products or obtain services from someone in a foreign country, and this threatens the company's U.S. intellectual property. Infringing imports are a common business problem even for business firms that do not intend to sell or expand their operations abroad. It is critical for an international business lawyer to understand the opportunities created and problems posed by international trade in and licensing of intellectual property.

Chapter 4 deals with the commercial transaction itself. Every international sale of goods or services involves a contract of some kind. International contracts differ from purely domestic contracts in some ways, and the laws regulating such contracts may be quite different as well. It is critical for the international business lawyer to understand how and why each differs. International shipping and insurance issues differ in some cases from their domestic analogs as well. The mechanics of transferring payment for the sale is usually quite different, because often the parties use different currencies, whose values fluctuate relative to each other over time. Also, the risk of nonpayment or other breach of contract in an international sale is much greater than the risk in a domestic sale, and business organizations have invented mechanisms to address that risk.

Chapter 5 introduces the basics of import and export regulation. Here we first encounter the legal mechanics of moving goods, software, technical information, and services across state borders. As these travel from one country to another, they face at least two basic kinds of state regulation. The exporting country may impose regulations on what kinds of goods, data, or services may be exported, and how and when and where and to whom they may be exported. The importing country will almost certainly impose regulations on how goods and sometimes services are imported and tax the importation in one way or another. The international business lawyer should understand at least the basic risks, costs, and administrative burdens associated with moving goods, data, or services from one country to another.

Chapter 6 explains the options for restricting the cross-border movement of goods using mechanisms called "trade remedies." In the United States and many other countries, there are laws to protect domestic industries against "unfair" foreign competition, including foreign competitors who use predatory pricing to drive domestic industries out of the market, or who receive government subsidies that give the foreign companies an advantage over their domestic competitors. The domestic companies seeking to stop such unfair foreign competition have certain powerful legal tools at their disposal, and the foreign companies that seek to import into the domestic market require representation to defend against charges of unfair competition.

In Chapter 7, we delve into the complex subject of direct foreign investment. It is of course possible to sell goods and some services in a foreign state without ever leaving your own country. A supplier can ship goods to a foreign purchaser or sell software or provide services over the Internet without ever crossing a border. But sometimes manufacturing, sales, or services are best done locally in the foreign country. For example, a company that builds power plants cannot simply build the plant domestically and ship it to a foreign country. The plant has to be built in the foreign country, employee training must be provided, and the plant must be connected to the electrical grid, all locally within the foreign country. Similarly, a company that wishes to open a retail store abroad can only do so by establishing facilities there.

Even with those goods and services that need not be provided locally, there may be both legal and business advantages to providing them locally. For example, a company may be able to reduce its tax burden or production costs by selling or manufacturing through a foreign subsidiary or joint venture. As a result, the company will have to choose between establishing a new venture in the foreign country or acquiring an existing foreign company. Such decisions carry important benefits and risks that an international business lawyer must understand. For example, raising capital for investment in a foreign state may involve risks and government assistance not available for purely domestic investments.

Chapter 8 discusses the problem of global corruption and its regulation by treaties and municipal laws. It may be difficult to set up a successful business in a foreign country without facing pressure to pay bribes or engage in other corrupt transactions, but strict laws, in some cases adopted in compliance with international treaties, forbid some kinds of payments to or favors for foreign officials.

Chapter 9 summarizes the techniques business lawyers use for planning dispute resolution in an international setting. International business transactions frequently involve large amounts of capital combined with risks that are difficult to foresee. Proper planning to prevent being haled before a hostile or inconvenient forum, or subjected to unfamiliar or disadvantageous laws, requires understanding the risks and options available to mitigate them. Whether the transaction is a simple, one-time cross-border sale of goods or a complex merger between two multinational corporations, serious disputes can never be ruled out. The problems of dispute resolution may be compounded by the fact that a customer or business partner is a foreign government agency that benefits from sovereign immunity. Fortunately, international business lawyers have some helpful legal tools at their disposal for minimizing litigation costs and risks that differ in many ways from what is typical in purely domestic transactions.

Finally, Chapter 10 deals with a constant consideration in international business law, namely, the extraterritorial application of national laws to foreign commerce. "Extraterritorial" means the laws apply to conduct or persons outside of the enacting state's sovereign territory. Many states have business regulations that apply beyond their national borders. Some of these will have been discussed in other chapters, such as Chapter 5 (especially export regulation) and Chapter 8 (relating to the regulation of corrupt business transactions). However, the doctrines and practices are sometimes complex and may carry implications for such diverse forms of regulation as securities offerings, competition law, and intellectual property protection. In the United States, there are general doctrines that apply across subject areas, but these do not entirely simplify the analysis, because the question of extraterritoriality depends in part on the nature of the statute at issue.

Of course, all of this is only part of the picture. There will be many business considerations that influence how a company structures its international transactions and operations, quite apart from questions of law. It is generally not the lawyer's responsibility to second-guess how a client weighs business factors. The lawyer's role is to apprise the client of legal risks and opportunities and to assist the client in realizing its business goals. Despite this relatively limited role, one lawyer could not possibly become an expert in all relevant fields of international business law. Most subjects introduced in this book are legal specialties unto themselves. The purpose of this course is not to impart expertise in each individual field, but rather to introduce you to these specialties and to make you aware of what kinds of legal issues can arise in, and what kinds of laws regulate, international business transactions.

Key Vocabulary

African Continental Free Trade Area
Common market
Customs union
EU Council of Ministers
EU Directive
EU Regulation
Euro (€)
Eurasian Economic Community (EAEC)
European Commission
European Parliament
European Union (EU)
Foreign Agents Registration Act (FARA)
Free trade agreement (FTA)
Free trade area
Intergovernmental organization (IGO)
International Chamber of Commerce (ICC)
Lobbying Disclosure Act (LDA)
MERCOSUR
Nongovernmental organization (NGO)
North American Free Trade Agreement (NAFTA)
United Nations (UN)
U.S.–Mexico–Canada Agreement (USMCA)
U.S. Trade Representative (USTR)
World Trade Organization (WTO)

Practice Exercises

#1 Where to Begin Research?

Your client, a New York corporation specializing in hotels and resorts, wishes to open a new vacation resort in the city of Puerto Vallarta, a coastal city in Jalisco, Mexico. Mexico is a federal republic like the United States, composed of thirty-one *estados* (states), of which Jalisco is one. What are the different legal systems you should review to determine whether and how they may affect the client's intended investment? (Hint: There are at least five).

#2 Government and Nongovernment Regulators

(a) Try to classify each of the following as a governmental actor, intergovernmental organization (IGO), or nongovernmental organization (NGO):

(i) U.S. Trade Representative
(ii) United Nations
(iii) International Chamber of Commerce
(iv) ASEAN
(v) U.S. Department of Justice
(vi) Greenpeace
(vii) European Union
(viii) World Trade Organization

(b) Why does it matter to a business enterprise whether a set of rules or guidelines ostensibly applicable to the enterprise's business activities is promulgated by a governmental actor, IGO, or NGO?

#3 What Kind of Trading Arrangement?

Freedonia, Sylvania, and Osterlich have negotiated a treaty whereby the parties agree that goods originating in any of the three countries may be imported into any other of the three countries duty-free. They maintain their present customs duties on imports from any country other than the three. Before the treaty, Freedonia levied a 10% customs duty on imports of peaches from anywhere in the world. Sylvania had a similar 15% customs duty on peach imports, and Osterlich had a 20% duty.

A. What kind of trading bloc is this, a free trade area, a customs union, or a common market?
B. What customs duty must Osterlich charge on imports of peaches grown in Sylvania?
C. Iago imports $10,000 in peaches from Zembia into Freedonia and

pays a $1,000 customs duty. He then resells them all to Roderigo, an importer in Sylvania. Must Roderigo pay a customs duty upon importing the peaches into Sylvania? If not, why not? If so, what duty?

Meanwhile, Grand Fenwick, Ruritania, Smalldonia, and Pottsylvania are also negotiating a treaty under which all goods originating in any of the four countries may be imported into any of the others duty-free. In addition, the treaty creates a commission that will harmonize all customs duties among the four states on products originating from outside the group. What kind of trading bloc is this, a free trade area, a customs union, or a common market?

Multiple Choice Questions

1. Which of the following terms most accurately characterizes the trading arrangement of the European Union?

   (a) Free trade area
   (b) Trading federation
   (c) Common market
   (d) Customs union
   (e) Union of republics

2. Which U.S. federal agency has the primary responsibility for negotiating foreign trade treaties?

   (a) U.S. Trade Representative
   (b) U.S. Ambassador to the relevant foreign state
   (c) Department of Commerce
   (d) Department of State
   (e) Department of Homeland Security

3. In what region is MERCOSUR located?

   (a) North America
   (b) Africa
   (c) The Middle East
   (d) South America
   (e) Eurasia

4. Which of the following forms of European Union legislation is directly binding on EU member states without the need for implementing

legislation?

(a) Directive
(b) Regulation
(c) Mandate
(d) Statute
(e) None of the above are directly binding

5. True or false?: Lawyers representing private business firms and industry groups directly negotiated the World Trade Organization Agreements under the supervision of the U.S. Trade Representative.

6. True or false?: U.S. lawyers representing foreign private business firms in U.S. administrative proceedings must disclose their representation to Congress under the Lobbying Disclosure Act even if they never lobby Congress on behalf of the foreign firm.

7. True or false?: The Court of Justice of the European Union is the highest appellate authority for any decision from the courts of EU member states.

Multiple Choice Answers

1. (c)
2. (a)
3. (d)
4. (b)
5. False
6. True
7. False

Chapter 2

International Business Treaties

What You Will Learn in This Chapter

This chapter will introduce you to the major international treaties that structure the regulation of international business law. The most important of these are the WTO Agreements, briefly mentioned in Chapter 1. The WTO Agreements are important for many reasons. Among them are their extremely broad subscription, the wide range of trade and investment-related transactions they govern, the extent of harmonization they prescribe, and their strong enforcement mechanisms.

There are other treaties that are very important to international business transactions as well. Some regional and bilateral free trade agreements have very broad scopes. Like the WTO Agreements, they frequently include not just the regulation of trade in goods, but of trade in services, regulation of intellectual property, telecommunications, and other matters. Regional agreements in particular may cover trade in a very large area, such as all of Europe or North America.

Finally, this chapter will introduce bilateral investment treaties, a common type of treaty that regulates direct foreign investment between the state parties. These treaties are especially important in international business, because they not only establish standards of protection for private investors, they also typically grant investors direct remedies in case of certain violations of the treaty commitments. As noted in the previous chapter, treaties are not binding on, and do not usually confer direct benefits to, private business firms. Investment treaties stand out as important exceptions to the rule.

1 The Need for International Trade Regulation

Throughout history, states have entered into trade agreements to facilitate the exchange of goods that they could not easily produce. Regular trade between civilizations is reflected in the earliest records of history. Evidence of formal trade treaties dates to the medieval age. The empires and principalities of Europe, Asia, and northern Africa engaged in vibrant trade within and between civilizations to secure such goods as Chinese silks, Burmese gemstones, and Indian teas and spices in exchange for European wool, iron, oil, wines, timber, and wax. These barters were sometimes governed by explicit agreements, such as the treaties between the sultanates of the Near East and the republics of Italy. Those instruments granted trading privileges to the foreign merchants, protection from interference with their business and property, and legal recognition of the enforceability of commercial contracts.*

However, formal trade treaties became common only in the nineteenth century. They were designed to remove administrative barriers to trade, reduce or abolish customs duties, and define the types of goods for which trade would be allowed or prohibited. Over time, they have become increasingly sophisticated and detailed.

2.1 Why Trade?

Why promote international trade in the first place? The simplest reason is that some products can be produced only in certain regions. A country without iron ore deposits needs trade to produce steel. The same applies to other natural resources, such as petroleum for gasoline, bauxite for aluminum, or trees for lumber. Not every state has an abundance of these. Similarly, landlocked states have no access to fish and seafood, states in cold climates cannot grow bananas, and states with highly alkaline soils cannot grow grapes for wine. To obtain these goods, states need to trade with other states.

Not all constraints on production are natural, however. Some states have expertise and technologies that others lack. Renaissance Italy and Flanders developed expertise in producing lace that other states lacked, whereas Germany had a special advantage in printing technologies. In the modern era, few states can produce commercial aircraft with the skill and efficiency of the United States or Europe, while Switzerland dominates watchmaking and Japan leads the world in electronics design. Aside from expertise, in some countries labor is cheaper than in others because of high long-term unemployment. In states of widespread poverty and high population density such as Bangladesh, China, and India, for example, wages are low, and so goods requiring intensive unskilled labor can be produced at lower costs than elsewhere. Because of these differences, states can benefit from importing goods that are produced abroad more efficiently. In these cases, states are said to have an **absolute advantage** in production.

Economists have developed arguments as to why international trade benefits states even in the absence of such advantages as these, however. The theory of **comparative advantage**, articulated by David Ricardo in the early

---

*See John Wansbrough, *Venice and Florence in the Mamluk Commercial Privileges*, 28 BULL. OF THE SCHOOL OF ORIENTAL & AFR. STUDIES, UNIV. OF LONDON 483 (1965); Pierre Moukarzel, *Venetian Merchants in Thirteenth-Century Alexandria and the Sultans of Egypt: an Analysis of Treaties, Privileges and Intercultural Relations*, 28 AL-MASĀQ 187 (2016).

nineteenth century, can only be understood in light of the idea of "opportunity cost." **Opportunity cost** is the loss of a potential gain from other alternatives when one alternative is chosen. For example, suppose a person has $1000 and could lend it out at a guaranteed average return of 5% real interest for one year (resulting in a $50 gain each year). Instead, the person buys a television set with the money, and after five years he resells the television for $400. Assuming no inflation, the direct cost of owning the television for five years was $600 ($1000 initial cost minus $400 recovered by resale). But the *opportunity cost* of buying the television was actually much more. Had he loaned the money out instead for the five years, he would have earned $276 in compound interest, which he sacrificed by buying the television. Therefore, his opportunity cost is much higher: $600 + $276 = $876. In other words, he would be $876 richer if he had invested the $1000 instead of buying a television.

Opportunity cost is the basis of many business decisions, and we will return to it in future chapters. Here, it is important for understanding the theory of comparative advantage, according to which states benefit from producing whatever goods they can at the lowest opportunity cost, regardless of whether they have an absolute advantage in producing those goods. A country therefore benefits from specializing in production of the goods it can turn out at the lowest cost, regardless of whether another country can produce the same goods at lower cost (as long as its trading partner produces some other good more efficiently). In short, countries should produce whatever they can grow, mine, or manufacture most efficiently, even though other states might produce the same thing more efficiently than they can do. When countries behave this way, according to the theory, trade will be to their mutual advantage.

If Ricardo's theory were correct, then specialization and free trade benefit all states. Other economists have sought to refine Ricardo's theory, and although sophisticated economists doubt its practical use (see the policy box: Is Comparative Advantage Real?), it has greatly influenced the trading policies of many states and remains the orthodoxy among most economists today.

2.2 A Brief History of the World Trading System

A. World Trade Before 1947

During the European colonial age, most European powers imposed high import duties, established exclusionary trading relationships with their colonies, subsidized manufacturing and exports, and the aggressively accumulated gold and silver. Technological advances in navigation and refrigeration had made international shipping much more profitable, but it was used relatively little between the colonizing powers. The theory that an empire best served its own interests by high exports, few or no imports, and the accumulation of precious metals came to be known as **mercantilism**, and it dominated economic policy until the liberal theories of Adam Smith and Ricardo gained ascendency.

In the mid-nineteenth century, these theories and the necessity of solving

Is Comparative Advantage Real?

The theory of comparative advantage is considered orthodox economics and, under its influence, most wealthy states today maintain a relatively open trade policy, except in agriculture. Yet, there are strong reasons to doubt its practical application to international trade. Like all general theories, comparative advantage relies on assumptions that do not always reflect reality. In fact, most of its assumptions never reflected the reality of world trade.

Among these, the theory of comparative advantage counterfactually assumes a world with only two states, instead of the 198 that exist today. It also assumes constant returns, meaning that production increases in direct proportion to an increase in labor. But in manufacturing, this is not generally true; costs of developing technology and production capacity are almost always highest at the beginning and decrease with experience. This gives the state that first develops an industry an advantage over other states. As a result, most countries with poorly developed economies must rely on agriculture, in which the opposite rule applies—greater investment leads to diminishing returns, as the land reaches its limit in crop productivity and available pasturage. Those countries that have historically produced mainly one crop, such as bananas, fish, or coffee, have consistently experienced economic decline. *See* JAMES K. GALBRAITH, THE PREDATOR STATE 68-69 (2008).

Ricardian theory and its progeny rely on many more fanciful assumptions. For example, they assume prices of commodities are constant, which is the opposite of the case. They also assume that states have access to similar technologies, and that goods from one country do not combine with goods from others to produce composite goods, like plastics, electronics, or machinery. As a result, comparative advantage can explain little about the benefits of free trade.

It is likely that free trade contributes to economic growth for other reasons, however, such as absolute advantage. A state with lower wages will undoubtedly tend to produce cheaper labor-intensive goods, and a state with a tropical climate will be more efficient at producing tropical fruits. Or it could be that comparative advantage causes free trade to be efficient among highly developed and diverse economies, but not for less developed economies with a narrow production base. Whatever the answer, simplistic economic theories cannot educate us about the best way to craft public policy. Complex economic interactions require much more nuanced theories.

the famine in Ireland influenced the United Kingdom to repeal many import tariffs and liberalize trade. The U.K. also began to negotiate free trade treaties with France, Germany, and other European states. Within a few decades, however, a European recession combined with increased competition in agriculture from outside of Europe led to a withdrawal from free trade and a resumption of high import duties in France and Germany. By 1880, only the U.K. maintained relatively free trade in Europe.* No change occurred in the United States, which had continuously maintained high trade barriers since independence.

The First World War (1914-18) predictably contributed nothing to trade liberalization, but following the Treaty of Versailles, the general atmosphere of mutual hostility and nationalism caused states to continue import barriers and competitively devalue their currencies in hopes of gaining an advantage over one another. As the world's economies fell into a Great Depression in the 1920s, opposition to free trade only increased.

The United States famously reacted to the Depression with the Smoot-Hawley Tariff of 1930, which raised import duties to an average of 60%. This trade strategy, called **protectionism**, uses import barriers like high customs duties to deter imports and encourage local manufacturing. The European powers quickly retaliated in the same way, and international trade ground nearly to a halt.** Contrary to the expectation of mercantilists and protectionists, the end of global trade did nothing to alleviate the depressions and may have prolonged them. In 1934, however, Congress authorized President Franklin Roosevelt to reverse course and negotiate free trade agreements with other countries, which he did energetically.

Toward the conclusion of the Second World War, the allied powers agreed at Bretton Woods, New Hampshire to form three institutions to assist in the world's economic recovery after the war. One Bretton Woods institution is the **International Monetary Fund**, whose role is to stabilize currency exchange rates so that states may productively borrow money and engage in trade with each other. Another is the **International Bank for Reconstruction and Development** (or **World Bank**), whose role is to provide loans and technical assistance to countries for economic development. The last was to be the **International Trade Organization**, which was intended to oversee the liberalization of global trade. Only the first two institutions were actually formed. Congress opposed the International Trade Organization as a potential constraint on its power to regulate U.S. commerce with foreign nations, and the institution never crystallized.

B. The General Agreement on Tariffs and Trade of 1947

Instead, the allies concluded a treaty that set the stage for progressive global trade liberalization. The **General Agreement on Tariffs and Trade** (**GATT**), adopted in 1947, created no supervisory institution or formal enforcement mechanism, but it became the basis for successive rounds of trade negotiations to lower import duties and reduce other barriers to trade. Originally, the GATT had only nineteen contracting parties. It would eventually expand

*Paul Bairoch & Susan Burke, *European Trade Policy, 1815-1914*, *in* 8 THE CAMBRIDGE ECONOMIC HISTORY OF EUROPE FROM THE DECLINE OF THE ROMAN EMPIRE 1, 51-52, 101 (Peter Mathias & Sidney Pollard eds. 1989).

**See JAMES FOREMAN-PECK, A HISTORY OF THE WORLD ECONOMY 215-16 (1983).

into one of the most widely subscribed treaties in the world.

The GATT 1947 established an unusually elaborate set of disciplines to govern international trade in goods, several of which became foundational to the world trading system. Among these were the principle of nondiscrimination among GATT parties in trade preferences and internal taxation; restrictions on market access barriers such as import quotas or burdensome import licensing procedures; limitations on shutting down trade to protect currency values; and limitations on the granting of export subsidies or the use of competition policy to restrict trade. It also harmonized some important procedures for importation, such as methods of appraising the value of imported goods for the purpose of calculating customs duties, and rules on determining and marking the country of origin of imports.

Finally, the GATT 1947 set forth **schedules of concessions** that significantly reduced the customs duties imposed by the state parties. The concessions were negotiated laboriously on a state-by-state and product-by-product basis for tens of thousands of products. At the end of the negotiations, each state published a list identifying the products for which duties would be reduced, their rates of import duties, special charges or other barriers to importation for each, and the concessions granted, if any, for each.

The original GATT left much for the future, however. The ever growing number of contracting parties therefore met regularly to reduce duties ever more by amending their schedules of concessions, and to develop additional disciplines to further liberalize trade. In 1947, when GATT negotiations commenced, import duties around the world averaged 40% of the value of the imports. Today, they sit at around 5%. But the GATT has not merely reduced tariff rates; world trade law has also evolved into a complex set of standards. At the Tokyo Round of negotiations in the 1970s, the parties agreed on numerous additional "codes" to govern such matters as trade in civil aircraft and dairy products, technical barriers to trade, and more favorable treatment for impoverished states, called **developing countries**.

3.1 The World Trade Organization Agreements

After the Tokyo Round came the **Uruguay Round**, a series of negotiations that lasted eight years. At the conclusion of this round in 1994, the contracting parties had established a revolutionary change to the world trading system. The package of agreements was more diverse and elaborate than any that had ever preceded it, with disciplines affecting much more than the trade in goods. Perhaps most importantly, it included a treaty establishing a supervisory institution for future trade negotiations—the **World Trade Organization (WTO)**—and a strong enforcement mechanism.

3.2 The World Trade Organization

The WTO is an intergovernmental organization headquartered in Geneva, Switzerland. It was created by a multilateral treaty, the Agreement Establishing the World Trade Organization. All WTO members are parties to this treaty.

The WTO provides a forum for states to negotiate new trade agreements and discuss the interpretation and enforcement of those currently in force. It consists of a Ministerial Conference composed of the representatives of each contracting party. The Conference runs its daily business through three bodies: the General Council, the Dispute Settlement Body, and the Trade Policy Review Body. It also has a Secretariat, composed of a Director-General and a number of other international civil servants who assist the WTO members in their negotiations and dispute resolution.

As of 2020, the WTO Agreements have 164 parties, including almost every major economy in the world. This makes the WTO one of the world's largest organizations by membership and economic impact. Those states not yet parties to the WTO Agreements are mostly in the Middle East, Central Asia, and Africa.

3.3 The Modern General Agreement on Tariffs and Trade

All members of the WTO also became parties to a package of binding agreements, one of which is the GATT. There are also some optional, or **plurilateral**, treaties. The core disciplines of the GATT now in force will be described here briefly. Other key agreements will be summarized in the following sections.

A. Tariff Bindings

The GATT continues to include schedules of "concessions" for the reduction of customs duties with regard to imports from all WTO members. The schedule lists and describes the goods, the reduced rate of duty granted to WTO members, and any other duties or charges on the goods. The bound duty rates are usually stated as a percentage of the value of the imported goods (so-called ***ad valorem* duties**).

Except under strictly limited circumstances, WTO members are prohibited from raising their customs rates beyond those listed in their schedule of concessions. They are of course free to reduce their duties below the scheduled amount at any time, either unilaterally or pursuant to a new round of trade negotiations.

Figure 2.1. Global trade in action. The cross-border trade in goods makes up a significant part of the national incomes of most countries. Most trade goods are shipped by cargo freighters like those here. This modern seaport in Barcelona has enough room to load and unload a dozen 290-meter cargo ships at once.
© 2010 by Aaron X. Fellmeth.

B. The Nondiscrimination Principles

Most Favored Nation Treatment

From its very beginnings, the GATT included disciplines to prevent contracting parties from differentiating between their trading partners. The **most favored nation** (**MFN**) principle prohibits states from granting better trade concessions to some WTO members than they do to others:

> 1. With respect to customs duties and charges of any kind imposed on or in connection with importation or exportation or imposed on the international transfer of payments for imports or exports, and with respect to the method of levying such duties and charges, and with respect to all rules and formalities in connection with importation and exportation * * * any advantage, favour, privilege or immunity granted by any contracting party to any product originating in or destined for any other country shall be accorded immediately and unconditionally to the like product originating in or destined for the territories of all other contracting parties.

GATT art. I.

Thus, if Ruritania agreed to reduce customs duties on imports of softwood lumber to 8% *ad valorem* under its schedule of concessions, every WTO member benefits from that rate of duty when exporting lumber to Ruritania. If Ruritania later unilaterally reduces the rate of duty on lumber imports to 6% for its neighbor Smalldonia, then it must automatically grant the same 6% duty rate to lumber imports from any and all WTO members. The same equal treatment duty would apply if Ruritania were to exempt Smalldonian imports from inspection or other formalities.

There are several exceptions to the MFN principle, most of which are limited and technical. One important exception relates to regional customs unions or free trade areas. Under Article XXIV of the GATT, contracting parties are permitted to conclude customs union treaties or free trade agreements that give lower customs duties or other preferential concessions to some WTO members and not others, as long as (1) the agreement does not increase customs duties over their previous rates, and (2) the agreement covers "substantially all trade" between the parties to the agreement. In other words, a WTO member may give preferential concessions to a subset of other WTO members through a "regional trading arrangement," and these concessions may be superior to those granted to other beneficiaries of MFN status, on the conditions specified.

Under another important exception to the MFN principle, imports from developing countries may benefit from customs duties lower than those imposed on other WTO members. In 1971, the General Council authorized a waiver of MFN principles under a **Generalized System of Preferences** (**GSP**) in favor of developing countries.* The WTO Agreements do not define "developing

---

*Decision BISD 18S/24 of June 25, 1971. The waiver was originally envisioned

country"; states self-designate to claim the benefits of GSP. More than two-thirds of the WTO members have claimed developing country status, including such exporting powerhouses as Brazil, Israel, and South Korea. States that choose to adopt a GSP program commit to unilaterally reducing customs duties on imports from such developing countries in order to promote economic growth in these states. At present, several dozen states, including the United States and the European Union, have adopted a GSP program despite the absence of reciprocal trade benefits.

The result of these exceptions is that, contrary to the MFN principle, WTO members do not uniformly give the same treatment to each other. Customs duties and other trade preferences vary considerably among WTO members, depending on whether they are classified as developed or developing countries, or are parties to a customs union or free trade agreement. A "most favored nation" does not necessarily receive the most favorable treatment under the GATT. A more accurate term might be "not-least-favored nation."

National Treatment

The second nondiscrimination principle is known as **national treatment**. The national treatment principle is designed to ensure that, after goods have cleared customs and entered the importing country, they do not suffer disadvantage through discriminatory municipal laws and regulations:

> 1. The contracting parties recognize that internal taxes and other internal charges, and laws, regulations and requirements affecting the internal sale, offering for sale, purchase, transportation, distribution or use of products, and internal quantitative regulations requiring the mixture, processing or use of products in specified amounts or proportions, should not be applied to imported or domestic products so as to afford protection to domestic production.
> 2. The products of the territory of any contracting party imported into the territory of any other contracting party shall not be subject, directly or indirectly, to internal taxes or other internal charges of any kind in excess of those applied, directly or indirectly, to like domestic products. Moreover, no contracting party shall otherwise apply internal taxes or other internal charges to imported or domestic products in a manner contrary to the principles set forth in paragraph 1.

GATT art. III.

Just as GATT article I prohibits import and export regulations that discriminate between products from different WTO member states, GATT article III prohibits *internal* regulations that discriminate against imported products in favor of domestic products. The scope of this provision is potentially very great, because regulations affecting the sale, transportation, and distribution

---

as temporary, but was made permanent by Decision of Nov. 28, 1979, GATT Doc. L/4903.

of goods in any given country may be varied and complex.

One problem sometimes arising in this context is that different states export different variants on similar goods, and because states levy disparate rates of duties on different variants, some states may face higher duty rates on imports from them than do other states, even though the goods may seem comparable. The following case, dealing with Japanese excise taxes on liquor, illustrates this problem in the context of the WTO dispute resolution system.

JAPAN — TAXES ON ALCOHOLIC BEVERAGES

World Trade Organization

Oct. 4, 1996 WT/DS8/AB/R, etc.

Report of the Appellate Body

A. Introduction

Japan and the United States appeal from certain issues of law and legal interpretations in the Panel Report, *Japan — Taxes on Alcoholic Beverages* (the "Panel Report"). That Panel (the "Panel") was established to consider complaints by the European Communities [now the European Union], Canada and the United States against Japan relating to the Japanese Liquor Tax Law (Shuzeiho), Law No. 6 of 1953 as amended (the "Liquor Tax Law").

[The Japanese Liquor Tax Law provided for taxes on the production or importation of liquors based on two factors: type of liquor and alcohol content. Higher alcohol contents resulted in higher taxes. However, the rates differed by type of liquor. For example, "shochu," a liquor widely made in Japan, was taxed at ¥155,700 or ¥102,100 per kilolitre at 25 degrees of alcohol strength (depending on the production process), whereas vodka with comparable alcohol strength was taxed at ¥367,300 per kilolitre, and whisky at ¥908,620. Neither vodka nor whisky is widely produced in Japan.]

The Panel Report was circulated to the Members of the World Trade Organization the "WTO") on 11 July 1996. It contains the following conclusions:

(i) Shochu and vodka are like products and Japan, by taxing the latter in excess of the former, is in violation of its obligation under Article III:2, first sentence, of the General Agreement on Tariffs and Trade 1994.

(ii) Shochu, whisky, brandy, rum, gin, genever, and liqueurs are "directly competitive or substitutable products" and Japan, by not taxing them similarly, is in violation of its obligation under Article III:2, second sentence, of the General Agreement on Tariffs and Trade 1994.

* * *

F. Interpretation of Article III

The WTO Agreement is a treaty—the international equivalent of a contract. It is self-evident that in an exercise of their sovereignty, and in pursuit of their own respective national interests, the Members of the WTO have made a bargain. In exchange for the benefits they expect to derive as Members of the WTO, they have agreed to exercise their sovereignty according to the commitments they have made in the WTO Agreement. * * *

The broad and fundamental purpose of Article III is to avoid protectionism in the application of internal tax and regulatory measures. More specifically, the purpose of Article III "is to ensure that internal measures 'not be applied to imported or domestic products so as to afford protection to domestic production.'" Toward this end, Article III obliges Members of the WTO to provide equality of competitive conditions for imported products in relation to domestic products. "[T]he intention of the drafters of the Agreement was clearly to treat the imported products in the same way as the like domestic products once they had been cleared through customs. Otherwise indirect protection could be given." Moreover, it is irrelevant that "the trade effects" of the tax differential between imported and domestic products, as reflected in the volumes of imports, are insignificant or even non-existent; Article III protects expectations not of any particular trade volume but rather of the equal competitive relationship between imported and domestic products. Members of the WTO are free to pursue their own domestic goals through internal taxation or regulation so long as they do not do so in a way that violates Article III or any of the other commitments they have made in the WTO Agreement.

The broad purpose of Article III of avoiding protectionism must be remembered when considering the relationship between Article III and other provisions of the WTO Agreement. Although the protection of negotiated tariff concessions is certainly one purpose of Article III, the statement in Paragraph 6.13 of the Panel Report that "one of the main purposes of Article III is to guarantee that WTO Members will not undermine through internal measures their commitments under Article II" should not be overemphasized. The sheltering scope of Article III is not limited to products that are the subject of tariff concessions under Article II. The Article III national treatment obligation is a general prohibition on the use of internal taxes and other internal regulatory measures so as to afford protection to domestic production. This obligation clearly extends also to products not bound under Article II. This is confirmed by the negotiating history of

Figure 2.2. Shochu competes with vodka in the "white spirit" market. Like vodka, shochu can be made from many food bases.

Article III.

G. Article III:1

The terms of Article III must be given their ordinary meaning—in their context and in the light of the overall object and purpose of the WTO Agreement. Thus, the words actually used in the Article provide the basis for an interpretation that must give meaning and effect to all its terms. The proper interpretation of the Article is, first of all, a textual interpretation. Consequently, the Panel is correct in seeing a distinction between Article III:1, which "contains general principles," and Article III:2, which "provides for specific obligations regarding internal taxes and internal charges." Article III:1 articulates a general principle that internal measures should not be applied so as to afford protection to domestic production. This general principle informs the rest of Article III. The purpose of Article III:1 is to establish this general principle as a guide to understanding and interpreting the specific obligations contained in Article III:2 and in the other paragraphs of Article III, while respecting, and not diminishing in any way, the meaning of the words actually used in the texts of those other paragraphs. In short, Article III:1 constitutes part of the context of Article III:2, in the same way that it constitutes part of the context of each of the other paragraphs in Article III. Any other reading of Article III would have the effect of rendering the words of Article III:1 meaningless, thereby violating the fundamental principle of effectiveness in treaty interpretation.* Consistent with this principle of effectiveness, and with the textual differences in the two sentences, we believe that Article III:1 informs the first sentence and the second sentence of Article III:2 in different ways.

H. Article III:2

1. First Sentence

Article III:1 informs Article III:2, first sentence, by establishing that if imported products are taxed in excess of like domestic products, then that tax measure is inconsistent with Article III. Article III:2, first sentence does not refer specifically to Article III:1. There is no specific invocation in this first sentence of the general principle in Article III:1 that admonishes Members of the WTO not to apply measures "so as to afford protection". This omission must have some meaning. We believe the meaning is simply that the presence of a protective application need not be established separately from the specific requirements that are included in the first sentence in order to show that a tax measure is inconsistent with the general principle set out in the first sentence. However, this does not mean that the general principle of Article III:1 does not apply to this sentence. To the contrary, we believe the first sentence of Article III:2 is, in effect, an application of this general principle. The ordinary meaning of the words of Article III:2, first sentence leads inevitably to this conclusion. Read in their context and in the light of the overall object and purpose of the WTO Agreement, the words of the first sentence require an examination of the conformity of an internal tax measure

*[Author's note: The principle of effectiveness, sometimes known by its Latin name, *ut res magis valeat quam pereat*, is a doctrine of treaty interpretation. Under it, no language in a treaty should be presumed superfluous; it should be read in a manner that makes it meaningful whenever reasonably possible.]

with Article III by determining, first, whether the taxed imported and domestic products are "like" and, second, whether the taxes applied to the imported products are "in excess of" those applied to the like domestic products. If the imported and domestic products are "like products", and if the taxes applied to the imported products are "in excess of" those applied to the like domestic products, then the measure is inconsistent with Article III:2, first sentence.

This approach to an examination of Article III:2, first sentence, is consistent with past practice under the GATT 1947. Moreover, it is consistent with the object and purpose of Article III:2, which the panel in the predecessor to this case dealing with an earlier version of the Liquor Tax Law, *Japan—Customs Duties, Taxes and Labelling Practices on Imported Wines and Alcoholic Beverages* ("*1987 Japan—Alcohol*"), rightly stated as "promoting non-discriminatory competition among imported and like domestic products [which] could not be achieved if Article III:2 were construed in a manner allowing discriminatory and protective internal taxation of imported products in excess of like domestic products."

(a) *"Like Products"*

Because the second sentence of Article III:2 provides for a separate and distinctive consideration of the protective aspect of a measure in examining its application to a broader category of products that are not "like products" as contemplated by the first sentence, we agree with the Panel that the first sentence of Article III:2 must be construed narrowly so as not to condemn measures that its strict terms are not meant to condemn. Consequently, we agree with the Panel also that the definition of "like products" in Article III:2, first sentence, should be construed narrowly.

How narrowly is a matter that should be determined separately for each tax measure in each case. We agree with the practice under the GATT 1947 of determining whether imported and domestic products are "like" on a case-by-case basis. The Report of the Working Party on *Border Tax Adjustments*, adopted by the CONTRACTING PARTIES in 1970, set out the basic approach for interpreting "like or similar products" generally in the various provisions of the GATT 1947:

> ... the interpretation of the term should be examined on a case-by-case basis. This would allow a fair assessment in each case of the different elements that constitute a "similar" product. Some criteria were suggested for determining, on a case-by-case basis, whether a product is "similar": the product's end-uses in a given market; consumers' tastes and habits, which change from country to country; the product's properties, nature and quality.

This approach was followed in almost all adopted panel reports after *Border Tax Adjustments*. This approach should be helpful in identifying on a case-by-case basis the range of "like products" that fall within the narrow limits of Article III:2, first sentence in the GATT 1994. * * *

No one approach to exercising judgement will be appropriate for all cases. The criteria in *Border Tax Adjustments* should be examined, but there can be no one precise and absolute definition of what is "like." The concept of "likeness" is a relative one that evokes the image of an accordion. The accordion of "likeness" stretches and squeezes in different places as different provisions of the WTO Agreement are applied. The width of the accordion in any one of those places must be determined by the particular provision in which the term "like" is encountered as well as by the context and the circumstances that prevail in any given case to which that provision may apply. We believe that, in Article III:2, first sentence of the GATT 1994, the accordion of "likeness" is meant to be narrowly squeezed.

The Panel determined in this case that shochu and vodka are "like products" for the purposes of Article III:2, first sentence. We note that the determination of whether vodka is a "like product" to shochu under Article III:2, first sentence, or a "directly competitive or substitutable product" to shochu under Article III:2, second sentence, does not materially affect the outcome of this case. * * *

2. Second Sentence

Article III:1 informs Article III:2, second sentence, through specific reference. Article III:2, second sentence, contains a general prohibition against "internal taxes or other internal charges" applied to "imported or domestic products in a manner contrary to the principles set forth in paragraph 1." As mentioned before, Article III:1 states that internal taxes and other internal charges "should not be applied to imported or domestic products so as to afford protection to domestic production." Again, *Ad* Article III:2 states as follows:

> A tax conforming to the requirements of the first sentence of paragraph 2 would be considered to be inconsistent with the provisions of the second sentence only in cases where competition was involved between, on the one hand, the taxed product and, on the other hand, a directly competitive or substitutable product which was not similarly taxed.

* * * Unlike that of Article III:2, first sentence, the language of Article III:2, second sentence, specifically invokes Article III:1. The significance of this distinction lies in the fact that whereas Article III:1 acts implicitly in addressing the two issues that must be considered in applying the first sentence, it acts explicitly as an entirely separate issue that must be addressed along with two other issues that are raised in applying the second sentence. Giving full meaning to the text and to its context, three separate issues must be addressed to determine whether an internal tax measure is inconsistent with Article III:2, second sentence. These three issues are whether:

> (1) the imported products and the domestic products *are "directly competitive or substitutable products" which are in competition with each other*;
>
> (2) the directly competitive or substitutable imported and domestic products *are "not similarly taxed"*; and
>
> (3) the dissimilar taxation of the directly competitive or substitutable imported domestic products *is "applied ... so as to afford protection to domestic production."*

Again, these are three separate issues. Each must be established separately by the complainant for a panel to find that a tax measure imposed by a Member of the WTO is inconsistent with Article III:2, second sentence.

(a) *"Directly Competitive or Substitutable Products"*

If imported and domestic products are not "like products" for the narrow purposes of Article III:2, first sentence, then they are not subject to the strictures of that sentence and there is no inconsistency with the requirements of that sentence. However, depending on their nature, and depending on the competitive conditions in the relevant market, those same products may well be among the broader category of "directly competitive or substitutable products" that fall within the domain of Article III:2, second sentence. How much broader that category of "directly competitive or substitutable products" may be in any given case is a matter for the panel to determine based on all the relevant facts in that case. As with "like products" under the first sentence, the determination of the appropriate range of "directly competitive or substitutable products" under the second sentence must be made on a case-by-case basis.

In this case, the Panel emphasized the need to look not only at such matters as physical characteristics, common end-uses, and tariff classifications, but also at the "market place". This seems appropriate. The GATT 1994 is a commercial agreement, and the WTO is concerned, after all, with markets. It does not seem inappropriate to look at competition in the relevant markets as one among a number of means of identifying the broader category of products that might be described as "directly competitive or substitutable".

Nor does it seem inappropriate to examine elasticity of substitution as one means of examining those relevant markets. The Panel did not say that cross-price elasticity of demand is "*the* decisive criterion" for determining whether products are "directly competitive or substitutable". The Panel stated the following:

> In the Panel's view, the decisive criterion in order to determine whether two products are directly competitive or substitutable is whether they have common end-uses, *inter alia*, as shown by elasticity of substitution.

We agree. And, we find the Panel's legal analysis of whether the products are "directly competitive or substitutable products" in paragraphs 6.28-6.32 of the Panel Report to be correct. * * *

(c) *"So As To Afford Protection"*

This third inquiry under Article III:2, second sentence, must determine whether "directly competitive or substitutable products" are "not similarly taxed" in a way that affords protection. This is not an issue of intent. It is not necessary for a panel to sort through the many reasons legislators and regulators often have for what they do and weigh the relative significance of those reasons to establish legislative or regulatory intent. If the measure is applied to imported or domestic products so as to afford protection to domestic production, then it does not matter that there may not have been any desire to engage in protectionism in the minds of the legislators or the regulators who imposed the measure. It is irrelevant that protectionism was not an intended objective if the particular tax measure in question is nevertheless, to echo Article III:1, "*applied* to imported or domestic products so as to afford protection to domestic production." This is an issue of how the measure in question is *applied*.

* * *

I. Conclusions and Recommendations

* * *

With the modifications to the Panel's legal findings and conclusions set out in this report, the Appellate Body affirms the Panel's conclusions that shochu and vodka are like products and that Japan, by taxing imported products in excess of like domestic products, is in violation of its obligations under Article III:2, first sentence, of the General Agreement on Tariffs and Trade 1994. Moreover, the Appellate Body concludes that shochu and other distilled spirits and liqueurs listed in HS 2208, except for vodka, are "directly competitive or substitutable products", and that Japan, in the application of the Liquor Tax Law, does not similarly tax imported and directly competitive or substitutable domestic products and affords protection to domestic production in violation of Article III:2, second sentence, of the General Agreement on Tariffs and Trade 1994.

The Appellate Body recommends that the Dispute Settlement Body request Japan to bring the Liquor Tax Law into conformity with its obligations under the General Agreement on Tariffs and Trade 1994.

Notes and Questions

1. In interpreting what goods are **like products** for purposes of determining whether differential taxes are discriminatory, the Appellate Body relied on a 1970 interpretation of the term by a working party established by the GATT General Council. The relevant factors identified by the Working Party were:

- the product's end-uses in a given market;
- consumers' tastes and habits, which change from country to country; and
- the product's properties, nature and quality.

The 1970 report said nothing about customs classifications, although presumably such classifications are established based on product similarity.

2. What kinds of factors might you consider in deciding whether vodka and shochu have the same or similar "end-uses?" The fact that they are both alcoholic beverages? Their percentage of alcohol by volume? Whether they are consumed on similar occasions (such as specific holidays, celebrations, ordinary meals)? Whether they are consumed in similar places (such as bars, restaurants, home)? How does consideration of these factors help determine whether a difference in treatment distorts competition?

3. Economists have developed a useful objective measure of how similar products are in the eyes of consumers. This is referenced in the Appellate Body Report as **cross-price elasticity of demand**, which is a measure of the responsiveness of demand for one good to a change in the price of another good. The more consumers consider the goods substitutable, the larger the change in consumption of one good when the price of the other good rises or falls. What does the Appellate Body consider to be the difference between "consumer tastes and habits," which are a factor in determining whether two products are "like products," and the separate question of whether goods are "directly competitive or substitutable?" Why would a trade treaty distinguish between the two?

C. Quantitative Restrictions

The laws of economics generally dictate that, as the price of a product rises, fewer units of the product will sell. This should be intuitive—as a product becomes more expensive, consumers are less able or willing to buy as many as they did when the product was cheaper. Customs duties raise the price of imported products, and so they reduce import competition. As customs duties rise, the price of the imports will rise in direct correlation, and fewer imports will be purchased by consumers in the importing country. By lowering import duties, the GATT helps make imports more competitive with domestically produced goods among WTO member states.

The relationship between the price of imports and the quantity imported means that states can also affect import competition by reversing the equation. In other words, by limiting the quantity of goods imported, the price of the goods in the country will increase (see Figure 2.2). It follows that another method that a state can use to limit the competition of imports with its

HOW CROSS-PRICE ELASTICITY OF DEMAND WORKS

Consider three goods: green apples, red apples, and automobile tires. If consumers are indifferent to buying green or red apples, then cross-price elasticity of demand will be very high. When the price of green apples rises just a little, consumption of red apples will increases a great deal and the consumption of green apples will decline somewhat proportionately. But consumers do not view tires as substitutes for green apples, and so no fall in the price of apples will decrease tire consumption appreciably, and no rise in green apple prices will increase tire consumption. Cross-price elasticity of demand between these two products will be very low. When product prices have no effect on the demand for each other, elasticity is said to be zero. When they are perfectly substitutable for one another, elasticity is 1. For most products, it varies between the two. Cross-price elasticity of demand is an extremely useful tool in measuring how goods compete with one another in a specific, real-world market.

domestically produced goods is by imposing a limit on the number of imports that admitted into that state.

Import quotas, also known as **quantitative restrictions**, set a maximum limit on the quantity of goods that may be imported into a county over a specific period, usually one year. They were historically used by many states to protect their domestic industries from foreign import competition. For example, in May 1982, the United States imposed country-by-country quotas on sugar imports to increase the price of domestically-produced sugar.

Not all quotas are absolute. States sometimes use a hybrid between import duties and quotas, called **tariff-rate quotas** (**TRQs**). TRQs permit a specific quantity of imported goods to enter the country at a reduced duty rate (or possibly duty-free), and quantities in excess of that amount enter at a higher duty rate. Once the quota has been reached, goods may still be imported, but at a higher rate of duty. For example, the TRQ may specify that the country will apply a 3% duty rate to foreign imports of electric fans up to 50,000 fans. After 50,000 fans have been imported, a 12% duty rate will be applied to any additional foreign imports of fans. The TRQ is very flexible; the quantities that trigger the increased tariff rate can be adjusted, the tariff rate itself can be

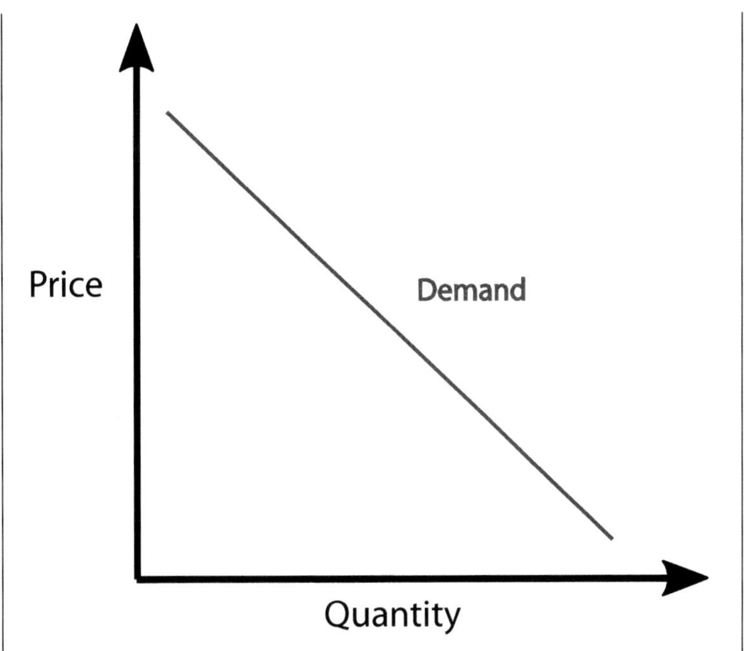

Figure 2.3. The demand curve illustrates the inverse correlation between the price of a product and the quantity of it demanded by consumers. Because of this relationship, states may use either price-control measures (duties) or quantity-control measures (quotas) to achieve similar trade outcomes.

adjusted, and it is even possible to create two or more TRQs for the same class of goods (e.g., the state may apply a 3% duty rate on the first 20,000 imported fans in a given year, a 6% duty rate on the next 20,000, and a 15% duty rate on fans imported after the first 40,000).

Because quantitative restrictions reduce international trade like import duties do, the GATT strictly limits their use by WTO members. GATT article XI:1 states:

> 1. No prohibitions or restrictions other than duties, taxes or other charges, whether made effective through quotas, import or export licences or other measures, shall be instituted or maintained by any contracting party on the importation of any product of the territory of any other contracting party or on the exportation or sale for export of any product destined for the territory of any other contracting party.

Other provisions of the GATT allow a small class of temporary exceptions for various reasons, some of which will be discussed in later chapters. Using these exceptions, many countries apply TRQs, mostly to agricultural and mined products. However, GATT article XIII provides that, if a state avails itself of any of these exceptions to the prohibition on quantitative restrictions, it must apply them in a nondiscriminatory manner consistent with MFN principles, meaning that a state cannot impose different quantitative restrictions on different WTO members. The goal of this provision is to help ensure that, to the extent quotas are permitted, they will be used in the least trade-distorting manner possible.

The question of what constitutes a quantitative restriction on imports, as opposed to merely a regulation of products for public safety and health, environmental, or other reasons, is not always clearly cut. The following excerpt from the report of an international trade panel grapples with this issue in the context of GATT and a free trade agreement.

LOBSTERS FROM CANADA

U.S.–CANADA FREE TRADE AGREEMENT
USA 89-1807-01 (May 25, 1990)

FINAL REPORT OF THE PANEL

* * *

2.1 On December 12, 1989, the United States enacted an amendment to the Magnuson Fishery Conservation and Management Act (the "Magnuson Act") to prohibit, among other things, the sale or transport in or from the United States of whole live lobsters smaller than the minimum possession size in effect under U.S. federal law ("subsized lobsters"). By that amendment (the "1989 amendment" or "U.S. measures"), lobsters originating in foreign countries or in states having minimum lobster size requirements smaller than the minimum limits imposed by U.S. federal law are prohibited, with effect from December 12, 1989, from entering into interstate or foreign commerce for sale within or from the United States. * * *

2.3 This 1989 amendment to the Magnuson Act was the latest of numerous initiatives by federal and state governments in the United States to [prevent the depletion of U.S. lobster stocks through harvesting young lobsters before they have had a chance to reproduce]. Until the 1989 amendment, lobsters harvested in federal waters could not be sold in interstate commerce if they failed to meet federal minimum size requirements, but Canadian lobsters could. Someone found selling sub-sized lobsters could, until the amendment, avoid conviction by showing evidence of purchase of the lobster from a jurisdiction, such as Canada, which did not impose the U.S. federal minima.

2.4 In December 1989, Canada advised the United States that the application of a minimum lobster size requirement to Canadian lobster exports to the United States was a GATT-illegal import prohibition [specifically, a quantitative restriction in violation of article XI]. * * *

3.2.5 Water temperature has a differential effect on the time lobsters will take to attain sexual maturity and reproductive capacity. It may take a lobster up to 10 years to attain sexual maturity in cold waters and only five years in warmer waters, where the lobster molts more frequently. Thus, reproductive maturity will occur at a smaller size in warmer waters.

3.2.6 Water temperature maxima and averages vary from area to area along the U.S. and Canadian coasts. [Testimony of biologists showed that the Canadian waters are warmer than are the Maine waters where most U.S. lobsters are caught, and that lobsters in Canadian waters are consequently smaller when they obtain sexual maturity than the lobsters in colder U.S. waters.] * * *

3.5.1 There has been intensive lobster harvesting in recent years and a large increase in the fishing effort. It was estimated in 1983 that only a tiny fraction (from 1 to 6 percent) of U.S. lobsters in the most-exploited areas avoided capture before reaching reproductive capacity. Scientists in both Canada and the United States have voiced alarm that this small percentage might be insufficient to avoid a catastrophic stock collapse although Canadian scientists believe Canadian stocks are now healthy. * * *

3.5.3 In view of this, the United States decided to adopt a range of conservation and management measures regarding its lobster industry. * * *

3.5.5 At the federal level, the United States first introduced a federal lobster size requirement with the adoption in 1985 of the American Lobster Fishery Regulations ("Federal Regulations") under the Magnuson Act. The federal minimum size requirement, set at 3 3/16 inches (81.0 mm), was established on the basis of the 1983 American Lobster Fishery Management Plan * * *.

3.5.14 The 1989 amendment * * * extended the prohibition on the marketing of sub-sized lobsters to lobsters harvested in foreign countries * * *. The 1989 amendment only applies to whole live lobsters and excludes frozen and canned lobsters, because the United States says, these are clearly labelled and readily identifiable according to origin.

3.5.15 The question for this Panel is whether the 1989 amendment constitutes a prohibition or restriction on the importation of Canadian lobster in conflict with U.S. obligations under GATT Article XI.

3.5.16 The legislative history of the 1989 amendment to the Magnuson Act indicates that there were three underlying objectives to extending the prohibition to imported sub-sized lobsters.

3.5.17 First, the 1989 amendment was expected to facilitate the enforcement and management of the federal program. According to U.S. enforcement officials, it was hard to catch violators under the Federal Regulations that went into effect in 1987. Unscrupulous lobster dealers might obtain fraudulent documentation to show Canadian origin of the lobsters or use, time after time, the same bills of lading or certificates attesting to the Canadian origin of sub-sized lobsters. Between 1987 and 1989 there were relatively few convictions involving falsified documents or fraudulent reuse of originally legitimate documents.

3.5.18 Secondly, the 1989 amendment was expected to strengthen the conservation of U.S. lobster stocks by removing the lure of the already illegal market for sub-sized U.S. lobsters.

3.5.19 Thirdly, the 1989 amendment was expected to redress a perception of unfairness in the application of the federal size minima only to U.S. lobsters; there was among many American lobstermen a sense of being forced to comply with minimum lobster size requirements which were not required of Canadian lobstermen, a situation perceived as a competitive imbalance.

* * *

[The United States argued that the measure was not a quantitative restriction, because Canada was free to export lobsters to the United States, as long as they met the minimum size conditions. It argued that the real question was whether Canada was receiving national treatment under GATT article III, and that, because the size restrictions on the possession and marketing of sub-sized lobsters applied regardless of the lobster's country of origin, the measure was nondiscriminatory. Canada argued to the contrary that the measure constituted a quantitative restriction on the importation of small lobsters, because customs authorities could entirely prevent the importation of such lobsters.]

7.3.2 Article XI is the principal GATT Article containing the general ban against the use of [quantitative restrictions, or QRs] to limit importation. The measures that are banned are those that would be applied to goods at the point or time of importation, the measures often being referred to as "border" measures. * * *

7.3.3 Article III is the principal GATT Article limiting the use of "border" and "internal" measures on imported goods. The rule of "national" treatment that it specifies to carry out the competition principle noted earlier bars a country from extending internal measures to imported goods in a way that bears more onerously on the imported products than on the like domestic products. The basic principle and operating rules of Article III are framed in terms of safeguarding a competitive relationship for an imported product—whether the measures are applied to the imported product at the "border" or in the "internal" market.

* * *

<u>7.5 Are the U.S. measures formulated as internal or border measures?</u>

7.5.1 The Panel sought clarification of the statutory phraseology in the Magnuson Act, as amended, "interstate or foreign commerce" to ascertain whether that would indicate action at the border, as well as internally. The United States replied that the language did not mean that intervention was to be made at the border, although there was authorization to permit the measures to be applied there. Rather, the term "interstate or foreign commerce" is embedded in U.S. constitutional law and, in common with much other legislation, was used in the statute formally to assert the jurisdiction that the American federal government has to regulate commerce. Moreover, it said, any examination of the statute in the context of the present proceeding would be the same whether the phrase was or was not included in the statute. * * *

7.6.3 While the measures could be applied at the border or internally, it was the intention, expectation, and current policy to apply the U.S. measures internally. * * *

7.7.5 The Panel noted that enforcement might at times entail the cooperation of U.S. customs officers. Although the United States reported that those officers would not be stopping any shipments at the border, enforcement might be considered as entailing some measure of activity at the border. The Panel considered that even if the measures were imposed fully at the border, the measures would apply to domestic and Canadian lobsters, and would therefore be nonprotectionist measures of the kind covered by Article III.

7.8 Does the trade effect of a measure determine whether it is covered by Articles XI or III?

7.8.1 As between Articles XI and III, the Panel considered whether the effect on trade attributed to a measure imposed on imported products determines whether the measure is covered by one of these Articles rather than the other.

7.8.2 Both Articles express principles and set forth specific rules to limit the use of measures that affect the trade of the importing country. Essentially, Article XI prohibits certain techniques for limiting the quantity of foreign goods that may be imported (or domestic goods that may be exported); Article III bans the use of a wide range of measures that can affect the internal marketing, and consequently the importation, of foreign goods.

7.8.3 The trade effects on Canadian lobsters will not differ if the U.S. measures are determined to fall under one of these Articles rather than the other. Whether as Article XI measures on importation or as Article III measures on internal marketing, the U.S. limits on Canadian lobsters will have identical effects: imports of sub-sized lobsters will be zero.

* * *

7.9 In deciding possible coverage under Article XI or III, does it matter that the measures are a prohibition rather than a restriction?

7.9.1 The Panel considered whether the fact that a measure applied to an imported product as a prohibition to its internal marketing (whether applied at the border or internally) called for a determination different from that concerning a lesser measure, that is, a measure restricting but not prohibiting the marketing of the product. * * *

7.9.4 The degree to which the marketing prospects for an imported product would be "affected" might be greater under a prohibition than under a restriction, but the imported product would still be "affected." Moreover, a restriction imposed on the internal marketing of an imported product, depending on the circumstances, could be just as fatal commercially as a prohibition. Putting an annual import quota on widgets at 10,000 units when trade has been 80,000, or requiring a marking or packaging specification, can make sales just as difficult—or impossible—as setting a quota at zero.

7.9.5 Accordingly, the Panel considered that, for determining the possible application of Article XI:1 or Article III, the relative intensity, or absoluteness, of a measure (notably, a prohibition or a restriction) would not itself determine under which of these GATT provisions the measure would fall. Further, they believed that a measure imposed on imports, otherwise eligible for coverage under Article III, would not be disqualified from that coverage because it was a prohibition rather than a restriction. Conversely, a measure does not escape the coverage of one of these provisions or the other by being partially limiting rather than totally limiting. (Consistent with this view, the trade effects of the measure might or might not differ depending on the degree of restrictiveness, but that aspect concerns the separate issue of nullification or impairment of benefits and of a trade effects assessment.) * * *

7.22.2 The Panel determined that the U.S. measures imposed on live U.S. and Canadian lobsters were covered by Article III and not by Article XI. In particular, they considered that the measures, as now applied in the U.S. internal market, or as they might be imposed at the border, came within the scope of "laws, regulations requirements affecting the internal sale, offering for sale, purchase, transportation, distribution or use of products." The Panel made no determination as to whether these Article III measures were consistent with the national treatment requirements of that Article, since such a determination was outside the terms of reference laid down by the Parties.

* * *

11.2 <u>The view of the Panel as represented by the majority</u>

11.2.1 The majority view is that the U.S. measures are covered by Article III. This view is based on the Panel majority's determinations that the U.S. measures are internal—affecting the internal marketing of U.S.-origin and Canadian lobsters—and, consequently, are not subject to Article XI, which, in paragraph 1 sets down a prohibition on measures that apply only to imports and that apply at the time or point of importation. The fact that the United States may shift administration of the measures, in so far as they apply to Canadian lobsters, partially or fully toward imposing them at the time or point of importation would not itself mean that the measures were no longer covered by Article III, imposition at the border being expressly permitted by Article III.

11.2.2 The Panel view, as represented by the majority, is based in part on the conclusion that, in so far as imported goods are concerned, the GATT distinguishes between the principles and obligations in Article XI:1 and those of Article III according to whether governmental measures apply, on the one hand, only to imported goods at the time or point of importation and, on the other hand, both to imported goods (at the border or internally) and to domestic goods. * * *

Notes and Questions

1. In determining whether a measure of the importing state is unduly trade restrictive, should it matter whether the measure is applied at the border versus after the goods have entered the country's internal market? Why or why not?

2. Because not all Canadian lobsters fell below the size threshold, Canada could not argue that the United States had imposed a quantitative restriction on all Canadian lobster imports. If Canada had prevailed in characterizing the dispute as relating to GATT article XI, its case would have partly turned on whether, when we speak of a quantitative restriction on imports, the relevant class of "imports" is a general category such as "lobsters" or a specific category such as "lobsters below a certain size threshold." What might be the consequences of accepting the latter approach to determining when a state has adopted a prohibited quantitative restriction? Can you think of a *reductio ad absurdum* that would help clarify the limits of Canada's argument?

D. Other Disciplines

The GATT contains many other disciplines that affect the global trade in goods, and that are properly covered in a course on the public international law of trade. But several of these disciplines merit mention here, and more extended treatment later in the book, because of their important effect on international business transactions.

Some GATT disciplines are designed to facilitate the international movement of goods and services by harmonizing importation procedures. A wide diversity of import practices among the trading states causes uncertainty and imposes potentially unnecessary costs on international business. Because most states assess customs duties as a percentage of the value of the imported goods, the method states use for valuing imports may significantly affect the customs duties payable. GATT article VII includes some rules prescribing how states may assess the value of imported goods. In addition, for those states requiring that imported goods be marked with their country of origin, article IX of the GATT includes some disciplines to ensure that marking measures are used in a nondiscriminatory and least trade restrictive manner. In 1994, the GATT parties also adopted agreements on valuation, rules for determining the country of origin of products manufactured in multiple countries, and import licensing procedures. These will be discussed in Chapter 5, dealing with import and export regulation.

Other GATT disciplines are designed to preserve open trade against state measures other than customs duties and quantitative restrictions. These are the most direct form of protectionism, but states pursue a wide variety of public policies that may affect international trade. Most prominently, some states have adopted trade remedies measures by which they suspend normal trade regarding certain designated products. Trade remedies may serve an important economic function. They may protect intellectual property rights, ameliorate the effects of anticompetitive conduct, and protect vulnerable domestic industries from serious harm caused by market fluctuations in the international trade context.

Whatever their purpose, trade remedies typically result in increased import duties, quantitative restrictions, or supplementary taxes on imported goods. As such, they tend to affect international trade negatively and are regulated by GATT disciplines. GATT article VI provides rules for states that adopt trade remedies known as antidumping duties and countervailing duties. These are additional duties intended to offset predatory pricing in the first instance and foreign government subsidies for the imported products in the second instance. Article XVI contains specific rules on states that grant subsidies to their domestic industries. In addition, GATT art. XIX contains an "escape clause" that allows WTO members to temporarily suspend trade concessions when certain imports injure or threaten to injure domestic producers of the same or similar products. The GATT parties adopted three side agreements in 1994 that further elaborate rules for states using these trade remedies. These provisions and agreements will be discussed in Chapter 6, which deals with trade remedies regulation.

E. General Exceptions

The WTO Agreements do not unconditionally limit the state's ability to restrict international trade across its borders. The GATT includes several exceptions, not only to the nondiscrimination rules, but to the trade concessions more generally. Article XX sets forth broad exceptions to the trade disciplines discussed above. Among other exceptions, it includes the following:

Article XX: General Exceptions

> Subject to the requirement that such measures are not applied in a manner which would constitute a means of arbitrary or unjustifiable discrimination between countries where the same conditions prevail, or a disguised restriction on international trade, nothing in this Agreement shall be construed to prevent the adoption or enforcement by any contracting party of measures:
>
> (a) necessary to protect public morals;
>
> (b) necessary to protect human, animal or plant life or health;
>
> * * *
>
> (d) necessary to secure compliance with laws or regulations which are not inconsistent with the provisions of this Agreement * * *.
>
> * * *
>
> (g) relating to the conservation of exhaustible natural resources if such measures are made effective in conjunction with restrictions on domestic production or consumption;

In addition, Article XXI provides that nothing in the GATT may be construed to prevent a party from taking any action necessary for the protection to its "essential security interests."

The WTO dispute settlement panels have frequently shown skepticism toward the invocation of these exceptions. For example, in *United States—Import Prohibitions of Certain Shrimp and Shrimp Products*, WTO Doc. WT/DS58/AB/R (Oct. 12, 1998), several southeast Asian countries had complained of a U.S. ban on imports of shrimp from countries that did not require designated turtle excluder devices in their shrimp fishing fleets. Shrimp fishing is a major cause of the gradual extinction of the sea turtles that hunt the shrimp and are caught and drowned in fishing nets. To ameliorate this risk, the United States had adopted a policy requiring U.S. shrimp fishing vessels to use certain turtle-safe techniques and prohibiting imports from countries lacking comparable requirements. In defense of its measure, the United States invoked GATT article XX, paragraphs (b) and (g).

The complainants argued that article XX did not authorize any state to adopt trade-restrictive measures to conserve any plant or animal not found exclusively within the state's borders. The United States countered that conservation of sea turtles is a shared responsibility of all states, because the range of sea turtles extends throughout international waters and the waters of many states, including the United States. The Appellate Body agreed that measures taken for the conservation of exhaustible natural resources fell within the purview of article XX, but nonetheless found the measure unjustifiably discriminatory, because it "coerced" other WTO members into adopting conservation policies. In effect, the Appellate Body denied that WTO members have an unqualified right to unilaterally exclude imports obtained by environmentally destructive methods. The decision was harshly criticized by environmentalists and hardened many in their opposition to free trade agreements generally.

3.4 The WTO Side Agreements

Aside from the revised GATT and the Agreement Establishing the WTO, the Uruguay Round resulted in twenty-two additional understandings and agreements binding on all WTO members, as well as five other optional agreements on liberalization of specific industries and trade modalities.

One consequential instrument is the **Agreement on Technical Barriers to Trade** (**TBT Agreement**). The other important agreements for purposes of this subject are the **General Agreement on Trade in Services** (**GATS**), the **Agreement on Trade-Related Investment Measures** (**TRIMS**), and **Agreement on Trade-Related Aspects of Intellectual Property Rights** (**TRIPS**). These will be summarized here, with more detailed discussions as the agreements become relevant to specific topics discussed in later chapters.

A. The Agreement on Technical Barriers to Trade

States regulate product quality and technical standards for many reasons, including consumer safety, product reliability, energy efficiency, conveying adequate information to consumers through product labeling requirements, etc. For example, different countries use different voltage and socket types in their public electricity systems, and they may understandably seek to ensure that electrical products sold in the country have compatible voltage inputs and plugs. The TBT Agreement imposes disciplines on national product specification rules that affect imports from other WTO contracting parties.

Most of these disciplines are concerned that such specifications do not artificially distort international trade. The main rules appear in article 2:

> **Article 2: Preparation, Adoption and Application of Technical Regulations by Central Government Bodies**
>
> With respect to their central government bodies:
>
> 2.1 Members shall ensure that in respect of technical regulations, products imported from the territory of any Member shall be accorded treatment no less favourable than that accorded to like products of national origin and to like products originating in any other country.
>
> 2.2 Members shall ensure that technical regulations are not prepared, adopted or applied with a view to or with the effect of creating unnecessary obstacles to international trade. For this purpose, technical regulations shall not be more trade-restrictive than necessary to fulfil a legitimate objective, taking account of the risks non-fulfilment would create. Such legitimate objectives are, *inter alia*: national security requirements; the prevention of deceptive practices; protection of human health or safety, animal or plant life or health, or the environment. In assessing such risks, relevant elements of consideration are, *inter alia*: available scientific and technical information, related processing technology or intended end-uses of products.
>
> 2.3 Technical regulations shall not be maintained if the circumstances or objectives giving rise to their adoption no longer exist or if the changed circumstances or objectives can be addressed in a less trade-restrictive manner.
>
> 2.4 Where technical regulations are required and relevant international standards exist or their completion is imminent, Members shall use them, or the relevant parts of them, as a basis for their technical regulations except when such international standards or relevant parts would be an ineffective or inappropriate means for the fulfilment of the legitimate objectives pursued, for instance because of fundamental climatic or geographical factors or fundamental technological problems.

The goal of these provisions is to ensure that technical regulations of products do not pose unnecessary barriers to international trade.

Like all of the WTO agreements, the TBT Agreement does not impose obligations directly on private manufacturers. Nothing in the treaty requires a business firm to conform its product to a specific international technical standard, for example. However, because the Agreement makes it more likely that states will adopt such standards into their domestic laws, manufacturing firms and agribusinesses are well advised to pay attention to them.

B. The General Agreement on Trade in Services

Before 1994, the world trading system applied only to the cross-border movement of goods. But services can be traded internationally as well, and the Uruguay Round brought services within the scope of the world trading system for the first time. The GATS imposes disciplines on WTO members relative to the cross-border transfer of services, regardless of whether the service is performed remotely or in the host state. Like the GATT, the GATS has a nondiscrimination obligation; it imposes an MFN obligation on member states with respect to foreign service providers in article II.

However, the GATS does not require automatic market access to all services that may cross state boundaries. Instead, the GATS is designed to allow WTO members to subject specific service sectors (such as higher education, retails sales, or courier services) to foreign market access and national treatment commitments. This means that WTO members may decide not to make market access or other trade concessions with respect to other service sectors.

The GATS does this by requiring WTO members to submit a "positive list" of service sectors to which foreign market access and national treatment obligations will apply, called a **Schedule of Commitments**. Each WTO member's Schedule of Commitments lists the service sectors that will be open to foreign trade and investment, and the limitations the member state intends to impose on foreign access to that market and on national treatment. A member state may provide in its Schedule for almost any limitations it wishes on access to a service sector, as long as these limitations are consistent with its article II MFN obligations and all regulations are administered "in a reasonable, objective, and impartial manner." GATS art. VI:1.

The GATS, unlike the GATT, does not necessarily require states to afford national treatment to imports of services from other WTO members. Although a commitment to provide market access without restrictions to foreign service providers in the Schedule of Commitments calls into play a national treatment obligation with regard to that specific service sector under article XVII, a WTO member can avoid a national treatment obligation either by (1) not listing a service sector on its Schedule in the first place, or (2) by expressly stating a denial of national treatment for that sector in the Schedule.

One common exception to national treatment, for example, is a local training or education requirement. Most states do not allow doctors, lawyers, or other professionals to practice within their territory until earning a degree from a local school or passing a qualifying examination. This practice ensures that foreign nationals have met the same training standards in the provision

HOW ARE SERVICES "TRADED" INTERNATIONALLY?

Services may be traded internationally in three ways: through the movement of *persons*, *products*, or *information*.

First, individuals provide international services whenever they travel from one state to another in order to provide the service in person. For example, if the government of Ruritania hires a Freedonian petroleum engineer to conduct oil exploration in Ruritania, the engineer must travel to Ruritania to perform the service. Ruritania has imported a service from Freedonia.

Second, cross-border services can be provided through products, such as when a Sylvanian design company hires a Zembian contract manufacturer to produce goods to the Sylvanian company's design that are owned by the design company throughout the process. Although goods may pass from Zembia to Sylvania, it is really the manufacturing service performed in Zembia that is being exported to Sylvania. Similarly, if an Osterlich airline delivers a commercial aircraft to Zembia for a modification, the modification is a service exported from Zembia to Osterlich.

Finally, when a business firm in Pottsylvania generates and sends information to a different firm in Smalldonia, it has exported a service as well. For example, a Pottsylvanian software engineer who remotely manages a Smalldonian Web server, or a Pottsylvanian customer service representative who assists customers of a Smalldonian business firm by telephone, are exporting services to Smalldonia in the form of transfers of information.

of services as domestic nationals. Such requirements may be specified in the Schedule of Commitments and are expressly allowed under GATS article VII. Nonetheless, any time a state lists a service sector in its Schedule of Commitments without any expressly qualification, it will be deemed to have agreed to market access commitments (GATS art. XVI) and national treatment obligations (GATS art. XVII) with regard to that sector.

Indeed, an unqualified commitment to open a sector listed in the Schedule of Commitments also entails multiple market access consequences. In case of such an unqualified commitment, the WTO member may not restrict:

- the number of foreign service suppliers or of their employees allowed to compete on its market;
- the value of foreign services provided, the amount of assets invested in the services, or the quantity of services provided;

- the type of legal entity or joint venture that the foreign service provider uses to provide the service, either from a foreign state or on the host state market; or
- the extent to which foreign investors may provide capital for the provision of services on the host state market.

Id. art. XVI(2). Again, WTO members are free to derogate from these obligations in the Schedule of Commitments, but only if any derogations are explicitly laid out in the Schedule. WTO members may modify their schedules from time to time following notice to other WTO members and the negotiation of offsetting trade concessions. *Id.* art. XXI.

The GATS requirement of reasonable, objective, and impartial administration of services regulations means that the GATS is concerned not just with promises of access to service markets, but fair and impartial enforcement of service regulations in practice. For example, in most countries, the government requires that service providers obtain some kind of local or national license to provide various kinds of services. A company wishing to provide banking services must comply with extensive licensing and supervision requirements by the finance ministry, central bank, or other regulatory authority in most states. In opening the banking sector to trade under its Schedule of Commitments, a WTO member must ensure that licensing requirements are transparent and unbiased against foreign service providers, that the grant or denial of a license is fairly expeditious, and that a denial includes an explanation. *Id.* art. VI.

Under the GATS, international trade has been liberalized for a wide range of services. However, most states also have declined to include many service sectors in the GATS Schedule, or have heavily qualified the market access right through exceptions and conditions listed in the Schedule. An international business lawyer always consults the GATS Schedule of Commitments in evaluating the risks and opportunities of a foreign investment involving the provision of services.

C. The Agreement on Trade-Related Investment Measures

The TRIMS Agreement is not a general international investment treaty. Instead, it limits the ability of WTO members to disadvantage foreign investment within their territories through certain kinds of trade restrictions and discrimination. Specifically, the TRIMS Agreement applies only to the state regulation of investment insofar as it affects international trade in goods.

The TRIMS Agreement contains only a few basic commitments. First, it requires WTO members to afford national treatment to foreign investments affecting trade. In other words, the TRIMs Agreement provides that, in regulating investments, a WTO member will not impose any regulation on foreign investors that is more burdensome than the regulations imposed on domestic investors.

For example, suppose Pottsylvania, the host state for a foreign investment, wanted to ensure that the profits from the foreign investment stayed within Pottsylvania. To achieve this objective, Pottsylvania enacts a law requiring foreign-owned or foreign-controlled enterprises operating within its territory to reinvest at least 50% of their net profits within Pottsylvania. Unless this requirement applied equally to local business firms in Pottsylvania, if it affects trade in goods, it would constitute unfavorable discrimination against investments originating in the investor state in violation of the national treatment obligation.

The TRIMS Agreement also prohibits quantitative restrictions on the importation of goods that may be used in the foreign investment, such as the inputs for use in manufacturing goods for export to other countries. An annex to the TRIMS Agreement gives examples of measures that might be inconsistent with TRIMS disciplines, including requiring that goods manufactured in the territory of a WTO member have a minimum percentage of local materials, components, or other content. The point of such measures is to ensure that states do not impose burdens on foreign investors that would distort trade flows between WTO members.

Unlike the GATT, the TRIMS Agreement does not require uniform MFN treatment. It is possible under the TRIMS Agreement for a state to give more preferential treatment to investments from some countries than others, as long as the state complies with the national treatment obligation. Any preferential treatment in the importation of goods, however, must comply with the GATT disciplines, which *are* subject to the general MFN obligation of GATT article I.

The TRIMs Agreement sets relatively low minimum standards of treatment for foreign investments. The reasons for the failure of TRIMs Agreement negotiations to create a strong and uniform standard of investment protection are complex, but the short explanation is that foreign investment is a sensitive issue for most countries, implicating their national pride and control over the domestic economy. And, especially when powerful foreign investors bring great wealth into an impoverished country for investment, there is the ever-present temptation for the investor to abuse its power in the local economy. These tensions illustrate the difficulty of finding a durable balance between the kinds of protection for foreign investments that would encourage the efficient international movement of capital and satisfy the sense of justice of capital-exporting states while encouraging healthy economic growth and political independence in capital-importing states.

D. The Agreement on Trade-Related Aspects of Intellectual Property Rights

The WTO Agreements also include the most comprehensive multilateral intellectual property (IP) treaty in the world, the TRIPS Agreement. The TRIPS Agreement will be discussed in some detail in the next chapter, but here it is helpful to mention the treaty's scope. Before the TRIPS Agreement, the multilateral treaties on IP protection dealt with only some fields of IP, such as copyright or trademarks. The TRIPS Agreement, in contrast, commits WTO members to adopt a broad range of IP protections and harmonizes those protections significantly. The treaty sets forth binding standards for copyright, trademarks, utility patents, industrial designs, trade secrets, and special topics such as geographical indications and semiconductor designs. It also includes standards for IP law enforcement both in courts and at the national border, as well as rules on anticompetitive practices in IP licensing.

Like the GATT, the TRIPS Agreement includes both an MFN (article 4) and national treatment (article 3) obligation to prevent discrimination in IP measures. Unlike the GATT, which sets maximum limits on customs duties, the TRIPS Agreement sets *minimum* standards for the protection of intellectual property (article 1). States are free to provide greater protection to IP, and some have done so. Finally, it is helpful to note that, unlike the TRIMS Agreement and GATS, the TRIPS Agreement does not entirely stand alone. Many of the provisions simply incorporate provisions of other, older IP treaties by reference. That is why, to really understand how the TRIPS Agreement works, it is important to study it in connection with the other major IP harmonization treaties, as we will do in Chapter 3.

3.5 Dispute Resolution under the WTO Agreements

One of the most remarkable innovations of the WTO Agreements was the adoption of a binding dispute settlement mechanism. Before the conclusion of the Uruguay Round, GATT parties resolved their disputes under the vague procedures of GATT article XXIII. That article provides for the submission of disputes to the GATT contracting parties, or a complaint panel consisting of a subset appointed by the chairman, if a state alleges that a benefit guaranteed by the treaty has been "nullified or impaired" by other party. The parties would consider the complaint and issue a recommendation, which the party complained of could choose to block, because such decisions were made by consensus. Moreover, because Article XXIII had no fixed timetable, disputes frequently dragged on for many years.

The long delays, ability of parties to block adverse recommendations, and consequent battles of tit-for-tat sanctions eventually began to undermine the very concessions that the GATT was designed encourage. To address these problems, the parties sought during the Uruguay Round a more stable mechanism for determining noncompliance and authorizing sanctions. The result is the Understanding on Rules and Procedures Governing the Settlement of Disputes, commonly known as the **Dispute Settlement Understanding** (**DSU**).

The DSU represented a radical change in how disputes are resolved under the GATT (and the other Uruguay Round agreements, such as the GATS and TRIPS Agreement). Under the DSU, consultations and complaint procedures follow a strict timetable. Parties unable to resolve their disputes amicably may request the appointment of a panel of the WTO's **Dispute Settlement Body (DSB)**. The panel will review the complaint and rebuttal, conduct a hearing, and eventually issue a binding report that cannot be blocked by the respondent. Only the DSB acting unanimously may block a panel report. If the report is adopted as a ruling, it will either find or not find a violation of WTO disciplines. If a violation should be found, there are no damages awarded to the complaining member. The remedies are all prospective; the DSB will merely recommend that the WTO member bring itself into compliance with its obligations. Each side may appeal the ruling to a panel of the DSB's **Appellate Body**, which may uphold, modify, or reverse the panel's legal findings. This ruling, should the DSB not unanimously reject it, is final and binding.

If the target of a complaint fails to adopt measure in conformity to a DSB ruling, the DSB may authorize the aggrieved WTO member to retaliate by withdrawing equivalent trade concessions until the other member complies. For example, when the United States was found in violation of its GATS obligations in the gambling sector, and it refused to alter its online gambling laws, the DSB authorized Antigua and Barbuda to retaliate by suspending equivalent intellectual property protection for U.S. companies.* The record of compliance with DSB rulings is very high at the WTO, though. In nearly every case in which the DSB has found a violation, the accused member has indicated its intention to comply with the DSB's ruling.** As a result, business firms can generally rely on WTO commitments as an indicator of how states will behave in regulating private international business transactions.

4 Regional and Bilateral Trade Agreements

Notwithstanding the complexity of the WTO system, that system represents only part of the international law that governs global trade, as Chapter 1 suggested. In addition to the global system is a network of regional and bilateral common markets, customs unions, and free trade agreements (FTAs) that further reduce trade barriers between specific parties.

It may seem odd, given GATT article I's MFN principle, that trade may be liberalized more between a subset of the WTO members than with respect to the WTO membership as a whole. After all, MFN by definition means that any concession a WTO member grants to any country must be granted to all WTO members equally. But, as noted in Section 3.3.B above, GATT article XXIV creates exceptions to MFN principles, among others for regional trading arrangements that lower trade barriers within the free trade area without raising them with regard to other WTO members.

**United States—Measures Affecting the Cross-Border Supply of Gambling and Betting Services*, DS285, Panel Decision of Jan. 28, 2013.

**Bruce Wilson, *Compliance by WTO Members with Adverse WTO Dispute Settlement Rulings: The Record to Date*, 10 J. INT'L ECON. L. 397 (2007).

Regional and bilateral trading arrangements are very common today. More than half of all WTO members are currently parties to three or more regional trading agreements. For example, the United States in 2020 had the USMCA, as well as bilateral FTAs with twenty countries. Chapter 1 of this book already introduced you to such regional trading arrangements as the EU, MERCOSUR, and ASEAN. These arrangements lower customs duties and grant other trade advantages beyond those in the WTO Agreements. The prevalence of such "WTO-plus" regional trading arrangements creates a kind of paradox. A WTO member benefiting from "most favored nation" status under GATT article I does not in fact receive the best trading concessions granted by most other WTO members. Other states with customs union agreements or FTAs with a WTO member will receive better treatment from the member.

How are regional FTAs different from the WTO Agreements? The general answer is that every FTA is individually negotiated by its parties, and so no two FTAs are entirely identical. However, there are strong trends. Like the GATT, regional and bilateral FTAs necessarily include nondiscrimination obligations, both MFN and national treatment. In addition, consistent with GATT article XXIV, they eliminate customs duties on the great majority (not necessarily all) imports originating in the parties to the treaty, and generally forbid the reintroduction of or any increase in existing customs duties. The GATT reduces customs duties between the contracting states; customs unions and FTAs mostly eliminate them. These are the most fundamental tenets of any FTA.

In addition, modern FTAs contain a plethora of provisions facilitating international trade, dealing with such topics as temporary imports, export restrictions, agricultural subsidies, port fees, and licensing of imports. Some FTAs, such as those of the United States, also include a large number of chapters on specific topics that liberalize trade beyond the disciplines of the WTO Agreements. These may include such topics as trade in services, trade remedies, government purchasing, antitrust and competition policy, measures to protect the environment and human health, and intellectual property protection. They also include special rules for politically sensitive industries such as textiles and apparel, telecommunications, financial services, and issues that may arise between the specific parties to the agreement. Some include general expressions of concern for labor, the environment, and human rights. Many of these topics are not covered by the WTO Agreements, because the parties to the Uruguay Round of negotiations could not agree on their inclusion.

Finally, unlike the WTO Agreements, modern FTAs frequently include a chapter on the protection of foreign investments. These chapters tend to replicate the provisions of existing bilateral investment treaties, and so they will be discussed together with that subject, below.

5 Foreign Investment Treaties

5.1 What Is Foreign Investment?

The laws of almost every state make it is possible for a foreign investor to set up a business within that state's territory through a local office, business organization, or joint venture* with a local firm. **Foreign direct investment** (**FDI**) means the active commitment and management of assets in a foreign country for purposes of earning a return.** More specifically, foreign investment is usually considered to have four elements:

(1) an investor's contribution of capital to an investment project,
(2) a time period during which a profit is expected to result,
(3) in which the investor undertakes operational risks, and
(4) with the result of contributing to the economic development of the host state.***

A contract for the sale of goods to a foreign country would not generally qualify as a foreign investment; a greater commitment of resources and acceptance of risk is necessary. The national recipient of foreign investment is called the **host state**, and the national source is the **investor state**.

When a business firm seeks to expand its operations to a foreign state through FDI, it has many options that range from setting up shop directly in the foreign state through a local branch office to setting up a complex network of foreign subsidiary companies to do business abroad. It may seek to commence foreign operations by itself, or it may partner with an unaffiliated local company through a "joint venture." It may orient its foreign operations toward manufacturing goods for importation or providing services back to its domestic market, or it may seek to fulfill demand for goods or services in the market of the host state itself, or in the global market more broadly.

Cross-border investment in economically developed countries has increased rapidly since the close of the Second World War. The United Nations estimates that total FDI worldwide exceeded $1.4 trillion in value in 2017, most of it in developed states.**** Every year, foreign business firms invest many billions of dollars in the United States, and U.S. firms invest similarly in foreign countries. Through foreign investment, business firms may manufacture goods

*A **joint venture** (**JV**) is a business firm owned by two or more unaffiliated parties, usually through the creation of a separate, jointly-owned subsidiary. A JV allows the parties to pool their resources in pursuit of a mutually beneficial enterprise.

***Malaysian Historical Salvors v. Malaysia*, Award of Apr. 16, 2009, ¶ 57, ICSID Case No. ARB/05/10, 48 I.L.M. 1086 (2009).

****See Salini Costruttori S.p.A. v. Morocco*, ICSID Case No. ARB/00/4, Decision of July 23, 2001 (Juris.).

****UNITED NATIONS CONFERENCE ON TRADE AND DEVELOPMENT, WORLD INVESTMENT REPORT 2018: KEY MESSAGES AND OVERVIEW at viii.

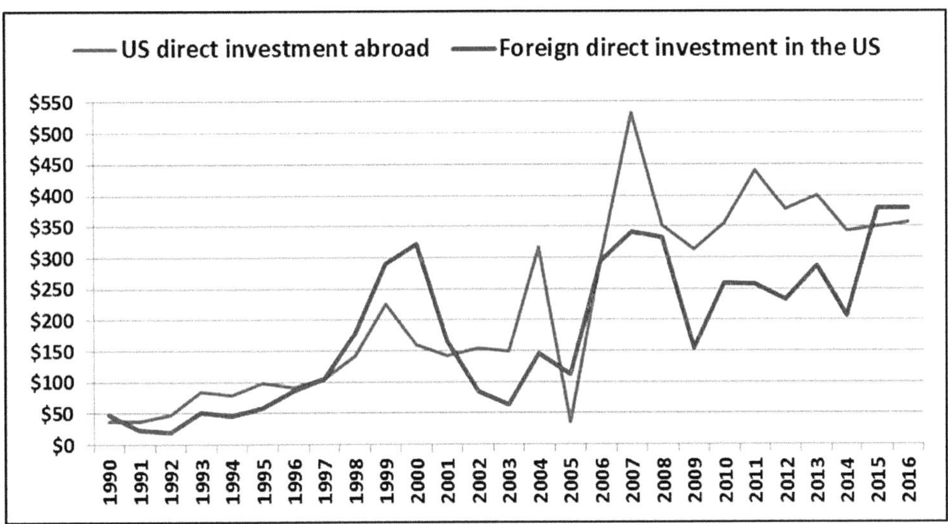

Source: U.S. Department of Commerce.

Figure 2.4. Foreign direct investment in the United States, and U.S. direct investment abroad in annual flows by billions of dollars, from 1990 to 2016.

abroad; build major infrastructure; extract and process natural resources; and provide services in such sectors as tourism, banking and finance, telecommunications, insurance, marketing, and computer programming.

Cross-border investment is often facilitated and sustained by international treaties designed to protect foreign investments from certain risks associated with doing business abroad. One problem facing both private investors and states seeking to attractive private investment is moral hazard. **Moral hazard** occurs when a person takes more risks or accepts greater costs because that person knows someone else will bear them. When he runs no risks himself and lacks any material incentive to act in the interests of others, a person (or state) may behave selfishly. The difficulty is that a private investor from one country may go to great effort and incur great expense to set up an investment in another. Once the efforts have been made and funds invested, the host state may adopt measures that cause the investor to lose some or all of the value of its investment. In the absence of international law to protect the investor, the host state knows the investor has no legal recourse except to its own courts, where the state may be biased against foreign investors, corrupt, or simply immune to judicial jurisdiction.

Suppose Investco Ltd., a Freedonian corporation, incorporates a subsidiary in Ruritania to distill schnapps. It calls its investment entity Investco Ruritania Ltd. (IRL). It contributes millions of dollars of its own capital to assist IRL to lease land, construct a distillery, acquire inputs, hire labor, and market its resulting schnapps. Further suppose the government of Ruritania, like many state governments, benefits from sovereign immunity before its own courts. If, after Investo has sunk its capital into its the distillery, the government of Ruritania were to decide that it wished to expropriate the plant for itself, what legal remedy would Investco have? Its only option would be to seek a remedy in the courts of another state, such as Freedonia. But these courts might decline to exercise municipal jurisdiction over a foreign sovereign as well. In this scenario, Investco could be left with no legal remedy, and Ruritania would have no immediate disincentive to harm Investco for its own benefit.

In practice, Ruritania does have some indirect disincentives to harm foreign investments. If foreign investors observe that Ruritania refuses to respect foreign-owned investments, then cautious investors will decline to risk their assets in Ruritania, and Ruritania will face difficulty in attracting new foreign investments in the future. Because foreign investment is desirable to all countries that seek economic growth, reputational risks put a natural constraint on selfish behavior toward foreign investors by rational host states.

The reputational constraint is imperfect, however, for several reasons. One is that host states sometimes act irrationally. In most countries, governments are temporary. A state government may harm a foreign investment for a short-term gain, knowing full well that it will reduce future foreign investment in the future, but caring little, because the negative consequences to the economy from reduced foreign investment will fall on a future government rather than on itself. Another is that a host state that selectively and unfairly harms only a few foreign investments may not raise a red flag high enough to deter investors who are less cautious, or who underestimate their chances of being victimized themselves by the government.

The most direct way to cope with the problem of moral hazard is to remove the host state's incentive for opportunism by imposing legal obligations to respect the investment and compensate any loss caused by breach of contract, discrimination, expropriation, or other act unfairly targeting foreign investments. States have an incentive to enter into credible legal commitments to respect foreign investment, because they know foreign investors will be reassured by such commitments and invest there more readily. States commonly use treaties to constrain themselves and other states in pursuit of long-term advantages.

Yet, there is no single multilateral treaty or convention that addresses foreign investment issues comprehensively. As you have seen, the TRIMS Agreement deals only with certain aspects of foreign investment that affect international trade. The year after the Uruguay Round of trade negotiations was concluded, therefore, the Organization for Economic Cooperation and Development (OECD) attempted to launch negotiations for a Multilateral Agreement on Investment (MAI). Its goal was to set a high standard for the protection of international investments in general. The MAI was based on the investment provisions of the North American Free Trade Agreement, but negotiations were discontinued in 1998 after the OECD's ambitious agenda

Policy Issue

The pros and cons of a global investment treaty

Proponents of a global investment treaty argue that it would bring many benefits to both developed and developing countries. First, it would simplify doing international business, because a single treaty could replace a network of thousands of treaties between various countries. This would increase the efficiency of international trade and investment with gains for everyone. Second, a global treaty would foster transparency in corporate regulation and protect investors from unfair government actions (such as nationalistic discrimination or expropriation) in host states that are not bound by a current investment treaty. Third, by leveling the playing field in investment risk, it would provide a framework to help global investors direct their capital to the most productive markets, which would tend to benefit developing countries where investors fear to commit their funds because of uncertain protections against government abuse. Finally, proponents claim that the increased foreign investment that would result from such a treaty would encourage technology transfer from advanced states to developing countries, as high technology firms invested their capital in new facilities and training local personnel.

Opponents view any such gains as doubtful and likely to subsumed by various harms. They contend, first, that a global treaty will be used by powerful corporations to prevent states from regulating the marketplace for the health and safety of consumers, fair wages for employees, and protection of the environment. They point to several cases in which such regulations have already been found inconsistent with the WTO Agreements. Second, because the proponents of a global investment treaty typically argue that the treaty should not address such matters as competition law, labor rights, minimum wages, or environmental protection, a global investment treaty will promote a "race to the bottom," as states compete for foreign investment capital by lowering standards of protection. Third, encouraging foreign investment necessarily will result in capital flight toward countries with low wages, resulting in more lost jobs and pressure to lower wages in developed countries.

In short, proponents of a global investment treaty base most of their arguments on economic efficiency and fairness to investors, while opponents base most of their arguments on protection of core democratic values such as human and worker rights, consumer safety, and environmental preservation for future generations. There will always be tradeoffs in international investment policy. Is there some way to achieve the aspirations of both sides?

failed to attract sufficient consensus in the international community. Developing countries import far more foreign investment capital than wealthy countries relative to their national incomes (which is why they are sometimes called **capital-importing states**) and would not agree to standards of investment protection demanded by states that export more investment than they receive from their wealthier counterparts (**capital-exporting states**). The MAI negotiations appear to have little immediate future, and so the FDI gap in multilateral treaties remains.

5.2 Bilateral Investment Treaties

This does not mean that there are no international treaties regulating the treatment of foreign investments. On the contrary, there are many such treaties, in some cases reaching back hundreds of years. **Treaties of friendship, commerce, and navigation** (**FCN treaties**)* are among the most venerable bilateral treaties dealing with foreign investment. They were in widespread use long before modern investment treaties became common. The first U.S. FCN treaty was concluded in 1778 with France, and the United States ratified its last FCN treaty in 1967. As of 2020, the United States remains a party to thirty-five separate FCN treaties.

Most FCN treaties contain diverse clauses relating to bilateral trade; access to territorial seas, ports, and inland waterways; and friendly diplomatic relations. More recent FCN treaties typically add provisions relevant to international investment, such as:

- a provision establishing a right of nationals of each state to own property in the other state;
- a prohibition on taking property without due process of law or payment of just compensation;
- a guarantee of protection and security of the property of the nationals of each state in the other; and
- a mutual prohibition of government discrimination against the nationals of the other state.

FCN treaties never became very widespread, with the consequence that much foreign investment around the world remained subject to moral hazard. Socialist states and developing countries did not always resist the temptation to seize the property of foreign nationals for themselves. In 1959, two major events changed the landscape of international investment law. The first was the Cuban Revolution, during which Prime Minister Fidel Castro expropriated all assets of U.S. companies in Cuba, valued at some $9 billion at the time (equivalent to $78 billion in 2020), and refused to compensate the dispossessed

*The FCN treaty goes by many names, such as Treaty of Amity and Commerce or Treaty of Amity and Cooperation. Here, we will call them FCN treaties for convenience.

owners. These companies had created jobs in Cuba, but Castro claimed they had acted "contrary to the interests of the revolution and the economic development of the country." The second event was the Brazilian seizure of a U.S. electricity company, also without compensation. In neither case could U.S. investors claim the benefits of a modern FCN treaty.

A. "Investors" and "Investments"

These takings deterred future foreign investment in the short term, and they galvanized aggrieved investor states, especially the United States and the European states, to develop new methods of investment protection through public international law. Since 1959, capital-exporting states have undertaken an active program of negotiating bilateral or regional treaties to protect investors and to ensure a more or less even playing field between their investors and the nationals of the host state. The most common form of treaty, the **bilateral investment treaty** (**BIT**), covers only investments between the nationals of the two state parties. BITs began to become common after 1959 as a means to encourage foreign investment. Although the great majority of global investment is between developed states, most of these already have strong legal protections for foreign investors. Consequently, most BITs are between capital-importing states on one side and capital-exporting states on the other.

Modern BITs are quite complex, but they have three main purposes. First, they establish nondiscrimination principles for the treatment of investments in the state parties. This is of course something the TRIMS Agreement does as well, but the latter is limited to measures that affect trade. Second, BITs guarantee a minimum standard of protection of foreign investments in the territory of the state parties to the treaty, even if they are not related to international trade in goods. The protection relates most obviously to state expropriation of the investment, but it also includes more general standards of fair treatment. Finally, BITs usually establish a mechanism to resolve disputes between the investor and the host state. This mechanism helps overcome the moral hazard with which foreign investment tempts host states, and it makes FDI sufficiently secure to protect foreign investors if a host state should violate its treaty commitments.

Who Qualifies as a Foreign Investor?

Because BITs are designed to reduce the risks of *foreign* direct investment, they do not protect citizens of the host state from measures by their own government. In other words, the "foreign-ness" of an investment relates to the foreign nationality of the investor rather than any attribute of the investment itself. When a foreign investment is undertaken by a business organization having independent personality, such as a corporation, what determines its nationality? Consider three scenarios for an investment operating in Smalldonia:

HOW COMMON ARE BITS?

More than a bit. The first modern BIT was signed in 1959 between Germany and Pakistan, and the use of BITs since then has ballooned. As of 2020, there were 2,369 BITs in effect, according to the United Nations Conference on Trade and Development. When you consider that there are fewer than 200 countries in the world, that means on average every country in the world is a party to BITs with about twelve other countries. This "spaghetti bowl" of treaties between the world's states creates a complex network of international investment obligations. The United States is a party to numerous BITs with countries from Albania to Ukraine, and it is negotiating more constantly. BITs are, in short, one of the most common forms of treaty in the world.

1. A corporation formed under the laws of Smalldonia has its headquarters in Grand Fenwick and is entirely owned by Ruritanian nationals.
2. A corporation formed under the laws of Grand Fenwick has its headquarters in Smalldonia and is entirely owned by Ruritanian nationals.
3. A corporation formed under the laws of Ruritania has its headquarters in Ruritania and is entirely owned by Smalldonian nationals.

In which of these examples is the investment entitled to protection as "foreign?" The answer depends in part on the specific treaty protecting the investment, but there are overarching principles of public international law, as well as definite trends in investment treaties, that guide the answer.

Most BITs define the nationality of a business firm as the place of its incorporation or where it has its head office. However, because foreign investment is often undertaken through a separate business entity incorporated in the host state, the question of nationality raises a potentially important problem. In *The Case Concerning Barcelona Traction, Light & Power Co., Ltd.*, 1970 I.C.J. REP. 3, the International Court of Justice held that, when a state harms a business firm in that state's own territory, only the state in which the firm was incorporated has the right to represent the interests of that firm under international law. The shareholders have no cognizable legal interest unless their direct rights as shareholders are harmed (for example, through an expropriation of their dividends). This holding implies that, if Ruritanian nationals invest in a corporation in Smalldonia, Ruritania has no authority to demand compensation when the Smalldonian government adopts a measure harmful to the corporation, because it is a case of Smalldonia harming a Smalldonian company.

BITs adopt the opposite approach. Because the very purpose of a BIT is to encourage foreign investment, it extends protection to the investors of each party as well as the investments themselves. Therefore, under a Ruritania-Smalldonia BIT, Ruritanian investors, even minority shareholders, have standing to complain of a harm to a separate business entity they incorporated in Smalldonia.*

That said, the international investment law jurisprudence is not perfectly consistent on all points. For example, in *Venoklim Holdings B.V. v. Venezuela*, ICSID Case No. ARB/12/22 (Apr. 3, 2015), an investment tribunal construed the Netherlands-Venezuela BIT to protect only "international investors" against acts by the Venezuelan government. The tribunal reasoned that "international investors" did not include a Dutch investor corporation owned by Venezuelan nationals. Although the treaty did not expressly exclude such entities from protection, the tribunal believed that any other interpretation would sacrifice substance to form. The BIT's protections, it held, were intended to resolve disputes between states and foreign investors, not between states and their own nationals, even if those nationals acted through a foreign intermediary.

Which approach do you think best balances the host state's interest in freely regulating the economic activities of its own nationals with the investor state's interest in protecting investment entities formed under its laws?

What Is a Foreign Investment?

Most BITs define the "investments" covered by the treaty to include a very wide variety of business enterprises run by the nationals of one state in the territory of another. Covered investments include newly formed business firms, securities such as stocks and bonds, tangible property, intellectual property rights, and certain intangible rights. Ordinary commercial transactions, such as purchases or sales of goods or services, are generally not considered investments per se.

Some international transactions, such as the construction or acquisition of manufacturing plants or the purchase of shares of a corporation, clearly qualify as "investments" in the host state. Others, such as the acquisition of a debt instrument, are harder to classify. The following case grapples with one such instance.

*See, e.g., Gemin v. Estonia, Award of June 25, 2001, para. 324, 6 ICSID Rep. 241; CMS v. Argentina, Decision on Juris. of July 17, 2003, paras. 48-51, 42 I.L.M. 2003.

DEUTSCHE BANK AG v. SRI LANKA

International Centre for the Settlement of Investment Disputes
Case No. ARB/09/02

Award of Oct. 31, 2012

* * *

6. The dispute has its origins in an oil Hedging Agreement dated 8 July 2008 (the "Hedging Agreement" or the "Agreement") between Deutsche Bank [a private German bank] and Ceylon Petroleum Corporation ("CPC"), Sri Lanka's national petroleum corporation.

7. Deutsche Bank submits that Sri Lanka has violated Articles 2, 3, 4 and 8 of the Treaty between the Federal Republic of Germany and the Democratic Socialist Republic of Sri Lanka concerning the Promotion and Reciprocal Protection of Investments of 7 June 2000 (the "BIT" or "Treaty"). This is disputed by Respondent.

[The Hedging Agreement was intended to protect Sri Lanka against deviations in the price of oil. Under the Agreement, if the monthly price of oil rose above a benchmark established in the Agreement, Deutsche Bank would pay the difference to CPC. However, if the price of oil fell below the benchmark, CPC was to pay the difference to Deutsche Bank. After the Agreement came into force, when the price of oil rose above the benchmark, Deutsche Bank duly made payments to the CPC. When prices fell, CPC made an initial payment to Deutsche Bank, but then stopped. Deutsche Bank invoked the dispute resolution provisions of the BIT, claiming expropriation of its investment in Sri Lanka. Sri Lanka denied that the Agreement qualified as an investment.]

* * *

130. The Treaty provides in its Article 1 that for the purposes of this Treaty:

> *"1. The term "investments" comprises every kind of asset, in particular: ...*
> *c) claims to money which has been used to create an economic value or claims to any performance having an economic value and associated with an investment; ...".*

* * *

219. According to Respondent, it is therefore not enough to have a claim to money, that claim must have been "used to create an economic value" or must have derived from "performance having an economic value," and it must be "associated with an investment." Respondent argues that by clear inference, claims to money under a contract are not, as such, investments under the BIT. In this case, the Hedging Agreement was not part of a larger aggregate of activities constituting an "investment." It was a stand-alone financial product.

* * *

132. According to Claimant, the Hedging Agreement satisfies the definition of investment under Article 1(1) of the Treaty. This Article provides that the term "investments"

comprises "every kind of asset" before setting out a list of illustrative categories. Claimant submits that the Hedging Agreement is an asset, it is legal property with economic value for Deutsche Bank that booked the Agreement as an asset at fair value in its accounts.

133. Claimant further submits that Article 1(1)(c) is simply an illustration of the reference to "every kind of asset". According to Claimant, the wording of Article 1(1)(c) cannot be read, as alleged by Respondent, as requiring the receivables or claims to performance to be associated with a separate investment in order to qualify for protection. Such an interpretation would render Article 1(1)(c) superfluous since it would depend on the existence of an independent investment. Claimant asserts that Sri Lanka has cited no case where a tribunal has read such language restrictively. According to Claimant, an illustrative list of "assets" is precisely that and does not imply the exclusion of assets which do not happen to be listed, or that the broad scope of protected investments should be constrained by a narrow and restrictive construction of those listed.

134. According to Claimant, Deutsche Bank's rights under the Hedging Agreement are definitely an "asset" and they comprise both "claims to money" and "claims to performance" within Article 1(1)(c). Claimant submits that no tribunal has read the circular language "associated with an investment" in the restrictive way that Sri Lanka intends. * * *

* * *

285. The Arbitral Tribunal considers that the Hedging Agreement is an asset. It is a legal property with economic value for Deutsche Bank. It is a claim to money which has been used to create an economic value.

286. The Arbitral Tribunal does not agree with Respondent that in order to qualify for protection the claim to money must be associated with a separate investment. The categories enumerated are just an illustrative list of "assets", every kind of which is considered to be an "investment". Defining an investment by reference to an investment would be a circular reasoning. The Tribunal does not see any reason to interpret Article 1(1)(c) in the restrictive way suggested by Respondent. Moreover, even if the terms "and associated with an investment" were to receive the meaning proposed by Respondent, the Tribunal considers that they would only apply to "claims to performance" and not to "claims to money".

* * *

295. The development of ICSID case law suggests that [three] criteria, namely [a substantial commitment or contribution, assumption of risk], and duration should be used as the benchmarks of an investment, without a separate criterion of contribution to the economic development of the host State and without reference to a regularity of profit and return. It should also be recalled that the existence of an investment must be assessed at its inception and not with hindsight.

296. The Arbitral Tribunal considers that the three above criteria are fulfilled in this case.

297. In the first place, the Tribunal agrees with Claimant that the Hedging Agreement

involved a contribution to Sri Lanka. A contribution can take any form. It is not limited to financial terms but also includes know-how, equipment, personnel and services * * *.

298. The record confirms that Deutsche Bank made a substantial contribution in connection with the Hedging Agreement. By concluding the Agreement on 8 July 2008, Deutsche Bank immediately committed to pay USD 2.5 million if CPC's costs of importing oil remained above [the benchmark price] per barrel. * * * [Because the price of crude oil at the time was well above that benchmark, the] immediate effect of the transaction was to allow CPC to purchase oil over the following twelve months at a price substantially below both the current market price and the forward curve.

* * *

300. Deutsche Bank also committed resources of substantial economic value to Sri Lanka. Deutsche Bank's employees engaged in over two years of regular meetings, negotiations and correspondence with CPC and the Central Bank. Furthermore, once it became clear that CPC would be required to make substantial payments pursuant to the Hedging Agreement, Deutsche Bank invested substantial resources in seeking to mitigate the costs to CPC. It organised a number of meetings between the Bank and CPC and examined various alternative structures which might reduce the required payment.

301. As far as risk is concerned, the Arbitral Tribunal takes note of Professor Schreuer's observation that "the very existence of the dispute is an indication of risk." Moreover, as assessed by the Tribunal in *Kardassopoulous v. Georgia*, "the risk component is satisfied in light of the political and economic climate prevailing throughout the period of the investment."

302. It cannot be seriously disputed that Deutsche Bank's investment involved a risk. The bank indeed faced a substantial risk that it would pay up to USD 2.5 million to CPC.

303. With respect to duration, the Tribunal once again agrees with Schreuer that "[duration] is a very flexible term. It could be anything from a couple of months to many years." * * *

304. The Arbitral Tribunal is persuaded that the duration criterion is satisfied in this case. The Hedging Agreement commitment was for twelve months. Moreover, Deutsche Bank had already spent two years negotiating the Agreement. The fact that it was terminated after 125 days is irrelevant.

* * *

308. Finally, the Arbitral Tribunal considers, contrary to Respondent's submission, that the Hedging Agreement was neither an ordinary commercial transaction nor a contingent liability.

* * *

Notes and Questions

1. What is the "economic value" created by the hedging agreement in this case, as the tribunal conceives it?

2. Should the amount of time spent in negotiating an agreement weigh in favor of its characterization as an "investment" subject to treaty protection? Why or why not?

3. A hedging agreement is a device commonly used as a kind of insurance to protect against risk from fluctuations in costs (in this case, of crude oil). In effect, a hedge is a gamble. Deutsche Bank was betting that the price of crude oil would stay stable or fall, and CPC was betting that it would stay high or rise. Is this the kind of transaction that requires treaty protection as an incentive for foreign investors? In other words, did Sri Lanka face a moral hazard from which Deutsche Bank had no reasonable means to protect itself?

4. How does the Hedging Agreement differ from an "ordinary commercial transaction," according to the tribunal? Do you agree? Why or why not?

5. Suppose a business firm in Zembia purchases a commercial liability insurance policy from an insurer in Osterlich. Under the tribunal's reasoning, is the insurance policy an "investment" by the insured firm in Osterlich? Is it an investment by the Osterlich insurer in Zembia?

One final important, but often overlooked, point about BITs is that, in modern practice, free trade agreements frequently include an investment chapter that is similar or identical to a freestanding BIT. Chapter 11 of the North American Free Trade Agreement, for example, is effectively a BIT incorporated into a larger trade treaty. These chapters may be quite as comprehensive in terms of scope and detail as any BIT. For the sake of simplicity, however, this chapter will usually refer to BITs alone, with the implicit understanding that equivalent commitments may be found in investment chapters of many FTAs.

B. Nondiscrimination

BITs almost always include national treatment and MFN treatment obligations with respect to foreign investments. Since 2004, the United States has published **Model BITs** that generally reflects preferred U.S. practice. The U.S. Trade Representative now uses the model as a template for negotiating investment treaties with other states. The current Model BIT contains typical nondiscrimination obligations:

2012 Model BIT (United States)

Article 3: National Treatment
1. Each Party shall accord to investors of the other Party treatment no less favorable than that it accords, in like circumstances, to its own investors with respect to the establishment, acquisition, expansion, management, conduct, operation, and sale or other disposition of investments in its territory.
2. Each Party shall accord to covered investments treatment no less favorable than that it accords, in like circumstances, to investments in its territory of its own investors with respect to the establishment, acquisition, expansion, management, conduct, operation, and sale or other disposition of investments. * * *

Article 4: Most-Favored-Nation Treatment
1. Each Party shall accord to investors of the other Party treatment no less favorable than that it accords, in like circumstances, to investors of any non-Party with respect to the establishment, acquisition, expansion, management, conduct, operation, and sale or other disposition of investments in its territory.
2. Each Party shall accord to covered investments treatment no less favorable than that it accords, in like circumstances, to investments in its territory of investors of any non-Party with respect to the establishment, acquisition, expansion, management, conduct, operation, and sale or other disposition of investments.

The USMCA has similar provisions. The Model BIT includes similar provisions in other clauses. These clauses prohibit such practices as requiring a minimum percentage of local content in products manufactured by a foreign-owned plant and requiring a minimum percentage of production to be exported outside of the host state.

The purpose of such provisions is to allow investors to make efficient decisions about how to allocate their capital between the state parties to the BIT. The BIT's nondiscrimination provisions ideally remove the incentive for states to impose costs on foreign investors that are not equally born by local business firms or firms from other countries. It is therefore logical to interpret the nondiscrimination provisions to prohibit measures that would affect investment decisions.

C. Standards of Investment Protection

Modern BITs almost always contain a set of disciplines to protect foreign investments from abuse or neglect by the host state. The substantive rules found in these treaties usually encompass three principles: compensation for expropriation of the investment; fair and equitable treatment for the investment; and full protection and security of the investment.

Expropriation

As noted, the TRIMS Agreement does not generally protect foreign investments from expropriation by the host state. **Expropriation** refers to a host state taking an entire firm, or substantially all of its business assets, for its own use, for the use of its own nationals, or simply in order to dissolve the foreign-owned business.

The consequences of an expropriation under public international law are subject to fierce debate among capital-exporting and capital-importing states. In general, an internationally wrongful act by a state gives rise to the obligation under customary international law to provide full compensation for the claimant's loss. In the *Factory at Chorzów* case, the Permanent Court of International Justice (the predecessor to today's International Court of Justice) held that a "breach of engagement involves an obligation to make reparation in an adequate form,"* and that such reparation "must, as far as possible, wipe out all the consequences of the illegal act and reestablish the situation which would, in all probability, have existed if that act had not been committed."** It further observed that a tribunal assessing damages must "determine the monetary value, both of the object which should have been restored in kind and of the additional damage, on the basis of the estimated value of the undertaking * * * together with any probable profit that would have accrued to the undertaking between the date of taking possession and that of the expert opinion."*** Yet, developing countries have long argued against expropriation being an "internationally wrongful act" in the first place and, even if it is, that it dictates this standard of compensation to the aggrieved foreign investor.

Historically, many capital-importing states adhered to a position expressed by Carlos Calvo, an Argentinian diplomat, that host states have exclusive jurisdiction over foreign investments in their territory and have no obligation under international law to compensate a private foreign investor for expropriation beyond what it considers reasonable in its discretion. This **Calvo Doctrine** was incorporated in some form into the laws, and sometimes even constitutions, of many post-colonial states in the mid-twentieth century.

Capital-exporting states predictably adopted a view more favorable to the interests of their investors. This view found its most popular expression in a formulation attributed to Cordell Hull, U.S. Secretary of State from 1933 to 1944. The **Hull Formula** states the position that international law requires a state that has expropriated a foreign national's investment to provide **prompt, adequate, and effective compensation** for the investment. While there are still some capital-importing states that adhere to the Calvo Doctrine,

---

*Factory at Chorzów (Ger. v. Pol.) (Claim for Indemnity—Jurisdiction), PCIJ Judgment No. 9, Series A, No. 9, at 21.

***Id.* (Claim for Indemnity—Merits), PCIJ Judgment No. 13, Series A, No. 17, at 47.

****Id.* at 52.

capital-exporting states have ultimately been able to persuade most developing countries to adopt some version of the Hull Formula in various BITs and FTAs.

Article 6 of the U.S. Model BIT exemplifies a provision incorporating and elaborating considerably on the Hull Formula:

2012 Model BIT (United States)

Article 6: Expropriation and Compensation

1. Neither Party may expropriate or nationalize a covered investment either directly or indirectly through measures equivalent to expropriation or nationalization ("expropriation"), except:
   (a) for a public purpose;
   (b) in a non-discriminatory manner;
   (c) on payment of prompt, adequate, and effective compensation; and
   (d) in accordance with due process of law and Article 5 [Minimum Standard of Treatment] (1) through (3).
2. The compensation referred to in paragraph 1(c) shall:
   (a) be paid without delay;
   (b) be equivalent to the fair market value of the expropriated investment immediately before the expropriation took place ("the date of expropriation");
   (c) not reflect any change in value occurring because the intended expropriation had become known earlier; and
   (d) be fully realizable and freely transferable.
3. If the fair market value is denominated in a freely usable currency, the compensation referred to in paragraph 1(c) shall be no less than the fair market value on the date of expropriation, plus interest at a commercially reasonable rate for that currency, accrued from the date of expropriation until the date of payment. * * *

A **direct expropriation** occurs when the host state fully deprives a foreign investor of ownership, control, or both, of its investment. Deprivation of ownership means that the host state transfers title to the investment to itself or its designee. Along with a transfer of title comes the right to the company's profits and (usually) the right to control the investment's business operations. An expropriation will also have occurred even though title remains with the investor, if the host state effectively deprives the investor of control over the investment. Without the ability to manage the business, the investor cannot protect its interests adequately.

But what if the host state does not deprive the investor of the full value of the investment? Whenever a state imposes any kind of regulation, there is some chance of the regulation impairing the investment and imposing costs on private actors. Taxes are an obvious example, but most regulations impose significant costs on private industry in one form or another. For example, the food labeling laws require food packagers to learn and comply with the labeling requirements. Regulations on the use of lead in paint for the safety of children

POLICY ISSUE
Do BITs Encourage Foreign Investment?

Economically developed countries like the United States persuade developing countries to adhere to bilateral investment treaties by arguing that such treaties reassure foreign investors and will lead to an inflow of funds to help develop the host state's economy. The evidence, however, does not unambiguously support such claims. Some research suggests that BITs do encourage foreign investment; other research suggests they have very little effect. *See* Jason W. Yackee, *Do Bilateral Investment Treaties Promote Foreign Direct Investment?*, 51 VA. J. INT'L L. 397, 405-14 (2011).

Can BITs be justified even if they do not promote much foreign investment in developing countries? Are legal protections against uncompensated expropriation, unfair or inequitable treatment, or nationality discrimination self-justifying? Or does it depend on how these protections are implemented? For example, suppose BITs tend to restrain developing countries from freely regulating their own economies as the price of conforming to a model of free-market capitalism. Or suppose BITs result in a net transfer of wealth from developing countries to wealthy foreign investors as the price of fairness to the foreign investor. Under what conditions should developing countries agree to BITs?

require paint manufacturers to develop lead-free alternatives at some cost to themselves. Any regulation can reduce the profitability of a business venture.

One of the more difficult conundrums of international investment law is how to determine when state regulation that imposes costs on a foreign investor causes an **indirect expropriation** of the protected investment, triggering the obligation to compensate that foreign investor, and when the regulation merely constitutes a permissible exercise of the state's police power. Although it is impossible to state a uniform rule for determining when state regulation rises to the level of indirect expropriation, the U.S. Model BIT contains some relevant standards in an Annex.

Annex B
Expropriation

The Parties confirm their shared understanding that:

1. Article 6 [Expropriation and Compensation](1) is intended to reflect customary international law concerning the obligation of States with respect to expropriation.
2. An action or a series of actions by a Party cannot constitute an expropriation unless it interferes with a tangible or intangible property right or property interest in an investment.
3. Article 6(1) addresses two situations. The first is direct expropriation, where an investment is nationalized or otherwise directly expropriated

through formal transfer of title or outright seizure.

4. The second situation addressed by Article 6(1) is indirect expropriation, where an action or series of actions by a Party has an effect equivalent to direct expropriation without formal transfer of title or outright seizure.

(a) The determination of whether an action or series of actions by a Party, in a specific fact situation, constitutes an indirect expropriation, requires a case-by-case, fact-based inquiry that considers, among other factors:

(i) the economic impact of the government action, although the fact that an action or series of actions by a Party has an adverse effect on the economic value of an investment, standing alone, does not establish that an indirect expropriation has occurred;

(ii) the extent to which the government action interferes with distinct, reasonable investment-backed expectations; and

(iii) the character of the government action.

(b) Except in rare circumstances, non-discriminatory regulatory actions by a Party that are designed and applied to protect legitimate public welfare objectives, such as public health, safety, and the environment, do not constitute indirect expropriations.

The U.S. Model BIT specifies more clearly what kinds of government regulation do *not* constitute an indirect expropriation than what kinds do qualify. The many international arbitration awards dealing with expropriation claims offer some general guidance, although tribunals frequently disagree about what standard should trigger a duty of compensation. At a minimum, the measures complained of must significantly impede the investor's control over, or substantially undermine the value of, the investment.* Many arbitral tribunals have emphasized that a merely temporary loss of the investor's control over the investment, or an incomplete deprivation of the value of the investment, will not trigger a duty of compensation.** In the words of one tribunal: "Interference with the investment's ability to carry on its business is not satisfied where the

*See, e.g., *Tippetts v. TAMS-AFFA Consulting Engineers of Iran*, Award No. 141-7-2, 6 Iran-U.S. Cl. Trib. Rep. 219, 225 (1984) ("A deprivation or taking of property may occur under international law through interference by a state in the use of that property or enjoyment of its benefits, even where legal title to that property is not affected."); *Starrett Housing Corp. v. Iran*, Award No. ITL-32-24-1, 4 Iran-U.S. Cl. Trib. Rep. 122, 23 I.L.M. 1090, 1115 (1983) ("[I]t is recognized by international law that measures taken by a State can interfere with property rights to such an extent that these rights are rendered so useless that they must be deemed to have been expropriated, even though the State does not purport to have expropriated them and the legal title to the property formally remains with the original owner.").

**See, e.g., *Tippetts*, 6 Iran-U.S. Cl. Trib. Rep. at 222 (holding that the assumption of control by a host state will be considered to rise to the level of expropriation if the state deprives the owner of "fundamental rights of ownership" for an indefinite period).

investment continues to operate, even if its profits are diminished."*

At the same time, legitimate state regulation of health, public safety, national security, or other important concerns will not be considered an indirect expropriation even though new regulations impose a significant economic burden on the foreign investor. The following influential case attempted to articulate some standards where the impairment did not fully deprive the foreign investor of the value of and control over the investment:

MARVIN FELDMAN v. MEXICO

International Centre for the Settlement of Investment Disputes
Case No. ARB(AF)/99/1, 7 ICSID Rep. 341
Award of Dec. 16, 2002

1. This case concerns a dispute regarding the application of certain tax laws by the United Mexican States (hereinafter "Mexico" or "the Respondent") to the export of tobacco products by Corporación de Exportaciones Mexicanas, S.A. de C.V. ("CEMSA"), a company organized under the laws of Mexico and owned and controlled by Mr. Marvin Roy Feldman Karpa (hereinafter "Mr. Feldman" or "the Claimant"), a citizen of the United States of America ("United States"). The Claimant, who is suing as the sole investor on behalf of CEMSA, alleges that Mexico's refusal to rebate excise taxes applied to cigarettes exported by CEMSA and Mexico's continuing refusal to recognize CEMSA's right to a rebate of such taxes regarding prospective cigarette exports constitute a breach of Mexico's obligations under Chapter Eleven, Section A of the North American Free Trade Agreement (hereinafter "NAFTA"). In particular, Mr. Feldman alleges violations of NAFTA Articles * * * 1105 (Minimum Level of Treatment), and 1110 (Expropriation and Indemnification). Mexico denies these allegations.

* * *

7. The case concerns the tax rebates which may be available when cigarettes are exported. Mexico imposes a tax on production and sale of cigarettes in the domestic market under the Impuesto Especial Sobre Producción y Servicios ("IESP") law, a special or excise tax on products and services. In some circumstances, however, a zero tax rate has been applied to cigarettes that are exported. According to the Respondent, the IEPS Law "has basically remained the same since its origins [in 1981], although the underlying methodology of the tax has changed several times." Review of the various versions of the IEPS law between 1990 and 1999 confirms this conclusion.

8. Under the 1991 IEPS law, certain activities generated liability for the tax, including, *inter alia*, selling domestically, importing and exporting the goods listed in Article 2, section I of the Law. The IEPS law also included the tax rate for each product. In the case of domestic sales and imports of cigarettes, the rates were 139.3% from 1990 through 1994, and 85% from 1995 through 1997. However, the IEPS rate on exports of

**LG&E Energy Corp. v. Argentine Rep.*, ICSID Case No. ARB/02/1, Decision on Liability, para. 191 (Oct. 3, 2006), 21 ICSID REV. 269 (2006).

cigarettes from 1990 through 1997 was 0%. From 1992, only exports to countries that were not considered low income tax jurisdictions (tax havens)—in general, countries with an income tax rate above 30%—were eligible for a 0% rate. In most instances, when cigarettes were purchased in Mexico at a price that included the tax, and subsequently exported, the tax amounts initially paid could be rebated.

9. The Claimant's firm, CEMSA, first began exporting cigarettes in 1990. According to the Respondent, the record shows that [the Mexican Ministry of Finance] paid the IEPS rebates to the claimant for 1990-1991 in full * * *.

10. According to the Claimant, an authorized producer of cigarettes in Mexico, Carlos Slim [a Mexican businessman who was for a time the richest man in the world] "protested [regarding Claimant's exports] and the government took administrative steps and passed legislation to cut off rebates to CEMSA in 1991." This assertion is contested by the Respondent. The 1991 legislation was apparently designed to provide IEPS rebates to exports undertaken by producers of cigarettes (such as Cigatam, a firm allegedly controlled by Carlos Slim), but to deny rebates for exports by resellers of cigarettes, such as CEMSA. * * * The Claimant, as a reseller, became ineligible for rebates.

* * *

89. In this proceeding, the Claimant's key contention is that the various actions of Mexican authorities, particularly [the Ministry of Finance], in denying the IEPS rebates on cigarette exports to CEMSA, resulted in an indirect or "creeping" expropriation of the Claimant's investment and were tantamount to expropriation under Article 1110. * * * Nor does the Claimant believe that the Mexican government policy of limiting cigarette exports is justified by public policy concerns, particularly in light of the stated purpose of the IEPS law in 1980, which was to encourage Mexican exports.

* * *

97. Expropriation under Chapter 11 is governed by NAFTA Article 1110, although NAFTA lacks a precise definition of expropriation. That provision reads in pertinent part as follows:

> 1. No Party may *directly or indirectly* nationalize or expropriate an investment of an investor of another Party in its territory *or take a measure tantamount to nationalization or expropriation* of such an investment ("expropriation"), except:
> (a) for a public purpose;
> (b) on a non-discriminatory basis;
> (c) in accordance with due process of law and article 1105(1); and
> (d) on payment of compensation in accordance with paragraphs 2 through 6.

The key issue, in general and in the instant case, is whether the Respondent's actions constitute an expropriation.

98. The Article 1110 language is of such generality as to be difficult to apply in specific cases. In the Tribunal's view, the essential determination is whether the actions of the Mexican government constitute an expropriation or nationalization, or are valid

governmental activity. If there is no expropriatory action, factors a-d are of limited relevance, except to the extent that they have helped to differentiate between governmental acts that are expropriation and those that are not * * *. If there is a finding of expropriation, compensation is required, even if the taking is for a public purpose, non-discriminatory and in accordance with due process of law and Article 1105(1).

* * *

100. Most significantly with regard to this case, Article 1110 deals not only with direct takings, but indirect expropriation and measures "tantamount to expropriation," which potentially encompass a variety of government regulatory activity that may significantly interfere with an investor's property rights. The Tribunal deems the scope of both expressions to be functionally equivalent. Recognizing direct expropriation is relatively easy: governmental authorities take over a mine or factory, depriving the investor of all meaningful benefits of ownership and control. However, it is much less clear when governmental action that interferes with broadly-defined property rights—an "investment" under NAFTA, Article 1139—crosses the line from valid regulation to a compensable taking, and it is fair to say that no one has come up with a fully satisfactory means of drawing this line.

101. By their very nature, tax measures, even if they are designed to and have the effect of an expropriation, will be indirect, with an effect that may be tantamount to expropriation. If the measures are implemented over a period of time, they could also be characterized as "creeping," which the Tribunal also believes is not distinct in nature from, and is subsumed by, the terms "indirect" expropriation or "tantamount to expropriation" in Article 1110(1). The Claimant has alleged "creeping expropriation." The Respondent has objected that the Claimant has in effect added a new element to the case which, among other things, should have been submitted to the Competent Authorities under Article 2103(6) for a determination as to whether it should be excluded from consideration as an expropriation. The *Restatement* [*of the Law (Third), The Foreign Relations Law of the United States*] defines "creeping expropriation" in part as a state seeking "to achieve the same result [as an outright taking] by taxation and regulatory measures designed to make continued operation of a project uneconomical so that it is abandoned." Since the Tribunal believes that creeping expropriation, as defined in the Restatement, noted above, is a form of indirect expropriation, and may accordingly constitute measures "tantamount to expropriation," the Tribunal includes consideration of creeping expropriation along with its consideration of these closely related terms.

102. Ultimately, decisions as to when regulatory action becomes compensable under article 1110 and similar provisions in other agreements appear to be made based on the facts of specific cases. This Tribunal must necessarily take the same approach.

103. The Tribunal notes that the ways in which governmental authorities may force a company out of business, or significantly reduce the economic benefits of its business, are many. In the past, confiscatory taxation, denial of access to infrastructure or necessary raw materials, imposition of unreasonable regulatory regimes, among others, have been considered to be expropriatory actions. At the same time, governments must be free to act in the broader public interest through protection of the environment, new or modified tax regimes, the granting or withdrawal of government subsidies, reductions or increases in tariff levels, imposition of zoning restrictions and the like. Reasonable

governmental regulation of this type cannot be achieved if any business that is adversely affected may seek compensation, and it is safe to say that customary international law recognizes this.

* * *

105. The "comments" to the Restatement are designed to assist in determining, *inter alia*, how to distinguish between an indirect expropriation and valid government regulation:

> A state is responsible for an expropriation of property under Subsection (1) when it subjects alien property to taxation, regulation, or other action that is confiscatory, or that prevents, unreasonably interferes with, or unduly delays, effective enjoyment of an alien's property or its removal from the state's territory... *A state is not responsible for loss of property or for other economic disadvantage resulting from bona fide general taxation, regulation, forfeiture for crime, or other action of the kind that is commonly accepted as within the police power of states, if it is not discriminatory* ....

* * *

108. The Tribunal has struggled at considerable length, in light of the facts and legal arguments presented, the language of Article 1110 and other relevant NAFTA provisions, principles of customary international law and prior NAFTA tribunal decisions, to determine whether the actions of the Respondent relating to the Claimant constituted indirect or "creeping" expropriation, or actions tantamount to expropriation. (There is in this case no allegation of a direct expropriation or taking under Article 1110.) The conclusion that they do not is explained below.

* * *

111. This Tribunal's rationale for declining to find a violation of Article 1110 can be summarized as follows: (1) * * * not every business problem experienced by a foreign investor is an expropriation under Article 1110; (2) * * * (3) at no relevant time has the IEPS law, as written, afforded Mexican cigarette resellers such as CEMSA a "right" to export cigarettes (due primarily to technical/legal requirements for invoices stating tax amounts separately and to their status as non-taxpayers); and (4) the Claimant's "investment," the exporting business known as CEMSA, as far as this Tribunal can determine, remains under the complete control of the Claimant, in business with the apparent right to engage in the exportation of alcoholic beverages, photographic supplies, contact lenses, powdered milk and other Mexican products—any product that it can purchase upon receipt of invoices stating the tax amounts—and to receive rebates of any applicable taxes under the IEPS law. While none of these factors alone is necessarily conclusive, in the Tribunal's view taken together they tip the expropriation/regulation balance away from a finding of expropriation.

112. First, the Tribunal is aware that not every business problem experienced by a foreign investor is an indirect or creeping expropriation under Article 1110, or a denial of due process or fair and equitable treatment under Article 1110(1)(c). As the *Azinian* tribunal observed, "It is a fact of life everywhere that individuals may be disappointed in their dealings with public authorities... It may be safely assumed that many Mexican parties can be found who had business dealings with governmental entities which were not to their satisfaction..." (*Azinian v. United Mexican States*, Award, November

1, 1999, para. 83, 14 *ICSID Review—FILJ* 2, 1999.) To paraphrase *Azinian*, not all government regulatory activity that makes it difficult or impossible for an investor to carry out a particular business, change in the law or change in the application of existing laws that makes it uneconomical to continue a particular business, is an expropriation under Article 1110. Governments, in their exercise of regulatory power, frequently change their laws and regulations in response to changing economic circumstances or changing political, economic or social considerations. Those changes may well make certain activities less profitable or even uneconomic to continue.

113. Here, it is undeniable that the Claimant has experienced great difficulties in dealing with [Mexican Ministry of Finance] officials, and in some respects has been treated in a less than reasonable manner, but that treatment under the circumstances of this case does not rise to the level of a violation of international law under Article 1110. Unfortunately, tax authorities in most countries do not always act in a consistent and predictable way. The IEPS law on its face (although not necessarily as applied) is undeniably a measure of general taxation of the kind envisaged by Restatement Comment g. As in most tax regimes, the tax laws are used as instruments of public policy as well as fiscal policy, and certain taxpayers are inevitably favored, with others less favored or even disadvantaged.

* * *

For these reasons, the Tribunal

209. Finds that the Respondent has not violated the Claimant's rights or acted inconsistently with the Respondent's obligations under NAFTA Article 1110 * * *.

Notes and Questions

1. Feldman pursued claims not only of "creeping expropriation" against the Mexican government, but a breach of the obligation of fair and equitable treatment (discussed below). The fact that the tribunal found no expropriation in this case does not necessarily mean that the same measure by the host state did not run afoul of other duties in the NAFTA. The award dealt separately with these other issues.

2. If the IEPS law had granted a clear right to tax rebates and the Mexican Ministry of Finance had denied them to the claimant arbitrarily, would that have justified treating the decision as an expropriation? Why or why not? If not, would it change your mind if the denial had effectively made it impossible for the claimant to profit from his investment in Mexico? Why or why not?

Minimum Standards of Treatment

Expropriation is the most extreme example of host state interference in a foreign investment. BITs also commonly include a higher order of security for foreign investments relating to harm by act or neglect of the host state. These standards are typically phrased as guarantees of **fair and equitable treatment** and **full protection and security** for the investments. The U.S. Model BIT exemplifies a widely used approach to these standards:

2012 Model BIT (United States)

> **Article 5: Minimum Standard of Treatment**
> 1. Each Party shall accord to covered investments treatment in accordance with customary international law, including fair and equitable treatment and full protection and security.
> 2. For greater certainty, paragraph 1 prescribes the customary international law minimum standard of treatment of aliens as the minimum standard of treatment to be afforded to covered investments. The concepts of "fair and equitable treatment" and "full protection and security" do not require treatment in addition to or beyond that which is required by that standard, and do not create additional substantive rights. The obligation in paragraph 1 to provide:
>   (a) "fair and equitable treatment" includes the obligation not to deny justice in criminal, civil, or administrative adjudicatory proceedings in accordance with the principle of due process embodied in the principal legal systems of the world; and
>   (b) "full protection and security" requires each Party to provide the level of police protection required under customary international law.
> 3. A determination that there has been a breach of another provision of this Treaty, or of a separate international agreement, does not establish that there has been a breach of this Article. * * *

The requirement of "full protection and security" is fairly clear; it merely requires the host state take reasonable policing measures to protect the foreign investor and its investment against crime and lawlessness.

In contrast, "fair and equitable treatment" has a broader and more ambiguous scope. In an influential 1926 arbitration between a U.S. investor and Mexico, *Neer v. United Mexican States*, 4 R.I.A.A. 60 (1926), the tribunal held that "the propriety of government acts" harming an alien "should be put to the test of international standards," and

> that the treatment of an alien, in order to constitute an international delinquency, should amount to an outrage, to bad faith, to wilful neglect of duty, or to an insufficiency of governmental action so far short of international standards that every reasonable and impartial man would readily recognize its insufficiency.

Many international arbitral tribunals have elaborated the concept in their jurisprudence. One tribunal has clarified that the standard requires "transparency and the protection of the investor's legitimate expectations [based on specific representations by the host state to the investor], freedom from coercion and harassment, procedural propriety and due process, and good faith." *Philip Morris Brands Sarl v. Oriental Rep. of Uruguay*, ICSID Case No. ARB/10/7, ¶ 320 (July 8, 2016). Concomitantly, a NAFTA tribunal ruled that a governmental act would qualify as unfair and inequitable only if "sufficiently egregious and shocking—a gross denial of justice, manifest arbitrariness, blatant unfairness, a complete lack of due process, evident discrimination, or a manifest lack of reasons—so as to fall below accepted international standards." *Glamis Gold, Ltd. v. United States*, NAFTA Ch. 11 Arb. Trib., June 8, 2009, ¶ 616, 48 I.L.M. 1038 (2009).

The following award explores the boundaries of this provision.

METALCLAD CORP. v. MEXICO

International Centre for the Settlement of Investment Disputes
Case No. ARB(AF)/97/1, 16 ICSID Rev. 168 (2001)
Award of Aug. 20, 2000

1. This dispute arises out of the activities of the Claimant, Metalclad Corporation (hereinafter "Metalclad"), in the Mexican Municipality of Guadalcazar (hereinafter "Guadalcazar"), located in the Mexican State of San Luis Potosi (hereinafter "SLP"). Metalclad alleges that Respondent, the United Mexican States (hereinafter "Mexico"), through its local governments of SLP and Guadalcazar, interfered with its development and operation of a hazardous waste landfill. Metalclad claims that this interference is a violation of the Chapter Eleven investment provisions of the North American Free Trade Agreement (hereinafter "NAFTA"). In particular, Metalclad alleges violations of NAFTA, Article 1105, which requires each Party to NAFTA to "accord to investments of investors of another Party treatment in accordance with international law, including fair and equitable treatment and full protection and security" * * *.

2. Metalclad is an enterprise of the United States of America, incorporated under the laws of Delaware. [Metalclad formed a wholly-owned Mexican subsidiary corporation, ECONSA]. In 1993, ECONSA purchased the Mexican company Confinamiento Tecnico de Residuos Industriales, S.A. de C.V. (hereinafter "COTERIN") with a view to the acquisition, development and operation of the latter's hazardous waste transfer station and landfill in the valley of La Pedrera, located in Guadalcazar. COTERIN is the owner of record of the landfill property as well as the permits and licenses which are at the base of this dispute.

* * *

28. In 1990 the federal government of Mexico authorized COTERIN to construct and operate a transfer station for hazardous waste in La Pedrera, a valley located in Guadalcazar in SLP. * * * Approximately 800 people live within ten kilometers of the site.

29. On January 23, 1993, the National Ecological Institute (hereinafter "INE"), an independent sub-agency of the federal Secretariat of the Mexican Environment, National Resources and Fishing (hereinafter "SEMARNAP"), granted COTERIN a federal permit to construct a hazardous waste landfill in La Pedrera (hereinafter "the landfill").

30. Three months after the issuance of the federal construction permit, on April 23, 1993, Metalclad entered into a 6-month option agreement to purchase COTERIN together with its permits, in order to build the hazardous waste landfill.

31. Shortly thereafter, on May 11, 1993, the government of SLP granted COTERIN a state land use permit to construct the landfill. * * *

32. One month later, on June 11, 1993, Metalclad met with the Governor of SLP to discuss the project. Metalclad asserts that at this meeting it obtained the Governor's support for the project. In fact, the Governor acknowledged at the hearing that a reasonable person might expect that the Governor would support the project if studies confirmed the site as suitable or feasible and if the environmental impact was consistent with Mexican standards.

* * *

35. On August 10, 1993, the INE granted COTERIN the federal permit for operation of the landfill. On September 10, 1993, Metalclad exercised its option and purchased COTERIN, the landfill site and the associated permits.

36. Metalclad asserts it would not have exercised its COTERIN purchase option but for the apparent approval and support of the project by federal and state officials.

37. Metalclad asserts that shortly after its purchase of COTERIN, the Governor of SLP embarked on a public campaign to denounce and prevent the operation of the landfill.

38. Metalclad further asserts, however, that in April 1994, after months of negotiation, Metalclad believed it had secured SLP's agreement to support the project. Consequently, in May 1994, after receiving an eighteen-month extension of the previously issued federal construction permit from the INE, Metalclad began construction of the landfill. Mexico denies that SLP's agreement or support had ever been obtained.

39. Metalclad further maintains that construction continued openly and without interruption through October 1994. Federal officials and state representatives inspected the construction site during this period, and Metalclad provided federal and state officials with written status reports of its progress.

40. On October 26, 1994, when the Municipality ordered the cessation of all building activities due to the absence of a municipal construction permit, construction was abruptly terminated. * * *

* * *

45. Metalclad completed construction of the landfill in March 1995. On March 10,

1995, Metalclad held an "open house," or "inauguration," of the landfill which was attended by a number of dignitaries from the United States and from Mexico's federal, state and local governments.

46. Demonstrators impeded the "inauguration," blocked the entry and exit of buses carrying guests and workers, and employed tactics of intimidation against Metalclad. Metalclad asserts that the demonstration was organized at least in part by the Mexican state and local governments, and that state troopers assisted in blocking traffic into and out of the site. Metalclad was thenceforth effectively prevented from opening the landfill.

* * *

50. On December 5, 1995, thirteen months after Metalclad's application for the municipal construction permit was filed, the application was denied. In doing this, the Municipality recalled its decision to deny a construction permit to COTERIN in October 1991 and January 1992 and noted the "impropriety" of Metalclad's construction of the landfill prior to receiving a municipal construction permit.

51. There is no indication that the Municipality gave any consideration to the construction of the landfill and the efforts at operation during the thirteen months during which the application was pending.

* * *

59. On September 23, 1997, three days before the expiry of his term, the Governor issued an Ecological Decree declaring a Natural Area for the protection of rare cactus. The Natural Area encompasses the area of the landfill. Metalclad relies in part on this Ecological Decree as an additional element in its claim of expropriation, maintaining that the Decree effectively and permanently precluded the operation of the landfill.

* * *

62. The landfill remains dormant. Metalclad has not sold or transferred any portion of it.

* * *

74. NAFTA Article 1105(1) provides that "each Party shall accord to investments of investors of another Party treatment in accordance with international law, including fair and equitable treatment and full protection and security." For the reasons set out below, the Tribunal finds that Metalclad's investment was not accorded fair and equitable treatment in accordance with international law, and that Mexico has violated NAFTA Article 1105(1).

75. An underlying objective of NAFTA is to promote and increase cross-border investment opportunities and ensure the successful implementation of investment initiatives. (NAFTA Article 102(1)).

76. Prominent in the statement of principles and rules that introduces the Agreement is the reference to "transparency" (NAFTA Article 102(1)). The Tribunal understands this to include the idea that all relevant legal requirements for the purpose of initiating, completing and successfully operating investments made, or intended to be made, under the Agreement should be capable of being readily known to all affected investors of another Party. There should be no room for doubt or uncertainty on such matters. Once the authorities of the central government of any Party (whose

international responsibility in such matters has been identified in the preceding section) become aware of any scope for misunderstanding or confusion in this connection, it is their duty to ensure that the correct position is promptly determined and clearly stated so that investors can proceed with all appropriate expedition in the confident belief that they are acting in accordance with all relevant laws.

77. Metalclad acquired COTERIN for the sole purpose of developing and operating a hazardous waste landfill in the valley of La Pedrera, in Guadalcazar, SLP.

78. The Government of Mexico issued federal construction and operating permits for the landfill prior to Metalclad's purchase of COTERIN, and the Government of SLP likewise issued a state operating permit which implied its political support for the landfill project.

79. A central point in this case has been whether, in addition to the above-mentioned permits, a municipal permit for the construction of a hazardous waste landfill was required.

80. When Metalclad inquired, prior to its purchase of COTERIN, as to the necessity for municipal permits, federal officials assured it that it had all that was needed to undertake the landfill project. Indeed, following Metalclad's acquisition of COTERIN, the federal government extended the federal construction permit for eighteen months.

* * *

85. Metalclad was led to believe, and did believe, that the federal and state permits allowed for the construction and operation of the landfill. Metalclad argues that in all hazardous waste matters, the Municipality has no authority. However, Mexico argues that constitutionally and lawfully the Municipality has the authority to issue construction permits.

86. Even if Mexico is correct that a municipal construction permit was required, the evidence also shows that, as to hazardous waste evaluations and assessments, the federal authority's jurisdiction was controlling and the authority of the municipality only extended to appropriate construction considerations. Consequently, the denial of the permit by the Municipality by reference to environmental impact considerations in the case of what was basically a hazardous waste disposal landfill, was improper, as was the municipality's denial of the permit for any reason other than those related to the physical construction or defects in the site.

* * *

89. Metalclad was entitled to rely on the representations of federal officials and to believe that it was entitled to continue its construction of the landfill. In following the advice of these officials, and filing the municipal permit application on November 15, 1994, Metalclad was merely acting prudently and in the full expectation that the permit would be granted.

* * *

92. The Town Council denied the permit for reasons which included, but may not have been limited to, the opposition of the local population * * * and the ecological concerns regarding the environmental effect and impact on the site and surrounding communities. None of the reasons included a reference to any problems associated

with the physical construction of the landfill or to any physical defects therein.

93. The Tribunal therefore finds that the construction permit was denied without any consideration of, or specific reference to, construction aspects or flaws of the physical facility[, the sole grounds on which the Municipality could legally regulate it].

* * *

97. The actions of the Municipality following its denial of the municipal construction permit, coupled with the procedural and substantive deficiencies of the denial, support the Tribunal's finding, for the reasons stated above, that the Municipality's insistence upon and denial of the construction permit in this instance was improper.

* * *

99. Mexico failed to ensure a transparent and predictable framework for Metalclad's business planning and investment. The totality of these circumstances demonstrates a lack of orderly process and timely disposition in relation to an investor of a Party acting in the expectation that it would be treated fairly and justly in accordance with the NAFTA.

100. Moreover, the acts of the State and the Municipality–and therefore the acts of Mexico–fail to comply with or adhere to the requirements of NAFTA, Article 1105(1) that each Party accord to investments of investors of another Party treatment in accordance with international law, including fair and equitable treatment. This is so particularly in light of the governing principle that internal law (such as the Municipality's stated permit requirements) does not justify failure to perform a treaty. (*Vienna Convention on the Law of Treaties*, Arts. 26, 27).

101. The Tribunal therefore holds that Metalclad was not treated fairly or equitably under the NAFTA and succeeds on its claim under Article 1105. * * *

Notes and Questions

1. Under NAFTA article 1114, state parties were allowed to adopt and enforce regulations to ensure that investment activities in their territory are "undertaken in a manner sensitive to environmental concerns." Why did the tribunal not find these concerns sufficient to justify Mexico's decision to deny Metalclad a permit to operate the site?

2. What precisely did the Mexican government do, or fail to do, that denied the claimant "fair and equitable treatment?" Does its reasoning define the full extent of protection under this treaty provision?

3. The *Metalclad* award emphasized the importance of transparent and self-consistent government decisionmaking. On the other hand, governments cannot be expected never to change policies, even if the change should affect a foreign investment adversely. One tribunal noted that "no investor may reasonably expect that the circumstances prevailing at the time the investment is made remain totally unchanged," *Saluka Investments v. Czech Rep.*, UNCITRAL Award of Mar. 17, 2006, ¶ 305, and many have held that investors are not entitled to expect that the host state will never alter general legislation. E.g., *Philip Morris Brands*, *supra*, ¶¶ 429-30. Should the foreseeability of changes to laws and regulations to a diligent investor play a role in determining which changes are unfair and inequitable? Or should only those changes that are unforeseeable to any investor regardless of their diligence qualify as unfair? See *MTD Equity Sdn. Bhd. v. Chile*, ICSID Case No. ARB/01/7, ¶ 178 (May 25, 2004). Is any state measure unforeseeable to that extent?

D. Dispute Resolution under Investment Agreements

Treaty-Based Dispute Resolution

As a general rule, treaties between sovereign states do not confer rights on private parties to enforce the treaty. Modern BITs generally stand as an exception. They frequently include a provision specifically authorizing private investors to invoke international arbitration against the host state, if the host state violates one of the treaty guarantees. The U.S. Model BIT is against exemplary:

2012 Model BIT (United States)
SECTION B

Article 23: Consultation and Negotiation
In the event of an investment dispute, the claimant and the respondent should initially seek to resolve the dispute through consultation and negotiation, which may include the use of nonbinding, third-party procedures.

Article 24: Submission of a Claim to Arbitration
1. In the event that a disputing party considers that an investment dispute cannot be settled by consultation and negotiation:
(a) the claimant, on its own behalf, may submit to arbitration under this Section a claim
(i) that the respondent has breached
(A) an obligation under Articles 3 through 10,
(B) an investment authorization, or
(C) an investment agreement;
and
(ii) that the claimant has incurred loss or damage by reason of, or arising out of, that breach; and
(b) the claimant, on behalf of an enterprise of the respondent that is a juridical person that the claimant owns or controls directly or indirectly, may submit to arbitration under this Section a claim

(i) that the respondent has breached
(A) an obligation under Articles 3 through 10,
(B) an investment authorization, or
(C) an investment agreement;
and
(ii) that the enterprise has incurred loss or damage by reason of, or arising out of, that breach,

provided that a claimant may submit pursuant to subparagraph (a)(i)(C) or (b)(i)(C) a claim for breach of an investment agreement only if the subject matter of the claim and the claimed damages directly relate to the covered investment that was established or acquired, or sought to be established or acquired, in reliance on the relevant investment agreement. * * *

3. Provided that six months have elapsed since the events giving rise to the claim, a claimant may submit a claim referred to in paragraph 1:
(a) under the ICSID Convention and the ICSID Rules of Procedure for Arbitration Proceedings, provided that both the respondent and the non-disputing Party are parties to the ICSID Convention;
(b) under the ICSID Additional Facility Rules, provided that either the respondent or the non-disputing Party is a party to the ICSID Convention;
(c) under the UNCITRAL Arbitration Rules; or
(d) if the claimant and respondent agree, to any other arbitration institution or under any other arbitration rules. * * *

Article 25: Consent of Each Party to Arbitration

1. Each Party consents to the submission of a claim to arbitration under this Section in accordance with this Treaty. * * *

Notes and Questions

1. The Model BIT sets forth detailed rules for the appointment of the arbitrators, conduct of the arbitration, and the governing law. When the claim is based on a violation of the treaty, international law governs the interpretation and application of the treaty. In most other cases, the applicable law is the law chosen by the parties to govern their agreement or, if there is no choice of law clause, the law of the host state. Article 34.7 provides that each state party to the BIT will provide for enforcement in its territory. If a host state fails to satisfy an arbitral award against it, the state-to-state dispute resolution procedures of the Model BIT take effect and the investor state will take up the investor's claim *parens patriae* against the host state.

2. Notice also that article 24(1)(b) of the Model BIT expressly provides that an individual or company from the investor state may submit a claim to arbitration on behalf of a business entity formed under the laws of the host state. This provision is especially important because, if a business organization formed under the laws of the host state by a foreign investor suffers an injury in the host state, the host state could otherwise refuse to submit to arbitration on the theory that it offers protections only to foreign investors themselves, not to local business entities that happen to be owned by foreign investors under the ICJ's *Barcelona Traction* rule.

3. Finally, consider that article 24(3) offers the claimant four options for initiating arbitration. These options will be considered in greater detail in Chapter 9, on planning for international disputes.

USMCA has specific provisions for investor-state dispute resolution as well. These provisions are found in Annex 14-D and parallel those of the U.S. Model BIT in many ways. Like the Model BIT, USMCA allows an investor to initiate arbitration against a foreign host state. Annex 14.D.3. Also like the Model BIT, USMCA Annex 14-D sets forth detailed procedural requirements in addition to rules for the formation of the arbitral tribunal and conduct of arbitration. Although all three parties to NAFTA were bound by this dispute resolution provision, Canada opted out in negotiating the USMCA. Therefore, Annex 14-D applies only to investment disputes arising between the United States and Mexico.

An investor seeking to set aside or revise a USMCA Annex 14-D arbitral panel award is likely to face great difficulty. In the United States, the **Federal Arbitration Act** establishes a strong policy in favor of recognition of foreign arbitral awards by U.S. courts. This policy applies to USMCA panel awards as well. Although a domestic court may refuse to recognize and enforce a USMCA panel award under limited circumstances, such situations are rare. As the District of Columbia district court noted in a NAFTA arbitration review case:

> Courts have long recognized that judicial review of an arbitration award is extremely limited. * * * A court may vacate an award only if there is a showing that one of the limited circumstances enumerated in the Federal Arbitration Act ("FAA") is present, or if the arbitrator acted in manifest disregard of the law. * * * [The party challenging the award] bears the heavy burden of establishing that vacatur of the arbitration award is appropriate.
>
> * * * Manifest disregard of the law "means more than error or misunderstanding with respect to the law." * * * Thus, a party seeking to have an arbitration award vacated on this ground must at least establish that "(1) the arbitrators knew of a governing legal principle yet refused to apply it or ignored it altogether and (2) the law ignored by the arbitrators was well defined, explicit, and clearly applicable to the case."

International Thunderbird Gaming Corp. v. United Mexican States, 473 F.Supp.2d 80, 83-84 (D.D.C. 2007). A panel award, then, is likely to be upheld in court absent extreme circumstances.

Key Vocabulary

Agreement on Trade-Related Investment Measures (TRIMS Agreement)
Bilateral Investment Treaty (BIT)
Dispute Settlement Body (DSB)
Dispute Settlement Understanding (DSU)
Expropriation
Fair and equitable treatment
Foreign direct investment (FDI)
Free trade agreement (FTA)
Full protection and security
General Agreement on Trade in Services (GATS)
General Agreement on Tariffs and Trade (GATT)
Hull Formula
International Centre for the Settlement of Investment Disputes (ICSID)
Indirect expropriation
Joint venture (JV)
Most favored nation (MFN)
National treatment
North American Free Trade Agreement (NAFTA)
Treaty of Friendship, Commerce and Navigation (FCN treaty)
U.S.-Mexico-Canada Agreement (USMCA)
U.S. Model BIT
World Trade Organization (WTO)
WTO Agreements

Practice Exercise

Your client, Darkseed Productions, is a California-based entertainment company wholly owned by Dirbleglass, Inc. a major liquor distributor headquartered in Japan. Darkseed was considering locations for the construction and operation of a chain of tourist-friendly nightclubs and received a letter from the city council of Disco, Pottsylvania, offering full city cooperation with Darkseed's plans, including police assistance for security; two free translators; and a full municipal trade tax exemption for the first 18 months of the club's operation in Disco if Darkseed would establish two or more clubs in Disco. The trade tax normally applies to any company doing business in Disco and is generally equal to 15% of the company's income. Darkseed would nonetheless be subject to a liquor distribution tax (the "LDT") of 30% *ad valorem* that applies to the domestic sale of any alcoholic beverage. Darkseed considered the offer sufficiently attractive that it entered into an agreement with the Disco city council to set up clubs there. Darkseed then formed a Pottsylvanian subsidiary company, Darkseed Pottsylvanique Ltd., capitalized at $15 million, and started construction.

After completing construction of the first club, Darkseed began importing liquor into Pottsylvania from Dirbleglass distilleries in Japan, the United States, and Europe. It had opened its doors and begun operating successfully for two months when a conjunction of events brought business to a halt.

First, the governor of California, Jeffrey Spicoli, made a widely reported joke in the press about being able to invade Pottsylvania single-handedly with nothing more than a scalding pot of coffee. The comment sparked anti-Californian protests throughout Pottsylvania, including the city of Disco, where the Pottsylvanian police were unable to prevent the dangerous protests from shutting down the first nightclub and delaying construction of the second for several months. Darkseed closed the doors of its nightclub in Disco, and the costs of keeping employees on payroll, paying rent and taxes, and servicing debt, plus equipment leasing costs, is rapidly draining the company's capital.

Next, Pottsylvania passed two new laws. The first, the National Liquor Adjustment Act ("NLAA") increased the LDT on liquor from its historic 30% rate to a new 45% rate. This rate is applicable only to sales imported liquor, however. Sales of domestically produced liquor are still taxed at the 30% rate. The second law, called the Anti-Drunk Driving Act ("ADDA"), prohibits the operation of any nightclub after midnight unless the nightclub owners provide free shuttle service to transport all patrons home. The increased tax and the cost of the shuttle service have rendered Darkseed's nightclub in Disco no longer profitable, and it has no incentive to open an equally unprofitable second club. It is now contemplating it potential remedies.

Pottsylvania and the United States are both parties to the WTO Agreements, and the United States and Pottsylvania have a BIT, identical to the U.S. Model BIT.

Analyze for Darkseed its rights under the relevant international treaties, and its options for pursuing a remedy. Be sure to address the following questions:

(a) What provisions of the WTO Agreements, if any, can Darkseed claim Pottsylvania has violated?

(b) If any provisions of the WTO Agreements have been violated, what remedies are available to Darkseed?

(c) Under the U.S.-Pottsylvania BIT, what claims might Darkseed credibly advance against Pottsylvania for

(1) the closing of its Disco club due to protests,
(2) the NLAA, and
(3) the ADDA?

(d) What remedies, if any, are available to Darkseed under the BIT?

(e) What defenses might Pottsylvania credibly assert to Darkseed's claims under the WTO Agreements and BIT?

Multiple Choice Questions

1. Which of the following theories posits that all states benefit from specializing in whatever goods they can produce most efficiently and trading them freely with other states?

   (a) Mercantilism
   (b) Protectionism
   (c) Supply and demand
   (d) Comparative advantage
   (e) Rational choice

2. Which of the following is an exception to most favored nation status under the General Agreement on Tariffs and Trade?

   I. Generalized System of Preferences
   II. Article XXIV regional trading arrangements
   III. National treatment
   IV. Quantitative restrictions

   (a) I and II only
   (b) II and III only
   (c) III and IV only
   (d) I, II and III only
   (e) II, III, and IV only

3. The General Agreement on Trade in Services would *not* generally apply to state measures respecting which of the following transactions between two WTO member states?

   (a) An underwriting company in one state insures a manufacturing plant in the other state.
   (b) An engineer in one state designs a product to be manufactured in that state and sold exclusively in the other state.
   (c) An Internet service provider in one state manages the Web site of a company with Internet servers in the other state.
   (d) A law firm in one state advises and represents a client in the other state, reporting back by telephone and email.
   (e) An engineer in one state travels to the other state to repair machinery located in the other state.

4. Which of the following factors need *not* generally be satisfied to show a violation of the national treatment obligation under the General Agreement on Tariffs and Trade?

(a) The imported products and domestic products are directly competitive with each other or like products.
(b) The imported and domestic products receive disparate treatment under internal laws or taxation measures.
(c) The measure is intended to discriminate against the imported products.
(d) The measure affects trade in goods rather than services or investment.
(e) The measure is applied so as to afford protection to domestic production.

5. Which of the following would most probably qualify as a foreign investment under a typical bilateral investment treaty between Grand Fenwick and Ruritania?

(a) A Grand Fenwick company's purchase of real property in Ruritania to gift to its Chief Executive Officer as a vacation home as a perquisite.
(b) A Ruritanian company's purchase of a manufacturing plant in Ruritania from a Grand Fenwick seller.
(c) A Grand Fenwick company's acquisition of the Ruritanian patents of a different Grand Fenwick company for the purpose of manufacturing the patented goods in Ruritania.
(d) A contract between a Grand Fenwick manufacturer and a Ruritanian distributor for the distribution of the former's goods in Ruritania.
(e) A Grand Fenwick company's long-term lease of a tract of land in Grand Fenwick for natural gas extraction, and for which it hires exclusively Ruritanian managers, engineers, and other employees.

6. Which of the following is *not* a requirement for host states exercising their right of expropriation of a foreign investment under the U.S. Model BIT?

(a) Compensation must be paid without undue delay.
(b) Compensation must be paid in a convertible currency or its equivalent.
(c) Compensation must be in an amount equivalent to the fair market value of the investment prior to expropriation.
(d) The expropriation must be for a public purpose.
(e) The expropriation must follow a fair and adequate trial before an impartial tribunal.

7. True or false?: Under most bilateral investment treaties, an investor can never prevail on a claim for the violation of the duty of fair and equitable treatment merely because the host state government materially misrepresents a regulatory requirement applicable to the investment, because governments commonly change their laws and regulations to

make certain activities less profitable or even uneconomic, and this is a risk of doing business in a foreign jurisdiction.

8. True or false?: Under most bilateral investment treaties, a foreign investor from one state party cannot invoke a private right of action against the host state party directly without the cooperation of the investor's own national government.

Multiple Choice Answers

1. (d)
2. (a)
3. (b)
4. (c)
5. (c)
6. (e)
7. False
8. False

Chapter 3

Protecting Intellectual Assets Across Borders

What You Will Learn in this Chapter

One of the first considerations in planning business abroad is the protection of intellectual property (IP). IP is broadly divided into four categories: copyrights, patents, trademarks, and trade secrets. Each kind of IP is different and calls for different considerations in ensuring their protection in international business, but they also share some common traits.

One common trait is potentially high value. Companies that regularly develop new technologies invest a great deal in their patents and frequently rely on them for the success of their business. Firms in every industry may depend on patented technologies, but in some fields, such as pharmaceuticals, communications, electronics, defense, and aerospace, patent protection can be a central part of a company's business strategy. The same is true of copyrights for business firms in the fields of entertainment and communication. Their software, apps, games, music, texts, sports, and motion pictures rely heavily on copyright to maintain profitability.

Business firms in all industries tend to rely on trademarks and trade secrets. Trademarks help the firms develop good will to cultivate customer loyalty and attract business by a strong reputation. Trade secrets are valuable information that a business firm may need to survive and thrive, such as information about actual and potential customers, product ingredients and recipes, manufacturing methods, and selling techniques.

In short, when doing business internationally, a firm needs to understand what kind of IP protection it can expect in whatever country it operates. It also needs to know what it can do to maximize the protection of its IP. Timing is often an important factor here. Some kinds of IP are more sensitive on the timing of protective measures than others in international business. Protecting trademarks, patents, and trade secrets internationally requires planning ahead, or at least prompt action, when the firm first trades or invests abroad. Copyright is less time sensitive, but copyright-reliant industries face different challenges in foreign jurisdictions.

Once the IP has been properly protected in a foreign state, its commercial exploitation can begin, such as by manufacturing or selling a patented device, publishing or selling a copyrighted work, or affixing a trademark to a product for sale. Exploitation also encompasses contracts providing others with the full or a limited right to manufacture, publish, sell, or otherwise use the protected IP in commerce through a licensing arrangement.

Before discussing IP protection, it is helpful to put the international system into perspective by outlining the treaties that impose uniform minimum requirements on states to protect IP. Often, U.S. and foreign IP legislation directly reference these treaties, so that it is difficult to explain domestic procedures without some idea of the treaties involved. The network of detailed IP treaties, both multilateral and bilateral, to which the United States and many of its trading partners are a party creates a nearly global baseline of protection on which a business firm can rely. In this chapter, you will learn how the international community has used treaties to harmonize their laws protecting IP. There is, of course, variation in what kinds of IP are protected and how they are protected from country to country. No international treaty creates complete harmonization among national IP laws, much less in enforcement of the laws. But it is helpful to have some idea of what most states have agreed are the minimum standards of protection that can be expected by IP owners.

We will then turn to the mechanics of registering IP to ensure that it is properly protected and enforceable in foreign countries. Because IP is normally protected on a state-by-state basis, states must coordinate with one another through treaties in order to simplify IP registrations internationally and to facilitate international business involving IP rights.

Once a business firm has registered its IP in foreign markets, it has taken one of the first steps toward expanding its commercial horizons globally. But further steps are needed to protect IP abroad, and to protect domestic IP rights from foreign acts that may diminish its value, primarily by using special administrative procedures.

In this chapter you will learn:

- the terms of the most important treaties harmonizing national IP laws for international business purposes;
- the basic treaty-based procedures for registering IP rights in multiple countries using a single application;
- how some groups of states have adopted regional treaties to allow multinational registration of IP rights within specific geographic areas;
- how an intellectual property owner can stop the importation of infringing products at the border using administrative mechanisms such as customs recordation and trade remedies; and
- what a "grey market import" or "parallel import" is, and the circumstances under which an IP owner can control competition in imported goods bearing or embodying its intellectual property.

1.1 The Development of International Legal Protection for Intellectual Property

The European powers recognized long ago that the facility of moving books, maps, and new inventions across national boundaries made their unauthorized copying or manufacture in other countries inevitable. Advances in mechanized transportation technology during the nineteenth, especially the invention of steamships and the spread of railroads, made the world seem ever smaller. Consequently, these states perceived an opportunity to secure the control of new literary and artistic works and of advances in technology beyond national borders for the benefit of their authors and inventors.

Multilateral treaties for the protection of IP followed, beginning in the late nineteenth century. These treaties were designed to address the general problem of international "free riding." It was thought that an authors, artists, and inventors should have the right not only within national boundaries to prevent others from using their expressive works and inventions without authorization. Under the treaties, creators of IP were to have a right to prevent their unauthorized use in foreign countries as well. After all, an author of a novel or map, and an inventor of a new technology, might be the first to produce it anywhere in the world. The creator confers a benefit on anyone who might use his or her work, wherever the user might be located. Why, it was thought, should the creator not be compensated for that benefit, regardless of the country where the work's benefits are enjoyed?

What followed was a major treaty providing some rules on the international protection of trademarks and utility patents on "industrial designs," meaning useful inventions, in 1883. Three years later, the European powers adopted a treaty for the international protection of expressive works by copyright, at the instigation of the French novelist and poet Victor Hugo. Each of these treaties was revised many times in subsequent years. In their wake came a few scattered IP treaties, but progress in the field was interrupted by the two world wars.

The year 1970 saw a rebirth of the IP treaty-making process with the conclusion of the Patent Cooperation Treaty. A constellation of treaties dealing with both traditional and new aspects of IP were concluded in subsequent years, and an important IGO, the World Intellectual Property Organization, now oversees both negotiation and implementation of most of these. Despite the profusion and complexity of these treaties, there are only a few key instruments and principles that every lawyer should know in planning and executing international business transactions.

1.2 The Major Intellectual Property Treaties

Intellectual property treaties follow the general rule that only states may invoke their protections. However, they usually do something else that can affect private actors—they impose minimum standards of IP protection, thereby giving private actors significant assurance that foreign states will meet the promised standards. The greater the international harmonization of IP rules, the more efficient it is for private actors to obtain multinational protection of the IP and enjoy the consequent ability to commercialize it in foreign countries.

The status of a foreign state as a party or nonparty to an international IP treaty can help a business firm to determine the ease of registration as well as the scope and reliability of protection in that state. That a private IP owner cannot usually invoke the treaty directly to challenge a foreign state's failure to fulfill its treaty obligations does not undermine the treaty's value as a signal of the state's protection of IP rights, because any state party to the IP treaty can invoke any other state party's breach to pressure the breaching state to conform to its treaty obligations. The result is that states usually comply with treaties of all kinds, allowing business firms to rely on treaty adherence as an indicator, if a sometimes imperfect or incomplete one, of its prospects for protecting its IP in the foreign market.

To illustrate the extent to which states have harmonized their IP laws through international treaties, and thereby facilitated international trade and investment by companies that rely on their IP in their business model, it will be helpful to review the main terms of the most widely-subscribed IP treaties. The focus will be on treaties of especially general adherence and broad scope. Regardless of whether the treaty is bilateral, regional, or global, it is important to emphasize that these treaties almost always set a *floor* beneath which standards of protection may not sink. They rarely create a ceiling that limits any state's decision to protect IP more vigorously than the treaty requires. Some of these treaties deal with one kind of IP only; while others deal with multiple kinds.

A. The TRIPS Agreement

The **Agreement on Trade-Related Aspects of Intellectual Property Rights** (**TRIPS Agreement**) was introduced in the last chapter as one of the World Trade Organization (WTO) Agreements. It is today the most important single IP treaty in the world. This is partly because all WTO members are automatically parties to the TRIPS Agreement. But it is also because of its very broad scope. It is the only multilateral treaty that sets detailed substantive and procedural standards for all of the general categories of IP, and others as well.

The TRIPS Agreement's substantive provisions are divided into four parts. The first lays out general principles such as the duties of national treatment and most-favored-nation treatment, and general exceptions to the treaty's obligations. Part II sets forth the substantive standards of IP protection. This part is divided into eight subparts, most dealing with a specific kind of IP. These include the four major divisions (copyright, patent, trademark, and trade secret), but some specific protections as well for design patents, geographical indications, and semiconductor layout designs. This part includes rules about what kinds of expressive works and inventions and copyrightable and patentable, respectively; conditions for the grant of IP protection and minimum periods of protection; and acceptable reasons for denying protection. The eighth subpart sets forth general principles for regulating IP licensing practices that implicate competition (antitrust) law.

Part III deals with enforcement obligations, including the availability of provisional measures to protect IP, the remedies that must be made available, civil and criminal infringement procedures for adjudication and administrative review, and measures for the prevention of import infringement taken at the border. This includes the consequential and innovative article 51:

> Article 51
>
> *Suspension of Release by Customs Authorities*
>
> Members shall, in conformity with the provisions set out below, adopt procedures[13] to enable a right holder, who has valid grounds for suspecting that the importation of counterfeit trademark or pirated copyright goods may take place, to lodge an application in writing with competent authorities, administrative or judicial, for the suspension by the customs authorities of the release into free circulation of such goods. * * *
>
> [13] It is understood that there shall be no obligation to apply such procedures to imports of goods put on the market in another country by or with the consent of the right holder, or to goods in transit.

The subsequent articles define the procedures for applying for the suspension of importation.

Finally, Article 64 of the TRIPs Agreement incorporates the WTO Dispute Settlement Understanding (DSU) by reference. Under the DSU, WTO members claiming that another WTO member has failed to fulfill its obligations under the TRIPs Agreement may consult with one another with the objective of resolving the dispute amicably. Should negotiation fail, a complaining state may refer the dispute to the WTO Dispute Settlement Body (DSB), which may issue a decision on compliance that binds the parties.

The WTO's dispute settlement mechanism greatly enhances the reliability of the TRIPs Agreement for IP owners. Although a private party cannot invoke the DSU, if any WTO member should fail to fulfill its TRIPs Agreement obligations, the IP owner may seek assistance from its government to use the dispute settlement mechanism to convince its trading partner to honor its TRIPs Agreement obligations. DSB decisions furnish a useful source of interpretive law relating to the TRIPs Agreement.

B. The Paris Convention

The 1883 **Paris Convention for the Protection of Industrial Property** (the **Paris Convention**, for short) commits state parties to protecting "industrial property," an archaic term that included both utility and design patents, as well as trademarks and trade names. The Paris Convention does not create any obligations with respect to copyright.

For patentable inventions, the Paris Convention imposes minimum substantive standards of protection, establishes some basic procedures for grant, takes steps to ensure equal treatment based on the nationality of inventors, and also creates a system to prevent inventors who apply for a patent in their own country before applying in foreign countries from losing the right to obtain foreign patents based on their domestic filing. For trademarks, the Paris Convention creates a similar right of priority and prohibits canceling the mark for certain commercial uses unlikely to confuse consumers. Almost every state in the world today is a party to the Paris Convention, which is today the product of well over a century of development and amendment.

Most of the important substantive provisions of the Paris Convention are incorporated by reference into the TRIPS Agreement. This means that the TRIPS Agreement cannot be entirely understood without also reviewing much of the Paris Convention. It also means that, even if a WTO member is not a party to the Paris Convention, by joining the WTO it commits itself to the Paris Convention's most important provisions. On the other hand, the Paris Convention has a few more parties than the TRIPS Agreement, and so the former may be operative even when the TRIPS Agreement does not apply between state parties.

C. The Berne Convention

The 1886 **Berne Convention for the Protection of Literary and Artistic Works** (**Berne Convention**) creates the basic international obligations of recognition and protection of expressive works through copyright law. The Convention encompasses most kinds of visually or audibly perceptible expressive work capable of recordation, including not only art and entertainment such as novels, music, paintings, sculptures, and cinematic works, but also—importantly for international business firms in general—any written work product (including reports, multimedia presentations, and memoranda), illustrations, maps, schematics, architectural plans, engineering blueprints, and 3-dimensional models. The Berne Convention provides quite detailed substantive and procedural standards for the protection of copyrighted works internationally.

The Berne Convention has many parties, but its significance is not limited to them. As with the Paris Convention, most of the important substantive provisions of the Berne Convention are incorporated by reference into the TRIPS Agreement, and so its key provisions apply to all WTO members.

D. Other Important IP Treaties

Most members of the international community have adopted several other important multilateral treaties relating to intellectual property law. Many of these were negotiated under the auspices of the **World Intellectual Property Organization (WIPO)**.

The WIPO is an intergovernmental organization established as a United Nations agency in 1967 and headquartered in Geneva, Switzerland. Its mission is to serve as a global forum for cooperation in the promotion of IP through the progressive development of international law, education on the uses and benefits of IP, and facilitation of the IP treaty systems.

Among the many treaties administered by WIPO, four stand out as particularly important. Two of them, the WIPO Patent Law Treaty and WIPO Trademark Law Treaty, harmonize and simplify procedures for applying for patents and trademarks, respectively. These treaties neither harmonize nor elevate substantive standards of protection. They simply make getting IP protection easier and more predictable in state parties.

In contrast, the **WIPO Copyright Treaty**, adopted in 1996, does require state parties to adopt specific copyright protections. These include protection for computer programs and compilations of data such as databases. In addition, it includes specific rights for copyright owners relating to the distribution and communication of protected works to the public through such means as rental, Internet posting, and streaming.

Figure 3.1. WIPO Headquarters in Geneva.
Credit: © 2011 by Mercedes Martinez, CC License.

The **WIPO Performances and Phonograms Treaty**, adopted in 2002, protects the rights of record labels to distribute protected music by the same means. In addition, it protects the rights of audio and visual performers to record and distribute their performances to the public. This treaty was considered necessary because copyright only applies to expressive works that are "fixed in a tangible medium," meaning recorded in a manner that allows for future viewing or listening. Before this treaty was adopted, there was no major international treaty protecting live performances such as music concerts, plays, and dance performances from unauthorized recordation.

Finally, some regional and bilateral trade agreements also establish standards of IP protection. These treaties are important not only because they affect the parties bound by them. The most-favored-nation clause of the TRIPS Agreement (discussed below) means that, when a WTO member increases IP protection with respect to any country in the world, it must grant an identical increase to all WTO members. Aside from the European Union's harmonized IP systems, which will be discussed later, these **TRIPS-plus** disciplines are most commonly found in the IP chapter of bilateral free trade agreements. For example, most modern FTAs negotiated by the United States extend the term of copyright protection from 50 years after death of the author (required by the Berne Convention and TRIPS Agreement) to 70 years after death.

Thus, while the major multilateral IP conventions can give a business

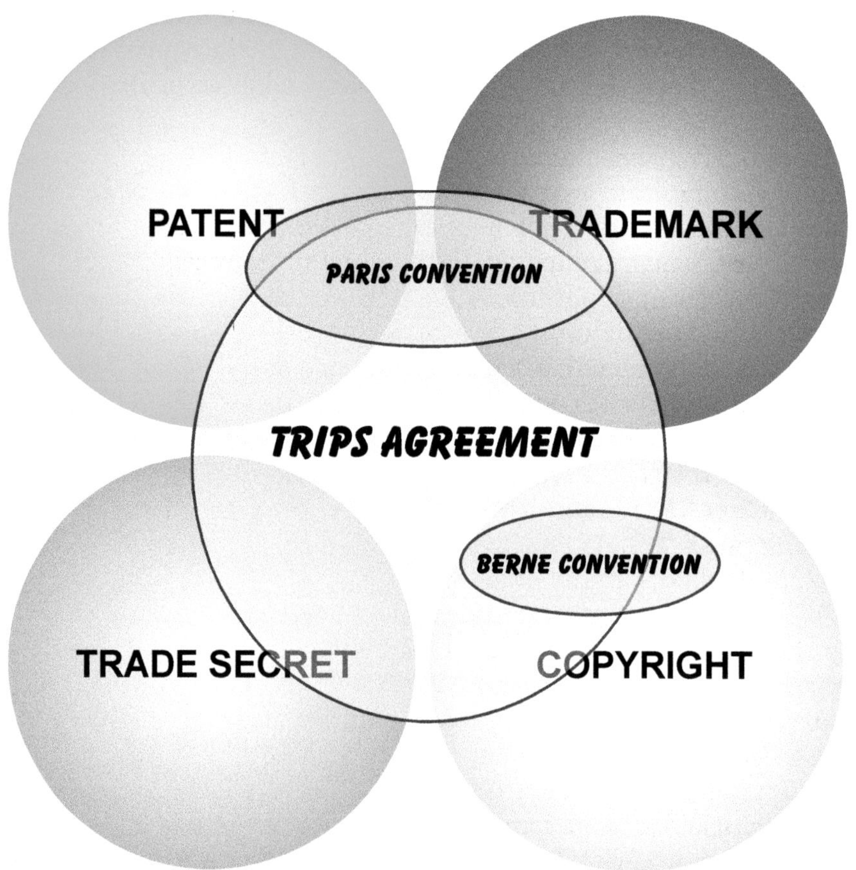

Figure 3.2. A schematic representation of the scope of the major substantive IP treaties.

firm a good idea of the minimum standards of IP protection that they may expect when exporting to or investing in other countries, the picture is complicated by the fact that standards may be even higher in some countries, depending on the existence of bilateral or regional treaties. In determining the international legal obligations of states to protect IP, then, it is important to review all applicable treaties and not just the major multilateral conventions.

1.3 General Treaty Principles

Before getting to the substantive doctrines of global IP protection, there are some important basic principles in the treaties discussed above that apply to IP protection generally. This section will describe the three most consequential: the territorial independence of IP rights, nondiscrimination principles, and priority rights.

A. Territorial Independence

The **territorial independence** of IP refers to the fact that, with a few exceptions to be discussed later, every sovereign state grants IP rights valid within its territory only. A patent or trademark issued by a state, and a copyright recognized in that state, are valid in that same state only. Other countries do not necessarily grant the same rights to the same IP. Even when two states grant identical patents, trademarks, or copyrights on identical subject matter, they have granted separate protections. The reason is that states generally cannot grant IP rights outside their territories under international law. At the same time, states are usually very reluctant to recognize and enforce IP rights granted in foreign countries.

An example can illustrate the principle best. Suppose Ruritania and Grand Fenwick have nearly identical copyright laws. Each simultaneously grants a copyright to Wanda Warbler for her popular song "Fulsome Love." The cancellation of Warbler's copyright on Fulsome Love in Ruritania has no effect on the validity of the song's copyright in Grand Fenwick. By the same token, if Warbler transfers her Ruritanian copyright to a third party, it does not affect her continued ownership of the Grand Fenwick copyright to the song.

Infringement works the same way. Suppose a sampling artist in Grand Fenwick, Ynot, allegedly infringed Warbler's copyright by using excerpts from Fulsome Love in his own song. Ynot's song was played solely in live performances and on the radio in Grand Fenwick. Warbler may have a copyright infringement cause of action in Grand Fenwick, but there is no reason to assume she can sue Ynot for copyright infringement in Ruritania.

The general legal basis for IP's territorial independence is that IP law is the creature of the domestic laws of states; it is not created by international treaties. Treaties merely obligate states to adopt certain standards of and procedures for protection. These principles are recognized in Paris Convention articles 4*bis* (respecting patents) and 6 (respecting trademarks), both of which are incorporated into the TRIPS Agreement by reference.

In the case of copyright, there is one minor wrinkle. Under article 5 of the Berne Convention (also incorporated into the TRIPS Agreement), all state parties must grant copyright protection without any formalities to qualifying expressive works. That means an expressive work entitled to copyright protection in any Berne Convention state or WTO member automatically receives copyright protection in every other Berne Convention state and WTO member. Nonetheless, the uniformity of a right to protection does not compromise the territorial independence principle. The rights conferred are "governed exclusively by the laws of the country where protection is claimed." Berne Convention art. 5(2).

B. Nondiscrimination

You have already been introduced to the concepts of **national treatment** and **most-favored-nation (MFN) treatment**. The Paris and Berne conventions each include a national treatment obligation but no MFN principle. The TRIPS Agreement applies both principles.

Article 3 of the TRIPS Agreement articulates a general national treatment duty relating to all of the Agreement's IP commitments. It provides that, subject to certain exceptions, "Each [WTO] Member shall accord to the nationals of other Members treatment no less favourable than that it accords to its own nationals with regard to the protection of intellectual property * * *."

In addition, the TRIPS Agreement article 4 is a standard MFN clause. It provides, subject to certain exemptions:

> With regard to the protection of intellectual property, any advantage, favour, privilege or immunity granted by a Member to the nationals of any other country shall be accorded immediately and unconditionally to the nationals of all other Members.

In other words, by granting concessions to another state, a WTO member *ipso facto* grants the same concession to all other WTO members. This commitment differs from a national treatment obligation, because it is possible that a WTO would give more favorable IP treatment to nationals of a foreign country than it does to its own nationals. In such cases, nationals of all other WTO members benefit from whichever treatment (national or MFN) is most favorable.

C. Priority Rights

The Paris Convention and, by extension, TRIPS Agreement create what is called a right of priority for patents and trademarks. Under a **right of priority**, the date a patent or trademark application was filed in one Paris Convention party or WTO member will be considered the date of application in all other Paris Convention parties or WTO members for a limited period of time.

Applicants thus receive a "grace period" to complete their foreign applications without losing priority. The right of priority thereby ameliorates the risk of a patent or trademark applicant applying in one country and, while preparing a foreign application, a third party registers the same or a similar patent or trademark in the foreign country, thereby seizing seniority in that foreign country from the first registrant.

Specifically, Paris Convention article 4 provides that, when an inventor files a utility patent application in any Paris Convention party, the inventor must be given at least 12 months from that date to apply for a patent application in every other contracting party. During that time, the parties will treat the applicant's filing date in the first country as the filing date for their own country.

For example, suppose inventor Earle filed a patent application in WTO member Freedonia on January 1, 2018, and inventor Lait filed a patent application claiming the same invention in WTO member Osterlich on June 1, 2018. Earle then filed a patent application in Osterlich on July 1, 2018. Under the TRIPS Agreement via the Paris Convention, the fact that Lait filed a patent application in Osterlich before Earle did so does not mean that Lait is entitled to the patent. Instead, Earle will be deemed to have filed a patent application in Osterlich on the same day he filed the application in Freedonia (January 1, 2018), provided he states in his Osterlich patent application that he is relying on a Paris Convention right of priority. Of course, if Earle had waited until January 2, 2019 to file a patent application in Osterlich, he would have no right of priority, because he exceeded the 12-month period.

The Paris Convention and TRIPS Agreement similarly establish a right of priority for trademark applicants. Such applicants have a six-month priority period. As with the patent priority right, if any other party applies to register a trademark during the priority period, it must prove use in commerce before

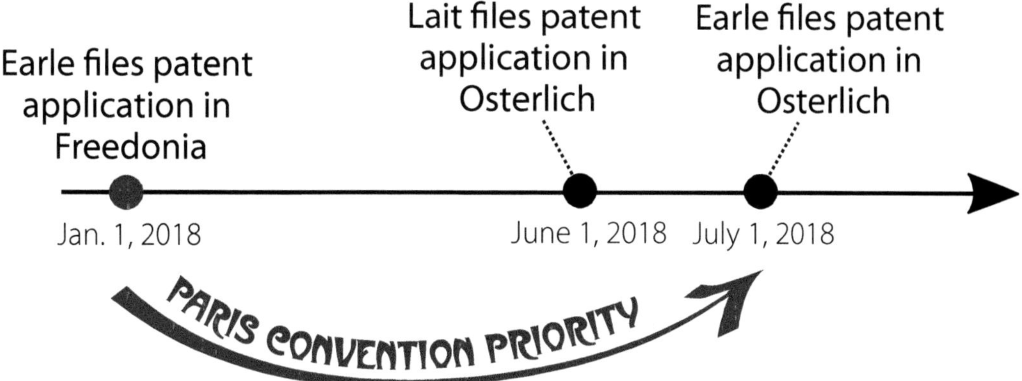

Figure 3.3. An example of international priority in the patent field under the Paris Convention.

the priority date established by the filer.

In contrast, neither the Berne Convention nor the TRIPS Agreement include a priority right for copyrights. The reason for this omission is that, under these treaties, copyrightable works are automatically entitled to protection in all Berne Convention and WTO Agreement contracting parties without the need for any formalities such as registration. There is no time lag between the creation of the work in one Berne or WTO country and its protection in all the others. Moreover, because two individuals who created very similar expressive works each can have a copyright in her own work if they were created entirely separately, there is no need for priority. Copyright law prohibit unauthorized copying; it does not prevent two unrelated creators from each owning rights in independently created similar works, no matter in what sequence they were produced.

Now that you are familiar the general treaty principles relating to international IP protection, we will move on to the minimum standards of international protection established by the treaties discussed here for the four principle kinds of IP: patents, trademarks, copyrights, and trade secrets.

1.4 International Utility Patent Protection

Due to the territorial independence principle, patents are generally granted and enforced on a state-by-state basis. However, to a degree, the Paris Convention and TRIPS Agreement globally harmonize the conditions for obtaining a patent and the protections afforded by patents. Only in those few states that are neither Paris Convention parties nor WTO members do these treaties not require the minimum standards discussed here. Because the TRIPS Agreement is more comprehensive than the Paris Convention, and because almost all economically important countries are WTO members, we will focus on the requirements of the TRIPS Agreement.

Utility patents protect "inventions," which may defined as new and useful variations in technology that require some significant insight. Technologies that would have been obvious to any scientist, engineer, or other expert in the field do not qualify for a patent. A novel pharmaceutical compound, a creatively conceived mechanical device or semiconductor chip, and an unexpectedly useful new alloy of metals are all the kind of inventions eligible for patent protection. Patents protect inventions by granting a legal right to exclude other persons from making or using the patented invention without the patent owner's permission.

Patents must be obtained by an application to the appropriate government agency. In the application, the inventor will describe the patented invention, including how to make and use it. If this application process is successful, the inventor will receive a certificate of patent, and the information about the invention will be published for the public to see. Public disclosure of the invention is commonly considered one of the benefits to the public of patents in compensation for the inventor's right to exclude others from benefiting from that invention for the period of patent protection.

The Paris Convention establishes some minimum procedural and substantive standards for the patent law of each state party, but these are not extensive. TRIPS Agreement Section 5 expands on the Paris Convention by including several important requirements for the content of patent laws in WTO member states. These include the following:

- Article 27: Patents must be granted in all fields of technology without discrimination as to the place of invention or place where the patented products are manufactured. However, certain specified classes of inventions may be excluded from patentable subject matter, such as inventions that threaten the public order or morality; animal or plant life; the environment; or human health. Also, medical diagnostic, therapeutic, or surgical methods for humans and animals need not be patentable. Nor must WTO members allow patents on animals themselves. Plants must either be patentable or protectable by some alternative regime.

- Article 28: Patents must grant a right to exclude others from making, using, selling, offering to sell, or importing the patented item into the protecting state without a license. Patent owners must also have the right to assign or license the patent to others.

- Article 31: Strict limitations are imposed on the ability of member states to use or grant compulsory licenses. These are licenses granted by the state to third parties to make or sell the patented invention without the patent owner's consent. The limitations are sufficiently stringent that the TRIPS Agreement has in practice precluded states from using compulsory licenses in all but the rarest cases.

- Article 33: The term of the patent must be at least twenty years, starting from the date the application was filed.

Taken together, these provisions ensure that states will grant patent protection to a very broad scope of technology, the protection will include a fairly comprehensive list of rights to profit from the patented invention, and the patent protection will last long enough to give most patent owners a chance to earn that profit.

1.5 Trademark Protections

Trademarks are words, slogans, logos, and other identifiers to help consumers distinguish a producer's goods or services from the similar goods or services of others. They are sometimes called "brand names." NIKE and its swoosh logo are both trademarks registered worldwide for athletic shoes and clothing. APPLE, IPHONE, and the apple logo are trademarks for electronic products and services. Here we will focus on products. By authorizing trademark owners to prevent unauthorized parties from using the mark, trademark law prevents consumers from confusing the source of the marked products. They also encourage trademark owners to invest in building the reputation of their products through continuous improvement and marketing campaigns. Public recognition of the mark and interest in the goods or services designated by the mark is commonly called **good will**. All trademarks are potentially commercially useful, but good will is what makes marks commercially valuable.

A. Scope of Protection

The substantive and procedural standards of trademark law established by the Paris Convention are comparatively detailed and extensive. The most important of these are the following:

- Article 5(C): A state party may not cancel a registered mark for non-use except (1) after a reasonable period of time and (2) unless the owner cannot justify the delay in use. Nor may a state invalidate a mark because its owner uses variants of the mark in commerce, unless these variants harm the distinctive character of the mark.

- Article 6*quinquies*: States must allow the registration of marks that are already registered in other state parties, unless (1) such registration would infringe a preexisting right, (2) the mark lacks distinctive character, or (3) the mark is "contrary to morality or public order and, in particular, of such a nature as to deceive the public." The fact that the mark sought to be registered differs from a mark owned by the same person in a foreign country cannot constitute grounds for denial or invalidation of registration.

- Article 9: State parties are obligated to seize goods bearing a counterfeit trademark when manufactured within the state. They are further required to seize, exclude, or at least provide damages, injunctions, or other remedies when infringing goods are imported into the state.

Remember that these provisions are incorporated by reference into the TRIPS Agreement. The TRIPS Agreement expands on the Paris Convention by adding several important provisions:

- Article 15(2): WTO members may not condition the registration of a trademark on actual use in commerce, as long as the registrant does in fact use the mark in commerce within three years after applying to register the mark. Thus, WTO members must allow **intent-to-use**

applications for trademarks. This provision allows business firms to register a mark in a foreign state before beginning commerce there.

- Article 16: A likelihood of confusion is presumed and registration of a confusingly similar mark should be denied when identical marks are used to designate identical goods or services.
- Articles 18 & 19: The initial term of protection of a trademark must be at least seven years. Marks must be renewable indefinitely, unless the trademark owner has stopped using the mark in commerce for an uninterrupted period of three years.
- Article 21: No WTO member state may force a trademark owner to license its mark to anyone else. Also, owners of a registered mark have the right to assign the mark without transferring the business to which the mark belongs. This allows multinational corporations to shift ownership of their trademarks and associated good will among affiliated companies without having to sell other assets, such as office buildings or manufacturing equipment.

Together, these provisions ensure that business firms have wide latitude to use their trademarks internationally without interference from state governments. The right to register marks before they are used in commerce is especially important, because it means a business firm need not wait until it is prepared to enter a foreign market before it can reserve the right to use its trademark in that market. Combined with the six-month priority right, business firms have significant flexibility in timing their entry into foreign markets without forfeiting their trademarks.

B. Famous Marks

Because almost all countries grant a trademark to the first applicant, firms that own famous trademarks are exposed to a significant risk in international business. Suppose General Widget Corp. has developed a product called Sodisco in its home state of Freedonia. One year after introducing Sodisco in Freedonia (and registering the SODISCO mark there), the product has become so explosively popular that its reputation and demand have circled the globe. Unfortunately, General Widget is only a moderately-sized company and does not have the immediate resources to register its marks and market its products worldwide. It will have to raise capital to expand its commerce abroad, which takes time. While it does that, various small competitors in the foreign states of Smalldonia and Zembia immediately capitalize on the popularity of General Widget's products by registering the SODISCO mark in those two countries and offering imitations of General Widget's products under that mark.

Assuming the three countries are WTO members or parties to the

Paris Convention, General Widget cannot take advantage of the priority period, because six months has already elapsed since it applied for registration in Freedonia. Because Smalldonia and Zembia grant trademark rights to the first registrant, it seems others in those countries can free ride on General Widget's reputation and deceive consumers. Unless, that is, international treaties protect General Widget in some way.

The Paris Convention offers a solution in article 6*bis*, which requires state parties to deny or cancel registration of any mark that is liable to create confusion with a famous or well-known mark in the country, even though the famous mark has not yet been registered. The mark must be well-known only among the relevant consuming public; it does not need to be famous to everyone in the country. In the example, this means that General Widget's competitors in Smalldonia and Zembia cannot preempt General Widget in those countries by registering the SODISCO trademark.

TRIPS Agreement article 16(3) expands this protection to encompass product categories other than the ones for which General Widget registered the SODISCO mark. No company in Smalldonia or Zembia can register the SODISCO mark for *different* goods, if relevant consumers are likely to infer a connection between those different goods and General Widget. Famous marks are thus given strong protection against would-be trademark squatters.

That said, like other treaty-based obligations, consistent enforcement at the national level is not guaranteed. For example, the U.S. Patent and Trademark Office has put the United States in violation of its obligations under the Paris Convention and TRIPS Agreement by refusing to cancel domestic registrations that replicate a famous foreign mark.* Some foreign states do the same.

C. Geographical Indications

The TRIPS Agreement also creates detailed rules relating to **geographical indications**, also known as "appellations of origin." A geographical indication is not a trademark. It is instead a designation of the geographic origin of a product, such as "Parma" ham, "Champagne" sparkling wine, or "Wisconsin" cheese. These provisions, not present in the Paris Convention, are designed to protect interests in famous products originating in specific localities, like Roquefort, France or Kona, Hawai'i. TRIPS Agreement article 22 provides in relevant part:

*Bayer Consumer Care AG v. Belmora LLC, 90 U.S.P.Q.2d 1587, 1589-91 (T.T.A.B. 2009). *But cf.* Fiat Grp. Auto. S.p.A. v. ISM, Inc., 94 U.S.P.Q.2d 1111, 1113-15 (T.T.A.B. 2010) (suggesting that, "in an unusual case, activity outside the United States related to a mark could potentially result in the mark becoming well-known within the United States, even without any form of activity in the United States," thereby giving rise to a dilution claim).

Article 22: Protection of Geographical Indications

> 1. Geographical indications are, for the purposes of this Agreement, indications which identify a good as originating in the territory of a Member, or a region or locality in that territory, where a given quality, reputation or other characteristic of the good is essentially attributable to its geographical origin.
>
> 2. In respect of geographical indications, Members shall provide the legal means for interested parties to prevent:
>
> (a) the use of any means in the designation or presentation of a good that indicates or suggests that the good in question originates in a geographical area other than the true place of origin in a manner which misleads the public as to the geographical origin of the good;
>
> (b) any use which constitutes an act of unfair competition within the meaning of Article 10*bis* of the Paris Convention (1967).
>
> 3. A Member shall, *ex officio* if its legislation so permits or at the request of an interested party, refuse or invalidate the registration of a trademark which contains or consists of a geographical indication with respect to goods not originating in the territory indicated, if use of the indication in the trademark for such goods in that Member is of such a nature as to mislead the public as to the true place of origin. * * *

Attempts to expand and strengthen protections of geographical indications through additional treaties have not met with widespread success.

Figure 3.4. Some geographical indications: Egyptian cotton, French champagne, Darjeeling tea from India, Parma prosciutto from Italy, Tahitian mono'i oil, Roquefort cheese from France, Colombian coffee, and Wisconsin cheese.

1.6 Copyright Protections

As noted, copyrights protect expressive works from unauthorized reproduction and distribution. With digital technology has come the ability to quickly and inexpensively reproduce almost any kind of expressive work. The ease of production creates economies of scale for copyright-based industries, such as the music, book publishing, and software industries. Companies in these industries can exploit a global market with ever-increasing ease, distributing content around the world at relatively little cost. The global scope of the Internet and increased use of satellite communications has created the potential for massive increases in distribution of copyrighted works.

But the low cost of reproduction also tempts the unscrupulous to reproduce the expressive works of others without paying license fees. Because such copyists did not incur the cost of developing, marketing, and popularizing the copyrighted work, they can actually sell the reproduced work at a much lower cost than the copyright owner itself, thereby undercutting the incentive to produce the work. To avoid or at least ameliorate this undesirable result, it must not be made overly burdensome for a publisher or studio to protect its work in foreign countries. Facilitating such protection is one of the major goals of international treaties dealing with copyright.

The most important accomplishment of the Berne Convention is to require all state parties to offer a minimum standard of protection to all authors who are either a national of, or who create a copyrightable work in, any member state without any necessity of registration or other formalities. This means that any person who creates an original expressive work in any of the Berne Convention or WTO member states enjoys automatic copyright protection in all of the Berne and WTO member states. There is no necessity even to designate the work as copyright protected with the copyright symbol: ©.*

The Berne Convention also provides control to the copyright owner over the reproduction and distribution of the protected works, as well as certain kinds of derivative works:

> Article 8
>
> Authors of literary and artistic works protected by this Convention shall enjoy the exclusive right of making and of authorizing the translation of their works throughout the term of protection of their rights in the original works.
>
> Article 12
>
> Authors of literary or artistic works shall enjoy the exclusive right of authorizing adaptations, arrangements and other alterations of their works.

* In a handful of countries, however, the copyright symbol is still necessary to ensure protection. These countries are neither members of the WTO nor parties to the Berne Convention, but may be parties to the Universal Copyright Convention, which allows states to require copyright symbol as a condition for protection.

Article 14 further provides that authors of literary and artistic works have the exclusive right of film adaptation of their works. Pursuant to Articles 2(3) and 14*bis*, these "derivative works" are separately copyrightable, but their commercial distribution and exploitation must be controlled by the copyright owner of the original work. In the context of international business transactions, translations and adaptations of copyrighted works (for example, a motion picture based on a novel) can be especially important sources of international revenue to the copyright owner.

Other important minimum standards mandated by the Berne Convention include the following:

- Article 7: The copyright must generally endure for at least fifty years after the death of the author or date of publication.
- Article 16: Infringing copies of copyright-protected works must be seized upon importation or distribution within any member state. Article 16 does not state what must happen to the copies after seizure—whether they must be destroyed or may be returned to foreign or domestic channels of commerce in some form.

The TRIPS Agreement incorporates these provisions of the Berne Convention, but expands on them significantly:

- Article 10: Member states are obligated to grant copyrights on computer programs and some kind of protection for certain databases.
- Article 11: Member states are obligated to ensure that authors of computer programs and "cinematographic works" such as motion pictures have the exclusive right "to authorize or to prohibit the commercial rental to the public of originals or copies of their copyright works."
- Article 14(1): Musicians, dancers, singers, actors, and other live performers are given the right to prevent the recordation or broadcasting of their performances without their permission.
- Article 14(2)-(4): Musical recording ("phonogram") producers and television or radio broadcasters are ensured the right to control the recordation, rebroadcasting, reproduction, and rental of their broadcasts and recordings.

As noted earlier, the WIPO Copyright Treaty further expands these provisions with respect to rental, distribution, and broadcasting rights.

1.7 Unfair Competition and Trade Secrets

A. Unfair Competition

The Paris Convention requires states to prohibit "unfair competition," which it defines as any "act of competition contrary to honest practices in industrial or commercial matters." By way of elaboration, it obligates states specifically to prohibit:

> 1. all acts of such a nature as to create confusion by any means whatever with the establishment, the goods, or the industrial or commercial activities, of a competitor;
> 2. false allegations in the course of trade of such a nature as to discredit the establishment, the goods, or the industrial or commercial activities, of a competitor;
> 3. indications or allegations the use of which in the course of trade is liable to mislead the public as to the nature, the manufacturing process, the characteristics, the suitability for their purpose, or the quantity, of the goods.

Paris Convention art. 10*bis*. The focus is on protecting consumers from false advertising or similar claims in a commercial context, and from practices that might cause them to confuse one product or manufacturer for another.

B. Trade Secret Protection

The TRIPS Agreement incorporates Paris Convention article 10*bis*, but it also expands on it by specifically including protections for "undisclosed information." It is consequently the first multilateral treaty to define a clear standard of trade secret protection. In particular, the TRIPS Agreement provides:

> 2. Natural and legal persons shall have the possibility of preventing information lawfully within their control from being disclosed to, acquired by, or used by others without their consent in a manner contrary to honest commercial practices so long as such information:
>
> (a) is secret in the sense that it is not, as a body or in the precise configuration and assembly of its components, generally known among or readily accessible to persons within the circles that normally deal with the kind of information in question;
>
> (b) has commercial value because it is secret; and
>
> (c) has been subject to reasonable steps under the circumstances, by the person lawfully in control of the information, to keep it secret.

TRIPS Agreement art. 39(2).

1.8 Enforcement Obligations Under the TRIPS Agreement

One very important new element found in Part III of the TRIPS Agreement, is the addition of IP enforcement obligations for all WTO members respecting. To comply with the TRIPs Agreement, it is not enough to enact laws protecting IP by minimum standards; WTO member states must enforce their laws according to the modalities prescribed in Part III. These obligations extend to all IP protected by the TRIPs Agreement.

In general, Part III requires WTO members to adopt fair and equitable procedures to allow IP owners to enforce their rights. Such procedures must not be complicated, costly, or unduly protracted. Decisions on infringement must be based on evidence presented in a hearing of some kind and must be in writing and reasoned. The state must also provide an opportunity for appeal to a higher authority.

In civil and administrative cases, authorities must have the power to enjoin future IP infringement. Injunctions were uncommon in many civil law jurisdictions before 1994. Under the TRIPS Agreement, the injunctive authority must include the ability to order provisional measures such as a preliminary order to prevent infringing goods from entering the channels of commerce by sale or importation, and the power to seize, destroy, or otherwise prevent goods from harming the IP owner. Part III also includes detailed provisions requiring border enforcement against infringing imports. Available remedies must also include damages sufficient to compensate fully the IP owner for injuries caused by the infringement. Such measures were not required by any IP treaty prior to the TRIPS Agreement.

1.9 IP Treaties in Summary

The substantive and procedural IP rights, and the enforcement obligations imposed on states, in the treaties discussed here provide strong protections, at least on paper. They ensure respect for all four types of IP. The minimum protection standards define a broad range of inventions, expressive works, branded products and services, and trade secrets that must be protected.

The protection obligations are no longer limited to traditional IP subject matter. Patents must encompass new technologies such as pharmaceuticals, nanomaterials, and some kinds of biotechnology. Copyrights must be granted for computer software; live performers have the right to prevent others from recording their performances; and broadcasters must be granted exclusive recording and rebroadcasting rights. Trademarks must be granted before the marked goods or services have entered commerce, and foreign famous trademarks must be protected by countries in which the owner of the famous mark has never done business or even intends to do business in the foreseeable future. States must adopt measures to protect trade secrets from dishonest use by competitors or public disclosure.

The treaties also expand the kinds of protection available for these IP rights. They set minimum terms of protection for patents, copyrights, and trademarks that nearly every country in the world must adopt. They harmonize many of the procedures and requirements for obtaining patent and trademark protection. They ensure copyrightable works will benefit from nearly global protection as soon as they are recorded.

However, as might be expected, actual enforcement practices vary greatly among states. The TRIPS Agreement builds on previous treaties by requiring states to adopt private administrative or judicial remedies, including injunctions and damages. It also requires states to seize imports of counterfeit or other infringing goods at the border. But, in practice, some states enforce IP rights vigorously and others more sporadically.

The disparity can be partly explained by the fact that the wealthiest states have more resources to devote to IP enforcement than developing countries. It can also partly be explained by self-interest; developing countries have much less to lose by tolerating widespread IP infringement than have the wealthier countries that produce and export most of the world's lucrative IP.

There is not a great deal that a multinational business firm can do about variations in enforcement among states. However, it can inform itself about which states pose a risk of chronic IP infringement. Every year, the **U.S. Trade Representative** (**USTR**) publishes a report on the global state of IP rights protection and enforcement. This publication, called the **Special 301 Report**, gives a country-by-country analysis of significant deficiencies in IP protection and enforcement. By reviewing the Special 301 Report before investing in or trading with a foreign country a business firm can better predict the risks of IP infringement even in states that have committed to extensive treaty obligations for IP protection.

2 Registering Intellectual Property Multinationally

The IP harmonization obligations in the treaties discussed so far make the process of obtaining and enforcing IP rights globally more uniform and predictable. However, the treaties do relatively little to facilitate the international registration of trademarks or patents. Under them, states remain free to require each trademark or patent applicant to apply individually for protection in every state in which the applicant seeks protection. Because the trademark and especially patent application process can be expensive and time-consuming, the possibility of applying to register trademarks and patents in many countries at once would greatly reduce the burdens of global IP protection. Fortunately, there are several important treaties that do just that. For both trademarks and patents, there are multilateral treaties that allow applicants to apply for rights in multiple countries with a single application. In addition, there are regional treaties for the same purpose, and some that even allow an applicant to obtain a single patent or trademark valid in multiple countries.

2.1 Multinational Patent Registration

Almost all countries of any size have a patent office that records patent registrations. In the United States, the **U.S. Patent & Trademark Office** (**PTO**) performs that function. In Mexico it is the Mexican Institute of Industrial Property. In Japan, it is the Japan Patent Office, and so forth. The patent office receives applications from inventors or their agents and, if it determines that the claimed invention merits a patent, will grant and publish the patent for public information in an official gazette, on a website, or in some other manner.

As noted earlier, the territorial independence principle means that each state's patents are valid and enforceable only within its borders. However, many countries have adopted treaties to allow a single patent application to be submitted to multiple states. Although the result will be separate patents in each state, the applicant needs to file only one "international" application to start the process. In addition, some states have agreed by treaty to abandon the territoriality principle and allow multinational IP protection. One patent may be issued for and valid and enforceable in multiple countries. Today, all such treaties are regional in scope; there is no such thing as a global patent.

A. The Multilateral Patent Registration System

To save time and expense in applying for patents in diverse geographical locations, a patent applicant may be able to make use of the 1970 **Patent Cooperation Treaty** (**PCT**). The PCT is a treaty administered by the WIPO. The purpose of the PCT is to facilitate obtaining separate patents in multiple countries covering the same invention. This is especially helpful when patents on the same invention will be sought globally, because the patent applicant can designate every contracting state as a designated country where he or she seeks a patent. As of 2020, the PCT has 152 contracting states.

Although there is no single global patent that is good in every contracting state, the PCT does streamline the patent application process and avoid some unnecessary repetition when multiple states are involved. In short, using the PCT can save a great deal of time and money for an inventor seeking patents abroad.

When an inventor files an international patent application, she begins what is called the **international phase** or **international stage** of the prosecution. She can file this application (designating it as a PCT application) with any national or regional patent agency, such as the U.S. PTO or the European Patent Office. This patent agency is called the **receiving office**. In the international application, the inventor need not designate the PCT state parties for which she seeks a patent; she is presumed to apply for patents in all PCT countries and can select the specific target states later.

The receiving office then forwards the international application to what is called an **International Searching Authority**, which is another name for a national patent agency chosen to search for conflicting patents and other prior art that might preempt a patent under the laws of any state in which the applicant seeks a patent.

For example, suppose Ivan Inventor is a citizen of Sri Lanka. The National Intellectual Property Office of Sri Lanka is not an authorized receiving office, so Ivan must choose a designated receiving office. Ivan can choose the nearby Indian IP Office (which is a receiving office) intending to seek patents in Sri Lanka, India, the United States, and eleven other countries. Alternatively, Ivan could have submitted his application directly to the WIPO's International Bureau as the receiving office. In either case, the receiving office will forward the application to one of the international searching authorities. (If Ivan had filed the international application with a patent office that *is* an international searching authority, then the searching authority will generally perform the international search itself.)

The international searching authority will publish an **international search report** along with a nonbinding written opinion indicating the countries in which invention is likely not to qualify for a patent. The international search report and written opinion indicate the searching authority's preliminary conclusions as to whether the invention meets the patentability requirements in each country designated by Ivan. The international application, search report, and written opinion will then be sent to WIPO's International Bureau within two months. Ivan then designates the states in which he wishes to seek patent protection, which will receive the international application and search report.

At this point, the applicant has some options. The international search report and written opinion will contain information about prior technologies in the designated countries that may prevent a patent from issuing in any given country, but it will not include a thorough analysis of the extent to which the invention fulfills the legal requirements of the various designated countries. If the applicant is confident that his invention is patentable in most or all designated countries, he can proceed directly to the **national phase** or **national stage**, at which point he will begin dealing with the separate national patent agencies directly. Alternatively, if the applicant wants more information about whether the patent is likely to be valid in the designated countries, he may request an **international preliminary examination**.

If the inventor requests a preliminary examination, WIPO's International Bureau will request a national patent agency to perform a patentability analysis for all designated states, including determining whether each country's patentability requirements have been satisfied. The agency performing that analysis is called an **International Preliminary Examining Authority (IPEA)**. What patent agencies are designated as IPEAs? The same ones that are qualified to act as International Searching Authorities, which keeps matters simple.

The applicant will have the opportunity to submit arguments to the IPEA

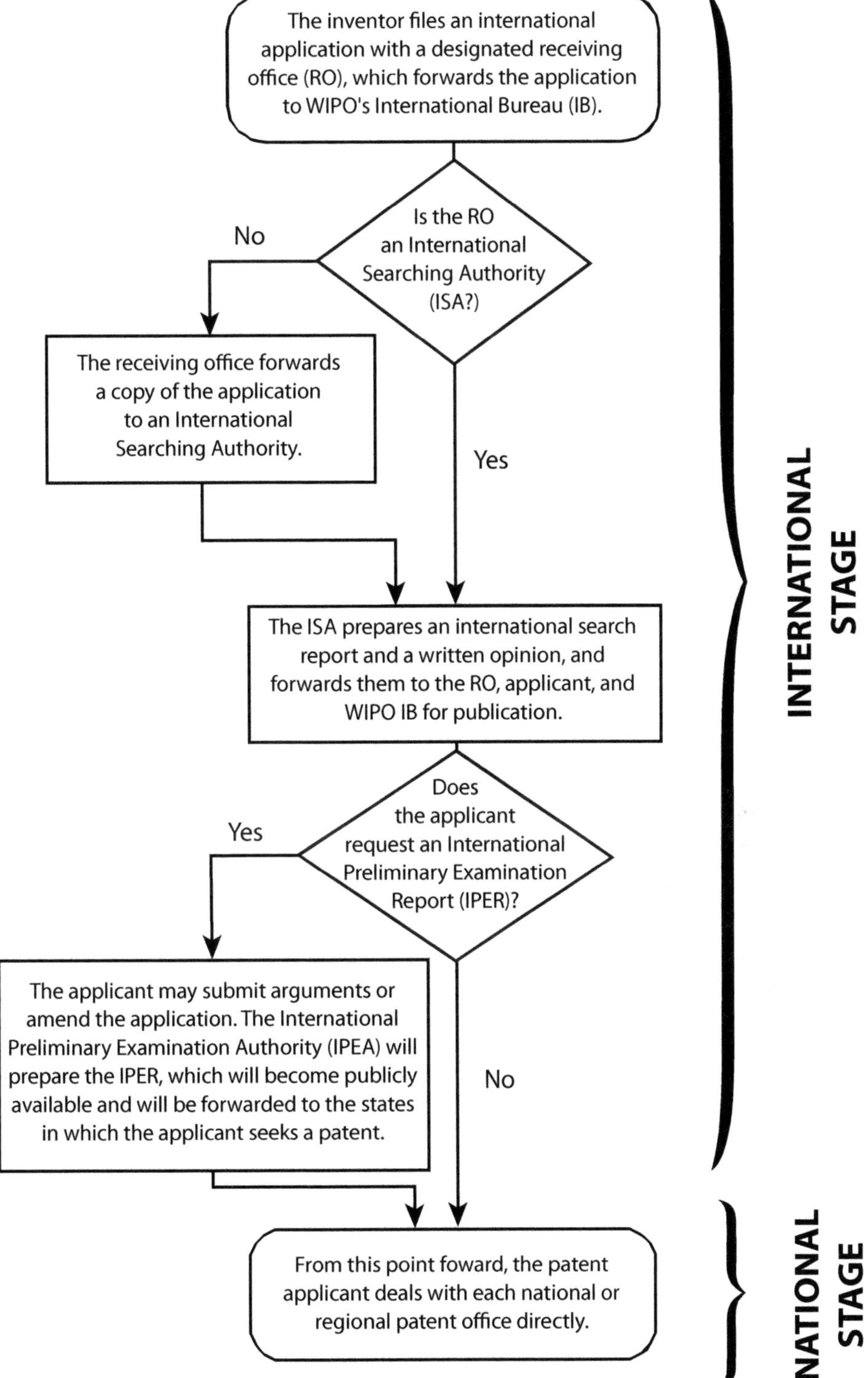

Figure 3.5. The Patent Cooperation Treaty application process.

Policy Issue

Should there be a global patent law system?

Most of the world's economically and technologically advanced countries have long sought to harmonize their patent laws and to impose on developing countries a model for patent laws that would represent the developed countries' interests. The advantages of a harmonized, global patent system could be significant. Such a system could simplify the task of obtaining patent protection in many countries, thereby reducing wasteful administrative expenses and encouraging research-intensive inventions that require a multinational market to justify research, development, and production expenses. It could also assist inventors in developing countries to exploit their inventions on an international level on par with inventors from developed countries, who have great advantages under the current system.

On the other hand, the kinds of patent rules that play to the advantage of inventors in developed countries may not be the same as those that best serve inventors in developing countries. Because most important patents are held by business firms in the developed world, strong worldwide patent protection would facilitate the transfer of wealth to them from licensees in the developing world. Weak patent protection, in contrast, would assist companies in developing countries to use technology from the developed world without the burden of compensating foreign patent owners exorbitantly. Moreover, the costs of setting up a patent system of complexity comparable to the systems in the developed world, with their well trained administrators and specialized courts systems, is beyond the capacity of many developing countries, which are struggling to provide basic governmental services and infrastructure, such as safety from crime, functional roads, clean water, and basic medical care, to their respective populations. Protecting foreign inventions from patent infringement is understerstandably not their first priority.

One compromise might be to create a multi-tiered patent law system, in which patent protection in developed countries is very strong, and protection in the developing world is more relaxed. Another would be to compensate the developing countries with financial aid and transfers of technology to offset the costs of maintaining the patent system and to counterbalance the transfer of wealth to patent owners in the developed countries. What do you think might be the advantages and disadvantages of each approach? Can you think of an alternative solution that would be fair to inventors and consumers in both developed and developing countries?

to convince it to publish a report favorable to the invention's patentability. He can later use this report to persuade the various national patent offices that they should grant a patent on the invention. Although it is not binding on any state's patent office, the report may constitute persuasive authority. If the applicant cannot convince the IPEA of the patentability of his invention, on the other hand, he can still amend the international patent application to make the application more likely to be granted. When the IPEA has considered all arguments and amendments, it will issue an **international preliminary examination report**.

When the applicant receives the examination report, it will also have been sent to all states designated by the applicant and become publicly available as well. If the results of the report do not look promising, the applicant can opt to amend the patent application to increase its chances of getting patents. In any case, this concludes the international stage, and the application moves on to the national stage.

At the national stage, the applicant pays a fee to each designated country's patent agency, translates any prior art cited in the application into each national language (if required), and appoints a patent agent (again, if required) in each designated country. Each national or regional patent agency will then process the patent application according to its own procedures, granting or denying the patent under its national law. There may, of course, be further negotiation and revision of the application in each individual country, so that a single international application may result in several patents in different states having varying claims even though they all relate to the same invention.

WHO USES THE PCT?

The most active national patent offices, meaning the ones that receive the most PCT applications and grant the most patents, are in economically developed states such as Japan, the United States, and Europe. Most inventors seeking patents are located in these same countries. Although some inventors live in developing countries in Africa, Latin America, and south and central Asia, they have to date obtained only a negligible percentage of the patents in either the developed or developing world. The PCT is especially popular among large multinational business firms in states with an advanced technology base. In 2017, the WIPO received 243,500 PCT applications. Most of these applications come from large business firms in the United States, China, Japan, and Germany.

B. Regional Patent Registration Systems

There are four major regional patent organizations. Each is established by a regional treaty, and each has its own collective patent office that coordinates its activities with the national patent offices of member states. Two are located in Africa, one is in Europe, and one in Central Europe and Asia. There are none in East Asia or the Americas.

Two of the organizations do not grant multinational patents; instead, like the PCT, they allow the patent applicant to "prosecute" (that is, pursue an application for) patents in multiple countries using a single application in a single language instead of individual patent applications in every member state. In contrast, the ***Organisation Africaine de la Propriété Intellectuelle*** (**OAPI**) ("the African Intellectual Property Organization") grants a single regional patent for multiple francophonic African states. Cameroon, the Central African Republic, Congo, Mali, and Senegal are members. The OAPI patent is possible because a single substantive patent law applies to all OAPI members, so that individual national examination and registration is unnecessary.

The European Patent System

The **European Patent Convention** (**EPC**) establishes a regional patent registration system. As of 2020, there are thirty-eight parties to the EPC, all of which are European states, but many of which are not members of the European Union, such as Iceland, Norway and Turkey.

The Convention performs three main functions. First, it creates a **European Patent Office** (**EPO**) that administers most of the treaty's provisions. The EPO is headquartered in Munich, Germany with a branch in The Hague, Netherlands.

Second, the EPC harmonizes the patents laws of state parties to a degree. Part II of the Convention sets forth substantive rules on the requirements for obtaining a European patent, rules for establishing inventorship, the term of the patent and rights conferred by it, and the effect of and limitations on licenses and assignments.

Finally, since 2013, the Convention, together with an EU Council regulation on the community patent and a separate 2009 Agreement on the European and Community Patents Court, authorizes the EPO to accept patent applications for two kinds of European patents: a single application resulting in multiple national patents (similar to the PCT process, but confined to the EPC parties), and a European **unitary patent** with effect throughout the EU. The treaties also establishes a Board of Appeal within the EPO to resolve disputes regarding proper application form, patentability, priority of inventors, and a **Unified Patent Court** to hear appeals from decisions of the EPO and patent revocation and infringement proceedings relating to the unitary patent. The Unified Patent Court is actually divided into two organs, a Court of First Instance (trial court) and a Court of Appeal.

To apply for a European patent *without* unitary effect, the application may be filed through one of the EPO's offices or the patent office of a Convention member state. To apply for a patent *with* unitary effect, the applicant must apply directly to the EPO. The applicant need not be a resident or citizen of an EPC state party or even be located in Europe. The applicant must merely be represented by an agent licensed to practice before the EPO.

2.2 Multinational Trademark Registration

Like patents, trademarks are generally protected on an individual country basis. In the United States and other common law countries, a business firm may acquire a legal right to exclude others from using a trademark based on its use of the mark in commerce. But many countries grant no rights to a trademark unless and until it is registered. Registration is an important step in protecting a company's marks when engaging in international business transactions. Multinational trademark registrations tend to cost less than patent registrations and involve fewer risks of accidentally forfeiting rights in some countries by actions taken in other countries. Nonetheless, like multinational patent registration, trademark registration on a country-by-country basis can be time-consuming and expensive. Treaties can help alleviate these problems as well.

A. The Multilateral Trademark Registration System

The first international system for a single trademark application for multiple countries was established in 1891 by the **Madrid Agreement Concerning the International Registration of Marks**. The Madrid Agreement provided a method of international trademark registration, allowing a single application to establish a priority date in multiple countries. However, the Madrid Agreement proved unpopular with the companies most active in filing trademarks in Europe, Japan, and the United States, and was consequently doomed to relative obscurity by lack of support. The Agreement is therefore not an important instrument in multinational trademark registration practice.

In 1996, however, a protocol to the Madrid Agreement came into force with much greater success. The **Madrid Protocol** allows a trademark applicant to file a single trademark application with its national or regional trademark office and to designate multiple countries for trademark protection. The Protocol is, therefore, the trademark counterpart to the PCT. Just as the PCT does not create the possibility of a single international patent, an international application under the Madrid Protocol does not result in a true international trademark. It does, however, make applying for a trademark in multiple countries much easier, and the international filing establishes a priority date for all countries designated in the application against a third party in one of the designated countries who tries to register the same mark locally.

Not only does this international registration allow applicants to establish a single priority date for multiple countries, it also creates a rule of default registration. In other words, if any specific state party designated in the trademark application fails to refuse registration within a specific period of time, the mark is deemed registered and protected in that state. The Protocol also simplifies rights management by allowing a trademark owner to record changes in ownership or to renew registration through a single procedure. The Madrid Protocol, also like the PCT, is administered by the WIPO's International Bureau in Geneva. As of 2020, the members of the Madrid Protocol, known as the **Madrid Union**, number 103 states, including the United States, the EU, and most other economically important states, such as China, Japan, and Russia.

To file an international trademark application under the Madrid Protocol, the applicant must be a national of, or have a commercial establishment in, a member of the Madrid Union and must have first applied for or obtained the trademark in the Madrid Union country. The national registration office of this first application is known as the **office of origin**, and the application is known as the **basic application** or, if granted, the **basic registration**.

Like a PCT application, a Madrid Protocol application has both international and national stages. When the office of origin receives an international application under the Madrid Protocol, it first verifies that the applicant is seeking to register the same mark for the same goods or services in each designated country, and, if so, it then forwards the application to the WIPO's International Bureau. WIPO will check that the goods or services are correctly classified and that the filing requirements are met. If so, it will record the mark in its International Trademark Register and notify the various trademark registration offices of the countries designated in the international application. This is the end of the international stage; WIPO does not examine the mark to determine whether it qualifies for registration in the designated countries.

Instead, it now moves to the national stage, during which the application will be examined by each designated country on an individual basis. The registration will either be granted or denied in each country based on its municipal trademark laws. If a national office fails to take action within a certain time period, the mark is deemed registered in that country. It is important to remember that, at the national stage, registrations in various countries (except the country of the basic application) are independent of each other. The fact that a registration is refused in one designated state will have no effect on its qualifications for registration in any other state.

As convenient as the Madrid Protocol makes filing trademark applications in multiple countries, there is a small risk to using the Madrid Protocol rather than filing separate trademark applications in each country. Specifically, for the first five years after the multinational application is filed, WIPO will cancel the Madrid Protocol registration if the basic registration is denied by or withdrawn from the office of origin. This rarely used procedure, known as a **central attack** on the Madrid Protocol registration, can be disastrous to a company that relies heavily on its trademarks for international marketing and sales. To mitigate the risks of a central attack, the applicant can break the international application down into multiple national applications in the designated countries without sacrificing the priority date of the basic application.

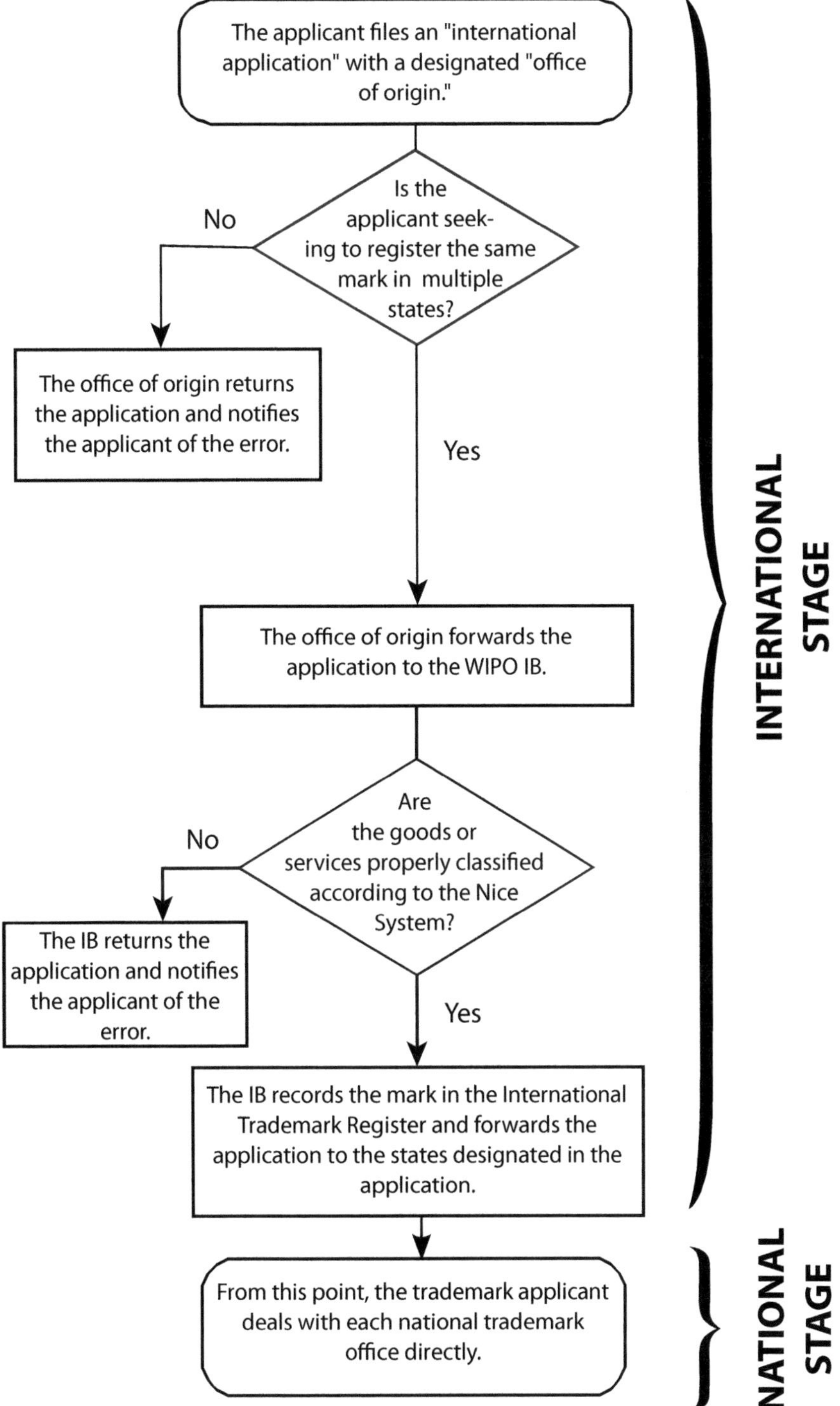

Figure 3.6. The Madrid process for multinational trademark registration.

In any case, after the five year period, the international registration becomes immune to central attack and cancellation of the registration by the office of origin will have no effect on registrations in the other designated countries.

B. Regional Trademark Registration Systems

Just as some states have created regional organizations to ameliorate the problems of multinational registration of patents, so have many states adopted regional treaties or collective decisions allowing private parties to apply for multiple national trademarks with a single application. There are several such regional arrangements. In the case of OAPI, a single regional trademark may be granted in much the same manner as applies with patents. The only other unitary trademark system belongs to the European Union.

The European Union Trademark System

In 1988, the European Community Council adopted a Community Trade Mark Regulation to partially harmonize the trademark laws of what are now the European Union (EU) member states. In 1993, the Council went further and adopted a Community Trade Mark Regulation providing for the grant of a single **Community Trade Mark** (**CTM**) that is valid in all EU member states.

The CTM Regulation provided for the creation of a central EU trademark office in Alicante, Spain, called the **Office for Harmonization in the Internal Market** (**OHIM**). OHIM is charged with executing registration procedures for the CTM, maintaining a public register of CTMs, and deciding on challenges to the validity of registered CTMs. The CTM itself does not replace national trademarks within the EU; rather, it adds the CTM as an alternative or complementary option. The CTM lasts for an initial period of ten years but may be renewed indefinitely. Any WTO member or applicant with its seat in an EU country can obtain one. The following excerpts from OHIM's description of the CTM explain more:

Office for Harmonization in the Internal Mark, Ten Good Reasons for Using the Community Trade Mark (1999)

1° Unitary nature and protection of exclusive rights

The Community trade mark is unitary in nature, i.e. it is valid everywhere in the European Union, and gives proprietors exclusive rights enabling them to prohibit any third parties from using the sign in their commercial or industrial activities.

2° Simplified formalities and management

The unitary nature of the Community trade mark, which covers all the countries of the European Union, means that formalities and management can be kept simple:

- a single application;

- a single language of procedure;
- a single administrative centre;
- a single file to be managed.

It is a simple procedure and applications may be made both at national industrial property offices or directly to the Office for Harmonization in the Internal Market in Alicante.

3º Reduced costs

This simplification results in considerably reduced costs as compared with the overall costs of national registration in all or many of the countries of the European Union. Filing a Community trade mark application is not expensive. The registration fee only needs to be paid once no obstacles remain to the trade mark being granted.

4º Option of claiming the seniority of national trade marks

The Community trade mark has been designed to complement the national systems of protection. If applicants or proprietors of a Community trade mark already hold a prior identical national trade mark for identical goods and services they may claim the seniority of that mark. This allows them to preserve their prior rights even if they surrender their national trade mark or do not renew it.

5º Right of priority

The Community trade mark complements the national systems of trade mark protection. The filing date accorded to a Community trade mark is recognised as constituting a date of priority for both national and international trade marks. This applies equally where applicants decide to convert their application or registered Community trade mark into national applications. There is therefore no risk involved in deciding immediately to opt for a Community trade mark.

6º Obligation of use which is easy to meet

A Community trade mark may be maintained in all the countries of the European Union by using it effectively and genuinely in a single Member State. Any company, even if it wishes to use its trade mark in one or in a few Member States only, may therefore validly obtain a Community trade mark without having to fear revocation proceedings on the grounds of lack of use.

7º Broadened legal protection which is accessible to all

Infringement proceedings may be brought before the Community trade mark courts, which are national courts designated by the Member States to have jurisdiction in respect of Community trade marks. Decisions have effect throughout the EU. This avoids the need to prosecute infringers in each Member State. Only the Community trade mark has such protection in the whole of the European Union.

8º An extended range of options for exercising rights under the trade mark

The option to transfer and assign Community trade marks is essential for the management of companies. A Community trade mark may be transferred, separately from any transfer of the undertaking which is its proprietor, in respect of some or all of the goods or services for which it is registered. A Community trade mark may also be licensed for the whole or part of the European Union. A licence may be exclusive or non-exclusive.

9° Community trade marks as prior rights in all the countries of the EU

Community trade marks constitute prior rights in relation to all subsequent trade marks and other conflicting rights in all Member States. This allows proprietors of Community trade marks not only to protect their exclusive rights at Community level but also to prevail over later national rights.

10° The prospect of enlargement

The enlargement of the European Union to include new Member States [has resulted in] a European Union of [28] Member States [and may expand further]. It is provided for the automatic extension of all existing Community trade mark applications and registrations, while limiting the possibility to attack them on grounds that become applicable merely as a result of the accession.

The Community trade mark therefore is not only a gateway to the existing single market but also to a market in the process of expansion.

Notes and Questions

1. When OHIM receives a CTM application, it examines the application to determine whether it complies with all formal requirements. OHIM then conducts a search for conflicting Community or national trademarks and issues a search report for the applicant's information. OHIM then publishes the mark in the *Community Trade Marks Bulletin*. OHIM is also empowered to adjudicate opposition proceedings. An **opposition proceeding** is an administrative litigation in which a third party with an identical or similar mark (either a CTM or a national trademark in an EU member state) challenges a pending trademark application by filing a notice of opposition with OHIM. At the conclusion of the submissions of evidence and observations, OHIM will decide the case on the merits. Adverse decisions may be appealed to the OHIM Board of Appeal and, from there, to the General Court, which is empowered to hear all cases relating to a CTM, and ultimately to the Court of Justice of the European Union (CJEU).

2. OHIM's assertion that the use of a mark in a single EU member state can support a CTM may be based on a joint statement by the EU Council and Commission to that effect.* The reality is not so simple. In January 2010, a regional IP office for Belgium, the Netherlands, and Luxembourg ("Benelux") issued a decision that a CTM could not stand if used in only one EU country. *Leno Merken BV v. Hagelkruis Beheer BV*, Dec. No. 2004448 (Benelux Off.

---

* Joint Statement No. 10 Regarding Article 15 of Council Regulation (EC) No. 40/94 of 20 Dec. 1993 on the Community Trade Mark (O.J. 1994, L 11, at 1).

NOTE FROM THE FIELD

Managing a Worldwide Intellectual Property Portfolio

Heidi L. Sachs, Esq. & Chun M. Ng, Esq.
Perkins Coie LLP

Intellectual property is one of the most valuable assets of a company—the Coca-Cola brand, Disney's Star Wars and Marvel Universe characters, and Google's technology patents account for most of the value of the companies themselves. The tremendous resources devoted to R&D and branding make worldwide IP protection paramount in any business strategy.

Patent protection around the world can be expensive, and counsel, working with the client, needs to prioritize which innovations and national markets are the most important. Considering that a patent in a single country may cost upwards of \$50,000-\$75,000 over the life of the patent, strategic use of resources is crucial. Even with the use of multi-jurisdictional patent treaties, such as the Patent Cooperation Treaty and the European Patent Convention, patents are still very country specific.

The patent attorney must also understand the procedures and enforceability in many different countries. The patent attorney must be well versed in litigation and licensing strategy. Many countries do not have a strong tradition of patent infringement enforcement. As such, sensitivities to the practical enforcement remedies in each country are indispensable.

Trademarks are much less expensive to register and copyrights require no registration. International trademark filing strategies must take into consideration applicable treaties, as well as the client's business, marketing objectives, and budget. Trademark attorneys work with foreign counsel throughout the world on registration and enforcement matters. A trademark lawyer shepherds the clients' trademarks through their life cycle, analyzing infringement risks and, once a mark is chosen, registering the mark internationally, as well as policing against infringers. The trademark attorney is actively involved in domestic and international enforcement efforts, working with trademark counsel throughout the world. A trademark practice also involves domain name and advertising issues.

Copyright practice has exponentially expanded as a result of the Internet. Issues such as linking, copying, framing, and modifying the websites of others present situations in which the law lags behind the technology. In all fields of IP, licensing is important to international commercialization.

Heidi L. Sachs has chaired or co-chaired the Perkins Coie Trademark & Copyright practice group since its inception. Chun M. Ng is the Chair of the Perkins Coie Intellectual Property practice.

Intell. Prop., Jan. 15, 2010). In 2012, a chamber of the Court of Justice of the European Union heard the dispute. The CJEU reversed the Benelux office by admitting the possibility that use in a single state could qualify as a "genuine use" of the mark in the EU "in certain circumstances," such as when "the market for the goods or services for which a [CTM] has been registered is in fact restricted to the territory of a single member state." *Leno Merken BV v. Hagelkruis Beheer BV*, Ct. Just. Eur. Union Case C-149/11, Judgment of Dec. 19, 2012, ¶ 50. Beyond this, the CJEU punted, saying only that use of a CTM in a single state would support a CTM if used in accordance with its "essential function and for the purpose of maintaining or creating market share within the [EU] for the goods or services covered by it." *Id.* ¶ 58.

If the market for a good or service is limited to a single EU country, why should a company be able to exclude others from using the trademark in all the other EU countries? Might it be somehow related to the fluid movement of persons and goods across national borders within the EU?

3 Border Protection Against Imports Infringing IP Rights

National registration is a precondition for the protection of some kinds of IP. However, the actual enforcement of IP rights poses a significant problem in the international business context, especially for famous brand names, recording studios, movie studios, and software developers. Ideally, these IP owners would like to prevent foreign infringing goods from even entering the country to prevent them from cutting into the IP owner's market share or degrading the reputation of its goods.

Any infringing imports may present a problem to IP owners, but the most pressing problems of IP import infringement come from counterfeit and piratical goods. A **counterfeit** good is one sold under the false pretense of being manufactured with the trademark owner's authority. Counterfeit Rolex® wristwatches, which are sold in many countries, are made by persons and companies completely alien to the Swiss company that owns the Rolex trademarks. Yet, they mimic the look of the Rolex watch and bear the ROLEX trade name and logo of a stylized crown. They are invariably made of inferior materials and technologies, so that, in the absence of the trademark infringement, they would sell at a very low price on the market. However, they command a higher price because of their superficial resemblance to the genuine goods. Other kinds of trademarked goods, from clothing to popular pharmaceuticals to complex electronics, are routinely counterfeited as well.

When a copyright-protected work is intentionally reproduced without the authorization of the copyright owner, the resulting work is called a **piratical good**. It is usually a simple matter to copy a music, software, or cinematic work; as a result, piratical goods are a multi-billion dollar industry that crosses international boundaries freely, unless the IP owner takes adequate preventive steps.

Figure 3.7. Fakin' it. Counterfeit (left) and genuine (right) Rolex® watches.
Credit: © 2016 by Mark Sirianni

There are several ways for an IP owner to prevent unlicensed imports by foreign counterfeiters, pirates, and other infringers. Litigation is one option. You may recall that Part III of the TRIPs Agreement requires WTO members to provide for injunctions against the sale or importation of infringing items. A lawsuit allows the IP owner to recover damages caused by the infringement, which in some countries will include statutory or punitive damages. Local laws may also allow the IP owner to seek an injunction to prevent future sales and importations of the infringing goods. Litigation has a further advantage; a court order enjoining future infringement may be backed with sanctions, such as a contempt order.

But infringement litigation has significant down sides. First, it is costly, slow, and uncertain. In countries that do not award attorneys' fees to the victorious party, the costs of the litigation itself can overshadow the damages awarded or recovered, especially if the infringer is impecunious. Moreover, infringement may seriously undermine the IP owner's ability to capitalize on her IP. The lengthy delays caused by litigation could, by the time a judgment is obtained, impair the value of the IP or even render it nugatory. In addition, very few states allow *in rem* litigation against infringing imports. Usually, the IP owner must identify a specific defendant. But where many small and fugitive defendants are infringing the IP, changing business names to avoid detection and starting and stopping importation sporadically, litigation is not an especially useful avenue of redress. Finally, an IP owner may be unable to collect on a judgment against a foreign importer if the infringer has no assets in the United States and a court in a country in which the infringer does have assets refuses to enforce a U.S. judgment (which is normally the case).

A second possibility, often used in conjunction with the first, is to cooperate with the governmental customs authority to stop the goods from entering the country. Under the TRIPS Agreement, WTO members must make a procedure available for informing customs authorities of infringing imports and having the offending goods seized or turned back at the border through administrative proceedings. In some countries, border interdiction can be an effective preventive measure.

Exclusion or seizure of infringing goods at the border has substantial advantages for the IP owner:

- It may be automatic, partly relieving the IP owner of the need to expend constant effort and funds attempting to identify foreign infringing goods released on the domestic market.
- A border enforcement measure may be *in rem* with respect to the infringing imports rather than *in personam* with respect to the importer. This would allow the exclusion of goods being entered by multiple importers, the names of whom the IP owner need not know in advance.
- A government agency (usually, the customs authority) absorbs most of the cost of policing the infringement.
- If the goods are stopped at the border, no harm to the IP itself or to the IP owner's reputation will arise from unauthorized goods circulating on the domestic market.

The third option, unique to the United States, is to initiate what is called a "Section 337 investigation" to stop the goods at the border. Section 337 is a quasi-judicial administrative procedure that is much faster than litigation in a court. The following subsections will discuss the customs recordation and Section 337 options in more detail.

3.1 Customs Recordation and Enforcement

The customs authorities of most countries make a practice of seizing counterfeit or piratical imports at the border when they happen to be identified as such by customs officials. For example, such seizures are mandated in the European Union by Regulation (EU) No. 608/2013. However, customs officials are not always able to identify imports protected by IP rights or to verify that imports embodying copyrighted works or patented technologies, or bearing protected trademarks, are in fact infringing. As a result, this system in many countries is haphazard and generally ineffective at preventing the importation of infringing goods.

In some countries, it is possible to exclude the importation of counterfeit or piratical merchandise without the need for litigation by identifying infringing imports and requesting that such goods be seized by the customs authorities. The United States has an effective system for automatically identifying and seizing counterfeit and piratical goods at the border through the prior **customs recordation** of IP rights. Using customs recordation, it is possible

Figure 3.8. A CBP officer inspects counterfeit Christian Louboutin shoes imported into Los Angeles from China in 2012. Over 20,000 fake pairs were discovered in the single shipment.
Credit: © 2012 by Nick Ut, Associated Press. All rights reserved.

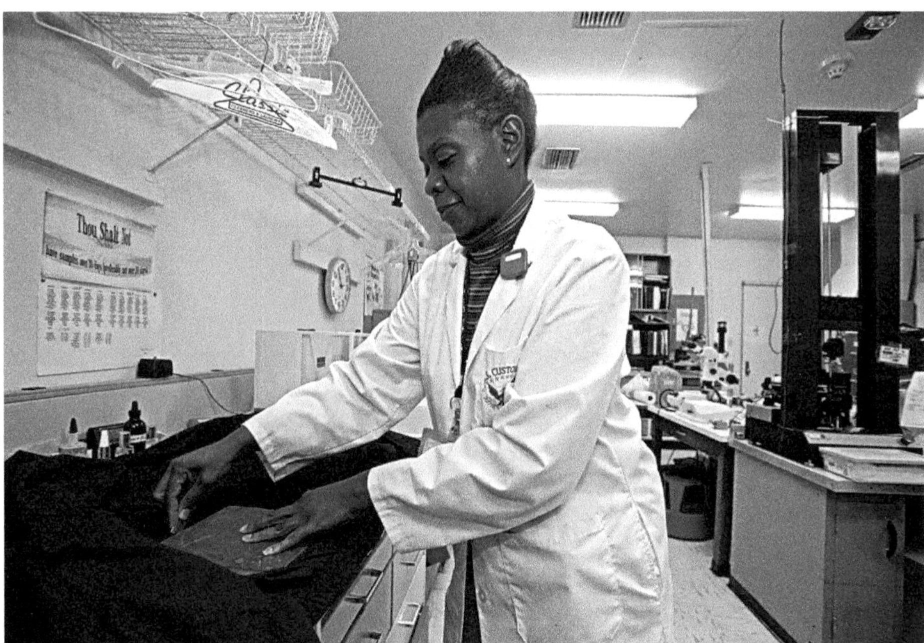

Figure 3.9. A CBP technician tests imported fabric to determine whether its trademark is genuine or counterfeit.
Credit: James Tourtelotte, U.S. Customs & Border Protection

to record a trademark or copyright with **Customs and Border Protection (CBP)**, a bureau of the **U.S. Department of Homeland Security (DHS)**. DHS is one government department charged with protecting the United States from dangerous persons, goods, and technologies. CBP is responsible *inter alia* for inspecting and collecting import duties on all goods imported into the United States from foreign countries.

Section 526 of the 1930 Tariff Act authorizes CBP to exclude infringing goods in the course of enforcing the customs laws:

> (a) Importation prohibited. Except as provided in subsection (d) of this section,* it shall be unlawful to import into the United States any merchandise of foreign manufacture if such merchandise, or the label, sign, print, package, wrapper, or receptacle, bears a trademark owned by a citizen of, or by a corporation or association created or organized within, the United States, and registered in the Patent and Trademark Office by a person domiciled in the United States * * * and if a copy of the certificate of registration of such trademark is filed with the Secretary of the Treasury,** in the manner provided in section 106 [*sic*: 1124] of said title 15, unless written consent of the owner of such trademark is produced at the time of making entry.
>
> (b) Seizure and forfeiture. Any such merchandise imported into the United States in violation of the provisions of this section shall be subject to seizure and forfeiture for violation of the customs laws.
>
> (c) Injunction and damages. Any person dealing in any such merchandise may be enjoined from dealing therein within the United States or may be required to export or destroy such merchandise or to remove or obliterate such trademark and shall be liable for the same damages and profits provided for wrongful use of a trademark * * *.

19 U.S.C. § 1526.

Section 42 of the Lanham Trademark Act elaborates by providing for customs recordation of any trade name or trademark registered in the United States:

> * * * [N]o article of imported merchandise which shall copy or simulate the name of any domestic manufacture, or manufacturer, or trader, or of any manufacturer or trader located in any foreign country which, by treaty, convention, or law affords similar privileges to citizens of the United

*[Coursebook author's note: Subsection (d), omitted here, lists a limited exception to the general rule for importations of trademarked items in a traveler's baggage for personal use.]

**[Coursebook author's note: Until 2004, CBP was known as the U.S. Customs Service and was part of the Department of the Treasury. You will still sometimes see references to the Treasury Department or the Secretary of the Treasury in statutes that Congress has not updated. These references should properly name the DHS and Secretary of Homeland Security instead.]

> States, or which shall copy or simulate a trademark registered in accordance with the provisions of this chapter or shall bear a name or mark calculated to induce the public to believe that the article is manufactured in the United States, or that it is manufactured in any foreign country or locality other than the country or locality in which it is in fact manufactured, shall be admitted to entry at any customhouse of the United States; and, in order to aid the officers of the customs in enforcing this prohibition, any domestic manufacturer or trader, and any foreign manufacturer or trader, who is entitled under the provisions of a treaty, convention, declaration, or agreement between the United States and any foreign country to the advantages afforded by law to citizens of the United States in respect to trademarks and commercial names, may require his name and residence, and the name of the locality in which his goods are manufactured, and a copy of the certificate of registration of his trademark, issued in accordance with the provisions of this chapter, to be recorded in books which shall be kept for this purpose in the Department of the Treasury, under such regulations as the Secretary of the Treasury shall prescribe, and may furnish to the Department facsimiles of his name, the name of the locality in which his goods are manufactured, or of his registered trademark, and thereupon the Secretary of the Treasury shall cause one or more copies of the same to be transmitted to each collector or other proper officer of customs.

15 U.S.C. § 1124. This is a complex way of saying that the owner of a U.S. trademark (usually regardless of whether the owner is a U.S. or foreign company) can record its mark with CBP, so that CBP will inspect imported articles bearing the trademark.

The 1976 Copyright Act also provides for the exclusion of infringing copyrighted works:

> **Importation prohibitions: Enforcement and disposition of excluded articles**
>
> (a) The Secretary of the Treasury [*sic*: DHS] and the United States Postal Service shall separately or jointly make regulations for the enforcement of the provisions of this title prohibiting importation.
>
> (b) These regulations may require, as a condition for the exclusion of articles under section 602—
>
> (1) that the person seeking exclusion obtain a court order enjoining importation of the articles; or
>
> (2) that the person seeking exclusion furnish proof, of a specified nature and in accordance with prescribed procedures, that the copyright in which such person claims an interest is valid and that the importation would violate the prohibition in section 602; the person seeking exclusion may also be required to post a surety bond for any injury that may result if the detention or exclusion of the articles proves to be unjustified.
>
> (c) Articles imported in violation of the importation prohibitions of this

> title are subject to seizure and forfeiture in the same manner as property imported in violation of the customs revenue laws. Forfeited articles shall be destroyed as directed by the Secretary of [DHS] or the court, as the case may be.

17 U.S.C. § 603.

The procedures for customs recordation of a copyright or registered trademark are set forth in part 133 of the Customs Regulations. The recordation includes information that will be helpful to CBP in determining whether imports of trademarked or copyrighted goods are legitimate or infringing, and in contacting the IP owner to verify legitimacy or to report a seizure of imports. Trademark owners may also request the investigation and seizure of infringing imports by describing the physical characteristics of goods authorized for importation so that CBP can distinguish them from unauthorized goods having different physical attributes.

If CBP has reason to believe questionable imports do not have permission of the trademark or copyright owner, it will contact the owner and provide a sample of the goods after the owner posts a bond guaranteeing return of the sample in the condition it was furnished. 19 C.F.R. §§ 133.21, 133.42. If the IP owner confirms that the goods are counterfeit, CBP will seize the articles and they will be forfeited to the U.S. government for violation of customs laws. 19 U.S.C. § 1526(e). In addition, CBP may impose a fine on the importer. 19 C.F.R. §§ 133.27, 133.42(c). The U.S. Court of Appeals for the Federal Circuit has held that this fine may not be appealed, leaving CBP with nearly unfettered discretion to impose penalties for importations of counterfeit merchandise. See *Sakar International, Inc. v. United States*, 516 F.3d 1340 (Fed. Cir. 2008).

If the imports merely infringe a trademark without being counterfeit, such as when the imports bear a mark confusingly similar to a recorded trademark,

DOES CUSTOMS RECORDATION ACTUALLY WORK?

Each year, CBP confiscates massive quantities of allegedly counterfeit, piratical, or infringing goods. In 2018, CBP seized 33,810 shipments that would have been valued at approximately $1.4 trillion if the goods had been genuine. The most common kinds of counterfeit or piratical goods by far are shoes and clothes, but computers and consumer electronics are also commonly seized. Media such as DVDs and CDs typically make up less than 10% of seizures in the U.S., but are commonly pirated in developing countries. The great majority of counterfeit and piratical goods imported into the United States originate in East Asia, with more than three-quarters coming from China and Hong Kong alone.

Source: Office of Trade, U.S. Customs & Border Protection, Intellectual Property Rights: Fiscal Year 2018 Seizure Statistics, CBP Pub. # 0917-0719.

the goods will not be forfeited, but they will be denied entry into the United States unless the importer removes or obliterates the offending mark from the imported goods. 19 C.F.R. § 133.22.

In the case of nonpiratical imports that infringe a copyright, such as a book that includes unlicensed copyrighted pictures or a recorded song that contains excessive samples from another copyrighted and unlicensed song, the copyright owner has two options. The first is to sue the importer for infringement in a U.S. court and seek a preliminary court order instructing CBP to exclude the imports until a final adjudication has been made. The other is to file a request to exclude the imports directly with CBP along with a bond (usually equivalent to the total value of the imports) to compensate the importer for the delay caused by the accusation of infringement should the goods be found non-infringing. The latter procedure will trigger a brief administrative litigation before the CBP. Each side will file briefs and present evidence of infringement or noninfringement to the director of the port in which the importer sought to enter the allegedly infringing goods. The copyright owner carries the burden of persuading the port director that the goods do in fact infringe the copyright. Each side may then file a rebuttal brief, and the port director will then forward the entire file to CBP Headquarters, which will make a final decision. If the goods are found infringing, they will be seized and forfeited, and the copyright owner's bond will be released. If the goods are found noninfringing, CBP will approve the goods for entry and the copyright owner's bond will be forfeited and given to the importer. Either side may appeal this decision to a federal court of competent jurisdiction. 19 C.F.R. §§ 133.43-.44.

Owners of trade secrets, trade dress rights, or patents cannot record them with CBP to detain potentially infringing goods at the border. Such infringement would be too difficult to identify. Patent infringement is especially challenging to verify and may require disassembling and comparing complex products or conducting expensive and time-consuming laboratory tests. For this reason, CBP will only exclude imports that potentially infringe a U.S. patent through a court injunction, or an exclusion order issued by the International Trade Commission through the procedure described in the next section.

3.2 The Section 337 Investigation

The **Section 337** investigation is authorized by the 1930 Tariff Act (19 U.S.C. § 1337) to provide a remedy to U.S. industries against unfair competition from foreign importers and to prevent the importation of goods that infringe a valid U.S. copyright, trademark, patent, or trade secret. The primary reason Congress added this remedy was because, as noted, lawsuits to challenge unfair competition from infringing foreign imports are slow and expensive, and imports may already have circulated in the market before a judgment is obtained. Congress believed U.S. IP owners should have an avenue for fast action to stop infringing imports at the border.

Customs recordation and enforcement under Section 526 of the 1930 Tariff Act overcomes some of these problems, but, as noted, it cannot be used to stop imports that infringe a U.S. patent or trade secret. Moreover, CBP has no power to order or enjoin a foreign exporter to cease attempting to export infringing goods; it is more like a goalie that blocks infringing goods from entering the United States without disabling the exporter's ability to try again later and through other front companies and through different ports of entry. Section 337 resolves many of these problems.

The rights, remedies, and procedures defined in Section 337 look complex at first glance, but Section 337 is simple to summarize. It makes unlawful:

> (a)(1) * * * (A) Unfair methods of competition and unfair acts in the importation of articles * * * into the United States, or in the sale of such articles by the owner, importer, or consignee, the threat or effect of which is—
>
> (i) to destroy or substantially injure an industry in the United States;
>
> (ii) to prevent the establishment of such an industry; or
>
> (iii) to restrain or monopolize trade and commerce in the United States.
>
> (B) The importation into the United States, the sale for importation, or the sale within the United States after importation by the owner, importer, or consignee, of articles that—
>
> (i) infringe a valid and enforceable United States patent or a valid and enforceable United States copyright registered under title 17; or
>
> (ii) are made, produced, processed, or mined under, or by means of, a process covered by the claims of a valid and enforceable United States patent.
>
> (C) The importation into the United States, the sale for importation, or the sale within the United States after importation by the owner, importer, or consignee, of articles that infringe a valid and enforceable United States trademark registered under the Trademark Act of 1946. * * *
>
> (2) Subparagraphs (B), (C), (D), and (E) of paragraph (1) apply only if an industry in the United States, relating to the articles protected by the patent, copyright, trademark, mask work, or design concerned, exists or is in the process of being established.

In plain language, the owner of a U.S.-registered copyright or patent, or a U.S. trade secret or trademark, may file a petition with the **U.S. International Trade Commission** (**ITC**), an independent federal agency, to stop the importation of infringing goods, but only if the owner of the patent, copyright, trademark, or trade secret is part of an existing or developing industry in the United States, called a **domestic industry** in technical parlance.

Unlike a IP infringement litigation, a Section 337 investigation is fast and results in an order to CBP to exclude any infringing goods at the border.

Moreover, unlike customs recordation, a Section 337 order can apply not just to imports of copyrighted and trademarked goods, but to patented goods and goods embodying trade secrets as well. However, Section 337 does have some requirements and limitations that do not apply in litigation.

WHO USES SECTION 337?

Section 337 is heavily used by small and medium-sized companies that depend upon their intellectual property for their business success and face competition from less expensive products from developing countries. In fact, more than half of all respondents in Section 337 actions are based in East Asia.

A. Domestic Industry

Section 337(a) makes it a precondition to requesting an investigation that there must be a significant presence of research and development, design, engineering, manufacturing, repair, or licensing facilities in the United States to justify a Section 337 action. A foreign company with no significant industrial or commercial presence in the United States will, therefore, have a difficult time invoking Section 337, even if imports into the United States infringe its IP rights.

Suppose a Japanese light chemical company, 2Dye4 Co., owns the U.S. trademark MISOTRENDI® on its line of clothing. 2Dye4 manufactures the fiber for its clothing in Japan and ships them to the People's Republic of China to be woven, cut, and assembled into clothing. The assembled clothing is then reshipped to Japan for labeling and packaging. 2Dye4 has a small subsidiary corporation in the United States, 2Dye4 USA Inc., that acts as sales agent for the parent company. 2Dye4 USA is staffed by a dozen employees whose job is to solicit sales and coordinate marketing of MISOTRENDI brand clothing in the United States.

If 2Dye4 USA, learns that clothing is being imported into the United States from the Philippines with a counterfeit MISOTRENDI label, 2Dye4 cannot use Section 337 to halt the importation of the counterfeit clothing unless it can establish that the activities of 2Dye4 USA qualify it as a "domestic industry."

Courts have never held that a domestic industry cannot exist unless manufacturing is performed in the United States. However, as the following case shows, manufacturing is a very important component of domestic industry analysis.

SCHAPER MANUFACTURING CO. v. U.S. INTERNATIONAL TRADE COMMISSION

U.S. Court of Appeals, Federal Circuit, 1983
717 F.2d 1368

DAVIS, Circuit Judge.

Schaper Manufacturing Company (Schaper) and A. Eddy Goldfarb, d/b/a A. Eddy Goldfarb and Associates (Goldfarb), seek review of the October 15, 1982 order of The United States International Trade Commission (ITC or Commission) which terminated the investigation in *In the Matter of Certain Miniature, Battery-Operated, All-Terrain, Wheeled Vehicles* on the ground that there is no domestic "industry" affected by the alleged unfair trade practices. * * *

I

The investigation was initiated by appellants' filing of a complaint with the Commission on April 23, 1982, under Section 337 of the Tariff Act of 1930 (19 U.S.C. § 1337). The complaint alleged unfair methods of competition and unfair acts in the importation into the United States, or sale here, of certain miniature, battery-operated, all-terrain wheeled vehicles (toy vehicles or Stomper vehicles), involving (1) infringement of U.S. Letters Patent 4,306,375 (the '375 patent) and (2) false designation of source by reason of the copying of appellants' vehicles. The complaint further alleged that the effect or tendency of the unfair methods of competition and unfair acts is to destroy or substantially injure an industry, efficiently and economically operated, in the United States.

The Commission published a notice of investigation on May 19, 1982. On October 15, 1982, the Commission issued its final determination that a section 337 violation did not exist, and filed an opinion supporting that determination four days later. The Commission concluded that "there is no violation of section 337 in this investigation because, given the particular facts of this case, complainants do not constitute 'an industry ... in the United States' within the meaning of that phrase as used in section 337."

The sole issue before us is whether the Commission properly so concluded, thus terminating the investigation.

II

Schaper is located in Minneapolis, Minnesota, and is engaged in the developing, manufacture and marketing of toy products. Goldfarb, situated in Northridge, California, invents toys and games which are then licensed to toy manufacturers. The toy vehicles here, marketed by Schaper under the trade name Stomper, were invented in 1979 by Goldfarb. The '375 patent was obtained for these toy vehicles on December 22, 1981. Schaper was granted an exclusive license in 1979 to manufacture, use and sell the Stomper toy vehicles and accessories[5] (also created and designed by Goldfarb).

[5]The accessories, such as toy logs, mountains, and racetracks, were designed to

Goldfarb has continued to develop successive lines of Stomper vehicles and accessories.

Schaper arranged for the manufacture of the Stomper vehicles by Kader Industrial Company (Kader), an unrelated firm in Hong Kong, from which Schaper procures the toys. After Schaper receives a new design from Goldfarb, it prepares specifications for the toy and engineering drawings for the tooling to be used in the manufacture of that design. These specifications and drawings are forwarded to Kader, which manufactures the tooling and the vehicles according to Schaper's specifications. Schaper pays for, and retains ownership of, the tooling made and used by Kader in its production of the vehicles. Schaper maintains regular communication with Kader regarding the manufacturing of the toy vehicles. After Kader conducts a quality control program of the toys in Hong Kong, designed by Schaper, they are shipped to the United States on procurement by Schaper. Most are shipped to Schaper already packaged and essentially ready for sale in blister packs; the remaining are shipped in cellophane poly bags and become component parts of Stomper play sets along with accessories. On receipt from Kader, Schaper conducts more quality control testing.

Appellee Soma Traders, Ltd. (Soma) also imports toy vehicles from Hong Kong—allegedly copies of the Stomper toy vehicles—sold under the names "Super Climbers" and "Military Super Climber." The Soma toy vehicles are sold by toy wholesalers, including appellees * * *.

III

Though the overall problem is whether appellants' domestic business activities constitute an "industry ... in the United States," giving appellants the protections of section 337, the initial inquiry is what parts of these activities are to be considered, in this investigation, as included in an "industry ... in the United States." We hold that the Commission properly disposed of that preliminary question.

First, the Commission correctly stated that the definition of "United States" is geographical and not based on citizenship. Section 337(j) defines "United States" as "the customs territory of the United States as defined in general headnote 2 of the Tariff Schedules of the United States (TSUS)." 19 U.S.C. § 1337(j). General headnote 2 of TSUS defines United States Customs territory as "the States, the District of Columbia, and Puerto Rico." In order to meet the threshold requirement of being an "industry ... in the United States," the "industry" must be geographically located in the United States.

Second, we agree with the Commission that that portion of the appellants' business activities relating to production of the Stomper accessories, all of which occurs in the United States, cannot be considered part of any domestic Stomper toy vehicle industry for the purpose of meeting the "industry ... in the United States" requirement. In cases under § 337 involving United States article patents, the relevant domestic "industry" extends only to articles which come within the claims of the patent relied on. This is a well-settled rule of longstanding. The House of Representatives committee report on section 337, when it was reconfirmed in 1974, supports this definition:

> In cases involving the claims of U.S. patents, the patent must be exploited by production in the United States, and the industry in the United States

---

"enhance the play value" of the vehicles by demonstrating their climbing and pulling abilities. Some of the accessories are the subject of pending patent applications.

> generally consists of the domestic operations of the patent owner, his assignees and licensees devoted to such exploitation of the patent.

H.Rep. No. 93-571, 93rd Cong. 1st Sess. 78 (1973).

Appellants' complaint alleged infringement of the '375 patent, which covers only the Stomper toy vehicles. The fact that the existence of the accessories derives from the toy vehicles does not make their domestic production by Schaper—regardless of the extent of Schaper's activities in manufacturing and producing them—a part of a toy vehicles industry in this action under section 337. The accessories are not a necessary part of the vehicles, nor are they integral to them. Most of the appellants' vehicles are sold without the accessories; the latter do not come within the claims of the '375 patent; nor do they have the claimed product configuration of the Stomper toy vehicle. The Commission could rightly conclude from these facts that "the Stomper accessories cannot be part of any domestic industry in this investigation."

Third, we also agree with the Commission that appellant Goldfarb's activities cannot be considered part of any domestic "industry" relevant to this case. His activity concerning the Stomper toy vehicles is the design and licensing of the toy vehicles and accessories, and the collection of royalties; Goldfarb is not involved in the manufacture or selling of the vehicles.

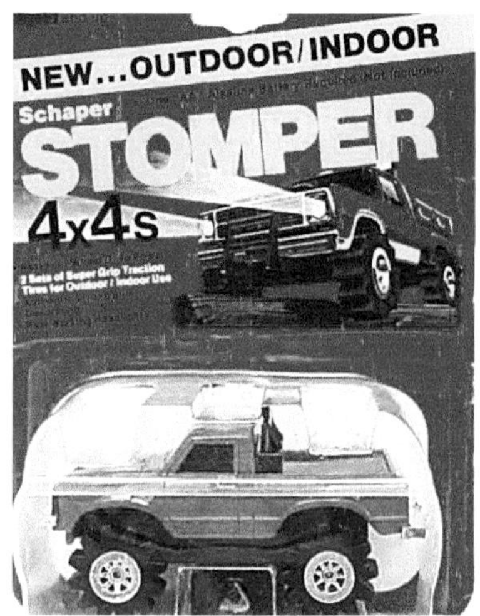

Figure 3.10. The Stomper 4x4, 1980s.

The record shows that Goldfarb's activities with respect to the patented toy vehicles amount to nothing more than that of any inventor. There is nothing in the statute or its legislative history to indicate that such activities, which do not involve either manufacture or production or servicing of the patented item, are meant to be protected by section 337. As noted by the Commission in *Certain Ultra-Microtome Freezing Attachments*, 195 USPQ 653, 656 (ITC 1976), "[t]he wording of the statute itself adds to the conclusion that the statute protects only parties producing under the patent. To find a section 337 violation, the statute requires that the industry be 'efficiently and economically operated.' 'If the statute were addressed to the patent rights per se of a patentee, there would be no need for the test of efficiency and economy of operation.'" As we have pointed out, this has been the consistent, long-established Commission rule, and there is no reason to disturb it.[7]

[7]Appellants rest on Goldfarb's general business of designing and inventing many kinds of toys (he has some 50-60 projects a year and has created over 1000 toys) for many firms, but most of this activity is, of course, unrelated in any way to the Stomper toy vehicle. Insofar as the claim is that Goldfarb was engaged in general "research and development" for the toy industry, the answers are that (a) in an investigation based on alleged infringement of a particular United States patent, the patentee's other activities are irrelevant, (b) the Commission has never considered "research and development" activities, standing alone, to constitute an "industry" under § 337, and (c) Schaper's activities together with Goldfarb's very different activities do not together

IV

Having joined with the Commission that both the accessories and Goldfarb's activities should be eliminated from consideration, we focus on Schaper's domestic activities related to the Stomper toy vehicles. Section 337 does not expressly define an "industry ... in the United States" for the purpose of determining whether a domestic industry has been injured. Both the legislative history of section 337 and past Commission decisions on those section 337 investigations that have been based on claims of patent infringement indicate that, in order to constitute an "industry ... in the United States," the patent must be exploited by production in the United States. As quoted above, the House report accompanying the Trade Act of 1974 states that "the patent must be exploited by production in the United States, and the industry in the United States generally consists of the domestic operations of the patent owner, his assignees and licensees devoted to such exploitation of the patent." The Commission in *Certain Ultra-Microtome Freezing Attachments*, *supra*, 195 USPQ at 656, likewise said that "[p]ast Commission decisions * * * have defined 'industry' in section 337 investigations as the domestic manufacture or production of the patented product by the patentee or his licensee."

On this view, the nature and the extent of Schaper's domestic activities (in relation to the total production process of the Stomper toy vehicles) are insufficient to constitute an "industry ... in the United States." The entire manufacturing of the toy vehicles occurs in Hong Kong, as does most of the packaging and quality control. Schaper purchases from Kader the toy vehicles, the great bulk of which are already packaged for sale in blister packs, and imports them into the United States. Those that are not already in blister packs are imported in plastic bags, which are then placed in some of the boxes containing accessories. Schaper's inspection activities upon receipt in this country appear to involve ordinary sampling techniques. They are nothing like those in *Certain Cube Puzzles*, USITC Pub. 1334 (Jan. 1983), in which Ideal Toy's quality control, repair and packaging of imported cube puzzles was determined to constitute an "industry ... in the United States." Unlike Ideal's large inspection and packaging operation in which half of the puzzle's value was added by Ideal's United States activities, Schaper has not shown its United States inspection activities to be substantially different from the random sampling and testing that a normal importer would perform upon receipt (and Schaper does no repairs). Also, Schaper's very large expenditures for advertising and promotion cannot be considered part of the production process. Were we to hold otherwise, few importers would fail the test of constituting a domestic industry. In addition, Schaper's monitoring[10] of Kader's manufacturing cannot be considered part of a domestic industry; it occurs in Hong Kong.

Nor are Schaper's activities comparable to the servicing and installation activities accepted in *Certain Airtight Cast Iron Stoves*, USITC Pub. 1126 (Jan. 1981) and *Certain Airless Paint Spray Pumps and Components Thereof*, USITC Pub. 1199 (Nov. 1981), in which substantial domestic repair and installation activities necessarily associated with imported stoves (in *Stoves*), and frequent domestic product servicing under warranties as well as some domestic production (in *Spray Pumps*), were found by the

constitute an "industry." * * *

[10]Not shown to be substantially different from that of an ordinary importer ordering and purchasing foreign goods to be manufactured abroad for importation into the United States.

Commission sufficient to warrant determinations that the "industry" requirement was met. Although we agree that in proper cases "industry" may encompass more than the manufacturing of the patented item, we also believe that the Commission did not err in deciding that Schaper's activities in the United States are too minimal to be considered an "industry" under section 337. There is simply not enough significant value added domestically to the toy vehicles by Schaper's activities in this country (including design, inspection and packaging). The result is that the Commission's determination, which is consistent with its other holdings, is not erroneous as a legal matter or unsupported by substantial evidence, nor arbitrary or capricious (to the extent the question is within the agency's discretion).

We do not have to deal in this case, more precisely, with the limits of section 337's use of "industry ... in the United States." The Commission has not adopted appellant's proposed general definition that a "significant employment of American land, labor and capital for the creation of value" constitutes such an "industry," and the words, purposes, and history of section 337 do not compel that reading if it is meant to downplay the role of production and servicing in this country. As the statute now stands, Congress did not mean to protect American importers (like Schaper) who cause the imported item to be produced for them abroad and engage in relatively small nonpromotional and non-financing activities in this country—*i.e.*, they engage in design and a small amount of inspection and packaging in this country.[12] If, as appellants suggest, present-day "economic realities" call for a broader definition to protect American interests (apparently including many of today's importers) it is for Congress, not the courts or the Commission, to legislate that policy.

The Commission's order is *Affirmed*.

Notes and Questions

1. It is probable that sales of the Stomper accessories depended heavily on sales of the Stomper toy. Why did the court exclude evidence of U.S. manufacturing of accessories in the determination of whether a domestic industry exists? Do you find what reasoning you can infer compelling? Why or why not?

2. Do you read *Schaper* to hold that there can be no "domestic industry" in the United States for a product that is manufactured in Hong Kong? If manufacturing in the United States is unnecessary, what other kinds of activities might qualify as a domestic industry? Why? What is the common thread tying together the activities that qualify as a domestic industry?

3. If Section 337 creates a remedy for patent infringement, why might the research and development that went into inventing the Stomper toy in the United States have no legal significance to the question of whether there is a

---

[12] In this case, the bulk of the land, labor and capital used for the creation of the value of the toy vehicles was utilized in Hong Kong, not the United States.

domestic industry? Doesn't inventive activity create valuable employment?

B. Section 337 Investigation Procedure

If the complainant can establish the existence of a domestic industry and protected intellectual property, the ITC will commence an investigation by appointing an administrative law judge to hear the case. An **administrative law judge** (**ALJ**) is an employee of the ITC and not a general judge provided for in Article III of the U.S. Constitution. The ALJ decides administrative litigations independently, but the Commission may overrule or amend the ALJ's decision.

Also, unlike in normal courtroom litigation, in every Section 337 investigation before the ITC, a separate organ of the ITC known as the **Office of Unfair Import Investigations** (**OUII**) participates. OUII lawyers are independent of the ITC Commissioners and ALJs alike, and they are charged with

Case Study

President Obama Overturns a Section 337 Exclusion Order

Although U.S. presidents rarely reverse a decision of the ITC following a Section 337 investigation, it does sometimes happen. An example occurred in August 2013, when President Obama overturned an exclusion order issued against imported Apple iPhones® and iPads®. The ITC had determined these infringed U.S. patents owned by Samsung Electronics Co. ITC No. 337-TA-794. The U.S. Trade Representative explained that the President's decision did not call into question the ITC's legal analysis, but was based solely on policy considerations.

The main policy consideration was that the U.S. Department of Justice, Federal Trade Commission, and PTO all had formed the opinion that Samsung's patents embody standards essential to a wide variety of consumer electronic products. If the patents were exercised to exclude competing imports, Samsung could undermine the interoperability of many kinds of consumer electronic devices. If a wide variety of consumer electronics must use the Samsung patents to be mutually compatible, an exclusion order would give Samsung too much power to block desirable electronics imports. Samsung could still seek patent infringement remedies before a court, but a court may decide not to order an injunction to prevent the importation or sale of infringing products. It might simply award a reasonable royalty to Samsung.

Figure 3.11. The Apple iPhone® 11.

representing the public interest. They participate fully in the case as a party, and they seek their own evidentiary discovery, separately examine witnesses, and file their own briefs. The OUII lawyers may pressure the complainant to present a full case when a small or inexperienced foreign respondent does not have the resources to defend itself vigorously. After all, if the complainant succeeds in the investigation, U.S. consumers will be denied access to imported goods of which the complainant seeks exclusion.

Beyond these differences, a Section 337 investigation is much like any other IP infringement litigation, except that the schedule is considerably compressed. Most Section 337 investigations are concluded within 18 months. Afterward, the defeated party may appeal, but not to a district court. Instead, appeals go directly to the **U.S. Court of Appeals for the Federal Circuit**, located in Washington, D.C. The Federal Circuit is a specialized appellate court that handles trade remedies appeals, patent prosecution appeals, customs appeals, and certain other specialized matters. 28 U.S.C. § 1295(a)(6). Appeals from the Federal Circuit go to the U.S. Supreme Court.

C. Section 337 Remedies

Section 337 does not authorize an aggrieved IP owner to recover damages from infringing importers. For that, recourse to a court is necessary. However, Section 337 authorizes some unique and very powerful remedies.

Most importantly, the ITC may, early in the investigation, issue a preliminary exclusion order. An **exclusion order** is an instruction to CBP to deny entry of the goods subject to the investigation into the United States at all customs ports of entry until a final determination has been made.

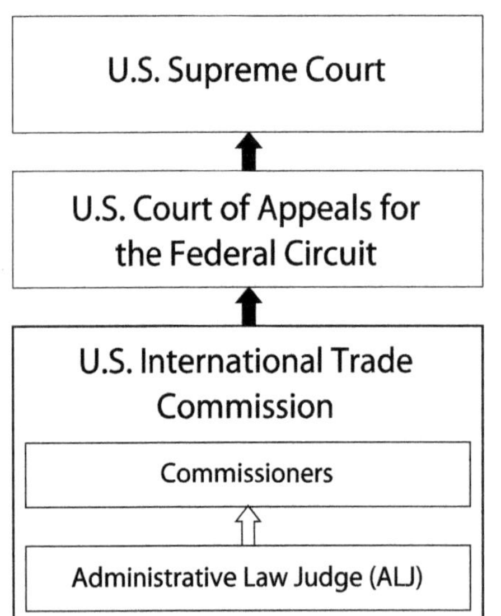

Figure 3.12. The flow of appeals in a Section 337 investigation.

A **limited exclusion order** applies to the respondents' imports specifically. Alternatively, a **general exclusion order** may prohibit the importation of all infringing goods of a specific kind, regardless of the identity of the importer. Because IP infringement litigation must generally be directed at identified defendants, Section 337 offers a potent remedy when the identity of importers of infringing merchandise are unknown, extremely numerous, or highly mutable. However, to obtain a general exclusion order, the complainant must post a bond to cover any damages that may result to the respondent importers if the complainant should lose the case.

The ITC may also issue a **cease and desist order** directly against the

NOTE FROM THE FIELD

Being a Section 337 Trade Remedies Litigator

F. David Foster, Esq. & James B. Altman, Esq.
Foster, Murphy, Altman & Nickel, PC

Litigating a Section 337 case is much like litigating a major IP infringement case in a district court, but on steroids. It's exciting, often involving bet-the-company products, with discovery done on multiple tracks, at lightning speed (trial within nine months), and with compressed trials of one to two weeks. And it's done under a trade remedy statute with its own set of international trade and policy issues and procedures.

Section 337 is used by a wide range of companies, from mom and pop to the largest multinationals, in many industries, from electronics to biotechnology, from heavy manufacturing to consumer products. Although Section 337 cases are technically *in rem* (filed against the imported products themselves), the companies responding in Section 337 investigations include both foreign companies and U.S. companies that manufacture abroad.

A petitioner in a Section 337 investigation has the benefit of being able to prepare and file the case on its own schedule. Because of the speed of the cases and their draconian remedies, Section 337 gives petitioners enormous leverage over respondents. Woe to the disorganized or unprepared.

In contrast, a typical respondent may find itself unprepared and in shock. Literally within weeks it will have to find counsel, determine its litigation positions and strategy, start intensive discovery, find experts, and prepare for trial. Many foreign companies have a limited understanding of U.S. IP law and little or no understanding of U.S. litigation, especially the breadth of discovery and the detailed sensitive information they will have to produce. Educating the client can be the single most important part of the representation.

Section 337 litigation also requires familiarity and working closely with U.S. Customs & Border Protection, which enforces the ITC's exclusion orders—the primary remedy issued under Section 337.

Section 337 litigation is not for everyone. It is intense at times and requires a tolerance for working under pressure. The most important skills are simply those of a good litigator—the ability to communicate and to work with occasionally complex issues. It takes a team with a multitude of talents to successfully litigate a Section 337 case.

David F. Foster is a former Attorney-Advisor and Assistant to the Chairman at the ITC. Mr. Altman has 30 years of experience litigating Section 337 and trade remedy cases. Both are former presidents of the ITC Trial Lawyers Association.

respondents in the investigation. Whereas an exclusion order is directed to CBP, a cease and desist order instructs the respondents to stop attempting to import the infringing goods under penalty of an intimidating fine of $100,000 *per day* or twice the value of the goods imported in violation of the order. 19 U.S.C. § 1337(f).

At the conclusion of the investigation, if the ITC determines that the respondent is seeking to import goods in violation of U.S. protected IP rights and is thereby injuring or threatening to injure a domestic industry, it will issue a permanent exclusion order or cease and desist order, or both. Despite its name, these orders are not really permanent; they merely last indefinitely. They may be rescinded if the ITC finds "that the conditions which led to such exclusion" no longer exist. 19 U.S.C. § 1337(k). For example, if the exclusion order was based on a claim of patent infringement, the order may be rescinded when the patent expires, or if the order was based on trademark infringement, it may be revoked if the importer removes the offending mark from the goods subject to the exclusion order.

Any ITC order under Section 337 takes immediate effect unless the President exercises his authority to veto the order within sixty days. The President has very great discretion to overturn the ITC; he may veto a decision for "policy reasons" without regard to legal considerations. 19 U.S.C. § 1337(g)(2). The Federal Circuit has held that courts lack jurisdiction to review an executive action of this character in the field of foreign affairs.

POLICY ISSUE

Is Section 337 consistent with the WTO Agreements?

Both article III:4 of the GATT and article 3 of the TRIPS Agreement require national treatment of imports from other WTO members. Section 337 grants a powerful remedy for IP infringement, but it can be used by domestic industries only. Foreign IP owners without manufacturing or other labor-intensive facilities in the United States cannot benefit from Section 337. Yet, they may be the target of a Section 337 investigation.

The EU challenged Section 337 in 2000, but the case settled before the DSB heard the request. Why? One explanation is that many large non-U.S. patentees have sufficient U.S. manufacturing facilities to qualify as domestic industries. These powerful firms may discourage their governments from objecting to the discrimination, because they actually benefit from Section 337. If that explanation is right, it leaves small foreign IP owners lacking U.S. manufacturing facilities at a disadvantage relative both to U.S. manufacturers and to their larger foreign competitors. How might such a problem be redressed?

4 Parallel Imports

As Section 1 of this chapter explained, most states are required by international treaties to protect owners of copyrights, patents, and trademarks from the infringing imports. However, many IP owners market their wares not only in their home country, but internationally as well. To understand how this can give rise to a conflict between the purchaser of such a product abroad and the domestic IP owner, picture two different scenarios.

In the first scenario, Widget Masters, Inc. (WMI) is a Delaware corporation that manufactures and sells its widgets globally bearing the WIDMAST trademark. Some of its widgets it sells in the United States; others it sells in foreign countries. All are manufactured in the United States, whether for domestic sale or exportation. WMI sells its widgets to distributors in the United States at $20 per widget. Sylvania Logistics Co. (SLC) is a company that imports WMI's widgets for sale in Sylvania. SLC notes that, because Sylvanian incomes are much lower than U.S. incomes, WMI sells the widgets to SLC for only $10 per widget, one half of the price at which it sells the same widgets to U.S. distributors. SLC decides that it can reap great profits by re-importing the widgets into the United States for sale there. The widgets being re-imported into the United States are called **gray market goods** or **parallel imports**.

Although both terms mean the same thing, they have different connotations. The term "gray market goods" refers to the fact that the importation of the goods does not violate any criminal laws (and thus they are not "black market goods"), but at the same time they potentially infringe IP laws of the importing state, tainting them with dubious legality. The more neutral term "parallel imports" suggests the possibility that such goods may be imported into the IP owner's state in competition with goods imported expressly with the IP owner's authorization. They are, in consequence, imported in parallel with these authorized goods. Different countries have different rules on the legality of parallel imports under their respective IP laws, and so one cannot assume that parallel imports always violate IP rights.

The second scenario tracks the first scenario with one minor but very consequential change. Instead of manufacturing all of WIDMAST marked goods in the United States, WMI's Sylvanian subsidiary, Widget Masters Sylvania, manufactures in Sylvania the widgets intended for sale in Sylvania. Third parties purchase the goods in Sylvania, then resell them at a profit in the United States. Does the fact that the goods were first manufactured and sold from Sylvania alter their legality? These goods are still considered parallel imports, because they are being imported into the IP owner's country (in this example, the United States) without the owner's consent. Again, however, different countries have different rules on the legality of parallel imports. Moreover, in each case, the rule may differ depending on the kind of IP at issue. Trademarked goods and patented goods, for example, may not be treated the same in any given country.

Scenario 1: Domestic Manufacture

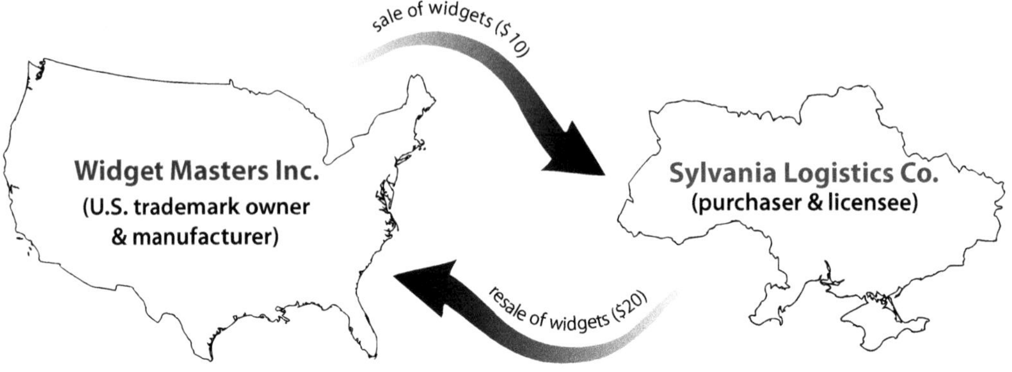

Scenario 2: Foreign Manufacture

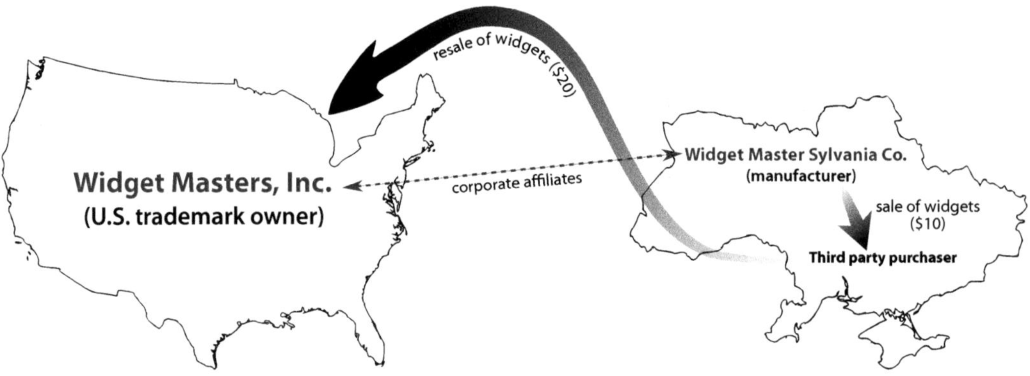

Figure 3.13. Two parallel import scenarios. In the first, Widget Masters, Inc. manufactures widgets in the United States for sale in Sylvania. Sylvania Logistics Co. purchases the widgets in Sylvania and, in defiance of a trademark license restriction prohibiting resale of the widgets outside Sylvania, resells them at a profit to various purchasers in the United States. This is the "round trip" scenario. In the second scenario, Widget Masters Sylvania Co., a corporate subsidiary of the Delaware corporation Widget Masters, Inc., manufactures the widgets in Sylvania for sale in Sylvania. A third party purchaser buys the widgets in Sylvania and resells them at a profit to various purchasers in the United States.

One of the factors that may bear on the question of whether an IP owner has a legal right to prevent the importation is the **exhaustion doctrine**, also known as the **first sale doctrine**. The exhaustion doctrine is a rule adopted by some states for some kinds of IP. According to it, the IP owner "exhausts" his exclusionary right or right to control future dispositions of a patented, trademarked, or copyrighted good once he has transferred ownership of the good to another person. In other words, when the exhaustion doctrine applies, the purchaser of a copyrighted, trademarked, or patented good need not seek permission from the IP owner to resell the good. Note that this doctrine applies only to goods or other tangible items. It does *not* apply to a license or assignment of the right to manufacture goods embodying a patented technology or copyrighted work, or bearing a protected trademark. Note also that article 6 of the TRIPs Agreement expressly disclaims any harmonization of the exhaustion doctrine. Each state is free to apply or not apply the exhaustion doctrine to imports, as it sees fit.

For example, suppose a U.S. company called Mobilia Connections, Inc. holds U.S. and Finnish patents on a mobile phone technology and U.S. and Finnish trademarks on the mark MOBILIA as applied to mobile telephones and telephone service. Mobilia Connections has an agreement with a Finnish company, Finectron Corp., to manufacture and sell mobile phones using Mobilia's patented technology and bearing the MOBILIA mark. You might expect that if, while in Finland, a U.S. company purchased these mobile phones and brought them from Finland to the United States, this would not constitute an infringing importation of the mobile phone in violation of Mobilia's U.S. patent or trademark rights. If so, you would be assuming implicitly that the exhaustion doctrine protects the importer's right to bring the mobile phone into the United States. Because of the territorial independence of IP rights, discussed earlier, that assumption could well be incorrect.

Parallel importation will be explored here in the U.S. context. Because the international exhaustion rules in this country are not entirely uniform for different types of IP, we will examine each field of IP law separately.

4.1 Trademarks and Parallel Imports

The Lanham Trademarks Act is not especially clear about whether exhaustion applies to a foreign sale. It prohibits the unauthorized "use in commerce" of a registered trademark, 15 U.S.C. § 1114(1), and forbids the importation of goods bearing a copy or simulation of a registered trademark, without the registrant's permission, *id.* § 1124, but it does not specify whether permission given abroad through a contract of sale constitutes permission to import goods bearing the mark, or whether a genuine trademark licensed abroad constitutes a "copy" or "simulation" of an identical U.S. trademark, or whether it should be considered the same trademark. The following case explores this issue.

LEVER BROTHERS CO. v. UNITED STATES

U.S. Court of Appeals, D.C. Circuit, 1989
877 F.2d 101

STEPHEN F. WILLIAMS, Circuit Judge:

Two affiliated corporations, one operating in the United States and one in the United Kingdom, use the same words, SHIELD and SUNLIGHT, as trademarks for products that differ materially in the two countries. The products differ because the manufacturers have adjusted them to the countries' differing tastes and conditions. Third parties have directly or indirectly acquired the UK Shield and Sunlight products and imported them to the United States over the objection of the US affiliate, the domestic markholder. Two principles of trademark law—acceptance of manufacturers' interest in signalling the character of their products and consumers' interest in trusting those signals, and the recognition that trademarks may be regional—point toward prohibiting these importations. Deference to the views of the agency entrusted with enforcement of the statute points the other way. The matter ultimately turns, however, on the interpretation of § 42 of the Lanham Act of 1946, 15 U.S.C. § 1124 (1982), and we remand to the district court for it to complete that interpretation with the benefit of any further light that § 42's legislative history and any related administrative practice may disclose.

Lever Brothers Company is a domestic corporation which we shall refer to as either Lever or Lever US. Lever Brothers Ltd. is an English corporation, affiliated with Lever US through the latter's corporate grandparent, and here referred to as Lever UK. Both Lever US and Lever UK manufacture a deodorant soap under a SHIELD trademark and a liquid dishwashing detergent under a SUNLIGHT trademark.

The Shield logo on the wrapper of the two different products is virtually identical and the only difference in the appearance of each wrapper lies in fine print revealing the country of origin and, on the US version, the ingredients. But US Shield contains a higher concentration of coconut soap and fatty acids, and thus more readily generates lather. The manufacturing choice evidently arises in part out of the British preference for baths, which permit time for lather to develop, as opposed to a US preference for showers. Moreover, Britons interested in a soap's lathering properties turn to "beauty and cosmetic" soaps rather than to deodorant soaps. Further, US Shield contains an agent that inhibits growth of bacteria; Lever accounts for this difference in terms of some mix of "differing consumer preferences, climatic conditions and regulatory standards." Finally, the two bars contain differing perfume formulas and colorants.

The two versions of Sunlight use the same word in similar lettering. Their external appearances differ more than the two Shields, however. The UK product comes in a cylindrical drum rather than the flattened hourglass shape employed by the US version. The UK version carries the designation, "washing up liquid" rather than the US's "dishwashing liquid," and it displays at the top a royal emblem, along with the legend "By Appointment to Her Majesty the Queen." The contents of the packages differ materially. UK Sunlight is designed for water with a higher mineral content than is generally found in the United States, and therefore does not perform as well as US

Sunlight in the "soft water" typical of US metropolitan areas.

Consumers are apparently capable of detecting the differences between the contents of the UK and US products—once they start using them. In support of its request for a preliminary injunction, Lever US submitted letters it received from consumers expressing their rage or disappointment with what they had believed, at the time of purchase, to be a discounted version of the familiar US product. Lever argues that these letters evidence consumer confusion, imperiling its reputation for quality.

Third parties import UK Shield and UK Sunlight without authorization by Lever US or, so far as appears, by Lever UK. Despite requests by Lever US, the Customs Service will not halt the importation. It declines to do so only because the trademarks are used abroad by an affiliate of Lever US.

Lever rests its claim that Customs is bound to seize such imports on § 42 of the Lanham Act of 1946, which provides that

> no article of imported merchandise which shall *copy or simulate the name* of the any [*sic*] domestic manufacturer, or manufacturer, or trader, ... or which shall *copy or simulate a trademark* registered in accordance with the provisions of this chapter or shall bear a name or mark calculated to induce the public to believe that the article is manufactured in the United States, or that is manufactured in any foreign country or locality other than the country or locality in which it is in fact manufactured, shall be admitted to entry at any customhouse of the United States....

15 U.S.C. § 1124 (1982) (emphasis added). At its core, Lever's contention is that where affiliated domestic and foreign firms produce goods bearing the same trademark, but different in physical content, the foreign products "copy or simulate" the domestic trademark, so that § 42 forbids their importation, notwithstanding the fact of affiliation.

The Customs Service rests on a regulation whose substance evidently dates back to 1936. While its regulations call as a general matter for seizure of foreign-made articles bearing a trademark identical with one owned and recorded by a US corporation, they make a number of exceptions:

> (c) *Restrictions not applicable*. The restrictions set forth in paragraphs (a) and (b) of this section do not apply to imported articles when:
>
> (1) Both the foreign and the U.S. trademark or trade name are owned by the same person or business entity;
>
> (2) The foreign and domestic trademark or trade name owners are parent and subsidiary companies or are otherwise subject to common ownership or control * * *.

19 C.F.R. § 133.21(c). The critical clause for our purposes is subsection (c)(2), the affiliate exception.

In the Customs Service's view, as embodied in the affiliate exception, goods are genuine—and thus neither copy nor simulate a domestic trademarked good—when they bear trademarks valid in their country of origin and the foreign manufacturer is affiliated with the domestic trademark holder. Where the affiliation between producers exists, Customs regards as irrelevant both physical differences in the products and the domestic markholder's non-consent to importation.

Lever sought a preliminary injunction against the Customs Service's continued application of the affiliate exception on the ground that it violated § 42 of the Lanham Act. The district court essentially agreed with the Customs Service's interpretation of § 42. * * * Lever US filed a timely appeal. * * *

The plain language and general sweep of the Lanham Act undeniably bespeak an intention to protect domestic trademark holders from foreign competitors who seek a free ride on the goodwill of domestic trademarks. But neither § 42 nor the Lanham Act as a whole draws an explicit line between goods that "copy or simulate" a trademark and ones that do not—known as "genuine" goods. We will address first the origins of the exception and a Customs claim of ratification, then the relevant judicial authority, and finally turn to factors bearing upon the correct construction but not addressed earlier. * * *

Case Authority

We turn first to the trio of Supreme Court cases, all revolving around face-powder, which bear upon § 42's predecessor, the almost identical § 27 of the Trademark Law of 1905. Although the cases do not control the present one, they demonstrate the Court's understanding of trademark law as intended to protect a manufacturer's reputation and goodwill and to prevent confusion among consumers. They also reflect and enforce trademark territoriality.

In [*Bourjois & Co. v. Katzel*, 260 U.S. 689 (1923)], the plaintiff (A. Bourjois & Company) was a US corporation that had purchased the US business of a French company * * *, including its goodwill and trademarks. The defendant found that the exchange rate would enable her to buy "Java" face-powder from the French company, and repackage and resell it in the United States under a label almost identical to the plaintiff US firm's and bearing the trademarked names "Java" and "Bourjois." The Second Circuit considered § 27 but construed it not to protect plaintiff because the goods were in its view "genuine." The Supreme Court reversed, but without explicit discussion of § 27.

As Justice Holmes put it, "There is no question that the defendant infringes the plaintiff's rights unless the fact that her boxes and powder are the genuine product of the French concern gives her a right to sell them in the present form." But the goods' being "the genuine product of the French concern" was not enough. Holmes analogized trademarks to patents. If goods were patented in the US, one who brought them abroad from someone entitled to manufacture and sell them there could not on that account sell them here over the opposition of the US patent holder. "The monopoly in that case is more extensive, but we see no significant reason for holding that the monopoly of a trade mark, so far as it goes, is less complete." Holmes was insistent on the inaccuracy of the representation made by the trademark. To the argument that the representation was true because the face-powder actually came from the French firm, he replied:

> But that is not accurate. It is the trade mark of the plaintiff only in the United States and indicates in law, and, it is found, by public understanding, that the goods come from the plaintiff although not made by it.... It stakes the reputation of the plaintiff upon the character of the goods. It was sold and could only be sold with the good will of the business that the plaintiff bought.

Holmes' failure to mention § 27 of the 1905 Act at all, and his reliance in the last quoted sentence on the infeasibility of the French firm's both selling and retaining the US goodwill, leave the case's bearing on § 27 uncertain. But the second case of the trilogy, *A. Bourjois & Co. v. Aldridge*, 292 F. 1013 (2d Cir.1922) (*per curiam*), forges a link to § 27, albeit a vulnerable one. *Aldridge* appears to involve the same business transfer as lay at the root of *Katzel*. The Second Circuit described the US firm A. Bourjois & Co. as having acquired the "exclusive right to manufacture and sell in the United States any and all toilet preparations now made by [the plaintiff]." The sale included the trademark "Manon Lescaut," used in selling a face-powder. As in *Katzel*, an unaffiliated importer bought Manon Lescaut face-powder from the French firm and resold it in the United States under that label. The only noticeable difference between the products' packaging was small print identifying the seller. (The ingredients of plaintiff's own Manon Lescaut powder, though chemically the same as the French version, were not always bought from the French firm.) The action was brought against the Collector of Customs, however, seeking to force him to exclude the third party's product. The Second Circuit certified two questions to the Supreme Court:

> (1) Is the sale in the United States of Wertheimer's Manon Lescaut powder an infringement of plaintiff's registered trade-marks?
> (2) Is the collector, by section 27 of the Trade-Mark Law, required to exclude from entry genuine Manon Lescaut powder so as aforesaid made in France?

The government's three-page brief conceded that *Katzel* controlled. The Court replied that "[t]he two questions certified by the Circuit Court of Appeals for Second Circuit are answered in the affirmative, upon the authority of *Bourjois & Co. v. Katzel*, 260 U.S. 689, the defendant not objecting."

While *Aldridge* reads § 27 to protect a domestic trademark holder from imports of trademarked merchandise that are "genuine" abroad, its precedential force is obviously weakened by the defendant's lack of opposition. Cases dealing with "parallel importation" or "gray goods" have relied on this weakness in discounting *Aldridge*. In such cases, both the holder of a domestic trademark and another party import goods manufactured at the same plant abroad and physically identical. But we think the case for exclusion far stronger here than in that context: here the goods imported are not physically identical to the goods sold by the US trademark holder, and the misrepresentation implicit in the use of the US trademark is far stronger than any present in the sale of gray goods.

The defendant further stresses that in *Aldridge* there was no affiliation between the French manufacturer and the US trademark holder. It persuaded the district court that the presence of affiliation here undercut equities that it viewed as having been determinative there. We shall return to the significance of this point in addressing Customs' policy arguments for its interpretation.

The third of the trilogy, *Prestonettes, Inc. v. Coty*, 264 U.S. 359, 44 S.Ct. 350 (1924), emphasizes truthfulness. The defendant purchased genuine "Coty" products, including face-powder, repackaged them with its own binder, and sold them with clearly distinguishable labels. The Court assumed defendant's conduct to be that which was permitted by a district court decree secured by plaintiff and acquiesced in by defendant. The decree permitted defendant to use the trademarked name in the sale of its products, but only in an explanatory 18-word message, with all words in equal size, color, type and general distinctiveness, stating truthfully that the primary ingredient was Coty's and that the packer and seller, Prestonettes, was "not connected with Coty." Justice Holmes, again writing for the Court, said that this did not amount to actionable infringement:

> The plaintiff could not prevent or complain of [defendant's] stating the nature of the component parts and the source from which they were derived if it did not use the trade mark in doing so.... If the compound was worse than the constituent, it might be a misfortune to the plaintiff, but the plaintiff would have no cause of action, as the defendant was exercising the rights of ownership and only telling the truth.... A trade mark only gives the right to prohibit the use of it so far as to protect the owner's good will against the sale of another's product as his. There is nothing to the contrary in *Bourjois & Co. v. Katzel*, 260 U.S. 689. When the mark is used in a way that does not deceive the public we see no such sanctity in the word as to prevent its being used to tell the truth. It is not taboo.

264 U.S. at 368, 44 S.Ct. at 351.

Prestonettes would aid the defendant only if one denied the fact that language is a social artifact, the meaning of words determined by their use in a particular social context. In Britain a request for "beer" will yield "bitter," a sort of ale with no exact equivalent here; an American seeking our "beer" over there must ask for "lager." Because of the differing conditions in the United States and United Kingdom, and the Lever affiliates' response to these conditions in the design of their products, Shield and Sunlight likewise have different meanings in the two countries. Thus the use of the trademarks for the UK versions in the United States is simply not truthful. The reasons that persuaded Holmes to deny relief in *Prestonettes* point toward granting it here.

We do not essay any grand resolution of the face-powder trilogy's legal message. None of the cases addresses the problem of affiliates generally, nor the special problem of affiliates using identical trademarks to sell products tailored for specific national conditions and tastes. On the other hand, the cases clearly view trademarks as having specific territorial scope, and are at least consistent with the view that § 27 of the 1905 Act protects a domestic trademark holder from goods genuinely trademarked abroad but imported here by parties hoping to exploit consumer confusion between the domestic and foreign products.

The Customs Service relies heavily on a variety of "parallel importation" or "gray market" cases, where a US trademark holder and a third party import goods that are not only identical in physical characteristics but are manufactured by the same firm abroad. * * *

Where the goods bearing a foreign trademark valid abroad are physically different from the US trademarked goods, however, courts have indicated a readiness to find infringement. In *Original Appalachian Artworks, Inc. v. Granada Electronics, Inc.*, 816 F.2d 68 (2d Cir.1987), the American trademark holder licensed a Spanish firm to make Cabbage Patch dolls and to sell them in Spain, the Canary Islands, Andorra and Ceuta Mellila. While the dolls of the US trademark owner contained English-language "adoption papers," which could be filled in and would lead to receipt of a birthday card from the US firm on the doll's "birthday," those of the Spanish licensee had Spanish-language "adoption papers" and seemingly lacked any equivalent of the birthday card system. A third-party imported and sold the Spanish version at about half the price of the US doll. The court found a violation of § 32(1)(a) of Lanham Act, 15 U.S.C. § 1114(1)(a) (1982), which prohibits use of a trademark where it "is likely to cause confusion, or to cause mistake, or to deceive." * * *

One may distinguish *Artworks* and *Dial* on several grounds, but only one seems of much weight here. First, there the goods were produced by a foreign licensee rather than by an affiliate. But this distinction shows only that while in *Artworks* * * * the foreign production was with the explicit consent of the US trademark holder, here it was with a consent inferred from the affiliation. The absence of consent to *importation* is the same. Second, *Artworks* * * * rest[s] on § 32 rather than § 42 of the Lanham Act. But the deceit that the Second Circuit found controlling in *Artworks* * * * seems, under the face-powder trilogy, equally relevant under § 42. * * *

Remaining Interpretative Concerns

Customs' central thesis, that affiliation between the foreign producer and domestic markholder automatically defines the foreign goods as genuine, draws on an important truth—that a trademark holder cannot infringe its own mark. Thus, if a US markholder itself imports goods (or licenses another to do so), the markholder's conduct of or authorization of the importation makes the goods authentic, whether they are better, worse, or the same as the US markholder's domestic products. To the extent that the affiliate exception extends this principle to goods imported into the US by companies affiliated with the US markholder, it does nothing more than treat the two companies as being constructively one for infringement purposes. As such it seems unobjectionable.

But the exception contained in 19 C.F.R. § 133.21(c)(2) does more. Merely on the basis of affiliation between the US markholder and the foreign *producer*, it extends the non-violation that is implicit in importation by the markholder or with its consent to a radically different matter, imports *by third parties*. Inferring non-violation from that relation seems no more plausible than an inference of consent to import from the US markholder's licensing production abroad, which the *Artworks* * * * court[ ] obviously rejected.

Apart from its attempted reliance on authority and the impossibility of self-infringement, the Customs Service asserts some policy arguments. First, it contends that because of the affiliation, the dispute is better suited for resolution "in the boardroom" than the court room. As often proves true of pleasing rhetorical phrases, this seems largely irrelevant to the issue. Even if all the Lever affiliates were collapsed into a single corporate entity, its board could not single-handedly implement a decision to limit sales of UK Shield and UK Sunlight to the United Kingdom. So long as it uses third-party middlemen and retailers, it must launch those products into the stream of commerce, with the risk that some purchasers may seek to exploit the opportunity to ride on the US trademarks' value. Indeed, at some exchange rates an arbitrageur could buy Shield and Sunlight at retail from a completely vertically integrated Lever UK and profitably resell them here. We are not told how either the US markholder or the foreign affiliate is to prevent this without invoking governmental authority, either in the form of Customs Service action or trademark-based injunctions against the importer.

Of course the "boardroom" that evidently controls both Lever US and Lever UK could solve the problem by abandoning use of the Shield and Sunlight trademarks in the United Kingdom, or at least by abandoning their use for physically distinct products. But this solution is obviously costly. The Lever affiliates have succeeded in attaching to products designed for their respective markets ordinary words that have both a favorable "spin" and a natural link to those products. Customs has offered us no shadow of a reason why it would serve any public interest implicit in § 42 to compel Lever to abandon the resulting goodwill, or (looking ahead) to refrain in the first place from establishing such goodwill by use of identical words. The resources of English are finite and the quest for an apt word costly.

Second, Customs suggests there is a consumer interest in access to the lower-priced UK products. But trademark law inherently denies consumers access to cheap goods sailing under false colors. Further, even if we were to accept Customs' dubious premise, it points to nothing supporting the idea that the mere fact of affiliation makes it more likely than in the general case that this potential consumer loss would exceed the gain from accurate signalling of quality by means of trademarks.

Third, Customs suggests that its interpretation of the Lanham Act is an administrative necessity. The alternative to the exception, it claims, is that "Customs Service agents [would be] required to assess at the border the amount of consumer confusion and/or loss of goodwill likely to result from the importation of goods bearing genuine foreign trademarks." We think this greatly overstates the problem. No one is suggesting that Customs assess the degree of consumer confusion or loss of goodwill, only that it distinguish between identical and non-identical goods. If Lever US's submissions here are correct, that would not be difficult in a case such as this. It is hard to see why Customs' arguments calls for more than allowing it room to choose inactivity in marginal cases.

Lever argues that the administrative problem is completely non-existent: that US markholders will seek to block the imports of goods produced by affiliates only when in fact they are different and therefore likely to erode the US holder's goodwill. We think this somewhat oversimplifies. [*K Mart Corp. v. Cartier, Inc.*, 486 U.S. 281 (1988)] upheld the affiliate exception as applied to parallel imports (but only in reference to plaintiffs' Tariff Act challenge), approving (for example) Customs' decision to permit third-party purchasers to buy goods produced abroad by a foreign subsidiary of a US firm and import them over the US firm's opposition * * *. If we were to hold that Customs must bar goods produced by a US firm's affiliate when the US and foreign goods differ, and *K Mart* is extended to permit Customs to apply the affiliate exception where a US firm's *domestically* manufactured goods are identical to the imports, then US firms would have an incentive to raise false claims of non-identity.

Nonetheless, we find that the specter of false claims that possible future extensions of *K Mart* might generate is not enough to validate Customs' administrative inconvenience theory. First, *K Mart* did not evaluate the affiliate exception as against an attack under § 42. Second, the *K Mart* Court never addressed the issue of foreign surrogates competing with domestically produced trademarked goods. We hesitate here to evaluate the probabilities of these two extensions of *K Mart*, neither of which is before us or has been briefed. We do note, however, that if the two extensions occur and if Customs' administrative practicality argument is controlling, § 42 will have become a dead letter for a surprisingly wide range of cases, the gray-goods tail wagging the dog of flat-out deception. We hesitate to impute such broad effects to *K Mart*, even in the face of the Service's disclaimer of ability to identify what is genuine.

We think the natural, virtually inevitable reading of § 42 is that it bars foreign goods bearing a trademark identical to a valid US trademark but physically different, regardless of the trademarks' genuine character abroad or affiliation between the producing firms. On its face the section appears to aim at deceit and consumer confusion; when identical trademarks have acquired different meanings in different countries, one who imports the foreign version to sell it under that trademark will (in the absence of some specially differentiating feature) cause the confusion Congress sought to avoid. The fact of affiliation between the producers in no way reduces the probability of that confusion; it is certainly not a constructive consent to the importation. The cases are entirely congruent with this view. Customs' assertion of administrative difficulties appears overdrawn, and in any event would seem to justify no more than inaction in those cases that are close on the factual issue of product identity. Thus, despite the deference we owe Customs under *Chevron*, we believe that the affiliate exception does not square with § 42.

For now, however, our conclusion must remain provisional. Neither party has briefed the legislative history nor administrative practice in any detail. * * * [W]e adopt a reading of the statute tentatively, and reverse and remand to the district court so that the parties may join issue on those points. Subject to some persuasive evidence running against our tentative conclusion, we must say that Lever's probability of success on its legal argument is quite high; at this preliminary stage we go no further. * * *

Notes and Questions

1. On remand, the district court in the *Lever Brothers* case held that Customs did not succeed in showing that a broad "affiliate exception" to the Lanham Trademark Act existed without reference to any physical differences between the U.S. and gray-market goods. The government appealed this ruling again. On the second appeal, *Lever Brothers Co. v. United States*, 981 F.2d 1330, 1338 (D.C. Cir. 1993), the appellate court affirmed that:

> Section 42 on its face appears to forbid importation of goods that "copy or simulate" a United States trademark. * * * [T]he issue of materially different goods was not addressed either in the legislative history or the administrative record. It is not enough to posit that silence implies authorization, when the authorization sought runs counter to the evident meaning of the governing statute. Therefore, we conclude that section 42 of the Lanham Act precludes the application of Customs' affiliate exception with respect to physically, materially different goods.

2. Why do you think the Supreme Court in the face powder trio of cases treated parallel imports of trademark-protected items differently than such imports of patented items? Could it have something to do with the nature of what trademarks, as opposed to patents, protect? Trademark protection is generally intended to protect consumers against confusing uses of the trademarks that affect their purchasing decisions. Patent law, in contrast, removes a market-based disincentive to inventors seeking to develop new technologies, and it also requires them to disclose the invention to the public in the patent application as a condition for protection.

3. Look back to Figure 3.13. In *Lever Brothers*, Scenario 2 was involved. What if the plaintiff's foreign affiliate had sold the goods to a U.S. third-party purchaser? Would the outcome have been the same or different? Why?

4. After the *Lever Brothers* cases, Customs amended its regulations to define restricted gray market goods as "foreign-made articles bearing a genuine trademark or trade name identical with or substantially indistinguishable from one owned and recorded by" a U.S. citizen or company without the trademark owner's license, and to authorize seizure and forfeiture of goods bearing a legitimate trademark that are "physically and materially different from the articles authorized by the U.S. trademark owner for importation or sale in the U.S." 19 U.S.C. § 133.23(a),(c). On the other hand, the Customs Regulations create a way for gray market importers to import even these goods:

> (b) *Labeling of physically and materially different goods.* Goods determined by [CBP] to be physically and materially different under the procedures of this part, bearing a genuine mark applied under the authority of the U.S. owner, a parent or subsidiary of the U.S. owner, or a party otherwise subject to common ownership or control with the U.S. owner * * *, shall not be detained * * * where the merchandise or its packaging bears a conspicuous and legible label designed to remain on the product until the first point of sale to a retail consumer in the United States stating that: "This product is not a product authorized by the United States trademark owner for the importation and is physically and materially different from the authorized product." The label must be in close proximity to the trademark as it appears in its most prominent location on the article itself or the retail package or container. Other information designed to dispel consumer confusion may also be added.

19 C.F.R. § 133.23(b). Why do you think Customs adopted this rule? Is it consistent with the rule announced by the D.C. Circuit in *Lever Brothers*? Is it consistent with the policy the D.C. Circuit was seeking to promote? Is it consistent with the territorial independence principle? Why or why not?

5. The ITC has also had to deal with parallel imports in the context of Section 337 investigations. One case raised the question of whether the differences between the parallel imports and the U.S. goods had to be physical, as stated in *Lever Brothers*. In *SKF USA Inc. v. ITC*, 423 F.3d 1307 (Fed. Cir. 2005), the U.S. trademark owner alleged that numerous respondents were importing into the United States ball bearings with SKF's trademark but without its authorization in violation of the Lanham Act. SKF did not allege, however, that the imported bearings had any physical attributes different from the SKF bearings authorized for sale in the United States. Instead, the imported bearings were sold without the benefit of a distribution agreement that would guarantee technical and engineering services to accompany the sale. Purchasers of the imported products, unlike purchasers of domestic products, were therefore not entitled to SKF's post-sale customer service support. The court held that the differences between the parallel imports and the domestic product need not be physical to justify excluding the imports after all. However, the court also found that the plaintiff:

> must establish that all or substantially all of its sales are accompanied by the asserted material difference in order to show that its goods are materially different. If less than all or substantially all of a trademark owner's products possess the material difference, then the trademark owner has placed into the stream of commerce a substantial quantity of goods that are or may be the same or similar to those of the importer, and then there is no material difference. Indeed, if it cannot be said that substantially all of a trademark owner's goods are accompanied by the asserted characteristic, then it may properly be concluded that, in effect, there exists no material difference between the trademark owner's goods and the allegedly infringing goods.

Does this rule allow U.S. trademark owners to offer warranty service on their U.S.-manufactured products that differs from what is offered on their identical foreign-manufactured products, and thereby to avoid *Lever Brothers*?

A few years later, in *Beltronics USA Inc. v. Midwest Inventory Distrib. LLC*, 90 U.S.P.Q.2d 1228 (10th Cir. 2009), the Tenth Circuit found that physically identical unauthorized imports did not benefit from the exhaustion doctrine when the trademark owner had a policy of refusing to offer warranty services, software upgrades, and rebates for the imported goods. To the importers' objections that this interpretation "would permit any trademark owner to eliminate the resale of its goods, shut down its competitors, and ultimately fix the price of its product simply by limiting its warranty coverage and service commitments to those who buy from it directly," the court replied that the importer could protect itself by eliminating consumer confusion, such as by disclosing to consumers that the goods would not benefit from the manufacturer's warranty and service. In deciding whether to exclude an infringing import, how can Customs distinguish between physically identical imports with different warranty or other contract conditions?

4.2 Copyright and Parallel Imports

A copyright owner has the right to exclude others from reproducing, selling, or otherwise distributing copies of the work. In the United States, the exhaustion doctrine is a statutory exception to that right, but it does not clearly specify whether it applies only to copies lawfully sold in the United States or also applies to copies first sold abroad. It merely provides in relevant part:

> the owner of a particular copy or phonorecord lawfully made under this title, or any person authorized by such owner, is entitled, without the authority of the copyright owner, to sell or otherwise dispose of the possession of that copy or phonorecord.

17 U.S.C. § 109(a). Section 602 of the Copyright Act superficially seems to resolve the issue. It provides in relevant part:

> (a) Importation into the United States, without the authority of the owner of copyright under this title, of copies or phonorecords of a work that have been acquired outside the United States is an infringement of the exclusive right to distribute copies or phonorecords under section 106 * * *.
>
> (b) In a case where the making of the copies or phonorecords would have constituted an infringement of copyright if this title had been applicable, their importation is prohibited. In a case where the copies or phonorecords were lawfully made, the United States Customs Service has no authority to prevent their importation unless the provisions of section 601 are applicable. * * *

17 U.S.C. § 602.

What if the copies were "lawfully made" in the United States under license of the copyright owner and then exported? May the owner then reimport the goods into the United States without the permission of the copyright owner? This is Scenario 1 from Figure 3.13. In *Quality King Distributors v. L'anza Research International*, 523 U.S. 135 (1998), the Supreme Court held that the copyright owner had no right to prevent such copies making a "round trip," because under Section 109(a) of the Copyright Act, the owner's rights were exhausted when the goods were lawfully made in the United States and title to the copies was transferred to another party with the owner's authorization.

What about Scenario 2? Because Section 602 says nothing about whether the imported copies were lawfully made under a foreign copyright covering the same work, it may seem to follow that the exhaustion doctrine does *not* apply to the imported copies, and the copyright owner may exclude their importation into the United States even though they were made and sold outside of the United States with the consent of the copyright owner. Yet, it seems this reading of the Copyright Act is contestable, as the following case illustrates.

KIRTSAENG v. JOHN WILEY & SONS, INC.

Supreme Court of the United States, 2013
568 U.S. 519

Justice BREYER delivered the opinion of the Court.

Section 106 of the Copyright Act grants "the owner of copyright under this title" certain "exclusive rights," including the right "to distribute copies . . . of the copyrighted work to the public by sale or other transfer of ownership." 17 U.S.C. § 106(3). These rights are qualified, however, by the application of various limitations set forth in the next several sections of the Act, §§ 107 through 122. Those sections, typically entitled "Limitations on exclusive rights," include, for example, the principle of "fair use" (§ 107), permission for limited library archival reproduction, (§ 108), and the doctrine at issue here, the "first sale" doctrine (§ 109).

Section 109(a) sets forth the "first sale" doctrine as follows:

> "Notwithstanding the provisions of section 106(3) [the section that grants the owner exclusive distribution rights], the owner of a particular copy or phonorecord *lawfully made under this title* . . . is entitled, without the authority of the copyright owner, to sell or otherwise dispose of the possession of that copy or phonorecord." (Emphasis added.)

Thus, even though § 106(3) forbids distribution of a copy of, say, the copyrighted novel *Herzog* without the copyright owner's permission, § 109(a) adds that, once a copy of *Herzog* has been lawfully sold (or its ownership otherwise lawfully transferred), the buyer of *that copy* and subsequent owners are free to dispose of it as they wish. In copyright jargon, the "first sale" has "exhausted" the copyright owner's § 106(3) exclusive distribution right.

What, however, if the copy of *Herzog* was printed abroad and then initially sold with the copyright owner's permission? Does the "first sale" doctrine still apply? Is the buyer, like the buyer of a domestically manufactured copy, free to bring the copy into the United States and dispose of it as he or she wishes?

* * * [Section] 602(a)(1) makes clear that importing a copy without permission violates the owner's exclusive distribution right. But in doing so, § 602(a)(1) refers explicitly to the § 106(3) exclusive distribution right. As we have just said, § 106 is by its terms "[s]ubject to" the various doctrines and principles contained in §§ 107 through 122, including § 109(a)'s "first sale" limitation. Do those same modifications apply—in particular, does the "first sale"modification apply—when considering whether § 602(a)(1) prohibits importing a copy?

* * * This case is like *Quality King* but for one important fact. The copies at issue here were manufactured abroad. That fact is important because § 109(a) says that the "first sale" doctrine applies to "a particular copy or phonorecord lawfully made under this title." And we must decide here whether the five words, "lawfully made under this title," make a critical legal difference.

Putting section numbers to the side, we ask whether the "first sale" doctrine applies to protect a buyer or other lawful owner of a copy (of a copyrighted work) lawfully manufactured abroad. Can that buyer bring that copy into the United States (and sell it or give it away) without obtaining permission to do so from the copyright owner? Can, for example, someone who purchases, say at a used bookstore, a book printed abroad subsequently resell it without the copyright owner's permission? * * *

I

A

Respondent, John Wiley & Sons, Inc., publishes academic textbooks. Wiley obtains from its authors various foreign and domestic copyright assignments, licenses and permissions—to the point that we can, for present purposes, refer to Wiley as the relevant American copyright owner. Wiley often assigns to its wholly owned foreign subsidiary, John Wiley & Sons (Asia) Pte Ltd., rights to publish, print, and sell Wiley's English language textbooks abroad. Each copy of a Wiley Asia foreign edition will likely contain language making clear that the copy is to be sold only in a particular country or geographical region outside the United States.

For example, a copy of Wiley's American edition says, "Copyright © 2008 John Wiley & Sons, Inc. All rights reserved.... Printed in the United States of America." J. WALKER, FUNDAMENTALS OF PHYSICS, p. vi (8th ed.2008). A copy of Wiley Asia's Asian edition of that book says:

> "Copyright © 2008 John Wiley & Sons (Asia) Pte Ltd[.] All rights reserved. This book is authorized for sale in Europe, Asia, Africa, and the Middle East only and may be not exported out of these territories. Exportation from or importation of this book to another region without the Publisher's authorization is illegal and is a violation of the Publisher's rights. The Publisher may take legal action to enforce its rights.... Printed in Asia." J. WALKER, FUNDAMENTALS OF PHYSICS, p. vi (8th ed. 2008 Wiley Int'l Student ed.).

Both the foreign and the American copies say:

> "No part of this publication may be reproduced, stored in a retrieval system, or transmitted in any form or by any means ... except as permitted under Sections 107 or 108 of the 1976 United States Copyright Act." [...]

The upshot is that there are two essentially equivalent versions of a Wiley textbook, each version manufactured and sold with Wiley's permission: (1) an American version printed and sold in the United States, and (2) a foreign version manufactured and sold abroad. And Wiley makes certain that copies of the second version state that they are not to be taken (without permission) into the United States.

Petitioner, Supap Kirtsaeng, a citizen of Thailand, moved to the United States in 1997 to study mathematics at Cornell University. He paid for his education with the help of a Thai Government scholarship which required him to teach in Thailand for 10 years on his return. * * * While he was studying in the United States, Kirtsaeng asked his friends and family in Thailand to buy copies of foreign edition English-language textbooks at Thai book shops, where they sold at low prices, and mail them to him in the United States. Kirtsaeng would then sell them, reimburse his family and friends, and keep the profit.

B

In 2008 Wiley brought this federal lawsuit against Kirtsaeng for copyright infringement. Wiley claimed that Kirtsaeng's unauthorized importation of its books and his later resale of those books amounted to an infringement of Wiley's § 106(3) exclusive right to distribute as well as § 602's related import prohibition. Kirtsaeng replied that the books he had acquired were "'lawfully made'" and that he had acquired them legitimately. Thus, in his view, § 109(a)'s "first sale" doctrine permitted him to resell or otherwise dispose of the books without the copyright owner's further permission.

The District Court held that Kirtsaeng could not assert the "first sale" defense because, in its view, that doctrine does not apply to "foreign-manufactured goods" (even if made abroad with the copyright owner's permission). The jury then found that Kirtsaeng had willfully infringed Wiley's American copyrights by selling and importing without authorization copies of eight of Wiley's copyrighted titles. And it assessed statutory damages of $600,000 ($75,000 per work).

On appeal, a split panel of the Second Circuit agreed with the District Court. It pointed out that § 109(a)'s "first sale" doctrine applies only to "the owner of a particular copy ... *lawfully made under this title*." And, in the majority's view, this language means that the "first sale" doctrine does not apply to copies of American copyrighted works manufactured abroad. A dissenting judge thought that the words "lawfully made under this title" do not refer "to a place of manufacture" but rather "focu[s] on whether a particular copy was manufactured lawfully under" America's copyright statute, and that "the lawfulness of the manufacture of a particular copy should be judged by U.S. copyright law." (opinion of Murtha, J.).

We granted Kirtsaeng's petition for certiorari to consider this question in light of different views among the Circuits.

II

We must decide whether the words "lawfully made under this title" restrict the scope of § 109(a)'s "first sale" doctrine geographically. The Second Circuit, the Ninth Circuit, Wiley, and the Solicitor General (as *amicus*) all read those words as imposing a form of *geographical* limitation. The Second Circuit held that they limit the "first sale" doctrine to particular copies "made in territories *in which the Copyright Act is law*," which (the Circuit says) are copies "manufactured domestically," not "outside of the United States." (emphasis added). Wiley agrees that those five words limit the "first sale" doctrine "to copies made in conformance with the [United States] Copyright Act *where the Copyright Act is applicable*," which (Wiley says) means it does not apply to copies made "outside the United States" and at least not to "foreign production of a copy for distribution exclusively abroad." Similarly, the Solicitor General says that those five words limit the "first sale" doctrine's applicability to copies "'*made subject to* and in compliance with [the Copyright Act],'" which (the Solicitor General says) are copies "made in the United States." (emphasis added). And the Ninth Circuit has held that those words limit the "first sale" doctrine's applicability (1) to copies lawfully made in the United States, and (2) to copies lawfully made outside the United States but initially sold in the United States with the copyright owner's permission.

Under any of these geographical interpretations, § 109(a)'s "first sale" doctrine would not apply to the Wiley Asia books at issue here. And, despite an American copyright owner's permission to *make* copies abroad, one who *buys* a copy of any such book or other copyrighted work—whether at a retail store, over the Internet, or at a library sale—could not resell (or otherwise dispose of) that particular copy without further permission.

Kirtsaeng, however, reads the words "lawfully made under this title" as imposing a non-geographical limitation. He says that they mean made "in accordance with" or "in compliance with" the Copyright Act. In that case, § 109(a)'s "first sale" doctrine would apply to copyrighted works as long as their manufacture met the requirements of American copyright law. In particular, the doctrine would apply where, as here, copies are manufactured abroad with the permission of the copyright owner.

In our view, § 109(a)'s language, its context, and the common-law history of the "first sale" doctrine, taken together, favor a non-geographical interpretation. We also doubt that Congress would have intended to create the practical copyright-related harms with which a geographical interpretation would threaten ordinary scholarly, artistic, commercial, and consumer activities. We consequently conclude that Kirtsaeng's non-geographical reading is the better reading of the Act.

A

The language of § 109(a) read literally favors Kirtsaeng's nongeographical interpretation, namely, that "lawfully made under this title" means made "in accordance with" or "in compliance with" the Copyright Act. The language of § 109(a) says nothing about geography. The word "under" can mean "[i]n accordance with." 18 OXFORD ENGLISH DICTIONARY 950 (2d ed.1989). See also BLACK'S LAW DICTIONARY 1525 (6th ed.1990) ("according to"). And a nongeographical interpretation provides each word of the five-word phrase with a distinct purpose. The first two words of the phrase, "lawfully made," suggest an effort to distinguish those copies that were made lawfully from those that were not, and the last three words, "under this title," set forth the standard of "lawful[ness]." Thus, the nongeographical reading is simple, it promotes a traditional copyright objective (combatting piracy), and it makes word-by-word linguistic sense.

The geographical interpretation, however, bristles with linguistic difficulties. It gives the word "lawfully" little, if any, linguistic work to do. (How could a book be *un*lawfully "made under this title"?) It imports geography into a statutory provision that says nothing explicitly about it. And it is far more complex than may at first appear.

To read the clause geographically, Wiley, like the Second Circuit and the Solicitor General, must first emphasize the word "under." Indeed, Wiley reads "under this title" to mean "in conformance with the Copyright Act where the Copyright Act is applicable." Wiley must then take a second step, arguing that the Act "is applicable" only in the United States. And the Solicitor General must do the same. * * *

One difficulty is that neither "under" nor any other word in the phrase means "where." See, e.g., 18 OXFORD ENGLISH DICTIONARY, *supra*, at 947–952 (definition of "under"). It might mean "subject to," but as this Court has repeatedly acknowledged, the word evades a uniform, consistent meaning. See *Kucana v. Holder*, 558 U.S. 233, 245, 130 S.Ct. 827 (2010) ("'under' is chameleon"); *Ardestani v. INS*, 502 U.S. 129, 135, 112 S.Ct. 515 (1991) ("under" has "many dictionary definitions" and "must draw its meaning from its context").

A far more serious difficulty arises out of the uncertainty and complexity surrounding the second step's effort to read the necessary geographical limitation into the word "applicable" (or the equivalent). Where, precisely, is the Copyright Act "applicable"? The Act does not instantly *protect* an American copyright holder from unauthorized piracy taking place abroad. But that fact does not mean the Act is *inapplicable* to copies made abroad. As a matter of ordinary English, one can say that a statute imposing, say, a tariff upon "any rhododendron grown in Nepal" applies to *all* Nepalese rhododendrons. And, similarly, one can say that the American Copyright Act is *applicable* to *all* pirated copies, including those printed overseas. Indeed, the Act itself makes clear that (in the Solicitor General's language) foreign-printed pirated copies are "subject to" the Act. § 602(a)(2) (referring to importation of copies "the making of which either constituted an infringement of copyright, or which would have constituted an infringement of copyright if this title had been applicable").

The appropriateness of this linguistic usage is underscored by the fact that § 104 of the Act itself says that works "*subject to protection under this title*" include unpublished works "without regard to the nationality or domicile of the author," and works "first published" in any one of the nearly 180 nations that have signed a copyright treaty with the United States. §§ 104(a), (b) (emphasis added); § 101 (defining "treaty party"). Thus, ordinary English permits us to say that the Act "applies" to an Irish manuscript lying in its author's Dublin desk drawer as well as to an original recording of a ballet performance first made in Japan and now on display in a Kyoto art gallery.

The Ninth Circuit's geographical interpretation produces still greater linguistic difficulty. As we said, that Circuit interprets the "first sale" doctrine to cover both (1) copies manufactured in the United States and (2) copies manufactured abroad but first sold in the United States with the American copyright owner's permission.

We can understand why the Ninth Circuit may have thought it necessary to add the second part of its definition. As we shall later describe * * *, without some such qualification a copyright holder could prevent a buyer from domestically reselling or even giving away copies of a video game made in Japan, a film made in Germany, or a dress (with a design copyright) made in China, *even* if the copyright holder has granted permission for the foreign manufacture, importation, and an initial domestic sale of the copy. A publisher such as Wiley would be free to print its books abroad, allow their importation and sale within the United States, but prohibit students from later selling their used texts at a campus bookstore. We see no way, however, to reconcile this half-geographical/half-nongeographical interpretation with the language of the phrase, "lawfully made under this title." As a matter of English, it would seem that those five words either do cover copies lawfully made abroad or they do not.

In sum, we believe that geographical interpretations create more linguistic problems than they resolve. And considerations of simplicity and coherence tip the purely linguistic balance in Kirtsaeng's, nongeographical, favor.

B

Both historical and contemporary statutory context indicate that Congress, when writing the present version of § 109(a), did not have geography in mind. * * *

Finally, we normally presume that the words "lawfully made under this title" carry the same meaning when they appear in different but related sections. But doing so here produces surprising consequences. Consider:

> (1) Section 109(c) says that, despite the copyright owner's exclusive right "to display" a copyrighted work (provided in § 106(5)), the owner of a particular copy "lawfully made under this title" may publicly display it without further authorization. To interpret these words geographically would mean that one who buys a copyrighted work of art, a poster, or even a bumper sticker, in Canada, in Europe, in Asia, could not display it in America without the copyright owner's further authorization.
>
> (2) Section 109(e) specifically provides that the owner of a particular copy of a copyrighted video arcade game "lawfully made under this title" may "publicly perform or display that game in coin-operated equipment" without the authorization of the copyright owner. To interpret these words geographically means that an arcade owner could not ("without the authority of the copyright owner") perform or display arcade games (whether new or used) originally made in Japan.
>
> (3) Section 110(1) says that a teacher, without the copyright owner's authorization, is allowed to perform or display a copyrighted work (say, an audiovisual work) "in the course of face-to-face teaching activities"—unless the teacher knowingly used "a copy that was not lawfully made under this title." To interpret these words geographically would mean that the teacher could not (without further authorization) use a copy of a film during class if the copy was lawfully made in Canada, Mexico, Europe, Africa, or Asia.
>
> (4) In its introductory sentence, § 106 provides the Act's basic exclusive rights to an "owner of a copyright under this title." The last three words cannot support a geographic interpretation.

Wiley basically accepts the first three readings, but argues that Congress intended the restrictive consequences. And it argues that context simply requires that the words of the fourth example receive a different interpretation. Leaving the fourth example to the side, we shall explain in Part II–D, *infra*, why we find it unlikely that Congress would have intended these, and other related consequences.

C

A relevant canon of statutory interpretation favors a nongeographical reading. "[W]hen a statute covers an issue previously governed by the common law," we must presume that "Congress intended to retain the substance of the common law." *Samantar v. Yousuf*, 560 U.S. __, n. 13 (2010) (slip op., at 14, n. 13).

The "first sale" doctrine is a common-law doctrine with an impeccable historic pedigree. * * * American law too has generally thought that competition, including freedom to resell, can work to the advantage of the consumer.

The "first sale" doctrine also frees courts from the administrative burden of trying to enforce restrictions upon difficult-to-trace, readily movable goods. And it avoids the selective enforcement inherent in any such effort. Thus, it is not surprising that for at least a century the "first sale" doctrine has played an important role in American copyright law.

The common-law doctrine makes no geographical distinctions; nor can we find any in [*Bobbs-Merrill Co. v. Straus*, 210 U.S. 339 (1908)] (where this Court first applied the "first sale" doctrine) or in § 109(a)'s predecessor provision, which Congress enacted a year later. Rather, as the Solicitor General acknowledges, "a straightforward application of *Bobbs-Merrill*" would not preclude the "first sale" defense from applying to authorized copies made overseas. And we can find no language, context, purpose, or history that would rebut a "straightforward application" of that doctrine here.

The dissent argues that another principle of statutory interpretation works against our reading, and points out that elsewhere in the statute Congress used different words to express something like the non-geographical reading we adopt. *Post*, at 8-9 (quoting § 602(a)(2) (prohibiting the importation of copies "the making of which either constituted an infringement of copyright, or which would have constituted an infringement of copyright if this title had been applicable" (emphasis deleted))). Hence, Congress, the dissent believes, must have meant § 109(a)'s different language to mean something different (such as the dissent's own geographical interpretation of § 109(a)). We are not aware, however, of any canon of interpretation that forbids interpreting different words used in different parts of the same statute to mean roughly the same thing. Regardless, were there such a canon, the dissent's interpretation of § 109(a) would also violate it. That is because Congress elsewhere in the 1976 Act included the words "manufactured in the United States or Canada," which express just about the same geographical thought that the dissent reads into § 109(a)'s very different language.

D

Associations of libraries, used-book dealers, technology companies, consumer-goods retailers, and museums point to various ways in which a geographical interpretation would fail to further basic constitutional copyright objectives, in particular "promot[ing] the Progress of Science and useful Arts." U.S. Const., Art. I, § 8, cl. 8.

The American Library Association tells us that library collections contain at least 200 million books published abroad (presumably, many were first published in one of the nearly 180 copyright-treaty nations and enjoy American copyright protection under 17 U.S.C. § 104); that many others were first published in the United States but printed abroad because of lower costs; and that a geographical interpretation will likely require the libraries to obtain permission (or at least create significant uncertainty) before circulating or otherwise distributing these books.

How, the American Library Association asks, are the libraries to obtain permission to distribute these millions of books? How can they find, say, the copyright owner of a foreign book, perhaps written decades ago? They may not know the copyright holder's present address. And, even where addresses can be found, the costs of finding them, contacting owners, and negotiating may be high indeed. Are the libraries to stop circulating or distributing or displaying the millions of books in their collections that were printed abroad?

* * *

Technology companies tell us that "automobiles, microwaves, calculators, mobile phones, tablets, and personal computers" contain copyrightable software programs or packaging. Many of these items are made abroad with the American copyright holder's permission and then sold and imported (with that permission) to the United States. A geographical interpretation would prevent the resale of, say, a car, without the permission of the holder of each copyright on each piece of copyrighted automobile software. Yet there is no reason to believe that foreign auto manufacturers regularly obtain this kind of permission from their software component suppliers, and Wiley did not indicate to the contrary when asked. Without that permission a foreign car owner could not sell his or her used car.

Retailers tell us that over $2.3 trillion worth of foreign goods were imported in 2011. American retailers buy many of these goods after a first sale abroad. And, many of these items bear, carry, or contain copyrighted "packaging, logos, labels, and product inserts and instructions for [the use of] everyday packaged goods from floor cleaners and health and beauty products to breakfast cereals." The retailers add that American sales of more traditional copyrighted works, "such as books, recorded music, motion pictures, and magazines" likely amount to over $220 billion. A geographical interpretation would subject many, if not all, of them to the disruptive impact of the threat of infringement suits.

* * *

Thus, we believe that the practical problems that petitioner and his *amici* have described are too serious, too extensive, and too likely to come about for us to dismiss them as insignificant—particularly in light of the ever-growing importance of foreign trade to America. See The World Bank, Imports of goods and services (% of GDP) (imports in 2011 18% of U.S. gross domestic product compared to 11% in 1980). The upshot is that copyright-related consequences along with language, context, and interpretive canons argue strongly against a geographical interpretation of § 109(a).

III

Wiley and the dissent make several additional important arguments in favor of the geographical interpretation. *First*, they say that our *Quality King* decision strongly supports its geographical interpretation. In that case we asked whether the Act's "importation provision," now § 602(a)(1) (then § 602(a)), barred importation (without permission) of a copyrighted item (labels affixed to hair care products) where an American copyright owner authorized the first sale and export of hair care products with copyrighted labels made in the United States, and where a buyer sought to import them back into the United States without the copyright owner's permission. 523 U.S., at 138-139.

We held that the importation provision did *not* prohibit sending the products back into the United States (without the copyright owner's permission). That section says:

> "Importation into the United States, without the authority of the owner of copyright under this title, of copies or phonorecords of a work that have been acquired outside the United States *is an infringement* of the exclusive right to distribute copies or phono-records *under section 106*." 17 U.S.C. § 602(a)(1) (emphasis added).

We pointed out that this section makes importation an infringement of the "exclusive right to distribute ... *under 106*." We noted that § 109(a)'s "first sale" doctrine limits the scope of the § 106 exclusive distribution right. We took as given the fact that the products at issue had at least once been sold. And we held that consequently, importation of the copyrighted labels does not violate § 602(a)(1).

In reaching this conclusion we endorsed *Bobbs-Merrill* and its statement that the copyright laws were not "intended to create a right which would permit the holder of the copyright to fasten, by notice in a book ... a restriction upon the subsequent alienation of the subject-matter of copyright after the owner had parted with the title to one who had acquired full dominion over it." 210 U.S., at 349-350.

We also explained why we rejected the claim that our interpretation would make § 602(a)(1) pointless. Those advancing that claim had pointed out that the 1976 Copyright Act amendments retained a prior anti-piracy provision, prohibiting the importation of pirated copies. *Quality King, supra*, at 146. Thus, they said, § 602(a)(1) must prohibit the importation of lawfully made copies, for to allow the importation of those lawfully made copies after a first sale, as *Quality King*' s holding would do, would leave § 602(a)(1) without much to prohibit. It would become superfluous, without any real work to do.

We do not believe that this argument is a strong one. Under *Quality King*'s interpretation, § 602(a)(1) would still forbid importing (without permission, and subject to the exceptions in § 602(a)(3)) copies lawfully made abroad, for example, where (1) a foreign publisher operating as the licensee of an American publisher prints copies of a book overseas but, prior to any authorized sale, seeks to send them to the United States; (2) a foreign printer or other manufacturer (if not the "owner" for purposes of § 109(a), e.g., before an authorized sale) sought to send copyrighted goods to the United States; (3) "a book publisher transports copies to a wholesaler" and the wholesaler (not yet the owner) sends them to the United States; or (4) a foreign film distributor, having leased films for distribution, or any other licensee, consignee, or bailee sought to send them to the United States. See, *e.g.*, 2 NIMMER ON COPYRIGHT § 8.12[B][1][a], at 8-159 ("Section 109(a) provides that the distribution right may be exercised solely with respect to the initial disposition of copies of a work, not to prevent or restrict the resale or other further transfer of possession of such copies"). These examples show that § 602(a)(1) retains significance. * * *

In *Quality King* we rejected the "superfluous" argument for similar reasons. But, when rejecting it, we said that, where an author gives exclusive American distribution rights to an American publisher and exclusive British distribution rights to a British publisher, "presumably *only those [copies] made by the publisher of the United States edition would be 'lawfully made under this title'* within the meaning of § 109(a)." 523 U.S., at 148 (emphasis added). Wiley now argues that this phrase in the *Quality King* opinion means that books published abroad (under license) must fall outside the words "lawfully made under this title" and that we have consequently already given those words the geographical interpretation that it favors.

We cannot, however, give the *Quality King* statement the legal weight for which Wiley argues. The language "lawfully made under this title" was not at issue in *Quality King*; the point before us now was not then fully argued; we did not canvas the considerations we have here set forth; we there said nothing to suggest that the example assumes a "first sale"; and we there hedged our statement with the word "presumably." Most importantly, the statement is pure *dictum*. It is *dictum* contained in a rebuttal to a counterargument. And it is unnecessary *dictum* even in that respect. Is the Court having once written *dicta* calling a tomato a vegetable bound to deny that it is a fruit forever after?

To the contrary, we have written that we are not necessarily bound by *dicta* should more complete argument demonstrate that the *dicta* is not correct. * * * And, given the bit part that our *Quality King* statement played in our *Quality King* decision, we believe the view of *stare decisis* set forth in these opinions applies to the matter now before us.

Second, Wiley and the dissent argue (to those who consider legislative history) that the Act's legislative history supports their interpretation. But the historical events to which it points took place more than a decade before the enactment of the Act and, at best, are inconclusive. * * *

But to ascertain the best reading of *§ 109(a)*, * * * we would give greater weight to the congressional report accompanying § 109(a), written a decade later when Congress passed the new law. That report says:

> "Section 109(a) restates and confirms the principle that, where the *copyright* owner has transferred ownership of a particular copy or phonorecord of a work, the person to whom the copy or phonorecord is transferred is entitled to dispose of it by sale, rental, or any other means. Under this principle, which has been established by the court decisions and ... the present law, the copyright owner's exclusive right of public distribution would have no effect upon anyone who owns 'a particular copy or phonorecord lawfully made under this title' and who wishes to transfer it to someone else or to destroy it. * * *

This history reiterates the importance of the "first sale" doctrine. It explains, as we have explained, the nongeographical purposes of the words "lawfully made under this title." And it says nothing about geography. Nor, importantly, did § 109(a)'s predecessor provision. This means that, contrary to the dissent's suggestion, any lack of legislative history pertaining to the "first sale" doctrine only tends to bolster our position that Congress' 1976 revision did not intend to create a drastic geographical change in its revision to that provision. We consequently believe that the legislative history, on balance, supports the nongeographical interpretation.

Third, Wiley and the dissent claim that a nongeographical interpretation will make it difficult, perhaps impossible, for publishers (and other copyright holders) to divide foreign and domestic markets. We concede that is so. A publisher may find it more difficult to charge different prices for the same book in different geographic markets. But we do not see how these facts help Wiley, for we can find no basic principle of copyright law that suggests that publishers are especially entitled to such rights. * * * We have found no precedent suggesting a legal preference for interpretations of copyright statutes that would provide for market divisions.

To the contrary, Congress enacted a copyright law that (through the "first sale" doctrine) limits copyright holders' ability to divide domestic markets. And that limitation is consistent with antitrust laws that ordinarily forbid market divisions. Cf. *Palmer v. BRG of Ga., Inc.*, 498 U.S. 46, 49-50, 111 S.Ct. 401 (1990) (*per curiam*) ("[A]greements between competitors to allocate territories to minimize competition are illegal"). Whether copyright owners should, or should not, have more than ordinary commercial power to divide international markets is a matter for Congress to decide. We do no more here than try to determine what decision Congress has taken.

Fourth, the dissent and Wiley contend that our decision launches United States copyright law into an unprecedented regime of "international exhaustion." But they point to nothing indicative of congressional intent in 1976. The dissent also claims that it is clear that the United States now opposes adopting such a regime, but the Solicitor General as *amicus* has taken no such position in this case. In fact, when pressed at oral argument, the Solicitor General stated that the consequences of Wiley's reading of the statute (perpetual downstream control) were "worse" than those of Kirtsaeng's reading (restriction of market segmentation). And the dissent's reliance on the Solicitor General's position in *Quality King* is undermined by his agreement in that case with our reading of § 109(a). Brief for United States as *Amicus Curiae* in *Quality King*, O.T.1996, No. 1470, p. 30 ("When ... Congress wishes to make the location of manufacture relevant to Copyright Act protection, it does so expressly"); *ibid*. (calling it "distinctly unlikely" that Congress would have provided an incentive for overseas manufacturing).

Moreover, the exhaustion regime the dissent apparently favors would provide that "the sale in one country of a good" does not "exhaus[t] the intellectual-property owner's right to control the distribution of that good elsewhere." But our holding in *Quality King* that § 109(a) is a defense in U.S. courts even when "the first sale occurred abroad," 523 U.S., at 145, n.14, has already significantly eroded such a principle.

IV

For these reasons we conclude that the considerations supporting Kirtsaeng's nongeographical interpretation of the words "lawfully made under this title" are the more persuasive. The judgment of the Court of Appeals is reversed, and the case is remanded for further proceedings consistent with this opinion.

It is so ordered.

Notes and Questions

1. Much of this case turns on the words "lawfully made under this title" in Section 109(a) of the Copyright Act. The Court effectively interprets the words to mean a copy "not made in violation of" U.S. copyright law. But, due to the principle of territorial independence discussed earlier in this chapter, a copy made in Thailand is protected by a Thai copyright and a U.S. copyright separately. In finding "no basic principle of copyright law that suggests" that copyright owners are entitled to treat U.S. and Thai copyrights as legally separate, is the Court respecting that principle?

2. The *Kirtsaeng* Court makes much of the inconvenience to which a territorially limited exhaustion doctrine would put U.S. purchasers of foreign books, art works, and other copies. However, because of the territorial independence principle, the owner of the U.S. copyright could be a completely different person unrelated to the owner of the Thai copyright. Suppose that these two copyright owners had opposing interests. Should the United States allow the owner of a copy purchased from the Thai copyright holder to import copies into the United

States in competition with the U.S. copyright owner? Why or why not?

3. The Court majority's statement in *Kirtsaeng* that U.S. antitrust law forbids market divisions is misleading. U.S. antitrust law discourages certain kinds of *domestic* market segmentation. But there is no general U.S. antitrust prohibition on segmenting markets internationally, except where the effects of market segmentation rebound and adversely affect competition on the U.S. market. Does John Wiley's segmentation of U.S. and foreign markets harm competition in the U.S. market? Should it matter?

4. The majority opinion is partly based on the claim that the Copyright Act is "applicable" to a piratical copy of a U.S.-protected work made in a foreign country. Is a copy made outside the United States without the U.S. copyright owner's permission piratical? Doesn't the foreign publisher have to do some additional act, such as importing the copies into the United States without the U.S. copyright owner's permission, in order to make the Copyright Act "applicable" to the copies? If not, in what sense is the Copyright Act applicable to the foreign copy? If so, how does this affect the persuasiveness of the Court's reasoning?

5. As will be discussed in Chapter 10, the Supreme Court has repeatedly applied a presumption against extraterritorial interpretations of U.S. statutes. See, e.g., *Morrison v. National Australia Bank*, 561 U.S. 247 (2010); *Equal Employment Opportunity Comm'n v. Arabian Am. Oil Co.*, 499 U.S. 244 (1991). In *Kirtsaeng*, the Supreme Court fails to cite this precedent, despite its apparent relevance. Is the Court simply ignoring weaknesses in its own argument, or is the opinion that the Copyright Act "applies" to "an Irish manuscript lying in its author's Dublin desk drawer" consistent with the presumption against extraterritoriality? If so, how?

4.3 Patents and Parallel Imports

In the United States, until very recently, the exhaustion doctrine generally applies to the sale or other transfer of a patented good first made in the United States, *Adams v. Burke*, 84 U.S. (17 Wall.) 453, 456 (1873), but not to transfers of goods first made outside the United States. *Jazz Photo Corp. v. International Trade Commission*, 264 F.3d 1094, 1105 (Fed. Cir. 2001) ("United States patent rights are not exhausted by products of foreign provenance. To invoke the protection of the first sale doctrine, the authorized first sale must have occurred under the United States patent.").

In the 2017 case *Impression Products Inc. v. Lexmark International Inc.*, 581 U.S. __, 137 S. Ct. 1523 (2017), the Court put U.S. patent law into alignment with U.S. copyright law on the subject of international exhaustion of rights. The Patent Act provides the patent owner with the right to prevent others from

Policy Issue

Should States Allow IP Market Segmentation Internationally?

Intellectual property owners attempt to segment markets internationally in order to extract the maximum profits. The economics of geographic market segmentation are fairly simple. The prices of goods on a competitive market are determined by two main market forces: supply and demand. Greater supply and lower demand tend to lower prices. Higher demand and reduced supply raise them.

Demand for any given product or service varies from country to country. This means the profit-maximizing price for a good or service is not the same in every country, so business firms can often maximize their profits by charging different rates in different countries for the same good or service. International market segmentation facilitates price discrimination, among other things.

Consumers in rich countries may be willing and able to pay more for a product or service than are consumers in poor countries. In addition, in some countries producers face effective competition and must lower their prices to compete, while in others they may face little competition and can raise their prices. Charging different prices for the same product in different countries helps maximize the manufacturer's profits by increasing the number of sales made internationally. Market segmentation also serves consumers in poorer countries; if products could only be sold at the rich country prices, then fewer consumers in poor countries would be able to afford the product. The lower prices paid by such consumers means that consumers in richer countries pay higher prices than they otherwise might have, but, on the whole, more products are sold globally with market segmentation than in the absence of market segmentation, so both the manufacturer and many consumers benefit.

In summary, from the producer's perspective, international market segmentation increases profits. From the perspective of consumers in countries where prices are low, international market segmentation is also helpful, because it makes products and services available that might otherwise be beyond their reach. The main consumers who do not benefit from market segmentation are the ones in wealthier countries, who pay somewhat more than they would if international market segmentation were prohibited. In addition, consumer expectations about the mobility of their copies of protected works may be upset if they wish to move the works to a foreign country. Given the foregoing, what factors should be considered in determining whether market segmentation has more benefits than costs?

importing the patented invention, 35 U.S.C. § 154(a), just as the Copyright Act does for copyright owners. However, unlike the Copyright Act, the Patent Act has no explicit exhaustion doctrine. That doctrine, wrote the Court, arose from the common law's "borderless" antipathy to restraints on alienation of property. Citing *Kirtsaeng*, and the "historic kinship between patent law and copyright law," the Court concluded that patent rights are exhausted on a legitimate sale regardless of the whether the patent owner includes a license provision prohibiting resale, and regardless of whether the sale is made from the United States (Scenario 1) or a foreign country (Scenario 2). As in *Kirtsaeng*, the Court ignored the fact that a U.S. patent and a foreign patent grant two entirely separate legal rights. Instead, it focused on the tangible article embodying the patent: "A purchaser buys an item, not patent rights."

Does that seem correct? In making a purchase, does not a purchaser acquire *both* the physical good and the legal right to use it in certain ways, but not others? For example, under U.S. law, the owner of a patented item is entitled to repair it if it breaks, but cannot rebuild it when it utterly wears out from use. If so, it would be more accurate to say that the purchaser acquires the good and certain patent rights together.

4.4 Foreign Regulation of Parallel Imports

No provision of the TRIPs Agreement deals expressly with parallel imports; as noted, the treaty specifically provides in Article 6 that it should not be read to address the exhaustion of IP rights. States are at liberty to adopt whatever parallel import rules suit them, subject to the national treatment and most-favored-nation obligations.

In several countries, including Argentina, India, Japan, New Zealand, South Africa, Thailand, and the United Kingdom, transfers of patented goods first made abroad benefit from the patent exhaustion doctrine in the absence of a contractual restraint on importation or retransfer. The default rule in these countries is that the patent owner has no right to exclude parallel imports, because patent rights can be exhausted internationally. Nonetheless, a patent owner who wishes to prevent the unlicensed importation of patented goods manufactured abroad may even in these countries have options for prohibiting parallel imports. Most typically, the patent owner may impose a contractual restriction on parallel importation, which in some countries turns such importation into infringement. This rule is followed in England, Japan, and several other states. Other countries, such as Brazil and China, generally prohibit parallel imports and do not recognize international exhaustion. In still others, the law regarding parallel imports remains unsettled.

The exhaustion doctrine generally applies within the EU with respect to parallel imports of goods first transferred within the EU. See *Merck & Co. v. Stephar BV*, Case 187/80, [1992] F.S.R. 57 (Eur. Ct. Just.). The EU competition law regulations play an important role in limiting the power of companies to restrict parallel imports in the common market. A seller or licensor attempting to segment markets within the EU in order to charge higher prices in one EU member state than in another is by definition disrupting the common market. The problem is more acute when the licensor maintains a dominant market position (meaning that the firm controls a large percentage of the market for the goods or services licensed). These regulations trouble firms with highly international business models, because states in the EU vary significantly in *per capita* income.* It may be efficient for business firms to charge different prices in different EU countries, and allowing parallel imports obstructs such price discrimination.

However, in *Boehringer Ingelheim, KG v. Dowelhurst Ltd.*, Case C-348/04, OJ C 273 (June 11, 2004), the ECJ interpreted EU law as allowing a trademark owner to restrict parallel imports between EU member states, even when the importer has truthfully added its own label to the imports ("overstickered") to distinguish the imports from product authorized for domestic sale, except when all of the following conditions are fulfilled:

> [I]t is established that reliance on trade mark rights by the proprietor in order to oppose the marketing of the overstickered product under that trade mark would contribute to the artificial partitioning of the markets between Member States; it is shown that the new label cannot affect the original condition of the product inside the packaging; the packaging clearly states who overstickered the product and the name of the manufacturer; the presentation of the overstickered product is not such as to be liable to damage the reputation of the trade mark and of its proprietor; thus, the label must not be defective, of poor quality, or untidy; and the importer gives notice to the trade mark proprietor before the overstickered product is put on sale, and, on demand, supplies him with the a specimen of that product.

The burden of proving these conditions rests on the parallel importer.

The exhaustion doctrine does not generally apply with respect to goods first transferred outside the EU. See *Zino Davidoff v. A&G Imports*, C-414/99, [2002] R.P.C. 20 (ECJ). The Commission is concerned with protecting the unity of the European market, not preserving competition in non-EU markets.

---

*For example, in 2017, Poland's average *per capita* income (US$ 28,000), was just over one-half of that in the Netherlands (US$ 52,000), and one-third of that in Luxembourg (US$ 72,700). WORLD BANK, GROSS NATIONAL INCOME PER CAPITA, PPP (2017).

Key Vocabulary

Berne Convention for the Protection of Literary & Artistic Works
Cease and desist order
Community Trade Mark (CTM)
Counterfeit
Customs recordation
Domestic industry
Exclusion order (limited, general)
Exhaustion doctrine / First sale doctrine
Famous mark
Geographical indication
Gray market goods
International Preliminary Examining Authority (IPEA)
International Searching Authority
Office for Harmonization in the Internal Market (OHIM)
Madrid Protocol
Most favored nation (MFN) treatment
National treatment
Parallel imports
Paris Convention for the Protection of Industrial Property
Patent Cooperation Treaty (PCT)
Piratical good
Receiving office
Right of priority
Section 337 investigation
Special 301 Report
Territorial independence
TRIPs Agreement
TRIPs-plus
Unitary patent
U.S. Court of Appeals for the Federal Circuit
U.S. International Trade Commission (ITC)
U.S. Patent & Trademark Office (PTO)
U.S. Trade Representative (USTR)
World Intellectual Property Organization (WIPO)

Practice Exercises

#1 Protecting IP Rights in Foreign Trade and Investment

Your client, Phantastic Productions, Inc. (PPI), is a small U.S. production company that is preparing to distribute its first major motion picture, *Scooter the Macaw.* While PPI has distributed its films to local art houses in the United States in the past, *Scooter the Macaw* is its first film with sufficient production value that PPI has had it translated into the Ruritanian language in preparation for its first international distribution. Ruritania is a large and populous country in which PPI expects the film to be successful, and PPI is currently researching potential distributors there.

PPI predicts that, if the film is successful in the United States and Ruritania, PPI will license the trademark SCOOTER THE MACAW and copyrighted images of the movie's eponymous protagonist to toy manufacturers in a third country, Smalldonia, for distribution to the United States and Ruritania. It is even possible that, if the movie is sufficiently popular, derivative toy sales will outstrip revenues from the movie itself.

PPI seeks your assistance in ensuring that its IP rights will be sufficiently protected when it makes its move to international distribution. Remember that both copyrightable works and trademarks are involved. In preparation for responding to PPI's request, answer the following questions:

(a) What specific information do you need to evaluate the probability that PPI can proceed in its distribution and licensing plans with confidence that its IP rights will be protected internationally? What information will help PPI determine the extent of IP protection it can expect?

(b) What steps can PPI take better to protect its IP before or during its commercialization of *Scooter the Macaw* and licensing of rights to toy manufacturers?

(c) How can PPI know whether it needs to use a copyright symbol, register its copyright, or comply with other formalities in Ruritania to be entitled to copyright protection?

#2 The Exportation of IP-Sensitive Goods

Skookum Inc. is a medium-sized Canadian pharmaceutical developer that relies on patents and trademarks to protect its new drugs. It has recently developed and fully tested a treatment for Type 1 Diabetes that resets the body's autoimmune system to recognize insulin-producing cells in the pancreas. The treatment, which involves two different patentable pharmaceuticals and a patentable treatment procedure, will be marketed under the name Imunofixin. It has obtained government food and drug agency approval to market the drugs in the United States, Canada, and Pottsylvania. Pottsylvania is a developing country with a moderate per capita national income.

Type 1 Diabetes is a life-threatening disease that was previously considered treatable but incurable. Over 300,000 Canadians, 1 million Americans, and 500,000 Pottsylvanians have it. As a result, the treatment is likely to become very lucrative for Skookum.

Skookum is preparing to apply for Canadian patents on its two drug molecules and treatment method, and for a Canadian trademark on the name IMUNOFIXIN. It considers it likely that it will wish to market Immunofixin in the United States within the next four months, and in Pottsylvania in about one year. At some point, it will consider expanding to other markets, such as Zembia and Osterlich.

In addition, Skookum has conducted additional tests on the drugs and treatment method that are not necessary for obtaining a patent or getting government approval to market the drug in any of the countries, because they relate to possible "secondary indications" of the drugs, meaning that they might be used to treat medical conditions other than Type 1 Diabetes. It wishes to retain the test results as a trade secret for now, but it would like to communicate the trade secret to its marketing representatives in the United States and Pottsylvania in order to prepare them for future, more expansive marketing.

Skookum now seeks your advice on its plans to expand abroad, specifically in terms of what IP issues its plans might raise. Assume that Canada, the United States, and Pottsylvania are all parties to the TRIPs Agreement, the Patent Cooperation Treaty, the Madrid Protocol, and no other relevant IP treaty. How do you respond to the following questions posed by Skookum's general counsel?

(a) Are there any timing issues relating to Skookum's patent or trademark applications in the United States, Pottsylvania, or anywhere else in the world?

(b) What assurance does Skookum have that Pottsylvania has no policy of refusing to grant patents on pharmaceutical molecules? How do you know?

(c) What assurance does Skookum have that the United States and Pottsylvania will protect its trade secrets, if it communicates them to its marketing representatives in those countries under a nondisclosure agreement?

(d) Is it possible to use a single patent application for each invention or single trademark application for IMUNOFIXIN to get patents or trademarks in Canada, the United States, and Pottsylvania? If so, how?

(e) Is it possible to get a single patent for each invention or single trademark on IMUNOFIXIN that is valid in Canada, the United States, and Pottsylvania? If so, how?

(f) If Skookum decides that it wishes to apply for patents and trademarks throughout Europe, would it be possible to obtain a single patent for each invention or single trademark on IMUNOFIXIN that is valid throughout the European Union? If so, how?

#3 Coping with Infringing Imports

Ynos Corp. is a large U.S.-based multinational electronics and media company with a rich and and diverse IP portfolio. Its portfolio includes many U.S. patented electronic devices; copyrighted software, motion pictures, and music; and hundreds of trademarks. Ynos manufactures the components for its electronics devices mostly in the Republic of Korea and ships some directly to foreign distributors. However, for those sold in the United States, the devices come unassembled, and Ynos does assembly, quality control, and packaging in the United States.

Ynos also sells its products worldwide, but it maintains strict territorial exclusivity with its distributors. It has separate distributors for the United States, East Asia, Latin America, Africa, Europe, and Central Asia/Middle East. Each distributor is authorized and licensed to sell the products only in its assigned territory. Sales outside of the territory would violate the licensing portion of the distribution agreements and constitute not only breach of contract, but infringement of the patents, copyrights, and trademarks embodied in the products. In addition, electronics devices manufactured for foreign markets do not benefit from a U.S. warranty (a fact that the purchaser would detect only after opening the box and examining the warranty card).

Ynos' General Counsel has approached you because the company's IP managers have detected three kinds of transnational infringement.

First, bootleg movies, software, and music bearing Ynos trademarks and including its copyright-protected materials are being imported into the United States by the tens of thousands through dozens of small importers that seem to disappear immediately after the goods are imported, only to reappear under different names a few weeks later. They are sold at flea markets, by hawkers on street corners, and sometimes over the Internet.

Second, Ynos has determined that one of its U.S. competitors, GL Inc., is manufacturing smart phones in China that seem to infringe Ynos' electronics patents. They also include software that at least partly copies Ynos' software as well. These competing smart phones are now being imported into the United States in ever-increasing amounts. The Christmas season is approaching, and if GL manages to market its electronic devices in competition with Ynos, the effect on Ynos' profits (and stock price) could be devastating.

Finally, Ynos has learned that electronic devices that it has sold to its distributor in Latin America are being imported into the United States for resale. Because the distributor sells the electronics in Latin America at approximately half the price charged in the United States, the foreign imports are threatening its sales and will soon force Ynos to trim its U.S. assembly and marketing staff. Ynos has confirmed that its Latin American distributor has not violated the distribution agreement; instead, a third party named ReRouter LLC is buying the devices from the distributor and importing them into the United States.

(a) What remedies are available to Ynos with respect to the fly-by-night importers of bootleg movies, music, and software? Explain the advantages and limitations of each remedy.

(b) What remedies are available against GL Inc.? Explain the advantages and limitations of each of these as well.

(c) Can Ynos prevent ReRouter's importation of its own electronics into the United States? If so, how? What are its best arguments? If not, why not? What major obstacles does it face?

Multiple Choice Questions

1. Which of the following principles is ***not*** embodied in the TRIPS Agreement?

   (a) National treatment
   (b) Right of priority for copyrights
   (c) Territorial independence of IP rights
   (d) Most favored nation treatment
   (e) Right of priority for patents

2. True or false?: Under the TRIPS Agreement, a state must grant patents to the inventions of foreign inventors, and it may not refuse to enforce the patent for products manufactured outside of the state.

3. True or false?: The TRIPS Agreement requires states to grant patents for a maximum of 20 years, starting from the date of application.

4. Under the TRIPS Agreement, after applying for a trademark in any WTO state, the applicant maintains priority for applying to register the same trademark in other WTO states. How long is the applicant's grace period?

   (a) Six weeks
   (b) Two months
   (c) Six months
   (d) One year
   (e) One year, with an additional year's extension for good cause

5. True or false?: Under the TRIPS Agreement, a contracting party can compel a trademark owner to license his mark to a third party only in extreme circumstances.

6. True or false?: The TRIPS Agreement forbids contracting states to require the use of the copyright symbol © as a condition for offering copyright protection.

7. Which of the following does the TRIPS Agreement require contracting states to do with regard to unfair competition?

   (a) Allow foreign nationals of WTO contracting parties to register their trade secrets with a government agency.
   (b) Prohibit unfair licensing practices by trademark and patent owners.
   (c) Compel someone who uses another's trade secret dishonestly and without consent to pay damages equivalent to a reasonable royalty to a trade secret owner.
   (d) Compel someone who uses another's trade secret dishonestly and without consent to cease use of the trade secret.
   (e) None of the above

8. Under which of the following treaties can a patent applicant obtain a single patent valid in every state that is a party to the treaty?

   (a) European Patent Convention
   (b) Madrid Protocol
   (c) Patent Cooperation Treaty
   (d) All of the above
   (e) None of the above

9. True or false?: The Community Trademark allows a trademark applicant to apply for separate trademarks in every country in the EU with only a single application.

10. Which of the following types of intellectual property can be recorded with U.S. Customs and Border Protection to facilitate customs seizures of infringing imports at the border?

    I. Copyrights
    II. Trademarks
    III. Patents

    (a) I only
    (b) II only
    (c) III only
    (d) I and II only
    (e) II and III only

11. Which of the following types of intellectual property can be the basis of an unfair import investigation under Section 337 of the 1930 Tariff Act?

I. Copyrights
II. Trademarks
III. Patents

(a) III only
(b) I and II only
(c) I and III only
(d) II and III only
(e) I, II, and III

12. Which of the following is ***not*** a remedy available to an intellectual property owner under Section 337 of the 1930 Tariff Act?

(a) A cease and desist order directed at a respondent importer
(b) An exclusion order directed at the imports of a respondent importer
(c) An exclusion order directed at all infringing imports from any importer, named or unnamed
(d) Preliminary relief
(e) Monetary damages

13. According to the U.S. Court of Appeals for the Federal Circuit in *Schaper Manufacturing v. U.S. ITC*, which of the following appears to be least relevant to finding a domestic industry in a Section 337 investigation?

(a) Installation, warranty service, and repair services in the United States
(b) Manufacturing activity in the United States
(c) Labor-intensive cleaning, sorting, and packaging in the United States
(d) Creative research leading to the patented invention or copyrighted expressive work in the United States

14. True of false?: Under current law, the owner of a U.S. patent may exclude the importation of patented goods solely authorized by it for sale abroad, as long as the imported goods were not previously sold in or sold for export from the United States with its authorization.

15. Under the D.C. Circuit's decision in *Lever Bros. v. United States* and subsequent precedents and CBP practice, which of the following statements regarding parallel imports of trademarked goods is most accurate?

The owner of a U.S. trademark may exclude the importation of goods bearing an authentic trademark:

(a) as long as the imported goods were not previously sold in, or sold for export from, the United States with its authorization.

(b) as long as they were not first sold abroad by a company affiliated with the U.S. trademark owner.

(c) as long as they are physically materially different from the goods offered under a U.S. trademark.

(d) as long as the imported goods do not cause consumer confusion about any material characteristics or features of the goods.

(e) as long as they are physically different in any way from the goods offered under a U.S. trademark, and the owner is part of a domestic industry.

16. True or false?: Under the Supreme Court decisions in *Quality King v. L'anza* and *Kirtsaeng v. John Wiley & Sons*, a copyright owner can prevent the importation of copies first published and sold abroad, but not of copies exported from the United States for sale abroad.

Multiple Choice Answers

1. b
2. True
3. False
4. c
5. False
6. True
7. d
8. a
9. False
10. d
11. e
12. e
13. d
14. False
15. d
16. False

Chapter 4

The International Commercial Exchange

What You Will Learn in This Chapter

Commercial sales agreements are the most basic form of international business transaction, but they come in many varieties and may be subject to rules that differ from those applicable to purely domestic agreements. One important aspect of commercial agreements—planning for dispute resolution—is covered in Chapter 9 of this coursebook. In this part, you will be learning about some of the unique aspects of formation, interpretation, performance, rescission, and enforceability of international commercial agreements. The focus in this chapter is on the sale or purchase of goods and services. These may take the form of a one-time sale or an ongoing supply arrangement. More complex arrangements involving significant foreign investment and major construction or service agreements are taken up in Chapter 7. One unique aspect of international commercial transactions is the widespread adoption of an international convention to regulate purely private sales of goods across national borders.

This part also deals with some kinds of problems special to international commercial agreements relating to such matters as international shipping and insurance and ongoing supply relationships. Some of the legal issues raised in international transactions differ significantly from their domestic counterparts for business rather than legal reasons, but may have important legal consequences. One prominent difference is that the carriage of goods internationally tends to involve greater expense, delay, and risk. As a result, both public and private legal measures have been adopted to cope with the vicissitudes of international shipping.

In addition, payment on an international sale of goods can pose unique problems. If the seller and purchaser are in countries using different currencies, as is often the case, one of the parties (typically the purchaser) must convert its own currency to the currency of the other party. It is important for the parties to specify the currency of the transaction, but even this is not enough; because currency exchange rates fluctuate constantly, the purchaser may bear the risk of the cost of the goods rising because of currency fluctuations or the seller may bear the risk of the value of the purchaser's payment falling for the same reason. The parties may be well advised to allocate this risk expressly

Figure 4.1. A cargo airplane loads freight into the top half of the hold using an electric lift. The hold in a cargo plane comprises most of the fuselage and is divided into upper and lower halves. Notice how the cargo container is rounded on top to fit in the top half of the airplane's cylindrical fuselage. © 2019 by Aaron X. Fellmeth

in the contract or to hedge the risk through financial instruments. Another challenge is that, in international sales between parties unfamiliar with each other, the seller may be uncertain that the purchaser will pay for the goods once they are received, and the purchaser may be unsure that the seller will ship conforming goods once it has received payment, so neither party may want to assume the risk of performing its side of the bargain first.

Another aspect of international transactions not present in the domestic context is the use of multiple currencies. Except in states with unpredictable levels of inflation, payment in a single currency facilitates domestic commercial transactions because, at the time the parties enter into an agreement, the purchaser knows just what it will be paying, and the seller knows what it will be paid. If the parties are in different countries with different currencies, and if the exchange rate between the currencies varies over time, then it is more difficult to predict the value to the seller or the cost to the buyer. Moreover, the longer the period of time between the execution of the contract and the time the payment is due, the less predictable the value or cost of the payment and the greater the risk and cost of the transaction.

This chapter introduces these varied sources of international commercial law primarily from the perspective of a U.S.-based international commercial lawyer. Specifically, this chapter discusses:

- the different kinds of basic sales, service, and lease agreements common in international business transactions;
- how agency and distributorship agreements differ in offering a supplier options for selling products or services in a foreign state;
- the United Nations Convention on the International Sale of Goods (CISG), including those circumstances under which the CISG applies and how its rules differ from those that may be more familiar to a U.S. lawyer;
- alternative international commercial rules that parties may choose to apply to their agreements, such as the UNIDROIT principles;
- the unique international regime for determining the meaning of shipping and delivery terms, and why special rules are necessary;
- the rules of carrier liability and the roles of various contract documents in setting the terms of carriage;
- basic concepts of international insurance for goods in international commerce;
- some ways in which both services agreements and natural resource extraction agreements differ from supply or purchase agreements;
- how laws governing ongoing commercial supply relationships, such as franchise agreements, may change in an international setting;
- why traditional domestic payment mechanisms are generally unsuited to international transactions;
- what a commercial letter of credit is, how it works, and what advantages

it offers; and

- how business firms engaged in international transactions can plan for and deal with exchange risk in their payment terms.

Keep in mind that, apart from the mechanics and unique problems of international payments, international sales often involve some kind of financing or payment guarantee. Export sales financing and insurance are discussed in a later chapter.

1.1 An Introduction to International Commercial Agreements

When planning to expand business internationally, a firm must begin by deciding how to structure the transactions. If the firm expects to sell or lease goods internationally on occasion, it is likely to rely on a simple direct sale agreement with the purchaser. If it expects foreign business to be more regular and substantial, it will seek some form of local representation, either through an independent distributor or a commercial agent. The options available to the supplier will be introduced here.

A. Commercial Sale and Purchase Agreements

The simplest form of international commercial agreement is a one-time sale of goods. A **sale agreement** (also called a **purchase agreement** if drafted by the buyer) merely transfers title of goods from the seller to the purchaser. An international sale agreement differs from a purely domestic sale agreement in several ways. First, the seller will need to consider registering its intellectual property (IP) in the purchaser's state to protect it from foreign infringement, and avoiding infringing the IP rights of others in the purchaser's country. In other words, the seller's trademarks, copyrights, or patents may already be registered to another person in the purchaser's country, in which case a sale will risk infringing the IP rights of others. Assuming no prior conflicting IP rights exist in the purchaser's country, the seller should obtain IP protection of its trademarks and patents before selling products in that country, as discussed in Chapter 3. This is especially important regarding patents; in most countries, a prior sale of products embodying a patented invention will result in the inventor forfeiting the right to patent protection.

Internationally sold goods also must by definition be exported from the country of manufacture and imported into the purchaser's country. Such sales must satisfy any regulations on exports and imports as well. Import and export regulations will be discussed in Chapter 5; the key question in an international sales context is whether the seller or purchaser has the obligation to comply with export and import formalities and to pay any customs duties. This matter is typically settled in the sale agreement. Similarly, the agreement should specify whether the purchaser or seller has the obligation to comply with the health, safety, national security, and other regulations of the respective importing state and exporting state. For example, if the purchase agreement is for the sale of automobiles, the importing state may impose safety, polluting emissions, and fuel efficiency standards. The importer must demonstrate that the automobiles comply with these standards prior to importation. Such regulations make it all the more important that the agreement specify the respective responsibilities of the parties to the contract.

Another peculiarity of international product sales is that shipping and insurance terms take on greater significance than in the domestic context. International shipping tends to be riskier, costlier, and more time-consuming than domestic shipping, so the parties need to pay special attention to determining when liability for the sold products passes from the seller to the purchaser, which party is responsible for arranging and paying for shipping and insurance, and when risk of loss of the goods passes from the seller to the buyer. This subject is taken up in Part 1.4, below.

Additionally, planning for the resolution of disputes arising from international sales agreements differs from planning for domestic dispute resolution. An international sale may be subjected to a law and court system foreign to either the seller or purchaser, or possibly both. The seller of goods may find that the purchaser's state considers its own law to govern the sale absent a contractual choice of law clause. If the seller sells its products in a dozen different states, and the products prove to have defects, the seller may find itself the defendant in lawsuits in a dozen foreign countries with the purchase agreement being governed by ten different foreign laws. A contractual choice of law to govern the contract and choice of country whose courts will have exclusive jurisdiction over any dispute become far more important in international purchase agreements for reasons discussed in Chapter 9. Indeed, the parties may wish to avoid the courts of each others' respective states altogether and resolve their differences in a more neutral forum, such as private mediation or arbitration.

Finally, there is an important international treaty that may apply to international sales of goods that does not generally apply in a domestic setting. This treaty, the UN Convention on Contracts for the International Sale of Goods, is the subject of Part 2, below.

B. Commercial Leases

A **commercial lease agreement** differs from a sale agreement in that the lessor retains title to the leased products, vehicles, or machinery and expects the lessee to return them after a set period of time. The leased goods will still have to clear customs in the country of importation (although import duties paid may be recoverable—see Chapter 5) and the goods must still comply with the health, safety, national security, and other regulations of the importing and exporting states.

However, an international lease agreement carries risks to the lessor usually absent from domestic leases, because the leased property will be transported to a foreign country with its own laws and court system, and in the event of damage to the property, bankruptcy of the lessee, or a dispute arising relating to the agreement, it may become difficult for the lessor to recover its property. The lessor may be able to protect its interests through insurance or using financial instruments, such as a standby letter of credit. In other respects, an international lease agreement is subject to many of the same concerns as an international sales agreement, such as choice of law and forum.

C. Independent Distribution and Agency Relationships

The Buy-Seller Distribution Arrangement

Many international sales of goods take place through long-term relationships between a supplier and a reseller. The most common kind of international buy-sell arrangement is the distribution agreement. A **distribution agreement** creates an ongoing relationship between the supplier of the goods—usually (but not always) the manufacturer—and a distributor who resells the goods to third-party retailers or consumers. Such arrangements are extremely common. Indeed, more than half of all international trade in goods is handled through distribution arrangements of some kind.

In a **buy-sell distribution agreement**, the distributor agrees to purchase certain identified goods from the supplier and the supplier agrees to supply them for a specific period of time or until terminated by notice of one of the parties. In an international distributorship, the distributor normally stores the goods in a local warehouse and resells them in a specified territory to third parties. Because a buy-sell distributor might purchase goods before it has procured contracts for their resale, the distributor takes certain risks in adopting this arrangement. If it is unable to resell the goods at a profit, it must absorb the loss itself, absent some provision in the contract allowing it to return the items to the supplier for a refund.

In an independent distribution agreement, the parties must define several important aspects of their relationship. First, assuming that the supplier has copyright, trademark, or patent rights in its products in the distributor's foreign territory or territories, the distribution agreement should include a license for the resale of the goods. Otherwise, the resale of the goods might violate the distributor state's IP laws. Also, if the supplier intends to rely on the distributor to market and sell the goods using its own expertise and resources, a trademark license for marketing purposes will be necessary, because the distributor will presumably identify the goods in its advertising using the supplier's registered marks. In order to ensure that the marketing efforts are consistent with the product and company image that the supplier wishes to project, the supplier may choose to include a contract provision requiring all marketing materials using the supplier's trademarks to be submitted to the supplier for prior approval.

The supplier is very likely to have superior information about the quality of and risks involved with the product. The distributor did not design or manufacture them, and it is not generally responsible for engineering, quality control, or searching for conflicting IP rights (unless the contract so specifies). Consequently, in a distribution arrangement, the distributor normally will insist that the supplier indemnify and hold the distributor harmless in case the products have any design or manufacturing defects, or if they infringe any third party's IP.

Because a distribution agreement provides a framework for future product sales, it may or may not include such terms as the price of the goods or the quantity to be supplied. Much depends on whether the supplier and distributor share a corporate affiliation or are unrelated. In any case, an international distribution agreement will include most of the same general terms as a one-time sale agreement, discussed above, such as providing for shipping terms, timing the risk of loss, and establishing a choice of law and forum for any disputes that may arise between the parties.

The Commercial Agency Arrangement

There are other possible distribution arrangements that do not involve a buy-sell relationship between the parties. Under a commercial agency agreement, an independent agent may represent the seller and assist it in identifying and negotiating with third party purchasers. Such a representative is a **sales agent**. Alternatively, the agent may represent a buyer, which it assists in identifying and negotiating with third party sellers who can supply the buyer's needs. Such a representative is a **purchasing agent**. In neither case does the agent actually buy or sell (that is, take title in, or transfer title to) the goods. It merely assists the principal in buying or selling.

There are several variants on the commercial agency relationship, depending on the terms of the agreement and the applicable agency laws. If the agency agreement gives the agent the power to solicit orders or bids, but not to commit the principal to a binding contract, the agent is usually called a **broker**. If the agent has the power to bind the principal, the agent is typically called a **commission agent**. In either case, however, the contract is between the principal and the buyer or seller; the agent is not a direct party to the purchase or sale.

Sales agencies are much more common than purchasing agencies. Sales agency agreements may involve services other than assisting in making sales; they may involve marketing efforts, representation of the principal at trade shows, assistance in securing credit or obtaining government regulatory approvals, and similar tasks, but commission sales agents deal primarily with soliciting sales for the principal, for which the agent receives a commission, usually based on the value of the sale. Normally, the commission agent takes no possession of the goods (and it never takes title); instead, the seller ships the goods directly to the customer. Alternatively, the agent might take possession of the goods without taking title to them and store them in a local customs warehouse (see Chapter 5). The agent can then sell the goods to third parties upon the principal's authorization and remit payment to the principal, minus its commission. Because the agent never takes title to the goods, the seller bears the risk of a failure to sell all of the goods; upon instructions of the seller, the agent will return any unsold goods to the seller or sell them at a discount, with the seller rather than the agent absorbing the loss.

A final common form of commercial agency is the **commissionaire** (the term used in civil law jurisdictions) or **factor** (the term used in common law jurisdictions). The rules governing each vary slightly depending on the state law governing the relationship. In general, though, the commissionaire/factor acts as a liability shield between the purchaser and the principal. The agent enters into contracts with the purchaser in its own name, even though by agreement it is acting on behalf of the principal. As an agent, the commissionaire/factor remits the full profit of the sale (minus its commission) to the principal and owes fiduciary and other duties to the principal. The principal, lacking privity with the purchaser, cannot be held liable for breach of contract or defect in the goods, unless the principal is the manufacturer and the governing law allows the purchaser to pursue a manufacturer in tort. The position of a commissionaire or factor is much more precarious from a liability viewpoint than the position of a commission sales agent; as a result, commissionaires and factors generally receive higher commission rates and are usually corporate affiliates of the principal.

Many of the duties of the agent to the principal, and the principal to the agent, are determined by the law of the contract. The parties to the agreement may generally choose any law that bears a reasonable relationship to the agreement, subject to potential mandatory provisions discussed below. Under the law of most states, the agent will by default have at least the following duties to the principal:

- to exercise care and diligence in executing its contractual duties;
- to comply with the specific instructions of the principal if such instructions are lawful and within the scope of the agency agreement;
- to act in good faith on the principal's behalf and in the principal's interests (also known as **fiduciary duty**), including a duty not to accept bribes or to put its own interests in conflict with or above the principal's;
- to maintain the confidentiality of the principal's trade secrets and non-public communications with the agent; and
- not to delegate its duties to others without the principal's consent.

Special Contract Terms

Distribution and agency agreements create potentially long-term relationships of a kind absent from most one-time purchase agreements. As a result, they may contain some special terms to protect the parties and define their relationship clearly. In the context of international distribution, several provisions of the agreement will be especially important for avoiding misunderstandings and eventual disputes. These include most prominently clauses defining:

- the scope of the supplier's product line that may be the subject of a purchase order, and whether it will encompass new products automatically;
- the country or countries within which the distributor or agent is authorized to sell the goods;
- whether the distributorship will be exclusive within the territory or nonexclusive (that is, whether the supplier can sell the same products to other, competing distributors in the same geographical area); conversely, whether the distributor or agent must carry or offer the supplier's goods exclusively to its customers, or whether it may offer competing goods as well;
- the amount of inventory the distributor or agent must keep stored and ready to deliver within its territory;
- which party bears the risk of loss and responsibility of insuring any goods held by a distributor or agent on consignment;
- any indemnification owed by the supplier to the distributor or agent in case of product manufacturing or design defects;
- a definition of the duties the distributor or agent has to advertise and market the goods within its territory, or what duty it owes to assist the supplier in marketing the goods within the territory;
- a license of trademark rights to the distributor or agent for advertising the products within its territory;
- any duty of the distributor or agent to assist the supplier in registering or otherwise protecting its IP and detecting or punishing IP infringement within the distributor's or agent's country or countries;
- the term of the contract, renewal provisions, the notice required by each party prior to termination, and any compensation due to the distributor or agent upon termination; and

- many of the provisions found in a one-time international sale agreement, such as choice of law and forum for dispute resolution, an arbitration clause if desired, and payment terms for goods sold to the distributor, or commission terms for goods sold by the agent.

Nonderogable Rights

One important difference between an independent distributor and a sales agent is that, under the laws of many countries, a supplier takes on special responsibilities to its agent that do not apply to an independent distributor. Frequently, a sales agent operating within the country's territory is entitled to certain nonderogable rights. In other words, a principal may carry certain duties to the agent regardless of the terms of their agreement and regardless of the fact that the parties chose a foreign law to govern the contract. These may include any or all of the following:

- a right to indemnification for any losses or liabilities incurred by reason of the agent's good faith representation;
- the right to a certain period of notice prior to termination;
- in some countries, the right not to be terminated at all without sufficient cause, except in limited circumstances;
- the right to receive commissions on sales realized due to the agent's efforts but occurring after termination; and
- a right to compensation following termination in an amount dependent on the length of time for which the agent represented the principal.

In some states, the agent is actually precluded from waiving these rights by contract, from concern that the principal will exercise its superior bargaining power to undermine or negate the state's protection for commercial agents.

These rights generally do not apply to independent buy-sell distributors because independent distributors do not generally carry any responsibility to represent the seller to third parties. Moreover, by virtue of their independence, distributors tend to rely less on the supplier for the success of their business, and, lacking a strict fiduciary duty, they have means to protect themselves that are unavailable to an agent. For example, an independent distributor may ignore the supplier's interests when it benefits the distributor, to the extent compatible with its contractual obligations. Nonetheless, some countries impose mandatory notice (but not compensation) obligations on a principal even when it terminates an independent distribution agreement.

Because each state has its own law establishing which agent rights are nonderogable and the extent of these rights, nothing more specific can be said about them. However, it is important for business firms seeking to expand their sales network abroad to be aware that local law may impose such limitations in commercial agency relationships.

Which Model to Choose?

Does this mean independent distribution is the best model for selling goods internationally? Not necessarily. Direct sales to foreign consumers, international distributorship networks, and foreign commercial sales agencies each have advantages and disadvantages. Direct sales are structurally simple, involve no "middle-man" costs, and allow sellers maximum control over how, when, and where they sell their goods. However, the seller may lack expertise in catering to the specific foreign market, it may lack preexisting business connections, and it may have no established credit rating there. Moreover, because international shipping is much slower than domestic shipping, the seller may be obliged to maintain warehouses in the foreign country to fill orders promptly, and it will accordingly bear the cost of maintaining the warehouse and supplying it without too much or too little stock.

In contrast, independent distributors and agents may have an existing reputation in, and experience with, the foreign market. They may already have relationships with purchasers, government contacts, a local credit rating, and knowledge of local trade customs and consumer culture. In addition, foreign governments may have laws favoring the purchase of goods from locally owned companies, for which a distributor of that nationality alone may qualify. Finally, as noted above, some forms of distribution, such as the commissionaire/factor, may help protect the supplier from foreign liability.

Independent distributorships and agents have disadvantages as well. As noted, in many countries, commercial agents may have certain nonderogable rights that limit the ability of the seller to structure the relationship as it wishes. Independent distributors may also be protected by franchise laws, discussed below. In addition, because distributors and agents are independent companies, they can be controlled only by legal means, much of which must be defined by contract. Because no contract can provide for every eventuality, troublesome disputes may arise between the seller and its distributor or agent that would not occur in the case of direct sales. A carefully drafted contract, cannot guarantee the parties will never engage in practices prejudicial to the interests of the other, imposing costs and inconvenience and possibly damaging the other party's reputation. It is even possible for an agent to engage the supplier's criminal liability in the foreign state. Reliability and good faith are accordingly at a premium in independent distribution and agency agreements.

1.2 The UN Convention on Contracts for the International Sale of Goods

Regardless of what business model the seller chooses, it will need some form of sale agreement to govern the relationship between the parties. In international sales of goods, the seller and buyer may exist under very different legal codes. They may accordingly have divergent expectations about such questions as when the contract is formed, what are its terms, what actions qualify as performance, how the agreement may be amended or terminated, and what remedies are available for breach of contract. For example, although in common law countries compensation for a breach is the normal remedy, and specific performance is available only under very limited circumstances, in some civil law countries such as Germany, specific performance is a normal remedy for breach.

You are probably familiar with the Uniform Commercial Code (UCC) that almost all U.S. states have adopted in some form to harmonize their laws relating to private contracts for the sale of goods. The benefits of such harmonization are easy to understand. If parties in two different U.S. states wish to enter into a sale agreement, and each state has a different law respecting the rights and duties of buyers and sellers, the parties will naturally seek to minimize uncertainty about what rules will apply to the formation, interpretation, and enforcement of the agreement. Parties to a sale agreement are likely to solve this problem by negotiating a **choice of law clause** into the contract (see Chapter 9) that specifies the governing law in the event of a dispute. However, if the parties cannot agree on which law will apply, negotiations may be time-consuming. Even sophisticated international business firms may decide not to include a choice of law clause to avoid complicating the sale or in the belief that a dispute is unlikely to arise.

If the parties do not select a law to govern the contract, they might not know what their precise rights and obligations are in cases where the contract is silent, vague, or ambiguous. The seller may think the law of the seller's state governs the contract (and the seller's state may have conflict of laws rules that specify that the seller's state law governs), while the buyer may think the opposite (and the buyer's state may have conflict of laws rules giving priority to the law of the buyer's state). On the other hand, if the contract law in the buyer's state is the same as the law in the seller's state, it does not much matter which law applies—the outcome will probably be the same in either case. The UCC achieves this happy result by creating relative uniformity in U.S. state laws governing commercial agreements.

Because the UCC homogenizes the contract law of U.S. states, it is familiar to every U.S. commercial lawyer. Non-U.S. business firms, however, may be unfamiliar with the UCC and more accustomed to their own national laws regulating commercial contracts. Because foreign commercial laws may differ from the UCC rules substantially, the same problem that the UCC was designed to address presents itself anew.

Some countries have harmonized their commercial laws through regional negotiations. Besides the EU's significant achievements in this field, the most prominent example is the **Organization for the Harmonization of Business Laws in Africa (OHADA)**. OHADA, created in 1995 by sixteen francophonic African states that have adopted identical commercial codes, even includes a regional court (the **OHADA Common Court of Justice and Arbitration**) to help resolve disputes by issuing advisory opinions and reviewing appeals on business law matters to ensure a uniform interpretation of the common commercial code. But the EU and OHADA are exceptions. State commercial laws differ significantly throughout most of the world.

To help address this problem, an intergovernmental organization called the **United Nations Commission on International Trade Law** (**UNCITRAL**) adopted an important draft treaty in 1980, the **UN Convention on Contracts for the International Sale of Goods** (**CISG**). The purpose of CISG is to promote uniform rules in international sales law globally. The CISG establishes a general code of legal rules governing international contracts for the sale of goods and has been in force since 1988. It is intended to be a complete contract code and is accordingly fairly detailed. As of 2020, CISG has ninety-one parties, including almost all of Europe, as well as Australia, Canada, China, Japan, Russia, the United States, and many African, Middle Eastern, and Latin American states. On the other hand, several major states, such as the United Kingdom, South Africa, and Thailand, are not parties.

A. When Does the CISG Apply?

The terms of the CISG apply automatically to certain contracts for the international sale of goods and not to others. Article 1 of the CISG provides in relevant part:

> **Article 1**
>
> (1) This Convention applies to contracts of sale of goods between parties whose place of business are in different States:
>
> (*a*) when the States are Contracting States; or
>
> (*b*) when the rules of private international law lead to the application of the law of a Contracting State. * * *

Clearly, if a manufacturer in Egypt (a party to the CISG) were to sell goods to a purchaser in Estonia (also a party to the CISG), the contract would by default be governed by the CISG. In contrast, if a manufacturer in Egypt were to sell goods to a purchaser in Indonesia (not a party to the CISG), the CISG would normally be irrelevant to the contract under Article 1(1)(a).

However, under Article 1(1)(b), the CISG also applies when the **conflict of laws** rules (which the CISG calls **private international law**) applicable to a contract dispute would result in the law of a state party to the CISG governing the contract, even if one party to the contract has its place of business in a nonparty to the CISG. In the example just given, if a court determined that Egyptian law governs the contract under conflict of laws rules, it would apply the CISG to the contract even though Indonesia is not a party to the CISG. Conflict of laws principles are discussed in Chapter 9; here it suffices to note that these are rules of international law adopted by states to determine whether their own law, or another state's law, applies to a private arrangement such as a commercial contract. If Indonesian law were found to govern the contract, in contrast, the CISG would not apply, because Indonesia is not a contracting state.

A few state parties to the CISG, such as the United States and China, entered a reservation stating that they disagree with and will not apply article 1(1)(b), as they are entitled to do under article 95 of the CISG. In those states, the CISG is considered to apply only when both parties to the contract have their place of business in CISG state parties. Most contracting states do, however, accept article 1(1)(b).

WHAT ROLE DOES UNCITRAL PLAY IN INTERNATIONAL BUSINESS?

UNCITRAL was established by vote of the United Nations General Assembly in 1966 to reduce obstacles to international trade and harmonize state laws governing trading relations. To that end, UNCITRAL provides technical advice on trade and commercial regulation to developing countries; collects statistics; and drafts texts such as model laws, treaties, and guidelines for adoption by UN members, such as the CISG. Several of the organization's treaties and model laws will be discussed in this book.

Article 1 also specifies that the CISG applies only to contracts for the sale of goods. Like the UCC, it does not apply to contracts in which a "preponderant part of the obligations" of the supplier are for the provision of services. CISG art. 3(2). Also like the UCC, the CISG does not deal with criminal or tort issues such as conversion or personal injury caused by defective products. *Id.* arts. 4-5. The CISG is further limited in applying only to commercial sales of existing goods or goods to be manufactured. It does not usually apply to retail sales for personal use, nor does it apply to sales of most intangible goods, such as electricity or securities. *Id.* art. 2.

The CISG is not exceptionally detailed in its definitions of the kind of sales agreements to which it applies. The CISG clearly does not apply to commission sales agency agreements, because the agent never purchases goods. However, it would seem to apply in international buy-sell distribution arrangements, because the distributor does indeed purchase goods from a supplier in another state. But does the CISG apply to the distribution agreement itself, or merely to individual purchase orders? The following case explores whether the CISG applies to a buy-sell distribution agreement in which the distributor purchases goods on its own account, but the price and quantity to be purchased are left open for specification in future orders on a case-by-case basis.

AMCO UKRSERVICE v. AMERICAN METER CO.

U.S. District Court, Eastern District of Pennsylvania, 2004
312 F.Supp.2d 681

DALZELL, District Judge.

Plaintiffs Amco Ukrservice and Prompriladamco are Ukrainian corporations seeking over $200 million in damages for the breach of two joint venture agreements that, they contend, obligated defendant American Meter Company to provide them with all of the gas meters and related piping they could sell in republics of the former Soviet Union.

After extensive discovery, American Meter and Prompriladamco filed the cross-motions for summary judgment now before us. American Meter asserts that it is entitled to judgment against both plaintiffs as a matter of law because the joint venture agreements are unenforceable under both the United Nations Convention on Contracts for the International Sale of Goods ("CISG") and Ukrainian commercial law. Prompriladamco claims that its agreement is enforceable, that there is no genuine issue of material fact as to whether American Meter is in breach of that agreement, and that the only remaining issue is the extent of the damages it has sustained. * * *.

I. FACTUAL AND PROCEDURAL HISTORY

The origins of this action lie in the collapse of the Soviet Union and the newly-independent Ukraine's fitful transition to a market economy. American Meter began to explore the possibility of selling its products in the former Soviet Union in the early 1990s, and in 1992 it named Prendergast as Director of Operations of C.I.S. [Commonwealth of Independent States] Projects. Sometime in 1996, a Ukrainian-born American citizen named Simon Friedman approached Prendergast about the possibility of marketing American Meter products in Ukraine.

Ukraine was a potentially appealing market for American Meter at that time. During and immediately after the Soviet era, Ukrainian utilities had not charged consumers for their actual consumption of natural gas but instead had allocated charges on the basis of total deliveries to a given area. That system penalized consumers for their neighbors' wastefulness and saddled them with the cost of leakage losses. In 1997, the Ukrainian government enacted legislation requiring utilities to shift toward a usage-based billing system. Prendergast's early prediction was that implementation of the legislation would require the installation of gas meters in millions of homes and apartment buildings.

After some investigation, Prendergast and his superiors at American Meter concluded they could best penetrate the Ukrainian market by forming a joint venture with a local manufacturer. To this end, American Meter Vice-President Andrew Watson authorized Friedman on June 24, 1997 to engage in discussions and negotiations with Ukrainian organizations, and the corporation also hired a former vice-president, Peter Russo, to consult on the project. Prendergast, Russo, and Friedman began to identify potential joint venture partners, and by late 1997, they had selected

Promprilad, a Ukrainian manufacturer of commercial and industrial meters based in Ivano-Frankivsk, the industrial capital of western Ukraine. On December 11, 1997, Prendergast (representing American Meter), Friedman (representing his firm, Joseph Friedman & Sons, International, Inc.), and representatives of Promprilad and American-Ukrainian Business Consultants, L.P. ("AUBC") met in Kyiv (the current preferred transliteration of "Kiev") and entered into the first of the agreements at issue here.

The agreement provided for the establishment of a joint venture company, to be called Prompriladamco, in which the four signatories would become shareholders. Prompriladamco would work in conjunction with its principals to develop the market for American Meter products in the former Soviet Union and, most important for the purposes of this action, the agreement committed American Meter to the following obligations:

9. AMCO shall grant Joint Venture PrompryladAmco exclusive rights to manufacture and install Meters within the former Soviet Union....
10. AMCO shall grant Joint Venture PrompryladAmco exclusive rights to distribute the products manufactured by PrompryladAmco and all products manufactured by AMCO in the former Soviet Union....
13. AMCO will deliver components and parts for Meters taking into account 90% assembly.
14. PrompryladAmco (at the first stage) shall perform 10% of the work required to assembl[e] the Meters using components and parts delivered by AMCO.
15. AMCO will deliver the components and parts for Meters by lots in containers, payments for the delivery being subject to at least a 90-day grace period.
16. The number of the components and parts for Meters to be delivered to Ukraine shall be based on demand in the former Soviet Union.
17. Orders for the components and parts for Meters, with the quantities and prices according to paragraph 16 above shall be an integral part of this Agreement.

After executing the agreement, the parties incorporated Prompriladamco in Ukraine, and Friedman became its Chief Executive Officer. The new corporation set out to obtain Ukrainian regulatory approval for American Meter products, which required bringing Ukrainian officials to the United States to inspect American Meter's manufacturing process, and it sponsored a legislative measure that would give those products a competitive advantage in the Ukrainian market.

On April 20, 1998, Friedman and a representative of AUBC executed a second joint venture agreement for the purpose of marketing the gas piping products of Perfection Corporation, a wholly-owned subsidiary of American Meter. Again, the parties agreed to create and fund a corporation, this one to be called Amco Ukrservice, and American Meter committed itself to deliver, on credit, a level of goods based on demand in the former Soviet Union. The parties duly formed Amco Ukrservice, and Friedman became its Chief Executive Officer.

By early summer, Prompriladamco and Amco Ukrservice had begun submitting product orders to American Meter. In late June or early July, however, American Meter President Harry Skilton effectively terminated the joint ventures by stopping a shipment of goods that was on its way to Ukraine and by refusing to extend credit to either Prompriladamco or Amco Ukrservice. Finally, at a meeting on October 27, 1998, American Meter Vice-President Alex Tyshovnytsky informed Friedman that the corporation had decided to withdraw from Ukraine "due to unstable business conditions and eroding investment confidence in that country."

On May 23, 2000, Prompriladamco and Amco Ukrservice filed parallel complaints claiming that American Meter had breached the relevant joint venture agreement by refusing to deliver the meters and parts that the plaintiffs could sell in the former Soviet Union. Prompriladamco's complaint alleges that the breach caused it to lose $143,179,913 in profits between 1998 and 2003, and Amco Ukrservice claims lost profits of $88,812,000 for the same period. We consolidated the actions on August 18, 2000.

II. AMERICAN METER'S MOTION FOR SUMMARY JUDGMENT

American Meter argues that summary judgment is warranted here because the joint venture agreements are invalid under the CISG and Ukrainian law. * * *

A. The CISG

The United States and Ukraine are both signatories to the CISG, which applies to contracts for the sale of goods where the parties have places of business in different nations, the nations are CISG signatories, and the contract does not contain a choice of law provision. American Meter argues that the CISG governs the plaintiffs' claims because, at bottom, they seek damages for its refusal to sell them goods and that, under the CISG, the supply provisions of the agreements are invalid because they lack sufficient price[4] and quantity terms.

Apart from a handful of exclusions that have no relevance here, the CISG does not define what constitutes a contract for the sale of goods. See CISG art. 2. This lacuna has given rise to the problem of the Convention's applicability to distributorship agreements, which typically create a framework for future sales of goods but do not lay down precise price and quantity terms.

In the few cases examining this issue, courts both here and in Germany have concluded that the CISG does not apply to such contracts. In *Helen Kaminski Pty. Ltd. v. Marketing Australian Products, Inc.*, 1997 WL 414137 (S.D.N.Y. July 23, 1997), the court held that the CISG did not govern the parties' distributorship agreement, but it suggested in dictum that the CISG would apply to a term in the contract that

---

[4]It is not entirely clear whether an open price term invalidates a contract for the sale of goods under the CISG. Article 14(1) of the Convention provides that a proposal is sufficiently definite to constitute an offer if "it indicates the goods and expressly or implicitly fixes or makes provision for determining the quantity and the price." However, Article 55 states that "[w]here a contract has been validly concluded but does not expressly or implicitly fix or make provision for determining the price, the parties are considered ... to have impliedly made reference to the price generally charged at the time of the conclusion of the contract for such goods sold under comparable circumstances in the trade concerned." The relationship between Articles 14 and 55 is the subject of a long-simmering academic controversy. Some commentators claim that Article 55 obviates the need for a specific price term. Others argue that this approach begs the question whether the parties have "validly concluded" a contract—a question that can only be answered by reference to Article 14—and surmise that Article 55 applies where a Contracting State has opted out of the CISG's provisions on contract formation.

addressed specified goods. Three years later, Judge DuBois of this Court followed *Helen Kaminski* and held that the CISG did not govern an exclusive distributorship agreement, an agreement granting the plaintiff a 25% interest in the defendant, or a sales commission agreement. *Viva Vino Import Corp. v. Farnese Vini S.r.l.*, No. 99-6384, 2000 WL 1224903, at *1-2 (E.D.Pa. Aug. 29, 2000). Two German appellate cases have similarly concluded that the CISG does not apply to distributorship agreements, which they termed "framework agreements," but does govern sales contracts that the parties enter pursuant to those agreements.

American Meter argues that this line of cases is inapplicable here because the plaintiffs do not claim damages for breach of what it terms the "relationship" provisions of the joint venture agreements,[5] but instead seek to enforce an obligation to sell goods. In other words, American Meter claims that the supply and credit provisions are severable and governed by the CISG, even if the Convention has no bearing on the remainder of the two agreements.

There are a number of difficulties with this argument, both in its characterization of the plaintiffs' claims and its construction of the CISG. To begin with, Promprilladamco and Amco Ukrservice are not seeking damages for American Meter's refusal to fill particular orders. Instead, they are claiming that American Meter materially breached the joint venture agreements when it refused to sell its products on credit, and as the *ad damnum* clauses of their complaints make clear, they seek damages for their projected lost profits between 1998 and 2003.

American Meter's construction of the CISG is equally problematic. It is premised on an artificial and untenable distinction between the "relationship" and supply provisions of a distributorship agreement—after all, what could be more central to the parties' relationship than the products the buyer is expected to distribute? American Meter's rhetorical view would also render it difficult for parties to create a general framework for their future sales without triggering the CISG's invalidating provisions. Such a construction of the Convention would be particularly destabilizing, not to mention unjust, in the context of the joint venture agreements at issue here. On American Meter's reading of the CISG, it could have invoked ordinary breach of contract principles if the plaintiffs had failed to exercise their best efforts to promote demand for its products, all the while reserving the right to escape its obligation to supply those products by invoking Article 14's price and quantity requirements. The CISG's provisions on contract formation do not compel such an expectation-defeating result.

We therefore join the other courts that have examined this issue and conclude that, although the CISG may have governed discrete contracts for the sale of goods that the parties had entered pursuant to the joint venture agreements, it does not apply to the agreements themselves. * * *

---

[5]In this category, American Meter would place terms dealing with such matters as quality control, the use of registered trademarks, and the parties' advertising and marketing obligations.

Notes and Questions

1. The court in this case concludes that, if it were to find the distribution agreement to be a contract "for the sale of goods" subject to the CISG, the contract could be invalid for failure to specify price and quantity terms. Is the court faced with a simple choice between finding the contract a "sale of goods" agreement subject to (and quite possibly invalid under) the CISG on one hand (as American Meter argues) and finding it outside the scope of the CISG on the other? Is it possible to view the distribution agreement as part of a unified network of contracts comprising the distribution agreement and each individual purchase order placed by the distributor under that agreement? If each purchase order is not a complete contract except when taken in combination with the distribution agreement, then how can the distribution agreement itself not be part of an agreement for the sale of goods? Assume for the moment that the court were to accept the logic of this argument; what problems in applying the CISG to the distribution agreement might arise?

2. In footnote 4, the court finds the CISG unclear on a critical point of law regarding contract formation. The resolution of this point under the contract law of a U.S. state would be straightforward—the absence of a price term is usually not fatal to contract formation; the court may infer a "reasonable price at the time of delivery" to be included if the intent of the parties to be bound by the contract is sufficiently clear, under UCC § 2-305. The uncertainty of CISG law is an important factor motivating many sophisticated business firms to exclude the CISG from their international sales agreements and to use instead some well-developed national law. For example, does the CISG clearly resolve whether the sale of uncut timber growing on private forest lands, or the sale of unharvested crops still in the field, would constitute a sale of goods under the Convention? What about the sale of electronically transmitted music files?

3. What is the significance of the prior German court opinions to the court's opinion in this case? See Article 7(1) of the CISG, reproduced below.

4. The breach of contract action in *AMCO Ukrservice* arose from joint ventures between a Ukrainian company and a U.S. company. Joint venture agreements, unlike simple buy-sell distribution agreements, are intended to create an identity of interests between the parties to facilitate cooperation. They accordingly require good will on both sides if they are to function effectively and profitably.

Opting Out

Perhaps the most important point about the scope of the CISG's application is that parties may decide they do not wish parts of the CISG, or even any of the CISG at all, to apply to their contract:

Article 6

The parties may exclude the application of this Convention or * * * derogate from or vary the effect of any of its provisions.

Why is Article 6 so important? A general reason is that some provisions of a sales agreement may contradict terms of the CISG. To respect the parties' freedom to set the terms of their own commercial relationship, it is important that parties be allowed to contract out of general CISG rules. In other words, even when the CISG rules apply, if a contract term and the CISG conflict, the contract term prevails (with a few specific exceptions).

In practice, the CISG does not apply to the great majority of commercial contracts involving U.S. purchasers or suppliers, and many contracts involving other contracting states,* when the parties have excluded application of the CISG.** In practice, the great majority of contracts involving U.S. parties do expressly exclude application of the CISG.*** Thus, for purposes of commercial law involving either the representation of U.S. clients or the representation of foreign clients doing business with U.S. companies, the CISG is usually not applicable. A typical opt-out provision might appear in a choice of law clause (along with the positive choice of law and forum), for example:

> The parties agree that the United Nations Convention on Contracts for the International Sale of Goods shall not govern or in any way affect the rights and obligations of the parties under this agreement, including the existence, validity, or interpretation of this agreement.

Lawyers opt out of the CISG for several reasons, some more convincing than others. First, companies that do a good deal of international business eventually become familiar with the nuances of the commercial laws of their major partners and do not necessarily object to their sales agreements being governed by English, French, or Japanese law. Their foreign trading partners may feel the same about U.S. law. Having become familiar with the UCC, many foreign sellers and purchaser have no objection to subjecting the contract to the law of New York or California, the two most common laws governing international contracts with U.S. parties. For these companies, the CISG is

*See, e.g., Justus Meyer, *UN–Kaufrecht in der deutschen Anwaltspraxis*, 69 RABELS ZEITSCHRIFT FÜR AUSLÄNDISCHES UND INTERNATIONALES PRIVATRECHT 457, 458 (2005) (Ger.).

**In some countries and U.S. states, merely including a choice of law clause in the contract will operate to exclude the CISG. In others, the contract must explicitly disclaim application of the CISG. For greater certainty, the parties to an international sales agreement are well advised to exclude or include the CISG expressly in the agreement.

***Empirical support for the regular exclusion of the CISG from both U.S. and foreign contracts has been assembled in John F. Coyle, *Rethinking the Commercial Law Treaty*, 45 GA. L. REV. 343, 374-83 (2011).

unnecessary and merely adds a complicating set of rules.

Another reason the CISG may be excluded, especially in sales agreements between sophisticated companies, is that the parties draft the contract to cover all matters of importance to them and to forestall disputes in a manner agreeable to them. In other words, the sale agreement is elaborated to the point at which it becomes a microcosm of an entire code of commercial law. In some cases, one party is sufficiently powerful that it can impose a comprehensive set of rules on the weaker party. In other cases, the parties negotiate a mutually beneficial compromise that includes all of the most important elements that the CISG, UCC, or any other body of commercial law would cover. In such cases, the CISG could be superfluous at best and potentially confusing at worst.

Still another reason that parties opt out of the CISG is that the CISG is less detailed than the UCC and various national commercial codes on many important matters. Contracting parties typically contemplate any disputes being decided in local courts, and the case law of most countries regarding commercial matters is far more developed than its case law interpreting the CISG. Although courts in any given country are expected to do their best to interpret the CISG in a manner that comports with interpretations by courts in other countries (CISG art. 7(1)), different countries (and, indeed, different U.S. states) do sometimes vary in their interpretations of the CISG, thereby creating potential uncertainty about how the rules will apply.

In any case, the number of U.S. cases interpreting the CISG is small, which creates its own brand of uncertainty even when the forum in which the dispute will be decided is agreed upon in advance. There is no single international commercial court that harmonizes dissonant national interpretations of the CISG. Moreover, judicial decisions in one CISG state party do not formally bind courts in other CISG state parties. The relatively rich legal precedents interpreting the various national and U.S. state commercial codes are more reassuring to these companies than risking an unexpected interpretation of the CISG. Of course, this creates a vicious circle. If business firms regularly exclude the CISG because of the lack of interpretive cases, case law interpreting the Convention will develop extremely slowly, which in turn justifies continuing to exclude the Convention. Moreover, there is in fact a good deal of foreign precedent interpreting the CISG; if U.S. courts were willing to draw on it for guidance, as they sometimes do, the task of interpretation might be made more predictable, at least regarding those provisions the interpretation of which has engendered relatively strong global convergence.

Finally, many companies feel uncomfortable applying an unfamiliar law and insist on local law, not because it is better, but merely because it is more familiar. Their lawyers may be unable to marshal arguments to overcome a reluctance to rely on strange legal rules. When the choice is between applying the local law of a commercially sophisticated country and applying the CISG, the CISG is usually considered to offer few compelling advantages.

Whether these reasons are cogent is immaterial, unless the parties to

Figure 4.2. International sales of manufactured goods are big business in the United States. The United States buys more foreign manufactured goods than any country in the world, and it is the second largest exporter after China.

a commercial contract have trouble agreeing on the applicable law. After all, there is usually very little reason for either party to the contract to object to the application of New York, German, or other law. With help from competent local counsel, the unexpected or objectionable provisions of foreign laws can be ascertained and, if necessary, excluded in the contract. But if choice of law becomes an issue, the CISG may present a viable alternative.

B. CISG Rules of Interpretation

Even when the CISG applies to a contractual relationship, it does not clearly resolve all questions of law, as *AMCO Ukrservice* illustrates. In such cases, the CISG provides two general rules of interpretation:

Article 7

> (1) In the interpretation of this Convention, regard is to be had to its international character and to the need to promote uniformity in its application and the observance of good faith in international trade.
> (2) Questions concerning matters governed by this Convention which are not expressly settled in it are to be settled in conformity with the general principles on which it is based or, in the absence of such principles, in conformity with the law applicable by virtue of the rules of private international law.

In other words, if the CISG does not settle a question of law, and the "general principles" on which the CISG is based give no assistance or incomplete assistance, the law of some state will supplement the CISG rules. Which state? Article 7 provides that the rules of private international law—which also are used to determine whether the CISG itself applies under Article 1—will decide.

Case law from courts around the world interpreting the CISG has proliferated over the years, and the body of law now reaches into the thousands of cases. Unfortunately, many of these decisions are made by private arbitral tribunals that do not publish their decisions. Nonetheless, the range of persuasive precedents upon which national courts may rely has been developing gradually. Aside from international variance in the interpretation of the CISG, the major obstacle to making use of this diverse interpretive guidance is the fact that national courts render judgments in their own national languages. It is highly inefficient for a court to survey case precedents in dozens of different languages to arrive at a consistent interpretation of the CISG.

Many private NGOs, as well as UNCITRAL itself, have undertaken initiatives to assist in the development and harmonization of international precedents relating to the CISG. Most importantly, UNCITRAL has developed a digest of interpretive national cases, arranged by article of the CISG that it publishes annually.

In addition, Pace Law School's Institute of International Commercial

Law has undertaken the task of translating cases from national courts and international arbitral tribunals interpreting and applying the CISG. The result is an article-by-article database to supplement the UNCITRAL digest:

http://www.cisg.law.pace.edu/cisg/text/case-annotations.html

These resources can assist national courts in interpreting vague or ambiguous provisions of the CISG. Although they do not by themselves create greater international harmonization in the case law, they do facilitate harmonization and increase the probability of the CISG becoming more widely used in the future.

C. Substantive Rules

The CISG has many provisions on the formation and interpretation of commercial contracts that seem similar or parallel to those found in the UCC. Provisions of the CISG are far more detailed than the UCC in some matters and far less detailed in others (omitting, for example, any provisions dealing with title to the goods). The CISG incorporates many principles of contract interpretation not found in the UCC, because the UCC leaves such matters to be decided under principles of common law in the United States. For example, the CISG provides:

> **Article 8**
>
> (1) * * * [S]tatements made by * * * a party are to be interpreted according to his intent where the other party knew * * * what the intent was.
>
> (2) If the preceding paragraph is not applicable, statements made by * * * a party are to be interpreted according to the understanding that a reasonable person of the same kind as the other party would have had in the same circumstances.
>
> (3) In determining the intent of a party or the understanding a reasonable person would have had, due consideration is to be given to all relevant circumstances of the case including the negotiations, any practices which the parties have established between themselves, usages and any subsequent conduct of the parties.
>
> **Article 9**
>
> (1) The parties are bound by any usage to which they have agreed and by any practices which they have established between themselves.
>
> (2) The parties are considered, unless otherwise agreed, to have impliedly made applicable to their contract or its formation a usage of which the parties knew or ought to have known and which in international trade is widely known to, and regularly observed by, parties to contracts of the type involved in the particular trade concerned.

Although various provisions of the UCC may reference such concepts as the intent of the parties, objective interpretation of contract language, or trade usages, the UCC itself has no comparably explicit provisions on these subjects. On the other hand, the UCC contains many detailed provisions governing contract formation and interpretation and duties of performance that are absent from the CISG. For example, the UCC provides that a contract may be formed even though some terms are left open. The CISG does not specify under what circumstances the absence of specific terms in an agreement may nullify it as indefinite.

Many provisions of the CISG differ substantially from U.S. commercial law, and some issues typically addressed by state commercial law are left unaddressed in the CISG. Nonetheless, many provisions of the UCC and CISG appear superficially similar. Consider this side-by-side comparison with the UCC:

UCC	CISG
Section 1-203 Every contract or duty within this Act imposes an obligation of good faith in its performance or enforcement.	**Article 7** (1) In the interpretation of this Convention, regard is to be had to its international character and to the need to promote uniformity in its application and the observance of good faith in international trade. * * *
Section 2-204 (1) A contract for sale of goods may be made in any manner sufficient to show agreement, including offer and acceptance [and] conduct by both parties which recognizes the existence of a contract * * *.	**Article 11** A contract of sale need not be concluded in or evidenced by writing and is not subject to any other requirement as to form. * * *
Section 2-209 (1) An agreement modifying a contract within this Article needs no consideration to be binding. * * *	**Article 29** (1) A contract may be modified or terminated by the mere agreement of the parties. * * *

While the meanings of the provisions may seem somewhat comparable, the apparent similarity can be deceptive. Different legal principles sometimes govern how the UCC and CISG are interpreted, and they draw on a different set of precedents. The CISG, unlike the UCC, is not supported by a rich background of common law. General rules of contract law must be spelled out through judicial or arbitral interpretation of the "general principles" on which the Convention is based or, in case these cannot be ascertained, by resort to the applicable municipal law governing the contract. It would therefore not be accurate to view the CISG as a "substitute" for a municipal choice of law.

Most provisions of the CISG are not even superficially similar to those UCC. This is partly because the UCC and CISG approach contract regulation from different perspectives. The UCC defines rights and obligations for the seller and buyer, and tries to reproduce the manner in which business firms typically do business. This means that the positions of sellers and buyers, being different, are defined in a different manner. The CISG, in contrast, resembles a general and rationalized approach to defining obligations that mostly treats sellers and buyers alike. The CISG also tends to impose more general rules in deference to the variance in approaches to commercial law in different states. This sometimes results in vague rules that leave much to interpretation.

Both the UCC and the CISG deal with what kind of evidence of agreement is admissible before a court or other tribunal. Section 2-201 of the UCC sets forth a classic statute of frauds, but it recognizes certain exceptions. Section 2-202 sets forth a classic parol evidence rule that precludes oral or prior written agreements from modifying a written contract. In contrast, Article 11 of the CISG renounces the statute of frauds and provides that an oral contract is generally binding and enforceable. It makes no exceptions and is textually unclear on whether it accepts the parol evidence rule. Consider the following articles side-by-side.

UCC	CISG
Section 2-201 (1) A contract for the sale of goods for the price of $5,000 or more is not enforceable by way of an action or defense unless there is some record sufficient to indicate that a contract for sale has been made between the parties and signed by the party against which enforcement is sought * * *. **Section 2-202** (1) Terms with respect to which the confirmatory records of the parties agree or which are otherwise set forth in a record intended by the parties as a final expression of their agreement with respect to such terms as are included therein may not be contradicted by evidence of any prior agreement or of a contemporaneous oral agreement * * *.	**Article 11** A contract of sale need not be concluded in or evidenced by writing and is not subject to any other requirement as to form. It may be proved by any means, including witnesses.
Section 2-205 An offer by a merchant to buy or sell goods in a signed record that by its terms gives assurance that it will be held open is not revocable, for lack of consideration, during the time stated or if no time is stated for a reasonable time; but in no event may the period of irrevocability exceed three months. Any such term of assurance in a form supplied by the offeree must be separately signed by the offeror.	**Article 16** (1) Until a contract is concluded an offer may be revoked if the revocation reaches the offeree before he has dispatched an acceptance. (2) However, an offer cannot be revoked: (a) If it indicates * * * that it is irrevocable; or (b) if it was reasonable for the offeree to rely on the offer as being irrevocable and the offeree has acted in reliance on the offer.

UCC	CISG
Section 2-716 (1) Specific performance may be decreed if the goods are unique or in other proper circumstances. In a contract other than a consumer contract, specific performance may be decreed if the parties have agreed to that remedy. * * *	**Article 28** If, in accordance with the provisions of this Convention, one party is entitled to require performance of any obligation by the other party, a court is not bound to enter a judgement of specific performance unless the court would do so under its own law in respect of similar contracts of sale not governed by this Convention.

Does CISG Article 11 mean that the *existence* of the contract may be proved by any means, such as witnesses, or that the *terms* of the contract may be proved by any means? If the former, as seems most likely, then the CISG does not appear to address the parol evidence issue at all. If the latter, then the parol evidence rule is arguably rejected, and oral evidence may be introduced to contradict the terms of a written agreement.

The absence of explicit terms regarding this issue makes this provision of the CISG more dependent on judicial interpretation, which, in spite of the CISG's interpretive rules, sometimes varies from state to state and may in some cases defeat the treaty's purpose of promoting uniformity. Consider the following case:

MCC–MARBLE CERAMIC CENTER, INC. v. CERAMICA NUOVA D'AGOSTINO, S.p.A

U.S. Court of Appeals, Eleventh Circuit, 1998
144 F.3d 1384

BACKGROUND

The plaintiff-appellant, MCC–Marble Ceramic, Inc. ("MCC"), is a Florida corporation engaged in the retail sale of tiles, and the defendant-appellee, Ceramica Nuova d'Agostino S.p.A. ("D'Agostino") is an Italian corporation engaged in the manufacture of ceramic tiles. In October 1990, MCC's president, Juan Carlos Monzon, met representatives of D'Agostino at a trade fair in Bologna, Italy and negotiated an agreement to purchase ceramic tiles from D'Agostino based on samples he examined at the trade fair. Monzon, who spoke no Italian, communicated with Gianni Silingardi, then D'Agostino's commercial director, through a translator, Gianfranco Copelli, who was himself an agent of D'Agostino. The parties apparently arrived at an oral agreement on the crucial terms of price, quality, quantity, delivery and payment. The parties then recorded these terms on one of D'Agostino's standard, pre-printed order forms and Monzon signed the contract on MCC's behalf. According to MCC, the parties also entered into a requirements contract in February 1991, subject to which D'Agostino agreed to supply MCC with high grade ceramic tile at specific discounts as long as MCC purchased sufficient quantities of tile. MCC completed a number of additional order forms requesting tile deliveries pursuant to that agreement.

MCC brought suit against D'Agostino claiming a breach of the February 1991 requirements contract when D'Agostino failed to satisfy orders in April, May, and August of 1991. [In its reply brief, D'Agostino invoked the terms of its standard contract referenced in its order forms, which it argued justified the refusal to fill the orders. MCC argued that the parties had no intention to override the oral agreement with the written agreement referenced on the order form.] * * *

DISCUSSION

* * *

Contrary to what is familiar practice in United States courts, the CISG appears to permit a substantial inquiry into the parties' subjective intent, even if the parties did not engage in any objectively ascertainable means of registering this intent. Article 8(1) of the CISG instructs courts to interpret the "statements ... and other conduct of a party ... according to his intent" as long as the other party "knew or could not have been unaware" of that intent. The plain language of the Convention, therefore, requires an inquiry into a party's subjective intent as long as the other party to the contract was aware of that intent. * * *

II. Parol Evidence and the CISG

Given our determination that the magistrate judge and the district court should have considered MCC's affidavits regarding the parties' subjective intentions, we must address a question of first impression in this circuit: whether the parol evidence rule, which bars evidence of an earlier oral contract that contradicts or varies the terms of a subsequent or contemporaneous written contract, plays any role in cases involving the CISG. We begin by observing that the parol evidence rule, contrary to its title, is a substantive rule of law, not a rule of evidence. * * * As such, a federal district court cannot simply apply the parol evidence rule as a procedural matter * * *.

The CISG itself contains no express statement on the role of parol evidence. It is clear, however, that the drafters of the CISG were comfortable with the concept of permitting parties to rely on oral contracts because they eschewed any statutes of fraud provision and expressly provided for the enforcement of oral contracts. Moreover, article 8(3) of the CISG expressly directs courts to give "due consideration ... to all relevant circumstances of the case including the negotiations ..." to determine the intent of the parties. Given article 8(1)'s directive to use the intent of the parties to interpret their statements and conduct, article 8(3) is a clear instruction to admit and consider parol evidence regarding the negotiations to the extent they reveal the parties' subjective intent.

Despite the CISG's broad scope, surprisingly few cases have applied the Convention in the United States, see *Delchi Carrier SpA v. Rotorex Corp.*, 71 F.3d 1024, 1027–28 (2d Cir. 1995) (observing that "there is virtually no case law under the Convention"), and only two reported decisions touch upon the parol evidence rule, both in dicta. One court has concluded, much as we have above, that the parol evidence rule is not viable in CISG cases in light of article 8 of the Convention. In *Filanto*, a district court addressed the differences between the UCC and the CISG on the issues of offer and acceptance and the battle of the forms. See 789 F.Supp. at 1238. After engaging in a thorough analysis of how the CISG applied to the dispute before it, the district court tangentially observed that article 8(3) "essentially rejects ... the parol evidence rule." Another court, however, appears to have arrived at a contrary conclusion. In *Beijing Metals & Minerals Import/Export Corp. v. American Bus. Ctr., Inc.*, 993 F.2d 1178 (5th Cir. 1993), a defendant sought to avoid summary judgment on a contract claim by relying on evidence of contemporaneously negotiated oral terms that the parties had not included in their written agreement. The plaintiff, a Chinese corporation, relied on Texas law in its complaint while the defendant, apparently a Texas corporation, asserted that the CISG governed the dispute. Without resolving the choice of law question, the Fifth Circuit cited *Filanto* for the proposition that there have been very few reported cases applying the CISG in the United States, and stated that the parol evidence rule would apply regardless of whether Texas law or the CISG governed the dispute. The opinion does not acknowledge *Filanto*'s more applicable dictum that the parol evidence rule does not apply to CISG cases nor does it conduct any analysis of the Convention to support its conclusion. In fact, the Fifth Circuit did not undertake to interpret the CISG in a manner that would arrive at a result consistent with the parol evidence rule but instead explained that it would apply the rule as developed at Texas common law. As persuasive authority for this court, the *Beijing Metals* opinion is not particularly persuasive on this point.

Our reading of article 8(3) as a rejection of the parol evidence rule, however, is in accordance with the great weight of academic commentary on the issue. As one scholar has explained:

> [T]he language of Article 8(3) that "due consideration is to be given to all relevant circumstances of the case" seems adequate to override any domestic rule that would bar a tribunal from considering the relevance of other agreements.... Article 8(3) relieves tribunals from domestic rules that might bar them from "considering" any evidence between the parties that is relevant. This added flexibility for interpretation is consistent with a growing body of opinion that the "parol evidence rule" has been an embarrassment for the administration of modern transactions.

[John O.] Honnold, *Uniform Law [for International Sales under the 1980 United Nations Convention]* § 110 at 170–71. Indeed, only one commentator has made any serious attempt to reconcile the parol evidence rule with the CISG. [He] argues that the parol evidence rule often permits the admission of evidence discussed in article 8(3), and that the rule could be an appropriate way to discern what consideration is "due" under article 8(3) to evidence of a parol nature. He also argues that the parol evidence rule, by limiting the incentive for perjury and pleading prior understandings in bad faith, promotes good faith and uniformity in the interpretation of contracts and therefore is in harmony with the principles of the CISG, as expressed in article 7. The answer to both these arguments, however, is the same: although jurisdictions in the United States have found the parol evidence rule helpful to promote good faith and uniformity in contract, as well as an appropriate answer to the question of how much consideration to give parol evidence, a wide number of other States Party to the CISG have rejected the rule in their domestic jurisdictions. One of the primary factors motivating the negotiation and adoption of the CISG was to provide parties to international contracts for the sale of goods with some degree of certainty as to the principles of law that would govern potential disputes and remove the previous doubt regarding which party's legal system might otherwise apply. See Letter of Transmittal from Ronald Reagan, President of the United States, to the United States Senate, *reprinted at* 15 U.S.C. app. 70, 71 (1997). Courts applying the CISG cannot, therefore, upset the parties' reliance on the Convention by substituting familiar principles of domestic law when the Convention requires a different result. We may only achieve the directives of good faith and uniformity in contracts under the CISG by interpreting and applying the plain language of article 8(3) as written and obeying its directive to consider this type of parol evidence.

This is not to say that parties to an international contract for the sale of goods cannot depend on written contracts or that parol evidence regarding subjective contractual intent need always prevent a party relying on a written agreement from securing summary judgment. To the contrary, most cases will not present a situation (as exists in this case) in which both parties to the contract acknowledge a subjective intent not to be bound by the terms of a pre-printed writing. In most cases, therefore, article 8(2) of the CISG will apply, and objective evidence will provide the basis for the court's decision. Consequently, a party to a contract governed by the CISG will not be able to avoid the terms of a contract and force a jury trial simply by submitting an affidavit which states that he or she did not have the subjective intent to be bound by the contract's terms. Moreover, to the extent parties wish to avoid parol evidence problems they can do so by including a merger clause in their agreement that extinguishes any and all prior agreements and understandings not expressed in the writing.

* * *

Notes and Questions

1. The purposes of the parol evidence rule are twofold. First, it inhibits the factfinder from using perjured or unreliable testimony to vary the terms of a written agreement. Second, it avoids conflicting interpretations of an agreement. It does this by presuming that the parties intended the integrated written contract would supersede statements made or intentions expressed during negotiations that were later rejected or altered in the written document. Does the court suggest that the CISG should be interpreted to mandate or allow courts to give more evidentiary weight to written agreements than to oral statements of the parties?

2. It is curious that Eleventh Circuit, after acknowledging the dearth of U.S. case authority on the question of whether the CISG endorses a parol evidence exclusionary rule, did not choose to survey how courts in other contracting states interpret the CISG. Although the court referred to article 7, it did not seem willing to promote uniformity of the Convention's application by harmonizing its interpretation with that of foreign courts. In contrast, non-U.S. courts frequently cite to the judicial decisions of foreign jurisdictions in interpreting the CISG. Nor did the court refer to the *travaux préparatoires* (negotiating history) of the CISG. If the Eleventh Circuit had followed either practice, it would have found that both support its decision to reject application of the parol evidence rule in CISG cases.

As the UCC–CISG comparison chart shows, both instruments set the terms for the revocation of firm offers to form a contract for the sale of goods. Section 2-205 of the UCC sets forth a clear rule: an irrevocable offer must be kept open for the period of time stated regardless of lack of consideration for the irrevocability, but only if it is in writing and for no longer than three months. The CISG provides a very general rule that an offer specified as irrevocable may not be revoked. It gives no definite guidance on whether the guarantee of irrevocability must be in writing (probably not, in light of Article 11), nor does it specify the maximum period of irrevocability. Thus, if an offeror states that his offer is "irrevocable" without specifying a term, it is uncertain whether the offer will ever become revocable and, if it does, after what period revocation will be permitted. Note also that Article 11 provides for promissory estoppel to prevent even a revocable offer from being revoked if the offeree acted in reasonable reliance on the offer. The UCC contains no such provision.

Finally, note that the UCC and CISG both contain rules regarding specific performance in a contract setting. UCC Section 2-716 provides that specific performance may be ordered only under certain limited conditions. Article 28 of the CISG leaves it to the courts to determine whether to require performance. Courts differ in their approaches to specific performance, leaving parties to an international contract potentially uncertain of whether specific performance can be obtained. Moreover, although Article 28 states that it only applies where a party is entitled to require performance "in accordance with the provisions of this Convention," the CISG does not in fact require the availability of specific performance.

These are just a few examples of the differing approaches that the UCC and CISG take to commercial contracts. They do not of course exhaust the differences between the two, but they illustrate that the decision to embrace or exclude application of the CISG in an international commercial agreement may be consequential to many aspects of contract formation, interpretation, enforceability, and remedies.

2 International Sales of Services

Just as international sales agreements differ from their domestic counterparts, international agreements to provide services differ from domestic services agreement. There are many kinds of services agreements, and it is difficult to generalize beyond a certain point. In an international context, service agreements may be divided into three basic classes: (1) agreements involving a provider in one country offering services to a purchaser in another; (2) agreements involving a provider in one country that establishes a local presence in another country to provide services there; and (3) agreements involving a provider in one country that establishes a local presence in another country to provide services back in the provider's own home country. When the establishment of a presence in another country is involved, foreign investment issues come to the fore. These are discussed in Chapter 7. Here, we will focus on the commercial aspects of the arrangements.

As explained in Chapter 2, services may be traded across state borders in three ways. They may involve (1) information moving across borders, (2) goods embodying a service exported to another country, or (3) persons traveling to a foreign country to provide the service. The contractual arrangements for each kind of service will differ significantly, because different costs, risks, and responsibilities are involved in each category.

2.1 Direct Service Agreements

When the international sale of a service consists of a cross-border provision of information, it may be a case of information simply being transmitted from one country to another, or it may relate to a complex interaction between experts in the selling and purchasing countries. An example of the former would be an enterprise in one country that backs up its data to a cloud server located in another country. An example of the latter would be a music composer in one country writing a score for a movie producer in another country based on discussions between them about mood, instrumentation, and other factors. Similarly, attorneys and tax advisers who represent clients in foreign states are providing a service internationally through information exchange, although the work may be largely performed in the consultant's home state. In each case, the service consists of data being transmitted between actors in different countries.

Direct services of this type may also be provided *in situ*, such as when the service provider sends its employees or agents across state borders to perform the services in a foreign state at the customer's request. For example, a communications technician working for a Smalldonian company who is sent to consult with a telecommunications company in Freedonia will be providing an international service, even though the actual service takes place entirely in Freedonia. In such cases, the work is performed in a state other than the service provider's home state.

Parties may agree on a one-time or recurrent provision of services by itself or as part of a purchase agreement. For example, a sale of goods to a buyer in a different state may be accompanied by a warranty clause providing that the seller will service and repair the warrantied product in the purchaser's country, or if the sale is of complex machinery or facilities, the seller might agree to install the product at the purchaser's foreign facilities. Such *in situ* service agreements require international travel of the service provider's employees or agents.

Many of the same issues that arise in international purchase agreements equally arise in international service agreements, although with some variation. Just as international product sales will be subject to the regulations of the importing state as well as the exporting state, the international provision of services may be subject to regulation in both states as well. At the very least, the sale of services will be subject to regulation in the importing state, which may require special training or licenses for the provision of certain kinds of services. The state may also impose nationality requirements on the provision of some services, if permitted by its schedule of commitments to the GATS (discussed in Chapter 2).

Unlike in a purchase agreement, however, it is the service provider who will be solely responsible for complying with import regulations; the obligations rarely can be delegated to the purchaser by contract. For example, if the importing state prohibits anyone from providing insurance services in its territory without an insurer's license and bond, and further prohibits majority foreign-owned companies from providing insurance services in its territory, it is the responsibility of the service provider to comply with these regulations.

Taxation, choice of law, and choice of forum issues arise in service agreements in manners very similar to those that arise in purchase agreements. Generally, a service provider can expect that the "default" law governing the provision of services internationally is the law of the state in which the services are performed—the so-called ***lex loci solutionis***. When a service provider provides services in multiple countries, contractual choice of law and choice of forum clauses are as important as, if not more important than, they are in international sales agreements.

2.2 Contract Manufacturing

One type of service particularly common in international business is contract manufacturing. A contract manufacturer is a company that manufactures goods according to specifications provided by the customer. It generally never owns title to the goods it makes; it merely manufactures them for its client. Offshore contract manufacturing is sometimes confused with an international purchase of goods, because the two are alternative business models. To explain how contract manufacturing works, it is helpful to understand why it is actually a service, and what need it fulfills that would not be satisfied by a direct purchase of goods.

A company that wishes to purchase goods from a foreign state on a regular basis is likely to find that the risks and costs of doing business internationally are reduced considerably when it has a record of experience with a foreign supplier. When the goods to be imported are fungible, the international supply agreement will not look much different from a one-time international purchase agreement. It may involve a framework agreement setting the general terms of sale, followed by purchase orders for specific quantities of goods. Sometimes, however, a company may wish to purchase goods are not fungible, but that are designed and manufactured to its specifications.

One option for such a company is to manufacture the product itself. However, there are many reasons why a company might prefer to rely on another company for its manufacturing needs. Most prominently, the business firm might specialize in product design and marketing and have no manufacturing facilities and may not wish to invest in expensive manufacturing plants and equipment. Or it may have simply determined that other firms can manufacture the products more efficiently than the company itself. When a firm decides to rely on contract manufacturing, it will often choose a manufacturing firm located in a different country, where wages and other costs are lower, or where expertise in the industry are especially high (or, ideally, both). For this reason, much contract manufacturing is international in character.

When a company delegates the task of manufacturing to a foreign contractor, especially when doing so after having manufactured its products itself, it is sometimes referred to as **outsourcing** its production. Much outsourcing of production to foreign countries results from lower foreign wage rates, lack of unions, weaker environmental regulation, tax incentives, and other factors that make manufacturing abroad more profitable. For this reason, outsourcing is often directed toward developing countries with very low wages and limited business regulation.

Outsourcing inevitably creates short-term unemployment in the outsourcing company's country, and so it is a controversial practice. Much of the opposition to free trade between wealthy countries and developing countries has centered over predictions or allegations of job loss caused by product outsourcing. On the other hand, by lowering production costs, the outsourcing company reduces the costs to consumers of the outsourced goods and contribute to the economic development of poor countries.

Whatever the net economic effect of outsourcing, it is a popular production strategy. Contract manufacturing is very common in consumer discretionary industries such as clothing and shoes, toys, and other low-value goods. It is also now common in high technology industries such as semiconductors, computers, and automobile parts. Many foreign firms in developing countries specialize in contract manufacturing various goods for developed country markets.

A contract manufacturer usually does not design the goods that it manufactures (although it may coordinate with and give advice to its client), nor does it market or sell the goods. As noted, in most cases, contract manufacturers never own title to the goods they manufacture or the components or materials from which the products are made, so that what they provide is more in the nature of a manufacturing service than a supply contract.

The nature of a business relationship between a contract manufacturer and its foreign client company raises issues that are not addressed by any existing international treaty. The closest relevant multilateral treaty is the TRIMS Agreement, discussed in Chapter 2, but even that agreement does not relate to ordinary contract manufacturing, because it usually involves no direct foreign investment. The relationship is sufficiently different from a standard supply agreement or intercompany manufacturing relationship that it demands consideration of several special aspects.

One such aspect is the risk present when the client supplies the contract manufacturer with designs, schematics, production techniques, and materials and technologies that may be copyrighted, patented, or protected as a trade

Figure 4.3. An old debate that keeps resurfacing. The negotiation of the North American Free Trade Agreement, the first major trade agreement between the United States and a developing country, provoked extensive debate over expected U.S. job losses caused in part by product outsourcing to Mexico Criticism eventually, led NAFTA to be renegotiated as the U.S.–Mexico–Canada Agreement, with mostly minor changes.

secret. Alternatively or in addition, the manufacturer may be printing trademarked names or logos on the manufactured articles. As discussed in Chapter 3, care must be taken to register the IP where appropriate in the country of manufacture and to define clearly in the license agreement who owns the IP and what rights it is necessary to grant to the contract manufacturer. There is always a risk that IP entrusted to the manufacturer may be leaked or used for illicit purposes, and, unless the manufacturer is highly reputable, some form of verification practice may be necessary to help the client prevent or detect any infringement of its IP rights. Clarity is especially important if the contract manufacturer will be coordinating the design or development of a product with the client, because it may be possible in some circumstances for the contract manufacturer to claim joint ownership of any resulting IP contrary to the intentions of the client.

A second problem relates to the client's supply of materials or components to the contract manufacturer. If the client assists the manufacturer in this way, the agreement will need to spell out clearly who owns the materials or components and which party is liable for insuring them at any given point. For example, suppose *X* Corp. supplies its contract manufacturer, *Y* Co., in *Y*'s country with fabric to be used in cutting and sewing blouses to be imported to *X*'s country. While the fabric is stored in *Y* Co.'s warehouse, a fire destroys all stock. Who is responsible for having arranged insurance, *X* Corp. or *Y* Co., and who is liable for the loss? The expectations of the parties should be made clear in the agreement.

Another, very prominent, issue is that of liability. If the contract manufacturer is producing goods according to the client's designs, the manufacturer may reasonably wish to be indemnified and held harmless against the possibility that the product design infringes a third party's IP rights. It may also expect the same rights in case of product defects arising from design or even manufacture. At the same time, the client may seek indemnification for manufacturing defects. Liability rules must be negotiated with the manufacturer as well.

Still another issue is raised by the ownership of the manufactured goods, alluded to above. Does the client own the goods at all times? Or will the contract manufacturer assume initial ownership of the goods and transfer ownership to the client at some point? This decision can have consequences for tax liabilities, customs duty, risk of loss, shipping and insurance obligations, bankruptcy, and other important matters. As this discussion should have made clear, there are many potential flashpoints of controversy in a contract manufacturing arrangement that may arise between the parties, with third parties, and with government regulators in one or the other country.

2.3 Service Outsourcing Agreements

For many years, the popularity of outsourcing was exclusive to manufacturing, but the outsourcing of services to developing countries has become increasingly common as well. Mostly these services involve unskilled labor such as customer service or data entry, but technical support or other skilled tasks may also be outsourced. Most of this outsourcing is done through third-party subcontractors who undertake to hire and train employees who are willing to perform services at a cost far below the minimum legal wage in the United States, European states, and other developed countries.

When services are outsourced to an unaffiliated contractor, the outsourcing company may implement a bidding process to obtain the lowest possible cost for the services. The supplier selected to provide the services will then enter into a service contract with the outsourcing company. The outsourcing company will retain primary liability to its customers for damages caused by the service provider. Even a contract by which the service provider agrees to indemnify the outsourcing company for any damages caused by faulty service will not fully protect the outsourcing company, because the service provider will typically operate under the trademarks and service marks of the outsourcing company.

Among other things, this means that, when something goes wrong in the

WHAT KINDS OF SERVICES CAN BE OUTSOURCED?

Outsourcing of services has occurred in a wide variety of fields, but has been most popular in customer service, records and data entry/processing, and information technology. Many airlines, travel agencies, banks, software publishers, and other service providers have partially or completely outsourced customer service to subcontractors in developing countries. For companies in the United States and U.K., India and Sri Lanka have been popular choices because English is commonly spoken there. Software publishers now commonly outsource routine programming and information processing tasks as well. Some companies even outsource network maintenance, using the computer experts in foreign countries to manage network tasks such as installing software and troubleshooting problems. In addition, companies that make heavy use of databases, such as hospitals, may outsource data entry functions to service providers in developing countries. Many other services, including engineering or pharmaceutical research and development; medical services such as radiological analysis; and animation are increasingly outsourced to China, India, and other developing countries. Even legal services are not immune. Since 2001, General Electric Corp. has outsourced some of its routine in-house legal work to India.

"We found someone overseas who can drink coffee and talk about sports all day for a fraction of what we're paying you."

Figure 4.4. Gallows humor. As skilled labor in services industries increasingly joins unskilled manufacturing jobs in being outsourced to developing countries, it creates socioeconomic tension. And where there is tension, humor is not far behind.

Case Study

Early Animation Outsourcing to Mexico

The practice of outsourcing servies to foreign countries with lower average wages is not entirely new. As far back as 1959, Jay Ward Productions outsourced the drafting work for a U.S. cartoon television series, *The Rocky & Bullwinkle Show*, to an animation studio in Mexico, Gamma Productions. The decision to outsource was strongly supported by the program's sponsor, General Mills, Inc., as a cost-saving measure. However, because Gamma emphasized low fees at the expense of quality, the graphics were crude and the show was plagued by mistakes, such as mustaches appearing and disappearing, colors changing in the middle of a scene, and so forth. Nonetheless, the show ran for five years before being canceled in 1964. It is unclear how much the poor quality caused by outsourcing contributed to Rocky and Bullwinkle's demise.

Today, animation outsourcing in the motion picture, television, and video game industries is extremely common. Animation can be extremely time-intensive, and animators in India, the Philippines, and other developing countries accept a small fraction of the wages of their U.S. or European counterparts.

services, customers will blame the outsourcing company rather than the service provider, of whose identity they may be unaware. Common problems include insufficient training or supervision of service provider personnel; lack of adequate skill in the relevant language (e.g., a U.S. company using a service provider in Ruritania to give technical support to its customers might find that the Ruritanian support personnel have trouble communicating in English with U.S. customers); cost overruns by the service provider; and fraud on the customers practiced by service provider personnel. Proper training and supervision of the service provider personnel by the outsourcing company and careful attention to restraining service costs by contract are essential to the success of the outsourcing. To control costs and ensure that the expected quality and quantity of services are provided, companies may enter into a **service level agreement** (**SLA**), which sets standards for the services, provides incentives to meet the standards, and imposes penalties (such as a fee) for falling short. Providing numerical benchmarks in the SLA helps simplify and clarify the outsourcing company's ability to assess whether the contractor is performing as expected, but some kinds of service (such as customer service) are very difficult to quantify. In such cases, the SLA may contain provisions allowing the outsourcing company to audit or review the contractor's performance periodically.

3 Shipping and Delivery Terms

International sales of services do not normally require shipping; telecommunications usually suffice. At most, they may involve travel between countries by the service provider, which may raise immigration issues (see Chapter 7 on corporate migration) and possibly export issues (see Chapter 5 on "deemed exports"). But the costs and risks of transporting service providers between countries is typically a marginal part of the business arrangement.

In contrast, the international sales of goods raises legal issues relating to transportation that may be quite complex. At the outset, one problem frequently confronted in international commercial agreements for the sale of goods is ambiguity about the mode and manner of shipping and delivery of the goods. Ideally, a sales agreement should make clear the following important points:

- Which party is responsible for arranging and paying for shipping?
- Which must arrange and pay for insurance on the goods while in transit?

Figure 4.5. Using foreign contractors to provide customer service requires careful contract planning to ensure that the service reflects the principal's business culture.

- Which is responsible for complying with customs law in the country of importation and paying any customs duties owed?
- Which is responsible for complying with export control law in the country of exportation and obtaining any export licenses necessary?
- Where will the goods be delivered to the purchaser or the purchaser's freight forwarder or agent? (At the port of entry? At the purchaser's warehouse? etc.)
- When does risk of loss for the goods pass from the seller to the buyer?
- When must the purchaser pay for the goods?

These terms can be very important. For example, suppose Sellco in South Carolina agrees to sell a shipment of widgets to Buyco in Freedonia and ships the goods out of the port of Charleston, S.C. Suppose the goods are damaged while being loaded onto the ship. Which party bears the risk of loss will depend on whether risk of loss passes from Sellco to Buyco before or after the goods are loaded onto the ship. Similarly, if the goods are lost at sea while in transit from Charleston to Port City, Freedonia, the questions arises whether risk of loss passed to Buyco when the goods were loaded onto the ship or when they are unloaded in Port City. The risks of ocean shipping are quite real. Over 1600 cargo containers on average are lost in ocean shipping each year.

Normally, we would expect this problem to be resolved either in the contract itself or, in the absence of a clear specification, under the law governing the contract. If South Carolina law governs the contract, for instance, South Carolina's version of the UCC will apply. UCC Article 2 includes shipping terms that may be used to resolve some or all of the above-mentioned questions. A **shipping term** is a brief phrase (or, more commonly, an acronym symbolizing the phrase) specifying which party is responsible for arranging shipping and insurance, where risk of loss passes, and other matters detailed above.

For example, suppose the parties specify in the sales agreement:

> Goods to be shipped FOB Port of Charleston on or before June 1, 2020.

Here, the shipping term is **F.O.B.**, meaning **free on board**. UCC § 2-319 provides that, if the contract specifies F.O.B. as the shipping term followed by the place of shipment (Charleston), the seller bears the expense and risk of getting the goods aboard ship, while the buyer must arrange and pay for ocean shipping and absorb the risk of loss until the goods arrive in Port City, Freedonia. Section 2-319 further provides that the purchaser must pay when the required documents, such as a bill of lading and packing list, are tendered. The UCC provides similar definitions for other shipping terms that the parties may choose to use.

There are, however, certain problems associated with relying on national legal systems to define the meaning of shipping terms in international commerce. First, the parties may be unaware that different countries define the same shipping terms in a different manner. Continuing the example above, suppose the term "F.O.B." is interpreted differently under Freedonian and South Carolina law. If the sales agreement specifies that South Carolina law governs the contrast, Buyco may not be aware that, under the UCC, Buyco bears the risk of loss during shipment and that Sellco has no obligation to purchase shipping insurance. Buyco might assume that the term F.O.B. is used everywhere in the same way it is used in Freedonia. Unfamiliarity with the way shipping terms are interpreted in foreign laws increases the uncertainty and, therefore, the costs and risks associated with international sales. In addition, if the parties fail to specify which law governs the contract, it may not be clear under which country's law the shipping term will be interpreted. In such cases, if the states whose laws potentially apply differ in their interpretations of shipping terms, the meaning of the shipping term is in doubt. This compounds the uncertainty associated with international sales.

Another potential problem with relying on municipal law for international shipping terms is that national legal systems may define shipping terms in an incomplete manner. UCC Article 2 is an excellent example. Because it was drafted with domestic rather than international commerce in mind, it does not include all of the shipping terms commonly used in international commerce. The UCC, like many local legal systems, contains gaps where important matters, such as which party is responsible for paying customs duties or whether one or the other party must arrange for insurance, would ideally be specified.

3.1 Incoterms

To address these shortcomings, the **International Chamber of Commerce** (**ICC**) has adopted a set of standardized shipping terms for use in international commercial agreements. The ICC is a Paris-based nongovernmental organization that coordinates lobbying for, standard-setting by, and dispute resolution between business firms globally. Its membership includes private business firms from around the world in virtually every industrial and service sector. The ICC's standard shipping terms, known as **Incoterms**, are not a code of law; they are rules that apply only if the parties agree voluntarily to incorporate them into their contract. But parties to international sales very commonly incorporate Incoterms into their agreements to ensure a predictable shipping term that is defined specifically with the problems unique to international sales in mind and that reflects the practical considerations that businesses prefer. The most recent version of Incoterms, adopted in the year 2020, is referred to as **Incoterms 2020** to distinguish it from earlier versions. Thus, in the example above, Sellco and Buyco could have incorporated a reference to Incoterms into their agreement expressly:

Goods to be shipped FOB Port of Charleston (Incoterms 2020) before June 1, 2021.

By specifying that "F.O.B. Charleston" is defined according to Incoterms 2020, the shipping term will be interpreted according to a standard international usage regardless of whether the law of the buyer's or seller's state governs the agreement.

The introduction to Incoterms 2020 explains the policies underlying their adoption.

INTERNATIONAL CHAMBER OF COMMERCE, INCOTERMS® 2020: ICC OFFICIAL RULES FOR THE INTERPRETATION OF TRADE TERMS, ICC Pub. No. 723E

* * *

I. What the Incoterms® rules do

4. The Incoterms® rules explain a set of eleven of the most commonly-used three-letter trade terms * * * reflecting business-to-business practice in contracts for the sale and purchase of goods.

5. The Incoterms® rules describe:

- *Obligations*: Who does what as between seller and buyer, e.g. who organises carriage or insurance of the goods or who obtains shipping documents and export or import licenses;
- *Risk*: Where and when the seller "delivers" the goods, in other words where risk transfers from seller to buyer; and
- *Costs*: Which party is responsible for which costs, for example transport, packaging, loading or unloading costs, and checking or security-related costs.

The Incoterms® rules cover these areas in a set of ten articles, numbered A1/B1 etc., the A articles representing the seller's obligations and the B articles representing the buyer's obligations. * * *

II. What the Incoterms® rules do NOT do

6. The Incoterms® rules are NOT in themselves—and are therefore no substitute for—a contract of sale. They are devised to reflect trade practice for no particular *type* of goods—and for *any*. They can be used as much for the trading of a bulk cargo of iron ore as for five containers of electronic equipment or ten pallets of airfreighted fresh flowers.

7. The Incoterms® rules do NOT deal with the following matters:

- whether there is a contract of sale at all;
- the specifications of the goods sold;
- the time, place, method or currency of payment of the price;
- the remedies which can be sought for breach of the contract of sale;
- most consequences of delay and other breaches in the performance of contractual

obligations;
- the effect of [trade or economic] sanctions [imposed by any government]; * * *
- export or import prohibitions;
- *force majeure* or hardship;
- intellectual property rights; or
- the method, venue, or law of dispute resolution in case of [breach of contract].

Perhaps most importantly, it must be stressed that the Incoterms® rules do NOT deal with the transfer of property/title/ownership of the goods sold.

8. These are matters for which the parties need to make specific provision in their contract of sale. Failure to do so is likely to cause problems later if disputes arise about performance and breach. In essence, the Incoterms® 2020 rules are *not* themselves a contract of sale; they only become *part* of that contract when they are incorporated into a contract which already exists. Neither do the Incoterms® rules provide the law applicable to the contract. There may be legal regimes which apply to the contract, whether international, like the [CISG]; or domestic mandatory law relating, for example, to [consumer] health and safety or the environment.

* * *

There are eleven shipping terms in Incoterms 2020. It would be impractical to try to memorize them all, but it is helpful to consider how three commonly used terms differ in their allocation of risks, responsibilities, and rights between the buyer and seller. The terms we will compare by way of example are **Ex Works**; **Cost, Insurance and Freight**; and **Free on Board**.

EXW—Ex Works

The Ex Works term (also known as "Ex Factory") minimizes the seller's risk and responsibilities by committing the seller to little more than making the goods available for pickup at the seller's premises. The buyer must arrange and pay for carriage from the seller's premises to the buyer's and must ensure that any export license is obtained and customs duties paid. The risk of loss of the goods passes as soon as the seller puts the goods at the buyer's disposal and notifies the buyer. If the goods are damaged while being transferred from the seller's place of business to the purchaser's truck, the purchaser bears the entire risk of loss. Because control over carriage rests with the purchaser, EXW can apply regardless of whether the goods are transported by sea, inland waterway, air, or land.

CIF—Cost, Insurance and Freight

The CIF shipping term imposes far more risks and costs on the seller. The seller is responsible for arranging and paying for the main carriage and shipping insurance to the named port of destination. The seller is also responsible for obtaining any necessary export licenses. The buyer is responsible for picking the goods up at the port and having them delivered to the buyer's premises. The buyer is also responsible for ensuring that the goods clear customs and that any customs duty is paid. The seller assumes the risk of loss until the goods are aboard the ship at the port of shipment, at which point the risk passes to the buyer. Technically, risk of loss passes after the consigned goods are fully loaded onto the vessel. Notice that the risk of loss passes from seller to buyer at the port of shipment, but the seller is responsible for paying for carriage to the port of destination.

FOB—Free on Board

The final shipping term, FOB, falls between EXW and CIF in terms of the allocation of costs, risks, and responsibilities between the seller and buyer. Its terms are presented in detail to give you a sense of a complete definition of an Incoterm.

INTERNATIONAL CHAMBER OF COMMERCE, INCOTERMS® 2020: ICC OFFICIAL RULES FOR THE INTERPRETATION OF TRADE TERMS, ICC Pub. No. 723E

FOB | Free On Board

FOB (insert named port of shipment) Incoterms® 2020

* * *

1. **Delivery and risk**—"Free on Board" means that the seller delivers the goods to the buyer

- on board the vessel
- nominated by the buyer
- at the named port of shipment
- or procures the goods already so delivered.

The risk of loss or damage to the goods transfers when the goods are on board the vessel, and the buyer bears all costs from that moment onwards.

2. **Mode of transport**—This rule is to be used only for sea or inland waterway transport where the parties intend to deliver the goods by placing the goods on board a vessel. Thus, the FOB rule is not appropriate where goods are handed over to the carrier before they are on board the vessel, for example where goods are handed over to a carrier at a container terminal. Where this is the case, parties should consider using the FCA rule rather than the FOB rule. * * *

4. **Export/import clearance**—FOB requires the seller to clear the goods for export, where applicable. However, the seller has no obligation to clear the goods for import or for transit through third countries, to pay any import duty or to carry out any import customs formalities.

A THE SELLER'S OBLIGATIONS

A1 General obligations

The seller must provide the goods and the commercial invoice in conformity with the contract of sale and any other evidence of conformity that may be required by the contract.

Any document provided by the seller may be in paper or electronic form as agreed or, where there is no agreement, as is customary.

A2 Delivery

The seller must deliver the goods either by placing them on board the vessel nominated by the buyer at the loading point, if any, indicated by the buyer at the named port of shipment or by procuring the goods so delivered.

The seller must deliver the goods

1. on the agreed date or
2. at the time within the agreed period notified by the buyer under B10, or
3. if no such time is notified, then at the end of the agreed period and
4. in the manner customary at the port.

If no specific loading point has been indicated by the buyer, the seller may select the point within the named port of shipment that best suits its purpose.

A3 Transfer of risks

The seller bears all risks of loss of or damage to the goods until they have been delivered in accordance with A2, with the exception of loss or damage in the circumstances described in B3.

A4 Carriage

The seller has no obligation to the buyer to make a contract of carriage. However, the seller must provide the buyer, at the buyer's request, risk and cost, with any information in the possession of the seller, including transport-related security requirements, that the buyer needs for arranging carriage. If agreed, the seller must contract for carriage on the usual terms at the buyer's risk and cost.

B THE BUYER'S OBLIGATIONS

B1 General obligations

The buyer must pay the price of the goods as provided in the contract of sale.

Any document to be provided by the buyer may be in paper or electronic form as agreed or, where there is no agreement, as is customary.

B2 Taking delivery

The buyer must take delivery of the goods when they have been delivered under A2.

B3 Transfer of risks

The buyer bears all risks of loss of or damage to the goods from the time they have been delivered under A2. * * *

B4 Carriage

The buyer must contract at its own cost for the carriage of the goods from the named port of shipment, except when the contract of carriage is made by the seller as provided for in A4.

The seller must comply with any transport-related security requirements up to delivery.

A5 Insurance

The seller has no obligation to the buyer to make a contract of insurance. * * *.

B5 Insurance

The buyer has no obligation to the seller to make a contract of insurance.

A6 Delivery/transport document

The seller must provide the buyer, at the seller's cost, with the usual proof that the goods have been delivered in accordance with A2.

Unless such proof is a transport document, the seller must provide assistance to the buyer, at the buyer's request, risk and cost, in obtaining a transport document.

B6 Delivery/transport document

The buyer must accept the proof of delivery provided under A6.

A7 Export/import clearance

a) Export clearance. Where applicable, the seller must carry out and pay for all export clearance formalities required by the country of export, such as:

- export licence;
- security clearance for export;
- pre-shipment inspection; and
- any other official authorisation.

b) Assistance with import clearance. Where applicable, the seller must assist the buyer, at the buyer's request, risk and cost, in obtaining any documents and/or information related to all transit/import clearance formalities, including security requirements and pre-shipment inspection, needed by any country of transit or the country of import.

B7 Export/import clearance

a) Assistance with export clearance. Where applicable, the buyer must assist the seller at the seller's request, risk and cost in obtaining any documents and/or information related to all export clearance formalities, including security requirements and pre-shipment inspection, needed by the country of export.

b) Import clearance. Where applicable, the buyer must carry out and pay for all formalities required by any country of transit and the country of import, such as:

- import licence and any licence required for transit;
- security clearance for import and any transit;
- pre-shipment inspection; and
- any other official authorisation.

A8 Checking/packaging/marking

The seller must pay the costs of those checking operations (such as checking quality, measuring, weighing, counting) that are necessary for the purpose of delivering the goods in accordance with A2.

B8 Checking/packaging/marking

The buyer has no obligation to the seller.

The seller must, at its own cost, package the goods, unless it is usual for the particular trade to transport the type of goods sold unpackaged. The seller must package and mark the goods in the manner appropriate for their transport, unless the parties have agreed on specific packaging or marking requirements.

A9 Allocation of costs

The seller must pay:

a) all costs relating to the goods until they have been delivered in accordance with A2, other than those payable by the buyer under B9;
b) proof to the buyer under A6 that the goods have been delivered;
c) where applicable, duties, taxes and any other costs related to export clearance under A7(a); and
d) the buyer for all costs and charges related to providing assistance in obtaining documents and information in accordance with B7(a).

B9 Allocation of costs

The buyer must pay:

a) all costs relating to the goods from the time they have been delivered under A2, other than those payable by the seller under A9;
b) the seller for all costs and charges related to providing assistance in obtaining documents and information in accordance with A4, A5, A6 and A7(b); [and]
c) where applicable, duties, taxes and any other costs related to transit or import clearance under B7(b) * * *.

A10 Notices

The seller must give the buyer sufficient notice either that the goods have been delivered in accordance with A2 or that the vessel has failed to take the goods within the time agreed.

B10 Notices

The buyer must give the seller sufficient notice of any transport-related security requirements, the vessel name, loading point and, if any, the selected delivery date within the agreed period.

The completeness of the Incoterms in defining the seller's and purchaser's respective obligations in a very brief reference, evident from the FOB entry above, makes them extremely useful in contract negotiations. Incoterms are accordingly used widely in international and even domestic commerce.

There are ways to divide up the Incoterms to illustrate how they differ and why parties to an international contract might choose one term over another. First, the terms might be organized on the basis of the relative obligations of the seller and the buyer. The terms run the gamut from imposing minimal obligations on the seller and maximal obligations on the buyer (EXW) to the reverse, with maximal obligations allocated to the seller and minimal obligations to the buyer (DDP). The terms may be grouped into four groups based on their starting letter—E, F, C, and D—with the classification of each term depending on the core responsibilities of, and risks assumed by, the seller:

Group E	Departure	
	EXW	Ex Works (... named place)
Group F	**Main carriage unpaid**	
	FCA	Free Carrier (... named place)
	FAS	Free Alongside Ship (... named place of shipment)
	FOB	Free On Board (... named place of shipment)
Group C	**Main carriage paid**	
	CFR	Cost and Freight (... named destination)
	CIF	Cost, Insurance and Freight (... named destination)
	CPT	Carriage Paid To (... named place of destination)
	CIP	Carriage and Insurance Paid To (... named destination)
Group D	**Arrival**	
	DAP	Delivered at Place (... named place)
	DPU	Delivered at Place Unloaded (... named place)
	DDP	Delivered Duty Paid (... named destination)

The second manner of organizing the Incoterms is to separate them into two categories—those used exclusively for shipments made by sea and inland waterways (which are navigable rivers and lakes), and those used for any kind of transportation method, land sea or air. These allow the use of truck, rail, air freight, water freight, or any combination of them. **Multi-modal transport** means transportation of the goods by a combination of two or more transportation methods. Goods carried from a manufacturing plant to a domestic seaport by train, and from there to a foreign seaport by ocean freighter, would qualify as multi-modal. Similarly, goods taken by truck to a river port, and from there floated on a barge for delivery at a downstream port, would qualify as multi-modal. The following chart illustrates the kinds of transport modalities to which each Incoterm applies.

Any mode of transport, including multi-modal

Group E	Departure	
	EXW	Ex Works (... named place)
Group F	**Main Carriage Unpaid**	
	FCA	Free Carrier (... named place)
Group C	**Main Carriage Paid**	
	CPT	Carriage Paid To (... named destination)
	CIP	Carriage and Insurance Paid To (... named destination)

Group D	Arrival	
	DAP	Delivered at Place (... named place)
	DPU	Delivered at Place Unloaded (... named place)
	DDP	Delivered Duty Paid (... named destination)

Maritime and inland waterway transport only

Group F	Main Carriage Unpaid	
	FAS	Free Alongside Ship (... named port of shipment)
	FOB	Free On Board (... named port of shipment)

Group C	Main Carriage Paid	
	CFR	Cost and Freight (... named destination)
	CIF	Cost, Insurance and Freight (... named destination)

You may have observed that Incoterms deal with the transfer of risk of loss, but not with transfer of title to the goods. Usually, these two go hand-in-hand, but, under the Incoterms, the parties to the contract remain free to decide when title transfers independently of when risk of loss transfers. The time and place where transfer of title takes place may be important, but is resolved by the law of the contract, not Incoterms. The place where title transfers may affect, for example, which party is responsible for the importation of goods that infringe any IP in the country of importation, which state has jurisdiction to tax the sale, or which state's law governs the transaction.

3.2 The Shipper-Carrier Legal Relationship

Even if the seller and purchaser have arranged between themselves who is to bear the risk of loss for goods in transit and who is to arrange for insurance, this does not settle the extent to which, if goods are indeed damaged or lost in transit, the carrier is liable to compensate the party bearing the risk of loss. The **cargo carrier** is the company charged with transporting the cargo from the point of shipment to the point of destination. Usually, the carrier is a shipping, air transportation, railway, or trucking company. The **shipper** is the person who puts the goods to be shipped into the charge of the carrier; the shipper is typically the seller of the goods or the seller's freight forwarding agent, but the sale contract may instead provide that the buyer is fully or partly responsible for shipping the goods. The **consignee** is the person who is authorized to receive the goods from the carrier at the conclusion of the carrier's transportation service. The consignee is usually the buyer or the buyer's freight forwarding agent.

The shipper and the carrier enter into the contract for the carriage of the goods. Under the carriage contract, the shipper and carrier agree on such matters as the date and port of cargo loading, the name and registry of the vessel that will carry the goods, the manner in which the shipper will deliver the goods to the named vessel for loading, the date and port of cargo unloading, and the consignee of the goods in the port of unloading. If the carriage contract fails to specify one of these terms, the law governing the contract might supply the missing term. For example, under English law, if a seagoing freight contract does not specify the manner of delivery of the goods to the carrier, it is presumed that the goods will be delivered at the dock alongside the ship and within reach of the dock's loading tackle.

A. Ocean Freight

Upon delivery of the goods to the carrier along with a draft bill of lading, the ship's tally clerks will inspect the goods and note the quantity, weight, and measurements of the packages; the condition of the packaging and goods (including any observable damage); and the date of loading. These details will be recorded on a **mate's receipt**, which the carrier will then issue to the shipper as an acknowledgment of having received the goods in the condition and on the date described. The mate's receipt is not a document of title to the goods shipped, but it does give the possessor the right to demand a bill of lading. A **bill of lading** *is* a document of title issued by the carrier to the shipper as a receipt to evidence that the carrier has received the merchandise to be shipped. The bill of lading includes the data on the mate's receipt, as well as other pertinent information such as the destination of the goods, the payment terms for freight, and the

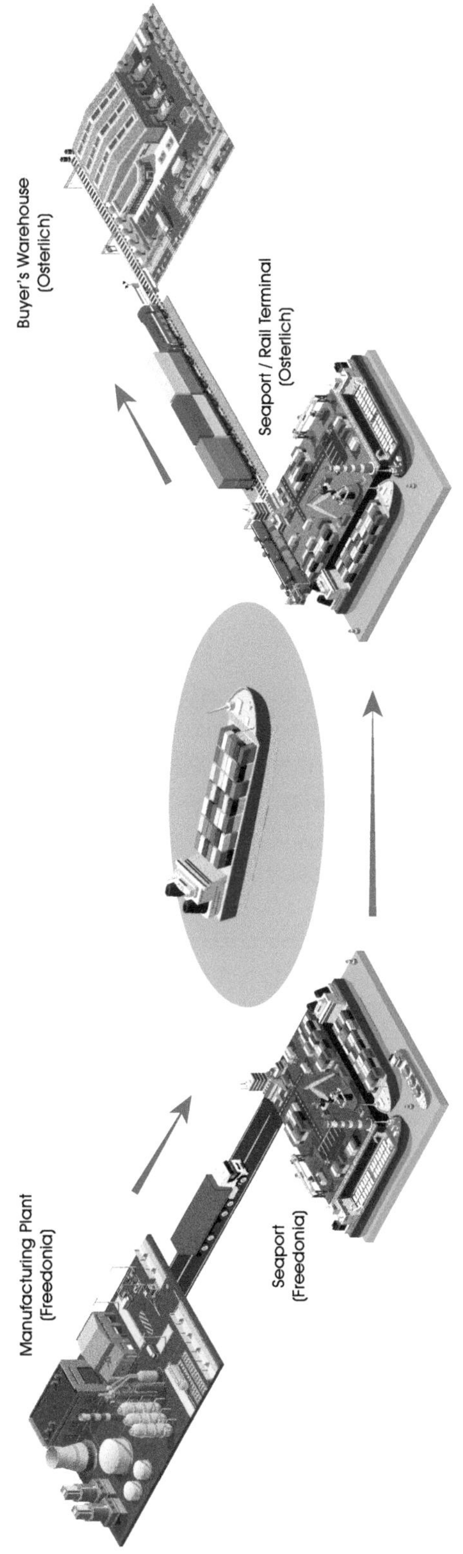

Figure 4.6. Illustration of a shipment conveyed by multimodal transport from a Freedonian factory to an Osterlich warehouse.

condition of the goods or their packaging. Although the carrier need not make more than a superficial inspection of the goods,* it is in the carrier's interest to note on the bill any evident damage to the goods prior to loading. The bill of lading is a key document for use in customs import procedures (see Chapter 5) and an integral part of the payment mechanism in an international sale of goods by virtue of it being evidence of ownership of the goods.

The bill of lading is usually negotiable, meaning that anyone in possession of the bill has the right to take possession of the goods. A bill of lading may be made out as non-negotiable, however. The possessor of a negotiable bill is bound by the terms of the carriage contract and the bill itself. If the bill of lading is issued in electronic format, however, it is typically non-negotiable, meaning that the only person authorized to receive the goods is the consignee named in the bill. Consequently, an electronic bill of lading, unlike a paper bill, is not necessarily a document of title.

The bill of lading may contain terms intended to explain or limit the carrier's liability to the shipper or owner of the goods. To harmonize rules on carrier liability, many states adhere to the **International Convention for the Unification of Certain Rules of Law Relating to Bills of Lading**, better known as the 1924 **Brussels Bills of Lading Convention**. The Brussels Convention was originally adopted by the members of the League of Nations (mostly the states of Europe and the United States, but including a few in Latin America), and was revised in 1968 by a protocol to create what are known as the **Hague-Visby Rules**. The Convention and Rules establish the minimum information required on bills of lading and specify their legal effects, as well as the rules on carrier liability for international sea transport.

INTERNATIONAL CONVENTION FOR THE UNIFICATION OF CERTAIN RULES OF LAW RELATING TO BILLS OF LADING

Signed at Brussels, Aug. 25, 1924; Entered into force June 2, 1931
As amended by the Brussels Protocol of 1968

[The parties:]

HAVING RECOGNIZED the utility of fixing by agreement certain uniform rules of law relating to bills of lading,

HAVE DECIDED to conclude a convention with this object and have appointed the following Plenipotentiaries: * * * who, duly authorized thereto, have agreed as follows:

---

*When the shipper or the shipper's agent has packed the goods, the carrier will examine the packaging but will not open the packaging to examine the goods. In such cases, the carrier will note "FCL" or "Full Container Load" on the bill to indicate that the goods were received on board the vessel prepackaged.

Article 1. In this Convention the following words are employed with the meanings set out below:
(a) "Carrier" includes the owner or the charterer [of the shipping vessel] who enters into a contract of carriage with a shipper.
(b) "Contract of carriage" applies only to contracts of carriage covered by a bill of lading or any similar document of title, in so far as such document relates to the carriage of goods by sea * * *. * * *
(e) "Carriage of goods" covers the period from the time when the goods are loaded on to the time they are discharged from the ship.

Article 2. Subject to the provisions of Article 6, under every contract of carriage of goods by sea the carrier, in relation to the loading, handling, stowage, carriage, custody, care and discharge of such goods, shall be subject to the responsibilities and liabilities, and entitled to the rights and immunities hereinafter set forth.

Article 3.
1. The carrier shall be bound before and at the beginning of the voyage to exercise due diligence to:
   (a) Make the ship seaworthy.
   (b) Properly man, equip and supply the ship.
   (c) Make the holds, refrigerating and cool chambers, and all other parts of the ship in which goods are carried, fit and safe for their reception, carriage and preservation.
2. Subject to the provisions of Article 4, the carrier shall properly and carefully load, handle, stow, carry, keep, care for, and discharge the goods carried.
3. After receiving the goods into his charge the carrier or the master or agent of the carrier shall, on demand of the shipper, issue to the shipper a bill of lading showing among other things:
   (a) The leading marks necessary for identification of the goods as the same are furnished in writing by the shipper before the loading of such goods starts, provided such marks are stamped or otherwise shown clearly upon the goods if uncovered, or on the cases or coverings in which such goods are contained, in such a manner as should ordinarily remain legible until the end of the voyage.
   (b) Either the number of packages or pieces, or the quantity, or weight, as the case may be, as furnished in writing by the shipper.
   (c) The apparent order and condition of the goods.

Provided that no carrier, master or agent of the carrier shall be bound to state or show in the bill of lading any marks, number, quantity, or weight which he has reasonable ground for suspecting not accurately to represent the goods actually received, or which he has had no reasonable means of checking.
4. Such a bill of lading shall be *prima facie* evidence of the receipt by the carrier of the goods as therein described in accordance with paragraph 3(a), (b) and (c).
5. The shipper shall be deemed to have guaranteed to the carrier the accuracy at the time of shipment of the marks, number, quantity and weight, as furnished by him, and the shipper shall indemnify the carrier against all loss, damages and expenses arising or resulting from inaccuracies in such particulars. The right of the carrier to such indemnity shall in no way limit his responsibility and liability under the contract of

carriage to any person other than the shipper.

6. Unless notice of loss or damage and the general nature of such loss or damage be given in writing to the carrier or his agent at the port of discharge before or at the time of the removal of the goods into the custody of the person entitled to delivery thereof under the contract of carriage, or, if the loss or damage be not apparent, within three days, such removal shall be *prima facie* evidence of the delivery by the carrier of the goods as described in the bill of lading. If the loss or damage is not apparent, the notice must be given within three days of the delivery of the goods. The notice in writing need not be given if the state of the goods has, at the time of their receipt, been the subject of joint survey or inspection. In any event the carrier and the ship shall be discharged from all liability in respect of loss or damage unless suit is brought within one year after delivery of the goods or the date when the goods should have been delivered. * * *

* * *

8. Any clause, covenant, or agreement in a contract of carriage relieving the carrier or the ship from liability for loss or damage to, or in connexion with, goods arising from negligence, fault, or failure in the duties and obligations provided in this Article or lessening such liability otherwise than as provided in this Convention, shall be null and void and of no effect. A benefit of insurance in favour of the carrier or similar clause shall be deemed to be a clause relieving the carrier from liability.

Article 4

1. Neither the carrier nor the ship shall be liable for loss or damage arising or resulting from unseaworthiness unless caused by want of due diligence on the part of the carrier to make the ship seaworthy and to secure that the ship is properly manned, equipped and supplied, and to make the holds, refrigerating and cool chambers and all other parts of the ship in which goods are carried fit and safe for their reception, carriage and preservation in accordance with the provisions of paragraph 1 of Article 3. Whenever loss or damage has resulted from unseaworthiness the burden of proving the exercise of due diligence shall be on the carrier or other person claiming exemption under this Article.

2. Neither the carrier nor the ship shall be responsible for loss or damage arising or resulting from:

(a) Act, neglect, or default of the master, mariner, pilot, or the servants of the carrier in the navigation or in the management of the ship. * * *

[what follows is a list of *forces majeures* beyond the control of the carrier, such as war, natural disasters, quarantine restrictions, insufficiency of packing by the shipper, etc.]

(q) Any other cause arising without the actual fault or privity of the carrier, or without the actual fault or neglect of the agents or servants of the carrier, but the burden of proof shall be on the person claiming the benefit of this exception to show that neither the actual fault or privity of the carrier nor the fault or neglect of the agents or servants of the carrier contributed to the loss or damage.

3. The shipper shall not be responsible for loss or damage sustained by the carrier or the ship arising or resulting from any cause without the act, fault or neglect of the shipper, his agents or his servants.

4. Any deviation in saving or attempting to save life or property at sea or any reasonable deviation shall not be deemed to be an infringement or breach of this Convention or of the contract of carriage, and the carrier shall not be liable for any loss or damage

resulting therefrom.
5. Neither the carrier nor the ship shall in any event be or become liable for any loss or damage to or in connexion with goods in an amount exceeding 100 pounds sterling per package or unit, or the equivalent of that sum in other currency unless the nature and value of such goods have been declared by the shipper before shipment and inserted in the bill of lading. This declaration if embodied in the bill of lading shall be *prima facie* evidence, but shall not be binding or conclusive on the carrier. By agreement between the carrier, master or agent of the carrier and the shipper another maximum amount than that mentioned in this paragraph may be fixed, provided that such maximum shall not be less than the figure above named. Neither the carrier nor the ship shall be responsible in any event for loss or damage to, or in connexion with, goods if the nature or value thereof has been knowingly misstated by the shipper in the bill of lading. * * *

Article 5. A carrier shall be at liberty to surrender in whole or in part all or any of his rights and immunities or to increase any of his responsibilities and obligations under this Convention, provided such surrender or increase shall be embodied in the bill of lading issued to the shipper * * *.

Article 6. [This article allows carriers to enter into contracts with shippers to modify their rights and liabilities only in non-standard conditions that would "reasonably justify a special agreement."]

Article 7. Nothing herein contained shall prevent a carrier or a shipper from entering into any agreement, stipulation, condition, reservation or exemption as to the responsibility and liability of the carrier or the ship for the loss or damage to, or in connexion with, the custody and care and handling of goods prior to the loading on, and subsequent to, the discharge from the ship on which the goods are carried by sea. * * *

Article 10. The provisions of this Convention shall apply to all bills of lading issued in any of the contracting States. * * *

Among the most important provisions of the Hague-Visby Rules are the requirement that the carrier provide a seaworthy vessel and exercise due care for the goods during carriage. The rules provide for exceptions to carrier liability in case of *force majeure* and in certain other cases in which the carrier can show it is not at fault for any loss to the goods, but the general rule of liability rests on the carrier. The Convention has been updated periodically since 1931 with protocols for the modernization of the liability rules.

The Hague-Visby Rules have attracted widespread adherence. It is estimated that some 80% of the world's shipping is done under flag states that adhere to the Brussels Convention. In addition, several major shipping companies have voluntarily incorporated the Hague-Visby Rules into their bills of lading, making them binding by force of contract between the carrier and shipper. Generally, however, the Hague-Visby Rules are treaty provisions and, as such, bind states only rather than private parties. The purpose of the Rules is

Figure 4.7. Dock workers called stevedores, or longshoremen, unload cargo containers from freight vessels using giant gantry cranes that grasp the containers with a "spreader." The spreader lifts the containers over the ship rail and shuttles them to the dock. Ports of Seattle, Washington (above) and Barcelona, Spain (below).

to harmonize state laws, so state parties to the treaty have generally incorporated the rules into their laws through national legislation.

In 1936, soon after the Brussels Convention entered into force, the U.S. Congress implemented it through the **Carriage of Goods by Sea Act** (**COGSA**), 46 U.S.C. app. §§ 1300-15. COGSA provides in Section 1300 that "Every bill of lading or similar document of title which is evidence of a contract for the carriage of goods by sea to or from ports of the United States, in foreign trade, shall have effect subject to the provisions of this chapter." The remainder of its provisions substantially reproduce the 1924 Brussels Convention on Bills of Lading.

In addition, the **Bill of Lading Act**, 49 U.S.C. §§ 80101-116, contains provisions governing the use of bills of lading in domestic and export commerce. It does not apply to shipments of foreign imports into the United States or its territories. Among other things, the Bill of Lading Act:

- defines negotiable and non-negotiable bills of lading;
- provides rules on the negotiation and validity of bills of lading;
- sets forth rules on warranties and liability attaching to a person presenting or transferring a bill of lading to another;
- describes the circumstances under which the carrier must deliver the goods and the carrier's liability for damage to the goods or any variance between the goods delivered and their description on the bill of lading;
- specifies the carrier's liability for misdelivery of the goods to the wrong consignee which, in the case of a negotiable bill of lading, means anyone other than the holder of the negotiable bill;
- explains the consequences of a lost, stolen, or destroyed bill of lading; and
- sets forth criminal penalties for creating a fraudulent bill of lading, altering a bill of lading with fraudulent intent, or presenting a fraudulent bill to a carrier.

The Bill of Lading Act is supplemented by rules limiting the carrier's liability in certain ways and constraining the contract options available to shift and limit liability in other ways. These include rules limiting the liability of the owner of any inland or seagoing vessel, whether of foreign or U.S. registration, for most losses to the vessel's cargo. Such liability is limited to the value of the vessel and its freight, 46 U.S.C. app. § 183(a). In addition, the 1893 **Harter Act**, 46 U.S.C. app. §§ 190-96, includes certain mandatory rules governing bills of lading and liability in international shipping that may not be waived by contract. The key provisions of the Harter Act are the following:

> **§ 190. Stipulations relieving from liability for negligence**
> It shall not be lawful for the manager, agent, master, or owner of any vessel transporting merchandise or property from or between ports of the United

Figure 4.8. On the waterfront. In smaller ports, like Irakleio, Crete (Greece), derrick jib cranes rather than large gantry cranes are used to load and unload cargo.

States and foreign ports to insert in any bill of lading or shipping document any clause, covenant, or agreement whereby it, he, or they shall be relieved from liability for loss or damage arising from negligence, fault, or failure in proper loading, stowage, custody, care, or proper delivery of any and all lawful merchandise or property committed to its or their charge. Any and all words or clauses of such import inserted in bills of lading or shipping receipts shall be null and void and of no effect.

§ 191. Stipulations relieving from exercise of due diligence in equipping vessels

It shall not be lawful for any vessel transporting merchandise or property from or between ports of the United States of America and foreign ports, her owner, master, agent, or manager, to insert in any bill of lading or shipping document any covenant or agreement whereby the obligations of the owner or owners of said vessel to exercise due diligence [to] properly equip, man, provision, and outfit said vessel, and to make said vessel seaworthy and capable of performing her intended voyage, or whereby the obligations of the master, officers, agents, or servants to carefully handle and stow her cargo and to care for and properly deliver same, shall in any wise be lessened, weakened, or avoided.

§ 192. Limitation of liability for errors of navigation, dangers of sea and acts of God

If the owner of any vessel transporting merchandise or property to or from any port in the United States of America shall exercise due diligence to make the said vessel in all respects seaworthy and properly manned, equipped, and supplied, neither the vessel, her owner or owners, agent, or charterers, shall become or be held responsible for damage or loss resulting from faults or errors in navigation or in the management of said vessel nor shall the vessel, her owner or owners, charterers, agent, or master be held liable for losses arising from dangers of the sea or other navigable waters, acts of God, or public enemies, or the inherent defect, quality, or vice of the thing carried, or from insufficiency of package, or seizure under legal process, or for loss resulting from any act or omission of the shipper or owner of the goods, his agent or representative, or from saving or attempting to save life or property at sea, or from any deviation in rendering such service.

Other states (e.g., the U.K.) have either adopted COGSA-like laws and bill of lading acts along similar lines or have simply adopted the Brussels Convention into their national laws (e.g., France and Egypt). In either case, because of the widespread international adherence to the Hague-Visby Rules, the form and use of bills of lading in international commerce has become highly standardized.

As shipping practices have evolved, however, the Hague-Visby Rules have become outdated. The Hague-Visby provisions do not deal with many shipping practices unknown in the 1920s but common today. Beginning in 2002,

Date: **BILL OF LADING** Page 1 of ______

SHIP FROM

Name:
Address:
City/State/Zip:
SID#: FOB: ☐

Bill of Lading Number:________________

BAR CODE SPACE

SHIP TO

Name: Location #:____
Address:
City/State/Zip:
CID#: FOB: ☐

CARRIER NAME: ________________________
Trailer number:
Seal number(s):

SCAC:
Pro number:

BAR CODE SPACE

THIRD PARTY FREIGHT CHARGES BILL TO:

Name:
Address:
City/State/Zip:

Freight Charge Terms: *(freight charges are prepaid unless marked otherwise)*
Prepaid _______ Collect ______ 3rd Party _____

SPECIAL INSTRUCTIONS:

☐ (check box) Master Bill of Lading: with attached underlying Bills of Lading

CUSTOMER ORDER INFORMATION

CUSTOMER ORDER NUMBER	# PKGS	WEIGHT	PALLET/SLIP Y	or N	ADDITIONAL SHIPPER INFO
GRAND TOTAL					

CARRIER INFORMATION

HANDLING UNIT		PACKAGE		WEIGHT	H.M.	COMMODITY DESCRIPTION	LTL ONLY	
QTY	TYPE	QTY	TYPE		(X)	Commodities requiring special or additional care or attention in handing or stowing must be so marked and packaged as to ensure safe transportation with ordinary care *See Section 2(e) of NMFC Item 360*	NMFC #	CLASS
							RECEIVING	
							STAMP SPACE	
						GRAND TOTAL		

Where the rate is dependent on value, shippers are required to state specifically in writing the agreed or declared value of the property as follows

"The agreed or declared value of the property is specifically stated by the shipper to be not exceeding

per

COD Amount: $__________________

Fee Terms: Collect: ☐ Prepaid: ☐
Customer check acceptable: ☐

NOTE Liability Limitation for loss or damage in this shipment may be applicable. See 49 U.S.C. - 14706(c)(1)(A) and (B).

RECEIVED, subject to individually determined rates or contracts that have been agreed upon in writing between the carrier and shipper, if applicable, otherwise to the rates, classifications and rules that have been established by the carrier and are available to the shipper, on request, and to all applicable state and federal regulations

The carrier shall not make delivery of this shipment without payment of freight and all other lawful charges.

______________________________Shipper Signature

SHIPPER SIGNATURE / DATE

This is to certify that the above named materials are properly classified, packaged, marked and labeled, and are in proper condition for transportation according to the applicable regulations of the DOT

Trailer Loaded:
☐ By Shipper
☐ By Driver

Freight Counted:
☐ By Shipper
☐ By Driver/pallets said to contain
☐ By Driver/Pieces

CARRIER SIGNATURE / PICKUP DATE

Carrier acknowledges receipt of packages and required placards. Carrier certifies emergency response information was made available and/or carrier has the DOT emergency response guidebook or equivalent documentation in the vehicle. *Property described above is received in good order, except as noted.*

Figure 4.9. A sample bill of lading form used by an ocean carrier. Today, electronic bills of lading are becoming common.

UNCITRAL parties negotiated a new update to maritime carriage rules. The **United Nations Convention on Contracts for the International Carriage of Goods Wholly or Partly by Sea**, also known as the **Rotterdam Rules**, was opened for signature in 2009 in the Netherlands. The Rotterdam Rules expand on and modernize the Hague-Visby Rules by allowing for electronic instead of paper shipping documents (especially electronic bills of lading); providing rules for "door-to-door" carriage contracts that involve multimodal transport; and addressing the now prevalent practices of containerized shipping (much of which is carried on the deck of the vessel rather than in the hold).* The Rotterdam Rules also include more detailed provisions regarding the liability of various parties, delivery and nondelivery, and default rules in case of missing contract provisions. Finally, the Rotterdam Rules include provisions specifying judicial jurisdiction over carriage disputes and providing for arbitration of such disputes. As of 2020, the Rotterdam Rules have not yet entered into force, with only a handful of states having ratified the convention.

B. Air Freight

The terms of freight carriage by air are even more treaty-bound than those for ocean freight. The main treaty governing international air freight was long the **Convention for the Unification of Certain Rules Relating to International Carriage by Air**, 137 U.N.T.S. 11, more commonly known as the **Warsaw Convention**. The Warsaw Convention was initially adopted in 1929 and supplemented or amended in 1955 and again in Montreal in 1999.

The system set up by the Convention creates uniform international rules for the rights, obligations, and liabilities of parties supplying or receiving commercial air service. It accordingly applies to "all international transportation of persons, baggage, or goods performed by aircraft for reward." Art. 1(1). Chapter II, Section III of the Convention deals with air freight documentation. The first requirement of the Convention is that the carrier normally issue an air waybill. *Id.* art. 5. An **air waybill** serves as a receipt to prove when and where shipping occurred, but unlike a maritime bill of lading, it is not a title document for the freight. Air transportation is so fast that a security document like a bill of lading is unnecessary; the shipper is unlikely to resell the goods to a third party while they are in transit. Also unlike a bill of lading, an air waybill is non-negotiable and need not be presented to the carrier to receive the goods. Instead, the carrier may deliver the goods to the designated consignee upon proof of the latter's identity.

An air waybill is made out in sets—one for the carrier, one for the shipper

---

*Under the Hague-Visby Rules, for example, it was unclear whether a carrier who lost a cargo container containing several sub-packages was liable for 100 pounds sterling per container or per package; the Rotterdam Rules clarifies that the relevant unit for calculating liability is the package enumerated in the contract of carriage, and if not, it is the cargo container (art. 59(2)).

Figure 4.10. Air freight being loaded into a commercial freight airplane's cargo bay.

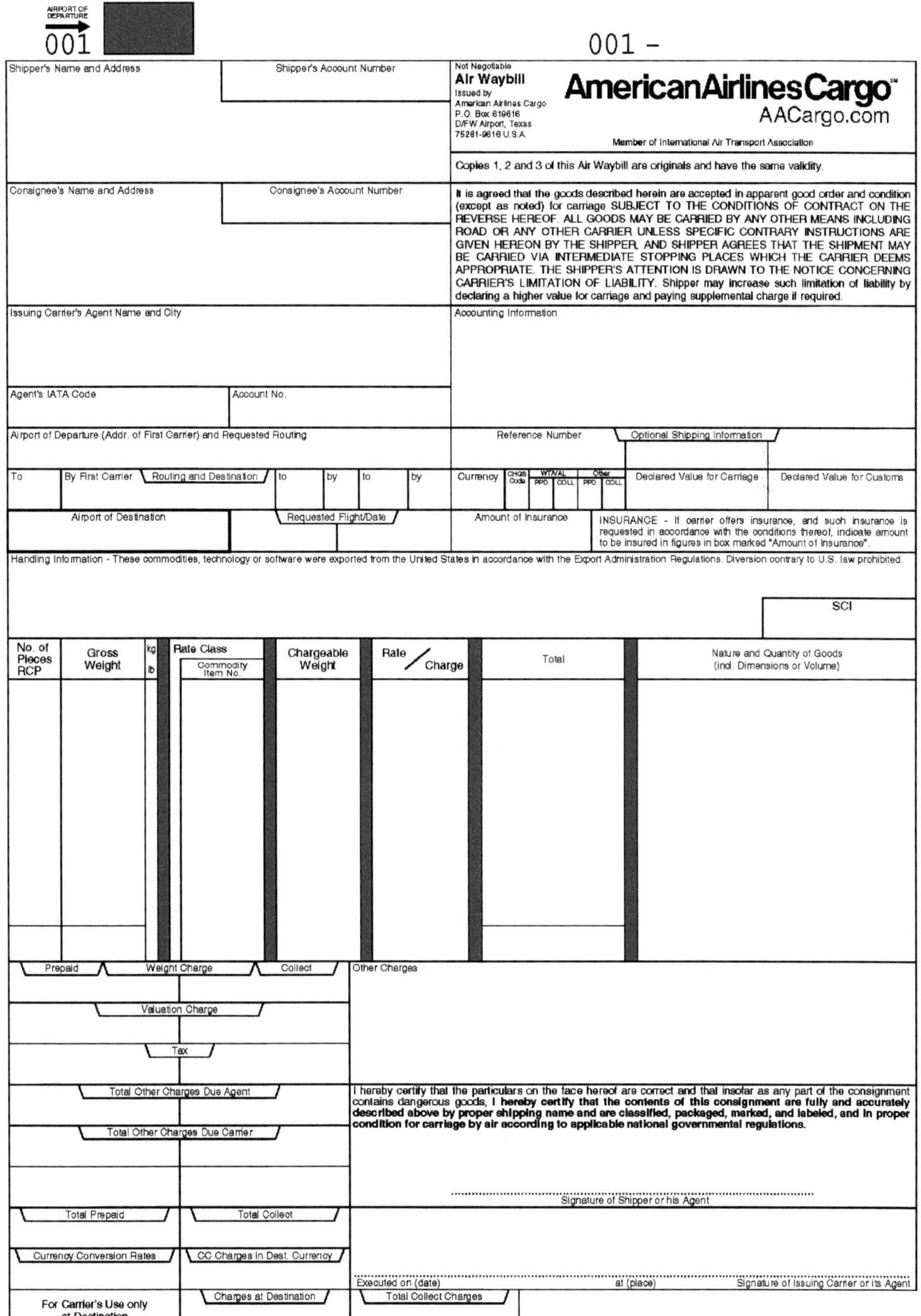

AIRPORT OF DEPARTURE → 001

001 -

Shipper's Name and Address | Shipper's Account Number

Not Negotiable
Air Waybill
Issued by
American Airlines Cargo
P.O. Box 619616
D/FW Airport, Texas
75261-9616 U.S.A.

AmericanAirlinesCargo℠
AACargo.com

Member of International Air Transport Association

Copies 1, 2 and 3 of this Air Waybill are originals and have the same validity.

Consignee's Name and Address | Consignee's Account Number

It is agreed that the goods described herein are accepted in apparent good order and condition (except as noted) for carriage SUBJECT TO THE CONDITIONS OF CONTRACT ON THE REVERSE HEREOF. ALL GOODS MAY BE CARRIED BY ANY OTHER MEANS INCLUDING ROAD OR ANY OTHER CARRIER UNLESS SPECIFIC CONTRARY INSTRUCTIONS ARE GIVEN HEREON BY THE SHIPPER, AND SHIPPER AGREES THAT THE SHIPMENT MAY BE CARRIED VIA INTERMEDIATE STOPPING PLACES WHICH THE CARRIER DEEMS APPROPRIATE. THE SHIPPER'S ATTENTION IS DRAWN TO THE NOTICE CONCERNING CARRIER'S LIMITATION OF LIABILITY. Shipper may increase such limitation of liability by declaring a higher value for carriage and paying supplemental charge if required.

Issuing Carrier's Agent Name and City | Accounting Information

Agent's IATA Code | Account No.

Airport of Departure (Addr. of First Carrier) and Requested Routing | Reference Number | Optional Shipping Information

To | By First Carrier | Routing and Destination | to | by | to | by | Currency | CHGS Code | WT/VAL PPD COLL | Other PPD COLL | Declared Value for Carriage | Declared Value for Customs

Airport of Destination | Requested Flight/Date | Amount of Insurance | INSURANCE - If carrier offers insurance, and such insurance is requested in accordance with the conditions thereof, indicate amount to be insured in figures in box marked "Amount of Insurance".

Handling Information - These commodities, technology or software were exported from the United States in accordance with the Export Administration Regulations. Diversion contrary to U.S. law prohibited.

SCI

No. of Pieces RCP	Gross Weight	kg lb	Rate Class / Commodity Item No.	Chargeable Weight	Rate / Charge	Total	Nature and Quantity of Goods (incl. Dimensions or Volume)

Prepaid | Weight Charge | Collect | Other Charges

Valuation Charge

Tax

Total Other Charges Due Agent

I hereby certify that the particulars on the face hereof are correct and that insofar as any part of the consignment contains dangerous goods, **I hereby certify that the contents of this consignment are fully and accurately described above by proper shipping name and are classified, packaged, marked, and labeled, and in proper condition for carriage by air according to applicable national governmental regulations.**

Total Other Charges Due Carrier

Signature of Shipper or his Agent

Total Prepaid | Total Collect

Currency Conversion Rates | CC Charges in Dest. Currency

Executed on (date) | at (place) | Signature of Issuing Carrier or its Agent

For Carrier's Use only at Destination | Charges at Destination | Total Collect Charges

Figure 4.11. A sample air waybill.

(which in air freight practice is often called the **consignor**), and one for the consignee (usually the purchaser or, if the purchaser has arranged for inland transportation, the purchaser's inland carrier). Usually, a separate air waybill is issued for each package.

The consignor bears primary responsibility for filling in the details on the waybill about the goods shipped, and owes to the carrier a duty to ensure that these details are correct. If the details on the air waybill are inaccurate, causing damage to the carrier or anyone else, the consignor bears the liability. For example, if the consignor understates the weight of the packages shipped, causing the aircraft to emergency land, the consignor must indemnify the carrier, the owners of any other cargo aboard the aircraft, and any third parties or their property harmed by the landing. *Id.* art. 10(1)-(2). The consignor is also fully responsible for ensuring that the goods clear customs at the port of destination. *Id.* art. 16. The carrier, for its part, must deliver the goods as stipulated in the air waybill and any additional carriage contract. *Id.* art. 13(3). The consignee is responsible for inspecting the goods received; acceptance of delivery is treated as *prima facie* evidence that the goods were delivered in proper condition. *Id.* art. 26(1). If damage is not apparent upon immediate inspection, the consignee nevertheless must notify the carrier of the damage discovered in writing within fourteen days of receipt or all claims are waived except in case of fraud. *Id.* art. 26(2)-(4).

Chapter III of the Convention provides rules for the carrier's liability. In general, the carrier is responsible for damage to the cargo only if the damage occurred while the aircraft was airborne or the goods were otherwise "in the charge of the carrier." For example, if the carrier is responsible for loading the goods on board the aircraft, as it frequently is, it assumes liability for any damage that occurs during loading. The carrier is not responsible for damage caused by a defect in the goods themselves, acts of third parties, or damage sustained due to an armed conflict. The carrier is liable for any damages caused by delay in delivery of the goods, unless the carrier took "all necessary measures" to avoid the delay or resulting damage.

Air carrier liability for lost or damaged cargo is not unlimited under the Convention. The Montreal Convention establishes a formula limiting the carrier's liability to a certain amount per kilogram of merchandise shipped (in 2020, about US$ 26.00 per kilogram) unless the consignor pays a supplemental insurance fee. Any term of a contract or air waybill purporting to limit the air carrier's liability below this formula is void.

As of 2020, 152 states and territories adhered to the Warsaw Convention, and 136 states are parties to the more modern rules of the Montreal Convention. Many of these, including the United States, enforce the Convention directly as binding law when cases involving air carrier liability come before their courts.

Figure 4.12. Train yards like this one in Vancouver, Canada, frequently run directly through a major port. Cranes or lifts load the isotainers from the dock onto special train cars designed to hold the isotainers. To save space, isotainers may be stacked two high, as here.

C. Ground Carriage by Rail and Truck

There is no general international convention governing the carriage of goods across national borders by truck, train, or other ground transportation with adherence as universal as that of the Hague-Visby Rules or the Warsaw and Montreal Conventions. Liability and other legal matters are governed by the law governing the carriage contract. In the United States, international carriage of goods by truck or rail is governed by federal law and regulated by the U.S. **Department of Transportation** (**DoT**). 49 U.S.C. § 13501.

As in air and sea carriage contracts, rail carriage contracts disallow the carrier to limit liability except in certain defined ways. Specifically, the parties to a rail carriage agreement may not limit the carrier's liability for lost or damaged cargo below the statutory amount. 49 U.S.C. § 11706(c)(1),(3). In contrast, most federal liability rules in truck cargo transportation contracts are subject to waiver by the parties. *Id.* § 14101(b)(1). The major exception is that a truck cargo carrier's liability may be limited only to maximum amounts that are "reasonable under the circumstances surrounding the transportation," and the filing period for a civil action against either a truck or rail carrier may not be

Figure 4.13. An air cargo isotainer being loaded onto a truck for ground delivery out of Sky Harbor Airport, Phoenix, Arizona.
© 2013 by Aaron X. Fellmeth

limited to less than two years. *Id.* §§ 11706(e) (rail), 14706(c)(1)(A),(e) (truck).

The default rules of ground carrier liability in the United States are broadly worded. Carriers are generally subject to liability to any injured party for the failure to observe federal transportation law or the DoT regulations. *Id.* §§ 11704(a) (rail), 14704(a)(2) (truck). Carriers and freight forwarders must issue a waybill to the consignor for property received and maintain liability for any actual damage to the property. *Id.* §§ 11706(a) (rail), 14706(a)(1) (truck). An aggrieved consignor or consignee must commence any action for damages against the carrier within two years for truck cargo and three years for rail cargo "after the claim accrues," defined as the date of delivery or tender for delivery. *Id.* §§ 11705(a),(g) (rail), 14705(c),(g) (truck).

In Europe, Central Asia, and the Middle East, there are broad treaties establishing cargo carriage rules for ground transportation. The 1956 **Convention on the Contract for the International Carriage of Goods by Road** (known as the **CMR**), 399 U.N.T.S. 189 applies to international road carriage, defined as carriage in which the place where the carrier takes possession of the goods and the place designated for delivery are different countries. The CMR rules apply automatically and cannot be waived by contract. However, matters that are not regulated in the CMR are governed by the state law chosen in the waybill or contract. Truck cargo carriers under the CMR maintain strict liability for loss or damage to their cargo between taking possession of the goods until their delivery. Damage occurring in transit is imputed to the carrier as a matter of law. As in the United States, liability under the CMR is generally limited to actual damages to the goods, plus carriage and other costs.

Much freight is also transported by rail within Europe. There is accordingly a **Convention Concerning International Carriage by Rail** (commonly known as **COTIF**), adopted in 1980 by most states in Europe. Appendix B to the COTIF comprises the **Uniform Rules Concerning the Contract of International Carriage of Goods by Rail** (commonly known as **CIM**), 1397 U.N.T.S. 76. The CIM provisions run parallel to those of the CMR. Most fundamentally, the CIM, like the CMR, regulates cargo traffic between state parties when the state in which the carrier takes possession of the goods is not the state where delivery will occur. In other words, it applies to international carriage only. The CIM rules also parallel those of the CMR in holding the carrier to a standard of strict liability for damage to or loss of the goods, with the usual exceptions. *Id.* art. 23. The CIM does limit the carrier's liability for damage or loss to an arbitrary amount determined by the weight of the goods, unless the parties express agree to a different amount.

3.3 The Role of Carriage Insurance in International Sales

Given the extremely low liability limits that shield cargo carriers under the international treaties discussed here, carriage insurance is usually considered critical in international sales. Many Incoterms accordingly impose an obligation on one of the parties to procure insurance on the carriage of the goods.

Insurance is a form of indemnity. The insurer, also known as an **underwriter**, undertakes to compensate the insured for a loss to specified goods under certain circumstances up to a specified amount. Usually, shippers seek to insure all or nearly all of the value of the goods being shipped. Here, we will focus on insurance in the most common form of international carriage of goods—seagoing freight.

Marine insurers may offer several options for the insurance of international freight. The most common choices are the voyage policy and the time policy. A **voyage policy** insures the freight from one point in a voyage to another. The portion of the voyage covered can include both water and land transportation, and it can cover the goods while awaiting loading onto the transportation vessel or only after loading. A **time policy** insures the goods for a definite period of time, during which they may be in transit from one port to another.

In either case, cargo insurance may cover "all risks" or merely specific, "named perils." An "all risks" policy covers all risks common to the cargo arising from ocean navigation except those specifically excluded in the policy (typically, improper packing, abandonment of cargo, defects in the goods themselves, and similar risks). Once the insured establishes that a loss occurred while the goods were in the carrier's possession, the burden shifts to the insurer to prove that the loss arose from a non-covered cause. An insurance policy covering "named perils," in contrast, protects the insured cargo only against the specific dangers named in the agreement, such as loss by fire or collision. For example, the shipper of a flammable chemical who procures fire insurance will not be covered for damage resulting from the chemical being contaminated with sea-water during ocean carriage. The burden of proving that the cause of the loss was a named peril rests on the insured rather than the insurer.

The shipper may procure insurance directly, or it may delegate the task to its freight forwarder or insurance broker. The shipper or its agent will normally contact an insurer with a reputation for expertise in the specific kind of coverage sought. The shipper will approach the insurer with the basic terms of coverage it seeks in a memorandum of agreement, known as a **slip**. Together, the shipper and insurer will negotiate any amendments to the slip and agree on a premium. The insurer will then initial the agreed slip and state the percentage of risk it is willing to bear; if the amount is less than 100%, the shipper must either bear the risk, or it must seek additional insurance from another insurer. Once the required coverage is reached, the slip is "closed" and the insurer will issue a formal policy in which the terms of the slip will be incorporated into a standard industry insurance form.

The insurer will also issue a **certificate of insurance**, which serves as evidence that the cargo is insured, which the shipper may be contractually required to present to the consignee, as will be discussed below. Although the formal policy may issue some time after the slip is closed, the closed slip itself is generally considered to constitute a binding contract between the agent and insurer. See *Ionides v. Pacific Fire & Marine Ins. Co.*, (1871) L.R., 6 Q.B. 674; (1872) L.R., 7 Q.B. 517 (U.K.).

As a mere risk-spreading tool, insurance of international cargo is not strictly necessary. It is a service provided to exporters and importers that wish to avoid the risk of the goods being lost, damaged, or delayed in transit. These risks are accentuated in international trade because of the greater distances involved in shipment and the greater perils to which the cargo is subjected. Maritime shipping is especially subject to dangers such as fire, leakage, jostling or crushing in extreme weather, collision, pilferage or barratry (embezzlement of cargo by a ship's master or other serious misconduct), piracy, or the need to jettison cargo to avoid the vessel sinking in rough weather.

Insurance for at least some of the damage to goods in transit may be duplicative, because the carrier may be liable for part or all loss to the exporter or importer. But strict limits on the amount of damages collectible from the carrier by law—such as those in the Warsaw Convention, CMR, and CIM—make insurance useful for any loss that exceeds the carrier's legal liability. Moreover, insurance claims tend to be paid more promptly and with less hassle than claims against a carrier, who may resist paying on a claim based on the alleged fault of the shipper or freight forwarder. Insurance either avoids the need for litigation entirely, or at least transfers its burdens to a later time and a third party (the insurer) while allowing the injured party to collect damages immediately. Moreover, the costs of shipping insurance are usually minimal in comparison to the value of the goods and freight costs. In view of these advantages, most business firms engaged in international trade purchase shipping insurance as a matter of course.

International shipping presents particular challenges for insurance companies because of the difficulty of assessing risk in international shipments by any of a tremendous number of freight forwarders, carriers, exporters, and importers, and a variety of risks from extreme weather to theft to civil or international armed conflict. To improve their prospects of assessing risk accurately, an insurer may reserve special rights to itself, especially in ocean freight insurance contracts, such as a right:

- to inspect and approve any ship or dock loading equipment, often at the insured's expense;
- to inspect and approve packing, loading, stowing and securing, and unloading of the goods;
- to approve transportation routing or carriage method (ocean, inland waterway, rail, air, or road) decisions; or
- to stipulate acceptable season or weather criteria for shipping or handling operations.

Needless to say, onerous conditions are much more likely to be imposed in high value shipments than in lower value ones.

There is no detailed treaty or convention that harmonizes national laws governing marine cargo shipping insurance. Instead, each state regulates insurance agreements according to its own national law. A worldwide survey of national laws relating to international shipping insurance is obviously beyond the scope of our subject matter, and in any case is unnecessary; international business lawyers typically delegate insurance matters to a specialist in the applicable national insurance law. Instead, we will here discuss U.S. and U.K. insurance rules—the legal regimes that a U.S. international business lawyer is most likely to confront.

In the United States, there is no general federal contract law; contracts are interpreted according to the applicable state law. International marine cargo insurance contracts differ from other insurance contracts under U.S. law, however. Article III, Section 2 of the U.S. Constitution confers "federal judicial Power" over "all cases of admiralty and maritime jurisdiction." The federal judiciary has accordingly developed a federal law of admiralty that affects the interpretation of insurance contracts respecting sea freight. Although state law governs most aspects of even a maritime insurance contract, see *Wilburn Boat Co. v. Fireman's Fund Ins. Co.*, 348 U.S. 310, 75 S.Ct. 368 (1955), federal admiralty law trumps conflicting state rules of state contract law.* *Calhoun v. Yamaha Motor Corp., U.S.A.*, 40 F.3d 622, 627 (3d Cir. 1994). In contrast, the U.K. has had a unified national marine insurance law—the Marine Insurance Act—since 1906.

Under both U.S. state and U.K. common law, the plain language of the insurance contract will usually govern the relationship between the parties absent some ambiguity. See, e.g., *Shahan v. Shahan*, 988 S.W.2d 529, 535 (Mo. 1999) (en banc). Most states also follow the common law rule of *contra proferentem*, by which ambiguous terms are construed in the manner least favorable to the contract drafter, which is usually the insurer. See, e.g., *Ingersoll Milling Machinery Co. v. M/V Bodena*, 829 F.2d 293, 306 (2d Cir. 1987). Some U.S. state laws mandate the inclusion of specific terms, imply terms into the contract as a matter of law, or prohibit the inclusion of other terms, in insurance contracts. For example, a U.S. state law may provide for punitive damages against an insurer that denies payment in bad faith on a valid claim.

Federal admiralty law, too, may imply terms in the contract. A consequential rule of the admiralty law in both U.S. and U.K. practice that is applicable to marine cargo insurance is the duty of good faith and greatest candor that the insured owes to the insurer, sometimes known by its Latin name ***uberrimae fidei***. As one court explained:

> *Uberrimae fidei* requires that an insured fully and voluntarily disclose to the insurer all facts material to a calculation of the insurance risk. See * * * G. Gilmore & C. Black, *The Law of Admiralty* 62 (2d ed. 1975) ("[T]he highest degree of good faith is exacted of those entering [a marine insurance contract], for the underwriter often has no practicable means of checking on either the accuracy or the sufficiency of the facts furnished him by the assured before the risk is accepted and the premium and conditions set."). The duty to disclose extends to those material facts not directly inquired into by the insurer. See * * * *Cigna Property & Cas. Ins., Co. v. Polaris Pictures Corp.*, 159 F.3d 412, 420 (9th Cir. 1998) ("Whether or not asked, an applicant for marine insurance is bound to reveal every fact within his knowledge that is material to the risk.").
>
> Under *uberrimae fidei*, a material misrepresentation on an application for marine insurance is grounds for voiding the policy. [A] misrepresentation, even if it is a result of "mistake, accident, or forgetfulness, is attended with the rigorous consequences that the policy never attaches and is void." A misrepresentation is material if "it might have a bearing

*Federal courts have applied their admiralty jurisdiction to multimodal carriage contracts covering an ocean shipment discharged at a port and then picked up by inland railway for transportation to a noncoastal destination city. In one case, the Tenth Circuit found that federal courts should exercise admiralty jurisdiction whenever a judicially fashioned admiralty rule could apply or there was a need for uniformity in admiralty practice. *Commercial Union Ins. Co. v. Sea Harvest Seafood Co.*, 251 F.3d 1294, 1299 (10th Cir. 2001).

NOTE FROM THE FIELD

Being an International Commercial Transactions Lawyer

Michael E. Santa Maria
Baker & McKenzie

An international commercial transactions lawyer is both a specialist and a generalist in helping companies expand their businesses into foreign markets. While commercial law has long been a staple of international business, multinational production, trade wars, and other complicating factors make the global sale of products an ever more intricate and demanding process. Modern commercial agreements govern a wide range of transactions, including sales, distribution, agency, IP licensing, franchising, and consulting or other services.

The "generalist" nature of this work relates to helping clients expand their sales of products or services to foreign markets. This requires lawyers to develop expertise in three layers of law, namely, a strong grounding in contract drafting and negotiating; a grounding in the issues of the local law in the foreign jurisdiction that need to be anticipated; and, finally, "cross-border' issues such as transfer pricing, creating a "permanent establishment" for tax purposes, or anticipating treaty-related complications that affect the negotiation of a commercial agreement.

The "specialist" nature of this work is that it is all cross-border, so that you must become an expert on the nuances of each of the above layers of commercial agreements and understand how to anticipate issues in the drafting and negotiating of the agreements in question with regard to your client's specific industry and needs.

The lawyer also needs to understand that some commercial arrangements may touch on multiple and diverse legal issues, such as labor laws, IP laws, and local regulatory laws governing specific business types. For example, the act of entering into a franchise agreement may implicate compliance with foreign laws that require the registration of a franchisor, disclosure of IP licenses, or the delivery of a pre-contractual disclosure document to the prospective franchisees.

This brief summary cannot give a full sense of the varied issues and fields of law relevant in international commerce, but always keep in mind that most lawyers are licensed only in their home country of residence, so an integral part of international commercial practice is consulting lawyers licensed in the relevant foreign states for expert advice on local law.

Michael E. Santa Maria is a principal of Baker & McKenzie, based in Dallas, and a member of the firm's Global Executive Committee.

> on the risk to be assumed by the insurer." * * * *Kilpatrick Marine Piling v. Fireman's Fund Ins. Co.*, 795 F.2d 940 (11th Cir. 1986) (materiality is "that which could possibly influence the mind of a prudent and intelligent insurer in determining whether he would accept the risk").

HIH Marine Services, Inc. v. Fraser, 211 F.3d 1359, 1362-63 (11th Cir. 2000). An insurance policy may become void by either a positive and material misrepresentation or a material omission when there was a duty of disclosure. Both U.S. and U.K. practice agree that an innocent misrepresentation may void the policy if material and relied upon by the insurer. See THOMAS J. SCHOENBAUM & JESSICA L. MCCLELLAN, 2 ADMIRALTY & MAR. LAW § 19-14 (4th ed. 2009).

Another principle implied in marine insurance contracts by both U.K. and U.S. admiralty law is that any warranties by the insured that a specific act will be performed or not performed must be strictly and literally fulfilled by the insured. "There generally is no excuse if the warranty is breached: pleas of due diligence, good faith, and inevitable accident are not admissible. If the warranty is breached, the insurer is discharged." *Id.* § 19-15. Such warranties include any express or implied undertaking by the insured for the benefit of the insurer, such as an undertaking to obtain additional insurance or to package the cargo competently. A breach of the warranty may discharge the insurer of liability to compensate any loss caused by the breach, and in some U.S. cases (but rarely if ever in U.K. cases) losses unrelated to the breach.

4 Payment Options in International Commerce

When you purchase goods or services at a local retail store, you normally have three options for paying the proprietor. You might pay in cash, by personal check, or by credit card. Cash is the most secure form of transaction for the seller.

A check is your promise that your bank will pay the seller the amount printed on the check. When you pay by check, the seller has two options; it must either trust that both you and your bank can and will honor the check, or else it will take steps to verify that your bank account is legitimate and has funds to cover the check by contacting the bank.

A credit card payment is a promise by the credit card company that it will pay the amount charged subject to certain conditions. When you pay by credit card, the seller will already know and trust the card issuer, and can verify electronically that your account is valid during the transaction.

Consider how transporting the payment options into an international setting creates risks and potential problems for the seller. Sales of goods and services in an international setting usually take place at a distance; it is not like the retail purchase in which the seller and purchaser meet at the seller's place of business and exchange goods for cash simultaneously. The distance means either that the seller has to ship its goods or provide its services before receiving payment, or else that the purchaser must pay the seller for the goods or services before receiving them.

If the buyer and seller have no established relationship or special reason to trust each other, they must be careful. How can either know whether, once it has performed its part of the bargain, the other will perform its own part of the bargain? Trust is hazardous in a business relationship unless well founded. Moreover, even if the parties could trust one another, there are risks to transporting cash across borders. The cash could get lost, pilfered, embezzled, or destroyed. Cash payments are, accordingly, extremely rare in legitimate international business.

4.1 Sales on Open Account

When the purchaser and seller have long done business together, or when the purchaser is a company of confirmed reputation for paying its debts, the seller may be willing to arrange an open account with the buyer. An **open account** is an extension of credit by the seller to the purchaser. It means that the seller will bill the buyer later; the invoice must be paid after a certain number of days (often thirty). The purchaser will usually pay by check or **electronic transfer** from the buyer's bank account to the seller's bank account. A seller will only ship goods on an open account basis to purchasers it has sound reason to trust. A purchaser, for its part, will only pay by electronic transfer in advance of shipment if it has sound reason to trust the seller. Because of the minimal financial services required, open account is one of the least costly forms of payment available. Today, with international credit information widely available and the proliferation of established trading relationships, approximately half of all global sales are made on open account.

The advantages of open account and payment by electronic transfer are the very low cost of the payment transaction, the simplicity of the transaction, and the minimal delay between the buyer's payment order and the actual transmission of the funds to the seller. However, such credit and payment arrangements carry a significant risk to the seller. If the purchaser fails to remit payment after the goods ship and the bill of lading is in the purchaser's hands, it will have no recourse to recover what is owed except by the costly, time-consuming, and risky process of litigation.

4.2 The Commercial Letter of Credit

When the goods will be in transit for a significant period of time and the seller and buyer do not have an established relationship of trust, what can the parties do to mitigate such risks? The seller may be justifiably concerned that, after it ships the goods, the purchaser will refuse to pay, either because it becomes insolvent or else by falsely claiming that the goods arrived damaged or are nonconforming. The purchaser, for its part, may not wish to pay before the goods are received for fear that the seller will fail to ship the goods, will ship nonconforming goods, or will divert or transfer the goods to a third party while in transit. There must be some mechanism to effectuate payment at minimal risk to both the seller and purchaser. Bankers have developed just such a mechanism, called a **commercial letter of credit** (**L/C**).

A. How the Letter of Credit Works

The most general description of a commercial letter of credit, also called a documentary letter of credit, is an agreement by a bank or other financial institution on behalf of one party, called the **account party** or **applicant**, to pay another party, called the **beneficiary**, a specific sum of money when certain documents are presented to the bank by the beneficiary. In an international trade context, the account party is usually the buyer or importer of goods, and the beneficiary is usually the seller or exporter of goods. In other words, the buyer's bank agrees to pay the seller (or the seller's bank) if the seller ships the right goods in the right way to the buyer. It is called a "letter" because it takes the form of a notification to the beneficiary that, if it performs certain acts, it will be paid a stated amount. The rationale for such an instrument is that, in an international context, the seller's bank (called the **advising bank**, because it advises the seller when the L/C is opened) is more likely to know whether a foreign bank is trustworthy, or more accurately creditworthy (because banks have established and well known credit reputations), than a private seller. The process is most easily understood if explained step by step.

First, upon conclusion of the sale agreement, the account party (the purchaser) will request a bank, called an **issuing bank** because it issues (or "opens") the L/C, to open a L/C in favor of the beneficiary (the seller). In opening the L/C, the purchaser will give his bank:

- a description of the nature of the transaction;
- the identity of the beneficiary (the seller or exporter);
- the amount to be paid;
- a brief description of the merchandise to be shipped to the purchaser;
- a description of the documents that the beneficiary will need to present in order to obtain payment; and
- an expiration date for the L/C.

The issuing bank does not have all of the details of the underlying sale transaction between the account party and the beneficiary. Most prominently, it will not receive a copy of the sale agreement. This is because the L/C process relates to the presentation of the proper documentation as specified by the purchaser, not to the sale transaction itself. The issuing bank in no way becomes a party to the sale agreement or concerns itself with the terms of the sale agreement.

Once the issuing bank has opened the commercial L/C, it will usually supply the bank of the seller/beneficiary, the advising bank, with a copy of the

ADVICE OF IRREVOCABLE CREDIT
45TH INDUSTRIAL BANK OF NEW ENGLAND
12345 MAIN ST.
NEW HAVEN, CT 06510, U.S.A.

⇦ *seller's bank*

OUR ADVICE NO.: 45IBNE-54321

Issuing bank: ABC Deutsche Industriebank AG
Käthe-Kollwitz Str. 1234, 04109 Leipzig
Germany

⇦ *purchaser's bank*

Issuing date: 23 June 2018

Beneficiary: Euphony of New England, Inc.
1234 E. Haydn Rd.
New Haven, CT 06511, U.S.A.

⇦ *seller*

Account Party: Das Wohltemperierte Clavier AG
Bachstraße 123, 04109 Leipzig, Germany

⇦ *purchaser*

Sir or Madam:

We have been requested by ABC Deutsche Industriebank AG to advise that they have opened with us their irrevocable documentary credit number ABCDI-123456 in your favor in the amount of not exceeding One Hundred Forty-Five Thousand U.S. Dollars (US$145,000.00), to be made available by your request for payment at sight for full invoice value accompanied by the following documents:

1. Signed commercial invoice in three (3) copies indicating the buyer's Purchaser Order No. ABC-123 dated June 2, 2018.
2. Packing list in three (3) copies.
3. Full set clean on board ocean bill of lading, plus two (2) non-negotiable copies, issued to the order of ABC Deutsche Industriebank AG, marked "freight prepaid," dated July 15, 2018, and showing documentary credit number.
4. Insurance policy in duplicate for 110% CIF value covering Institute Cargo Clauses (A), Institute War and Strike Clauses, evidencing that claims are payable in the United States.

Covering: 15,000 Model XYZ-890 electronic metronomes
20,000 Model ZZT-001 electronic tuners

Shipment from New Haven, Connecticut, U.S.A. to Leipzig, Germany
Partial shipment prohibited Transshipment permitted

We confirm this credit and hereby undertake that all drafts drawn under and in conformity with the terms of this credit will be duly honored upon delivery of documents as specified, if presented at this office on or before November 30, 2018.

This letter of credit is issued subject to the Uniform Customs and Practice for Documentary Credits, 2007 Revision, ICC Publication No. 600.

By: ______________________

Figure 4.14. Confirmed advice of an irrevocable commercial letter of credit.

L/C, which looks like the document in Figure 4.14. The issuing bank may also request that the advising bank confirm that the advising bank will honor the letter of credit as well. In such cases, the L/C is called a **confirmed letter of credit**. Next, the advising bank informs its client, the beneficiary, about the L/C and its terms. The advising bank also lacks any information about or involvement in the underlying sale transaction. The advising bank deals only with the issuing bank; it takes its instructions from the beneficiary and issuing bank and never communicates directly with the purchaser.

The seller/beneficiary will review the terms of the L/C as represented in its bank's advice letter and, if it agrees that the payment terms conform to what the parties negotiated, it will arrange a transportation company, or cargo **carrier**, and consign the goods to the carrier for delivery to the purchaser by water, air, train, or truck. The seller may arrange shipping with a carrier directly, or more commonly it will use a **freight forwarder**, to make shipping and delivery arrangements. Freight forwarders usually have a relationship with a **customs broker** to assist in clearing foreign customs; with carriers; and with insurers. They assist the seller in all of the logistics involved in packing the goods to be exported; arranging cargo space on the freighter, aircraft, train, or truck; negotiating fees with carriers and insurance companies; preparing and reviewing documentation; and determining the shipping, insurance, customs, and other costs the exporting seller must pay.*

The shipper will draft, and the carrier will issue and approve, a document called a **bill of lading** (if the shipment will be made by sea) or a **waybill** (if carriage is by airplane) or **consignment note** (if by truck or rail), often prepared with the help of the freight forwarder. You may recall that the bill constitutes evidence that the carrier received, and the seller shipped, the goods specified on the bill, on the date and in the condition specified. The bill states who the exporter is, the name of the vessel on board of which the goods are being shipped; a description of the goods; the date shipped; the ports of shipment and destination; and the consignee or other parties to be notified on arrival of the goods at the port of destination. The bill of lading plays a crucial role in the L/C process, because it must be presented to the carrier by the person accepting delivery of the goods. Unless the purchaser has the bill, the carrier will not deliver the goods to the purchaser. The paper bill of lading is usually negotiable, or **to order**, meaning that anyone presenting the bill of lading to the carrier can accept delivery of the goods. An electronic bill of lading, in contrast,

---

*All U.S. freight forwarders are licensed either by the International Air Transport Association to handle air freight or the Federal Maritime Commission to handle ocean freight. An exporter is ill-advised to rely on the freight forwarder and its customs broker for determining complex questions of export or customs compliance, but sellers do commonly rely on the freight forwarder to ensure that the bill of lading conforms to the terms of the L/C. The shipper must be able to rely upon the freight forwarder to perform its services competently; if the bill of lading does *not* conform to the terms of the L/C, the issuing bank will not pay the seller.

is usually nonnegotiable, or **straight**, meaning that only the consignee named in the bill may take delivery of the goods.

A waybill or consignment note is always straight, and need not necessarily be presented to obtain delivery of the goods. The reason ground and air freight makes do with a waybill or consignment note instead of a bill of lading is that air or ground transportation time is much shorter. This greatly reduces the risk of fraudulent delivery or of the seller reselling the goods in transit and having them delivered to someone other than the rightful consignee at an intermediate port while pocketing payment on the L/C. Instead, the named consignee may take delivery merely by providing proof of identity unless the contract of carriage stipulates that the carrier must procure the waybill or note from the consignee prior to delivery.

To facilitate the use of bills of lading in international commercial transactions, many states adhere to the Hague-Visby Rules. Recall that the Rules harmonize the minimum information that must be included in a bill of lading; provide for the legal effect of a bill of lading as evidence that the carrier has received the goods described on the bill and that the holder of the bill is the presumptive owner of the goods; and specify the period of time during which the recipient of the goods may claim damage by fault of the carrier.

In modern practice, electronic shipping documents are increasingly used in place of paper documents. In such cases, the buyer and seller (or freight forwarder) must agree with the cooperation of the involved banks and carriers to make use of an electronic system for creating, delivering, and verifying the electronic bill of lading. Such systems are maintained by private organizations that charge a fee for the service. Besides making document storage and retrieval more efficient, these systems use digital encryption and digital signatures to further reduce the risk of fraud. It is much more difficult to forge an electronic bill of lading than it is to forge a paper bill of lading.

The parties to the transaction may also choose to incorporate special terms into their agreement to ensure the proper use and acceptance of an electronic bill of lading. An organization called the ***Comité Maritime International*** (**CMI**) has drafted a popular set of rules for electronic shipping documents called the **Rules for Electronic Bills of Lading**. The CMI is a NGO, headquartered in Belgium, that is devoted to unifying national maritime laws and facilitating international maritime commerce. Because CMI is a private organization, the Rules apply only when the parties incorporate them by reference into the contract. The CMI Rules establish standards and procedures to ensure that the electronic bill of lading is not fraudulent or forged (by mandating the use of encryption technology), is legally effective, and actually transmits the required information between the relevant parties.

Once in receipt of the bill of lading and other documents, the seller/beneficiary will take the carrier's bill of lading and other documents required by the letter of credit (such as a commercial invoice, packing list, and certificate of insurance) to the advising bank and present it for inspection. A **commercial invoice** is a nonnegotiable bill issued by the seller to the purchaser requesting payment for the exported goods. The advising bank will review the commercial invoice and other documents to ensure they strictly conform with the requirements of the bill of lading. If there is any discrepancy, the advising bank may reject the documents and refuse to pay the shipper. For example, the L/C will almost always require that the bill of lading be **clean**, meaning that the carrier has not noted any evident damage to the packaging or the goods prior to shipment. If the carrier has noted damage, the bill will be deemed **claused**, in which case the issuing or confirming bank must reject the L/C. But any discrepancy in the documents may suffice to justify rejecting the presentation.

The beneficiary will also present the advising bank with a **time draft**, also known as a **bill of exchange**, which is a negotiable demand for payment from the issuing bank. If all the documents conform to the requirements of the L/C, the advising bank will stamp the draft "accepted" and sign it, then notify the buyer that it has received the conforming documents. The beneficiary is now entitled to payment from the bank on the date specified in the time draft. The advising bank then transmits the documents and the draft to the issuing bank. The issuing bank will, in turn, verify that the documents conform to the terms in the L/C and, if so, it will honor the draft by repaying the advising bank.

The buyer obtains these documents from its bank by paying the amount due to the seller. At this stage, the roles of the banks and the L/C itself end. It is for this reason that the L/C advice letter in Figure 4.14 states: "We * * * undertake that all drafts drawn under and in conformity with the terms of this credit will be duly honored upon delivery of documents as specified * * *." This is the advising bank's way of saying that, if all of the seller's documents conform to the L/C, the advising bank will purchase the draft from the seller, thereby paying the seller, and undertake to collect on the draft from the issuing bank itself.

Finally, when the goods arrive at the place of delivery, the consignee will take delivery. It is at this point that the importance of the bill of lading becomes clear, because the carrier will refuse to deliver the goods to anyone unless that person presents it with its own bill of lading. The consignee must give the conforming bill of lading to the carrier in order to take delivery of the goods. The carrier, for its part, has no legal obligation to inquire as to whether the holder of the bill of lading is legitimately entitled to it, so long as the bill of lading itself is facially valid. In exchange for the bill of lading, the carrier gives the consignee a **delivery order**, which is a document that entitles the holder to demand delivery of the goods either immediately or at some point in the future. At this point, the transaction is complete; the seller has its payment and the purchaser or its agent has the right to take possession of the goods.

The process described above and represented in Figure 4.15 is for a

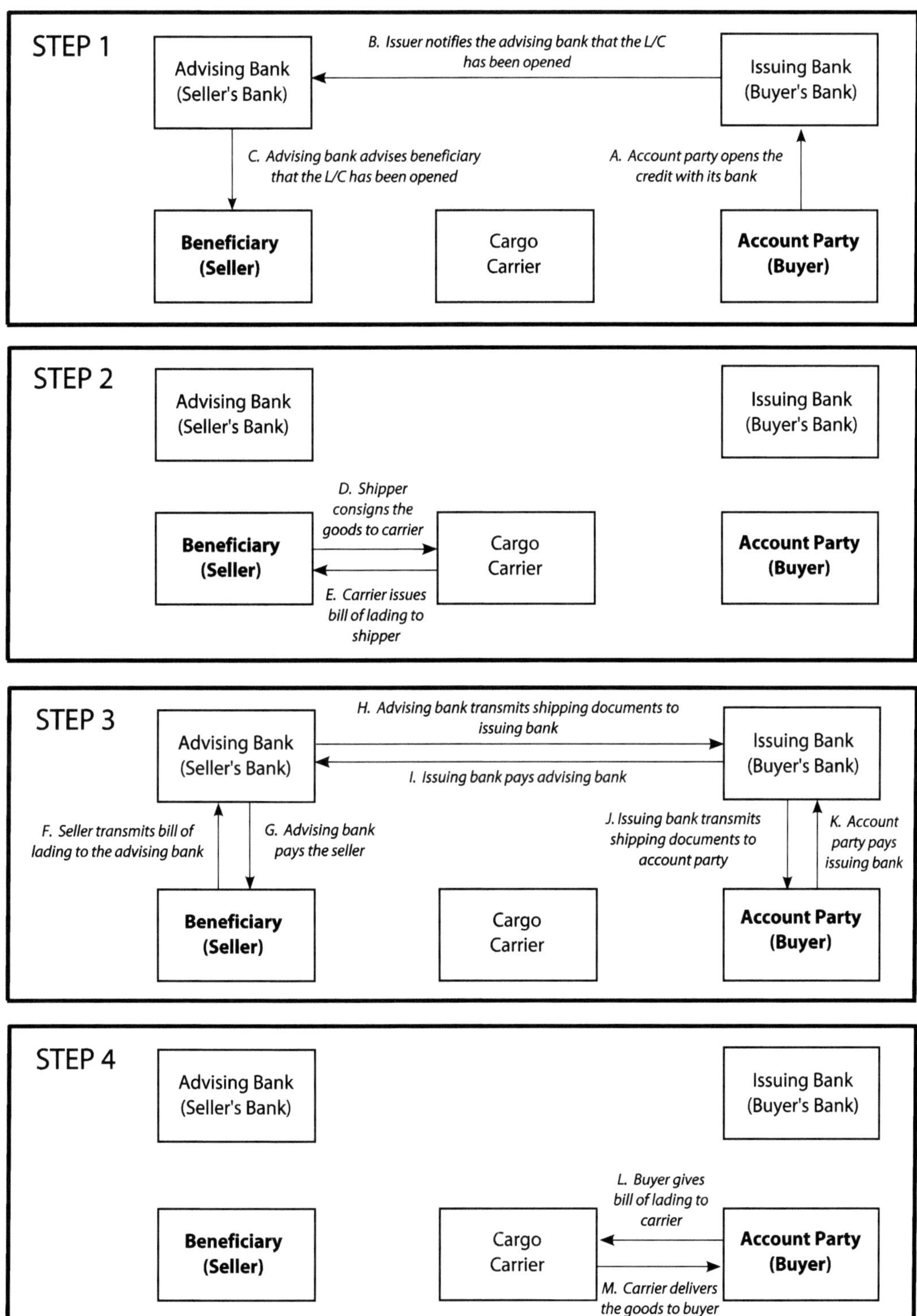

Figure 4.15. The use of a typical confirmed letter of credit.

confirmed letter of credit (hence, the language in the advice letter in Figure 4.14 stating: "We confirm this credit"), in which the seller's bank agrees to act as an intermediary between the seller and the buyer's bank. Confirmed L/Cs are common whenever the seller wishes to deal with a bank in its own country rather than a foreign bank.

It is also possible for the L/C to be **unconfirmed**, in which case all of the seller's interactions are directly with the buyer's bank. If the buyer's bank is sufficiently well known internationally, the seller will usually not require confirmation. In an unconfirmed L/C, the advising bank's only role is to notify the beneficiary that the L/C has been opened in the beneficiary's favor. This simplifies matters and cuts expenses by minimizing the number of banks involved, but it requires that the seller both trust the buyer's bank and find it convenient to transact business in a foreign country.

As the foregoing discussion implies, the L/C has several characteristics that make it extremely appealing in international commercial transactions. First, the bill of exchange and L/C are usually negotiable, meaning that the seller can assign the right to collect on the L/C to its bank or anyone else it nominates. This makes it easier for the seller to deal with a foreign bank, because the seller's own bank will be more capable of dealing with a bank in a foreign country than the seller itself.

Second, the L/C is usually irrevocable, meaning that it cannot be closed or amended without the consent of the seller/beneficiary, the advising bank, and of course the issuing bank. In other words, as long as the bill of lading is presented to the issuing bank before the date on which the L/C expires, the bank must pay on an irrevocable L/C upon proper presentation of the required documents regardless of any objections or opposition by the account party. This preempts the possibility that the issuing bank will revoke the L/C between the time that the seller ships the goods and presents the bill of lading to the issuing bank for payment. Such a possibility would negate all the security that the L/C is supposed to provide!

It is important to remember that the roles of the issuing and advising banks do not include evaluating whether the seller and purchaser have complied with or breached the underlying sale agreement. The sale agreement is a matter entirely between the seller and purchaser. The letter of credit is its own contract, and the banks are solely concerned with whether the seller and purchaser have complied with the terms of the L/C. Thus, if the seller breaches the sale agreement but complies with all of the terms of the L/C, it is entitled to full payment on the L/C, even if the purchaser must later recover for the breach through litigation. Similarly, if the seller complies with substantially all of the terms of the contract and delivers the goods as promised, but fails to comply with all of the terms of the L/C, it is not entitled to draw on the L/C and must instead look to the purchaser for compensation. In other words, if the account party instructs the issuing bank to refuse to pay on nonconforming documents, the bank must comply with the account party's instructions, because the bank will not examine the underlying sales contract and compare it to the beneficiary's performance. A bad faith refusal to pay on a letter of credit may constitute a breach of the purchaser's payment obligation under the sales agreement. This puts the seller in the difficult situation of having to litigate the breach of contract, possibly in a foreign forum, which is precisely what the L/C was designed to avoid. This highlights the importance of ensuring that all of the formalities are observed in the shipping documents and that they conform precisely to the terms of the L/C, but it also protects the banks from being pulled into litigation over contracts in whose drafting they were not involved and in whose subject matter they have no expertise.

The fact that a bill or other required document is nonconforming means that the issuing bank may refuse to honor the L/C. In fact, in practice some 60% to 70% of all letters of credit are initially rejected on the first presentation because of discrepancies between the credit and the presented documents. It does not follow, however, that the account party is relieved of the duty of paying for conforming goods received. Because the L/C is concerned only with documents and not actual performance of the underlying contract, a mere defect in the shipping documents does not mean that the beneficiary has breached the contract. It simply means that the beneficiary is not entitled to payment *on the letter of credit*. In such cases, if the account party is satisfied that the beneficiary has performed the contract (by shipping substantially conforming goods within the time frame contemplated by the contract, for example), the account party can waive discrepancies between the shipping documents and the L/C, causing the issuing bank to pay the beneficiary anyway. If the account party considers the beneficiary to have breached the contract (because the goods are significantly nonconforming or arrived too late, for example), it can refuse to waive the discrepancies. In that case, the obligation of the account party to pay the beneficiary will be settled by negotiation or litigation, to which the banks will not generally be parties.

B. International Standards Governing Letters of Credit

In purely domestic transactions in the United States, the terms and background law governing letters of credit are found in the state law implementation of UCC art. 5, which addresses L/Cs specifically. International documentary credits, in contrast, usually incorporate a different set of rules, as the advice letter in Figure 4.14 does.

To increase the uniformity of international practice relating to commercial L/Cs, the **International Chamber of Commerce** (**ICC**) has established **Uniform Customs and Practice for Documentary Credits** (**UCP 600**). The ICC is a nongovernmental organization whose members are national chambers of commerce, business organizations, and business professionals. The organization serves the role of advocating for international business and promulgating practices for the benefit of multinational enterprises and cross-border trade. One of its functions is to draft rules reflecting standard business-friendly customs that parties can incorporate into their contracts for the sake of simplicity. One of these sets of rules is the UCP 600.

ICC Uniform Customs and Practices for Documentary Credits UCP 600, ICC Pub. No. 600LE

Article 1 - Application of UCP
The [UCP] are rules that apply to any documentary credit ("credit") * * * when the text of the credit expressly indicates that it is subject to these rules. They are binding on all parties thereto unless expressly modified or excluded by the credit.

Article 2 - Definitions
Advising bank means the bank that advises the credit at the request of the issuing bank.
Applicant means the party on whose request the credit is issued. * * *
Beneficiary means the party in whose favour a credit is issued. * * *
Confirmation means a definite undertaking of the confirming bank, in addition to that of the issuing bank, to honour or negotiate a complying presentation. * * *
Credit means any arrangement, however named or described, that is irrevocable and thereby constitutes a definite undertaking of the issuing bank to honour a complying presentation.
Honour means:

a. to pay at sight if the credit is available by sight payment.
b. to incur a deferred payment undertaking and pay at maturity if the credit is available by deferred payment.
c. to accept a bill of exchange ("draft") drawn by the beneficiary and pay at maturity if the credit is available by acceptance.

Issuing bank means the bank that issues a credit at the request of an applicant or on its own behalf.
Negotiation means the purchase by the nominated bank of drafts (drawn on a bank other than the nominated bank) and/or documents under a complying presentation, by advancing or agreeing to advance funds to the beneficiary * * *.
Nominated bank means the bank with which the credit is available or any bank in case of a credit available with any bank.
Presentation means either the delivery of documents under a credit to the issuing bank or nominated bank or the documents so delivered. * * *

Article 3 - Interpretations
* * * A credit is irrevocable even if there is no indication to that effect. * * *

Article 4 - Credits v. Contracts
a. A credit by its nature is a separate transaction from the sale or other contract on which it may be based. Banks are in no way concerned with or bound by such contract, even if any reference whatsoever to it is included in the credit. Consequently, the undertaking of a bank to honour, to negotiate or to fulfil any other obligation under the

credit is not subject to claims or defences by the applicant resulting from its relationships with the issuing bank or the beneficiary.
A beneficiary can in no case avail itself of the contractual relationships existing between banks or between the applicant and the issuing bank.
b. An issuing bank should discourage any attempt by the applicant to include, as an integral part of the credit, copies of the underlying contract, *pro forma* invoice and the like.

Article 5 - Documents v. Goods, Services or Performance
Banks deal with documents and not with goods, services or performance to which the documents may relate.

Article 6 - Availability, Expiry Date and Place for Presentation

* * *

d. **i.** A credit must state an expiry date for presentation.

* * *

Article 7 - Issuing Bank Undertaking
a. Provided that the stipulated documents are presented to the nominated bank or to the issuing bank and that they constitute a complying presentation, the issuing bank must honour if the credit is available by:

i. sight payment, deferred payment or acceptance with the issuing bank;
ii. sight payment with a nominated bank and that nominated bank does not pay;
iii. deferred payment with a nominated bank and that nominated bank does not incur its deferred payment undertaking or, having incurred its deferred payment undertaking, does not pay at maturity; * * *

b. An issuing bank is irrevocably bound to honour as of the time it issues the credit.
c. An issuing bank undertakes to reimburse a nominated bank that has honoured or negotiated a complying presentation and forwarded the documents to the issuing bank.
* * *

Article 8 - Confirming Bank Undertaking
a. Provided that the stipulated documents are presented to the confirming bank or to any other nominated bank and that they constitute a complying presentation, the confirming bank must:

i. honour, if the credit is available by * * * sight payment, deferred payment or acceptance with the confirming bank;
* * *.

b. A confirming bank is irrevocably bound to honour or negotiate as of the time it adds its confirmation to the credit. * * *

Article 9 - Advising of Credits and Amendments
a. A credit and any amendment may be advised to a beneficiary through an advising bank. An advising bank that is not a confirming bank advises the credit and any amendment without any undertaking to honour or negotiate.
b. By advising the credit or amendment, the advising bank signifies that it has satisfied itself as to the apparent authenticity of the credit or amendment and that the advice accurately reflects the terms and conditions of the credit or amendment received. * * *

Article 10 - Amendments
a. Except as otherwise provided in article 38, a credit can neither be amended nor cancelled without the agreement of the issuing bank, the confirming bank, if any, and the beneficiary. * * *

Article 14 - Standard for Examination of Documents
a. A nominated bank acting on its nomination, a confirming bank, if any, and the issuing bank must examine a presentation to determine, on the basis of the documents alone, whether or not the documents appear on their face to constitute a complying presentation.
b. A nominated bank acting on its nomination, a confirming bank, if any, and the issuing bank shall each have a maximum of five banking days following the day of presentation to determine if a presentation is complying. * * *
d. Data in a document, when read in context with the credit, the document itself and international standard banking practice, need not be identical to, but must not conflict with, data in that document, any other stipulated document or the credit.
e. In documents other than the commercial invoice, the description of the goods, service or performance, if stated, may be in general terms not conflicting with their description in the credit. * * *

Article 15 - Complying Presentation
a. When an issuing bank determines that a presentation is complying, it must honour.
b. When a confirming bank determines that a presentation is complying, it must honour or negotiate and forward the documents to the issuing bank. * * *

Article 16 - Discrepant Documents, Waiver and Notice
a. When a nominated bank acting on its nomination, a confirming bank, if any, or the issuing bank determines that a presentation does not comply, it may refuse to honour or negotiate.
b. When an issuing bank determines that a presentation does not comply, it may in its sole judgment approach the applicant for a waiver of the discrepancies. * * *

Article 27 - Clean Transport Document
A bank will only accept a clean transport document. A clean transport document is one bearing no clause or notation expressly declaring a defective condition of the goods or their packing. The word "clean" need not appear on a transport document, even if a credit has a requirement for that transport document to be "clean on board." * * *

Notes and Questions

1. In Articles 18 through 25 and 28, the UCP 600 sets forth standards with which the shipping documents, such as the commercial invoice, bill of lading, or waybill, must comply. These standards include rules about whether the documents must be signed, the extent of precise conformity with the L/C required, and what minimum information must be included on each shipping document.

It is, therefore, important for shippers and carriers to be familiar with the UCP 600 rules when preparing shipping documents; discrepancies may cause the issuing bank to refuse to honor the L/C.

2. The UCP 600 is commonly incorporated into commercial L/Cs by the issuing bank with a reference to the following effect:

> This credit is issued subject to the Uniform Customs and Practice for Documentary Credits (2007 Revision), International Chamber of Commerce Publication No. 600.

As this proviso implies, the UCP is periodically revised and updated to reflect evolving commercial practices. It is important to specify which version of the UCP applies, then, in case the relevant rules have changed between the time of the L/C was opened and the time it is presented for payment.

3. The UCP 600 makes clear that, in issuing or confirming a L/C, the bank assumes no liability for the genuineness, accuracy, sufficiency, or legal effect of any document. Nor does the bank in any way guarantee that the goods being shipped conform to the documents. UCP 600, art. 34. If the beneficiary presents falsified documents, the bank cannot be expected to investigate allegations of fraud; its role is limited to examining the documents and comparing them to what is required by the L/C. Only if the bank can prove fraud or forgery, must it deny payment on the L/C. See, e.g., *United City Merchants (Investments) Ltd. v. Royal Bank of Canada*, [1983] 1 A.C. 168 (U.K.); *Prutscher v. Fidelity Int'l Bank*, 502 F. Supp. 535 (S.D.N.Y. 1980). The bank must have solid proof, however; mere suspicion or even partial evidence will not suffice.

The UCP also exonerates banks from liability for their inability to honor a L/C due to *force majeure*, which include weather catastrophes, riots, war, acts of terrorism, or strikes. UCP 600 art. 36. This provision creates a definite risk for the beneficiary wherever disasters or political instability are likely, because the bank need not honor the L/C if it has expired during the interruption of its business. If the account party has become insolvent or bankrupt during the disruption, or if the court system in the account party's state ceases its regular functioning, the beneficiary may be left without recourse. Wherever such risks are present, exporters typically obtain insurance to guarantee payment in case of *force majeure*.

4. The possibility that a beneficiary, or someone posing as the beneficiary, might present falsified documents poses a definite risk to the applicant/account party that the UCP 600 does not address. Most courts consequently allow the account party who becomes aware of fraud to bring an action to prevent the issuing bank from paying on the L/C. See, e.g., *Mid-America Tire, Inc. v. PTZ Trading Ltd.*, 768 N.E.2d 619, 632-37 (Ohio 2002). In such cases, the account party typically brings the action in the courts of its own state, and this state's domestic law relating to fraud on the letter of credit will usually apply. However, forgery and fraud remain a serious problem, because even if a seller suspects that its bank, or a confirming bank, has been presented with falsified documents, rarely does it have the means to prove the fraud before the bank becomes obligated to honor the presentation.

The UCP 600 does not expressly address the question of whether the issuing bank may give an implied waiver on a nonconforming presentation. Article 16(b) permits an issuing bank to seek a waiver of a nonconforming presentation from the account party, but it does not specify under what circumstances, if any, the bank's own actions may be construed to waive a nonconformity. The following case addresses this question.

BANCO GENERAL RUNIÑAHUI, S.A.
v.
CITIBANK INTERNATIONAL

U.S. Court of Appeals for the 11th Circuit, 1996
97 F.3d 480

BLACK, Circuit Judge:

Appellants Citibank International (Citibank) and Banco General Runiñahui, S.A. (Banco) appeal the district court's entry of summary judgment in favor of R.M. Wade & Co. (Wade), arguing the court improperly concluded Citibank had wrongfully dishonored nonconforming documents Wade presented under the second of two letters of credit issued by Banco in favor of Wade and subsequently confirmed by Citibank. * * *

I. BACKGROUND

Commercial Letter of Credit

The commercial letter of credit is a payment device often used in international trade which permits a buyer in a transaction to substitute its financial integrity with that of a stable credit source, usually a bank. *Alaska Textile Co., Inc. v. Chase Manhattan Bank, N.A.*, 982 F.2d 813, 815 (2d Cir.1992). As described by the Second Circuit:

> In its classic form, the letter of credit is only one of three distinct relationships between three different parties: (1) the underlying contract for the purchase and sale of goods between the buyer ("account party") and the seller ("beneficiary"), with payment to be made through a letter of credit to be issued by the buyer's bank in favor of the seller; (2) the application agreement between the [issuing] bank and the buyer, describing the terms the issuer must incorporate into the credit and establishing how the bank

> is to be reimbursed when it pays the seller under the letter of credit; and (3) the actual letter of credit which is the bank's irrevocable promise to pay the seller-beneficiary when the latter presents certain documents (e.g., documents of title, transport and insurance documents, and commercial invoices) that conform with the terms of the credit.

Id. In some letters of credit, another bank, known as the confirming bank, assumes the same obligations as the issuing bank.

The key to the commercial vitality of the letter of credit is its independence: it is wholly separate and distinct from the underlying contract. When the beneficiary submits documents to the issuing/confirming bank, the bank's only duty is to examine the documents and determine whether they are in accordance with the terms and conditions of the credit. If the bank finds the documents to be conforming, it is then obligated to honor a draft on the credit, independent of the performance of the underlying contract for which the credit was issued.

The Uniform Customs and Practices for Documentary Credits (UCP), first issued in 1930 by the International Chamber of Commerce and revised approximately every ten years since, is a compilation of internationally accepted commercial practices which may be incorporated into the private law of a contract between parties. Although it is not the law, the UCP applies to most letters of credit because issuers typically incorporate it into their credits.

Facts

Wade engages in the business of manufacturing and marketing irrigation products. In September 1991, Ribadalgo Agro Consultores CIA Ltd. (Ribadalgo), Wade's Ecuadorian distributor, entered into a contract with Wade for the purchase of a Wade irrigation system. The parties agreed that a commercial letter of credit governed by the UCP, Int'l Chamber of Commerce Pub. No. 400 (1983 Revision) (UCP 400) would be used to finance Ribadalgo's purchase of the irrigation system from Wade.

First Letter of Credit

On November 14, 1991, Ribadalgo obtained an irrevocable letter of credit from Banco, a banking institution with its principal place of business in Quito, Ecuador. The letter of credit was in the amount of $446,000, and named Wade as the beneficiary. The material terms of the letter of credit were that Wade was to ship certain of the irrigation equipment by December 31, 1991; Wade was to present the request for payment, including all the requisite documents "no later than 15 days after shipment, but within the validity of the credit"; and the letter of credit was valid through January 28, 1992, the expiry date. Citibank, which does business in Miami, Florida, confirmed the letter of credit upon Wade's request after Banco deposited $446,000 cash as collateral.

Wade shipped the goods on December 31, 1991, and subsequently presented the requisite documents to Citibank for payment on January 14, 1992. The documents contained numerous discrepancies, but Citibank honored Wade's request for payment on January 22, 1992, without noting any deficiencies.

Second Letter of Credit

In April 1992, Banco issued another irrevocable letter of credit to Ribadalgo in the amount of $400,000, again naming Wade as the beneficiary. The terms of this letter of credit were that Wade was to ship certain of the irrigation equipment by June 30, 1992; Wade was to present the request for payment, including all the requisite documents "no later than 15 days after shipment, but within the validity of the credit"; the expiry date of the credit was August 4, 1992; and partial shipments were acceptable. After Banco deposited $400,000 cash as collateral, Citibank confirmed the letter of credit. Thereafter, the letter of credit was amended to extend the shipment date to July 30, 1992, and the expiry date to August 21, 1992, and change the port of discharge. All remaining terms were unchanged.

Wade timely shipped a portion of the goods on July 7, 1992. On July 21, 1992, one day before the document presentment deadline, Wade presented the requisite documents to Citibank, requesting payment under the terms of the credit for the shipped merchandise. Two days later, on July 23, 1992, Citibank informed Wade that the documents submitted contained numerous discrepancies and that it therefore would not honor Wade's request for payment. In response, Wade forwarded amended documents to Citibank on July 24, 1992, and July 27, 1992. Although Citibank conceded the documents as amended contained no discrepancies, it nevertheless rejected them as untimely because they were not received within 15 days of shipment as required under the terms of the credit.

II. ISSUES PRESENTED

There are three issues raised by the parties in this appeal which merit our consideration: (1) whether Wade is entitled to payment under the second letter of credit because it submitted conforming documents before the expiry date of the credit; (2) whether the district court erred in finding Citibank waived its right to require that Wade submit conforming documents under the second letter of credit; * * *.

III. STANDARD OF REVIEW

We review district court rulings on summary judgment *de novo*, applying the same legal standards that bound the district court in rendering its decision.

IV. DISCUSSION

A. *Document Presentment*

Appellants contend Citibank rightfully dishonored Wade's demand for payment under the second letter of credit because Wade did not submit conforming documents as required under the terms of the credit. The letter of credit provided that documents had to be presented "no later than 15 days after shipment, but within the validity of the credit." It is this provision which is the source of dispute.

This Court has recognized and applied the "strict compliance" standard to requests for payment under commercial letters of credit:

> Under Florida law, letters of credit are subject to a rule of "strict compliance." Documents presented for payment must precisely meet the

> requirements set forth in the credit.... If the documents do not on their face meet the requirements of the credit, the fact that a defect is a mere "technicality" does not matter.

Kerr-McGee Chem. Corp. v. FDIC, 872 F.2d 971, 973 (11th Cir.1989) (citations omitted).

Wade does not challenge the applicability of this standard, but disputes *when* the submitted documents had to be in strict compliance with the terms of the credit. Wade argues the documents did not have to be conforming before the presentment deadline, but only before the expiry date of the credit. Specifically, Wade interprets the phrase "no later than 15 days after shipment, but within the validity of the credit" to mean it was required to initially submit documents "no later than [July 22, 1992]," but that between the presentment deadline and the expiry date of the credit there was a "cure period" during which it could remedy any deficiencies contained in the initial presentment. Since Wade initially submitted its documents within the 15-day presentment period and thereafter cured the discrepancies before the expiry date, it maintains it was entitled to receive payment.[7]

A rule such as that suggested by Wade would reduce the function of the document presentment deadline to a mere benchmark for the initial submission of documents, no matter how discrepant. It would permit beneficiaries to make only half-hearted presentments, forcing banks to waste time reviewing discrepant documents submitted in anticipation of the opportunity to cure defects before the "real deadline," the expiry date. Enabling a beneficiary to enjoy an unrestricted right to cure deficiencies before the expiration of the credit would render the document presentment deadline virtually meaningless and effectively subvert the strict compliance standard.

Moreover, "the terms and conditions of a letter of credit must be strictly adhered to...." *Corporacion de Mercadeo Agricola v. Mellon Bank Int'l*, 608 F.2d 43, 47 (2d Cir.1979), and the terms of the letter of credit in this case made no provision for a "cure period" entitling Wade to limitless attempts at remedying deficiencies until the expiry date. Accordingly, under the terms of the credit in this case, we conclude that conforming documents had to be submitted by the presentment deadline in order to satisfy the strict compliance standard followed in this Circuit. Any right to cure would have arisen only if the documents had been submitted promptly enough to permit bank examination, notification of discrepancies, and a second submission all before the presentment deadline. Since Wade failed to submit conforming documents by the presentment deadline, Citibank was justified in dishonoring Wade's demand for payment.

B. *Waiver*

The district court found that although Citibank had a right to demand conforming documents in strict compliance with the terms of the second letter of credit, it waived its right in this case by its previous one-time acceptance of discrepant documents submitted by Wade under the first letter of credit. We disagree.

---

[7]No court has considered the question of when submitted documents must be in strict compliance with the terms of the credit in the event such terms provide for a document presentment deadline in advance of the expiry date. * * * In this case * * *, the terms of the letter of credit clearly provided for a document presentment deadline in advance of the expiry date.

The text of the UCP does not support the application of common law equitable doctrines such as waiver in letter of credit cases.[9] Although we have observed that "equitable doctrines such as waiver and estoppel apply to these types of [letter of credit] transactions" under the Uniform Commercial Code (UCC), courts have been reluctant to accept claims of waiver in such cases. Against this background, there is no need for us to determine whether common law equitable doctrines such as waiver are applicable under letters of credit governed by the UCP,[13] because even were we to so find, the facts of this case simply would not support a waiver claim.

We conclude that a significant showing would have to be made before parties to a letter of credit governed by the UCP would be found to have waived its express terms, and such a showing has not been made here. It would severely hamper large institutions, dealing in a myriad of complex international transactions, if a single failure to apply the strict compliance standard under a letter of credit were to result in the loss of the right to demand conforming documents in subsequent transactions with the same beneficiary. Citibank's single instance of accepting discrepant documents under the first letter of credit did not extinguish its right to demand conforming documents from Wade under the second letter of credit. * * *

V. CONCLUSION

For the foregoing reasons, we reverse the judgment of the district court in finding Citibank barred from dishonoring Wade's nonconforming presentment under the second letter of credit. In all other respects, we affirm the district court's judgment. We remand the case for further proceedings consistent with this opinion.

Notes and Questions

1. Banco General Runiñahui refused to pay on the letter of credit because, on July 17, 1992, the Ecuadorian government determined that Ribadalgo was involved in the narcotics trade and issued an order freezing all of Ribadalgo's assets. The frozen assets included Ribadalgo's credit line with Banco, and so Banco was forbidden by Ecuadorian law from paying on the letter of credit. Citibank, in order to avoid paying on a letter of credit it could not recover from the issuing bank, broke with its past practice of overlooking minor discrepancies in Wade's presentation. Does this fact change your view about whether Citibank

[9]Indeed, nothing in the UCP obligates or even permits a bank to examine documents presented under a letter of credit in relation to similar documents previously examined under a different letter of credit. Such a practice would undermine the UCP goals of certainty, promptness and finality in the context of an international banking system.

[13]Since courts have been hesitant to find waiver under letters of credit incorporating the UCC, they will be as reluctant, if not more so, to find waiver under letters of credit governed by the UCP. The UCC, which is supplemented by common law equitable doctrines, and the UCP "adopt vastly different approaches" to nonconforming demands. * * *

should have been obligated to honor the belated presentation?

2. Does the court seem receptive to an equitable theory of waiver or estoppel in L/C transactions? What policies of the UCP does the court imply would be undermined by holding a confirming bank to an established practice of honoring a defective presentation?

3. Suppose a bank had accepted dozens of presentations with minor defects from the plaintiff in the past without comment or objection. Would allowing the bank to suddenly require strict conformity serve or disserve the UCP goals of "certainty, promptness and finality" identified by the court? Why?

4. In *J.H. Rayner & Co. v. Hambro's Bank Ltd.*, [1943] K.B. 37 (U.K.), an English court heard a complaint from a shipper who had tendered a bill of lading for "machine-shelled groundnut kernels" when the L/C described the goods as "Coromandel groundnuts," causing the bank to refuse to honor the L/C. Although it was well known in the nut industry that these terms were synonymous (both refer to peanuts), the court exonerated the bank. A banker, the court concluded, could not be expected to know "the customs and customary terms of every one of the thousands of trades for whose dealings he may issue a letter of credit." With the advent of the Internet, does this holding still seem justifiable?

4.3 Planning for Foreign Exchange Risk

An electronic transfer of currency between countries that use the same currency is straightforward. As of 2020, nineteen EU member states have abandoned their national currencies and adopted the euro (€). Between these countries, a seller and purchaser can pay in euros with no need to exchange currencies. Similarly, eight countries use the West African CFA franc, and six use the Central African CFA franc,* so cash sales within these groups of countries can also take place without any complication. Many international sales, however, take place between states using different currencies.

Suppose a U.S. company entered into an agreement with a German company to purchase 5000 automobile engines. The agreement will specify the price for the engines and the currency in which the price is payable. Most obviously, the agreement will specify payment in euros or U.S. dollars. If payment is to be in dollars, the German exporter will probably rely on its bank to

*"CFA" in West Africa stands for *Communauté financière d'Afrique*—African Financial Community. "CFA" in Central Africa stands for *Coopération financière en Afrique centrale*—Financial Cooperation in Central Africa.

convert the dollars into euros for a small fee. If the payment is to be in euros, the U.S. importer bears the burden of arranging and paying for the currency conversion.

Between the time when the parties enter into the contract and the time the payment comes due, the value of the currencies relative to one another may shift. Suppose that, in the foregoing example, when the companies agree upon the sale of engines, they agree that payment will be made in the amount of US$ 5 million. A **foreign exchange** (also called a **forex** or **FX**) rate is the amount of one currency that can be bought with one unit of another currency. If one U.S. dollar can buy 0.6 euros, we say the exchange rate is US$ 1 to € 0.6 (or conversely € 1 to US$ 1.67). In our example, suppose this is the dollar to euro exchange rate at the time of the sale agreement. The German exporter

HOW DO FOREIGN EXCHANGE MARKETS WORK?

Currencies are exchanged on many international financial markets, especially those in New York, London, Tokyo, Frankfurt, Zurich, and Milan. Purchases and sales on the markets are coordinated by computer systems linking the foreign exchange market with banks, brokers, governments, and corporations. Banks and other actors on the exchange market may purchase one currency in exchange for another, for immediate delivery or delivery at some future date. They may also sell or purchase **currency derivatives**, which are financial instruments whose value derives from changes in the value of the underlying currency. The speed and ease with which currency exchanges take place on world markets usually makes acquiring needed currencies very easy. The effect of this market liquidity is that forex rates vary constantly and sometimes significantly. More than one hundred currencies are traded on forex markets, but most currency transactions by far (more than 80% on average in any given day) involve the U.S. dollar. Other common currencies exchanged are the euro, the Japanese yen, the U.K. pound sterling, the Swiss franc, and the Australian dollar. The frequency of trading does not, however, necessarily increase the variability of the currency value. Much trading in the major currencies is attributable to **arbitrage**, which is the practice of buying and selling currencies in different markets to take advantage of small differences in their prices on the markets. For example, if euros are offered at a rate of € 1 to US$ 1.41 on the London market and € 1 to US$ 1.40 on the Frankfurt market, a currency trader might buy euros on the Frankfurt market and trade them for dollars on the London market. It may seem that the resulting profit is not much, but if the trader buys and sells € 10 million in the transaction, it will clear a profit of US$ 100,000 minus fees. Arbitrage ensures that the price of a currency is approximately the same everywhere currency is traded and so contributes to a uniform worldwide exchange rate.

would calculate the sale revenue in euros at € 3 million (5,000,000 x 0.6).

In some cases, currencies are **pegged** or **fixed** to other currencies; for example, the Panamanian currency, the balboa, has been pegged to the U.S. dollar at a 1:1 exchange rate since Panama's independence in 1904. However, such cases are exceptions to the general rule; exchange rates between two currencies typically vary or **float** against each other over time. The change in value of one currency against another is called **exchange rate fluctuation**. When the value of a currency rises relative to other currencies, it is said to **appreciate**. When it falls relative to other currencies, it **depreciates**. Exchange rate fluctuation can be highly unpredictable, and this can affect the profitability of an international sale of goods or services in a way that does not occur in purely domestic sales.

A. What Is Exchange Risk?

Continuing with the example of German engines, suppose that, when payment comes due, the dollar to euro exchange rate has become US$ 1 to € 1. In other words, the dollar rose in value relative to the euro, so that now one dollar is worth one euro instead of € 0.6. Because, in our example, the buyer agreed to pay in U.S. dollars, the German exporter still gets US$ 5 million, but it is now worth € 5 million instead of € 3 million. Because most of the German exporter's expenses (such as labor costs, material inputs, rents, debts) will be payable in euros, this confers a windfall on the German exporter. Its revenues from the sale rose by 40% entirely by serendipity! Moreover, the exchange rate fluctuation cost the U.S. importer no extra, because it paid exactly as many dollars as it expected to pay.

In contrast, suppose alternatively that the U.S. importer had agreed at the time of sale to pay € 3 million instead of US$ 5 million. When the time comes for payment, the importer must purchase euros with its dollars. It had expected to pay US$ 5 million for the € 3 million it needs to pay the exporter. But because one dollar at the time payment is due is now worth one euro instead of only a fraction of a euro, it will only cost US$ 3 million to buy € 3 million instead of the US$ 5 million that it expected to pay. Under this scenario, the windfall goes to the U.S. importer, which saved US$ 2 million by serendipity. The fluctuation in each case is neutral to the other party in the context of the transaction. But the choice of currency in which the purchaser must pay determines which party gets the windfall.

Finally, suppose that the euro, instead of falling against the dollar, rises against the dollar. In this scenario, at the time the price becomes payable to the German exporter, the value of the euro has risen from US$ 1 = € 0.6 to US$ 1 = € 0.4. The dollar now buys fewer euros. If the price is payable in U.S. dollars, the value of the US$ 5 million in euros has fallen to € 2 million. This hurts the German exporter, because it expected to receive the dollar equivalent of € 3 million and is now receiving one-third fewer euros for the same exported

WHY DO EXCHANGE RATES FLUCTUATE?

The most influential factor causing exchange rate fluctuation is the relative international demand for the goods and services of the states whose currencies are being compared. Currencies are traded on international financial markets, just like commodities, such as oil and gold futures, are exchanged. Like other commodities, the price of the currency varies with supply and demand. When the demand for one currency rises relative to the demand for another currency, it alters the exchange rate between the two currencies.

For example, imagine two states: Farinia and Melaland. Farinia's main export is wheat, which it supplies to Melaland every summer when it ripens. Melaland's main export is apples, which it supplies to Farinia every winter when they ripen. Suppose the exchange rate begins at 1 unit of Farinia currency (the farollar) to 1 unit of Melalander currency (the mela). In the summer, Melaland importers will require fardollars to buy wheat. Demand for fardollars will accordingly increase in summer relative to melas (which Farinians do not need at the moment, because they cannot buy apples yet).

As demand for fardollars rises relative to melas, the exchange rate will increase in favor of fardollars (say, 1 fardollar = 2 melas). As winter comes, however, Farinia stops exporting wheat and starts importing apples from Melaland. Now Farinians demand melas, but Melalanders no longer demand farollars. The exchange rate will accordingly shift in favor of the mela (say, 1 fardollar = 0.5 melas). In the following summer, when the wheat ripens again, the exchange rate can revert to 1 fardollar = 2 melas.

As you can see, the exchange rate can fluctuate back and forth over time. But these changes are not just cyclical. Imagine that, over several years, the Farinians sell more wheat by value to Melalanders than Melalanders sell to Farinians. The exchange rate will gradually shift so that more and more melas are needed to buy one fardollar.

Of course, exchange rate markets are much more complex than this simple illustration suggests, and governments have ways of shifting the exchange rate proactively through manipulating interest rates, printing currency, and by other techniques, but the point is that wheat farmers in Farinia and apple ranchers in Melaland do not control the exchange rate—currency markets and macroeconomic forces do. How exchange rates will vary is usually very difficult to predict accurately, which is why exchange rate risk poses a constant challenge in international business transactions.

engines. On the other hand, if the price is payable in euros, the loss will fall to the importer. The importer must procure € 3 million. At the time of concluding its contract with the seller, it expected those € 3 million to cost US$ 5 million, but now it finds that the same amount of euros costs US$ 7.5 million due to the falling value of the dollar relative to the euro. As the example illustrates, exchange rate fluctuation can not only lead to a windfall to one party; it can also lead to a disastrous loss.

As you can see, the parties to the agreement, in deciding to make the price payable in one currency or another, are effectively wagering that the value of the currencies will rise or fall relative to one another, according to the terms of the agreement. One party may receive an unexpected gain or loss. As the table below should make clear, the benefit of (or loss from) exchange rate fluctuation depends on which currency rises and which currency is payable to the exporter.

The risk that exchange rate fluctuation in the course of an international purchase or sale will result in a loss to the importer or exporter is called, naturally enough, **exchange risk**. Because the exchange risk attendant upon an international sale of goods or services is often difficult to predict accurately, part of planning an international commercial transaction includes coping with exchange risk.

	Exporter's currency appreciates relative to importer's currency	**Importer's currency appreciates relative to exporter's currency**
Price payable in importer's currency	Exporter loses No effect on importer	Exporter gains No effect on importer
Price payable in exporter's currency	No effect on exporter Importer loses	No effect on exporter Importer gains

In the usual case, the price is payable in the exporter's currency (second row), because the exporter pays for its production expenses in its own currency. The importer therefore bears the exchange risk in most commercial transactions.

In international commerce, finance experts have developed several ways to mitigate exchange risk. Here, we will deal with the two most common: forward purchase and currency trading options.

Forward Purchase

One way of eliminating exchange risk is for the purchaser who must pay in a foreign currency to make a **forward purchase** of the currency (also called a **forward exchange contract** or **forward contract**) at the time the underlying sales or service contract is concluded. In a forward purchase, the party buying the foreign currency pays ahead of time and receives delivery of the currency later. The purchaser or seller will then be able to lock in the current exchange rate. If traders on the currency exchange market believe that the currency will appreciate in the future, they might charge a premium on the forward purchase. If they believe that the currency will depreciate in the future, they might give a discount on the forward purchase. In either case, the exchange risk is reduced. A forward exchange contract can provide for the delivery of currency in a few days or, in some cases, up to ten years for long-term projects contracts such as those involved in major construction.

Why doesn't the party needing to make a currency exchange acquire the currency immediately when the contract is concluded? This does sometimes occur, but it is rare for several reasons. First, business firms record their accounts and report their assets to shareholders in local currency. If a large amount of foreign currency must be acquired and held for a significant period of time, the fluctuation in the value of the foreign currency relative to domestic currency

WHAT IS OPPORTUNITY COST?

The concept of **opportunity cost** was introduced in Chapter 1. You may recall that it is the cost of choosing one course of action relative to the benefits that could have accrued, or the expenses avoided, from an alternative course of action. It is a more sophisticated way of understanding the time-value of money and is commonly used in making business decisions. It is therefore crucial that an international business lawyer understand opportunity cost. Two examples will be helpful for explaining the importance of the concept.

First, consider the cost of buying a foreign currency one month before payment actually comes due. For simplicity, assume the exchange rates of the domestic and foreign currency stay stable during that month and that inflation is nonexistent. Further assume that the real interest rate on low-risk investments is 0.5% per month. A business firm that holds onto its currency for a month, doing nothing with it while it waits to use it, sacrifices the 0.5% of its value that it could have earned in interest. The opportunity cost of not investing the currency is therefore at least 0.5% of its value. So, for example, if the amount of currency held is $200,000, then the opportunity cost of holding it is $10,000.

Similarly, suppose a business firm predictably earns a 6% net annual return on its investments. If that firm can delay paying $150,000 in customs duties for one year, then the opportunity cost of paying the duties immediately, as opposed to waiting twelve months, is $9000 ($150,000 x 6%). In short, it is worth $9000 to the firm to take advantage of an opportunity to delay paying duties for a year.

A well-considered legal strategy enables clients to use their funds freely for as long as possible, so that the funds sit idle as little as possible, and are remitted to a creditor or government authority at the latest possible date.

will create administrative and accounting burdens. In addition, it is always risky to keep large amounts of any currency on hand, as it could be stolen or lost. Finally, currency that is not invested earns no returns, and any money (foreign or domestic) that is not currently earning a return is, in an economic sense, a loss to the company. The larger the amount of money at stake and the longer it remains uninvested, the greater the loss to the company holding the currency from lost interest or other opportunity cost.

Currency Trading Options

An alternative for dealing with exchange risk is a **currency trading option**, which is a derivative instrument that can be used as a kind of exchange rate insurance. Some commercial banks allow companies to purchase an option to buy a specified amount of a foreign currency at a predetermined exchange rate during a specified future time period. The company can then exercise the right to purchase the currency if the foreign currency holds its value or rises relative to its own currency, and can decline to use the option if the foreign currency falls against the company's currency. While there is always a fee for purchasing an option, the option locks in an exchange rate that the company can exercise if necessary without being penalized if the foreign currency should fall in value, which may make the option more advantageous than a forward purchase. As a result, fees for currency options tend to be higher than fees for a forward purchase. Options are an important means of hedging exchange risk in large forex transactions.

B. Exchange Rates and Debt Repayment

One key component of planning for exchange risk is understanding in advance exactly when the currency exchange will take place. Because exchange rates fluctuate on a daily basis, this calculation may be complicated by the fact that different states have different rules about which exchange rate is applicable. In most, the rate in effect on the day payment is made is the relevant rate. In others, though, the relevant rate can be the rate in effect on day the debt comes due, the day a judgment for the creditor is entered in a court or by an arbitral tribunal, or some other day. Almost half of all U.S. states have adopted some form of the **Uniform Foreign-Money Claims Act**, a model law drafted by the National Conference of Commissioners of Uniform State Laws. A "foreign-money claim" is a claim based on a debt expressed or measured in a foreign currency. When the creditor seeks to recover the debt, the Act provides guidance on how to determine the applicable exchange rate. As of 2020, twenty U.S. states and the District of Columbia have adopted the Uniform Act.

UNIFORM FOREIGN-MONEY CLAIMS ACT

* * *

SECTION 2. SCOPE.

(a) This [Act] applies only to a foreign-money claim in an action or distribution proceeding.*

(b) This [Act] applies to foreign-money issues even if other law under the conflict of laws rules of this State applies to other issues in the action or distribution proceeding.

SECTION 3. VARIATION BY AGREEMENT.

(a) The effect of this [Act] may be varied by agreement of the parties made before or after commencement of an action or distribution proceeding or the entry of judgment.

(b) Parties to a transaction may agree upon the money to be used in a transaction giving rise to a foreign-money claim and may agree to use different moneys for different aspects of the transaction. Stating the price in a foreign money for one aspect of a transaction does not alone require the use of that money for other aspects of the transaction.

SECTION 4. DETERMINING MONEY OF THE CLAIM.

(a) The money in which the parties to a transaction have agreed that payment is to be made is the proper money of the claim for payment.

(b) If the parties to a transaction have not otherwise agreed, the proper money of the claim, as in each case may be appropriate, is the money:

(1) regularly used between the parties as a matter of usage or course of dealing;

(2) used at the time of a transaction in international trade, by trade usage or common practice, for valuing or settling transactions in the particular commodity or service involved; or

(3) in which the loss is ultimately felt or will be incurred by the party claimant. * * *

SECTION 6. ASSERTING AND DEFENDING FOREIGN-MONEY CLAIM.

(a) A person may assert a claim in a specified foreign money. If a foreign-money claim is not asserted, the claimant makes the claim in United States dollars.

(b) An opposing party may allege and prove that a claim, in whole or in part, is in a different money than that asserted by the claimant.

(c) A person may assert a defense, set-off, recoupment, or counterclaim in any money without regard to the money of other claims.

(d) The determination of the proper money of the claim is a question

*[Coursebook author's note: A "distribution proceeding" is defined in Section 1 of the Act as a judicial or nonjudicial proceeding for the distribution of a fund against which a foreign-money claim is asserted. It thus includes bankruptcy and estate funds.]

Case Study

Currency Hyperinflation in Zimbabwe

Because the material value of currency is nothing more than the paper on which it is printed, inflation of free-floating currencies is potentially limitless. The Republic of Zimbabwe from 2007 until 2009 furnishes a stark example of how far hyperinflation can go.

Zimbabwe's economy is primarily agrarian, and during the 30-year reign of Robert Mugabe (1987-2017), a combination of corruption and incompetent policymaking sent the economy into an abyss. Beginning in the 1990s, Mugabe began arbitrary land redistribution using race, political loyalty, and nepotism as the primary considerations. Agricultural output, the main factor in Zimbabwe's economy, predicably plummeted.

As unemployment rose and exports fell, the Zimbabwean dollar responded. Having no other way to pay its debts, the government began printing vast quantities of currency in 1991. Annual inflation climbed from 17% to 48% that year. By 2007, 80% of the population was unemployed and inflation had reached 66,212%. The following year, inflation reached 500 billion percent. The government soon began mass printing million, then billion, then trillion dollar notes.

In 2009, the government stopped printing currency altogether, and the country switched to using foreign currencies. This ended the inflation, because there was no currency to inflate.

For someone in Zimbabwe who owed a US$ 1000 debt in September 2006, it cost 1 million Zimbabwe dollars to repay the principal that same month. To repay the same amount one year later cost 1.5 billion Zimbabwe dollars, and the year after that, 669 trillion dollars. Clearly, currency conversion was a major issue for any company doing business or having debts in Zimbabwe.

of law.

SECTION 7. JUDGMENTS AND AWARDS ON FOREIGN-MONEY CLAIMS; TIMES OF MONEY CONVERSION; FORM OF JUDGMENT.

(a) Except as provided in subsection (c), a judgment or award on a foreign-money claim must be stated in an amount of the money of the claim.

(b) A judgment or award on a foreign-money claim is payable in that foreign money or, at the option of the debtor, in the amount of United States dollars which will purchase that foreign money on the conversion date at a bank-offered spot rate.

* * *

(d) Each payment in United States dollars must be accepted and credited on a judgment or award on a foreign-money claim in the amount of the foreign money that could be purchased by the dollars at a bank-offered spot rate of exchange at or near the close of business on the conversion date for that payment. * * *

SECTION 14. UNIFORMITY OF APPLICATION AND CONSTRUCTION.

This [Act] shall be applied and construed to effectuate its general purpose to make uniform the law with respect to the subject of this [Act] among states enacting it. * * *

The Uniform Act also provides for unusual or unforeseeable situations, such as when a country revalorizes or begins using new currency in place of an old currency. For example, if Hungary substituted the European Union's "euro" for its current currency, the "forint," a decision would need to be made as to the applicable exchange rate for an existing U.S. judgment on a contract payable in Hungarian forints. The Uniform Act resolves such problems by deferring to the exchange rate adopted by the issuing government (here, Hungary).

The commentary to the Act explains the policies that the drafters hoped to promote:

UNIFORM FOREIGN-MONEY CLAIMS ACT

PREFATORY NOTE

This Act facilitates uniform judicial determination of claims expressed in the money of foreign countries. It requires judgments and arbitration awards in these cases to be entered in the foreign money rather than in United States dollars. The debtor may pay the judgment in dollars on the basis of the rate of exchange prevailing at the time of payment.

A Uniform Act governing foreign-money claims has become desirable because:

> These claims have increased greatly as a result of the growth in international trade.
> Values of foreign moneys as compared to the United States dollar fluctuate more over shorter periods of time than was formerly the case.
> United States jurisdictions treat recoveries on foreign-money claims differently than most of our major trading partners.
> A lack of uniformity among the states in resolving foreign-money claims stimulates forum shopping and creates a lack of certainty in the law.

American courts historically follow one of two different rules in selecting a time during litigation for converting foreign money into United States dollars. These are called the "breach day rule"—the date the money should have been paid—and the "judgment date rule"—when judgment is entered. Many other countries use the "payment day rule"—when the judgment is paid. See *Miliangos v. George Frank (Textiles) Ltd.*, (1976) A.C. 1007 [U.K.]. The merits of this approach have begun to be recognized in this country. The payment day rule is endorsed by this Act.

The three rules produce wildly disparate results in terms of making an injured person whole. This is illustrated by the following example:

> An American citizen (A) owes £18,790 to a British corporation (BCo) suing in New York, and the pound is falling against the dollar. Due to the declining value of the pound, the three rules worked out as follows:

Date	**Rate of Exchange**	**BCo Gets**
Breach day	1£ = $2.20	$41,338
Judgment day	1£ = $1.50	$28.185
Payment day	1£ = $1.20	$22,548

* * * This example is adapted from an actual case. See *Comptex v. LaBow*, 783 F.2d 333 (2d Cir. 1986). The facts are simplified.

If conversion is delayed until the date of actual payment, the creditor is recompensed with its own money or the financial equivalent in United States dollars; the debtor bears the risk of a fall in the debtor's money or reaps the benefit of a rise therein. If conversion is made at breach or judgment date, the risk of fluctuation in value of a money not of its selection falls on the creditor.

The real issue is where the risk of exchange rate fluctuation should be placed. This Act recognizes the right of the parties to agree upon the money that governs their relationship. In the absence of an agreement, the Act adopts the rule of giving the aggrieved party the amount to which it is entitled in its own money or the money in which the loss was suffered. * * *

The payment day rule, on which the Act is based, meets the reasonable expectations of the parties involved. It places the aggrieved party in the position it would have been in [*sic*] financially but for the wrong that gave rise to the claim. States which adopt it will align themselves with most of the major civilized countries of the world.

5 Export Financing

One potential obstacle to international commerce is the foreign buyer's inability to pay for the exported goods or services within the relatively brief time usually allotted for sales on credit or a commercial letter of credit. The need for credit tends to be especially acute when the buyer is located in a developing country or is making a purchase of considerable size. The buyer may be unable to secure financing in the country of importation and, unless the exporter can find a way to assist the buyer, the sale may prove infeasible. The exporter itself may be unwilling to risk extending credit to an unknown buyer or a buyer in a politically or economically volatile country.

5.1 The Ex-Im Bank

The U.S. government has adopted a means of assisting U.S. exporters to sell goods or services in overcoming this problem through the **Export-Import Bank of the United States (Ex-Im Bank**). The Ex-Im Bank is the general export credit agency in the United States. It is an independent federal agency that provides insurance to exporters that extend credit to foreign purchasers. Ex-Im Bank does not itself make loans directly to U.S. exporters or foreign purchasers of U.S. goods. Instead, induces the exporter to offer extended credit to risky foreign purchasers by absorbing the risk of nonpayment by the foreign purchaser for 90% of the value of the loan.

Most loans insured by Ex-Im Bank relate to exports to developing countries, but the Ex-Im Bank provides loan guarantees for exports to almost all countries. Because the Ex-Im Bank's export insurance is intended to assist exporters in short term financing, loans guaranteed by Ex-Im Bank typically have one year or shorter term, but may last as long as three years in some cases. Because the Ex-Im Bank substitutes its own solid creditworthiness for the creditworthiness of the foreign purchaser, the exporter is likely to grant the purchaser credit on favorable terms.

The Ex-Im Bank's insurance covers a variety of commercial risks, including the buyer's insolvency or bankruptcy, and *forces majeures* such as wars or revolutions, ecological disasters, and currency inconvertibility. The Ex-Im Bank may guarantee payment to the exporter when the buyer fails to perform,. The Ex-Im Bank may also insure an unconfirmed letter of credit against the risk that the issuing bank refuses or fails to pay on the commercial credit after the seller performs.

The advantages to an exporter of securing Ex-Im Bank guarantees in this manner are substantial. There is no minimum or maximum transaction amount eligible for coverage, and the Ex-Im Bank will generally guarantee 90% of the credit, including interest as well. The cost of the insurance ranges from 1% to 1.5% of the total loan amount. Finally, Ex-Im Bank pre-qualifies some commercial lenders to allow for expedited processing of the export credit insurance application.

The Ex-Im Bank's export credit insurance is subject to three general requirements:

1. The exporter must be a U.S. national or an organization formed under the laws of a U.S. state.
2. The goods to be exported must have at least 50% U.S. content. If they have less than 50% U.S. content, the Ex-Im Bank may guarantee credit for the value of the U.S. content only.
3. The exports must be shipped from the United States. Credit relating to the exportation of U.S. origin goods being shipped from foreign countries are not covered. In addition, if the exportation involves installation, training, or other services, these must be performed by U.S.-based personnel.

The Ex-Im Bank imposes several other conditions as well. The exporter must have been in business for at least one year and have a positive net worth (in other words, it must not carry more debt than assets). This rule helps reduce the probability that the exporter will default on its debt after the foreign purchaser fails to pay, forcing the Ex-Im Bank to repay the loan itself. In addition, for policy reasons, the Ex-Im Bank will not insure credit for the exportation of military items or exports to most military purchasers, such as foreign defense ministries or armed forces.

An exporter wishing to take advantage of an Ex-Im Bank guarantee may use either of two methods for applying for export credit insurance. If a private commercial lender is pre-approved for Ex-Im Bank credit insurance, it may apply for Ex-Im Bank insurance on behalf of the exporter when the exporter seeks a loan. Alternatively, the exporter may apply directly to the Ex-Im Bank for its preliminary commitment to extend credit to the foreign purchaser.

Other countries have their own governmental banks that perform functions similar to the Ex-Im Bank's. Many Asian states have set up national export-import banks, including Bangladesh, China, India, Malaysia, and Thailand. The rules and credit limits of each bank respecting working capital loan guarantees and export credit insurance vary, but the banks are primarily intended to benefit local companies seeking to export or invest abroad. Like the Ex-Im Bank of the United States, these non-U.S. export-import banks permit loan guarantees only to companies formed under their laws or owned by their nationals.

DO SMALL BUSINESSES ENGAGE IN FOREIGN TRADE?

Given the complexity of exporting from commercial, financial, and regulatory perspectives, it may seem unlikely that small businesses export much. In fact, the reverse is true. In any given year, approximately 230,000 U.S. business firms having fewer than 500 employees export goods. On average, more than 95% of all U.S. exporters are small firms and some 70% of exporters by number are businesses with 20 or fewer employees. Most exportation by value is still attributable to large firms, however. On average, less than one third of U.S. exports by value are attributable to small business firms. Nonetheless, the amount of small business exports by both number and value is significant. From an international trade perspective, small business is big business.

5.2 The U.S. Small Business Administration

The Ex-Im Bank offers especially favorable terms to small businesses having export sales on credit of less than $5 million annually, but it is not the only U.S. government agency that assists small businesses seeking to expand abroad. The **Small Business Administration (SBA)** is an independent federal agency that advises and assists small business firms. The SBA has special programs to assist small businesses seeking to begin or expand exports.

Like the Ex-Im Bank, the SBA provides credit insurance for exporting business firms, but SBA's assistance is limited to independently owned and operated business firms that are not dominant in their field of operation. In its regulations, the SBA defines eligible firms more specifically either by (1) their annual income, (2) their total assets, or (3) the number of individuals employed by the firm. 13 C.F.R. pt. 121. There is no one business size that determines eligibility for SBA assistance; size standards vary according to the industry in which the business firm operates. Generally, a manufacturing firm must have fewer than 500 employees and a wholesaler must have fewer than 100 employees to qualify for assistance.

The SBA's **Export Working Capital Program (EWCP)** provides credit insurance very similar to that provided by Ex-Im Bank. Like the Ex-Im Bank, SBA will guarantee 90% of the value of export credit for one to three years. Also like Ex-Im Bank loan guarantees, the SBA can assist exporters in using accounts receivable, commercial letters of credit, and other soft collateral to guarantee the loan.

However, the SBA is more flexible on several requirements. Most prominently, unlike the Ex-Im Bank, the SBA will provide export credit insurance regardless of whether the exporter is selling U.S.-origin or foreign-origin merchandise. In other words, the SBA has no U.S. content requirement as a precondition to guaranteeing a loan for the exporter. Similarly, the SBA's EWCP does not require that exports be shipped directly from the United States.

Unlike the Ex-Im Bank, the SBA has size limits on the loan amounts that it can guarantee; SBA will only guarantee credit of $1.5 million or less.

Ex-Im Bank and SBA Export Credit Insurance Compared		
	Ex-Im Bank	**SBA**
Eligible exporters	U.S. firms in operation for at least one year	U.S. firms having fewer than 500 production or 100 wholesale employees
Loan term	Usually one year	Usually one year
Maximum loan	No limit	$1.5 million
U.S. content	At least 50% U.S. content	No limitation
Port of shipment	Must ship from a U.S. port	No limitation
Fee	1% to 1.5% of loan amount	0.25% of loan amount

Key Vocabulary

Account party / Applicant
Advising bank
Air waybill
Bill of lading
Bill of Lading Act
Brussels Convention on Bills of Lading
Carriage of Goods at Sea Act (COGSA)
Certificate of insurance
Commission agent
Commissionaire / Factor
Consignee
Consignor
Contract manufacturer
Convention on Contracts for the International Sale of Goods (CISG)
Currency fluctuation / appreciation / depreciation
Currency trading option
Distribution Agreement
Exchange risk
Foreign exchange (FX)
Forward purchase
Freight forwarder
Hague-Visby Rules
Incoterms
International Chamber of Commerce (ICC)
Issuing bank
Letter of credit (L/C)
Multi-modal transport
Opportunity cost
Outsourcing
Sale (purchase) agreement
Uniform Customs and Practice for Documentary Credits (UCP)
Uniform Foreign-Money Claims Act
Warsaw Convention

Practice Exercises

#1 Commercial Production Options

Your client, Phathreds Corp., assembles clothing from imported fabrics in its state of incorporation, South Carolina, and sells it through several U.S. retail stores that it operates. While the Phathreds' clothing lines have become extremely popular, Phathreds has determined that the high cost of labor and strict environmental standards in the United States are rendering it unable to compete with foreign clothing brands, so that it will eventually have to cease production if it does not cut costs significantly.

Given the low customs duties on imported clothing, Phathreds has determined that its best solution is to cut and assemble the clothing abroad for importation into the United States. In addition, it has determined that the cost savings will allow it to begin exploring the possibility of expanding its sales into foreign markets.

Phathreds seeks your advice in response to the following questions:

(a) Phathreds is not yet comfortable investing in establishing its own foreign manufacturing plant. Is there another production option available to it? What are its advantages, disadvantages, and risks?

(b) What are the three most prevalent options for structuring the sale of its clothing line beyond the United States? Explain the advantages and disadvantages of each.

(c) With regard to each option discussed in your answer to (b) above, explain under what circumstances the CISG will apply to the relevant contract.

#2 Arranging the International Sale and Carriage of Goods

Your law firm's longstanding client, Cheatham Daley, Inc. (CDI), is a New Jersey manufacturer of casino equipment such as craps tables, roulette tables, and slot machines. CDI recently received its first international order from a new casino in Egypt, called Ancient Evenings, and has several questions. The casino equipment is heavy and fragile, and CDI is concerned about the costs and risks of ocean shipping, which is the only realistic carriage option.

CDI is also concerned about securing payment. CDI's standard purchase order says nothing about payment on credit, and CDI prefers not to extend credit to Ancient Evenings, which is not a longstanding customer. Ancient Evenings has an account with Crédit Agricole, a well-known bank in Egypt, but Ancient Evenings itself is a new company and its credit risk unknown.

Answer the following questions for CDI:

(a) Ancient Evenings has requested that CDI quote a price for delivery to the port of Cairo. CDI does not object to arranging shipping, but it wants to know whether, by undertaking to arrange and pay for shipping, it will bear the risk of damage or loss in transit. It also wishes to know whether it will be responsible for calculating and paying Egyptian customs duties and complying with any Egyptian import regulations on gambling equipment. What is your advice?

(b) If CDI does assume the risk of loss and the goods are damaged in transit through the fault of the carrier, can CDI recover its loss from the carrier? Under what circumstances and to what extent? If not, what can CDI to protect itself from liability for damage to or loss of the shipment?

(c) What method of payment should CDI request?

#3 Political Instability and Letter of Credit Performance

You represent Universal Bank Corp. (UBC), a commercial bank existing under the laws of New York. A few weeks ago, UBC opened an unconfirmed, irrevocable letter of credit on behalf of account party Clearcutters Unlimited Corp. (CUC), an Oregon-based logging and timber company. CUC had placed an order of industrial chainsaws with a Ruritanian company, Rurisaw, and had agreed in the contract to open an irrevocable, confirmed letter of credit in favor of Rurisaw as beneficiary. Rurisaw is a private company majority owned by the brother of Ruritanian dictator, President Skipjack. By its terms, the letter is payable on presentation to UBC of a bill of lading and certificate of insurance indicating that five hundred "model GPC500" chainsaws have been shipped to CUC at the seaport of Portland, fully insured. The letter is governed by the UCP 600. As of yesterday, the goods had not yet been shipped, but the letter of credit does not expire for another two weeks.

Yesterday, a notoriously corrupt colonel in the Ruritanian army, Col. Bonito, staged a coup and deposed President Skipjack. Skipjack and his family fled from Ruritania, while Col. Bonito proceeded to expropriate and nationalize all of the property of Skipjack and his family, including the shares of Rurisaw.

CUC is concerned that Col. Bonito is likely either to breach the contract or to falsify a bill of lading in order to obtain payment for saws that he never intends to ship. Advise UBC on the following questions:

(a) Explain step-by-step how payment for the shipment of goods is made under a confirmed commercial letter of credit.

(b) Can CUC revoke the letter of credit on the strength of a reasonable belief that Bonito will cause Rurisaw to breach the contract?

(c) If Rurisaw does breach the contract, must UBC pay on the letter of credit, or can it withhold payment pending verification by CUC that conforming goods were received per the contract? Explain your answer.

(d) If Rurisaw does indeed ship goods to CUC, but the bill of lading is materially nonconforming to the terms of the letter of credit, must UBC decline payment on the letter of credit? If not, what alternatives are available to it?

#4 Dealing with Forex Risk

Your client, The Pink Panda, LLC (TPP), owns a chain of U.S. restaurants specializing in Chinese cuisine. TPP has historically purchased the spices for its food from a U.S. grocery supplier, but it has determined that, in the future, it will be more reliable and less costly to procure the spices from a supplier in Indonesia. The Indonesian supplier requires payment in Indonesian rupiah. Unfortunately, the rupiah has been fluctuating wildly against the U.S. dollar recently, and TPP is concerned that it cannot plan its budget with such continued uncertainty about the cost of its spices.

(a) Name two options available to TPP to deal with exchange risk and explain the advantages and disadvantages of each.

(b) Suppose that, after TPP paid in advance for a shipment of spices, the Indonesian supplier sent nonconforming goods. If TPP sued in a U.S. court to recover damages, in what currency will the court require payment of the assessed damages?

Multiple Choice Questions

1. True or false?: "Commissionaire" is just the French term for a commission agent. They are essentially the same thing.

2. In entering into an international distribution agreement with an independent buy-sell distributor, which of the following need the seller *not* consider?

   (a) The defined territory of the distributorship
   (b) The product line to be distributed
   (c) The allocation of product liability risks
   (d) The intellectual property rights licensed to the distributor
   (e) Any mandatory compensation obligations upon termination of the distribution agreement imposed by local law

3. According to the court in *Amco Ukrservice*, for what reason the Convention on Contracts for the International Sale of Goods (CISG) does not govern a product distribution agreement?

   (a) The agreement does not contain a price term.
   (b) The agreement deals with quality control and trademark licensing.
   (c) The agreement governs the relationship between the parties and not specific sales of goods.
   (d) German appellate courts have established a binding precedent that such contracts are not sales agreements under the CISG.
   (e) All of the above.

4. True or false?: The CISG may govern a sales agreement between parties even though only one of them is located in a party that has ratified the CISG.

5. Which of the following does *not* qualify as an international sale of a service?

   (a) An agreement by which an architecture firm in Ruritania will purchase custom-designed 3-D printers from an electronics manufacturer in Freedonia, which it will use for designing skyscrapers to be built all over the world.
   (b) An agreement by which a hospital in Ruritania will temporarily ship its equipment to the country of manufacture, Freedonia, for warranty repairs.
   (c) An agreement by which customer service for a Ruritanian company is outsourced to a call center located in the Freedonia.
   (d) An agreement by which a manufacturer in Ruritania will manufacture widgets to be exported to Freedonia.
   (e) An agreement by which a videographer in the Ruritania will travel to Freedonia to film a documentary about Freedonian wildlife for distribution solely in Freedonia.

6. Incoterms defines the responsibilities of the parties for which of the following aspects of an international shipment of goods?

   I. Paying any customs duties
   II. Opening a letter of credit
   III. Purchasing any shipping insurance
   IV. Packaging the goods safely

   (a) I and II only
   (b) I and III only

(c) II and III only
(d) I and IV only
(e) III and IV only

7. Masco Line is a cargo carrier specializing in container shipping. In January, it entered into a shipping agreement with Smallmart to transport five full cargo containers of bicycles from across the Atlantic Ocean, Zembia to Smalldonia, on a container ship, the MV *Slyjester*. The *Slyjester* was a seaworthy vessel, but unfortunately, the Ship's Master hired two unqualified Deck Officers who had no experience in maritime navigation. During the voyage, the Ship's Master became inebriated and made a navigation planning error, which the Deck Officers failed to notice due to their lack of training. As a result, the *Slyjester* drove toward a shallow reef and, although the Chief Officer eventually noticed the error, the rudder unexpectedly jammed, causing the vessel to strike the reef. The collision caused the vessel to pitch steeply, and three of Smallmart's cargo containers went overboard, resulting in a total loss of their contents.

   Under the Hague-Visby Rules, for which of the following acts could Smallmart invoke Masco's liability?

   (a) Failure to hire a competent crew
   (b) Negligent navigation by the Ship's Master
   (c) Failure to guarantee the vessel remained seaworthy throughout the voyage
   (d) All of the above
   (e) None of the above

8. Which of the following most accurately summarizes the concept of *uberrimae fidei*?

   (a) It obligates a commercial agent to act with the highest standard of fiduciary duty in representing the interest of his principal.
   (b) It obligates a commercial agent to voluntarily inform the principal of any potential conflict of interest between the agent and a prospective purchaser.
   (c) It obligates a shipper to answer in the highest good faith any question regarding risk of cargo loss posed by the insurance underwriter.
   (d) It obligates a shipper to disclose voluntarily to his insurance underwriter any fact the shipper knows that could materially affect the risk to the cargo.

9. A commercial letter of credit is concerned with which of the following?

(a) Performance of the sale agreement.
(b) Presentation of the proper shipping documents.
(c) Performance of the cargo carriage agreement.
(d) Performance of the export credit agreement.
(e) All of the above.

10. Which of the following was a holding of the Eleventh Circuit in *Banco General Runiñahui v. Citibank* regarding the issuer of a documentary credit?

(a) The issuer violates its obligations under the UCP if it honors a nonconforming presentation.
(b) The issuer may never be estopped from rejecting a conforming presentation due to its own past action.
(c) The issuer must accept a conforming presentation if it falls within the validity period of the credit.
(d) The issuer need not accept a conforming presentation even if it falls within the validity period of the credit.
(e) None of the above.

11. True or false?: The global treaty governing international rail transportation that binds the United States and Europe limits the liability of rail carriers to a certain amount of money per kilogram of cargo.

12. Which of the following is a difference between a forward purchase and a currency trading option?

(a) A forward purchase tends to result in higher fees due to the certainty that a currency purchase can be made.
(b) A forward purchase allows the purchaser to bid on a currency and commits the purchaser to buy on the best bid received; a currency trading option requires the purchaser to make an exchange offer at a specified rate to a bank, which has the option of accepting or rejecting the offer.
(c) A forward purchase commits the purchaser to acquire the currency at the agreed exchange rate; a currency trading option allows the purchaser to decline to make the exchange.
(d) A forward purchase reduces exchange risk for the bank; a currency trading option shifts exchange risk to the purchaser.

13. The Uniform Foreign-Money Claims Act establishes which of the following rules for determining the exchange rate for a debt in a foreign currency on which a judgment will be paid in U.S. dollars?

(a) The exchange rate on the date the debt came due.

(b) The exchange rate on the date the judgment was rendered.
(c) The exchange rate on the date the defendant satisfies the judgment.
(d) None of the above. The judge has discretion to determine the exchange rate based on what he or she determines will grant the plaintiff full compensation.

14. True or false?: All U.S. states and the District of Columbia have adopted some form of the Uniform Foreign-Money Claims Act.

Multiple Choice Answers

1. False	5. a	9. b	13. c
2. e	6. b	10. d	14. False
3. c	7. a	11. False	
4. True	8. d	12. c	

Chapter 5

Import and Export Regulation

What You Will Learn in this Chapter

Every state has its own laws and agencies that regulate the importation of goods and sometimes intangibles, such as transfers of technology or money. Many states also have laws and regulatory agencies to control the exportation of certain politically, militarily, environmentally, or culturally sensitive goods, services, and technologies. The global fragmentation of border control measures adds costs, delays, and risk to international sales of goods and services. States tend to take border control measures very seriously for a variety of reasons, which aggravates the risks should a business firm fail to comply. Moreover, because such measures are policy tools, states differ significantly in the kinds of measures they impose, and these measures tend to morph over time in response to changing political exigencies. In short, you will find state regulation of imports and exports to be at once important, highly technical, risk-laden, and protean. Fortunately, both import and export laws have seen a good deal of international harmonization in the past few decades. This homogenization is still incomplete, but it nonetheless has greatly facilitated the transnational movement of goods, services, and information by business firms.

This part of the coursebook deals with two general classes of border regulation. The first is import and customs regulation. Import regulations serve many functions, from helping states control their trade balances to protecting domestic industries from foreign competition to raising revenue by taxing imports. The complexity of these policy goals is usually reflected in the customs regulations themselves. This is an important topic in international business, because every transnational sale of goods, and some transnational transfers of information or provisions of services, will be subject to at least one state's customs regulation.

Export regulation tends to serve more limited purposes than does import regulation. Most export regulation is undertaken pursuant to multilateral commitments to prevent the spread of arms, munitions, and dangerous items. In some cases, export regulation may be more concerned with solving specific problems, such as punishing an unfriendly foreign state or impeding a foreign state's sanctions against a third, friendly foreign country. Because of these limited goals, export regulation is typically directed at specific kinds of goods, services, and technologies or at specific states, organizations, or persons. Like import regulation, it is a highly technical subject in those states where it is used. In no state does export regulation match import regulation in the scope of transactions regulated or the prevalence of application, but companies doing transnational business must nevertheless be conversant with the basic rules of export regulation. The regulations may cover a surprising range of items, and apply to many foreign states, organizations, and individuals. The sanctions for noncompliance are at least as severe as are those imposed for violating import regulations.

In addition to the main international trade regulation regimes, in some countries there are specific regimes for certain kinds of regulated products and services. Products and services may be subjected to special forms of regulation for many reasons. In some cases, states may impose import or export restrictions when unregulated trade is thought to pose a threat to public health. Two examples are quarantines on the importation of livestock or other animals, and licensing requirements for the importation or exportation of pharmaceuticals. In other cases, environmental integrity may be the primary concern. For example, licensing requirements for the international shipment of hazardous wastes, or maximum pollution emission standards for imported automobiles, serve these functions. In short, the policy goals such regulation serve are many and varied, from the protection of domestic industries considered vital to national security to the preservation of economic, religious, or cultural interests. Because each special trade regulatory regime is unique, we will here focus on the broadest forms of import and export regulation.

In this chapter, you will learn specifically:

- why states regulate imports and exports;
- the international regimes that harmonizing import and export regulation by states;
- how customs duties are assessed, and the measures that importers may take to reduce or avoid the payment of customs duties;
- what requirements the United States imposes for the labeling of imported goods with the country of origin and why labeling requirements exist;
- the difference between the various kinds of export regulations and the policies underlying them;
- how to determine which exports of goods, technology, software, and services are regulated;
- the basic steps for applying for an export license;
- the consequences of violating the export regulations and how to minimize the risks and consequences of such violations; and
- how to recognize and avoid violating the rules relating to foreign boycotts of U.S. allies.

1 An Introduction to Import Regulation

Importing something means bringing it from outside of the borders of a state into that state. The most obvious example is when someone in a first state purchases a product manufactured or situated in a second state and arranges for it to be transported from the second country to the first. But it is not only goods that can be imported. Software, technical data, and even services can be imported as well. For example, someone who downloads a software application from the Internet can be "importing" the application if the software server (which is the computer that makes the application accessible) is located in a foreign country. Similarly, when a Japanese engineering company sends employees to France to assist in the design and construction of a railway, France is "importing" services (and, in a sense, labor) from Japan. As you will learn, some legal regimes, such as customs law, typically deal only with importations of tangible products, while others, such as trade sanctions, may also apply to intangible imports of software, data, and services.

1.1 A Brief History of Import Regulation

> BARABAS: Why, then, go bid them come ashore,
> And bring with them their bills of entry:
> I hope our credit in the custom-house
> Will serve as well as I were present there.*

Some of the earliest administrative laws known to humankind relating to foreign affairs are customs rules. In ancient Greece and Egypt, as early as the 14th century B.C.E., customs duties were levied on imports through shipping ports, and in some periods customs revenues comprised the chief source of public funds.** Each ancient Roman province, and sometimes large cities, similarly levied customs duties on imports.*** In the Tang Dynasty (618 C.E.–907 C.E.), all legitimate imports into and exports from China were funneled through the Canton Province, where they were inspected by a Bureau of Merchant Shipping that collected customs duties and investigated smuggling.**** In short, customs procedures and duties have existed for almost as long as foreign trade has existed and were adopted at opposite ends of the globe.

The longevity of customs laws has not diminished their popularity. Today, every state has an agency that monitors and regulates the importation of goods originating in other countries. In the United States, it is an agency called

*Christopher Marlowe, *The Jew of Malta*, act I, scene I (1590).

**3 AUGUSTUS BOECKH, THE PUBLIC ECONOMY OF ATHENS 313-29 (Ayer Co. Pub. 1976) (1842); Ladislav Balko, *The Position of the Customs Law in the Legal System*, 12 TRANSITION STUD. REV. 551, 556-58 (2005).

***A DICTIONARY OF GREEK AND ROMAN ANTIQUITIES 944, 944-45, 978-79 (William Smith ed., 1875) (entries on *portorium* and *quadragesima*); Balko, *supra*, at 557.

****JOANNA WALEY-COHEN, THE SEXTANTS OF BEIJING 27 (1999).

Customs and Border Protection (**CBP**) in the **Department of Homeland Security** (**DHS**), introduced in the previous chapter. In Canada, it is the Canada Border Services Agency. In Japan, it is Japan Customs in the Ministry of Finance. In Mexico, it is an agency called Hacienda that is also responsible for collecting Mexican income tax. The Europe Union (EU) currently has no single customs agency, although the European Commission is responsible for coordinating customs policy in the EU. Instead, each EU member state administers its own harmonized customs procedures.

States regulate imports for a variety of reasons, the most common being the following:

- the collection of taxes on imported goods as a form of national revenue;
- the protection of domestic industries from competition from foreign industries;
- the enforcement of quota limits on foreign imports;
- the detection of unauthorized imports (contraband) such as illegal narcotics or endangered species of animals or plants;
- the prevention of terrorism;
- the capture of persons seeking unauthorized entry into the country;
- the protection of the environment; and
- the prevention of threats to public health and safety.

With so many important functions, customs authorities play a visible and challenging role in government regulation. The volume of international trade has raised the importance of customs regulation as well. Imports of goods into the United States, for example, have tripled since 1965. Fortunately for customs authorities, they usually regulate only the importation of tangible goods. Trade in services, foreign investment not involving the transborder movement of goods, and the licensing of intellectual property for production abroad are excluded from the purview of customs law.

Historically, the primary role of customs regulation was the collection of revenue for the government. In other words, **customs duties**, also called **tariffs**, are a form of taxation—specifically, a consumption tax. For the first hundred years of the United States' existence, customs duties were the most important source of federal revenue; there was no income tax yet. With the advent of general income and value added taxes in most countries, customs revenue began to assume a role of diminishing importance to the national treasury. Customs duties remain the second largest form of federal tax revenue in the United States today, but the revenue generated by customs is dwarfed by the income tax revenue. Customs duties have developed into a form of protection against foreign import competition feared to create unemployment in the United States. In many countries, however, especially developing countries, customs revenue remains a major source of government income. In some African states, for example, customs duties and other import taxes account for half of all government revenue.

Customs duties raise the cost of buying foreign-produced goods, and so they shelter domestic industries from foreign competition. This is sometimes thought desirable to preserve domestic employment, which may be harmed by the relocation of labor-intensive industries to countries in which workers cannot or do not unionize and are paid much less than U.S. workers. The goal of high customs duties is to make importing articles sufficiently expensive that, if an article of commerce is in demand in a country, suppliers will choose to manufacture the article domestically, because it is cheaper than importing the article. No duties are imposed if the article is not imported. As noted in Chapter 2, trade **protectionism** through high import duties, **import quotas**, and **tariff-rate quotas** (**TRQs**) was routine before the advent of the GATT in 1947.

As common as customs duties, quotas, and TRQs may be among the states of the world, these measures raise the price of imported goods, thereby reducing transnational competition and making goods more expensive to consumers in the importing state. As a rule, then, most economists believe that customs duties and other import barriers tend to reduce the overall wealth of all states in most circumstances. In some cases, the cost of maintaining domestic employment through the use of import barriers is so high that it would be much less costly for consumers to pay displaced workers not to work, or to pay to train them in a more competitive industry, rather than maintaining a few uncompetitive jobs at the cost of more expensive goods for everyone. This consensus has led the great majority of states to enter into trade treaties of the kind discussed in Chapter 2.

Customs law remains as important as ever, however, because, while customs duties in most states are lower than ever before in history, they are still common and are far more complex. This complexity is multiplied by the many new roles that import regulation has assumed. What follows here is a relatively simple explanation of the importation process from the perspective of a company engaging in

Figure 5.1. I'm on a boat! The U.S. Revenue Cutter *Bear* on patrol in the Bering Sea, depicted around 1890. Credit: James Archibald Mitchell, III

transnational trade in goods.

1.2 The Importation Process

Before describing the importation process, it may be helpful to explain the key actors and steps involved in the importation of goods. The most important actor in this context is the **importer of record**. The importer of record is responsible for ensuring that the goods properly clear customs and any customs duty owed to the customs authority is paid. The importer may be the company *selling* or *exporting* the goods, although the buyer or its agent more often acts as importer. In either case, the importer may hire a **customs broker**, also known as a **customs agent**, to conduct these transactions as importer of record on her behalf. Customs brokers are typically licensed by the customs authority to transact customs business on behalf of importers and exporters. The importer of record is responsible for complying with the laws of the importing country and paying customs duties. Another agent that may act as an importer on behalf of the buyer is a **freight forwarder**. A freight forwarder, also called a **forwarding agent**, is an agent that arranges shipping, transport insurance, customs clearance, and related needs on behalf of an importer or exporter.

Commercial importers are often required to post a customs bond with the customs authority in case they fail to make full payment of import duties. In the United States and many other countries, posting a customs bond is a normal prerequisite for importing commercial goods. 19 U.S.C. § 1623. A **customs bond** is a contract by which a party to a transaction (the **principal**) obtains a guarantee from a third party (the **surety**) that an obligation will be performed for the benefit of the other party to the transaction (the **beneficiary**). In a customs bond, the transacting parties are the importer and a customs authority such as CBP, and the surety is usually an insurance company that guarantees payment of customs duties owed in case the importer fails to do so. The

WHO AND WHAT ARE CUSTOMS BROKERS?

In some countries, including the United States, customs brokers are the only nonlawyers authorized to act as agents for importers in their customs transactions. In the United States, customs brokers must pass a license examination administered by CBP. As of 2020, there are some 14,500 businesses and individuals active as licensed customs brokers. Because customs brokers often advise their clients about compliance with customs law, they must be familiar with the complex requirements of customs regulations. Very few customs brokers are licensed to practice law, but, as a result, they tend to cost significantly less than using customs lawyers for routine transactions.

Figure 5.2. The office of a freight forwarder in Ybor City, Tampa, Florida.
© 2017 by Aaron X. Fellmeth

bond must specifically provide that, in case the importer fails to pay the proper customs duties to CBP, the bond will be forfeited to CBP. The bond effectively allows the consignee to take possession of the imported goods before customs authorities are certain that all appropriate duties have been paid.

An importer may post a bond for each individual shipment of imports, called a **single entry bond**, if it wishes. But this can be inconvenient for large volume importers, who may import hundreds or thousands of shipments each year. In such cases, the importer posts a much larger bond, called a **continuous bond** because it does not have to be renewed but continues in force indefinitely, to cover a stream of imports.

The **consignee**, who receives the shipment, is usually the purchaser of the goods in the importing country or the purchaser's freight forwarder. The consignee may have no customs-related responsibilities, but it must usually be identified on the customs forms in any case. The importer and the consignee may be the same person.

Finally, the **carrier** is the air, sea, or ground cargo transport company hired by the importer or exporter (or either party's freight forwarder) to transport the goods from the point of shipment to the point of delivery. The great bulk of international trade (about 90% of total world trade, in fact) is packed by the shipper, freight forwarder, or carrier in cargo containers called **isotainers**.

WHAT ARE THE SOURCES OF U.S. IMPORTS?

On average, about 9.5 million isotainers filled with imported goods, worth around $2.3 trillion, arrive at U.S. ports every year. In 2018, about 48% of these imports originated in China (21%), Mexico (14%), or Canada (13%). Other countries exporting significant quantities of goods to the United States include Japan, Germany, the U.K., South Korea, Ireland, and India.

Source: U.S. International Trade Commission, Interactive Tariff and Trade DataWeb.

Because they are stackable and of uniform size, isotainers can be loaded onto a ship or train and transported in bulk across the ocean cheaply and efficiently. Maritime shipping is the most popular method of long-distance international trade carriage, although trains and trucks are important transportation means as well.

In most countries, the importation of goods involves six steps: entry, inspection, classification, determination of the country of origin, valuation, and liquidation. We will consider what is involved in each step in turn, with special focus on the United States. Before we do, it is helpful to review the main sources of U.S. customs law.

The general law regulating the importation of goods is known as the **1930 Tariff Act**, codified in Title 19 of the U.S. Code. The 1930 Tariff Act, as frequently amended, provides general import rules and authorization for what used to be called the U.S. Customs Service of the Department of the Treasury, and is now the CBP, to promulgate and enforce regulations governing the importation of goods into the United States. These customs regulations are set forth conveniently in Title 19 of the Code of Federal Regulations (C.F.R.).

The customs laws and regulations provide quite detailed guidance on import procedures. But this is not the only source of customs law. Judicial decisions interpreting the statute and regulations are important sources of authority as well. In addition, there are two courts that have special authority to decide customs issues. The first is the U.S. **Court of International Trade** (**CIT**) in New York City. The CIT hears mainly cases in which decisions of CBP or the trade remedies authorities are challenged. Appeals from decisions of the CIT are heard by the U.S. Court of Appeals for the Federal Circuit. The Federal Circuit was created by Congress in 1982 to replace the **Court of Customs and Patent Appeals** (**CCPA**), but in customs law it performs essentially the same function as its predecessor. The U.S. Supreme Court has sometimes issued important customs decisions on certiorari from the CCPA and Federal Circuit as well.

Finally, CBP itself sometimes issues formal guidance to importers. These formerly took the form of **Treasury decisions**, many of which are still

Figure 5.3. Isotainers on the deck of an ocean freighter off the coast of Auckland, New Zealand. Cargo freighters like this one can carry hundreds or even thousands of 40-foot cargo containers at a time.

Figure 5.4. Isotainers at Barcelona Harbor, Spain, waiting to be loaded onto an ocean freighter.

considered authoritative today, and now take the form of **CBP directives**. In addition, importers may specifically request **customs rulings** from Customs Headquarters to resolve specific legal questions (see 19 C.F.R. pt. 177). These decisions are usually published and available in the **Customs Rulings Online Search System** (**CROSS**) at the CBP Web site (http://rulings.cbp.gov/). Although customs rulings only apply to the facts submitted to CBP in the ruling request, they can serve as useful sources of guidance.

A. Entry

The term **entry** means that the goods have arrived at a customs port in the country of importation. A **customs port** or **port of entry** is an airport, harbor, railway station, or other place that customs authorities have authorized to receive and process imported goods. Every major city has a customs port at its airport, river or sea harbor, train station, or other commercial transportation link. The United States, for example, has over 300 official ports of entry, including at least one in every major metropolis.

Imported goods are not legally entered into the United States until after the shipment has arrived within the port of entry, the customs authority has received the proper information, and delivery of the merchandise has been authorized by the customs authority. The information must normally be submitted electronically to the customs authorities within a few days after the goods arrive at the customs port and must be accompanied by a payment of customs duties. The required information generally includes the following:

(1) an entry manifest;
(2) a bill of lading or air waybill;
(3) a commercial invoice;
(4) packing lists; and,
(5) following release of the goods, an entry summary and payment of customs duties.

In the United States, CBP has adopted the **Customs Automated Forms Entry System** and the **Automated Broker Interface**, which allow electronic filing of customs information.

An **entry manifest** is reproduced in Figure 5.5. This document summarizes the basic customs information and requests liquidation of the entry. It identifies the port of lading (where the goods were loaded onto the ship, truck, train, or airplane); the port of entry (where the goods will first enter the country of importation); the ultimate port of destination (where the goods will be finally delivered to the consignee); a full description of the goods imported; the country of origin of the goods; and the price of the goods, including freight, insurance, packing, and other charges.

A **bill of lading** is a shipping document issued by the carrier, acknowledging that specific goods have been received as cargo for conveyance to a named place for delivery to a designated consignee. The bill of lading serves three main functions. First, it provides evidence that the seller or exporter has entered into a contract for transportation of the goods to the port of entry. Second, because the bill of lading lists the goods delivered to the carrier, it serves as evidence that the goods shipped are the same as those described on the entry form and in the sales contract, if any. Third, the bill of lading is used by the consignee as a document of title, as discussed in Chapter 4. By presenting the bill of lading to customs authorities and the carrier, the consignee can show that she is authorized to receive the goods at the port of entry. A bill of lading is usually used only when goods are transported by sea. A **waybill** or **consignment note** is used instead when the carrier will transport the goods by air or land, respectively.

A **commercial invoice** is a document issued by the seller of the goods describing the goods by name, quantity, and price (including shipping charges), and identifying the purchaser or other consignee. An invoice is essentially an itemized demand for payment issued by the seller to the purchaser. A sample commercial invoice is reproduced below as Figure 5.6. The commercial invoice is used by the government to appraise the imported goods. Notice how, on the form, different elements of the cost of the goods are listed separately. This is because some elements are included in the dutiable value of the imports (such as packing costs), while others are not (such as international freight and insurance costs).

A **packing list** is a document prepared by the packer (usually the shipper, freight forwarder, or carrier) that describes what is in each package prepared for shipment by commercial invoice line item number. A packing list helps customs authorities identify the shipping containers to which the customs documents relate by the dimensions and weight of each container, the type (box, crate, bale, full container, etc.); and the exterior marks and numbers on each.

Once the importer has submitted the necessary information to the customs authority, the importer will wait to be notified by the carrier of the goods that the shipment has arrived at the port of entry. Upon entry of the goods at the port, the customs authority will have an opportunity to inspect the imported goods.

B. Inspection

Customs authorities inspect goods crossing national borders for a number of reasons. They seek to identify illegal narcotics, weapons, goods infringing U.S. intellectual property rights, or other contraband for seizure; to find mismarked or unmarked goods; to ensure that certain classes of goods subject to special regulation (such as food and beverages or children's toys) meet applicable regulatory requirements; and to ensure that the goods conform with

U.S. DEPARTMENT OF HOMELAND SECURITY
Bureau of Customs and Border Protection

Approved OMB No. 1651-0001
Exp. 12/31/2008

INWARD CARGO MANIFEST FOR VESSEL UNDER FIVE TONS, FERRY, TRAIN, CAR, VEHICLE, ETC.

(INSTRUCTIONS ON REVERSE)

19 CFR 123.4, 123.7, 123.61

CBP Manifest/In Bond Number

Page No.

1. Name or Number and Description of Importing Conveyance	2. Name of Master or Person in Charge	
3. Name and Address of Owner	4. Foreign Port of Lading	5. U.S. Port of Destination
6. Port of Arrival	7. Date of Arrival	

Column No. 1	Column No. 2	Column No. 3	Column No. 4	Column No. 5
Bill of Lading or Marks & Numbers or Address of Consignee on Packages	Car Number and Initials	Number and Gross Weight (in kilos or pounds) of Packages and Description of Goods	Name of Consignee	For Use By CBP only

CARRIER'S CERTIFICATE

To the Port Director of CBP, Port of Arrival:

The undersigned carrier hereby certifies that ______________________ of ______________

is the owner or consignee of such articles within the purview of section 484, Tariff Act of 1930.

I certify that this manifest is correct and true to the best of my knowledge.

Date ______________ Master or Person in charge ______________________________

(Signature)

Previous Editions are Obsolete **CBP Form 7533 (05/00)**

Figure 5.5. A customs entry manifest.

COMMERCIAL INVOICE

Invoice No
Date

Invoice Address:	Delivery terms (Incoterms) Put delivery terms (Incoterms) as per trade contract
Ship to: Contact person: Phone:	Delivered under: Put number and date of trade contract Payment terms

No item	Description	Country of origin	Net weight/kg	HTS Code	Qty (pieces)	Unit price, USD	Total price, USD
1.							
2.							
						Total, USD	

Insurance cost, USD:	
Freight cost, USD:	Put transportation cost amount (for Incoterms DAT, DAP, DDP, CPT, CIP, CIF, CFR)
Total for payment, USD:	Put total amount: total price plus insurance amount (if insured), and transportation cost above

Gross Weight, kg (total) :	Put total gross weight of the shipment (should match weight on bill of lading or air waybill)

Signed by:	

Figure 5.6. A commercial invoice.

the description, quantity, country of origin, and valuation declared on the entry documents. Any attempt to smuggle contraband or intentionally misidentified goods into the United States is a criminal offense. Smuggled imports are subject to confiscation, and the importer becomes liable for penalties and possible prison time. Even accidentally misidentified goods can subject the importer to fines (called oxymoronically "civil penalties") and interest on underpaid duties.

Inspection itself rarely delays the imports at the port for very long. However, in most countries, so many goods are imported on any given day that customs authorities could never hope to inspect every shipment. Customs authorities typically inspect a random sample of imported goods, which may hold up delivery of some or all of the goods to the consignee. It is therefore in the importer's interest to reduce the incidence of detailed customs inspections whenever possible.

In the United States, importers can reduce the probability of inspection by cooperating with CBP through various programs that ensure cargo security and accurate documentation. These programs primarily rely on the importer to self-police using a regulatory regimen prescribed by CBP in order to increase CBP confidence in the reliability and security of their shipments and shipping documentation by decreasing the regularity of border inspections. Adhering to such compliance programs can be costly and inconvenient, but for many importers, especially those who import large volumes of goods regularly, minimizing port delays justifies the expense and extra labor.

C. Tariff Classification

The activities of the various national customs agencies are coordinated by the **World Customs Organization** (**WCO**), which is headquartered in Brussels, Belgium. The WCO maintains a list called the **Harmonized Tariff Schedule** (**HTS**). The HTS is a nearly comprehensive system for classifying goods of every type by dividing them into various categories and subcategories. Each specific type of good is identified by a six-digit number called a **tariff classification**, and similar goods are grouped together into broad ranges of classification numbers.

WORLD CUSTOMS ORGANIZATION
ORGANISATION MONDIALE DES DOUANES

The HTS makes selling goods to foreign countries much easier for importers, because every major state has adopted the Harmonized Tariff System of classification. This greatly increases the probability that goods classified as one thing in the manufacturer's state are classified the same way in the state of importation. Imagine how difficult international trade was when every state had its own classification scheme for imported goods, so that an importer had to figure out how to classify the same goods separately in every state in which it did business. With the adoption of the HTS, it has become much more likely that goods assigned a classification number in any one country will be treated as having

Figure 5.7. Customs and Border Protection uses an advanced X-ray to scan isotainers. Credit: James Tourtellotte, U.S. Customs & Border Protection

the same classification number in every other country. Using the same classification number cuts down a great deal on the costs of importing goods, especially in fees paid to customs experts around the world to perform classification.

The HTS is divided most generally into sections and chapters. Each section covers a large variety of goods and includes notes to help importers determine how to classify their goods. For example, Section I covers live animals and animal products. Section XI covers textiles, clothing, and similar items. Section XXI covers art works and antiques. Most sections contain several chapters, and each chapter covers a more specific, but still very general, group of goods. For example, Chapter 1 (in Section I) includes livestock, live fowl, and animals such as might be imported for use as personal companions. Chapter 3 (also in Section I) covers fish and crustaceans. Chapter 60 (in Section XI) includes knitted or crocheted fabrics such as sweaters. Nuclear reactors are found in Chapter 84.

Now that you understand how the HTS is broadly organized, it will be easier to understand how to use a tariff classification. Within each chapter, goods are further broken down into smaller groups with four-digit **headings**. The first step to determining how much duty, if any, is owed to the state of importation is to figure out which heading best describes the imported goods. The first two numbers of every heading are the chapter number in which the goods are found. Thus, all headings in Chapter 60 start with "60," and all headings in Chapter 3 start with "03." When you see heading 6006, then you know it is found in Chapter 60, and when you see heading 0304, you know it is found in Chapter 3. But this is not the end of the classification, because the HTS further breaks down goods into 6-digit **subheadings**, which include the next two digits following the four-digit heading. So the next step in classifying imported goods is to determine which subheadings apply to the imports. This requires knowing further details about the characteristics of the goods. In some countries, including the United States, tariff classifications are listed in even more detail, and include an additional 2-digit subheading, making the classification number a total of eight digits long.

WHAT IS THE WCO?

The World Customs Organization (WCO) was established in 1952 as the Customs Co-operation Council. Its mission is to establish, maintain, support, and promote international harmonization and uniform application of simplified customs procedures among member states through drafting treaties and providing technical advice and assistance. In 1994, the organization changed its name to the WCO to reflect its almost universal membership (183 countries as of 2020). WCO members account for more than 98% of all international trade in the world.

Goods may be classified on the HTS in several ways. First, an HTS entry may actually name the items it covers. These are known as ***eo nomine*** ("by name") provisions. For example, an HTS entry that covers "surfboards" names exactly what is included. Second, an HTS entry may describe the goods covered generally. For example, an HTS entry that covers "stringed musical instruments" might include both guitars and violins. Third, an HTS entry may identify the goods covered by a component material. For example, "silver jewelry" might encompass rings, bracelets, and necklaces made primarily of silver. Finally, an HTS entry may describe goods according to their actual or principal use. For example, "ski equipment" might cover any goods designed or primarily used for skiing, such as poles that could also be used for trekking.

All this is very abstract, so let's use an example. Suppose you represent a Smalldonian sports gear company trying to import its snowshoes into the United States. The United States' version of the HTS is called the **Harmonized Tariff Schedule of the United States** (**HTSUS**) and is maintained and periodically updated by the U.S. International Trade Commission (ITC), an independent federal Executive Branch agency that you may recall from its role in Section 337 investigations. You start with the table of contents of the HTSUS and see that it contains two possibly relevant chapters: Chapter 64 ("Footwear, gaiters and the like") and Chapter 95 ("Toys, games and sports requisites"). Suppose you look at Chapter 64 and rule it out. Now you examine Chapter 95.

The sections may contain notes from the WCO to assist in classification;

in this case, Chapter 95 is found in Section XX, which has no **section notes** to help interpret the scope of Section XX. However, Chapter 95 does have some explanatory notes—**chapter heading notes**—from the WCO. Some chapters also include additional U.S. notes that the ITC has prepared to assist you in determining how to classify goods that could (at least, theoretically) be classified in more than one way. The additional U.S. notes include other U.S.-specific information, such as whether there are import quotas on any goods in that chapter, and similar information. In this case, no chapter heading notes are relevant.

You will now search through the "article descriptions" to see if you can locate something that sounds like your client's product. Figure 5.8 is the relevant sample page from a recent version of the HTSUS. As you see, on the leftmost part of Figure 5.8 are the headings and subheadings used for classification right next to article descriptions. You have chosen heading 9506 ("Articles and equipment for general physical exercise * * * or outdoor games not specified elsewhere in this chapter") as the most likely to contain snowshoes, working on the hypothesis that if snowshoes are not classified as footwear on the HTS, they must be some kind of exercise or outdoor sporting equipment.

You're in luck—snowshoes are explicitly described under heading 9506. In this case, they are identified as 9506.99.50.* In other words, HTSUS 9506.99.50 is an *eo nomine* provision, because it identifies the goods it covers by name. Now you have the classification number for your snowshoes, and your client, the importer, will enter this number in the appropriate box of the entry form.

Now consider a different scenario. What if the imported goods could be described under more than one provision of the HTS? Suppose, for example, the imported goods are a set composed of colored sand, a pipette, and several glass bottles. The set is intended for use as a toy for children to make sand crafts. Such a set is not classified by name anywhere on the HTS. It could theoretically be classified as an article of stone or mineral substances (Chapter 68 HTS) because of the sand, or an article of glass (Chapter 70 HTS) because of the bottles and pipette, or a children's toy (Chapter 95 HTS) because that is its intended use. Which classification is correct?

Or suppose we are trying to classify Smucker's Goober Grape®—a sandwich spread composed half of peanut butter and half of grape jelly. Grape jelly is properly classified under HTSUS 2007.99.70 ("Fruit jellies: Currant and berry," because grapes are berries), while peanut butter is classified as HTSUS 2008.11.05. Which classification is correct?

When two or more provisions seem to cover the same merchandise, the prevailing provision is determined first in accordance with the section notes and

---

*The "00" under the "Stat. Suffix" column is known as the **statistical suffix**. The statistical suffix does not affect the amount of customs duties owed on imported goods; it must be reported so that CBP can help keep track of U.S. trade trends.

Harmonized Tariff Schedule of the United States (2019)

Annotated for Statistical Reporting Purposes

XX
95-10

Heading/ Subheading	Stat. Suf- fix	Article Description	Unit of Quantity	Rates of Duty 1 General	Rates of Duty 1 Special	Rates of Duty 2
9506 (con.)		Articles and equipment for general physical exercise, gymnastics, athletics, other sports (including table-tennis) or outdoor games, not specified or included elsewhere in this chapter; swimming pools and wading pools; parts and accessories thereof: (con.)				
		Other: (con.)				
9506.99 (con.)		Other: (con.)				
		Sleds, bobsleds, toboggans and the like and parts and accessories thereof:				
9506.99.40	00	Toboggans; bobsleds and luges of a kind used in international competition	No.	Free		Free
9506.99.45	00	Other, including parts and accessories	No.	2.8%	Free (A, AU, BH, CA, CL, CO, D, E, IL, JO, KR, MA, MX, OM, P, PA, PE, SG)	45%
9506.99.50	00	Snowshoes and parts and accessories thereof	No.	2.6%	Free (A, AU, BH, CA, CL, CO, D, E, IL, JO, KR, MA, MX, OM, P, PA, PE, SG)	33 1/3%
9506.99.55	00	Swimming pools and wading pools and parts and accessories thereof	No.	5.3%	Free (A, AU, BH, CA, CL, CO, D, E, IL, JO, KR, MA, MX, OM, P, PA, PE, SG)	80%
9506.99.60		Other		4%[9/]	Free (A*, AU, BH, CA, CL, CO, D, E, IL, JO, KR, MA, MX, OM, P, PA, PE, SG)	40%
	40	Nets not elsewhere specified or included	kg			
	80	Other	No.			

Figure 5.8. Sample page from Chapter 95 of the HTSUS.

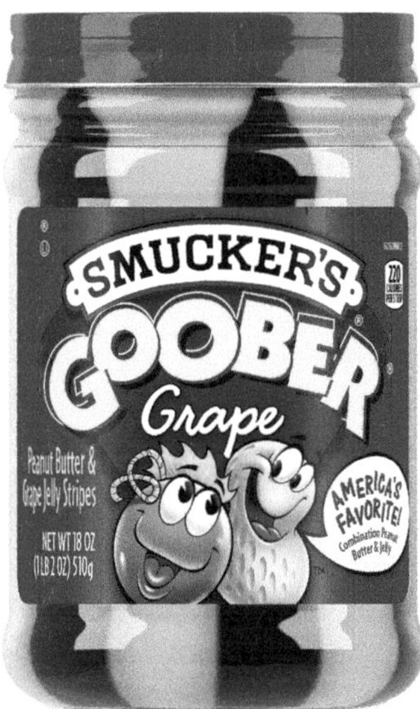

Figure 5.9. Goober Grape® is combined peanut butter and jelly. © The J.M. Smucker Company, used with permission.

chapter heading notes of the HTS. These sometimes provide helpful guidance as to what kinds of goods are or are not covered in the section or chapter at issue. If these do not resolve the question, the next step is to apply what are known as the **General Rules of Interpretation** (**GRI**) adopted by the WCO members for the HTS. The GRI is a list of six principles to help customs authorities and importers decide how to classify goods that appear to be described by more than one heading.

GENERAL RULES OF INTERPRETATION

Classification of goods in the tariff schedule shall be governed by the following principles:

1. The table of contents, alphabetical index, and titles of sections, chapters and sub-chapters are provided for ease of reference only; for legal purposes, classification shall be determined according to the terms of the headings and any relevant section or chapter notes and, provided such headings or notes do not otherwise require, according to the following provisions:

2. (a) Any reference in a heading to an article shall be taken to include a reference to that article incomplete or unfinished, provided that, as entered, the incomplete or unfinished article has the essential character of the complete or finished article. It shall also include a reference to that article complete or finished * * *, entered unassembled or disassembled.

(b) Any reference in a heading to a material or substance shall be taken to include a reference to mixtures or combinations of that material or substance with other materials or substances. Any reference to goods of a given material or substance shall be taken to include a reference to goods consisting wholly or partly of such material or substance. The classification of goods consisting of more than one material or substance shall be according to the principle of rule 3.

3. When, by application of rule 2(b) or for any other reason, goods are, *prima facie*, classifiable under two or more headings, classification shall be effected as follows:

(a) The heading which provides the most specific description shall be preferred to the heading providing a more general description. However, when two or more headings each refer to part only of the materials or substances contained in mixed or composite goods or to part only of the items in a set put up for retail sale, those headings are to be regarded as equally specific in relation to those goods, even if one of them gives a more complete or precise description of the goods.

(b) Mixtures, composite goods consisting of different materials or made up of different components, and goods put up in sets for retail sale, which cannot be classified by reference to 3(a), shall be classified as if they consisted of the materials or component which gives them their essential character, insofar as this criterion is applicable.

(c) When goods cannot be classified by reference to 3(a) or 3(b), they shall be classified under the heading which occurs last in numerical order among those which equally merit consideration.

4. Goods which cannot be classified in accordance with the above rules shall be classified under the heading appropriate to the goods to which they are most akin.

5. [omitted]

6. For legal purposes, the classification of goods in the subheadings of a heading shall be determined according to the terms of those subheadings and any related subheading notes and, *mutatis mutandis*, to the above rules, on the understanding that only subheadings at the same level are comparable. For purposes of this rule, the relative section, chapter and subchapter notes also apply, unless the context otherwise requires.

There are a few important themes running through the GRIs. The first is that the most relevant sources of interpretive authority are the section notes, chapter notes, and the 4-digit headings themselves.

The second is that headings should be compared with other headings, not subheadings. But, within a heading, 6-digit subheadings should be compared with other 6-digit subheadings, not 8-digit subheadings, and so forth.

The third is that, when goods seem to be classifiable under two different headings because they contain a mixture of materials or are assembled from different components that are each separately classified, the GRIs favor classifying the goods under the heading applicable to the material or component that gives the goods their "essential character." How would this resolve the case of Goober Grape? There are separate headings for both peanut butter and fruit jelly. GRIs 3(a) and 3(b) dictate that, in such a situation, the product should be classified as peanut butter if it gives Goober Grape its essential character and grape jelly if jelly gives it its essential character. But how do we know which gives the product its essential character? After all, the peanut butter gives the product protein and a dense, creamy texture while the jelly adds sweetness, fruit flavor, and moisture. Both of these characteristics may be an essential characteristic for the product's use as a sandwich spread.

In such circumstances, the importer would typically turn to sources of interpretive authority relating to GRI 3, such as customs rulings and court decisions, discussed below. For example, there may be decisions of the CIT or the Federal Circuit stating that the proper heading for combination products like sandwich spreads is the one applicable to the most expensive ingredient, or the ingredient that makes up the greatest weight. If none of these sources of authority can help the importer decide which heading applies, GRI 3(c) gives the importer the simple expedient of using the heading with the highest number. In this example, both peanut butter and jelly are found in chapter 20. The former is classified under heading 2008, while grape jelly is under heading 2007. In the absence of any other source of authority, Goober Grape would be classified as peanut butter under heading 2008, the higher number.

In summary, the section and chapter notes, the headings and subheadings themselves, and the GRIs together constitute the basic legal texts, known in customs circles as the **nomenclature**, of the HTS.

Finally, as mentioned earlier in this Chapter, judicial decisions of the CIT and the U.S. Court of Appeals for the Federal Circuit may provide guidance on classification where the GRIs do not lead to a clear result. There are not very many of these cases relative to the large diversity of classification problems that can arise in import transactions. Therefore, the most common source of authority used to answer classification questions not resolved by the GRIs are CBP directives and customs rulings.

Returning to the snowshoe scenario, you now have the HTS classification for your imports. But you still do not know how much duty to pay. To learn that, the next step is determining whence the goods come. Although they come most directly from Smalldonia, that merely makes Smalldonia the country of shipment or lading. Ascertaining the country of origin requires a deeper inquiry.

D. Country of Origin

Most merchandise is manufactured with inputs and processing steps involving more than one country. A pair of shoes may be designed in the United

States, with the outer parts made from rubber formed in Switzerland and leather cured in Argentina, the insole and laces made from synthetic fabric woven, cut, sewn, and dyed in China. In which of these countries do these shoes originate? The literal answer is of course "all of them," but every country requires that importers designate just one country as the **country of origin** of imported goods. The country of origin will help determine what duties are owed on the goods and may also determine whether any antidumping duties, countervailing duties, or quotas apply to the goods.

Let's continue our example of the Smalldonian snowshoes. Returning to Figure 5.8, you will notice that under "Rates of Duty," there is a "2.6%" under "1—General," some gobbledygook under "1—Special," and a "33 1/3%" under "2." For now, ignore everything but the column headings under "Rates of Duty." These tell us how much duty is payable on any given classification of goods if we know the country of origin. But countries are not listed in the HTSUS. So how do we know what duty rate applies to goods from Smalldonia? The short answer is that countries are classified by the United States into groups. One group pays the highest rate of duty, because countries in that group benefit from no trade treaties or unilateral concessions from the United States. This highest duty rate is called the **nonpreferential duty rate**. In the HTSUS, the nonpreferential rate of duty is listed under column 2 (here, 33 1/3%). If you ever forget which column is which, just remember that the nonpreferential duty rate is always the highest rate, as its name implies.

Other groups of countries benefit from various **preferential duty rates**. The largest group belongs to the World Trade Organization (WTO). The "1—General" column sets forth rates of duty for goods originating in most WTO member states. Notice that it is much lower (2.6%) than the nonpreferential duty rate. Trade with these countries is called **permanent normal trade relations (PNTR)** or **most favored nation (MFN)** status trade. This is labeled the "general" rate because most states are WTO members and benefit from that rate. However, suppose that Smalldonia is not yet one of those states. In that case, we must look elsewhere to determine its rate of duty. Maybe Smalldonia belongs to a third group of states, so that it will not have to pay the highest duty rate.

Turning to the "1—Special" column, there are a number of abbreviations following the remark "Free." This column sets forth preferential duty rates for many countries and groups of countries that receive special treatment from the United States, regardless of whether they are WTO members. These rates are usually more favorable even than those given to WTO members—often duty free, as here for snowshoes. The General Notes to the HTSUS include explanations of each of these abbreviations. For example, "IL" stands for Israel, which receives special benefits under the bilateral U.S.-Israel Free Trade Agreement. You may recall that the United States has entered into many such bilateral and regional **free trade agreements (FTAs)**, including among others with Canada and Mexico (USMCA) (designated on the HTSUS as "CA" for Canada and "MX" for Mexico), with Singapore ("SG"), and with Morocco ("MA"). In addition, the United States has unilaterally enacted several laws that provide for non-reciprocal (that is, unilateral) preferential treatment for less developed countries, such as the Andean Trade Preferences Act (covering Bolivia, Colombia, Ecuador, and Peru) ("J"), the African Growth and Opportunity Act (covering most of Africa) ("D"), and the Caribbean Basin Economic Recovery Act, also known as the Caribbean Basin Initiative (covering most of the Caribbean and parts of Central and South America) ("E"). In all, there are several dozen statutory schemes granting preferential duty rates to various countries, groups of countries, and classes of goods. Note that the abbreviations are sometimes intuitive, but often they are not.

The most important non-reciprocal trade preference program—because it is the most extensively used—is the **Generalized System of Preferences** (**GSP**), symbolized on the HTSUS by the letter "A". As discussed in Chapter 2, GSP is authorized expressly for WTO members by a waiver issued by the WTO General Council. As adopted by the United States, the GSP is a statutory program that allows the President to designate certain developing countries to benefit from duty-free treatment for a fairly wide variety of imports. 19 U.S.C. §§ 2461 *et seq*. By making it less costly to export goods to wealthy countries, the GSP program effectively puts imports from certain developing countries at a competitive advantage relative to imports from other states.

At any given time, approximately one hundred states and various territories and country groups are designated as eligible for GSP treatment by the U.S. President. The President periodically adds or removes states from GSP eligibility, depending on whether they continue to meet the statutory criteria (such as rising or falling *per capita* income, the openness of the country to U.S. imports and investment, and whether the country has adopted and enforces laws protecting U.S. intellectual property). As a result, the list of GSP-eligible states changes over time, making such programs too malleable for long-term planning.

Keep in mind that not *all* imports from GSP-eligible countries actually benefit from duty-free treatment; the President decides which articles from each developing country will be imported into the United States duty free. Often excluded from GSP eligibility are imports in industries in which the United States was once internationally competitive, but is no longer, such as textiles and clothing, steel, certain electronics, and other items that U.S. companies and trade unions succeed in lobbying the Executive Branch to exempt. In addition, the President must exclude goods from GSP eligibility when the state exporting them has had unusual success on the U.S. market, such as when a developing country is the source of 50% or more of the value of U.S. imports of the good. Only the very poorest countries, almost all in Africa, are exempt from this limitation.

Because the GSP program is intended to benefit specific developing countries, it is important that imports receiving duty-free treatment under the GSP are in fact mined, harvested, or manufactured in the beneficiary country. The GSP program, like most unilateral U.S. trade promotion programs, uses the normal rules of origin to determine whether imported goods originate an a GSP-eligible country, subject to one exception: The cost or value of materials produced in the beneficiary developing country or the direct cost of processing performed there must always represent at least 35% of the appraised value of the goods.

Applying GSP analysis to our snowshoe example, the snowshoes may enter the United States duty-free if the following criteria are satisfied:

(1) the goods originate in Smalldonia under the normal U.S. rules of origin; and
(2) Smalldonia is designated as GSP-eligible; and
(3) at least 35% of the value of the goods is attributable to Smalldonia.

Why? Because there is an "A" (meaning all GSP-eligible countries) next to "Free" in the "1—Special" column next to the classification number for snowshoes (HTSUS 9506.99.50 in Figure 5.8). This would be good news for the importer, because goods imported into the United States duty-free can be sold at a lower price than if a duty were charged, meaning they are more likely to be bought by U.S. consumers.

Unfortunately, we now have to complicate things a bit. As noted, the fact that the snowshoes are being exported from Smalldonia does not necessarily mean Smalldonia is the country of origin of the snowshoes. Suppose, for example, that the snowshoes had been manufactured in Finland, sold to a Smalldonian wholesaler, and the Smalldonian wholesaler now seeks to resell them to retailers in the United States. In that case, Finland would be the country of origin, not Smalldonia. Or, what if the aluminum snowshoe frame was manufactured in Smalldonia, then the frame was sent to Finland where a fabric platform and bindings were attached, then returned to Smalldonia for packaging. Is the country of origin Smalldonia or Finland?

Under the customs laws of all countries, including the United States, if the product is **wholly produced** in a single country, the product originates in that country. That means that all industrial inputs into the product must originate in that country. For example, if the product is a steel pipe, that pipe must not only be shaped or molded in the country, but the iron from which it is made must be mined in the country; the steel rolled there; and the pipe formed, cut, and polished there. Or, if the product is a loaf of bread, the wheat must be grown in the country, the flour milled in the country, the yeast produced in the country, the dough beaten there, and the loaf baked there.

The Non-Preferential Rule of Origin

Of course, relatively few goods are wholly produced in a single state. For goods produced through materials from or operations in more than one state, The **WTO Agreement on Rules of Origin** dictates the use of a **substantial transformation test**. Specifically, the treaty requires WTO members to provide by law that a product originates in *the country in which the last substantial transformation of all of the materials, components, and parts of the product took place*. The Agreement on Rules of Origin does not, however, specify in detail how to judge whether a particular manufacturing process causes a substantial transformation of the product. As a result, states sometimes use different standards for determining when a sufficient transformation has occurred. The following case applies the "default" U.S. rules of origin, also called the **nonpreferential rule of origin**, because it applies to trading partners with which the United States does not have a special treaty arrangement.

SUPERIOR WIRE v. UNITED STATES

United States Court of Appeals, Federal Circuit, 1989
867 F.2d 1409

ARCHER, Circuit Judge.

Superior Wire (Superior) appeals the judgment of the United States Court of International Trade * * * that wire drawn in Canada from Spanish wire rod is not "substantially transformed" for purposes of determining the country of origin * * *.

I

Superior began importing wire rod from Spain into Canada in 1984 following the imposition of preliminary anti-dumping and countervailing duties on wire rod imported from Spain into the United States. In a newly-established wire drawing facility in Canada, Superior drew the wire rod into wire before shipping the wire to its wire mesh operation in Michigan. It claimed Canada as the country of origin instead of Spain.

* * * In March 1987, the Customs Service * * * determined that the drawing of wire from wire rod does not constitute a substantial transformation. Based on this ruling, Superior's imports of drawn wire from Canada were classified as being of Spanish origin. * * *

The Court of International Trade further determined on the merits that the drawing of wire rod into wire does not substantially transform wire rod into a new product for the purpose of determining the country of origin * * *.

II

The trial court's findings of fact are reviewed under the clearly erroneous standard of review. Findings of fact may be overturned only when "the reviewing court on the entire evidence is left with the definite and firm conviction that a mistake has been committed." The court is not so restricted with respect to legal conclusions and will reverse those conclusions found to be in error. * * *

IV

On the country of origin issue, Superior contends that the wire imported into the United States is a product of Canada, not Spain, because the Spanish wire rod was "substantially transformed" in Canada. Substantial transformation requires that "[t]here must be transformation; a new and different article must emerge, 'having a distinctive name, character, or use.'" Anheuser-Busch Brewing Ass'n v. United States, 207 U.S. 556, 562 (1908). Whether such a transformation occurred involves findings of fact by the trial court. These findings may not be set aside unless clearly erroneous. "This standard plainly does not entitle a reviewing court to reverse the finding of the trier of fact simply because it is convinced that it would have decided the case differently. . . . If the district court's account of the evidence is plausible in light of the record viewed in its entirety, the court of appeals may not reverse it." Anderson v. City of Bessemer City, 470 U.S. 564, 573-74 (1985).

The Court of International Trade considered the "transformation of wire rod to wire to be minor rather than substantial." The court found that there was no significant change in use or character, but there was a change in name, see *Anheuser-Busch Brewing Ass'n*, 207 U.S. at 562, and concluded that "wire rod and wire may be viewed as different stages of the same product."

Although noting that "[t]he wire emerges stronger and rounder after" drawing the wire rod, the court found "[i]ts strength characteristic * * * is * * * metallurgically predetermined * * * through the fabrication of the wire rod." The court explained that "[t]he chemical content of the rod and the cooling processes used in its manufacture * * * determine the properties that the wire will have after drawing." These findings are "plausible" in light of the record viewed in its entirety and are not clearly erroneous. See *Anderson*, 470 U.S. at 573-74. There was evidence of record to show that the rod producer determines the tensile strength of the drawn wire by the chemistry of the steel, particularly by the mix of carbon and manganese in the molten steel rods, and that the properties desired in the drawn wire dictate the selection of scrap grade.

We are not persuaded by Superior's argument that because wire is "cleaner, smoother * * * and cross-sectionally more uniform" than the wire rod it has a different character. Such changes appear to be primarily cosmetic in the light of the predetermined qualities and specifications of the wire rod.

There was also ample evidence from which the Court of International Trade could determine that there is no change in use between the wire rod and the wire. The end use of wire rod is generally known before the rolling stage and the specifications are frequently determined by reference to the end product for which the drawn wire will be used. Thus, rod used for the production of concrete reinforcing mesh is known as "mesh-grade" or "mesh-quality rod." Moreover, the evidence indicates that if the rod is produced improperly for its intended application, the wire drawing process is incapable of making the product suitable for such use.

With respect to the third of the *Anheuser-Busch* factors, the trial court noted that the two products have different names: wire and wire rod. This is the least persuasive factor and is insufficient by itself to support a holding that there is a substantial transformation. See United States v. International Paint Co., 35 CCPA 87, 93-94 (1948) ("a change of name alone would not necessarily result in a product being regarded as 'manufactured or produced'").

The Court of International Trade also cited a number of other considerations influencing its decision that a substantial transformation had not occurred in the drawing process, including the fact that there was "no transformation from producers' to consumers' goods * * * no complicated or expensive processing," and "only relatively small value * * * added."

In view of the court's findings and conclusions, we are convinced of the correctness of its decision. The drawing of wire rod into wire is, as the Court of International Trade concluded, not the manufacture of a new and different product as required by *Anheuser-Busch Brewing Ass'n*, 207 U.S. at 562.

The judgment of the Court of International Trade is

AFFIRMED.

Notes and Questions

1. One of the best known articulations of the substantial transformation test originates in *United States v. Gibson-Thomsen*, 27 C.C.P.A. 267 (1940). In that case, wooden toothbrush and hair brush handles were imported from Japan into the United States, where bristles were implanted. In evaluating whether the addition of bristles worked a substantial transformation of the brush handles, the Court of Customs and Patent Appeals held that the handles would be substantially transformed in the United States—and thus become U.S.-origin goods—if the imported materials or components are "so processed in the United States that each loses its identity in a tariff sense and becomes an integral part of a new article having a new name, character, and use." On the facts before it, the CCPA concluded: "the involved articles—toothbrush handles and wood brush blocks—are mere materials to be used in the United States in the manufacture of new articles—toothbrushes and hairbrushes, respectively." The substantial transformation test has accordingly sometimes been called the **name, character, and use test** or the ***Gibson-Thomsen* test**.

2. A change in character and a change in use are often interdependent. For example, in *Ferrostaal Metals Corp. v. United States*, 664 F. Supp. 535 (Ct. Int'l Trade 1987), the CIT considered whether steel sheet that had been annealed and galvanized (i.e., dipped in molten zinc) in New Zealand by a process known as "continuous hot-dip galvanizing" using hard cold-rolled steel sheet from Japan worked a "substantial transformation" of the Japanese steel sheet in New Zealand. The court considered whether the processes in New Zealand changed the "chemical composition and dimensions" of the steel sheet. Although annealing only affected the distribution of some of the chemical elements rather than the underlying chemical structure of the sheet, the court found relevant that galvanization irreversibly changes the electrochemical properties of the sheet, adding strength and ductility that "significantly affects the character by dedicating the sheet to uses compatible with the strength and ductility of the steel." Cold-rolled steel sheet cannot be used in the same industrial applications for which annealed and galvanized steel sheet is typically used, meaning that the processes performed in New Zealand had changed the "uses" of the Japanese sheet. The court considered this change in the "end uses" as "itself indicative of a change in the character of the product."

The court in *Ferrostaal Metals* did not focus solely on the change in physical characteristics and use, however. It also noted that galvanization "is substantial in terms of the value it adds to full hard cold-rolled steel sheet. The evidence showed that the Japanese product is sold for approximately $350 per ton, while the hot-dipped galvanized product is sold for an average price of $550 to $630 per ton." Thus, differences in the value of the good before and after the process may be relevant to determining whether a substantial transformation has occurred. Finally, the court noted that both the product's name and its tariff classification on the HTS were changed by the annealing and galvanizing processes. This, too, was considered relevant in determining that a substantial transformation had occurred.

3. Every country recognizes that the concept of "substantial transformation" should be decisive in determining the country of origin of imported goods. However, only a few use the "name, character, and use" test. Some focus on the percentage of the value of the good added in each country and consider the country contributing the highest value to be the country of origin, for example. Others define as a "substantial transformation" certain specified manufacturing or processing operations. Still others require that the tariff classification of the goods have changed as a result of the processing performed on the goods in the purported country of origin.

Preferential Rules of Origin

As complex as the nonpreferential rule of origin seems, it is only the tip of the iceberg. The United States has entered into numerous bilateral and regional free trade agreements, by which the United States and its treaty partners agree to apply special rules of origin in determining whether goods originate in the territory of treaty parties. The rationale for these rules is partly that, because most goods between these treaty parties can be imported duty-free, it is important to be certain and avoid disputes about which goods originate where.

For example, the U.S.–Chile Free Trade Agreement has its own rules of origin for goods originating in the territory of the two countries. First, instead of the "wholly produced" rule applying on an individual country basis, any good that was wholly produced in any one or both of the United States and Chile will enter any of them with preferential treatment. Continuing with the loaf of bread example, if the wheat was grown and milled in the United States, and the dough beaten and baked in Chile, the loaf can be imported into the United States under the FTA's preferential treatment, generally meaning duty-free.

In addition, U.S.-Chile FTA does not rely on the *Gibson-Thomsen* test. Instead, it substitutes three types of substantial transformation rules on an HTS heading by HTS heading basis: (1) a **tariff shift**; (2) **regional value content**; or (3) some combination of (1) and (2). This list of HTS headings is set forth in Annex 4.1 to the FTA. These headings typically specify one of three types of rules of origin that applies to goods indicated in the heading.

Under a tariff shift rule, goods classified as tariff heading or subheading *X* on the HTS are considered to originate in country *A* if all of the foreign materials or components are transformed in country *A* from goods classified under other tariff headings or subheadings (sometimes specified) to goods classified under the *X* heading or subheading.

For example, suppose you are a company seeking to import into the United States gas barbecues made partly with Chinese ceramic plates and manufactured in Chile. You wish to know whether the barbecues will be classified as originating in China or Chile. Looking up barbecues (HTS heading 7321.11) in U.S.–Chile FTA Annex 4.1, you find the following options:

> A change to subheading 7321.11 * * * from any other heading; or
> A change to subheading 7321.11 * * * from subheading 7321.90, whether or not there is also a change from any other heading, provided there is a regional value content of not less than:
> (a) 35 percent when the build-up method is used, or
> (b) 45 percent when the build-down method is used.

The build-up and build-down methods are explained in Article 4.2 of the Agreement and offer alternative ways of calculating value content based on either the value of materials originating in the United States and Chile (build-up) or the value of materials originating outside the two countries (build-down).

The ceramic plates might be classified under heading 6901 (which covers ceramic tiles) or under subheading 7321.90 (which covers barbecue parts). If the Chinese plates are properly classified under heading 6901, the tariff shift rules apply (because the plates are *not* found in heading 7321) and the barbecues originate in Chile under the FTA rules of origin. If, however, the plates are classified under subheading 7321.90, we move on to the second type of FTA rule of origin—a regional value content rule.

A regional value content rule specifies that goods classified as tariff heading or subheading *X* on the HTS are considered to originate in country *A* if at least a specified percentage of the total value of the goods is attributable to materials, components, or manufacturing processing in any FTA country (here, in Chile or the United States, or some combination of the two). Continuing with the example above, suppose the ceramic plates are properly classified under subheading 7321.90, and we use the build-up method. In that case, Annex 4.1

UNITED STATES - CHILE FREE TRADE AGREEMENT
TRATADO DE LIBRE COMERCIO CHILE - ESTADOS UNIDOS
CERTIFICATE OF ORIGIN

Page 1 of 1

1. EXPORTER NAME AND ADDRESS: TAX IDENTIFICATION NUMBER:	2. BLANKET PERIOD (MM/DD/YYYY) FROM: TO:
3. PRODUCER NAME AND ADDRESS: TAX IDENTIFICATION NUMBER:	4. IMPORTER NAME AND ADDRESS: TAX IDENTIFICATION NUMBER:

5. DESCRIPTION OF GOOD(S)	6. HS TARIFF CLASSIFICATION NUMBER	7. PREFERENCE CRITERIA	8. PRODUCER	9. REGIONAL VALUE CONTENT	10. COUNTRY OF ORIGIN

I CERTIFY THAT:

- THE INFORMATION ON THIS DOCUMENT IS TRUE AND ACCURATE AND I ASSUME THE RESPONSIBILITY FOR PROVING SUCH REPRESENTATIONS. I UNDERSTAND THAT I AM LIABLE FOR ANY FALSE STATEMENTS OR MATERIAL OMISSIONS MADE ON OR IN CONNECTION WITH THIS DOCUMENT;
- I AGREE TO MAINTAIN, AND PRESENT UPON REQUEST, DOCUMENTATION NECESSARY TO SUPPORT THIS CERTIFICATE, AND TO INFORM, IN WRITING, ALL PERSONS TO WHOM THE CERTIFICATE WAS GIVEN OF ANY CHANGES THAT COULD AFFECT THE ACCURACY OR VALIDITY OF THIS CERTIFICATE;
- THE GOODS ORIGINATED IN THE TERRITORY OF ONE OR MORE OF THE PARTIES, AND COMPLY WITH THE ORIGIN REQUIREMENTS SPECIFIED FOR THOSE GOODS IN THE UNITED STATES - CHILE FREE TRADE AGREEMENT, AND UNLESS SPECIFICALLY EXEMPTED IN ARTICLE 4.11, THERE HAS BEEN NO FURTHER PRODUCTION OR ANY OTHER OPERATION OUTSIDE THE TERRITORIES OF THE PARTIES; AND
- THIS CERTIFICATE CONSISTS OF [1] PAGES, INCLUDING ALL ATTACHMENTS.

11.	11a. AUTHORIZED SIGNATURE:		11b. COMPANY:	
	11c. NAME (PRINT OR TYPE):		11d. TITLE:	
	11e. DATE (MM/DD/YYYY):	11f. TELEPHONE NUMBER:	(Voice)	(Facsimile)

Figure 5.10. A U.S.-Chile Certificate of Origin (U.S. version).

provides that if 35% of the value of the barbecues is attributable to either the United States or Chile, then the barbecue originates in U.S.–Chile territory and qualifies for preferential treatment. If the barbecues are entirely made in Chile from Chilean parts and materials except for the ceramic plates, then this rule means the barbecues originate in Chile so long as the plates do not comprise more than 65% of the value of the barbecues. So, if the barbecues are sold to U.S. importers for $1000 each, the barbecues will be considered to originate in Chile so long as the ceramic plates in each barbecue are worth no more than $650 (i.e., 65% of $1000).

Almost all other U.S. FTAs use rules of origin similar to those in U.S.–Chile FTA. In addition, most FTAs require that importers obtain from the manufacturer a **certificate of origin** to show that the goods satisfy the FTA's country of origin rules and qualify for preferential treatment.* For illustrative purposes, a Certificate of Origin for the U.S.–Chile FTA is reproduced as Figure 5.10.

E. Appraisal (Valuation)

Sometimes under the "1—General" or "1—Special" column it says "Free." That means that some goods of that classification enter duty free—the importer need pay no customs duties on the imported items—but only if they come from certain countries. For other countries, duties will be assessed. Frequently, the numbers under the "1—General" and "2" columns are expressed as percentages. That means customs duty is assessed as a percentage of the value of the goods. Duties assessed as a percentage of the value of the goods are called ***ad valorem* duties** (*ad valorem* is a Latin term meaning "on the value").

Appraisal (also known as **valuation**) means determining the value of the goods themselves. In the United States, it is the importer's responsibility to determine the value of goods, although CBP may check to ensure the importer has appraised the goods properly. If not, the importer may be penalized, so it is important to get valuation right consistently. To determine how much duty is owed, it is frequently necessary to know the value of the goods. The U.S. appraisal rules are set forth in 19 U.S.C. § 1401a and 19 C.F.R. pt. 152.

Import duties are usually calculated on an *ad valorem* basis. There is nothing unusual about the Smalldonian snowshoes being subjected to an *ad valorem* duty. For example, suppose that your client's first shipment of snowshoes into the United States is worth a total of $100,000. If the United States imposes a customs duty of 2.6% *ad valorem* on imported snowshoes from Smalldonia, then the duty payable will be:

2.6% × $100,000 = $2,600

*Some countries require a certificate of origin for their own purposes. For example, some members of the European Economic Area (EEA) require a certificate of origin for goods that allegedly originate in the EEA and qualify for duty-free treatment.

Customs duties on some classes of goods may not be based on the value of the goods. In some cases, duties are calculated based on the weight (e.g., $ *z* per kilogram), volume (e.g., $ *z* per kiloliter), or number (e.g., $ *z* per piece or dozen). If we suppose that a shipment of 1000 kiloliters of the chemical sulfuric acid is being imported into Ruritania, and Ruritania calculates duties on sulfuric acid based on volume rather than value, then the value of the acid is irrelevant. Suppose Ruritania charges duties on sulfuric acid at a rate of 60 cents per kiloliter. In that case, because 1000 kiloliters are being imported, it does not matter whether the shipment of the acid is worth $1000 or $1 million, the duty is the same:

60¢/kiloliter x 1000 kiloliters = $600

For some imports, duty may be calculated based on a combination of *ad valorem* duty and some other method. For example, duty might be levied at 15 cents per kilogram plus 2% *ad valorem.*

Normally, goods are worth different things to different classes of people under different circumstances. For example, suppose Widgico is a Zembian corporation that manufactures widgets. Widgico manufactures 100,000 widgets each year at an average cost to Widgico of US$ 5 per widget. Widgico might find that it can sell the widgets in Zembia at a wholesale price of $7 per widget and in the United States at a wholesale price of $9 per widget. Zembian retailers might purchase the widgets for $12 each and resell them to consumers for $24 per widget. Meanwhile, U.S. retailers purchase them from U.S. wholesalers for $16 per widget and resell them to consumers for $32 per widget. With all these "values" from which to choose, which one will CBP prefer for appraising the goods?

The United States uses appraisal methods that conform to its international treaty obligations. Article VII of the General Agreement on Tariffs and Trade (GATT) and the Agreement on Implementation of Article VII of the GATT, commonly known as the **WTO Customs Valuation Agreement**, together establish a general appraisal methodology used in all of the WTO member states. This code sets forth a list of acceptable and unacceptable appraisal methods and describes how each generally may be used.

The preferred method for appraisal under the WTO Customs Valuation Agreement, and the one accordingly preferred by CBP, is based on the **transaction value** of the imports. Simply put, the transaction value is the price the purchaser in the country of importation actually pays (or is required by contract to pay) for the imported goods, assuming the parties are dealing at "arm's length" with each other—that is, neither is doing the other a special favor by charging a lower price because they are affiliated companies. Packing costs, selling commissions, royalties paid to the seller, and similar costs are included in the transaction value, even if not paid directly to the seller. However, freight, insurance, and related costs are not included, because these relate not to the value of the goods themselves, but to their transportation to the country of importation. The transaction value establishes the value of the goods for purposes of determining the amount of *ad valorem* customs duties owed by the importer.

If transaction value cannot be used (e.g., because the seller and purchaser are affiliated companies not selling at arm's length), a hierarchy of other appraisal techniques are used. These are, in the order of preference:

1. The **transaction value of identical merchandise** between parties doing business at arm's length.

2. The **transaction value of similar merchandise** between parties doing business at arm's length. This may be necessary where the imported goods are unique in some way. Obviously, this appraisal technique can only be used when the differences between the imported goods at issue and the reference goods are economically insubstantial, or when those differences can be adequately accounted for in assessing the value of the imports.

3. **Deductive value**. Basically, deductive value is the resale price in the United States after importation of the goods (as opposed to the price the importer paid), with deductions for certain items such as transportation costs or sales commissions.

4. **Computed value**. Computed value attempts to recreate the producer's cost of making the good plus the normal profit the producer expects to derive from selling the good. It is usually the sum of the materials, fabrication, and other processing used in growing, extracting, or manufacturing the imported merchandise, plus profit, general expenses, and packing costs.

The WTO Customs Valuation Agreement provides that these appraisal methods should be used in the order presented. Thus, if the transaction value of the imports presented for entry cannot be used, then the transaction value of identical or similar merchandise is used. Failing that, deductive value is used. If all else fails, the goods will be appraised according to a computed value.

F. Liquidation

Liquidation means that the customs authorities have accepted the importer's assessment of the duties owed and released the goods into the U.S. customs territory for consumption. Within ten days after release of the goods, the importer will present an **entry summary** (reproduced in Figure 5.11) to CBP. This document summarizes the necessary information to determine the customs duties owed, including the classification, value, and country of origin. It also includes information about the relevant ports of lading and entry and actors (shipper, carrier, and consignee). Along with the entry summary, the importer will pay the import duties owed. Failure to pay the duties will result in the forfeiture of the importer's customs bond. If CBP subsequently determines that the importer has overpaid, it will typically refund the excess amount.

Within a limited period of time after the goods are imported and inspected by customs authorities (in the United States, within 30 days), the importer must arrange to have the imports picked up from the customs port and delivered elsewhere. They may be transported to a customs warehouse or Foreign Trade Zone, they may undergo further transportation by inland freight, or they may be transported straight to the consignee by truck. If the consignee fails to pick up with goods by the deadline, customs authorities may confiscate the goods or put them in a warehouse and charge the importer for storage.

G. Binding Rulings, Protest, and Appeal

In the United States, if an importer is unsure how specific goods are properly classified or appraised, or needs advice on determining their country of origin, it may get advance information from the port director or from CBP headquarters by sending a letter requesting either informal advice or a binding ruling. Informal advice is just that, but a binding **customs ruling** can be relied upon for placing or accepting orders or otherwise making firm business arrangements, because once a ruling has been issued it is binding at all customs ports, and CBP cannot change its mind except by a formal revocation giving advance notice. A request for a binding ruling is typically drafted by a customs lawyer and gives all relevant details about the intended shipment of goods. The ruling applies only to the facts presented in the request; if the shipment deviates from those facts, the ruling cannot be relied upon.

After liquidation, if the importer disagrees with the customs authorities about the amount of duties owed, in most countries it may request an administrative or judicial review of the decision of the customs authorities. The importer would first file a **protest** with CBP, which will review the decision at its New York headquarters. If CBP denies the protest, the importer may appeal to the U.S. Court of International Trade. The CIT also sits in New York City and hears all customs appeals, as well as some other international trade-related cases. Appeals from final decisions of the CIT go to the U.S. Court of Appeals for the Federal Circuit and, ultimately, to the U.S. Supreme Court.

1.3 Duty Minimization or Avoidance

Customs duties are a form of taxation and, depending on the duty rate and the value of the goods, they may present some disincentive to what might otherwise be the most efficient allocation and use of manufacturing resources. Customs duties can thereby discourage an optimal international investment of capital. Consider three examples.

Form Approved OMB No. 1651-0022

DEPARTMENT OF HOMELAND SECURITY
U.S. Customs and Border Protection

ENTRY SUMMARY

1. Filer Code/Entry No.		2. Entry Type	3. Summary Date
4. Surety No.	5. Bond Type	6. Port Code	7. Entry Date

8. Importing Carrier	9. Mode of Transport	10. Country of Origin	11. Import Date
12. B/L or AWB No.	13. Manufacturer ID	14. Exporting Country	15. Export Date

16. I.T. No.	17. I.T. Date	18. Missing Docs	19. Foreign Port of Lading	20. U.S. Port of Unlading

21. Location of Goods/G.O. No.	22. Consignee No.	23. Importer No.	24. Reference No.

25. Ultimate Consignee Name and Address	26. Importer of Record Name and Address
City State Zip	City State Zip

27. Line No.	28. Description of Merchandise 29. A. HTSUS No. B. ADA/CVD No.	30. A. Grossweight B. Manifest Qty.	31. Net Quantity in HTSUS Units	32. A. Entered Value B. CHGS C. Relationship	33. A. HTSUS Rate B. ADA/CVD Rate C. IRC Rate D. Visa No.	34. Duty and I.R. Tax Dollars Cents

Other Fee Summary for Block 39	35. Total Entered Value $	**CBP USE ONLY**		TOTALS
	Total Other Fees $	A. LIQ CODE	B. Ascertained Duty	37. Duty
		REASON CODE	C. Ascertained Tax	38. Tax
			D. Ascertained Other	39. Other
			E. Ascertained Total	40. Total

36. DECLARATION OF IMPORTER OF RECORD (OWNER OR PURCHASER) OR AUTHORIZED AGENT

I declare that I am the ☐ Importer of record and that the actual owner, purchaser, or consignee for CBP purposes is as shown above, **OR** ☐ owner or purchaser or agent thereof. I further declare that the merchandise ☐ was obtained pursuant to a purchase or agreement to purchase and that the prices set forth in the invoices are true, **OR** ☐ was not obtained pursuant to a purchase or agreement to purchase and the statements in the invoices as to value or price are true to the best of my knowledge and belief. I also declare that the statements in the documents herein filed fully disclose to the best of my knowledge and belief the true prices, values, quantities, rebates, drawbacks, fees, commissions, and royalties and are true and correct, and that all goods or services provided to the seller of the merchandise either free or at reduced cost are fully disclosed.
I will immediately furnish to the appropriate CBP officer any information showing a different statement of facts.

41. DECLARANT NAME	TITLE	SIGNATURE	DATE

42. Broker/Filer Information (Name, address, phone number)	43. Broker/Importer File No.
	PaperWork Reduction Act Notice CBP Form 7501 (04/05)

Figure 5.11. An entry summary (CBP Form 7501).

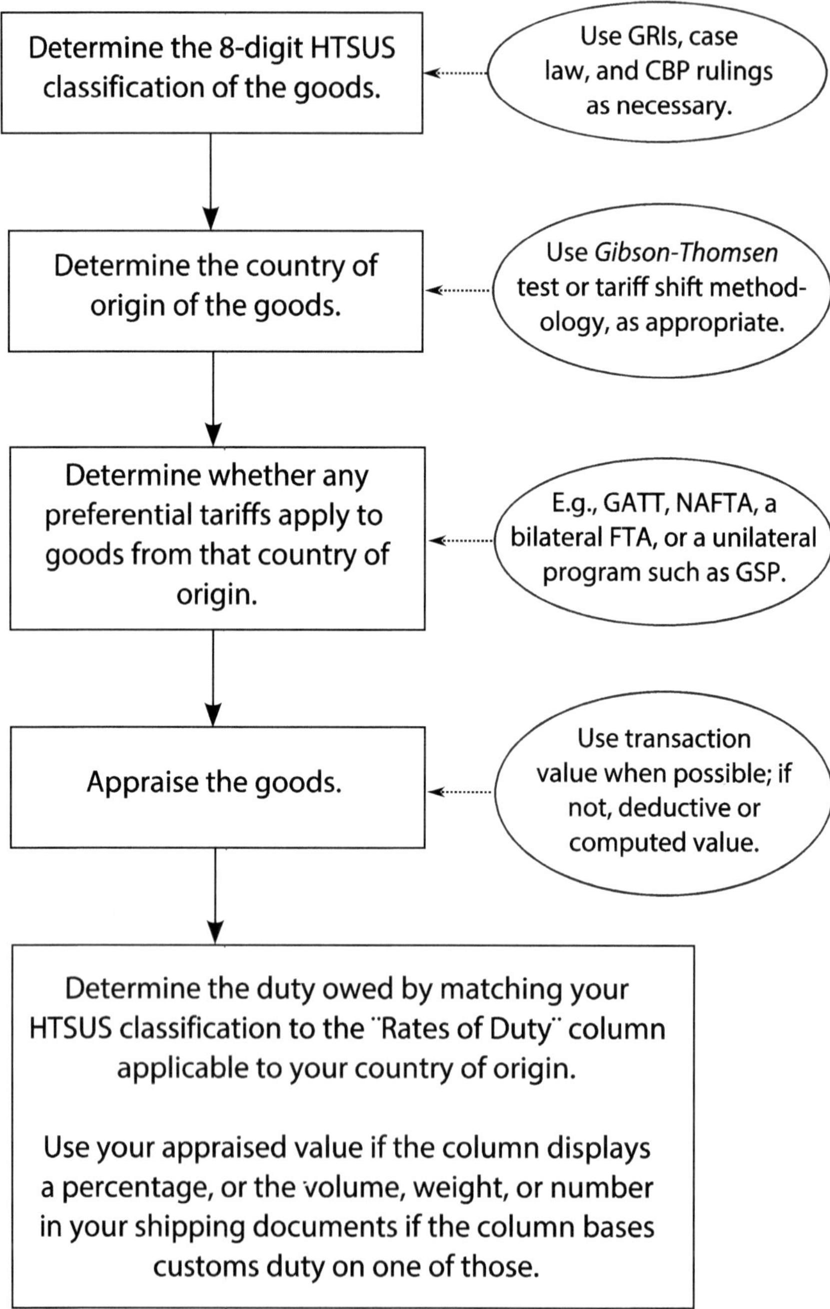

Figure 5.12. Flow chart of the basic steps for calculating the customs duties owed on imports into the United States.

Example 1: Unpredictable Demand. A purchaser may face unpredictable demand for the imported products. It can deal with this problem in several ways. First, it can order large stocks of imported merchandise and keep them in a warehouse until needed to fill consumer demand. But there are at least three major costs associated with extensive warehousing: (1) the cost of renting or buying warehouse space for the stockpiled merchandise; (2) the opportunity cost of the money spent on the stockpiled merchandise as it waits to be used or resold; and (3) the opportunity cost of the duties paid on the goods while they are sitting in the warehouse. The purchaser may find itself importing large quantities of the goods, paying import duties, and then letting the goods sit in a warehouse for months or even years before using them or putting them at the disposal of customers. During this time, had the purchaser not paid customs duties, it could have used the money to invest or earn interest. Instead, it loses the use of the money it paid in merchandise and duties even if it has not yet used or resold any of the imported products.

Second, the purchaser could wait to order goods, or cut back on the size of its orders, until it was relatively certain of its needs or of consumer demand, as appropriate. When the foreign supplier is in an adjacent country or the merchandise is of high value relative to its weight, this model is fairly common and is called **just-in-time shipping**. The problem with this approach is that international shipping will likely be slow if the supplier is distant and the items are too heavy or bulky to ship by air. Even in the best case scenario, the foreign supplier may need some advance notice before it can fill the order. Moreover, there may be unexpected delays at the customs port that the carrier cannot control. So the purchaser may find itself short of stock during an unpredicted upswing in demand. This could cause it to miss out on the chance to fill lucrative orders. Neither of these options may be very attractive to importers.

Example 2: Assembly for Export. In many cases, a manufacturer will import goods into a country with no intention of selling them there. It may merely wish to import industrial inputs (materials and components); assemble or otherwise process them; and then export them to overseas markets. This business model is fairly common and is known in the U.S.-Mexico trade context as a *maquila* arrangement. It is attractive to foreign manufacturers as well, because they can take advantage of inexpensive labor, low taxes, or lax foreign environmental or other regulatory standards to lower costs of production. But, because customs duties raise the cost of importing goods into the country for further processing, they may discourage desirable foreign investment.

Example 3: Nonconforming or Damaged Imports. Finally, consider the company that imports foreign-made merchandise into the United States under a sales agreement, only to learn that the goods have arrived damaged or nonconforming. The importer would like to send the goods back (or, if that is too expensive, destroy them), but has already paid customs duties before discovering the problem. It is inconsistent with the nature of customs duties as a consumption tax that the importer should be taxed on goods it cannot consume.

NOTE FROM THE FIELD

Being a Customs Lawyer

David R. Hamill, Esq.
Arent Fox

I have practiced customs law both as a government lawyer and in private firms. My own work included helping the U.S. Customs Service (now CBP) draft what would ultimately become the 1993 Customs Modernization Act, landmark legislation that rewrote many of the customs requirements for importers. Later, I worked on revising U.S. customs regulations to comply with the NAFTA Implementation Act. Other tasks assigned to customs lawyers include drafting CBP directives and ruling letters when members of the importing community request CBP's advice on specific questions about classification, valuation, drawback, and similar matters. DHS lawyers working with CBP consult with representatives of private importers frequently to help them understand the practical effects of CBP regulations and customs law enforcement on real world business firms.

A government customs lawyer typically knows well in advance that he or she will be asked to draft or interpret regulations, while in private practice a customs lawyer's work may begin when CBP agents are literally at the client's doorstep seeking to audit records. Similarly, a private customs lawyer may be told by his or her client that CBP is holding at the border goods needed urgently for production or distribution to customers. Entering the merchandise quickly requires understanding the customs regulations thoroughly, but it also means knowing how to deal with the CBP.

In the recent past, private customs practice has evolved to focus less on sporadic problem-solving and more on "compliance practice," while entails evaluating how clients do business to preempt violations of customs regulations. CBP relies increasingly on importers to self-police. This means working not just with the client's legal department, but with its finance, procurement, distribution, logistics, warehousing, and other departments as well. Each department must be aware of and conform to its customs law obligations to ensure that the client avoids trouble with CBP.

In consequence, customs lawyers do not just deal with problems as they arise, but spend their time training the client's personnel in how to comply with customs regulations and conducting practice audits of the client's records.

David R. Hamill is a partner at Arent Fox. He previously worked for nine years as Senior Counsel and Attorney-Advisor to the Department of the Treasury, Office of the General Counsel.

These examples illustrate how the simple payment of customs duties may result in inefficient, unfair, or otherwise undesirable outcomes. Fortunately for importers, in most states, including the United States, customs regulations permit several forms of duty minimization to help importers to delay the payment of duties until the goods are ready to be sold to consumers, to encourage the use of labor in the importing country, and to avoid penalizing importers when the goods are imported but are never consumed in the country.

A. Customs Bonded Warehouses

The opportunity cost of paying duties before the imports are entered into the country for consumption may be quite high. If an importer or consignee wishes to postpone the entry of the goods and the payment of customs duties, many countries allow the importer to place the goods temporarily in a **bonded warehouse**. The warehouse is called "bonded" because the operator must post a bond for the benefit of the customs authorities to guarantee the payment of duties if the imported goods stored in the warehouse are withdrawn for consumption into the importing country.

As early as the medieval era, the Florentine writer Boccaccio was describing customs warehouses maintained by the state:

> After presenting a written description of the cargo and its value to the officers in charge, he is given a storeroom where his merchandise is placed under lock and key; the officers then record all the details in their register under the merchant's name, and whenever the merchant removes his goods from bond, either wholly or in part, they make him pay the appropriate [duties].*

At least as far as Boccaccio described customs warehousing, not much has changed in over six centuries.

In modern practice, however, warehouse regulations have become highly nuanced. The goods generally may remain in the bonded warehouse for a limited time. In the United States, they must be exported or released for consumption within five years of importation. At any time during that period, warehoused goods may be re-exported without paying duty, or they may be withdrawn for consumption upon paying duty at the duty rate in effect on the date of withdrawal. If the goods are destroyed, no duty at all is payable.

While the goods are in the bonded warehouse, they may usually be manipulated by cleaning, sorting, repacking, or otherwise changing their condition by processes short of "manufacturing" the imported goods into new articles of commerce. After such manipulation, and within the warehousing period, the goods may be exported without the payment of duty, or they may be withdrawn

*Giovanni Boccaccio, The Decameron VIII: 10 (G.H. McWilliam trans. 1971) (1353).

for consumption upon payment of duty at the rate applicable to the goods classified as of the time of withdrawal. The warehouse allows the importer to delay paying customs duties for goods to be entered into the country, and to avoid paying duties entirely on goods to be exported.

In the United States and Europe, there are several types of bonded warehouses authorized for use by importers. Some may be operated by government agencies—called "public" warehouses—and others by private warehousing companies or even the importer itself. Some warehouses are used exclusively for storage of merchandise, while others can be used for cleaning, sorting, or other manipulation of the kind described above. Still other types of bonded warehouses may be exclusively dedicated to the manufacture in bond of specially regulated goods such as tobacco or alcohol, which are subject to excise taxes in many countries.

HAVE YOU BEEN IN A CUSTOMS BONDED WAREHOUSE?

If you've ever been in the international terminal of an airport, you have probably been in (or at least seen) a bonded warehouse. Many countries allow importers to set up bonded warehouses, known as duty-free stores, right in airports or other ports of entry. Under this arrangement, goods imported for sale in a duty-free store avoids the payment of customs duties on condition that the merchandise will be exported or taken abroad by the purchaser. So the next time you see an airport store with a DUTY-FREE sign, you will know you are looking at a Class 9 customs bonded warehouse.

B. Foreign Trade Zones

Most states wish to encourage foreign investment in their economies, because foreign investment tends to create jobs and bring tax revenues, among other benefits. Foreign investment may also bring with it costs to the host state, however. A potential disadvantage of foreign investment in manufacturing is that a foreign investor may sell the goods produced in the local economy and remove the profits of the sales to its state of nationality. When a state's consumers purchase goods from a foreign investor, some of the resulting revenues contribute to a negative trade balance between the host state and the investor state. The ideal situation for the host state, then, is to encourage job-creating foreign investment that does not result in the sale of significant foreign products on the host state market. To achieve this ideal, many states have instituted special measures to attract foreign investment in manufacturing for goods that will be exported from the host state. Such measures allow importers to take advantage of cheap or highly expert foreign labor without burdensome customs rules.

One common measure for attracting desirable foreign investment of this kind is known as a foreign trade zone. A **foreign trade zone** (**FTZ**) is a secured area operated by either a private company or a government agency and considered to be outside a state's territory for customs purposes. In other words, the FTZ acts as a region within the state that is carved out of its customs territory. This means that an importer who brings foreign goods into an FTZ does not incur the immediate responsibility of paying customs duties. It may also be exempt from taxation in the host state. The purpose of the FTZ is to allow an importer to make use of local labor to process or assemble imported goods with no payment of duty. In some states, the importer may then enter the processed goods into the state's domestic tariff area and pay customs duties at that time; an advantage of the FTZ in these states is that it allows for a delay in the payment of customs duties, like a bonded warehouse. The difference is that manufacturing in an FTZ is always allowed.

In some states, most or all goods processed in an FTZ must be exported; the state's purpose of increasing domestic employment without increasing imports would otherwise be undermined. For example, India requires operators in a Special Economic Zone to be net earners of foreign currency, meaning that a majority of their output by value must be exported. In such states, the manufacturer imports materials and parts into the FTZ duty-free, assembles or otherwise processes them in the FTZ, and then exports the product for sale elsewhere. The FTZ achieves the goal of encouraging the use of local labor without harming the state's trade balance by importing goods for sale by a foreign company.

The U.S. Department of Commerce is empowered to authorize FTZs in the United States by the 1934 Foreign-Trade Zones Act, 19 U.S.C. §§ 81a-81u. Many other states, especially in Europe and Asia, but some in Latin America as well, have authorized FTZs. In those states, FTZs are also known by many names, such as "free trade zone" (e.g., the Philippines), "free zone" (e.g., Ireland, Jamaica, the United Arab Emirates), "export processing zone" (e.g., Brazil), or the much older term "freeport" (e.g., Bermuda). Usually, FTZs are located in border or coastal cities, but they may also be located inland, especially near airports or in economically depressed areas in need of greater employment. In most countries that authorize FTZs, a government agency is charged with administering the FTZ approval process and supervising their use by importers.

FTZs are usually operated like public accommodations, with published rates applicable to any importer that wishes to lease space in the FTZ. Goods brought into FTZs may usually be stored, sold, exhibited, assembled, distributed, sorted, graded, cleaned, repacked, mixed with other foreign or domestic goods, or otherwise manipulated or manufactured without the payment of customs duties unless and until they enter the customs territory of the state. Although the imported goods may be "consumed" in the sense of being incorporated into another good or otherwise used up, they incur no customs duties until they leave the FTZ and enter the state for sale to the ultimate consumer.

THE *MAQUILADORA*

A ***maquiladora*** or *maquila* for short, is similar to an FTZ in some ways. In modern times, it has given birth to the term *maquilar*, meaning "to assemble." A *maquila* is an assembly plant in Mexico intended mostly for making exports (frequently for the United States). Imports of raw materials and other manufacturing inputs into Mexico typically receive a total or near total exemption from customs duties. The United States, in turn, may make *maquilas* more attractive for companies using U.S. materials in the manufacturing process by imposing customs duties only on the value added in Mexico when the finished products are exported to the United States for consumption. For example, if a *maquila* assembles furniture from wooden parts manufactured in the United States, CBP may impose customs duties (which are already assessed at preferential rates under the USMCA) only on the value added by the Mexican labor rather than on the furniture as a whole. This encourages *maquila* operators to use U.S. materials and parts in their manufacturing operations.

As of 2020, there are over 3000 *maquilas* in Mexico, most of them near the northern border and owned by U.S. companies. *Maquilas* employ about a million Mexican workers and are used in a wide variety of industries. They are common in the garment, electronics and electrical, and furniture industries.

Maquilas are generally managed and owned by non-Mexicans, but the *maquila* operator must abide by Mexican employment laws, including making payments into the socialized medical care system on behalf of the employees and paying Mexican employment and income taxes. The low cost of Mexican labor makes *maquilas* an attractive option for developed countries to avoid paying the (currently $7.25) minimum wage to workers in the United States. The average hourly wage in Mexico hovers around US$ 2.40.

Duties on the foreign goods mixed with domestic goods to create a new article of commerce are usually assessed on the actual quantity of foreign goods incorporated rather than on the finished article. For example, suppose an importer wanted to make sailboats in the United States from fiberglass imported from Osterlich but with all other materials originating in the United States. Suppose the rate of duty on boats from Osterlich is 12% *ad valorem*, but the duty rate on fiberglass is only 6% *ad valorem*. The importer could import the fiberglass into an FTZ, apply to the port director to have the dutiable status of the fiberglass permanently fixed, then mold the fiberglass and combine it with the other materials to make the boat hull in the FTZ; add the engine and other parts there; and then store it until ready for sale in the United States. The importer would not have to pay any duty until the boats were withdrawn from the FTZ for consumption in the United States and, even then, it would only

Policy Issue

Why do developing countries exempt FTZs from customs duties?

It may seem that, by exempting foreign manufacturers from customs duties, developing countries are depriving themselves of valuable customs revenue. But developing countries may consider such arrangements advantageous because, by exempting imported industrial inputs from customs duties, they are encouraging foreign investors to come and use their labor, thereby creating employment opportunities and possibly transferring valuable business knowhow or technology. But such arrangements may also lead to the exploitation of developing country populations by reinforcing low wages and unemployment in higher wage countries, thereby forcing wages down worldwide. In addition, lax or underenforced environmental or worker health and safety standards may result in developed countries "exporting" their pollution and worker injuries or maladies to developing countries. For this reason, environmental and pro-labor groups in both developed and developing countries often oppose such arrangements. There are ways for developing countries and developed countries to use FTZs to their mutual benefit without harming the environment, worker rights, or creating high unemployment among the unskilled or semi-skilled in high-wage developed countries. However, such a compromise would require significant investment in education, job retraining, and worker relocation. Is the problem an absence of better solutions, or an absence of incentives for politicians to adopt sound long-term public policies that benefit unskilled workers?

pay 6% duty on the value of the fiberglass used in the boats, not on the boats themselves. In other words, domestic merchandise can go in and out of the FTZ without paying duty even if it is transformed into a new article by combining it with foreign materials or components.

FTZs have several advantages for importers. First, goods may be brought into an FTZ and stored there as if the FTZ were a customs warehouse without the need to pay duties until the goods are withdrawn for consumption in the importing state. In fact, even beyond the ability to manufacture, an FTZ may be preferable to a customs warehouse, because in some countries (such as the United States) there is no time limit as to how long foreign merchandise may be stored in a zone, or when it must be entered into customs territory, reexported, or destroyed. Also, in some countries, if any unrecoverable waste results from manufacture or manipulation (for example, if part of the fiberglass is rendered worthless in the process of manufacture), no duty is paid on that waste, thereby eliminating payment of duty except on the articles that actually enter the customs territory of the importing state.

C. Drawback

In the United States, if the customs inspectors determine that imported goods entirely lacked commercial value at the time of arrival in the United States because of damage or deterioration, the goods are treated as a "nonimportation." In other words, no duties are assessed on the imported goods. But what if the customs inspectors and the consignee do not notice the damage or deterioration until after the goods have been liquidated? Or what if the imported goods are incorporated into other goods that are subsequently destroyed or exported without being used in the United States? In each case, no end-user consumption has occurred in the United States, and so it seems no import duty should be paid.

The 1930 Tariff Act provides for such cases through the drawback procedure. **Drawback** is a refund to the importer of 99% of the customs duties on imported goods that, for one reason or another, could not be consumed but had to be destroyed or else reexported. One drawback of drawback is that CBP keeps 1% as an administrative fee. The Act provides for many kinds of drawback that can be classified into three broad categories: manufacturing drawback, unused-merchandise drawback, and rejected-merchandise drawback. 19 U.S.C. § 1313.

Manufacturing drawback is a refund of duties paid on imported merchandise used in the manufacture of goods that are either exported or destroyed. For example, an importer may obtain drawback on foreign salt imported to cure fish in the United States. The imported merchandise must be used up in the manufacturing process and the resulting goods exported within five years from the date of importation of the merchandise. The importer may obtain drawback only if the manufacturing arrangement has received prior approval from CBP.

Unused-merchandise drawback, also known as **substitution drawback**, is a refund of duties paid on imported merchandise that is simply destroyed or exported in the same condition in which it was imported. The merchandise must not have been used in any way in the United States and must be exported within three years from the date of importation. It does not have to be the exact same merchandise that was imported, so long as the merchandise is commercially interchangeable. This spares the importer from having to separate fungible industrial inputs such as steel or sugar that are imported from those procured domestically.

Rejected-merchandise drawback is a refund of duties on imported merchandise that is exported because it was nonconforming to the sales contract or was otherwise shipped without the consent of the consignee. Such merchandise must be returned to CBP within three years of the date of its importation and must be reexported to another state, usually the place of origin, rather than destroyed.

The official justification given by CBP for allowing drawback is to assist U.S. importers, manufacturers, and exporters to compete on international markets. This explains manufacturing drawback, but the other two kinds can be justified much more simply. Because customs duty is a consumption tax, it is improper to require importers to pay the customs duty on imported goods that could not be consumed.

D. Temporary Imports and the ATA Carnet

Sometimes, a company may wish to import goods into a country temporarily, without consuming them, and reexport them in substantially the same condition. For example, the company may wish to send one of its employees or agents to a trade show in a foreign country with sample products to demonstrate. Or a machine manufacturer may send a team of technicians to visit a foreign purchaser and repair his machine using valuable tools. In these cases, the goods—the demonstration products in the first scenario and the technicians' tools in the second—are not being imported for consumption, but merely for temporary use. The importer in each case expects to reexport the goods upon conclusion of the trade show or repair service. Here, too, customs duties are not properly applicable, because consumption has not occurred.

In many countries, importers may import such items temporarily if they first post a bond guaranteeing that, if the goods are not exported in a reasonable time, the importer will pay all customs duties due. In the United States, this procedure is called **temporary import under bond** (**TIB**). Goods that can be imported duty-free using the TIB procedure include those intended to be:

- repaired, altered, or processed for exportation;
- demonstrated as samples to solicit sales;
- used as advertising materials;
- used in experimental testing; or
- employed as professional tools of the trade

subject to the requirement that they be exported from the United States within one year of importation.

In addition to domestic regulations allowing duty-free temporary imports, many states are parties to the **Customs Convention on ATA Carnet for Temporary Importation of Goods** or the Istanbul Convention on Temporary Admission. This treaty establishes a procedure for the temporary admission of certain classes of goods duty-free using an internationally recognized document called an **ATA carnet**. The "ATA" stands for "*admission temporaire*—temporary admission" (the French and English versions were combined into a single acronym). The carnet acts as evidence that the importer has posted a bond guaranteeing that the temporarily imported goods will be exported within one year. The carnet can be used by business travelers to transport commercial samples; tools of the trade; advertising devices and materials; and audiovisual, medical, scientific, and other professional equipment.

The main advantages of using an ATA carnet over TIB are:

(1) some countries that accept ATA carnets have no other temporary importation procedures;

(2) TIB procedures require formal entry of the goods, which requires the posting of an individual bond for each importation and much electronic reporting each time the goods are imported, whereas goods carrying an ATA carnet may be entered as many times as desired during the carnet's validity without having to post bond or make formal entry; and

(3) the same ATA carnet may be used in multiple countries, so long as they are signatories to the Convention.

As of 2020, 80 countries and territories, including the United States and the European Union, accept ATA carnets. Notable, however, is the nearly complete absence of Latin American countries from this group.

The ATA Convention is administered by the World Customs Organization, but ATA carnets are issued by local carnet associations, which are responsible for collecting the importer's bond and making sure the importer honors its export obligation before the one-year term of the carnet expires. Every country designates its own carnet association. In the United States, the **U.S. Council for International Business** is the authorized issuer.

1.4 Country of Origin Marking

You may recall that determining the country of origin of imported goods is a necessary step in calculating customs duties owed on the imports. But it is also necessary because many countries require that all imported goods be labeled, engraved, or otherwise marked with their country of origin to inform consumers of where the goods were made. For example, the manufacturer of an acetate scarf may attach a label to the scarf with a statement such as "MADE IN CHINA" or "PRODUCT OF PARAGUAY" to comply with these **marking requirements**.

The U.S. marking rules are set forth in Section 304 of the 1930 Tariff Act:

---

19 U.S.C. § 1304

(a) Marking of articles. Except as hereinafter provided, every article of foreign origin (or its container, as provided in subsection (b) hereof) imported into the United States shall be marked in a conspicuous place as legibly, indelibly, and permanently as the nature of the article (or container) will permit in such manner as to indicate to an ultimate purchaser in the United States the English name of the country of origin of the article. The Secretary of the Treasury [*sic*: of DHS] may by regulations—

* * *

(3) Authorize the exception of any article from the requirements of marking if—

(A) Such article is incapable of being marked;

(B) Such article cannot be marked prior to shipment to the United States without injury;

(C) Such article cannot be marked prior to shipment to the United States, except at an expense economically prohibitive of its importation;

(D) The marking of a container of such article will reasonably indicate the origin of such article;

(E) Such article is a crude substance;

(F) Such article is imported for use by the importer and not intended for sale in its imported or any other form;

(G) Such article is to be processed in the United States by the importer or for his account otherwise than for the purpose of concealing the origin of such article and in such manner that any mark contemplated by this section would necessarily be obliterated, destroyed, or permanently concealed;

(H) An ultimate purchaser, by reason of the character of such article or by reason of the circumstances of its importation, must necessarily know the country of origin of such article even though it is not marked to indicate its origin;

* * * ; or

(K) Such article cannot be marked after importation except at any expense which is economically prohibitive, and the failure to mark the article before importation was not due to any purpose of the importer, producer, seller, or shipper to avoid compliance with this section.

(b) Marking of containers. Whenever an article is excepted under subdivision (3) of subsection (a) of this section from the requirements of marking, the immediate container, if any, of such article, or such other container or containers of such article as may be prescribed by the Secretary of the Treasury [*sic*: of DHS], shall be marked in such manner as to indicate to an ultimate purchaser in the United States the English name of the country of origin of such article, subject to all provisions of this section, including the same exceptions as are applicable to articles under subdivision (3) of subsection (a) of this section.

* * *

(*i*) Additional duties for failure to mark. If at the time of importation any article (or its container, as provided in subsection (b) of this section) is not marked in accordance with the requirements of this section * * *, there shall be levied, collected, and paid upon such article a duty of 10 *per centum ad valorem*, which shall be deemed to have accrued at the time of importation, shall not be construed to be penal, and shall not be remitted wholly or in part nor shall payment thereof be avoidable for any cause. Such duty shall be levied, collected, and paid in addition to any other duty imposed by law and whether or not the article is exempt from the payment of ordinary customs duties. * * *

(j) Delivery withheld until marked. No imported article held in customs custody for inspection, examination, or appraisement shall be delivered until such article and every other article of the importation (or their containers), whether or not released from customs custody, shall have been marked in accordance with the requirements of this section or until the amount of duty estimated to be payable under subsection (*i*) of this section has been deposited. * * *

In summary, Section 304 of the 1930 Tariff Act requires each imported article produced abroad to be marked in a conspicuous place "as legibly, indelibly, and permanently as the nature of the article permits," with the name of the country of origin. Although the language of the customs laws seems exacting, the reality is that CBP only requires the goods to be marked in such a manner that the ultimate consumer will be notified of the country of origin. In other words, the marking is sufficiently permanent if it will remain on the imported article until it reaches the ultimate consumer. With a few specific exceptions, it is not actually necessary to mold or engrave the country of original in all imported metal items if a sturdy sticker label will reliably adhere and be legible to the ultimate consumer.*

Section 304 also addresses the problem of imported goods that cannot themselves be marked. After all, how do you "mark" a shipment of wheat or iron ore? Or how do you mark high precision ball bearings or frozen chicken breasts without ruining them? The answer given by Section 304 is that, where such unmarkable goods will be delivered to the ultimate purchaser in a package, box, or other container, the container may be conspicuously labeled with the country of origin. For example, a box of imported wood screws may state the country of origin of the screws on the box label. Where there is no package that will reach the ultimate consumer, no marking is required.

Marking requirements for imported goods may begin with customs law, but they do not end there. Many different laws require special marking for specific types of goods. In the United States and several other states, for example, processed foods must contain information about the ingredients and nutritional content on the package, and clothing must contain information about

*Article IX:4 of the GATT prohibits WTO members from requiring marking that would seriously damage the products, materially reduce their value, or unreasonably increase their cost.

the fibers used. Every country has its own requirements, so it is important to know about the labeling regulations of each country into which the client is importing goods.

For those importing goods into the United States, it is also important to be aware of special marking laws relating to the use of the phrase "Made in the U.S.A." and similar language. The **Federal Trade Commission** (**FTC**) has adopted its own rules separate from the customs marking rules for the use of this phrase. Under the customs marking rules, articles manufactured in the United States do not need to be marked with the country of origin, but many manufacturers voluntarily mark products originating in the United States in hopes of gaining a patriotic edge on sales in the U.S. marketplace. The problem for manufacturers is that even though some goods would be considered as originating in the United States for customs purposes, this does not mean they qualify to be labeled as made in the U.S.A. under the FTC regulations!

The FTC has adopted the rule that only those products that are "all or virtually all" made in the United States may be labeled as "Made in the U.S.A." (or similar language) without qualification. This rule is similar to the customs "wholly produced" rule—the product only originates in the United States for labeling purposes if the foreign content or value in the product is negligible. If the product contains more than negligible foreign content, the FTC allows the importer or manufacturer to make carefully-crafted, accurate claims of U.S. content. For example, a sofa may be labeled "Assembled in the United States from Italian leather and a Mexican wooden frame," or an electronic device may state "75% U.S. content," if these claims are accurate.

Finally, it is important to recall that Section 42 of the Lanham Trademark Act (15 U.S.C. § 1124) prohibits the importation of articles of foreign origin bearing a name or mark calculated to induce the public to believe that it was manufactured in the United States or in any place other than its country of origin. Section 43 of the Lanham Act (15 U.S.C. § 1125) also prohibits the entry of goods marked with a false designation of origin or any other false representation. These sections of the Lanham Act go beyond prohibiting imports that infringe a U.S. trademark; they are designed to protect consumers from misleading labels regardless of the absence of infringement.

1.5 Penalties for Noncompliance

Article VIII:3 of the GATT prohibits WTO members from imposing substantial penalties for minor breaches of customs regulations. In the United States, penalties range from fines equal to 10% of the dutiable value of the merchandise for failure to properly mark imported goods with the country of origin to imprisonment for trying to smuggle imports into the country without declaring them to CBP. Penalties also may include confiscation of the imported goods; because an imported shipment may be very valuable, confiscation is sometimes the harshest form of economic penalty.

The general penalties for failure to comply with the import laws are set forth in Section 592 of the 1930 Tariff Act. This section breaks down fines into categories that depend on the mental state of the importer.

§ 1592. Penalties for fraud, gross negligence, and negligence

(a) Prohibition

(1) General rule. Without regard to whether the United States is or may be deprived of all or a portion of any lawful duty, tax, or fee thereby, no person, by fraud, gross negligence, or negligence—

(A) may enter, introduce, or attempt to enter or introduce any merchandise into the commerce of the United States by means of—

(i) any document or electronically transmitted data or information, written or oral statement, or act which is material and false, or

(ii) any omission which is material, or

(B) may aid or abet any other person to violate subparagraph (A).

(2) Exception. Clerical errors or mistakes of fact are not violations of paragraph (1) unless they are part of a pattern of negligent conduct. The mere nonintentional repetition by an electronic system of an initial clerical error does not constitute a pattern of negligent conduct.

* * *.

(c) Maximum penalties

(1) Fraud. A fraudulent violation of subsection (a) of this section is punishable by a civil penalty in an amount not to exceed the domestic value of the merchandise.

(2) Gross negligence. A grossly negligent violation of subsection (a) of this section is punishable by a civil penalty in an amount not to exceed—

(A) the lesser of—

(i) the domestic value of the merchandise, or

(ii) four times the lawful duties, taxes, and fees of which the United States is or may be deprived, or

(B) if the violation did not affect the assessment of duties, 40 percent of the dutiable value of the merchandise.

(3) Negligence. A negligent violation of subsection (a) of this section is punishable by a civil penalty in an amount not to exceed—

(A) the lesser of—

(i) the domestic value of the merchandise, or

(ii) two times the lawful duties, taxes, and fees of which the United States is or may be deprived, or

(B) if the violation did not affect the assessment of duties, 20 percent of the dutiable value of the merchandise.

As you see, there are in effect three classes of violations: fraud (intentional violation of the law), gross negligence (disregard of the law), and

POLICY ISSUE
Why do special rules apply to MADE IN THE U.S.A. labels?

Compare the reasons why CBP and FTC have adopted different marking rules. The FTC rules are allegedly designed to protect consumers from deceptive or confusing statements as to the origin of the goods. CBP claims that the customs marking rules are designed for a similar purpose—to inform the ultimate purchaser of the goods of their country of origin. If both regulations have similar purposes, why are the rules for marking the country of origin of U.S. goods so much stricter than those for marking the country of origin of other goods? If 80% of the value of a product originates in Peru, and 80% of the value of a similar product originates in the United States, how can we say it *does not* mislead consumers to say the first product is MADE IN PERU and *does* mislead consumers to say the second is MADE IN THE U.S.A.?

One possible answer is that, if products labeled MADE IN THE U.S.A. benefit from a "patriotic price premium," perhaps the FTC's labeling rules are not designed to protect consumers, but rather to use the higher price of U.S. goods to influence manufacturers to locate as much of their manufacturing operations as possible in the United States. If so, FTC rules play a subtle role in a selectively protectionist trade policy. Whether patriotism does in fact influence consumers is an empirical question.

An alternative explanation may be that consumers believe products labeled MADE IN THE U.S.A. are made from 100% U.S. content, but they believe products labeled as made in other countries may not have all content from the designed country. Or, perhaps more likely, they may not care about how much foreign content is in a foreign-marked product, because they are concerned with sponsoring U.S., not foreign, industry and employment.

If so, is the rule really designed to prevent misleading labels, or is it designed to facilitate protectionism? Or both? If a study found that MADE IN THE U.S.A. labels do not significantly increase U.S. consumer willingness to pay more for the labeled item, how would that affect your answer? See Thomas J. Maronick, *An Empirical Investigation of Consumer Perceptions of "Made in the USA" Claims*, 12 INT'L MKTG. REV. 15 (1995).

Figure 5.13. Made in whatnow?

negligence (failure to take reasonable care to observe the law). These subject the importer to a hierarchy of penalties starting at the appraised value of the goods and ending, in the last category, with the lesser of doubled customs duties or the value of the goods.

CBP interprets negligence in light of the importer's **duty of reasonable care** to ensure compliance with all customs laws and regulations. In *United States v. Golden Ship Trading Co.*, 25 C.I.T. 40 (2001), the U.S. importer had misdesignated the country of origin of T-shirts on customs entry forms. The T-shirts had been assembled in the Dominican Republic from fabric woven in China, making the country of origin under special textiles rules China. The importer, who erroneously reported the country of origin of the shirts as the Dominican Republic, claimed that she should not be found negligent under Section 592(c)(3) of the Tariff Act, because she relied on the exporter's repeated assertions that the T-shirts were made in the Dominican Republic. In rejecting this argument, the Court of International Trade held that the importer had "the responsibility to at least undertake an effort to verify the information on the entry documents. There is a distinct difference between legitimately attempting to verify the entry information and blindly relying on the exporter's assertions." *Id.* at 47.

The penalties are not entirely unforgiving. Most enforcement of any law is self-enforcement, and Congress wanted to give importers an incentive to disclose violations of the customs laws whenever they are discovered. 19 U.S.C. § 1592(c)(4) accordingly provides for the reduction of penalties in case of **prior disclosure** by the importer or other relevant person to CBP of the violation. If this person discloses the circumstances of a violation before CBP commences a formal investigation of the violation, or informs CBP of the violation without having any reason to know that CBP has started an investigation, penalties are reduced significantly.

2 Import Regulation in the European Union

As members of the World Customs Organization, the EU has adopted a version of the Harmonized Tariff System. In fact, prior to the integration of the import regimes of the European states, their customs laws were harmonized with each other and not especially different from those of the United States. The EU member states had also adopted the same customs duties schedule, so that, at least in theory, an importer in one EU member state would pay the same duties as if it had entered the same goods in any other EU member state. EU member states cannot alter their customs duty rates unless the entire EU does so. European customs law enforcement, however, is undertaken by the individual states; each EU member state uses its own customs agency.

In 1993, the EU adopted a system of mutual recognition of tariff rulings of EU member states. If one EU member state issues a binding tariff ruling, other EU member states must recognize the classification, appraisal, or country

Figure 5.14. Customs penalties are no joke, until they are.

of origin decision with respect to the same goods imported into their own territories. In 1994, the EU adopted a **Common Customs Code** to homogenize the customs entry procedures; entry bond procedures; rules on classification, appraisal, and country of origin; and rules on warehouses and FTZs, temporary entry of goods, and drawback. This further reduced the risks of discrepancies in EU members states' customs rulings. Ultimately, the Court of Justice of the European Union is empowered to resolve discrepancies in customs treatment, but an appeal is expensive, and the Court's docket is crowded.

EU customs procedures do not differ greatly from U.S. procedures. EU appraisal methods are much like U.S. methods; both conform to the WTO Customs Valuation Agreement, as do the appraisal methods of most other countries. EU states consequently use transaction value to appraise imported goods whenever possible. EU rules of origin do not use a tariff shift methodology, but they do use a test somewhat similar to the U.S. *Gibson-Thomsen* substantial transformation test. Under EU rules, the country of origin is the state in which the "last substantial process or operation" economically justified by the market was performed on the product, resulting in a new and important stage in the creation of the product, or the transformation of the product to a new product entirely.

Also like the United States, many countries, including the EU, use a generalized system of preferences to reduce duties on imports from developing countries, although criteria for GSP benefits, and the rules and beneficiary countries to which they apply, vary from those used by the United States.

3 An Introduction to Export Regulation

To export something means to send it beyond the borders of the country in which it is currently situated. As with importing, it is possible to export goods, services, software, and technology to a foreign country. However, much import regulation is related primarily to the collection of customs duties, whereas export regulation is not about raising revenue or protecting domestic industries from foreign competition through financial impositions. Very few states levy export duties on goods shipped to foreign countries for a simple reason. To impose taxes on exports would create a disincentive to export, and states wish to encourage rather than discourage exports of goods manufactured in the state. Such exports create domestic jobs and taxable income. In the United States, export taxes are even explicitly prohibited by the Constitution: "No Tax or Duty shall be laid on Articles exported from any State." U.S. CONST. art. I, sec. 9, cl. 5.

It is also important to be aware that, at least in the modern day, very few countries impose onerous and complex regulations on the exportation of every item. While every exportation carries some duties to comply with various legal rules, most states tend to limit the most complex and restrictive regulations to specific kinds of exports. For example, states in possession of nuclear technologies are usually very restrictive about who can export nuclear items where and to whom. Similarly, a state in which petroleum is in short supply may restrict the exportation of oil to other states to prevent economic problems, such as fuel shortages and inflation, at home.

Export regulation has a long history but was never practiced as universally as import regulation. For centuries, the Ptolemaic Egyptians banned the exportation of cats, which were considered sacred animals. In Tang and Song China (618 C.E. - 1279 C.E.), the law forbade the exportation of products that could be used to make weapons, while medieval Japan exported its famous swords to China by the tens of thousands. The ninth century Emperor Charlemagne forbade the exportation of Frankish steel swords to prevent Viking raiders from using them against his empire. Later medieval blacksmiths were able to export their weapons and armor throughout Europe. Unregulated exports of weapons technology led to the disastrous fall of Constantinople, and the end of the eastern Roman Empire in 1453, when a Hungarian technician helped the Ottoman Turks learn European cannon technologies that could batter down the city's formerly impregnable walls.*

Today, war technologies are exponentially more deadly, and international coordination of arms control efforts has become imperative. There are several multilateral treaties and informal arrangements by which states coordinate their efforts to prevent the global spread of arms, munitions, and weapons of mass destruction. Among these are treaties that commit parties to control the international dissemination of nuclear weapons and materials that could be used to make them, deadly biological and chemical materials that may be used in weapons of mass destruction, and goods and technologies having military uses.

---

* Carlos A. Driscoll *et al.*, *The Taming of the Cat*, SCIENTIFIC AM., June 2009, at 68, 72; JOANNA WALEY-COHEN, THE SEXTANTS OF BEIJING 40 (1999); Herbert Maryon, *Pattern-Welding and Damascening of Sword-Blades—Part I: Pattern-Welding*, 5 STUD. IN CONSERVATION 25, 25-26 (1960); DAVID EDGE & JOHN MILES PADDOCK, ARMS AND ARMOUR OF THE MEDIEVAL KNIGHT 92-93, 134-35 (1996); JOHN P. MCKAY, BENNETT D. HILL & JOHN BUCKLER, A HISTORY OF WESTERN SOCIETY: VOLUME B: FROM THE RENAISSANCE TO 1815, at 472 (3d ed. 1987).

Different modern states use different systems to control exports. Most concentrate export licensing authority in the hands of a single agency. Canadian export regulations, for example, are generally administered by International Trade Canada's Export Controls Division. Similarly, the Netherlands delegates most export regulatory authority to the Trade Policy Instruments and Export Control Division of the Ministry of Economic Affairs. The United States is unusual in having three regulatory systems for controlling the exportation of goods, services, and technologies on homeland security and foreign policy grounds.

One U.S. export regulatory system applies to the exportation only of **dual-use items**, which are defined as goods, software, and technology that have "civil applications as well as terrorism and military or weapons of mass destruction" applications. 15 C.F.R. § 730.3. Exports of these items are controlled by the **Export Administration Regulations** (**EAR**), administered and enforced by the **Bureau of Industry and Security** (**BIS**) in the Department of Commerce. Such exports are regulated for a variety of reason to be described below.

A second system regulates the exportation of **defense articles** and **defense services**. These regulations apply only to items designed or modified for military use, and they are mainly intended to prevent the spread of war technologies and to foreclose the possibility that foreign countries and organizations, which may some day become hostile to the United States or its allies, could match U.S. military technology. Exports of defense items are governed by the **International Traffic in Arms Regulations** (**ITAR**), administered by the **Directorate of Defense Trade Controls** (**DDTC**) of the Department of State. An exported item may be regulated by the EAR or by the ITAR, but it cannot be regulated by both at the same time. Imports of defense articles and services, unlike imports of dual-use items, are also regulated, as discussed in the previous chapter.

Finally, states from time to time flatly prohibit unlicensed trade in goods, services, or technology with a foreign state, organization, or person. They may also require a freeze on the assets of, or monetary or credit transactions with, the target. These **trade sanctions** and **economic sanctions** are intended to punish the foreign subject for pursuing a policy or course of action repugnant to the sanctioning state. The United States maintains several sanctions programs at any given time, and these are mostly administered by the **Office of Foreign Assets Control** (**OFAC**) in the Department of the Treasury. A more detailed description of each program follows.

3.1 Foreign Trade Statistics Reporting

The most basic form of export regulation is simple reporting of export transactions to the government. Most countries like to keep track of what goods, and how much of them, are being exported by private industries, just as they keep track of imports. This data allows governments to calculate their foreign trade balances, learn what kind of goods the country is importing and exporting, and understand what kinds of challenges customs ports face in regulating traffic in general and hazardous materials specifically. In the United States, exporters use a document called the **shipper's export declaration** (**SED**) to report exports to the federal government. The shipper must file the SED with Customs and Border Protection at the port of exportation. The information required for an SED is reproduced in Figure 5.15. Exporters are now required to file the SED electronically through the **Automated Commercial Environment**. The SED is required for nearly all exports, but not all. Only certain exports of very low value or destined for Canada (except controlled items) require no SED.

The SED requires the exporter to report the date of shipment, destination, type, weight, and value of the exported merchandise. The U.S. Department of Commerce's **Bureau of the Census** uses this information to compile its foreign trade statistics, which are made available to Congress and the public. 13 U.S.C. § 301. The specific regulations governing when and how an SED must be completed and filed are called the **Foreign Trade Statistics Regulations** (**FTSR**). The FTSR are found in 15 C.F.R. pt. 30. The FTSR require that exporters keep copies of their SEDs for no less than five years after exportation to assist the Census Bureau in verifying its statistics.

Although the SED serves the basic purpose of helping the Census Bureau to compile official U.S. export statistics, it is also used to alert the Department of Commerce and the Department of State to exports of certain regulated items. As will be discussed, the exportation of some products may require a license from either the Commerce Department, depending on the type of product and the destination or purchaser of the product. The SED form requires exporters to report to the government the shipment of such controlled items, which can in turn determine whether a license was obtained or, if not, should have been obtained. Specifically, fields 27 and 28 of the SED require reporting of export license information for controlled exports. In short, the SED helps the government to keep tabs on potential violations of U.S. export restrictions.

In compiling its foreign trade statistics, the Census Bureau faces a problem. The United States, like most countries, exports a bewildering variety of products, from raw materials and agricultural products to complex electronics and heavy machinery. How can it conveniently group exports into comprehensible classes to give the government a general idea of what kinds of goods are being exported in what quantities? You may recall that, whenever goods are imported into the United States, the importer must report the HTSUS classification number of the goods to assist CBP in determining the customs duties owed. CBP reports the HTSUS number to the Census Bureau to compile its foreign trade statistics respecting imports. But for export purposes, the HTSUS number is not reported on the SED—at least, not technically.

Instead, a very similar number, called a **Schedule B** number, is used.

Schedule B numbers are reported on the SED. The Schedule B number is almost always identical to the HTSUS number, but because the former is administered by the Census Bureau and the latter by the U.S. International Trade Commission, it is important to consult Schedule B, even if the HTSUS number is known, in case of any discrepancy between the two classification schemes. The first six digits of a ten-digit product classification in the HTSUS and Schedule B are always the same, but sometimes the last four digits differ because the HTSUS is more detailed than Schedule B. For example, the HTS number for umbrellas in the EU is 6603.20.0000, but their Schedule B classification is 6603.20.3000. A Belgian importer would report the former number to the Belgian customs authority, but the U.S. exporter would report the latter number to the Census Bureau.

WHAT ARE THE DESTINATIONS OF U.S. EXPORTS?

On average, U.S. companies export about $1.5 trillion in goods every year. The same countries that export to the United States also tend to import from the United States. In 2018, about 41% of U.S. exports were destined for Canada (18%), Mexico (16%), or China (7%). Other countries importing significant quantities of U.S. goods include Japan, Germany, the U.K., and South Korea.

Source: U.S. Census Bureau

Other countries also require a declaration to customs authorities or other government agencies of classification, quantity, value, and other information prior to the exportation of general merchandise. Japan, for example, requires exporters to note the statistical classification of the exports on the Export Statistical Schedule, much like the U.S. Schedule B, as well as the quantity and value of the goods on an export declaration, similar to the U.S. SED. Japanese customs officials may inspect the exports and their invoice to ensure consistency with the reported information.

In addition to collecting customs duties and statistical information about international trade, the U.S. government imposes export and import regulation for other purposes as well. As noted above, one purpose of export regulation is to prevent the spread of technologies that could be used to promote terrorism, war, civil strife, or violations of human rights. Another goal may be to prevent the exportation of scarce resources such as rare minerals that, it may be thought, are needed to fill domestic demand. Still another purpose of international trade controls may be to punish foreign states, organizations, or persons for activities that threaten the national security or foreign policy interests of the sanctioning state.

3.2 "Dual-Use" Exports

Exports of sensitive goods, services, and technologies can be roughly divided into two types. The first are defense articles and related services and

U.S. DEPARTMENT OF COMMERCE – Economics and Statistics Administration – U.S. CENSUS BUREAU – BUREAU OF EXPORT ADMINISTRATION

FORM **7525-V** (7-18-2003)

SHIPPER'S EXPORT DECLARATION

OMB No. 0607-0152

1a. U.S. PRINCIPAL PARTY IN INTEREST (USPPI)(Complete name and address)

ZIP CODE

2. DATE OF EXPORTATION

3. TRANSPORTATION REFERENCE NO.

b. USPPI'S EIN (IRS) OR ID NO.

c. PARTIES TO TRANSACTION ☐ Related ☐ Non-related

4a. ULTIMATE CONSIGNEE *(Complete name and address)*

b. INTERMEDIATE CONSIGNEE *(Complete name and address)*

5a. FORWARDING AGENT *(Complete name and address)*

5b. FORWARDING AGENT'S EIN (IRS) NO.

6. POINT (STATE) OF ORIGIN OR FTZ NO.

7. COUNTRY OF ULTIMATE DESTINATION

8. LOADING PIER *(Vessel only)*

9. METHOD OF TRANSPORTATION *(Specify)*

14. CARRIER IDENTIFICATION CODE

15. SHIPMENT REFERENCE NO.

10. EXPORTING CARRIER

11. PORT OF EXPORT

16. ENTRY NUMBER

17. HAZARDOUS MATERIALS ☐ Yes ☐ No

12. PORT OF UNLOADING *(Vessel and air only)*

13. CONTAINERIZED *(Vessel only)* ☐ Yes ☐ No

18. IN BOND CODE

19. ROUTED EXPORT TRANSACTION ☐ Yes ☐ No

20. SCHEDULE B DESCRIPTION OF COMMODITIES *(Use columns 22–24)*

D/F or M (21)	SCHEDULE B NUMBER (22)	QUANTITY – SCHEDULE B UNIT(S) (23)	SHIPPING WEIGHT (Kilograms) (24)	VIN/PRODUCT NUMBER/ VEHICLE TITLE NUMBER (25)	VALUE (U.S. dollars, omit cents) (Selling price or cost if not sold) (26)

27. LICENSE NO./LICENSE EXCEPTION SYMBOL/AUTHORIZATION

28. ECCN *(When required)*

29. Duly authorized officer or employee

The USPPI authorizes the forwarder named above to act as forwarding agent for export control and customs purposes.

30. I certify that all statements made and all information contained herein are true and correct and that I have read and understand the instructions for preparation of this document, set forth in the **"Correct Way to Fill Out the Shipper's Export Declaration."** I understand that civil and criminal penalties, including forfeiture and sale, may be imposed for making false or fraudulent statements herein, failing to provide the requested information or for violation of U.S. laws on exportation (13 U.S.C. Sec. 305; 22 U.S.C. Sec. 401; 18 U.S.C. Sec. 1001; 50 U.S.C. App. 2410).

Signature

Confidential – Shipper's Export Declarations (or any successor document) wherever located, shall be exempt from public disclosure unless the Secretary determines that such exemption would be contrary to the national interest (Title 13, Chapter 9, Section 301 (g)).

Title

Export shipments are subject to inspection by U.S. Customs Service and/or Office of Export Enforcement.

Date

31. AUTHENTICATION *(When required)*

Telephone No. (Include Area Code)

E-mail address

Figure 5.15. A shipper's export declaration. The same information in this form is now filed electronically through the Automated Commercial Environment.

WHY ARE TRADE BALANCES IMPORTANT?

A state's trade balance is the ratio of the value of the state's annual imports to the value of its annual exports. States keep a close watch on their trade balance because it affects their national wealth over time. To understand why, consider that those who purchase foreign goods must pay in the currency of the exporting state, and those who sell to foreign state receive payment in their own currency. A state with a consistently positive trade balance (that is, more exports than imports by value) accumulates foreign currency, which it can then invest by, for example, making loans to the foreign state whose currency is held. These loans bring in interest and thereby create wealth. If the positive trade balance continues, it stimulates demand for the state's currency, which in turn makes the currency more expensive relative to other currencies. As the currency becomes more expensive (a process called **appreciation**), the state's goods and services become less attractive to purchasers in other states, which tends to discourage the continuation of the positive trade balance. If a state has a consistent negative trade balance (more imports than exports), it tends to lose wealth to foreign lenders and its currency tends to lose value relative to other currencies (**depreciation**). Depreciation contributes to currency inflation. These negative consequences can be mitigated by a high rate of household savings in the state, but some states with a consistent negative trade balance have a low rate of savings. Since 2010, the U.S. personal savings rate has averaged only 7%. Eventually, profligate consumption and a negative trade balance decrease economic growth, and contribute to inflation and unemployment. This does not mean that imports harm a state, but imports and exports should be roughly balanced in the long term with a reasonable rate of savings.

technologies, which are designed or adapted for use by the military. Such defense items include artillery, fighter and bomber jets, fully automatic machine guns or shotguns, and explosive ordnance. The other class of sensitive exports encompasses dual-use items. In this section, we will focus on dual-use items, because they make up a much larger portion of international trade.

Dual-use items are items that have both military and civilian uses. Often they are technologies originally developed for military use, but have been widely adapted over time to commercial or industrial uses. For example, an extremely powerful computer can be used to coordinate flight data and passenger reservations for thousands of people by a commercial airline, but it can also be used to simulate explosions for the purpose of developing an nuclear weapon.

Similarly, certain naturally occurring biotoxins may be used in medical research or therapy (for killing cancer cells, for example), but could also be used to poison a town's water supply. The exportation of these items may be regulated to prevent their falling into the wrong hands and to ensure that their use does not threaten any country's national security or foreign policy interests, or to undermine international peace.

It is important to be aware that not every item regulated as a dual-use export presents any evident dangers to national security. For example, the United States regulates the exportation of boats, underwater cameras, paraffin wax, video game consoles, and even life jackets. Other items regulated for exportation may seem innocuous, but to a technician would have significant military or terrorist uses.

A. International Coordination of Dual-Use Export Controls

During the Second World War, many states made unprecedented efforts to develop technologically sophisticated and powerful weapons, including **atomic, biological, and chemical weapons** (so-called **ABC weapons**, also known less accurately as **weapons of mass destruction**, or **WMD**), precision munitions, armor-piercing munitions, and long-range missiles. In many cases, countries allied during the Second World War shared weapons and technology in their cooperative effort to defeat a common enemy. The end of the war reopened and aggravated the ideological schism between communist China and the Soviet-controlled states of Eastern Europe on one hand, and the democracies of Western Europe and North America on the other.

Figure 5.16. The international symbols for regulated ABC substances. From left to right, atomic, biological, and chemical substances. Credit: Vardion, Andux, Simon Eugster.

Once the Axis powers no longer presented a common enemy to unify these blocs, the erstwhile allies turned their animosity toward each other, creating a long period of tension known as the Cold War (1945-1991). In preparation for a possible military confrontation, both sides of the Cold War continued their fervent efforts to develop more powerful and effective weapons and technologies, both offensive and defensive in nature. A key part of each country's strategy was, of course, to monopolize the most effective weapons and technologies for itself and its allies, which required stringent controls to prevent their transfer or retransfer to the opposing power. This was easier in the Eastern Bloc, where totalitarian dictatorships strictly controlled all military research and testing. In contrast, the open nature of democracy and the decentralized production methods of capitalism made complete control over arms and military technology much more challenging. This problem was aggravated by the fact that the Cold War fomented tensions, and sometimes civil wars or rebellions, in many countries, creating a global demand for arms and military technologies that promised great profits to whoever could deliver them.

To ensure that the Western democracies did not undermine each other's efforts to stem the spread of their weapons and technologies to the Soviet Union and its satellite states, a group of countries led by Australia, Japan, the United States, and most of Western Europe created an informal consultation institution called the **Coordinating Committee for Multilateral Export Controls**, or **CoCom**. CoCom members met periodically from the group's foundation in 1947 to agree upon a list of munitions and technologies that should be withheld from Soviet bloc states and other undesirables. The controlled items included not only conventional weapons like tanks, missiles, and submarines, but dual-use goods and technologies such as powerful computers, air navigation equipment, riot gear, and certain kinds of industrial chemicals or biological materials, all of which, it was thought, could be used to give a military or technological advantage to an enemy country or facilitate the suppression of human rights.

After the disintegration of the Soviet Union, CoCom was replaced in 1996 by the **Wassenaar Arrangement on Export Controls for Conventional Arms and Dual-Use Goods and Technologies**. The Wassenaar Arrangement has a secretariat located in Vienna, Austria, where the members meet periodically. Like the CoCom before it, the Wassenaar Arrangement is an informal organization of states intended to promote coordination in ensuring that international transfers of military and dual-use goods and technologies do not threaten international peace and security. The list of controlled items is much the same as it was under CoCom, updated to include present-day technologies. Unlike CoCom, however, the Wassenaar Arrangement is not oriented toward depriving communist dictatorships of advanced arms and technologies, but rather toward preventing their transfer to warmongers, oppressive dictatorships, or terrorists. This is most evident from the fact that Russia, the former target of CoCom, is now a member of the Wassenaar Arrangement. The Wassenaar Arrangement's much expanded membership encompasses 42 countries having advanced military and dual-use technologies as of 2020, including most of Europe, as well as Argentina, Australia, Canada, India, Japan, the Republic of Korea, South Africa, Switzerland, and the United States. Notably absent among major arms exporting states are China and Israel.

Wassenaar Arrangement countries share information on their export controls and foreign transfers (and denials of transfers) of arms and dual-use items. They meet periodically in Vienna to discuss global security threats and to update the lists of controlled items to account for new technologies and new experience. All decisions are made by consensus.

The Wassenaar Arrangement's informality means that there is no treaty provision or agency responsible for enforcing its terms. The decision to license the exportation of any item on a Wassenaar control list to any person or state is left to the discretion of each Wassenaar member. Wassenaar members are,

Figure 5.17. Scope of the three main trade control regimes.

however, expected to enact domestic legislation to regulate goods and technologies agreed upon by the members and included in a control list. Thus, the legislation and regulations governing dual-use exports will differ from country to country, but the list of items controlled will be more or less similar among the countries. In all cases, the objective is to prevent the uncontrolled spread of dangerous weapons and technologies to irresponsible hands without unnecessarily impeding manufacturers and researchers from selling their wares.

The **Australia Group** is another informal IGO to which the United States belongs. Its mission is specifically to coordinate enforcement of two treaties designed to control the proliferation of non-atomic WMD: The 1993 Convention on the Prohibition of the Development, Production, Stockpiling and Use of Chemical Weapons and on Their Destruction, also known as the **Chemical Weapons Convention** (**CWC**), and the 1972 Convention on the Prohibition of the Development, Production and Stockpiling of Bacteriological and Toxin Weapons and on Their Destruction, also known as the **Biological Weapons Convention** (**BWC**). All members of the Australia Group are parties to both treaties, although not all parties to the treaties are members of the Australia Group. Both treaties are designed to control the spread of indiscriminate weapons of the kind used in the First World War, such as the blister agent mustard gas, and those used in terrorist attacks on civilians, such as the nerve agent sarin released in the Tokyo subway system by a religious cult in 1995.

The CWC classifies chemical toxins into three groups: Schedule 1 chemicals, which have few or no nonmilitary uses; Schedule 2 chemicals, which have no major industrial uses but may have small-scale uses; and Schedule 3 chemicals, which may be used in military applications but also have common and legitimate industrial uses, as in the manufacture of plastics or as herbicides. Chemicals grouped in Schedule 1 may be used for medical or protective research only. Schedule 2 and 3 chemicals are subject to decreasingly strict controls, but they are nonetheless subject to inspection by the CWC's international inspection body, the Organization for the Prohibition of Chemical Weapons.

The BWC has over 150 parties and prohibits the creation or storage of weapons using pathogenic microorganisms and biochemicals, such as the Anthrax bacterium and Ebola virus. It also obligates parties to destroy any such weapons prior to ratifying the BWC. These organisms and substances may be used for legitimate medical, industrial, and protective research and use, but their distribution must be strictly controlled.

The Australia Group was formed in 1985 after United Nations investigators reported that Iraq had used chemical weapons against Iran in the Iran-Iraq War in violation of the international law of armed conflict, and that it had acquired at least some precursor chemicals through legal trade with American and European companies. But export regulations are always ineffective unless every supplier country participates and controls the exports with similar rigor. If one country refuses a license to export a dangerous chemical or microorganism to a potential abuser, but another issues an export license for the same substance to the same potential abuser, the system will be ineffective. To improve cooperation, Australia proposed a meeting among the fifteen participating countries and the European Commission to harmonize export controls and licensing regimes. Since 1985, the Australia Group has met annually in Paris to discuss methods of controlling the proliferation of chemical and biological weapons. Australia Group decisions help member states to coordinate export controls on weapons and precursor chemicals and technologies and to render the controls more effective by sharing their regulatory expertise. Learning from experience, the Australia Group has also tightened security by progressively including within its export controls new technologies and equipment that could be used to develop chemical or biological weapons.

Australia Group decisions, like those made pursuant to the Wassenaar Arrangement, are not legally binding, but, as with Wassenaar, there are informal mechanisms the parties may use to bring wayward members back to the fold, such as diplomatic pressure and the threat of expulsion. As a result, all Australia Group members have enacted export licensing requirements for numerous chemical weapons precursors and technologies, plant and animal pathogens, pathogenic microorganisms, and dual-use equipment.

The third informal group of countries that meets to coordinate export control policy is known as the **Nuclear Suppliers Group** (**NSG**). The NSG was first formed in 1974 and now includes most countries capable of supplying enriched uranium, plutonium, and nuclear fission technologies to others, including most of Europe, China, Japan, the United States, Canada, South Africa, Russia, and Argentina. Members must demonstrate a commitment to the purpose of the body, which is to prevent the proliferation of nuclear weapons by the uncontrolled transfer of nuclear devices, software, materials, and technologies. Controlled items may relate to nuclear weapons or to nuclear power generation and other dual civilian-military use nuclear items. The NSG maintains guidelines on export controls and licensing to which NSG members voluntarily adhere.

The last noteworthy informal, international export coordinating body is known as the **Missile Technology Control Regime** (**MTCR**). The MTCR membership overlaps greatly with the NSG and Australia Group membership, and it extends their basic principles and techniques to export controls on missile technology such as launch vehicles, rocket engines, rocket fuel, guidance systems and software, and their related materials and technologies. The MTCR is designed especially to coordinate export controls and licensing for the means of delivery of ABC weapons. As with the other regimes, there is an agreed-upon list of controlled items (the MTCR Annex) and guidelines on the export control and licensing policy, to which all members voluntarily adhere. MTCR partners meet annually and consult regularly to update the guidelines and annex. In 2001, the member states drafted an International Code of Conduct Against Ballistic Missile Proliferation. Since that time, over 110 countries have agreed to abide by the Code of Conduct.

In summary, these international coordinating groups do not require or even advise members to control the exportation of all goods, services, or technologies. Instead, they focus on those with potential military, paramilitary, or terrorist uses. They do not create law directly applicable in participating states. For an export lawyer in any of the Wassenaar, MCTR, NSG, and Australia Group states, however, the coordinating groups have three useful functions.

First, to the extent that negotiations in the groups are made public, these negotiations can serve as a regulatory barometer to give lawyers some indication of the future directions of export regulation in the participating states.

Second, because participating states can be expected to implement the export policies adopted by the group, these groups give some assurance of a certain minimum level of uniformity in export regulation among participating states. This helps alert trade lawyers to the possibility that a product, technology, or service whose exportation is regulated in one participating state in the group should also be examined for export controls in every other participating state. If a U.S. license is required to export a chemical from the United States, for example, a Czech license may be required to export the same chemical from the Czech Republic, because both states participate in the Australia Group. Moreover, some organizations have an anticircumvention policy, by which the participating states agree that if one state denies an export license to ship a controlled good to a specific country or end-user, the other states will consult with the denying state before granting a license similar to the denied one.

Third, the guidelines, background papers, and published negotiations of these groups may be used as sources of interpretation of vague or ambiguous state regulations. Because these sources are not technically law or formal congressional or regulatory guidance, they must be used with caution. They may, however, provide insight into the motivations underlying the regulation and serve as interpretive sources to that limited extent.

Wassenaar Arrangement	**Australia Group**	**Nuclear Suppliers Group**	**Missile Technology Control Regime**
dual-use items; conventional defense items	dangerous biological and chemical materials	nuclear fission technologies; uranium; plutonium	rocket and missile materials and technologies

B. Introduction to U.S. Regulation of Dual-Use Exports

In the United States, the primary law authorizing the Executive Branch to regulate the exportation of dual-use items is currently the **International Emergency Economic Powers Act** (**IEEPA**), 50 U.S.C. §§ 1701-07. The IEEPA authorizes the President to identify international emergencies and to impose economic and trade sanctions on foreign states, organizations, and individuals. These sanctions are permitted whenever necessary to protect U.S. national security from hostile foreign states and organizations, and from anyone considered by the Executive Branch to threaten U.S. foreign policy objectives. In relevant part, the IEEPA reads:

§ 1702. Presidential authorities

(a) In general

(1) At the times and to the extent specified in section 1701 of this title, the President may, under such regulations as he may prescribe, by means of instructions, licenses, or otherwise—

(A) investigate, regulate, or prohibit—

(i) any transactions in foreign exchange,

(ii) transfers of credit or payments between, by, through, or to any banking institution, to the extent that such transfers or payments involve any interest of any foreign country or a national thereof,

(iii) the importing or exporting of currency or securities,

by any person, or with respect to any property, subject to the jurisdiction of the United States;

(B) investigate, block during the pendency of an investigation, regulate, direct and compel, nullify, void, prevent or prohibit, any acquisition, holding, withholding, use, transfer, withdrawal, transportation, importation or exportation of, or dealing in, or exercising any right, power, or privilege with respect to, or transactions involving, any property in which any foreign country or a national thereof has any interest by any person, or with respect to any property, subject to the jurisdiction of the United States; and * * *

(2) In exercising the authorities granted by paragraph (1), the President may require any person to keep a full record of, and to furnish under oath, in the form of reports or otherwise, complete information relative to any act or transaction referred to in paragraph (1) either before, during, or after the completion thereof, or relative to any interest in foreign property, or relative to any property in which any foreign country or any national thereof has or has had any interest, or as may be otherwise necessary to enforce the provisions of such paragraph. In any case in which a report by a person could be required under this paragraph, the President may require the production of any books of account, records, contracts, letters, memoranda, or other papers, in the custody or control of such person. * * *

(b) Exceptions to grant of authority. The authority granted to the President by this section does not include the authority to regulate or prohibit, directly or indirectly—

(1) any postal, telegraphic, telephonic, or other personal communication, which does not involve a transfer of anything of value;

(2) donations, by persons subject to the jurisdiction of the United States, of articles, such as food, clothing, and medicine, intended to be used to relieve human suffering, [unless the President objects on specified grounds]. * * *

(3) the importation from any country, or the exportation to any country, whether commercial or otherwise, regardless of format or medium of transmission, of any information or informational materials, including but not limited to, publications, films, posters, phonograph records, photographs, microfilms, microfiche, tapes, compact disks, CD ROMs, artworks, and news wire feeds * * * or

(4) any transactions ordinarily incident to travel to or from any country, including importation of accompanied baggage for personal use, maintenance within any country including payment of living expenses and acquisition of goods or services for personal use, and arrangement or facilitation of such travel including nonscheduled air, sea, or land voyages. * * *

§ 1704. Authority to issue regulations

The President may issue such regulations, including regulations prescribing definitions, as may be necessary for the exercise of the authorities granted by this chapter.

§ 1705. Penalties

(a) A civil penalty of not to exceed $10,000 may be imposed on any person who violates, or attempts to violate, any license, order, or regulation issued under this chapter.

(b) Whoever willfully violates, or willfully attempts to violate, any license, order, or regulation issued under this chapter shall, upon conviction, be fined not more than $50,000, or, if a natural person, may be imprisoned for not more than ten years, or both; and any officer, director, or agent of any corporation who knowingly participates in such violation may be punished by a like fine, imprisonment, or both.

As discussed in the following article excerpt, the main U.S. statutes authorizing regulation of dual-use exports were historically a series of very specific and detailed laws, each called the **Export Administration Act** (**EAA**), or some variant on that name. Members of Congress have periodically proposed a new EAA for many decades, but consensus has continually eluded it. In the meantime, the IEEPA serves as the main legislative authority for regulation of dual-use exports. It is helpful, however, to understand the historical development of dual-use export regulatory laws better to understand why the current system delegates to much discretion to the President and how the system may evolve in the future.

Aaron Xavier Fellmeth, *Cure Without a Disease: The Emerging Doctrine of Successor Liability in International Trade Law*, 31 YALE J. INT'L L. 127 (2006)

* * *

3. Dual-Use Export Controls

Before considering the current peacetime export administration law, some history of export regulation will be helpful here to illustrate the nature and purposes of the current export regulatory statute, IEEPA. The first general act authorizing the President to regulate exports in time of peace was enacted in 1949. The 1949 Export Control Act was designed to protect the U.S. economy "by limiting exports of scarce materials, and to channel exports to countries where need is greatest and where our foreign-policy and national security interests would be best served." The 1949 Act delegated to the Secretaries of Commerce and Agriculture the power to determine which items would be controlled and to fix export quotas. The 1949 Act was not directed at controlling arms or military exports for national security reasons so much as to prevent shortages of important supplies, including food and textiles, to ensure that U.S. allies were given first priority in the allocation of such supplies after the Second World War and to prevent inflation caused by abnormally high international post-war demand. Nonetheless, national security played a role in the law, as Congress sought to prevent shipments of items having "direct or indirect military significance" to the newly expanded Soviet bloc.

Congress undertook a major revision to the U.S. export control law two decades later. By this time, the post-war scarcity had long since evaporated, and the United States had experienced two decades of economic expansion. Meanwhile, the Soviet Union had grown in power and was perceived as an increased threat to U.S. national security. The 1969 Export Administration Act (1969 EAA), which replaced the 1949 Export Control Act, dealt almost exclusively with national security and foreign policy concerns rather than scarcity of supply. The 1969 EAA was designed to "restrict exports which would make a significant contribution to the military potential of any other nation or nations which would prove detrimental to the national security of the United States." The export controls were instituted in cooperation with the Coordinating Committee on Multilateral Export Controls (COCOM), a group of NATO countries, Australia, New Zealand, and Japan, which jointly determined the outlines of export control policy to deny weapons and technological advances to the Soviet bloc.

The 1969 EAA expired on September 30, 1979 and, that year, was replaced with the last major revision to the U.S. export control statutes. Congress enacted the 1979 EAA to clarify exporter obligations while preserving the primary purpose of U.S. export law as restricting exports that may make a "significant contribution to the military potential of individual countries or combinations of countries [that] may adversely affect the national security of the United States,"[200] and, of lesser importance, complying with U.S. foreign policy obligations, protecting the domestic economy from excessive drain of scarce materials, and reducing the serious inflationary impact of foreign demand. In enacting the 1979 EAA, Congress expected the Department of Commerce to balance the competing goals of exploiting U.S. technological and commercial superiority by encouraging exports without affording access to breakthrough technologies to communist countries or other destinations that might harm U.S. national security. Like its predecessors, the 1949 Export Control Act and the 1969 EAA, the 1979 EAA vested the Executive Branch with broad authority to enumerate items of potential military significance and to institute export licensing controls, including outright prohibitions. Relatively few classes of goods, other than agricultural commodities, exceeded the purview of executive discretion.

* * * The 1979 EAA provided for civil as well as criminal penalties for violations of its terms and regulations enacted under it, but both were punitive in nature. Criminal penalties were divided into sanctions for willful violations, which could result in fines up to $100,000 or five times the value of the exports per violation, whichever is greater, and imprisonment up to five years for "whoever" committed the violation "knowingly" or conspired or attempted to violate the 1979 EAA or regulations issued pursuant to it. "Willful violations" applied to "[w]hoever willfully" committed such a violation and "[a] ny person" who willfully failed to report a military or intelligence use by a controlled country, and could result in harsh penalties: fines up to $250,000 or five times the value of the exports, whichever is greater, and imprisonment up to ten years for individuals, and fines up to $1,000,000 or five times the value of the exports, whichever is greater,

[200] 50 U.S.C. app. § 2401(5); see §§ 2401(8), 2402(2)(A) (2000).

for legal entities. Civil penalties were limited to $10,000, imposed by the Secretary of Commerce "for each violation" of the 1979 EAA or its regulations, and increased to $100,000 for national security violations. In addition, knowing or willful violations of the Export Administration Regulations could result in the forfeiture of exported goods or funds and debarment from exporting goods and technologies subject to the EAR.

The 1979 EAA was last reauthorized by Congress in 1990. Congress extended its authority for one-year intervals in 1993, 1994, and 2000. The 1979 EAA lapsed most recently on August 20, 2001, and has not been reenacted since, although a major revision is currently under consideration by Congress. During the several years of lapsed authority, the President has fallen back several times upon IEEPA[209] to continue the EAR [Export Administration Regulations] in effect.

* * *

The main federal agency responsible for enforcing the IEEPA is the **Bureau of Industry and Security** (**BIS**), in the U.S. Department of Commerce. Before 2001, BIS was called the Bureau of Export Administration (BXA) and was responsible for enforcing the EAA. Its successor, BIS, is headed by the ponderously titled Under Secretary of Homeland Security for Industry and Security and is composed of several offices, each charged with pursuing a different aspect of BIS's mission. That mission is primarily to protect U.S. national security and foreign policy interests by regulating the exportation of dual-use goods and technologies. In service of the mission, the Office of National Security and Technology Transfer Controls, for example, updates those parts of the export control regulations dealing with national security to comply with the periodic recommendations of the Wassenaar Arrangement members. The Office of Exporter Services issues export licenses and counsels exporters on compliance with the dual-use export regulations. The Office of Export Enforcement investigates possible violations of the law and arrests suspected violators. Its special agents are criminal investigators who carry firearms, execute search warrants, and seize goods being exported illegally. The **Office of Antiboycott Compliance** (**OAC**) promotes another of BIS's missions, which is to prevent U.S. companies and their foreign subsidiaries from cooperating in foreign boycotts of U.S. allies—a role to be explored later.

Pursuant to congressional authorization, the Secretary of Commerce has delegated to BIS the task of drafting, implementing, and enforcing the regulations issued under the EAA, IEEPA, and other dual-use export laws. These rules are known as the **Export Administration Regulations** (**EAR**). The EAR are codified in Title 15, Chapter 7 of the Code of Federal Regulations.

---

[209]International Emergency Economic Powers Act of 1977, Pub. L. No. 95-223, 91 Stat. 1626 (1977), codified as amended at 50 U.S.C. §§ 1701-06 (2001). IEEPA was originally enacted as title II to the Trading with the Enemy Act Reform Legislation.

The EAR regulate exports of all "controlled" items that are subject to the EAR. Generally, an item is **subject to the EAR** if it satisfies one or more of the following conditions:

- it originates in the United States though it may now be anywhere in the world;
- it contains a nontrivial amount of U.S.-origin parts or materials;
- it is based on certain U.S.-origin technology or software; or
- it is currently located in the United States.

If an item is subject to the EAR *and* is listed on the EAR's **Commerce Control List** (**CCL**), found at 15 C.F.R. pt. 774 supp. 1, then exportation or reexportation of the item is controlled. Notice that, under these rules, an item may be subject to the EAR even though it was manufactured in a foreign country by a foreign company and is currently not in the United States (nor indeed has ever entered the United States). On the other hand, a Freedonian company wishing to sell its Freedonia-made boat hulls (containing no U.S.-origin parts or materials), currently located in Ruritania, to a purchaser in Grand Fenwick need not concern itself with an export license from BIS, because its boat hulls are not "subject to the EAR." The exporter may need to obtain an export license from the Freedonian government, but that is a different matter.

Items subject to the EAR but not listed on the CCL are classified as **EAR99** items. An exporter is generally free to export EAR99 items to almost any country without a license, except to a specific and very short list of sanctioned countries, organizations, or persons (see the discussion of "End-User Controls") or for prohibited purposes (see the discussion of "End-Use Controls"). In other words, an exporter may need a license to export *anything*, whether a dual-use good or not, that originates in the United States, is located in the United States, or contains more than *de minimis* U.S.-origin parts or materials or technology. For now, we will focus on the general category of items listed on the CCL.

On the CCL, each controlled item is assigned an **Export Control Classification Number** (**ECCN**). The exporter carries the burden of determining whether any given export requires a license from BIS. Once the exporter has ascertained that an item is subject to the EAR, it is its responsibility to identify the proper ECCN of each exported item, because this is the next step in determining whether an export license is required. The following excerpt from a BIS publication explains how the ECCNs are assigned and organized.

U.S. Department of Commerce, Bureau of Industry & Security, Introduction to the Commerce Department's Export Controls (Nov. 2018)

What are you exporting?

The Export Control Classification Number and the Commerce Control List

A key in determining whether an export license is needed from the Department of Commerce is knowing whether the item you are intending to export has a specific Export Control Classification Number (ECCN). The ECCN is an alpha-numeric code, *e.g.*, 3A001, that is made up of the item category, its product group, and primary reason for control. The ECCN entry describes the item and specifies licensing requirements. All ECCNs are listed in the Commerce Control List (CCL) (Supplement No. 1 to Part 774 of the EAR) * * *. The CCL is divided into ten broad categories, and each category is further subdivided into five product groups.

Commerce Control List Categories

0 = Nuclear materials, facilities, and equipment (and miscellaneous items)
1 = Special Materials and Related Equipment, Chemicals, "Microorganisms" and "Toxins"
2 = Materials Processing
3 = Electronics
4 = Computers
5 = Telecommunications and "Information Security"
6 = Sensors and Lasers
7 = Navigation and Avionics
8 = Marine
9 = Aerospace and Propulsion

Classifying Your Item

The proper classification of your item is essential to determining any licensing requirements under the Export Administration Regulations (EAR). You may classify the item on your own, check with the manufacturer, or submit a classification request to have BIS determine the ECCN for you. When reviewing the CCL to determine if your item is specified by an ECCN, you will first need to determine in which of the ten broad categories of the Commerce Control List your item is included and then consider the applicable product group.

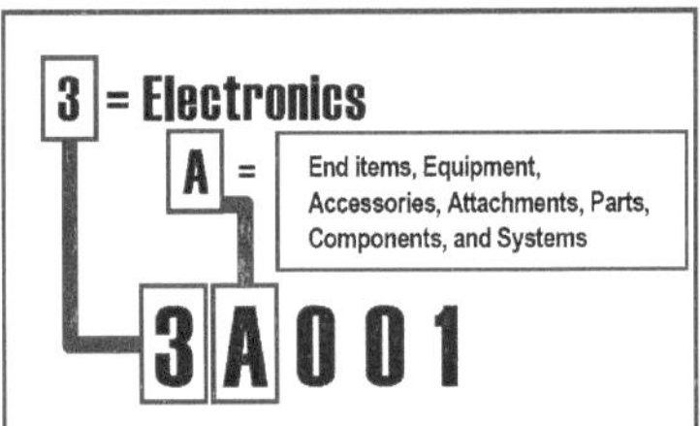

Example

Assume that you have polygraph equipment that is used to help law enforcement agencies. What would be your ECCN? Start by looking in the Commerce Control List under the category of electronics (Category 3) and product group which covers equipment (Product Group A). Then read through the list to find whether your item is included in the list. In this example, the ECCN for the item is 3A981, as shown below.

If Your Item is Not on the Commerce Control List – EAR99

If your item falls under U.S. Department of Commerce jurisdiction and is not listed on the CCL, it is designated as EAR99. The following EAR99 entry is found at the end of each CCL category:

3A981 Polygraphs *(except biomedical recorders designed for use in medical facilities for monitoring biological and neurophysical responses); fingerprint analyzers, cameras and equipment, n.e.s.; automated fingerprint and identification retrieval systems, n.e.s.;* * * *

License Requirements
Reason for Control: CC

Control(s)
CC applies to the entire entry

Country Chart
CC Column 1

List-Based License Exceptions
LVS: N/A
GBS: N/A
CIV: N/A

List of Items Controlled
Related Controls: See ECCN 0A982 * * *
Related Definitions: N/A
Items: The list of items controlled is contained in the ECCN heading.

EAR99 items generally consist of less sensitive consumer goods and do not require a license in most situations. However, if you plan to export an EAR99 item is to an embargoed country, to an end-user of concern or in support of a prohibited end-use, you may be required to obtain a license.

EAR99—Items subject to the EAR that are not elsewhere controlled by this CCL Category or in any other category in the CCL are designated by the number EAR99.

Where are you exporting?

How to cross-reference the ECCN with the Commerce Country Chart

Once you have classified the item, the next step is to determine whether you need an export license based on the "Reasons for Control" and the country of ultimate destination. You begin this process by comparing the "Reason for Control" found in the ECCN

Commerce Country Chart
Reason for Control

Countries	Chemical & Biological Weapons			Nuclear Nonproliferation		National Security		Missile Technology	Regional Stability		Firearms Convention	Crime Control			Anti-Terrorism	
	CB 1	CB 2	CB 3	NP 1	NP 2	NS 1	NS 2	MT 1	RS 1	RS 2	FC 1	CC 1	CC 2	CC 3	AT 1	AT 2
Guyana	X	X		X		X	X	X	X	X	X	X		X		
Haiti	X	X		X		X	X	X	X	X	X	X		X		
Honduras	X	X		X		X	X	X	X	X	X	X		X		
Hong Kong	X	X		X		X	X	X	X	X		X		X		
Hungary	X					X		X	X							
Iceland	X					X		X	X							
India	X			X		X		X	X							

entry with the Commerce Country Chart (Supplement No. 1 to Part 738).
Below the main heading for each ECCN entry, you will find "Reason for Control" (*e.g.*, NS for National Security, AT for Anti-Terrorism, CC for Crime Control, etc.). Below this, you will find the "Country Chart" designator, which shows the specific export control code(s) for your item (*e.g.*, NS Column 2, AT Column 1, CC Column 1). These control codes for your ECCN must be cross-referenced against the Commerce Country Chart.

If there is an "X" in the box based on the Reason(s) for Control of your item and the country of destination, a license is required, unless a License Exception is available. Part 742 of the EAR sets forth the license requirements and licensing policy for most reasons for control.

If there is no "X" in the control code column(s) specified under your ECCN and country of destination, you will not need an export license unless you are exporting to an end-user or end-use of concern.

Example

Question: You have polygraph equipment classified as 3A981 for export to Honduras. Would you be required to obtain an export license from the Department of Commerce before selling and shipping it to your purchaser?

Answer: Yes. 3A981 is controlled for Crime Control (CC) reasons under CC Column 1 and the Country Chart shows that such items require a license for Honduras.

Example

Question: You have polygraph equipment classified as 3A981 for export to Iceland. Would you be required to obtain an export license from the Department of Commerce before selling and shipping it to your purchaser?

Answer: No. 3A981 is controlled for Crime Control (CC) reasons under CC Column 1 and the Country Chart shows that such items do not require a license for Iceland. Therefore, a license is not required unless you are exporting to an end-user or end-use of concern.

Although a relatively small percentage of all U.S. exports and reexports require a BIS license, virtually all exports and many reexports to embargoed destinations and countries designated as supporting terrorist activities * * * are more restricted and require a license. Part 746 of the EAR describes embargoed destinations and refers to certain additional controls imposed by the Department of the Treasury's Office of Foreign Assets Control.

Notes and Questions

1. In the polygraph ECCN (3A981) example discussed by BIS, the "n.e.s." means "not elsewhere specified." In other words, the item described falls within the ECCN at issue if it is not specifically described in any other ECCN. A fingerprint analyzing device, for example, would fall under 3A981 unless described under some other ECCN.

2. Note that, unlike customs regulations, which apply only to physical goods, the CCL has product groups for software (D) and technology (E). Sending software and technical information listed on the CCL to a person in another country would therefore trigger the export regulations. Continuing the example above, sending abroad diagnostic software for a polygraph machine, or a technical design for such a machine, would qualify as a controlled export.

In summary, determining whether an item requires an export license involves several steps:

(1) The exporter determines whether the item is "subject to the EAR." If not, no export license is required.
(2) The exporter classifies the item on the CCL. If the item is not found on the CCL, the item is EAR99 and no export license is required unless an end-user or end-use control applies.
(3) The exporter checks the "reason for control" listed under the item's ECCN and determines whether the country of destination is checked on the Commerce Country Chart under that "reason for control column." If not, no license is required, and the exporter writes "NLR" (no license required) on its shipper's export declaration unless an end-user or end-use control applies. If the box is checked, that means a license may be required for the export.
(4) The exporter looks again at the ECCN entry to determine whether any license exception might apply.
(5) If an end-user or end-use control applies (see sections D and E, below), an export license is required for any item subject to the EAR.
(6) If no license is required, the exporter may ship the item without further ado. If a license is required, the exporter must apply to BIS for an export license and delay shipping the item until the license is granted.

Of course, in some cases the license will be denied and no exportation will be possible. For this reason, it is always a good idea for an international sale contract to include a clause providing that the contract may be cancelled without any right to damages by either party if the exportation should require a government license and the license application is denied. Otherwise, the denial of an export license could leave the exporter liable to the would-be purchaser for breach of contract!

Most exporters rely on export lawyers to classify their goods on the CCL, but if an exporter or its counsel has trouble determining the ECCN of an item, it may request an official classification from BIS through BIS's electronic licensing system known as the **Simplified Network Application Process Redesign** (**SNAP-R**). In the request, the exporter will describe the item in full technical detail, including its capabilities and uses. Sometimes an exporter will include photographs, schematics, sales brochures, or other supplementary information to help BIS in its classification. Most importantly, the exporter's legal counsel will submit a legal opinion to persuade BIS that the item should be classified in the least export-restrictive manner.

It is important to be aware that the export regulations described here apply regardless of how the item is to be sent out of the United States (e.g., by airplane, seagoing vessel, truck, email, or Internet transmission) and regardless of whether it is sent as a sale, gift, or lease. Moreover, as noted above, an export of an item subject to the EAR from a foreign country to another foreign country will require an export license just as if it were sent from the United States itself.

Reexports

A related point is that the EAR regulates not only exports, but reexports as well. A **reexport** is an item that was produced in and exported from the United States to one state (State *X*), and that will at some point be exported again to another state (from State *X* to State *Y*). The EAR defines the term "reexport" in relevant part as follows:

> (4) *Definition of reexport.* "Reexport" means an actual shipment or transmission of items subject to the EAR from one foreign country to another foreign country; or release of technology or software subject to the EAR to a foreign national outside the United States, as described in paragraph (b)(5) of this section.
> (5) *Reexport of technology or software.* Any release of technology or source code subject to the EAR to a foreign national of another country is a deemed reexport to the home country or countries of the foreign national. * * *

15 C.F.R. § 734.2(b)(4)-(5). Reexports have the same licensing requirements from BIS as exports. Software and technology released by a person in one foreign country to a person in another foreign country is also considered a reexport of the software or technology.

Generally, then, the steps to determining whether a reexport license is necessary are identical to the steps for determining whether an export license is necessary. This rule is very important, because it subjects the foreign purchaser of U.S.-origin goods, software, or technology, as well as certain foreign-origin goods, software, or technology, to the EAR's licensing requirements. It is the obligation of the foreign purchaser to know and comply with the EAR, but the exporter is also obligated to include on the commercial invoice and the bill of lading, air waybill, or other shipping document a **destination control statement** to notify the consignee or purchaser of its obligation not to reexport in violation of the EAR:

> The Destination Control Statement (DCS) must be entered on the invoice and on the bill of lading, air waybill, or other export control document that accompanies the shipment from its point of origin in the United States to the ultimate consignee or end-user abroad. The person responsible for preparation of those documents is responsible for entry of the DCS. The DCS is required for all exports from the United States of items on the Commerce Control List that are not classified as EAR99, unless the export may be made under [certain license exceptions]. At a minimum, the DCS must state: "These commodities, technology or software were exported from the United States in accordance with the Export Administration Regulations. Diversion contrary to U.S. law is prohibited."

15 C.F.R. § 758.6.

C. License Exceptions

Some exports and reexports are exempt from licensing requirements under a specified **license exception**. The license exceptions are listed in 15 C.F.R. pt. 740. License exceptions do not generally apply to end-user and end-user controls or to embargoed destinations, but they otherwise apply with certain narrow exceptions (see 15 C.F.R. § 740.2). Generally, the CCL specifies which license exceptions, if any, may apply to any specific ECCN.

Each license exception is designated by a three-letter code that must be entered on the SED or electronic export record along with the ECCN of the items being exported. There are more than a dozen license exceptions, some very narrow and others fairly general. To illustrate how they work be helpful to summarize a few of the most commonly used: STA, CIV, and TMP.

The Strategic Trade Authorization, or STA, license exception was adopted in 2011 and authorizes two distinct classes of exports and reexports. The first applies to most controlled export and reexports for most controlled purposes to any of a list of countries considered stable, democratic, and closely allied to the United States. The second authorization allows any item controlled for national security purposes only to be exported or reexported to a slightly larger list of countries. In both cases, some condition are imposed on the exporter to ensure the controlled items are not diverted to prohibited uses. See 15 C.F.R. § 740.20.

The Civil End-Users (CIV) license exception applies to exports and reexports to non-military end-users and end-uses of items controlled for national security reasons only and to specific countries only. This exception applies only to items in which the ECCN entry provides: "CIV: Yes." See 15 C.F.R. § 740.5.

Case Study

Another Use for Fertilizer

The exportation of standard farm fertilizer is regulated by the United States and several other countries for national security purposes. Why? Some fertilizers contain chemicals that burn quickly enough to cause an explosion if ignited. In 1995, two U.S. citizens, angry at the federal government for its harsh treatment of private militias and dangerous cult groups, detonated 3 tons of ammonium nitrate—a common farm fertilizer—mixed with diesel fuel and packed into a truck. Both items were acquired from common sources. The terrorists had parked the truck in front of a 9-story federal office building in Oklahoma City and ignited the load.

The resulting blast, measuring 3.0 on the Richter scale, wiped out a third of the building and created a 30-foot wide, 8-foot deep crater at the blast site. The collapse of the building and shock to surrounding buildings caused the deaths of 168 adults and children, over 800 injuries, and hundreds of millions of dollars in property damage. The Oklahoma City bombing illustrates how a seemly harmless substance in everyday civilian use can be turned into a deadly weapon by terrorists.

Figure 5.18. The Oklahoma City Federal Building, Post-Bombing
Credit: U.S. Army Corps of Engineers

Finally, the TMP license exception allows the temporary exportation or reexportation of goods or software abroad subject to the requirement that they be returned to the exporting country within one year. Only certain kinds of goods and software are eligible for this exception, such as tools of the trade, news-gathering equipment for the media, containers for shipping, and sent to affiliated companies in certain stable democracies. This exception excludes a detailed list of specific items, but TMP can be used even if the ECCN does not explicitly state that exception TMP applies. See 15 C.F.R. § 740.9.

D. End-User Controls

The previous sections described how items are classified on the CCL and how to determine whether a license is generally needed before exporting the item to a specific foreign destination. However, even if this analysis results in a determination that no license is required, it is important to know that exports to some specific individuals and organizations require a license or are even forbidden outright, with no license possible. These **end-user controls** apply not only to items listed on the CCL, but to all items subject to the EAR, even if they do not normally require an export license. That includes all EAR99 items—everything from writing paper to trousers to window panes—if located in the United States or containing a nontrivial amount of U.S.-origin parts or materials. Most end-user regulations are set forth in Part 744 of the EAR (15 C.F.R. pt. 744). There are four groups of persons and organizations to whom no exports are possible without a specific license.

The first, called the **Entity List**, is published at 15 C.F.R. pt. 744 supp. 4. The Entity List contains a list of organizations identified by BIS as engaging in the proliferation of weapons of mass destruction or otherwise thwarting U.S. foreign policy interests. Historically, nearly all of the organizations on the Entity List have been located in China, the Middle East, and Russia. These may include universities and government-operated laboratories as well as private companies. No export of anything, including uncontrolled software or technical data, to an organization on the Entity List may be made without a prior license from BIS. None of the license exceptions described above may be used with respect to organizations on the Entity List.

The second, called the **Denied Persons List**, is also maintained by BIS. This list includes all individuals and organizations that have been denied the right to engage in any export or reexport transaction with U.S. persons or involving U.S.-origin goods. Usually, this denial is the result of an actual or suspected violation of U.S. export or reexport regulations. Some denied persons and organizations are located in the United States, but most are foreign. No U.S. person may engage in export transactions with denied persons.

In addition, the BIS keeps a list of names, countries, and addresses of foreign persons involved in export transactions with respect to which BIS is uncertain of the security of the transaction for various reasons. For example,

BIS may have been unable to verify the existence or identity of the end-user, an intermediate agent, or some other party involved in the transaction. In such cases, BIS may place the foreign person on this **Unverified List** to alert exporters that transferring controlled goods or technologies to such persons raises a "red flag." A **red flag** is an indicator that a transaction may violate U.S. export regulations even though it superficially appears to comply with all relevant laws and regulations. As with the Entity List, most companies on the Unverified List are found in China, the Middle East, and Russia.

The fourth list is maintained by the Treasury Department and is discussed later. All four groups are included in a single, consolidated list maintained on the U.S. government's export promotion Web site for ease of reference (http://www.export.gov/).

E. End-Use Controls

Part 744 of the EAR also contains so-called end-use controls. These regulations prohibit any exports subject to the EAR that the exporter knows or has reason to know will be used in the proliferation of nuclear or other dangerous technologies without a prior license from BIS. An example of end-use controls is found in 15 C.F.R. § 744.2:

> **§ 744.2 Restrictions on certain nuclear end-uses.**
>
> (a) *General prohibition.* In addition to the license requirements for items specified on the CCL, you may not export or reexport to any destination, other than countries in the Supplement No. 3 to this part, any item subject to the EAR without a license if at the time of the export or reexport you know [or have reason to know] the item will be used directly or indirectly in any one or more of the following activities described in paragraphs (a)(1), (a)(2), and (a)(3) of this section:
>
> (1) *Nuclear explosive activities.* Nuclear explosive activities, including research on or development, design, manufacture, construction, testing or maintenance of any nuclear explosive device, or components or subsystems of such a device.
>
> (2) *Unsafeguarded nuclear activities.* Activities including research on, or development, design, manufacture, construction, operation, or maintenance of any nuclear reactor, critical facility, facility for the fabrication of nuclear fuel, facility for the conversion of nuclear material from one chemical form to another, or separate storage installation, where there is no obligation to accept International Atomic Energy Agency (IAEA) safeguards at the relevant facility or installation when it contains any source or special fissionable material (regardless of whether or not it contains such material at the time of export), or where any such obligation is not met. * * *

Other end-uses that might trigger a license requirement include missile and rocket development, the design and manufacture of high-technology seagoing vessels and aircraft, and the development or use of strong software encryption.

F. The Deemed Export Rule

Imagine that, instead of exporting technical data listed on the CCL to someone in a foreign country, a U.S. company revealed the data to a foreign national visiting the United States. If the foreign national memorized the information and brought it back to his or her home country abroad, it would defeat the purpose of controlling the exportation of the data.

For example, assume that CCL heading 1E001 states that a license is required for the exportation of any technology for the development or production of the deadly tick-borne encephalitis virus (heading 1C360) to a country restricted for the prevention of the proliferation of biological weapons (CB column 1 on the country chart). Beardsley University in the midwestern United States has admitted several foreign graduate students to study medicine at its medical school. Among these students is Lolita, a national of Zembia. A faculty member at the Beardsley Medical School, Dr. Cuddler, has offered Lolita the opportunity to assist in his research on using recombinant techniques to synthesize the encephalitis virus artificially for the production of an inoculating vaccine. Thanks to the efforts of the General Counsel of Beardsley to educate the faculty on export control laws, Dr. Cuddler knows enough about the export laws to be aware of the illegality of allowing Lolita to take a sample of the controlled virus back to Zembia. He may also be aware that Lolita is forbidden to carry back to Zembia any copies of Dr. Cuddler's technical data on production of the virus. But what Dr. Cuddler, and the Beardsley Medical School faculty in general, should also know is that the very act of training Lolita and giving her access to the technical data necessary to perform the research in the United States violates the EAR unless Dr. Cuddler has obtained a prior license from BIS.

The EAR defines the exportation of technology quite broadly in 15 C.F.R. § 734.2(b):

> (b) Export and reexport
>
> (1) Definition of export. "Export" means an actual shipment or transmission of items subject to the EAR out of the United States, or release of technology or software subject to the EAR to a foreign national in the United States, as described in paragraph (b)(2)(ii) of this section. * * *
>
> (2) Export of technology or software. * * * "Export" of technology or software * * * includes:
>
> (i) Any release of technology or software subject to the EAR in a foreign country; or
>
> (ii) Any release of technology or source code subject to the EAR to a foreign national. Such release is deemed to be an export to the home country or countries of the foreign national. This deemed export rule does not apply to persons lawfully admitted for permanent

> residence in the United States and does not apply to persons who are protected individuals under the Immigration and Naturalization Act (8 U.S.C. § 1324b(a)(3)). * * *
>
> (3) Definition of "release" of technology or software. Technology or software is "released" for export through:
>
> (i) Visual inspection by foreign nationals of U.S.-origin equipment and facilities;
>
> (ii) Oral exchanges of information in the United States or abroad; or
>
> (iii) The application to situations abroad of personal knowledge or technical experience acquired in the United States.

In other words, communicating technical data to a foreign national even within the United States, or even giving that national access to the data, is considered equivalent to exporting the data to a foreign country. BIS deems the communication or access to be an export even if the data never actually leaves the country. For that reason, such communications are called **deemed exports** and the license requirement is called the **deemed export rule**. Transmitting controlled technical data out of the United States is an export potentially requiring a license. Transmitting the same data to a foreign national *within* the United States is a "deemed" export that may also require a license.

Observe that, under the EAR's definition of a "release" of technology, the mere visual inspection of U.S.-origin equipment or facilities by a foreign national can be an "export" of the technology to the foreign person's country of nationality. Similarly, merely discussing the technology, either in person or on the telephone, can qualify as an export. This broad definition requires companies developing or using U.S.-origin controlled technologies to exercise extreme caution when interacting with foreign nationals, even if the foreign national is the company's own employee. Unless the company has obtained a prior export license from BIS, allowing a foreign national to tour a manufacturing plant, access the company computers, or discuss business over a cup of coffee with company engineers or sales personnel could each violate the EAR. Violations expose the company to civil penalties, adverse publicity, unwelcome attention from BIS and other regulatory agencies, and possibly even criminal fines and imprisonment.

G. Advisory Opinions

The complexity of the EAR may render the regulations subject to some uncertainty. The IEEPA itself grants broad powers to the President, and very little case law interpreting the IEEPA or EAR exists. To assist exporters in interpreting the EAR, BIS will issue nonbinding **advisory opinions** regarding the key questions that confront an exporter:

- Is the proposed export subject to the EAR?
- Is the proposed product, software, or technology listed on the CCL and,

if so, under which ECCN? (This is called a **classification request**.)

- Is an export license necessary for the product?
- Does a license exception apply?

The procedures for requesting an advisory opinion are set forth in EAR §§ 734.6 and 748.3. Requests must be in writing or through BIS's electronic system and must include all pertinent information. Generally, BIS responds to classification requests within fourteen days and other advisory opinion requests within thirty days. 15 C.F.R. § 750.2.

Technically, an advisory opinion does not bind BIS; it is merely guidance. However, there are no known cases in which an export made in conformity with an advisory opinion has resulted in penalties for the exporter. Of course, BIS does not commit to issuing future licenses for exportation in an advisory opinion, but if BIS takes the position that an exportation requires no license, the exporter can generally rely on the opinion.

H. Grant or Denial of the Export License

If the exporter or reexporter determines that a license is necessary, it may apply for a license by submitting a request through BIS's automated export system, SNAP-R. Each application includes an application control number that allows the exporter and BIS to identify the application in their communications. Upon receipt, BIS will consider the application:

> (a) *Review by BIS.* In reviewing specific license applications, BIS will conduct a complete analysis of the license application along with all documentation submitted in support of the application. In addition to reviewing the item and end-use, BIS will consider the reliability of each party to the transaction and review any available intelligence information. To the maximum extent possible, BIS will make licensing decisions without referral of license applications to other agencies, however, BIS may consult with other U.S. departments and agencies regarding any license application.

15 C.F.R. § 750.3.

If required information is missing, the application will be returned without action. Otherwise, BIS will eventually approve or reject the application. In general, BIS decides what action to take within ninety days from receipt of all required information, although longer processing times may be required. 15 C.F.R. § 750.4. The delay typical in the processing of an export application puts U.S. exporters at some disadvantage in procuring and fulfilling international sales contracts involving controlled items to controlled destinations. To minimize the disadvantage, exporters typically forewarn purchasers of expected delays and apply for an export license immediately upon conclusion of the sales agreement (and sometimes beforehand, if the sale is expected to be sufficiently large).

If BIS denies the application, it will notify the exporter promptly of its "intent" to deny the application, to which the exporter may respond with arguments and evidence. Should the exporter fail to convince BIS to change its decision, the denial will issue. 15 C.F.R. § 750.6. The exporter may appeal the denial to the Deputy Under Secretary of Commerce for Industry and Security. 15 C.F.R. §§ 756.1-.2. The Deputy Under Secretary's decision is not further appealable, either administratively or judicially. Courts generally decline jurisdiction over decisions of this nature in deference to the President's foreign affairs power and the express congressional grant in IEEPA of regulatory discretion to the President.

If the application is granted, it will authorize only the specific transaction, or series of transactions, described in the application. It does not constitute a general authorization to export goods of the kind described in the application to destinations described in the application in the future. The license will bear a license number that must be entered on the SED, and will impose specific conditions on the exporter with respect to the export. Most commonly, the license will include an expiration date, and so will require exportation within a specified period after the license grant, usually within two years. However, other restrictions are usual, such as limitations on the quantity or value of the exports authorized.

I. Penalties for Noncompliance

Penalties for violating any provision of the EAR are exceptionally heavy. Under the 2007 revisions to the IEEPA, any violation of, attempt to violate, or conspiracy to violate the EAR may result in a "civil penalty" in an amount of $250,000 per violation or "an amount that is twice the amount of the transaction that is the basis of the violation." 50 U.S.C. § 1705(b). A **civil penalty** is a criminal fine, except that no *mens rea* (intent to commit the illegal act) is required; the government's burden of proof is a "preponderance of the evidence" standard instead of the criminal "beyond a reasonable doubt" standard; and other constitutional protections applicable in criminal cases are denied the accused.

In addition, a "willful" violation, attempt to violate, or conspiracy to violate the EAR may result in a criminal fine up to $ 1 million per violation and up to 20 years imprisonment. In cases of criminal penalties, the accused benefits from the usual constitutional protections applicable in criminal cases, including the protection of a "reasonable doubt" burden of proof standard. 50 U.S.C. § 1705(c). It is important to be aware that most federal regulations define a "willful" violation to include not only intentional or knowing violations, but also acts committed with **reason to know** a regulatory violation will result.

Any violation of the EAR may also result in a denial of export privileges, at BIS's discretion. A **denial of export privileges** for a certain period means that the person or company sanctioned may not export any controlled item; it will be systematically denied an export license. Such denials typically last up to ten or twenty years. For a company heavily reliant upon exports for revenue, a denial of export privileges can be crippling. For this reason, such denials are typically imposed in practice against individuals, foreign companies, and very small U.S. companies. Such violators are included in the denied persons list, discussed in section D above.

Finally, BIS administers an unofficial sanction in the form of adverse publicity. In pursuit of its mission of deterring violations of the EAR, BIS routinely publishes press releases when it obtains a court judgment or even a voluntary settlement by an accused exporter. These press releases may affect a sanctioned company's stock prices, insurance rates, or credit rating. Sanctions imposed on an individual may affect his or her employment prospects and business reputation. To compound the difficulties, BIS regularly publishes a manual, ominously titled *Don't Let This Happen to You!*, in which all of its major favorable settlements, judgments, and convictions are recapitulated for public edification. In short, BIS makes every effort to publicize its successful enforcement actions.

BIS has substantial discretion in the choice of which penalties to apply to any given violation. Because the EAR contain both reporting and recordkeeping requirements, BIS sometimes "multiplies" penalties, resulting in tremendous fines if the exporter has committed a series of violations. For example, suppose an exporter negligently misclassified a product that it exported to various foreign customers ten times within a one-year period. Suppose that each exportation properly required a license and that, as a result of the exporter's misclassification, each exportation was made without a license in violation of the EAR.

You might think that the maximum fine for these accidental violations—$250,000 multiplied by ten, or $2.5 million—is extreme. But, because of the mistake, the exporter will have failed to report on the SED the proper ECCN of the export and to report that it required a license. BIS considers that this constitutes a separate violation of the EAR, although it may have been unavoidable under the circumstances. Moreover, the exporter's records will be inaccurate as well, which might be considered as constituting a *third* violation of the EAR. The already exceptionally heavy $2.5 million dollar "civil" penalty has now become $7.5 million (3 counts per violation × 10 violations × $250,000 per count). According to BIS: "Frequently, a single transaction can give rise to multiple violations. Depending on the facts and circumstances, BIS may choose to impose a smaller or greater penalty per violation." 15 C.F.R. § 766 supp. 2(d)(1)(iii). BIS commonly seeks multiple sanctions of this kind in order to inflate the threatened penalty, which in turn helps it negotiate a higher settlement from the violator. This practice has not been judicially tested, but BIS's ongoing regulatory authority over most exporters discourages judicial challenges to BIS practices.

In theory, BIS penalties may be appealed. They are first appealed to an administrative law judge (ALJ) within the Department of Commerce. You may recall that the ALJ is not an independent judge, but rather an employee of the Executive Branch. In the unusual case that the ALJ alters or annuls his employer's decision, the Secretary of Commerce may override the ALJ's judgment. Decisions of the Secretary of Commerce may be appealed through the regular

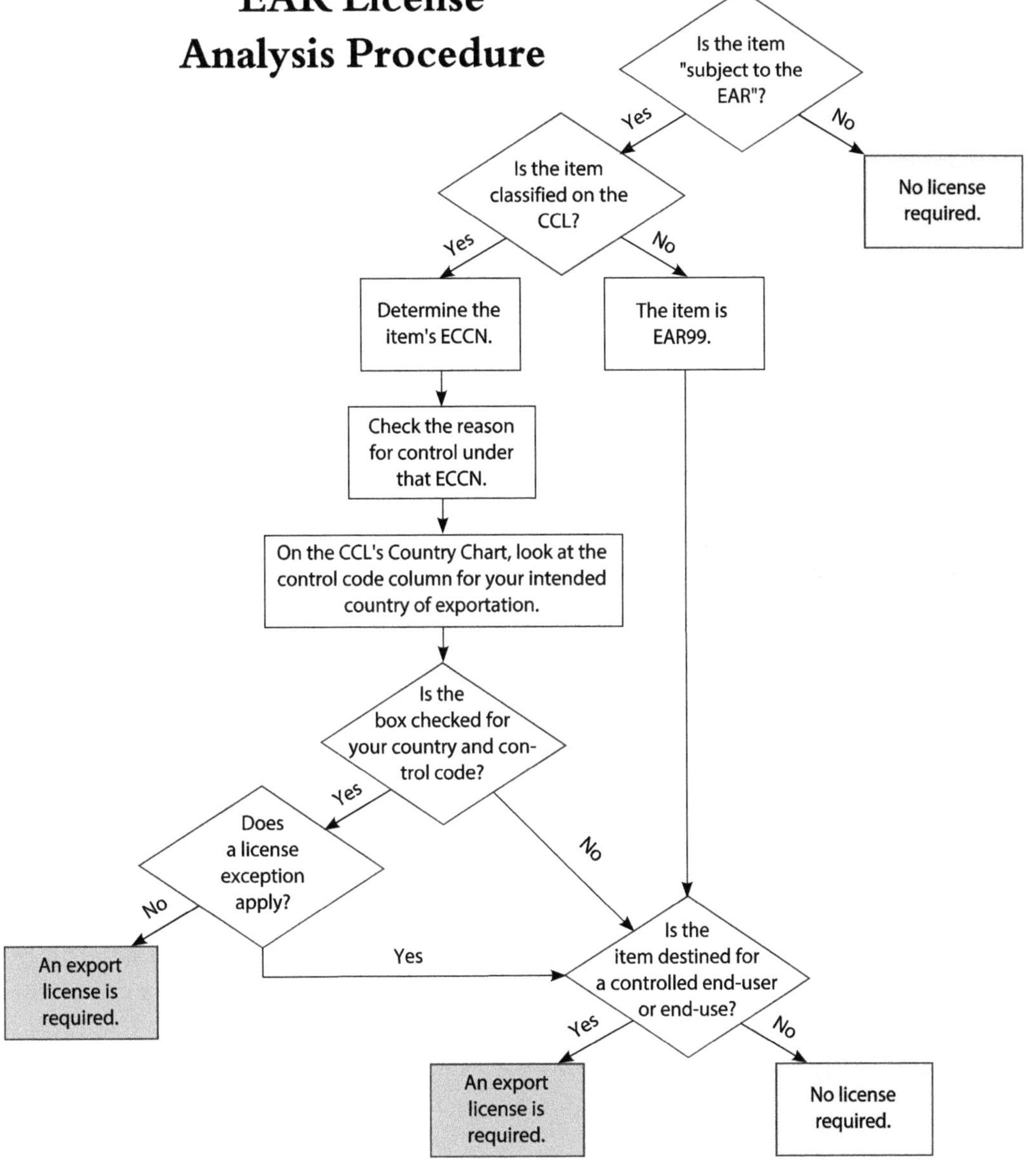

Figure 5.19. Flow chart of the basic procedures for determining whether an export license is required under the Export Administration Regulations.

court system (generally going through the federal courts of the District of Columbia). However, federal courts give substantial deference on foreign policy questions to the Executive Branch, and courts are further bound to defer to federal agencies on questions within the agency's statutory competence. Thus, successful appeals are sufficiently rare that exporters rarely even bother to appeal BIS penalties.

J. Voluntary Self-Disclosure

These deterrents to an impartial assessment of the merits of any accused violation of the EAR make cooperation with BIS very attractive to repeat exporters. Preserving a cordial relationship with the agency reduces the chance of crippling penalties. One way an exporter demonstrates its willingness to cooperate with BIS is to report its own violations of the EAR before BIS discovers them. BIS, like CBP, encourages **voluntary self-disclosure** of any violation of the regulations. Such disclosures reduce the violation detection and enforcement burden on BIS. In return, voluntary self-disclosures might mitigate penalties significantly or even avoid them altogether. See 15 C.F.R. § 764.5; 15 C.F.R. pt. 766 supp. 1. BIS is not obligated to mitigate penalties when the exporter self-discloses, however, and there are known cases in which a self-disclosure has resulted in little or no mitigation.

4.2 Arms Export Controls

If U.S. law regulates the exportation of items having both civilian and military uses, you can well imagine that it would regulate *a fortiori* items primarily having a military use. The Wassenaar Arrangement, MTCR, NSG, and Australia Group coordinate international trade policy for military as well as dual-use items. In the United States, exports of items primarily for military use are currently regulated separately from exports of dual-use items.

A. U.S. Munitions Export Controls

The **Arms Export Control Act** (**AECA**), 22 U.S.C. §§ 2778-80, authorizes the President to control international and domestic trade in arms and munitions. The following excerpt summarizes the AECA and its purpose.

Aaron Xavier Fellmeth, *Cure Without a Disease: The Emerging Doctrine of Successor Liability in International Trade Law*, 31 YALE J. INT'L L. 127, 161-62 (2006)

* * * The AECA authorizes the Executive Branch to regulate the export and import of "defense articles and services," such as armaments, ordnance, spacecraft and space equipment, and technical data about articles and services that are "inherently military." It also permits the Executive Branch to require the licensing of the manufacture

and trans-border movement of the foregoing. The licensing scheme centers on the Munitions Control List (also known as the U.S. Munitions List, or USML), a cryptic enumeration of items that the Department of State has determined constitute defense articles, services and data, the exportation or importation of which must be duly licensed.

The purported goals of the AECA are to deter activities detrimental to U.S. homeland security and foreign policy. Congress has stated that the purposes of the AECA are the promotion of "a world which is free from the scourge of war and the dangers and burdens of armaments," the subordination of the use of force to the rule of law, the assurance of peaceful adjustments in a changing world, the encouragement of regional arms control and disarmament agreements, and the discouragement of arms races. To these ends, the AECA delegates to the Secretary of State the task of creating and maintaining the Munitions List and of supervising and regulating the sale of arms on the List to foreign countries. The AECA also contains several provisions that encourage the Executive Branch to monitor and limit the foreign sale of weapons by the federal government and to enter into arms control and disarmament agreements. The provisions relating to presidential control of arms exports and imports are designed to authorize and encourage the President "to check and control the international sale and distribution of conventional weapons of death and destruction" to advance "world peace and the security and foreign policy of the United States." * * *

The AECA's provisions are fairly vague and leave much administrative discretion to the President. The President, in turn, has delegated the regulation of the importation, exportation, and domestic sale of munitions to the **Directorate of Defense Trade Controls** (**DDTC**) of the Department of State. The DDTC has adopted rules known as the **International Traffic in Arms Regulations** (**ITAR**), 22 C.F.R. pts. 120-30, to implement the AECA. To regulate trade in munitions, implements of war, and related technical data and services, it is first necessary to define what munitions are and how they differ from the "dual-use" goods discussed previously in this chapter. To that end, the DDTC has adopted what is called the **U.S. Munitions List** (**USML**) to clarify those articles and services that fall within the jurisdiction of DDTC as opposed to the jurisdiction of BIS. The USML is located at 22 C.F.R. pt. 121. The USML classifies defense articles and services into twenty-one categories designated by roman numerals.

As with the EAR, the ITAR defines controlled services to include providing training, assistance, or technical data to any foreign person "in the United States or abroad." Remember the **deemed export rule** applied by BIS? The same prohibition applies to the ITAR. Thus, if a U.S. arms manufacturer gave a factory tour or unrestricted computer access to a foreign national in the United States—even one employed by the manufacturer's foreign subsidiary—that tour or computer access might be considered an "exportation" of a defense service to the foreign national's country of citizenship requiring a license from DDTC. This interpretation is confirmed by the ITAR's definition of "export," which includes not only sending controlled munitions to foreign countries or providing defense services abroad, but also:

> (3) Disclosing (including oral or visual disclosure) or transferring in the United States any defense article to an embassy, any agency or subdivision of a foreign government (e.g., diplomatic missions); or
> (4) Disclosing (including oral or visual disclosure) or transferring technical data to a foreign person, whether in the United States or abroad; or
> (5) Performing a defense service on behalf of, or for the benefit of, a foreign person, whether in the United States or abroad.

22 C.F.R. § 120.17(a).

Not all items that meet the definitions of defense article or defense service are considered subject to the ITAR. Only defense articles and services specifically listed on the USML cannot be manufactured or exported without a license. According to the ITAR, the Department of State, in consultation with the Department of Defense, lists an item on the USML if it is specifically designed, developed, modified for a military application and:

- neither has a predominant civilian application nor is equivalent to a civilian article or service in its form, fit, or function; nor
- has significant military or intelligence applicability.

The relevant question, then, is not how any specific item is intended to be used, but rather how it was designed and what its capabilities are. Exporting paper clips to a foreign armed force does not make them defense articles subject to the ITAR any more than exporting a combat tank to a foreign motion picture studio for entertainment purposes relieves the exporter of the obligation to obtain an export license from DDTC.

B. Defense Trade Registration and Licensing

If you represented the government of a militarily sophisticated state wishing to prevent the unsupervised spread of powerful weapons around the world, you would want to be aware of which companies intend to manufacture or export munitions. The AECA accordingly requires all manufacturers and exporters of munitions and defense services listed in the USML to register with the DDTC prior to manufacturing or exporting the controlled items. This condition allows the State Department to keep an eye on companies dealing in dangerous munitions. Merely registering with DDTC does not, of course, automatically mean that the registered company can export its munitions at will; the registered company must also obtain a separate export license from DDTC for each controlled shipment it intends to export. However, registration is a precondition to obtaining an export license.

To register as an arms manufacturer or exporter, a company must fill in a DDTC form called a **Statement of Registration** and submit it to the DDTC.

The form is reproduced as Figure 5.20. Through the statement, the company provides DDTC with information about its owners, responsible directors and officers, any affiliated companies such as subsidiaries or parent companies, and the kinds of articles and services the company intends to distribute. Only U.S. companies may register as arms manufacturers and exporters with DDTC.

Registration itself does not authorize any specific shipment of items listed on the USML; it only makes it possible to apply for export licenses. License applications must generally be filed through DDTC's electronic system, called **D-TRADE**. In the license application, the company must:

- fully describe the products or services to be exported in technical detail, including the appropriate USML classification;
- provide a copy of the purchase order or sales/service agreement;
- provide evidence of prior registration with DDTC;
- identify the manufacturer of any USML-listed articles to be exported;
- identify the foreign consignee and/or end-user of articles or services; and
- explain the intended purposes to which the articles or services will be put by the end-user.

If DDTC grants the license, the defense articles may be exported or defense services provided abroad in accordance with the terms of the license. If the license is denied, the company must forego the sale. There is no possibility of appealing a license denial. For this reason, it is always wise to make contracts for the sale of controlled items, services, or technologies contingent upon approval by both the government of the exporter and the government of the importer.

C. The Commodity Jurisdiction Procedure

Imagine that you represent Air Superiority, Inc. (ASI), a California corporation that builds small private jet airplanes. ASI, a DDTC-registered defense manufacturer, has designed and begun production of a new small passenger jet called the Redtail 100. ASI began designing the Redtail 100 in response to a notice posted by the Department of Defense, which is seeking a fast, lightweight, and fuel-efficient aircraft for surveillance or officer transportation. The Redtail 100 has a hybrid solar motor and kerosene engine that gives it a much longer range and lower fuel consumption than comparable jets. In designing the Redtail, ASI perceived both a potential civilian and military market for the product. It accordingly made two basic design variations. Both variations are based on the same airframe design and use the same engine and other technology, with only a few differences. One design, the Redtail 100c, is intended as a private jet for use by corporate executives and wealthy individuals for business or entertainment purposes. The other, the Redtail 100m, is intended for use by military officers for transportation on or off the battlefield. The Redtail 100m

U.S. Department of State

STATEMENT OF REGISTRATION

(SEE INSTRUCTIONS PAGE)
(Attach additional sheet if necessary)

OMB APPROVAL NO 1405-0002
EXPIRATION DATE 09/30/2008
*ESTIMATED BURDEN 2 Hours

PM/DDTC Date Received *(mm-dd-yyyy*

New Registrant Code

1. Registrant's Name and Address

Telephone Number

2. Current Registrant Code

3. ____________ Enclosed For 1 2 *(Circle One)* Year*(s)* Registration

4. Registrant Is: ☐ Individual ☐ Partnership ☐ Company ☐ Corporation

5. Registrant Is:
☐ Manufacturer ☐ Exporter of Hardware/Technical Data
☐ Exporter of Defense Service ☐ Broker

6. Incorporation or Commencement of Business: Date*(mm-dd-yyyy* ____________
In ____________
City, County, and State

7. Directors, Officers, Partners, Owners:

Name *(Last, First, MI)*	Position	Date of Birth *(mm-dd-yyyy)*	Place of Birth	Social Security Number	Home Address	Citizenship

8. U.S. Munitions List Articles Manufactured and/or Exported, or Defense Services Provided:

Category	Commodity/Service	Purchasing U.S. Government Agency *(If Any)*

9. Names and Addresses of Registrant's Wholly- and Partially-Owned U.S. Subsidiaries: ☐ Yes *(Specify)* ☐ No

10. Names and Addresses of Registrant's Wholly- and Partially-Owned Foreign Subsidiaries: ☐ Yes *(Specify)* ☐ No

11. Name, Address and Telephone Numbers of Registrant's Parent Company *(if any)*

12. Is The Registrant ☐ Owned ☐ And/Or Controlled By Foreign Persons *(22 CFR 122.2(c))* ☐ Yes *(Specify)* ☐ No

13. Does Registrant Submit Federal Income Tax Forms Separately From Company In Block 11? ☐ Yes ☐ No

14. Registrant's Statement:
Under Penalty According To Federal Law *(see 22 CFR 127; 22 U S C 2778, 18 U.S.C. 1001)*

I, ______________________ Warrant The Truth of All Statements Made Herein
Type Full Name

______________________ Signature ____________ Date *(mm-dd-yyyy)*

______________________ Title/Position

DS-2032
10-2005

(DESTROY PREVIOUS EDITIONS)

Page 1 of 1

Figure 5.20. A DDTC Statement of Registration.

is identical to the 100c, except that its fuselage surface is coated with a low-radar-profile material, it has more powerful radar, and it comes equipped with electronic countermeasures to distract incoming anti-aircraft missiles.

Assume the Redtail 100m falls within the USML as an aircraft specifically designed or modified for military purposes. But what about the 100c? CCL category 9 covers "aerospace and propulsion," and ECCN 9A991.b includes "aircraft n.e.s." (not elsewhere specified), which would include most civilian aircraft. USML Category VIII(a) includes aircraft "specially designed to incorporate a defense article for the purpose of performing an intelligence, surveillance, and reconnaissance function." Which classification applies to the Redtail 100c? On one hand, the 100c has a predominant civilian application and no significant military use in its finished form. On the other, its airframe and engines were designed in response to a perceived need of the U.S. military, and its unusually long range means that it has performance characteristics that are not equivalent to similar civilian aircraft.

As this example illustrates, it is not always clear whether a specific product or service is encompassed by the USML or the CCL administered by BIS. When a manufacturer or exporter is unsure whether registration and licensing is required for a specific product or service, it may request that DDTC clarify the point. BIS, you may recall, may issue an advisory opinion on classification, but this is limited to items classified on the CCL. The question of whether a good or technology is subject to the EAR and CCL on one hand, or the ITAR and USML on the other, is a matter that only DDTC can resolve. When a company requests that DDTC issue an authoritative opinion on whether an item is included in the USML, it is called a **commodity jurisdiction (CJ) request**. In response to a proper CJ request, DDTC will issue a binding determination that conclusively resolves whether the article or service at issue is included in the USML or the CCL. A CJ determination does not, of course, in itself grant permission to export the article or service at issue, but it does clarify which export list contains the item and, accordingly, which agency (BIS or DDTC) is the proper addressee of an export license application.

There is no specific government form to fill in when filing a CJ request. Instead, the company wishing to export the article or service sends a letter to DDTC describing in full technical detail the product or service at issue, how it works, for what purposes it is designed, and how and to whom it is marketed. It is also common to include marketing literature and sales data showing the kinds of end-users who have ordered or purchased the article or service in the United States.

Upon receipt of a proper CJ request, DDTC consults with the Department of Defense, BIS, and other relevant federal agencies before deciding on whether the item is classified on the USML or CCL. Because a CJ request typically requires the evaluation of detailed data by technical experts and negotiation among two or more agencies, it normally takes two to three months after submission of the CJ request to obtain a final determination.

The advantage of obtaining a CJ determination is the security it gives to the exporter. The determination is binding. If the exporter obtains a CJ determination stating that its product is listed on the CCL rather than the USML, and the exporter subsequently exports the product pursuant to a license from BIS instead of DDTC, DDTC cannot then change its mind and punish the exporter for exporting the product without a license from DDTC. On the other hand, the time needed for preparing a CJ request and the waiting required for a response can deter exporters from using the CJ procedure whenever a long delay would significantly undermine the chance of a foreign sale. In such cases, the exporter may be willing to rely on its legal counsel's best judgment as to whether the article or service is properly classified on the CCL or USML in order to expedite export clearance.

D. License Exceptions

The ITAR does not have general license exceptions like those found in the EAR. However, the United States has signed a few **Defense Trade Cooperation Treaties** with certain close allies that relax the export controls on certain defense items to those states for certain purposes, such as use by the U.S. military in the foreign country or for joint defense exercises. Under the treaties, no prior DDTC license is required to export listed items on the USML to treaty states for listed purposes, subject to the usual reexport controls. At present, the United States is a party to only a few such treaties.

E. Penalties for Noncompliance

Willful violations of the AECA or ITAR carry criminal sanctions up to $1 million and ten years imprisonment per violation, plus forfeiture of the unlicensed goods or disgorgement of illegal profits. 22 U.S.C. § 2778(c). Civil penalties of $500,000 per violation may be imposed for unintentional violations. 22 U.S.C. § 2778(e). In addition, goods involved in any ITAR violation may be confiscated, and the exporter may be denied export privileges in DDTC's discretion. 22 C.F.R. §§ 127.6-.7. Just as BIS does with violations of the EAR, DDTC encourages voluntary self-disclosure of ITAR violations and promises to mitigate penalties in the event of such disclosure. 22 C.F.R. § 127.12.

The DDTC has internal ALJs to review agency decisions to deny an export or import license or to impose penalties on an accused ITAR violator. These ALJs function similarly to Department of Commerce ALJs, reviewing agency decisions to deny a license or impose civil penalties on an exporter or importer. Decisions of the ALJ may be appealed to the Under Secretary of State for Arms Control and International Security. See 22 C.F.R. pt. 128. As with alleged violations of the EAR, any final DDTC decision on ITAR sanctions may be appealed to the federal courts of the District of Columbia.

DILBERT, I HIRED SOME CONTRACT EMPLOYEES FROM NORTH ELBONIA TO HELP ON YOUR PROJECT.
NORTH ELBONIA IS AN EVIL TOTALITARIAN REGIME. MY PROJECT WILL CREATE TOP SECRET MILITARY TECHNOLOGY TO USE AGAINST THEM.
SURE, BUT YOU HAVE TO WEIGH THAT AGAINST THE FACT THAT THEY'RE WILLING TO WORK FOR FREE.
www.unitedmedia.com
© 1997 United Feature Syndicate, Inc.
12/5/97

I'M A LITTLE CONCERNED ABOUT YOUR HIRING COMMUNIST NORTH ELBONIAN CONTRACTORS TO HELP ON MY TOP SECRET MILITARY PROJECT.
E-mail: SCOTTADAMS@AOL.COM

DON'T WORRY. WHAT'S THE WORST THING THAT COULD HAPPEN?
I COULD BE EXECUTED FOR TREASON.

TALK TO OUR LEGAL DEPART-MENT.
COULD I OPT FOR THE EXECUTION INSTEAD?
© 1997 United Feature Syndicate, Inc.
12/6/97

THE COMPANY LAWYER
I'M WORKING ON A TOP SECRET MILITARY PROJECT. MY BOSS HIRED SOME NORTH ELBONIANS TO HELP ME.
www.unitedmedia.com

THEY'RE COMMUNISTS. IF I GIVE THEM ANY INFORMATION, I COULD BE GUILTY OF TREASON. I COULD BE EXECUTED.

CAN YOU HELP?
SURE. WHAT WOULD I HAVE TO DO — PULL A LEVER?
© 1997 United Feature Syndicate, Inc.
12/17/97

DON'T WORRY THAT WE'LL TAKE ANY MILITARY TECHNOLOGY SECRETS BACK TO NORTH ELBONIA.
E-mail: SCOTTADAMS@AOL.COM

WE SIGNED THESE LITTLE AGREEMENTS THAT SAY WE WON'T.

HA HA HA HA HA!!
MOVING ON...
© 1997 United Feature Syndicate, Inc.
12/18/97

Figure 5.21. Even Dilbert has to deal with deemed arms exports on occasion. Presumably, the "Helen Reddy song" is *I Am Woman*. Although the cartoon is largely inaccurate on the law, a deemed export license may well require foreign employees to sign "little agreements" not to use the U.S. technology in violation of the AECA or ITAR. Credit: **DILBERT** © 1997 by Scott Adams/United Features Syndicate, Inc.

Parallel Export Control Regimes		
	DUAL-USE ITEMS	DEFENSE ARTICLES & SERVICES
STATUTORY AUTHORITY	International Emergency Economic Powers Act (IEEPA)	Arms Export Control Act (AECA)
AGENCY	Department of Commerce Bureau of Industry & Security	Department of State Directorate of Defense Trade Controls
REGULATIONS	Export Administration Regulations	International Traffic in Arms Regulations
LIST OF ITEMS	Commerce Control List (CCL)	U.S. Munitions List (USML)
CRIMINAL PENALTIES	$1 million per violation and/or 20 years imprisonment	$1 million per violation and/or 10 years imprisonment
CIVIL PENALTIES	$250,000 per violation Denial of export privileges	$500,000 per violation Debarment Seizure & Forfeiture

5 Trade and Economic Sanctions

Trade sanctions are laws that prevent one state's citizens from buying from or selling to another state or its citizens under specified circumstances. Trade sanctions that prohibit substantially all trade with a foreign state are sometimes called an **embargo**, although not all sanctions are intended to halt trade completely between the states. They may instead be directed toward specific classes of goods or technologies that the state is considered in danger of abusing, or specific targeted regions, organizations, or persons within a state. In any case, trade sanctions are usually an attempt by one state to influence another state, organization, or class of individuals, to weaken their economies, and to prevent them from obtaining WMD and advanced military or related technologies.

Economic sanctions serve the same purposes, but they do not necessarily involve trade in goods or services *per se*. Instead, economic sanctions usually include an asset freeze or a blocking order, or both. An **asset freeze** prohibits banks, debtors, and others in possession of funds owed to the target individual, organization, or state from disbursing those funds to the target. For example, after evidence appeared that Libya was involved in a terrorist attack on a European passenger jet in 1988, the United States froze all assets of the Libyan government in the United States. If the Libyan government or any of its agencies held an account in any U.S. bank, that bank was prohibited from allowing the Libyan government to withdraw or transfer any funds while the freeze was in effect. Similarly, any U.S. person owing money to the Libyan government was prohibited from paying it, but instead had to put the funds into a trust account or disburse them to the federal government. The embargo on Libya was lifted in 2004, after the Libyan government extradited to the U.K. the persons accused of conspiring in the bombing.

A **blocking order** prohibits any U.S. person from doing business with or entering into financial or commercial transactions with the target individual, organization, or state (called the **blocked person**). The blocking order prohibits such transactions in both export and import commerce, and in purely domestic transactions as well. It may also prohibit any transactions relating to property owned by the blocked person or in which the blocked person has some ownership interest. For example, the Iranian sanctions prohibited the sale to anyone of any U.S. property in which the Iranian government owns an interest.

Sanctions may be multilateral or unilateral. **Multilateral sanctions** are imposed by the international community as a whole, or by some group within the community. Often, multilateral sanctions result from action by the United Nations Security Council. The 1945 United Nations Participation Act, 22 U.S.C. § 287c, authorizes the U.S. President to implement economic and trade sanctions in compliance with a UN Security Council resolution. The Security Council periodically imposes sanctions to pressure or punish certain states or organizations for violating internationally protected human rights, undermining democracy, or resorting to military force or terrorism in violation of international law. For example, when Iraq invaded and attempted to annex Kuwait in 1990, the Security Council adopted a resolution instructing all UN members to cease trade and economic relations with Iraq and occupied Kuwait. The United States, like other UN members, may impose sanctions pursuant to a Security Council resolution. Indeed, as one of the permanent members of the Security Council, the United States can be expected always to comply with Security Council sanctions because, if it opposed the sanctions, it would have vetoed the measure.

Unilateral sanctions are imposed by a single country without international support. Unilateral trade and economic sanctions are usually designed to deprive disfavored foreign countries of the advantages of selling to or buying from the sanctioning state's market; to withhold advanced military technologies from terrorist-sponsoring states; and to punish and isolate terrorist organizations, terrorists, narcotics traffickers, and their associates.

The United States is by far the most active user of economic and trade sanctions in the world. Some U.S. sanctions have endured for decades. Since 1963, for example, the U.S. Executive Branch has maintained an almost complete embargo against Cuba and Cuban nationals. The United States also periodically imposes and retracts sanctions on various other countries. In the past, these have included among others Iran, Iraq, Libya, North Korea, and Syria. In some cases, sanctions are imposed not on the country as a whole, but on specific regions or individuals. For example, in 2018, the U.S. President invoked IEEPA to order trade and economic sanctions against certain Russians involved in a massive campaign to manipulate U.S. elections. In still other cases, sanctions take a more complex form. For example, since 2002, the United States and forty-seven other states have regulated the trade in rough diamonds because they were being sold by African warlords to fund civil war and various atrocities in Angola, Sierra Leone, and elsewhere in Africa (where many of the world's diamonds originate). As noted, many other states have similar regulations.

5.1 U.S. Sanctions Programs

There are many statutes empowering or requiring the Executive Branch to impose economic and trade sanctions on various countries, organizations, and individuals. The two main authorizing statutes of general application, however, are the IEEPA, which also provides the authority for the dual-use export sanctions, and the **Trading with the Enemy Act** (**TWEA**), 12 U.S.C. § 95a, 50 U.S.C. App. §§ 1-39, 41-44. The following article excerpt explains the nature and basic purpose of the TWEA.

Case Study

Night-Vision Goggle Exports

Figure 5.22. Night vision goggles. Credit: Ministère de la Défense de France

In 2001, a U.S. multinational corporation exported components of infrared night-vision goggles to China, Singapore, and the United Kingdom without obtaining a DDTC export license. The goggles are used by soldiers in the field to see enemies at nighttime. The exporter further failed to report the goggle part exports in its periodic report to the DDTC. After discovering the violations, the company reported them voluntarily, but the Department of Justice still filed a criminal complaint for violation of the AECA.

The DoJ claimed that company's exportations "jeopardized our national security and the safety of our military men and women on the battlefield." After negotiating a plea bargain, the exporter in 2007 pled guilty to only one count of an unlicensed exportation and one count of failure to report an exportation. The exporter agreed to pay one of the largest fines in the history of export regulation, $100 million.

This figure greatly overstates the amount the exporter had to pay in fact, however. The $100 million included $2 million as a criminal fine, forfeiture of $28 million in revenues from the goggle part sales, and a $20 million civil penalty paid to the DDTC. The remaining $50 million fine was suspended for five years, but even so the exporter was allowed to spend it in research for the development and production of more advanced night-vision technology that would ultimately profit the exporter itself. Forcing the company to invest in improving its own technology is the regulatory equivalent of forcing a child to eat broccoli. It may subjectively be perceived as a punishment, but the net result is a benefit.

The case illustrates how companies accused of violating export regulatory laws can reduce penalties by negotiating with the government and agreeing to concessions that cost it little but create value for the regulators. Regulators may be willing to reduce penalties actually paid in exchange for an increase in the penalties they can report to the news media. After all, regulators realistically can only detect and prosecute a small percentage of the actual export violations that occur. If regulators can deter many future violations by headline-grabbing penalties, the fact of actually collecting a smaller amount matters little.

Aaron Xavier Fellmeth, *Cure Without a Disease: The Emerging Doctrine of Successor Liability in International Trade Law*, 31 YALE J. INT'L L. 127, 164 (2006)

* * * TWEA was adopted in 1917 to "define, regulate, and punish trading with the enemy" or an "ally of the enemy" during time of war. TWEA is intended to accomplish this purpose by prohibiting any U.S. citizen or any person within the United States from buying from, selling to, paying, or entering into or performing contracts with any individual, entity or government with knowledge or reason to believe that the trading partner is an "enemy" or ally of an enemy. An "enemy" was originally defined as a state with which the United States is at war, but the statute was amended in 1933 to accommodate peacetime national emergencies. TWEA also prohibits exports of any tangible form of information directly or indirectly to the enemy or an ally of the enemy. Finally, TWEA authorizes the President to implement these provisions by, *inter alia*, regulating or prohibiting transactions in foreign exchange. The President invoked his authority under TWEA to impose embargoes against Germany during the First World War; against Japan prior to the attack on Pearl Harbor; against communist China; against Cuba after Fidel Castro seized power; and in the Korean and Vietnam Wars.

* * * TWEA provides for criminal sanctions. These sanctions include $1 million fines for legal entities and, for individuals, fines and imprisonment up to ten years; the penalties are to be applied against "[w]hoever shall willfully violate any of the provisions of this Act, or of any license, rule or regulation issued thereunder, and whoever shall willfully violate, neglect, or refuse to comply with any order of the President issued in compliance with the provisions of the Act." TWEA additionally provides for a nominally civil penalty up to $50,000 against "any person who violates any license, order, rule, or regulation issued in compliance with the provisions of this Act." In case of either a civil or criminal violation of TWEA, all property, funds, securities, vessels, furniture, equipment, and other items "concerned in any violation" may be forfeited to the U.S. government. * * *

In addition, Congress from time to time passes statutes authorizing or instructing the President to impose sanctions on specific countries or classes of organizations or individuals, such as terrorists or foreign terrorist organizations. Most sanctions are imposed, however, by executive order. An **executive order** is a presidential directive instructing one or more U.S. executive departments or other agencies to act in a specified manner pursuant either to the President's constitutional authority or to a statutory authorization or mandate. In the realm of economic and trade sanctions, an executive order typically instructs the Department of Commerce, the Department of the Treasury, Department of State, or CBP to adopt and enforce sanctions against specified states, regions, organizations, or individuals pursuant to statutory authorization such as that provided by IEEPA, the TWEA, or other laws.

Most of the more comprehensive economic and trade sanctions are administered by the Department of the Treasury's **Office of Foreign Assets Control** (**OFAC**). OFAC administers a variety of somewhat similar sanctions programs codified in Title 31, Chapter 5 of the Code of Federal Regulations. These programs include regulations that block and freeze the assets of several countries, regions within countries, and organizations; prohibit trade with them; and implement other sanctions, such as the U.N. sanctions. To give you some idea of the range of these sanctions, the following is a sample of sanctions programs administered by OFAC in 2020:

- *Iranian Sanctions Regulations* (31 C.F.R. pts. 535, 560-62) block and freeze the assets of the government of Iran, most Iranian citizens, and Iran-registered organizations; and comprehensively prohibit commercial trade with the government of Iran, and most trade with Iranian citizens and Iran-registered organizations. Moreover, the sanctions extend to non-U.S. financial institutions that assists Iran in developing WMD or supporting global terrorism.
- *Somalia Sanctions Regulations* (31 C.F.R. pt. 551) block and freeze the assets of, and prohibit all trade with, certain listed persons and organizations in Somalia determined to threaten the stability of that country. Somalia itself is not a target of the sanctions.
- *Rough Diamonds Control Regulations* (31 C.F.R. pt. 592) prohibit trading in unregulated rough diamonds that could fuel civil strife in Africa. Adopted pursuant to a U.N. embargo with which the United States cooperates, the regulations forbid U.S. persons to trade in any rough diamonds except those that comply with a certification scheme to ensure they originate from a legitimate source.
- *Cuban Assets Control Regulations* (31 C.F.R. pt. 515) block and freeze the assets of the government of Cuba, Cuban citizens, and Cuba-registered organizations. The regulations also comprehensively prohibit commercial trade with these targets.

Federal statutes generally authorize the Executive Branch to prohibit various kinds of imports as well as exports. The 1985 International Security and Development Cooperation Act (22 U.S.C. § 2349aa-9) authorizes the President to ban the importation into the United States of goods or services from any country that supports or harbors terrorists or terrorist organizations. The President has authorized such embargoes periodically since 1985, most prominently against Iran. See 31 C.F.R. pt. 560. The Iranian Transactions Regulations prohibit the importation of any goods and services (other than informational materials) from Iran or Iranian nationals into the United States with only a few exceptions. 31 C.F.R. § 560.201.

Other countries are periodically targeted with import sanctions as well. For example, in 1997, the Clinton Administration introduced trade sanctions against Burma (Myanmar) in response to the repressive actions of the military dictatorship in control of the Burmese government. The sanctions included a comprehensive ban on imports from Burma. See 31 C.F.R. pt. 537. By instituting this import ban, the United States government expressed its outrage against the violations of human rights taking place in Burma and, by denying Burma the economic benefits of selling to the United States, the Clinton Administration also hoped to pressure the Burmese government to change its policies.

The Iranian sanctions provide a convenient example of a relatively comprehensive set of sanctions. The first U.S. asset freeze of Iranian property was instituted in 1979 in response to the new Islamic fundamentalist government seizing hostages at a U.S. embassy in violation of international law. The Iranian Assets Control Regulations resulted, and these were eventually expanded into a full trade embargo against Iran. Most of the embargo and asset freeze were lifted two years later when the hostages were released, but these were soon reinstituted. Both Iraq and Iran, in the course of the Persian Gulf War (lasting from 1980 to 1988), had attacked hundreds of neutral ships in the Gulf, in violation of international law. Included in these attacks were vessels flying the U.S. flag. Although both Iraq and Iran were culpable, U.S. hostility to Iran caused it to take a strong stance against Iran's violations only. On October 29, 1987, President Ronald Reagan invoked his statutory authority to impose sanctions on Iran by executive order (these became the Iranian Transactions Regulations). These sanctions were gradually tightened until, by 1995, various executive orders had barred virtually all trade with and investment in Iran by any U.S. person, no matter where in the world located. In other words, the Iran sanctions apply beyond the borders of the United States. These **extraterritorial sanctions** apply not only to anyone within the United States (citizen or alien), but to U.S. citizens resident in foreign countries. This is evident from the definition of "United States person" subject to the prohibitions in the Iranian Transactions Regulations:

> **United States person.** The term United States person means any United States citizen, permanent resident alien, entity organized under the laws of the United States (including foreign branches), or any person in the United States.

31 C.F.R. § 560.314. Notice how the provision distinguishes between a "United States citizen" and "any person in the United States." Clearly, if the former term is not to be redundant of the latter, U.S. citizens must be subject to the regulations even when they are in foreign countries.

The Iranian Assets Control Regulations go still further. These define "Person subject to the jurisdiction of the United States" as follows:

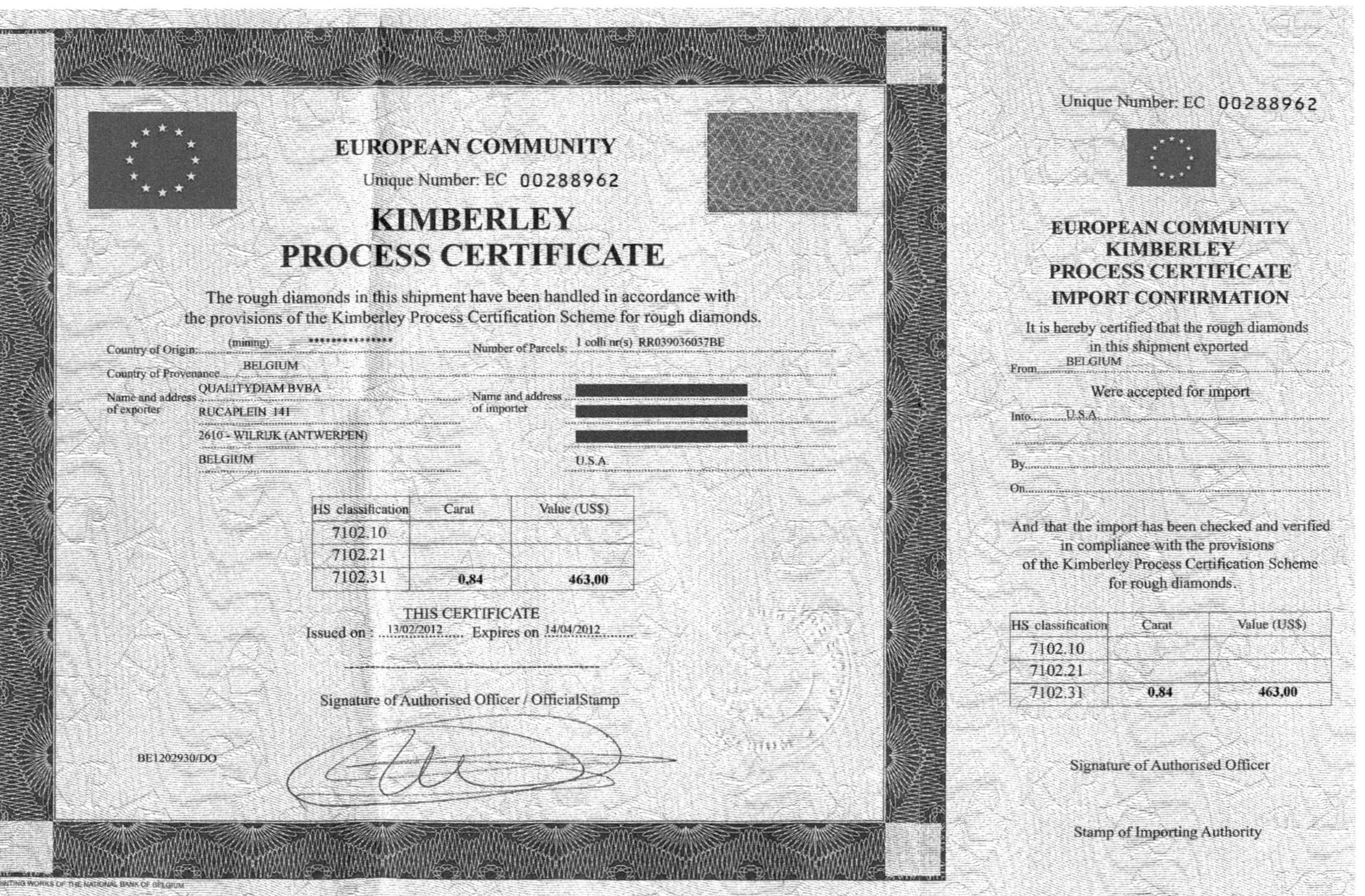

EUROPEAN COMMUNITY

Unique Number: EC 00288962

KIMBERLEY PROCESS CERTIFICATE

The rough diamonds in this shipment have been handled in accordance with the provisions of the Kimberley Process Certification Scheme for rough diamonds.

Country of Origin: (mining) *************** Number of Parcels: 1 colli nr(s) RR039036037BE

Country of Provenance: BELGIUM

Name and address of exporter: QUALITYDIAM BVBA, RUCAPLEIN 141, 2610 - WILRIJK (ANTWERPEN), BELGIUM

Name and address of importer: U.S.A

HS classification	Carat	Value (US$)
7102.10		
7102.21		
7102.31	0,84	463,00

THIS CERTIFICATE

Issued on: 13/02/2012 Expires on 14/04/2012

Signature of Authorised Officer / OfficialStamp

BE1202930/DO

PRINTING WORKS OF THE NATIONAL BANK OF BELGIUM

Unique Number: EC 00288962

EUROPEAN COMMUNITY
KIMBERLEY
PROCESS CERTIFICATE
IMPORT CONFIRMATION

It is hereby certified that the rough diamonds in this shipment exported

From BELGIUM

Were accepted for import

Into U.S.A.

By

On

And that the import has been checked and verified in compliance with the provisions of the Kimberley Process Certification Scheme for rough diamonds.

HS classification	Carat	Value (US$)
7102.10		
7102.21		
7102.31	0,84	463,00

Signature of Authorised Officer

Stamp of Importing Authority

Figure 5.23. A Kimberley Process Certificate, used to certify that rough diamonds in international trade comply with United Nations-mandated trade controls.

> **Person subject to the jurisdiction of the United States.** The term *person subject to the jurisdiction of the United States* includes:
>
> (a) Any person wheresoever located who is a citizen or resident of the United States;
>
> (b) Any person actually within the United States;
>
> (c) Any corporation organized under the laws of the United States or of any state, territory, possession, or district of the United States; and
>
> (d) Any partnership, association, corporation, or other organization wheresoever organized or doing business which is owned or controlled by persons specified in paragraph (a), (b), or (c) of this section.

31 C.F.R. § 535.329.

Look carefully at paragraph (d). The term "wheresoever organized or doing business" means that the sanctions regulations apply even to foreign companies doing business entirely in foreign countries if they are owned or controlled by U.S. citizens or companies. In other words, although only U.S. citizens, U.S. companies, and anyone on U.S. soil is prohibited from exporting to or importing from Iran by the Iranian Transactions Regulations, the Iranian Assets Control Regulations (which forbid dealing in property in which "Iran has any interest of any nature whatsoever") prohibit even *foreign companies* from dealing with Iran if owned or controlled by U.S. partners, U.S. shareholders, or a U.S. parent company. That means a French or Japanese company may be prohibited from doing business in Iran based purely on its ultimate U.S. ownership. The Cuban Assets Control Regulations have a similar definition of U.S. persons.

Not only are the regulations often far-reaching, they are frequently complex. The Sudan sanctions present a helpful illustration. In November 1997, the Clinton Administration imposed sanctions by executive order on Sudan in response to the UN Security Council's condemnation of Sudanese government-sponsored atrocities against African civilians. E.O. 13067 (Nov. 3, 1997). These sanctions included a country-wide freeze on assets and blocking of all property interests of the Sudanese government and the implementation of license requirements for all trade transactions with Sudan. Ultimately, the sanctions were codified in the Code of Federal Regulations (31 C.F.R. pt. 538), known as the Sudanese Sanctions Regulations. In 2006, the Bush Administration modified the order to exempt the "regional government" of southern Sudan from the sanctions, to allow most exports by U.S. persons or from the United States directly to southern Sudan without license, and to add a prohibition on transactions by U.S. persons relating to Sudan's petroleum industry, except for designated cities and regions in Sudan. E.O. 13412 (Oct. 13, 2006).

Sanctions programs come and go. For many years, as mentioned earlier, the United States imposed trade and economic sanctions on Libya in retaliation for the Libyan government's sponsorship of the terrorist bombing of a

European passenger jet. The sanctions were lifted after Libya agreed to pay compensation to the survivors of its victims, renounce terrorism, surrender the Libyans suspected of planning the murders, and abandon its program of trying to acquire nuclear weapons. In February 2011, President Obama reimposed more sanctions on the Libyan government and its dictator, Colonel Muammar Qadhafi, to punish his violent suppression of the demands of Libyan nationals for recognition of their human rights. The sanctions were lifted again after rebels overthrew the Qadhafi government and established a precarious democratic government later that year.

Similarly, at one time or another, the United States has imposed sanctions on certain groups and individuals and their associates who threaten world peace, such as UNITA rebels causing civil war in Angola, the Japanese Yakuza gangsters, or Slobodan Milosevic, the former president of the Federal Republic of Yugoslavia, who supported Bosnian Serbs slaughtering non-Serbs in Bosnia-Herzegovina. On the other hand, some of these sanctions programs, such as those relating to Cuba and Iran, have been around for several decades. Although they have changed over time, they have retained some stable features, such as the continuing prohibition on trade with or investment in the countries.

Some sanctions programs do not comprehensively prohibit trade with the target country, but may instead impose license requirements for shipments of all items subject to the EAR. These countries are typically those supporting international terrorism but against whom the U.S. President has decided a total embargo would be excessive. BIS, not OFAC, administers these sanctions. Examples of such programs include the longstanding sanctions on North Korea and Syria.

5.2 Specially Designated Nationals and Blocked Persons

Like the EAR, the sanctions administered by OFAC apply some special end-user prohibitions to transactions not only with foreign states, but to nationals of the sanctioned state. In addition, the Executive Branch imposes sanctions on designated organizations and individuals acting contrary to U.S. national security and foreign policy interests that are *not* necessarily nationals of any sanctioned state. These include:

- individuals who have acted on behalf of a sanctioned state (so-called **specially designated nationals** (**SDNs**) of the sanctioned state);
- individuals who have violated U.S. sanctions and are punished by OFAC by being cut off from trading on the U.S. market (**blocked persons**);
- organizations and individuals identified by the Departments of State or Treasury as subject to sanctions, such as terrorists or their supporters; persons engaged in or supporting cyber attacks against the U.S. government or U.S. business firms; and persons who traffic significantly in

narcotics in or to the United States.

OFAC maintains the **Specially Designated National and Blocked Persons List**, published at 15 C.F.R. pt. 764 supp. 3, as a resource for identifying sanctioned organizations and individuals. This list includes persons and organizations whom OFAC considers:

- to pose a risk of diverting goods and technology to terrorists; terrorist-sponsoring states; or other states, persons, and organizations against which the United States maintains economic and trade sanctions;
- to engage in or to mastermind international narcotics trafficking; or
- to pose a risk of diverting goods and technology for the proliferation of WMD.

Exports to or through listed persons or organizations (indeed, any transactions dealing with money or other property) are prohibited without an OFAC license, which is very unlikely to be granted.

The designation of a person or organization as an SDN, specially designated global terrorist, FTO, etc. is a discretionary decision of the Executive Branch. Federal courts give the President such deference in his determinations that judicial review is minimal. See, e.g., *Paradissiotis v. Rubin*, 171 F.3d 983, 987 (5th Cir. 1999) (holding that OFAC in designating a person a SDN must merely act in a way not "plainly inconsistent" with its own regulations and not "clearly forbid[den] by" statute); *Office of Foreign Assets Control v. Voices in the Wilderness*, 329 F.Supp.2d 71, 80 (D.D.C. 2004).

However, more recently, the Ninth Circuit has required OFAC to observe due process of law in its designations to the extent consistent with national security. In that case, OFAC had designated the plaintiff a "foreign terrorist organization" without notice or opportunity to be heard. The court held: "OFAC violated [the plaintiff's] Fifth Amendment right to due process by failing to provide constitutionally adequate notice and a meaningful opportunity to respond, and by failing to mitigate the use of classified information" by, for example, preparing and disclosing an unclassified summary. *Al Haramain Islamic Found., Inc. v. U.S. Dep't of Treasury*, 660 F.3d 1019 (9th Cir. 2011).

In contrast, the Court of Justice of the EU has held that it may exercise "full review" over EU Council decisions to block the assets of an individual. See *Kadi v. Council of the European Union*, Eur. Ct. Just. Case Nos. C402/05P & C415/05P, Judgment of Sept. 3, 2008, 47 I.L.M. 923 (2008).

6 International Boycotts and Blocking Statutes

6.1 What Is a Boycott?

In 1996, the U.S. Congress enacted the Cuban Liberty and Democratic Solidarity (LIBERTAD) Act, 22 U.S.C. §§ 6021-91, commonly known as the

Helms-Burton Act, after its sponsors. Title I of the Act prohibits not only U.S. persons and companies, but foreign subsidiaries of U.S. companies as well, from importing into the United States any goods or services of Cuban origin or containing materials or goods originating in Cuba either directly or through third countries; dealing in merchandise that is or has been located in or transported from or through Cuba; dealing in Cuban assets; and engaging in any financial dealings with Cuba. Because the law applies to persons that are not U.S. citizens or located in the United States, the law has extraterritorial application.

Titles III and IV of the Helms-Burton Act forbid U.S. companies and their foreign subsidiaries to "traffic" in property that was formerly owned by U.S. persons (including Cubans who have obtained U.S. citizenship) and was expropriated illegally (i.e., without compensation) by the revolutionary Cuban government. **Trafficking** is a broad term encompassing use, sale, exportation, transfer, control, management, and similar activities. The Act actually authorizes legal proceedings in the United States by any U.S. person whose property was illegally expropriated by the Cuban government against any U.S. or foreign persons who "traffic" in the expropriated property. In addition, the Act provides that any person who traffics in such property will be refused an entry visa into the United States, as well as that person's spouse and minor children. The Helms-Burton Act sets up a kind of boycott of Cuba.

A **boycott** is a refusal to do business with the target of the boycott. There are several kinds of boycotts. A **primary boycott** means a refusal to do business with specified persons. When a country refuses to buy goods or services from, or sell goods or services to, a target country (or the target country's citizens and business associations), this is a primary boycott. The United States imposes primary boycotts on disfavored states from time to time; most of the OFAC embargoes discussed above are examples of primary boycotts. Such boycotts do not regulate compliance with by non-U.S. nationals acting outside of the United States. A **secondary boycott** means a refusal to do business with anyone who does business with persons subject to a primary boycott. A secondary boycott usually means that the boycotting country keeps a "blacklist" of companies and persons who deal with the boycotted country. The Helms-Burton Act and the Iranian Financial Sanctions Regulations both impose secondary boycotts, which by their nature have extraterritorial effects on non-citizens. Some states even go so far as to impose a **tertiary boycott**, which is a boycott against anyone who does business with a blacklisted person or country. As you can imagine, at this level boycotts can become quite complicated. Figure 5.24 illustrates primary, secondary, and tertiary boycotts graphically.

6.2 U.S. Antiboycott Regulations

Although the United States sometimes imposes secondary boycotts, it has laws prohibiting U.S. persons and even foreign persons from complying with certain secondary boycotts by foreign countries. To that end, it maintains two overlapping and regimes dealing with foreign boycotts against U.S. allies. BIS administers one regime through its **Office of Antiboycott Compliance** (**OAC**). The OAC implements executive orders issued under the authority of IEEPA relating to foreign "restrictive trade practices or boycotts" and maintains regulations published in the EAR. The other regime is maintained by the Department of the Treasury's **Internal Revenue Service** (**IRS**). The IRS administers the Internal Revenue Code, or IRC (Title 26 of the U.S. Code). **IRC Section 999** regulates U.S. taxpayer cooperation with international boycotts.

The reason these regulations exist is simple to describe, although the political history is a much longer story. The short version is that several Arab states that have adopted Islam as an official national religion claim to be deeply offended that the world powers created a Jewish homeland, Israel, in a region that had been dominated by Muslims for centuries. These states accordingly have refused to trade with, or to allow their citizens to trade with, Israel. This in itself would present little problem for non-Israeli business firms, but many of these states have also implemented secondary and, in some cases, tertiary boycotts against those who do business with Israel. These states include, among others, Iraq, Kuwait, Lebanon, Libya, Saudi Arabia, and Syria. The United States objects to any country establishing a secondary or tertiary boycott against Israel or any other U.S. ally, and so it keeps track of these boycott activities and punishes U.S. companies that comply with the boycott to the disadvantage of Israel through the two sets of regulations.

A. Department of Commerce Antiboycott Regulations

The Commerce Department rules are found in part 760 of the EAR (15 C.F.R. pt. 760), commonly known as the **Antiboycott Sanctions Regulations**. The regulations prohibit "U.S. persons"—meaning U.S. citizens, companies

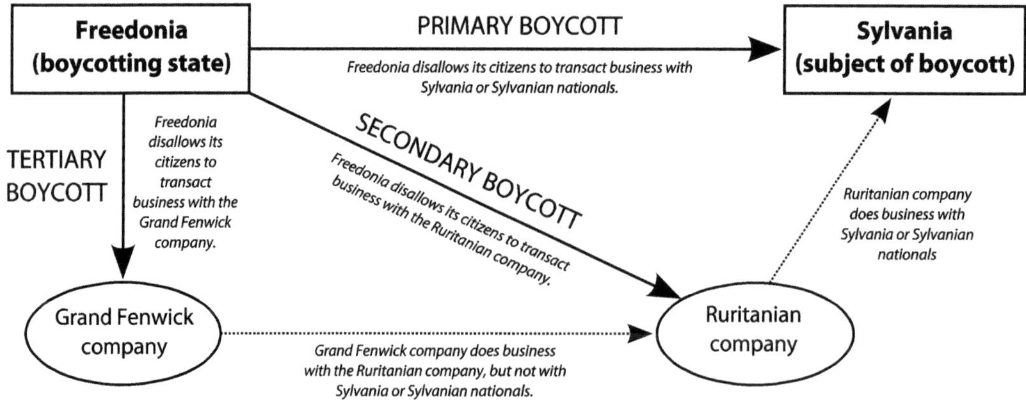

Figure 5.24. Freedonian primary, secondary, and tertiary boycotts against Sylvania.

formed under the laws of a U.S. state, or foreign companies owned or controlled by U.S. persons or companies—from complying with, or agreeing to comply with, an **unapproved foreign boycott**. 15 C.F.R. §§ 760.1(b), 760.2. In other words, the U.S. antiboycott regulations have extraterritorial effect, and foreign companies must comply with them if they are controlled by a U.S. parent company or U.S. shareholders.

An unapproved foreign boycott is any foreign boycott against a U.S. citizen or company, or against a foreign country friendly to the United States. The regulations further prohibit complying with a request for information by a third party that would assist in the enforcement of an unapproved foreign boycott. Finally, the regulations require such persons to file quarterly reports with the OAC detailing any request to comply with a foreign boycott, and to keep records of any such request for five years after the request was received. 15 C.F.R. § 760.5. In summary, the Antiboycott Sanctions Regulations prohibit:

- complying or agreeing to comply with an unapproved foreign boycott;
- complying with a request for information that would assist an unapproved foreign boycott;
- failing to file quarterly reports in any quarter in which a boycott-related request was received; and
- failing to keep records of such requests and their related transactions for a period of five years.

The OAC enforces these regulations with the help of CBP, the Federal Bureau of Investigation, and other law enforcement agencies. Should OAC accuse any person of violating the antiboycott regulations, it may seek to impose a substantial civil penalty on the violator. In addition, an intentional violation of the OAC's antiboycott regulations carries a criminal penalty of gravity comparable to penalties imposed for other violations of the EAR.

OAC, like BIS more generally, has great discretion in assessing fines and penalties for violations of its regulations. In practice, penalties can range from a warning letter for minor accidental, first-time offenses, to maximum fines multiplied by BIS's practice of double- or triple-counting violations of the EAR, to a referral of the matter to the Department of Justice for criminal investigation.

Not all boycott requests come in the straightforward form of a request by a customer, supplier, or other business partner not to do business with a specific country or business firm. Most are less direct. Figure 5.25 provides an example of what a typical boycott-related letter from a foreign customer might look like. Requests to comply with a foreign boycott or to furnish boycott-related information may not even be presented as conspicuously as the sample letter suggests. They may be integrated into the boilerplate language of a purchase order or a letter of credit. Therefore, it is important for companies doing business in foreign states, especially in the Middle East, to have a compliance program to help them establish procedures to ensure that unreported boycott requests do not slip through. Someone trained to find such requests should always review any documents originating from a foreign customer, supplier, agent, carrier, or insurer.

B. Internal Revenue Service Antiboycott Regulations

The second set of antiboycott regulations, administered by the IRS, basically contains a reporting requirement and a prohibition against cooperation with an unapproved foreign boycott. Regarding the former, U.S. taxpayers are required to file periodic reports with the IRS describing any business activities they have undertaken in a list of countries known to boycott Israel or other U.S. allies. Such activities include the purchase of goods or services from, or the sale of goods or services to, persons in such countries, as well as direct investment in the listed countries through the establishment of an ongoing business there. Section 999 also requires U.S. taxpayers to report each time they are requested to participate in, or to cooperate with, a boycott of a U.S. ally. The IRS uses these reports to help it keep an eye on companies that might be covertly complying with a prohibited boycott.

Section 999 further prohibits actually complying with a foreign boycott. Specifically, it prohibits activity defined in Section 999(b)(3):

> (3) Definition of boycott participation and cooperation
>
> For purposes of this section, a person participates in or cooperates with an international boycott if he agrees—
>
> (A) as a condition of doing business directly or indirectly within a country or with the government, a company, or a national of a country—
>
> (i) to refrain from doing business with or in a country which is the object of the boycott or with the government, companies, or nationals of that country;
>
> (ii) to refrain from doing business with any United States person engaged in trade with a country which is the object of the boycott or with the government, companies, or nationals of that country;
>
> (iii) to refrain from doing business with any company whose ownership or management is made up, all or in part, of individuals of a particular nationality, race, or religion, or to remove (or refrain from selecting) corporate directors who are individuals of a particular nationality, race, or religion; or
>
> (iv) to refrain from employing individuals of a particular nationality, race or religion; or
>
> (B) as a condition of the sale of a product to the government, a company, or a national of a country, to refrain from shipping or insuring that product on a carrier owned, leased, or operated by a person who does not participate in or cooperate with an international boycott (within the meaning of subparagraph (A)).

Dear Sirs:

You are kindly requested to complete the enclosed questionnaire in duplicate and have both copies legalized by the chamber of commerce or industry or similar organization or Arab chamber of commerce and duly attested by the commercial attaché or his representative, and return it to us as soon as possible.

This arrangement shall facilitate for you the immediate presentation of your shipping documents (consisting of the invoices and bills of lading only) to the bank at your end of collection of amounts due to you without having to await the legalization formalities of the documents in conformity with the Israel boycott rules and regulations.

We would appreciate an early response.

Yours faithfully,

Head of Materials and Purchasing
ALL-MIDEAST PETROLEUM ORGANIZATION

Questionnaire:

1. Have you ever had a branch, subsidiary, parent company, factory, or assembly plant in Israel? Have you ever sold one to Israel?
2. Have you ever licensed the right of using your trademarks, patents, copyrights, or trade secrets, or any of the foregoing of your subsidiaries, to Israeli persons or firms?
3. Have you ever participated in or owned shares in an Israeli firm?
4. Have you ever rendered any services or technical assistance to any Israeli firm for consideration?
5. Have you ever represented any Israeli firm in Israel or abroad?
6. Of what companies do you own shares? Please state the name and nationality of each company and the percentage share of their total capital.
7. What companies own shares of your capital? Please state the name and nationality of each company and the percentage share of your total capital.

The above questions should be answered on behalf of your company itself, and all subsidiaries or branches, if any.

Figure 5.25. Sample letter from a boycotting country.

In other words, Section 999(b) forbids compliance with both a secondary boycott (i.e., U.S. taxpayers refusing to trade with Israel, Israeli companies, or Israeli nationals) and compliance with a tertiary boycott of blacklisted U.S. companies and with shipping or insurance companies. This prohibition does not, however, apply if the United States itself participates in the boycott, such as a boycott imposed by authority of the United Nations Security Council.

Thus, if a U.S. company's business partner in Yemen demanded that the company should refrain from trading with Israel or Israelis, or with blacklisted companies that have done business with Israel or Israelis, that U.S. company is required both to report the request to the IRS and to refuse to comply. The Treasury Department periodically publishes a list of countries that may require participation in a boycott of U.S. allies, most or all of which are found in the Middle East. The list is not exhaustive, but is intended to alert taxpayers to the heightened probability of being required to comply with the reporting requirements.

The IRS antiboycott report is filed on a special form (Form 5713—International Boycott Report) that requires detailed disclosures about the reporting entity, its international operations, relations with foreign states known or believed to boycott Israel or any other state friendly to the United States, and the kinds of boycott-related requests that have been directed to the reporting entity.

Unlike the Department of Commerce antiboycott sanctions, Section 999 applies to all "U.S. taxpayers," which does not include foreign corporations unless majority controlled by a U.S. company. It also requires non-portfolio U.S. shareholders (that is, any U.S. person who holds more than 10% of the voting shares of a foreign company) to report to the IRS if the foreign company has operations in a boycotting country. That means merely owning a small minority stake in a foreign business firm could subject a U.S. person to IRC § 999 reporting obligations.

Section 999 imposes a somewhat complex tax penalty on those who do comply with an unapproved foreign boycott. Basically, the penalties for violating the IRS antiboycott regulations are mostly limited to a denial of tax benefits, such as a denial of foreign tax credits or deferral rights with respect to boycott-related income, or a denial of the benefits of foreign sales corporations. These tax benefits may be substantial, and in some cases may even have greater economic significance to a company than the imposition of a heavy fine. In addition, the willful failure to file a required report can result in criminal penalties, including a fine of $25,000 per violation and imprisonment up to one year. 26 U.S.C. § 999(f).

NOTE FROM THE FIELD

Being an Export Regulatory Lawyer

Stanley J. Marcuss, Esq.
Bryan Cave, Leighton Paisner LLP (retired)

At the core of an international regulatory practice is everyday news: controlling the spread of national security technology, affecting the policies of other countries by the imposition of economic sanctions and, increasingly, defining the limits of executive action. Much of this involves dealing with governments. Much involves white-collar criminal defense.

Clients in the export regulatory arena tend to consist of major multinational corporations, U.S. and foreign-based, with far-flung interests in many parts of the world.

On a typical day, an export regulatory lawyer might be asked by one client to help determine whether an exportation of goods to China is permissible, by another to determine whether a foreign subsidiary's investment in Iran is allowed, or whether compliance with a request for information from Saudi Arabia is a violation of U.S. antiboycott law.

Other clients may have received a subpoena to produce documents in an investigation of dealings with Syria or been subjected to a search pursuant to court-issued warrant for documents. Some may even have been subjected to searches and seizures in foreign lands pursuant to a request from the U.S. government. They want help in knowing what to do.

The needs of clients like these for help in dealing with subpoenas and search warrants present is immediate. A wake-up call at 6 a.m. from a client in Switzerland that is being subjected to a dawn raid requires fast thinking and fast action and will make the following twenty-four hours anything but typical. Dealing with issues like these requires an awareness of the laws of local jurisdictions. It requires sophistication in thinking.

Compliance with the vast array of international laws that confront major corporations also places a high premium on preventive maintenance. This typically takes the form of sophisticated compliance programs that require for their effectiveness a thorough understanding of how the company operates and who is responsible for what. Devising such programs, thus, requires the practitioner to know his client intimately and understand the practical realities of corporate life.

An export lawyer is truly a renaissance person.

Stanley J. Marcuss has served as Counsel to the U.S. Senate's International Finance Subcommittee and Deputy Assistant Secretary, U.S. Department of Commerce. He was also a Senior Fellow at Harvard's Kennedy School.

6.3 Blocking Statutes

The Helms-Burton Act is a kind of secondary boycott insofar as it sanctions foreign persons and companies, having no U.S. connection whatsoever and who deal or "traffic" in property expropriated from U.S. citizens by the Cuban government in violation of international law, meaning *inter alia* without adequate compensation to the victim of the expropriation. Such traffickers may be subject to harsh sanctions. This exercise of U.S. jurisdiction over foreign transactions between foreign persons involving foreign property was viewed by the international community as contrary to public international law respecting state jurisdiction.

In response to the Helms-Burton Act and other U.S. extraterritorial and extranational legislation, Canada and the EU both enacted **blocking statutes** designed to nullify or counteract the effects of an offensive foreign (in this case, U.S.) law. In 1996, the EU enacted Regulation No. 2271/96, which requires companies threatened with the enforcement of a secondary boycott to report the matter to the European Commission. Such companies are forbidden to comply with the secondary boycott and are given a right of action to sue in the EU any person that seeks to enforce a secondary boycott against them. In 2018, the EU amended the regulation to apply to other U.S. extraterritorial sanctions adopted in 2012 and 2018.

The simultaneous adoption of a U.S. law forbidding subsidiaries of U.S. companies to deal in the Cuban property and Canadian and EU laws forbidding these same companies and persons to refuse to deal in the Cuban property can put MNEs that receive purchasing orders or service requests from Cuba between the proverbial Scylla and Charybdis. There would seem to be no way to avoid violating the law of one or another jurisdiction short of some very creative lawyering. If a Canadian or EU company receives an order for goods from a prospective purchaser that traffics in Cuban property illegally taken from U.S. citizens, and it fills the order, it violates U.S. sanctions laws. If it refuses to fill the order so as to avoid violating U.S. law, it violates the Canadian or EU blocking statute.

Some U.S. sanctions laws contain a presidential waiver clause, which allows the President to choose not to apply some of the more severe extraterritorial sanctions, such as the right to sue the trafficker in U.S. courts and the provisions barring entry into the United States for family members of the trafficker. Nonetheless, the Act, like other extraterritorial U.S. laws, continues to generate friction between the United States and its trading partners, and business firms remain caught in the middle.

Key Vocabulary

1930 Tariff Act
Air waybill
Antiboycott Sanctions Regulations
Appraisal / Valuation
Arms Export Control Act (AECA)
ATA carnet
Atomic, Biological, and Chemical (ABC) weapons
Australia Group
Bill of lading
Blocked person
Blocking statute
Bonded warehouse
Boycott (primary/secondary/tertiary)
Bureau of the Census
Bureau of Customs & Border Protection (CBP)
Bureau of Industry & Security (BIS)
Cargo carrier
CBP directive
Certificate of origin
Civil penalty
Commerce Control List (CCL)
Commodity jurisdiction (CJ)
Country of origin
Customs bond
Customs port
Deemed export
Defense article / Defense service
Denied person's list
Destination Control Statement
Directorate of Defense Trade Controls (DDTC)
Drawback
Dual-use item
EAR99
End-use controls
End-user controls
Entry
Eo nomine classification
Export Administration Regulations (EAR)
Export Control Classification Number (ECCN)
Foreign Trade Statistics Regulations (FTSR)
Foreign trade zone (FTZ)
Freight forwarder / Forwarding agent
General Rules of Interpretation (GRI)
Generalized System of Preferences (GSP)
Gibson-Thomsen Test
Harmonized Tariff Schedule (HTS)
Import quota
Importer of record
Internal Revenue Service (IRS)
International Emergency Economic Powers Act (IEEPA)
International Traffic in Arms Regulations (ITAR)
IRC Section 999
Isotainer
License exception
Liquidation
Maquiladora
Marking
Missile Technology Control Regime (MTCR)
Multilateral sanctions
Nonpreferential duty rate
Nuclear Suppliers Group (NSG)
Office of Antiboycott Compliance (OAC)
Office of Foreign Assets Control (OFAC)
Port of entry
Preferential duty rate
Prior disclosure
Protectionism

Reasonable care
Regional value content
Schedule B
Shipper
Shipper's Export Declaration (SED)
Specially designated national (SDN)
Statement of Registration
Substantial transformation
Tariff classification
Tariff rate quota (TRQ)
Tariff shift methodology
Temporary import under bond (TIB)
Trade and economic sanctions
Transaction value
U.S. Court of Appeals for the Federal Circuit
U.S. Court of Customs & Patent Appeals (CCPA)
U.S. Court of International Trade (CIT)
U.S. Munitions List (USML)
Voluntary self-disclosure
Wassenaar Arrangement
Weapons of mass destruction (WMD)
Wholly produced
World Customs Organization (WCO)
WTO Customs Valuation Agreement

Practice Exercises

#1 Classifying a Dog Treadmill

Your client, Therapet Technologies Co. (TTC) has come to you for help in classifying a new invention that it intends to import into the United States from a manufacturing plant in Pottsylvania. The invention is a "hydrotherapy" treadmill for pet dogs recovering from injuries or surgical operations called the Aquadog®. Basically, the Aquadog consists of a 100-gallon plexiglass water tank with a water nozzle into which warm water flows. When the tank is partially full, the dog is placed in the tank and a motorized treadmill at the bottom of the tank begins turning, causing the dog to walk with its legs submerged in the water. With this machine, veterinarians and physical therapists may speed the recovery of injured dogs. The warm water increases blood circulation while providing resistance that strengthens muscles and promotes orthopedic healing. The client wishes to know how CBP would classify the Aquadog for customs purposes.

After conferring with the client about the product specifications, you learn that the Aquadog has no means for causing the water to whirlpool, leading you to conclude that it could not be classified as a jacuzzi or hydromassager. You also learn that it is not suitable for use by humans.

The question is whether the Aquadog is properly classified as a mechanical conveyor system or a medical device and, if the latter, whether it is a therapy appliance for animals or an orthopedic appliance. After reviewing the HTSUS, you conclude that the relevant Sections are XVI (covering, among other things, "machinery and mechanical appliances; electrical equipment"), XVIII (covering, among other things, "medical or surgical instruments and apparatus"), or XX (covering "miscellaneous manufactured articles").

You begin by reading the official notes to Sections XVI, XVIII, and XX. Note 1 to Section XVI states:

> 1. This section does not cover:
> (a) Transmission, conveyor or elevator belts or belting, of plastics of chapter 39 * * *
> (e) Transmission or conveyor belts or belting of textile material (heading 5910) * * *
> (m) Articles of chapter 90

Because the Aquadog is not simply a conveyor belt, notes 1(a) and 1(e) do not seem to apply. Within Section XVI, the relevant chapter seems to be Chapter 84 (covering *inter alia* "machinery and mechanical appliances").

Sections XVIII and XX contain no section notes. Within Section XVIII, the relevant chapter seems to be Chapter 90 (covering *inter alia* "medical and surgical instruments and apparatus"). But Section XVI states that it does not cover articles of Chapter 90. What does this mean? After all, merchandise cannot be classified both in Section XVI and Chapter 90 (which falls within Section XVIII) at the same time. Note 1(m) to Section XVI offers little help in this case. Within Section XX, the relevant chapter is Chapter 95 (covering, among other things, "sports equipment"). You now move on to the chapter notes for Chapters 84, 90 and 95 to see if they offer any useful guidance, and find that none contains relevant information (although note 4 observes that the "toys" covered in that chapter do not include pet toys).

Now look at the pertinent headings within each chapter you identified:

> 8428 Other lifting, handling, loading or unloading machinery (for example, elevators, escalators, conveyors, teleferics)
> 9019 Mechano-therapy appliances; massage apparatus; psychological aptitude-testing apparatus; * * * .
> 9506 Articles and equipment for general physical exercise, gymnastics, athletics, other sports * * * or outdoor games, not specified or included elsewhere in this chapter; swimming pools and wading pools; parts and accessories thereof:

Each heading contains subheadings that seem to describe the Aquadog more or less accurately:

> 8428.90 Other continuous-action elevators and conveyors, for goods or materials: Other machinery
> 9019.10 Mechano-therapy appliances and message apparatus; parts and accessories thereof
> 9506.91 Articles and equipment for general physical exercise, gymnastics

or athletics; parts and accessories thereof

You now review the Explanatory Notes to the HTS published by the WCO. None of the notes to headings 8428, 9019, or 9506 specifies that they apply to animals, but neither do they say the headings cannot be applied to animals.
What are your next steps for classifying the Aquadog on the HTSUS?

#2 Minimizing Customs Duties

Your law firm has recently been hired to represent the U.S. subsidiary of an Italian business firm, Placcatoro Srl, in customs matters. The client, Placcatoro USA Corp. (PUC), has been importing into the United States from its parent company in Italy components of electroplating machines used to deposit metallic coatings such as gold or nickel over hard surfaces. PUC adds a U.S.-origin power conductor and in some cases a power converter, then exports approximately one half of the finished electroplating machines to another Placcatoro subsidiary, Placcatoro Distribuzione Srl—an Italian company that does no manufacturing, but that sells the machines throughout Europe and the Middle East. PUC sells the remaining devices in the United States. PUC seeks your assistance in reducing its customs duties. U.S. customs duties on the components from Italy are 2.6% *ad valorem* (assume you have already determined the classification of the components and that the country of origin is indeed Italy). The machine components that PUC imports from Italy are delicate, and ocean transportation is slow; consequently, PUC keeps a large stock of components on hand in case of unexpected delays in shipment from Placcatoro.
Because PUC pays customs duties when the components first enter the United States, there is often a long delay between the time duties are paid and the time the components are used in the manufacturing process. Moreover, a certain number of the components arrive in damaged or unusable condition, and PUC objects to paying duties on these components. Finally, because Italy imposes its own customs duties of 6% *ad valorem* on the finished electroplating machines imported from the United States, PUC pays duties twice on the machine components imported from Italy—once to CBP and once to Italy's *Agenzia delle Dogane* (Customs Agency). PUC seeks your advice on how to minimize its worldwide customs duties. What advice can you offer PUC?

#3 Determining Whether an Export License Is Required

You have been retained by Space Solutions, Inc. (SSI), a Florida corporation, to assist it in expanding its business operations to foreign markets. SSI manufactures global positioning systems (GPS) of extraordinary accuracy and reliability. SSI is registered with DDTC as an arms manufacturer; the

U.S. Department of Defense has purchased several thousand of SSI's newest GPS, the AngelEye1000®. SSI has received interest in its system from the government of Ruritania, and SSI wishes to know whether an export license is required. SSI has requested that you describe the sequential steps that you would take to determine whether an exportation of the AngelEye1000 to Ruritania requires an export license, and from which agency or agencies such a license might be necessary.

#4 Dealing with a Possible Intangible Exportation

Your client, GloboRocket Inc., is a U.S. corporation that designs missile guidance systems primarily for use in the defense industry. All of GloboRocket's products and designs are listed in the USML and, therefore, subject to regulation under the AECA and ITAR. Pursuant to export licenses from DDTC, GloboRocket has sold its guidance systems to various governments of foreign countries allied to the United States, including that of Freedonia. These licenses cover only the exportation of the equipment itself and do not cover any services or technical data.

One day, GloboRocket receives a telephone call from an officer in the Freedonian Army, Colonel Julius, who is responsible for the country's missile defense. Col. Julius informs GloboRocket that the guidance systems purchased from the latter have malfunctioned in a series of tests, and he requests that GloboRocket send an engineer to Freedonia to coordinate with his staff and determine the source of the problem. GloboRocket agrees to send one of its senior engineers, Mary Cury, to assist the Freedonian Army.

GloboRocket's Vice President consults you as GloboRocket's export counsel to determine whether any further export license is required from DDTC for the proposed trip of GloboRocket's engineer to Freedonia. Based on what you have learned in this chapter, answer the Vice President's questions:

(a) Ms. Cury knows a great deal of technical data on the controlled guidance systems. Is Ms. Cury's travel to Freedonia *ipso facto* an exportation of technical data under the ITAR definition that may require an export license?

(b) If Ms. Cury communicates any technical data to Freedonian Army engineers while in Freedonia, would that constitute an exportation of technical data under the ITAR definition? Does it matter that she will be in Freedonia, not the United States, when she discloses the data?

(c) If Ms. Cury never discloses any technical data to any Freedonian national, but instead merely performs the technical acts necessary to integrate the GloboRocket guidance system with the Freedonian missiles, would that avoid the necessity of a DDTC export license?

#5 Deciding How to Respond to Suspicious Requests

Your client, Gigertron Studios, Inc., produces and sells reproduction art posters to retailers. Gigertron is a small Canadian corporation 60% owned by a U.S. parent company (Gigermania Enterprises, Inc.) and 40% owned by Canadian nationals. Despite its small size, Gigertron has a global clientele; it sells its posters directly to wholesalers in sixty-three countries on four continents.

Gigertron recently received three unusual requests from new purchasers in Yemen, Saudi Arabia, and Kuwait, respectively:

- The Yemeni purchaser requested that Gigertron certify that its posters do not originate in Israel or contain any Israeli parts or materials.
- The Saudi purchaser requested that Gigertron state whether it is owned or operated by any persons of Jewish ancestry.
- The Kuwaiti purchaser requested that Gigertron certify that it has not traded and will not trade with a list, supplied by the Kuwaiti government, of persons blacklisted for having traded with Israel in the past.

Advise Gigertron on the following matters:

(a) the legality of responding to each request, respectively;

(b) whether these requests have triggered a duty to file any reports, and if so, with what agency; and

(c) whether the requests have triggered any recordkeeping requirement, and, if so, of what nature.

Multiple Choice Questions

1. Which of the following is Customs & Border Protection's preferred appraisal methodology?

   (a) Computed value of the actual imported goods
   (b) Computed value of similar imported goods
   (c) Deductive value
   (d) Transaction value
   (e) None of the above

2. For which of the following steps does an importer of goods, rather than Customs & Border Protection, bear ultimate responsibility under the 1930 Tariff Act and applicable customs regulations?

   I. Inspection
   II. Appraisal

III. Classification
IV. Liquidation

(a) I and IV only
(b) II and III only
(c) I, II, and III only
(d) I, III, and IV only
(e) I, II, III, and IV

3. Which of the following statements regarding customs marking rules is most accurate, as practiced by Customs & Border Protection and the Federal Trade Commission?

(a) All imported goods must be marked with the country of origin as legibly, conspicuously, and permanently as possible. This includes products originating in the USA under customs rules of origin.
(b) All imported goods must be marked with the country of origin as legibly, conspicuously, and permanently as physically possible, with the exception of goods originating in the USA, which may not be marked with a country of origin.
(c) All imported goods must be marked with the country of origin as legibly, conspicuously, and permanently as necessary to be viewed with reasonable certainty by the ultimate consumer. This includes products originating in the USA under U.S. customs rules of origin.
(d) All imported goods must be marked with the country of origin as legibly, conspicuously, and permanently as necessary to be viewed with reasonable certainty by the ultimate consumer, with the exception of goods originating in the USA, which must not be marked at all.
(e) None of the above.

4. True or false?: When composite goods or mixtures containing two or more materials or substances are *prima facie* classifiable under two or more headings of the HTSUS, the first step in interpretation is to classify the goods under the heading with the more specific description.

5. Which of the following is *not* a relevant source of law in classifying imports under the HTSUS?

(a) Section and chapter notes
(b) The 4-digit headings
(c) The 8-digit subheadings
(d) World Customs Organization rulings
(e) Treasury decisions

6. In determining the country of origin of imports, which of the following statements is accurate?

   (a) The *Gibson-Thomsen* substantial transformation test is the default method for determining country of origin in all WTO contracting parties.
   (b) The country of origin of goods wholly produced in one country is always that country.
   (c) Most U.S. free trade agreements use the *Gibson-Thomsen* test as the basis for determining country of origin.
   (d) All U.S. free trade agreements provide that, when the regional value content of an import is 50% of higher, the good is considered to originate in the treaty region and enters the customs territory of either state party duty-free.
   (e) The WTO Agreements do not include any specific treaty setting forth rules for determining country of origin.

7. Which of the following is *not* a program available to U.S. importers for delaying or avoiding the payment of customs duties?

   (a) Drawback
   (b) Foreign Trade Zones
   (c) Customs Refund Program
   (d) Bonded warehouses
   (e) ATA carnet

8. True or false? With only a few exceptions, the U.S. Foreign Trade Statistics Reporting regulations require U.S. exporters to file a Shipper's Export Declaration with the description, quantity, value, and HTSUS classification of the exported goods.

9. Which of the following intergovernmental organizations coordinates state export policy with respect to military items?

   (a) Australia Group
   (b) NSG
   (c) Wassenaar Arrangement
   (d) MTCR
   (e) All of the above

10. Which of the following is the most accurate definition of a "dual-use item" for purposes of U.S. export law?

   (a) An item that capable of use by both the military and civilians

(b) An item that is actually used by both the military and civilians
(c) An item originally specially designed or adapted for military use that has been widely adopted for civilian use
(d) An item that is listed on the Commerce Control List
(e) None of the above

11. True or false?: EAR 99 is a classification used by the Treasury Department's Office of Foreign Assets Control to designate items that may be freely exported without an export license.

12. The Export Administration Regulations are currently authorized by which statutory authority?

    (a) International Emergency Economic Powers Act
    (b) Export Administration Act of 1979
    (c) Trading with the Enemy Act
    (d) Arms Export Control Act
    (e) None of the above

13. You represent Darkbloom Corp., a Smalldonian manufacturer of electronics with a U.S. subsidiary company. Darkbloom has developed a new line of consumer drones for photography and videography, and it wishes to know if an export license is required for sales outside of Smalldonia. Which of the following will you *not* need to know in order to determine whether an export license is required from BIS?

    (a) The sources of all of the drone's materials, parts, and components
    (b) The sources of all the software and technology incorporated into the drone or used in its design
    (c) Whether Darkbloom Corp. is owned or controlled by a U.S. person
    (d) To what countries the drones will be exported
    (e) Whether the drones will be shipped to the United States before exportation to other countries

14. Your client, DeRivia Co., is an independent automobile manufacturer headquartered and having its sole business operations in the state of Temeria. Several years ago, it purchased a continuous-wave laser generators made in the Kingdom of Poviss used for drilling holes in steel fuel injection nozzles. The laser, classified on the CCL under 6A005, includes more than *de minimis* U.S.-origin designs and operation software. This year, DeRivia began buying pre-made fuel injection nozzles from a company in neighboring Nilfgaard, and it wishes to resell its generators to the Poviss Army, which intends to use it for cutting

ventilation holes in machine guns. Which of the following statements most accurately describes DeRivia's obligations under U.S. EAR?

(a) It has no such obligations, because it is not a U.S. company, nor owned by a U.S. company, nor headquartered in the United States.
(b) It has no such obligations, because the laser machines were made in Poviss and being returned to Poviss.
(c) It has no such obligations, because it owns the generators and has the right to freely dispose of its property under the first sale doctrine.
(d) It may be obligated to seek a license from BIS to reexport the generators, because it will be used for a controlled end-use.
(e) It may be obligated to seek a license from BIS to reexport the generators, because all reexports of items listed on the CCL containing more than *de minimis* U.S. software or technology are subject to licensing requirements.

15. True or false?: An item listed on the CCL and subject to the EAR requires no export license if the country chart shows no license is required, unless the item will be exported to a controlled end-user or will be used in the development of nuclear, missile, or other controlled end-use.

16. True or false?: If a U.S. person in the United States emails schematic designs of technology listed on the CCL to a person in a foreign country, it will be considered a "deemed export."

17. Which of the following is an accurate statement about the commodity jurisdiction request procedure?

(a) Its primary use is to determine whether the item is properly classified on the CCL or USML.
(b) The request may be directed to either BIS or DDTC.
(c) The CJ results in a license by either BIS or DDTC, as appropriate.
(d) The government bears the burden of producing evidence that an item subject to a CJ request requires an export license from BIS or DDTC.
(e) Exporters cannot rely on a CJ decision, because they are not binding on the government.

18. True or false?: The fact that the foreign purchaser of an item is a military organization means the U.S. seller must secure a export license from the Directorate of Defense Trade Controls.

19. True or false?: The Directorate of Defense Trade Controls is an agency

within the U.S. Department of Defense.

20. Which of the following statements about trade and economic sanctions is or are accurate?

    I. The sanctions programs administered by OFAC impose a nearly complete trade embargo on some states.
    II. If a U.S. company receives a purchase order from a company in a state subject to U.S. sanctions, a reliable way to legally avoid violating the sanctions is to redirect the sale to a non-U.S. subsidiary company that does no business in the USA.
    III. A person charged with violating U.S. trade and economic sanctions may be subjected to a harsh civil penalty, but only if the violation was committed by someone knowing or having reason to know that the transaction was prohibited.

    (a) I only
    (b) II only
    (c) III only
    (d) I and III only
    (e) II and III only

21. Which of the following correctly describes a specially designated national (SDN)?

    (a) A person blacklisted by a country maintaining an unapproved boycott against a U.S. ally
    (b) A person reported by OFAC as owned or controlled by, or acting on behalf of, a country subject to trade or economic sanctions
    (c) A person on OFAC's entity list
    (d) A person convicted of violating OFAC sanctions regulations in the past
    (e) A person convicted of violating the EAR in the past

22. True or false?: Having complied with the EAR antiboycott sanctions regulations does not guarantee compliance with the IRS antiboycott sanctions regulations in IRC § 999.

Multiple Choice Answers

1. d	7. c	13. c	19. False
2. b	8. False	14. e	20. a
3. e	9. e	15. True	21. b
4. True	10. d	16. False	22. True
5. d	11. False	17. a	
6. b	12. a	18. False	

Chapter 6

Trade Remedies

What You Will Learn in This Chapter

You will learn here about some ways in which states protect their domestic industries from foreign competition considered unduly market-distorting or "unfair." There are several kinds of unfair competition, but this chapter deals specifically with three that are commonly invoked in the context of international trade. The first occurs when a foreign company or industry exports goods for sale on the domestic market at a price below fair market value in the exporter's country—a practice called "dumping." The second occurs when a foreign company or industry receives assistance in the form of subsidies from a foreign government, which allows the company or industry to export goods to a local market for sale at a lower price than would otherwise be possible. The third occurs when an unexpected increase in import competition threatens a domestic industry that claims it cannot adjust without temporary protection. In each case, the laws provide what are called "trade remedies" to shield a local industry from foreign competition.

In this chapter, you will learn specifically:

- why the United States and other countries regulate the importation of foreign-produced merchandise using "unfair trade practices";
- how the international trade treaty system deals with national trade remedies regulation;
- the circumstances under which a U.S. industry may petition the federal government to impose duties and other restrictions on foreign-produced merchandise to reduce competition with domestically-produced merchandise;
- what emergency measures are available to U.S. industries threatened by an unforeseen surge in import competition;
- the basic procedures for filing a petition for trade remedies and pursuing the investigation to its conclusion; and
- the options for appealing decisions on trade remedies by the federal regulators.

Trade remedies law is a vibrant practice in many countries. In the United States, it is practiced almost exclusively out of Washington, D.C., where the regulatory agencies are located. Because the practice mixes litigation, administrative law, microeconomics, business, and international relations, it tends to appeal to lawyers who have an interest or background in economics and business and are attracted to international issues.

1 Fair and Unfair Competition

Companies sometimes accuse their competitors of "unfair trade practices" or "unfair competition." This may seem like a strange phrase to use when discussing market competition; after all, capitalism values efficiency, and what is efficient, if it is not dishonest, is fair to a capitalist. It may seem unfair to a U.S. manufacturer employing unskilled workers, and the workers themselves, that a Mexican or Chinese company can manufacture the same merchandise at a lower cost due to lower employee wages in those countries. But the sword of "fairness" is double-edged. In a free market, what affects consumers directly in either country is that they can obtain the merchandise more cheaply if it is manufactured in a developing country than in the United States. This outcome may seem to consumers more "fair" than forcing them to pay more for the same merchandise so that some U.S. employees may continue to receive higher pay.

Of course, not all competition partakes of the same character. Presumably, "fair competition" would involve different companies trying to sell rival products to the same group of consumers, and competing for greater profits by trying to cut costs legitimately. Such measures might include, for example, cutting down unnecessary expenses; finding cheaper sources of labor, parts, and materials; and taking advantage of new ideas and technologies to increase efficiency. What, then, does "unfair competition" really mean?

In a domestic setting, it is often a claim that a competitor has infringed the company's intellectual property or engaged in consumer deception. This is not precisely the meaning of unfair trade practices in international law, however. In that context, it more often means either or both of two things: (1) that a competitor has unduly benefitted from foreign government subsidies, or (2) that it is offering products in the domestic market at prices below those it offers in its own home market. To understand why such practices might be considered objectionable, we will consider each in turn.

1.1 Why Object to Foreign Government Subsidies?

Sometimes, governments give their industries special cash grants, low interest loans, tax breaks, or other benefits to encourage the industry to flourish. These are called **subsidies**. The government's goal may be to grow the industry to the point at which it can compete on the international market. Or the government may be promoting a politically powerful industry that is unable to compete effectively on the international market. Alternatively, and

ARE GOVERNMENT SUBSIDIES COMMON?

Governments of developing countries can sometimes afford to subsidize certain domestic industries, but this practice is rare. In wealthy states, in contrast, government subsidies are common. Some subsidies come in the form of direct payments. In 2018, government subsidies to agriculture alone in rich countries amounted to $232 billion, or 18% of total farm income. Each year, the U.S. Department of Agriculture hands out at least $20 billion in direct subsidies to U.S. agribusinesses, and more in indirect subsidies. The U.S. Agency for International Development further subsidizes food exports to developing countries through export contracts to U.S. agribusinesses worth $2.6 billion each year. Farmers in Japan and Korea receive a full 60% of their income from government subsidies.

Many states give indirect subsidies to businesses as well. For example, farms typically are charged less for water, and factories are charged less for electricity, than are consumers. The U.S. federal government allows media corporations to broadcast on the public airwaves and send advertising at a lower cost than regular mail, and it permits privately owned cattle to graze on public lands at public expense. U.S. state and municipal governments hand out some $45-$80 billion a year to corporations. Canada charges lumber companies very low fees for cutting timber on public lands. Such practices transfer public money to business firms to privilege them over foreign (and domestic) firms that receive no such subsidies.

Sources: Alyssa R. Casey, *U.S. International Food Assistance: An Overview*, CRS Rep. R45422, Dec. 6, 2018; Chris Edwards, *Reforming Federal Farm Policies*, CATO Inst. Tax & Budget Bull. No. 82, Apr. 12, 2018; Daniel A. Summer, *Agricultural Subsidy Programs*, Library of Econ. & Liberty, www.econlib.org; NATHAN M. JENSEN & EDMUND J. MALESKY, INCENTIVES TO PANDER 95-121 (2018).

probably rarely, the government may be trying to boost an already competitive industry into worldwide dominance. Whatever the reason for subsidies, they are extremely common in developed countries like Japan, the United States, and western Europe.

Subsidies can be direct or indirect. Cash grants are the most obvious example of a direct subsidy. For example, suppose a state believes that nanotechnology is the key to future economic success for the country. If the state starts distributing cash grants to companies to perform research in nanotechnology, it is directly subsidizing its industries. In other words, it is taking money from taxpayers and giving it to companies as an incentive to do research that is likely to help the companies themselves, perhaps on the theory that what is good for the companies is good for their society as a whole. This gives the companies receiving the subsidy an advantage over competitors in other countries not receiving such a subsidy. It also benefits consumers who purchase the subsidized products, because the subsidy represents a transfer of wealth from the taxpayers of the subsidizing country to the purchasers of the subsidized goods.

Indirect subsidies transfer wealth to industries in other, less obvious, forms. Suppose a state's water monopoly arranged its prices so that persons using large amounts of water paid less per kiloliter than persons using small amounts. Because farmers use much more water than other citizens, they will pay less per kiloliter. This is an indirect way of taking money from the general populace and giving it to farmers. This gives the farmers an advantage not enjoyed by farmers in states charging all users the same price for water.

To a domestic company that receives few or no subsidies, it may seem unfair that a foreign company that competes with the domestic company on the domestic company's market receives subsidies. These subsidies may allow the foreign company to sell its products at a price below what would be available on a free market. Because, in most states, the state budget dwarfs the assets of any of its companies or even industries, it will seem to the domestic industry that the assistance the foreign state offers to its own foreign companies gives those companies an unfair advantage when competing with the domestic company. To offset the effect of certain foreign subsidies, many states impose countervailing duties on imports benefitting from foreign subsidies to nullify the domestic effect of the subsidies.

B. Why Object to Dumping?

Dumping in the context of international trade law is the practice of selling merchandise in the domestic market at a price below the price at which the same or similar merchandise is sold on the foreign producer's market. For example, if the market price for electric fans produced in Smalldonia averages $40 on the Smalldonian market, and Smalldonia exports these same fans to Freedonia to be sold at an average price of $30, the Smalldonian fan industry may be "dumping" its fans on the Freedonian market.

Producers and consumers are likely to have very different perspectives on dumping. First, consider the effect of dumping on consumers. Continuing the example above, Smalldonian consumers are paying $40 each for fans, while Freedonian consumers are paying $30 each. Clearly, Freedonian consumers have no cause for complaint. They are getting fans cheaply—it is the Smalldonian consumers who should be unhappy. So why would the Freedonian government object to Smalldonian manufacturers effectively giving a $10 per fan gift to Freedonian consumers? If the Freedonian government were primarily concerned with its consumers, it would not object to lower prices at all.

Consider now the perspectives of Freedonian manufacturers and workers. Why would Smalldonian manufacturers choose to sell products in a foreign country at a lower cost than in their own country? There are two salient reasons. First, the Smalldonian and Freedonian markets may have different characteristics. For example, the fan market may be more competitive in Freedonia than in Smalldonia, forcing Smalldonian manufacturers to lower the price of fans on the Freedonian market to avoid being shut out of the market. Or, even if there is little competition on the Freedonian market, it may be that the costs of supplying fans to consumers in Smalldonia is higher than the cost of supplying them in Freedonia due to better sales infrastructure. Or perhaps Freedonian consumers have on average lower incomes than Smalldonian consumers, so that the profit-maximizing price of fans on the Freedonian market is lower than the profit-maximizing price of fans on the Smalldonian market.

The practice of selling at different prices to different groups of consumer is called **market segmentation**—a concept introduced in Chapter 3 in the context of gray market goods. Here, as there, the segmentation is along geographic lines. Market segmentation is a common profit-maximizing strategy in both international and domestic business practices. You may have noticed, for example, that service stations sell gasoline at higher prices in some cities than in others. Similarly, many pharmaceuticals are sold at higher prices in the United States than in other countries, sometimes because consumers in other countries cannot afford to pay the prices that relatively wealthy Americans can pay. These are both forms of geographic market segmentation, and many countries, including the United States, have no general objection to such practices when it is considered to promote efficiency in world markets.

Now suppose the different prices in Smalldonia and Freedonia do not result from differences in either distribution costs or consumer demand. Instead, Smalldonian manufacturers are selling fans on the Freedonian market at lower prices because they know that Freedonian fan manufacturers cannot match the prices, and by trying they will eventually be driven out of business. Such a practice is called **predatory pricing**. It can only be used by a business with better capitalization than its target. In other words, a company with a greater quantity of liquid funds or more ready credit can practice predatory pricing against another company having a lesser quantity of liquid funds or less credit, but not the other way around. Why? Because the predatory company is selling below its profit-maximizing price, and possibly even at a loss. It does this in hopes that it can sustain losses long enough so that its target industry will go bankrupt or leave the market from trying to match the low prices. A Smalldonian company might try to accomplish this by financing its lower priced sales on the Freedonian market through higher priced sales on the Smalldonian market. Or it might simply use its cash reserves or borrow money for the purpose. Eventually, in theory at least, consumers will buy only Smalldonian fans because they are cheaper than Freedonian fans until, at last, the Freedonian fan manufacturers have lost so much money they go out of business.

At that point, of course, the Smalldonian fan manufacturers have no Freedonian competition. And, when there is less competition, the Smalldonian fan manufacturers will presumably raise their prices quite a bit higher than they were before they faced competition in Freedonia. Freedonian consumers will have little reason to thank Smalldonian manufacturers when reduced competition results in increased prices. To prevent such trade practices, many states have adopted **antidumping** laws that impose additional import duties on imported goods that have been dumped on the domestic market to the detriment of a domestic industry.

2 Antidumping and Countervailing Duties

2.1 The Treaty Regime

In many countries, including Canada, China, Japan, Mexico, the United States, and throughout the EU, when a company or union believes its foreign competitors are engaging in dumping or have received certain kinds of subsidies, it can seek to initiate a trade remedies action. **Antidumping duty** (**ADD**) investigations and **countervailing duty** (**CVD**) investigations are the most common forms of trade remedies. An antidumping duty is, as its name suggests, a levy imposed on the importation of foreign goods that have been sold at less than fair value on the domestic market. The duty is intended to raise the price of the imports to match their price on the exporter's own market. A countervailing duty is a levy, imposed on the importation of foreign goods that have benefitted from certain state-granted subsidies, designed to raise the price of the imported goods to offset the benefit of the subsidy. The WTO Agreements, which set limits on and harmonize the trade laws of the WTO contracting parties, allow ADD and CVD investigations and measures subject to certain conditions designed to prevent member states from using these investigations too aggressively to restrict trade.

The General Agreement on Tariffs and Trade (GATT) makes clear that some subsidies are flatly inconsistent with GATT obligations. Most prominently, GATT Article XVI prohibits states from giving subsidies to domestic firms or industries if the subsidies are tied to, or for the purpose of, encouraging exports to other countries.

GATT Article VI sets forth a general rule that contracting parties may "condemn" dumping if it causes or threatens material injury to one of its industries, or threatens to prevent a party from establishing a domestic industry. Article VI sets forth rules on the conditions under which antidumping duties may be applied and permits additional duties to be assessed on dumped products in an amount necessary to offset the dumping. Article VI also limits the application of countervailing duties to certain kinds of subsidies and to amounts commensurate with foreign government subsidies granted to an exporting industry for the manufacture or export of its products. Domestic price stabilization measures taken by states, which might be necessary to slow down rapid currency inflation or deflation, are considered to be excluded from the scope of dumping even though such measures may result in export prices temporarily dropping below domestic prices.

In 1994, the WTO members agreed to supplement the GATT with an

Policy Issue

Does punishing dumping restore competition?

There are several reasons to doubt whether the predatory pricing scenario is at all common. First, effective predatory pricing is only possible when the costs of starting up a new business are very high. If they are not, once the foreign manufacturers raise their prices on the domestic market to take advantage of reduced competition, a new competitor can enter the domestic market and undersell the foreign manufacturers. Second, the foreign manufacturers must have more capital or credit than the domestic manufacturers. This is possible when the target is a market in a developing country, but the scenario is less likely in highly developed markets like the United States and Europe. Yet, wealthy countries account for a large majority of the antidumping petitions filed every year, and developing countries themselves are usually the targets of these petitions. It seems unlikely that a manufacturer in, say, Ukraine could successfully destroy a U.S. industry through predatory pricing, yet Ukraine is the subject of numerous antidumping orders imposed by developed countries, such as the United States and European Union.

Moreover, in some countries, including the United States, the potential effects of an ADD on competition are excluded from consideration in the investigation. The government may issue an ADD order even though it establishes a domestic monopoly to the detriment of consumers.

A counterargument is that some industries do have high start up costs, and even in wealthy countries with ready capital some **infant industries** are very sensitive to competition as they are being formed. Although foreign manufacturing may face the necessity of expensive international shipping, infant industries facing high labor and regulatory compliance costs might face difficulty in competing with the much lower manufacturing costs in developing countries. This explanation may justify ADDs in some circumstances, but it does not apply to the great majority of real world antidumping cases. Most industries that regularly bring antidumping petitions are well established and not in an early developmental phase.

Is there some way to limit antidumping petitions to industries that could realistically be harmed by predatory pricing? The U.S. 1916 Dumping Act required petitioning industries to prove that foreign producers specifically intended to harm competition on the U.S. market, but this was difficult to prove and ultimately abandoned. Would it be feasible to limit petitions to infant industries or industries outclassed in capital or liquidity by their foreign competitors?

additional treaty called the **Agreement on Implementation of Article VI of the GATT 1994**. This treaty further limits the methodology by which a WTO member may determine whether dumping has occurred, the procedures for conducting an ADD investigation, the question of when and how provisional ADDs may be imposed pending the outcome of the investigation, and the method for calculating a dumping margin.

The **dumping margin** is the difference between the price the exporter would have charged for its goods in the importing state under normal market conditions and the price it did in fact charge. Among other things, the Agreement on Implementation of article VI requires a clear showing that the exporting industry's dumping caused an injury or threatens to cause injury to a **domestic industry**, which the Agreement generally defines as "the domestic producers as a whole of the like products." *Id.* art. 4. The Agreement further prohibits an ADD investigation if producers accounting for a majority (more than 50%) of domestic production *that adopt a position on the petition* do not support it, provided that producers accounting for less than 25% of the total domestic production must explicitly support the petition. *Id.* art. 5.4.

Even if causation is proven, if the injury is negligible—as the Agreement puts it, ***de minimis***—the investigation must be promptly terminated. *Id.* art. 5.8. Among the Agreement's procedural requirements are a right of public notice, a right of all affected industries to participate in the investigation, and a right of judicial or administrative appeal of the outcome of the investigation.

The WTO Agreements also include a separate **Agreement on Subsidies and Countervailing Measures** (**SCM Agreement**). The SCM Agreement sets forth disciplines that supplement GATT article XVI and relate to subsidies available to a specific company, group of companies, or industry in the subsidizing state's territory. The SCM Agreement classifies most specific subsidies into two categories:

Prohibited subsidies, which are those contingent on the export performance of the subsidized companies or industry. In other words, the SCM Agreement prohibits most subsidies that specifically encourage exports to other WTO members or encourage domestic manufacturing to prevent imports from other members. These are sometimes called **red box** or **red light** subsidies. Red box subsidies may be challenged before the WTO Dispute Settlement Body as well as in national CVD investigations.

Actionable (or **specific**) subsidies, which are subsidies explicitly limited to specified enterprises and harm, threaten to harm, or cause "serious prejudice to" the industries of other WTO members or undermine world trade"nullify or impair") the trade benefits that the WTO Agreements were intended to grant. Certain subsidies, such as those totaling 5% or more *ad valorem* of the subsidized products, are presumed to distort markets and cause "serious prejudice" to the affected WTO member's industries. In such cases, the subsidizing state carries the burden of showing that the subsidies at issue do not harm other WTO members. Such subsidies are called "actionable" because they may justify a CVD investigation in an affected WTO member. These subsidies are sometimes called **amber box** or **yellow light** subsidies.

General or specific subsidies for industrial development, such as to promote research in some technology, give assistance to underdeveloped regions of the state, or adapt facilities to new environmental or health and safety regulations, were formerly considered non-actionable or **green box** or **green light** subsidies, but this class expired in 2000 pursuant to article 31 of the SCM Agreement. Nonetheless, such measures are rebuttably presumed WTO-compliant.

There are exceptions to these classifications, most prominently for agricultural subsidies, but these are the general categories defined by the SCM

ARE TRADE REMEDIES WIDELY DISPUTED?

Trade remedies actions supply the most fruitful source of WTO litigation bar none. At any given time, ADD, CVD, and safeguards measures comprise much of the subject matter of the WTO's dispute resolution docket. For example, from 2018:

- Peru—Antidumping & Countervailing Measures on Biodiesel from Argentina
- Kyrgyz Republic—Antidumping Measures on Steel Pipes
- Armenia—Antidumping Measures on Steel Pipes
- United States—Safeguard Measure on Imports of Crystalline Silicon Photovoltaic Products
- United States—Safeguard Measures on Imports of Large Residential Washers
- United States—Antidumping Measures on Fish Fillets from Vietnam

Trade remedies actions are common because, as import barriers such as customs duties gradually fall pursuant to GATT negotiations, companies in the member states become vulnerable to foreign competition. WTO member resort to ADD and CVD investigations to protect their domestic industries indirectly from free trade. The United States has been the most aggressive user of these measures. On average, the United States conducts 40 ADD and 16 CVD investigations every year. ADD/CVD authorities in other countries, such as Mexico, India, and Thailand, have followed the U.S. example and have increasingly used trade remedies to restrict foreign competition.

Agreement.

The SCM Agreement also sets forth more detailed standards for CVD investigations in the same way that (and to some extent parallel to the way that) the Agreement on the Implementation of article VI creates more detailed standards for ADD investigations. Like the article VI Agreement, the SCM Agreement requires WTO members to terminate a CVD investigation promptly upon determining that the amount of a countervailable subsidy is *de minimis* (less than 1% *ad valorem* of the goods), or when the volume of the subsidized goods imported into the complaining state is insignificant. In addition, the SCM Agreement requires that CVD investigations must be terminated within one year after initiation under normal circumstances, and that countervailing duties imposed following an investigation must **sunset**, meaning that they must automatically terminate within five years unless the state affirmatively finds that the subsidy and injury will continue beyond the five year period.

Through these investigations, petitioners representing a state's domestic industry seek to persuade their governments that they should impose additional import duties to offset the effects of dumping and countervailable subsidies, respectively. The duties are "additional" in the sense that they are added to the normal customs duties applicable to the imports. So if widgets from Smalldonia imported into the United States are typically assessed 5% *ad valorem* duty, but the U.S. government has assessed a 20% antidumping duty on the widgets, then importers of widgets from Smalldonia will have to pay a 25% combined duty. In some cases, the government may find that a foreign exporter is *both* dumping the product on the U.S. market and receiving a countervailable subsidy and may impose both an ADD and a CVD on the imported merchandise. Thus, if the U.S. government assessed both a 20% ADD and a 10% CVD on Smalldonian widgets, importers of such widgets would have to pay a 35% duty (5% normal duty + 20% ADD + 10% CVD) on the imported widgets.

2.2 The U.S. ADD and CVD Investigation Procedure

The first U.S. countervailing duty law was passed in 1897, and the first antidumping law was enacted in 1916. The standards of "unfair competition" in these laws differed significantly from those in modern U.S. law. The CVD law, for example, did not require any showing that a domestic industry was injured or threatened with injury by a foreign subsidy before a countervailing duty could be imposed on the foreign imports. The 1916 antidumping law required, as the precondition to the imposition of an antidumping duty, that the foreign manufacturer had intended to dump goods on the U.S. market.

The most commonly used U.S. antidumping and countervailing duty laws today are found in Title VII of the **1930 Tariff Act** (19 U.S.C. §§ 1671 *et seq.*), as amended. The 1930 Tariff Act incorporates many changes resulting from international trade negotiations involving the WTO Agreements. The Department of Commerce's **International Trade Administration** (**ITA**) and the independent Executive Branch agency, **International Trade Commission (ITC** or Commission) jointly investigate claims of dumping and actionable subsidies under the Tariff Act. If these agencies determine that dumping or countervailable subsidies have injured or threaten to injure a U.S. industry, they will order CBP to impose offsetting duties on imports of the dumped or subsidized merchandise from the countries found to be dumping or subsidizing the goods.

Why two agencies? Because they each play a partial role in a trade remedies investigation. The ITA, sometimes referred to less precisely by its department name, "Commerce," must determine whether the merchandise is sold at less than fair value or is subsidized. The ITA also determines the amount of duties that must be assessed. The ITC's role is to determine whether any dumping or subsidy identified by the ITA is causing or threatens to cause an injury to a U.S. industry.

As you may recall from Chapter 3, the ITC is an independent Executive Branch agency. It is led by six commissioners who are nominated by the President and confirmed by the U.S. Senate. No more than three commissioners may be of any one political party at any time, so that three Democrats and three Republicans always serve as commissioners. The commissioners serve overlapping terms of nine years. Of these six commissioners, one is designated Chairman and another Vice Chairman for two-year terms, with each necessarily belonging to a different political party and each alternating in political party. At any given time, then, the Chairman belongs to a different political party than the Vice Chairman and to the Chairman immediately preceding him or her. The ITC staff consists of some 350 employees, including trade analysts, economists, attorneys, and technical support personnel.

A. The Petition for Relief

When a U.S. company, labor union, or industry organization wishes to complain of unfair import competition, it may file a petition for ADD or CVD relief. The petitioner simultaneously files the petition with the ITA and the ITC. The petition must:

(1) allege the existence dumping or actionable subsidies;
(2) identify the country or countries that are the source of the allegedly dumped or subsidized goods;
(3) specify the imported goods complained of; and
(4) allege that such dumping or subsidies materially injure or threaten to materially injure the domestic industry.

The petition must also allege that the petitioner is a company, trade association, labor union, or other interested party in the affected domestic industry with standing to file on behalf of that industry. In other words, the petitioner does not merely represent itself, but is considered to speak on behalf of a substantial part of the entire domestic industry. If the petitioner requests advice on filing the petition, the ITC or ITA will inform the petitioner of any defects in the petition and how to remedy them.

The petition looks much like a complaint brief, but it is customized for the procedures, laws, and facts unique to trade remedies investigations. If the petition satisfies the requirements just stated, the ITA and the ITC will initiate separate investigations. The investigations involve a set of preliminary determinations followed by final determinations, resulting in one of the following findings:

- the absence of dumping or actionable subsidies;
- the absence of a U.S. industry;
- the absence of injury or threat of injury to a domestic industry; or
- the presence of all three foregoing conditions and an order to the CBP to impose ADDs or CVDs.

One reason investigations are divided into preliminary and final determinations is that a preliminary determination allows the agencies to grant faster relief to the U.S. industry. This division also potentially benefits importers of foreign-made products; if a preliminary determination by either agency is negative, then the importer need not post a bond to cover additional duties on its imports during the course of the investigation.

B. Preliminary Determinations

The first preliminary determination is made by the ITC. The ITC begins by ascertaining whether there is a likelihood of injury to a U.S. industry caused by the imports. It must first define the scope of the investigation by determining which imports are sufficiently like the domestically produced goods to qualify as the same product. The ITC then makes three separate determinations:

(1) **domestic industry**: that a U.S. industry for the production of goods like the identified imports exists or is in the process of being created;
(2) **harm / threat of harm**: that the industry is currently being harmed or is threatened with harm by foreign imports; and
(3) **causation**: that the cause of the injury or threat is the unfair imports.

To make these determinations, the ITC will consider the evidence submitted by the petitioners and respondents. It will supplement this information by sending out questionnaires to U.S. and foreign producers and U.S. importers of the products under investigation to gather data independently on, for example, whether the domestic industry supports or opposes the petition, and how the domestic and foreign industries are faring economically. The ITC will typically hold a public conference during the investigation to hear the testimony of experts and brief oral arguments from the petitioners and respondents. Non-parties to the proceeding may also submit brief statements with the ITC's permission. The ITC does not inquire deeply into whether there have been illegal dumping or countervailable subsidies; this is for the ITA to decide. The ITC merely determines whether the imports harmed the domestic industry. If any of the three determinations is negative, the ITC will terminate the investigation and the petition will be denied.

If the ITC makes all three determinations in the affirmative, the ITA then issues its own preliminary determination with respect to:

(4) the existence of **dumping** or **subsidization** of the relevant goods; and
(5) the amount of the dumping or subsidization.

If the ITA's determination is positive, it will direct CBP to suspend the liquidation of any imports of merchandise subject to the investigation, effectively putting the imports on hold unless the importers post a bond equal to the amount of estimated dumping margin (again, the difference between the "fair market value" and the U.S. price) or the net subsidy found by the ITA. A **bond** is a form of financial guarantee offered by a third party—usually an insurance company—that the importer will pay any duties assessed. If the ITA's preliminary determination is negative, the investigation is not closed; rather, the ITA will still move on to its final determination, but the importer will not be required to post any bond.

C. Final Determinations

After the preliminary determinations, the petitioner and respondent have an opportunity to submit further evidence and arguments. Based on this evidence, the ITA will make its final determination. In the rare case that the ITA finds no dumping or countervailable subsidy, the case will be terminated. If the ITA finds dumping or a countervailable subsidy, it calculates the final dumping margin or countervailable subsidy. The ITC then makes its own further investigation of injury or threat of injury to a U.S. industry.

To that end, the ITC assigns a six-person team to gather information by drafting questionnaires for U.S. and foreign producers and U.S. importers of the like products similar to the questionnaires used in the preliminary investigation. Questionnaires will also be sent to all significant purchasers or to a representative sample of consumers of the like products in the United States. Based on the answers to the questionnaires, the ITC will prepare a prehearing staff report analyzing the state of the U.S. industry and the competition it faces. The petitioner and respondent file briefs arguing the various legal issues to the ITC soon after the issuance of the staff report, using the report as the factual basis for their arguments.

The ITC will then hold another public hearing, with all Commissioners attending. The purpose of the hearing is to allow all interested parties to present arguments about the facts found in the staff report and alleged by the parties, and to give the Commissioners an opportunity to ask questions for the further development of the factual record. Witnesses may give testimony for either side. Each party is typically given an hour to present its case, followed by extensive questioning by the Commissioners. Following the hearing, the ITC will prepare a final staff report for the Commissioners and parties, after which the ITC will close the factual record and cease gathering or accepting new factual information, although it will accept final comments on the

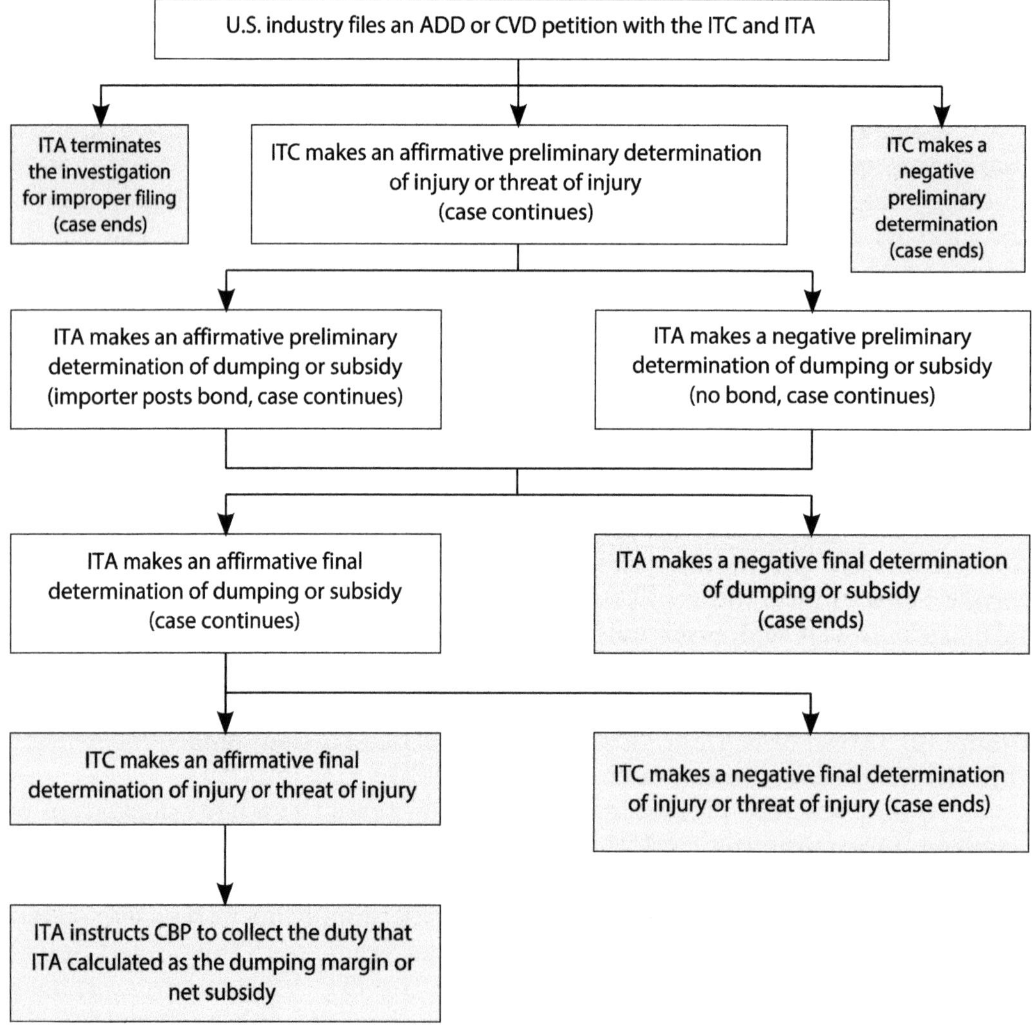

Figure 6.1. A simplified schematic of the U.S. ADD/CVD investigation process.

accuracy, reliability, or probative value of the information presented to the ITC.

The ITC will evaluate the testimony and other evidence and will arrive at a final determination of injury or threat of injury at a brief public hearing based on a majority vote of the Commissioners. If the ITC majority's final determination is affirmative, it will communicate this to the ITA, which will in turn either confirm its ADD or CVD order, or revise the order to account for its ultimate determination of the dumping margin or net subsidy. At that time, the ITA will order the collection of any additional duties due from foreign importers based on the preliminary affirmative determination (if any) and will direct CBP to require cash deposits of estimated duties prior to any further importation. Both agencies announce their determinations, including orders, in the *Federal Register*.

D. Appeals

Administrative Appeals

If either the ITA or ITC terminates an investigation for failure to find a requisite element of dumping or countervailable subsidies, the domestic industry may appeal the decision to a federal court. Similarly, a foreign industry may appeal an affirmative ADD or CVD order to a federal court. The court of immediate appeal from the ITA or ITC is a specialized court located in New York City called the **U.S. Court of International Trade (CIT)**. You may recall the CIT from Chapter 5—it also handles all customs appeals. 28 U.S.C. § 1581. From a decision of the CIT, appeal may be made to the **U.S. Court of Appeals for the Federal Circuit**, located in Washington, D.C. The Federal Circuit specializes in customs, trade remedies, patent, trademark, and a few other specific categories of cases. See 28 U.S.C. § 1295(a)(5). Appeals from the Federal Circuit go to the U.S. Supreme Court.

U.S. Supreme Court

U.S. Court of Appeals for the Federal Circuit

U.S. Court of International Trade

U.S. International Trade Commission or Department of Commerce

Figure 6.2. The flow of appeals available for ADD and CVD determinations.

Although appeals from either agency go to the same courts, attorneys representing the domestic or foreign industry will face different lawyers, depending on which agency's determination they are appealing. The U.S. Department of Justice handles appeals from decisions of the ITA, but the ITC's own general counsel handles appeals from Commission determinations.

USMCA Chapter 10 Appeals

In most forms of litigation, the plaintiff has a choice of forum in which to file a complaint or petition, and this choice automatically determines where any appeal may be filed. For example, a choice of bringing an action in a federal court in California usually means that any appeal must be filed in the U.S. Court of Appeals for the Ninth Circuit. Similarly, a decision to file a claim in the *tribunal de commerce de Paris* means that any appeal must go to the regional *cour d'appel de Paris*. In contrast, parties to an ADD or CVD case in the United States may have a choice of forum to which appeal may be made.

If the accused imports originate in one of the three parties to the U.S.-Canada-Mexico Agreement (USMCA), then a different appeals mechanism can be invoked by the respondent. USMCA Chapter 10, formerly NAFTA Chapter 19, provides for binational panels to review final determinations made by government agencies in ADD and CVD cases. These binational review panels are composed of five persons chosen by the parties from a roster of qualified international trade experts and judges. The panel will establish its own procedures unless the parties themselves agree on applicable procedures.

The panel will conduct a binding arbitration to determine whether the ADD or CVD order conforms with the procedural and substantive law of the country that issued the order. The panels do not assess whether the order conforms with USMCA, because USMCA does not limit the ability of parties to adopt, change, and enforce their ADD and CVD laws: "Each Party reserves the right to apply its antidumping law and countervailing duty law to goods imported from the territory of any other Party." Thus, if Canada issues a final dumping determination against goods from Mexico, a Mexican manufacturer who was a respondent in the Canadian antidumping action can invoke USMCA Chapter 10 to convene a panel composed of arbitrators from Canada and Mexico to adjudicate the consistency of the Canadian antidumping measure with Canadian law. The final decision of the panel becomes binding on the parties.

USMCA Chapter 10 also provides for appeals in case one of the parties to the dispute believes that the panel both (1) materially violated the rules of conduct (for instance, by failing to disclose a conflict of interest) or a fundamental rule of procedure, or manifestly exceeded its powers; and (2) this action both materially affected the panel's decision and threatened the integrity of the review system.

In such cases, a three-person **Extraordinary Challenge Committee** will be convened. The members of the Committee are selected by the parties from a fifteen-person roster comprised of judges or former

HOW IMPORTANT ARE USMCA CHAPTER 10 DISPUTES?

Under NAFTA, Chapter 19 appeal was the most widely used of the seven different dispute resolution procedures in the Agreement. As of 2019, there had been 120 such appeals. Like NAFTA Chapter 19, USMCA Chapter 10 is also the only dispute resolution procedure that provides for appeal to a higher tribunal, the Extraordinary Challenge Committee.

judges of certain U.S., Canadian, or Mexican courts. The Committee can affirm the panel's decision or reverse and remand it to the panel for further consideration. In either case, the Committee's decision is binding on the parties before it.

The decision to resort to one forum or another in a case involving imports from a USMCA member state involves some foresight and understanding of the advantages and disadvantages of each potential forum. Moreover, the dispute can trigger the involvement of governments on an international legal or political level.

2.3 Requirements for an Affirmative Determination

The 1930 Tariff Act defines dumping and countervailable subsidies very specifically. To qualify as such, the petitioner must present evidence sufficient to sustain the agency findings mentioned in the previous discussion. We will now review the conditions for an affirmative determination in greater detail.

A. Domestic Like Products

When a petitioner claims that imported goods are unfairly harming or threatening to harm the domestic industry, it must of course describe what kinds of goods are causing the harm. If the imported merchandise is essentially identical to the domestically-made merchandise, that task will be easy. If the domestic manufacturer makes professional soccer balls and the imported goods are professional soccer balls, the ADD or CVD petition will specify professional soccer balls as the petition's subject merchandise.

The imported products complained of by the domestic industry representative need not, however, be identical to the domestically produced or manufactured goods. According to Section 771(10) of the 1930 Tariff Act, 19 U.S.C. § 1677(10), merchandise that is "like, or in the absence of like, most similar in characteristics and uses with, the article subject to an investigation" can be included in the scope of the ADD or CVD investigation. Thus, one critical question that the petitioner must decide in drafting the petition, and the ITC must decide in evaluating it, is how to determine when one kind of merchandise is a **domestic like product** to another, different kind of merchandise.

Like product issues are very typical in ADD and CVD cases. Are canned peas "like" frozen peas? Is a digital zoom camera "like" a digital camera without a zoom feature? Is Queen Anne-style hardwood furniture "like" Shaker-style softwood furniture? Such questions require consideration of many facts, and they are consequently decided on a case-by-case basis.

Why does this matter? On a policy level, it matters because, if the imports are so different from the domestically produced merchandise that the two do not compete with each other, there is no risk that the imports can harm the domestic industry. Continuing with the example of canned peas and frozen peas, both canning and freezing are used to store peas over a long period

NOTE FROM THE FIELD

Being an Attorney in the Office of the General Counsel, U.S. ITC

Stephen A. McLaughlin, Esq.
U.S. International Trade Commission

The U.S. International Trade Commission employs attorneys in a wide variety of offices, including the Office of the General Counsel, Office of Unfair Import Investigations, Office of the Administrative Law Judges as judicial clerks, and staff counsel for each individual commissioner.

In the Office of the General Counsel, staff attorneys work in four areas: (1) as investigative attorneys in import injury investigative teams (in ADD and CVD investigations); (2) as staff attorneys advising the Commission regarding IP cases (in Section 337 investigations); (3) as appellate litigators representing the Commission before the Court of International Trade and the Federal Circuit; and (4) as administrative law advisors providing legal support to various offices of the Commission on a variety of matters, much as a corporate general counsel would do for his or her employer.

The typical new staff attorney has three to five years of experience in the field after law school, preferably in the trade area. The Office of the General Counsel has hired staff straight out of law school on occasion, however, as well as staff with over ten years of experience. Most attorneys in the Office are generalists and work in all four practice areas, but there are a few that specialize in patent law.

A general attorney in the Office of the General Counsel can expect to have four to five simultaneous active assignments. Juggling these assignments requires initiative and independence. Attorneys work with little daily supervision. The staff attorney must track their own deadlines, conduct their own research, prepare their own drafts, and meet with relevant Commission staff and private parties. Staff attorneys participate in investigative proceedings and argue their own cases in federal court.

As in most areas of the law, it is critical that staff attorneys have strong oral and written communication skills. An interest in business and commerce is helpful. They also need strong analytical skills, particularly regarding business and microeconomic issues. In addition, they have to be able to work well in inter-disciplinary investigative teams, as they rely on data collection and analysis of investigators, economists, and accountants. They must be objective in Commission proceedings but zealous advocates in judicial appeals.

Stephen A. McLaughlin is the Director of the International Trade Commission's Office of Administration and former Senior Legal Counsel.

without spoliation. Canned peas require no refrigeration and cannot suffer from frost burn. Frozen peas taste fresher than canned peas and retain more nutrition.

Suppose the U.S. vegetable industry only produced frozen peas and never canned peas. When U.S. consumers wish to purchase peas for storing and eventually eating, will they purchase either frozen or canned peas indifferently, or will they only purchase frozen peas? If they purchase indifferently, then imported canned peas dumped on the U.S. market will drive down the price of U.S.-produced frozen peas, harming the U.S. preserved vegetable industry. If they will purchase frozen peas only, then dumped canned peas may have little effect on the sales of frozen peas packed by U.S. vegetable companies. In that case, there is no need to raise the price of imported canned peas through an antidumping duty to protect the U.S. vegetable industry.

On a practical level, determining what is a like product matters because the range of products subject to the investigation will decide two things. First, which companies should be included in the scope of the "domestic industry" for purposes of determining whether the domestic industry is sufficiently represented by the petitioners? Second, what kinds of imported merchandise will be the subject of the investigation and, if found to be dumped or subsidized, subject to an ADD or CVD order?

The ITA initially determines the scope of merchandise subject to investigation when it commences the investigation, but it is the ITC that identifies domestic like products. The ITC looks for a clear distinction between products in determining whether they should be grouped together as like products, focusing on the following factors:

a. the similarity of their physical appearance;
b. whether one article is functionally interchangeable with another;
c. the similarity of their channels of distribution;
d. customer perceptions about the interchangeability of the articles; and
e. whether manufacturers can use the same manufacturing facilities and production employees for both articles.

None of these factors is typically dispositive by itself; they are considered as a whole, as the following case illustrates.

TORRINGTON CO. v. UNITED STATES

U.S. Court of International Trade, 1990
747 F. Supp. 744

OPINION

TSOUCALAS, Judge:

Plaintiff brings this action pursuant to Rule 56.1 of the Rules of this Court to challenge the finding by the International Trade Commission ("ITC" or "Commission") of six separate "like products" and "domestic industries" in its investigations of antidumping and countervailing duty injuries involving imports of antifriction bearings. *Antifriction Bearings (Other than Tapered Roller Bearings) and Parts Thereof From the Federal Republic of Germany* * * * ("Final Determinations"). * * *

Background

Torrington filed an antidumping and countervailing duty petition on March 31, 1988 on behalf of the domestic industry which produces antifriction bearings. In the petition, Torrington described one class or kind of merchandise, to wit, all antifriction bearings (except tapered roller bearings). Torrington also requested that the ITC find a single like product and a single domestic industry.

In May, 1988, the ITC issued a preliminary determination which stated that there was reason to believe that six domestic industries were materially injured, or threatened with such injury, because of unfairly imported bearings from nine countries. The Commission differentiated among bearings based on the type of rolling element each bearing contains. As a result, the ITC found that each of the following comprised a different like product produced by a different industry: (1) ball bearings; (2) spherical roller bearings; (3) cylindrical roller bearings; (4) needle roller bearings; (5) plain bearings; and (6) other antifriction devices, such as ball screws and linear guides.

The Commission issued its final determinations in May 1989 and found that there were six like products. Five of the like products corresponded to the classes or kinds of merchandise found by the International Trade Administration ("ITA"); they are ball bearings, spherical roller bearings, cylindrical roller bearings, needle roller bearings and plain bearings. However, the Commission found that slewing rings constituted a separate, sixth, like product.

Subsequently, the ITC rendered negative injury determinations for spherical roller bearings, needle roller bearings and slewing rings, and affirmative determinations for ball bearings, cylindrical roller bearings and spherical plain bearings. Plaintiff asserts that the Commission's approach "substantially narrowed the scope of the ultimate antidumping and countervailing duty orders, and thereby adversely affected Torrington."

Discussion

I. ITC's Authority to Determine Like Products

Torrington contends that the ITC must accept the definition of like product and domestic industry provided by the petition, and does not possess the authority to modify that description.

The Commission is authorized by statute to make a determination based on the evidence before it as to whether a domestic industry has been materially injured (or is threatened with such injury) by reason of imports at less than fair value ("LTFV"). The imports under investigation must cause material injury or threaten such injury to a domestic industry which produces like products, that is, products which are "like, or in the absence of like, most similar in characteristics and uses with, the article subject to an investigation under this subtitle."

Torrington's complaint is that the ITC should have made its determination based on Torrington's assertion that all antifriction bearings (except tapered roller bearings) constitute one like product and one domestic industry. It is well settled that the ITC has the authority to determine whether or not one or more domestic industries have been injured by reason of LTFV imports. This Court repeatedly has upheld the ITC when its determinations have deviated from the contentions made in the petition, provided those determinations were supported by substantial evidence.

Plaintiff also claims that the ITC's like product determination must be consistent with the ITA's class or kind finding. It is settled law that the ITC's like product determination is separate and distinct from the ITA's determination of the class or kind of merchandise. While the ITC does not have the authority to modify the ITA's finding of class or kind, it has the right to make its own determination as to what should be considered a like product. Inconsistencies in the agencies' determinations are not, *per se*, contrary to law. Indeed, the possibility that they will reach inconsistent conclusions is "built into the law." Hence, the ITC was within its discretion when it found that there were six different like products in the instant investigation.

II. ITC's Interpretation of "Like Product"

Torrington also asserts that the Commission "applied an impermissibly narrow construction of the 'like product' and industry."[2] In support of its position, Torrington cites the legislative history to the Trade Agreements Act of 1979, which states that

> [t]he requirement that a product be "like" the imported article should not be interpreted in such a narrow fashion as to permit minor differences in physical characteristics or uses to lead to the conclusion that the product and article are not "like" each other, nor should the definition of "like product" be interpreted in such a fashion as to prevent consideration of an industry adversely affected by the imports under investigation.

S.Rep. No. 249, 96th Cong., 1st Sess. 90-91. Essentially, plaintiff is contending that,

[2]The determinations of like product and domestic industry are inextricably intertwined, since industry is defined in terms of like product. Hence, "the like product determination is the industry determination."

in finding that there were six like products in the investigation of antifriction bearings, the Commission "impermissibly" relied on minor differences in characteristics and uses.

It appears that plaintiff has misunderstood the mandate of the statute and its legislative history. The Senate Report cited above warns against permitting minor differences between domestic products and imported articles from keeping them from being compared to each other. In the present action, the ITC has found distinctions "among the domestic products, not between domestic products and imported products."

Nonetheless, there is no question that differences exist among antifriction bearings. Whether the differences among the various bearings are minor or significant is a factual issue for the Commission to decide. This Court recently held that "[i]t is up to [the] ITC to determine objectively what is a minor difference." Provided the determination is reasonable and supported by the evidence, the Court will affirm the Commission. Given the vast differences among the products investigated by the ITC, it would be impossible for the Court to give specific directives as to what would constitute a minor difference.[3] The issue for the Court is whether the evidence used by the ITC to make its determination rises to the level of substantial evidence and supports the conclusion.

III. Substantial Evidence

The Court will uphold a determination by the Commission unless it is not supported by substantial evidence in the administrative record or is otherwise not in accordance with law. A decision by the ITC will not be overturned merely because the Court would have decided the issue differently, had the issue come before the Court *de novo*. The function of the Court is to determine whether there is substantial evidence to support the ITC's conclusions.

In making its determination as to what domestic products constitute like products, the ITC considers similar, but not identical, factors to those considered by the ITA in its class or kind determination.[4] These consist of "(1) physical appearance, (2) interchangeability, (3) channels of distribution, (4) customer perception, (5) common manufacturing facilities and production employees, and where appropriate, (6) price." The use of these factors by the ITC in its like product determinations has been upheld by this Court.

---

[3]In *Exportadores*, the Court affirmed the ITC's determination that the differences among carnations, chrysanthemums and gerberas were not minor and thus those flowers were separate like products. [*Asociacion Colombiana de Exportadores de Flores v. United States*] 693 F.Supp. [1165,] 1170 (Ct. Int'l Trade 1988). But in *Sony Corp. of America v. United States*, the Court found that Trinitron color picture tubes were not separate like products from other color picture tubes, despite certain unique qualities. 712 F.Supp. 978, 983 (1989). These dissimilar results demonstrate that every like product determination "must be based on the particular record at issue" and the "unique facts of each case." *Exportadores*, 693 F.Supp. at 1169.

[4]The criteria upon which Commerce relies include "the general physical characteristics of the merchandise, the expectation of the ultimate purchasers, the channels of trade in which the merchandise moves, the ultimate use of the merchandise, and cost."

In the final determinations in the present action, the ITC determined that antifriction bearings did not all comprise one like product. Rather, the Commission distinguished the bearings on the basis of the rolling element each type of bearing contains, and found that the bearings actually constitute six like products. The six like products found by the Commission are: (1) ball bearings, (2) spherical roller bearings, (3) cylindrical roller bearings, (4) needle roller bearings, (5) plain bearings, and (6) slewing rings.

The Commission's final determinations examine the differences among antifriction bearings due to different rolling elements, using the six criteria outlined above. The Commission found that most of the products within the scope of the investigation share four physical characteristics. They are an inner ring, an outer ring, some kind of rolling element and a cage or separator which holds the rolling elements in place. Furthermore, all bearings function to reduce friction between moving parts and are manufactured by the same processes.

However, the Commission concluded that those similar characteristics did not, in and of themselves, determine the character of a bearing. Instead, the Commissioners found that within the category of antifriction bearings there are separate like products depending on the type of rolling element in the bearing. This is due to the fact that "[t] he type of rolling element, or lack of a rolling element, is the key physical characteristic that determines the functional capability of the bearing and the use to which it is put."

The differing physical characteristics for ball bearings, spherical roller bearings, cylindrical roller bearings, needle roller bearings and spherical plain bearings are discussed at length by the Commission. Ball bearings have ball-shaped rolling elements while cylindrical roller bearings contain cylindrical rollers. Needle roller bearings also have cylindrical roller elements, but have a higher length-to-diameter ratio than cylindrical roller bearings. Spherical roller bearings employ spherical rollers. Finally, spherical plain bearings do not have balls or rollers; they "consist of a spherically shaped inner ring that is self-aligning in an outer ring."

Slewing rings, which were added to the ITA investigation late in the process, were found by the ITC to constitute a sixth like product. The evidence distinguishing slewing rings from the other bearings is substantial. Slewing rings have inner and outer rings and balls or rollers but normally are considerably larger than other bearings. Unlike other bearings, they also contain gears, cut on either the inner or outer ring.

Slewing rings are used primarily in heavy equipment and "perform a 'turntable' function in cranes, tank turrets, radio telescopes, hoisting equipment, and the like." For instance, slewing rings can support both the load hanging from a crane as well as radial and thrust loads, while other bearings "cannot accommodate tilting loads." Also, they are custom made for each end user and therefore are sold almost exclusively to end users, making their channels of distribution distinct from those of other bearings. Because of their atypical applications and designs, slewing rings are differentiated from other bearings in the perceptions of customers as well. Equally as important, slewing rings are produced one at a time, whereas other bearings normally are mass-produced on assembly lines. Accordingly, the Court holds that the Commission's determination that slewing rings constitute a separate like product is supported by substantial evidence.

As for the other factors considered by the ITC, the evidence indicates that interchangeability of bearings at the design stage is extremely limited. For instance, as the buyer for Caterpillar, Inc., a major purchaser of antifriction bearings, explained, "there is no way that the ball bearings which are needed for alignment, not load carrying, could be used instead of needle bearings, which have high load bearing capacity for small envelope size."[8] While some interchangeability is a theoretical possibility, in reality substitution of one type of bearing for another requires redesign of the product to conform it to the new bearing's functional capabilities. The evidence convincingly supports the conclusion that the six like products are not commonly interchangeable.

The third factor is the channels of distribution for the bearings. Plaintiff contends that the evidence demonstrates that "the channels of distribution, whether to [original equipment manufacturer] buyers or replacement distributors are the same for different types of bearings." There is evidence that bearings are marketed through one of two channels, direct sales to end users or through independent distributors to the end users. But there is little evidence to support the Commission's conclusion that bearings move through different channels of distribution based on their rolling elements.[10]

At least one foreign maker of bearings, NSK Corp., admitted that no such distinction is made in the distribution channels of bearings. While catalogues and price lists may be segregated by type of bearing, the channels through which bearings are distributed are not. However, the fact that one of the six criteria does not support the determination is not dispositive. If the balance of the evidence constitutes substantial evidence, then the determination will be affirmed.

The next factor considered by the ITC is customer perceptions. Torrington asserts that "[a]ll customers expect the bearings they purchase will function to reduce friction between moving parts." Such a broad and all-inclusive description of customer perceptions might be expected from a casual, superficial observer, but it is not a credible statement from a member of the industry.

If a purchaser of parts for heavy construction equipment considered ball bearings to be equivalent to spherical plain bearings, it is difficult to imagine that purchaser would remain on the job for long. The testimony of Caterpillar's buyer makes this point perfectly clear. He states that "[c]ertain bearings are required to perform certain mechanical tasks. And the limitations imposed by a dimension on capacity strengths dictate which bearing must be used for a specific application." Clearly, purchasers of bearings are aware of the differences among bearings and their functional capabilities.

Lastly, the Commission examined the manufacturing facilities, equipment and processes used in the production of antifriction bearings. The Commission found that "many producers make only one type of bearing," but even those who make more than one type generally used a separate manufacturing facility for different types of bearings. Plaintiff argues that antifriction bearings share "common manufacturing facilities, equipment and production employees."

The record indicates that "[m]any companies rationalize their production by size, precision, and/or type of rolling element." Thus, plaintiff claims, the rolling element is not the only distinguishing feature in the rationalization of bearings production. Yet, of those producers who make more than one type of bearing, only the petitioner reported common manufacturing facilities for assorted types of bearings.

---

[8]Caterpillar's buyer added that "engineers agree that it is ludicrous to suggest that bearings of different types are readily substitutable."

[10]For example, there is no evidence that ball bearings are sold directly to end users while needle roller bearings are sold through distributors. The exception is slewing rings, which, as discussed above, generally are sold directly to end users.

Figure 6.3. To help you get your bearings. Shown left to right: ball bearing, spherical roller bearing, cylindrical roller bearing, needle roller bearing, and plain bearing.

At the Commission Hearing, NSK's spokesman went so far as to criticize Torrington for its common production facilities because of the advantages in capacity utilization of "dedicated equipment that produces a particular type of bearing within a very small size range." He added that "[y]ou would not see that in Japan ... [or] Europe." The President of SKF confirmed that his company's domestic facilities "are in fact dedicated" to producing one type of bearing each. INA's Chief Executive Officer concurred, asserting that INA has separate plants for ball bearings, cylindrical roller bearings and needle bearings.

This argument was further buttressed by NTN's Marketing and Sales Manager who maintained that "you never produce a ball bearing on a needle bearing line or produce a spherical bearing on a ball bearing line. All of the equipment is specially designed for just that production line." Hence, while some factories may produce more than one type of bearing, there is substantial evidence to support the conclusion that within a factory, separate facilities are used for different bearings based on their rolling elements.

The production of antifriction bearings involves four major processing steps which are the same for all the bearings subject to this investigation. They are: green machining, heat treating, finishing, and assembly and inspection. The Commission explained that the same green machining equipment may be used to manufacture the components of several different types of bearings. This is because the size and the form of raw material (not the type of bearing) are the key factors that determine the type of machine to be used for green machining. Also, the same heat treatment machinery is used for all types of bearings, except tapered roller bearings.

It is in the finishing and assembly stages that there are significant distinctions based on the type of bearing. Finishing consists of grinding (and sometimes, honing) the bearing components. In grinding, "most machines are specifically designed for one or two types of bearings, although certain machines can be used to grind a wider variety of bearing types." Nevertheless, the grinding *process* is distinct for each type of bearing.

The evidence in the record indicates that the manufacturing facilities and equipment used to produce the six like products found by the ITC differ at certain levels on the basis of the rolling element. While the same machinery may be used at certain stages of production for different types of bearings, there is substantial evidence to support the conclusion that, in general, the facilities and equipment are different. It is clear, however, that the same processing *steps* are used in the manufacture of all antifriction bearings subject to this investigation.

The finding of some similarities among the products delineated by the Commission is not sufficient to overturn the determinations when there is otherwise substantial evidence to support its findings. Substantial evidence does not require that the overwhelming weight of the evidence support the Commission's conclusions. It requires that the evidence be more than a "mere scintilla." Undeniably, that standard has been met in this case. * * * Accordingly, those determinations of the ITC are affirmed. * * *

Notes and Questions

1. On appeal, the Federal Circuit laconically affirmed:

> Because the trial court performed a thorough and correct analysis of the facts and arguments raised, we affirm its decision and adopt its opinion as our own. Moreover, we note that the Commission is charged with administering the involved sections of the antidumping and countervailing duty laws. We will not disturb its interpretation unless it is unreasonable, and we conclude that it is not. We have considered all of appellant's arguments and find no reason to reverse the Court of International Trade.

Torrington Co. v. United States, 938 F.2d 1278 (Fed. Cir. 1991).

2. Under the Supreme Court's guidance in *Chevron v. NRDC*, courts tend to defer to a regulatory agency like the ITA or ITC when the agency interprets the statute that it is charged by Congress with interpreting and administering:

> If Congress has explicitly left a gap for the agency to fill, there is an express delegation of authority to the agency to elucidate a specific provision of the statute by regulation. Such legislative regulations are given controlling weight unless they are arbitrary, capricious, or manifestly contrary to the statute. Sometimes the legislative delegation to an agency on a particular question is implicit rather than explicit. In such a case, a court may not substitute its own construction of a statutory provision for a reasonable interpretation made by the administrator of an agency.

Chevron U.S.A. Inc. v. Natural Resources Defense Council, Inc., 467 U.S. 837, 843-44, 104 S.Ct. 2778, 2782 (1984).

3. Why would the U.S. industry representatives want the ITC to consider all six types of bearings "like products?" How might aggregating the products into a single category help or hurt their case for dumping or subsidies?

4. Which factors did the CIT seem to weigh most heavily in determining whether the bearings of one class or another were like products? How would you explain the preference given to some factors over others?

B. Domestic Industry

In addition to being subsidized or sold at less than fair value, the imported merchandise must also materially injure or threaten to injure a **domestic industry**. The standard of "material injury" is discussed below; first, it is necessary to discuss what qualifies as a domestic industry. After all, if a domestic industry does not exist, or is at least in the process of being established, it cannot be injured and no "remedy" is necessary or even possible.

Section 771(4)(A) of the 1930 Tariff Act (19 U.S.C. § 1677(4)(A)) defines the domestic industry as "the producers as a whole of a domestic like product, or those producers whose collective output of a domestic like product constitutes a major proportion of the total domestic production of the product." Thus, once the range of like products has been determined, the ITC will typically define the domestic industry as including all U.S. producers of the like products.

It was observed above that the petitioner is considered to file the petition on behalf of the entire domestic industry. In some cases, a single firm or association does in fact represent all or substantially all domestic production. But if not, the petitioner must convince the ITA, first, that the petitioner represents at least 25% of the total domestic production of products like the imported product subject to investigation and, second, that at least half of the domestic industry does not oppose the petition. 19 U.S.C. §§ 1671a, 1673a. For this reason, when many domestic firms manufacture products comparable to the allegedly dumped or subsidized imported product, often the largest few companies will file an ADD or CVD petition and seek the support of their domestic competitors to prevent the petition from being denied.

It is possible in some cases for a petitioner to prevail on a petition even though no domestic industry exists, if the petitioner can show that the dumping or subsidies "materially retard" the formation of a domestic industry. Evidence of material retardation can include a showing that the petitioner is unable to obtain financing to build new manufacturing plants or could otherwise not afford to compete on the domestic market because of import competition.

Because the manufacturing process ever more frequently involves processing or assembly steps in multiple countries, the question often arises whether a company that has both U.S. and foreign operations should be considered part of the domestic industry. The purpose of the ADD and CVD laws is to protect U.S. jobs and investments from unfair foreign competition. But if the "domestic" industry performs a significant portion of its operations abroad, the question naturally arises whether the ADD and CVD laws would effectively be protecting U.S. jobs and investments, or protecting foreign jobs and investments contrary to their purpose. The following final determination of the ITC explores this issue.

DRAMs AND DRAM MODULES FROM KOREA

U.S. International Trade Commission, Aug. 2003
Inv. No. 701-TA-431 (Final), USITC Pub. 3616

* * *

VIEWS OF THE COMMISSION

Based on the record in this investigation, we determine that an industry in the United States is materially injured by reason of imports of dynamic random access memory semiconductors ("DRAMs") and DRAM modules from the Republic of Korea ("Korea") sold in the United States that the U.S. Department of Commerce ("Commerce") has found to be subsidized by the Government of Korea. * * *

II. DOMESTIC INDUSTRY AND RELATED PARTIES

The domestic industry is defined as "the producers as a [w]hole of a domestic like product whose collective output of a domestic like product constitutes a major proportion of the total domestic production of the product." In defining the domestic industry, the Commission's general practice has been to include in the industry all domestic production of the domestic like product, whether toll-produced, captively consumed, or sold in the domestic merchant market.

Based on the current record, during at least part of the period of investigation eight firms performed wafer fabrication in the United States, five firms performed DRAM casing ("assembly"), and two of those firms which performed both fabrication and assembly also stuffed ("packaged") DRAMs into DRAM modules domestically. During at least some part of the period of investigation, Micron, Infineon, Hynix, Samsung, Dominion Semiconductor, Fujitsu, IBM, and NECELAM fabricated uncased DRAMs. Hynix and Samsung export all of their U.S.-fabricated wafers to Korea for final assembly into DRAMs. During the period of investigation, Micron, Infineon, NECELAM, and IBM had operations to assemble DRAMs in the United States. In addition, Kingston Technology Co., Inc. ("Kingston"), a domestic module packager, has a[n affiliate] * * * ("Payton") that assembles DRAMs in the United States. The record also indicates that [one party] imported uncased DRAMs fabbed in third countries and assembled them in the United States for sale as DRAMs or DRAM modules. There are also some DRAMs and DRAM modules sold in the United States that are from DRAMs fabbed in the United States, but assembled in third countries. Finally, the record suggests that some companies, including PNY, Simple Technologies, and Smart Modular package DRAMs into DRAM modules, but these companies neither fabricate wafers nor assemble DRAMs.

A. What Constitutes Sufficient Production-Related Activities

1. Fabbers, Module Packagers, and Fabless Design Houses

In previous investigations and in its preliminary determination in this investigation, the Commission concluded that the domestic industry producing DRAM products consists of those producers that fabricate DRAMs in the United States, and those producers that assemble DRAMs in the United States, but that the industry does not include module "packagers" or fabless design houses. With respect to each of those operations, the Commission identified the relevant inquiry as whether the operations in question constituted sufficient production-related activities in the United States. In assessing the nature and extent of production-related activities in the United States associated with a particular operation, the Commission generally considers six factors:

(1) source and extent of the firm's capital investment;
(2) technical expertise involved in U.S. production activities;
(3) value added to the product in the United States;
(4) employment levels;
(5) quantity and type of parts sourced in the United States; and
(6) any other costs and activities in the United States directly leading to production of the like product.

No single factor is determinative and the Commission may consider any other factors it deems relevant in light of the specific facts of any investigation. All of the parties agree with the Commission's findings in the preliminary phase of this investigation that fabrication of uncased DRAMs constitutes sufficient production-related activities to qualify as domestic production and that companies that only package DRAMs into DRAM modules and fabless design houses do not engage in sufficient production-related activities. In light of the parties' agreement and the absence of factual information on the record in the final phase of this investigation contradicting the Commission's analysis in the preliminary determination or in previous investigations, we again find that fabrication of uncased DRAMs in the United States constitutes sufficient production-related activities to include producers that fabricate uncased DRAMs in the domestic industry. For the same reasons, we also find that companies that only package DRAMs into DRAM modules and fabless design houses do not engage in sufficient production-related activities to warrant their inclusion in the domestic industry.

2. DRAM Assembly Operations

a. Parties' Arguments

Hynix [a respondent] argues that DRAMs and DRAM modules containing DRAMs that are fabbed in the United States and assembled in the United States should be considered domestic production, but that DRAMs and DRAM modules containing DRAMs that are fabbed in third countries and assembled in the United States should be considered non-subject imports. Hynix does not dispute that assembly operations comprise sufficient production-related activities to constitute domestic production if the product being assembled was fabbed in the United States. Hynix, however, argues that the Commission's approach of treating fabrication as determinative of country of origin in all cases except where DRAMs and DRAM modules contain DRAMs that are fabbed in third countries and assembled in the United States is internally inconsistent. It also alleges that this approach masks the role of non-subject imports on the condition of the domestic industry, and is inconsistent with U.S. proposals in WTO negotiations on non-preferential rules of origin, and with the practices of Commerce, the European

Union, Japan, and Korea. Hynix argues that it is legally possible both to recognize that assembly is a legitimate U.S. production-related activity and that fabrication controls country-of-origin for shipments (market share) and pricing purposes. Hynix states that its research has not yielded any case in which the Commission was faced with the same situation.

[Petitioners] Micron and Infineon argue that shipments of DRAMs and DRAM modules containing DRAMs that were either fabbed in the United States or assembled in the United States from dice fabbed anywhere but by Hynix in Korea should be treated as domestic shipments, consistent with the Commission's practice in other investigations. They argue that both fabbing and assembly operations are significant production-related activities, such that if either or both operations are performed in the United States, shipments of the resulting DRAMs or modules containing those DRAMs should be considered domestic shipments. Although there may be some inconsistency to the Commission's approach, they argue that the results are correct based on application of the usual test and the statutory purpose of the Commission's inquiry—to identify domestic production operations of a like product and to analyze the impact of unfairly traded imports on such operations.

b. Analysis and Finding

For Customs' purposes, the country of origin of DRAMs is considered to be the country where the DRAMs were assembled because Customs has determined that assembly operations constitute a substantial transformation of the merchandise. For purposes of determining the scope of subject merchandise in this investigation (as well as in other investigations of DRAM and SRAM products), Commerce determined the country of origin of DRAMs and DRAM modules based on the country where the DRAMs were fabbed. For the Commission's purposes, the statute requires that a company be a producer of a domestic like product to be included in the domestic industry. There is no dispute that uncased DRAMs as well as cased DRAMs are part of the domestic like product, as indicated above. Although assembly operations are not as sophisticated a process as fabrication, we again find that both operations involve sufficient production-related activities to constitute domestic production.

Source and Extent of Capital Investment. The cost of a new fabrication facility (and equipment) is estimated to be more than $2 billion, whereas the cost of a new assembly facility is estimated to be approximately $300 million. Both fabbing operations and assembly operations warrant continuing research and development and capital spending to keep up with the latest product and process developments.

Technical Expertise involved in U.S. Production Activities. The fabrication process is highly automated, takes two to three months to complete, is the stage where the electrical and technical characteristics of the individual dice are developed, and is the process on which Commerce bases its country of origin determinations in Title VII investigations. Assembly operations are somewhat more labor intensive than fabrication, but are nevertheless a highly automated and technologically sophisticated process that takes an estimated seven to fourteen days; Customs uses assembly operations as the basis for country of origin determinations for DRAMs. Whereas a fabrication plant requires a Class 1 clean room and involves more than 100 different material inputs and 180 operations, respondents report that a DRAM assembly plant only requires a Class 1,000 clean room, 10 material inputs, and 10 operations.

Value Added to the Product in the United States. While fabrication involves greater value added than assembly operations, total value added by the assembly process is more than minimal in absolute terms, and particularly over the life of DRAM products. A Micron representative testified at the staff conference that at the beginning of a product's life cycle, 80 to 90 percent of the cost of production is accounted for by fabrication, but that ultimately, fabrication declines to account for only 30 to 40 percent. * * *

Employment Levels. Assembly operations employ a significant number of domestic production and related workers ("PRWs"). * * *

Quantity and Type of Parts Sourced in the United States. [This information was considered confidential and, therefore, not published.]

Because the record in the final phase of this investigation continues to demonstrate that DRAM assembly operations, although not as sophisticated as fabrication operations, involve a moderate degree of technological sophistication, require continuing research and development and capital spending to keep up with the latest product and process developments, involve more than minimal value added particularly over the life of DRAM products, employ a significant number of domestic PRWs, * * * we again find that assembly operations involve sufficient production-related activity to constitute domestic production.

Hynix argues that shipments of DRAM products that were fabricated in third countries but assembled in the United States should be considered non-subject imports. In effect, what respondents request is for the Commission to give determinative weight to the "quantity and type of parts sourced in the United States" factor on a transaction-by-transaction basis. * * *

The Commission has never given determinative weight to an individual factor in previous investigations, including previous investigations of DRAM and SRAM products, nor has it examined any individual factor on a company-specific basis, let alone on a transaction-specific basis for each company. * * * Although the identities and activities of the various companies in the U.S. market have fluctuated over the years, the Commission has consistently treated assembly operations as domestic production activities, and therefore the output of those operations, cased DRAMs, must be treated as domestic shipments.

B. Related Party Analysis

We must further determine whether any producer of the domestic like product should be excluded from the domestic industry pursuant to section 771(4)(B) of the Act. That provision of the statute allows the Commission, if appropriate circumstances exist, to exclude from the domestic industry producers that are related to an exporter or importer of subject merchandise or which are themselves importers. Exclusion of such a producer is within the Commission's discretion based upon the facts presented in each case.

Micron and Infineon argue, and Hynix concedes, that Hynix Semiconductor Manufacturing America ("HSMA") is a related party. HSMA, which has fabrication operations in the state of Oregon, is a wholly-owned subsidiary of Hynix Semiconductor America, an importer of subject merchandise * * *. Hynix Semiconductor America, in turn, is a wholly-owned subsidiary of Hynix Semiconductor Inc., a Korean producer of subject merchandise. Because importer Hynix Semiconductor America and exporter Hynix Semiconductor, Inc. are legally or operationally in a position either directly or indirectly to exercise restraint or direction over HSMA, we find HSMA is a related party.

With respect to whether appropriate circumstances exist to exclude HSMA from the domestic industry, the evidence is mixed. Several factors weigh in favor of exclusion. HSMA is not equipped to assemble DRAMs or package DRAM modules, and it sends all uncased DRAMs to Korea for assembly. The corporate headquarters in Korea control decision-making for HSMA, including decisions about what to produce, production operation levels, capital expenditures, research and development, capacity, and process technology, but seek input from HSMA on these issues. Other assembly and packaging operations exist outside Korea, so in theory HSMA could send its uncased DRAMs elsewhere, but as a factual matter, it does not do so. As a practical matter, * * * it would not be economical for the single fabrication facility in the United States to produce the broader product range required by purchasers in the U.S. market. Hynix opposes the petition * * *.

On the other hand, several factors weigh against exclusion. HSMA has operated a wafer fab in Eugene, Oregon[;] * * * production began in 1998. * * * [O]ngoing investments in the Eugene facility indicate a continuing commitment to maintaining a presence in the United States.

* * * [I]t is true that HSMA was not the corporate entity responsible for subject imports, but rather the importer of record was a different entity of the same corporate family.

No party now argues that appropriate circumstances exist to exclude HSMA from the domestic industry, and on the whole, we find that appropriate circumstances do not exist to do so. * * *

Notes and Questions

1. The ITC considers a list of six nonexclusive factors in determining whether a domestic industry for a product exists. Are there any other factors that the ITC considered in this case? That it should have considered but did not?

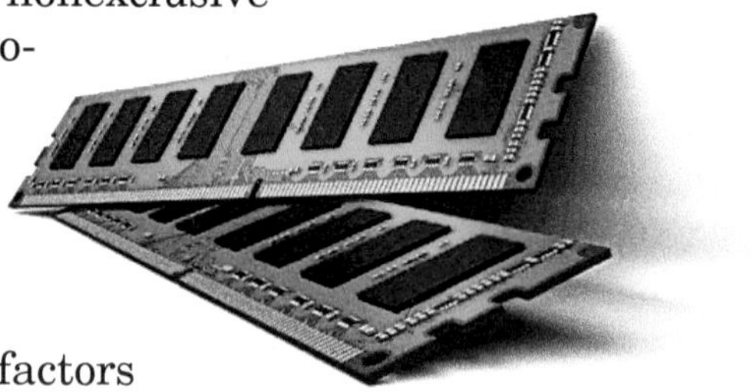

2. What policy goals do each of the factors listed above serve? Are they consistent with the mission of trade remedies law of protecting U.S. jobs and investment from unfair foreign competition?

Figure 6.4. DRAM modules.
Credit: © Micron Corp. Reproduced with permission.

3. One of the respondents in the *DRAMs and DRAM Modules from Korea* investigation, Hynix, argued that whether a DRAM module was "produced" in the United States should depend on the customs rules of origin being proposed by the United States in its international trade negotiations. However, under

U.S. rules of origin at the time, assembly of DRAMs into modules in the United States apparently qualified to make the DRAM modules U.S.-origin goods, even though the wafers themselves were fabricated in South Korea. As discussed in Chapter 5, customs rules of origin in the United States use either the *Gibson-Thomsen* substantial transformation test, or a tariff shift and/or regional value content methodology. Is an ADD/CVD "domestic industry" determination intended to serve the same purposes as a country of origin determination? If so, which rule of origin should the Commission use: the one currently in use by CBP or the one the U.S. Trade Representative is proposing be adopted in international treaties? If not, how do the determinations differ?

4. Does the Commission hold that the foreign ownership of a company is a factor in determining whether the company is part of the domestic industry? Should it be a factor?

C. Existence of Dumping or Subsidy

Dumping occurs when imported products are sold at **less than fair value (LTFV)** on the domestic market. 19 U.S.C. § 1673. The word "fair" has a technical meaning in the trade remedies context. It means the price at which the imported goods are sold on the domestic market (the "normal" market value) is less than the price at which the same goods are sold on the foreign market (the export price). Thus, if Smalldonian widgets typically sell for US$ 10 each on the U.S. market and the Smalldonian currency equivalent of US$ 15 each on the Smalldonian market, the widgets are considered to be sold on the U.S. market at LTFV.

A **countervailable subsidy** occurs when "the government of a country or any public entity within the territory of a country is providing, directly or indirectly," a benefit "with respect to the manufacture, production, or export of a class or kind of merchandise imported, or sold (or likely to be sold) for importation, into the United States" to the detriment of a U.S. industry. 19 U.S.C. § 1671(a). All red box and amber box subsidies under the SCM Agreement qualify as potentially countervailable.

The fact that a foreign company receives some kind of benefit from its government cannot *ipso facto* mean that every other country can impose additional duties on imports from the subsidizing country to offset the benefit. If they could, there would be no end to CVD investigations, because government subsidies to businesses in the form of tax exemptions and credits, direct payments, discounted utilities, and other benefits—all forms of so-called "corporate welfare"—are common. In order for a subsidy to be countervailable, it must discriminate in favor of a specific foreign industry or company and must in addition significantly harm or threaten to harm a domestic industry.

Keep in mind that the GATT prohibits imposing ADDs and CVDs that are duplicative of each other:

> No product of the territory of any contracting party imported into the territory of any other contracting party shall be subject to both anti-dumping and countervailing duties to compensate for the same situation of dumping or export subsidization.

GATT art. VI.5. However, if dumped products separately benefit from countervailable subsidies, it is possible, and not uncommon, for the goods to be subjected to simultaneous ADD and CVD investigations and remedies in the United States.

D. Injury and Causation

The 1930 Tariff Act defines a "material injury" tautologically as a "harm which is not inconsequential, immaterial, or unimportant." 19 U.S.C. § 1677(7). How does a domestic industry show that it has suffered a material injury or will soon suffer one, and that the injury was caused by the dumped or subsidized foreign imports? If the data gathered by the ITC shows that sales of the domestically produced merchandise have recently fallen or grown more slowly than might be expected, that the industry has significant unused capacity, that unemployment is on the rise in the industry, that profits or **return on investment** have fallen relative to sales or that losses are mounting, or any other indicia of economic harm, the ITC may conclude that the industry has suffered a material injury.

Proving causation is more difficult. To understand why, consider the following reasons that domestic sales could drop or fail to grow as quickly as the domestic industry might expect:

- A domestic industry's key product could become obsolete because of new advances in technology. For example, fiber optic cable manufacturers could see a fall in demand during the rise of wireless communications.
- Consumer tastes could change.
- New government regulation could create disincentives to use the product. For example, high cigarette taxes will not only decrease cigarette sales; they will also incidentally decrease sales of disposable lighters if there is a correlation between cigarette and lighter consumption.
- Exogenous market forces could make the product less attractive. For example, a long-term rise in the price of oil tends to decrease sales of large, fuel-inefficient cars.
- The national economy as a whole could experience a slump, so that sales of all products decrease.

As these examples illustrate, there are many explanations for why domestic sales might drop or fail to grow that have nothing to do with foreign trade practices, fair or unfair.

To show causation, the ITC must be presented with evidence that tends to link the injury to the domestic industry to the dumped or subsidized products. This can best be done by showing, for example, significant underselling of domestically produced products by foreign like products; an increase in the number of relevant foreign imports over time relative to domestically produced like products; a decrease in the price of foreign imports relative to domestic products; and, of course, the absence or relative unimportance of the kinds of factors listed above, which might offer an alternative explanation for the decreased relative or absolute sales of domestic products.

In determining the effect of foreign imports on the U.S. industry, the ITC has historically considered imports from all countries named in the petition collectively rather than on a country-by-country basis, a practice called **cumulation**. Cumulation may greatly affect the outcome of a determination of injury. It is possible that dumping or subsidies attributable to any single country will have no appreciable effect on a U.S. industry, but the effects of dumping or subsidies from numerous countries might combine to injure or threaten to injure a U.S. industry. The 1930 Tariff Act provides that the ITC must cumulatively assess the volume and effect of the subject imports from all countries when making an injury determination. 19 U.S.C. § 1675.

2.4 Remedies and Review

A. Dumping Margin and Net Subsidy

At the conclusion of an ADD investigation, if dumping is found, the ITA will typically calculate the difference between the normal price at which the subject merchandise is sold on the foreign market (the fair market value) and the domestic market, and impose additional duties to close the gap. The difference between the domestic price and the fair market price of the goods is the **dumping margin**. 19 U.S.C. § 1677(35). Each exporter is usually subject to a separate dumping margin calculation.

WHAT IS "RETURN ON INVESTMENT" AND WHY DOES IT MATTER?

Return on investment (ROI), is the amount of money an investor makes expressed as a percentage of his or her initial investment. To use a simplistic example, if an investor builds a factory at a cost of $10 million and makes an annual profit of $1 million from the factory, her ROI is 10%. ROI is a rough measure of the profitability of an investment or enterprise. Along with other financial indicators, it can be useful for assessing a company's or industry's economic success.

A determination of countervailable subsidies causing harm to a domestic industry will result in an order to CBP to impose a duty on the importation of the products subject to the investigation equal to the amount of the **net subsidy** found to exist. 19 U.S.C. § 1671e(a)(1). The calculation of dumping margin or net subsidy is typically a matter of intense dispute between the parties, as it directly affects the ADD or CVD payable on the importation into the United States of the goods subject to the investigation.

A finding of dumping or countervailable subsidies is not in any way equivalent to a criminal conviction, a civil penalty, or even civil damages. The formal purpose of ADDs and CVDs is not to punish foreign exporters or even to compensate the domestic industry for the harm caused by dumping or subsidy.* Their ostensible purpose is to "level the playing field" between foreign and U.S. producers by counteracting predatory pricing (dumping) and foreign government-granted advantages (subsidies). This is one reason why they are commonly called "trade remedies" laws—they are supposed to remedy a problem through the imposition of additional duties. Thus, there is no possibility of a criminal action by either the Department of Commerce or the ITC against a foreign exporter that has dumped its goods on the U.S. market or benefitted from a foreign subsidy, nor can a U.S. party sue a foreign exporter in a civil action before a court for violating the antidumping or countervailing duty provisions of the 1930 Tariff Act. That said, a foreign exporter or group of exporters that attempts to monopolize the U.S. market or otherwise engage in trade distorting behavior may run afoul of a different set of laws—U.S. antitrust laws.

CBP collects antidumping and countervailing duties and remits them to the U.S. Treasury like any other customs duty. To do this, CBP will indicate which goods, by HTS classification, from which countries, are subject to additional duties, then assess duties in addition to any normal import duties. It is the importer's responsibility in the first instance to determine whether an antidumping or a countervailing duty applies to its imports, to declare this fact to CBP, to calculate the amount of additional duties owed, to increase its import bond accordingly, and to pay these additional duties.

B. Review

An ADD or CVD order is not permanent. It is designed to counteract unfair competitive practices, and if the importers cease these practices with no intention to resume them later, the duty becomes unnecessary. Therefore, each year, in the anniversary month of the order, importers or their customers have

*Congress did once try to convert the 1930 Tariff Act to a "compensatory" purpose in 2000 through an act known as the "Byrd Amendment." The Byrd Amendment provided for the annual distribution of ADDs and CVDs to "affected domestic producers." An "affected domestic producer" was defined as a petitioner in the ADD or CVD investigation. In 2005, a WTO dispute settlement panel found the Byrd Amendment to violate WTO disciplines, and Congress repealed it in 2006.

Thomas N. Thompson, *Dumping on Trade*, WASHINGTON POST, July 18, 1994, at A19

Americans spend an inordinate amount of time hypocritically proclaiming the virtues of free trade: NAFTA, APEC, GATT, MFN and "market access" are now a big part of our foreign policy vocabulary. The sad reality, however, is that the virtues of free trade are contradicted almost daily with one petty protectionist trade dispute after another.

Trade disputes, in fact, have becomes something of a new Cold War battlefield with Washington, D.C.-based trade attorneys and an assortment of private spies often doing so-called "market research," leading the protectionist charge to ensnare foreigners in the quicksand of U.S. trade law. These disputes don't always make the headlines, but they have become more than run-of-the-mill business news. One of those spies was recently found murdered, face down in a drainage ditch on the outskirts of Seoul.

As a spy for several U.S. law firms until my recent retirement, I traveled throughout Asia, North and South America collecting information on basic industries in otherwise friendly countries. When my research was carefully packaged by trade attorneys and presented to an all-too-receptive U.S. Department of Commerce, more often than not it resulted in punitive import tariffs to protect U.S. manufacturers from foreign competition.

The key to understanding this new phenomenon is protectionism's current weapon of choice: U.S. antidumping law and the investigatory process, or lack of it, at the Department of Commerce. * * * Just how much the penalty tariff might be has mostly to do with how imaginative the petitioning U.S. industry through its attorneys has been in presenting its case to Commerce and how minimally and unobjectively Commerce reviews that petition.

If a foreign exporter fails to respond within 30 days in computer-readable format to a 100-page English-language questionnaire, Commerce Department trade bureaucrats are willing to turn to their well-known, alternative "best information available"—in other words, the petitioning U.S. industry's data and analysis. Too often Commerce's relatively young and inexperienced analysts have meager, if any, accounting/financial background, and their industry expertise is even worse. In a recent antidumping case involving manhole covers from China, one of the Commerce Department's analysts valued foundry sand higher than pig iron!

Not surprisingly, the petitioning U.S. industry often succeeds at portraying the foreign exporter to be particularly villainous—in other words, product cost data, transportation costs or actual export sales are presented in such a way as to suggest to Commerce that the exporter is spending as much as possible to manufacture a product that it is selling at the least cost possible, all of which bolsters the appearance of unfair, and even irreparable, damage done to the U.S. industry. What possible motive a foreign exporter might have to do this is never asked. Nor is the data submitted by a U.S. industry usually questioned.

Yet, the petitioner's analysis doesn't have to be very well substantiated, thanks to the Commerce Department's helpful double standards. The administrative burden simply of furnishing the required information within the required time in the required form to the Department of Commerce has become so overwhelmingly difficult that more and more foreign companies are either unable or unwilling even to try. The fact that companies of the stature of Matsushita, SKF and Toshiba find compliance with the Commerce Department's demands impossible suggests that the unfair trade practices are often Commerce's, not a foreign exporter's. Yet when the foreign exporter does provide manufacturing or financial data to Commerce, it is typically met by an on-site verification visit by a Commerce analyst.

Not so for the petitioning U.S. industry's analysis of its foreign competition. In concocting the worst picture of injury to one U.S. industry after another—with aerial photos, database searches, interviews with domestic competitors and various clandestinely collected information from inside a plant (photos, inventories, invoices and shipping records, for example)—not once was I ever contacted by a Commerce investigator to verify any data I collected. Even if the current environment wasn't so bad for a U.S. industry, its petitions always underscore the at least potential predatory future intentions of various foreign firms.

Criticisms of this unfair and inequitable process falls on deaf ears. The Commerce Department is judge, jury, prosecutor and executioner for dumping allegations. Commerce officials are quick to point out that Congress gives them broad discretion to apply antidumping laws, and it's true. So broad is the Commerce Department's discretion in pursuing anti-dumping charges, that it routinely shuts down U.S. companies importing foreign products targeted by anti-dumping investigations through the application of retroactive duties.

But Commerce's success can also be measured by how often its practices are being copied by other countries that want to limit American exports. In fact, most of the requests I receive these days for "market research" come from overseas for possible assignments here in the United States.

The writer is president of Overseas Trade Corp. in Seattle.

the opportunity to request a review of the order on an importer-by-importer basis. If a review is requested, the ITA and ITC carry out a review similar to its original investigation and issue revised rates for assessment and deposits.

In addition, both the ITA and ITC must automatically conduct **sunset reviews** of outstanding ADD and CVD orders every five years as required by the WTO Agreements. 19 U.S.C. §§ 1675-75c. During these reviews, the agencies must decide whether the revocation of an order would likely lead to continued or recurring dumping or subsidies that would injure a domestic industry. This evaluation proceeds much like the ITA and ITC's initial ADD or CVD determination, although any changes in the domestic industry or in foreign import practices that have occurred since the original order, as well as likely future developments, will be considered. For example, if the domestic industry continues to decline relative to the performance of the economy as a whole in spite of the ADD or CVD order, this may indicate that foreign dumping or subsidies were not the main cause of the injury to the domestic industry.

The sunset review process is public. Interested parties, including the domestic and foreign industries, are invited to submit evidence and observations that may affect the agencies' determinations. The ITC may hold either an expedited or a full review. A full review, unlike an expedited review, often includes a public hearing. If the ITA determines that dumping or subsidies continue, or would likely recur, and if the ITC determines that such dumping or subsidies continue to injure U.S. industry (or is likely to injure a U.S. industry in the future), the agencies will instruct CBP to continue to enforce the ADD or CVD order. If either agency makes a negative determination, however, the ADD or CVD order will be revoked.

Dave Barry, *Clinton Ignores Accordion-Repair Crisis*, MIAMI HERALD, Apr. 4, 1993

In these days of rising taxes, job insecurity and soaring medical costs, more and more Americans are asking themselves a chilling question: "What happens if, God forbid, I have to get my accordion repaired?"

This is certainly on my mind. I own an accordion. I used to own two of them. I bought them years ago at an auction for $25, which worked out to $12.50 per accordion, which struck me as an unbelievable deal. It's hard to describe the look on my wife's face when I brought them home. It reminded me of her reaction to "natural" childbirth.

One of my accordions was destroyed when I made the common consumer mistake of leaving it outdoors for 14 months. But I still have the other one, a Hohner "Student" model. It sits on a filing cabinet in my office, and sometimes, when I'm having trouble thinking up major issues to have opinions about, I amuse myself by causing it to make a scary wailing noise and swoop down at my two dogs, Earnest and Zippy, who jump up violently and bang their heads against the table they sleep under. Earnest and Zippy hate the Hohner "Student." It's an instinctive reaction they have, dating back millions of years, to when their wild dog ancestors often fell prey to larger, hairier prehistoric accordions.

But I like my accordion, although it is not in the best of shape, a fact that has me deeply concerned, in light of an article from *The Winona* (Minn.) *Daily News* sent in by alert reader Mike Jones. This article states that the board of Red Wing/Winona Technical College has voted to eliminate, because of low enrollment, the college's accordion-repair program—which happens to be the only such program in the entire United States.

I can't believe we would let this happen. We're talking about a vital part of our nation's history, dating back to the early 1800s, when each generation would seek to pass the secrets of accordion repair on to the next.

FATHER: Son, it's time for me to pass along the secrets of accordion repair.
SON: I'm moving to Utah.

That's right: Without accordion repair, Westward Expansion might never have occurred. And let's not forget the critical role that an unrepaired accordion played at the Battle of Gettysburg ("Have the accordion player sound the charge!" "He can't, sir! He took a bullet in the bellows during 'Lady of Spain!'" "Good!").

I could go on, but I am clearly lying. This is why, in an unusual effort to include actual facts in this column, I called Red Wing/Winona Technical College and spoke with the accordion-repair instructor, Helmi Harrington. She told me there are "eight or nine million" accordions in the United States, and that accordion repair can be "eminently lucrative." Right now, she said, "there are only a handful of certified accordion technicians," the result being that many accordions are being repaired by unqualified people.

"There are a lot of butchers out there," said Harrington.

I don't know about you, but when I look at the beautiful and innocent young people of today, laughing gaily and tossing their used Slurpee containers on my lawn, it pains me to think that they could grow up in a country where they would be forced to take their broken accordions to some back-alley practitioner.

In an effort to find out what the federal government is doing about this, I called U.S. Sen. Bob "Bob" Graham of Florida, who is—and I mean this as a compliment—the weirdest major politician I have ever met. I first interviewed him back when he was governor of Florida. In an effort to throw him off base, I asked him what I thought was a ridiculous question, demanding to know what he had done, as governor, to promote harmonica safety. Without a moment's hesitation, he delivered a two-minute, well-organized and extremely persuasive speech, featuring statistics, in which he claimed that his predecessor was responsible for most of Florida's harmonica-related deaths.

So I figured Sen. Graham was the man to call about this issue. I had barely got the words "accordion-repair crisis" out of my mouth when he launched into a lengthy, impassioned oration, from which I got the following quotes, which I swear I am not making up:

— "Just last night I ate at an Italian restaurant which, like thousands of other Italian restaurants across America, is now without music, because their accordion is in disrepair and has been returned from Winona, Minn., with postage due."

— "We are preparing an anti-dumping order against Liechtenstein, which has become the center of accordion repair on a global basis and has developed some ferociously anti-competitive practices."

— "I don't know whether the actual use of nuclear weapons is called for, but I do think we need a credible military threat."

(Bear in mind that this man is on the Senate Intelligence Committee.)

So some leaders are aware of the crisis. But so far, the failed Clinton administration has said NOTHING about it, despite proposing MILLIONS for saxophone repair, and despite the fact that accordion repair could provide jobs for thousands of unemployed Americans who have no useful skills, not that I am singling out Dan Quayle. What we need is for ordinary Americans like yourself, but with more spare time, to "get involved." Write to your congressperson. Write to the board of Red Wing/Winona Technical College. Write (what the heck) to your mom. Future generations will thank you. My dogs will hate you.

NOTE FROM THE FIELD

Being an ADD/CVD Trade Remedies Litigator

James B. Altman, Esq.
Foster, Murphy, Altman & Nickel PC

John R. Magnus, Esq.
Tradewins LLC

Trade remedy litigation lies at the intersection of law, trade policy, economics, and accounting. As a rule, the injury side of the case, before the ITC, is heavily economic and involves working closely with industry personnel and economists to provide the needed background and data.

The role of counsel for a petitioner is different from the role of counsel for a respondent. The petitioner is typically a trade industry association or group of companies. Petitioner's counsel may need to help organize and work with a group of clients with varying interests and agendas. The petitioner is responsible for initially providing to the ITC and ITA the data and information on which the request for import relief is based. If the case is initiated, petitioner's counsel turns to analyzing the data provided by the respondents and arguing about its sufficiency and implications.

Respondent's counsel, representing foreign manufacturers, generally will have to cope with differences in language and culture, records and accounting systems, ways of doing business, and expectations about the nature of legal proceedings and trade rules.

Trade remedy cases are fast-paced and intense. Both the ITC and ITA proceedings are subject to procedural rules and deadlines, many imposed by statute. For a respondent, gathering the needed data with sufficient accuracy from companies that do not keep information in the format demanded by the ITA and that may not keep records to U.S. standards can be quite difficult in the limited time available.

Most trade remedy lawyers do not have an extensive accounting or economics background. Most pick up what they need through experience and learn the rest from the expert consultants. A good trade remedy lawyer is a good litigator who can analyze complex factual situations and legal precedent and explain those clearly to the agencies and courts. Trade remedy litigation requires considerable organization and management skills. There are frequent critical deadlines and little margin for error.

Trade remedies cases are fun and interesting, however, because they often arise from trade policy developments that dominate the news and may be critically important to the client. Counsel also gain expertise in diverse industries, products, and manufacturing methods.

James B. Altman is a former president of the ITC Trial Lawyers Association. John R. Magnus is president of Tradewins LLC in Washington, D.C.

3 Safeguard Measures

Suppose a U.S. manufacturer had been competing with foreign imports on the domestic market with reasonable success for many years, but the manufacturer's sales have begun declining while imports are increasing. Suppose further that, after a careful review of foreign practices, the U.S. manufacturer determines that foreign imports are being sold on U.S. and foreign markets at the same low prices, and the exporters of these goods are not receiving any direct or indirect government subsidies, so antidumping or countervailing duty investigations are unlikely to alleviate the problem. After lowering prices as much as possible, the manufacturer still finds itself in dire straits. It tightens production and lays off all nonessential employees, but it continues losing ground in the U.S. market. Is there anything the government can do to help the manufacturer?

If the state wished to keep the manufacturer afloat, the most obvious options would be either direct subsidization or raising import duties. Direct subsidization is in fact often used by states, but there are political limits to their proliferation. Corporate welfare is generally unpopular among the taxpaying public, who may object to being coerced into diverting their income toward support someone else's uncompetitive private company. Even subsidies funded by national debt rather than increased taxes may be politically objectionable, because increases in national debt merely shift the burden of higher taxation onto future generations.

As for increases in import duties, these are, as you know, constrained by the WTO Agreements and other trade treaties. The whole point of these agreements is to foster free competition in international trade rather than state intervention and protectionism. However, the trade treaties do leave one option for shielding the domestic industry from import competition on a temporary basis.

This is known as a **safeguard measure**, and it is designed to give the industry time to adjust to the increased foreign competition. Unlike an ADD or CVD investigation, there is no need for the foreign imports to be anticompetitive or unfair. On the contrary, the reason domestic industries object to the foreign imports is that they have become *too* competitive. The theory behind the safeguard measure is that, if some unpredictable event causes foreign imports to become cheaper, the domestic industry could be mortally wounded by the unforeseen increase in foreign imports before it has time to react, resulting in unemployment and, eventually, harm to consumers, because the erstwhile domestic industry can no longer offer competition to the foreign imports.

For example, suppose a certain kind of computer memory chip sells in the United States for $40 each, regardless of whether it was manufactured in the United States or abroad. In every country, the cost of manufacturing the chip is about $20. One year, the discovery of a new process for making the chips much more cheaply leads manufacturers in Osterlich to invest in massive manufacturing plants, which churn out the chips at $15 each, allowing them to sell at $30. Because no U.S. manufacturer holds a license to this new technology, the U.S. industry cannot compete effectively, and its share of the U.S. market plummets. Soon, U.S. chip manufacturers will have to lay off workers and sell or scrap their manufacturing equipment. Through a safeguard investigation, they may be able to petition the U.S. government to increase import duties on foreign chips to bring the price of imports up to $40 temporarily. This may give the U.S. chip industry time to develop a comparable manufacturing technology or otherwise find some way to lower the price of domestically manufactured chips. The U.S. safeguard measure will decidedly not help the U.S. industry to compete on foreign markets, but if the U.S. market for their goods is sufficiently capacious, increased domestic sales could sustain them during the adjustment period.

Note that the rationale for allowing safeguard measures does not justify a permanent restriction on foreign imports. The argument that unexpected foreign competition imposes on the domestic industry the need for relief while it adjusts to new market conditions can only justify a safeguard for the time required by the domestic industry to adjust. If the domestic industry is simply incapable of adjusting, it is in the interests of competition for it to disappear and for its assets to be redeployed to a different use in which they will be more productive. Similarly, the argument that intense foreign competition will harm consumers in the long run if it drives the domestic competitors from the marketplace is only convincing if the domestic industry eventually contributes effectively to competition.

3.1 International Trade Treaties and Safeguards

A. The WTO Agreements

The GATT, you will recall, requires contracting parties to submit to various trade disciplines, including lowering their import duties on products originating in other WTO member states. Article XIX of the GATT authorizes safeguard measures under specific circumstances. Article XIX is sometimes called the **escape clause**, because it allows treaty parties to escape temporarily from their binding commitments to lower international trade barriers.

Article XIX

Emergency Action on Imports of Particular Products

1. (a) If, as a result of unforeseen developments and of the effect of the obligations incurred by a contracting party under this Agreement, including tariff concessions, any product is being imported into the territory of that contracting party in such increased quantities and under such conditions as to cause or threaten serious injury to domestic

producers in that territory of like or directly competitive products, the contracting party shall be free, in respect of such product, and to the extent and for such time as may be necessary to prevent or remedy such injury, to suspend the obligation in whole or in part or to withdraw or modify the concession. * * *

2. Before any contracting party shall take action pursuant to the provisions of paragraph 1 of this Article, it shall give notice in writing to the CONTRACTING PARTIES as far in advance as may be practicable and shall afford the CONTRACTING PARTIES and those contracting parties having a substantial interest as exporters of the product concerned an opportunity to consult with it in respect of the proposed action. * * * In critical circumstances, where delay would cause damage which it would be difficult to repair, action under paragraph 1 of this Article may be taken provisionally without prior consultation, on the condition that consultation shall be effected immediately after taking such action.

3. (a) If agreement among the interested contracting parties with respect to the action is not reached, the contracting party which proposes to take or continue the action shall, nevertheless, be free to do so, and if such action is taken or continued, the affected contracting parties shall then be free * * * to suspend * * * the application to the trade of the contracting party taking such action, or, in the case envisaged in paragraph 1(b) of this Article, to the trade of the contracting party requesting such action, of such substantially equivalent concessions or other obligations under this Agreement the suspension of which the CONTRACTING PARTIES do not disapprove.

(b) Notwithstanding the provisions of subparagraph (a) of this paragraph, where action is taken under paragraph 2 of this Article without prior consultation and causes or threatens serious injury in the territory of a contracting party to the domestic producers of products affected by the action, that contracting party shall, where delay would cause damage difficult to repair, be free to suspend, upon the taking of the action and throughout the period of consultation, such concessions or other obligations as may be necessary to prevent or remedy the injury.

Observe that article XIX imposes important conditions on the withdrawal of a trade concession:

(1) new market conditions must cause a quantitative increase in imports;
(2) these developments must have been "unforeseen";
(3) the increase in import quantities must "cause or threaten serious injury" to the domestic industry;
(4) the safeguard may be imposed only "to the extent and for such time as may be necessary to prevent or remedy such injury"; and
(5) before imposing the safeguard, the GATT party must first notify any other parties whose exports may be affected by the withdrawal of trade concessions to allow an opportunity to negotiate a resolution, unless the delay caused by the prior notification would cause damage to the domestic industry that would be "difficult to repair."

In addition, there is an important consequence of a WTO member imposing a safeguard measure. Under article XIX(3), whenever a WTO member employs a safeguard measure, all WTO members that export the restricted goods to that WTO member are justified in withdrawing equivalent concessions from the WTO member imposing the safeguard. In other words, the use of a safeguard by any WTO member may result in a tit-for-tat withdrawal of trade concessions.

The WTO Agreements adopted in 1994 include additional restrictions on the use of safeguard measures through the **WTO Agreement on Safeguards**. Its most important provisions are the following:

- Article 2(2): When a WTO member imposes a safeguard measure, it must do so regardless of the source of the imports, so that all imports will be affected rather than those from any one state or group of states.
- Article 3(1): A safeguard measure may only be imposed following public notice and a public hearing in which importers and exporters may present their views.
- Article 5: If safeguard measures include a quantitative restriction such as absolute maximum import quotas, the quantitative limit generally may not be less than the typical number of annual imports of the merchandise in recent years before the unforeseen increase in imports.
- Article 7: Safeguards may not be imposed for a period exceeding four years, unless the state authority finds that the domestic industry is successfully adjusting to the new market conditions and an extension is necessary. In that case, the safeguards may last no longer than a total of eight years. In any case, if the safeguard lasts more than one year, import restrictions must progressively relax. Moreover, if safeguards on a product are removed, they may not be reapplied to that product within 2 years or the period of time during which the safeguards were previously in place, whichever is longer.
- Article 8: WTO members imposing safeguards must try to negotiate with affected WTO members to offset the trade-limiting effects of the safeguard by granting additional trade concessions with respect to other imports. If no agreement can be reached, then other WTO members may suspend some of their own trade concessions to the member imposing the safeguard measure after the third year during which the safeguard measure has continued in force.
- Article 9: WTO members may not impose safeguard measures against a developing country unless the developing country's imports make up a nontrivial share (generally, more than 3%) of the imports at issue.
- Article 11: WTO members are forbidden to use the escape clause to seek or agree to a **voluntary export restraint (VER)**, which is an agreement between the importing and exporting states to limit the quantity of exports of a certain article to the importing state.

VERs were in common usage before 1994, when some countries—the United States especially—used them to negotiate limits to foreign competition from states like Japan that had a high volume of exports but maintained formal or informal limitations on imports. An exporting country would typically agree to negotiate a VER to convince the importing state not to impose harsher, unilateral measures. To ensure that VERs are not used to bypass the limitations set forth in GATT Article XIX and the Agreement on Safeguards, VERs are no longer permitted.

Safeguard measures were never intended to be common trade remedies. According to a panel of the WTO dispute settlement body, safeguard measures "constitute an *extrema ratio*, applicable only when positive demonstration by the applying Member is given as to the unsuitability of the other tariff-based measures (tariff increases or tariff-rate quotas)." *United States—Definitive Safeguard Measures on Imports of Wheat Gluten from the EC*, WTO Doc. WT/DS166/R, at 155, 190 (July 31, 2000). Nonetheless, safeguard measures are fairly common in international practice.

B. Bilateral and Regional Free Trade Agreements

In addition to Article XIX of the GATT and the WTO Agreement on Safeguards, safeguard measures are permitted in some bilateral and regional trade treaties. The USMCA incorporates treaty provisions on the use of safeguards in Chapter 10. This chapter includes special restrictions similar to those in the WTO Agreements. USMCA does not prohibit the imposition of global safeguard measures, but it does provide that any such measure must exclude imports from other USMCA members unless imports from a USMCA member "considered individually, account for a substantial share of the total imports" of the product at issue and that such imports, again "considered individually," "contribute importantly to the serious injury, or threat thereof, caused by the imports." USMCA art. 10.2. USMCA also includes standards for evaluating what constitutes a "substantial share" of imports and what might "contribute importantly" to a serious injury. Chapter 10 also includes procedural standards

WHO IMPOSES SAFEGUARD MEASURES ON WHICH IMPORTS?

The WTO members reporting the most active in using safeguard measures from 1995 to 2017 are India, Indonesia, Turkey, Chile, and Jordan. The imports most frequently subjected to safeguard measures are those especially important to the national economies of the imposing state—chemicals, agricultural products and foodstuffs, and metals (especially steel). Safeguard measures are almost never imposed on manufactured goods, because specific manufactured products rarely make up a significant portion of any state's national income.

specifying how an emergency action may be initiated and conducted.

The United States has adhered to other free trade agreements with many states. These bilateral free trade agreements (FTAs) may also contain provisions requiring either party to exempt imports of the other party from safeguard measures except when conditions similar to USMCA Article 10.2 are met. In the *United States—Safeguard Measures on Wheat Gluten* case discussed earlier, the Appellate Body held that exempting FTA partners (including NAFTA member states) from the scope of safeguard measures was inconsistent with the GATT. WTO Doc. WT/DS166/AB/R, ¶¶ 95-96 (Dec. 22, 2000). Provisions such as USMCA Article 10.2 are, therefore, inoperative under international law.

3.2 Safeguard Measures in the United States

The United States has long included escape clauses in its trade agreements with other states. Even before the GATT, the United States had negotiated treaties of friendship, commerce, and navigation with major trading partners, and these typically included some provision allowing derogation from each party's commitments to reduce import duties from the other whenever "unforeseen developments" caused imports to increase to the point of causing or threatening to cause serious injury to the domestic industry. Because these treaties lacked any formal mechanism for evaluating claims of import injury, however, their use rested entirely in the discretion of a very busy President, and they were rarely invoked.

In 1947, President Truman tried to remedy this problem by delegating to an independent federal Tariff Commission (a predecessor of the modern U.S. International Trade Commission) the task of evaluating claims of injuries caused by import surges and recommending remedies to the President. Exec. Order No. 10004, 3 C.F.R. § 819 (1943-48 compilation). That same year, the United States and its trading partners concluded the first GATT, which included the article XIX escape clause.

In the ensuing years, the U.S. treatment of escape clause measures became increasingly sophisticated and in some ways complex and confused. In 1974, Congress finally undertook major trade law reform on the recommendation of President Nixon, and the resulting law, with minor amendments, still largely governs safeguard measures today.

In effect, the standards for obtaining escape clause relief were relaxed, and the procedures for investigating complaints of import surges have been formalized and regularized through the **Section 201 investigation**. The term "Section 201" is shorthand for sections 201 through 204 of the Trade Act of 1974, codified at 19 U.S.C. §§ 2251-54. Actually, the most important provision is Section 202 (19 U.S.C. § 2252), but the term "Section201" has become idiomatic. Using Section 201, a U.S. company, trade association, or union may petition the by-now-familiar U.S. ITC to initiate an investigation to determine whether certain imports threaten to be, or actually are, a substantial cause of serious injury to a domestic industry.

A Section 201 investigation is usually commenced through a petition filed by a U.S. business firm, trade association, or trade union.* When a U.S. business firm or trade association initiates the investigation, it typically collects thorough data on the domestic supply and consumption of the imported product and on the rate of importation over the past five years. Much of this data can be obtained from the U.S. Department of Commerce, although private companies specializing in market analysis may also provide useful information. If the data show either an absolute decline in domestic sales or a decline relative to market growth, the company or association may file a petition for relief under Section 201.

The ITC Rules of Practice and Procedure require that the petition contain the following pertinent information:

(1) descriptions of the imported product and the domestically produced product;
(2) the names and locations of the domestic firms represented in the petition and the manufacturing facility, mill, farm, mine, or other place in which the domestic product is produced;
(3) the names of all domestic producers of the product known to the petitioner;
(4) the respective volumes of domestic production and of imports of the product for each of the last five years;
(5) any quantitative data that demonstrates injury to the domestic injury;
(6) any evidence that the domestic injury was caused by the imports;
(7) a description of the import relief sought by the petitioner;
(8) a description of the efforts that domestic business firms and labor have made to compete with the imports; and
(9) any "critical circumstances" that would justify taking expedited action to prevent a serious injury to the domestic producers.

19 C.F.R. § 206.14.

The ITC will consider the data presented in the petition or, if the industry cannot afford to gather the data for the investigation, the Commission may conduct a factfinding investigation of its own—called a **Section 332 investigation**. 19 U.S.C. § 1332.

In either case, if the Commission determines that a certain class of goods is being imported in such increased quantities that a U.S. industry is in fact

*A petition for investigation may also be made by Congress, the President, or the U.S. Trade Representative. Alternatively, the ITC may initiate an investigation *sua sponte*. The great majority of petitions are brought by private companies and industry representatives, however.

injured or threatened with injury, it will recommend to the President some remedy—a safeguard measure, such as the imposition of additional duties to make the imports more expensive or a quantitative restriction to diminish the effect the imports will have on the U.S. industry. Section 201 requires the ITC to do this fairly quickly—within 4 to 5 months of having received the petition, depending on the complexity of the case.

A. Statutory Requirements

The best way to understand safeguard measures in U.S. practice is to review the relevant provisions of the 1974 Trade Act:

---

§ 2251. Action to facilitate positive adjustment to import competition.

(a) Presidential action
If the United States International Trade Commission (hereinafter referred to in this part as the "Commission") determines under section 2252(b) of this title that an article is being imported into the United States in such increased quantities as to be a substantial cause of serious injury, or the threat thereof, to the domestic industry producing an article like or directly competitive with the imported article, the President, in accordance with this part, shall take all appropriate and feasible action within his power which the President determines will facilitate efforts by the domestic industry to make a positive adjustment to import competition and provide greater economic and social benefits than costs. * * *

§ 2252. Investigations, determinations, & recommendations by Commission.

(a) Petitions and adjustment plans

(1) A petition requesting action under this part for the purpose of facilitating positive adjustment to import competition may be filed with the Commission by an entity, including a trade association, firm, certified or recognized union, or group of workers, which is representative of an industry.

(2) A petition under paragraph (1)—

(A) shall include a statement describing the specific purposes for which action is being sought, which may include facilitating the orderly transfer of resources to more productive pursuits, enhancing competitiveness, or other means of adjustment to new conditions of competition; and

(B) may [request provisional relief].

(3) Whenever a petition is filed under paragraph (1), the Commission shall promptly transmit copies of the petition to the Office of the United States Trade Representative and other Federal agencies directly concerned.

(4) A petitioner under paragraph (1) may submit to the Commission and the United States Trade Representative (hereafter in this part referred to as the "Trade Representative"), either with the petition, or at any time within 120 days after the date of filing of the petition, a plan to facilitate positive adjustment to import competition.

* * *

(6) (A) In the course of any investigation under subsection (b) of this section, the Commission shall seek information (on a confidential basis, to the extent appropriate) on actions being taken, or planned to be taken, or both, by firms and workers in the industry to make a positive adjustment to import competition. * * *

(b) Investigations and determinations by Commission

(1) (A) Upon the filing of a petition under subsection (a) of this section, the request of the President or the Trade Representative, the resolution of either the Committee on Ways and Means of the House of Representatives or the Committee on Finance of the Senate, or on its own motion, the Commission shall promptly make an investigation to determine whether an article is being imported into the United States in such increased quantities as to be a substantial cause of serious injury, or the threat thereof, to the domestic industry producing an article like or directly competitive with the imported article.

(B) For purposes of this section, the term "substantial cause" means a cause which is important and not less than any other cause. * * *

(c) Factors applied in making determinations

(1) In making determinations under subsection (b) of this section, the Commission shall take into account all economic factors which it considers relevant, including (but not limited to)—

(A) with respect to serious injury—

(i) the significant idling of productive facilities in the domestic industry,

(ii) the inability of a significant number of firms to carry out domestic production operations at a reasonable level of profit, and

(iii) significant unemployment or underemployment within the domestic industry;

(B) with respect to threat of serious injury—

(i) a decline in sales or market share, a higher and growing inventory (whether maintained by domestic producers, importers, wholesalers, or retailers), and a downward trend in production, profits, wages, productivity, or employment (or increasing underemployment) in the domestic industry,

(ii) the extent to which firms in the domestic industry are unable to generate adequate capital to finance the modernization of their domestic plants and equipment, or are unable to maintain existing levels of expenditures for research and development,

(iii) the extent to which the United States market is the focal point for the diversion of exports of the article concerned by reason of restraints on exports of such article to, or on imports of such article into, third country markets; and

(C) with respect to substantial cause, an increase in imports (either actual or relative to domestic production) and a decline in the proportion of the domestic market supplied by domestic producers.

(2) In making determinations under subsection (b) of this section, the Commission shall—

(A) consider the condition of the domestic industry over the course of the relevant business cycle, but may not aggregate the causes of declining demand associated with a recession or economic downturn in the United States economy into a single cause of serious injury or threat of injury; and

(B) examine factors other than imports which may be a cause of serious injury, or threat of serious injury, to the domestic industry. * * *

(6) For purposes of this section:

(A) (i) The term "domestic industry" means, with respect to an article, the producers as a whole of the like or directly competitive article or those producers whose collective production of the like or directly competitive article constitutes a major proportion of the total domestic production of such article. * * *

(B) The term "significant idling of productive facilities" includes the closing of plants or the underutilization of production capacity.

(C) The term "serious injury" means a significant overall impairment in the position of a domestic industry.

(D) The term "threat of serious injury" means serious injury that is clearly imminent.

(d) Provisional relief

[Note: This subsection provides for provisional relief lasting up to two years for domestic producers of perishable agricultural products, such as fruits, vegetables, and grains injured or threatened by an increase in foreign imports.] * * *

(e) Commission recommendations

(1) If the Commission makes an affirmative determination * * *, the Commission shall also recommend the action that would address the serious injury, or threat thereof, to the domestic industry and be most effective in facilitating the efforts of the domestic industry to make a positive adjustment to import competition.

(2) The Commission is authorized to recommend under paragraph (1)—

(A) an increase in, or the imposition of, any duty on the imported article;

(B) a tariff-rate quota on the article;

(C) a modification or imposition of any quantitative restriction on the importation of the article into the United States;

(D) one or more appropriate adjustment measures, including the provision of trade adjustment assistance under part 2 of this subchapter; or

(E) any combination of the actions described in subparagraphs (A) through (D).

(3) The Commission shall specify the type, amount, and duration of the action recommended by it under paragraph (1). The limitations set forth in section 2253(e) of this title are applicable to the action recommended by the Commission. * * *

(5) For purposes of making its recommendation under this subsection, the Commission shall—

(A) after reasonable notice, hold a public hearing at which all interested parties shall be provided an opportunity to present testimony and evidence; * * *.

(f) Report by Commission

(1) The Commission shall submit to the President a report on each investigation undertaken under subsection (b) of this section * * *. * * *

(3) The Commission, after submitting a report to the President under paragraph (1), shall promptly make it available to the public (with the exception of the confidential information obtained under subsection (a)(6)(B) of this section and any

other information which the Commission determines to be confidential) and cause a summary thereof to be published in the *Federal Register*.

§ 2253. Action by President after determination of import injury.

(a) In general

(1) (A) After receiving a report under section 2252(f) of this title containing an affirmative finding regarding serious injury, or the threat thereof, to a domestic industry, the President shall take all appropriate and feasible action within his power which the President determines will facilitate efforts by the domestic industry to make a positive adjustment to import competition and provide greater economic and social benefits than costs. * * *

(3) The President may, for purposes of taking action under paragraph (1)—

(A) proclaim an increase in, or the imposition of, any duty on the imported article;

(B) proclaim a tariff-rate quota on the article;

(C) proclaim a modification or imposition of any quantitative restriction on the importation of the article into the United States;

(D) implement one or more appropriate adjustment measures, including the provision of trade adjustment assistance under part 2 of this subchapter;

(E) negotiate, conclude, and carry out agreements with foreign countries limiting the export from foreign countries and the import into the United States of such article;

(F) proclaim procedures necessary to allocate among importers by the auction of import licenses quantities of the article that are permitted to be imported into the United States;

(G) initiate international negotiations to address the underlying cause of the increase in imports of the article or otherwise to alleviate the injury or threat thereof;

(H) submit to Congress legislative proposals to facilitate the efforts of the domestic industry to make a positive adjustment to import competition;

(I) take any other action which may be taken by the President under the authority of law and which the President considers appropriate and feasible for purposes of paragraph (1); and

(J) take any combination of actions listed in subparagraphs (A) through (I). * * *

(e) Limitations on actions

(1) (A) Subject to subparagraph (B), the duration of the period in which an action taken under this section may be in effect shall not exceed 4 years. Such period shall include the period, if any, in which provisional relief under section 2252(d) of this title was in effect.

(B) (i) Subject to clause (ii), the President, after receiving an affirmative determination from the Commission under section 2254(c) of this title * * *, may extend the effective period of any action under this section if the President determines that—

(I) the action continues to be necessary to prevent or remedy the serious injury; and

(II) there is evidence that the domestic industry is making a positive adjustment to import competition.

(ii) The effective period of any action under this section, including any extensions thereof, may not, in the aggregate, exceed 8 years.

(2) Action of a type described in subsection (a)(3)(A), (B), or (C) of this section may be taken * * * only to the extent the cumulative impact of such action does not exceed the amount necessary to prevent or remedy the serious injury.

(3) No action may be taken under this section which would increase a rate of duty to (or impose a rate) which is more than 50 percent *ad valorem* above the rate (if any) existing at the time the action is taken.

(4) Any action taken under this section proclaiming a quantitative restriction shall permit the importation of a quantity or value of the article which is not less than the average quantity or value of such article entered into the United States in the most recent 3 years that are representative of imports of such article and for which data are available, unless the President finds that the importation of a different quantity or value is clearly justified in order to prevent or remedy the serious injury.

To summarize, for a U.S. petitioner to obtain the ITC's recommendation for Section 201 import relief, the ITC's investigation must result in three findings:

(1) As in an antidumping duty (ADD) or countervailing duty (CVD) investigation, a "domestic industry" for the goods must exist. Also like an ADD or CVD investigation, the domestic industry is defined as the "producers as a whole of the like or directly competitive article." Section 201 provides that the petitioner must account for a "major proportion" of the domestic production of the goods, which term the ITC has generally interpreted as consistent with ADD and CVD standards of 25% or more of the industry.

(2) The industry is suffering from or threatened with "serious injury," meaning a significant overall impairment in the economic position of a domestic industry, as evidenced by an increase in foreign imports relative to domestic sales, the existence of unused domestic productive capacity, an increase in unemployment in the industry, and similar factors.

(3) Such injury is "substantially" caused by the increase in identified foreign imports. A "substantial cause" is defined as "a cause which is important and not less than any other cause." According to the legislative history, this establishes a two-part test: "increased imports must constitute an important cause and be no less important than any other single cause." S. Rep. No. 93-1298, at 7264 (1974).

The ITC's safeguard investigation regulations are set forth in 19 C.F.R. pt. 206, but its interpretation of Section 202 of the 1974 Trade Act is better developed in the ITC's decisions. As noted, the Commission's interpretation of "domestic industry" mirrors that of the ADD and CVD provisions of the 1930 Tariff Act. Similarly, the standard of serious injury runs parallel to the ADD and CVD standard. The causation standard has developed its own jurisprudence, however.

In *Certain Motor Vehicles*, Inv. No. TA-201-44 (Dec. 1980), USITC Pub. 1110, the ITC noted that Congress had revised the Section 202 causation standard to clarify that the imports need not account for more than 50% of the injury to the domestic injury; on the other hand, if other causes account for the injury better than do the imports, the imports should not be considered a substantial cause of the injury. On the fact before it in *Certain Motor Vehicles*, the Commission found that some 80% of the cause of declining U.S. auto sales was attributable to such factors as a general economic recession and other factors, and only 20% of the injury was attributable to the imports themselves. Such a cause was not considered "substantial" within the meaning of Section 202.

B. Remedies

Upon an affirmative determination, the ITC will recommend a remedy to the President, who can choose to adopt, modify, or reject the remedy. The ITC's options for recommended relief are listed in Section 203 of the 1974 Trade Act. The options generally include one or more of the following measures:

(1) increasing import duties on the subject merchandise;
(2) imposing a tariff-rate quota on the subject merchandise (explained below);
(3) imposing or increasing a quantitative restriction on the imports; or
(4) trade adjustment assistance (explained below) or some other form of adjustment measure.

As you will recall, a **tariff-rate quota** (**TRQ**) is a kind of combination of a quantitative restriction and increased customs duties. Under a TRQ, some quantity of foreign imports of the subject merchandise may enter either duty-free or at the normal rate of duty. Amounts imported above the fixed quantity will be subjected to a higher rate of duty. There may be more than two tiers to a TRQ, and the highest tier may include a lofty import duty. For example, a two-tiered TRQ on imported widgets might look something like this:

Quantity of Widgets Imported	Tariff Rate
≤ 150,000 widgets	12% *ad valorem*
> 150,000 widgets	20% *ad valorem*

A combination TRQ and quantitative restriction (numerical quota) prohibits imports beyond a maximum, such as the following:

Quantity of Widgets Imported	Tariff Rate
≤ 150,000 widgets	12% *ad valorem*
150,001 to 300,000 widgets	20% *ad valorem*
> 300,000 widgets	imports prohibited

The reference in Section 203 to "appropriate adjustment measures" refers to trade adjustment assistance, which usually takes the form of financial assistance given by the government to workers in companies in the industry affected by the imports. Subsidies given to companies under Section 203 may be used to adjust to increased competition or transition to a new industry. Aid given to workers may be used for supporting them during temporary unemployment, providing them with training in new careers, paying for relocation to places with more job opportunities, and related expenses. Trade adjustment assistance is further discussed below.

As noted, the President need not act on the ITC's recommendations. He or she can choose to take no action or to take a different course of action to the extent permitted by 19 U.S.C. § 2253(a)(3) and subject to the limitations of § 2253(e). In short, the President has additional options for protecting the domestic industry and helping it adjust to changing market conditions. The President may also determine that, notwithstanding the ITC's recommendation, no remedy is warranted.

Whatever remedy the President grants, there are limitations on its scope and duration. No remedy may last longer than eight years, and no increase in customs duties may exceed 50% *ad valorem* more than the customs rate prior to the safeguard action. For example, suppose that in 2017, the normal (MFN) duty rate on widgets for WTO members is 14% *ad valorem*. If, in 2020, the President were to authorize an increase in customs duties on widgets as a safeguard measure under Section 201 procedures, the duty rate could rise to no higher than 64% *ad valorem* (= 14% + 50%). Of course, if the President wished to restrict imports more severely, he may still impose a quantitative restriction.

However, Section 201 also limits the President's ability to restrict trade through numerical quotas. Specifically, it provides that the President may not set quantitative restrictions lower than the amount of imports prior to the surge that triggered the safeguard investigation, assuming that the surging imports are of the same kind as previous imports. For example, if from 2015 through 2017, the average quantity of widgets imported into the United States was 350,000 per year, and a surge in imports occurred in 2018, the President is not authorized to impose a safeguard measure limiting imports to quantities less than 350,000 annually.

Finally, as required by WTO disciplines, all safeguard measures of whatever kind must be gradually phased out beginning three years after their initial imposition. Continuing the example above, suppose that, in 2018, in response to a surge of imports to two million in 2017, the President imposed a quantitative restriction of 350,000 annual imports of widgets. In 2021, the President must begin relaxing the quantitative restriction on an annual basis. For example, he might raise the quantitative restriction in 2021 to 450,000 widgets, and again in 2022 to 550,000 widgets, until the restriction disappears altogether within eight years after the initial safeguard measure (which would, in this example, occur in 2023).

To give you a sense of what the affirmative result of a safeguard action looks like, consider the following extract from the President's proclamation of a safeguard for steel bar, slab, plate, sheet, and wire.

The White House
President George W. Bush
March 5, 2002

STEEL PRODUCTS PROCLAMATION

To Facilitate Positive Adjustment to Competition From Imports of Certain Steel Products by the President of the United States of America, a Proclamation

1. On December 19, 2001, the [ITC] transmitted to the President a report on its investigation under Section 202 of the Trade Act of 1974, as amended (the "Trade Act") (19 U.S.C. 2252), with respect to certain steel product.

2. The ITC reached affirmative determinations under section 202(b) of the Trade Act that the following products are being imported into the United States in such increased quantities as to be a substantial cause of serious injury, or threat of serious injury, to the domestic industries producing like or directly competitive articles: (a) certain carbon flat-rolled steel, including carbon and alloy steel slabs ("slabs"); plate (including cut-to-length plate and clad plate) ("plate"); hot-rolled steel (including plate in coils) ("hot-rolled steel"); [etc.] * * * The ITC commissioners were equally divided with respect to the determination required under section 202(b) regarding whether (i) carbon and alloy tin mill products ("tin mill products") and (j) stainless steel wire. * * *

4. Section 330(d)(1) of the Tariff Act of 1930, as amended (19 U.S.C. 1330(d)(1)), provides that, when the ITC is required to determine under section 202(b) of the Trade Act whether increased imports of an article are a substantial cause of serious injury, or the threat thereof, and the commissioners voting are equally divided with respect to such determination, then the determination agreed upon by either group of commissioners may be considered by the President as the determination of the ITC. Having considered the determinations of the commissioners with regard to tin mill products and stainless steel wire, I have decided to consider the determinations of the groups of commissioners voting in the affirmative with regard to each of these products to be the determination of the ITC.
* * *

6. The ITC commissioners voting in the affirmative under section 202(b) of the Trade Act also transmitted to the President their recommendations made pursuant to section

202(e) of the Trade Act (19 U.S.C. 2252(e)) with respect to the actions that, in their view, would address the serious injury, or threat thereof, to the domestic industries and be most effective in facilitating the efforts of those industries to make a positive adjustment to import competition.

7. Pursuant to section 203 of the Trade Act (19 U.S.C. 2253) * * *, I have determined to implement action of a type described in section 203(a)(3) (a "safeguard measure") with regard to the following steel products:

(a) certain flat steel, consisting of: slab provided for in the superior text to subheadings 9903.72.30 through 9903.72.48 in the Annex to this proclamation; [etc.];
(b) hot-rolled bar provided for tin the superior text to subheadings 9903.73.28 through 9903.73.38 in the Annex to this proclamation;
(c) cold-finished bar * * * ;
(d) rebar * * * ; [etc.]
* * *

9. Pursuant to section 203 of the Trade Act (19 U.S.C. 2253), the actions I have determined to take shall be safeguard measures in the form of:

(a) a tariff quota on imports of slabs described in paragraph 7, imposed for a period of 3 years plus 1 day, with annual increases in the within-quota quantities and annual reductions in the rates of duty applicable to goods entered in excess of those quantities in the second and third years; and

(b) an increase in duties on imports of certain flat steel, other than slabs (including plate, hot-rolled steel, cold-rolled steel and coated steel), hot-rolled bar, cold-finished bar, [etc.], as described in paragraph 7, imposed for a period of 3 years plus 1 day, with annual reductions in the rates of duty in the second and third years, as provided in the Annex to this proclamation. * * *

11. These safeguard measures shall apply to imports from all countries, except for products of Canada, Israel, Jordan, and Mexico. * * *

14. Pursuant to section 203(a)(1)(A) of the Trade Action (19 U.S.C. 2253(a)(1)(A)), I have further determined that these safeguard measures will facilitate efforts by the domestic industry to make a positive adjustment to import competition and provide greater economic and social benefits than costs. If I determine that further action is appropriate and feasible to facilitate efforts by the pertinent domestic industry to make a positive adjustment to import competition and to provide greater economic and social benefits than costs * * * I shall reduce, modify, or terminate the action established in this proclamation accordingly. In addition, if I determine within 30 days of the date of this proclamation, as a result of consultations between the United States and other WTO members pursuant to Article 12.3 of the WTO Agreement on Safeguards that it is necessary to reduce, modify, or terminate a safeguard measure, I shall proclaim the corresponding reduction, modification, or termination of the safeguard measures within 40 days. * * *

Notes and Questions

1. In the steel products safeguard measure referenced above, the commissioners of the ITC were evenly split on the question of whether a few of the steel products should be included in the safeguard measure. In such cases, section 330 of the 1930 Tariff Act gives the President the choice of adopting either the affirmative or negative view. In this case, he adopted the affirmative and included all of the steel products subject to investigation in the safeguard measure. He did not, however, decide to adopt the commissioners' affirmative findings with respect to certain steel products imported from Canada and Mexico. This means that the TRQs and increased duties imposed on imported steel products under the proclamation will not apply to steel products originating in Canada or Mexico, as paragraph 11 states explicitly. Also in paragraph 11, the President has made clear that steel imports from Israel and Jordan would not be subject to the tariff increase or quotas. Why? Because, by 2002, the United States had bilateral free trade agreements with Israel and Jordan that discourage such safeguards. However, remember that exemptions like those in paragraph 11 have been ruled GATT-illegal by the WTO Appellate Body.

2. Notice also how, in paragraph 7 of the proclamation, the President has listed the items subject to the safeguard by their Harmonized Tariff System nomenclature (see Chapter 5). This is a convenient way to specify precisely which products are included in, and excluded from, the safeguard measure.

3. You may wonder why the ITC would recommend, and the President would adopt, a TRQ on steel slab, but only an increase in customs duties on other steel products such as wire and bars. The short answer is that TRQs afford more customized, and therefore often greater, protection to the domestic industry than increased customs duties. Increased duties decrease the quantity of imports by making it more expensive to import relative to manufacturing domestically. But the government cannot foresee exactly how foreign importers will cope with increased duties. They may find a way to cut costs and continue to import in only slightly decreased quantities, thereby undermining the protective effect of the tariff hike. TRQs impose a multilevel system of duties, so that the government can impose customs duties so high after a designated quantity of the goods has been imported that foreign manufacturers realistically cannot hope to sell their goods on the local market beyond that quantity.

4. Consider why the President ordered annual increases in the quota amount of imported steel slabs and decreases in the tariff rates of slabs and other steel products in paragraph 9. This means that every year more foreign steel slabs can be imported at the lowest duty rates, and the duty rate for non-slab imports will be lower every year as well.

The proclamation was not the end of the steel products saga. Like all U.S. Section 201 safeguards since 1994, this one was found inconsistent with the World Trade Organization (WTO) agreements by a WTO dispute settlement panel. The following article excerpt explains how the WTO dealt with this safeguard measure:

Eliza Patterson, *WTO Rules Against US Safeguard Measures on Steel*, ASIL INSIGHTS, Nov. 2003

* * * On June 3, 2002, a WTO dispute settlement panel was established at the request of the European Communities to examine the consistency of the US safeguard measures with WTO rules. Complaints on the same matter by Japan, Korea, China, Norway, Switzerland, New Zealand and Brazil were subsequently submitted to the same Panel.

The Agreement on Safeguards and Article XIX of GATT 1994 provide that a WTO member may apply safeguard measures only if, following an investigation by competent authorities, it determines that imports have increased, that the increase was a result of unforeseen developments and that the increased imports have caused, or threatened to cause, its domestic industry to suffer serious injury. The Agreement further provides that the competent authorities must issue a "report setting forth their findings and reasoned conclusions reached on all pertinent issues of fact and law."

The Panel concluded that all ten US safeguard measures were inconsistent with the Agreement on Safeguards and the GATT 1994. Specifically, the Panel found that the US had failed to "provide a reasoned and adequate explanation of their conclusion" (1) that imports had increased; (2) that a causal link existed between the increased imports and serious injury to the domestic industry; and (3) that the increased imports had resulted from "unforeseen developments." The Panel recommended that the Dispute Settlement Body request that the US bring all the safeguard measures into conformity with its WTO obligations.

On August 14, 2003, the US appealed the Panel ruling.

The Appellate Body's ruling on November 10 largely upheld the initial Panel's conclusions, specifically its focus on the inadequacy of the US explanation of how the facts supported the conclusion that each of the elements of a safeguard case had been met. It is noteworthy that the WTO violation resulted from the inadequacy of explanation and not from a fault in US law. The Appellate Body emphasized throughout its report that safeguard measures were considered extraordinary measures and that consequently WTO members had an obligation to clearly set forth the rationale for their determinations.

On the question of increased imports, the Appellate Body ruled that the USITC failed to provide a reasoned and adequate explanation of how the facts supported its determination that the increase in imports had been recent enough, sudden enough, sharp enough and significant enough to cause serious injury.

On the issue of "unforeseen developments," the Appellate Body similarly concluded that the USITC report was wanting in reasoning. The USITC had found that the Asian and Russian financial crisis, together with the strong US dollar and economy, were the cause of the increased imports and that those economic developments were "unforeseen." The Appellate Body did not question the existence of those developments or the claim that they were unforeseen. Neither did it question that the developments might have caused the import surge. Rather, it ruled that USITC had failed to provide a logical explanation of how such causation actually occurred. * * *

As a result of the WTO Appellate Body report, President Bush revoked the proclamation and its safeguard measures on December 4, 2003. However, because WTO decisions award damages that apply prospectively only, and never retrospectively, the President effectively transferred millions of dollars from U.S. consumers to the U.S. steel industry over the course of eighteen months. From the U.S. steel industry's perspective, the U.S. safeguard measure was worthwhile despite the WTO's ultimate rejection of the measure.

C. Trade Adjustment Assistance

Theoretically, there are several kinds of **trade adjustment assistance** that the **U.S. Trade Representative** (**USTR**) may propose to assist U.S. industries and companies adversely affected by foreign competition. One possibility is temporary direct subsidies (e.g., cash grants). More commonly, the USTR has proposed tax reductions or rebates to affected industries.

In addition to assistance given directly to the companies themselves, the USTR can rely on a scheme implemented by the U.S. Congress to assist workers laid off or otherwise displaced from their jobs by import competition. This scheme is found in the 1974 Trade Act, as amended by the Trade Adjustment Assistance Reform Act of 2002, Pub. L. 107-210 (2002), 116 Stat. 933, and several other acts. Upon a petition by a group of three or more U.S. workers to the U.S. Department of Labor, the Department may grant training or reemployment assistance, job search allowances, relocation funds, income support, and tax credits for health insurance premiums to the workers if it is satisfied that they have suffered job loss due to import competition. Specifically, the Department must be satisfied that:

(1) workers have been laid off or work hours have been reduced from full time to part time, and
(2) industry sales or productions have declined, and
(3) increased imports have contributed "importantly" to worker layoffs.

Negative determinations by the Department may be appealed either to the Secretary of Labor for reconsideration or to the U.S. Court of International Trade.

The most common benefit offered is training (or tuition assistance for training) to transition into a new industry. The program is increasingly offering assistance with new job placement as well. When the worker must move to a new geographic location to pursue employment, such costs as travel and

POLICY ISSUE

Do safeguard measures promote long-term competition?

To answer this question, it is necessary to know whether the measures apply when an increase in imports results from more cost-effective overseas production. What if the domestic industry is shrinking—Americans are losing their jobs, imports are increasing and exports decreasing, etc.—because the U.S. has lost its technological edge or U.S. manufacturers have ignored consumer preferences? What if, for example, U.S. automobile manufacturers have lost market share because foreign manufacturers have simply performed better at anticipating consumer demand for larger cup holders? Section 201 does not distinguish between injury caused by normal foreign competition and "unfair" practices. A surge in "fair" foreign imports may harm the domestic industry, but only because competition is working properly and benefiting consumers.

Unlike other trade remedies, Section 201 relief makes no pretense of preserving competition between U.S. and foreign manufacturers. The rationale for imposing such hardships on consumers and foreign manufacturers is that the relief is temporary; it is designed to allow the domestic industry to adjust to intense foreign competition. If it fails to adjust before the relief expires, it is doomed in any case. If the domestic industry does adjust, however, it may be saved from extinction.

Yet, the question remains, in a wealthy and technologically advanced country with a highly developed manufacturing base and ready credit, whether foreign competition can ever so threaten to injure a U.S., Japanese, or European industry that it would not be able to adjust without government assistance. There are few examples since the Second World War of any viable industry in a wealthy, highly industrialized state that required such assistance to adjust to foreign competition, and that would not have survived without such assistance. In any case, the industries that have used Section 201 the most—agriculture and steel—rank among the oldest and best established.

One certain consequence of safeguard measures is an increased cost of goods for domestic consumers, in most cases beyond the net benefit conferred on the industry itself. How is this different from simply taxing consumers, turning over most of the proceeds to companies in the protected industry, and burning the rest? Are there circumstances under which even well established industries could need temporary government protection against foreign competition? Or should safeguards be limited to protecting nascent industries? Could a new foreign breakthrough in technology devastate a domestic industry before the domestic industry had time to develop a comparable, competing technology?

moving expenses may be reimbursed.

The amount of money Congress has historically allocated to the program is normally small, but it has varied greatly over the years. In 2016, the budget for Trade Adjustment Assistance was a trivial $8 million. But in 2017, the Trump Administration obtained an increase to $673 million due to hardships on workers caused by his trade policy.

The great majority of the money has been spent in industries hardest hit by international trade competition, such as textiles and apparel, electronics and computers, lumber and paper, agriculture, and heavy equipment manufacturing. Almost all U.S. workers who have benefitted from TAA have been manufacturing workers lacking a college degree. Nevertheless, empirical evidence seems to suggest that TAA has not significantly increased the employment prospects of displaced workers.*

3.3 Section 301 Investigations

A. Introduction to Section 301

If Section 201 of the Trade Act of 1974 protects U.S. industries from increased import competition, the U.S. government sometimes uses sections 301 through 310 of the same act (19 U.S.C. §§ 2411-19) to respond to foreign government practices that burden or restrict U.S. exports to foreign countries.

Pursuant to these provisions of the Act, the USTR is authorized to conduct an investigation in response to a complaint by U.S. exporters against foreign "unfair" trade practices. At the conclusion of a **Section 301 investigation**, the USTR may attempt to negotiate the abolition of the offending trade practice with the subject country and, if these negotiations do not arrive at a satisfactory result, may decide to suspend trade concessions previously granted to the country subjected to the complaint or take other adverse action. For example, the USTR may suspend the **permanent normal trade relations** (**PNTR**) rate of customs duty, which is the normal tariff rates afforded to WTO members (see Chapter 5), and substitute a substantially higher rate of duty on designated products from the foreign country if it is found to be discriminating against U.S. products. Section 301 reads, in relevant part, as follows:

---

19 U.S.C. § 2411. Actions by the United States Trade Representative

(a) Mandatory action

(1) If the United States Trade Representative determines under section 2414(a)(1) of this title that—

(A) the rights of the United States under any trade agreement are being denied; or

---

*See Kara M. Reynolds & John S. Palatucci, *Does Trade Adjustment Assistance Make a Difference?*, 30 CONTEMP. ECON. POL'Y. 43 (2012).

(B) an act, policy, or practice of a foreign country—

(i) violates, or is inconsistent with, the provisions of, or otherwise denies benefits to the United States under, any trade agreement, or

(ii) is unjustifiable and burdens or restricts United States commerce;

the Trade Representative shall take action authorized in subsection (c) of this section, subject to the specific direction, if any, of the President regarding any such action, and shall take all other appropriate and feasible action within the power of the President that the President may direct the Trade Representative to take under this subsection, to enforce such rights or to obtain the elimination of such act, policy, or practice. Actions may be taken that are within the power of the President with respect to trade in any goods or services, or with respect to any other area of pertinent relations with the foreign country.

(2) The Trade Representative is not required to take action under paragraph (1) in any case in which—

(A) [the WTO Dispute Settlement Body has formally determined that the foreign state's practice is consistent with the WTO Agreements]; or

(B) the Trade Representative finds that—

(i) the foreign country is taking satisfactory measures to grant the rights of the United States under a trade agreement,

(ii) the foreign country has—

(I) agreed to eliminate or phase out the act, policy, or practice, or

(II) agreed to an imminent solution to the burden or restriction on United States commerce that is satisfactory to the Trade Representative,

(iii) it is impossible for the foreign country to achieve the results described in clause (i) or (ii), as appropriate, but the foreign country agrees to provide to the United States compensatory trade benefits that are satisfactory to the Trade Representative,

(iv) in extraordinary cases, where the taking of action under this subsection would have an adverse impact on the United States economy substantially out of proportion to the benefits of such action, taking into account the impact of not taking such action on the credibility of the provisions of this subchapter, or

(v) the taking of action under this subsection would cause serious harm to the national security of the United States.

(3) Any action taken under paragraph (1) to eliminate an act, policy, or practice shall be devised so as to affect goods or services of the foreign country in an amount that is equivalent in value to the burden or restriction being imposed by that country on United States commerce.

(b) Discretionary action

If the Trade Representative determines under section 2414(a)(1) of this title that—

(1) an act, policy, or practice of a foreign country is unreasonable or discriminatory and burdens or restricts United States commerce, and

(2) action by the United States is appropriate, the Trade Representative shall take all appropriate and feasible action authorized under subsection (c) of this section, subject to the specific direction, if any, of the President regarding any such action, and all other appropriate and feasible action within the power of the President that the President may direct the Trade Representative to take under

this subsection, to obtain the elimination of that act, policy, or practice. Actions may be taken that are within the power of the President with respect to trade in any goods or services, or with respect to any other area of pertinent relations with the foreign country.

(c) Scope of authority

(1) For purposes of carrying out the provisions of subsection (a) or (b) of this section, the Trade Representative is authorized to—

(A) suspend, withdraw, or prevent the application of, benefits of trade agreement concessions to carry out a trade agreement with the foreign country referred to in such subsection;

(B) impose duties or other import restrictions on the goods of, and, notwithstanding any other provision of law, fees or restrictions on the services of, such foreign country for such time as the Trade Representative determines appropriate;

* * * or

(D) enter into binding agreements with such foreign country that commit such foreign country to—

(i) eliminate, or phase out, the act, policy, or practice that is the subject of the action to be taken under subsection (a) or (b) of this section,

(ii) eliminate any burden or restriction on United States commerce resulting from such act, policy, or practice, or

(iii) provide the United States with compensatory trade benefits that—

(I) are satisfactory to the Trade Representative, and

(II) meet the requirements of paragraph (4). * * *

(3) The actions the Trade Representative is authorized to take under subsection (a) or (b) of this section may be taken against any goods or economic sector—

(A) on a nondiscriminatory basis or solely against the foreign country described in such subsection, and

(B) without regard to whether or not such goods or economic sector were involved in the act, policy, or practice that is the subject of such action. * * *

(d) Definitions and special rules. For purposes of this subchapter—

(1) The term "commerce" includes, but is not limited to—

(A) services (including transfers of information) associated with international trade, whether or not such services are related to specific goods, and

(B) foreign direct investment by United States persons with implications for trade in goods or services. * * *

(3) (A) An act, policy, or practice is unreasonable if the act, policy, or practice, while not necessarily in violation of, or inconsistent with, the international legal rights of the United States, is otherwise unfair and inequitable.

(B) Acts, policies, and practices that are unreasonable include, but are not limited to, any act, policy, or practice, or any combination of acts, policies, or practices, which—

(i) denies fair and equitable—

(I) opportunities for the establishment of an enterprise, * * * or

(IV) market opportunities, including the toleration by a foreign government of systematic anticompetitive activities by enterprises or among enterprises in the foreign country that have the effect of restricting, on a basis that is inconsistent with commercial considerations, access of United States goods or services to a foreign market,

(ii) constitutes export targeting, or

(iii) constitutes a persistent pattern of conduct that [violates basic labor rights] * * *

(E) The term "export targeting" means any government plan or scheme consisting of a combination of coordinated actions (whether carried out severally or jointly) that are bestowed on a specific enterprise, industry, or group thereof, the effect of which is to assist the enterprise, industry, or group to become more competitive in the export of a class or kind of merchandise. * * *

(4) (A) An act, policy, or practice is unjustifiable if the act, policy, or practice is in violation of, or inconsistent with, the international legal rights of the United States. * * *

(5) Acts, policies, and practices that are discriminatory include, when appropriate, any act, policy, and practice which denies national or most-favored-nation treatment to United States goods, services, or investment. * * *

If the USTR affirmatively finds a violation of U.S. trade benefits or an unjustifiable burden or restriction on U.S. exports or foreign investment, the Representative is authorized to implement action to terminate the foreign practices. As Section 301(c) makes clear, this can include a suspension or withdrawal of trade concessions previously granted to the offending country, an increase in U.S. customs duties for imports from that country, or the negotiation of a settlement of the dispute that entails the cessation of the practice by the foreign trading partner.

There is, however, a complicating factor. If the USTR seeks to impose a unilateral sanction on a country that the USTR has determined discriminates unfairly against U.S. exports, the action must comply with the WTO Agreements. The WTO Agreements generally prohibit any WTO member such as the United States from imposing quantitative restrictions, increasing duties, or suspending trade concessions except following a ruling by the WTO dispute settlement body that the impugned foreign practice violates the WTO Agreements. See, e.g., GATT arts. XI & XIII; WTO Dispute Settlement Understanding art. 23.2(a). While Article XX of the GATT lists several general exceptions to these obligations, "unfair treatment" by a trading partner is not a listed ground for the suspension or withdrawal of concessions. Article XXIII does permit parties to suspend or withdraw concessions with respect to other GATT parties that have failed to carry out their GATT obligations or otherwise taken GATT-inconsistent action, but only with the prior assent of a majority of GATT parties. Unilateral sanctions are nowhere permitted. Instead, the states must resort to negotiations and possibly formal WTO dispute settlement.

In 1998, the EU challenged Section 301 as inconsistent with the WTO Agreements. *United States—Sections 301-310 of the Trade Act of 1974*, WTO

Doc. WT/DS152/R (Dec. 22, 1999). The EU argued that Section 301 obligated the USTR to apply unilateral sanctions without a favorable ruling by a panel of the Dispute Settlement Body (DSB) if the USTR found a foreign state to have treated U.S. business firms unfairly or inconsistently with WTO obligations. The WTO panel agreed that the language of Section 301 could be construed as facially inconsistent with the U.S. obligations under the WTO Agreements. However, the panel noted the USTR's broad discretion to find a foreign act unjustifiable or a violation of treaty obligations or not, and even broader discretion to fashion sufficient remedies. Moreover, in submitting the WTO Agreements for congressional approval, President Clinton published a "Statement of Administrative Action" in which he took the position that all Section 301 determinations should in the future be based on a decision of the WTO Dispute Settlement Body. Accordingly, the USTR now tends to use Section 301 mainly as a basis for invoking the WTO's disputing procedures under the DSU.

B. The Section 301 Petition

Why are Section 301 investigations potentially important to companies that do business internationally? Because, if the USTR does not initiate an investigation *sua sponte*, Section 302 specifically provides an avenue for U.S. companies, industries, workers, and labor and business associations to petition the USTR to commence an investigation under Section 301. 19 U.S.C. § 2412(a). The USTR has discretion to grant or deny the petition to initiate an investigation, but it must do so within forty-five days. If the petition is denied, the denial will be published in the *Federal Register*. If the petition is granted, the USTR's investigation will be publicly announced, also in the *Federal Register*, and the USTR will hold a public hearing on the position's merits.

A Section 301 investigation is a tool that U.S. industries can use to obtain assistance from the federal government in challenging a foreign trade practice disadvantageous to U.S. export business. Because the Section 301 investigation is conducted by the USTR, and because the United States government is required to comply with the WTO Agreements in adopting a unilateral remedy, the involvement of U.S. companies and their private lawyers is limited to calling the USTR's attention to the problem and providing any information the USTR might find helpful. For that reason, Section 301 practice requires some sophistication in dealing with the government. One trade lawyer has offered the following bit of wisdom to companies considering filing a Section 301 complaint with the USTR on behalf of an exporter client:

> A well-counseled firm approaches the USTR before submitting its petition. The USTR reviews and comments on draft petitions before recommending that one be filed. If the USTR believes that the Section 301 process is not the most effective way to have the barrier removed, it will so indicate. For this reason, the USTR has rarely had to formally reject a petition in Section 301's twenty-eight-year history.

GREGORY C. SHAFFER, DEFENDING INTERESTS: PUBLIC-PRIVATE PARTNERSHIPS IN WTO LITIGATION 45 (2003).

In 1999, for example, the USTR began a Section 301 investigations concerning the EU's directive on meat hormones, which bans the importation into Europe of meat from animals that had been treated with specified hormones. Because these hormones were used by most U.S. cattle ranchers to speed cattle growth artificially, the ban effectively shut most U.S. beef out of the European market. The USTR, on the prompting of U.S. cattle ranchers, had unsuccessfully sought to negotiate a termination of the ban with the EU Commission. The USTR then invoked the WTO dispute settlement procedure in 1995, in which the United States prevailed in 1997. *EC—Measures Concerning Meat and Meat Products (Hormones)*, WTO Doc. WT/DS26/R/USA (Aug. 18, 1997). The DSB (and the Appellate Body on appeal) agreed that the EU's meat hormones directive violated the WTO Agreements.

This was not, however, the end of the U.S. beef industry's challenges. The EU refused to implement the WTO's recommendations, and so the USTR sought and received WTO authorization to increase import duties to 100% on some $117 million worth of food products from Europe annually as a retaliatory measure. The affected European products included pork, mustard, truffles, Roquefort cheese, cereals, and mineral waters. Although the EU amended the directive in 2006 and again in 2009, the USTR considered the amendments inadequate, and by agreement of the parties increased U.S. duties remained in effect as of 2020—more than two decades later. The U.S. beef industry obtained some (incomplete) relief from the EU, but the biggest winners were other U.S. food industries, which received import protection for reasons completely unrelated to any European trade measure affecting them.

C. Special 301

The United States puts great pressure on its trading partners to protect and enforce intellectual property rights for the benefit of U.S. IP owners. The remedies afforded to such owners, such as customs recordation and enforcement, Section 337 investigations, and court-based litigation, generally ensure IP owners a strong chance of protecting their rights from infringement within the United States. However, the infringement of IP owned by U.S. nationals in foreign markets continues to pose a significant problem. The various IP treaties discussed in Chapter 3 are generally designed to address the most salient threats to the international commerce for IP owners, but some states are not parties to these treaties, and others are parties but do not devote significant resources to enforcement of foreign IP rights.

U.S. nationals are not entirely on their own in trying to protect and enforce their IP rights outside of the United States. Congress has passed legislation to ensure that the U.S. government takes a direct interest in the protection and enforcement of IP by U.S. trading partners. In 1988, President Reagan

Case Study

Section 301 and the U.S. Trade War Against China

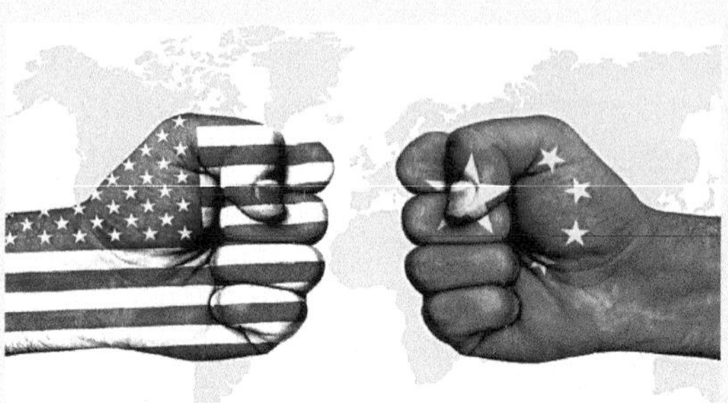

Acting on a campaign promise to punish China for unfair trade practices, President Donald Trump ordered the USTR in 2017 to commence a Section 301 investigation of China. In announcing his decision to impose tariffs on China, Trump tweeted: "trade wars are good, and easy to win." In 2018, the USTR concluded that China had adopted a practice of refusing to allow U.S. investment in China unless investors transfer technology to Chinese firms. The USTR also found that the Chinese government "directs and unfairly facilitates" the systematic acquisition of U.S. companies and assets by Chinese companies, in order to obtain new technologies and IP.

Although the impugned Chinese practices related to investment and IP rights, the USTR recommended imposing new punitive duties on Chinese imports under Section 301, without invoking WTO dispute settlement. The tariffs added 25% to some 1333 line items from the HTSUS and netted several hundred billion dollars. Chinese exports to the United States accordingly decreased annually, beginning in 2017.

Few of the alleged practices by China would have violated the WTO Agreements. However, the Trump Administration's additional duties on China did violate U.S. obligations under those treaties, as well as past U.S. assurances that Section 301 would not be used in violation of U.S. WTO obligations. No provision of the WTO Agreements allows a contracting party to escape its tariff bindings by unilateral sanctions. China accordingly requested the establishment of a panel of the WTO's dispute settlement body and sought $2.4 billion in retaliatory sanctions.

China also immediately imposed tariffs on $130 billion of U.S. imports. As a result of the Section 301 action and retaliation, U.S. exports declined and domestic manufacturing costs rose, resulting in the bankruptcy of some small U.S. manufacturers. By 2019, the U.S. trade deficit had risen to a 10-year high of $617 billion. Instead of reconsidering, Trump further escalated, and China retaliated by allowing its currency to depreciate. Global markets weakened as the trade war intensified. Although Section 301 can be used to pressure other states that treat U.S. exporters and investors unfairly, it is plainly a double-edged sword.

Figure 6.5. Who's winning? Unilateral tariff increases under Section 301 may provoke disputes within the WTO, as well as retaliation that can harm U.S. industries, farmers, and consumers. These results in turn may provoke satire.
Credit: © 2019 by Carla Millar

proposed legislation to amend Section 301 of the 1974 Trade Act, which instructs the USTR to monitor the trade practices of other countries, to issue reports on these practices to Congress, and to recommend or take steps to pressure foreign governments to terminate discrimination against U.S. imports. The 1988 amendments created a procedure, known as the Special 301 procedure, to identify foreign practices prejudicial to U.S.-owned IP rights.

The **Special 301** provisions of the 1974 Trade Act (19 U.S.C. § 2242) require the USTR to identify foreign countries that deny "adequate and effective protection" of IP or "fair and equitable market access" for U.S. citizens and companies that rely on IP protection to do business in the foreign country. Some of these provisions appear in the authorization to the USTR to protect U.S. exporting and foreign investment interests:

---

19 U.S.C. § 2411. Actions by the United States Trade Representative

* * *

(d)(3)

(A) An act, policy, or practice is unreasonable if the act, policy, or practice, while not necessarily in violation of, or inconsistent with, the international legal rights of the United States, is otherwise unfair and inequitable.

(B) Acts, policies, and practices that are unreasonable include, but are not limited to, any act, policy, or practice, or any combination of acts, policies, or practices, which—

(i) denies fair and equitable—

* * *

(II) provision of adequate and effective protection of intellectual property rights notwithstanding the fact that the foreign country may be in compliance with the specific obligations of the Agreement on Trade-Related Aspects of Intellectual Property Rights referred to in section 3511(d)(15) of this title,

(III) nondiscriminatory market access opportunities for United States persons that rely upon intellectual property protection, or

(IV) market opportunities, including the toleration by a foreign government of systematic anticompetitive activities by enterprises or among enterprises in the foreign country that have the effect of restricting, on a basis that is inconsistent with commercial considerations, access of United States goods or services to a foreign market, * * *.

(F) (i) For the purposes of subparagraph (B)(i)(II), adequate and effective protection of intellectual property rights includes adequate and effective means under the laws of the foreign country for persons who are not citizens or nationals of such country to secure, exercise, and enforce rights and enjoy commercial benefits relating to patents, trademarks, copyrights and related rights, mask works, trade secrets, and plant breeder's rights.

(ii) For purposes of subparagraph (B)(i)(IV), the denial of fair and equitable nondiscriminatory market access opportunities includes restrictions on market access related to the use, exploitation, or enjoyment of commercial benefits derived from exercising intellectual property rights in protected works or fixations or products embodying protected works. * * *

(4) * * *

(B) Acts, policies, and practices that are unjustifiable include, but are not limited to, any act, policy, or practice described in subparagraph (A) which denies national or most-favored-nation treatment or the right of establishment or protection of intellectual property rights. * * *

As you mentioned in Chapter 3, the TRIPS Agreement requires almost all U.S. trading partners to provide a specific minimum level of intellectual property law protection. But the Special 301 provisions specify that even if a foreign country complies with its WTO obligations, it may still be found to deny adequate IP protection. For example, the USTR may use Special 301 to identify a foreign country that discriminates against U.S. IP owners in a manner that technically complies with the WTO Agreements, or that fails to enforce WTO-compliant laws against IP infringement. A WTO member may, for example, have adequate laws for the protection of IP consistent with the TRIPs Agreement but fail to adopt a policy of systematic enforcement of the laws.

The purpose of the Special 301 provisions was to establish:

> a comprehensive and effective program to address the growing problem of piracy and counterfeiting faced in foreign markets by United States firms and industries. This problem is not an isolated one affecting just one or two industries. It is a problem confronted by virtually all sectors of the U.S. economy, including manufacturers of semiconductors and other high technology products, motion pictures, computer software, books, records, auto parts, pharmaceuticals, and chemicals. It also is a problem encountered in developed and developing countries alike.

H.R. Rep. No. 40, 100th Cong., 1st Sess. 163 (1987).

The Special 301 provisions direct the USTR to identify any foreign countries that deny "adequate and effective protection of intellectual property rights" or "fair and equitable market access to United States persons who rely upon intellectual property protection." 19 U.S.C. § 2242(a)(1). To that end, the USTR publishes an annual **Special 301 Report** that classifies foreign countries denying adequate IP protection into three categories. The list of countries is published in the *Federal Register*, and the report is submitted to Congress. *Id.* § 2242(g).

The first category of countries is explicitly mandated by the Special 301 provisions, which require the USTR to designate **priority foreign countries**, defined as those:

> (A) that have the most onerous or egregious acts, policies, or practices that—
>
> (i) deny adequate and effective intellectual property rights, or
>
> (ii) deny fair and equitable market access to United States persons that rely upon intellectual property protection,
>
> (B) whose acts, policies, or practices described in subparagraph (A) have the greatest adverse impact (actual or potential) on the relevant United States products, and
>
> (C) that are not—
>
> (i) entering into good faith negotiations, or
>
> (ii) making significant progress in bilateral or multilateral negotiations,
>
> to provide adequate and effective protection of intellectual property rights.

Id. § 2242(b)(1). Within thirty days of identifying a country as a priority foreign country, the USTR is required to initiate an investigation of the offending foreign policies or practices. *Id.* § 2412(b)(2)(A). Within six months, the USTR must negotiate a termination of the practice. *Id.* § 2414(a)(3)(A)-(B). Failing an acceptable resolution, the USTR is authorized to retaliate by increasing duties or imposing other restrictions on imports or invoking the formal dispute resolution provisions of the WTO Agreements. *Id.* § 2416(b). The USTR may designate a country as a priority foreign country at any time, and may revoke the designation as well. Such designations are fairly rare, however.

The other two categories used by the USTR do not trigger any statutory obligations, but merely provide warning to IP owners and foreign states of the practices deemed unacceptable. The **watch list** includes countries whose practices the USTR would like to see conform more closely to U.S. standards of IP protection. The **priority watch list** includes countries at risk of being designated priority foreign countries if they do not reform their IP polices or practices. In the USTR's words:

> Placement of a trading partner on the Priority Watch List or Watch List indicates that particular problems exist in that country with respect to IPR protection, enforcement, or market access for persons relying on IP. Provisions of the Special 301 statute, as amended, direct USTR to develop action plans for each country identified as a Priority Watch List country that has been on the Priority Watch List for at least one year.

Case Study

The USTR Designates Ukraine as a Priority Foreign Country

Figure 6.6. USTR accused Ukraine of tolerating piracy of films and music.

In 2001, the USTR identified Ukraine as a "priority foreign country" under the Special 301 provisions of Section 301 due to Ukraine's allegedly inadequate IP protections. At the conclusion of its investigation, the USTR found that Ukraine had failed to take sufficient enforcement measures to prevent the piracy of U.S. optical media (at the time, CDs and DVDs). Invoking Section 301, the USTR unilaterally raised customs duties on certain products from Ukraine and suspended Ukraine's eligibility for reduced customs duties under the Generalized System of Preferences (see Chapter 5 for more on GSP). This decision, which significantly increased U.S. customs duties on Ukrainian imports, did not require WTO approval, because the GSP grants trade concessions over and above what is required by the WTO agreements. In 2005, Ukraine amended its Laser-Readable Disc Law to strengthen its antipiracy enforcement capabilities, causing the USTR to revoke the increased customs duties and restore Ukraine's GSP eligibility.

In 2013, various failures by the Ukrainian government to enforce IP rights, including the government's own piracy of U.S. software, caused its redesignation as a priority foreign country.

Office of the U.S. Trade Representative, *2018 Special 301 Report*, at 7.

The USTR tends to initiate negotiations with foreign countries placed on the Priority Watch List to remedy the perceived inadequacies of that country's IP protection. The Watch List serves more as a warning that the USTR has identified some problems with IP enforcement that may, if continued or aggravated, lead the USTR to upgrade the country to Priority Watch List status. The EU has adopted a similar practice of listing countries having inadequate protections of IP rights, including by issuing an annual "Report on Barriers to Trade and Investment in the United States."

The Special 301 Report does not afford any specific rights to the U.S. IP owners aggrieved at insufficient IP protection in foreign countries. It does, however, give them the indirect ability to influence foreign practices through the USTR. The USTR relies very heavily on private industry organizations to gather facts and make recommendations on which countries protect intellectual property adequately and which do not. In practice, the most politically powerful trade associations representing IP owners submit a proposed report annually to the USTR, and the USTR's final Special 301 Report reflects private lobbying efforts.*

In addition, the Special 301 Report alerts U.S. IP owners to significant lapses in IP protection in the listed foreign countries. The Report can be used, along with the advice of local counsel in the foreign country where the IP will be exploited, to help predict the probability that the IP owner will be able to protect its intellectual property in the foreign country.

The Special 301 Report may be especially important to business firms heavily reliant on IP rights seeking to invest in foreign countries. The Report gives reliable guidance on the kinds of obstacles IP owners face in obtaining protection and enforcement of their IP rights. Although the Special 301 Report confers no rights or powers on the owner, it does provide useful information about the extent to which foreign states are complying with their TRIPs Agreement and other treaty obligations and any weaknesses in protection that may not be evident from their treaty commitments, such as a lack of enforcement resources dedicated to detecting, stopping, and prosecuting IP piracy or counterfeiting. For that reason the Special 301 Report is one useful resource for advising clients on the kinds of protection that can be expected of their IP in foreign countries.

---

*See GREGORY C. SHAFFER, DEFENDING INTERESTS: PUBLIC-PRIVATE PARTNERSHIPS IN WTO LITIGATION 35-36 (2003).

Key Vocabulary

Antidumping duty (ADD)
Bond
Countervailing duty (CVD)
Court of International Trade (CIT)
Domestic industry
Domestic like product
Dumping
Dumping margin
Escape clause
International Trade Administration (ITA)
International Trade Commission (ITC)
Less than fair value (LTFV)
Material injury
Predatory pricing
Priority Foreign Country
Priority Watch List
Quantitative restriction
Return on investment (ROI)
Safeguard measure
Section 201 investigation
Section 301 investigation
Special 301
Subsidy
Sunset review
Tariff-rate quota (TRQ)
Trade adjustment assistance (TAA)
USMCA Chapter 10 panel
USMCA Extraordinary Challenge Committee (ECC)
Voluntary export restraint (VER)
Watch List
WTO Dispute Settlement Understanding (DSU)
WTO Agreement on Safeguards

Practice Exercises

#1 Choosing The Appropriate Trade Remedies

You work in the office of the general counsel of a Netherlands-based multinational corporation, Hipils Nederlands BV (HN). HN's U.S. subsidiary, Ordinary Objects, Inc. (OOI), manufactures aluminum ladders in the United States for distribution in the United States, Canada, and Mexico. It is the sole manufacturer of fiberglass ladders in the United States. The main other countries that manufacture aluminum ladders are Argentina, Brazil, Norway, and Russia.

Recently, there has been a surge in aluminum ladder imports into Canada and the United States from Brazil and Russia. OOI has hired an economic consultant, who reports that the same model ladders manufactured by the Brazilian and Russian exporters are being sold at slightly lower cost in Brazil and Russia, respectively, than the price at which the imports are sold in the United States. The consultant also reports that the Russian government provides a tax credit to Russian ladder manufacturers for all import duties paid to foreign governments.

While ladder imports from neither Argentina nor Norway have increased significantly over the last few years, Brazilian and Russian imports have forced down U.S. prices to the point where OOI estimates that, within three years, OOI will cease U.S. ladder production entirely to maintain profitability.

Advise OOI on the availability of trade remedies. In your answer, be sure to:

(a) list each trade remedy available to OOI for each country;

(b) list the elements that OOI will need to show to establish a right to each trade remedy you identify;

(c) describe the actions that the U.S. or other government might take on its behalf, and which specific remedies OOI should advocate; and

(d) describe any statutory limitations on the remedies available to OOI.

#2 Responding to Competitive Foreign Imports

You have been approached for legal advice and representation by the largest Pottsylvanian fruit company, Prizes Co. Prizes exports its fruit worldwide, including to the United States, and reports that it has received notice that gold kiwifruit imports from Pottsylvania are the subject of a U.S. antidumping and countervailing duty investigations initiated by a petition of the American Fruit Growers Association (AFGA). Prizes is confused by the petition, because no gold kiwifruit are commercially grown in the United States. Many AFGA member sell *green* kiwifruit grown in California, and several AFGA members are wholesale distributors who import gold kiwifruit from New Zealand to the United States, where they are cleaned and sorted, spoiled kiwifruit are removed, and they are packed for transportation to U.S. grocery stores and restaurants. Gold kiwifruit are milder, sweeter, and less acidic than green kiwifruit. In addition, their skin is smoother and less fuzzy, which makes them more palatable to eat without peeling. In terms of nutrition, green kiwifruit has slightly less sugar and more fiber, while gold kiwifruit has slightly more vitamins and minerals.

Regarding the antidumping investigation, Prizes represents that it sells the kiwifruit to retailers in the United States at the same price it sells the fruit to other foreign states. The price in Pottsylvania is slightly higher than the price at which the fruit are sold outside of Pottsylvania (including in the United States), but Prizes explains this as being a result of the fact that, because no transportation across oceans is needed, the fruit for domestic consumption are picked later and therefore are naturally riper and sweeter. They therefore command a higher price.

Regarding the subsidies investigation, Prizes represents that it does receive loan guarantees from the Pottsylvanian government as well as discounts on water and energy from the state-owned Pottsylvanian public utilities. In addition, Pottsylvanian agribusinesses and farmers receive a 10% tax credit on all income derived from sales of agricultural products, whether the sale is made in Pottsylvanian or foreign markets. U.S. kiwifruit growers receive identical subsidies from the U.S. government, however.

Figure 6.7. Yellow and green varieties of kiwifruit.

Advise Prizes on the following matters relating to the ADD and CVD petition:

(a) Is the fact that gold kiwifruit is not grown in the United States fatal to the ADD and CVD petitions? Why or why not?

(b) Assuming the ADD and CVD petitions could go forward, does this case does involve dumping?

(c) Does any of the assistance Prizes receives from the Pottsylvanian government qualify as countervailable subsidies?

Multiple Choice Questions

1. Which of the following treaties includes provisions regulating the use of ADD or CVD measures?

   I. Agreement Establishing the World Trade Organization
   II. SCM Agreement
   III. Agreement on Implementation of Article VI of GATT 1994

   (a) I only
   (b) II only
   (c) I and II only
   (d) II and III only
   (e) I, II, and III

2. Which of the following is a remedy available after an affirmative finding in an antidumping investigation under the 1930 Tariff Act?

(a) The imposition of additional duties equal to the lesser of twice the import duties or the domestic value of the imported merchandise.
(b) The imposition of additional duties equal to the difference between the foreign market price and the domestic market price.
(c) The imposition of quantitative restrictions on the dumped imports.
(d) Compensatory damages equal to the harm caused to the domestic industry.
(e) Compensatory damages equal to the harm caused to the domestic industry plus punitive damages for intentional dumping.

3. True or false?: Any direct or indirect subsidy that a foreign government grants to one of its industries or business firms can give rise to a countervailing duty under the 1930 Tariff Act.

4. True or false?: To obtain relief under an ADD or CVD investigation, it is not necessary to show actual harm to a domestic industry.

5. In an ADD or CVD investigation, what is the consequence of a negative preliminary determination by the Department of Commerce?

(a) The investigation is referred to the ITC for its preliminary determination.
(b) The investigation is terminated with prejudice.
(c) The investigation is terminated without prejudice.
(d) The importer posts a bond, and the investigation is referred to the ITC for its final determination.
(e) None of the above.

6. True or false?: A petitioner or respondent may appeal from a final determination by the ITC or Department of Commerce directly to the U.S. Court of Appeals for the Federal Circuit.

7. True or false?: A panel formed under USMCA Chapter 10 offers an alternative to domestic courts in the U.S., Canada, or Mexico for appealing a final antidumping or countervailing duty determination that allegedly violates USMCA trade remedies disciplines.

8. Which of the following is not a factor used by the International Trade Commission in evaluating whether an imported good and domestically produced good are "like products?"

(a) whether the products have similar HTSUS classifications
(b) whether the products appear physically similar

(c) whether the products are functionally similar
(d) whether customers perceive the products as interchangeable
(e) whether the products have the same channels of distribution

9. Which of the following is not a factor used by the International Trade Commission in evaluating whether a business firm is part of a domestic industry?

(a) whether technical expertise is involved in its U.S. production activity
(b) whether the U.S. production activities of the firm add significant value to the product
(c) whether the business firm sources its components and materials from the United States
(d) whether the business firm is owned by U.S. or foreign nationals
(e) whether the U.S. production activities of the firm employ significant numbers of employees

10. True or false?: In an ADD or CVD investigation, if neither production nor sales of a domestic industry is falling or has ever fallen, the ITC must issue a negative determination because there is no harm to the domestic industry.

11. Last year, the average price of thingamajigs imported into the United States from Zembia fell by 28%, and imports increased by 25%. The U.S. thingamajig manufacturing industry, composed of a single company (U.S. Thingamajig Corp.), responded with efficiency-increasing measures, but it was unable to reduce costs (and correlative prices) by more than 9%. As a result, U.S. Thingamajig Corp. had to reduce production by one-third and layoff several hundred workers. U.S. Thingamajig has approached you for advice about whether it might succeed in obtaining relief under Section 201 of the 1974 Trade Act. Which of the following additional facts, if true, would preclude a safeguard measure under the WTO Agreements?

(a) Import prices by other exporting countries did not fall at all, and import volumes from these countries into the United States remained stable.
(b) Zembia is a developing country and, even after the increase in imports, Zembian imports only account for 16% of the U.S. market.
(c) The United States already imposes a 20% antidumping duty on Zembian thingamajig imports.
(d) Zembia is the only importer of Thingamajigs into the United States, so that a safeguard measure would result a nearly complete lack of competition in Thingamajigs on the U.S. market,
(e) The increase in Zembian imports was the direct result of a U.S. de-

crease in import duties pursuant to recent GATT negotiations.

12. True or false?: If, after a full Section 201 investigation by the ITC, the ITC determines that no protective measures are justified under the 1974 Trade Act, the U.S. President may freely disregard the ITC determination and order the imposition of safeguard measures such as increased import duties or tariff rate quotas.

13. True or false?: Section 301 of the 1974 Trade Act requires a trading partner to have adopted a discriminatory or unreasonable measure harmful to a U.S. industry in violation of the WTO Agreements, a free trade agreement, or other trade treaty obligation in order to authorize retaliatory measures on that partner.

14. To take action under Section 301, the U.S. Trade Representative must find which of the following?

    (a) a foreign practice that is unreasonable and burdens or restricts U.S. commerce
    (b) a foreign practice that discriminates against U.S. business firms and burdens or restricts U.S. commerce
    (c) a foreign practice that violates a trade treaty with the United States
    (d) All of the above
    (e) Any of the above

15. The U.S. Trade Representative does which of the following through the Special 301 review process?

    (a) Identifies and imposes sanctions on any state that fails to protect the IP rights of U.S. owners under the TRIPS Agreement or other IP treaty with the United States.
    (b) Identifies and imposes sanctions on any state that violates its obligations under the TRIPS Agreement or other IP treaty with the United States.
    (c) Assesses and reports on the practices of any state that fails to protect the IP rights of U.S. owners to the extent deemed acceptable solely in the judgment of the USTR.
    (d) Assesses and reports on the practices of any state that violates its obligations under the TRIPS Agreement or other IP treaty with the United States.
    (e) Applies the Section 301 procedure specifically to IP laws and enforcement among U.S. trading partners.

Multiple Choice Answers

1. d
2. b
3. False
4. True
5. e
6. False
7. False
8. a
9. d
10. False
11. e
12. True
13. False
14. e
15. c

Chapter 7

Foreign Direct Investment

What You Will Learn in This Chapter

This chapter explains the process of forming, financing, and operating a new foreign company. Foreign direct investment is a complex and risky venture, requiring analysis in diverse fields of law. Some of the analyses involved in foreign investment, such as planning for the protection of intellectual property or the crafting of international commercial agreements, have already been discussed in previous chapters. Here, we will be exploring the considerations unique to forming and operating a foreign investment.

One aspect of foreign investment in particular requires special attention: investment financing. Building or acquiring a foreign manufacturing plant, utility plant, resort, natural resource extraction operation, or similarly large business involves a variety of risks not common with purely domestic investments. These include political instability, currency conversion problems, and the risk of direct or indirect expropriation. To help investors cope with these risks, national governments and intergovernmental organizations have created special arrangements unique to foreign investment.

In this chapter, you will specifically learn:

- what motivates business enterprises to invest in foreign states;
- what forms a foreign investment might take, and the advantages and disadvantages of each form;
- what kinds of treaties may affect the feasibility, security, and profitability of a foreign investment;
- how regulatory approval or notification processes of the investor's state and host state may apply to foreign investments;
- how foreign exchange regulations may affect a foreign investment;
- some special considerations in dealing with employment decisions;
- how immigration regulations affect foreign investment and employment decisions;
- what role U.S. and foreign securities regulation may play in financing

and structuring a foreign investment;
- the financial sources that business firms use to expand their operations internationally or to purchase from foreign exporters;
- the kinds of financial instruments and techniques they use to fund large-scale international sales and foreign direct investment;
- how various government agencies and programs may give local businesses assistance in expanding internationally, and what kinds of assistance may be offered; and
- how business firms cope with the risk inherent in international project financing.

1 Incorporating Abroad

1.1 Why Expand Internationally?

A **multinational enterprise** (**MNE**) is a business entity composed of multiple separate companies that are organized under the laws of more than one state. An MNE is not monolithic; it is a network of companies, each technically having its own goals and interests, that are ultimately owned and controlled by a single company. Each company comprising the MNE is formed under the law of some specific state, so that different companies have different nationalities, and each company's internal affairs will be subject to different laws. What makes the MNE a single business is the common ownership of all companies by the same **ultimate parent company**. In other words, the ultimate parent company must directly or indirectly own at least 50% of all of the shares or other ownership interest of every company in the MNE. The companies so owned or controlled are called **subsidiary companies**. Any company not majority owned (directly or indirectly) by that parent company is not part of the MNE, although, if the MNE owns a minority share in a company, that company is one of the MNE's investments.

The fact that an MNE is owned and controlled by a single company does not mean that all of the subsidiary companies act in unison or even in harmony. It is common for different directors and officers to manage different companies within the MNE, and they may sometimes coordinate their efforts badly or work at cross-purposes. Ideally, they all work for the common good of their shareholder, ultimate parent company and its own shareholders, but the parent company may sometimes encounter difficulty in closely supervising all of its subsidiaries. The larger the MNE becomes, and the more subsidiaries in more countries that it owns and controls, the more it must rely on regional executives to operate different divisions of the MNE. Quite a few MNEs have multiple divisions and subsidiaries or branches in dozens of countries. Others have a business presence in two countries only.

International trade requires at a minimum a seller in one country and a buyer in another. Complicating this scenario by establishing a foreign presence can bring many advantages to a business firm. The type of foreign presence is a function of the business problem the company is trying to solve or the specific advantage that it is trying to capture. As circumstances require, the foreign presence may range from a supply warehouse or the hiring of a single agent for making sales or purchases to a large network of manufacturing plants, service centers, and research laboratories.

A company may wish to establish a permanent presence in a foreign country, called the **host state** of the investment, for very simple reasons. Suppose a U.S. manufacturer has several buyers throughout a foreign region, such as Europe, that periodically place orders for unpredictable quantities for delivery on short notice. Given the vicissitudes of international shipping, the manufacturer may find that the most reliable and efficient means of supplying its customers is to purchase or lease a customs warehouse in Europe for storage and quick delivery of its products to its European customers. Suppose the company chooses Brussels for its warehouse. The warehouse is simply property owned or leased by the U.S. company, subject to Belgian law because it is in Belgian territory.

If the manufacturer has ongoing business with European customers, it may find it convenient to have a local branch office in Brussels to promote sales and handle customer service. A **branch office** is an extension of a business into a new jurisdiction through a physical location such as leased property. It is not a legal person separate from the company that owns it; it is merely an operational unit of the company. For example, the U.S. manufacturer might lease an office or office building in Brussels and hire Brussels sales representatives or service technicians for the convenience of its European customers.

Unlike a separate entity, any tort, contractual, criminal, tax, or other liability of the branch office is directly imputable to the company that owns the branch. There is, in short, no "corporate veil" between the owner of the office and the office itself. In different countries, a branch office may have different names with different attributes and be subject to different rules, such as "representative office" (e.g., the People's Republic of China or the Russian Federation) or "liaison office" (e.g., India). Some countries have more than one form. Both France and Japan, for example, have a concept of branch office as well as representative office. Here, we will just use the term "branch office" generically to apply to all such offices, because they share their most important features in common.

It is important to be aware that, whatever the form of the foreign investment, the investor must comply with the host state's laws regulating both foreign investment and the establishment of business organizations. In most cases, the investor must also comply with the laws of its own country—the **investor state**—relating to foreign investments as well. Some countries set strict limits on the kinds of activities in which a branch office may engage that do not apply to separate business entities like corporations. For example, Japan does not allow representative offices to make sales, open a bank account, or manufacture goods, but a branch office may do so.

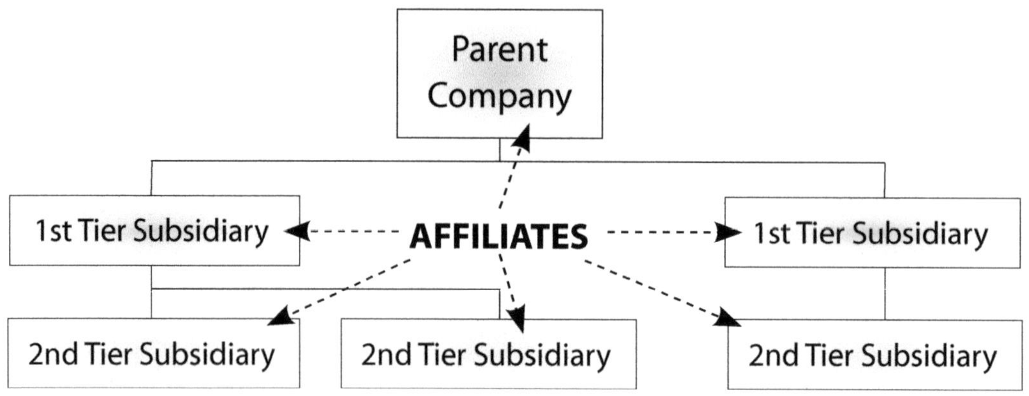

Figure 7.1. Intercompany relationships and affiliation.

As foreign activities become more extensive, such as when a company engages in significant research and development, sales promotion, manufacturing, or other activities in a foreign state, the risks of liability to the company and the nuances of tax minimization strategies may make a separate business entity in the host state a much more appealing option. In such cases, the investor may choose to create a subsidiary company instead of a branch office. A subsidiary is a separate company with its own legal personality. All companies majority owned by the same parent company are **affiliates** of one another, meaning that they are ultimately owned by the same investors.

The establishment of an ongoing business presence in a foreign state through a branch office or subsidiary company is a form of foreign direct investment. The process of incorporating a subsidiary tends to be somewhat more involved and costly than registering a branch office. Nonetheless, separate legal personality offers substantial advantages, and subsidiaries are consequently a much more common form of foreign investment than are branch offices.

A. Administrative Convenience

For some companies, delegating responsibility for foreign operations to a separate legal entity facilitates and simplifies the administration of the organization's business. Directors and executive officers of the parent company need not maintain careful scrutiny of and control over the daily operations of the foreign part of the business because this responsibility is delegated to the directors and executive officers of the subsidiary itself. As the company expands multinationally, the task of centrally monitoring business activities in an ever increasing number of foreign jurisdictions becomes progressively more burdensome. By incorporating foreign subsidiaries, the parent company may decentralize administration of its foreign business activities.

B. Limitation of Liability

Because a subsidiary is a separate legal person, it may be possible to limit liabilities incurred by a foreign subsidiary to the amount of the foreign investment. In other words, if a foreign subsidiary incurs any sort of debt, whether arising by commercial loan, tort action, criminal penalty, or tax liability, the investor's exposure to liability may be limited to the amount of the foreign investment put into the subsidiary and no more. Of course, the question of liability is governed by the law of the host state, but most states provide in their law for a form of business entity, the liability of which is generally limited to the entity's own assets.

In the United States and Canada, the most common form of limited liability entity is a corporation. In other countries, the analogous concept has different names. For example:

Australia, India, Ireland, Israel, Pakistan, Singapore, South Africa, U.K.	public limited company (PLC) private limited company (Ltd.)
Belgium, France, Morocco	*société anonyme* (S.A.)
Italy	*società per azioni* (s.p.a.)
Spain, Latin America	*sociedad anónima* (S.A.)
Austria, Germany	*Aktiengesellschaft* (A.G.)
Japan	*kabushiki kaisha* (KK)

Other forms of limited liability entity include the **limited liability company** (**LLC**) and **limited liability partnership** (**LLP**), both of which are distinguished from corporations by having special tax and other attributes. Many countries have some business forms analogous to LLCs and LLPs.

Of course, a subsidiary need not be a limited liability entity. Every state in the world provides for at least one kind of a business entity that lacks limited liability. In the United States, for example, owners of a general partnership or sole proprietorship do not benefit from limited liability. In France, investors may form a *société en participation* (SP) or *société en nom collectif* (SNC) with unlimited liability. In Germany, an *Offene Handelsgesellschaft* performs a similar function.

C. Foreign Direct Investment versus Commercial Relationships

A company seeking the advantages of foreign manufacturing must decide between using, on one hand, a commercial relationship with an independent contract manufacturer and, on the other, investing directly in the foreign state by establishing its own manufacturing subsidiary or branch there. Each choice has its relative advantages and disadvantages.

One advantage of a commercial relationship is that it requires minimal foreign investment, which means a limited need to understand and comply with foreign regulations, reduced exposure to liability, and relatively little concern with complications to the company's tax strategy caused by income earned in multiple jurisdictions. Another advantage is that it may be relatively easy to enter and exit the foreign market, because most commercial agreements are relatively easily made and terminated.

A foreign investment, in contrast, involves extensive advanced planning and a substantial outlay of capital and effort to comply with foreign regulations; to enter into leases; to hire and commit to employment contracts; and to acquire equipment, materials and components, utility services, and other necessities. In some cases, an independent contractor will also be more experienced and efficient in its line of business than the company itself could be. Finally, establishment of a foreign subsidiary may subject the investor to risks of civil disturbance, government interference, and economic instability in the host state.

Foreign direct investment in a subsidiary or branch office has its own notable advantages, however. First, the investor will retain all profits from the foreign operations and not need to share them with an unaffiliated contractor. Second, the investor will have maximal control over the foreign operations, because it hires the managers of its own foreign subsidiary or branch office. Whenever reliability and trust are crucial business factors, the investor's control over its own subsidiary or office allows that investor to ensure that customer service meets its own quality standards, supply remains reliable, and intellectual property is unlikely to be infringed. These advantages will be sufficient to outweigh competing considerations in many cases. If the host state and investor state have a bilateral investment treaty, the investment treaty protections, discussed in Chapter 2 of this book, will facilitate establishing a foreign presence by mitigating some of the political risks.

1.2 Forms of Foreign Investment

The decision to form a foreign subsidiary usually begins with a few fairly simple legal procedures; but, as the firm develops its business, regulation becomes more intricate. This section will begin by describing the steps involved in choosing a wholly-owned or jointly-owned business entity and setting up basic business operations.

A. Wholly-Owned Subsidiary Companies

The modern process of forming a foreign subsidiary is not in itself especially complex, as long as none of the subsidiary's stock will be publicly traded. A company seeking to incorporate abroad usually has two options. It can either incorporate from scratch or purchase an existing corporation. The process of incorporation involves several steps. First, the investor must determine which business form to use. As noted, in most countries, there are several forms of limited and unlimited liability business entities, and a decision will be made with the assistance of corporate counsel in the host state and international tax counsel as to which form best suits the investor's needs.

In the host state, different forms of business entities may have different requirements, capabilities, and characteristics, such as:

- the minimum and maximum number of directors, officers, or shareholders required to form and operate the entity;
- the minimum necessary capitalization of the business entity;
- the minimum funds that the company must keep on hand to meet operating expenses and to pay taxes;
- the fields of commerce or industry in which the entity can engage;
- whether the company may offer and sell an equity interest to the public market through a stock exchange; and
- the relative ease with which the company may change its management structure, basic charter, or bylaws.

Every country has at least one government agency empowered to register the incorporation of a business entity. For example, in the United Kingdom, the Companies House is charged with registering business entities. In Sweden, it is the Corporation Commission (*Bolagsverket*), and in Japan, the Ministry of Economy, Trade and Industry. In some federal states like Brazil and Mexico, registration may be regional rather than federal, or both federal and regional.

In some countries, such as Sweden, this process can be expedited through the purchase of a pre-formed company. A **shelf company** is a business entity that has been registered and formed but has no business operations or assets. Some business firms create and maintain shelf companies to sell to investors to allow the company to begin business more rapidly, because all of the formalities of registration and approval have already been completed. If the shelf company has been in existence for a significant period of time, it may also carry other advantages, such as allowing the investor to bid on contracts that are open only to a company that has existed in the jurisdiction for a defined minimum period of time, or making it easier to obtain credit because of its longevity. However, some countries, such as France, do not permit the use of shelf companies.

B. Joint Ventures

Many foreign investments are fully owned by the investor. The investor bears all of the risk and reaps all of the reward of the investment. However, some kinds of investments require cooperation with a partner to achieve success. Consider the following examples:

- the investor may have insufficient funds to support a large investment and to sustain its risks without the assistance of another investor;
- the investor may need intellectual property that the owner refuses to license to anyone except a business partner;
- the investor would like to begin manufacturing or providing services on a foreign market immediately and needs a partner on that market with an existing manufacturing plant or other facilities;
- the investor may wish to do business on a foreign market in which it has little experience or knowledge and seeks long-term assistance from a company that is already well established on that market, has a well-known reputation and contacts, and has a credit rating on the local market that can facilitate loans from local banks; or
- the law of the host state may require part or majority ownership by local nationals of certain kinds of businesses within its territory, or it may simply require some projects to be undertaken with local nationals.

Notice that, in some of these scenarios, the fact that an intended investment is taking place in a foreign market weighs especially heavily in a decision to collaborate with another business firm.

When an investor decides to cooperate with another, unaffiliated investor in forming a foreign company, a **joint venture (JV)** is commonly chosen as the business model. The usual form of JV is an **equity joint venture**, in which all of the parties to the JV receive stock or another ownership interest in a newly formed or acquired company. An equity JV typically includes a contract between the participating companies, but it almost always involves either the formation of a new, jointly-owned company, or the purchase by one of the participating companies of an ownership interest in another participating company, so that the parties ultimately share ownership of a company operating within the host state. This arrangement is common when the foreign investor wishes to establish a business presence in the host state to take advantage of laws favoring companies formed under the laws of the host state and to limit liability.

Equity joint ventures are frequent in international collaborations involving the building and operation of a manufacturing plant in the host state; in major construction and infrastructure projects in foreign countries, and in long-term service investments, such as hotels, resorts, casinos, and theme parks. One attraction of equity ownership is that it reassures the JV partners that they will not lose control of the business or any IP they contribute to it. Equity ownership also gives each partner a stake in the success of the business venture, which creates an incentive to perform contractual obligations in good faith. In some countries, part or majority local ownership of the company can also create business opportunities that would not be available to companies wholly-owned by foreign investors. For example, some states will not award government contracts to companies having less than a specified percentage of local ownership. A JV company can allow a foreign investor to take advantage of such important business opportunities.

The equity JV process usually begins with a search for a suitable JV partner that will perform its part of the bargain reliably and shares the investor's business goals. When the investor has found a willing partner that seems right for the project, the parties typically sign a nonbinding letter of intent, followed by the negotiation and execution of a joint venture agreement.

An equity JV agreement will specify the capital that each investor will contribute to the JV company; the percentage of its capital may or may not be reflected in its relative ownership interest. For example, one investor might contribute 80% of the capital to the JV in cash while being entitled to only a 50% ownership interest, because the other investor is contributing its services and knowhow to the JV. Capital contributions are necessary at the beginning of the JV because no business can operate without money to hire labor, rent facilities, purchase equipment and manufacturing inputs, and obtain services such as utilities and legal advice.

In addition to the JV agreement, the parties will also typically negotiate several other key documents defining the respective rights and obligations of the investors, such as:

- articles of incorporation and bylaws of the JV company, which will define voting rights, procedures for the election of directors and officers, the JV's reporting obligations to its owners, and rules about when it may declare dividends;
- license agreements for any IP that the investors will license to the JV;
- consulting, management, marketing services, research, or similar agreements to define how the investors will contribute their expertise and resources to the JV;
- a noncompetition agreement to ensure that the investors do not work at cross-purposes to the JV;
- a confidentiality agreement to protect the trade secrets that the investors may reveal to one another in the course of the JV; and
- in some cases, a distribution or purchase agreement in case one or more investor has agreed to guarantee the purchase of products manufactured by, or services provided by, the JV.

These documents will help the investor deal with four key variables governing their relationship:

(1) the scope of each investor's duties and rights, including their contributions to the formation and operation of the JV;
(2) the relative percentage of the company's profits to which each investor will be entitled;
(3) the kinds and amounts of risk to which each investor will be subjected; and

(4) the kinds and amounts of control that each investor will have over the JV.

Although the basic terms of a JV agreement will be similar in cases of both domestic and foreign investment, foreign investment presents special risks and challenges that make a precise delimitation of these factors particularly important.

C. International Merger or Acquisition

Instead of forming a new company, the investor may choose to purchase or merge with an existing one. To understand international mergers and acquisitions (sometimes called **M&A**), it is first necessary to understand the difference between ownership of a company and ownership of assets. **Assets** are anything of recognizable value. A company's assets include its tangible property, such as real estate, buildings, equipment, stock, and products. Assets also include intangibles such as IP, trade secrets, good will, ownership interest in other companies (e.g., stock) and accounts receivable (debts owed to the company). When one company acquires another's assets, it may or may not acquire its liabilities as well, depending on the contract terms and the national law governing the transaction. In any case, keep in mind that assets can include an ongoing business, so that, by buying the assets, the acquiring company buys the business, but this does not mean that the acquiring company has acquired another company. A company and its business are two different things; a company is a legal person, but the business is just a collection of assets, such as equipment, IP, customer good will, etc.

Ownership of a company usually means the entitlement to profits of the company and at least some control over the company. One can own a small percentage of a company or all of the company, but usually when we say that a person "owns" a company we mean not just that they own a few shares of its stock, but that they own at least 50% of the company's voting stock or other ownership interest.

When one company purchases at least a majority of the voting shares of another company, it has effectively acquired that company. An **acquisition** of a company merely means that the **acquiring company** has assumed most of the ownership and control of the **target company**, which then becomes the acquiring company's subsidiary. In other words, an acquisition places the acquired company in a subordinate position to the acquiring company, with both companies continuing to exist after the acquisition. The parent company does not directly own the assets of the subsidiary; the subsidiary continues to own them. Nor does the parent company typically acquire responsibility for the subsidiary's liabilities; the subsidiary keeps those as well.

A **merger** between two companies differs significantly. When two companies merge, each company is absorbed into the other and ceases to exist, and a new company replaces both. All of the assets of both companies are absorbed by the new company, and the merging companies cease to exist independently. The new company issues stock to the shareholders of both merging companies, so that the former owners of each merging company are now owners of the new merged company. In most states, the liabilities of the merging companies pass to the new merged entity. The foregoing is a description of a **merger of equals**, which is a "pure" merger, although not an especially common form of reorganization.

In domestic transactions, mergers and acquisitions serve many purposes, such as benefiting from economies of scale, reducing supply costs, acquiring exclusive assets such as desirable contracts or important IP, acquiring tax credits, and attenuating competition. In the international business arena, mergers and acquisitions occur for all of these same reasons, plus an additional

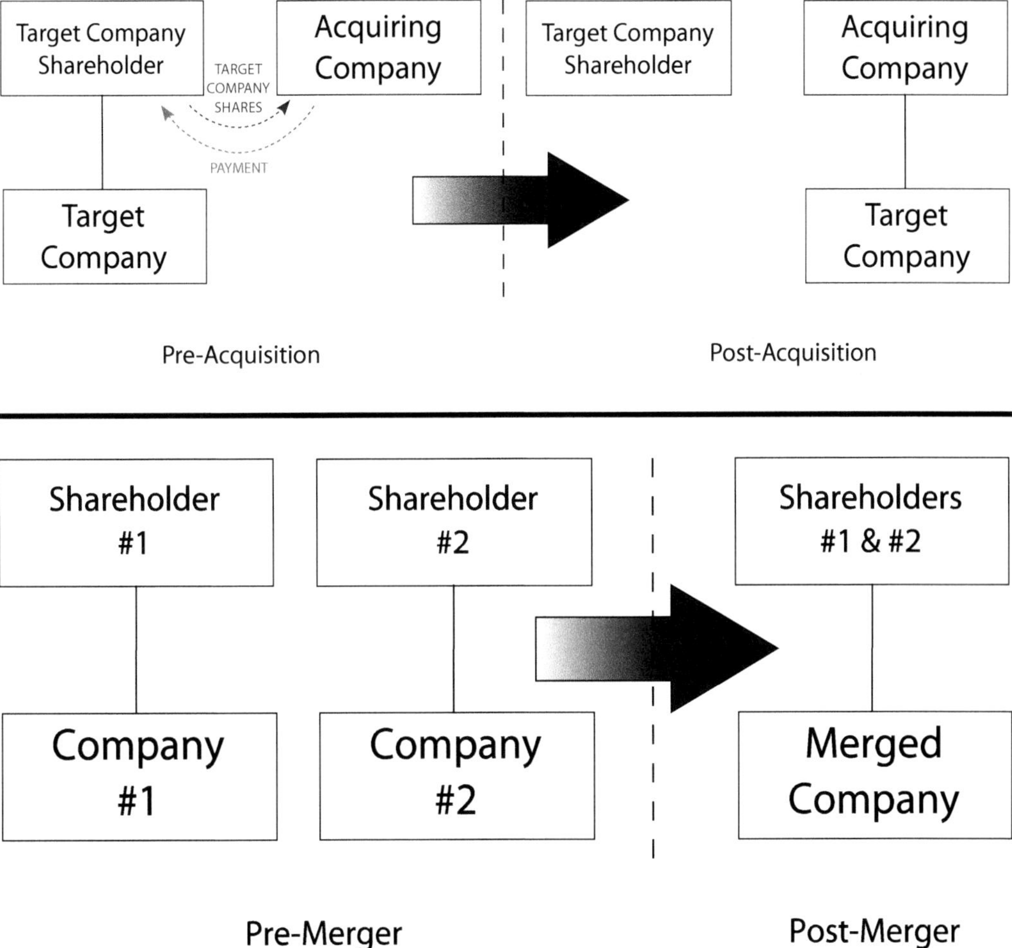

Figure 7.2. An acquisition of a company (top) and a merger of equals (bottom).

important one: acquisition of an established foothold in a foreign market. This is the same reason for which companies seek joint ventures in foreign markets, but in the case of a merger or acquisition, there is no risk of divided loyalties. In a merger, both sets of shareholders will own the merged entity and so have the same interest in its success. In an acquisition, the acquiring company will have sole control over the acquired company, and it will not have any independent partner about which to worry.

Mergers and acquisitions sometimes involve two parties with different countries of corporate formation, as when the Japanese *zaibatsu** Sumitomo Corporation acquired the U.S.-based automotive tire manufacturer TBC Corporation in 2005, or when German chemical leviathan Bayer AG acquired U.S. agribusiness giant Monsanto Co. in 2018. Even when business entities with the name nationality merge, if they are MNEs, they will have foreign subsidiaries, and the transaction will be transnational and involve requirements to comply with foreign as well as domestic laws.

Before acquiring or merging with a foreign company, care must be taken to ensure that the target company that will be acquired or absorbed into the acquiring company is as prosperous and promising as it superficially appears. There are always risks associated with buying an existing business firm. Any target company may have latent liabilities for defective products, undiscovered breaches of contracts or IP infringement, regulatory violations (for example, of corporate or securities laws, export or import rules, environmental protection laws, or labor laws), or even criminal liability that are not readily apparent.

In such cases, the purchaser of an unaffiliated company runs a risk of buying not the company or business it expects, but unforeseen lawsuits, fines, and other liabilities. These risks are elevated in an international transaction, because, aside from difficulties of translation, foreign companies may use unfamiliar business approval and recordkeeping procedures and may be subject to regulations quite different from those in the client's jurisdiction. These include rules about the registration or reporting of foreign investments in the host state market.

2 Regulation of Foreign Investments

2.1 Foreign Investment Registration and Reporting

Many states require foreign investors to notify the government prior to, or soon after, creating or acquiring an interest in a domestic business entity.

*A *zaibatsu* is a large and influential Japanese corporate conglomerate with financial and industrial holdings, currently or formerly controlled by a single family. Sumitomo, Mitsubishi, and Yasuda are all well known *zaibatsu*. The modern descendent of the *zaibatsu* is the *keiretsu*, which is a more general term encompassing a group of related companies with integrated business relationships centered around a major bank.

NOTE FROM THE FIELD

Being a Cross-Border Mergers and Acquisitions Attorney

Brian Hoffmann, Esq.
McDermott, Will & Emery LP

The globalization of business has caused a dramatic increase in the number of cross-border mergers and acquisitions around the world. Beyond simply acting for purchasers and sellers, M&A lawyers represent various other participants in M&A transactions. These include financial advisors, lenders, and others.

- When acting for the purchaser or seller, a lawyer's role can be summarized as follows:
- negotiating the key business terms of the merger or acquisition;
- structuring the transaction to take account of tax, corporate, competition, and securities laws;
- conducting due diligence;
- drafting documents which effectuate the transaction; and
- implementing the transaction by complying with the regulations of various states and obtaining necessary licenses and permissions.

M&A lawyers must have detailed experience in all relevant corporate disciplines necessary to consummate a successful deal. However, given the complexity of M&A transactions, they are often supported by experts from other practice areas of the firm, including finance, antitrust, tax, employment, and environmental law. All components must blend smoothly to address all aspects of the transaction, and to ensure relevant issues in each area have been addressed in the transaction structure and documentation. To do this, M&A lawyers must have a general understanding of specialist areas and be able to synthesize the advice in discussions with their clients.

In cross-border deals, advice in each of the various fields of law will usually be required across several applicable jurisdictions in order to ensure the transaction complies with local laws and is structured in a tax and commercially efficient manner. Foreign jurisdictions often have different requirements to register ownership changes, asset transfers, and approvals needed to effect a closing. Ensuring that these occur smoothly at closing can require intense and sustained focus, flawless organizational skills, and the ability to juggle diverse legal problems in multiple jurisdictions.

Brian Hoffmann is a partner in the New York office of McDermott, Will & Emery and former Co-Chair of the Mergers and Acquisitions group at the law firm Clifford Chance.

ARE INTERNATIONAL MERGERS AND ACQUISITIONS COMMON?

International M&A vary from year to year, but they are never rare. On average, between 2010 and 2020, about 13,000 cross-border mergers and acquisitions worth about $1.3 trillion have occurred worldwide every year. The top ten states most frequently involved in international mergers and acquisitions are all in Western Europe except one: the United States. Cross-border M&A accounts for about one-third of all M&A activity around the globe in any given year.

In 2018, U.S. companies alone accounted for nearly 30% of all international mergers in terms of both value and number of deals. The great majority of mergers and acquisitions occur within and between wealthy countries. Developing countries account for a very small percentage of global M&A in the average year. Of these, Brazil, Russia, India, and China account for the greater part.

Source: Institute for Mergers, Acquisitions & Alliances

In some cases, they may even require more prior government approval. Some states also require foreign investors, or local companies partly owned or controlled by foreign investors, to report periodically on their activities and ownership. Such registration and reporting regulations may apply universally or to certain industries only.

In the United States, foreign investment registration and reporting is somewhat complex. At the federal level, the International Investment and Trade in Services Survey Act, 22 U.S.C. §§ 3101-08, requires that all foreign investments in a U.S. business enterprise must be reported to the **Bureau of Economic Analysis** (**BEA**) of the U.S. Department of Commerce, if the foreign investor owns a significant interest in the enterprise. The most basic report is the initial investment report. In addition, foreign investors must file periodic reports of their activities. Specifically, the Act imposes three periodic reporting requirements. The accidental failure to file any of these reports subjects the investor to civil penalties; willful refusal to file the report can result in criminal fines and imprisonment for the responsible officer.

A. U.S. Initial Investment Report

The initial investment report is intended to ensure that the federal government is made aware of all significant new investments, direct or indirect, by a foreign person in a U.S. business enterprise. An investment can be "indirect" if the investor is a U.S. company, but it is owned or controlled by a foreign individual or parent company.

Any time such a foreign enterprise acquires a 10% or greater voting interest in a U.S. enterprise, the reporting requirement is triggered, and the U.S. entity must file a report with the BEA shortly thereafter. A report is also required if a foreign investor acquires an ownership interest in U.S. real property.

The initial investment report must include a variety of information that the federal government may use in measuring the extent of foreign investment in United States business and real estate, such as the percentage of ownership interest the foreign investor will have in the U.S. business and the assets and income of the U.S. business.

No *approval* by BEA is necessary; the purpose of the initial investment report is merely to keep the government apprised of foreign investment in the United States.

B. Periodic Reports

The BEA also tracks transfers of money between foreign investors and their U.S. investment companies. A U.S. company owned in part by one or more foreign investors is required to file **quarterly reports** on all financial transfers to and from its foreign parent company if the U.S. affiliate has more than $40 million in total assets or annual gross revenues. Smaller U.S. companies are not required to report their transfers quarterly.

In addition, U.S. companies of which a foreign investor owns more than a 10% interest must file **annual reports** with BEA revealing key information about the investment, such as its assets, income, and the value of its imports and exports. Similarly, U.S. investors owning more than 10% of a foreign company's voting stock are required to file similar reports with BEA. Based on the information received from these companies, BEA compiles statistics on the economic significance and effect of foreign direct investment in the United States and U.S. investment abroad, and reports both to Congress.

The final foreign investment report required is a **quinquennial benchmark survey report**. This report must be filed every five years by all U.S. investors owning 10% or more voting interest in a foreign business entity and all foreign investors owning 10% or more voting interest in a U.S. business firm. This report is a comprehensive survey and covers much of the same information as that required to be reported in the annual surveys.

2.2 Exon-Florio Review

Finally, in the United States, the **Exon-Florio provision** of the Defense Production Act of 1950, 50 U.S.C. App. § 2170, authorizes the President to block the foreign acquisition of, or a foreign company's merger with, a U.S. corporation to protect national security. Specifically, the President is authorized to prohibit the acquisition or merger if he finds that:

- there is credible evidence that the foreign entity exercising control

might take action that threatens national security, and
- the provisions of law, other than the International Emergency Economic Powers Act (IEEPA), do not provide adequate and appropriate authority to protect the national security.

The United States is not unique in requiring national security reviews of proposed foreign direct investment. Some other countries, such as Canada,* have similar laws. We will focus here on U.S. law.

To assist the President in making this determination, any acquisition of or merger with a U.S. corporation that would result in foreign persons or organizations obtaining control over the U.S. corporation may voluntarily be reported to the **Committee on Foreign Investment in the United States** (**CFIUS**), an inter-agency committee chaired by the U.S. Secretary of the Treasury.

Before filing a voluntary notice with CFIUS, the parties to the investment transaction may consult with CFIUS or submit a rough draft to CFIUS to try to elicit and respond to any objections that the Committee is likely to raise. After the notice is officially filed, CFIUS will determine whether the notice complies with all formalities. If not, it will require amendment or correction. If the notice does comply, CFIUS will have thirty days to review it. The contents of the notice are described in the Title 31, Part 800 of the Code of Federal Regulations, the relevant parts of which follow.

---

31 C.F.R. § 800.402 Contents of voluntary notice.

(a) If the parties to a transaction file a voluntary notice, they shall provide in detail the information set out in this section, which must be accurate and complete with respect to all parties and to the transaction.

* * *

(c) A voluntary notice * * * shall describe or provide, as applicable:

(1) The transaction in question, including

(i) A summary setting forth the essentials of the transaction, including a statement of the purpose of the transaction, and its scope, both within and outside the United States;

(ii) The nature of the transaction, for example, whether the acquisition is by merger, consolidation, the purchase of voting interest, or otherwise;

(iii)-(vi) [the identities of the foreign acquirer and U.S. acquired entity, and the parent companies or owners of the foreign acquirer];

(vii) The expected date for completion of the transaction, or the date it was completed;

(viii) A good faith approximation of the net value of the interest acquired in the U.S. business in U.S. dollars, as of the date of the notice; and

(ix) The name of any and all financial institutions involved in the

* Investment Canada Act, R.S.C. 1985, c. 28 (1st Supp.) (Can.).

transaction, including as advisors, underwriters, or a source of financing for that transaction;

(2) With respect to a transaction structured as an acquisition of assets of a U.S. business, a detailed description of the assets of the U.S. business being acquired, including the approximate value of those assets in U.S. dollars;

(3) With respect to the U.S. business that is the subject of the transaction and any entity of which that U.S. business is a parent (unless that entity is excluded from the scope of the transaction):

(i) Their respective business activities, as, for example, set forth in annual reports, and the product or service categories for each, including an estimate of U.S. market share for such product or service categories and the methodology used to determine market share, and a list of direct competitors for those primary product or service categories;

* * *;

(iii) Each contract (identified by agency and number) that is currently in effect, or was in effect within the past five years with any agency of the United States Government involving any [U.S. government classified] information, technology, or data * * *;

(v) Any products or services (including research and development):

(A) That it supplies, directly or indirectly, to any agency of the United States Government * * *,

(4) Whether the U.S. business that is being acquired produces or trades in:

(i) Items that are subject to the EAR and, if so, a description * * * of the items and a list of the relevant commodity classifications set forth on the CCL * * *; and

(ii) Defense articles and defense services, and related technical data covered by the USML in the ITAR, and if so, the category of the USML; articles and services for which commodity jurisdiction requests * * * are pending; and articles and services (including those under development) that may be designated or determined in the future to be defense articles or defense services * * *;

(iii) [Nuclear materials and technologies];

(iv) Select Agents and Toxins * * *;

(5) Whether the U.S. business that is the subject of the transaction:

* * *

(ii) Has technology that has military applications (if so, an identification of such technology and a description of such military applications shall be included); and

(6) With respect to the foreign person engaged in the transaction and its parents:

(i) The business or businesses of the foreign person and its ultimate parent * * *;

(ii) The plans of the foreign person for the U.S. business with respect to:

(A) Reducing, eliminating, or selling research and development facilities;

(B) Changing product quality;

(C) Shutting down or moving outside of the United States facilities that are within the United States;

(D) Consolidating or selling product lines or technology;
(E) Modifying or terminating contracts * * *; or
(F) Eliminating domestic supply by selling products solely to non-domestic markets;

(iii) Whether the foreign person is controlled by or acting on behalf of a foreign government, including as an agent or a representative, or in some similar capacity, and if so, the identity of the foreign government;
(iv) Whether a foreign government or a person controlled by or acting on behalf of a foreign government [has any ownership interest or control over the acquiring foreign person]; * * *
(vi) [Personal and professional information about each director, officer, or manager of the acquiring foreign person engaged in the transaction and its parent companies, and any nonportfolio investors in either company].

* * *

(j) Persons filing a voluntary notice shall include:

(1) An organizational chart illustrating all of the entities or individuals above the foreign person that is a party to the transaction up to the person or persons having ultimate control of that person, including the percentage of shares held by each * * *.

An Exon-Florio notification must be accompanied by a certification of compliance, accuracy, and completeness, as in Figure 7.3.

In addition, beginning in October 2018, there is now a mandatory notification filing for any foreign acquisition, no matter how small, of U.S. businesses involved in listed "critical technologies" if the acquisition could result in a foreign person gaining access to nonpublic technical information. Most of these critical technologies relate to avionics, metallurgy and materials processing, electronics, telecommunications, and defense items such as those listed on the U.S. Munitions List.

After CFIUS has received a complete notification, it begins a review of the notified transaction. During the review period, CFIUS members may request additional information from the parties, which they must address within three business days. In some cases, the Committee may undertake an extended review or "investigation." An investigation is required by law whenever:

(1) the acquirer is controlled by or acting on behalf of a foreign government; or
(2) the acquisition "could result in control of a person engaged in interstate commerce in the U.S. that could affect the national security of the U.S."

50 U.S.C. App. § 2170(b). In other cases, an investigation is discretionary. Any investigation will begin within thirty days after receipt of a notice and must usually be completed within forty-five days of initiation. Upon completion, CFIUS will determine whether the transaction creates a national security

EXON-FLORIO CERTIFICATION

Pursuant to subsection (n) of Section 721 of the Defense Production Act of 1950, I hereby certify that I am [the Chief Executive Officer] or [the duly authorized designee] of the person(s) submitting the foregoing [Notice] or [information], and that, to the best of my knowledge and belief:

1. The foregoing [Notice] or [information] fully complies with the requirements of Section 721 of the Defense Production Act, 31 C.F.R. Part 800, and any agreement or condition entered into with the Committee on Foreign Investment in the United States or any agency acting on its behalf; and

2. The foregoing [Notice] or [information] is accurate and complete in all material respects.

Signature: ______________________
(include printed name of signer)

Title: ______________________

Submitter: ______________________
(identify person or persons submitting foregoing Notice or information)

Date: ______________________

Figure 7.3. An Exon-Florio certification form.

concern. Alternatively, the CFIUS may simply refer the case to the President for a determination following the conclusion of its investigation.

Assuming that CFIUS does not refer the case to the President at the conclusion of the review period, if the transaction presents no national security concerns, CFIUS will so advise the parties. If it does present concerns, then CFIUS will either impose conditions on the parties to mitigate the risks to national security (it may do so simply by letter or it may reach an agreement with the parties) or it will refer the case to the President for action.

If the President decides not to act, then the parties are free to conclude the transaction. However, the President may prohibit the transaction altogether, which rarely happens, or, like the CFIUS, he or she may impose conditions on the parties. Why file a voluntary notice if such problems may result? Because it preempts the potentially disastrous possibility that the President will evaluate and prohibit the investment after the time, effort, and expense of concluding the merger or acquisition.

In assessing the national security consequences of a foreign investment, the Exon-Florio provision lists the following factors that the President may consider in determining the effects of a foreign acquisition on national security:

- domestic production needed for national defense requirements, relative to the capacity of domestic industries to meet those requirements;
- the control of domestic industries and commercial activity by foreign citizens as it affects the capability and capacity of the U.S. to meet the requirements of national security;
- the potential effects of the transaction on the sales of military goods, equipment, or technology to a country that supports terrorism or proliferates missile technology or chemical and biological weapons; and
- the potential effects of the transaction on U.S. technological leadership in areas affecting U.S. national security.

50 U.S.C. App. § 2170(f).

As these factors indicate, the primary concerns in CFIUS or the President's analysis are the energy industry; defense industry; industries on which the defense industry depends, such as industries controlling key materials, technologies, and research; health care; and telecommunications infrastructure. The concern that these factors are intended to address is that foreign investors may not prioritize U.S. interests because they lack a sense of loyalty to the United States or its government, and at a critical moment of national security they may act, or be required by the national governments to act, in a manner harmful to U.S. national interests.

The Defense Production Act provides that the President's decision "shall not be subject to judicial review." 50 U.S.C. App. § 2170(e). Nonetheless, federal discretion to require the divestment of assets acquired by a foreign company is not limitless. In *Ralls Corp. v. Committee on Foreign Investment in the United States*, 758 F.3d 296 (D.C. Cir. 2014), the U.S. Circuit Court for the District of Columbia held that, notwithstanding the President's statutory discretion, the Exon-Florio provision does not clearly bar a U.S. company's claim that a blocking order violates constitutional due process. Specifically, the plaintiff claimed that CFIUS had failed to disclose the nature of the national security threat that the acquisition allegedly posed. If CFIUS or the President were to present a credible allegation that a proposed merger or acquisition threatens U.S. national security interests, however, it is unlikely that a court would interfere.

2.3 Competition Law Notification and Approval

When one business firm merges with or acquires an unaffiliated firm or its business assets, there is a possibility that the resulting reduction in independent economic entities will decrease competition in the marketplace.

Case Study

An Extraterritorial Exon-Florio?

Figure 7.4. An Aixtron machine for depositing thin films on semiconductor wafers. Credit: © 2015 by Aixtron SE

On December 5, 2016, U.S. President Obama issued an executive order blocking Fujian Grand Chip Investment Fund, a private Chinese firm, from acquiring Aixtron SE, a German semiconductor manufacturer.

Why? Aixtron SE controls semiconductor manufacturing technology used in sensitive military applications. Its U.S. subsidiary accounted for about 20% of Aixtron's global revenues. The Obama Administration was concerned that, by gaining access to this technology, China could control the availability of products necessary for the U.S. military edge.

Chinese foreign direct investment in the United States increased dramatically between 2010 and 2018. According to BEA, the value of Chinese investment increased from $1.6 billion in 2009 to $7 billion in 2012, to $27 billion in 2016. This has caused concern among national security experts, because the Chinese government is a human-rights-violating dictatorship that has committed acts hostile to the United States in the past. Although China never owned Fujian Grand Chip, as a communist state, it could in the future nationalize the company or adopt laws to prevent Fujian Grand Chip from supplying equipment to the U.S. Department of Defense.

The December 2016 order represents the first time in history that a U.S. President entirely blocked a prospective transaction using Exon-Florio. Although the parties appear to have offered to insulate Aixtron's U.S. operations from Chinese control through a trust arrangement, the Obama Administration determined that no mitigation efforts could remove the threat to U.S. national security.

There is no evidence of a general U.S. policy of blocking Chinese investment in U.S. technology industries. Most Exon-Florio notifications involving Chinese foreign investment provoke no adverse reaction from CFIUS. However, the fact that the Exon-Florio provision was used to block an acquisition of a company whose operations are predominantly outside the United States demonstrates the long reach of U.S. investment regulation.

Although fewer business firms does not necessarily mean less competition, eliminating competitors can result in reductions in output and increases in consumer prices.

To detect mergers or acquisitions that would have a negative effect on competition, states with developed economies require such acquisitions to be submitted to the government for review if the firms or assets involved surpass a certain size threshold. **Premerger notification** rules are part of U.S. antitrust law. They typically require either notification or approval of mergers or acquisitions that risk significantly reducing competition.

In considering how competition regulation of international M&A transactions may affect business plans, three important questions must be considered:

1. To what extent is notification or approval of a merger or acquisition necessary in states in which the client or its acquisition target are *not* located? In other words, to what extent to do states exercise extraterritorial regulation of M&A?

2. In those states requiring notification of mergers or acquisitions, when must notification be filed? Before the transaction or afterward?

3. In those states, what criteria govern the determination of which mergers and acquisitions must be notified and which are exempt from notification requirements?

Here, we will focus on U.S. and EU practice, because these enforce the regulations most likely to affect a cross-border transaction.

A. U.S. Premerger Notification Rules

General Notification Thresholds

In the United States, Section 7 of the Clayton Act, 15 U.S.C. § 18, prohibits any person engaged in commerce to acquire the assets of another person engaged in commerce where "the effect of such acquisition may be substantially to lessen competition, or to tend to create a monopoly." Section 7A of the Act, commonly known as the **Hart-Scott-Rodino Act**, 15 U.S.C. § 18a, requires both acquiring and target companies to file a premerger notification with the **Federal Trade Commission** (**FTC**) and the Antitrust Division of the U.S. Department of Justice (DoJ) before completing a merger or acquisition of a certain size. After filing, the parties to the transaction must observe a waiting period of thirty days to allow the FTC to assess the competitive impact of the acquisition.

To avoid burdensome reviews of economically insignificant acquisitions, the Hart-Scott-Rodino Act limits the notification requirement to large transactions. Generally, these thresholds require the combined value of the parties to equal at least $100 million, and possibly much more. The threshold are adjusted upward each year to account for inflation and the increased size of the U.S. economy.

If the FTC or DoJ determines that a proposed merger or acquisition will have a sufficiently negative effect on competition, the DoJ may file an action to enjoin the transaction as a violation of Section 7 of the Clayton Act. Failure to comply with any resulting injunction may result in significant civil penalties for each day that the violation continues. Injunctions are not especially common, however. More typically, the agencies will recommend that the companies offset the market concentration expected to result from the acquisition by divesting some assets (typically, one or more divisions, subsidiaries, or manufacturing facilities). In this way, increased concentration in one market, meaning decreased competition, is counterbalanced by decreased market concentration, meaning greater competition, in another.

Notifications in Cross-Border Transactions

The Hart-Scott-Rodino Act does not specify whether the notification requirement applies any differently when a U.S. company acquires foreign assets. However, because the purpose of U.S. antitrust law is to protect U.S. markets from anticompetitive conduct, the fact that the target business firm or assets is not located in the United States may mitigate the risk of the merger or acquisition harming competition in the United States. The FTC has accordingly adopted special exemptions for acquisitions of foreign assets and shares that do not apply in purely domestic transactions.

Under 16 C.F.R. §§ 802.50-802.51, when a U.S. person acquires foreign assets or the voting securities of a foreign business firm, no premerger notification must be filed unless, after the acquisition, the acquirer would hold total foreign assets that generate very considerable assets or annual sales (in 2020, at least $90 million) into the United States. Moreover, these thresholds are considerably higher when both the parties, or the acquiring person and the acquired assets, are foreign. The value of U.S. assets and the amount of sales in the United States are the determining factors, not the value of the foreign assets or company themselves.

The natural corollary of these principles is that, even when one non-U.S. business firm buys another non-U.S. firm, or a non-U.S. firm buys assets located entirely outside the United States, U.S. premerger notification may still be required under the Hart-Scott-Rodino Act. The fact that the parties to the transaction are foreign does not mean the merger or acquisition will not have an effect on competition in the United States, if they have assets on the U.S. market or make sales to the United States. In this context, "assets" in the United States includes owning subsidiary companies in the United States.

A concrete example might help explain how the agencies react to mergers and acquisitions between foreign companies affecting the U.S. market. In

2007, the DoJ's Antitrust Division required a Netherlands steel producer with a steel plant in Baltimore to divest one of its U.S. steel plants in order to obtain approval of a merger with a Luxembourg company. The foreign nationalities of the merging parties and foreign locations of some of their subsidiary companies did not deter the DoJ from requiring the divestiture, because of the significant potential effects of the merger on the U.S. steel market:

U.S. Department of Justice, Press Release, Feb. 20, 2007

JUSTICE DEPARTMENT REQUIRES MITTAL STEEL TO DIVEST SPARROWS POINT STEEL MILL

Divestiture Will Preserve Competition in the Tin Mill Products Industry

WASHINGTON—The Department of Justice today announced that it will require Mittal Steel Company N.V. to divest its Sparrows Point facility located near Baltimore, Md., to remedy the competitive harm arising from Mittal's recent $33 billion acquisition of Arcelor S.A. The Department said the acquisition, as originally proposed, would have substantially lessened competition in the market for tin mill products in the eastern United States.

On Aug. 1, 2006, the Department's Antitrust Division filed a civil lawsuit in U.S. District Court in Washington, D.C., to block Mittal's proposed acquisition of Arcelor. At the same time, the Department filed a proposed consent decree that, if approved by the court, would resolve the lawsuit and the Department's competitive concerns.

To remedy the Department's competitive concerns, the proposed consent decree required Mittal to divest a steel mill that supplied tin mill products to the eastern United States. Mittal's first obligation was to attempt to divest Dofasco Inc., a Canadaian company owned by Arcelor. * * *

The Department has determined after a thorough review that * * * the divestiture of Sparrows Point will most reliably remedy the anticompetitive effects of the acquisition. The Department said that Sparrows Point is a profitable and diversified facility that has the capacity to produce more than 500,000 tons of tin mill products annually. Sparrows Point currently operates as an integrated facility that produces the steel slabs used in the manufacture of tin mill products * * *.

"With the divestiture of Sparrows Point, competition in the market for tin mill products in the eastern United States will be preserved," said Thomas O. Barnett, Assistant Attorney General in charge of the Department's Antitrust Division.

Background

Tin mill products are finely rolled steel sheets normally coated with tin or chrome. Tin mill products are used primarily in the manufacture of sanitary food cans and general line cans used for aerosols, paints and other products.

Prior to Mittal's acquisition of Arcelor, two large firms—Mittal and one other integrated steel producer—accounted for more than 74 percent of all tin mill product sales in the eastern United States. Prior to the merger, Arcelor, together with its subsidiary Dofasco, which operates a large integrated mill in Ontario, provided a significant competitive constraint on these two firms. By removing those constraints on anticompetitive pricing, the acquisition likely would have resulted in price increases of tin mill products to can manufacturers and other customers in the eastern United States.

B. European Union Competition Notification

In the EU, each member state has regulatory authority over mergers and acquisitions involving business entities formed under the member state's laws or having its head office in the member state. EU states may require notification or approval of M&A under differing circumstances, depending on the sizes of the companies and other factors. However, there is a general merger law at the European Union level as well. Council Regulation 139/2004 sets forth general EU merger regulations.

Under the EU regulation, the Commission will generally examine a merger or acquisition only where the combined "turnover" (sales) of all of the business entities involved exceeds a certain threshold of tens of million euros or more. The individual EU member states lack jurisdiction to review mergers and acquisitions for competition purposes with respect to transactions larger than these Commission thresholds, subject to a few exceptions. National premerger review authority generally applies only beneath the EU thresholds.

A merger or acquisition that meets this threshold must be notified to the Commission after the formation of a definite intent to engage in the merger or acquisition, but before its implementation. Failure to notify the Commission when the threshold is met subjects all of the non-notifying entities involved in the transaction to large fines. The Commission is charged with considering whether the merger will result in a significant reduction of EU competition.

The Commission has the power to inspect company records and facilities and to interview company personnel on the record. It backs this power with the authority to impose significant fines on any company that refuses to produce records at the Commission's request or that produces inaccurate or misleading information. The concerned parties have a right to make representations to the Commission in order to plead their cases. Based on the information submitted to it and its own investigation, the Commission will form a judgment of the proposed transaction's compatibility with the common market based on the existing degree of market concentration, the position of the relevant companies relative to each other as competitors or not, and related factors. It will then declare the proposed transaction compatible or incompatible with the common European market. If the Commission declares the transaction incompatible, it will commence proceedings to block the merger or acquisition unless the parties agree to modify the transaction in a manner satisfactory to the Commission. An adverse Commission decision or fine may be appealed to the Court of Justice of the European Union.

Just as the FTC or DoJ may review a merger or acquisition exclusively involving foreign companies, the EU Commission has sometimes exercised its power to review and block mergers between entirely foreign companies that do significant business on the European market. Unlike the FTC regulations, the EU regulation does not contain detailed exemptions for foreign transactions. Evaluation of the foreign element is left to the Commission's discretion. In 1999, the EU Court of First Instance (called today the "General Court") ruled that the Commission had proper jurisdiction over any merger or acquisition, regardless of where in the world it occurs, if it has "the substantial effect of creating or strengthening a dominant position" in the EU market "as a result of which effective competition or a substantial part thereof will be significantly impeded." *Gencor v. Commission of the European Community*, Case T-102/96, 1999 E.C.R. II-753, 785.

The Commission has sometimes exercised its discretion to achieve a result at odds with the U.S. government views on the same transaction. In 2001, for example, the Commission blocked the merger of two U.S. companies, General Electric Co. and Honeywell International, Inc., even though the U.S. antitrust authorities had cleared the merger, as described in the following excerpt.

Raymond J. Ahearn, Congressional Research Service, Issue Brief for Congress: U.S.-European Union Trade Relations: Issues and Policy Challenges, May 1, 2006, at 15-16

GE-Honeywell Case

As M&A activity has accelerated in the 1990s among U.S. and European companies, the U.S. Justice Department and the European Union's competition directorate have worked closely in passing judgment on proposed deals. Pursuant to a 1991 bilateral agreement on antitrust cooperation between the European Commission and the United States, the handling of these cases has been viewed generally as a successful example of transatlantic cooperation. In reviews of several hundred mergers over the past 10 years, there has been substantial agreement between regulators in Brussels and Washington on antitrust decisions. However, the EU's 2001 rejection of General Electric's $43 billion merger with Honeywell International has highlighted major differences in antitrust standards and processes employed by the EU and the United States. In the process, some observers have argued that the GE-Honeywell case points to a need for closer consultations or convergence in antitrust standards.

The GE-Honeywell merger would have combined producers of complementary aircraft components. GE produces aircraft engines and Honeywell makes advanced avionics such as airborne collision warning devices and navigation equipment. GE and Honeywell do not compete over any large range of products. The combined company arguably would have been able to offer customers (mostly Boeing and Airbus) lower prices for a package that no other engine or avionics company could match. In its review, the U.S. Justice Department concluded that the merger would offer better products and services at more attractive prices than either firm could offer individually, and that competition would be enhanced.

With regard to the European Commission's merger review (which occurs over any merger between firms whose combined global sales are more than $4.3 billion and that do at least $215 million of business in the European Union), the legal standard employed for evaluating mergers is whether the acquisition creates or strengthens a company's dominant position as a result of which effective competition would be significantly impeded. The commission's Task Force on Mergers concluded that, together, GE-Honeywell's "dominance" would be increased because of the strong positions held by GE in jet engines and by Honeywell in avionics products.

EU antitrust regulators relied, in part, on the economic concept of "bundling" to reach its decision. Bundling is the practice of selling complementary products in a single, discounted package. The combined company makes more profits than the pre-merger companies and prices are lower, making consumers better off. But the EU concluded that the lower prices and packages of products that could be offered by the merged entity would make competition a lot more difficult for [European] producers of airplane equipment such as Rolls Royce * * *. In the long run, European regulators had concerns that the merger could force weaker competitors out of the market, thereby leaving GE-Honeywell free over time to raise prices.

GE officials countered that the commission relied on a theory that is not supported by evidence, particularly in the aerospace industry. Boeing and Airbus, for example, tend not to be weak or passive price takers, but are strong and sophisticated customers that negotiate all prices. And even if the new company offered discounted "bundled" packages, the winners would be the airlines and, ultimately, their customers.

In short, the GE-Honeywell case crystallized differences in standards and processes employed by antitrust regulators in Washington and Brussels. In terms of standards, in the United States, a merger could be acceptable if it results in efficiencies that regulators were convinced would lower prices to consumers, even if competition in the marketplace might adversely be affected. In Europe, however, the governing regulation requires the competition commissioner to block a merger if he determines that it will "create or strengthen a dominant position." This is based on a concern that "dominance" increases the likelihood of "consumer abuse." Regarding process, one of the most striking differences is that the European process clearly affords competitors more leeway to oppose mergers by allowing for testimony behind closed doors and places more weight on economic models that predict competition will be reduced and competitors eliminated in the long-run. In contrast, U.S. antitrust regulators tend to presume that any post-merger anti-competitive problems can be taken care of later by corrective antitrust enforcement action. * * *

C. Other Countries

Outside of Europe, notification thresholds differ from state to state, but most use either an absolute size limit to dictate which transactions require filing and which do not (as the United States does), or an either/or rule requiring reporting if the transaction either exceeds a size ceiling or exceeds a market share percentage ceiling. Argentina, an example of the former, requires notification whenever, as a result of the merger or acquisition, the resulting entity would have an annual worldwide revenue above a certain amount. Canada also has absolute monetary thresholds, but based on Canadian rather than worldwide revenues, and on assets in Canada as well as revenues from Canada. Brazil and Israel are examples of states using an either/or rule.

Of course, a state has jurisdiction to review only those mergers or acquisitions that are somehow connected to the state's market. Not all states have a clear policy on what kinds of foreign mergers and acquisitions require competition notification and review. While it is not easy to generalize, it can be said that relatively few states are as extraterritorially aggressive as the United States and the EU. In most other countries, mergers and acquisitions will require notification only if the transaction will have "some effect" or "significant effect," depending on the country, on the local market and the threshold is met.

Many states follow the U.S. and EU practice of requiring pre-merger notification to facilitate antitrust review. This group of countries is geographically diverse. Still other countries require not only prior notification of a merger or acquisition, but positive governmental approval if the threshold effect on the market is met. Other states, mostly developing countries, conduct no antitrust review of mergers and acquisitions at all. Still others perform a competition review *sua sponte*, without requiring premerger notification.

Finally, some states that do require notification to conduct M&A competition law reviews do not require *prior* notification. Some will accept notification, either within a certain period after the transaction has been completed or during the transaction (e.g., after the bid to acquire the assets or stock has been publicly announced but before the transaction is completed). Some even require both premerger and postmerger notification. The disadvantage of a postmerger evaluation is that, after the transaction has been completed the state government may require a divestiture or other alteration to the agreement that the parties did not expect and that makes the deal much less desirable for the acquiring company.

2.3 International Labor and Employment Law Issues

A. Foreign Investment and Employment Regulation

A foreign subsidiary must usually hire at least some foreign managers and employees. In most countries, employers have distinct obligations to employees that do not apply to independent agents or contractors. For example, in Belgium, employees must be given a mandatory year-end bonus. In England, employees have the right to sick pay and paid holidays. Independent contractors have no such right in either country. On the other hand, some rights or benefits apply to both employees and independent contractors. Argentina, for example, has dealer termination laws and requires compensation to employees and independent agents alike if dismissed without cause.

National laws may differ slightly in how they define an "employee." In some countries, the key determinant is whether the employer is contractually or impliedly entitled to exercise supervisory authority over the content and performance of the employee's work. The fact that the employee does not work on the employer's premises, or is not forbidden to work for other employers simultaneously, or is not paid a fixed salary, may or may not affect whether an employment relationship has arisen.

Rules defining an employment relationship can be very complex and might define the employment relationship very broadly. France has adopted rules commonly used in civil law countries. Under French law, a hired person is considered an employee unless an analysis of the following factors weigh in favor of considering the person an independent contractor:

(1) the agreement between the principal and laborer provides for specific, detailed services to be performed within a limited period of time;
(2) the laborer has discretion about and control over the means to perform the results that the principal seeks;
(3) the laborer is directly and solely responsible for the results of the services, so that the principal cannot discipline or dismiss the laborer's subordinates;
(4) the laborer provides his/her own tools, vehicles, and other material means;
(5) the laborer's subordinates or employees are not generally integrated with those of the principal; and
(6) payment to the laborer is lump-sum and not calculated according to the number of hours worked.

In other countries, such as Germany, the characterization of the relationship in the agreement between the parties plays a greater role in determining whether an employment relationship has arisen. However, even in Germany the presence or absence of an employment contract will be disregarded and the individual treated as an employee if the structure of compensation, exclusiveness of the relationship, and level of supervision and control of the individual's activities rise to the level of an employment relationship.

The consequences of classification as an employee in most countries entails a variety of legal duties on the employer's part that would not generally apply in independent contractor relationships. These can include *inter alia* the following:

- Employers are required to withhold income taxes and remit them to the state government in almost every country.

- Employers may be required to pay into social security, unemployment insurance, pension plans, and disability plans. In most countries, contributions to a social security fund at a minimum are mandatory for all employees.

- Employers may be required to comply with prohibitions on discrimination on grounds of race, ethnicity, age, gender, religion, disability, sexual orientation, and other status.

- The employer may be required to comply with employee protection laws such as workplace safety rules, maximum working hours, minimum wage, mandatory vacations, and similar regulations. These regulations vary widely. For example, in 2020, the maximum work week for nonprofessionals in Mexico was 48 hours, but in France, 35 hours. In Belgium, employees are entitled to take 10 paid public holidays per year, plus 20 days of vacation. In Brazil, employees are entitled to 30 days of paid vacation with a bonus of 33% of their monthly salary.
- Employees may be entitled by law to a defined notice period prior to termination and to compensation unless terminated for cause. For example, in Brazil, dismissal without cause requires 30 days prior notice. In Japan, the compensation owed to an employee for dismissal without cause varies from three months' to one year's salary.

Many of these regulations are nonwaivable and grant employee rights regardless of the terms of the employment agreement.

For most employment law purposes, the nationality of the employer is irrelevant. The place of the employment determines the law that governs the relationship. See, e.g., *Ventress v. Japan Airlines*, 486 F.3d 1111 (9th Cir. 2007) (applying California whistleblower protection laws to a Japanese airline operating in California).

In addition, two kinds of employment regulations tend to be especially consequential for business firms expanding internationally. The first relates to employee unions and other legally-recognized employee organizations. The second relates to antidiscrimination law, which in some countries, including the United States, has potentially extraterritorial application. This last issue will be discussed in Chapter 10.

B. Foreign Investment and Organized Labor

One of the most important consequences of characterizing a laborer as an employee is the necessity in some states of recognizing and bargaining with unions. A **labor union** is an organization of workers who collectively bargain with employers on behalf of the workers. They are usually led by democratically elected representatives who negotiate for the workers with employers at a company, group of companies in a region, or even an entire industry over salary, hours, benefits, terms of employment, workplace safety, and other issues.

The rights to organize a union, to bargain collectively, to organize a strike without retaliation, and to protection from dismissal based on union membership are internationally recognized human rights under several widely-subscribed treaties, including the International Covenant on Civil and Political

Rights (art. 22); the International Covenant on Economic, Social and Cultural Rights (art. 8); and multiple conventions supervised by the International Labor Organization.

In addition, some countries, particularly in Europe, obligate employers to create and negotiate with a works council. A **works council**, like a union, helps strengthen the hands of employees by bargaining collectively with employers. Unlike a union, works councils do not represent the laborers of an entire industry or market sector, but rather the employees in a specific company. In most states with laws requiring works councils, unions exist separately from works councils.

It is the employer that is responsible for creating a works council whenever its number of employees exceeds a certain amount (typically fifty employees). The relationship between the employer and works council is closely regulated by law. Works council members are usually elected directly, by secret ballot, from lists of candidates drawn up by employees within the company either in consultation with industrial unions or not. The employer is obliged to provide the council and its committees with facilities for consultation meetings and time for training. The dismissal of works council members is prohibited in many countries except under very narrow circumstances.

Under the laws of most European countries, the employer must obtain the council's consent for any decision introducing, amending, or withdrawing the rules on defined classes of labor-related matters. These include rules on working hours and holidays, payment systems and job evaluation schemes, health and safety at work, and the enterprise's works rules. Other powers include the council's right to prior consultation on transfer of control of the company and on the retrenchment, expansion, or significant alteration of its activities, together with the right to regular consultation meetings with the employer and the right to information. A duty of secrecy may be imposed on the council with respect to certain types of information supplied to it in order to protect company trade secrets.

In some countries, the respective powers of the works council and the industrial unions may overlap. For example, in the Netherlands, an employer that is contemplating a merger with another company is required both to consult the works council and to give the unions the opportunity to express their view. This does not mean that either has a veto on the merger, but they must be given an opportunity to reflect and comment on the proposed transaction. In addition, the union may be required by law to appoint a delegation as a grievance council in medium-sized or larger employer organizations that exists alongside the works council.

In 1994, the Council of the EU adopted a directive requiring MNEs employing significant numbers of employees (at least 300) in more than one EU member state to set up and negotiate with an EU-wide works council. The central management of the MNE is obligated to negotiate with the European works council at least once every year to discuss EU-wide business and labor concerns. The works council also has a right to be informed of developments that will significantly affect employment, such as manufacturing plant or office closures, relocation, or large scale layoffs.

Under Council Directive 2001/23/EC, EU member states must take certain measures to safeguard employee rights in case the employer sells or otherwise transfers all or part of its business to another firm. In general, the directive provides that, when the employer transfers the business, the transfer must include all employment contracts, with both firms remaining jointly and severally liable to the employees for the fulfillment of the employment contract. The transferee is further responsible for honoring the transferor's collective bargaining agreements with unions or works councils.

There are, of course, states that do not require any kind of bargaining with unions or works councils. China, for example, does not require negotiation with either. It is important to understand, however, that, in those states in which unions and works councils are common, employment terms may be subject to collective bargaining agreements that obligate employers to give their employees more liberal benefits or protections than what is required by national law. In other words, the standard of employee protection afforded by national law is a floor below which an employer may not fall, but the law does not guarantee that the employer may not be subjected to greater obligations under a collective bargaining agreement.

3 Corporate Immigration

Multinational enterprises often need to move employees and independent contractors between countries for temporary and even long term tasks. For example, consider the following three scenarios:

1. A U.S. manufacturer of specialty video displays, Plasmoid Technologies, Inc. (PTI) has recently formed a French branch office for the purpose of marketing and distributing PTI's displays in Europe. The company wishes to hire nationals of certain European states instead of Americans to conduct the local marketing and sales, because European sales experts are more likely to be familiar with local market conditions and business needs. But PTI would also like its European sales associates to be thoroughly familiar with the technical process of display manufactured and how they can be customized for the needs of business customers. Therefore, all new European sales associates must work for PTI in the United States for three to four months before taking up their foreign sales positions.

2. PTI has also recently acquired a small South Korean computer processor developer, Visual Bits Corp. (VBC). VBC engineers have much needed expertise in digital processing technologies that PTI wishes to incorporate into its displays. However, to ensure effective integration of the technologies, it is necessary for VBC engineers to come to the United States and

work with PTI for approximately one year to learn about PTI technologies and to assist PTI's engineers to incorporate VBC technologies into the displays.

3. Finally, PTI wishes to hire an Indian engineer, Shivukamar, to create and run a secure wide-area network between itself and its French branch and Korean subsidiary. Shivukamar is one of relatively few affordable people with the necessary skills, and given that the network will need ongoing maintenance and improvement, PTI wishes to hire Shivukamar for an indefinite duration.

How will it be possible for PTI to arrange for its own foreign employees, the employees of its South Korean subsidiary, and the Indian engineer to come work for it in the United States?

Every state regulates to some extent how individuals pass through its borders going into and out of its territory. In distinguishing between foreign nationals and their own citizens, who are entitled to enter and usually leave the country at will, states often require nationals of some or all other states to obtain permission prior to entry, called an **entry visa**.

States differentiate in their terms of entry for foreign nationals coming into the country for different reasons. Separate visas may be needed for entry as a tourist, for management of an investment, for employment, or other purposes. In many states, including the United States, no foreign national, or **alien**, may be employed in the state's territory without a visa that specifically authorizes employment. Any employer that hires a foreign national to work within the state without proper work authorization may be subjected to fines and restrictions on the future hiring of foreign nationals. As for the employee, a foreign national who falsifies information on any immigration form, including a visa application, may be excluded or deported from the state.

Returning to the scenarios above, PTI will need to arrange temporary entry visas for its European sales associates and VBC engineers, and an entry visa of indefinite duration for Shivukamar. A visa for temporary use is called a **nonimmigrant visa**. An **immigrant visa** is granted to aliens who intend to reside indefinitely in the state or to seek to become citizens—a process called **naturalization**. There may be significant differences between the two classes of visas.

In the United States, the great advantage of a nonimmigrant visa for an employer is that it is usually processed much more quickly than an immigrant visa. Most kinds of nonimmigrant visas take no more than two to three months to obtain. An immigrant visa, in contrast, can take anywhere from eight months to twenty years to process. For this reason, most U.S. employers apply for a nonimmigrant visa on behalf of their employees and, if it appears that the employee will remain employed in the United States indefinitely, the employer may later apply for an immigrant visa.

The fact that a nonimmigrant visa is temporary does not mean that it necessarily is limited to a brief duration. Most U.S. nonimmigrant visas can be reissued and extended, although all but a few have a cap of five to seven years. This gives the employer a buffer of time to evaluate whether an immigrant visa will be necessary for the employee. Some U.S. nonimmigrant visas can even be renewed indefinitely.

Most U.S. immigration policy is governed by the **Immigration and Nationality Act** of 1952, as amended by the Immigration and Nationality Act of 1965 and codified in Title 8 of the U.S. Code. The immigration regulations are found in Title 8 of the Code of Federal Regulations, except those administered by the Department of State (Title 22 of the CFR).

Four federal agencies are involved in the administration and enforcement of U.S. immigration regulations. The U.S. Department of State evaluates and either grants or denies visa requests in coordination with an agency of the U.S. Department of Homeland Security (DHS) known as **U.S. Bureau of Citizenship and Immigration Services** (**USCIS**). Once within the United States, a petition for authorization to work in the United States, extend the stay, or adjust the alien's status must be evaluated by USCIS.

The **Bureau of Customs and Border Protection** (**CBP**), with which you are already familiar, ensures that all visas are proper at the time the alien enters the United States. Finally, enforcement of visa conditions is primarily delegated to DHS's **Bureau of Immigration and Customs Enforcement** (**ICE**).

3.1 U.S. Nonimmigrant Visas

With very few exceptions, any non-U.S. national entering the United States must procure an entry visa. There are many kinds of nonimmigrant work visas that are used by international business firms, but we will focus here on the five most common.*

The B-1 Visa—Temporary Visitors

A business visitor wishing to enter the United States to negotiate a contract, to inspect a potential investment, to receive professional training, or for similar activities may apply for a **B-1 visa**. The B-1 visa is appropriate for a wide range of business-related activities, but it does not authorize the visitor to seek or obtain employment or to provide paid services in the United States. The B-1 visa may be valid for up to one year.

*Other kinds of nonimmigrant visas may be important in specific industries or economic sectors. For example, the H-2B visa, which allows U.S. employers in industries with seasonal or intermittent needs to augment their existing labor force with temporary workers, is commonly used in the construction and food service industries.

The H-1B Visa—Specialty Occupations

An employer may apply for an **H-1B visa** on behalf of an employee employed in "specialty occupations" that require at least a bachelor's degree or its foreign equivalent, and highly specialized knowledge. An H-1B visa may be granted for an initial period up to three years and may be extended an additional three, for a total of six years.

To obtain an H-1B visa, the employer is required to submit a **Labor Condition Application** (**LCA**) to the **U.S. Department of Labor**, whose approval is a prerequisite for the grant of an H-1B visa. In the LCA, the employer must certify that the foreign employee will be paid wages comparable to similarly situated employees, that hiring the foreign employee will not adversely affect working conditions, and that, in effect, the employee is not being hired in order to break a strike or undermine a union. In essence, the LCA is intended to assist USCIS to ensure that a foreign employee is being hired to fill a genuine need and not to exert downward pressure on the salaries of U.S. employees.

The only significant disadvantage to the H-1B visa is that each year Congress sets a numerical cap to the number of H-1B visas that may be granted. At present, the quota is 20,000 per year for graduates of U.S. master's degree programs or higher, and an additional 65,000 per year for holders of bachelor's degrees. The visas are granted to eligible applicants through an annual lottery held by USCIS in April. In most years, applicants greatly outnumber the available visas. Therefore, a U.S. employer that waits until after April to apply for an H-1B visa may have to wait an additional year to hire its foreign workers.

The L-1 Visa—Intracompany Transferees

Multinational enterprises may have ongoing needs to transfer employees—especially executives and managerial-level employees—between countries on a temporary basis. The **L-1 visa** was created specifically to permit aliens previously employed in foreign countries as executives or managers requiring expertise, and who are being transferred to the United States to work directly for the same employer or its U.S. affiliated company—whether a subsidiary, sister company, or parent company—in a similar capacity.

There are two main types of L-1 visas, the L-1A and L-1B. To be eligible for an L-1A visa:

(1) The employee must have worked in a "managerial capacity" or "executive capacity" outside the United States.
(2) The employee must have held the managerial or executive position at an affiliate of the U.S. company recently and for at least one year.
(3) The employer must continue to do business in both the United States and at least one foreign country during the employee's stay in the United States.

The L-1B visa allows foreign employees who have *not* worked in a managerial or executive capacity, but who meet the other requirements for the L-1 visa and have "specialized knowledge." Specialized knowledge means knowledge of the organization's products, services, research, equipment, techniques, management, or other interests and its application in international markets, or an advanced level of knowledge or expertise in the company's organization, practices, and procedures.

For multinational enterprises that require intracompany transfers on short notice, there is a procedure called a **Blanket L-1 Petition** that allows a business firm to establish itself as qualifying for L-1 visas and, at an unspecified future time, designate a foreign employee as a transferee for L-1 visa purposes on relatively short notice. The maximum period of stay is seven years for an L-1A visa and five years for an L-1B visa.

E Visas—Treaty Traders or Investors

There is another category of entry visas, the E category, available only to business owners, investors, and employees who need to remain in the United States for lengthy periods to oversee or work in a business firm that represents a major investment in, or substantial trade with, the United States. An **E visa** is only possible under a very specific set of circumstances:

(1) The employer and employee must both be nationals of the same foreign country.
(2) The United States has a treaty providing for preferential trade or investment rights with that country. The treaty may be a FTA, a BIT, or a treaty of friendship, commerce and navigation.
(3) The employee must be coming to the United States to serve the employer as a manager, executive, or highly trained and specially qualified employee (a so-called **essential employee**). Whether an employee is essential is determined by several factors, such as experience, degree of expertise, uniqueness of skills, and whether U.S. workers are available for the position.

Although an E visa is technically a nonimmigrant visa, there is no limit to the length of time for which an E visa maybe granted and renewed.

3.2 The Immigrant U.S. Visa

An immigrant visa, known colloquially as a **green card**, grants an alien the right to reside indefinitely in the United States. A foreign national who has obtained an immigrant visa is called a **lawful permanent resident** (**LPR**) of the United States. In order to obtain LPR status, an immigrant will be classified according to preference categories for foreign nationals. These categories are ranked according to the perceived need for, or desirability of, specific kinds

NOTE FROM THE FIELD

Being a Corporate Immigration Lawyer

C. Matthew Schulz, Esq.
Dentons

Corporate immigration attorneys assist companies in hiring and transferring personnel within MNEs between their offices in different countries. This work ranges from temporary and permanent visas to structuring employment agreements, compensation and benefits packages for such assignments. An example is preparing the secondment agreement and securing the visa to temporarily transfer a Canadian national employed in the United States on an American nonimmigrant visa for an assignment at a Japanese parent company.

Clients tend to be large MNEs. They may be based anywhere in the world, but tend to do business in two or more of the world's financial centers. We also represent banks, investors, and other entrepreneurs.

Another aspect of corporate immigration work involves the development and implementation of programs to ensure company compliance with immigration laws. This work includes affirmative training on government requirements and best practices to comply with mandated recordkeeping, as well as representing clients before government agencies in enforcement actions. An example is representing a U.S. employer during a work site raid by Immigration & Customs Enforcement (ICE). This type of work may also involve collaboration with litigation and criminal defense specialists.

When companies merge or acquire new subsidiaries, corporate immigration lawyers may also help conduct due diligence to ensure the acquired entity has complied with relevant immigration laws and advice on workforce reduction. This work involves coordinating with corporate and tax colleagues who are managing merger and acquisition projects to ensure that the proposed new company structures take into account immigration-related legal requirements for specific visa classifications and that layoffs do not violate the visa status of any foreign worker and take into account future visa requests by the employer.

One of the benefits of corporate immigration law is that expertise in the field creates opportunities for work *pro bono publico*. Corporate immigration attorneys have the privilege of providing *pro bono* assistance to individual immigrants and families unable to afford representation.

C. Matthew Schulz is a partner at Dentons in the Palo Alto office. He is a past president and of the Immigration Legal Resource Center and current chair of its Audit Committee.

of foreign nationals. The higher the preference for a class of foreign national, the more likely LPR status will be granted.

If an employer applies for an immigrant visa on behalf of its employee, the employer must file a **Petition for Alien Worker** with USCIS. The preference category that must be specified on the petition is not a type of visa. All immigrant visas are the same. The preference category simply helps USCIS evaluate the priority of the visa applicant.

The highest preference, called the **first preference** (**EB-1**) is for priority workers. Priority workers are divided into three categories:

- Workers of extraordinary ability;
- Outstanding professors and academic researchers; and
- Multinational executives and managers.

Workers of extraordinary ability are the rare individuals who have risen to the top of their field, as demonstrated by U.S. or international acclaim and extensive, documented recognition. The typical example of a worker of extraordinary ability would be the recipient of a Nobel. However, classification as EB-1 is a discretionary decision of a USCIS adjudication officer. For some, lesser indications of achievement might be accepted as well, such as membership in the National Academy of Sciences or some similarly selective and prestigious organization.

Executives and high level managers of foreign companies who are being transferred to the United States for employment may also qualify as priority workers. The prerequisites for this category of employees are similar to those required to qualify for an L-1A nonimmigrant visa for intracompany transferees. Basically, the employee must have had at least three years of executive or managerial experience with the same company (or an affiliated company) to the U.S. employer prior to entry into the United States, and the U.S. employer must have been doing business for at least one year in the United States. Overall, fewer than 1% of all immigrant visas are granted based on the applicant's EB-1 classification.

The **second preference** (**EB-2**) is for professionals with advanced degrees (master's degree or above) and aliens of exceptional abilities in the arts, sciences, or business. Employers generally file for LPR status on behalf of a second preference workers. Along with the petition, the employer must file a labor certification request known as an **Application for Alien Employment Certification**. This form is filed with the Department of Labor, except in the unusual circumstance that USCIS grants a "national interest waiver."

The **third preference** (**EB-3**) is for skilled or professional workers. This category encompasses foreign professionals with a bachelor's degree or equivalent but no higher degree; foreign skilled workers with at least two years of training and experience; and in some cases foreign unskilled workers. A labor certification is required for these workers as well. There is also a fourth preference (EB-4) for "special immigrants" who do not qualify for a higher preference category, but this category is rarely used in international business. A **fifth preference** (**EB-5**) is reserved for foreign investors who invest a significant amount of money in a new commercial enterprise (usually $1 million) and create at least ten new full-time jobs.

Visa Type	Scope of Visa	Duration
H-1B	Professionals for employment in the U.S. The number of such visas granted annually is capped.	Up to 3 years, renewable up to 6 years.
L-1	(A) Intracompany transferees working in an executive or managerial capacity; or (B) "specialized knowledge" workers.	Up to 7 years for L-1A visa; Up to 5 years for L-1B visa.
E	Traders and investors from a state party to a BIT or FCN treaty with the U.S. coming as "essential" employees to oversee U.S. trade or investments.	No maximum.
LPR	Lawful permanent resident, admitted according to preference category.	Permanent, with no renewal required.

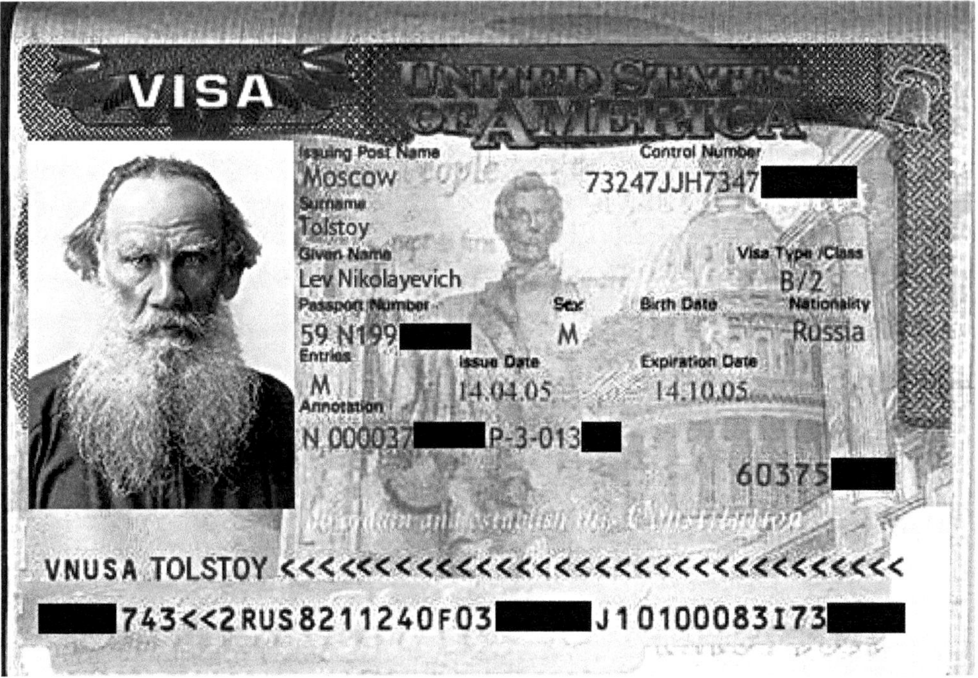

Figure 7.5. A sample U.S. nonimmigrant visa.

4 Corporate Social Responsibility

Some international corporate investment takes place in states in which democracy and human rights are still aspirational goals. When there is no legal prohibition on foreign investment in such states, MNEs may be lured to invest by the prospect of large profits, low labor costs, lax environmental regulation, convenient location, or other reasons. In the course of a foreign investment, an investor may sometimes find itself cooperating with or encouraging foreign government action repressive of human rights or damaging to the natural environment.

MNEs are not, of course, usually responsible for the political system, values, or governmental proclivities of a foreign country. But, by virtue of the MNE's economic influence, they may abet or encourage extrajudicial killings, kidnapping, torture, coerced labor, environmental devastation, or simply unsavory employment practices such as deterring unionization or providing an unsafe workplace in pursuit of profits.

As long as MNEs comply with both local laws and the laws of their place of incorporation, it may seem that their obligations are fulfilled. After all, international human rights laws and environmental treaties directly bind states, not private companies. However, some international human rights law is directly binding on individuals, such as the obligation not to engage in genocide, enslavement, or other crimes against humanity. Corporate executives and employees are bound by these prohibitions to the same extent as everyone else. Moreover, acting ethically is a moral imperative everywhere in the world for everyone at all times; no profit can justify infringing or ignoring human dignity:

> Will we rate our prudence and business so high? . . . . I have no objection,
> I rate them as high as the highest . . . . but a child born of a woman and man
> I rate beyond all rate.*

4.1 Evolving International Human Rights Law

The concept of international **corporate social responsibility (CSR)** is an attempt to inculcate into MNEs responsibility for behaving in a pro-social manner through respect for human rights and the environment, compliance with law, and contributing to the economy of developing countries. Here, we will focus on the first concerns listed, because ensuring their universal protection is the most urgent and compelling aspect of CSR.

At the international level, there is currently no general, multilateral treaty unambiguously requiring states to monitor the extraterritorial activities of their business organizations for the protection of human rights and the environment. Instead, as the Council of Europe has observed:

---

*Walt Whitman, *A Song for Occupations*, LEAVES OF GRASS (1855).

> [T]he current international framework for governing businesses in relation to human rights is extremely weak. It is almost entirely based on a mixed bag of soft law principles, voluntary corporate social responsibility initiatives and toolkits, without any effective judicial mechanism to ensure that businesses respect human rights.

Council of Europe, Committee on Legal Affairs and Human Rights, *Report on Human Rights and Business* (Sept. 27, 2010).

The "mixed bag" described by the Council of Europe includes attempts by NGOs and IGOs to promote voluntary guidelines. Most prominently, in 2011, the **United Nations Human Rights Council** unanimously adopted **Guiding Principles on Business and Human Rights**. The Human Rights Council is the UN's main organ for addressing human rights violations and making recommendations for the development of human rights. The Guidelines set forth thirty-one principles for the protection of human rights against abuses by MNEs, many of which supposedly apply directly to business firms.

These duties include, "at a minimum," basic human rights obligations set forth in the Universal Declaration of Human Rights; the International Covenant on Civil and Political Rights; the International Covenant on Economic, Social, and Cultural Rights; and the International Labor Organization's Declaration on Fundamental Principles and Rights at Work. These instruments abolish child labor and establish the following universal human rights, among others:

- to life, security of person, and health;
- to work without discrimination and to receive equal pay for equal work;
- to reasonably limited working hours and periodic paid vacations;
- to free speech, assembly, and association (including collective bargaining);
- to protection from torture and inhumane treatment;
- to freedom from servitude or compulsory labor; and
- to liberty of movement and residence within the person's state.

According to the Guiding Principles, business firms of all sizes and in all industries must not only avoid causing or contributing to human rights violations in their operations, but should seek to prevent or mitigate such violations that are "directly linked to their operations, products, or services . . . even if they have not contributed to those impacts." The Guiding Principles further suggest that business firms announce high-level policy commitments to respecting human rights and implement a "human rights due diligence" program. Such a program would set up processes to systematically detect, prevent, and mitigate the negative effects of their operations on human rights.

Many IGOs and NGOs have drafted similar nonbinding guidance on how business organizations should behave with respect to human rights and the environment. Such instruments include, among many others, the UN Draft

Norms on the Responsibilities of Transnational Corporations with Regard to Human Rights; the Organization for Economic Cooperation and Development's Guidelines for Multinational Enterprises; and the UN Global Compact, by which many business executives have made a public commitment to respect human rights and implement principles that will lead to sustainable development.

Technically, none of these principles reflect international law. They are instead the basis for the future solidification and elaboration of rules that may some day apply directly to business firms operating internationally. Promotion of these voluntary commitments may be the first in a long series of steps leading in the distant future to the adoption of an international treaty regulating business firms in their international operations.

4.2 Domestic Legal Regulation of Foreign Human Rights Violations

In the absence of public international law binding business organizations, MNEs nonetheless face practical risks when participating in activities that threaten human rights and environmental integrity. In general, states are hesitant to exercise jurisdiction over acts occurring in the territory of other states. The EU and a few states have adopted legislation requiring MNEs based in their territories to publicly report on their global human rights policies or steps taken to ensure the company does not violate certain human rights.

However, the publication of official human rights policies cannot be equated to legislated prohibitions on complicity with foreign human rights violations or environmental devastation. Such legal prohibitions are exceedingly rare. For the most part, victims of human rights violations must try to rely on local legislation and courts for redress, which may offer no remedies at all when the state government does not itself respect human rights.

For a time, the United States provided a prominent avenue of legal redress for victims of human rights violations committed by MNEs. The basis for liability was the **Alien Tort Claims Act**, 28 U.S.C. § 1350, also called the **Alien Tort Statute**, a law adopted in 1789 and never afterward amended.

This statute provides in its entirety:

> The district courts shall have original jurisdiction of any civil action by an alien for a tort only, committed in violation of the law of nations or a treaty of the United States.

Between 1789 and 1980, this statute was accepted by only two courts as a basis for jurisdiction. However, because a human rights violation is a tort committed in violation of both the law of nations—an archaic term for customary international law—and human rights treaties ratified by the United States, foreign plaintiffs began suing both U.S. and foreign corporations in federal courts for alleged violations of their human rights with some frequency beginning in the 1980s.

Notice that the Alien Tort Statute does not specify a territorial limitation or a limitation on the nationality of the defendant. It nowhere states that the tort must have been committed within the United States or by a U.S. person.

Accordingly, in many cases brought under the Alien Tort Statute, foreign plaintiffs sought compensation from foreign defendants for alleged human rights violations committed entirely outside the United States. These are sometimes referred to as F-cubed claims. Because, as noted above, it is states rather than private business organizations that are bound by international law not to violate most human rights, many of these claims relied on a theory of corporate conspiracy or complicity in human rights violations by the governments of the foreign states in which they operate.

These cases raised numerous legal questions, most saliently:

- Was the Alien Tort Statute intended to address acts committed outside U.S. jurisdiction by a foreign national?
- Is conspiracy to violate or complicity in violating international human rights law a recognized "tort . . . committed in violation" of international law?
- Can business organizations be liable for human rights violations under international law?

For several decades, U.S. case law regarding these questions remained unsettled and sometimes contradictory. U.S. courts sometimes held that an MNE that provides substantial assistance to a foreign government with the intention of facilitating a violation of fundamental human rights may face liability for the consequences of wrongful government acts under the Alien Tort Statute.

In several cases, federal appellate courts entertained the possibility of a lawsuit proceeding against U.S. or foreign private corporations for collusion with or aiding foreign governments to violate human rights in foreign lands. See, e.g., *Wiwa v. Royal Dutch Petroleum Co.*, 226 F.3d 88 (2d Cir. 2000); *Doe VIII v. Exxon Mobil Corp.*, 654 F.3d 11 (D.C. Cir. 2011); *Flomo v. Firestone Natural Rubber Co.*, 643 F.3d 1013 (7th Cir. 2011); *Bauman v. DaimlerChryster Corp.*, 644 F.3d 909 (9th Cir. 2011); *Baloco v. Drummond Co.*, 631 F.3d 1350 (11th Cir. 2011). Sometimes, these cases resulted in U.S. or foreign business firms paying multimillion dollar settlements to the foreign plaintiffs.

In 2013, the U.S. Supreme Court effectively shut down much of this line of litigation. In *Kiobel v. Royal Dutch Petroleum Co.*, 569 U.S. 108 (2013), the Court began its analysis from the presumption that Congress legislates solely with respect to U.S. territory unless the relevant statute gives a clear indication of a contrary intent—a presumption to be discussed in greater detail in Chapter 10 of this book. The Court noted that "nothing in the text of the statute suggests that Congress intended causes of action recognized under it to have extraterritorial reach," *id.* at 118.

The Court majority further interpreted the historical background of the Alien Tort Statute not to support application outside of the United States. This conclusion was problematic, because the Court acknowledged that the statute was intended to provide a jurisdictional basis for claims against acts of piracy, and such acts by definition occur on the high seas, outside of U.S. territory. The Court majority implied that piracy was *sui generis*, however, because the high seas were outside the territorial jurisdiction of every state. *Id.* at 121.

Kiobel did not entirely close the door on the possibility that the Alien Tort Statute could reach foreign human rights violations, if some of the "relevant conduct" took place within the United States. On that question, the Court merely made a general observation:

> where the claims touch and concern the territory of the United States, they must do so with sufficient force to displace the presumption against extraterritorial application. Corporations are often present in many countries, and it would reach too far to say that mere corporate presence suffices.

Id. at 124-25.

In 2017, the Supreme Court heard another case relying on the Alien Tort Statute, this time alleging a significant connection to the United States in the behavior of the alleged human rights violator.

JESNER v. ARAB BANK, PLC

United States Supreme Court, 2017
584 U.S. ___, 138 S.Ct. 1386

Justice KENNEDY announced the judgment of the Court and delivered the opinion of the Court with respect to Parts I, II-B-1, and II-C, and [a minority opinion] with respect to Parts II-A, II-B-2, II-B-3, and III, in which THE CHIEF JUSTICE and Justice THOMAS join.

Petitioners in this case, or the persons on whose behalf petitioners now assert claims, allegedly were injured or killed by terrorist acts committed abroad. Those terrorist acts, it is contended, were in part caused or facilitated by a foreign corporation. Petitioners now seek to impose liability on the foreign corporation for the conduct of its human agents, including its then-chairman and other high-ranking management officials. The suits were filed in a United States District Court under the Alien Tort Statute, commonly referred to as the ATS. See 28 U.S.C. § 1350.

The foreign corporation charged with liability in these ATS suits is Arab Bank, PLC; and it is respondent here. Some of Arab Bank's officials, it is alleged, allowed the Bank to be used to transfer funds to terrorist groups in the Middle East, which in turn enabled or facilitated criminal acts of terrorism, causing the deaths or injuries for which petitioners now seek compensation. Petitioners seek to prove Arab Bank helped the terrorists receive the moneys in part by means of currency clearances and bank transactions passing through its New York City offices, all by means of electronic transfers.

It is assumed here that those individuals who inflicted death or injury by terrorism committed crimes in violation of well-settled, fundamental precepts of international law, precepts essential for basic human-rights protections. It is assumed as well that individuals who knowingly and purposefully facilitated banking transactions to aid, enable, or facilitate the terrorist acts would themselves be committing crimes under the same international-law prohibitions.

Petitioners contend that international and domestic laws impose responsibility and liability on a corporation if its human agents use the corporation to commit crimes in violation of international laws that protect human rights. The question here is whether the Judiciary has the authority, in an ATS action, to make that determination and then to enforce that liability in ATS suits, all without any explicit authorization from Congress to do so.

The answer turns upon the proper interpretation and implementation of the ATS. The statute provides: "The district courts shall have original jurisdiction of any civil action by an alien for a tort only, committed in violation of the law of nations or a treaty of the United States." § 1350. The Court must first ask whether the law of nations imposes liability on corporations for human-rights violations committed by its employees. The Court must also ask whether it has authority and discretion in an ATS suit to impose liability on a corporation without a specific direction from Congress to do so.

I

A

Petitioners are plaintiffs in five ATS lawsuits filed against Arab Bank in the United States District Court for the Eastern District of New York. The suits were filed between 2004 and 2010.

A significant majority of the plaintiffs in these lawsuits—about 6,000 of them—are foreign nationals whose claims arise under the ATS. These foreign nationals are petitioners here. They allege that they or their family members were injured by terrorist attacks in the Middle East over a 10–year period. * * *

Arab Bank is a major Jordanian financial institution with branches throughout the world, including in New York. * * * Petitioners allege that Arab Bank helped finance attacks by Hamas and other terrorist groups. Among other claims, petitioners allege that Arab Bank maintained bank accounts for terrorists and their front groups and allowed the accounts to be used to pay the families of suicide bombers.

Most of petitioners' allegations involve conduct that occurred in the Middle East. Yet petitioners allege as well that Arab Bank used its New York branch to clear dollar-denominated transactions through the Clearing House Interbank Payments System. That elaborate system is commonly referred to as CHIPS. It is alleged that some of these CHIPS transactions benefited terrorists.

Foreign banks often use dollar-clearing transactions to facilitate currency exchanges or to make payments in dollars from one foreign bank account to another.

Arab Bank and certain amici point out that CHIPS transactions are enormous both in volume and in dollar amounts. The transactions occur predominantly in the United States but are used by major banks both in the United States and abroad. The CHIPS system is used for dollar-denominated transactions and for transactions where the dollar is used as an intermediate currency to facilitate a currency exchange. In New York each day, on average, about 440,000 of these transfers occur, in dollar amounts totaling about $1.5 trillion. The "clearance activity is an entirely mechanical function; it occurs without human intervention in the proverbial 'blink of an eye.'" There seems to be no dispute that the speed and volume of these transactions are such that individual supervision is simply not a systemic reality. As noted below, substantial regulations govern these transactions, both in the United States and in Jordan.

In addition to the dollar-clearing transactions, petitioners allege that Arab Bank's New York branch was used to launder money for the Holy Land Foundation for Relief and Development (HLF), a Texas-based charity that petitioners say is affiliated with Hamas. According to petitioners, Arab Bank used its New York branch to facilitate the transfer of funds from HLF to the bank accounts of terrorist-affiliated charities in the Middle East. * * *

B

[The Court here begins by reciting its interpretation of the history of the Alien Tort Statute, which was in its view adopted to provide a federal remedy for such cases as a private assault on an foreign ambassador or legate to the United States.]

The ATS is "strictly jurisdictional" and does not by its own terms provide or delineate the definition of a cause of action for violations of international law. But the statute was not enacted to sit on a shelf awaiting further legislation. Rather, Congress enacted it against the backdrop of the general common law, which in 1789 recognized a limited category of "torts in violation of the law of nations."

In the 18th century, international law primarily governed relationships between and among nation-states, but in a few instances it governed individual conduct occurring outside national borders (for example, "disputes relating to prizes, to shipwrecks, to hostages, and ransom bills"). There was, furthermore, a narrow domain in which "rules binding individuals for the benefit of other individuals overlapped with" the rules governing the relationships between nation-states. As understood by [William] Blackstone [in his 1769 Commentaries on the Laws of England], this domain included "three specific offenses against the law of nations addressed by the criminal law of England: violation of safe conducts, infringement of the rights of ambassadors, and piracy." "It was this narrow set of violations of the law of nations, admitting of a judicial remedy and at the same time threatening serious consequences in international affairs, that was probably on the minds of the men who drafted the ATS."

This history teaches that Congress drafted the ATS "to furnish jurisdiction for a relatively modest set of actions alleging violations of the law of nations." The principal objective of the statute, when first enacted, was to avoid foreign entanglements by ensuring the availability of a federal forum where the failure to provide one might cause another nation to hold the United States responsible for an injury to a foreign citizen.

Over the first 190 years or so after its enactment, the ATS was invoked but a few times. Yet with the evolving recognition—for instance, in the Nuremberg trials after World War II—that certain acts constituting crimes against humanity are in violation of basic precepts of international law, courts began to give some redress for violations of international human-rights protections that are clear and unambiguous. In the modern era this began with the decision of the Court of Appeals for the Second Circuit in *Filartiga v. Pena-Irala*, 630 F.2d 876 (1980).

[In *Filartiga*, the Second Circuit held that the survivors of a Paraguayan man tortured and murdered in Paraguay by Paraguayan police officers could invoke the Alien Tort Statute against one of the police officers resident in New York State, because official torture is universally recognized as a violation of international human rights law.] * * * This Court did not review that decision. * * *

After *Filartiga* * * *, ATS lawsuits became more frequent. Modern ATS litigation has the potential to involve large groups of foreign plaintiffs suing foreign corporations in the United States for alleged human-rights violations in other nations. For example, in *Kiobel* the plaintiffs were Nigerian nationals who sued Dutch, British, and Nigerian corporations for alleged crimes in Nigeria. The extent and scope of this litigation in United States courts have resulted in criticism here and abroad.

In *Sosa* [*v. Alvarez-Machain* in 2004], the Court considered the question whether courts may recognize new, enforceable international norms in ATS lawsuits. The *Sosa* Court acknowledged the decisions made in *Filartiga* and similar cases; and it held that in certain narrow circumstances courts may recognize a common-law cause of action for claims based on the present-day law of nations, in addition to the "historical paradigms familiar when § 1350 was enacted." The Court was quite explicit, however, in holding that ATS litigation implicates serious separation-of-powers and foreign-relations concerns. Thus, ATS claims must be "subject to vigilant doorkeeping." * * *

II

With these principles in mind, this Court now must decide whether common-law liability under the ATS extends to a foreign corporate defendant. * * *

Before recognizing a common-law action under the ATS, federal courts must apply the test announced in *Sosa*. An initial, threshold question is whether a plaintiff can demonstrate that the alleged violation is "of a norm that is specific, universal, and obligatory." And even assuming that, under international law, there is a specific norm that can be controlling, it must be determined further whether allowing this case to proceed under the ATS is a proper exercise of judicial discretion, or instead whether caution requires the political branches to grant specific authority before corporate liability can be imposed. "[T]he potential implications for the foreign relations of the United States of recognizing such causes should make courts particularly wary of impinging on the discretion of the Legislative and Executive Branches in managing foreign affairs." * * *

With that introduction, it is proper now to turn first to the question whether there is an international-law norm imposing liability on corporations for acts of their employees that contravene fundamental human rights.

* * * [Section II-A of the opinion represents a minority opinion and is here omitted. In it, Justice Kennedy noted that the Nuremberg Tribunal created to try war criminals after the Second World War did not hold any corporations directly liable for war crimes, but instead convicted their corporate officers. He further noted that the *ad hoc* international criminal courts in Rwanda and the former Yugoslavia, and the modern International Criminal Court, were all given jurisdiction over individuals but not

corporations for war crimes and, in the latter case, human rights violations. From this, he concluded that the Court should be reluctant to hold corporations directly liable for human rights violations.]

B

1

Sosa is consistent with this Court's general reluctance to extend judicially created private rights of action. The Court's recent precedents cast doubt on the authority of courts to extend or create private causes of action even in the realm of domestic law, where this Court has "recently and repeatedly said that a decision to create a private right of action is one better left to legislative judgment in the great majority of cases." That is because "the Legislature is in the better position to consider if the public interest would be served by imposing a new substantive legal liability." Thus, "if there are sound reasons to think Congress might doubt the efficacy or necessity of a damages remedy, ... courts must refrain from creating the remedy in order to respect the role of Congress."

This caution extends to the question whether the courts should exercise the judicial authority to mandate a rule that imposes liability upon artificial entities like corporations. * * *

Neither the language of the ATS nor the precedents interpreting it support an exception to these general principles in this context. In fact, the separation-of-powers concerns that counsel against courts creating private rights of action apply with particular force in the context of the ATS. The political branches, not the Judiciary, have the responsibility and institutional capacity to weigh foreign-policy concerns. That the ATS implicates foreign relations "is itself a reason for a high bar to new private causes of action for violating international law."

In *Sosa*, the Court emphasized that federal courts must exercise "great caution" before recognizing new forms of liability under the ATS. In light of the foreign-policy and separation-of-powers concerns inherent in ATS litigation, there is an argument that a proper application of *Sosa* would preclude courts from ever recognizing any new causes of action under the ATS. But the Court need not resolve that question in this case. Either way, absent further action from Congress it would be inappropriate for courts to extend ATS liability to foreign corporations.

* * *

[In subparts B-2 and B-3, which failed to command a majority, Justice Kennedy noted that Congress created a cause of action for foreign torture under the 1992 Torture Victims Protection Act (TVPA) with respect to individual defendants and not to corporations. Justice Kennedy concluded that the TVPA's exclusion of corporate liability should be "all but dispositive of the present case." He appears to infer that Congress would have amended the Alien Tort Statute to apply specifically to corporations if it had desired such a result. He then argued that other prudential considerations, such as the availability of alternative remedies and the possibility of foreign retaliation, argued against corporate liability under the ATS.]

C

The ATS was intended to promote harmony in international relations by ensuring foreign plaintiffs a remedy for international-law violations in circumstances where the absence of such a remedy might provoke foreign nations to hold the United States accountable. But here, and in similar cases, the opposite is occurring.

Petitioners are foreign nationals seeking hundreds of millions of dollars in damages from a major Jordanian financial institution for injuries suffered in attacks by foreign terrorists in the Middle East. The only alleged connections to the United States are the CHIPS transactions in Arab Bank's New York branch and a brief allegation regarding a charity in Texas. * * *

At a minimum, the relatively minor connection between the terrorist attacks at issue in this case and the alleged conduct in the United States well illustrates the perils of extending the scope of ATS liability to foreign multinational corporations like Arab Bank. For 13 years, this litigation has "caused significant diplomatic tensions" with Jordan, a critical ally in one of the world's most sensitive regions. "Jordan is a key counterterrorism partner, especially in the global campaign to defeat the Islamic State in Iraq and Syria." [Brief for the United States as amicus curiae.] The United States explains that Arab Bank itself is "a constructive partner with the United States in working to prevent terrorist financing." Jordan considers the instant litigation to be a "grave affront" to its sovereignty. See Brief for Hashemite Kingdom of Jordan as Amicus Curiae ("By exposing Arab Bank to massive liability, this suit thus threatens to destabilize Jordan's economy and undermine its cooperation with the United States").

This is not the first time, furthermore, that a foreign sovereign has appeared in this Court to note its objections to ATS litigation. These are the very foreign-relations tensions the First Congress sought to avoid.

Petitioners insist that whatever the faults of this litigation—for example, its tenuous connections to the United States and the prolonged diplomatic disruptions it has caused—the fact that Arab Bank is a foreign corporate entity, as distinct from a natural person, is not one of them. That misses the point. As demonstrated by this litigation, foreign corporate defendants create unique problems. And courts are not well suited to make the required policy judgments that are implicated by corporate liability in cases like this one.

Like the presumption against extraterritoriality, judicial caution under *Sosa* "guards against our courts triggering ... serious foreign policy consequences, and instead defers such decisions, quite appropriately, to the political branches." If, in light of all the concerns that must be weighed before imposing liability on foreign corporations via ATS suits, the Court were to hold that it has the discretion to make that determination, then the cautionary language of *Sosa* would be little more than empty rhetoric. Accordingly, the Court holds that foreign corporations may not be defendants in suits brought under the ATS.

* * *

The judgment of the Court of Appeals is *affirmed*. * * *

Notes and Questions

1. In an omitted part of Justice Kennedy's opinion not commanding a majority, he argued that the Torture Victims Protection Act, which does not authorize claims against corporations, is a "suitable model" for the Alien Tort Statute. What might be the relevance of an act of Congress adopted in 1992 to the interpretation of an act adopted in 1789? Why do you think most of the justices found this reasoning unpersuasive?

2. Although the majority opinion in *Jesner* left open the possibility of claims under the Statute against individual corporate officers and employees, the decision in *Kiobel* requiring a forceful connection to the United States further narrows the range of cases in which the Alien Tort Statute can be used against corporate acts affecting human rights abroad. Moreover, even when there is significant U.S. activity, it is unlikely that one corporate officer, or even several of them, have the resources to satisfy a compensatory judgment for widespread and serious human rights violations. For example, in *Jesner* itself, six thousand plaintiffs were seeking "hundreds of millions of dollars in damages." After *Jesner*, are the doors of U.S. federal courts now effectively closed to holding business actors responsible for complicity in violating human rights outside the United States?

3. In another part of the decision not joined by the majority, Justice Kennedy argued that allowing human rights lawsuits against foreign corporations could set a precedent for foreign courts to hold U.S. corporations liable for complicity in human rights violations:

> In other words, allowing plaintiffs to sue foreign corporations under the ATS could establish a precedent that discourages American corporations from investing abroad, including in developing economies where the host government might have a history of alleged human-rights violations, or where judicial systems might lack the safeguards of United States courts. And, in consequence, that often might deter the active corporate investment that contributes to the economic development that so often is an essential foundation for human rights.

Justice Sotomayor in dissent called this argument an alarmist conjecture. But might there be a deeper problem with it? One possible interpretation of the quoted statement is that Justice Kennedy believes that, even though a foreign investment may cause or facilitate human rights violations in the host state, the investment actually promotes human rights by promoting economic development. Another possible reading is that he believes that there is a high risk that foreign courts will fraudulently hold innocent U.S. corporations liable for human rights violations abroad. Would either claim be defensible?

4. In dissent, Justice Sotomayor and three other justices pointed out that the *Sosa* decision did not require a clear international consensus with regard to the mechanisms of enforcement of international law, but merely of the norms of law themselves. For example, international law forbids states to sponsor terrorism or to allow their territories to be used as a base for terrorist acts against other states. Indeed, one treaty specifically requires states to forbid corporations to finance terrorism. However, international law does not necessarily specify the manner by which states should prohibit and punish complicity in terrorism. Do these observations lead inevitably to the conclusion that the Alien Tort Statute should be interpreted to allow lawsuits against corporations? Why or why not?

4.3 Other Business Consequences of Human Rights Violations

One potential constraint on human rights abuses by MNEs is the risk of adverse publicity that could lead to consumer boycotts or increased municipal regulation. The negative repercussions to the accused company's profitability caused by public perceptions of corporate human rights violations can occasionally be significant.

This is a lesson the world's largest diamond supplier, the De Beers Group, learned. The background of the De Beers incident can be traced to the threat to peace in Africa caused by the unregulated mining of raw diamonds. Rebel groups that control diamond-rich territories in Africa frequently mine the diamonds, sometimes using slave labor, and barter or sell the diamonds on the black market to fund arms purchases that prolong or aggravate internal armed conflicts.

In 1998, the NGO Global Witness documented how these "conflict diamonds" or "blood diamonds" were being funneled to De Beers to fund sanguinary conflict in Africa. After a UN Security Council resolution condemning the effects of the black market in diamonds, some consumer groups began a campaign to boycott diamonds. The uproar embarrassed DeBeers sufficiently to motivate it to cooperate in setting up a global diamond certification process. See Thomas W. Dunfee & Timothy L. Fort, *Corporate Hypergoals, Sustainable Peace, and the Adapted Firm*, 36 VAND. J. TRANSNAT'L L. 563, 605-10 (2003).

Other companies have sometimes been subjected to costly negative publicity campaigns based on their alleged participation or complicity in human rights abuses or indifference to environmental devastation. However, it is an unfortunate fact that lightly publicized abuses are unlikely to trigger serious negative consequences. Studies have shown that consumers make buying decisions mainly based on price and quality; corporations with bad ethical records do not generally suffer significant loss of business because of unethical conduct. See Louis A. Mohr et al., *Do Consumers Expect Companies to Be Socially Responsible?*, 35 J. CONSUMER AFF. 45, 67 (2001).

Nonetheless, many large MNEs have begun to cope with negative publicity by cooperating with labor rights initiatives like the Fair Labor Association, the Global March Against Child Labor, or the UN Global Compact. In compliance with applicable guidelines, they may adopt codes of ethical conduct for their own use and that of their foreign contractors, appoint compliance officers to supervise ethical trade and investment practices, and train employees in best practices for respecting international human rights law.

Empirically, such practices have had mixed success. Private codes of conduct vary in their rigor, and not all MNEs make vigorous efforts to monitor compliance by their foreign contractors. The frequent impotence of such codes may not result entirely from the MNE's economic self-interest. Some such codes face significant practical resistance in developing countries.

For example, the issues of child labor and excessive work hours are not as simple as they might at first appear. In especially poor countries, some parents cannot feed their families unless their children earn incomes. One UNICEF study found that dismissing children in Bangladesh from jobs making textiles for multinational enterprises merely drove the children into the "black market" for child labor, such as stone crushing, prostitution, and street crime.

Similarly, laborers working for contract manufacturers may actively seek to work illegally long hours in order to earn greater incomes, and their employers may collude because of the pressures the MNEs put on them, to meet strict production targets. Those pressures may take the seemingly neutral form of deadlines with penalties for failure to meet production targets. Foreign contractors may falsify their accounting books by underreporting hours and overreporting wages to appear to meet the MNE's standards, making verification especially difficult even for MNEs acting in good faith.

As a result, one study has found that corporate codes of conduct tend to highlight labor abuses without delivering sustained improvements in labor conditions. RICHARD LOCKE, BEYOND COMPLIANCE: PROMOTING LABOR RIGHTS IN A GLOBAL ECONOMY (2012). Even if MNEs can ultimately be persuaded to behave with consistently high ethical standards in international business, private business firms acting alone cannot reliably counteract the economic, political, and cultural forces impelling systematic labor abuses in developing countries. The most reliable way to reduce violations of human rights in international trade and investment necessarily couples ethnical behavior by MNEs with campaigns addressing the root causes of human rights abuses.

5 Financing Foreign Trade and Investment

5.1 Short-Term Working Capital for International Business

Frequently, one of the first business challenges to expanding sales to a foreign country or undertaking a foreign investment is to secure financing. A manufacturer's or distributor's sales of goods take on many new complexities with the transition from purely domestic sales to international sales. These complexities bring with them costs and risks. When a business firm seeks to transition from selling its merchandise on the domestic market to selling internationally, it usually must commit to investing a substantial amount of money into the expansion. The need for investment in order to expand beyond local borders may be daunting to small firms, and many firms lack the ready cash, sometimes called working capital, necessary to fund an expansion of this kind.

Case Study

The Wages of Deception

FAIR LABOR ASSOCIATION

Corporate complicity in human rights violations may result in liability through unexpected channels. In *Kasky v. Nike, Inc.*, 45 P.3d 243 (Cal. 2002), the California Supreme Court held that a U.S. consumer could seek recovery on behalf of the public for Nike's "unfair and deceptive business practices." The plaintiff alleged that Nike had made false public statements about the conditions under which its shoes and clothing were manufactured in Asia. According to the allegations, Nike knew its contractors abused worker rights systematically:

> [W]orkers were paid less than the applicable local minimum wage; required to work overtime; allowed and encouraged to work more overtime hours than applicable local law allowed; subjected to physical, verbal, and sexual abuse; and exposed to toxic chemicals, noise, heat, and dust without adequate safety equipment, in violation of applicable local occupational health and safety regulations.
>
> In response to this adverse publicity, and for the purpose of maintaining and increasing its sales and profits, Nike and the individual defendants made statements to the California consuming public that plaintiff alleges were false and misleading. Specifically, Nike and the individual defendants said that workers who make Nike products are protected from physical and sexual abuse, that they are paid in accordance with applicable local laws and regulations governing wages and hours, that they are paid on average double the applicable local minimum wage, that they receive a "living wage," that they receive free meals and health care, and that their working conditions are in compliance with applicable local laws and regulations governing occupational health and safety. Nike and the individual defendants made these statements in press releases, in letters to newspapers, * * * and in other documents distributed for public relations purposes. * * *

After losing the possibility of dismissal, Nike settled the case by agreeing to donate $1.5 million to a NGO called the Fair Labor Association, which globally monitors the apparel industry for human and labor rights violations. The settlement allowed Nike to avoid an adverse judgment or protracted litigation in which misdeeds associated with the firm are continually on display before consumers. At the same time, contributing to a human rights NGO publicized the firm's commitment to improving foreign labor conditions.

A **working capital loan** is short-term credit (usually lasting one year or less) for the purpose of expanding or improving the borrower's business operations.

Suppose a local Vermont pastry maker called Dancing Squirrel Bakery has had such success selling its packaged "artisan" cookies on a national scale that its owners believe the cookies would be popular in Europe as well. Dancing Squirrel merely wants to sell its cookies abroad; it has no current intention to establish a permanent foreign business presence. However, in order to expand into the European market even at this level, the following will first be necessary at a minimum:

- The bakery must hire international trade and tax counsel to deal with transnational commercial, regulatory, and other legal issues.
- International trade counsel will need to consult with local European lawyers on the bakery's behalf to comply with local European laws and regulations relating to food safety, purity, and labeling; advertising; importation; taxation; distributorship and agency issues; and other matters.
- The bakery will need to protect its trademark and possibly other intellectual property (e.g., if it holds a copyright on its logo or a patent on its cookie recipe).
- The bakery will need to develop business relationships with European distributors or retailers, advertising experts, freight forwarders, and other service providers.
- The bakery may wish to register European domain names and have Web sites specially designed in foreign languages for European use.
- Whether the bakery offers short-term credit to its foreign buyers or requires payment by letter of credit, there will be a delay between the manufacturing and shipping of the cookies and the receipt of payment. This puts the bakery in the position of having to make and deliver shipments a significant time before the purchaser has paid for them.

Moreover, if Dancing Squirrel expects to need increase production capacity to fill substantial foreign demand in addition to its domestic demand, a more sizeable outlay of capital may be required. The bakery may need to lease or buy new real estate and floor space, purchase and install more ovens, hire more employees, find new sources for ingredients and equipment, and otherwise invest large sums to fund the expansion.

If the loan required is not very large, there are several ways for a business firm to obtain capital for new foreign trade and investment projects, or to expand existing projects. Here, we will discuss the most common for modest financing needs: conventional direct loans from banks, venture capital, and government assistance programs. There is another form of financing—access to global securities markets—that is too complex and specialized to discuss here.

A. Private Banks and Export Working Capital

When a business firm finds that it requires a loan to expand operations or continue profitable operations, it will often seek a conventional direct loan from a commercial bank. A **commercial bank** is a bank that accepts deposits and makes loans to business firms, charging more interest on the loans it makes than what it pays to depositors.

In a **conventional direct loan**, the size, terms, and interest rate of the loan are based on the creditworthiness of the borrower. Creditworthiness in turn is based on many factors, most of which are personal to the borrower. In evaluating the borrower's creditworthiness, the lender will typically consider the assets and cash flow of the borrower and the availability of collateral to secure the loan in order to determine the probability that it will be able to service—that is, to pay the interest on—the loan. It will also consider other important factors, such as the borrower's reputation and history of servicing past loans, or a guarantee of repayment offered by a reliable third party, called a **surety**.

Direct loans may be virtually any size, but their key characteristics are the periodic payment of interest and a fairly short term for repayment. The creditworthiness of the borrower and the availability of satisfactory collateral are the key factors upon which lenders rely to determine whether to offer a loan, and, if so, what size loan should be offered and at what interest rate. If a loan is offered and accepted, the debt appears on the borrower's accounts, or balance sheet, as a liability until repaid, while the funds advanced appear as an asset until spent. The more and larger debt the borrower assumes relative to its assets and cash flow, the less creditworthy the borrower becomes with respect to future loans. It does not matter whether the borrower uses the borrowed funds to invest in its domestic business or to expand foreign operations; the direct loan procedures and outcome are mostly the same.

A potential disadvantage to such loans is that commercial lenders generally require the borrower to put up sufficient collateral to guarantee a loan. Lenders differ on what they will accept as collateral, but many commercial lenders require that the borrower own real estate or other hard collateral. If the borrower possesses insufficient collateral, it will be unable to secure a direct loan to fund its international expansion.

B. The Venture Capitalist as a Source of Working Capital

Another source of modestly sized working capital for foreign commerce and investment is a kind of investor called a **venture capitalist**. Venture capital firms may be formed by wealthy individuals, insurance companies, pension funds, or other investors. The venture capitalist is usually not a lender. Instead, it is a business firm that offers funding to investments with high growth potential in exchange for equity in the enterprise. The investment could be a startup, such as a new foreign investment, or an expansion of an existing

KEY INVESTMENT AND FINANCE TERMS

An **asset** is anything of positive value. A company's real estate, office building, and production equipment are all assets. Assets may be intangible as well. Shares of a company owned by an investor are assets, as is the company's IP. Even the good will a business accumulates from its customers may be an asset, because it creates an expectation that customers will continue to patronize the business. When a customer owes money to a business, this debt is an asset as well, called an **account receivable** by the creditor (but an **account payable** by the debtor). In a sense, the opposite of an asset is a **liability**, which includes any obligation to pay money or anything else of value to another person.

The term **capital** or **capital assets** refers to assets that are devoted to the production of goods or provision of services for profit. In a manufacturing enterprise, the plant, the land on which it stands, and its equipment are all capital. Long-term employment contracts may be capital as well. To help you distinguish, remember that not all assets are capital, but all capital is an asset.

Equity is an ownership right in property. An **equity investment** is, accordingly, an investment in the ownership of an asset. Because company shares can be assets, someone who makes an equity investment in a corporation acquires shares of the corporation, just as someone who owns an equity investment in a partnership is a partner.

Collateral is an asset that can be used to guarantee repayment on the loan. If the borrower fails to repay the loan, it forfeits the collateral to the lender, who may then sell the collateral to repay the loan. Collateral can be almost any asset that the lender is willing to accept to guarantee the loan. It may be real property, such as land or a building. It may be moveable property, such as equipment or inventory. Or it may be intangible property, such as IP, cash reserves, third party debts, or corporate stock.

Cash flow is the ongoing income and expenditures of a business enterprise. A positive cash flow means income exceeds expenditures over time, which indicates profitability. A negative cash flow means the opposite and indicates (at least short-term) unprofitability. Nonrecourse lenders use projected cash flow analysis to determine the probability that the project will be capable of repaying the loan.

business.

Venture capitalists provide an option for foreign expansion when the business firm lacks collateral or sureties for a conventional direct loan. Venture capitalists vary in their risk aversion. Most will refuse to invest in any project carrying significant risk of failure. Some have a high tolerance for risk, however, if the potential profit is sufficiently great.

Venture capital has certain limitations and disadvantages. Because the venture capitalist will own equity in the business firm, it may have some control over how the business is run. Moreover, the capitalist will certainly be entitled to a share of the profits, which could result in the deal costing more than a loan. Venture capitalists also tend to have limited capital they are willing to put at risk, and so they are more commonly used in small enterprises than in major investments.

Finally, with respect to international investments, venture capital has limited uses, because venture capitalists tend to be uncomfortable investing geographic regions with which they have no experience and knowledge. This may pose little problem in developed countries that have vibrant investment markets, but in developing countries, the sources of venture capital are distinctly limited.

C. U.S. Government Export Working Capital Loan Guarantees

You will recall the **Export-Import Bank of the United States** (**Ex-Im Bank**) from Chapter 4, where it was described as a U.S. agency that provides credit insurance to U.S. exporters. The Ex-Im Bank can also provide insurance to private lenders for exporters seeking to expand their business abroad. The Ex-Im Bank's working capital loan guarantees can help exporters and foreign investors buy materials, supplies and equipment, labor, or products for sale abroad. Private banks may be unwilling to finance the exporter's and investor's plans when hard collateral is lacking. The Ex-Im Bank can guarantee 90% of the loan, regardless of the size of the loan. Notwithstanding the bank's name, however, the loans cannot be used to purchase imports for resale abroad. The loans typically last for up to one year.

The **U.S. Small Business Administration** (**SBA**) also offers working capital and investment loan guarantees to business firms that fall below the size ceilings discussed in Chapter 4. As was the case with export credit insurance, SBA imposes fewer restrictions on eligibility than does the Ex-Im Bank. Although the SBA only guarantees loans to U.S. business firms, the loan can be used to purchase imports or to manufacture for shipment from a non-U.S. port.

Recall that neither Ex-Im Bank nor SBA provides direct loans to U.S. business firms wishing to expand their sales or operations abroad. Instead, they guarantee loans when private lenders otherwise refuse to make the desired loan.

5.2 Financing Major Foreign Investment Projects

The construction and operation of an overseas manufacturing plant, airport, seaport, public utility, hotel resort, or other sizable project can require tens or hundreds of millions of dollars up front to buy or lease land, purchase construction materials and pay construction crews, secure a supply of manufacturing components or materials, obtain legal advice and permits, hire workers, and other responsibilities. Even very large business firms may not keep sufficient cash available to undertake such a large investment. The opportunity cost of keeping large amounts of liquid capital on hand imposes a major deterrent.

When a firm seeks financing for a major investment project, conventional direct loans are rare. This is especially true in international investments, which entail costs and risks that may be absent from purely domestic investments. For such investments, business firms usually turn to project financing.

Project financing is the process of raising capital or obtaining credit for a major investment such as large scale manufacturing, mineral extraction, construction, operation of major infrastructure, or other costly projects. Often such projects require hundreds of millions of dollars in start-up capital. In order to undertake a project of such magnitude, a business firm may need to seek the assistance of lenders that are willing to base their decision to extend credit on something other than the assets and creditworthiness of the business firm itself, which may be insufficient for a very large loan. Even if these assets are sufficient, the investor may wish to share the risk with an unaffiliated bank or other source of capital to reduce its exposure, especially when investing in a foreign country.

In major foreign investment projects, the investors (also called in this context **project sponsors**) will nearly always form a foreign subsidiary business entity under the laws of the host state. This investment entity will usually be some form of limited liability entity wholly or majority owned by the sponsors.

In any large international project, the subject of the foreign investment, the **investment entity**, is likely to lack the collateral in amounts to justify a conventional direct loan of sufficient size to itself. This is especially the case with new investments, but it may also be true of an investment seeking to expand its operations significantly. When the investment entity lacks collateral sufficient to reassure lenders that they will be able to recover the principal if the borrower defaults on the loan, the sponsors may seek a lender that is willing to consider the potential future earnings of the investment entity as a basis for the loan. In other words, the lender will base its decision to lend not on the assets of the sponsor (or even necessarily on the sponsor's creditworthiness), but on the chances of success and profit potential of the investment itself.

This is a key aspect of project finance; the lender is financing the *project*, not its sponsors, and the primary source of interest and principal on the debt will come from the earnings of the investment entity rather than the sponsors. For this reason, major projects are typically financed with **nonrecourse debt**, meaning that in the event of a default on the payment of the loan, the lender must be content to recover the loan from the investment itself rather than the project sponsors. Any nonrecourse loan is risky to the lender, because the assets of the project available to satisfy the debt in the event of default are usually dwarfed by the size of the loan.

The lender must, therefore, evaluate the economic potential of the project itself by considering a variety of relevant factors. To this end, the lender will typically ask the following questions in assessing the risk associated with an international project:

- *Is the project technically feasible?* Is the necessary technology available at the project site, or can it be obtained? Is the necessary infrastructure in place in the place of investment? Can the project be assured of adequate and reliable power, water, and other utilities? Are seaports, airports, or other transportation available and consistently functioning?

- *Is the project economically sound?* Is long term demand for the contemplated products or services assured? Are the costs of building and operating the project sufficiently low to ensure profitability? Is an affordable long-term supply of input materials or components available?

- *Are the project sponsors capable of operating the project?* Do they have sufficiently promising track records of operating projects of similar scale and type? Is experienced management available? Can the needed employees be obtained and, if necessary, trained at the project site?

- *Are there any other risk factors that might endanger the long-term success of the project?* Have any necessary host state licenses or permits been obtained? Is the economic environment in the host state sufficiently stable? Is the host state willing to commit to treating foreign investors fairly by adhering to a BIT or FTA and submitting to binding arbitration? Is the political environment in the host state sufficiently stable and favorable to foreign investment? Is there any significant prospect of a major change in government policy, war, civil strife, or revolution? Is insurance available to cover expected risks?

This close evaluation and planning of the project requires that the lender be much more deeply involved in the project than would be typical in a commercial direct loan scenario.

Financial experts call projects **highly leveraged** or **heavily leveraged** when the debt significantly outweighs the equity. Project finance is usually a highly leveraged form of debt. Moreover, the lender typically commits to financing the project over a very long term, sometimes up to fifteen or twenty years. The lender must, therefore, protect its interests in the project through legal means. This will typically take the form of multiple security interests in the project, including:

- a mortgage or lien on the land, buildings, equipment, and inventory of the investment entity;
- an assignment to the lender of all or a portion of the investment entity's earnings;
- a pledge of the investment entity's bank deposits in the event of default; and
- an assignment of letters of credit, insurance disbursements, intellectual

property, or other potential revenue sources in favor of the lender.

If the investment entity defaults on its debts to the lender, the lender may be able to recover part of the debt by seizing and selling the mortgaged assets of the investment entity under the laws of the host state. The lenders may also impose detailed requirements on the sponsor to protect the lender's interests, such as requiring that the sponsor maintain a majority of the controlling interest in the investment until the loan has been paid off.

Most major international projects are financed by large banks, but there are other sources for such financing as well. Another common source of financing is through joint ventures. Through a JV, the lender may even be a partner in the investment in a legal sense. Far from being a burden on the sponsors, however, this is another potential advantage of project financing. Some projects are so significant in size that a single business firm, no matter how large, would not wish to bear the entire risk of failure by itself, even with the help of insurers. Project financing naturally shares risks between the sponsors and the lender, and is flexible enough that it can be tailored to allocate risk in any manner desired by the parties.

Beyond limiting the risk to the sponsor of a major investment project, project finance has substantial accounting benefits. Depending upon the structure of the financing, the sponsor may not be required by government accounting regulations to report any of the project's debt in its accounting books because of the nonrecourse or limited recourse character of the debt. Such **off-balance-sheet** treatment has three principal advantages to the sponsor from an accounting perspective. First, by limiting the debt on its books, the sponsor remains free to obtain loans on its own account, because the less debt an entity has, the more are lenders willing to loan to it. Second, if the sponsor has any covenants and restrictions in its current debts to other lenders that require lender approval before the sponsor assumes more debt, these covenants and restrictions will be unaffected by the project, because it is the investment entity, not the sponsor, that assumes the project financing debt. Third, if the sponsor is a publicly traded corporation, the absence of a debt related to the project reassures investors that the sponsor does not carry a large debt load, which in turn helps to buoy its stock price.

These characteristics make international project financing especially desirable for firms that have identified resources or products for which there is a very strong demand or a committed purchaser. These include projects where purchasers are willing to enter into firm, long-term purchase agreements, such as mineral extraction or pharmaceutical manufacturing. They may also include projects sought by host governments for the construction and operation of major infrastructure, such as a power plant; subway, train line, or other urban transit system; sports stadium; airport or seaport; water purification or desalination plant; or telecommunications system.

The project financing process begins when the sponsors submit an

offering memorandum to potential lenders or equity investors. The memorandum explains the proposed project and includes information lenders need to evaluate the project's prospects. This information typically includes:

- the identity, experience, and finances of the sponsors;
- the identity and experience of other participants such as construction contractors, suppliers, purchasers, and managers or operators;
- summaries of the project and construction contracts;
- information about the host state, including its government, infrastructure, resources, and economic condition;
- a description of the risks expected to carry significant potential of undermining the profitability or success of the project, and the sponsors' plans for dealing with such risks;
- the amount of equity to be contributed to the project, and the financial projections for the project's expected cash flow; and
- proposed financing terms, including the amount of debt expected to be incurred.

Once the lenders and equity owners have been determined, or sometimes beforehand, the project financing itself centers around a network of contracts. These may include the following key contracts:

1. between a construction company and the investment entity for the construction of any building, manufacturing plant, or other facility necessary for the operation of the project;
2. between the investment entity and its upstream suppliers, lessors, and service providers for the supply of necessary land, office space, equipment, supplies, and services to the investment entity;
3. between the investment entity and its downstream distributors, clients, or customers (or the sponsors themselves) to create a market for the investment entity's products or services;
4. between the sponsors, investment entity, and lenders of working capital;
5. between the sponsors, investment entity, lenders, and insurers for the guarantee that loans will be repaid;
6. between the investment entity and a management company to operate the project; and
7. between the investment entity and insurers.

Before committing to allowing the investment entity to draw on the loan, lenders typically require that the investment entity already have these contracts drafted and executed. The investment entity must also typically have already received all necessary government licenses and approvals to commence operations. The agreements themselves will be discussed individually below.

Engineering and Construction Agreement

Among the most common risks in engineering and construction agreements are delay and cost overruns. Unplanned construction delays especially, whether caused by weather, strikes, political turmoil, failure of a supplier, or other source, can be extremely costly to the project sponsor. Delays increase costs and may cause the investment entity to breach any time-sensitive supply contracts to downstream purchasers. For example, delay in the construction of a sewage treatment plant may mean that the community to be served will not receive the agreed services on time. To guard against the consequences of delays, the contractor may post a performance bond. This way, each party has a financial guarantee of the other's performance. Insurance or a *force majeure* clause in the contracts with downstream purchasers can help protect the project from the costs of construction delay.

Cost overruns, on the other hand, cannot be insured against and may not result from any *force majeure*. Because the contractor usually bids using an estimate rather than a firm price, the investment project will bear the risk of most cost overruns. Construction costs may rise unexpectedly for many reasons, including delay, unavailability of materials, extreme weather, flawed engineering, or inflation. In such cases, the sponsors may be required to contribute additional equity to the project or seek supplemental loans. In major joint venture projects, the engineering or construction company may be one of the sponsors, which also tends to spread the cost of overruns to more parties.

Supply Agreements

Contracts for the supply of raw materials, components, and other inputs for the investment entity are sometimes called **feedstock supply agreements**. These contracts tend to stipulate long terms in order to guarantee a source of supply for the project. To increase security of supply, the investment entity may require that the supply agreement be made on a **put-or-pay** basis, which requires the supplier to supply an agreed amount of products or services or else pay the investment entity the difference between the agreed price and the price that the investment entity must pay to procure its supply elsewhere.

Put-or-pay agreements make the supplier guarantee that the investment entity will receive the needed goods or services at a fixed price regardless of whether the supplier can successfully fulfill its contractual duties. Often the supplier will agree to such a guarantee only in exchange for very substantial consideration, or if the supplier is itself a project sponsor or one of a sponsor's affiliates. The supplier's equity investment in the project will help ensure its commitment to the project's success.

Lease or Land Purchase Agreement

The investment entity is likely to need a project site for its plant, building, warehouse, or other facilities. In some government contracts, such as for utility services or major construction, the land may be supplied or designated by the host state. In others, especially purely private projects, the investment entity or sponsor will need to choose a site, which the investment entity will then purchase or lease.

Product or Service Offtake Agreements

An excellent source of security for the investment entity's future profitability is a contract with one or more purchasers that guarantees that the investment's output or services will be purchased. These are sometimes called product or service **offtake agreements**. Lenders are most willing to loan to an investment project that has one of the following three types of offtake contracts:

- **Take-if-Offered** and **Take-or-Pay.** These types of contract obligate the purchaser to buy or pay for any goods or services offered by the investment entity, regardless of whether the purchaser has an immediate use for them.

- **Hell-or-High-Water.** This kind of contract obligates the purchaser to pay for all of the goods or services that the project is required by contract to furnish, regardless of whether the project actually delivers the goods or provides the services. In other words, even if the project fails to provide the expected goods or services because of a *force majeure* or poor planning, for example, the purchaser must still pay. Such agreements are also useful if the investment entity is primarily engaged in research and development, which may entail an unpredictable schedule of deliverables.

The reference to "all" of the project's supply of goods or services does not necessarily mean all that the project can or does produce. There may be a limit to the amount of goods or services the purchaser must take under the contract. Even in such cases, though, the project has a guaranteed market for a specified portion of its goods or services. This gives the lender security that the investment project stands a very good chance of achieving profitability, even if the sponsors do not profit. A profitable investment is, after all, most likely to repay its loan.

Usually, the project sponsors or their corporate affiliates are the parties most likely to be willing to accept such definite commitments. When this is not possible, the project sponsor may offer special incentives to purchasers to induce them to accept a firm offtake agreement. Incentives may include a guaranteed price below market rates, a steady supply, or exclusivity. Sometimes the best approach may be to offer the purchaser an equity stake in the investment, thereby making the purchaser a joint venturer with the project sponsors. A joint venture purchaser has a direct interest in the success of the project and will therefore be much more likely to agree to the potentially burdensome commitment of an offtake agreement.

Not all investments that benefit from project financing require a firm offtake agreement. When the market for the investment's products or services is sufficiently robust and reliable, the lenders may agree to forego the security of an offtake contract. Such an arrangement is common in oilfield development, mineral mines, and other commodity production investments. In most other cases, however, the lender expects an offtake agreement to include provisions that decrease the risks of project failure.

Loan Agreements

As noted above, the debt in a project financing arrangement will be nonrecourse. Typically, the loan agreement will define two key aspects of the lending relationship between the lenders on one hand and the investment entity and sponsors on the other. The first aspect is expressed in provisions to limit the risks of default or nonpayment that the lender must undertake. For example, the loan agreement may require:

- that the project sponsors make all necessary funds available for the completion of the project through loans or equity contributions;
- prior lender approval of any additional debt (even subordinate debt) to be undertaken by the project;
- prior lender approval of any contemplated amendment to the key supply, construction, offtake, or other agreements;
- prior lender approval of the investment entity's merger with, or acquisition by, another company, which could lead to a diversion of the loan funds to the new company for uses other than the original project;
- that the investment entity justify all draws on the loan by presenting invoices, supply agreements, or other evidence of the need to make expenditures in order to allow the lender to monitor the project's use of funds and satisfy itself that the funds are being used responsibly;
- that the investment entity maintain a minimum amount of working liquid capital to service the debt and pay for its feedstock; and/or
- that all interest and principal payments be made on time before the investment entity pays any dividends to the sponsors.

The second aspect of the loan agreement is the compensation that the lender can expect. This will typically take the form of one or more interest rates calculated as a percentage of the loan amount. This aspect will often be complicated by the need to capitalize interest. A new investment project may not become sufficiently profitable to pay interest on the loan until several years after investment has begun. In a normal commercial loan, interest becomes payable as soon as it starts accruing. The principal loan may become payable

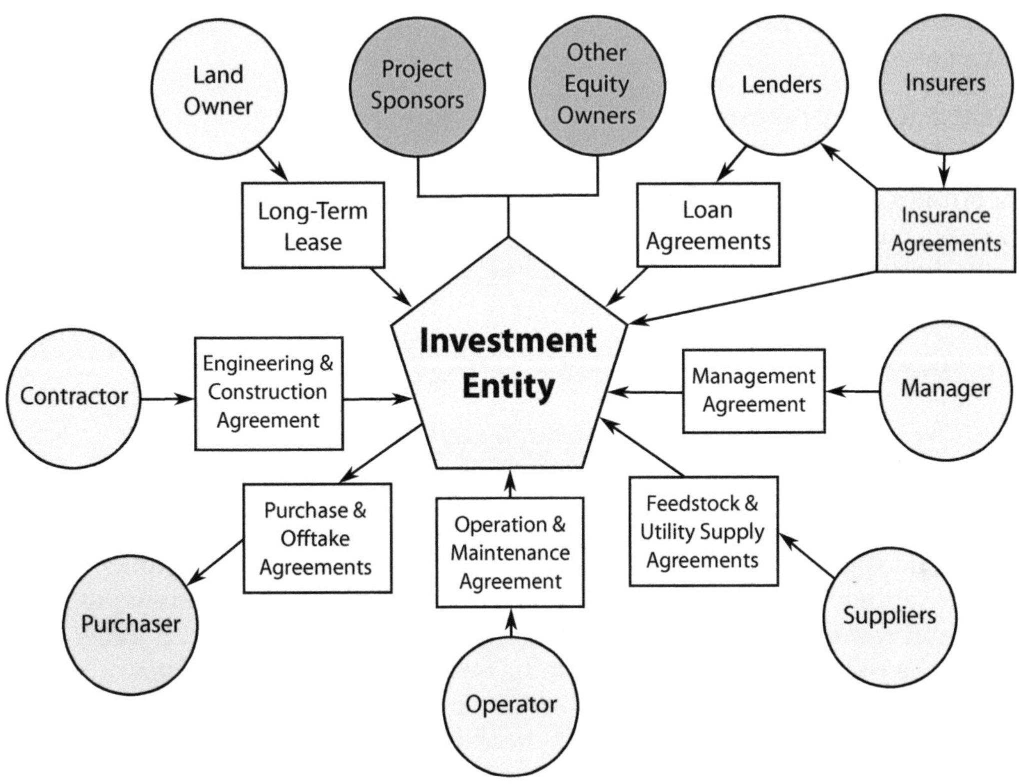

Figure 7.6. A graphic depiction of the major project financing participants.

in installments immediately as well. In project finance, interest and principal payments may not be possible for many months or years. To account for this trait of large international projects, it is common for the lender to capitalize or compound the interest in order to delay payment for a specified period. This gives the investment a chance to become profitable without having to give up earnings crucial to its future success in order to service debt.

Operations and Maintenance Agreement

The investment entity may in some cases hire its own managers and employees to run the project, whether it is a manufacturing plant, power plant, telecommunications service, airport, natural resource extraction, or some other operation. It is much more common, however, for the investment entity to enter into a long-term agreement with another company to manage and operate the project. The operator may be a project sponsor or one of its affiliates, or it may be an independent contractor with expertise in the project type. The agreement will typically commit the operator to managing project operations in exchange for agreed compensation. The agreement may include provisions for a bonus for unusually good project performance and a penalty for substandard performance.

Insurance Agreements

As a business enterprise, the project will need general commercial liability insurance, worker's compensation insurance, and umbrella coverage. But in international project finance, the loan itself will also need to be insured to give additional security to the lender. This special insurance is the subject of the next part.

5.3 Public Sources of International Project Finance

A. The International Finance Corporation

Although investment banks and other private lenders are a common source of project finance, it may be difficult for an investor to secure financing for a major project in a developing country. Private investment banks may be too unfamiliar with the political and economic climate to accurately judge the risks and rewards of the investment project. Even when they can judge accurately, the risks may seem to great to hazard a large, long-term loan.

Fortunately, private investment banks are not the only potential source of financing in developing countries. Investors may also make use of an intergovernmental organization known as the **International Finance Corporation (IFC)**. The IFC, headquartered in Washington, DC, is part of an important group of economic agencies known as the **World Bank Group**. The World Bank Group was organized to assist in the global economic recovery following the Second World War and to help developing countries achieve economic prosperity. Another organization in the World Bank Group is the International Bank for Reconstruction and Development, known colloquially as the World Bank. The World Bank loans money to developing countries or, less commonly, to private investment entities with a host state's guarantee of repayment; it plays a relatively small direct role in private international business transactions. But the IFC is the single largest source of project financing for private projects in developing countries.

The following excerpt describes the role of the IFC in project finance in the developing world:

Carol M. Mates, *Project Finance in Emerging Markets—the Role of the International Finance Corporation*, 18 TRANSNAT'L LAW. 165, 165-72 (2004)

* * * A short historical note is in order to assist the audience to better understand the role and functions of IFC. The World Bank and the International Monetary Fund ("IMF") were created as a result of the Bretton Woods Conference of 1944, when the soon-to-be victorious Allies decided that there must be a better way for countries to

solve problems without war. In the same spirit, countries adopted the United Nations ("UN") charter in 1945. The World Bank commenced business in 1946.

The IMF and the World Bank were structured as part of the post-war international financial architecture. The World Bank's initial focus was to implement post-war reconstruction efforts in Europe and Japan. Its development activities began in the late 1950s, when decolonization started. The World Bank Group is today composed of five institutions—three lend money, one provides political risk insurance, and one serves as an arbitration facility.

IFC, the second affiliated institution of the World Bank Group, was founded in 1956 by the shareholders of the World Bank as a separate legal entity, to allow the private sector to play a role in furthering economic development in developing countries. IFC invests in the private sector. * * * The fourth member of the World Bank Group, the Multilateral Insurance Guarantee Agency ("MIGA"), was establish in 1988 and also has an independent legal status and shareholding. * * *

The specific roles of the different World Bank Group institutions are: the IBRD lends to middle-income countries on the strength of a sovereign government guarantee, IFC invests in the private sector without any host government guarantee of its investment, and MIGA provides political risk insurance to private investors. * * *. MIGA provides political risk insurance through its guarantee contracts for debt and equity investments. IFC invests in private projects, while MIGA can insure private projects. * * *

IFC's mandate is to promote sustainable private sector development, and IFC's Articles of Agreement mandate that it fulfill its mission in conjunction with the World Bank. The World Bank plays a different role in development, because by its charter, it can only lend directly to governments, or to an entity other than the government with a host government guarantee. This government guarantee can support loans by the World Bank to a para-statal (a 100 percent government-owned corporation) or to a private project. The World Bank issued these guarantees only in the last few years for private infrastructure finance. With the exception of these partial guarantees, the World Bank finances governments and government-backed projects, and IFC finances private sector, privately-backed projects.

Since 1956, IFC has been involved in project finance. * * * [T]he term "project finance" * * * generally refers to private sector financing of large infrastructure projects, principally in emerging markets, on a non-recourse basis. Until the 1990s, this type of financing was not done often because most infrastructure projects in emerging markets were government related. From 1956 until the 1990s, prior to the activation of private financing of infrastructure in emerging markets, IFC engaged in mostly non-recourse financing of industrial and financial projects in emerging markets. Beginning in the late 1980s, IFC started financing private infrastructure projects in developing countries as well. The types of legal documentation used are fairly standard now for project financing. IFC enters into a loan agreement with the project company, which is almost always incorporated in the host country's jurisdiction in an emerging market. IFC might also enter into a subscription agreement in order to subscribe to shares in the project company and most likely would also enter into a completion agreement, or a project funds agreement, which is an agreement by the project's sponsor to provide the company with sufficient capital to complete the project. This completion agreement (or project funds agreement) enables IFC to avoid assuming completion risk. As a financier, IFC will take operational risk but not the risk of non-completion of the project.

IFC also generally requires a share retention agreement, which is the project sponsor's agreement that it will retain a negotiated number of shares—generally at least a controlling interest in the project—until repayment of IFC loan. These documents have been the core of IFC's standard documentation financing package.

However, in the 1990s, it seemed as though the whole world was being privatized. Market-based economies, or forms of capitalism, came more into vogue than state-controlled economies. IFC started getting involved in financing private infrastructure projects in the emerging markets, by developing a specialty in financing infrastructure projects in the 1990s. In order to tailor financing to these particular types of projects, additional documentation was developed to address the risks of these types of projects.

IFC provides loan and equity capital for viable projects by mobilizing capital from other sources, in several ways. * * * IFC's participation in a project gives a "good housekeeping" seal of approval to the project. Very often, an IFC Board approval to finance a project means that other lenders or potential equity investors will increase their interest in financing the project, because they know that IFC performed its due diligence.

IFC looks for good private sector projects, shares the same equity risks as other investors, and makes market-based loans. IFC cannot take a guarantee from the host government under its Articles of Agreement, and it can share the project risks only with other private investors. IFC's financing and presence in the deal reassures all parties—the local partners, the governments, and the foreign investors—and IFC calls this its "honest broker" role. The value-added by IFC is money to the project in the form of loans or equity, an intimate knowledge of the host county, and a different perspective. Probably seventy percent of IFC's staff are not from the United States, but rather are from seventy or eighty different countries. This gives IFC staff a very broad perspective. Since the host governments are shareholders of IFC, they have a greater trust in IFC than perhaps in a commercial bank. Because the private sector investor knows that IFC is investing with them and that IFC shares the same risks, they have faith in IFC's objectives. The local partners in the project may sometimes see IFC as more friendly to their project and their objective of making money than the partners' own government.

One thing that is difficult for many individuals raised in the United States to understand is the deep suspicion of capitalism in many developing countries. Many governments of developing countries are also suspicious of foreign investors, and may believe that such investors are simply "profiteers" coming to the country for a brief stay, only to earn a lot of money and then leave. As a result of this suspicion, all the parties in the project must reach a delicate balance so they feel that the other party is actually sharing the same risks and is not going to try and take advantage of them. Some of these fears are based in fact, because unfortunately sometimes private foreign investors have tried to take their profits and run. Very often, the governments in emerging markets may have taxed heavily the only project that is occurring in their country. Distrust from all sides remains, but often for good historical reasons. Institutions such as IFC and other development agencies * * *, such as the Asian Development Bank and the Overseas Private Investment Corporation [now the Development Finance Corporation], must serve as a catalyst to attract private money and provide a certain amount of political risk comfort to the investors. Also, development agencies need to show the host governments that the agencies will consider the government interests and structure a balanced deal. Therefore, when an investor requests IFC financing for a new project, IFC will analyze the deal to verify that all parties share equitably in the project. IFC believes that a good investment deal should balance out the interests of the investors, government, and the local community. For example, IFC may say that high management fees need to be reduced, or back-ended instead of front-loading them. All of this also assists country development.

IFC looks for sound environmental and social management in a project. * * * IFC attempts to set standards for environmental performance because this makes a project sustainable. A key tenet of IFC is that its projects must be "sustainable" from the perspective of environmental and social performance, corporate governance, and financially. * * *

IFC invests in a broad range of sectors, such as finance, insurance, infrastructure, oil, gas, primary metals, and education. The project sponsors who seek financing from IFC are local, foreign, or both because IFC is a multilateral organization and the world's largest source of private sector finance for emerging markets. * * * IFC does not impose any mandatory arrangements, so equipment does not have to be sourced from any particular countries or follow a particular "nationality." The only restriction is that equipment cannot be sourced from the few nonmember countries of the World Bank.

IFC strives for innovation and to meet its customers' demands in terms of financial products. Loans are made generally in hard currency, of the borrower's choice. IFC recently made some local currency loans, but such loans depend on the availability and depth of swap markets in the host country. * * *

IFC also makes equity investments but tends to be a passive investor due to interpretations of a charter restriction against exerting management control over an enterprise. IFC generally does not vote at shareholders meetings, except if there is a jeopardy situation or its vote is necessary. Many private sector sponsors welcome this lack of interference in management decisions.

IFC provides another advantage to project sponsors through its equity investments. Some emerging markets fear domination by foreign investors. As a result, there are rules on how much of any investment can be held by foreigners in specific sectors. Countries sometimes categorize IFC as a local investor, which encourages foreign sponsors because they know that IFC provides the foreign investor perspective. * * *

IFC has many investments in independent power producers which are generation projects, an increasing number in distribution projects, and even transmission projects.

IFC also finances a large amount of transportation infrastructure, including toll road developments, ports, and privatized airlines. Water, which is a utility, is a more difficult sector to finance. To deal with this challenge, IFC is now looking at sub-sovereign municipal finance. This is an area that requires a lot of creativity. IFC finances a lot of other infrastructure, such as telecommunications, information technology, and agribusiness.

Finally, to highlight IFC's environmental and social standards, IFC has contributed to upgrading development in developing countries by setting high standards. IFC's environmental and social standards for loans to projects in the developing world have recently been adopted, through the Equator Principles, by a substantial number of large, international commercial banks.

The IFC's emphasis on environmental standards is intended to deflect criticism of the World Bank Group for allegedly financing projects that have negative social and environmental consequences in developing countries. Economic development requires the generation of electricity on a greater scale and may create harmful ecological effects, such as the contamination of groundwater reservoirs, rivers, lakes, and oceans with polluting fertilizers, pesticides, and herbicides from agriculture; the development of "dirty industries" such as the chemical, petrochemical, pharmaceutical, metals, and other industries that generate air, soil, and groundwater pollution; the clear-cutting of ecologically critical forests; the destruction of wildlife habitat by flooding for the creation of dams and hydroelectric power plants; etc. Some forms of economic development are more environmentally harmful than others, but all economic development tends to be more or less at the expense of environmental integrity.

The governments of some countries are willing to sacrifice significant ecological health at the altar of economic growth. Creating jobs and increasing national income not only alleviates human suffering, it confers greater power and prestige on the state and its government. The World Bank Group has sometimes been criticized for failing to make environmentally and socially responsible decisions in funding economic development. The IBRD and IFC have responded by adopting principles to demonstrate a commitment to considering the environmental impact of development funded by them. This may affect a project sponsor's chances of receiving financing from the IFC if the project plan fails to consider the likely environmental or human rights effects of its proposed investment.

B. The Development Finance Corporation

In 1949, the U.S. Congress set up a new government agency for the purpose of encouraging U.S. business firms to invest in developing countries. It was thought that the best way to prevent newly decolonized states from resorting to Communism was to encourage the creation of jobs and the transfer of technology that would improve standards of living in those states. U.S. private investment in those countries, along with direct foreign aid to developing country governments, was considered an effective way to promote foreign economic growth while building familiarity and ties with U.S. culture, products, and services.

The resulting agency, the **Overseas Private Investment Corporation** (**OPIC**), had as its mission the encouragement of U.S. investment in developing countries. In 2019, OPIC was transformed into the **Development Finance Corporation** (**DFC**). DFC provides direct loans to investment entities that are at least 25% owned by U.S. persons. Like other forms of project finance, these loans are usually nonrecourse and serviced from the profits of the investment entity. To ensure that the project will be viable, DFC places conditions on the investment, such as a maximum debt-to-equity ratio, and adequate sponsor support. Like a private investment bank, DFC can take an equity stake in development projects it funds.

In addition, DFC provides loan guarantees to private lenders to help U.S. investors obtain private financing for projects in developing countries. Such a guarantee greatly decreases the risk to the private lender and thus makes private financing more probable and less expensive for foreign investments in developing countries.

C. Regional Credit Sources

Other countries offer project finance and foreign investment guarantees more or less like those available in the United States from DFC. In Europe, each EU member state has its own public export credit insurance system, but in 1998, the Council issued a directive (Council Directive 98/29/EC) mandating the harmonization of guarantee arrangements, premium rates, and coverage policies to avoid creating competition in export policies among EU member states. Therefore, although each EU member state maintains export credit for its own nationals, export credit insurance policies are relatively uniform throughout Europe.

In addition, there are several regional credit guarantee IGOs. The **Asian Development Bank**, for example, finances investment projects and provides

Figure 7.7. The World Bank headquarters in Washington, D.C.
Credit: © 2015 by Franz Mahr/The World Bank Group

investment guarantees in developing countries in Asia. The Asian Bank has sixty-seven member states, most of which are in Asia or the Pacific islands. The remainder are European states, Canada, and the United States, which contribute political and financial support to the bank. It is headquartered in Manila, Philippines and makes or guarantees several billion dollars in loans every year. The **African Development Bank**, headquartered in Abidjan, Côte d'Ivoire, performs a similar function for African development projects. The African Bank includes some supporters in Europe, North America, and Asia. A third IGO, the **Inter-American Development Bank Group**, supports investment projects in Mexico, Central America, South America, and the Caribbean Islands. This Group includes the **Inter-American Investment Corporation**, which offers financing and working capital loan insurance for development in that region. Most members are in the region, but Japan and several European states are supporting members.

6 Protecting the Foreign Investment

6.1 Special Foreign Investment Risks

When a business firm invests in a new foreign market, it faces several kinds of risks that may be absent from, or minimal in, its domestic market. These risks may be inherent in the concept of international business itself, or they may result from political or economic instability in the host state where the investment is being contemplated.

To forestall losses caused by unexpected instability, a foreign investor may seek insurance on its investment. Investment insurance typically covers three types of risks specific to foreign investment: currency inconvertibility coverage; expropriation coverage; and political violence coverage.

A. Foreign Exchange Controls and Convertibility Risk

Currency inconvertibility occurs when the host state places limitations on, or flatly forbids, the conversion of local currency into a foreign currency. A host state may impose restrictions on currency conversion to cope with uncontrolled currency inflation and other economic woes having nothing to do with the foreign investment. Although such restrictions are uncommon, they do sometimes occur.

As you will recall from the discussion of currency exchange risk in Section 8.3 of Chapter 4, a state that consistently imports more value in goods and services from other countries than it exports will ultimately face a problem. Because, in order to acquire these goods and services, the state or its nationals must purchase foreign currencies with the state's own currency, there will be greater demand for foreign currencies in the state than for the state's own currency in other countries. This means that the value of the state's currency relative to foreign currencies is likely to depreciate over time.

Case Study

OPIC and Mall for Africa

Chris Folayan is a Californian entrepreneur born in Nigeria. Every time Folayan flew to Nigeria to visit friends and family, he would be asked to bring back retail products from the United States. Eventually, he got so many requests that tried to check in with ten bags full of U.S. merchandise and was denied boarding.

Knowing this experience reflected the fact that some African countries have a growing middle class but limited options for shopping in person or online without fear of fraud, Folayan formulated a plan to create an e-commerce retail company servicing growing African states. To answer African demand for U.S. and European products, he would base his firm's warehouses in the United States and United Kingdom, accept African currencies, and ship in partnership with reliable courier services already operating in Africa, such as DHL.

Folayan presented his project to dozens of venture capitalists and was rejected each time. The investors he approached understood the risks of retail and investing in Africa, but they did not foresee the opportunities of African markets. They were skeptical that a middleman could earn a healthy return by charging fees for making shopping more convenient for African consumers and small business firms.

Folayan turned to OPIC for assistance. OPIC agreed to guarantee a large nonrecourse loan from an African equity investment consortium, and MallforAfrica.com opened its virtual doors in 2013. By 2019, it was already servicing fifteen African countries and featured online products in partnership with some of the largest retailers in the world, including Amazon, eBay, Macy's, and Walmart. To deal with the specific needs of African consumers, MallforAfrica.com features installment payments and local pickup options for consumers without a street address. The firm now has millions of dollars in annual revenue and is growing rapidly.

Several things happen when a state's currency depreciates relative to foreign currencies. First, the depreciation tends to put inflationary pressure on the state's economy. A small amount of inflation is not a problem. On the contrary, some inflation promotes economic growth. But rampant inflation can become disastrous. When the value of the currency is rapidly changing in a highly inflationary economy, it becomes very difficult to plan for long term loans or sales agreements, because the parties must guess what the value of the currency will be in the future. In addition, the need for retailers to constantly change prices to reflect the new value of the currency imposes costs on commerce.

Also important to the state, a high rate of inflation indicates to foreign creditors that the state lacks control over its economy and increases interest rates on new state debt. Many states have a large public debt, meaning that they borrow money from various sources—private investors, other states, and intergovernmental organizations—to pay for public projects and services. It becomes more expensive for these states to borrow if creditors suspect the state may default on its loan payments, and creditor confidence in a state is always shaken by high rates of inflation.

This points to the second problem with currency depreciation. Some of the interest payments on a state's debt may be payable in a stable foreign currency, such as the U.S. dollar, U.K. pound, euro, or Japanese yen. When the state's currency depreciates relative to foreign currencies, it becomes more expensive for the state to purchase the foreign currencies needed to service its foreign debt. This often creates a vicious circle: The more foreign currency the host state needs to service its debt, the more of its own currency it has to print in order to buy the foreign currency. But by printing more currency, the host contributes more to inflation, because it is increasing the supply of that currency while demand for the currency is not equivalently increasing.

Currency held in bank accounts loses its real value at the rate of inflation. When inflation is high enough, holding onto currency for even a short time results in a serious loss. Imagine that you are a Ruritanian citizen with retirement savings of 10,000 ruros in the bank today. If monthly inflation of the ruro is 25% per month, in six months your savings will be worth the equivalent of only 1780 ruros today. In order to maintain liquid assets, persons and companies seek to exchange the inflationary currency for a more stable currency, such as the U.S. dollar or euro, at the earliest opportunity. This further contributes to inflation by flooding the market with the currency and increasing demand for more stable foreign currencies.

When the rate of depreciation increases to the point at which the state has difficulty controlling inflation and servicing its foreign debts, a state may take currency inconvertibility measures to slow the rate of depreciation and inflation. By halting the exchange of inflationary currency for foreign currencies, it is no longer possible for holders of the inflationary currency to contribute to inflation through foreign exchange. By itself, currency inconvertibility cannot end inflation, but it can slow it. Regardless, such measures can have a dire effect on foreign investors, who now encounter significant obstacles to benefiting from their investments.

The reason is simple. An investor usually invests its capital into a foreign state with the intention of earning a profit and paying at least part of that profit back to the investor. The investment will earn profits in the host state's currency, but that currency may be useful only for purchasing goods or services in the host state itself. Typically, however, the investor wants its foreign-source profits paid in a currency that it can use in its home state or anywhere else

NOTE FROM THE FIELD
Being an International Project Finance Lawyer

Douglas J. Lanzo, Esq.
Breakout Capital, LLC

Project finance attorneys interact with a myriad of players, including the sponsor; future officers of the project company; project counterparties; financial, technical, insurance, marketing, and environmental advisors or consultants; insurance brokers; local counsel; intergovernmental agencies; and many others. A successful project finance attorney must have strong organizational, team management, and negotiating skills as well as sound judgment in identifying issues, attention to detail, cultural sensitivity, and the ability to draft with precision and consistency across documents. Practitioners will find language skills useful in reading and negotiating documents in the project country without translation. Education or background in accounting, finance, international law, securities, energy regulation, and corporate taxation are likewise useful.

The project finance attorney plays a crucial role throughout the life of the project, from the initial stages of project development to the completion of the financing and beyond. As pre-closing matters alone may entail months or even years of legal work, project finance attorneys may be analogized to marathoners running at a measured pace through the various stages of a project financing with determination, focus, and the ability to tactically or strategically make mid-course adjustments in response to unanticipated developments.

Given the project's critical role as the source of repayment and collateral for a project financing, one of the central roles of the practitioner is to help structure and negotiate a feasible deal. Practitioners assist their clients in assessing the risks and financial merit of a proposed project, recommending and interfacing with advisors and consultants, and drafting, negotiating, or commenting on the key project documents.

Project finance is less adversarial than most other practices in that the finance providers, sponsor, and project team share an interest in ensuring that a project will be able to be completed on time and on budget, operate as projected, and generate sufficient revenues. A project finance attorney must learn how to think like a businessperson in terms of spotting, understanding, and evaluating the importance of business issues, just as he or she does with respect to legal issues.

Douglas J. Lanzo is Executive Vice President and General Counsel of Breakout Capital, LLC, a working capital lender for emerging businesses.

in the world. It will need to issue dividends to equity owners in the investor state's currency, and it may need to service loans in that same currency. For example, suppose a Freedonian publicly traded corporation has a subsidiary investment in Ruritania. The Freedonian currency is the freedollar, and the Ruritanian currency is the ruro. The Ruritanian subsidiary will earn profits in ruros, but when it pays dividends to its parent company, the parent company will need to convert the ruros to freedollars in order to service any debt to Freedonian lenders and to issue dividends to its own Freedonian investors. If Ruritanian forbids converting ruros to freedollars, the investor loses most of the benefit of its investment.

A host state may choose to handle its currency depreciation problem in a different and even more problematic way but with similar effect. A currency convertibility restriction is usually applicable to both nationals of the host state and foreign nationals. But the host state may choose to prohibit or restrict only *foreign* investors from transferring any currency or other assets from the foreign investment back to the investor state or any other state. In other words, the host state may direct the foreign investment not to allow its profits or other assets to leave the host state.

Such a **capital repatriation restriction** achieves the same effect as currency inconvertibility, but it targets primarily foreign investments in the host state. Nationals of the host state may be unaffected by the law. States have sometimes adopted other convertibility restrictions as well, such as prohibiting the opening of bank accounts denominated in a foreign currency or requiring foreign investors to maintain a minimum account balance or fund reserve in the country in local currency.

The **International Monetary Fund** (**IMF**) is an intergovernmental lending and standard setting agency created to promote international monetary cooperation, exchange rate stability, and orderly exchange arrangements; to foster economic growth; and to provide temporary financial assistance to developing states. The IMF Articles of Agreement, which bind all IMF members, create a pool of currency resources. Member states may borrow from this pool to stabilize their currencies when necessary. With 189 member states as of 2019, the IMF has great influence over international monetary policy. The IMF does not loan to private companies, but its activities are important to investors because the IMF Articles curtail the ability of member states to restrict currency convertibility and capital repatriation without IMF approval. Article VIII of the IMF Articles of Agreement provides that, with some exceptions, no member state may:

- place currency restrictions on payments or transfers for trading, commercial, debt service, or other purposes;
- pursue discriminative practices depending on the currency chosen in a commercial transaction; or

- have multiple currencies or exchange rates (e.g., a currency for foreign transactions and a currency for domestic transactions).

In addition, BITs and free trade agreements may limit the ability of state parties to restrict currency convertibility and capital repatriation.

Nonetheless, states do sometimes seek and obtain IMF approval to impose temporary currency convertibility restrictions, and developing countries in particular sometimes resort to such measures. For example, until 1990, India tried to regulate currency exchange transactions by making it illegal to purchase or otherwise procure a foreign currency without government permission. In the past, states have also commonly imposed exchange restrictions to deal with economic crises and hyperinflation. Several Latin American states have imposed repatriation controls or currency exchange restrictions in the recent past in response to economic disasters. For example, in response to an economic crisis caused by government incompetence and corruption, Venezuela adopted currency restrictions in 2003 to prevent private, market-rate exchanges of Venezuelan bolivars for the U.S. dollar. These restrictions continue as of the printing of this book.

Finally, it is important to be aware that less direct restrictions on currency conversion may have a significant effect on a foreign investor. If a state suffering inflationary pressures has pegged its currency to another, harder currency (often the yen, U.S. dollar, or euro) to stabilize its own currency, a foreign investor may believe that payment in the foreign currency is acceptable because its stability is guaranteed. But, suffering from an economic recession or crisis, the government could unpeg the currency and allow it to float freely, which generally causes a significant fall in the value of that currency. A foreign investor that expected to convert its foreign profits to U.S. dollars or another hard currency will now be sorely disappointed to learn that, although it is free to convert one currency to the other, it will be receiving much less hard currency than expected.

B. Expropriation Risk

A second foreign investment risk is expropriation or nationalization. As you will recall from Part 5.2 of Chapter 2, **expropriation** occurs when a host state deprives the foreign investor of ownership or control over the investment. A state that has expropriated an investment may refuse to compensate the investor for his loss. Sometimes, it may compensate the investor, but in a manner that the investor feels to be insufficient. The compensation may be inadequate in amount if it fails to reflect the full value of the investment taken according to the investor's own valuation or the market value. Compensation may also take a form that limits its usefulness to the investor, as when it is made in an inconvertible currency. Finally, the payment of compensation may be delayed, sometimes for many years, which frustrates the investor's expectations.

A foreign investor may be able to invoke a bilateral investment treaty; free trade agreement; treaty of friendship, commerce and navigation; or other international instrument to claim full compensation for the expropriated investment. Some treaties confer a right directly on the investor to invoke a dispute settlement proceeding with the host state, as will be discussed in Chapter 9. At other times, the investor is left with no immediate remedy except to appeal to its own government to take up its case against the host state and demand compensation through diplomatic channels.

Expropriation insurance protects against confiscation, expropriation, and nationalization. Typically, the insurer will compensate the investor promptly upon a direct expropriation leading to loss of the investor's ownership or control of its investment. Depending on the insurance terms, the insurance may also protect against indirect expropriation, although the line between normal government regulation and indirect expropriation is often difficult to draw. This may create obstacles to a prompt recovery of insurance benefits and potential litigation with the insurer.

C. Political Instability Risk

A third common type of foreign investment risk is political instability in the host state. Wars, revolutions, insurrection, terrorism, riots, or other politically or economically motivated violence can damage the investment, disrupt the investment's operations, or even destroy the investment altogether. This risk is especially high in certain states with unstable forms of government. In such cases, political instability insurance can compensate the investor for the loss of profits or the investment itself.

Finally, there are risks specific to the investment project. The supplier of inputs or the purchaser of outputs may become insolvent and breach the supply or purchase agreement. Without a source of affordable materials or a purchaser for the products or services, the investment may become unprofitable. Or the purchaser may simply choose to breach the contract. This risk is especially great where the purchaser is the host state government.

For example, suppose the project sponsor had entered into a contract with a foreign host state government to build and operate a power plant. The host state government might commit to purchasing a minimum amount of the energy produced, and this guarantee would greatly facilitate the financing of the power plant construction. But suppose, after a few years in operation, the host state government repudiates the bargain and refuses to purchase the minimum amount of energy. It has not expropriated the investment, but it has diminished or removed a major source, if not the sole source, of revenue for the project.

Other risks, such as labor difficulties, consumer boycotts, or international sanctions against the host state can harm an otherwise profitable investment as well. Insurance can be obtained to forestall such risks. While private

Case Study

Argentina's Currency Exchange Restrictions

In 1983, the Argentinian government responded to runaway inflation by adopting a new currency, the austral. Unfortunately, the government continued amassing sovereign debt, mainly to foreign investors, to the point at which it became unable to keep up with interest payments. The economy soon collapsed, resulting in massive inflation. By 1989, annual inflation reached a stupefying 3000%.

A new government was elected to handle the debt crisis, and initially it controlled inflation by restoring the use of the old currency (pesos), reducing the printing of pesos, and pegging the exchange rate of pesos to the U.S. dollar. Sadly, a combination of growing sovereign debt and an unfavorable trade balance initiated a new economic crisis in the late 1990s. As U.S. dollars experienced a prolonged rise in value, so did the pegged peso, and Argentine exports became more costly, resulting in mounting trade deficits.

Despite assistance from the IMF, World Bank, and Inter-American Development Bank, the Argentine economy continued to deteriorate. In 2001, public panic caused wide scale withdrawals of cash from bank accounts for conversion to stable U.S. dollars. Fears of renewed inflation undermining the peso resulted in even purely local transactions being carried out with U.S. dollars. As the demand for dollars increased, so did peso inflation, which in turn increased the demand for dollars. Whenever pesos were accepted as payment, they were taken at a discount on the assumption that they would continue to lose value.

The government reacted by imposing restrictions on bank account withdrawals, provoking public protests, riots, and several changes of government. In 2002, Argentina converted all money in local bank accounts from dollars to pesos to prevent the use of dollars in local transactions. Argentina also unpegged the peso from the dollar, resulting in another drop in the peso's value. Because some foreign investors and exporters had contracts calling for payments in pesos, these lost much of their value and had to be renegotiated if the foreigners were not to suffer extreme losses. Some of them were unable to renegotiate successfully and simply lost their capital to the combination of inflation and exchange restrictions.

insurance is easily obtained for investments in wealthy and stable democracies, it is more difficult to secure for foreign investment risks in developing countries due to the specialized nature of foreign investment, the high variability of risks, and the large sums of money involved. Governmental and international agencies have filled the gap by offering insurance to private investors. However, they do not guarantee against every kind of risk, and only some kinds of investments may qualify for government or international agency guarantees.

6.2 Sources of Foreign Investment Insurance

A. The Development Finance Corporation

DFC does not only provide loan guarantees for investments in developing countries. It also provides expropriation and political risk insurance to investments and projects sponsored by U.S. companies in the developing world. DFC's criteria for "developing" countries is quite broad; it includes 160 states, which is more than three-quarters of the world.

DFC insures investments by all industries, with special emphasis on infrastructure projects such as building oil and gas pipelines, dams, and power plants; constructing highways, bridges, airports, seaports, and public buildings such as universities and government offices; and both heavy and light manufacturing. DFC can insure international investment transactions, from the very small to the large (up to $500 million) for up to 20 years. The insurance may cover not only the initial investment but expected profits as well. Generally, DFC will insure only 90% of the investment; the investor is required to bear 10% of the risk of loss, or to obtain private insurance to cover that portion of the risk.

Because DFC's mission is to encourage U.S. investment in developing countries, only U.S. investors, contractors, and financial institutions are eligible for its insurance. Foreign-registered business entities are ineligible unless at least 95% owned by U.S. nationals. U.S. business entities are generally eligible for DFC insurance if they are majority owned by U.S. investors.

DFC insurance covers all three types of investment risk described above, and it protects against not only direct expropriation, but indirect and creeping expropriation as well. It does not, however, compensate a loss of profitability in the foreign investment caused by a normal tax increase or other foreseeable regulations by the host state. It also excludes from protection losses caused by strikes and other labor disputes, although these may seriously impair the profitability of a foreign investment.

Consider the following real examples of how insurance from DFC's predecessor, OPIC, protected a foreign investor from each kind of investment risk:

> A U.S. company made an equity investment in a subsidiary in the Philippines in order to process coconuts. Sixteen years later, the subsidiary declared a dividend of over 9 million Philippine pesos payable to the U.S.

> parent company. The Central Bank of the Philippines had [in the meantime] adopted restrictions on foreign currency so that the subsidiary was unable to pay the dividend in dollars. The U.S. parent company filed an inconvertibility claim with OPIC and was compensated, since the Central Bank restrictions were not in effect when the U.S. parent company originally obtained its insurance.
>
> * * *
>
> A U.S. investor established a fishing venture in Somalia. After a military coup occurred, the new government began a series of repeated and continuous acts of harassment and interference against the U.S. investor's personnel and operations. For example, the U.S. investor's personnel were repeatedly threatened by military and police officials, arrested and, in one instance, deported from the country. In addition, the Government interfered with the company's operation of its aircraft, which was used to transport the fish, and ordered the company to permit a military observer to accompany all flights. The extra passenger displaced several hundred pounds of seafood products and added substantially to the cost of the company's operations. Viewing these and other government actions together, OPIC found that the Somalian Government had expropriated the investor's project and compensated the investor.
>
> * * *
>
> In 1988, a U.S. company made an investment in a Liberian subsidiary in order to operate a rubber plantation. Due to the Liberian civil war, the subsidiary's property was seized by rebels and then damaged and destroyed by the general military activities. OPIC found the claim to be valid and compensated the investor.

OPIC, *Insurance: Products: Coverage Types*, at www.opic.gov.

DFC investment insurance may accompany a project financing loan or loan guarantee from DFC itself. DFC can therefore provide most of the core financial services needed by a U.S. company investing in the developing world.

B. The Multilateral Investment Guarantee Agency

The World Bank Group, discussed earlier in this chapter, includes an IGO known as the **Multilateral Investment Guarantee Agency** (**MIGA**). MIGA, like the other main World Bank agencies, is headquartered in Washington, D.C. One of its primary functions is to provide political risk insurance for investments in developing countries. Another is to provide guarantees for project finance, especially if the IFC is the source of that finance. The developing countries in which foreign investments are eligible for MIGA guarantees are listed in Schedule A to the MIGA Convention as "Category 2" countries and include more than one hundred states. To qualify for a MIGA guarantee, the host state must first agree to MIGA's issuance of the guarantee for the specified risks that the guarantee will cover.

Case Study

Political Risk in Project Financing

Figure 7.8. The Dabhol Power Plant.
Credit: © 2015 by *Business Standard*

Enron Corp. was a U.S. energy company based in Houston, Texas. In 1992, the Indian national government invited Enron to bid on constructing and operating a power plant in Maharashtra state. With financial backing from major investment bankers, including GE Capital Corp., and the participation of Bechtel, a power plant design and construction company, Enron was awarded the project without a competitive bid process.

The projected cost of designing, building, and operating the plant, $2.8 billion, would make it the largest single foreign investment project in the history of India. The Indian national government had encouraged Enron throughout the planning and early construction phases, calling it a "showcase" foreign investor and leading the sponsors and lenders to optimistic estimates of the project's financial success.

Enron, GE Capital, and Bechtel jointly formed an Indian subsidiary company, Dabhol Power Co. In spite of criticism from the World Bank and India's Central Electricity Authority regarding the lack of competitive bidding, they proceeded with the project. Within a year, Dabhol Power Co. had signed a 20-year power purchasing agreement with Maharashtra state, with provisional approval of the Central Electric Authority. By 1995, the project sponsors had already invested $600 million in laying the foundation for three large generators and hiring three thousand workers.

In March, a new election was held, resulting in a change of state government. Maharashtra then repudiated the power purchasing agreement, pointing to the high price of the power and the absence of an environmental impact assessment. Construction of the plant ceased, leaving the project in considerable debt.

Although the local government eventually agreed to reopen negotiations with Enron on condition of a lower price for the power, the economic consequences of these events strained Enron's already precarious financial resources caused by its long history of accounting fraud and, before negotiations were completed, Enron went bankrupt in 2001 and was liquidated. GE Capital and Bechtel soon became entangled in costly litigation with the government of Maharashtra, and the project was completely nationalized by the Indian government in 2005.

Like DFC, MIGA can guarantee new foreign investments or expansions of existing foreign investments, and MIGA insurance protects against the three foreign investment risks (currency inconvertibility, expropriation, and political instability). Unlike DFC, MIGA also insures against a fourth risk—breach of contract by the host state. Such a guarantee is helpful when the investment project involves collaboration with the host state government, such as a natural resource extraction venture, or building or operating a public utility or transportation infrastructure.

If a BIT or FTA is in force between the host state and investor state, a breach of such contract will normally give rise to an arbitral remedy, as discussed in Chapter 9. However, there may be no investment treaty, or the host state may refuse to honor an adverse arbitration award, or even when a remedy is available and the host state is willing to comply with an arbitration award, the investment may be seriously undermined by the delay between the breach of contract and the announcement of the arbitration award.

MIGA insurance offers the investor an interim payment while the dispute is pending or full compensation if the host state repudiates an award in favor of the investor. MIGA will also insure investments in countries that are members of MIGA only, which, however, encompasses almost every country.

While DFC insures foreign investments by U.S. investors only, investors from any MIGA member state may be eligible for MIGA insurance, so long as they are not nationals of the host state itself. In other words, the investment must be truly transnational. For business entities, this means the company must have either been formed under the laws of a MIGA member state or have its principal place of business in one. Because MIGA insures only cross-border investments, a corporation seeking MIGA guarantees must both be incorporated in and have its principal place of business in a MIGA member state other than the host state. An exception may be made, however, for companies incorporated in the host state but majority owned by foreign nationals.

If the host state accepts the MIGA guarantee sought by the investor, MIGA will negotiate the guarantee with the investor based on its standard form contracts. MIGA may guarantee up to 95% of a project finance loan plus interest. It also may guarantee up to 90% of a foreign investment itself, plus an additional 450% for earnings. However, rarely will MIGA cover more than $180 million on a single project. For larger projects, MIGA may jointly insure the project with a commercial lender or government agency such as DFC.

The following example from 2008, involving a Spanish company investing in the Costa Rican transportation infrastructure, illustrates a typical MIGA project:

> MIGA has issued $152.96 million in guarantees for the development of a toll road in Costa Rica. The guarantees include $9 million in coverage for an equity investment by FCC Construcción S.A. and Itinere Infraestructura S.A., and $143.96 million in coverage for a shareholder loan by

Caja Madrid. MIGA is providing 15-year coverage for the equity against the risk of transfer restriction. The debt will be covered for up to 18 years against the risks of transfer restriction, expropriation, war and civil disturbance, and breach of contract.

The project consists of the design, construction and/or rehabilitation, operation and maintenance of portions of the toll road linking San José to Caldera. This 25-year concession will be the first highway concession in Costa Rica to successfully reach financial closing and begin operations.

The project is aligned with the World Bank Group's strategy for Costa Rica, which includes supporting, rehabilitating, and maintaining key trade corridors. The corridor connects the main industrial/business area of the country to one of the main ports. The project is expected to reduce transportation costs by reducing travel time by 1.5 hours for those who travel the full length of the corridor. It is also expected to reduce the number of road accidents and the costs associated with heavy traffic conditions, such as gasoline consumption and deterioration of vehicle parts and tires. By providing easier access to the port of Caldera, the investment will help improve the country's trade competitiveness and may reduce the price of imports.

MIGA's participation is critical for the project to proceed since it allows mobilization of commercial bank financing that might otherwise not be available. It also supports MIGA's commitment to catalyzing private sector investment in infrastructure.

MIGA, *Recently Guaranteed Projects*, at www.miga.org/projects.

In the event that one of the guaranteed risks occurs, MIGA will normally compensate the investor, whose claim against the host country will be subrogated to MIGA. In other words, MIGA will substitute for the investor as the claimant seeking recovery from the host state. MIGA will then negotiate with the host state to recoup the costs of the compensation paid to the investor. Should negotiations fail, MIGA will resolve the dispute with the host state through conciliation or arbitration pursuant to Annex II to the MIGA Convention. Arbitration is normally conducted through the World Bank's International Centre for the Settlement of Investment Disputes, which will be discussed in Chapter 9. Should these negotiations fail and arbitration lead to a loss by MIGA, MIGA will absorb the cost; the investor retains the benefit of the guarantee.

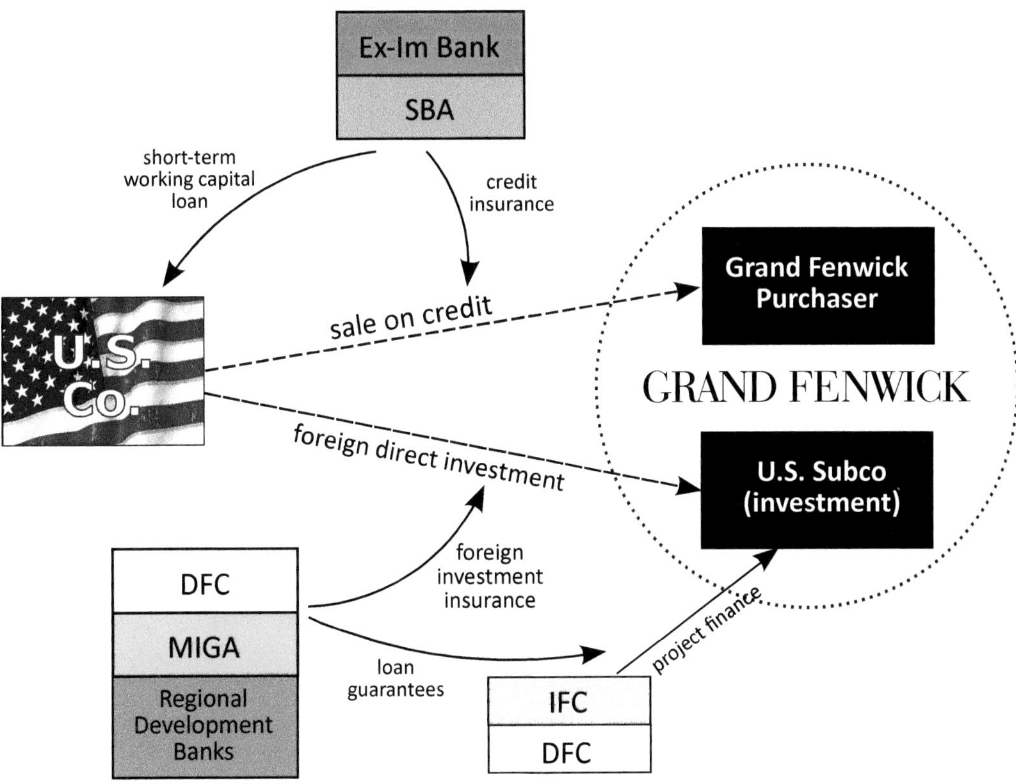

Figure 7.9. A graphical depiction of the roles of export credit and foreign investment insurance agencies in international trade and investment. Here, U.S. Co. has two connections with the fictitious country Grand Fenwick. First, it sells U.S. products to an independent purchaser in Grand Fenwick on credit. Second, it has incorporated a subsidiary in Grand Fenwick for the purpose of manufacturing products there. Each of the U.S., foreign, and international agencies could play a role in facilitating the sales and investment in Grand Fenwick. Be sure to note the difference between an agency providing a loan itself and providing credit insurance for a private loan.

Key Vocabulary

Asset
Branch office
Bureau of Economic Analysis (BEA)
Capital
Collateral
Committee on Foreign Investment in the United States (CFIUS)
Currency inconvertibility
Development Finance Corp. (DFC)
Direct loan
Entry visa
Equity
Exon-Florio review
Export-Import Bank of the United States (Ex-Im Bank)
Expropriation
Foreign direct investment (FDI)
Guiding Principles on Business and Human Rights
H-1B visa
Hart-Scott-Rodino Act
Host state
Immigrant visa
International Finance Corporation (IFC)
Investor state
Joint venture (JV)
L-1 visa
Lawful permanent resident (LPR)
Multilateral Investment Guarantee Agency (MIGA)
Naturalization
Nonimmigrant visa
Nonrecourse debt
Political risk
Project financing
Project sponsor
Shelf company
Small Business Administration (SBA)
Surety
U.S. Citizenship and Immigration Services (USCIS)
Venture capital
Working capital loan
World Bank Group

Practice Exercises

#1 Expanding Abroad for the First Time

Your client, Ginormous Rentals Co. (GRC), is a Delaware general partnership that rents construction equipment to land developers. GRC has made several cross-border leases of equipment to developers in Osterlich, and it is considering whether to establish a local presence there in order to facilitate future leases and possibly expand its business operations into the region. GRC seeks your advice on the options available to it regarding the planned expansion into the Osterlich market.

GRC has several concerns of special weight. First, the company wishes to maintain maximum control over its business operations in Osterlich. It is also concerned about liability for its Osterlich operations. Because GRC's ability to supervise the maintenance of the equipment and to service it in Osterlich will be limited for the first few years of local operations, it is concerned about whether it will be possible to protect the U.S. assets of the partners. Finally, GRC is concerned about competition from companies already renting construction equipment on the Osterlich market. While the U.S. rental companies, including GRC, outstrip their Osterlich competitors in terms of size and market power, some of GRC's key U.S. competitors are already operating with success on the Osterlich market, and its competitors there obtain a certain amount of business just from name recognition and established local ownership.

Assist the client by answering the following questions:

(a) What are the legal advantages and disadvantages to continuing to rent its equipment to developers in Osterlich from the United States, as opposed to establishing a local presence in Osterlich?

(b) If GRC does decide to establish a local presence in Osterlich, what are the basic advantages to GRC of a branch office versus a subsidiary? Are there some tasks or objectives one or the other is better suited to accomplish?

(c) Is there something GRC can do while in the process of expanding into the Osterlich market to gain an advantage over its competitors on the market? If you recommend a specific course of action, discuss any special regulatory concern your recommendation might raise, and any regulatory notifications or approvals that might be necessary.

#2 Financing an International Expansion

Your client, Seeduway, Inc., is a Missouri agribusiness that specializes in developing and selling new varieties of seeds, mostly for the core grains (rice, wheat, oats, and corn) to farmers. Seeduway provides its customers with annual bags of genetically modified seeds for sowing crops with improved characteristics such as high protein content, increased vitamins, resistance to pests, and early ripening. Seeduway has discovered that certain plants in South America and central Africa have valuable genes that, if transplanted into Seeduway's existing varieties of grain seeds, increase drought and heat tolerance.

Seeduway has approached you for assistance with two new international projects. Excited about the prospect of drawing on existing tropical plants for new insights into recombinant seed engineering, Seeduway wishes to establish high technology biological research centers in the South American state of Simonia and the African state of Mandelia.

Setting up a biological research center is extremely expensive. It requires the construction of a specialized building with closely controlled air conditioning; sealed, airtight rooms to contain the possible spread of contaminants and possibly toxins; a great deal of expensive research equipment; hazardous materials storage and disposal facilities such as an incinerator; green houses; and an independent power generator. In addition, the operation of the laboratory will require significant human resource efforts to identify and hire competent microbiologists, chemists, geneticists, botanists, and business management willing to work in foreign subsidiaries located in relatively poor and politically unstable countries. Seeduway estimates that each facility will require $200 million in startup capital. It has been unable to identify investment banks in either Simonia or Mandelia willing and able to lend to startup projects of this size, nor have U.S. investment banks shown interest in financing projects in these foreign countries.

Finally, Seeduway hopes to shorten its starting time by hiring some of its future Simonian and Mandelian employees before setting up the investment entities and training them in its Missouri headquarters for six to twelve months, with the expectation of then transferring their employment to the Simonian and Mandelian investment entities. In the future, it expects to hire employees in these countries directly, transfer them to Missouri headquarters for training, then transfer them back when finished.

Advise Seeduway on its options for:

(a) obtaining financing for its overseas expansion;

(b) protecting its overseas investments against any unexpected political or economic instability in Simonia or Mandelia; and

(c) obtaining an entry visa for Simonian and Mandelian employees?

Be sure to discuss both the advantages and disadvantages of each option you suggest, as well as any limitations on the option that might limit its availability or usefulness to Seeduway.

Multiple Choice Questions

1. In 2018, a U.S. company called Patriot Design Corp. acquired 18% of the shares of another U.S. company, Abfab Engineering LLC. Patriot Design Corp. is fully owned by a Zembian corporation. Abfab Engineering LLC is fully owned by a Pottsylvanian corporation. Which of the following statements relating to U.S. foreign investment reporting regulations administered by the Bureau of Economic Analysis (BEA) is most accurate?

   Abfab Engineering:

   (a) need not file an initial investment report with BEA, because less than a majority of its shares are being acquired by a foreign investor.
   (b) need not file an initial investment report with BEA, because the ac-

quired entity is already owned by a foreign corporation.

(c) need not file an initial investment report with BEA, because it is being acquired by a U.S. investor.

(d) need not file an initial investment report with BEA, because it is the foreign investor, not the investment entity, that must file the report.

(e) must file an initial investment report with BEA.

2. True or false? If the Committee on Foreign Investment in the United States (CFIUS) determines that a proposed merger between a foreign company and a U.S. company could result in a significant loss of U.S. jobs, it is authorized by the Exon-Florio Amendment to halt or impose conditions on the merger.

3. True or false? Even if a proposed acquisition of a U.S. company by a foreign investor is likely to result in a serious threat to U.S. national security, the Exon-Florio Amendment does not require the U.S. company to file a notification with CFIUS.

4. Your firm has been retained by Bokeh Imaging Co. (BIC), a Freedonian corporation, to advise it on its planned acquisition of several smaller corporations in competition with BIC. BIC currently has no U.S. assets or sales to the United States. For which of the following planned acquisitions is a premerger notification filing under the Hart-Scott-Rodino Act probably not necessary?

(a) BIC intends to acquire 100% of the shares of Ostco, an Osterlich corporation with no U.S. assets or sales to the United States. However, after the acquisition, BIC believes it will be positioned to begin making very significant sales to the United States.

(b) BIC intends to acquire the assets of F-Stoppers Corp., a U.S. corporation valued at $500 million, but it will not acquire any shares or control over F-Stoppers Corp.

(c) BIC intends to acquire 100% of the shares of Zemco, a Zembian corporation with no U.S. assets, but that makes $250 milllion in annual sales to the United States. BIC and Zemco have no product lines that compete with each other on any market in the world.

(d) BIC intends to acquire 51% of the shares of a U.S. company valued at $500 million, but the U.S. company only conducts research and development and makes no sales of goods.

(e) BIC intends to acquire 100% of the shares of a U.S. company valued at $500 million, but the U.S. company makes no sales to, and has no assets in, Freedonia.

5. True or false?: A merger between two U.S. companies with no subsidiary companies or branch offices in the European Union cannot be subject to the jurisdiction of EU competition law authorities, because they have no presence on the EU market.

6. Which of the following statements is ***not*** true of works councils in the European Union?

   (a) They are authorized to engage in collective bargaining on behalf of the company's employees.
   (b) They are initially organized by the company on behalf of its employees.
   (c) They may exercise a veto over proposed mergers or acquisitions that will result in dismissal of significant numbers of employees.
   (d) Company management has no right to delegate one or more members to sit on the works council.
   (e) If a company in the EU hires large numbers of employees in multiple EU states, it must have a single EU-wide works council.

7. Your client, Bowfinger Industries USA (BIA), is a U.S. production company wholly owned by Bowfinger Worldwide SA (BWS), a Nilfgaardian corporation. Both companies were formed in 1995. The United States and Nilfgaard are not parties to any investment or trade treaties. BIA wishes to hire one of its parent company's executives, Gern Blanston, on a yearly contract. Mr. Blanston holds an MBA degree and has worked for BWS for three years. Which of the following types of U.S. entry visas would be appropriate for BIA to seek for Mr. Blanston?

   I. B-1 visa
   II. H-1B visa
   III. L-1 visa
   IV. E visa

   (a) I and II only
   (b) II and III only
   (c) I and IV only
   (d) III and IV only
   (e) II, III, and IV only

8. True or false?: Under the UN Guiding Principles on Business and Human Rights, multinational enterprises are considered to have satisfied their obligations if they ensure that their officers and employees refrain from violating internationally protected human rights or from contributing to environmental degradation.

9. In light of the U.S. Supreme Court decisions in *Kiobel v. Royal Dutch Petroleum Co.* and *Jesner v. Arab Bank, PLC*, for which of the following claims would U.S. courts have jurisdiction under the Alien Tort Statute?

   (a) A group of Ruritanian citizens claims that a Smalldonian corporation conspired with the Ruritanian government to force them to work on the Smalldonian corporation's investment project in Ruritania without compensation.
   (b) A group of Pottsylvanian citizens claims that Royal Rock PLC, a Grand Fenwick company, conspired with the government of Pottsylvania to censor their protests against Royal Rock investments in Pottsylvania by refusing to grant demonstration permits and by arresting and confining demonstrators without due process of law.
   (c) A group of U.S. citizens who are journalists claims that, while they were investigating possible human rights violations by Dump & Son, a U.S. corporation operating in Zembia, the CEO of Dump & Son conspired with the Zembian government to try to kidnap and murder them.
   (d) A group of Osterlich citizens claims that, after they had protested against a foreign investment of a North Elbonian corporation, Dogbert Enterprises, in Osterlich, the CEO of Dogbert Enterprises conspired with the Osterlich government to assassinate the protesters while they were visiting the United States. They want to sue the CEO.
   (e) None of the above.

10. Which of the following could offer an export working capital guarantee to a U.S. business firm seeking to expand its business abroad?

   (a) The Export-Import Bank of the United States
   (b) The Development Finance Corporation
   (c) The Multilateral Investment Guarantee Agency
   (d) The International Bank for Reconstruction and Development
   (e) All of the above

11. Which of the following loans describes classic project financing with respect to Major Project Sponsors LLP (MPS), a U.S. limited liability partnership?

   (a) A loan to MPS to capitalize a foreign subsidiary in Freedonia. The foreign subsidiary will manufacture high-technology electronic parts for sale to MPS back in the United States.
   (b) A loan to MPS's new foreign subsidiary in Freedonia, partially secured by the subsidiary's assets and partially based on the expected future revenue stream of the subsidiary.
   (c) A loan to MPS's foreign subsidiary in Freedonia, which has been in operation for seven years, and which needs additional capital to expand

its manufacturing facilities. The loan will be fully collateralized by the lender's security interest in the subsidiary's manufacturing plant.

(d) A loan to MPS to capitalize a foreign subsidiary in Freedonia. The foreign subsidiary will build a new seaport in Freedonia in agreement with the Freedonian government.

(e) None of the above.

12. Which of the following does ***not*** directly offer nonrecourse loans to major foreign investment projects in the developing world?

(a) The International Finance Corporation
(b) The Export-Import Bank of the United States
(c) The Development Finance Corporation
(d) private investment banks
(e) regional development banks

13. Which of the following does ***not*** offer foreign investment insurance for major projects in the developing would?

(a) Private insurance companies
(b) The Development Finance Corporation
(c) The Multilateral Investment Guarantee Agency
(d) The International Finance Corporation
(e) All of the above offer foreign investment insurance.

14. In the following scenarios, which event could ***not*** be covered by MIGA foreign investment insurance? For the purpose of these scenarios, Ruritania is a developing country. The United States and Freedonia are both developed countries.

(a) A U.S. company owns a foreign subsidiary in Ruritania. In response to uncontrollable inflation in its currency, the ruro, the Ruritanian government obtains permission from the International Monetary Fund to impose currency controls. As a result, the U.S. company cannot convert its subsidiary's dividends to U.S. dollars.

(b) A U.S. company owns a foreign subsidiary that has a manufacturing plant in Ruritania. After the president of the Ruritanian subsidiary repeatedly makes insulting public statements about Ruritania and Ruritanians, a riot breaks out, and the manufacturing plant is burned to the ground.

(c) A Freedonian company owns a foreign subsidiary in Ruritania. Under the Freedonia-Ruritania Bilateral Investment Treaty (BIT), each country agreed not to expropriate investments by nationals of the other country. If a prohibited expropriation does occur, the host state agrees to arbitrate the dispute with the foreign investor and to abide by the decision. After Ruritania expropriates the Freedonian company's subsidiary, the Freedonian company invokes arbitration under the BIT. Meanwhile, it presses an insurance claim.

(d) A Freedonian company owns a foreign subsidiary in Ruritania. The Ruritanian subsidiary exists for the sole purpose of providing water treatment services for the Ruritanian government pursuant to a long-term agreement. However, the Ruritanian government breaches the services agreement by unilaterally reducing the fees paid for the subsidiary's services.

(e) A U.S. company owns a foreign subsidiary in Freedonia. The two countries have no bilateral investment treaty. After a change in government, Freedonia expropriates the U.S. company's subsidiary and refuses to pay any compensation whatsoever pursuant to the Calvo Clause of the Freedonian constitution.

Multiple Choice Answers

1. e
2. False
3. True
4. a
5. False
6. c
7. b
8. False
9. d
10. a
11. b
12. b
13. d
14. e

Chapter 8

The Regulation of Global Corruption

What You Will Learn in This Chapter

It is an unfortunate fact of international business that not every government official is impervious to the temptation to solicit or accept bribes, and not every business firm resists the temptation to offer them. Bribery and other forms of corruption tend to distort the efficient functioning of the market and to undermine public trust in the good faith of the implicated government. It also threatens to bring international commerce and investment into disrepute among the outraged population.

For these reasons, almost every state in the world has criminalized the payment or receipt of gifts or money by private persons to public officials. Yet, such laws are underenforced in many countries. In some, corruption is so rampant that the government is simply incapable of consistently deterring and punishing it. In others, corruption pervades the highest levels of government. The enticements of bribery are especially strong in international business transactions, where private firms and individuals may feel no loyalty to the host state, detection may be unlikely, and large sums of money may be at stake. As a result, the international community collectively, and capital exporting states individually, have undertaken measures to reduce corruption in international business.

This chapter discusses the treaties, laws, and regulations that both the global community and the United States have adopted to deal with problems of cross-border corruption and crime. Specifically, you will learn here:

- what kinds of problems corruption creates for those countries in which it proliferates;
- the treaties by which the international community has attempted to harmonize rules and coordinate action to reduce global corruption;
- how U.S. legislation regulates bribery and other forms of corruption in international business transactions; and
- how a business organization may protect itself from inadvertently violating antibribery prohibitions.

Although different countries have different regulations to control corruption, there is now significant international harmonization in this field. Corruption remains a serious problem in international business, and complying with anti-corruption laws requires moderate precautions.

1 The Problem of Global Corruption

There are both intergovernmental and nongovernmental organizations that include in their mission reducing global corruption. For some, such as the World Bank and the International Chamber of Commerce, anti-corruption efforts are just one part of a range of activities that fall within the organization's portfolio. Only a few focus exclusively on global corruption.

One of the most influential NGOs monitoring and advocating action on global corruption is **Transparency International**, a Berlin-based organization. Transparency International is fully dedicated to monitoring and promoting the reduction of global bribery and other forms of corruption in both government services and international business. As the organization's work demonstrates, international business corruption is common in wealthy states and developing countries alike.

TRANSPARENCY INTERNATIONAL

The following excerpt from the Transparency International source book gives a sense of the most common kinds of corruption affecting international business, and the reason that such corruption is considered objectionable:

JEREMY POPE, THE TRANSPARENCY INTERNATIONAL SOURCE BOOK 2000, at 2-7, 16-18

Defining corruption

Defined simply, corruption is the misuse of entrusted power for private benefit. Yet it is not so long ago that the word itself was completely taboo in professional and political environments. The word seldom appeared in newspapers and it was rarely mentioned by economists, although political scientists had begun to take an academic interest in it.

Normative statements about corruption require a point of view, a standard of "goodness" and a model of how corruption works in particular instances. For the purposes of this Source Book, "corruption" involves behaviour on the part of officials in the public sector, whether politicians or civil servants, in which they improperly and unlawfully enrich themselves, or those close to them, by the misuse of the power entrusted to them.

The Source Book concentrates on administrative rather than political corruption *per se*, focusing on the activities of individuals who, in their positions as public officials—as policymakers or as administrators—control various activities or decisions.

In the wake of privatisations and the transference into the private sector of tasks previously regarded as those of the state, with near or total monopolies for the supply of public goods in private hands (e.g. water, electricity), the concepts explored in this Source Book include corrupt conduct in the private sector—outside as well as within its interface with the public service—conduct that nonetheless has negative public consequences.

Administrative corruption

There are two quite separate categories of administrative corruption: the first occurs where, for example, services or contracts are provided "according-to-rule" and the second, where transactions are "against-the-rule."

In the first situation, an official is receiving private gain illegally for doing something which he or she is ordinarily required to do by law. In the second situation, the bribe is paid to obtain services which the official is prohibited from providing. "According-to-rule" and "against-the-rule" corruption can occur at all levels of the government hierarchy and range in scale and impact from "grand corruption" to small scale varieties.

In practice, public attitudes can overshadow legal definitions of administrative corruption, and public opinion can define corruption in ways which will override law. If public opinion and legal definitions do not conform, the likelihood is that officials will act in accordance with the public view, and in so doing transgress the law. It is therefore crucial that the public be informed and enlightened as to the damage that corruption can cause.

How is corruption damaging?

Corruption is damaging for the simple reason that important decisions are determined by ulterior motives, with no concern for the consequences for the wider community.

Dieter Frisch, former Director-General of Development at the European Commission, has observed that corruption raises the cost of goods and services; it increases the debt of a country (and carries with it recurring debt-servicing costs in the future); it leads to lowering of standards, as sub-standard goods are provided and inappropriate or unnecessary technology is acquired; and it results in project choices being made based more on capital (because it is more rewarding for the perpetrator of corruption) than on manpower, which would be the more useful for development. Frisch points out that when a country increases its indebtedness to carry out projects which are not economically viable, the additional debt does not only include the 10 to 20 percent extra cost due to corruption; rather the entire investment, all 100 percent of it, is attributable to dishonest decisions to proceed with unproductive and unnecessary projects.

If corruption cannot be brought under control, it can threaten the viability of democratic institutions and market economies. In a corrupt environment, resources will be directed towards non-productive areas—the police, the armed forces and other organs of social control and repression—as the elite move to protect themselves, their positions and their material wealth. Laws will be enacted (e.g., the Public Tranquillity Act 1982 in the Sudan) and resources otherwise available for socio-economic development will be diverted into security expenditure. This in turn can cause the withering of democratic institutions as corruption, rather than investment, becomes the major source of financial gain. This undermines the legitimacy of government, and ultimately the legitimacy of the state. * * *

Impact on private sector development

It is a generally held view around the modern world that much of government-led development efforts in the past have been mishandled, and have generated waste rather than development. A strong state is needed, but this needs to be clear in its tasks and its organisation. It needs to provide vital services essential if the private sector is to flourish, but it should not attempt to compete with the private sector, and nor should the state undertake tasks which the private sector can perform more efficiently and more effectively unless there are compelling social reasons for it to do so.

So if development is to be private-sector led, what is the impact of corruption on the environment in which the private sector must operate? First and foremost, it introduces uncertainty: will contracts be honoured? Can disputes be resolved by impartial and competent adjudicators? Can future decisions by officials be predicted with requisite certainty? Where corruption introduces uncertainty, it also increases risk. And as risk escalates, so must greater and faster returns be looked for by investors. Furthermore, corrupt relationships operate to keep newcomers out of the game, thereby inhibiting the growth of the private sector itself.

Corrupt regimes also impose extraordinary management obligations on the private sector. In the Ukraine, for example, in 1994 firms surveyed reported that they spent on average 28 percent of management time simply on dealing with the government. By 1996 this had risen to 37 percent. Eliminating unnecessary bureaucratic obstacles, of course, is not done simply to reduce corruption but rather also to induce more businesses to switch to the formal sector and to encourage new productive investment.

Impact on foreign direct investment

One of the most crucial elements for accelerating private sector development is an increasing flow of foreign direct investment (FDI). So what, if any, is the impact of corruption on FDI?

In a recent study, Professor Shang-Jin Wei, a professor at the Kennedy School of Government, Harvard University, examined bilateral investment from 14 traditional source countries into some 45 host countries during the period 1990-91, with startling results. He compares corruption levels with marginal tax rates and concludes that on the scale of zero to ten—as used in the TI Corruption Perceptions Index—a full one point increase in the corruption level is associated with a 16 percent reduction in the flow of FDI—or approximately equivalent to a three percentage point increase in the marginal rate of tax. In other words, a worsening of a host government's corruption level from that of Singapore (with a rating of near zero) to that of Mexico (with a rating of 6.75 at the time of the study) incurs a 21 percent increase in the marginal tax rate on foreigners. That, in turn, is sufficient to eliminate the country's expectations of FDI almost completely. Wei's work encourages us to see corruption as being an additional—if unofficial—tax on the private sector. And one to which international investors are sensitive and to which they react very negatively. * * *

His findings, too, have been confirmed by a survey of private sector leaders undertaken by Control Risks Group in October 1999, which showed that among US investors, a country's high level of corruption was three times as likely to deter them from investing than was a country's poor record in human rights.[19]

Is corruption always bad?

Some would argue that corruption can have beneficial effects such as non-violent access to government affairs and administration, when political channels are clogged, or as a means of lessening the potentially crippling tension between the civil servant and the politician by linking them in an easily discerned network of self-interest.

However, counter-arguments are more acceptable. They focus on the fact that corruption leads to economic inefficiency and waste, because of its effect on the allocation of funds, on production, and on consumption. Gains obtained through corruption are unlikely to be transferred to the investment sector as ill-gotten money is either used in conspicuous consumption or is transferred to foreign bank accounts. Such transfers represent a capital leakage from the domestic economy. Furthermore, corruption generates inefficiency in allocation, by permitting the least efficient contractor with the highest ability to bribe to be the recipient of government contracts. In addition, since the cost of bribes is included in the price of the goods produced, demand tends to be reduced, the structure of production becomes biased, and consumption falls below efficiency levels. Thus corruption lowers the general welfare of the populace.

The following points summarise the costs induced by corrupt practices:

- A corrupt act represents a failure to achieve the objectives which government seeks (e.g. corruption in appointments induces inefficiency and waste; corruption in the allocation of scarce university places results in best use not being made of a scarce opportunity, etc.);
- Corruption contaminates the environment in which the private sector has to operate, leading either to quick (and excessive) profit-taking in circumstances of unpredictability, or to inward investment being discouraged, and excluding new potential entrants thus reducing participation and private sector growth;
- Corruption represents a rise in the price of administration (the taxpayer must submit to bribery as well, thereby having to pay several times over for the same service);
- If corruption takes the form of a kickback, it serves to diminish the total amount available for public purposes;
- Corruption exerts a corrupting influence on the administrative apparatus, eroding the courage necessary to adhere to high standards of probity ("morale declines—each man asking himself why he should be the sole custodian of morality");
- Corruption in government, perceived by the people, lowers respect for constituted authority and therefore the legitimacy of government;
- If the elite politicians and senior civil servants are widely believed to be corrupt, the public will see little reason why they, too, should not help themselves;

[19]The survey was conducted by the Industrial Research Bureau (IRB) on behalf of Control Risks. Respondents were asked whether they had held back from an otherwise attractive foreign investment on account of a country's reputation for corruption, human rights, labour or environmental controversy. European companies ranked corruption (38%) ahead of labour (35%), environment (34%) and human rights (28%). By contrast, US corporations ranked corruption higher (40%), human rights (13%), environment (14%) and labour (16%) all significantly lower. 92% of US corporations "forbid bribes to obtain business" (Europe 85%), and 76% of US corporations forbid "grease payments" (Europe 62%).

- A barrier to development has been an unwillingness at the political level to take unpopular decisions ("a corrupt official or politician is a self-centred individual [unlikely] to jeopardise his prospects for the sake of prosperity for the whole country in the remote future");
- Corruption results in a substantial loss in productive effort as time and energy are devoted to making contacts to circumvent and outwit the system, rather than to enhancing credentials and strengthening one's case objectively;
- Corruption, as it represents institutionalised unfairness, inevitably leads to litigation and trumped-up charges with which even the honest official may be blackmailed; and,
- The most ubiquitous form of corruption in some countries—"speed money" or "grease payments"—causes decisions to be weighed in terms of money, not human need. * * *

Types of bribery

There is widespread agreement on the situations that are especially amenable to corruption. However, an effective effort to deal with corruption must begin with its root causes. We need to understand the incentives for potential bribers and those injured by the corruption of others. Four broad categories can be distinguished:

Category (1): Bribes may be paid for (a) access to a scarce benefit, or (b) avoidance of a cost.

Category (2): Bribes can be paid for receipt of a benefit (or avoidance of a cost) that is not scarce, but where discretion must be exercised by state officials.

Category (3): Bribes can be paid, not for a specific public benefit itself, but for services connected with obtaining a benefit (or avoiding a cost), such as speedy service or inside information.

Category (4): Bribes can be paid (a) to prevent others from sharing in a benefit or (b) to impose a cost on someone else.

Category (1) includes any bureaucratic decision where the briber's gain is someone else's loss: for example, access to import or export permits; foreign exchange; a government contract or franchise; concessions to develop oil or other minerals; public land allocation; the purchase of a newly privatised firm; access to scarce capital funds under state control; a license to operate a business when the total number of licenses is fixed; access to public services such as public housing; subsidised inputs; or heightened police protection for a business. In all these examples, there may be competition between bribers which can be manipulated or even created by bureaucrats or politicians. If public servants have the discretion to design programmes, they may be able to create scarcity for their own pecuniary benefit or over-allocate resources (a phenomenon known as 'supply stretching').

Examples of Category (2) include: reducing tax bills or extorting higher payments when no fixed revenue constraint exists; waiving of customs duties and regulations; avoidance of price controls; awarding a license or permit only to those who are deemed to "qualify"; access to open-ended public services (entitlements); receipt of a civil service job; exemption from enforcement of the law (especially for victimless and white collar crime); board approval for a building project; and lax enforcement of safety or environmental standards. Bureaucratic discretion can often lead to the extortion of bribes. Police can pay gangs to threaten businesses, while at the same time accepting bribes from these same businesses for their protection. Similarly, politicians can threaten to support laws that will impose costs or promise to provide specialised benefits in return for payoffs.

Category (3) are services related to the first two categories, rather than a benefit *per se*. For example, inside information on contract specifications (as was the case in Singapore, where a consortium of corporations from exporting countries bribed to obtain privileged information in connection with government contracts—the corporations were subsequently blacklisted by the Government of Singapore). Other aspects include faster service; reduced paperwork; advance notice of police raids; reduced uncertainty; or a favourable audit report that would keep taxes low. Bureaucrats can often generate the conditions that produce such bribes. Officials can introduce delays and impose rigid application requirements. For example, despite tough environmental protection laws in Russia, the condition of the environment suggests that the legal regime is focused more on providing opportunities for officials to extract bribes for non-compliance, than on actually protecting the environment.

Category (4), like (1), also includes winners and losers. Examples include cases where one operator of an illegal business might pay law enforcement agencies to raid his competitors. Owners of legal businesses might seek the imposition of excessive regulatory constraints on competitors, or attempt to induce officials to refuse to license a potential competitor. A Queensland Police Commissioner was bribed by illegal gaming interests to furnish a report to his government arguing strongly that the gaming industry should not be legalised.

In Categories (1) and (4), where there are direct losers, the organisation of the potential bribers may be important in determining the size and prevalence of corruption. If there is only a small number of potential beneficiaries, they may simply share the market monopolistically among themselves, rather than resort to bribery, and then present a united front to public officials. These cases demonstrate that the elimination of corruption is not an end in itself. A policy encouraging the monopolisation of an industry could reduce corruption, but would have few social gains. Instead of flowing in part to public officials, the benefits would flow into the pockets of monopolistic firms. In addition, if these companies are foreign-owned and repatriating profits, or international criminal concerns, the benefits will mostly flow out of the country. Examples like these illustrate how the problem might not be corruption *per se*, but the monopoly rents that give rise to payoffs.

The extraction of payments from people who are entitled to services but unable to get them (e.g. for the issuing of a driver's licence) is properly classified as "extortion" (and a crime in most countries), rather than a bribe. The test would be whether both payer and recipient were acting illegally, or whether the payer was an innocent victim of an offence by an official who would otherwise deny the payer his lawful entitlement.

Corruption and market inefficiency

Some commentators argue that bribery simply represents the operation of market forces within state programmes, and that, given the efficiency of the market, payoffs should be tolerated. Such cases might exist; however, this benign assessment must be treated with scepticism.

First, public programmes may be undermined when public servants allocate scarce resources to the highest bidder. Public housing, for instance, is designed for the poorest families, not those who can pay the most. In addition, the prospect of payoffs can lead officials to create artificial scarcity and red tape. Moreover, where bribes are paid to induce public officials to favour a firm at the expense of competitors, the highest bidder is often not the most efficient organisation in the marketplace; instead, it can be the organisation with the highest monopoly profits resulting from the elimination of competitors.

The illegality of corruption itself introduces costs that will limit the efficiency of bribery. First, because its perpetrators try to keep their illicit dealings secret, the price information that is essential for a well-operating market is not easily available, and may result in price inflexibility. Once an acceptable bribe rate (10% of the contract price) or fee (US$100 to get a driving license) has been set and is known in the relevant community, the price may remain constant, even in the face of changing market conditions over time. Corruption markets may be more influenced by habit and tradition than ordinary private markets. Large shocks may be needed, such as the fall of a corrupt government, to re-adjust bribe payments.

Second, to reduce the risk of detection, entry into the bribery market for both payers and receivers is limited to people who are known and trusted—relatives, close friends, members of the village or tribe. Third, the benefits of corruption are not widely distributed if some refuse to participate. Honest public servants may simply refuse to enter the corrupt marketplace. Fourth, given the illegality of bribes, contracts between beneficiaries and public officials cannot be enforced. Thus, the risk that one side or the other will not perform, will limit the number and type of deals and make it more likely that such transactions will only occur among people who are well known to one another. As a general rule, then, one can reject the claim that corruption allocates resources efficiently. * * *

As the excerpt suggests, in the past, business firms and their advocates sometimes argued that corruption is economically efficient, because it allows firms to avoid unnecessary bureaucratic red tape. However, the available evidence suggests that corruption more often does the opposite. See JOHANN GRAF LAMBSDORFF, THE INSTITUTIONAL ECONOMICS OF CORRUPTION AND REFORM 122-25 (2007). A government official who can erect regulatory barriers to doing business creates opportunities to extract bribes to evade those barriers. It is therefore in the self-interest of corrupt officials to create more, and more burdensome, unnecessary bureaucratic obstacles to efficient business as a means to demand ever greater bribes.

Transparency International engages in and disseminates research useful in helping international investors, law enforcement officials, public policy makers, and others measure the risks of bribery or other corruption in an international transaction. Among its activities is the publication of a **Corruption Perceptions Index** to indicate how business firms and country analysts evaluate governmental integrity in various countries. A high index score on a scale of 100 denotes high confidence in the integrity of public officials; a low index score indicates the opposite. In 2018, for example, the countries perceived as "cleanest" were Denmark (score of 88), New Zealand (87), and Finland (85),

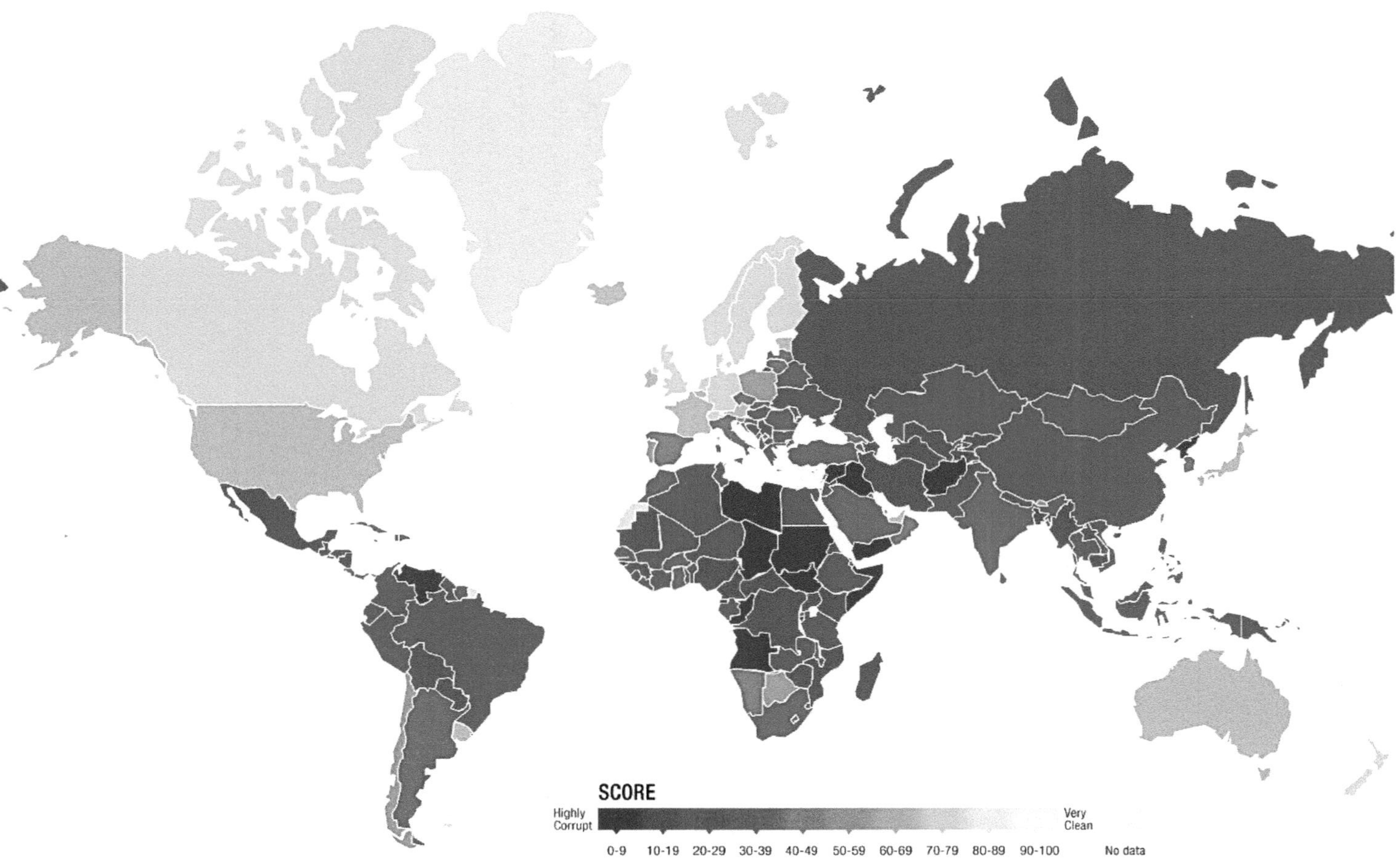

Figure 8.1. The Transparency International Corruption Perceptions Index 2018. Darker areas indicate a perception of greater corruption; lighter areas indicate less perceived corruption.
Credit: © 2020 by Transparency International. Reproduced with permission.

while the countries perceived as having the most corruption were South Sudan (13), Syria (13), and Somalia (10). Figure 8.1 illustrates a recent global map of perceived corruption.

Transparency International also periodically publishes a Bribe Payers Index, which evaluates the propensity of companies in the leading capital-exporting states to pay bribes in other countries. Using the same scale as the Corruption Perceptions Index, the Bribe Payers Index measures the average integrity of successful businesses, mostly in the developed world. In 2011, for example, Dutch, Swiss, and Belgian business firms came out the "cleanest," while Mexican, Chinese, and Russian businesses scored most poorly.

The Corruption Perceptions Index, like reports from other corruption-monitoring NGOs such as Global Witness, can be useful to a multinational enterprise seeking information about the risks of investing or otherwise doing business in a foreign country. One advantage of understanding perceived corruption in a potential investment host state is that it can help a business foresee the kinds of risks it may face and to take precautions against violating domestic or foreign anticorruption laws. A firm contemplating doing business in a country with a low index score, meaning a strong perception of corruption, may wish to give especially thorough training to its personnel and agents to prevent unintended involvement in a bribe or other corrupt act. In some cases, the firm may wish to refrain entirely from investing heavily in a market with a low index score because of the risks of the investment failing in the absence of bribe payments.

Another advantage of understanding a foreign state's perceived corruption is that firms doing business in high corruption countries may often expect to be monitored to some degree by law enforcement agencies and anticorruption regulators. The expectation of greater scrutiny is likely to lead the firm to take precautions against even an appearance of improper contact with foreign government officials. There is an additional risk of negative publicity in the event that the public media learns of a bribe or other corrupt act. Large companies with a salient public profile among consumers can be especially damaged by revelations of participation in corruption.

2 International Treaty-Based Responses

Almost all states formally prohibit at least some forms of corrupt payments to their public officials. Some go further and prohibit the use of former government officials as lobbyists or other representatives to the government. Many states are concerned, not only with bribery of their own officials, but with the participation of their nationals and business entities in foreign bribery.

For many years, the United States and only a few other capital-exporting states maintained strict anti-bribery laws relating to foreign business practices. But unless all capital-exporting states prohibit foreign bribery, a business firm not constrained by anti-bribery rules has a notable edge on its more

IF EVERYONE GIVES BRIBES, DOESN'T IT ALL BALANCE OUT?

Bribes paid to government officials by private contractors may seem relatively innocuous if the practice is widespread, because all firms know that they have to pay bribes and plan accordingly. But a bribery system results in awards of government contracts to the largest bribe payer rather than the best or lowest bidder. In the regulatory context, it may divert badly needed tax revenues from state coffers, resulting in dangerous under-regulation of business activity. Such practices may have disastrous consequences for persons who rely on competent government regulation of industries. International bribery has caused many scandalous hardships for the public:

> Fifty-one [persons] died from contaminated toothpaste manufactured abroad. Fake baby formula killed dozens of infants. Lead and other toxins are found in children's toys manufactured abroad. Dogs and cats died after consuming pet food poisoned with melamine. Vast amounts of imported drywall used in residential home construction in America turn out to be so contaminated with toxins that the homes are literally uninhabitable. Hundreds of children attending school died or were terribly injured, in Sichuan, China, and in Haiti, when shoddy construction resulted in their schools collapsing during earthquakes.

Elizabeth Spahn, *Nobody Gets Hurt?*, 41 GEO. J. INT'L L. 861, 894 (2010).

constrained competitors. By being the only firm to bribe foreign officials, it can secure advantages unavailable to honest firms. If even one capital-exporting state permits its business firms to bribe foreign government officials, corruption will continue. In such situations, there is continuous pressure to "race to the bottom." Companies prohibited to influence foreign governments corruptly will suffer in their overseas business, and so they will try to exert political pressure on their governments to relax anti-bribery regulations.

The control of international corruption can be dependable and effective only if all or nearly all capital-exporting states prohibit foreign bribery, and on approximately the same terms. In the late 1990s, the United States finally managed to convince most of Europe and other capital exporting states to adopt a convention prohibiting foreign bribery. Through an IGO known as the **Organization for Economic Cooperation and Development** (**OECD**), the ponderously titled **Convention on Combating Bribery of Foreign Public Officials in International Business Transactions**, also known as the **OECD Anti-Bribery Convention**, was concluded in 1997.

This treaty obligates state parties to adopt laws that prohibit offering, promising, or giving:

> any undue pecuniary or other advantage, whether directly or through intermediaries, to a foreign public official * * * in order that the official act or refrain from acting in relation to the performance of official duties, in order to obtain or retain business or other improper advantage in the conduct of international business.

OECD Anti-Bribery Convention art. 1(1). The OECD Convention states to impose require criminal penalties on individuals who engage in these prohibited acts, as well as conspiring to bribe a public official or inciting, aiding and abetting, attempting, or authorizing such bribery.

Because the OECD Convention reaches the bribery of foreign public officials only, it requires states to take measures necessary to establish jurisdiction over acts having effects beyond their borders. The Convention does not require states to impose criminal liability on corporations or other legal persons. However, articles 2 and 3(2) require states to "take such measures as may be necessary . . . to establish the liability" of legal persons for acts of bribery, such as civil fines.

The Convention includes several other important prohibitions and requirements, by which the parties agree:

- to adopt laws for the seizure and forfeiture of bribes paid to foreign government officials;
- to implement effective international anti-bribery enforcement efforts;
- to adopt uniform standards for criminalizing money laundering, which is a measure taken to hide the illegal source of funds;
- to coordinate extradition of offenders found outside the state in which the bribery took place; and
- to adopt laws requiring companies to keep accurate accounts and records in order to make concealing corrupt transactions more difficult.

As of 2020, the Convention has been ratified by forty-three states, including the United States and most other capital exporting countries. The United States modified its anticorruption laws to conform to the OECD Convention requirements in 1998.

A second major treaty was adopted by the United Nations General Assembly in 2003. The **UN Convention Against Corruption** (**UNCAC**) provides a still more comprehensive global framework for combating corruption. Unlike the OECD Convention, UNCAC requires state parties to adopt measures to prevent not just bribery of foreign officials by private industry, but corruption within their own private sector and among their own government officials as well. These measures include the establishment of an anticorruption detection and enforcement agency; ensuring transparency in hiring, licensing, and government procurement practices; and adopting codes of conduct for government officials. Like the OECD Convention, UNCAC requires the adoption of measures to criminalize money laundering. It further requires state parties to enact criminal laws prohibiting taking or receiving bribes in both the public and private sectors, money laundering, abuse of office, embezzlement, obstructing justice, and similar forms of corruption.

UNCAC does not require state parties to adopt criminal penalties for every corrupt act. It limits the criminalization requirement to promising, offering, or giving bribes to public officials, directly or indirectly "in order that the official act or refrain from acting in the exercise of his or her official duties." It also requires criminal penalties for public officials who solicit or accept bribes for the same purpose. Article 16 specifically requires criminal penalties for the bribery of foreign public officials. Certain other forms of corruption, such as embezzlement or trading in influence, must also be subject to criminal penalties.

These prohibitions, like those of the OECD Convention, apply not only to individuals, but to corporations, partnerships, and other business entities. Specifically, UNCAC provides:

Article 26
Liability of legal persons

> 1. Each State Party shall adopt such measures as may be necessary, consistent with its legal principles, to establish the liability of legal persons for participation in the offences established in accordance with this Convention.
> 2. Subject to the legal principles of the State Party, the liability of legal persons may be criminal, civil or administrative.
> 3. Such liability shall be without prejudice to the criminal liability of the natural persons who have committed the offences.
> 4. Each State Party shall, in particular, ensure that legal persons held liable in accordance with this article are subject to effective, proportionate and dissuasive criminal or non-criminal sanctions, including monetary sanctions.

In Article 31, UNCAC requires that states take measures to confiscate or freeze the proceeds of crimes of corruption, or the equipment or property used in committing the crimes. UNCAC also provides for the protection of whistleblowers and extradition of persons involved in a corrupt transaction if the alleged transaction was illegal in both the extraditing state and in the state seeking extradition.

Finally, an innovation in UNCAC is the requirement in Chapter V that states must assist one another in recovering assets obtained or stolen through corrupt transactions. Each state party must adopt laws permitting other state parties to bring a civil action against a party either engaged in embezzlement or a corrupt transaction, or that is otherwise holding assets derived from such a transaction, in order to recover the ill-gotten assets. UNCAC has 186 parties as of 2020, encompassing almost every state in the world, including the United States.

In addition, there are other anti-corruption treaties having different membership. These include the 1997 Inter-American Convention Against Corruption, which requires Organization of American States members (including the United States) to criminalize bribery, and the 1997 Convention on the Fight Against Corruption Involving Officials of the European Communities or Officials of Member States of the European Union, which prohibits the bribery of

WHAT IS MONEY LAUNDERING?

It's not as clean as it sounds. **Money laundering** is the practice of obfuscating the origins of illegally-obtained funds. For example, a money launderer might buy foreign currency with ill-gotten gains, deposit it in foreign banks, create shell corporations with no assets or active operations to hold the money, or purchase expensive goods like yachts or houses with illegal funds. The goal is to make the origin of the income difficult to trace by law enforcement agencies, by moving it between different forms of assets and between different companies and countries. As noted, both the OECD Anti-Bribery Convention and UNCAC require states to criminalize money laundering.

FATF

Many states have anti-money laundering legislation is designed to detect crime and corrupt. For example, they may require banks, stock brokers, and casinos to report deposits or exchanges of large sums of cash, or they may require sellers of expensive goods such as automobiles and jewelry to report on all sales. Self-reporting may also be required. The world's most economically powerful states coordinate anti-money laundering efforts through an informal group, the **Financial Action Task Force**. In the United States, the main anti-money laundering laws are the Money Laundering Control Act, 18 U.S.C. §§ 1956-57, and the Bank Secrecy Act, 31 U.S.C. §§ 5311-30.

You may have noticed that, whenever you enter or leave the United States, you are asked whether you are carrying $10,000 or more in cash. This is because all persons are required to report the movement of large sums into or out of the country. Failure to do so can result in forfeiture of the money and other penalties. That is the Bank Secrecy Act in action.

DO ANTI-CORRUPTION TREATIES WORK?

A treaty by itself, like any law, can accomplish very little unless accompanied by institutions to monitor and correct noncompliance, or a strong self-motivation to comply. So far, anti-corruption treaties have not been consistently backed by either force. According to a Transparency International report, most parties to the OECD Convention have undertaken "little or no" enforcement so far, largely due to a lack of political commitment to combat corruption. GILLIAN DELL & ANDREW MCDEVITT, TRANSPARENCY INTERNATIONAL, EXPORTING CORRUPTION: PROGRESS REPORT 2018, at 5. Only a few OECD parties, strongly led by the United States, regularly commence investigations and impose sanctions for foreign bribery. The same applies to UNCAC. In fact, some of the biggest exporting states, such as China, Japan, South Korea, and Singapore, do not enforce anti-bribery laws for foreign investment virtually at all. *Id.* at 10-11.

Because the OECD Convention and UNCAC lack any mechanism to punish states that shirk their enforcement duties, it seems that the exercise of extraterritorial jurisdiction by the United States and a handful of foreign states offers one of the few effective deterrents to global corruption.

The WTO's Dispute Settlement Understanding works well because states have a direct interest in the compliance of other states with international trade rules. But states generally lack an incentive for other states to punish their own corruption. How might an enforcement institution be crafted to capture the benefits of an international regulatory regime, while taking into account the different dynamic involved?

public officials within the EU. The African Union also adopted a Convention on Preventing and Combating Corruption in 2006.

3 U.S. Regulation of Transnational Corruption

As might be expected, U.S. federal law criminalizes the bribery of any federal official, 18 U.S.C. § 201, and every U.S. state makes bribing state or local public officials a crime as well. Supplementing these prohibitions are several laws designed to prevent companies subject to U.S. jurisdiction from engaging in transnational corruption specifically. The most important of these in general international business is the Foreign Corrupt Practices Act.

3.1 Introduction to the Foreign Corrupt Practices Act

Long before the OECD Anti-Bribery Convention and UN Convention Against Corruption were under negotiation by the international community, the United States forbade U.S. companies from bribing foreign officials to obtain an unfair business advantage.

In the early and mid-1970s the U.S. **Securities Exchange Commission** (**SEC**) discovered that hundreds of U.S. business firms had regularly been making payments worth hundreds of millions of dollars to foreign government officials and political parties in violation of foreign laws. Although most of the bribing firms were major U.S. defense and aerospace manufacturers, perhaps the most influential scandal was known as Bananagate.

In 1975, Eli Black, the chairman and president of United Brands Company, a major fruit importer, leapt out of a Manhattan skyscraper window. While investigating the suicide, the SEC discovered that United Brands had paid over $1 million in bribes to the then-president of Honduras to reduce the banana export tax. The tax had been doubled to help local banana plantations compete with U.S. fruit companies, which controlled most banana production

"Then we carefully disguise the bribes as legal fees by changing the word 'bribes' to 'legal fees.'"

Figure 8.2. Discovering corruption often requires looking past superficial records.

in Honduras. The bribe saved United Brands $7.5 million in taxes and crushed competition by local Honduran fruit exporters. Although bribing foreign governments violated no U.S. law at the time, publicly traded corporations like United Brands were required by U.S. securities laws to report such payments to the company's shareholders. Having concealed the bribes, and realizing he would be disgraced when the SEC discovered his secret, Black committed suicide.

The public outrage upon revelation of widespread foreign bribery motivated Congress in 1977 to enact the **Foreign Corrupt Practices Act** (**FCPA**), 15 U.S.C. §§ 78m, 78dd-1, 78dd-2, 78dd-3, 78ff. Because the FCPA is part of the U.S. securities regulation laws, it is generally enforced by the SEC as well as the U.S. Department of Justice (DoJ), which is primarily responsible for prosecuting federal crimes.

A. Persons Subject to the FCPA

The FCPA's mandates apply to persons in three general categories. First, they regulate issuers of securities listed on a U.S. stock exchange or required to file periodic reports to the SEC. Such **securities issuers** may be either U.S. firms or foreign firms that offer their securities on a U.S. stock exchange. In addition, some foreign companies that have significant U.S. shareholders must comply with certain provisions of the FCPA as well.

Second, all **domestic concerns** must comply with the FCPA. Domestic concerns are defined as any individual who is a citizen, national, or resident of the United States. The definition further encompasses any business organization, nonprofit entity, or sole proprietorship that has its principal place of business in the United States or that is organized under the laws of a U.S. state. This includes the U.S. subsidiaries of foreign parent companies.

Finally, any other person must comply with the FCPA while present in U.S. territory. 15 U.S.C. §§ 78dd-1, 78dd-2(h)(1).

It is important to be aware, then, that the FCPA binds not just U.S. companies, but foreign companies that issue stock in the United States or operate out of the United States. It is equally important to remember that the act applies to U.S. nationals wherever in the world they live and work.

B. Anti-Bribery Provisions

The FCPA prohibits companies registered on a U.S. securities exchange, and other companies required to file reports with the SEC, from making:

> (a) * * * use of the mails or any means or instrumentality of interstate commerce corruptly in furtherance of an offer, payment, promise to pay, or authorization of the payment of any money, or offer, gift, promise to give, or authorization of the giving of anything of value to—
>
> (1) any foreign official for purposes of—

(A)(i) influencing any act or decision of such foreign official in his official capacity,

(ii) inducing such foreign official to do or omit to do any act in violation of the lawful duty of such official, or

(iii) securing any improper advantage; or

(B) inducing such foreign official to use his influence with a foreign government or instrumentality thereof to affect or influence any act or decision of such government or instrumentality,

in order to assist such issuer in obtaining or retaining business for or with, or directing business to, any person;

(2) any foreign political party or official thereof or any candidate for foreign political office for purposes of—

(A)(i) influencing any act or decision of such party, official, or candidate in its or his official capacity,

(ii) inducing such party, official, or candidate to do or omit to do an act in violation of the lawful duty of such party, official, or candidate, or

(iii) securing any improper advantage; or

(B) inducing such party, official, or candidate to use its or his influence with a foreign government or instrumentality thereof to affect or influence any act or decision of such government or instrumentality,

in order to assist such issuer in obtaining or retaining business for or with, or directing business to, any person; or

(3) any person, while knowing that all or a portion of such money or thing of value will be offered, given, or promised, directly or indirectly, to any foreign official, to any foreign political party or official thereof, or to any candidate for foreign political office, for purposes of—

(A) (i) influencing any act or decision of such foreign official, political party, party official, or candidate in his or its official capacity,

(ii) inducing such foreign official, political party, party official, or candidate to do or omit to do any act in violation of the lawful duty of such foreign official, political party, party official, or candidate, or

(iii) securing any improper advantage; or

(B) inducing such foreign official, political party, party official, or candidate to use his or its influence with a foreign government or instrumentality thereof to affect or influence any act or decision of such government or instrumentality,

in order to assist such issuer in obtaining or retaining business for or with, or directing business to, any person.

15 U.S.C. § 78dd-1(a).

Consider the following important aspects of this provision:

1. The prohibitions include giving not just money but any "thing of value" to foreign officials.

2. The provision makes *offering* or *promising* anything of value to a foreign official for the prohibited purposes a crime as well as actually giving it. It also makes *authorizing* someone else to give something of value to a foreign official for the prohibited purposes a crime. In other words, the FCPA will not allow a principal or employer to shield itself from liability by having an agent or employee engage in the corrupt transaction on its behalf.

3. In order for the FCPA to prohibit a transaction, it is not necessary for the foreign recipient actually to be a government official. It is also illegal to bribe political parties, party officials, or candidates for office.

Title 15, sections 78dd-2 and 78dd-3 of the U.S. Code apply almost identical prohibitions to "domestic concerns" generally and to foreign persons in U.S. territory. The primary differences between these last two categories and securities issuers is that only securities issuers are subject to the reporting requirements of the FCPA, discussed further below.

C. "Thing of Value"

Cash is always considered a thing of value, even in very small amounts.* The expression "thing of value" is intended to catch non-cash as well as cash offers and exchanges. Obviously, previous metals, jewelry, vehicles, and other tangible valuables are included. Similarly, in the context of domestic laws prohibiting bribery of public officials, federal courts have held that stocks, bonds, and promises of loans are things of value.**

But what about things that are not normally the object of commercial exchange? In *United States v. Moore*, 525 F.3d 1033 (11th Cir. 2008), a federal court held that a prison guard who had sexual intercourse with a female inmate in exchange for violating an official duty had accepted a "thing of value." "[M]onetary worth," the court held, "is not the sole measure of value." *Id.* at 1048. In *United States v. Gorman*, 807 F.2d 1299 (6th Cir. 1986), an appellate court held that a promise of future employment would qualify as a thing of value, despite the fact that the obligations in an employment relationship are mutual. It seems likely that the FCPA's definition is intended to be similarly broad in defining what qualifies as valuable.

What about favors, the economic value of which is questionable? Suppose a U.S. business executive offers to write a letter of recommendation for admission to a prestigious university on behalf of the child of a foreign government official in exchange for the award of a government contract. Do you think the recommendation would qualify as a "thing of value" for anti-bribery purposes?

---

*E.g., United States v. Hsieh Hui Mei Chen, 754 F.2d 817, 822 (9th Cir. 1985) (payment of $100).

**E.g., United States v. Williams, 705 F.2d 603, 622-23 (2d Cir. 1983) (stocks).

D. The Mental Element of Corruption

To be criminally liable for violating the FCPA, a person must act "willfully." That term is not defined in the FCPA itself. The U.S. Supreme Court has adopted a problematical definition of "willfulness," holding that when that term is used in criminal law, it generally means "the Government must prove that the defendant acted with knowledge that his conduct was unlawful." *Bryan v. United States*, 524 U.S. 184 (1998). The problem with that interpretation is that it violates an important legal canon: *ignorantia legis neminem excusat*, meaning ignorance of the law does not excuse its violation. Several circuit courts have tried to mitigate the consequences of the Supreme Court's definition by holding that a defendant may act willfully even without knowing of the FCPA or that his or her conduct violated it.

Another important aspect of the mental component of the FCPA is that, although the Act sometimes phrases its prohibitions as relating to a person who "knows" the payment will be used for bribery, a firm or employee may not self-blind to a high probability that a payment will be used for illicit purposes. For example, if a company hires a sales agent to help market its goods to a foreign government knowing that the agent has a reputation for unethical business conduct, and the sales agent shares part of his commission with a government official in order to obtain business for the company, the company may be liable for a criminal violation of the FCPA even though it never actually knew with certainty that a bribe would or did occur.

Regulated persons are expected to maintain a reasonable level of diligence and supervision of the activities of their employees and agents. This includes foreign subsidiary companies whose activities the parent company directed or controlled. The legislative history of the Act states:

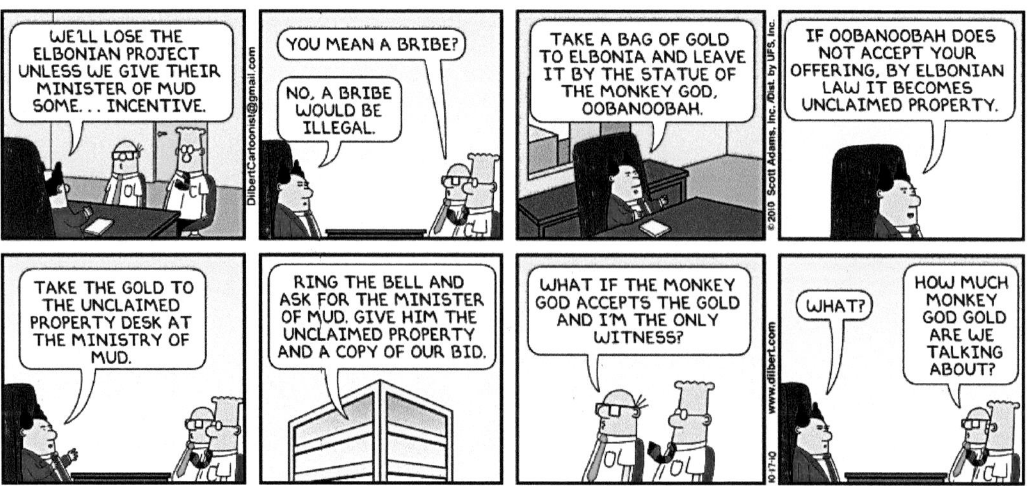

Figure 8.3. A manager who authorizes a bribe is as culpable as the employee paying it. Credit: DILBERT © 2010 Scott Adams/United Features Syndicate, Inc.

> [K]nowledge of a fact may be inferred where the defendant has notice of the high probability of the existence of the fact and has failed to establish an honest, contrary disbelief. The inference cannot be overcome by the defendant's "deliberate avoidance of knowledge," his or her "willful blindness," or his or her "conscious disregard," of the existence of the required circumstance or result.

H.R. Rep. No. 576, 100th Cong., 2d Sess., 920 (1988), 1988 U.S.C.C.A.N. 1949, 1953-54.

As an example, consider the business executive of Blip Radar Company (BRC), Ryan, who authorizes the hiring of a commission sales agent, Wayne, in Ruritania. Wayne is known as a commercially ambitious and effective sales agent who will do almost anything to get sales. He was formerly Assistant Defense Minister of Ruritania and has many high level contacts in the Ruritanian government. Ryan wishes Wayne to help BRC sell its radar to the Ruritanian Defense Ministry. To that end, BRC provides Wayne with a $20,000 expense account and does not require him to report his expenditures. In informal instructions, Ryan tells Wayne that selling radar to the Ruritanian government is very important to BRC and that he should "think creatively" about how to persuade Ruritanian officials to purchase BRC equipment. Wayne uses money from his expense account to bribe Ruritanian Defense Ministry employees and secure contracts for BRC.

In this scenario, BRC has neither bribed any official of the Ruritanian government, nor explicitly authorized Wayne to bribe any official. However, Ryan may be aware of a high probability that his instructions to Wayne implicitly authorize a bribe. This may be inferred from the large amount of money put at Wayne's disposal without any accounting controls and from the open-ended instructions to secure Ruritanian business. Moreover, the fact that Wayne works on commission gives him a substantial incentive to ensure that BRC gets its contract even at some risk. True, there are alternative interpretations to the events recounted in this scenario, but the point is that Ryan has exposed himself and BRC to potential criminal prosecution by failing to take precautions against bribery or the appearance of authorizing bribery.

E. Purpose of the Bribe

An offer, promise, or payment, etc. is made "corruptly" when it is intended to influence the recipient to do something contrary to a legal duty. This implies that the regulated person's act was intentional. But intentional to what end? The FCPA defines prohibited bribes to include only payments or gifts made for the purpose of "obtaining or retaining business" or directing business to another person. But bribes may be paid to government officials merely to make business more efficient or less expensive. The following case explores the extent to which the FCPA prohibits such bribes as well.

UNITED STATES v. KAY

U.S. Court of Appeals, Fifth Circuit, 2004
359 F.3d 738

WIENER, Circuit Judge:

Plaintiff-appellant, the United States of America ("government") appeals the district court's grant of the motion of defendants-appellees David Kay and Douglas Murphy ("defendants") to dismiss the Superseding Indictment ("indictment") that charged them with bribery of foreign officials in violation of the Foreign Corrupt Practices Act ("FCPA"). In their dismissal motion, defendants contended that the indictment failed to state an offense against them. The principal dispute in this case is whether, if proved beyond a reasonable doubt, the conduct that the indictment ascribed to defendants in connection with the alleged bribery of Haitian officials to understate customs duties and sales taxes on rice shipped to Haiti to assist American Rice, Inc. in obtaining or retaining business was sufficient to constitute an offense under the FCPA. Underlying this question of sufficiency of the contents of the indictment is the preliminary task of ascertaining the scope of the FCPA, which in turn requires us to construe the statute.

The district court concluded that, as a matter of law, an indictment alleging illicit payments to foreign officials for the purpose of avoiding substantial portions of customs duties and sales taxes to obtain or retain business are not the kind of bribes that the FCPA criminalizes. * * *

I. FACTS AND PROCEEDINGS

American Rice, Inc. ("ARI") is a Houston-based company that exports rice to foreign countries, including Haiti. Rice Corporation of Haiti ("RCH"), a wholly owned subsidiary of ARI, was incorporated in Haiti to represent ARI's interests and deal with third parties there. As an aspect of Haiti's standard importation procedure, its customs officials assess duties based on the quantity and value of rice imported into the country. Haiti also requires businesses that deliver rice there to remit an advance deposit against Haitian sales taxes, based on the value of that rice, for which deposit a credit is eventually allowed on Haitian sales tax returns when filed.

In 2001, a grand jury charged Kay with violating the FCPA and subsequently returned the indictment, which charges both Kay and Murphy with 12 counts of FCPA violations. As is readily apparent on its face, the indictment contains detailed factual allegations * * *. The indictment also spells out in detail how Kay and Murphy allegedly orchestrated the bribing of Haitian customs officials to accept false bills of lading and other documentation that intentionally understated by one-third the quantity of rice shipped to Haiti, thereby significantly reducing ARI's customs duties and sales taxes. In this regard, the indictment alleges the details of the bribery scheme's machinations, including the preparation of duplicate documentation, the calculation of bribes as a percentage of the value of the rice not reported, the surreptitious payment of monthly retainers to Haitian officials, and the defendants' purported authorization of withdrawals of funds from ARI's bank accounts with which to pay the Haitian officials, either directly or through intermediaries—all to produce substantially reduced Haitian customs and tax costs to ARI. * * *

In contrast, without any factual allegations, the indictment merely paraphrases the one element of the statute that is central to this appeal, only conclusionally accusing defendants of causing payments to be made to Haitian customs officials:

> for purposes of influencing acts and decisions of such foreign officials in their official capacities, inducing such foreign officials to do and omit to do acts in violation of their lawful duty, and to obtain an improper advantage, in order to assist American Rice, Inc. in *obtaining and retaining business* for, and directing business to American Rice, Inc. and Rice Corporation of Haiti. (Emphasis added).

Although it recites in great detail the discrete facts that the government intends to prove to satisfy each other element of an FCPA violation, the indictment recites no particularized facts that, if proved, would satisfy the "assist" aspect of the business nexus element of the statute, i.e., the nexus between the illicit tax savings produced by the bribery and the assistance such savings provided or were intended to provide in *obtaining or retaining business* for ARI and RCH. Neither does the indictment contain any factual allegations whatsoever to identify just *what* business in Haiti (presumably some rice-related commercial activity) the illicit customs and tax savings assisted (or were intended to assist) in obtaining or retaining, or just *how* these savings were supposed to assist in such efforts. In other words, the indictment recites no facts that could demonstrate an actual or intended cause-and-effect nexus between reduced taxes and obtaining identified business or retaining identified business opportunities.

In granting defendants' motion to dismiss the indictment for failure to state an offense, the district court held that, as a matter of law, bribes paid to obtain favorable tax treatment are not payments made to "obtain or retain business" within the intendment of the FCPA, and thus are not within the scope of that statute's proscription of foreign bribery. The government timely filed a notice of appeal.

II. ANALYSIS

* * *

B. *Words of the FCPA*

"[T]he starting point for interpreting a statute is the language of the statute itself." When construing a criminal statute, we "must follow the plain and unambiguous meaning of the statutory language." Terms not defined in the statute are interpreted according to their "ordinary and natural meaning ... as well as the overall policies and objectives of the statute." Furthermore, "a statute must, if possible, be construed in such fashion that every word has some operative effect." Finally, we have found it "appropriate to consider the title of a statute in resolving putative ambiguities." If, after application of these principles of statutory construction, we conclude that the statute is ambiguous, we may turn to legislative history. For the language to be considered ambiguous, however, it must be "susceptible to more than one reasonable interpretation" or "more than one accepted meaning."

The FCPA prohibits payments to foreign officials for purposes of:

> (i) influencing any act or decision of such foreign official in his official capacity, (ii) inducing such foreign official to do or omit to do any act in violation of the lawful duty of such official, or (iii) securing any improper advantage ... in order to assist [the company making the payment] in obtaining or retaining business for or with, or directing business to, any person.

None contend that the FCPA criminalizes every payment to a foreign official: It criminalizes only those payments that are intended to (1) influence a foreign official to act or make a decision in his official capacity, or (2) induce such an official to perform or refrain from performing some act in violation of his duty, or (3) secure some wrongful advantage to the payor. And even then, the FCPA criminalizes these kinds of payments only if the result they are intended to produce—their *quid pro quo*—will *assist* (or is intended to assist) the payor in efforts to get or keep some *business* for or with "any person." Thus, the first question of statutory interpretation presented in this appeal is whether payments made to foreign officials to obtain unlawfully reduced customs duties or sales tax liabilities can ever fall within the scope of the FCPA, i.e., whether the illicit payments made to obtain a reduction of revenue liabilities can *ever* constitute the kind of bribery that is proscribed by the FCPA. The district court answered this question in the negative; only if we answer it in the affirmative will we need to analyze the sufficiency of the factual allegations of the indictment as to the one element of the crime contested here.

The principal thrust of the defendants' argument is that the business nexus element, i.e., the "assist ... in obtaining or retaining business" element, narrowly limits the statute's applicability to those payments that are intended to obtain a foreign official's approval of a bid for a new government contract or the renewal of an existing government contract. In contrast, the government insists that, in addition to payments to officials that lead directly to getting or renewing business contracts, the statute covers payments that indirectly advance ("assist") the payor's goal of obtaining or retaining foreign business with or for some person. The government reasons that paying reduced customs duties and sales taxes on imports, as is purported to have occurred in this case, is the type of "improper advantage" that *always* will assist in obtaining or retaining business in a foreign country, and thus is always covered by the FCPA.

[The court then analyzed the statutory language and found it unclear on the question of whether a bribe paid to obtain more favorable customs treatment was made "to obtain or retain business."] * * *

C. *FCPA Legislative History*

As the statutory language itself is amenable to more than one reasonable interpretation, it is ambiguous as a matter of law. We turn therefore to legislative history in our effort to ascertain Congress's true intentions.

1. *1977 Legislative History*

Congress enacted the FCPA in 1977, in response to recently discovered but widespread bribery of foreign officials by United States business interests. Congress resolved to interdict such bribery, not just because it is morally and economically suspect, but also because it was causing foreign policy problems for the United States.[22] In particular, these concerns arose from revelations that United States defense contractors and oil companies had made large payments to high government officials in Japan, the Netherlands, and Italy. Congress also discovered that more than 400 corporations had made questionable or illegal payments in excess of $300 million to foreign officials for a wide range of favorable actions on behalf of the companies.

In deciding to criminalize this type of commercial bribery, the House and Senate each proposed similarly far-reaching, but non-identical, legislation. In its bill, the House intended "broadly [to] prohibit[ ] transactions that are *corruptly* intended to induce the recipient to use his or her influence to affect *any* act or decision of a foreign official...." Thus, the House bill contained no limiting "business nexus" element. Reflecting a somewhat narrower purpose, the Senate expressed its desire to ban payments made for the purpose of inducing foreign officials to act "so as to direct business to any person, maintain an established business opportunity with any person, divert any business opportunity from any person or influence the enactment or promulgation of legislation or regulations of that government or instrumentality."

At conference, compromise language "clarified the scope of the prohibition by requiring that the purpose of the payment must be to influence any act or decision of a foreign official ... so as to assist an issuer in obtaining, retaining or directing business to any person." In the end, then, Congress adopted the Senate's proposal to prohibit only those payments designed to induce a foreign official to act in a way that is intended to facilitate ("assist") in obtaining or retaining of business.

Congress expressly emphasized that it did not intend to prohibit "so-called grease or facilitating payments," such as "payments for expediting shipments through customs or placing a transatlantic telephone call, securing required permits, or obtaining adequate police protection, transactions which may involve even the proper performance of duties." Instead of making an express textual exception for these types of non-covered payments, the respective committees of the two chambers sought to distinguish permissible grease payments from prohibited bribery by only prohibiting payments that induce an official to act "corruptly," i.e., actions requiring him "to misuse his official position" and his discretionary authority, not those "essentially ministerial" actions that "merely move a particular matter toward an eventual act or decision or which do not involve any discretionary action."

In short, Congress sought to prohibit the type of bribery that (1) prompts officials to misuse their discretionary authority and (2) disrupts market efficiency and United States foreign relations, at the same time recognizing that smaller payments intended to expedite ministerial actions should remain outside of the scope of the statute. The Conference Report explanation, on which the district court relied to find a narrow statutory scope, truly offers little insight into the FCPA's precise scope, however; it merely

---

[22]The House Committee stated that such bribes were "counter to the moral expectations and values of the American public," "erode[d] public confidence in the integrity of the free market system," "embarrass[ed] friendly governments, lower[ed] the esteem for the United States among the citizens of foreign nations, and lend[ed] [*sic*] credence to the suspicions sown by foreign opponents of the United States that American enterprises exert a corrupting influence on the political processes of their nations." H.R.Rep. No. 95-640, at 4-5 (1977); S.Rep. No. 95-114, at 3-4 (1977), reprinted in 1977 U.S.C.C.A.N. 4098, 4100-01.

parrots the statutory language itself by stating that the purpose of a payment must be to induce official action "so as to assist an issuer in obtaining, retaining or directing business to any person."

To divine the categories of bribery Congress did and did not intend to prohibit, we must look to the Senate's proposal, because the final statutory language was drawn from it, and from the SEC Report on which the Senate's legislative proposal was based. In distinguishing among the types of illegal payments that United States entities were making at the time, the SEC Report identified four principal categories: (1) payments "made in an effort to procure special and unjustified favors or advantages in the enactment or *administration of the tax* or other *laws*" of a foreign country; (2) payments "made with the intent to assist the company in obtaining or retaining government contracts"; (3) payments "to persuade low-level government officials to perform functions or services which they are obliged to perform as part of their governmental responsibilities, but which they may refuse or delay unless compensated" ("grease"), and (4) political contributions. The SEC thus exhibited concern about a wide range of questionable payments (explicitly including the kind at issue here) that were resulting in millions of dollars being recorded falsely in corporate books and records.

As noted, the Senate Report explained that the statute should apply to payments intended "to *direct business* to any person, *maintain an established business opportunity* with any person, divert any business opportunity from any person or *influence the enactment or promulgation of legislation or regulations* of that government or instrumentality." We observe initially that the Senate only loosely addressed the categories of conduct highlighted by the SEC Report. Although the Senate's proposal picked up the SEC's concern with a business nexus, it did not expressly cover bribery influencing the administration of tax laws or seeking favorable tax treatment. It is clear, however, that even though the Senate was particularly concerned with bribery intended to secure new business, it was also mindful of bribes that influence legislative or regulatory actions, and those that maintain established business opportunities, a category of economic activity separate from, and much more capacious than, simply "directing business" to someone.

The statute's ultimate language of "obtaining or retaining" mirrors identical language in the SEC Report. But, whereas the SEC Report highlights payments that go toward "obtaining or retaining *government contracts*," the FCPA, incorporating the Senate Report's language, prohibits payments that assist in obtaining or retaining *business*, not just government contracts. Had the Senate and ultimately Congress wanted to carry over the exact, narrower scope of the SEC Report, they would have adopted the same language. We surmise that, in using the word "business" when it easily could have used the phraseology of SEC Report, Congress intended for the statute to apply to bribes beyond the narrow band of payments sufficient only to "obtain or retain government contracts." The Senate's express intention that the statute apply to corrupt payments that *maintain* business opportunities also supports this conclusion.

For purposes of deciding the instant appeal, the question nevertheless remains whether the Senate, and concomitantly Congress, intended this broader statutory scope to encompass the administration of tax, customs, and other laws and regulations affecting the revenue of foreign states. To reach this conclusion, we must ask whether Congress's remaining expressed desire to prohibit bribery aimed at getting assistance in retaining business or maintaining business opportunities was sufficiently broad to include bribes meant to affect the administration of revenue laws. When we do so, we conclude that the legislative intent was so broad.

Congress was obviously distraught not only about high profile bribes to high-ranking foreign officials, but also by the pervasiveness of foreign bribery by United States businesses and businessmen. Congress thus made the decision to clamp down on bribes intended to prompt foreign officials to misuse their discretionary authority for the benefit of a domestic entity's business in that country. This observation is not diminished by Congress's understanding and accepting that relatively small facilitating payments were, at the time, among the accepted costs of doing business in many foreign countries.[40]

In addition, the concern of Congress with the immorality, inefficiency, and unethical character of bribery presumably does not vanish simply because the tainted payments are intended to secure a favorable decision less significant than winning a contract bid. Obviously, a commercial concern that bribes a foreign government official to award a construction, supply, or services contract violates the statute. Yet, there is little difference between this example and that of a corporation's lawfully obtaining a contract from an honest official or agency by submitting the lowest bid, and—either before or after doing so—bribing a different government official to reduce taxes and thereby ensure that the under-bid venture is nevertheless profitable. Avoiding or lowering taxes reduces operating costs and thus increases profit margins, thereby freeing up funds that the business is otherwise legally obligated to expend. And this, in turn, enables it to take any number of actions to the disadvantage of competitors. Bribing foreign officials to lower taxes and customs duties certainly can provide an unfair advantage over competitors and thereby be of assistance to the payor in obtaining or retaining business. This demonstrates that the question whether the defendants' alleged payments constitute a violation of the FCPA truly turns on whether these bribes were intended to lower ARI's cost of doing business in Haiti enough to have a sufficient nexus to garnering business there or to maintaining or increasing business operations that ARI already had there, so as to come within the scope of the business nexus element as Congress used it in the FCPA. Answering this fact question, then, implicates a matter of proof and thus evidence.

* * * The congressional target was bribery paid to engender assistance in improving the business opportunities of the payor or his beneficiary, irrespective of whether that assistance be direct or indirect, and irrespective of whether it be related to administering the law, awarding, extending, or renewing a contract, or executing or preserving an agreement. * * *

2. *1988 Legislative History*

After the FCPA's enactment, United States business entities and executives experienced difficulty in discerning a clear line between prohibited bribes and permissible

[40]We recognize that all payments to foreign officials exist on a continuum in which any payment, even if only to connect telephone service in two days instead of two weeks, marginally improves a company's competitive advantage in a foreign country. Nevertheless, Congress was principally concerned about payments that prompt an official to deviate from his official duty, not necessarily payments that get an official to perform properly those usually ministerial duties required of his office. As explained *infra*, Congress enacted amendments in 1988 in an effort to reflect just how limited it envisioned the grease exception to be.

facilitating payments. As a result, Congress amended the FCPA in 1988, expressly to clarify its original intent in enacting the statute. Both houses insisted that their proposed amendments only clarified ambiguities "without changing the basic intent or effectiveness of the law."

In this effort to crystallize the scope of the FCPA's prohibitions on bribery, Congress chose to identify carefully two types of payments that are not proscribed by the statute. It expressly excepted payments made to procure "routine governmental action" (again, the grease exception), and it incorporated an affirmative defense for payments that are legal in the country in which they are offered or that constitute *bona fide* expenditures directly relating to promotion of products or services, or to the execution or performance of a contract with a foreign government or agency.

We agree with the position of the government that these 1988 amendments illustrate an intention by Congress to identify very limited exceptions to the kinds of bribes to which the FCPA does not apply. * * * Therefore, routine governmental action does not include the issuance of *every* official document or *every* inspection, but only (1) documentation that qualifies a party to do business and (2) scheduling an inspection—very narrow categories of largely non-discretionary, ministerial activities performed by mid- or low-level foreign functionaries. In contrast, the FCPA uses broad, general language in prohibiting payments to procure assistance for the payor in obtaining or retaining business, instead of employing similarly detailed language, such as applying the statute only to payments that attempt to secure or renew particular government contracts. Indeed, Congress had the opportunity to adopt narrower language in 1977 from the SEC Report, but chose not to do so. * * *

3. *1998 Legislative History*

In 1998, Congress made its most recent adjustments to the FCPA when the Senate ratified and Congress implemented the Organization of Economic Cooperation and Development's Convention on Combating Bribery of Foreign Public Officials in International Business Transactions (the "Convention"). Article 1.1 of the Convention prohibits payments to a foreign public official to induce him to "act or refrain from acting in relation to the performance of official duties, in order to obtain or retain business *or other improper advantage* in the conduct of international business." * * * Thus, as amended, the statute now prohibits payments to foreign officials not just to buy any act or decision, and not just to induce the doing or omitting of an official function "to assist ... in obtaining or retaining business for or with, or directing business to, any person," but also the making of a payment to such a foreign official to secure an "improper advantage" that will assist in obtaining or retaining business.

* * * The commentaries to the Convention explain that "'[o]ther improper advantage' refers to something to which the company concerned was not clearly entitled, for example, an operating permit for a factory which fails to meet the statutory requirements." Unlawfully reducing the taxes and customs duties at issue here to a level substantially below that which ARI was legally obligated to pay surely constitutes "something [ARI] was not clearly entitled to," and was thus potentially an "improper advantage" under the Convention. * * *

4. *Summary*

Given the foregoing analysis of the statute's legislative history, we cannot hold as a matter of law that Congress meant to limit the FCPA's applicability to cover only bribes that lead directly to the award or renewal of contracts. Instead, we hold that Congress intended for the FCPA to apply broadly to payments intended to assist the payor, either directly or indirectly, in obtaining or retaining business for some person, and that bribes paid to foreign tax officials to secure illegally reduced customs and tax liability constitute a type of payment that can fall within this broad coverage. * * *

Thus, in diametric opposition to the district court, we conclude that bribes paid to foreign officials in consideration for unlawful evasion of customs duties and sales taxes *could* fall within the purview of the FCPA's proscription. We hasten to add, however, that this conduct does not automatically constitute a violation of the FCPA: It still must be shown that the bribery was intended to produce an effect—here, through tax savings—that would "assist in obtaining or retaining business." * * *

REVERSED and REMANDED.

Notes and Questions

1. In *United States v. Kay*, the Fifth Circuit interpreted the FCPA's requirement that the bribe be paid to assist the payer in obtaining or retaining business to include more than payments to government officials to procure or keep supply or construction contracts with foreign governments. Do you think the court's interpretation of the language relating to securing an "improper advantage" is too broad, too narrow, or the best construction? Would a payment or gift given to a government official to earn his general good will, without any expectation of a specific and immediate business advantage, fall within the scope of payments prohibited by the FCPA under the *Kay* court's reasoning? Should it?

2. The *Kay* court recognizes that there may be cases in which the financial or other benefits of a bribe do "nothing other than increase the profitability of an already-profitable venture or ensure profitability of some start-up venture." Does the court conclude or imply that bribes in such cases would be consistent with the FCPA despite not qualifying as facilitating payments? If so, is such a conclusion consistent with the public policy underlying the FCPA, the OECD Anti-Bribery Convention, and UNCAC? Why or why not? Or does the court dodge the question?

3. The U.S. Supreme Court has often held that, when it is unclear whether a criminal prohibition applies to the defendant's conduct, the principle of lenity applies. E.g., *Hughey v. United States*, 495 U.S. 411, 422 (1990); *United States v. Bass*, 404 U.S. 336, 347-50 (1971) (holding that the rule of lenity is based on the concept that "'fair warning should be given to the world in language that the common world will understand, of what the law intends to do if a certain line is passed'" and that "legislatures and not courts should define criminal activity"). Given the Fifth Circuit's explicit recognition that the FCPA did not clearly apply to bribes paid without any motive of obtaining or retaining new business, what is your best argument for why the Fifth Circuit properly ignored the rule of lenity?

3.2 Exceptions and Defenses Under the FCPA

In *United States v. Kay*, the Fifth Circuit alluded to some important exceptions and defenses in the FCPA that may protect a person subject to U.S. jurisdiction who has made, or who intends to make, payments or gifts to foreign government officials:

> (b) Exception for routine governmental action. Subsections (a) and (g) of this section shall not apply to any facilitating or expediting payment to a foreign official, political party, or party official the purpose of which is to expedite or to secure the performance of a routine governmental action by a foreign official, political party, or party official.
> (c) Affirmative defenses. It shall be an affirmative defense to actions under subsection (a) or (g) of this section that—
> (1) the payment, gift, offer, or promise of anything of value that was made, was lawful under the written laws and regulations of the foreign official's, political party's, party official's, or candidate's country; or
> (2) the payment, gift, offer, or promise of anything of value that was made, was a reasonable and bona fide expenditure, such as travel and lodging expenses, incurred by or on behalf of a foreign official, party, party official, or candidate and was directly related to—
> (A) the promotion, demonstration, or explanation of products or services; or
> (B) the execution or performance of a contract with a foreign government or agency thereof. * * *
> (3)(A) The term "routine governmental action" means only an action which is ordinarily and commonly performed by a foreign official in—
> (i) obtaining permits, licenses, or other official documents to qualify a person to do business in a foreign country;
> (ii) processing governmental papers, such as visas and work orders;
> (iii) providing police protection, mail pick-up and delivery, or scheduling inspections associated with contract performance or inspections related to transit of goods across country;
> (iv) providing phone service, power and water supply, loading and unloading cargo, or protecting perishable products or commodities from deterioration; or
> (v) actions of a similar nature.

15 U.S.C. § 78dd-1(b),(c).

A. Facilitating Payments

Under paragraph (b), small payments made to ensure that a government official does the job he or she is required to do are commonly called **grease payments** or, more formally, **facilitating payments**. Facilitating payments are defined as payments to secure a nondiscretionary act that is "ordinarily and commonly performed" by the foreign official, such as processing a visa application or providing police protection during a civil disturbance. In such cases, the bribe is not supposedly intended to obtain an unfair advantage for the giver against the interests of the country for whom the official works, but rather is seen as necessary to get done some act that the official is required by law to do anyway, but will not do without a bribe.

Why? In many developing countries, wages given to government employees are low, and employees interacting with wealthy foreign companies may feel entitled to a side payment. In fact, in some countries, it is impossible reliably to get basic government services such as mail delivery or customs clearance without making facilitating payments. On the other hand, although such payments do not violate the FCPA, they may violate the law of the country in which they are given.

B. Lawful Under the Foreign Laws and Regulations

Paragraph (c) states an affirmative defense when it is lawful to give, offer, or promise something of value to a foreign official in the foreign official's country. Here, the FCPA is referring to the written and published laws of the country, not the customary practices. Given that different legal systems define law differently, what exactly qualifies as a written law for FCPA purposes? The following case examines that question.

UNITED STATES v. KOZENY

U.S. District Court, Southern District of New York, 2008
582 F.Supp.2d 535

SHIRA A. SCHEINDLIN, District Judge.

I. INTRODUCTION

This prosecution relates to alleged violations of the Foreign Corrupt Practices Act ("FCPA") by defendant Frederic Bourke, Jr. and others in connection with the privatization of the State Oil Company of the Azerbaijan Republic ("SOCAR"). Bourke has requested that the Court make determinations as to the content of applicable law in Azerbaijan and instruct the jury on certain defenses that might be available under the law of Azerbaijan. The Government and Bourke were unable to agree on the contents or applicability of that law. To resolve this disagreement, the Court held a hearing on September 11, 2008. This Opinion and Order contains the Court's determinations.

II. BACKGROUND

A. Facts

The Government's allegations in this case are complex, and it is unnecessary to recite them here. The relevant facts are as follows: SOCAR is the state oil company of the Republic of Azerbaijan. In the mid-1990s, Azerbaijan began a program of privatization. The program gave the President of Azerbaijan, Heydar Aliyev, discretionary authority as to whether and when to privatize SOCAR. Bourke and others allegedly violated the FCPA by making payments to Azeri officials to encourage the privatization of SOCAR and to permit them to participate in that privatization. Bourke argues that the alleged payments were legal under Azeri law and thus under the FCPA (which provides an affirmative defense for payments that are legal under relevant foreign law) because they were the product of extortion. He also argues that pursuant to Azeri law, any criminality associated with the payments was excused when he reported them to the President of Azerbaijan.

The Government and Bourke have submitted expert reports. * * * On September 11, 2008, the Court held a hearing in which the experts testified as to their interpretations of the relevant law.

B. The Legal System of Azerbaijan

Azerbaijan, a sovereign nation in the Caspian Sea region that borders Russia, was formerly integrated as a Republic of the Soviet Union. Azerbaijan declared independence in 1991. The current criminal code of Azerbaijan took effect in 2000. In Azerbaijan, decisions of most courts are not considered binding authority; however, the highest court in Azerbaijan has the authority to give official interpretations of the Azeri Constitution and laws.

III. LEGAL STANDARD

A. The FCPA

The FCPA prohibits giving something of value for the purpose of "(i) influencing any act or decision of [a] foreign official in his official capacity, (ii) inducing such foreign official to do or omit any act in violation of the lawful duty of such official, or (iii) securing any improper advantage ... to obtain[ ] or retain[ ] business for or with ... any person." The law provides an affirmative defense for payments that are "lawful under the written laws and regulations" of the country.

B. Foreign Law

"Though foreign law once was treated as an issue of fact, it now is viewed as a question of law and may be determined through the use of any relevant source, including expert testimony." Rule 26.1 of the Federal Rules of Criminal Procedure provides that "[a] party intending to raise an issue of foreign law must provide the court and all parties with reasonable written notice. Issues of foreign law are questions of law, but in deciding such issues a court may consider any relevant material or source—including testimony—without regard to the Federal Rules of Evidence."

IV. DISCUSSION

During the relevant period, Article 170 of the Azerbaijan Criminal Code ("ACC") provided that "[t]he receiving by an official ... of a bribe in any form whatsoever for the fulfillment or the failure to fulfill any action in the interest of the person giving the bribe which the official should have or might perform with the use of his employment position ... shall be punished by deprivation of freedom...." Professor Stephan [expert witness for the defendants] asserts that during the same period, Article 171 of the ACC provided that "[g]iving a bribe shall be punished by deprivation of freedom for a term of from three to eight years.... A person who has given a bribe shall be free from criminal responsibility if with respect to him there was extortion of the bribe or if that person after giving the bribe voluntarily made a report of the occurrence." Professor Butler [expert witness for the government] believes that a more accurate translation of the last clause is "[a] person who has given a bribe shall be relieved from criminal responsibility if extortion of the bribe occurred with respect to him or if this person after giving the bribe voluntarily stated what happened."

The Supreme Court of the U.S.S.R. interpreted Article 171 in a Resolution published in 1990. The parties agree that the Resolution is relevant to the Azeri courts' interpretation of the Article. It defines extortion as "a demand by an official for a bribe under the threat of carrying out actions that could do damage to the legal interests of the briber...." The Resolution further explains that "a voluntary declaration of having committed the crime absolves from criminal responsibility not only the bribe giver but his accomplices." Finally, the Resolution provides that "[t]he absolution of a bribe-giver from criminal responsibility because of extortion of the bribe or the voluntary declaration of the giving of the bribe ... does not signify an absence in the actions of such persons of the elements of an offense. For that reason, they cannot be considered victims and are not entitled to claim restitution of the items of value given as bribes."

As a threshold matter, I must determine the meaning of "relieved (or free) from criminal responsibility." Bourke contends that if an individual is relieved of criminal responsibility, his action was "lawful" and he may thus avail himself of the FCPA's affirmative defense. I disagree.

For purposes of the FCPA's affirmative defense, the focus is on the payment, not the payer. A person cannot be guilty of violating the FCPA if the payment was lawful under foreign law. But there is no immunity from prosecution under the FCPA if a person could not have been prosecuted in the foreign country due to a technicality (e.g., time-barred) or because a provision in the foreign law "relieves" a person of criminal responsibility. An individual may be prosecuted under the FCPA for a payment that violates foreign law even if the individual is relieved of criminal responsibility for his actions by a provision of the foreign law.

A. The Reporting Exception

As Professor Butler observes, the structure of the reporting exception to liability in Article 171 illustrates that the initial payment of a bribe was certainly not lawful. The ACC relieves the payer of a bribe from criminal liability if the bribe is properly reported not because such an action retroactively erases the stain of criminality, but because the state has a strong interest in prosecuting the government official who received the bribe. By waiving liability for reporting payers, the state increases the likelihood that it will learn of the bribery.

But at the moment that an individual pays a bribe, the individual has violated Article 171. At that time, the payment was clearly not "lawful under the written laws" of Azerbaijan. If the individual later reports the bribe, she can no longer be prosecuted for that payment. But it is inaccurate to suggest that the payment itself suddenly became "lawful"—on the contrary, the payment was unlawful, though the payer is relieved of responsibility for it. This is why the Resolution provides that the payer cannot receive restitution. Further, if the payment were retroactively lawful, the official who received the payment could not be prosecuted for receiving it. This cannot be correct because the purpose of the reporting exception is to enable the government to pursue the official. Thus, the relief from liability in Article 171 operates to excuse the payer, not the payment.

B. The Extortion Exception

The exception for extortion contained in the same sentence must operate in the same manner. A payment to an Azeri official that is made under threat to the payer's legal interests is still an illegal payment, though the payer cannot be prosecuted for the payment.

This conclusion does not preclude Bourke from arguing that he cannot be guilty of violating the FCPA by making a payment to an official who extorted the payment because he lacked the requisite corrupt intent to make a bribe. The legislative history of the FCPA makes clear that "true extortion situations would not be covered by this provision." Thus, while the FCPA would apply to a situation in which a "payment [is] demanded on the part of a government official as a price for gaining entry into a market or to obtain a contract," it would not apply to one in which payment is made to an official "to keep an oil rig from being dynamited," an example of "true extortion." The reason is that in the former situation, the bribe payer cannot argue that he lacked the intent to bribe the official because he made the "conscious decision" to pay the official. In other words, in the first example, the payer could have turned his back and walked away—in the latter example, he could not.

* * *

SO ORDERED

Notes and Questions

1. The court distinguishes between a criminal act and the defendant's criminal liability for purposes of the FCPA. Is the court suggesting that there can be a crime without a criminal? Or is there a more complex behind the court's reasoning?

2. If the law of the jurisdiction in which the bribe was paid exculpates the bribe payer, what could be the U.S. interest in holding the bribe payer criminally liable nonetheless?

C. Bona Fide Expenditures

The final affirmative defense is for two kinds of legitimate expenses. First, amounts paid for marketing and educating foreign government officials about the company's products or services, including travel and lodging expenses of the official, qualify as promotional expenses. For example, a foreign official soliciting bids on a dam building contract may wish to travel to see some of the bidder's other work. Even after the contract has been secured, it may be necessary to transport foreign government employees to another country for training in operating and maintaining the dam machinery. Any such expenses are considered permissible under the FCPA, so long as they are not intended to disguise a bribe or otherwise improperly influence the official.

The second kind of expense is any expense incurred in the performance of an existing contract with a foreign government agency. For example, suppose a U.S. company, Forvestco, enters into an agreement with the Ruritanian Ministry of Natural Resources that allows Forvestco to harvest timber in Ruritania in exchange for a stumpage fee of 10 ruros per tree. When Forvestco harvests 5000 trees and pays the Ministry of Natural Resources 50,000 ruros, that payment falls within the affirmative defense of section 78dd-1(c)(2)(B).

The difference between an exception and a defense can be important. An exception clarifies the scope of the prohibition. In other words, acts that fall within the exception are not considered to violate the anti-bribery prohibition of Section 78dd-1 in the first instance. Therefore, when the government accuses a person of violating the FCPA by offering, paying, or promising something of value to a foreign government official or candidate, it is the prosecution that must carry the burden of showing that the thing of value was not made merely to expedite or secure routine governmental action.

In contrast, an affirmative defense must be pled by the defendant at the trial stage, and the defendant accordingly bears the burden of persuasion. The defendant must therefore produce sufficient evidence of the payment's legality under written foreign laws, or that the thing of value was given as part of a bona fide promotional expense or performance of a contract, to avoid conviction.

3.3 FCPA Recordkeeping and Reporting Requirements

The FCPA includes accounting, recordkeeping, and reporting obligations for issuers of securities registered on a U.S. securities exchange market, such as the New York Stock Exchange. See 15 U.S.C. § 78m. Such issuers may be U.S. or foreign companies. Many foreign companies, such as Hitachi Ltd. (Japan), Brasil Foods SA, and L'Oréal SA (France), offer their shares for trade on U.S. stock exchanges.

These provisions require, first, that securities issuers make and keep

Case Study

Consequences of Bribery

On December 15, 2008, the German multinational corporation Siemens AG pled guilty to violations of the FCPA for bribing government officials in dozens of countries around the world. The scale of the corruption was the largest ever uncovered by the SEC up to that point (which has since been surpassed).

In announcing the plea agreement, the DoJ and SEC stated that, from the 1990s to 2007, Siemens had paid $1.4 billion in bribes to foreign government officials, and used off-the-books slush fund accounts, false entries on accounting records, and other illegal accounting techniques to hide the bribes.

The intrigue involved the use of "business consultants" who paid the bribes on the instructions of senior Siemens executives. Siemens recorded profits as liabilities on the accounting records and converted the funds to the "time-tested method of suitcases filled with cash." In exchange, Siemens received billions of dollars worth of foreign government contracts. Siemens Venezuela received a $340 million contract to build two city rail systems from the Venezuelan government. Siemens Bangladesh received a $40 million mobile phone service contract for its bribes to government officials. Siemens Argentina received a $1 billion contract with the Argentinian government to develop a national identity card for citizens.

The firms were ultimately forced to pay $1.6 billion in criminal and civil penalties—the largest FCPA settlement in U.S. history. $450 million was allocated to criminal fines to the U.S. government. Siemens also agreed to disgorge $350 million in ill-gotten gains to the SEC and pay $800 million in fines to the German government. Finally, the firm had to retain an independent auditor for four years to ensure non-repetition.

Siemens' own internal investigation of officer and employee misconduct cost almost as much. Siemens' lawyers and accountants conducted over 1,750 interviews in 34 countries, spending 1.6 million billable hours at a cost of $850 million. Moreover, the revelation of criminal charges contributed to a drop in Siemens' stock price to one-third of its former value.

Siemens is not a U.S. firm, no U.S. subsidiaries were implicated, and the target of the bribery was in each case a foreign government. How did the FCPA regulate the conduct? Siemens stock has been traded on the New York Stock Exchange since 2001. Siemens' acts of foreign bribery therefore fell squarely within SEC jurisdiction under the FCPA.

records in reasonable detail to "accurately and fairly reflect" all business and accounting transactions. In other words, issuers are required to create a paper trail that will help investigators discover how the company's funds were spent and to whom they were given. This means that any funds spent on a bribe or other corrupt transaction, no matter how small, must be reflected in records that the government can discover. The FCPA also requires issuers to implement an accounting system to "provide reasonable assurances" that all transactions are executed with the authorization of management. This provision is designed to ensure that the company's management is aware of, and maintains responsibility for, any illicit payments. International business transactions lawyers specializing in foreign corrupt practices law typically include in their compliance programs advice on how to comply with these regulations.

The recordkeeping and reporting provisions do not technically apply to privately held companies that do not trade their shares on a market, but there are risks to any company in the United States that does not comply with the regulations. If a violation of the FCPA does occur, the Department of Justice may use the absence of FCPA-compliant accounting and recordkeeping procedures as evidence of illegal intent. Therefore, non-issuing U.S. companies reduce the risk of a criminal enforcement action by complying with the accounting and recordkeeping provisions regardless of whether they qualify as issuers.

3.4 FCPA Enforcement and Penalties

The SEC enforces civil penalties with respect to issuers of U.S. securities, while the DoJ enforces the criminal penalties of the FCPA as well as civil penalties respecting non-issuers. Criminal penalties include fines up to $2 million for companies, and $100,000 and imprisonment for up to five years for individuals who violate the FCPA. 15 U.S.C. § 78dd-2(g). The SEC and DoJ take FCPA violations seriously, and have imprisoned both U.S. and foreign corporate executives for participating in violations in the recent past. Substantial civil penalties may also be assessed on accidental as well as intentional violations.

It may be counterintuitive that the civil penalties are sometimes much more consequential than the criminal penalties. This is because civil penalties may include punishments such as debarment from trading stock on a U.S. securities exchange, bidding on government contracts, or exporting controlled items. Such sanctions could ruin a company reliant on public funding, government business, or exports.

3.5 Informal Regulatory Guidance

The DoJ is responsible for pursuing criminal prosecutions for violations of the FCPA. Because the line between illegal bribes and permissible facilitating payments or payments legal in the foreign state is sometimes difficult to draw, the DoJ has adopted an **FCPA Opinion Procedure** by which any U.S. national or business entity, or any U.S. securities issuer, may present the DoJ with a proposed business transaction in order to ascertain the DoJ's opinion about its legality.

Under the FCPA Opinion Procedure, set forth in 28 C.F.R. pt. 80, the U.S. Attorney General will issue a formal opinion in response to such an inquiry within thirty days of receiving a request for advice containing all relevant details. The DoJ regulations specify what information must be included and when it should be made:

> **Section 80.3. Transaction.**
> The entire transaction which is the subject of the request must be an actual—not a hypothetical—transaction but need not involve only prospective conduct. However, a request will not be considered unless that portion of the transaction for which an opinion is sought involves only prospective conduct. An executed contract is not a prerequisite and, in most—if not all—instances, an opinion request should be made prior to the requestor's commitment to proceed with a transaction. * * *
>
> **Section 80.6. General requirements.**
> Each request shall be specific and must be accompanied by all relevant and material information bearing on the conduct for which an FCPA Opinion is requested and on the circumstances of the prospective conduct, including background information, complete copies of all operative documents, and detailed statements of all collateral or oral understandings, if any. The requesting issuer or domestic concern is under an affirmative obligation to make full and true disclosure with respect to the conduct for which an opinion is requested. Each request on behalf of a requesting issuer or corporate domestic concern must be signed by an appropriate senior officer with operational responsibility for the conduct that is the subject of the request and who has been designated by the requestor's chief executive officer to sign the opinion request. In appropriate cases, the Department of Justice may require the chief executive officer of each requesting issuer or corporate domestic concern to sign the request. All requests of other domestic concerns must also be signed. The person signing the request must certify that it contains a true, correct and complete disclosure with respect to the proposed conduct and the circumstances of the conduct.

The requirement that the transaction be prospective prevents a business firm from seeking *post hoc* ratification from the DoJ of questionable actions.

The Attorney General's opinion does not analyze in great detail the legal arguments for or against commencing an enforcement action against the proposed transaction. Instead, the opinion tends to assume a summary form. Nonetheless, the opinion can give significant reassurance to a business firm uncertain about the legality of a contemplated transaction. Although the opinion is not binding, approval does entitle the requester, and no other person, to a presumption that the approved transaction conforms to the FCPA's requirements in any enforcement action. 28 C.F.R. §§ 80.10-.11.

The Opinion Procedure has not been frequently used by U.S. business firms. In fact, between 2000 and 2014, the DoJ released only twenty-seven opinions, on average about two every year. The following is an example of an Opinion Procedure release:

No.: 07-01
Date: July 24, 2007
Foreign Corrupt Practices Act Review
Opinion Procedure Release

The Department has reviewed the FCPA Opinion request of a U.S. company (the "requestor") that was submitted on June 29, 2007. The company is both an "issuer" and a "domestic concern" within meaning of the FCPA.

The requestor proposes to cover the domestic expenses for a trip to the United States by a six-person delegation of the government of an Asian country for an educational and promotional tour of one of the requestor's U.S. operations sites. The stated purpose of the visit is to familiarize the delegates with the nature and extent of the requestor's operations and capabilities and to help establish the requestor's business credibility. The requestor is interested in participating in future operations in the foreign country similar to those it conducts in the U.S. The visit will last for four days and will be limited to domestic economy class travel to one U.S. operations site only. The requestor also intends to pay for the domestic lodging, local transport, and meals for the six officials. The foreign government plans to pay the costs of the international airfare. The requestor has asked for a determination of the Department's present enforcement intention under the FCPA.

The requestor has represented, among other things, that:

1. it does not currently conduct operations in the foreign country or with the foreign government, although it is interested in pursuing such opportunities in the future;
2. it has obtained written assurance, a copy of which has been provided to the Department of Justice, from an established law firm with offices in both the U.S. and the foreign country that the requestor's sponsorship of the visit and its payment of the expenses described in the request is not contrary to the law of the foreign country;
3. it did not select the delegates who will participate in the visit; rather, the foreign government selected the delegates;
4. to the requestor's knowledge, the delegates have no direct authority over decisions relating to potential contracts or licenses necessary for operating in the foreign country;
5. it will host only officials working for the relevant foreign ministries and one private government consultant;
6. it intends to pay all costs directly to the providers; no funds will be paid directly to the foreign government or the delegates;
7. it will not pay any expenses for spouses, family, or other guests of the officials;
8. any souvenirs that the requestor may provide to the delegates would reflect the requestor's name and/or logo and would be of nominal value;
9. apart from meals and receptions connected to meetings, speakers, or events the requestor is planning for the officials, it will not fund, organize, or host any

NOTE FROM THE FIELD
Being an Anti-Corruption Lawyer

Lucinda A. Low, Esq.
Steptoe & Johnson LLP

Dealing with corruption issues that arise in the course of business activities around the world exposes investors to the weaknesses in the legal systems in many nations. It also reveals the limits of the law and the countervailing and powerful pulls of culture and practice, societal expectations and pressure, poverty, and simple greed.

Although the legality of some situations is black and white, for most it is a shade of gray. The facts may be obscure and difficult to learn, but they determine the legality of the transaction. Assessing an issue often involves cross-disciplinary thinking about government and politics, economics, history, and sometimes social and psychological factors.

Anti-corruption work involves a diverse variety of services, including:

- developing an internal corporate compliance program (writing a compliance manual, implementing compliance procedures, training);
- assisting with due diligence to check out risks of dealing with specific customers, consultants, joint venture partners, acquisition candidates, or other business partners;
- rendering opinions on risks and risk-mitigation strategies;
- investigating alleged violations of law;
- defending companies in investigations and enforcement actions; and
- representing companies in parallel national proceedings or in cross-border evidence-gathering requests.

While the FCPA applies to all U.S. business firms and persons, it also covers an expanding group of foreign persons and companies as well. Clients often need someone who will travel or work odd or long hours, and who will be responsive in a crisis situation. Lawyers with FCPA experience can be found in various parts of the country, but the practice is concentrated in Washington, D.C., because most enforcement activity takes place there. The field of anti-corruption work has grown significantly in recent years, and expectations are that it will continue to grow due to increased enforcement around the world.

Lucinda Low is a partner at Steptoe & Johnson LLP, practicing from its Washington, DC office. She is a member of the Board of Directors of Transparency International USA.

entertainment or leisure activities for the officials, nor will it provide the officials with any stipend or spending money; and

10. all costs and expenses incurred by the requestor in connection with the visit will be properly and accurately recorded in the requestor's books and records.

Based upon all of the facts and circumstances, as represented by the requestor, the Department does not presently intend to take any enforcement action with respect to the proposal described in this request. This is because, based on the requestor's representations, consistent with the FCPA's promotional expenses affirmative defense, the expenses contemplated are reasonable under the circumstances and directly relate to "the promotion, demonstration, or explanation of [the requestor's] products or services."

The FCPA Opinion Letter referred to herein, and this release, have no binding application to any party which did not join in the request, and can be relied upon by the requestor only to the extent that the disclosure of facts and circumstances in its request is accurate and complete and continues to accurately and completely reflect such facts and circumstances.

From the facts, it is clear that the expenses relate directly to the promotion and explanation of the requester's products or services. However, notice that the Department of Justice does not explain its standard for "reasonable under the circumstances." The release offers no analysis of whether a six-person delegation is necessary to secure the business sought, especially if the delegates "have no direct authority over decisions relating to potential contracts." It tells nothing about whether the company's sponsorship of the delegates is a precondition for securing the business, given that most foreign governments can afford to pay for transportation of their officials on legitimate government business. And it offers no guidance on what kind of meals would be considered legitimate expenses, given that an individual meal can vary in price by many multiples. Nonetheless, the release gives some reassurance to the requester itself.

Key Vocabulary

Bona fide expenditure
Corruption Perceptions Index
Domestic concern
Facilitating payment / Grease payment
FCPA Opinion Procedure
Foreign Corrupt Practices Act (FCPA)
Money laundering
Organization for Economic Cooperation and Development (OECD)
OECD Anti-Bribery Convention
Securities Exchange Commission (SEC)
Securities issuer
Transparency International
UN Convention Against Corruption (UNCAC)

Practice Exercises

Forbidden or Permitted Bribery?

Your client, Phastphlo, Inc., is a Delaware provider of oilfield consulting services. Phastphlo has come to you with an urgent question. It has a wholly-owned Smalldonian subsidiary corporation, Phastphlo Smalldonia (PS), headquartered in Connecticut, that retains an independent agent in central Eurasia. PS uses its Smalldonian agent, Deja Viau, to solicit business from customers in that region. Deja is not an employee; she works on commission equivalent to an 8% fee on every service agreement she secures on behalf of PS. She is a citizen of Smalldonia and resident there.

PS has an ongoing contract with Slavikoil, from Slavikoil, the national, government-owned oil company of the Eurasian republic of Slavikistan. PS originally obtained this contract through Deja's representation. Pursuant to this contract, PS supplies Slavikoil with oil field consulting services at a cost of $7 million per month. Under the agreement, PS sends its employees to Slavikistan to live near the oil fields and train Slavikoil employees, advise Slavikoil on dealing with technical extraction challenges, and repair extraction equipment. The agreement, which has a five-year term, does not expire for several more years. One of the great economic attractions of the PS's business in Slavikistan is that, under a separate agreement with the Slavikistani Minister of Natural Resources, PS and its employees pay no income tax for the services provided in Slavikisan. The income tax rate in Slavikistan is a flat 28%.

Under the agreement, however, the Minister of Natural Resources has the right to withdraw the tax exemption after three months of prior notice. Recently a new Minister of Natural Resources, Mr. Badlee Shosun, was appointed.

Deja has met with Mr. Shosun and been given formal notice that he intends to withdraw the tax exemption. Although this withdrawal will make not eliminate the profits from Phastphlo's agreement with Slavikoil, it will drastically reduce those profits.

After consulting with local counsel in Slavikistan, you learn that it is customary and expected in Slavikistan for the Minister of Natural Resources to receive a percentage of the value of all oil-related contracts with the government. Although PS did not have to do this with the previous Minister, local counsel suggests that such "profit sharing" with Mr. Shosun will cause him to reverse his position on terminating the tax exemption.

Slavikistani law has no criminal prohibition on bribing government officials. However, under the Slavikistani Civil Code, such bribery gives Slavikistan a right to terminate employment of the government official, to sue both the briber payer and government official for restitution, and to debar the bribe payer from future government contracts.

What advice should you offer to Phastphlo? In responding, do not neglect to answer the questions:

(a) Would profit sharing with Minister Shosun violate the FCPA's anti-bribery prohibition? Why or why not?

(b) Assuming it did violate the FCPA, would any FCPA exception or defenses exonerate PS? Why or why not?

(c) What effect on legality under the FCPA does it have if Deja and not PS pays part of the profits to Minister Shosun?

(d) What effect does the fact that PS is a Smalldonian company with no publicly traded stock have on your analysis?

Multiple Choice Questions

1. How is the Corruption Perceptions Index best described?

   (a) United Nations regulatory guidance warning companies against doing business in low-index states.
   (b) A United States program that identifies red flags for companies doing business in low-index states.
   (c) A United Nations ranking of the most corrupt countries in the world.
   (d) An NGO indicator of the most corrupt countries in the world.
   (e) An NGO indicator of perceptions of corruption by private actors about the states of the world.

2. Which of the following measures are state parties to the OECD Bribery Convention ***not*** required to do?

(a) To impose criminal penalties on individuals giving bribes to foreign public officials.
(b) To impose criminal penalties on corporations giving bribes to foreign public officials.
(c) To impose criminal penalties on conspiracy or attempt to bribe foreign public officials.
(d) To require the seizure and forfeiture of bribes paid to foreign public officials.
(e) To require business organizations to keep accurate records of foreign financial transactions.

3. On which of the following acts are state parties to UNCAC ***not*** required to impose criminal penalties?

(a) When individuals offer or give bribes to domestic public officials.
(b) When individuals offer or give bribes to foreign public officials.
(c) When public officials demand or accept bribes.
(d) When corporations give bribes to foreign public officials.
(e) When individuals launder money to hide its criminal source.

4. True or false?: The available evidence shows that UNCAC and the OECD Anti-Bribery Convention have largely eliminated corruption in international business transactions.

5. In which of the following scenarios has the named person ***not*** violated a prohibition of the Foreign Corrupt Practices Act (FCPA), assuming each person has used an instrumentality of U.S. interstate commerce in the process?

(a) Darla is the Chief Financial Officer of Greenwater Ltd., a Freedonian corporation privately held solely by Freedonian investors. Darla is a national of Osterlich who is resident in Freedonia. Greenwater has a wholly owned U.S. subsidiary, Greenwater USA. While in Smalldonia, Darla bribes the Smalldonian Deputy Minister of Finance to avoid paying taxes on Greenwater Ltd.'s income derived from its operations in Smalldonia. Greenwater USA is not involved.
(b) Ronald is a Sylvanian national resident in the United States. Ronald intends to bribe the President of Sylvania to obtain business there. To avoid the application of the FCPA, he travels to Sylvania to pay the bribe.
(c) Ronald Jr. is the export manager of a small U.S. corporation. He offers a bribe to customs officials in North Elbonia to avoid customs duties, but they indignantly refuse to accept it. Ronald Jr. drops the subject and pays the required customs duties.
(d) Ivann Co. is a Ruzophilian corporation headquartered and solely op-

erating outside the United States. Ivann Co. is publicly listed on the New York Stock Exchange. Through its agents, Ivann Co. bribes the Defense Minister of the kingdom of Sud Rabbia to secure a government contract.

(e) Janet is the CEO of Dumpf Enterprises, a New York corporation. She authorizes Dumpf's sales agent in Zembia, Wanda Gettrich, to use Wanda's own personal funds to bribe the Zembian Minister of Education, in order to persuade her to award a contract to Dumpf. Neither Janet nor Dumpf directly reimburses Wanda.

6. According to the Fifth Circuit Court of Appeals' opinion in *United States v. Kay*, which of the following scenarios would qualify as a violation of the FCPA's prohibitions absent an applicable exception or defense?

(a) While Tony, president of a U.S. corporation is visiting Ruritania to scout out a possible foreign investment, a Ruritanian police officer arrests Tony on a questionable charge of public intoxication. To avoid the inconvenience of spending time in jail, Tony bribes the officer.

(b) Lynda, Chief Financial Officer of a U.S. partnership, is taking Velma, an important official in the Osterlich government, to dinner in Osterlich's capital to discuss how Lynda's company might serve the Osterlich government's needs. After the meal, she leaves an exceptionally large tip to the waitress in order to impress Velma.

(c) D'Arco Inc., a California corporation, has a wholly owned subsidiary in Pottsylvania, D'Arco Pottsylvania, that manufactures widgets. Donnie is a California resident who is the president of D'Arco and on the Board of Directors of D'Arco Pottsylvania. Donnie telephones the head of Pottsplant, the government-owned electrical utility of Pottsylvania, and offers him a large bribe to bill D'Arco Pottsylvania for a much smaller amount of energy than it actually uses.

(d) Ohayo Co., a Ruritanian corporation listed on the New York stock exchange, sells small electric vehicles used by government postal services and parking enforcement officers, as well as private tourism companies and hobbyists. Jane, the head of Ohayo's marketing division, is visiting Smalldonia. While there, Jane notices that the Smalldonian Ministry of Transportation has a program for selling advertisements in subway stations. Acting on behalf of Ohayo, she purchases the largest amount of advertising space in Smalldonian history to use for Ohayo's services, in the expectation of attracting business from the Smalldonian government itself.

7. Which of the following scenarios would qualify as a permissible facilitating payment by a U.S. corporation, USCo, under the FCPA?

(a) Tax authorities in Mohamia are required by law to conduct annual audits of all foreign companies doing business in Mohamia as a condition for granting any tax credits. USCo does business in Mohamia, but the Mohamian tax agents refuse to conduct the required audit, claiming they are too busy. USCo bribes the tax agents to conduct the audit.

(b) The Mohamian Minister of the Environment plans to seek bids on a project to develop an oil field in central Mohamia. USCo bribes the Minister to award the contract to USCo instead of undertaking the competitive bidding process.

(c) The Mohamian Minister of the Environment is seeking bids on a project to develop an oil field in central Mohamia. USCo is one of several companies bidding on the project. USCo bribes the Minister to use his discretion to award the contract to USCo.

(d) The Mohamian Minister of the Environment is seeking bids on a project to develop an oil field in central Mohamia. USCo is one of several companies bidding on the project. USCo bribes the Minister to use his discretion not to award the contract to USCo's biggest competitor.

8. According to the dominant interpretation of the FCPA's "lawful under the foreign laws" defense, in which of the following scenarios would the defense most likely be successful?

(a) The foreign law criminalizes the relevant payment, but it provides only a fine and no prison sentence for the crime.

(b) The foreign law forbids the relevant payment, but it does not specifically describe the payment as a crime.

(c) The foreign law criminalizes the relevant payment and provides for a prison sentence, but the president of the foreign state pardoned the public official who accepted the bribe.

(d) The foreign law criminalizes the relevant payment and provides for a prison sentence, but the president of the foreign state pardoned the bribe payer.

(e) The foreign law criminalizes the relevant payment and provides for a prison sentence, but the alleged bribe payer was found not guilty of paying an illegal bribe in a regularly constituted court of law.

9. A U.S. company has a contract to purchase rare minerals from a state-owned mining company of Freedonia. Under the contract, the U.S. company pays Freedonia a price slightly above the market value of the mineral to ensure a stable supply. True or false?: The payments to Freedonia probably do not violate the FCPA.

10. True or false?: The FCPA includes recordkeeping and reporting obligations that apply to all business firms subject to the FCPA.

11. True or false?: The FCPA opinion procedure allows business firms to request the Department of Justice's prior advice on whether the Department would consider a hypothetical transaction to violate the FCPA.

12. True or false?: Although the FCPA opinion procedure is set forth in binding federal regulations, a written opinion of the Department of Justice is not in fact binding on the U.S. government.

Multiple Choice Answers

1. e
2. b
3. d
4. False
5. a
6. c
7. a
8. e
9. True
10. False
11. False
12. True

Chapter 9

Planning for International Business Disputes

What You Will Learn in This Chapter

Cross-border litigation is a regrettable but nonetheless predictable concomitant of international business. Every business transaction carries the seeds of future dispute. The more complex the transaction and the greater the risks and sums of money involved, the more likely a serious dispute becomes. Responsible international business lawyers always consider from the early moments of planning how the risk of future disputes may be minimized and, if a dispute should arise, how to structure the transaction to reduce the attendant costs and risks.

The differences between international business disputes and domestic disputes are, of degree in some cases and, in others, of kind. A complication typical of international business litigation—that of dealing with multiple jurisdictions—is not unknown to lawyers in federal states like the United States. Concurrent jurisdiction, forum shopping, races to a local court, disputes about the applicable law, and the added expense of litigation in a distant forum arise in business transactions within federations, as in international commerce.

These problems are usually aggravated when the transaction moves from a domestic to an international context, however. For example, in international disputes, distances are usually increased, differences in local procedures and law are greater, and expenses are augmented by the need for lawyers in two or more jurisdictions. To these difficulties may be added several unique challenges in the international context. Translation of large volumes of documents to a foreign language may be necessary. Foreign laws and procedures may be unfamiliar, and less developed and predictable. Bias, corruption, or inefficiency in foreign courts may sometimes be a problem. And courts may refuse to defer to an existing assertion of jurisdiction by a foreign court, resulting in simultaneous litigation. Add to this the uncertainties of enforcing a court judgment in a foreign country, and proper planning for disputes becomes a paramount consideration in international business planning.

Finally, international commerce and investment sometimes involves doing business with foreign governments. Foreign sovereigns may have a substantial advantage in their own courts and immunity from the jurisdiction of foreign courts. As a result, transactions with a sovereign state involve unique challenges of both planning reliable dispute resolution and ensuring its enforcement.

To avoid or mitigate these risks and costs, international business lawyers have developed strategies for structuring business deals with an eye toward the efficient settlement of future disputes. In some cases, the simplest solution is to prepare for litigation in a mutually acceptable forum under mutually acceptable laws. In others, private dispute settlement serves the parties best. When a foreign government is involved in the dispute, special treaties, the application of certain national laws, or contract provisions may supply a means to overcome sovereign immunity.

This chapter explores the dispute resolution options available to lawyers planning international business transactions. Specifically, you will learn:

- the general principles that courts use to determine whether they may properly exercise jurisdiction over a dispute involving a foreign person, foreign property, or a transaction spanning more than one state;
- how courts deal with contractual choices of forum and law in international agreements;
- judicial practice in recognizing and enforcing foreign court judgments;
- the unique problems that arise in international commercial litigation involving a foreign government or state agency as a defendant;
- the uses and advantages of mediation, arbitration, and other alternative dispute resolution for settling international business disputes;
- how international investment disputes differ in nature from other kinds of international disputes; and
- the rights international treaties may provide to a foreign investor that assist in the resolution of an international investment dispute.

1 Dealing with Jurisdiction and Choice of Forum

1.1 General Principles of Jurisdiction to Adjudicate

When a dispute arises from an international business transaction, one or more parties to the transaction may wish to seek resolution in a national court. If the parties have not planned and negotiated a mutually agreeable forum for the resolution of the dispute, a significant problem confronts them; the courts of several states may accept jurisdiction over the dispute, and some potential jurisdictions may be disadvantageous to one of the parties.

Suppose a Thai company were to enter into a contract with a Delaware corporation whose head office is in Mexico to provide services to the Delaware corporation's branch office in the Philippines. If a contract dispute were to arise, it is theoretically possible that:

- a state or federal court in Delaware would accept jurisdiction over the dispute based on the purchaser's state of incorporation;
- a Mexican court would accept jurisdiction based on the purchaser's state of residence;
- a court in Thailand would accept jurisdiction based on the service provider's residence; and
- a court in the Philippines would accept jurisdiction based on the place where the services are to be rendered.

The multiplicity of potential courts, each of which may offer more advantages and fewer disadvantages to one side or the other, creates a potential secondary dispute between the parties about where to adjudicate the original dispute between them.

In the absence of a forum selection clause in an applicable contract, there is no global treaty harmonizing state rules regarding acceptable or unacceptable bases for jurisdiction. There are some general principles of customary international law relating to state jurisdiction, however, and there are also trends in national principles of jurisdiction. Notwithstanding these, concurrent state jurisdiction is common, and therefore so are contests about jurisdiction in international litigation.

When planning for international business transactions, it is important to bear in mind the possible forums that could assert jurisdiction over the dispute. Jurisdiction has two main aspects: personal and subject matter. Personal jurisdiction relates to authority over the parties to the dispute. Subject mattter jurisdiction relates to whether the municipal law of the state authorizes the court to hear the case.

A. Personal Jurisdiction

The courts of most countries will accept jurisdiction only over persons having some definite connection with the forum state. The limits of personal jurisdiction, also known as ***in personam*** or **personal jurisdiction**, vary from country to country. There is no international treaty harmonizing how states exercise jurisdiction over persons, whether natural or legal. However, the general trend is to require that the person must:

(1) be a national or resident of the state;
(2) have regularly engaged in commerce in the state; or
(3) purposefully direct some activity toward the state.

In the United States, courts may exercise personal jurisdiction over any defendant who has "continuous and systematic" contacts with the forum state. *International Shoe Co. v. Washington*, 326 U.S. 310 (1945). U.S. courts exercise "general jurisdiction" over such defendants and will entertain claims against them to the extent they consider reasonable under the Constitution.

In addition, a U.S. court may assert "specific jurisdiction" over a foreign person who has allegedy caused an injury "arising out of or relating to" the defendants' contacts with the forum state. *Goodyear Dunlop Tires Operations, S.A. v. Brown*, 564 U.S. 915 (2011). A complaint based on a service performed by the defendant in the United States, or a contract formed in the United States, would generally qualify as arising out of or relating to the defendant's contacts with the United States. However, if most of the defendant's relevant activities take place outside the United States and relatively few within, a U.S. court will be reluctant to assert specific jurisdiction over the defendant.

As for asserting jurisidiction over property, with some exceptions, courts will generally confine their *in rem* jurisdiction to property located within the territorial boundaries of the state, or property normally located within the state even if temporarily outside of it. United States judicial practice conforms to this trend.

The *Restatement (Third) of the Foreign Relations Law of the United States* set forth more specific rules for personal jurisdiction recognized by U.S. courts:

§ 421. Jurisdiction to Adjudicate.

(1) A state may exercise jurisdiction through its courts to adjudicate with respect to a person or thing if the relationship of the state to the person or thing is such as to make the exercise of jurisdiction reasonable.

(2) In general, a state's exercise of jurisdiction to adjudicate with respect to a person or thing is reasonable if, at the time jurisdiction is asserted:

(a) the person or thing is present in the territory of the state, other than transitorily;

(b) the person, if a natural person, is domiciled in the state;

(c) the person, if a natural person, is resident in the state;

(d) the person, if a natural person, is a national of the state;

(e) the person, if a corporation or comparable juridical person, is organized pursuant to the law of the state;

(f) a ship, aircraft or other vehicle to which the adjudication relates is registered under the laws of the state;

(g) the person, whether natural or juridical, has consented to the exercise of jurisdiction;

(h) the person, whether natural or juridical, regularly carries on business in the state;

(i) the person, whether natural or juridical, had carried on activity in the state, but only in respect of such activity;

(j) the person, whether natural or juridical, had carried on outside the state an activity having a substantial, direct, and foreseeable effect within the state, but only in respect of such activity; or

(k) the thing that is the subject of adjudication is owned, possessed, or used in the state, but only in respect of a claim reasonably connected with that thing.

(3) A defense of lack of jurisdiction is generally waived by any appearance

by or on behalf of a person or thing (whether as plaintiff, defendant, or third party), if the appearance is for a purpose that does not include a challenge to the exercise of jurisdiction.

Restatement section 421(2)(a) furnishes an example of jurisdictional practice considered exorbitant in many countries, so-called **tag jurisdiction**. However, it appears that this limitation is no longer applies in the United States. The Supreme Court approved tag jurisdiction over individuals (but not representatives of corporations) in a 1990 case. See *Burnham v. Superior Court*, 495 U.S. 604, 619 (1990). Accordingly this guidance, and indeed all of the guidance, in this section of the Restatement (Third) are omitted from the more recent Restatement (Fourth). However, section 422 does represent the general practice of most countries.

One important lesson about of these trends is that they define the circumstances under which it is likely or unlikely that a foreign state will exercise jurisdiction over a client doing business internationally. A second important lesson, not mentioned in either edition of the Restatement, is that parties over which a court would not normally have jurisdiction can consent to jurisdiction by agreement. This point is important in an international business agreement, which may designate a forum state to decide disputes relating to the agreement, even if the forum state would otherwise have no personal jurisdiction over one of the parties. The contract's forum selection clause is effectively consent to the personal jurisdiction of the forum state.

B. Subject Matter Jurisdiction

In addition to personal jurisdiction, the court must have jurisdiction over the subject matter of the dispute. Subject matter jurisdiction is jurisdiction to hear a cause of action brought before the court. As with personal jurisdiction, courts around the world differ in how they interpret statutes to confer subject matter jurisdiction. In general, municipal courts have subject matter jurisdiction only over causes of action authorized by statute. In common law countries, such as Australia, Canada, the United Kingdom, and the United States, courts also have subject matter jurisdiction over causes of action arising at common law.

In either case, public international law provides in general terms for the limits of the state's jurisdiction to legislate or apply common law. International law refers to the scope of a state's authority to regulate conduct as **prescriptive jurisdiction**. International law recgonizes three primary bases for prescriptive jurisdiction that states may exercise:

(1) **Territoriality jurisdiction**. States have primary jurisdiction to regulate persons, property, conduct, and events within their territorial boundaries.

(2) **Effects jurisdiction**. States have jurisdiction to regulate conduct that occurs outside of their territorial boundaries that has a direct, substantial, and reasonably foreseeable effect within their territorial boundaries.

(3) **Nationality jurisdiction**. States have jurisdiction to regulate their own nationals and permanent residents regardless of where in the world they are located at the time.

International law also recognizes a few other forms of jurisdiction, such as jurisdiction over conduct outside the state's territory that inflicts a serious harm on the state's nationals (called **passive personality jurisdiction**), but the three listed above are the most commonly used in international business law.

In the United States, there are certain nuances to how prescriptive jurisdiction is used by Congress and courts. These will be explored in greater detail in Chapter 10. For now, the important point is that the three bases of jurisdiction make it possible for the laws of multiple states to regulate the same business transaction.

If a dispute should arise from an international business transaction, it would not be surprising if one state's law favored one party's interests more than another. Therefore, both parties to an international business agreement may have reason to argue for the application of a specific choice of law that the other party opposes. The outcome depends on the jurisdictional rules applied by the court hearing the case. It is crucial that parties to an international business transaction understand both the potential forum states that might accept jurisdiction over the dispute and the applicable state laws that might govern any dispute that may arise between them.

1.2 The Role of *Forum Non Conveniens*

In international business transactions, the relevant parties and evidence are by definition located in more than one country. Should a dispute arise, the plaintiff can be expected to file its lawsuit the forum state most advantageous and convenient to itself. This forum state may or may not be the most efficient forum for resolution of the dispute, and it may be seriously inconvenient to the defendant.

In common law countries such as Australia, the United Kingdom, and United States, courts may invoke the doctrine of ***forum non conveniens*** ("the forum is inconvenient") to challenge and defeat a plaintiff's choice of forum. *Forum non conveniens* is a discretionary doctrine allowing a court to decline to exercise jurisdiction over a dispute if the court "is a seriously inconvenient forum for the trial of the action provided that a more appropriate forum is available to the plaintiff." RESTATEMENT (SECOND) OF CONFLICT OF LAWS § 84 (1971).

The classic case defining the U.S. approach to forum non conveniens in international disputes is *Piper Aircraft v. Reyno,* 454 U.S. 235 (1981). In Piper, a commuter airplane traveling from northern England to Scotland crashed in Scotland, killing all passengers. The defendants were aircraft and aircraft part manufacturers in Pennsylvania and Ohio, and the aircraft owner and operator, both subjects of Great Britain. The plaintiffs were all Scottish subjects. When the plaintiffs sued in Pennsylvania district court , the defendants sought removal to a court in Scotland based on an assertion of *forum non conveniens.*

The Court conceded that the plaintiff's choice of forum "should rarely be disturbed." The plaintiff's choice of U.S. courts was undoubtedly influenced by the fact that strict liability in tort is not available in Scotland, and punitive damages for wrongful death were likely to be higher in the United States. However, the plaintiff's choice of forum is not itself decisive.

In footnote 6, the Court summarized the public and private factors traditionally used in *forum non conveniens* analysis:

> The factors pertaining to the private interests of the litigants included the "relative ease of access to sources of proof; availability of compulsory process for attendance of unwilling, and the cost of obtaining attendance of willing, witnesses; possibility of view of premises, if view would be appropriate to the action; and all other practical problems that make trial of a case easy, expeditious and inexpensive." The public factors bearing on the question included the administrative difficulties flowing from court congestion; the "local interest in having localized controversies decided at home"; the interest in having the trial of a diversity case in a forum that is at home with the law that must govern the action; the avoidance of unnecessary problems in conflict of laws, or in the application of foreign law; and the unfairness of burdening citizens in an unrelated forum with jury duty.

Weighing these factors on the facts before it, the Court concluded that the majority of them strongly favored Scotland as the best forum for the dispute. The Court noted in particular that the aircraft wreckage, air traffic controllers, and accident investigators were all located in Great Britain. The Court expressly rejected the circuit court's holding that the plaintiff's choice of forum should never be disturbed when the alternative forum is less favorable to the plaintiff. The relative favorability of the alternative forum was not even entitled to substantial weight, the Court held, unless the remedy would be inadequate or unsatisfactory. The availability of a suitable alternative forum in Scotland sufficed to justify dismissal based on *forum non conveniens.*

An important lesson of *Piper Aircraft v. Reyno* is that, even when a plaintiff wins a race to its preferred court, and the court has jurisdiction over the dispute, there is no guarantee that the plaintiff's chosen court will accept jurisdiction over the dispute if the public and private factors weigh strongly in favor of a different forum state. However, in *Piper v. Reyno*, the relevant parties had no prior contract between them. A contract with a forum selection clause could have altered the outcome.

1.3 The Contractual Choice of Forum Clause

The consequence of losing a race to the preferred court, or being ousted from the preferred court, may be litigation in a forum state undesirable for the business firm. Any given foreign court may be undesirable for many reasons. The forum state may be distant, rendering litigation litigation cumbersome and expensive. Its docket may be crowded or its administration inefficient, resulting in excessive delays in the resolution of the dispute. Its procedures may be disadvantageous due to statutes of limitations that are too short or too long, absence of necessary discovery, unavailability of preliminary injunctions, and the like. It may conduct proceedings in a foreign language, requiring costly and time-consuming translation of the relevant agreements, communications, discovery, and other evidence. And, in the worst case, the courts may be inexpert, biased, or corrupt.

The most straightforward method of minimizing the risk of litigation in an undesirable state for whatever reason is to settle the forum having exclusive jurisdiction by agreement. But will courts recognize and enforce a **forum selection clause** in a private international contract?

A. U.S. Recognition of Forum Selection Clauses

In general, the answer is yes. Outside of the EU, each state's individual law governing choice of forum applies. Nonetheless, most states, including the United States, tend to defer to the parties' choice of forum in a valid contract unless the chosen forum has no significant relationship to the parties or the agreement. The 1988 revision to the *Restatement (Second) of Conflict of Laws* states the basic rule:

> **§ 80. Limitations Imposed By Contract of Parties**
> The parties' agreement as to the place of the action will be given effect unless it is unfair or unreasonable.

The parties presumably chose the forum for their own convenience, and this choice is entitled to significant weight in U.S. courts. Also, because the choice of forum is presumably a term that was the subject of contractual bargaining, it would be unfair if a party could escape the obligation to resort to the specified forum when the other party may have made concessions of its own to gain the commitment to use that forum exclusively.

If the court enforces a contract clause designating another jurisdiction as the exclusive forum, it will usually either dismiss the action or stay it, pending acceptance of jurisdiction by the designated forum. A U.S. court usually prefers to stay in case the designated forum declines to accept jurisdiction over

Your Honor, we hereby submit a motion to transfer this case to any country with a less impartial judicial system.

Figure 9.1. The choice of forum can be a consequential decision in contract drafting.
© 2020 by Jonathan Brown & Aaron X. Fellmeth

the dispute.

Soon after the *Restatement (Second)* was published, the U.S. Supreme Court decided a pivotal case on the enforceability of a forum selection clause in an international agreement.

M/S BREMEN v. ZAPATA OFF-SHORE CO.

Supreme Court of the United States, 1972
407 U.S. 1

Mr. Chief Justice BURGER delivered the opinion of the Court,

We granted certiorari to review a judgment of the United States Court of Appeals for the Fifth Circuit declining to enforce a forum-selection clause governing disputes arising under an international towage contract between petitioners and respondent. The circuits have differed in their approach to such clauses. * * *

In November 1967, respondent Zapata, a Houston-based American corporation, contracted with petitioner Unterweser, a German corporation, to tow Zapata's ocean-going, self-elevating drilling rig *Chaparral* from Louisiana to a point off Ravenna, Italy, in the Adriatic Sea, where Zapata had agreed to drill certain wells.

Zapata had solicited bids for the towage, and several companies including Unterweser had responded. Unterweser was the low bidder and Zapata requested it to submit a contract, which it did. The contract submitted by Unterweser contained the following provision, which is at issue in this case:

> Any dispute arising must be treated before the London Court of Justice.

In addition the contract contained two clauses purporting to exculpate Unterweser from liability for damages to the towed barge.[1]

After reviewing the contract and making several changes, but without any alteration in the forum-selection or exculpatory clauses, a Zapata vice president executed the contract and forwarded it to Unterweser in Germany, where Unterweser accepted the changes, and the contract became effective.

On January 5, 1968, Unterweser's deep sea tug *Bremen* departed Venice, Louisiana, with the *Chaparral* in tow bound for Italy. On January 9, while the flotilla was in international waters in the middle of the Gulf of Mexico, a severe storm arose. The sharp roll of the *Chaparral* in Gulf waters caused its elevator legs, which had been raised for the voyage, to break off and fall into the sea, seriously damaging the *Chaparral*. In this emergency situation Zapata instructed the *Bremen* to tow its damaged rig to Tampa, Florida, the nearest port of refuge.

On January 12, Zapata, ignoring its contract promise to litigate 'any dispute arising' in the English courts, commenced a suit in admiralty in the United States District Court at Tampa, seeking $3,500,000 damages against Unterweser *in personam* and the *Bremen in rem*, alleging negligent towage and breach of contract. Unterweser responded by invoking the forum clause of the towage contract, and moved to dismiss for lack of jurisdiction or on *forum non conveniens* grounds, or in the alternative to stay the action pending submission of the dispute to the 'London Court of Justice'. Shortly thereafter, in February, before the District Court had ruled on its motion to stay or dismiss the United States action, Unterweser commenced an action against Zapata

---

[1]The General Towage Conditions of the contract included the following:

> '1. . . . (Unterweser and its) masters and crews are not responsible for defaults and/or errors in the navigation of the tow.
> '2. . . .
> 'b) Damages suffered by the towed object are in any case for account of its Owners.'

In addition, the contract provided that any insurance of the Chaparral was to be 'for account of' Zapata. Unterweser's initial telegraphic bid had also offered to 'arrange insurance covering towage risk for rig if desired.' As Zapata had chosen to be self-insured on all its rigs, the loss in this case was not compensated by insurance.

seeking damages for breach of the towage contract in the High Court of Justice in London, as the contract provided. Zapata appeared in that court to contest jurisdiction, but its challenge was rejected, the English courts holding that the contractual forum provision conferred jurisdiction.[2]

In the meantime, Unterweser was faced with a dilemma in the pending action in the United States court at Tampa. The six-month period for filing action to limit its liability to Zapata and other potential claimants was about to expire, but the United States District Court in Tampa had not yet ruled on Unterweser's motion to dismiss or stay Zapata's action. On July 2, 1968, confronted with difficult alternatives, Unterweser filed an action to limit its liability in the District Court in Tampa. That court entered the customary injunction against proceedings outside the limitation court, and Zapata refiled its initial claim in the limitation action.

It was only at this juncture, on July 29, after the six-month period for filing the limitation action had run, that the District Court denied Unterweser's January motion to dismiss or stay Zapata's initial action. In denying the motion, that court relied on the prior decision of the Court of Appeals in *Carbon Black Export, Inc. v. The Monrosa*, 254 F.2d 297 (CA5 1958). In that case the Court of Appeals had held a forum-selection clause unenforceable, reiterating the traditional view of many American courts that 'agreements in advance of controversy whose object is to oust the jurisdiction of the courts are contrary to public policy and will not be enforced.' Apparently concluding that it was bound by the *Carbon Black* case, the District Court gave the forum-selection clause little, if any, weight. Instead, the court treated the motion to dismiss under normal *forum non conveniens* doctrine applicable in the absence of such a clause, citing *Gulf Oil Corp. v. Gilbert*, 330 U.S. 501 (1947). Under that doctrine 'unless the balance is strongly in favor of the defendant, the plaintiff's choice of forum should rarely be disturbed.' The District Court concluded: 'the balance of conveniences here is not strongly in favor of (Unterweser) and (Zapata's) choice of forum should not be disturbed.'

Thereafter, on January 21, 1969, the District Court denied another motion by Unterweser to stay the limitation action pending determination of the controversy in the High Court of Justice in London and granted Zapata's motion to restrain Unterweser from litigating further in the London court. The District Judge ruled that, having taken jurisdiction in the limitation proceeding, he had jurisdiction to determine all matters relating to the controversy. * * *

We hold * * * that far too little weight and effect were given to the forum clause in resolving this controversy. For at least two decades we have witnessed an expansion of overseas commercial activities by business enterprises based in the United States. The barrier of distance that once tended to confine a business concern to a modest territory no longer does so. Here we see an American company with special expertise contracting

---

[2]Zapata appeared specially and moved to set aside service of process outside the country. Justice Karminski of the High Court of Justice denied the motion on the ground the contractual choice-of-forum provision conferred jurisdiction and would be enforced, absent a factual showing it would not be 'fair and right' to do so. He did not believe Zapata had made such a showing, and held that it should be required to 'stick to (its) bargain.' App. 206, 211, 213. The Court of Appeal dismissed an appeal on the ground that Justice Karminski had properly applied the English rule. * * * (1968) 2 Lloyd's Rep. 158, 162-163.

with a foreign company to tow a complex machine thousands of miles across seas and oceans. The expansion of American business and industry will hardly be encouraged if, notwithstanding solemn contracts, we insist on a parochial concept that all disputes must be resolved under our laws and in our courts. Absent a contract forum, the considerations relied on by the Court of Appeals would be persuasive reasons for holding an American forum convenient in the traditional sense, but in an era of expanding world trade and commerce, the absolute aspects of the doctrine of the *Carbon Black* case have little place and would be a heavy hand indeed on the future development of international commercial dealings by Americans. We cannot have trade and commerce in world markets and international waters exclusively on our terms, governed by our laws, and resolved in our courts.

Forum-selection clauses have historically not been favored by American courts. Many courts, federal and state, have declined to enforce such clauses on the ground that they were 'contrary to public policy,' or that their effect was to 'oust the jurisdiction' of the court. Although this view apparently still has considerable acceptance, other courts are tending to adopt a more hospitable attitude toward forum-selection clauses. This view, advanced in the well-reasoned [appellate] dissenting opinion in the instant case, is that such clauses are *prima facie* valid and should be enforced unless enforcement is shown by the resisting party to be 'unreasonable' under the circumstances. We believe this is the correct doctrine to be followed by federal district courts sitting in admiralty. It is merely the other side of the proposition recognized by this Court in *National Equipment Rental, Ltd. v. Szukhent*, 375 U.S. 311 (1964), holding that in federal courts a party may validly consent to be sued in a jurisdiction where he cannot be found for service of process through contractual designation of an 'agent' for receipt of process in that jurisdiction. In so holding, the Court stated:

> '(I)t is settled . . . that parties to a contract may agree in advance to submit to the jurisdiction of a given court to permit notice to be served by the opposing party, or even to waive notice altogether.'

This approach is substantially that followed in other common-law countries including England. It is the view advanced by noted scholars and that adopted by the Restatement of the Conflict of Laws [§ 80]. It accords with ancient concepts of freedom of contract and reflects an appreciation of the expanding horizons of American contractors who seek business in all parts of the world. Not surprisingly, foreign businessmen prefer, as do we, to have disputes resolved in their own courts, but if that choice is not available, then in a neutral forum with expertise in the subject matter. Plainly, the courts of England meet the standards of neutrality and long experience in admiralty litigation. The choice of that forum was made in an arm's-length negotiation by experienced and sophisticated businessmen, and absent some compelling and countervailing reason it should be honored by the parties and enforced by the courts.

The argument that such clauses are improper because they tend to 'oust' a court of jurisdiction is hardly more than a vestigial legal fiction. It appears to rest at core on historical judicial resistance to any attempt to reduce the power and business of a particular court and has little place in an era when all courts are overloaded and when businesses once essentially local now operate in world markets. It reflects something of a provincial attitude regarding the fairness of other tribunals. No one seriously contends in this case that the forum selection clause 'ousted' the District Court of jurisdiction over Zapata's action. The threshold question is whether that court should have exercised its jurisdiction to do more than give effect to the legitimate expectations of the parties, manifested in their freely negotiated agreement, by specifically enforcing the forum clause.

There are compelling reasons why a freely negotiated private international agreement, unaffected by fraud, undue influence, or overweening bargaining power,[14] such as that involved here, should be given full effect. In this case, for example, we are concerned with a far from routine transaction between companies of two different nations contemplating the tow of a extremely costly piece of equipment from Louisiana across the Gulf of Mexico and the Atlantic Ocean, through the Mediterranean Sea to its final destination in the Adriatic Sea. In the course of its voyage, it was to traverse the waters of many jurisdictions. The *Chaparral* could have been damaged at any point along the route, and there were countless possible ports of refuge. That the accident occurred in the Gulf of Mexico and the barge was towed to Tampa in an emergency were mere fortuities. It cannot be doubted for a moment that the parties sought to provide for a neutral forum for the resolution of any disputes arising during the tow. Manifestly much uncertainty and possibly great inconvenience to both parties could arise if a suit could be maintained in any jurisdiction in which an accident might occur or if jurisdiction were left to any place where the *Bremen* or Unterweser might happen to be found.[15] The elimination of all such uncertainties by agreeing in advance on a forum acceptable to both parties is an indispensable element in international trade, commerce, and contracting. There is strong evidence that the forum clause was a vital part of the agreement, and it would be unrealistic to think that the parties did not conduct their negotiations, including fixing the monetary terms, with the consequences of the forum clause figuring prominently in their calculations. Under these circumstances, as Justice Karminski reasoned in sustaining jurisdiction over Zapata in the High Court of Justice, '(t)he force of an agreement for litigation in this country, freely entered into between two competent parties, seems to me to be very powerful.'

Thus, in the light of present-day commercial realities and expanding international trade we conclude that the forum clause should control absent a strong showing that it should be set aside. Although their opinions are not altogether explicit, it seems reasonably clear that the District Court and the Court of Appeals placed the burden on Unterweser to show that London would be a more convenient forum than Tampa, although the contract expressly resolved that issue. The correct approach would have been to enforce the forum clause specifically unless Zapata could clearly show that

---

[14]The record here refutes any notion of overweening bargaining power. * * *

[15]At the very least, the clause was an effort to eliminate all uncertainty as to the nature, location, and outlook of the forum in which these companies of differing nationalities might find themselves. Moreover, while the contract here did not specifically provide that the substantive law of England should be applied, it is the general rule in English courts that the parties are assumed, absent contrary indication, to have designated the forum with the view that it should apply its own law. It is therefore reasonable to conclude that the forum clause was also an effort to obtain certainty as to the applicable substantive law.

The record contains an affidavit of a Managing Director of Unterweser stating that Unterweser considered the choice-of-forum provision to be of 'overriding importance' to the transaction. * * *

enforcement would be unreasonable and unjust, or that the clause was invalid for such reasons as fraud or overreaching. Accordingly, the case must be remanded for reconsideration.

We note, however, that there is nothing in the record presently before us that would support a refusal to enforce the forum clause. The Court of Appeals suggested that enforcement would be contrary to the public policy of the forum under *Bisso v. Inland Waterways Corp.*, 349 U.S. 85 (1955), because of the prospect that the English courts would enforce the clauses of the towage contract purporting to exculpate Unterweser from liability for damages to the *Chaparral*. A contractual choice-of-forum clause should be held unenforceable if enforcement would contravene a strong public policy of the forum in which suit is brought, whether declared by statute or by judicial decision. It is clear, however, that whatever the proper scope of the policy expressed in *Bisso*, it does not reach this case. *Bisso* rested on considerations with respect to the towage business strictly in American waters, and those considerations are not controlling in an international commercial agreement. Speaking for the dissenting judges in the Court of Appeals, Judge Wisdom pointed out:

> '(W)e should be careful not to overemphasize the strength of the (*Bisso*) policy. . . . (T)wo concerns underlie the rejection of exculpatory agreements: that they may be produced by overweening bargaining power; and that they do not sufficiently discourage negligence. . . . Here the conduct in question is that of a foreign party occurring in international waters outside our jurisdiction. The evidence disputes any notion of overreaching in the contractual agreement. And for all we know, the uncertainties and dangers in the new field of transoceanic towage of oil rigs were so great that the tower was unwilling to take financial responsibility for the risks, and the parties thus allocated responsibility for the voyage to the tow. It is equally possible that the contract price took this factor into account. I conclude that we should not invalidate the forum selection clause here unless we are firmly convinced that we would thereby significantly encourage negligent conduct within the boundaries of the United States.'

428 F.2d, at 907-908.

Courts have also suggested that a forum clause, even though it is freely bargained for and contravenes no important public policy of the forum, may nevertheless be 'unreasonable' and unenforceable if the chosen forum is seriously inconvenient for the trial of the action. Of course, where it can be said with reasonable assurance that at the time they entered the contract, the parties to a freely negotiated private international commercial agreement contemplated the claimed inconvenience, it is difficult to see why any such claim of inconvenience should be heard to render the forum clause unenforceable. We are not here dealing with an agreement between two Americans to resolve their essentially local disputes in a remote alien forum. In such a case, the serious inconvenience of the contractual forum to one or both of the parties might carry greater weight in determining the reasonableness of the forum clause. The remoteness of the forum might suggest that the agreement was an adhesive one, or that the parties did not have the particular controversy in mind when they made their agreement; yet even there the party claiming should bear a heavy burden of proof. Similarly, selection of a remote forum to apply differing foreign law to an essentially American controversy might contravene an important public policy of the forum. For example, so long as *Bisso* governs American courts with respect to the towage business in American waters, it would quite arguably be improper to permit an American tower to avoid that policy by providing a foreign forum for resolution of his disputes with an American towee.

This case, however, involves a freely negotiated international commercial transaction between a German and an American corporation for towage of a vessel from the Gulf of Mexico to the Adriatic Sea. As noted, selection of a London forum was clearly a reasonable effort to bring vital certainty to this international transaction and to provide a neutral forum experienced and capable in the resolution of admiralty litigation. Whatever 'inconvenience' Zapata would suffer by being forced to litigate in the contractual forum as it agreed to do was clearly foreseeable at the time of contracting. In such circumstances it should be incumbent on the party seeking to escape his contract to show that trial in the contractual forum will be so gravely difficult and inconvenient that he will for all practical purposes be deprived of his day in court. Absent that, there is no basis for concluding that it would be unfair, unjust, or unreasonable to hold that party to his bargain. * * *

The judgment of the Court of Appeals is vacated and the case is remanded for further proceedings consistent with this opinion.

Notes and Questions

1. Although the Court technically limited its holding to cases arising under federal maritime jurisdiction, forum selection clauses are generally honored in the United States in all kinds of federal cases, whether arising under diversity jurisdiction or federal question jurisdiction. See, e.g., *Karl Koch Erecting Co. v. New York Convention Center Dev. Corp.*, 838 F.2d 656, 659 (2d Cir. 1988); *Mercury Coal & Coke, Inc. v. Mannesmann Pipe & Steel Corp.*, 696 F.2d 315, 317-18 (4th Cir. 1982); *Pelleport Investors Inc. v. Budco Quality Theatres Inc.*, 741 F.2d 273, 279 (9th Cir. 1984). Cf. *Stewart Org., Inc. v. Ricoh Corp.*, 487 U.S. 22, 28-30 (1988) (Kennedy, J., concurring) ("Although our opinion in *The Bremen v. Zapata Off-Shore Co.* . . . involved a Federal District Court sitting in admiralty, its reasoning applies with much force to federal courts sitting in diversity."). Forum selection clauses are also typically honored by U.S. state courts as well. That said, some U.S. states impose conditions on accepting jurisdiction under a forum selection clause, such as the dispute having a significant relationship to the state.

2. District courts generally have discretion to transfer cases to a different venue for the convenience of the parties. 28 U.S.C. § 1404(a). The Supreme Court has emphasized nonetheless that, although the district court maintains discretion under Section 1404 to disregard a forum-selection clause if other factors weigh heavily against the selected forum, the Court's decision in *Bremen* dictates that the clause "will be a significant factor that figures centrally in the district court's calculus." *Stewart Org.*, 487 U.S. at 29.

3. What factors does the *M/S Bremen* court weigh in favor of refusing to enforce a forum selection clause as "unreasonable," "unjust," or "invalid for such reasons as fraud or overreaching?" Are there any other factors that you would add?

4. Note that the Court rejected the applicability of *Bisso* because this case involved towage in international, not merely U.S. waters. Should U.S. courts be less concerned about excessive bargaining power and the failure of the contract to deter negligence merely because the contract is partly or even fully performed on the open sea? Is the U.S. interest in protecting its citizens and deterring maritime accidents somehow reduced by the fact that any injury would occur in international waters as opposed to U.S. waters? If so, how?

Another important function of the forum selection clause is to prevent transfer or dismissal of a case based on *forum non conveniens*. Except when duress or other exceptional circumstances can be shown, courts will usually respect a forum selection clause even though the forum would be considered seriously inconvenient under the public and private factors of *forum non conveniens* analysis. See *Atlantic Marine Const. Co. v. U.S. Dist. Ct. for W. Dist. of Tex.*, 571 U.S. 49, 59-60 (2013).

B. Recognition of Forum Selection Clauses in the EU

Within the EU, choice of forum is affected by Council Regulation No. 1215/2012 on Jurisdiction and the Recognition and Enforcement of Judgments in Civil and Commercial Matters (also called the **EEX Regulation**), which replaced previous rules and took effect in 2015. The EEX Regulation includes several clear rules on jurisdiction of courts over cross-border disputes involving parties domiciled in the EU.

Like all EU regulations, the EEX Regulation is directly applicable in all EU member states. It supersedes, but is substantially similar to, the Convention on Jurisdiction and the Enforcement of Judgments in Civil and Commercial Matters of 1968, commonly known as the **Brussels Convention** or **EEX Convention**. Generally speaking, a person's **domicile** under private international law is the fixed and principle place that the person regards as his or her home for the foreseeable future. A business organization's domicile is the place considered the center of its business affairs, usually the state in which its principal office may be found or its state of registration.

The EEX Regulation helps to settle disputes about where to litigate a case within the European Union by specifying in which EU member state or states a person domiciled in the EU may be sued for breach of contract, tort, and civil claims for restitution.

The provisions of the Regulation differ only slightly from those of the

Brussels Convention. It adds provisions for the enforcement of a forum selection clause under certain conditions:

Article 25

1. If the parties, regardless of their domicile, have agreed that a court or the courts of a Member State are to have jurisdiction to settle any disputes which have arisen or which may arise in connection with a particular legal relationship, that court or those courts shall have jurisdiction, unless the agreement is null and void as to its substantive validity under the law of that Member State. Such jurisdiction shall be exclusive unless the parties have agreed otherwise. The agreement conferring jurisdiction shall be either:

(a) in writing or evidenced in writing;
(b) in a form which accords with practices which the parties have established between themselves; or
(c) in international trade or commerce, in a form which accords with a usage of which the parties are or ought to have been aware and which in such trade or commerce is widely known to, and regularly observed by, parties to contracts of the type involved in the particular trade or commerce concerned.

2. Any communication by electronic means which provides a durable record of the agreement shall be equivalent to 'writing'.

3. The court or courts of a Member State on which a trust instrument has conferred jurisdiction shall have exclusive jurisdiction in any proceedings brought against a settlor, trustee or beneficiary, if relations between those persons or their rights or obligations under the trust are involved.

* * *

5. An agreement conferring jurisdiction which forms part of a contract shall be treated as an agreement independent of the other terms of the contract.

The validity of the agreement conferring jurisdiction cannot be contested solely on the ground that the contract is not valid.

Neither the Convention nor the Regulation applies to parties domiciled outside of the EU, even if they contractually select the courts of an EU member to resolve their disputes.

Even within the EU, the principle of ***lis alibi pendens*** might, at least temporarily, overcome a forum selection clause. According to this principle, set forth in article 29 of the Regulation, a court seised of a dispute that is already under consideration in another jurisdiction must defer its own consideration until the prior jurisdiction has decided the case. Granted, the first court, if not designated in a forum selection clause, will usually dismiss the case, but that decision may take time.

Some parties to a dispute in the EU have used *lis alibi pendens* to delay the resolution of disputes strategically. The commercial courts of certain states are notoriously slow; if *lis alibi pendens* overcomes a clear forum selection clause, a party to a dispute could file an action in the inefficient courts of a state having no possible jurisdiction in order to delay resolution of the dispute until the court eventually concedes that it lacks jurisdiction (assuming it comes to that decision). Nonetheless, the first court seised must be allowed the opportunity to rule on the case first. See *Erich Gasser GmbH v. MISAT Srl*, [2003] E.C.R. I-14693 (2003).

Indeed, the Court of Justice of the EU has not only found that the selected forum could not proceed to hear the case while a prior lawsuit in a non-selected forum was underway; it has also held that such courts could take no action to stop the improper litigation. In *Turner v. Grovit*, ECJ Case C-159/02, [2004] E.C.R. I-3565, the EcJ clarified that a court of an EU member state could not legally issue an anti-suit injunction against a party who had breached a forum selection agreement to stop it from litigating in a forum other than the one selected in the agreement. More recently, the Court has affirmed that the EEX Regulation forbids the courts of any EU member state to issue an anti-suit injunction to restrain judicial proceedings in another state "on the ground that such proceedings would be contrary to an arbitration agreement." *Allianz SpA v. West Tankers Inc.*, ECJ Case C-185/07 OJ C 82, 48 I.L.M. 488 (2009).

C. The Hague Conventions on Choice of Court Agreements

Outside of the EU, there is no single international authority to require states to recognize forum selection clauses. To help fill this gap, participants at the Hague Conference on Private International Law negotiated a treaty in 2005 setting forth rules for the treatment of choice-of-forum clauses in international commercial contracts and of judgments from courts selected by such a clause. The treaty, known as the **Hague Convention on Choice of Court Agreements**, has only thirty-two ratifications as of 2020. The United States is a signatory but not currently a party. However, if more widely accepted, the Hague Convention may solve some of the problems associated with litigating international commercial matters in national courts.

The Hague Convention applies only to business-to-business contracts; agreements involving consumers are excluded from its scope. Not every business agreement falls within the Convention; those dealing with carriage of goods or persons, IP rights, arbitration, and other listed matters are expressly excluded.

Also excluded are purely domestic contracts in which all contracting parties are "resident" in the same state and performance is contemplated in that state. A company is "resident" in any state in which it is incorporated or formed or has its principal office or place business. The Convention is designed, in other words, to apply when two companies in different states enter into a commercial or other business agreement and designate a specific court (or the courts of a specific state) as having exclusive jurisdiction over any dispute arising from the agreement.

In such cases, the Convention sets forth three basic rules:

1. The designated court is required to accept jurisdiction over any dispute referred to it relating to or arising from the agreement.
2. If the case is referred by either party to any other court, such other court is required to stay or dismiss the proceedings except in certain cases.
3. If the designated court issues a judgment, the judgment must be recognized and enforced in the courts of other state parties to the Convention.

Suppose Supplyco and Wholesaleco enter into an agreement for the sale of a certain quantity of widgets each year for the next three years. The Hague Convention will apply to the contract only if Supplyco and Wholesaleco are not incorporated in and do not have their principal offices in the same state. Suppose further that this is the case; Supplyco is incorporated in, and has its sole office in, Smalldonia, and Wholesaleco is incorporated in and has its main office in Freedonia.

Assuming both Smalldonia and Freedonia are parties to the Hague Convention, if the contract designates the courts of Freedonia as having exclusive jurisdiction over any dispute relating to the agreement, and Supplyco brings an action for breach of contract against Wholesaleco in the Smalldonian courts, the Smalldonian courts are obligated to dismiss the case unless one of the exceptions applies. Among the most important exceptions are the following.

Article 6 Obligations of a court not chosen

A court of a Contracting State other than that of the chosen court shall suspend or dismiss proceedings to which an exclusive choice of court agreement applies unless —

a) the agreement is null and void under the law of the State of the chosen court;

b) a party lacked the capacity to conclude the agreement under the law of the State of the court seised;

c) giving effect to the agreement would lead to a manifest injustice or would be manifestly contrary to public policy of the State of the court seised;

d) for exceptional reasons beyond the control of the parties, the agreement cannot reasonably be performed; or

e) the chosen court has decided not to hear the case.

If Wholesaleco were to bring an action in a Freedonian court, that court would be required to accept jurisdiction under the Hague Convention. Equally important, if Wholesaleco obtained an award in the Freedonian court against Supplyco, the Smalldonian courts would be required to recognize and enforce the award against Supplyco's assets in Smalldonia. This would prevent the Freedonia award from being worthless in the event that Supplyco had no assets in Freedonia on which Wholesaleco could execute the judgment. Indeed, even a settlement agreement between the parties, if approved by the designated court, must be enforced in other state parties to the Convention.

Paragraph (c) of Article 6 may seem to open the door to courts declining to recognize a contractual choice of a foreign court by invoking some regulatory regime that would be affected by a foreign decision, such as competition law or securities regulation. This may be the case in some countries. However, U.S. courts already tend to enforce forum selection agreements even in matters that seem clearly to affect U.S. public policy. See *Bonny v. Society of Lloyd's*, 3 F.3d 156 (7th Cir. 1993); *Roby v. Corporation of Lloyd's*, 996 F.2d 1353 (2d Cir. 1993).

Obviously, Articles 6 and 9 of the Convention provide sufficient opportunities for arguing, in any given instance, that a court other than the designated court should assume jurisdiction over the dispute, or that an award of the designated court should be refused recognition. However, any interpretation of these exceptions that would allow them to swallow the general rules of dismissal by non-designated courts and recognition of awards would be contrary to the intent and purpose of the Convention.

2 Which Law Governs an International Dispute?

2.1 The Substantive Law Governing the Dispute

The courts of a forum state do not necessarily apply their own state's law to a pending litigation. The choice of law depends on terms of any agreement between the parties and on a body of law known as **private international law**, or the **conflict of laws**. When the parties to a transaction are located in different countries and fail to agree on a law applicable to the resolution of disputes relating to the transaction, the conflict of laws rules of the forum state resolve the issue. Conflict of laws rules are part of the system of international law applicable to all states. Although states vary in their interpretations of these rules, practice is reasonably uniform among most commercially important states on many matters.

Nonetheless, there is sufficient divergence in state practice to leave the outcome of a contractual dispute up in the air in many cases. As one scholar has commented:

> [U]ncertainty about choice of applicable contract law is substantial, partly because the applicable choice-of-law rule itself depends on the forum in which a suit is brought and whether the forum's choice-of-law rule chooses a single nation's law for the whole contract or potentially applies rules

from different nations to different issues that arise in the contract dispute, and partly because of the indeterminacy inherent in the tests advanced in some approaches to choice of law.*

In U.S. practice, the applicable conflict of laws rules are described in the *Restatement (Second) of Conflict of Laws*. Sections 6 and 188 state the appropriate law in the absence of an agreed election by the parties to the dispute.

§ 6. Choice-Of-Law Principles

(1) A court, subject to constitutional restrictions, will follow a statutory directive of its own state on choice of law.

(2) When there is no such directive, the factors relevant to the choice of the applicable rule of law include

(a) the needs of the interstate and international systems,

(b) the relevant policies of the forum,

(c) the relevant policies of other interested states and the relative interests of those states in the determination of the particular issue,

(d) the protection of justified expectations,

(e) the basic policies underlying the particular field of law,

(f) certainty, predictability and uniformity of result, and

(g) ease in the determination and application of the law to be applied.

§ 188. Law Governing In Absence Of Effective Choice By The Parties

(1) The rights and duties of the parties with respect to an issue in contract are determined by the local law of the state which, with respect to that issue, has the most significant relationship to the transaction and the parties under the principles stated in § 6.

(2) In the absence of an effective choice of law by the parties (see § 187), the contacts to be taken into account in applying the principles of § 6 to determine the law applicable to an issue include:

(a) the place of contracting,

(b) the place of negotiation of the contract,

(c) the place of performance,

(d) the location of the subject matter of the contract, and

(e) the domicil, residence, nationality, place of incorporation and place of business of the parties.

These contacts are to be evaluated according to their relative importance with respect to the particular issue.

(3) If the place of negotiating the contract and the place of performance are in the same state, the local law of this state will usually be applied, except as otherwise provided in §§ 189-199 and 203.

Sections 189 to 197 of the *Restatement (Second)* provide specific choice of

*Charles R. Calleros, *Toward Harmonization and Certainty in Choice-of-Law Rules for International Contracts*, 28 WIS. INT'L L.J. 639, 653-54 (2011).

law rules according to the subject matter of the contract. Most significantly, Sections 189 and 190 provide that, in the absence of a choice of law, the law governing a dispute relating to an interest in real property is the law of the state in which the property is situated. Section 191 provides that the law governing a dispute relating to the sale of personal property is governed by the state in which the seller will deliver the property to the buyer (a matter that may depend on the shipping term used, as described in Chapter 4 of this book).

Section 196 provides that, when a contract relates to the provision of services, the law of the state where the services are to be performed generally governs the contract, unless the factors listed in section 6 weigh in favor of another state with a more significant relationship to the agreement.

Outside of the United States, some countries do not use balancing tests or rely on rules precisely tracking those in the *Restatement*. Even in the United States, many jurisdictions apply more rigid rules. For example, in some U.S. states and foreign countries alike, the law applicable to a contract in the absence of an express choice of law is the *lex loci contractus*—the law of the state in which the contract was concluded. In others, it is the *lex loci solutionis*—the law of the place of contractual performance.

Similarly, in tort actions, most states apply the *lex loci delicti*—the law of the place where the wrongful act occurred—but some apply the *lex loci damni*—the law of the place where the harm was felt. The relative diversity of approaches to conflict of laws rules makes designating a choice of law an important part of any international business agreement.

The following case serves as a cautionary tale when failing to specify a choice of law in the relevant contract or bill of lading:

ELI LILLY DO BRASIL, LTDA v. FEDERAL EXPRESS CORP.

U.S. Court of Appeals for the Second Circuit, 2007
502 F.3d 78

BARRINGTON D. PARKER, Circuit Judge:

Eli Lilly do Brasil ("Lilly") contracted with Federal Express ("FedEx") to ship drums of pharmaceuticals from Brazil to Japan. While being trucked in Brazil, the shipment was stolen. This appeal considers whether the limitation on liability in FedEx's waybill is enforceable and the answer depends on whether federal common law or Brazilian law applies.

The United States District Court for the Southern District of New York agreed with FedEx that federal common law applied, under which the limitation was enforceable. The District Court declined Lilly's invitation to apply Brazilian law, under which Lilly contended the clause would have been invalid if gross negligence were shown. The District Court concluded that to do so would serve "to invalidate the liability limitations to which the parties voluntarily bound themselves" and would disturb the parties' justified expectation that their contract was enforceable. * * *

In October 2002, Lilly contracted with Nippon Express do Brasil, who, in turn, subcontracted with FedEx to transport fourteen drums of Cephalexin from Lilly's factory in Guarulhos, Brazil to Narita, Japan, through FedEx's hub in Memphis. FedEx received the cargo and consigned it to Jumbo Jet Transportes Internacionais Ltda. for transportation by truck to Viracopos, Brazil. The truck was hijacked en route and the cargo, worth approximately $800,000, was stolen.

The waybill for the shipment limited FedEx's liability for stolen goods to $20 per kilogram. If a customer, such as Lilly, was dissatisfied with the limitation, it was given the option of securing additional coverage by declaring a higher value and paying additional charges.

The limitation of liability on the face of the waybill was conspicuous. Lilly did not elect to declare a higher value or to pay for additional coverage. The record is silent as to the circumstances of the theft. It is not disputed that, if the limitation applied, FedEx's exposure for the loss was approximately $28,000.

Lilly, a Brazilian firm, chose not to sue FedEx in Brazil but instead sued in the Southern District of New York. The parties cross-moved for partial summary judgment. FedEx sought to limit its liability in accordance with the waybill and Lilly sought to have Brazilian law applied, believing that the limitation might not be enforceable if it could prove that the trucking company acted with gross negligence. Both parties assumed that federal common law choice-of-law analysis applied but they disagreed as to the results of that analysis.

The District Court granted FedEx's motion, ruling that substantive federal common law, not Brazilian law, applied and, as a result, the limitation was valid. The court's choice-of-law analysis, relying on the *Restatement (Second) of Conflict of Laws* (the "Restatement"), determined that Brazil had an interest in "regulating the liability of—and corollary standards of care to be exercised by—carriers transporting goods within its borders." The court then reasoned that because of Brazil's numerous contacts with the transaction, it undoubtedly had a significant interest in regulating the transaction, while the United States had only a "general policy interest in limiting the liability of FedEx as a federally-certified air carrier."

After considering all the Restatement factors, however, including several that favored Lilly, the court concluded that federal common law, which accords primacy to vindicating the parties' justified expectations, trumped Brazilian law. Specifically, Judge Lynch found that because United States law would enforce the contract as written and Brazilian law might permit the contract to be disregarded, "Brazil's interests in defining the liability of carriers operating within its borders, even taking into account its considerable contacts with the transaction, are not so strong here as to occasion unsettling the private agreement of these particular parties, who, to the extent they were aware of Brazilian law, opted to contract around it." Heavily weighting this factor, the court concluded that the United States is "the jurisdiction with the most significant relationship to the transaction and the parties." After the parties stipulated the amount of damages, the court entered a judgment for Lilly in accordance with the limitation in the waybill. This appeal followed.

II. DISCUSSION

A. Standard of Review

We review *de novo* the district court's determination that federal law applies; the district court's determinations regarding questions of Brazilian law, as well as the district court's resolution of the cross-motions for summary judgment.

B. Choice of Law Analysis

Although the Supreme Court has cautioned that it is appropriate for courts to apply federal common law in only a "few and restricted" instances, this Court has recognized that cases involving the liability of air carriers for lost or damaged freight are controlled by federal common law. Because this appeal requires us to consider FedEx's liability for lost shipment of freight, and since the parties have conceded the issue, a federal common law choice-of-law analysis is appropriate.

As our prior cases indicate, when conducting a federal common law choice-of-law analysis, absent guidance from Congress, we may consult the *Restatement (Second) of Conflict of Laws.*

In general, "[t]he federal common law choice-of-law rule is to apply the law of the jurisdiction having the greatest interest in the litigation." As to the transportation of goods, § 197 of the Restatement provides:

> The validity of a contract for the transportation of passengers or goods and the rights created thereby are determined, in the absence of an effective choice of law by the parties, by the local law of the state from which the passenger departs or the goods are dispatched, *unless, with respect to the particular issue, some other state has a more significant relationship under the principles stated in § 6 to the contract and to the parties, in which event the local law of the other state will be applied.*

RESTATEMENT (SECOND) OF CONFLICT OF LAWS § 197 (emphasis added). * * *.

Brazil's interests in the contract and the parties are by no means insignificant. The contract was negotiated and executed in Brazil, between a Brazilian company and a United States company that regularly transacts business in Brazil. The purpose of the contract was to ship goods located in Brazil, out of Brazil to Japan. The goods did not enter the United States and would have done so only because Memphis is the FedEx transship center. These considerations are important ones to the § 6 analysis. As explained in the Restatement, the § 188 contacts serve to identify "[t]he states which are *most likely* to be interested," namely those states "which have one or more of the [section 188] contacts with the transaction or the parties." *Id.* § 188 cmt. e (emphasis added). Section 188, like § 197, thus establishes something akin to a default rule based on a non-exhaustive list of contacts. In moving beyond the default rule to a determination of what rule of law applies in a particular circumstance, the contacts are "to be taken into account in applying the principles of § 6." *Id.* § 188(2). However, they do not subsume those principles and are not determinative in themselves. To hold otherwise would render § 6 superfluous.

Thus, our recognition that Brazil's interest, based only on § 188 contacts, is greater than the United States' cannot be the end of our inquiry or determinative of its conclusion. The United States also has some interest in this transaction and the parties, being FedEx's domicile. Which state is most interested under § 188 is a different question from which state has the more significant relationship with the parties and the contract for purposes of § 197.

In this case, even taking account of Brazil's superior § 188 contacts, two of the § 6 factors emerge as determinative of United States venue: (1) the relevant policies of other interested states and the relative interest of those states in the determination of the particular issue in dispute, § 6(2)(c), and (2) protection of the parties' justified expectations, § 6(2)(d). Once Lilly—for whatever reason—asked a United States court to consider its contract, it invited application of the well-settled "presumption in favor of applying that law tending toward the validation of the alleged contract." * * *

The paramount importance of enforcing freely undertaken contractual obligations, especially in commercial litigation involving sophisticated parties, was obvious to the District Court and is obvious to us. The Restatement expressly provides that the justified expectation of enforceability generally predominates over other factors tending to point to the application of a foreign law inconsistent with such expectation. Comment b of § 188 of the Restatement provides:

> Parties entering a contract will expect at the very least, *subject perhaps to rare exceptions*, that the provisions of the contract will be binding upon them. Their expectations should not be disappointed by application of the local law rule of a state which would strike down the contract or a provision thereof unless the value of protecting the expectations of the parties is substantially outweighed in the particular case by the interest of the state with the invalidating rule in having this rule applied.

Id. § 188, cmt. b (emphasis added). Likewise, the comments to § 197 note that the default rule favoring the local law of the state of dispatch may not apply when the contract would be invalid under such law "but valid under the local law of another state with a close relationship to the transaction and the parties."[3] *Id.* § 197 cmt. c. In such a situation, the default shifts to favor the validating law "unless the value of protecting the expectations of the parties by upholding the contract is outweighed in the particular case by the interest of the state of departure or dispatch in having its invalidating rule applied." *Id.*

Under federal common law, the limitation in the waybill is valid. The "release value" doctrine recognizes the validity of provisions limiting the liability of carriers for lost or damaged cargo.

We have little difficulty concluding that this case does not present a rare exception and that the parties reasonably expected—or certainly should have expected—that their contract would be enforceable. As we noted, the contract contained not only a loss limitation clause, but offered Lilly the option of securing more insurance if it paid a higher premium—an option Lilly did not avail itself of. Lilly has offered no satisfactory

[3]The dissent suggests that the United States does not have a "significant" or "close" relationship with the contract for purposes of § 197. As we have already noted, the United States is the domicile of FedEx. Moreover, the § 197 comments suggest that the very fact that one interested state's laws would render a contract valid, while another's would not, bolsters the "significance" of the first state's relationship to the transaction and the parties. See RESTATEMENT § 197 cmt. c.

justification for expecting that it would be permitted to finesse this commitment.

Lilly's principal contention is that the District Court erred in attaching a presumption of validity to the contract because it is commonplace in the sphere of international common carriage, including in Brazil, that a carrier who acts with gross negligence will be precluded from relying on a contractual liability limitation. While acknowledging that the contractual limitation provision controls for simple negligence, Lilly, relying on § 6(2)(c) of the Restatement, contends that under the laws of Brazil—the other interested state—the limitation provision is void if FedEx acted with willful misconduct or gross negligence.

Lilly has not convinced us that this contention is correct. * * * Lilly's statements of Brazilian law prove too much. Brazilian law does not provide for any specific limitations on liability for losses occurring during truck carriage. * * * In the absence of such support, we are comfortable concluding that our own firmly grounded policy of enforcing contractual obligations assumed by sophisticated commercial entities should apply.[5]

The judgment of the District Court is *affirmed*.

MESKILL, Circuit Judge, dissenting:

I agree that we should apply the federal common law's choice of law rules to determine whether this contract is governed by Brazilian law or federal common law and that we may look to the Restatement (Second) of Conflict of Laws (1971) (the Restatement) for guidance. However, I disagree with the majority's conclusion that under federal common law and the Restatement the United States has a greater interest in this litigation than does Brazil. I believe that Brazil's strong interest in regulating commerce within its borders trumps any interest of the United States in enforcing this contract. Therefore, I respectfully dissent.

I. *The Restatement (Second) of Conflict of Laws*

The Restatement has four provisions that offer guidance as to how we should resolve this conflict between Brazilian law and federal common law. See Restatement §§ 6, 188, 197 and 207. My analysis begins with the Restatement provisions that specifically apply to conflicts in contract law because "a specific statute controls over a general one." *Bulova Watch Co. v. United States*, 365 U.S. 753, 758 (1961).

---

[5] * * * Confoundedly, the dissent argues that we need not concern ourselves with what Brazilian law is, in determining Brazil's policy interests. It seems obvious to us that whether or not Brazilian law has an invalidating rule governing ground transport is particularly relevant to whether Brazil, in fact, has a strong policy interest in this issue that is owed deference. The Restatement acknowledges that "[t]he content of the relevant local rule of a state may be significant in determining whether this state is the state with the dominant interest." RESTATEMENT (SECOND) OF CONFLICT OF LAWS § 6 cmt. f. In this case, the provisions of Brazilian law submitted by Lilly reflect policies that are either completely at odds with what the parties contracted for (i.e., would never allow a provision that limits ground carriage damages) or that have no relationship to the issue before us (i.e., would only apply to air carriage losses and not ground carriage).

A. *Section 197 of the Restatement Sets Brazil as the Default Jurisdiction Because the Goods Were Dispatched From Brazil*

The FedEx Air Waybill called for the transportation of Lilly's goods from Brazil to Japan. The Waybill contained no choice of law provision. Under Restatement § 197 contracts for the transportation of goods are governed "by the local law of the state from which ... the goods are dispatched." Section 197 sets Brazil as the default jurisdiction because the state of dispatch "will naturally loom large in the minds of the parties" and it "has a natural interest in the contract of transportation and in many instances has a greater interest in the contract than the state of destination, if for no other reason than that there can be no absolute certainty at the time of the departure that ... the goods will reach the latter state." Restatement § 197 cmt. b.

However, while § 197 sets Brazil as the default jurisdiction, it also provides for the possibility that another state may have "a more significant relationship under the principles stated in § 6 to the contract and to the parties." Furthermore, "[o]n occasion" the law of a state other than the state of dispatch might apply. Restatement § 197 cmt. c. This may occur if the contract is invalid under the law of the state of dispatch but valid under the law of a state with "a close relationship to the transaction and the parties." *Id.* Thus, Brazil's laws will govern this contract unless the United States has either a "more *significant* relationship" to the contract and to the parties than does Brazil, Restatement § 197 (emphasis added), or the contract is invalid under Brazilian law and the United States has a "*close* relationship" to the contract and to the parties, Restatement § 197 cmt. c (emphasis added). Leaving aside for the moment the issue of whether the FedEx Air Waybill is valid under Brazilian law, I turn to Restatement § 188 for guidance in determining whether the United States has a significant or close relationship to the contract or to the parties.

B. *Under § 188 of the Restatement Brazil Has the Most Substantial Contacts With the Contract and With the Parties*

Section 188 of the Restatement is designed to help courts resolve a conflict of laws that involves "an issue in contract." RESTATEMENT § 188(1). To determine which state has "the most significant relationship to the transaction and the parties," *id.*, the court evaluates the following five contacts: * * *

[Judge Meskill then pointed out that the places of (1) negotiation, (2) conclusion of the contract, and (3) performance were all in Brazil; that (4) the subject matter of the contract (the cargo) was located in Brazil, and (5) the parties were all either Brazilian companies or companies that "regularly conduct[] business in Brazil." In his analysis, Brazil was clearly the state with the most significant relationship to the parties and the transaction under Restatement § 6.]

The presumption in favor of applying the law that tends to validate a contract is important where the alternative is no contract at all. * * * In this case application of Brazilian law may invalidate one provision in the FedEx Air Waybill and then only under limited circumstances. * * *

Furthermore, while the federal common law's presumption in favor of applying the law that tends to validate contracts might mean that the United States has a general interest in validating contracts, the United States still does not have a "*significant*" or "*close*" relationship with this contract. Therefore, under § 197 Brazil remains as the default jurisdiction whose laws govern this contract of transportation regardless of whether the liability limitation is valid under Brazilian law. The Restatement does not elevate the forum state's interests above any other state's, nor should we.

I also disagree with the majority's conclusion that the protection of the justified expectations of the parties mandates application of federal common law. First, because choice of law is not expressed in the Waybill the justified expectations of the parties, like the other § 6 principles, must be analyzed in accordance with each state's § 188 contacts. The United States does not have any significant § 188 contacts with this contract. However, Brazil served as the place of negotiation and execution of the contract, the majority of the companies are domiciled in Brazil, and the contract called for the transportation of goods located in Brazil out of Brazil. Under these circumstances, I believe that the parties would be wholly justified in expecting that their contract was governed by Brazilian law.

Second, there has been no allegation by either party that the contract would be rendered completely invalid under Brazilian law. We are only concerned with the validity of the limitation of liability provision and then only under certain conditions. I agree with the Restatement commentary that while "the expectations of at least one of the parties would presumably be disappointed if the [damages] provision is found to be invalid[,] [o]n the other hand, a rule declaring such a provision invalid is likely to represent a strongly-felt policy which the forum would be hesitant to override if the state with the invalidating rule was the state with the dominant interest in the issue to be decided." RESTATEMENT § 207 cmt. c. Regardless of what the parties expectations were, Brazil is the state with the dominant interest in this litigation and by applying federal common law we are overriding Brazil's "strongly-felt policy" regarding the validity of the damages provision.

Third, while I agree with the majority that in many cases "the protection of the justified expectations of the parties is of considerable importance in contracts," I do not agree that to protect the justified expectations of the parties we should enforce blindly the contract as written where no choice of law is expressed and that choice might determine the damages allowed. If the majority's interpretation of the Restatement is correct, then §§ 188, 197 and 207 serve no purpose, and we need never consider whether the United States or any other interested state has any contacts with a contract. I do not believe that the presumption in favor of applying the law that tends toward the validation of the contract has supplanted the traditional choice of law analysis embodied in the Restatement.

Of course, where two states have significant interests in the contract the common law presumption in favor of applying the law of the state that tends to validate the contract might prove dispositive. However, this is not such a case. Brazil's interest in regulating commerce within its own borders heavily outweighs any interest the United States has in enforcing this contract. The Supreme Court has instructed courts to "construe[ ] ambiguous statutes to avoid unreasonable interference with the sovereign authority of other nations." *F. Hoffmann-La Roche Ltd. v. Empagran S.A.*, 542 U.S. 155, 164 (2004); *see also Murray v. The Schooner Charming Betsy*, 6 U.S. (2 Cranch) 64, 118 (1804) ("[A]n act of congress ought never to be construed to violate the law of nations if any other possible construction remains."). Here we are dealing only with a judicially created common law presumption and not an act of Congress, yet the majority somehow concludes that this presumption is an interest that trumps Brazil's sovereign authority.

* * * For the foregoing reasons, I respectfully dissent from the majority opinion. I would vacate the district court's judgment and remand this case to allow the district court to determine whether the limitation of liability provision in the FedEx Air Waybill is valid and enforceable under Brazilian law.

Notes and Questions

1. Would a choice of law provision in the waybill have preempted this dispute? What choice of law would you expect to find in a U.S. carrier's waybill? Would it be feasible for the carrier to tailor its choice of law to the nationality of the exporter on a case-by-case basis? Why do you suppose Eli Lilly do Brasil chose to file its complaint in a New York court rather than a Brazilian court?

2. What is the significance of the majority's decision to rely on U.S. case law and the *Restatement of Conflict of Laws* in deciding that the United States was the appropriate forum for resolving a dispute relating to a Brazilian contract? When a court is confronted by a conflict of laws issue, as the Second Circuit was in *Eli Lilly do Brasil*, it applies the ***lex fori*** to decide the outcome. *Lex fori* is a Latin term meaning "the law of the forum," in this case, the law of the Second Circuit. Yet, did the majority neutrally apply its conflict of laws rules? Or, by putting decisive weight on U.S. *substantive* law policies in favor of the enforceability of contracts as opposed to the many factors favoring Brazil's interest in the contract, did the majority put the cart before the horse and apply U.S. substantive law in the process of deciding whether U.S. substantive law should apply? Does it make sense to distinguish between applying federal law and putting U.S. public policy into practice?

3. On what grounds does the dissenting opinion take issue with the majority opinion? Does the United States have a significant interest in ensuring that every private contract in the world is enforced, regardless of its connection to the United States? Does the U.S. interest in or relationship to the specific contract in this case justify overriding Brazilian law? What exactly is that interest, and what might happen if it were disregarded? Do you think the majority opinion accurately reflects the expectations of the "parties?" Is it possible that Eli Lilly do Brasil expected that, because the contract was made in Brazil, FedEx's liability limiting provision would be unenforceable? If so, what result would the common law doctrine of *contra proferentem* (ambiguous clauses in contracts are construed against the interests of the party that drafted the contract) dictate, considering that the air waybill was written by FedEx and contained no choice of law clause by FedEx's omission?

2.2 The Contractual Choice of Law Clause

If the parties choose a specific state's substantive law in their agreement, the general rule is that this choice of law will be honored by any court seised of a dispute based on the agreement. In the United States, for example, the Uniform Commercial Code (UCC) makes a choice of law by the parties *prima facie* enforceable, as long as the chosen law has some reasonable relationship to the contract. U.C.C. §§ 1-105, 1-301(b).

The *Restatement (Second) of Conflict of Laws* includes a similar rule for contracts more generally.

> **§ 187. Law Of The State Chosen By The Parties**
>
> (1) The law of the state chosen by the parties to govern their contractual rights and duties will be applied if the particular issue is one which the parties could have resolved by an explicit provision in their agreement directed to that issue.
>
> (2) The law of the state chosen by the parties to govern their contractual rights and duties will be applied, even if the particular issue is one which the parties could not have resolved by an explicit provision in their agreement directed to that issue, unless either
>
> (a) the chosen state has no substantial relationship to the parties or the transaction and there is no other reasonable basis for the parties' choice, or
>
> (b) application of the law of the chosen state would be contrary to a fundamental policy of a state which has a materially greater interest than the chosen state in the determination of the particular issue and which, under the rule of § 188, would be the state of the applicable law in the absence of an effective choice of law by the parties.
>
> (3) In the absence of a contrary indication of intention, the reference is to the local law of the state of the chosen law.

Because parties to a commercial agreement are generally free to set the rules by which their relationship will be governed, paragraph 1 will usually allow them to designate the law of any state as applicable to their agreement, even when the designated state has no relationship to the contract, so long as the parties had a reasonable basis for choosing that law, such as when the law has a "substantial relationship" to the transaction. The fact that one of the parties is incorporated in, or has a principal office in, the state whose law is chosen to govern a contract involving that party is usually considered sufficient to justify the choice of law. See, e.g., *Nedlloyd Lines B.V. v. Superior Court*, 834 P.2d 1148, 1153 (Cal. 1992); *Hale v. Co-Mar Offshore Corp.*, 558 F. Supp. 1212, 1215 (W.D. La. 1984). Similarly, a U.S. insurer and a Zembian insured could determine that their insurance agreement should be governed by the laws of England because of the sophistication of English law in international insurance matters, even though neither party does business in England.

However, every state imposes some limits on the power of private parties to specify the terms of their contract. For example, suppose that, under the law of Smalldonia, a person can never by contract bind a third party of whom the person is not the agent. In contrast, in Ruritania, it is possible for a person to bind such a third party under some circumstances. If a Smalldonian person enters into a contract with a Freedonian in order to bind a Smalldonian third party, they cannot successfully choose the law of Ruritania to govern the contract in order to bind the Smalldonian party contrary to Smalldonian law.

Similarly, the Smalldonian and Freedonian parties cannot invoke Ruritanian law in their agreement to perform an act in Smalldonia that would be illegal under Smalldonian law. Because the parties are not free to opt out of the criminal laws of Smalldonia by contract, they cannot do so indirectly by choosing in their agreement the law of a jurisdiction in which the act is *not* illegal.

A contractual choice of law may be understood to include not only the substantive rules of law of the chosen state, but that state's choice-of-law rules as well, which may dictate that the substantive rules of *another* jurisdiction govern the dispute. In other words, although the parties to an agreement may expressly choose the law of one state to govern the agreement, the application of that state's conflict of laws rules may result in the application of a foreign law. The U.S. Supreme Court held, in *Klaxon v. Stentor Electric Mfg. Co.*, 313 U.S. 487 (1941), that a court ordinarily must apply the choice-of-law rules of the state in which it sits. To avoid the chosen law bouncing the agreement to a different law, a choice of law clause will typically include an exclusion of the chosen law's conflict of laws rules. For example, a choice of law clause might be phrased as follows:

> This agreement, including its existence, validity, and interpretation, will be governed by the law of Ruritania, except that Ruritanian conflict of laws rules shall not be applied.

Many states follow the tradition of deference to contractual choice of law. EU regulations provide for the enforceability of a choice of law clause in courts within the EU, for example.

A few states, however, show less deference to the choice of the parties. In China, a clear choice of law clause specifying non-Chinese law will not be enforced unless the law chosen is the one most closely connected with the transaction. Similarly, Brazilian courts have not consistently honored choice of law clauses in international commercial contracts.* It is therefore important for the contract to choose as the place of litigation a forum state whose law permits full and free choice of substantive law to govern the interpretation and enforcement of the contract. Otherwise, the parties to the agreement could find unexpectedly that the court seised of a contract dispute substitutes its

*See Dana Stringer, *Choice of Law and Choice of Forum in Brazilian International Commercial Contracts*, 44 COLUM. J. TRANSNAT'L L. 959 (2006).

own state law for the contractual choice of law, and interprets the contract in a manner inconsistent with the parties' intentions. Worse still, some provisions of the contract could be nullified by the court as inconsistent with the laws of the forum state.

2.3 Which Procedural Law Will Be Applied?

Regardless of what substantive law governs the dispute between private parties, a court seised of the dispute will tend to use its own procedures when hearing the dispute. In other words, courts distinguish between the procedural law applicable to a litigation and the substantive law governing the dispute underlying that litigation.

The procedural law is comprised of rules relating to the form, timing, and manner of pleading and litigating the dispute and related matters. Rules regarding the timing and sufficiency of the complaint, the proper response, conduct of hearings, discovery, and the availability of preliminary remedies all fall within the scope of procedural rules. The substantive law, in contrast, is the law that determines the legal rights and obligations of the parties and the remedies for any breach of an obligation. This is not to say that procedural rules cannot determine the outcome of a legal dispute. Some do, in certain situations. For example, a party that fails to file a complaint before the statute of limitations expires will sacrifice the right to enforce a valid legal right, even though a statute of limitations is generally considered a procedural rule.

The reason the distinction between procedural and substantive law is important in the context of international dispute resolution arises from their difference in treatment. As noted above, a court may apply the substantive law of a foreign jurisdiction in resolving a dispute if it appears to the court that the foreign law is more readily applicable than local law. However, courts almost never apply any procedural rules but their own. The procedural law is virtually always the *lex fori*. A French court will use French procedures, even if it is applying German law.

Thus, although parties may choose the substantive law to govern the resolution of their dispute, the procedural law will generally be determined by the choice of forum. It is not always clear which rules are procedural and which are substantive, so choosing a forum state different from the state whose law will apply to the dispute (or failing to specify a forum state in the contract) may create some risk of uncertainty.

3 Recognition and Enforcement of Foreign Court Judgments

There is no guarantee that the jurisdiction in which a plaintiff has obtained a judgment will be the same jurisdiction in which the plaintiff needs to enforce the judgment. If the judgment is obtained in a state in which the defendant has no assets, it may be difficult for the court to compel the defendant to honor the judgment.

There are many reasons why a plaintiff might seek a rememdy, or be required to sue, in a jurisdiction in which the defendant has no assets and does no regular business. For example, suppose that Sellco in Freedonia and Buyco in Osterlich have a contract with a forum selection clause designating Freedonia as the exclusive forum in case of a dispute. Obviously, Freedonia is the forum most convenient for Sellco. If a dispute arises, and Sellco obtains a judgment against Buyco, Buyco might refuse to satisfy the judgment. Why? If Buyco has no plans to do future business in Freedonia and has no assets in Freedonia, a Freedonian court has no way to compel Buyco to satisfy the judgment. Sellco may now have no alternative but to seek recognition and enforcement of the judgment in Osterlich, where Buyco has most of its assets and would not risk ignoring a court order.

However, Sellco, like all cross-border judgment creditors, faces a problem. Courts in many states are reluctant to recognize and enforce a foreign court judgment. Customary international law does not require any country to enforce the civil or criminal judgments of the courts of any other country. The absence of a binding commitment to respect foreign judgments could potentially leave a party to an international contract devoid of a meaningful remedy.

In the European Union, recognition and enforcement in EU states of judgments by courts in other EU states is generally not a problem. An EU regulation specifically provides for the recognition and enforcement of judgments in other EU states. Outside the EU, recognition and enforcement is less uniform. For purposes of this section, judgments within the EU should not be considered "foreign" in other EU courts.

Aside from EU rules, many states have entered into bilateral treaties providing for automatic recognition, or recognition upon registration, of each others' court judgments. The U.K., for example, has entered into such treaties with the Australia, Canada, and India, among others (but not the United States). Recognition is not automatic, however. Usually, bilateral recognition treaties allow the recognizing court to set aside the foreign judgment on certain grounds, such as lack of fair notice or proof of fraud.

Recognition of a foreign judgment should not be confused with its enforcement; the two procedures pose different problems to the litigant. A court recognizes a foreign judgment when it accepts the judgment as if the recognizing court had itself rendered it. Only a judgment that is recognized will be enforced. A judgment is enforced when a court orders the judgment debtor to pay the plaintiff or face a contempt order, seizure of assets, or other sanctions. A plaintiff bringing a foreign court judgment to the attention of a local court in hopes of collecting the foreign judgment initially needs recognition; it will need enforcement only if the debtor refuses to pay the recognized judgment.

3.1 Unilateral Recognition of Foreign Judgments

A. Recognition of Foreign Judgments Through Comity

The courts of most countries do not recognize foreign court judgments absent a treaty requiring such recognition. However, a few countries provide in their domestic laws for the recognition of certain kinds of court judgments of other countries under limited conditions, and others recognize foreign judgments under principles of judicial **comity**.

According to the U.S. Supreme Court, comity "refers to the spirit of cooperation in which a domestic tribunal approaches the resolution of cases touching the laws and interests of other sovereign states." *Société Nationale Industrielle Aérospatiale v. U.S. Dist. Ct. for the S.D. of Iowa*, 482 U.S. 522, 543 n.27 (1987). The Court has further noted:

> "Comity," in the legal sense, is neither a matter of absolute obligation, on the one hand, nor of mere courtesy and good will, upon the other. But it is the recognition which one nation allows within its territory to the legislative, executive or judicial acts of another nation, having due regard both to international duty and convenience, and to the rights of its own citizens or of other persons who are under the protection of its laws.

Hilton v. Guyot, 159 U.S. 113, 163-64 (1895).

The role of comity in judicial decisions has a complex and sometimes conflicted history. There is no simple rule that divides those cases in which comity will play a dominant role from those in which it is sidelined. The facts of each case are highly determinative. Generally, comity cannot be relied upon if the foreign judgment conflicts with a prior judgment, lacked fair notice or due process of law, or was obtained by fraud.

Another common requirement is **reciprocal recognition**. In some countries, such as Canada, China, Germany, Japan, and Mexico, a court will refuse recognition of a foreign award that otherwise might qualify for recognition if the courts of the foreign state would decline to recognize an award of the state in which recognition is being sought. Many jurisdictions, including Switzerland and some U.S. states, have no reciprocity requirement.

In general, comity is not a reliable means for obtaining recognition and enforcement of foreign court judgments for several reasons. First, as noted, some countries do not recognize comity as a judicial doctrine. Second, in those states where courts consider comity, courts may not view the recognition and enforcement of foreign judgments as a legitimate use of the comity doctrine. This is especially true wherever a law or statute governs the question of recognition of foreign judgments. In such cases, courts typically defer to the legislated procedure for foreign judgment recognition. Finally, because comity is a discretionary doctrine, it is difficult to predict when a court will choose to apply comity to recognize a foreign judgment. Such decisions tend to be highly fact-dependent.

States may also impose other limitations on recognition of foreign judgments. Some states are very liberal about what kinds of foreign judgments they will enforce, but most are not. For example, a U.K. court may unilaterally recognize a U.S. court judgment, but only on condition that:

- the defendant in the recognition and enforcement proceedings was a resident or had a place of business in the United States;
- the defendant was a plaintiff in the original litigation or asserted a counterclaim in that litigation;
- the defendant had agreed to submit to the jurisdiction of the U.S. court by taking an active step in the proceedings;
- the U.S. court judgment is final and not subject to appeal; and
- the judgment is for a definite amount of money.

B. U.S. Statutory Recognition of Foreign Judgments

In the United States, the rules governing recognition of foreign judgments depend on state law. As of 2020, twenty-four U.S. states and the District of Columbia have adopted the **Uniform Foreign-Country Money Judgments Recognition Act** (**UFCMJRA**), a draft law proposed by the Uniform Law Commission. The UFCMJRA, completed in 2005, provides in part:

UNIFORM FOREIGN-COUNTRY MONEY JUDGMENTS RECOGNITION ACT

* * *

SECTION 3. ***Applicability.***

(a) Except as otherwise provided in subsection (b), this [act] applies to a foreign-country judgment to the extent that the judgment:
  (1) grants or denies recovery of a sum of money; and
  (2) under the law of the foreign country where rendered, is final, conclusive, and enforceable.

(b) This [act] does not apply to a foreign-country judgment, even if the judgment grants or denies recovery of a sum of money, to the extent that the judgment [relates to taxes, fines, alimony, or spousal support].

(c) A party seeking recognition of a foreign-country judgment has the burden of establishing that this [act] applies to the foreign-country judgment.

SECTION 4. ***Standards for Recognition of Foreign-Country Judgment.***

(a) Except as otherwise provided in subsections (b) and (c), a court of this state shall recognize a foreign-country judgment to which this [act] applies.

(b) A court of this state may not recognize a foreign-country judgment if:

(1) the judgment was rendered under a judicial system that does not provide impartial tribunals or procedures compatible with the requirements of due process of law;

(2) the foreign court did not have personal jurisdiction over the defendant; or

(3) the foreign court did not have jurisdiction over the subject matter.

(c) A court of this state need not recognize a foreign-country judgment if:

(1) the defendant in the proceeding in the foreign court did not receive notice of the proceeding in sufficient time to enable the defendant to defend;

(2) the judgment was obtained by fraud that deprived the losing party of an adequate opportunity to present its case;

(3) the judgment or the [cause of action] [claim for relief] on which the judgment is based is repugnant to the public policy of this state or of the United States;

(4) the judgment conflicts with another final and conclusive judgment;

(5) the proceeding in the foreign court was contrary to an agreement between the parties under which the dispute in question was to be determined otherwise than by proceedings in that foreign court;

(6) in the case of jurisdiction based only on personal service, the foreign court was a seriously inconvenient forum for the trial of the action;

(7) the judgment was rendered in circumstances that raise substantial doubt about the integrity of the rendering court with respect to the judgment; or

(8) the specific proceeding in the foreign court leading to the judgment was not compatible with the requirements of due process of law.

(d) A party resisting recognition of a foreign-country judgment has the burden of establishing that a ground for nonrecognition stated in subsection (b) or (c) exists.

* * *

SECTION 7. ***Effect of Recognition of Foreign-Country Judgment.*** If the court [properly seised of a petition for recognition] finds that the foreign-country judgment is entitled to recognition under this [act] then, to the extent that the foreign-country judgment grants or denies recovery of a sum of money, the foreign-country judgment is:

(1) conclusive between the parties to the same extent as the judgment of a sister state entitled to full faith and credit in this state would be conclusive; and

(2) enforceable in the same manner and to the same extent as a judgment rendered in this state.

* * *

SECTION 10. ***Uniformity of Interpretation.*** In applying and construing this uniform act, consideration must be given to the need to promote uniformity of the law with respect to its subject matter among states that enact it.

SECTION 11. ***Saving Clause.*** This [act] does not prevent the recognition under principles of comity or otherwise of a foreign-country judgment not within the scope of this [act]. * * *

Notice that the UFCMJRA requires no reciprocity with the courts of the state where the judgment was rendered. Several U.S. states have adopted a reciprocity requirement in addition to the Uniform Act rules, however. The money judgments of any country that generally refuses to recognize U.S. money judgments are not recognized in these states.

The 2005 Act was based on an earlier project by the UCL, the 1963 **Uniform Foreign Money Judgments Recognition Act**. The 1962 version omits several of the advantages of the UFCMJRA. For example, the 1962 version does not:

- specify the burdens of proof;
- allow non-recognition when the integrity of the rendering court is in question;
- specify the procedure for obtaining recognition and enforcement;
- provide for a stay of proceedings during foreign appeals of the judgment;
- specify which jurisdiction's statute of limitations applies to enforcement of the foreign judgment.

As of 2020, there are still several U.S. states that use the 1962 Uniform Act, such as Florida, Missouri, New York, and Pennsylvania. This number will diminish over time as the remaining states shift to the 2005 version.

3.2 Multilateral Recognition Treaties

A. The Hague Convention on Choice of Court Agreements

You have already learned that the Hague Convention on Choice of Court Agreements was adopted to facilitate the enforcement of choice of forum clauses in international contracts. Although the Hague Convention is not yet widely subscribed, for those states that have ratified it, the Convention deals not only with choice of forum clasues, but with the recognition and enforcement of resulting court judgments as well.

HAGUE CONVENTION ON CHOICE OF COURT AGREEMENTS

* * *

Article 4 Other definitions

1. In this Convention, "judgment" means any decision on the merits given by a court, whatever it may be called, including a decree or order, and a determination of costs or expenses by the court (including an officer of the court), provided that the determination relates to a decision on the merits which may be recognised or enforced under this Convention. An interim measure of protection is not a judgment.
2. For the purposes of this Convention, an entity or person other than a natural person shall be considered to be resident in the State—
   a) where it has its statutory seat;
   b) under whose law it was incorporated or formed;
   c) where it has its central administration; or
   d) where it has its principal place of business. * * *

Article 8 Recognition and enforcement

1. A judgment given by a court of a Contracting State designated in an exclusive choice of court agreement shall be recognised and enforced in other Contracting States in accordance with this Chapter. Recognition or enforcement may be refused only on the grounds specified in this Convention.
2. Without prejudice to such review as is necessary for the application of the provisions of this Chapter, there shall be no review of the merits of the judgment given by the court of origin. The court addressed shall be bound by the findings of fact on which the court of origin based its jurisdiction, unless the judgment was given by default.
3. A judgment shall be recognised only if it has effect in the State of origin, and shall be enforced only if it is enforceable in the State of origin.
4. Recognition or enforcement may be postponed or refused if the judgment is the subject of review in the State of origin or if the time limit for seeking ordinary review has not expired. A refusal does not prevent a subsequent application for recognition or enforcement of the judgment. * * *

Article 9 Refusal of recognition or enforcement

Recognition or enforcement may be refused if —
   a) the agreement was null and void under the law of the State of the chosen court, unless the chosen court has determined that the agreement is valid;
   b) a party lacked the capacity to conclude the agreement under the law of the requested State;
   c) the document which instituted the proceedings or an equivalent document, including the essential elements of the claim,
      i) was not notified to the defendant in sufficient time and in such a way as to enable him to arrange for his defence, unless the defendant entered an

appearance and presented his case without contesting notification in the court of origin, provided that the law of the State of origin permitted notification to be contested; or

ii) was notified to the defendant in the requested State in a manner that is incompatible with fundamental principles of the requested State concerning service of documents;

d) the judgment was obtained by fraud in connection with a matter of procedure;

e) recognition or enforcement would be manifestly incompatible with the public policy of the requested State, including situations where the specific proceedings leading to the judgment were incompatible with fundamental principles of procedural fairness of that State;

f) the judgment is inconsistent with a judgment given in the requested State in a dispute between the same parties; or

g) the judgment is inconsistent with an earlier judgment given in another State between the same parties on the same cause of action, provided that the earlier judgment fulfils the conditions necessary for its recognition in the requested State. * * *

Article 11 Damages

1. Recognition or enforcement of a judgment may be refused if, and to the extent that, the judgment awards damages, including exemplary or punitive damages, that do not compensate a party for actual loss or harm suffered.

2. The court addressed shall take into account whether and to what extent the damages awarded by the court of origin serve to cover costs and expenses relating to the proceedings. * * *

The Hague Convention also sets forth the procedures for recognition and enforcement of a foreign judgment, including the documents that must be produced as evidence of the judgment, and it allows states to disclaim the recognition or enforcement of judgments on subject matter of special sensitivity.

As noted earlier, the Hague Convention has not yet become very widely subscribed. However, the number of ratifications and accessions grows annually, and between parties to the Convention, it is a useful tool for increasing the enforceability of judgments obtained in cross-border commercial litigation.

B. The Hague Convention on the Recognition and Enforcement of Foreign Judgments

Finally, in July 2019, members of the Hague Conference on Private International Law concluded a **Convention on the Recognition and Enforcement of Foreign Judgments in Civil or Commercial Matters**. The Convention has not yet entered into force, but, if it does, it will require contracting states to recognize and enforce certain judgments of other contracting states relating to commercial agreements. The Convention includes jurisdictional requirements and provides specific grounds for refusal to recognize or enforce a foreign judgment, such as that the judgment was obtained by fraud, is inconsistent with a prior judgment by a court having jurisdiction, or the defendant was not notified of the lawsuit in time to prepare its case.

4 Issues Unique to Disputes with Foreign Governments

A significant amount of international business involves foreign governmetns as parties. Doing business with governments involves challenges absent in purely private transactions. One such challenge might be the immunity of the foreign government from lawsuit. Another might be the immunity of a specific class of government acts from challenge in courts.

Immunity issues arise even when a company is not doing business directly with a government agency. A private foreign business partner might be fully or partially owned or controlled by the government. A company entering into a commercial relationship with a **state-owned enterprise** should first determine whether that firm qualifies as an organ or agency of the foreign government, with the government's legal privileges. Partial government ownership, or even control, of a firm does not necessarily make the firm an organ or agency of the state.

On the other hand, even private business firms minority-owned by a foreign government may have full immunity in courts of their own state. In most cases, the determinative factors are (1) the extent of government ownership of the firm (more than 50% ownership weighs in favor of finding it a sovereign entity); (2) the extent of government control over the firm; and (3) whether the firm serves a public function, such as ensuring public order, collecting taxes, or maintaining public infrastructure.

The courts of the private firm's own state of nationality may serve as a viable forum for resolving commercial disputes, but here, too, the litigant may encounter roadblocks. *Forum non conveniens*, discussed above, is one potential obstacle. Foreign sovereign immunity is another. Even when they are not immune to jurisdiction, a private corporation may be uncomfortable trusting to the objectivity of the state's courts in a dispute with the government of which the court itself is an organ. In such cases, successful vindication of the company's legal interests in the courts of the foreign state may not be realistic.

4.1 The Concept of Foreign Sovereign Immunity

One of the reasons why foreign investment or commerce may be more risky than purely domestic investment or commerce is the influence the government of the host state may exercise over the profitability of the investment. If a private party were to breach a contract or interfere with a foreign investment, the aggrieved party would normally be able to seek reparations in the courts of one state or the other, or both. But if a foreign government or its agency has caused the injury, suing the state in a court is not always so easy.

In some countries, national or municipal governments are immune from lawsuits in their own courts. Under the principle of **sovereign immunity**, a state government (including its agencies) is immune to lawsuit unless it consents to be sued. For example, under the Philippines constitution, the government is immune to lawsuit, and the U.S. federal and state governments are also immune to lawsuit without their consent. In most countries, foreign governments are also immune to lawsuit in the state's courts.

It was formerly common for states to grant no exceptions to this rule under an **absolute theory of sovereign immunity**. Not only was it impossible to sue one's own sovereign government, but courts would decline jurisdiction over foreign states out of respect for the concept of sovereignty under international law. The only possibility for suing a foreign sovereign under their theory was by consent of that sovereign. The absolute theory was accepted by virtually all states until the twentieth century. Yet, as states evolved in their political theories and economic activities, so did international law.

Specifically, state governments in the mid-twentieth century began to engage increasingly in the same kinds of business activities in which private companies could engage, such as the for-profit sale of goods or provision of services. Some governments began to consider it unfair to allow government actors to escape legal responsibility for acts that, if undertaken by a private actor, would routinely give rise to liability.

On the other hand, no state government would consent to being held liable in the courts of another state for the exercise of its sovereign functions. For example, a state government could not consent to being held liable for not putting a traffic light at every intersection, resulting in occasional automobile accidents, or for not adequately protecting a parade participant against an unforeseen, violent protest. If government actors could be held liable under such circumstances in foreign courts, their functions would be paralyzed by constant lawsuits. From the need to balance these competing concerns, capital exporting states such as Argentina, Australia, Canada, the United States, South Africa, and much of Western Europe developed a **restrictive theory of sovereign immunity**.

The restrictive theory distinguishes between acts of an essentially sovereign character, known as ***acta iure imperii*** ("acts of sovereign right"), and acts of a private character that could be performed by any actor whatsoever, known as ***acta iure gestionis*** ("acts of the right of normal behavior"). The former were generally considered to retain the benefit of immunity from lawsuit in foreign courts, but the latter forfeited sovereign protections and were considered suitable for judicial resolution.

An increasing number of states have adopted a restrictive theory of sovereign immunity. For example, in 2006, Japan's Supreme Court changed its longstanding practice and accepted that sovereign immunity does not apply with respect to *acta iure gestionis*.*

A restrictive theory of state sovereignty was adopted in the 2004 **United Nations Convention on Jurisdictional Immunities of States and Their Property**. Under the UN Convention, states and their agencies enjoy immunity except in a limited class of *acta iure gestionis*, such as ordinary commercial transactions, employment contracts, and IP infringement. However, the UN Convention has only 22 parties and has not yet entered into force as of 2020.

In any case, a few states continue to apply an absolute theory of sovereign immunity, such as Brazil and China. The number of adherents to an absolute theory is dwindling quickly, however, as ever more states transition to a restrictive theory.

4.2 The Foreign Sovereign Immunities Act

The United States codified the restrictive approach to immunity in the 1976 **Foreign Sovereign Immunities Act (FSIA)**, 28 U.S.C. §§ 1330, 1441, 1601-11. Two years later, the United Kingdom passed similar legislation known as the State Immunity Act 1978. Eventually, similar laws were passed throughout Europe.

The FSIA is a complex law; it confers original jurisdiction on the federal district courts to hear claims against foreign states and their governments, but only under specific circumstances. Its basic provisions are the following:

---

28 U.S.C. § 1602. Findings and declaration of purpose

The Congress finds that the determination by United States courts of the claims of foreign states to immunity from the jurisdiction of such courts would serve the interests of justice and would protect the rights of both foreign states and litigants in United States courts. Under international law, states are not immune from the jurisdiction of foreign courts insofar as their commercial activities are concerned, and their commercial property may be levied upon for the satisfaction of judgments rendered against them in connection with their commercial activities. Claims of foreign states to immunity should henceforth be decided by courts of the United States and of the States in conformity with the principles set forth in this chapter.

28 U.S.C. § 1603. Definitions

For purposes of this chapter —

(a) A "foreign state" * * * includes a political subdivision of a foreign state or an agency or instrumentality of a foreign state * * *.

(b) An "agency or instrumentality of a foreign state" means any entity —

(1) which is a separate legal person, corporate or otherwise, and

---

*Case No. 1231 [2003], 1416 Saibansho Jihō 8 (Jap. Sup. Ct., July 21, 2006).

(2) which is an organ of a foreign state or political subdivision thereof, or a majority of whose shares or other ownership interest is owned by a foreign state or political subdivision thereof, and
(3) which is neither a citizen of a State of the United States as defined in section 1332(c) and (d) of this title, nor created under the laws of any third country.

(c) The "United States" includes all territory and waters, continental or insular, subject to the jurisdiction of the United States.

(d) A "commercial activity" means either a regular course of commercial conduct or a particular commercial transaction or act. The commercial character of an activity shall be determined by reference to the nature of the course of conduct or particular transaction or act, rather than by reference to its purpose.

(e) A "commercial activity carried on in the United States by a foreign state" means commercial activity carried on by such state and having substantial contact with the United States.

28 U.S.C. § 1604. Immunity of a foreign state from jurisdiction

Subject to existing international agreements to which the United States is a party at the time of enactment of this Act a foreign state shall be immune from the jurisdiction of the courts of the United States and of the States except as provided in sections 1605 to 1607 of this chapter.

28 U.S.C. § 1605. General exceptions to the jurisdictional immunity of a foreign state

(a) A foreign state shall not be immune from the jurisdiction of courts of the United States or of the States in any case —

(1) in which the foreign state has waived its immunity either explicitly or by implication, notwithstanding any withdrawal of the waiver which the foreign state may purport to effect except in accordance with the terms of the waiver;

(2) in which the action is based upon a commercial activity carried on in the United States by the foreign state; or upon an act performed in the United States in connection with a commercial activity of the foreign state elsewhere; or upon an act outside the territory of the United States in connection with a commercial activity of the foreign state elsewhere and that act causes a direct effect in the United States;

(3) in which rights in property taken in violation of international law are in issue and that property or any property exchanged for such property is present in the United States in connection with a commercial activity carried on in the United States by the foreign state; or that property or any property exchanged for such property is owned or operated by an agency or instrumentality of the foreign state and that agency or instrumentality is engaged in a commercial activity in the United States;

* * *

(6) in which the action is brought, either to enforce an agreement made by the foreign state with or for the benefit of a private party to submit

to arbitration all or any differences which have arisen or which may arise between the parties with respect to a defined legal relationship, whether contractual or not, concerning a subject matter capable of settlement by arbitration under the laws of the United States, or to confirm an award made pursuant to such an agreement to arbitrate, if

(A) the arbitration takes place or is intended to take place in the United States, [or]

(B) the agreement or award is or may be governed by a treaty or other international agreement in force for the United States calling for the recognition and enforcement of arbitral awards * * *.

28 U.S.C. § 1606. Extent of liability

As to any claim for relief with respect to which a foreign state is not entitled to immunity under section 1605 or 1607 of this chapter, the foreign state shall be liable in the same manner and to the same extent as a private individual under like circumstances; but a foreign state except for an agency or instrumentality thereof shall not be liable for punitive damages; * * *.

As should be clear from these provisions, there is a general rule of foreign sovereign immunity. However, immunity is qualified under the FSIA. There are certain acts that can strip immunity and confer jurisdiction on U.S. courts over a foreign state. As with any statute, the scope of these limitations is not always clear. One way to prepare for or preempt problems of construction is to include a clause in the relevant agreements by which the foreign state expressly agrees to subject disputes arising under or relating to the contract to the exclusive jurisdiction of the courts of the private party's state of nationality or the courts of a third, neutral state. Most states with laws similar to the FSIA include an exception from sovereign immunity where the foreign state has waived immunity. 28 U.S.C. § 1605(a)(1). This is something governments are rarely willing to do, however.

The FSIA also clarifies that immunity applies not only to the state itself, but to governmental ministries and agencies, and to any "organ" of the state or private corporation majority-owned by a foreign state. The FSIA does not expressly discuss whether individual government officials enjoy immunity from lawsuit.

In 2010, the U.S. Supreme Court resolved a longstanding debate by holding that individual government officials do not benefit from sovereign immunity under the FSIA, even when acting on behalf of their government. *Samantar v. Yousuf*, 560 U.S. 305 (2010). However, the Court left open the door to such individuals claiming immunity under common law. In *Sosa v. Alvarez-Machain*, 542 U.S. 692, 732 (2004), the Supreme Court had held that federal common law reaches individual conduct that violates clearly defined, widely accepted rules of international human rights law. Whether private plaintiffs may successfully invoke international human rights law against a foreign official under the FSIA, and under what circumstances, are questions still unresolved.

A. The Commercial Activity Exception and "Direct Effect"

Of the exceptions to sovereign immunity, the most commonly invoked is the "commercial activity" exception of § 1605(a)(2). An activity is commercial "when a foreign government acts, not as regulator of a market, but in the manner of a private player within it." *Republic of Argentina v. Weltover, Inc.*, 504 U.S. 607, 614 (1992). It is the nature of the act as a type a private actor could perform, rather than the purpose of the act to serve a government need, that determines its character as commercial. In *Weltover*, the Court held that the issuance of bonds by the government of Argentina to address a currency crisis qualified as a commercial act, because the bonds were "garden-variety debt instruments."

Note that, for the commercial activity exception to apply, either the commercial act must have been performed in the United States, or it must cause a "direct effect" within the United States. As one court explained:

> An effect is "direct" for purposes of the commercial activity exception if it follows as an "immediate consequence" of the defendant's activity. However, mere financial loss by a person—individual or corporate—in the U.S. is not, in itself, sufficient to constitute a "direct effect." Rather, courts "often look to the place where legally significant acts giving rise to the

Figure 9.2. Immune to lawsuit? Most countries have at least some state-owned enterprises, primarily in transportation and public utility industries. Banks, oil companies, airlines, public utilities, and telecommunications service providers are often wholly or partly owned by governments. All of these companies whose logos are shown here are at least party owned by national or provincial governments.

> claim occurred' in determining the place where a direct effect may be said to be located." [S]ee also *Gregorian v. Izvestia*, 871 F.2d 1515, 1527 (9th Cir.1989) (to establish direct effect, plaintiff must show "something legally significant actually happened in the U.S.").

Adler v. Federal Rep. of Nigeria, 107 F.3d 720, 726-27 (9th Cir. 1997).

In the context of foreign investment, very rarely does the investor's injury arise directly from the foreign sovereign's commercial activity in the United States. Rather, it is typically the host state's regulation of its own market that injures the investor. Another exception to the FSIA addresses foreign investment expropriation.

B. The Expropriation Exception

The exception of § 1605(a)(3) relates to "rights in property taken in violation of international law." Property, in this case, primarily relates to a foreign investment expropriated by the host state. As discussed in Chapter 2, an expropriation is generally deemed to violate international law when the host state refuses to pay prompt, adequate, and effective compensation to the foreign investor.

This expropriation exception has some consequential limitations. U.S. courts have jurisdiction in an action against a foreign sovereign only if the expropriated property "or any property exchanged for such property is present in the United States in connection with a commercial activity carried on in the United States by the foreign state," or when the property or exchanged property is owned or operated by an agency of the foreign government engaged in a commercial activity in the United States.

To illuminate how these limitations might work, consider the following example. A U.S.-based multinational enterprise, Belchmor Beverages, owns a soft drink bottling plant in Sylvania. Following a change of government in Sylvania, the new government's Ministry of Trade expropriates the plant without compensating Belchmor. This act, by itself, does not create an exception under the FSIA. However, a few years later, a foreign investor in Osterlich, Burpop Bottlers, purchases the bottling plant from the Sylvanian Ministry of Trade for $8 million. Because the transaction is in U.S. dollars, Burpop pays the Sylvanian government by transferring the $8 million to the government's New York bank account.

In this scenario, the $8 million payment in the New York bank account is "property exchanged for" the expropriated property, present in the United States. If the Sylvanian Ministry of Trade carries on a commercial activity in the United States, the FSIA's expropriation exception applies.

C. The Arbitration Exception

When a foreign government agrees to submit disputes with a private party to arbitration, it is not a waiver of sovereign immunity with respect to any national court. It is merely a waiver with respect to the private arbitration itself. The FSIA therefore adds an exception as § 1605(a)(6) for the enforcement of an arbitration agreement or confirmation of an arbitral award.

This exception requires the fulfillment of either of two conditions. The first is that the seat of the intended or actual arbitration must be in the United States. Agreements to arbitrate outside the United States may nonetheless be enforceable, and the tribunal's awards confirmable, if an arbitration treaty to which the United States is a party makes the agreement and award enforceable.

The main relevant treaty to this provision is the New York Convention on the Recognition and Enforcement of Foreign Arbitral Awards. The New York Convention is a very widely subscribed treaty that will be discussed in more detail below.

D. Enforcement of a Judgment or Award Under the FSIA

Although it may be possible to obtain a judgment against a foreign sovereign under the FSIA in the right circumstances, it may be difficult or impossible to enforce the judgment. Some property of a foreign sovereign, such as military assets,* ambassadorial or consular property, and anything found within the embassy or consulate, are immune from attachment and execution under international law.** Other property may be available to satisfy a judgment, but only if it meets the criteria in the FSIA, set forth here:

28 U.S.C. § 1609. Immunity from attachment and execution of property of a foreign state

Subject to existing international agreements to which the United States is a party at the time of enactment of this Act the property in the United States of a foreign state shall be immune from attachment arrest and execution except as provided in sections 1610 and 1611 of this chapter.

28 U.S.C. § 1610. Exceptions to the immunity from attachment or execution

(a) The property in the United States of a foreign state, as defined in section 1603(a) of this chapter, used for a commercial activity in the United States, shall not be immune from attachment in aid of execution, or from execution, upon a judgment entered by a court of the United States or of a State after the effective date of this Act, if—

(1) the foreign state has waived its immunity from attachment in aid

*28 U.S.C. § 1611.

**Vienna Convention on Diplomatic Relations arts. 22(3), 30(2), Apr. 18, 1961, 500 U.N.T.S. 95.

> of execution or from execution either explicitly or by implication, notwithstanding any withdrawal of the waiver the foreign state may purport to effect except in accordance with the terms of the waiver, or
> (2) the property is or was used for the commercial activity upon which the claim is based, or
> (3) the execution relates to a judgment establishing rights in property which has been taken in violation of international law or which has been exchanged for property taken in violation of international law,
> * * *
> (6) the judgment is based on an order confirming an arbitral award rendered against the foreign state, provided that attachment in aid of execution, or execution, would not be inconsistent with any provision in the arbitral agreement. * * *

Section 1610(b) adds an additional condition; it provides that the property of an "agency or instrumentality" of a foreign sovereign is not immune to attachment and execution under most of the same circumstances that apply to the sovereign itself.

Because foreign governments very rarely waive immunity from attachment of their property, these conditions effectively limit the foreign government's susceptible assets to the same U.S. commercial assets upon which the claim was based, any payment for expropriated property held in U.S. banks, or any property used in commerce when an arbitral award was rendered in the United States or under the New York Convention.

In entering into commercial relations with the sovereign or foreign investment, a business firm should plan not only its routes to recovery for any breach of contract, expropriation, or other business injury, but it should also consider its ability to enforce the judgment where the sovereign holds susceptible assets. This calculation may affect the choice of forum.

4.3 The Act of State Doctrine

In the United States and United Kingdom, in addition to the concept of sovereign immunity there is an **act of state doctrine**. Originally, the doctrine was developed by common law courts to keep from fomenting trouble in international relations by trying to assert jurisdiction over a foreign state. The basis of the doctrine was the sovereign equality of states under public international law, expressed by the maxim *par in parem non habet iurisdictionem* (equals have no jurisdiction over each other). As explained by the U.S. Supreme Court:

> Every sovereign State is bound to respect the independence of every other sovereign State, and the courts of one country will not sit in judgment on the acts of the government of another done within its own territory. Redress of grievances by reason of such acts must be obtained through the means open to be availed of by sovereign powers as between themselves.

Underhill v. Hernandez, 168 U.S. 250, 252 (1897). The U.K. House of Lords has described the doctrine in fuller detail:

> Act of State is a confusing term. It is used in different senses in many different contexts. So it is better to refer to non-justiciability. * * * Non-justiciability is a principle of private international law. It goes to the substance of the issues to be decided. It requires the court to withdraw from adjudication on the grounds that the issues are such as the court is not competent to decide. State immunity, being a procedural bar to the jurisdiction of the court, can be waived by the state. Non-justiciability, being a substantive bar to adjudication, cannot.

R. v. Bow Street Metropolitan Stipendiary Magistrate ex parte *Pinochet Ugarte*, [2002] 1 A.C. 61, 90 (Berwick, L.J.) (U.K.).

The U.S. Supreme Court has characterized the act of state doctrine as neither a rule of customary international law nor a constitutional restriction on judicial jurisdiction. Instead, according to the Court, the doctrine is based on federal common law giving expression to a judicial conception of separation of powers. As the U.K. House of Lords has done, the Supreme Court characterized the act of state doctrine as a substantive defense on the merits to a claim, unlike a defense based on the FSIA, which is a jurisdictional statute. Specifically, a U.S. court will not interpret a U.S. statute to reach the official conduct (*acta iure imperii*) of a foreign state in its own territory.

However, the defense does not furnish a broad basis for U.S. courts to decline hearing cases in which foreign sovereign acts are merely involved. See *W.S. Kirkpatrick & Co. v. Environmental Tectonics Corp.*, 493 U.S. 400, 405-06 (1990) ("Act of state issues only arise when a court must decide—that is, when the outcome of the case turns upon—the effect of official action by a foreign sovereign. When that question is not in the case, neither is the act of state doctrine.").

In *Banco Nacional de Cuba v. Sabbatino*, 376 U.S. 398 (1964), the Supreme Court held that a plaintiff could not succeed on a claim in a U.S. court that the government of Cuba had violated Cuban, U.S., or international law by expropriating the defendant's sugar located in Cuba without compensation. When the Cuban government sold the defendants' sugar to a U.S. company, the U.S. company paid the former owner of the sugar instead of the Cuban government. The government of Cuba, through its national bank, then brought suit against the former owner. According to the Court, the act of state doctrine supplied Cuba with a full defense against a U.S. court's judgment that Cuba had violated international law through a sovereign act on its own territory. It followed that the payment for the sugar belonged to the government of Cuba, which had taken the very same sugar in violation of international law.

The *Sabbatino* decision outraged influential members of Congress, which soon afterward abolished the act of state doctrine as a defense to a claim of foreign expropriation undertaken in violation of international law, except when the President instructs the courts to refrain from deciding the case for political reasons. 22 U.S.C. § 2370(e)(2). While this law, known as the **Second Hickenlooper Amendment** to the 1965 Foreign Assistance Act, after its senatorial sponsor, abolishes the foreign government's act of state defense, U.S. plaintiffs must still navigate the FSIA's jurisdictional restrictions. Moreover, courts have interpreted the Second Hickenlooper Amendment to apply only with respect to property (or proceeds from the sale of the property) present in the United States (which was the case in *Sabbatino*); courts may continue to apply the act of state doctrine where the expropriated property remains in a foreign state.

The act of state doctrine does exert some influence, however, in cases not involving expropriation. For example, U.S. courts have dismissed antitrust claims against oil production companies owned by sovereign states (members of the Organization of Petroleum Exporting Countries, or OPEC) for colluding to limit oil output. *Spectrum Stores, Inc. v. Citgo Petroleum Corp.*, 632 F.3d 938 (5th Cir. 2011). Similarly, the courts of one state might decline to hear a claim regarding the validity of a patent or trademark granted in another state because to do so would put the court in the position of judging the act of another sovereign—here, the decision to grant a patent or trademark in its own territory under its own law. Similarly, a court might invoke the act of state doctrine to deny the justiciability of foreign government decisions to grant or withdraw government concessions (for instance, manufacturing subsidies or a decision to regulate an industry) that do not amount to expropriation.

Section 441 of the *Restatement (Fourth) of Foreign Relations Law of the United States* reflects the Court's traditional approach:

> (1) In the absence of a treaty or other unambiguous agreement regarding controlling legal principles, courts in the United States will assume the validity of an official act of a foreign sovereign performed within its own territory.
> (2) The rule stated in subsection (1) is subject to modification by act of Congress.

For purposes of modern investment dispute resolution, paragraph 2 of Section 441 is key. As noted, after the Supreme Court's decision in *Sabbatino*, Congress forbade courts to invoke the act of state doctrine with respect to expropriations of U.S. property in violation of international law, unless the President decides that the doctrine should apply. The FSIA revoked foreign sovereign immunity for such expropriations as well.

Because, in the judgment of the United States, any uncompensated or undercompensated taking of the property of a U.S. citizen by a foreign government violates international law, the act of state doctrine does not bar a U.S. investor from seeking to recover the value of its property in U.S. courts. However, plaintiffs seeking recovery against foreign governments for an uncompensated expropriation will still have to navigate the requirements of the FSIA.

5 Alternative Dispute Resolution in International Business

One advantage of litigation is that it is an "official" form of dispute resolution offered by a sovereign state. The state in most cases has well known procedures for enforcing the judgment in its own territory, and enforcement—except against the state itself, or another sovereign state or its officials—usually presents few problems, as long as the defendant's assets are located within the forum state.

Litigation has numerous disadvantages as well. One is that judicial proceedings are always conducted in the official language of the state in which the action is brought, and usually at place where the complaint was filed. As a result, a party to a dispute may initiate an action requiring time-consuming and costly translation of contracts and evidentiary documents and in a venue that is inconvenient to the other party or parties. In short, the parties do not choose the most convenient language and location to resolve the dispute by consensus.

There are many other downsides to litigation as well. If a dispute involves complex technical issues of law or fact that a generalist judge has difficulty understanding, the parties must rely on an unpredictable battle of the experts. A specialist judge appointed by the parties could have particular expertise in the field.

Another disadvantage of litigation is that, in some states, it involves an extremely slow and costly process, including expensive discovery, delays in docketing, interlocutory appeals, and post-trial appeals. Still another is that litigation usually is a public proceeding that may attract unwanted media attention or risk revealing the parties' business secrets.

Finally, if the defendant's assets are located in a state other than the forum state, and the Hague Convention on Choice of Court Agreements does not bind all relevant states, a court award may be difficult or impossible to enforce in the state in which the defendant's assets are located.

To avoid or mitigate these problems, international business lawyers rely on private alternatives to judicial litigation. The most simple and common alternative is, of course, a negotiated resolution or settlement of the dispute. But, in structuring a business transaction, the careful lawyer always prepares for the worst case, and it is impossible to rely in advance on an amicable settlement.

Alternative dispute resolution (**ADR**) is a term referring to the private settlement of a dispute using one or more third-party intermediaries. ADR comes in both nonbinding and binding forms, and an international commercial contract can provide for either or both.

5.1 Nonbinding Dispute Resolution

A. Forms of Nonbinding ADR

There are many forms of nonbinding dispute resolution available to firms engaged in international commerce, the best known of which is mediation. **Mediation** is the process of using an impartial third party, known as a **neutral** or **mediator**, to assist the parties in resolving their differences or settling a dispute. There is no requirement that the parties reach a binding settlement; the purpose of mediation is to facilitate rather than to compel dispute resolution.

A key characteristic of the mediator is neutrality; a mediator generally does not express an opinion on the merits of the dispute, but rather assists the parties to communicate productively with each other. He or she may meet separately with each party to a dispute, then use good offices to assist them in reaching a binding settlement agreement or reconciliation. Mediators tend to avoid shaping the issues for discussion or making concrete proposals. As explained by one authority:

> Depending on what seems to be impeding agreement, the mediator may attempt to encourage exchange of information, provide new information, help the parties to understand each others' views, let them know that their concerns are understood; promote a productive level of emotional expression; deal with differences in perceptions and interest between negotiations and constituents (including lawyer and client); help negotiators realistically assess alternatives to settlement, learn (often in separate sessions with each party) about those interest the parties are reluctant to disclose to each other and invent solutions that meet the fundamental interests of all parties.

STEPHEN B. GOLDBERG, FRANK E.A. SANDER & NANCY H. ROGERS, DISPUTE RESOLUTION 123 (3d ed. 1999). Consequently, a mediator need not be trained in law (although knowledge of law is usually preferred). Instead or in addition, a mediator may be trained in psychology or a technical field relating to the dispute, such as engineering, cargo carriage, or international business.

A similar form of nonbinding ADR is **conciliation**. Like mediation, conciliation does not require the parties to arrive at a binding agreement. The key difference between mediation and conciliation is generally that a conciliator takes a more active role in formulating terms of settlement than a mediator. A conciliator is expected to form an opinion on the merits of the dispute and propose terms of a settlement or modify the parties' individual proposals to reconcile them.

While the parties are not bound by the conciliator's opinion, the opinion of a neutral third party may influence them to abandon untenable legal positions and moderate extreme demands. The conciliator's objective assessment helps each party understand the weaknesses of its own case and the strengths of the other party's case, thereby facilitating agreement. A mediator tends to play a less obtrusive role, facilitating agreement by the parties without necessarily offering an opinion on the best settlement or the position most likely to prevail in a judicial or arbitral arena.

Some international business agreements specify that the parties will resort to negotiation, mediation, or conciliation prior to arbitrating or litigating a dispute. Such clauses are intended to avoid escalating disputes and to resolve them as quickly and inexpensively as possible. They also ensure that, if the dispute is resolved, the negotiations and resolution will remain confidential, as mediators and conciliators typically are bound not to disclose such matters to any third party or the public.

Because these forms of ADR are nonbinding, they may fail to resolve the dispute, but the parties may think it worthwhile to try in order to preserve amicable relations. The agreement need not provide for mediation or conciliation for the parties to use such measures, however. They may agree *ad hoc* to resort to any form of nonbinding ADR at any point after the dispute has arisen.

B. Supervising Authorities and Rules

The most informal mediation may take the form of the parties appointing an agreed mediator and, with the mediator's assistance, working out a schedule of meetings that they hope will end in a settlement. However, it is sometimes helpful to have preformulated guidelines and a supervising authority to assist in conducting the mediation. For this purpose, there are several sets of international mediation rules.

The **International Chamber of Commerce** (**ICC**), introduced in previous chapters, offers its good offices to facilitate mediation, conciliation, and other forms of ADR. It has published sets of rules that are generally used as mediation or conciliation procedures if the parties agree to incorporate them into the mediation. These rules are especially useful when the parties cannot agree on the basic form and conduct of the mediation. For example, when the parties fail to agree on a mediator, the ICC rules provide that the ICC itself may appoint a mediator. They also provide for allocation of the costs of the mediation, the confidentiality of the mediation, and termination procedures. Other dispute resolution organizations also provide rules and facilities for parties seeking international mediation or conciliation.

The **UN Commission on International Trade Law** (**UNCITRAL**), a subsidiary organ of the United Nations, has also adopted conciliation procedures that can be used in the absence of any supervising authority. These **UNCITRAL Conciliation Rules** provide a comprehensive set of guidelines for the conduct of a conciliation proceeding, from initiation to termination, that parties may choose to accept. Many of the basic provisions (for example, those respecting confidentiality or whether counsel may be present during the proceedings) are similar to those of other mediation or conciliation rules. The absence of a supervising authority, however, means that parties must agree on a conciliator (or conciliators), or at least on a person or organization to appoint a conciliator for them. There is no default appointing authority.

The exceptional detail found in the UNCITRAL Conciliation Rules makes them especially desirable for parties seeking a relatively structured proceeding. The parties are forbidden to resort to arbitration during the conciliation proceeding, except when necessary to preserve a party's rights (Article 16), and the rules on fees ensure a high degree of predictability in costs (Article 17). The Rules also include a clear prohibition on using information or views disclosed in the conciliation proceeding in later arbitral or judicial proceedings (Article 20), which encourages a frank discussion likely to be conducive to settlement. Finally, the Rule contain a model conciliation clause that parties may adopt by agreement:

MODEL CONCILIATION CLAUSE

> Where, in the event of a dispute arising out of or relating to this contract, the parties wish to seek an amicable settlement of that dispute by conciliation, the conciliation shall take place in accordance with the UNCITRAL Conciliation Rules as at present in force.

The reference to the Rules being "at present in force" is intended to prevent the parties from being surprised by some future change to the Rules that may bind the parties, if the clause does not clearly specify whether the original (1980) Rules or a future revision of the Rules apply.

5.2 Binding Private Dispute Resolution: Commercial Arbitration

If one or both parties have no interest in mediation or conciliation, or if they conduct either procedure without success, then binding dispute resolution is the preferred resort. **Arbitration** is a formal process of private, binding alternative dispute settlement under the authority of one or more formally neutral third parties.

Because arbitration is a private form of dispute resolution, unlike litigation before a court, the parties to an arbitration have a great deal of control over nearly every aspect of the process, including the rules of discovery and evidence, the seat and composition of the arbitral tribunal, the language of the proceedings, and the arbitration procedures.

Arbitration differs in many important ways from litigation. First, arbitrators, unlike judges, need not be lawyers. They may be experts in accounting, engineering, finance, insurance, or any other subject about which the parties would like the tribunal to have expertise. In addition, the terminology used is different even though the concepts may be parallel, as the following comparison illustrates.

LITIGATION	ARBITRATION
Judge	Arbitrator
Chief Judge	President or Chairman
Court	Tribunal
Plaintiff	Claimant
Defendant	Respondent
Complaint and Reply	Memorial and Counter-Memorial
Judgment	Award

The differences between arbitration and litigation extend far beyond semantics, however. Although both litigation and arbitration usually proceed by parties, represented by counsel, preparing written submissions, offering evidence, examining witnesses, and making oral arguments before the tribunal, many facets of arbitration are quite different from litigation. Figure 9.2 compares some of the major differences between adjudication and arbitration.

These differences are substantial and varied. Some characteristics of arbitration are quite desirable to businesses engaged in international transactions, such as the flexibility of the location of the arbitration. Even those characteristics that appear limiting, such as the limitations on discovery and the lack of jurisdiction over third parties whose participation may be necessary to resolving the dispute, are in some ways helpful. These limitations tend to simplify the proceedings, lower the costs of arbitration, and hasten the resolution of the dispute.

A. Why Arbitrate?

The advisability of arbitration depends on the needs and interests of the parties. For some parties, litigation offers an acceptable dispute resolution option. But commercial arbitration has become the norm in international business transactions, which strongly suggests that arbitration supplies some needs that litigation fails to fulfill, as the following excerpt discusses.

Peter D. Ehrenhaft, *Effective International Commercial Arbitration*, 9 L. & POL'Y IN INT'L BUS. 1191, 1191-94 (1977)

* * * Particularly in the context of business crossing national boundaries and, thus, involving at least two legal systems, two cultures, and two ways of looking at the world, arbitration in accordance with procedures which the parties previously have agreed upon seems inherently more sensible than resort to the vagaries of the judicial system of one of the parties or even an agreed-upon neutral country.

Litigation is generally a less desirable means for settling disputes arising from transnational transactions. Resolution of disputes by litigation tends to be expensive

	LITIGATION	ARBITRATION
Compulsory or voluntary?	Compulsory. If the court accepts jurisdiction, the defendant must appear and defend, or risk losing by default.	Voluntary at inception. Only parties that have agreed to submit to arbitration (usually in writing) may be compelled to arbitrate.
Joinder and intervention	In most countries, a court can allow or compel a nonparty to the contract to intervene in a litigation to protect its rights or to answer a claim.	Nonparties to the *compromis* may not be compelled to arbitrate and usually may not intervene except with the consent of both disputants.
Composition of tribunal	A trial court usually has a single judge employed by the state. There may be a right to a jury trial in common law countries.	The parties choose how many arbitrators will sit on the tribunal and choose the arbitrators themselves. There is no jury.
Seat of the tribunal	Usually, a court will hear a case in the country and city in which the complaint is filed if the dispute is sufficiently connected to the forum country.	An arbitral tribunal may conduct proceedings almost anywhere in the world designated by the parties.
Discovery	The court's procedural rules will determine how much and what kind of discovery is permitted.	No inherent right of discovery unless the parties agree or the arbitration rules provide for it.
Subpoena power	The courts of most states may compel any person within its jurisdiction to testify on a matter at bar.	An arbitral tribunal has no power of subpoena except over the parties to the arbitration.
Confidentiality	Pleadings and judgment are usually public information.	Pleadings and the award are usually confidential unless the parties otherwise agree.
Possibility of appeal	Usually a party may appeal by right to at least one higher court.	No right to appeal award, but most states permit appeal to courts on limited grounds.
Enforcement	Judgment is automatically enforceable in the state of origination. It is *not* automatically enforceable in other states unless local law so provides or the Hague Convention on Choice of Court Agreements applies.	Not automatically enforceable in any state unless the law of the state where enforcement is sought so provides, or unless the New York Convention on Recognition & Enforcement of Foreign Arbitral Awards applies.

Figure 9.3. A comparison of some of the important features of litigation and arbitration as dispute resolution options.

and protracted. Even in a case free of complications, the court calendars of many countries are so crowded that adjudication may be delayed for years. In some foreign systems the resolution of a dispute may be particularly protracted since trials are sometimes held in episodic sessions as the court is prepared to receive evidence. * * *

Litigation commenced by one party may stimulate lengthy and expensive battles over personal and subject matter jurisdiction. Even if the contract contains both choice of law and choice of forum clauses, the judicial road to resolution of disputes remains full of obstacles. The selected forum may decline jurisdiction over the dispute if adjudication at that location would cause undue hardship to one of the parties, or if there is an insufficient relationship between the forum nation's law and the transaction out of which the dispute arose. Even if the selected court were willing to decide the dispute, that nation's law on conflict of laws might direct the parties to another body of law and forum altogether. * * *

Another disadvantage of litigation is the publicity which often attends court proceedings. Publicity may retard resolution of a dispute by compelling the parties to take public positions that make settlement difficult or impossible. In addition, adverse publicity may hurt the parties' public images.

Finally, even when all these potential obstacles of litigation are successfully overcome, the victorious litigant may find enforcement of the court's judgment troublesome. No broad international convention, comparable to the United Nations convention on arbitral awards, assures the enforcement of judgments.

Of course, the disadvantages outlined may not all be present in a given case. Also, there are certain favorable aspects of litigation which arbitration may not be able to offer. In court, the dispute more likely will be decided by professional judges experienced in resolving contested issues. Arbitrators are often lawyers or businessmen without extensive adjudicatory experience and uncontrolled by judicial canons or standards. Discovery of documents may be facilitated in court, but be beyond the authority of arbitrators. * * *

Arbitration can be more expensive than litigation, particularly when the parties have decided to use a panel of arbitrators, and where each is paid *per diem* and requires translation of relevant documents. Judges, on the other hand, are not paid by the parties. Often no written record of an arbitration proceeding is prepared, as is usual in court, making the handling of a lengthy or complex case both more tedious and uncertain. An arbitration award may be more capricious than a judicial award because under many legal systems—notably that of the United States—an arbitrator need not have, much less explain, legal support for his decision and may take the simple approach of merely dividing the pie in half. As a rule, the arbitrator's award is both the first and last word; appeals are not contemplated. Finally, enforcement of an award may prove more difficult than enforcement of a judgment if a court called upon to enforce the award [either] regards * * * the dispute as nonarbitrable or [considers] its nonjudicial resolution as a contravention of a public policy to reserve such decisions for the courts.

The fundamental difference, and perhaps advantage, of arbitration, though, is that it may be custom-tailored to suit the parties' needs and desires. Litigation, on the other hand, locks the parties into preexisting channels, through which they must proceed to obtain resolution of their dispute. Arbitration is potentially a far more flexible instrument, by which the parties can choose as their judge a person knowledgeable in the particular business or legal issues involved. Their dispute can be resolved in the language of their contract or in a language familiar to both parties. Each party can be represented by its existing counsel. The arbitration can be informal, quick, and private; it may be comparatively cheap; and it can be held in a place best suited to resolution of the issues.

As Ehrenhaft observed, arbitral tribunals typically lack power to order the discovery of documents, testimony, and other evidence in the possession of third parties (or even the disputing parties themselves, depending on the arbitration rules), that can be useful or necessary for a just resolution of the dispute. The parties may view this as an advantage, however, because discovery can often be very expensive and time consuming.

Another difference between arbitration and adjudication is that courts in many countries are empowered to order equitable relief such as an injunction or restitution, whereas arbitrators may order such relief if authorized by the applicable arbitration rules, but rarely possess authority to compel a party to obey by, for example, holding a party in contempt. Equitable relief can be especially important in cases in which one party licenses its IP rights to another and wishes to compel the licensee to cease using the IP upon termination of the license agreement. For this reason, the arbitration clause often carves out an exception to allow the parties to seek equitable relief in a court.

Finally, many of the limitations on litigation are absent in arbitration. As discussed above, a court may decline to accept jurisdiction if the parties and the dispute lack any reasonable connection to the forum and another, more convenient forum is available. But parties may choose to arbitrate a dispute anywhere in the world; the arbitrators have no duty or even power to decline to convene in the designated forum state unless the forum state is dangerous or unstable, or the state refuses to admit the arbitrators or the parties.

B. The Arbitration Clause

The use of an arbitration clause in international commercial contracts is very common today. An international business lawyer should know how to draft such a clause with a view toward the efficient resolution of any dispute that may arise from the contract. One arbitration expert has cautioned that paying insufficient attention to the details of the procedures to be used in the conduct of arbitration during contract drafting may exacerbate the cost and trouble of a future dispute:

> Usually arbitration clauses will be 'cut and paste' jobs by transactional lawyers who have little relish for questions about evidence and briefing schedules. The corporate lawyers who write contracts are often out of touch with the procedural mishaps that occur during arbitration, and generally remain in the dark about how their arbitration clauses play out during litigation. This absence of any well-informed reflection about the

> consequences of the arbitration clause inhibits rational decision-making, which creates a market failure.
>
> Only after the dispute arises, when the transaction has gone sour, does the importance of [procedural] rules hit home. But at that stage of the business relationship each side will be seeking tactical advantage for its position, and thus, the litigants may not be able to agree on very much at all.*

Even when the parties have neglected to include an arbitration clause in their contract, they may, upon a dispute arising, agree to arbitrate in preference to litigation. In such cases, the parties execute a separate *ad hoc* contract called a ***compromis***,** or agreement to arbitrate.

The arbitration clause may designate a private organization with arbitration expertise under whose auspices, and pursuant to whose rules, the proceedings will take place. In private commercial disputes, the most common such organizations include the **ICC International Court of Arbitration**, the **American Arbitration Association** (**AAA**), and the **China International Economic and Trade Arbitration Commission** (**CIETAC**), among many others. These organizations publish arbitration rules governing such important questions as how arbitrators are to be appointed, whether the arbitral tribunal is authorized to make an interim award, what law governs the relationship of the parties, and whether the parties may apply to a court to obtain an injunction.

The ICC International Court of Arbitration

Different supervising authorities have different constraints. Among the least constrained is the ICC International Court of Arbitration. This is not technically a "court," but rather a secretariat and supporting bureaucracy established by the International Chamber of Commerce in 1923. ICC arbitration is an extremely popular choice for resolving international business disputes. Although the International Court of Arbitration has been described as having a European flavor and is headquartered in Paris, France, the Court may assist in the formation of a tribunal almost anywhere in the world, with arbitrators of any nationality, to conduct a proceeding in any language.

The American Arbitration Association

The AAA is another popular venue for international commercial arbitration, especially among

*William W. Park, *The 2002 Freshfields Lecture—Arbitration's Protean Nature*, 19 ARB. INT'L 279, 296 (2003).

**Pronounced "comb-pro-MEE." *Compromis* is the French term for compromise.

parties based in the United States. The AAA is a nonprofit corporation based in New York and was founded with the purpose of promoting dispute resolution through the use of mediation, arbitration, and other forms of ADR in both commercial and noncommercial contexts.

In commercial arbitration, the AAA's contribution as supervising authority takes the primary form of providing rules of procedure and helping the parties appoint members of the tribunal—either a single arbitrator or the chair of a three-member tribunal. Like the ICC International Court of Arbitration, the AAA itself does not resolve disputes, but rather assists in the formation and supervision of the arbitral tribunal. While a large preponderance of AAA-supervised arbitrations occur in the United States, the AAA may assist in arbitration in other countries as well.

The China International Economic & Trade Arbitration Commission

CIETAC was founded in 1956 in Beijing and has become an important arbitration supervisory authority for international business in Asia. CIETAC has facilities in several major cities in China, as well as a very popular site in Hong Kong. Although still less used than the ICC or AAA, CIETAC supervises hundreds of international arbitrations per year, and many more domestic arbitrations.

CIETAC

UNCITRAL Arbitration Rules

If the parties do not wish to rely on the services of a private arbitration authority, they can invoke the Model Arbitration Rules published by UNCITRAL. The **UNCITRAL Arbitration Rules** were adopted by the UN General Assembly in 1976 to facilitate the use of arbitration in international disputes. The were significantly revised in 2013.

The UNCITRAL Rules do not require supervision by any private organization, and thus they allow the conduct of an arbitration largely according to the parties' mutual agreement. On the other hand, a supervising authority such as the AAA or ICC may apply UNCITRAL rules instead of its own rules to an arbitration at the request of the parties. The absence of a supervising authority does, however, tend to make the arbitration less expensive and to maximize the ability of the parties to customize their arbitration. The fees charged by the supervising authorities vary, but they range from at least a few thousand dollars to close to $100,000 per case.

The UNCITRAL Rules are popular in *ad hoc* international commercial arbitration. These rules have exerted significant influence over institutional arbitration rules worldwide.

The Arbitration Clause

An arbitration clause, also called a **compromissory clause**, should ideally be phrased in such a manner that all disputes in any way relating to the contract, including its validity, will be resolved by the arbitral tribunal. In addition, it should specify the supervising authority (if any) and the rules that will govern the arbitration. Finally, other important information should typically be included in the clause. Several of the supervising authorities, or the rules themselves, specify a preferred compromissory clause. The ICC's preferred clause reads:

> All disputes arising in connection with the present contract shall be finally settled under the Rules of Conciliation and Arbitration of the International Chamber of Commerce by one or more arbitrators appointed in accordance with the said Rules.

The UNCITRAL model arbitration clause is more explicit:

> Any dispute, controversy or claim arising out of or relating to this contract, or the breach, termination or invalidity thereof, shall be settled by arbitration in accordance with the UNCITRAL Arbitration Rules.

Although phrased well, both clauses omit important details. Both the UNCITRAL Arbitration Rules and the ICC recommend including additional information, such as:

- the number of arbitrators (usually one or three) to compose the tribunal;
- the city and country where the arbitration will be conducted;
- the language in which the arbitration will proceed; and
- the law governing the contract.

If the parties fail to specify any of these in the contract itself and cannot agree at the time of arbitration, the default rules supplied by the supervising authority (or, in the case of the UNCITRAL Rules, the UNCITRAL Rules themselves) will fill in the gap.

Choosing Arbitration Rules

The rules promulgated by the various arbitration supervising authorities vary in some significant respects, so it is important to consider these differences when choosing which rules to adopt. To illustrate the similarities and differences in arbitration proceedings, Figure 9.3 compares the AAA International Arbitration Rules, ICC Rules of Arbitration, and UNCITRAL Arbitration Rules. Keep in mind that many of these are default rules that apply only when the parties have failed to agree otherwise.

As the comparison illustrates, the various rules coincide on several key points of procedure. On other points, the differences may be consequential in certain cases. Legal issues raised in international arbitration may also differ from those in otherwise similar domestic arbitrations. Many arbitration authorities have separate rules for international and domestic proceedings. For example, punitive damages may be available in domestic arbitration under the AAA domestic arbitration rules, but not under the AAA international rules.

There are several important principles of law that help prevent the use of delay tactics to reduce the convenience of arbitration. One is the **severability** or autonomy of the arbitration clause itself from the underlying agreement. In other words, the question of whether a contract between two parties is valid and enforceable is legally separate from the question of whether an arbitration clause in that agreement is valid and enforceable.

If the arbitration clause is properly drafted, it will usually survive a challenge to the validity of the agreement in which it is found. As one expert observed: "when the parties to an agreement containing an arbitration clause enter into that agreement, they conclude not one but two agreements, the arbitral twin of which survives any birth defect or acquired disability of the principle agreement."*

While this result may seem counterintuitive, consider the consequences of tying the validity of the arbitration clause to the validity of the underlying agreement. In that case, any party wishing to avoid arbitration would simply challenge the validity of the underlying agreement in court, which would result in a litigation over the very subject matter that the arbitral tribunal was to decide. Many of the advantages of arbitration would be compromised. A party wishing to avoid arbitration, then, must challenge the validity or enforceability of the arbitration clause itself rather than the underlying agreement.

This leads to consideration of a second, related principle. Under most arbitration rules, the tribunal has jurisdiction to determine whether it has jurisdiction over the parties and the case, including the validity of the underlying agreement and the arbitration clause itself. The tribunal's inherent authority to determine its own jurisdiction is commonly called ***compétence de la compétence***. I prefer to call it **metajurisdiction**. Some arbitral rules, including the UNCITRAL, ICC, and AAA rules, provide explicitly for metajurisdiction. The 2013 UNCITRAL Rules are exemplary:

> **Pleas as to the jurisdiction of the arbitral tribunal**
>
> **Article 23**
>
> 1. The arbitral tribunal shall have the power to rule on its own jurisdiction, including any objections with respect to the existence or validity of the arbitration agreement. For that purpose, an arbitration clause that forms part of a contract shall be treated as an agreement independent of the other terms of the contract. A decision by the arbitral tribunal that the contract is null shall not entail automatically the invalidity of the arbitration clause. * * *

---

*Steven M. Schwebel, International Arbitration: Three Salient Problems 1, 5 (1987).

Once the arbitral tribunal has determined that it has proper jurisdiction over the dispute, it may proceed to adjudicate in spite of any pending challenge against its jurisdiction in a national court.

Metajurisdiction is important to keeping arbitration a convenient, fast, and inexpensive forum. If a party could have recourse to a court of law to object to the underlying validity of a contract containing an arbitration clause or agreement, the benefits of arbitration would be seriously attenuated. Metajurisdiction allows the arbitral tribunal a clear opportunity to assess separately the validity of the underlying contract and of the arbitration agreement.

While the general principle of metajurisdiction is widely accepted, most states do not accept the principle of *exclusive* metajurisdiction when the validity or enforceability of the arbitration clause itself, as opposed to that of the underlying agreement, is challenged. See, e.g., *Rent-A-Center, West, Inc. v. Jackson*, 561 U.S. 63, 70-71 (2010).

Although the courts of many states will refuse to order a stay of arbitration while the court decides the validity or applicability of the arbitration clause, the court may nonetheless consider the validity of the *compromis* before, during, or after the arbitral tribunal has considered the same question. There is no unified, worldwide practice on whether it is permissible to examine arbitral jurisdiction before the arbitral tribunal itself has had a chance to rule on its own jurisdiction. As one expert has observed:

> [I]f German courts are asked to hear a matter which one side asserts is subject to arbitration, they decide immediately on the validity and scope of the arbitration agreement. In neighboring France, such challenges normally wait until an award has been made. Across the Channel in England, litigants have a right to declaratory decisions on arbitral authority, but only if they take no part in the arbitration. In Sweden and Finland, as in the United States, courts may entertain applications for jurisdictional declarations at any time.
>
> In Switzerland, courts asked to appoint an arbitrator will normally apply a *prima facie* standard in deciding whether the arbitration clause is valid but engage in full consideration of jurisdiction (at least as to law) in the context of award review. American courts, however, may order full examination of the validity of an arbitration clause at any stage of the arbitral process to determine whether, as a matter of fact and law, the parties have indeed agreed to arbitrate.*

If a national court determines that the *compromis* is invalid or inapplicable, its decision will deprive the tribunal of jurisdiction in the court's forum state. In such a case, any resulting arbitral award will be unenforceable in that state.

---

*William W. Park, *Determining an Arbitrator's Jurisdiction: Timing and Finality in American Law*, 8 NEV. L. REV. 135, 139 (2007).

Choice of Law

As with international business agreements generally, it is wise to designate the law applicable to a *compromis*. This choice of law binds the arbitral tribunal; the tribunal may not choose to apply a law other than the one the parties have selected to resolve the dispute. As in litigation before courts, however, it is important to specifically exclude the conflict of laws rules of the law selected. Excluding the conflict of laws rules ensures that the tribunal will honor the parties' choice of substantive law. If the parties failed to stipulate a choice of law in the *compromis*, then the tribunal must apply general conflict of laws rules to determine the substantive law to govern the dispute. The conflict of laws rules are discussed in the previous chapter.

As in choice of law clauses generally, it is important to be clear in the contract as to the distinction between choice of procedural and substantive law. In a *compromis*, as in any other agreement, language simply designating a specific country's law as the law of the agreement or dispute may be read as a reference to procedural or substantive law, at the reviewing court's preference. In one case, for example, a U.S. district court interpreted a contract clause providing for arbitration in London and stating that "the arbitration shall be in accordance with the laws of England" to mean that English law merely governs "the procedural aspects of the arbitration" based on the words "in accordance with" and the fact that a later article provided that the agreement would be "governed by" the laws of England. *PPG Indus. v. Pilkington plc*, 825 F. Supp. 1465 (D. Ariz. 1993). Consider how, if the parties had not really intended to make a choice of procedural law in that case, they could have made their intention less equivocal:

- "The procedural law governing the resolution of the dispute will be the law of Freedonia and the law governing the agreement will be the law of Grand Fenwick."
- "The arbitration will be conducted according to the UNCITRAL Arbitration Rules and the procedural law of Freedonia, and the rights and duties of the parties shall be governed by the law of Grand Fenwick."
- "The procedures governing the resolution of any dispute arising under this agreement will be the UNCITRAL Arbitration Rules supplemented by the law of Freedonia. The agreement, including the interpretation, validity, and enforceability thereof, will be governed by the law of Grand Fenwick."

Do any of these choices of phrasing seem clearer than others?

In the absence of a clear choice of procedural law, most institutional arbitration rules grant discretion to the arbitral tribunal to choose rules of procedure and evidence to the extent not specified in the institutional rules themselves. Most institutional rules allow the tribunal to establish the facts by "all

	ICC	AAA	UNCITRAL
No. of arbitrators	1 or 3	1 or 3	3
Method of choosing a sole arbitrator	If parties cannot agree, the ICC Court appoints the arbitrator.	If parties cannot agree, the AAA Administrator appoints the arbitrator.	If parties cannot agree, the Secretary-General of the Permanent Court of Arbitration (PCA) appoints arbitrators in consultation with parties.
Method of choosing multiple arbitrators	Each party appoints one arbitrator and the ICC Court appoints the third. If one party fails to appoint, the ICC Court does so instead.	No default method. If parties agree on a method but one party fails to appoint, the AAA Administrator does so instead.	Each party appoints one arbitrator. These two arbitrators appoint the third. If one party fails to appoint, the PCA Secretary-General does so.
Place of arbitration	Tribunal's choice.	Tribunal's choice.	Tribunal's choice.
Default language	Tribunal's choice.	The language "of the documents containing the arbitration agreement."	Tribunal's choice.
Oral hearing	Subject to the tribunal's discretion, but an oral hearing is usually included.	Subject to the tribunal's discretion, but an oral hearing is usually included.	Mandatory at the request of either party. Otherwise, discretionary.
Right to discovery	None.	None.	None, but the tribunal may require the parties to produce any evidence it deems helpful.
Provisional or interim measures	Authorized for the tribunal, or the parties can apply directly to judicial authorities.	Authorized for the tribunal, or the parties can apply directly to judicial authorities.	Authorized for the tribunal on a showing of necessity and "reasonable possibility" of success on the merits, or the parties can apply directly to judicial authorities.
Requirement for an award	Majority of arbitrators. If no majority, the chairman of the tribunal's award.	Majority of arbitrators. No provision in case no majority is achieved.	Majority of arbitrators. If no majority, the president of the tribunal's award.
Costs of arbitration	Allocated by the tribunal in its award.	Allocated by the tribunal in its award.	Allocated by the tribunal in its award.

Figure 9.4. A comparison of three leading sets of international arbitration rules.

appropriate means" (ICC Arbitration Rule 20), with the "widest discretion to discharge its duties" (London Court of International Arbitration Rule 14.2) and in "whatever manner [the tribunal] considers appropriate" (UNCITRAL Rule 18; AAA International Rule 16). Such matters as attorney-client privilege, the order of oral argument and number of times each side is entitled to present, and whether witness testimony may be written or oral, are typically resolved by the discretion of the tribunal unless otherwise specified in the *compromis*.

Choice of Venue

Theoretically, an arbitration may be conducted anywhere in the world. National courts are generally constrained to convene in a specific city, but the parties to a *compromis* can designate almost any city for their arbitration. The choice of venue depends on the convenience of the parties; it bears no necessary relation to the nationalities of the parties to the dispute, to the place of performance of the contract, or to the substantive law governing the dispute.

The parties will typically designate the place of arbitration in the *compromis*. An upfront contractual choice avoids wrangling over the venue after the dispute has arisen. In general, the decision of the parties receives great deference by courts and nearly total deference by the arbitral tribunal unless war, civil disturbance, extreme weather, or other *force majeure* renders the chosen venue inaccessible. In that case, if the parties are unable to agree on an alternative venue, the tribunal itself will choose the locale of its seat.

C. Enforcement and Appeal of an Arbitration Award

The fundamental challenge confronting a party invoking an arbitration clause is ensuring that, if the respondent resists going to arbitration, the claimant can prevent the respondent from initiating a lawsuit in a court, which would undermine one of the main advantages of the arbitration. In other words, for arbitration to be an efficient and effective recourse for parties to an international commercial agreement, there must be some assurance that the compromissory clause will be enforceable. There must be some assurance that a court seised of the dispute will dismiss any lawsuit brought by the other party within the scope of the arbitration clause, and refer the case to arbitration.

Of course, even if the *compromis* is enforced, a second challenge might confront a victorious claimant in an arbitration. The claimant must be able to enforce the award wherever the respondent has assets. Often a respondent will pay an arbitral award without the need for any external enforcement measures, but sometimes it refuses. For arbitration to be worthwhile, the claimant must be confident that courts will recognize and enforce the arbitral award in the states in which the respondent has valuable assets.

The enforcement of arbitral awards issued in foreign countries has been enormously facilitated by the **UN Convention on the Recognition and Enforcement of Foreign Arbitral Awards**, 330 U.N.T.S. 38 (1970), signed in 1958 in New York (commonly called the **New York Convention** or **NY Convention**). The NY Convention was intended to encourage the use of private international arbitration by increasing the enforceability of foreign arbitration clauses and awards, subject to certain limited exceptions. The NY Convention, drafted in part at the urging of the ICC, was designed to help overcome the traditional reluctance of many states to allow business firms to resolve their disputes by private means rather than through national court systems. The Convention commits state parties to recognizing and enforcing compromissory clauses providing for foreign commercial arbitration, and arbitral awards rendered in commercial disputes in other state parties to the Convention.

Article I

1. This Convention shall apply to the recognition and enforcement of arbitral awards made in the territory of a State other than the State where the recognition and enforcement of such awards are sought, and arising out of differences between persons, whether physical or legal. It shall also apply to arbitral awards not considered as domestic awards in the State where their recognition and enforcement are sought. * * *

Article II

1. Each Contracting State shall recognize an agreement in writing under which the parties undertake to submit to arbitration all or any differences which have arisen or which may arise between them in respect of a defined legal relationship, whether contractual or not, concerning a subject matter capable of settlement by arbitration.

2. The term "agreement in writing" shall include an arbitral clause in a contract or an arbitration agreement, signed by the parties or contained in an exchange of letters or telegrams.

3. The court of a Contracting State, when seized of an action in a matter in respect of which the parties have made an agreement within the meaning of this article, shall, at the request of one of the parties, refer the parties to arbitration, unless it finds that the said agreement is null and void, inoperative or incapable of being performed.

Article III

1. Each Contracting State shall recognize arbitral awards as binding and enforce them in accordance with the rules of procedure of the territory where the award is relied upon, under the conditions laid down in the following articles. * * *

As of 2020, 159 states, including the United States, adhere to the Convention, making it extremely attractive to resort to arbitration to settle international business disputes. You will recall that, although the courts of most states will enforce a forum selection clause, they will not generally enforce a foreign money judgment unless they are parties to the Hague Convention on Choice of Court Agreements or the newer Convention on the Recognition and Enforcement of Foreign Judgments. The NY Convention supplies the missing element of award enforceability due to its large number of parties.

In addition to the NY Convention, there are several other important regional arbitration conventions designed for the same purpose in Europe, the Americas, and elsewhere. The terms of these treaties are largely similar to those of the NY Convention, but some countries that are not parties to the NY Convention are parties to a regional treaty. It is important to determine which country is a party to which treaty before deciding on the forum state for the arbitration.

The U.S. Congress has implemented the NY Convention in chapter 2 of the **Federal Arbitration Act (FAA)**. The FAA as originally adopted, 9 U.S.C. §§ 1-14, provides that arbitration agreements are valid and enforceable in the United States except "upon such grounds as exist at law or in equity for the revocation" of the contract. 9 U.S.C. § 2. It further provides for a stay of judicial proceedings pending the outcome of the arbitration:

> **9 U.S.C. § 3. Stay of proceedings where issue therein referable to arbitration**
> If any suit or proceeding be brought in any of the courts of the United States upon any issue referable to arbitration under an agreement in writing for such arbitration, the court in which such suit is pending, upon being satisfied that the issue involved in such suit or proceeding is referable to arbitration under such an agreement, shall on application of one of the parties stay the trial of the action until such arbitration has been had in accordance with the terms of the agreement, providing the applicant for the stay is not in default in proceeding with such arbitration.

Upon conclusion of the NY Convention, Congress added a second chapter to the FAA (§§ 201-08) to implement the Convention.

Foreign and "Not Domestic" Arbitral Awards

Under article 1 of the NY Convention, the first condition to a state's enforcement obligation of an arbitral award is that the award must be "foreign"; in other words, the Convention applies only to the recognition and enforcement of award rendered in a state other than where the recognition and enforcement of the award is sought.

The Convention does not require Ruritania to recognize or enforce an arbitral award rendered in Ruritania. Of course, most states do indeed recognize and enforce their own domestic arbitral awards, but that is not the purpose of the NY Convention. Its main purpose is to encourage the international enforcement of arbitral awards.

In addition, the NY Convention requires the enforcement of a foreign arbitral award if the award is considered "not domestic" by the enforcing state. In other words, if under a state's law, an arbitral award made in its territory is considered "not domestic" because only foreign parties were involved, or because the dispute was governed by a foreign law, or for any other reason, the courts of the same state in which the award was rendered must enforce that award under the Convention.

In determining whether an arbitral award is "domestic," most states place the greatest weight on the nationality of the parties, their residence, or the place where the transaction is deemed to have occurred. Belgium, Switzerland, and the United Kingdom are examples of states that consider an award is "foreign" if all of the parties to the dispute have a foreign nationality or residence. Other states, such as France, balance various factors such as the residence and nationality of the parties, the place of execution and performance of the contract, and the law governing the contractual relationship, to determine whether the award is foreign or domestic.

In the United States, an arbitration agreement between U.S. citizens is generally not considered to result in a "foreign" award unless the agreement is reasonably related to a foreign state:

9 U.S.C. § 202

An arbitration agreement or arbitral award arising out of a legal relationship, whether contractual or not, which is considered as commercial * * * falls under the Convention. An agreement or award arising out of such a relationship which is entirely between citizens of the United States shall be deemed not to fall under the Convention unless that relationship involves property located abroad, envisages performance or enforcement abroad, or has some other reasonable relation with one or more foreign states. For the purpose of this section a corporation is a citizen of the United States if it is incorporated or has its principal place of business in the United States.

The kinds of "reasonable relation" with a foreign state that would justify treating an arbitration between U.S. citizens or companies as "foreign" is not entirely clear from the statute or its legislative history. Such factors as the place of arbitration (the United States versus a foreign country), the payment of consideration in a foreign state, the law applied in the arbitration (foreign versus domestic), or the fact that one or more corporate parties to the agreement is headquartered in a foreign country may be relevant. See, e.g., *Fuller Co. v. Compagnie des Bauxites de Guinée*, 421 F. Supp. 938 (W.D. Pa. 1976).

This opens the door to the possibility of an arbitration in a foreign country not qualifying as "foreign" under the Convention, as the following case illustrates.

WILSON v. LIGNOTOCK U.S.A., INC.

U.S. District Court, Eastern District of Michigan, 1989
709 F. Supp. 797

ZATKOFF, District Judge.

This case involves an employment dispute. Plaintiff is a manufacturer's representative with extensive experience in the automotive industry. Defendants sell automotive parts manufactured in Europe. This lawsuit originated in Wayne County Circuit Court on September 8, 1988. Thereafter, defendants moved for summary disposition alleging the matter should be referred to arbitration. On January 20, 1989, the state court denied summary disposition finding the matter not subject to arbitration. On February 1, 1989, defendants removed the case to this Court alleging jurisdiction pursuant to 9 U.S.C. § 205, which provides for the removal of cases subject to the Convention on the Recognition and Enforcement of Foreign Arbitral Awards.

On February 6, 1989, defendants filed a motion to direct arbitration in Zurich, Switzerland. Plaintiff responded that removal was improper because the dispute is not subject to the Convention on the Recognition and Enforcement of Foreign Arbitral Awards ("Convention"), 9 U.S.C. § 201 *et seq*. Resolution of this matter rests upon a single legal issue: Is this dispute subject to arbitration under the Convention? If the answer to this question is yes, the matter must be referred to arbitration in Zurich, Switzerland. If the answer is no, the matter must be remanded to state court for lack of jurisdiction. * * *

There are four prerequisites to finding a dispute subject to arbitration under the Convention. They are:

> (1) the existence of a written agreement to arbitrate the subject matter of the dispute;
> (2) the agreement must provide for arbitration within a territory of a signatory to the Convention on Foreign Arbitration;
> (3) the agreement must arise out of a commercial relationship; and
> (4) the agreement must be with a party that is not an American citizen—or—the commercial relationship must have some reasonable relationship with one or more foreign states.

If the above prerequisites are satisfied, the court must order arbitration unless the agreement is found to be "null and void, inoperative or incapable of being performed."

Applying the facts of this case to the above cited criteria there is no question but that the first three criteria are satisfied and that the parties to the employment agreement are American citizens.* Thus, the pivotal questions are whether the commercial

---

*There is a written agreement to arbitrate this dispute. Plaintiff's employment contract provides:

> Any controversy arising from, or related to this Agreement which cannot

relationship has some reasonable relationship with one or more foreign states and if so, whether the agreement is null and void, inoperative or incapable of being performed.

Defendants submit the commercial relationship is reasonably related to a European venue because plaintiff's employment contract contemplated performance and enforcement abroad.

The Court disagrees. During the course of his employment, plaintiff made several trips to Europe for business purposes. However, these trips were not required under plaintiff's employment contract. To the contrary, the employment contract defines a single duty on the part of plaintiff to:

> build up a sales and marketing organization for the distribution of LIGNOTOCK products and services in the metropolitan Detroit area.

The contract clearly calls for performance within the United States. Lignotock, an American corporation, maintained offices in Michigan. Plaintiff's sales market existed exclusively in the United States. Although it was plaintiff's duty to sell products manufactured abroad, all sales contracts generated by plaintiff were made in Michigan. The products sold by plaintiff were eventually installed in the United States in vehicles sold in the United States. Plaintiff's trips to Europe were incidental to the performance of plaintiff's contractual duty of selling Lignotock products to U.S. automobile manufacturers.

Defendants' argument with respect to European enforcement of the employment agreement is equally unavailing. While the contract contemplates arbitration in Zurich, Switzerland, the arbitration provision of the employment contract unequivocally provides that enforcement of the arbitration award shall be pursuant to U.S. law:

> the execution of any judgment of the arbitrators shall be done in accordance with U.S. law. The parties of the Agreement are agreed that it is a question, in the case of an arbitral award, of an U.S. arbitral award.

Since the employment contract dictates that U.S. law shall govern the enforcement of any arbitration award and further dictates that performance of plaintiff's contractual duties shall be within the United States, the Court finds no reasonable relation between the commercial relationship existing between the litigants and Zurich, Switzerland, the proposed cite of arbitration. Accordingly, this Court finds the employment contract is not subject to the Convention and this Court lacks jurisdiction over this dispute.

Assuming, *arguendo*, that the commercial relationship at issue was reasonably related to Europe, the Court would nonetheless find the arbitration agreement incapable of being performed. The arbitration agreement requires that arbitration be conducted "... in accordance with the rules of the International Arbitration Court in Paris, France." By defendants' admission, no such entity exists anywhere in Europe, and

---

> be amicably settled, shall be determined by arbitration in Zurich, Switzerland....

[Switzerland] is a signatory to the Convention. Furthermore, an employment contract is considered a commercial relationship for purposes of the Convention. Thus, the first three prerequisites to finding the contract subject to the Convention are satisfied.

thus, no rules exist to govern this dispute.

CONCLUSION

Finding no jurisdiction over this matter, defendants' motion to direct arbitration is DENIED. * * *

Notes and Questions

1. Although the court seems to imply that the New York Convention is a U.S. statute codified at 9 U.S.C. §§ 201-08, U.S. law actually provides for the enforcement of the Convention; it does not reproduce the Convention itself.

2. What standard did the district court announce in determining whether the contractual choice of arbitration venue would be enforced? In your judgment, did the court apply that standard optimally? Would you consider the result in this case fair and reasonable? Why or why not?

3. In *Jones v. Sea Tow Serv. Freeport NY Inc.*, 30 F.3d 360 (2d Cir. 1994), a federal appellate court was confronted with a more tenuous connection between the parties, the services performed under the contract, and the choice of venue. In the case, a New York company that salvages wrecked sea vessels (a "salvor") had presented the owner of a yacht, which had capsized and been beached in Long Island, with a six-page salvage agreement providing for arbitration in London under the English law of salvage. When a dispute arose regarding the costs of salvaging the vessel, the salvor invoked the arbitration clause. In refusing to enforce the clause, the court held that, because a salvage operation between U.S. parties in U.S. territorial waters bore no reasonable relationship to England, arbitration in England would not be compelled.

4. A compromissory clause specifying arbitration under nonexistent rules or supervised by a nonexistent authority is called a **pathological clause**. The court in *Wilson v. Lignotock* asserted in *dicta* that the clause at issue was pathological because the arbitration rules referred to an organization that does not exist "anywhere in Europe." Does it seem clear to you that the clause stating "International Arbitration Court in Paris, France" was meant to designate the arbitral rules of the "ICC International Court of Arbitration in Paris, France?" Was the court looking for an excuse to refuse to enforce the clause, or was the intent of the employer genuinely unclear?

What if the *Wilson v. Lignotock* facts were reversed, and an arbitration were conducted in the United States entirely between foreign parties? It would not be a foreign award, but would it be domestic? Consider the following case.

BERGESEN v. JOSEPH MULLER CORP.

U.S. Court of Appeals for the Second Circuit, 1983
710 F.2d 928

CARDAMONE, Circuit Judge:

The question before us on this appeal is whether the 1958 Convention on the Recognition and Enforcement of Foreign Arbitral Awards, 21 U.S.T. 2517, T.I.A.S. No. 6997, 330 U.N.T.S. 38, is applicable to an award arising from an arbitration held in New York between two foreign entities. * * *

In resolving the question presented on this appeal, we are faced with the difficult task of construing the Convention. * * *

I

The facts are undisputed and may be briefly stated. Sigval Bergesen, a Norwegian shipowner, and Joseph Muller Corporation, a Swiss company, entered into three charter parties in 1969, 1970 and 1971. The 1969 and 1970 charters provided for the transportation of chemicals from the United States to Europe. The 1971 charter concerned the transportation of propylene from the Netherlands to Puerto Rico. Each charter party contained an arbitration clause providing for arbitration in New York, and the Chairman of the American Arbitration Association was given authority to resolve disputes in connection with the appointment of arbitrators.

In 1972, after disputes had arisen during the course of performing the 1970 and 1971 charters, Bergesen made a demand for arbitration of its claims for demurrage and shifting and port expenses. Muller denied liability and asserted counterclaims. The initial panel of arbitrators chosen by the parties was dissolved because of Muller's objections and a second panel was selected through the offices of the American Arbitration Association. This panel held hearings in 1976 and 1977 and rendered a written decision on December 14, 1978. It decided in favor of Bergesen, rejecting all of Muller's counterclaims save one. The net award to Bergesen was $61,406.09 with interest.

Bergesen then sought enforcement of its award in Switzerland where Muller was based. For over two years, Muller successfully resisted enforcement. On December 10, 1981, shortly before the expiration of the three-year limitations period provided in 9 U.S.C. § 207, Bergesen filed a petition in the United States District Court for the Southern District of New York to confirm the arbitration award. * * * [The district court confirmed Bergesen's award and held that the Convention applied to arbitration awards rendered in the United States involving foreign interests.]

On appeal from this $90,883.73 judgment, Muller contends that the Convention does not cover enforcement of the arbitration award made in the United States because it was neither territorially a "foreign" award nor an award "not considered as domestic" within the meaning of the Convention. Muller also claims that the reservations adopted by the United States in its accession to the Convention narrowed the scope of its application so as to exclude enforcement of this award in United States courts, that the statute implementing the treaty was not intended to cover awards rendered within the

United States, and finally, that Bergesen's petition to obtain enforcement was technically insufficient under the applicable requirements of the Convention.

II

Whether the Convention applies to a commercial arbitration award rendered in the United States is a question previously posed but left unresolved in this Court. The two district courts that have addressed the issue have reached opposite conclusions, with little in the way of analysis.

To resolve that issue we turn first to the Convention's history. * * *

A proposed draft of the 1958 Convention which was to govern the enforcement of foreign arbitral awards stated that it was to apply to arbitration awards rendered in a country other than the state where enforcement was sought. This proposal was controversial because the delegates were divided on whether it defined adequately what constituted a foreign award. On one side were ranged the countries of western Europe accustomed to civil law concepts; on the other side were the eastern European states and the common law nations. For example, several countries, including France, Italy and West Germany, objected to the proposal on the ground that a territorial criterion was not adequate to establish whether an award was foreign or domestic. These nations believed that the nationality of the parties, the subject of the dispute and the rules of arbitral procedure were factors to be taken into account in determining whether an award was foreign. In both France and West Germany, for example, the nationality of an award was determined by the law governing the procedure. Thus, an award rendered in London under German law was considered domestic when enforcement was attempted in Germany, and an award rendered in Paris under foreign law was considered foreign when enforcement was sought in France. As an alternative to the territorial concept, eight European nations proposed that the Convention "apply to the recognition and enforcement of arbitral awards other than those considered as domestic in the country in which they are relied upon." Eight other countries, including the United States, objected to this proposal, arguing that common law nations would not understand the distinction between foreign and domestic awards. These latter countries urged the delegates to adopt only the territorial criterion.

A working party composed of representatives from ten states to which the matter was referred recommended that both criteria be included. Thus, the Convention was to apply to awards made in a country other than the state where enforcement was sought as well as to awards not considered domestic in that state. The members of the Working Party representing the western European group agreed to this recommendation, provided that each nation would be allowed to exclude certain categories of awards rendered abroad. At the conclusion of the conference this exclusion was omitted, so that the text originally proposed by the Working Party was adopted as Article I of the Convention. A commentator noted that the Working Party's intent was to find a compromise formula which would restrict the territorial concept. The final action taken by the Convention appears to have had the opposite result, i.e., except as provided in paragraph 3, the first paragraph of Article I means that the Convention applies to all arbitral awards rendered in a country other than the state of enforcement, whether or not such awards may be regarded as domestic in that state; "*it also applies to all awards not considered as domestic in the state of enforcement, whether or not any of such awards may have been rendered in the territory of that state*." (emphasis supplied).

To assure accession to the Convention by a substantial number of nations, two reservations were included. They are set forth in Article I(3). The first provides that any nation "may on the basis of reciprocity declare that it will apply the Convention" only to those awards made in the territory of another contracting state. The second states that the Convention will apply only to differences arising out of legal relationships "considered as commercial under the national law" of the state declaring such a reservation. These reservations were included as a necessary recognition of the variety and diversity of the interests represented at the conference, as demonstrated, for example, by the statement of the delegate from Belgium that without any right of reservation his country would not accede.

III

With this background in mind, we turn to Muller's contentions regarding the scope of the Convention. The relevant portion of the Convention, Article I, is set forth in the margin.[2] The territorial concept expressed in the first sentence of Article I(1) presents little difficulty. Muller correctly urges that since the arbitral award in this case was made in New York and enforcement was sought in the United States, the award does not meet the territorial criterion. Simply put, it is not a foreign award as defined in Article I(1) because it was not rendered outside the nation where enforcement is sought.

Muller next contends that the award may not be considered a foreign award within the purview of the second sentence of Article I(1) because it fails to qualify as an award "not considered as domestic." Muller claims that the purpose of the "not considered as domestic" test was to provide for the enforcement of what it terms "stateless awards," i.e., those rendered in the territory where enforcement is sought but considered unenforceable because of some foreign component. This argument is unpersuasive since some countries favoring the provision desired it so as to preclude the enforcement of certain awards rendered abroad, not to enhance enforcement of awards rendered domestically.

Additionally, Muller urges a narrow reading of the Convention contrary to its intended purpose. The Convention did not define nondomestic awards. The definition appears to have been left out deliberately in order to cover as wide a variety of eligible awards as possible, while permitting the enforcing authority to supply its own definition of "nondomestic" in conformity with its own national law. Omitting the definition made it easier for those states championing the territorial concept to ratify the Convention while at the same time making the Convention more palatable in those states which espoused the view that the nationality of the award was to be determined by the law governing the arbitral procedure. We adopt the view that awards "not considered as domestic" denotes awards which are subject to the Convention not because made abroad, but because made within the legal framework of another country, e.g., pronounced in accordance with foreign law or involving parties domiciled or having their principal place of business outside the enforcing jurisdiction. We prefer this broader construction because it is more in line with the intended purpose of the treaty, which

[2] "This Convention shall apply to the recognition and enforcement of arbitral awards made in the territory of a State other than the State where the recognition and enforcement of such awards are sought, and arising out of differences between persons, whether physical or legal. It shall also apply to arbitral awards not considered as domestic awards in the State where their recognition and enforcement are sought."

was entered into to encourage the recognition and enforcement of international arbitration awards, see *Scherk v. Alberto Culver Co.*, 417 U.S. 506, 520 n.15 (1974). Applying that purpose to this case involving two foreign entities leads to the conclusion that this award is not domestic. * * *

V

We now turn to the argument that the implementing statute was not intended to cover awards rendered within the United States. Section 202 of Title 9 of the United States Code which is entitled "Agreement or award falling under the Convention," provides in relevant part:

> An agreement or award arising out of such a relationship which is entirely between citizens of the United States shall be deemed not to fall under the Convention unless that relationship involves property located abroad, envisages performance or enforcement abroad, or has some other reasonable relation with one or more foreign states.

The legislative history of this provision indicates that it was intended to ensure that "an agreement or award arising out of a legal relationship exclusively between citizens of the United States is not enforceable under the Convention in [United States] courts unless it has a reasonable relation with a foreign state." H.R.Rep. No. 91-1181, 91st Cong., 2d Sess. 2, *reprinted in* 1970 U.S.Code Cong. & Ad.News 3601, 3602. Inasmuch as it was apparently left to each state to define which awards were to be considered nondomestic, Congress spelled out its definition of that concept in section 202. Had Congress desired to exclude arbitral awards involving two foreign parties rendered within the United States from enforcement by our courts it could readily have done so. It did not.

Additional support for the view that awards rendered in the United States may qualify for enforcement under the Convention is found in the remaining sections of the implementing statute. It has been held that section 203 of the statute provides jurisdiction for disputes involving two aliens. Section 204 supplies venue for such an action and section 206 states that "[a] court having jurisdiction under this chapter may direct that arbitration be held ... at any place therein provided for, *whether that place is within or without the United States*" (emphasis supplied). It would be anomalous to hold that a district court could direct two aliens to arbitration within the United States under the statute, but that it could not enforce the resulting award under legislation which, in large part, was enacted for just that purpose.

Muller's further contention that it could not have been the aim of Congress to apply the Convention to this transaction because it would remove too broad a class of awards from enforcement under the Federal Arbitration Act, 9 U.S.C. §§ 1-13, is unpersuasive. That this particular award might also have been enforced under the Federal Arbitration Act is not significant. There is no reason to assume that Congress did not intend to provide overlapping coverage between the Convention and the Federal Arbitration Act. Similarly, Muller's argument that Bergesen only sought enforcement under the terms of the Convention because it has a longer statute of limitations than other laws under which Bergesen could have sued is irrelevant. Since the statutes overlap in this case Bergesen has more than one remedy available and may choose the most advantageous. * * *

The judgment is *affirmed*.

Notes and Questions

1. Under the court's reading of the NY Convention and implementing act, could an arbitration between foreign parties rendered under a foreign law in the United States *ever* qualify as a "domestic" award? Under what circumstances?

2. In *Lander Co. v. MMP Investments, Inc.*, 107 F.3d 476 (7th Cir. 1996), *cert. denied*, 522 U.S. 811 (1997), a federal appellate court extended the *Bergesen* holding further still. Two U.S. companies had entered into contracts for the distribution in Poland of shampoos and other products manufactured in the United States. The contract provided for arbitration of all disputes in New York City under the ICC Arbitration Rules, which the distributor invoked after the manufacturer terminated the contract. When the distributor lost the arbitration, it refused to pay the award and sought to resist judicial recognition of the award, arguing that the NY Convention did not apply to an arbitration between two U.S. companies conducted in the United States. The Seventh Circuit disagreed, observing that performance of the contract was to take place in a foreign country. This foreign nexus was sufficient, the court held, to qualify the arbitration award as "nondomestic."

Grounds for Resisting Enforcement of an Arbitral Award

Just as state parties to the Hague Convention on Choice of Court Agreements are permitted to refuse enfordcement of a foreign judgment on specified grounds, there are several bases on which the courts of a state party to the NY Convention are authorized to refuse to enforce a foreign arbitral award.

Article 1(3) of the NY Convention provides that state parties may declare that they will not enforce awards made in the territory of any state not a party to the Convention. Many states, including the United States and most European countries, have adopted this "reciprocity" reservation to avoid the possibility that their courts would enforce arbitral awards made in a country whose courts refuse to enforce arbitral awards rendered outside their own territory.

In addition, Article 5 sets forth six other grounds for refusing to enforce a foreign arbitral award. These include the following:

1. the agreement is invalid under the ***lex contractus*** (the law chosen by the parties to govern the contract);
2. the party against whom the arbitration agreement was invoked did

not receive proper notice or was otherwise unable to present its case through no fault of its own;

3. the award goes beyond the scope of the agreement to arbitrate, so that the arbitrator acted *ultra vires*;
4. the arbitral tribunal was not composed as provided in the arbitration agreement, or it did not follow the procedures in that agreement;
5. the award was set aside by a court of the state whose law applies to the agreement or a court of the state in which the award was rendered; or
6. the subject matter of the dispute is "not capable of settlement by arbitration" under the laws of the country where enforcement is sought, or allowing private dispute resolution of the dispute would otherwise be contrary to public policy.

Most of these exceptions are clear, but the last seems very broad. What kinds of disputes are not capable of settlement by arbitration?

In some states, such as Germany, private parties may not resolve claims relating to competition law violations through private arbitration because of the public interest in ensuring free competition, at least unless the arbitrator takes adequate account of German competition laws. Still other states, such as the Netherlands, disallow arbitration of claims alleging patent invalidity.* More generally, many states do not allow arbitration to enforce a contract that contemplates one or both parties committing a criminal act.

A private resolution of such disputes is very likely to exclude considerations of what is good for the public generally or for unrepresented third parties, and to focus exclusively on the representations and arguments of the parties to the arbitration. On the other hand, there is rarely any legal obstacle to private parties settling such disputes out of court, so the value of precluding arbitration is open to question. Many states, including Algeria, China, Malaysia, and the United States, have simply limited the scope of the NY Convention to "commercial" matters. This may create some problems of consistency, as what is considered a "commercial" dispute in some countries may be considered primarily political or religious in others.

U.S. courts have shown increasing comfort in allowing matters of public importance to be decided in private arbitration, especially in international cases. The leading case on this point is *Scherk v. Alberto-Culver Co.*, 417 U.S. 506 (1974). In that case, Alberto-Culver, a publicly-traded Illinois company had purchased German and Liechtenstein businesses from Fritz Scherk, a German businessman living in Switzerland. The purchase agreement provided for arbitration of any dispute to be conducted in Paris under Illinois law, was signed in Vienna, and was concluded in Geneva. Following the purchase, Alberto-Culver discovered that some of the trademarks transferred by Scherk as part of the

---

*See M.A. Smith et al., *Arbitration of Patent Infringement and Validity Issues Worldwide*, 19 HARV. J.L. & TECH. 299, 333, 339 (2006).

POLICY ISSUE
Why privilege private over public dispute settlement?

It may seem paradoxical that states have proven more ready to recognize and enforce the awards of foreign arbitration tribunals than foreign courts. After all, arbitrators are merely private actors appointed by the parties or their delegate. Courts, in contrast, are the official dispute resolution bodies of state governments.

One reason states are reluctant to recognize and enforce the rulings of foreign courts is precisely because arbitration is private and, therefore, voluntary. A party cannot be compelled to arbitrate a dispute unless it has previously agreed to the proceeding. Moreover, the parties themselves agree upon the scope and limitations of the arbitration, and on arbitral procedures to be employed. In contrast, a foreign court may assert jurisdiction over a business firm despite the firm's best effort to avoid it.

Another reason for greater acceptance of foreign arbitral awards is that municipal courts are more likely than private arbitrators to allow their state's policy interests to influence the judgment. States may be reluctant to commit to their own courts giving a foreign court *carte blanche* to impose a foreign nation's public policies on their own citizens.

Do these considerations seem compelling to you? If parties agree to the jurisdiction of a foreign court in their contract, is the court's resulting judgment less "voluntary" than the award of an arbitral tribunal agreed upon by the parties? For what reason would one expect a foreign judge to be more likely to superimpose his state of nationality's public policies on a dispute than a foreign arbitrator? Does this seem like a serious concern in general?

businesses sold had undisclosed encumbrances. Disregarding the arbitration clause, Alberto-Culver sued Scherk in an Illinois federal district court for fraud in violation of the 1934 Securities Exchange Act. That Act prohibits (among other things) the use of any instrumentality of interstate commerce to engage in deception with regard to a security in violation of Securities Exchange Commission regulations.

The district court denied Scherk's motion to dismiss based on the compromissory clause. The court noted that the Securities Exchange Act serves the public function of protecting private investors on the U.S. securities markets from fraud. If companies could privately resolve disputes relating to fraud on these markets, there is no guarantee that the public interest in honest and reliable markets would be vindicated or even considered. The Seventh Circuit affirmed, partly on the strength of earlier Supreme Court jurisprudence holding that a securities purchase agreement could not constrain the buyer to arbitrate disputes relating to U.S. securities law. On *certiorari*, however, the Supreme Court reversed, finding that the international aspects of the agreement between Scherk and Alberto-Culver rendered arbitration more acceptable:

> A parochial refusal by the courts of one country to enforce an international arbitration agreement would not only frustrate these purposes, but would invite unseemly and mutually destructive jockeying by the parties to secure tactical litigation advantages. In the present case, for example, it is not inconceivable that if Scherk had anticipated that Alberto-Culver would be able in this country to enjoin resort to arbitration he might have sought an order in France or some other country enjoining Alberto-Culver from proceeding with its litigation in the United States. Whatever recognition the courts of this country might ultimately have granted to the order of the foreign court, the dicey atmosphere of such a legal no-man's-land would surely damage the fabric of international commerce and trade, and imperil the willingness and ability of businessmen to enter into international commercial agreements.

Analogizing the case to *The Bremen v. Zapata Off-Shore Co.*, the Court focused on the convenience of the parties and uncertainty in international commerce that would result if a party could avoid arbitration merely by invoking a U.S. statute embodying an important public policy.

> An agreement to arbitrate before a specified tribunal is, in effect, a specialized kind of forum-selection clause that posits not only the *situs* of suit but also the procedure to be used in resolving the dispute. The invalidation of such an agreement in the case before us would not only allow the respondent to repudiate its solemn promise but would, as well, reflect a 'parochial concept that all disputes must be resolved under our laws and in our courts. . . . We cannot have trade and commerce in world markets and international waters exclusively on our terms, governed by our laws, and resolved in our courts.'

Despite language in the Securities Exchange Act prohibiting the use of private agreements to avoid U.S. securities laws, the Court held the dispute arbitrable.

Following *Scherk*, the Supreme Court applied the same reasoning to antitrust cases. In *Mitsubishi Motors Corp. v. Soler Chrysler-Plymouth, Inc.*, 473 U.S. 614 (1985), for example, the Court upheld an arbitration clause in an international distribution and sales agreement against an argument that the respondent's Sherman Act counterclaims rendered the dispute incapable of being arbitrated. According to the Court:

> The mere appearance of an antitrust dispute does not alone warrant invalidation of the selected forum on the undemonstrated assumption that the arbitration clause is tainted. A party resisting arbitration of course may

> attack directly the validity of the agreement to arbitrate. Moreover, the party may attempt to make a showing that would warrant setting aside the forum-selection clause—that the agreement was "[a]ffected by fraud, undue influence, or overweening bargaining power"; that "enforcement would be unreasonable and unjust"; or that proceedings "in the contractual forum will be so gravely difficult and inconvenient that [the resisting party] will for all practical purposes be deprived of his day in court." But absent such a showing—and none was attempted here—there is no basis for assuming the forum inadequate or its selection unfair.

The *Mitsubishi Motors* decision thus leaves the door open to arguing that the agreement containing the clause itself is incapable of arbitration because it is invalid due to fraud or antitrust injury.

Another Supreme Court challenge to the arbitrability of an international dispute with public policy implications related to the Carriage of Goods by Sea Act (COGSA), discussed in Chapter 4. COGSA, you may recall, nullifies terms in a bill of lading that would reduce the liability of the carrier for acts of negligence.

In *Vimar Seguros y Reaseguros, S.A. v. M/V Sky Reefer*, 515 U.S. 528 (1995), a company engaged to transport citrus from Morocco to the United States had included in the bill of lading a clause specifying that all disputes would be resolved by arbitration in Tokyo under Japanese law. When the purchaser of the shipped citrus discovered the goods had been seriously damaged in transit, the purchaser, together with the insurer, brought an action in the United States to recover damages on the bill of lading. They resisted enforcement of the arbitration clause, arguing that it was a contract of adhesion and contrary to COGSA's prohibition on terms that would reduce the carrier's liability because, first, arbitrating in a remote forum under law totally irrelevant to the transaction would be inconvenient and unfair, and second, there is no guarantee that the Japanese arbitral tribunal would apply COGSA's liability standards. In rejecting these arguments and upholding the arbitration clause, the Court held that neither the inconvenience of the forum nor the mere possibility that the arbitrators would refuse to apply COGSA would necessarily reduce the carrier's liability.

It would be unrealistic to portray the NY Convention as having rendered arbitration a perfectly reliable and impartial means of resolving international commercial disputes. Nonetheless, judicial enforcement of foreign commercial arbitration awards is much more consistent and impartial in international practice than te enforcement of foreign court judgments.

6 Foreign Investment Arbitration

Due to the absence of a global foreign investment treaty, there is a great deal of fragmentation within international standards of investment protection. As discussed in Chapter 2, there are many bilateral and regional treaties, each with its own rules on investment protection. These do overlap significantly, but they also diverge on some points. Most provide for some forum to resolve investment disputes. These various forums, although belonging to different treaty regimes, tend to cite each others' decisions regularly. Through cross-fertilization, they have developed a loosely coherent jurisprudence on the protection of international investments. Nonetheless, the fragmentation is sufficiently salient to justify separate discussions of each treaty type.

6.1 Bilateral Investment and Trade Treaties

Chapter 2 of this book discussed **bilateral investment treaties** (**BITs**), and **free trade agreements** (**FTAs**), which may contain an investment chapter resembling a BIT. Such agreements include substantive protections for foreign investors in investments between the treaty parties, such as a requirement of compensation in the event of expropriation, fair and equitable treatment, as well as full protection and security, for the investment and investor.

The 2012 **U.S. Model Bilateral Investment Treaty**, which closely resembles all but a few U.S. BITs with its trading partners, exemplifies these protections. But the U.S. Model BIT also includes complex dispute resolution provisions that empower foreign investors to compel arbitration against the host state.

This means that, through BITs and sometimes FTAs, the host state effectively grants a limited waiver of its sovereign immunity with respect to all foreign investors from the other state party to the treaty. You may recall that article 24(3) of the U.S. Model BIT provides specifically for three kinds of arbitration:

> Provided that six months have elapsed since the events giving rise to the claim, a claimant may submit a claim referred to in paragraph 1:
>
> (a) under the ICSID Convention and the ICSID Rules of Procedure for Arbitration Proceedings, provided that both the respondent and the non-disputing Party are parties to the ICSID Convention;
>
> (b) under the ICSID Additional Facility Rules, provided that either the respondent or the non-disputing Party is a party to the ICSID Convention;
>
> (c) under the UNCITRAL Arbitration Rules; or
>
> (d) if the claimant and respondent agree, to any other arbitration institution or under any other arbitration rules. * * *

The UNCITRAL Arbitration Rules were introduced earlier in this chapter. But what is ICSID, and why are its rules listed first?

6.2 ICSID Arbitration

The **International Centre for the Settlement of Investment Disputes** (**ICSID**) is an organ of the World Bank Group, an intergovernment

NOTE FROM THE FIELD
Being an International Litigator

Marco E. Schnabl, Esq.
Skadden, Arps, Slate, Meagher & Flom LLP

Dispute resolution is no longer an afterthought in international commercial relations: it is now a central element in planning and executing the transactions that have become commonplace among peoples of the most diverse backgrounds and nationalities. That is the field in which international litigators now play such central role.

All of the talents of the domestic litigator are required of the international litigator. But the international litigator is also concerned with certain unique matters, loosely grouped into three categories:

- Understanding and predicting the ways in which the domestic legal system interacts with the legal systems of other jurisdictions that may have the power to affect a client's commercial or legal position;
- Understanding the client's international transactions in order to identify what dispute-resolution risks are inherent in it, how best to minimize such risks, and, once those risks materialize, how best to conduct and control the resulting dispute resolution process; and
- Understanding the cultural, linguistic, legal, and historical aspects that underlie other legal systems that may potentially affect the relevant transaction or dispute.

To be an outstanding practitioner in this area you need the same skills any good litigator needs to excel at his/her craft. However, in addition, you must become conversant with legal concepts with which your domestic colleagues may seldom come to grips, including jurisdictional issues; foreign sovereign immunity and act of state concepts; the extraterritorial reach of U.S. and foreign laws; international service of process and discovery treaties and practices; treaties and national rules on the recognition and enforcement of foreign court judgments and arbitral awards; the various arbitration organizations, treaties, and rules; and the international law governing the formation and interpretation of treaties.

Also unlike your domestic counterparts, an international litigator needs to develop the ability to engage in legal combat with the demeanor and style of a diplomat or foreign envoy. You need to be able to "tone down" what you learn in domestic litigation and adapt it to other languages, cultures, and environments. You have to understand how other peoples and legal systems approach disputes and their resolution. You have to be sensitive to the interpersonal struggle that is dispute resolution when the "soldiers" (and other actors) in that struggle come from very different backgrounds that may not share any of the common assumptions that bind even opponents in purely domestic litigation or arbitration.

Marco E. Schnabl, J.D., M.Phil., M.S., Lic., is a retired partner of the global law firm Skadden Arps, based in its New York City office.

organization introduced in Chapter 7. ICSID was established to promote a climate of mutual confidence between host states and investors that would be conducive to international investment flows to developing countries. This organization was created by the **Convention on the Settlement of Investment Disputes Between States and Nationals of Other States** (**ICSID Convention**), 575 U.N.T.S. 159, which establishes a secretariat to facilitate the resolution of international investor-state disputes by conciliation or formal arbitration.

ICSID arbitration never takes place entirely between two private parties; instead, it is designed solely for disputes between private investors and the host states. The ICSID Convention was intended specifically to help build foreign direct investment in developing countries by guaranteeing that any state party to the ICSID Convention will agree in advance to the impartial arbitration of any dispute arising from a foreign investor's investment in the host state. This is because, by becoming a party to the ICSID Convention, a state commits to arbitrating some classes of disputes with foreign investors from other Convention parties.

Article 25 of the ICSID Convention defines the applicable arbitral jurisdiction:

> (1) The jurisdiction of the Centre shall extend to any legal dispute arising directly out of an investment, between a Contracting State * * * and a national of another Contracting State, which the parties to the dispute consent in writing to submit to the Center. * * *
>
> (2) 'National of another Contracting State' means:
>
> (a) any natural person who had the nationality of a Contracting State other than the State party to the dispute on the date on which the parties consented to submit such dispute to conciliation or arbitration as well as on the date on which the request was registered * * *; and
>
> (b) any juridical person which had the nationality of a Contracting State other than the State party to the dispute on the date on which the parties consented to submit such dispute to conciliation or arbitration and any juridical person which had the nationality of the Contracting State party to the dispute on that date and which, because of foreign control, the parties have agreed should be treated as a national of another Contracting State for the purposes of this Convention.

The consent requirement is usually fulfilled before the investment takes place, and it need not appear specifically in a contract between the investor and the host state. Instead, to invoke ICSID arbitration against a state party to the ICSID Convention, an investor is usually able to rely on:

1. a BIT, FTA, or other treaty committing the state to arbitrating the relevant class of investment disputes with foreign investors;
2. a specific agreement between the investor and host state to arbitrate the dispute; or
3. legislation in, or a declaration by, the host state committing itself to arbitrate the relevant class of investment disputes with investors. Article 25 of the Convention allows states unilaterally to publish a notification that a defined class of disputes may or may not be submitted to arbitration, such as those relating to a specific sector or industry.

ICSID itself does not arbitrate disputes. Instead, it has two sets of procedural rules to facilitate arbitration before qualified experts in international investment law. The **ICSID Arbitration Rules** apply when both the host state and investor state are parties to the ICSID Convention. If one of the three conditions listed above applies, ICSID is empowered to facilitate resolution of the dispute under its Arbitration Rules. When only the host state or investor state (not both) is a party to the Convention, the **ICSID Additional Facility Rules** are used. ICSID arbitration under the Arbitration Rules may only proceed if the dispute arises directly out of an international "investment." In contrast, the Additional Facility Rules may be used regardless of whether the dispute arises from an investment.

As of 2020, the ICSID Convention has 153 state parties, including all economically developed states except the Russian Federation, and the great majority of developing countries as well. Almost all modern bilateral and multilateral investment agreements authorize ICSID arbitration to resolve investment disputes. As a result, dozens of ICSID cases are pending resolution at any given time.

An ICSID award is final and binding on the parties. In practice, most ICSID awards are made public, and ICSID tribunals commonly cite these prior awards, as well as awards by *ad hoc* arbitration panels and mixed claims commissions, as sources of persuasive authority. Decisions are not generally subject to review by national courts, unlike other forms of arbitration. The ICSID Convention specifically requires all state parties, whether or not parties to the dispute, to recognize and enforce ICSID arbitral awards. Thus, if a host state refuses to honor an adverse arbitral award, the victorious investor may attach and execute on the host state's assets in any ICSID member state in the world. This makes ICSID arbitration a very powerful tool for both promoting foreign investment and protecting foreign investors. You will learn more about how ICSID arbitration works in Chapter 9, on planning for international disputes.

A. ICSID Arbitration Rules: Basic Provisions

The ICSID Arbitration Rules have much in common with the commercial arbitration rules of the ICC, UNCITRAL, and others, but they do differ in a few respects. ICSID arbitrations generally use a panel of three arbitrators. Each party appoints one arbitrator and proposes a third as the president of the tribunal. ICSID Arb. R. 3(1). If the parties cannot agree on the third arbitrator, the Chairman of the ICSID Administrative Council appoints the third. *Id.* rule 4.

One important safeguard to prevent the possibility of perceived bias is the rule prohibiting each disputing party from appointing an arbitrator of its own nationality without the consent of the other party. *Id.* rules 1(3), 3(1). For example, suppose a Freedonian national were to complain of the violation of BIT obligations with respect to his investment in Sylvania, and both Sylvania and Freedonia are parties to the ICSID Convention. The BIT provides for ICSID arbitration with a panel of three arbitrators. The Freedonian investor could not appoint a Freedonian arbitrator, and Sylvania could not appoint a Sylvanian arbitrator, without the other party's consent.

Upon appointment of a tribunal, the tribunal will consult with the parties and issue orders setting forth the procedures to be observed in the arbitration. Generally, a pre-hearing conference will follow in which the parties will stipulate the facts not in contention. The parties will then submit written memorials and counter-memorials pleading the facts and arguing for a favorable outcome under their respective interpretations of the applicable law. The "applicable law" is the one agreed upon by the parties, such as a BIT or FTA, supplemented by the rules of customary international law. If there is no BIT or FTA, or if the BIT or FTA so provides, the law of the host state will generally apply. ICSID Convention art. 42(1).

Article 47 of the ICSID Convention expressly authorizes arbitral tribunals to recommend provisional measures to preserve the rights of either party. ICSID tribunals have interpreted these recommendations as "legally compulsory."* Arbitration rule 39 makes clear that the tribunal may order provisional measures either upon the motion of a party or *sua sponte*. Because articles 16 and 26 of the ICSID Convention provide that an ICSID arbitration panel will be the exclusive mode of dispute resolution between the host state and the foreign investor, there is usually no expectation that the parties will resort to courts for provisional measures in addition to, or instead of, the ICSID tribunal. If a party does resort to courts—for example, if a host state commences an action in its own courts against the investor, or if the investor initiates an action in the courts of a third state—one provisional measure the ICSID tribunal might adopt would be to request the litigating party to cease pursuing parallel court litigation.

In *Maritime International Nominees Establishment (MINE) v. Guinea*, Trib. de Première Instance, Geneva, Judgment of Mar. 13, 1986, 1 ICSID REV. 383 (1986), a Swiss trial court confronted just such a situation. The defendant,

**Tokios Tokelės v. Ukraine*, ICSID Case No. ARB/02/18, Proc. Order of July 1, 2003, 11 ICSID REP. 310 (2007).

the government of the Republic of Guinea, had entered into a joint venture (JV) contract in 1971 with the plaintiff, MINE, a Liechtenstein company, to arrange the transportation and sale of bauxite mined in Guinea to purchasers around the world. The JV contracts included agreements to submit all disputes to ICSID arbitration. When the JV company proved unable to secure transportation for the bauxite, the collaboration broke down and the parties arbitrated voluntarily before a panel convened by the American Arbitration Association, which rendered an award favoring MINE in 1980. However, MINE then initiated ICSID arbitration in 1984. During this time, MINE applied to a Swiss trial court for interim enforcement of the AAA arbitral award under the New York Convention.

In dismissing MINE's request for provisional measures, the Swiss court first noted that Switzerland was a party to the ICSID Convention, and that the Convention was incorporated into Swiss law. The court then observed that article 26 of the ICSID Convention provides in relevant part that "[c]onsent of the parties to arbitration under this Convention shall, unless otherwise stated, be deemed consent to such arbitration to the exclusion of any other remedy." The ICSID tribunal before which the parties were then arbitrating had already held that MINE's request for provisional measures directed to the Swiss court violated article 26 of the ICSID Convention and had granted Guinea provisional relief by requesting that MINE withdraw from and discontinue the Swiss litigation. The Swiss court considered itself bound by this decision.

Even if the ICSID tribunal had not made such a ruling, the court would likely have dismissed the case as contrary to article 26. As for the AAA arbitral award, the court held that, by initiating ICSID litigation, MINE had effectively asserted that the AAA award had no binding effect. In other words, the court implicitly held that the exclusivity of ICSID arbitration is such that, by resorting to ICSID arbitration, MINE nullified any past arbitral award in its own favor.

Upon conclusion of an arbitration, the tribunal deliberates in private and arrives at a decision by a majority vote of all members. ICSID Convention art. 48 & rules 15-16. The award must be in writing and will typically include an allocation of costs between the parties at the tribunal's discretion. In most cases, the award is made publicly available, although some awards go unpublished by agreement of the parties under article 48(5) of the Convention.

Following the award, another unusual feature of ICSID arbitration becomes available. Article 50 of the ICSID Convention and chapter VII of the Arbitration Rules provide that either party may apply to the ICSID Secretary-General for an interpretation; revision in case of the discovery of some new and important fact after the issuance of the award; or even the annulment of the award on specified grounds, such as failure to state the reasoning on which the award was based or corruption of the tribunal. Such requests are, however, very rarely granted.

B. Exhaustion of Local Remedies

Under customary international law, an individual is generally required to "exhaust local remedies" in a state before seeking redress against that state in an international forum. Exhaustion of local remedies means pursuing all reasonably available remedies in the state's domestic legal system, such as litigation before municipal courts to final, nondiscretionary appeal. For example, the International Court of Justice will decline to hear a case brought by a claimant state on behalf of its own national until that national has sought and been denied a remedy in the respondent state's courts. See *Interhandel Case* (Switz. v. U.S.), Prelim. Objections, 1959 I.C.J. REP. 6, at 27.

To use ICSID arbitration, an investor is generally not required to exhaust local remedies, unless the relevant BIT or FTA requires it, or the host state has otherwise conditioned consent to arbitrate on exhaustion of local remedies. ICSID Convention art. 26; see also *Saipem SpA v. Bangladesh*, Award of June 30, 2009, ¶ 181, ICSID Case No. ARB/05/7, 48 I.L.M. 999 (2009) ("[E]xhaustion of local remedies does not constitute a substantive requirement of a finding of expropriation by a [host state's] court."). Some BITs or FTAs do require exhaustion of local remedies before invoking ICSID arbitration, however.

C. Attribution of Conduct to the Host State

One important question sometimes raised in investment disputes is whether the injury of which the investor complains can be attributed to the host state government. In general, the host state cannot be held liable for injuries caused by the acts of private third parties, even if those private acts deprive the investor of some or all of the benefit of the investment. For example, a consumer boycott of a foreign investor's products or services in the host state can severely undermine the value of the investment, but if the host state government did nothing to foment or prolong the boycott, it cannot be held responsible on a theory of indirect expropriation or denial of national treatment or fair and equitable treatment.

All state governments have various departments and agencies with varying levels of autonomy. In federal states, government functions may be exercised by regional or city governments rather than the national governments. Some governments also own, control, or have some economic interest in private corporations. Norway and the Russian Federation both have civil laws providing for government-owned private corporations with limited liability. Such companies may perform private functions, such as supplying electric power or manufacturing, or they may serve essentially public functions, such as promoting tourism or economic development. In addition, the state government may employ contractors who are not technically employed as government officials, but who exercise some government functions by delegation. Whether acts of private companies owned and persons employed by the host state may be attributed to the host state government sometimes raises difficult legal issues.

In *Tokios Tokelès v. Ukraine*, ICSID Case No. ARB/02/18, Decision of Apr. 29, 2004 (Juris.), 20 ICSID REV. 205 (2005), an arbitral tribunal constituted under the ICSID rules addressed this issue. The claimant was a Lithuanian company that had created a wholly owned subsidiary in Ukraine for the purpose of advertising, publishing, and printing in Ukraine and elsewhere. The claimant alleged that, after it had invested several million dollars in the subsidiary, the "governmental authorities" of Ukraine violated the Lithuania-Ukraine BIT through a series of tax investigations, seizures of documents, and lawsuits to invalidate the subsidiary's contracts, because the subsidiary had published a book that favorably portrayed a leading Ukrainian opposition politician.

Ukraine objected to the tribunal's jurisdiction on the ground that the alleged Ukrainian wrongdoers were "local governmental authorities in Kyiv" rather than the Ukrainian government, and that the Kyiv local authorities were not authorized to act on behalf of the government of Ukraine. In rejecting this objection to jurisdiction, the tribunal noted in dicta that the conduct of an "organ" of the state—which includes a territorial unit of the state—is attributable under international law to the state itself. Moreover, the tribunal noted that public international law also precludes the state from pleading its internal division of authorities as a defense to an international claim.

In *Salini Costruttori S.p.A. v. Morocco*, ICSID Case No. ARB/00/4, Decision of July 16, 2001 (Jurisdiction), 42 I.L.M. 609 (2003), an ICSID tribunal addressed a slightly different issue. There, the claimant had entered into a construction contract to work on a highway in Morocco for a private, limited liability company (ADM). After the conclusion of its construction performance, the claimant applied to the president of ADM, for additional payments. When the request was denied, the claimant initiated ICSID arbitration pursuant to a provision in the Italy-Morocco BIT.

The government of Morocco objected to the ICSID tribunal's jurisdiction on the ground that ADM was a private company whose acts could not be attributed to the government. The tribunal noted several factors, some relating to the structure of ADM and others relating to its function, that together weighed in favor of attributing ADM's actions to the Moroccan government:

- ADM's shares were majority owned by Moroccan government agencies;
- because of this majority ownership, the state controlled a majority of the seats on ADM's Board of Directors;
- the president and Chairman of the Board of ADM was the Moroccan Minister of Infrastructure; and
- the purpose of ADM was to fulfill a sovereign function—"the construction, maintenance and operation of the highways and communication routes" of the state.

Based on these factors, the tribunal concluded that there was no legal ground for distinguishing between ADM and the government of Morocco itself.

D. Withdrawal from the ICSID Convention

A host state that has consented to ICSID arbitration may at some point decide to withdraw its consent to future arbitrations. Despite the withdrawal, current foreign investors continue to benefit from the protection of the state consent to arbitrate. ICSID tribunals have consistently held that a withdrawal of consent to arbitrate investment disputes may not apply retroactively. See, e.g., *Alcoa Minerals of Jamaica v. Jamaica*, ICSID Case No. ARB/74/2, Decision of July 6, 1975, 4 Y.B. COMM. ARB. 206 (1979).

However, such a withdrawal acts as a signal to future foreign investors that the state probably intends to take future actions adverse to their interests. In 2007, Bolivia became the first state ever to withdraw from the ICSID Convention. In 2009, Ecuador followed suit, and in 2012, Venezuela joined them. Companies considering new investment in these states now lack an international institutional guarantee that an impartial and expert tribunal will protect their investments from arbitrary measures by the host state governments. How would this affect your advice to a client contemplating a foreign investment in such countries.

6.3 Human Rights Tribunals and Foreign Investment

Other sources of redress may be available in some investor-state disputes, and this is a factor that an international lawyer may consider in planning remedies in case problems arise.* Several international human rights instruments guarantee human rights to own property and to be free from arbitrary deprivation of that property. Most prominently, the right is announced in the Universal Declaration of Human Rights art. 17, G.A. Res. 217A(III), U.N. Doc. No. A/810 at 71 (1948), and several binding regional human rights treaties.

One tribunal called upon to address expropriation claims with increasing frequency is the **European Court of Human Rights**. The Court is an international court based in Strasbourg, France and part of an intergovernmental organization known as the **Council of Europe**. The Council of Europe is unrelated to the European Union, although all EU members belong to the Council of Europe.

As of 2020, the Council is composed of forty-seven European states—ranging from Iceland in the west to Russia in the east, and from Norway in the north to Spain, Georgia, and Turkey in the south—with a few nonvoting observer states, including Canada, Japan, Mexico, and the United States. All

*The most commonly used is public or private investment insurance. Regardless of whether the investor succeeds in obtaining compensation for loss caused by a breach of the host state's obligations, its insurer may determine that, notwithstanding a contrary decision by an arbitral tribunal or claims commission, the investor did suffer a compensable harm. The insurance contract rather than a treaty may govern this relationship.

members of the Council have adopted the Convention for the Protection of Fundamental Rights and Freedoms, commonly known as the **European Convention on Human Rights** (**ECHR**). The role of the Strasbourg Court is to decide cases in which individuals have complained of a violation of the human rights protections set forth in the ECHR and its various protocols.

Specifically, an individual or private organization that considers that a Council of Europe member state has violated any of its human rights guaranteed by the ECHR may apply to the court for a judgment and remedy. It must first exhaust local remedies in the state of which it complains.

Any individual or organization, including a business firm, of whatever nationality may file an application for relief with the Court with respect to a state measure that has affected the applicant personally. The acts of which the applicant complains must have been committed by a Council member state, usually within its own territory. The Strasbourg Court does not hear appeals from national courts; the applicant must apply directly to the court. The judgment of the Strasbourg Court is binding on the member state against which it is directed, and may include an injunction, compensation, a declaration that some state conduct violates its obligations under the ECHR, or some combination of these.

The ECHR itself provides no significant protection to private property. However, in 1952 the Council members negotiated a side agreement, **Protocol No. 1 to the European Convention on Human Rights** (E.T.S. No. 009). Protocol No. 1 adds three rights to the ECHR, the first of which is the right to protection of private property.

Article 1—Protection of property

> Every natural or legal person is entitled to the peaceful enjoyment of his possessions. No one shall be deprived of his possessions except in the public interest and subject to the conditions provided for by law and by the general principles of international law.
>
> The preceding provisions shall not, however, in any way impair the right of a State to enforce such laws as it deems necessary to control the use of property in accordance with the general interest or to secure the payment of taxes or other contributions or penalties.

Parties to the ECHR need not accede to Protocol No. 1, but forty-five of the forty-seven have done so as of 2020 (all but Monaco and Switzerland). Protocol No. 1, then, is at least theoretically a viable option for investors from any country in the world to seek compensation for direct or indirect deprivations of property in Europe. A large number of applications relating to alleged expropriations have been heard by the Court.

The Court's decisions on expropriation and other interference with private property employ a proportionality test that examines whether the host state struck "a fair balance * * * between the demands of the general interest of the community and the requirements of the protection of the individual's fundamental rights." *Sporrong & Lönnroth v. Sweden*, 5 E.H.R.R. 35, ¶ 1(c) (1983). If the host state imposes a burden on the individual investor that the court considers excessive relative to the benefit to the host state, the measure will run afoul of Protocol No. 1.

On the other hand, the Strasbourg Court's jurisprudence gives the state the benefit of a certain **margin of appreciation** in deciding which regulations are necessary or advisable for the public good and how much compensation to award for an expropriation. The proportionality test and margin of appreciation both have historically tended to weigh against a finding of compensable expropriation except in fairly clear cases of an excessive burden imposed on the property-owner and a benefit to the state questionable in nature or degree. However, the Court has increasingly awarded compensation for regulatory takings in recent years, and its standard for expropriation has now come to resemble the standard of customary international law adopted by international arbitral tribunals.

The protection of investments through human rights tribunals has not been widely replicated elsewhere in the world. Although there are some precedents in the Inter-American Court of Human Rights, the human right to the protection of property offers no reliable guarantee of foreign investment protection in the Africa, the Middle East, Asia, or Oceania.

Figure 9.5. The European Court of Human Rights in Strasbourg, France.

Key Vocabulary

Act of state doctrine
Acta iure gestionis
Acta iure imperii
Alternative dispute resolution (ADR)
Arbitration
Choice of law clause
Comity
Compétence de la compétence / Metajurisdiction
Compromis
Compromissory clause
Conciliation
Conflict of laws
Domesticated judgment
Domicile
European Convention on Human Rights (ECHR) & Protocol No. 1
European Court of Human Rights (ECtHR)
Expropriation
Fair and equitable treatment
Federal Arbitration Act (FAA)
Foreign Sovereign Immunities Act (FSIA)
Forum non conveniens
Forum selection clause
Full protection and security
Hague Convention on Choice of Court Agreements
ICSID Convention
ICSID Additional Facility Rules
ICSID Arbitration Rules
Indirect expropriation
International Centre for the Settlement of Investment Disputes (ICSID)
International Chamber of Commerce (ICC)
Jurisdiction to adjudicate
Jurisdiction to prescribe
Lex arbitri
Lex contractus
Lex fori
Mediation
New York Convention on the Recognition and Enforcement of Foreign Arbitral Awards
Pathological arbitration clause
Prescriptive jurisdiction
Private international law
Second Hickenlooper Amendment
Sovereign immunity
Uniform Foreign-Country Money Judgments Recognition Act
UN Commission on International Trade Law (UNCITRAL)
U.S. Model BIT
World Bank Group

Practice Exercises

#1 Which Forum, Which Law?

D'arcy Corp. is a popular multinational clothing retail chain that operates out of its headquarters in Niagara Falls, New York. D'arcy licenses its trademarks and sells its "I LUV NYC" line of clothing through independent franchisees in the United States and Canada. Recently, D'arcy decided to take steps toward seeking potential franchisees in Europe. D'arcy has already set up a subsidiary corporation in Greece (D'arcy Europa SA) to handle its European licensing and distribution operations, and appointed Douglass as the Chief Executive Officer.

D'arcy had no immediate plans to begin franchise operations in Europe, but an unfortunate miscommunication occurred between Douglass and D'arcy's Chief Financial Officer, Sylvester, in which Douglass erroneously believed Sylvester wished him to begin franchise operations. Douglass accordingly entered into a franchise agreement on behalf of D'arcy Europa with a local Cypriot entrepreneur, Anna Cyrilla, using D'arcy's standard franchise agreement. Anna has already set up a D'arcy store in Cyprus. More unfortunately still, Douglass, lacking experience in international business law, did not consult a lawyer before concluding the agreement.

The franchise agreement contains the following provision:

> 81. The law governing this agreement and any dispute arising from or related to this agreement shall be the law of the state of New York. The courts of New York shall have exclusive jurisdiction over any claim, dispute, or controversy arising from or relating to this agreement.

Sylvester now seeks your counsel on the following questions:

(a) Is the forum selection and choice of law clause enforceable in the United States? What facts might pose obstacles to its enforcement?

(b) If a dispute arose between Anna and D'arcy Europa, is there a serious risk that a court in New York might dismiss the case based on *forum non conveniens*?

(c) If Anna filed a lawsuit against D'arcy Europa in Cyprus before D'arcy Europa commenced litigation in New York, would a Cyprus court be required to stay or dismiss the case immediately in deference to the forum selection clause? Under what circumstances?

(d) If a Cyprus court held against D'arcy Europa and awarded monetary compensation to a plaintiff despite the forum selection clause, would a New York court recognize and enforce the award against D'arcy Europa?

#2 Planning for a Foreign Government Contract

The United States is a party to a bilateral investment treaty with Freedonia that is substantially identical to the U.S. Model BIT. Your client, International Duty-Free Enterprises (IDFE), is a Delaware corporation with its head office in Florida. IDFE has recently won a bid to develop a shopping mall inside Spaulding International Airport in the capital of Freedonia. The airport is owned and operated by a corporation wholly owned and controlled by the government of Freedonia, Firefly Industries Corp. (FIC). IDFE has requested your advice regarding the possibility of FIC failing to perform its portion of the airport development agreement. The agreement contains no forum selection or choice of law clause. Freedonia is a party to the Hague Convention on Choice of Court Agreements. Advise IDFE on the following questions:

(a) If IDFE were to bring an action in a Florida court against FIC, assuming a Florida court could assert personal jurisdiction over FIC, could FIC have the lawsuit dismissed based on its sovereign ownership? Why or why not?

(b) What problems might FIC encounter in enforcing a judgment obtained against FIC in a Florida court?

(c) Suppose the Florida court declined jurisdiction over the dispute based on FIC's sovereign immunity, and Freedonian courts did the same. Does IDFE have any alternative dispute resolution options based on the fact described?

(d) Suppose you could renegotiate the agreement between IDFE and FIC from the beginning. Draft three different forum selection clauses that would be enforceable and that FIC might realistically be willing to accept.

#3 Choices for Resolving an International Dispute

You recently represented Popeye's Olive Oil Co. (Popeye's), an Illinois food products distributor, in its negotiations with a Spanish supplier—Comidas Wimpidas S.L.—of olives, olive products, and cheese that Popeye's intended to distribute in the United States. After several months of satisfactory performance, however, Popeye's has begun complaining that Wimpidas had repeatedly failed to preserve its cheese shipments against spoilage in packing and arranging shipping. Although Popeye's has complained, the spoiled cheese shipments continue. Popeye's is satisfied with the quality of Wimpidas' other products and does not wish to terminate the relationship, but it believes itself entitled to refunds for the spoiled cheese shipments and insists that Wimpidas take greater care in future shipments. Wimpidas has thus far proved impervious to persuasion.

Popeye's seeks your advice on how to approach Wimpidas with stronger demands. Popeye's sales agreement with Wimpidas provides that the courts of La Rioja, Spain will have exclusive jurisdiction over any dispute arising under the contract. Popeye's has four main reasons for not invoking the dispute resolution clause of the contract: (1) the unfamiliarity of the Spanish judicial system, (2) the necessity of conducting proceedings in Spanish there, (3) the great distance between Illinois and Spain, and (4) Popeye's desire to maintain friendly relations with Wimpidas, which public litigation before a court would likely harm.

Bearing in mind that Spain is a party to the New York Convention on the Recognition and Enforcement of Foreign Arbitral Awards, write a memorandum to Popeye's answering the following questions:

(a) What are the advantages and disadvantages of seeking mediation or conciliation of the dispute? How might Popeye's find a suitable neutral?

(b) If mediation should fail, is it possible to arbitrate the dispute? If so, what are the advantages and disadvantages of arbitration compared with litigation? What are some of Popeye's options in terms of supervising authorities and choice of procedural rules?

(c) The local government of La Rioja, an autonomous province in Spain, has expressed interest in purchasing a majority stake in Wimpidas. If this does occur, how will it affect Popeye's ability to enforce a *compromis* executed by both parties? To enforce an arbitral award?

(d) If Wimpidas insists on arbitration in Spain, and Wimpidas wins an award against Popeye's, what arguments are available to Popeye's to resist the enforcement in the United States? If Popeye's prevails, what arguments are available to Wimpidas to resist enforcement in Spain?

#4 Drafting an International Commercial Arbitration Clause

You are incorporating an arbitration clause into an international distribution and license agreement. List each of the variables that the arbitration agreement should ideally resolve.

Multiple Choice Questions

1. In which of the following scenarios would the legislature of Osterlich definitely ***not*** be legitimately exercising prescriptive jurisdiction under international law? The legislature adopts a law:

(a) forbidding any person, anywhere in the world, from attempting to monopolize Osterlich markets.
(b) forbidding citizens of Osterlich, including those permanently resident in other countries, from selling alcohol anywhere in the world.
(c) requiring non-citizens of Osterlich to pay income taxes while visiting or resident in Osterlich.
(d) forbidding any person, anywhere in the world, from refusing to do business with an Osterlich business firm.
(e) forbidding any person, anywhere in the world, from registering an Osterlich domain name on the Internet unless they are resident in Osterlich.

2. True or false?: In the absence of a contractual choice of forum clause, the doctrine of *forum non conveniens* authorizes the court chosen by the plaintiff to decline to hear a case over which the court has jurisdiction.

3. Which of the following was ***not*** a factor that, according to the U.S. Supreme Court, weighed in favor of dismissing the case in *M/S Bremen v. Zapata Off-Shore Co.*?

(a) The courts of the chosen forum are adequately neutral and expert in the subject matter of the dispute.
(b) The parties were not attempting to oust U.S. courts of their legitimate jurisdiction.
(c) The relevant contract was negotiated by experienced and sophisticated business actors in an arm's length transaction.
(d) The subject matter of the case is international in nature.
(e) The contractual choice of forum is not so inconvenient that it deprives the defendant of a reasonable chance to present its case.

4. Freedonia and Smalldonia are both parties to the Hague Convention on Choice of Court Agreements. Freesport Enterprises is a Freedonian corporation that owns the broadcasting and intellectual property rights of a popular Freedonian soccer team, Freedonia United. Freesport owns a subsidiary corporation in Smalldonia, Freesmallco. Freesmallco owns the broadcasting and IP rights of Freedonia United in Smalldonia. Freesmallco entered into a trademark license agreement with Smalldistrib, a Smalldonian partnership that manufactures sports-related clothing and equipment. Under the agreement, Freesmallco authorizes Smalldistrib to produce soccer jerseys, shirts, and other gear bearing the FREEDONIA UNITED trademark in exchange for a 30% royalty on each authorized item sold by Smalldistrib.

The agreement includes a forum selection clause designating the courts of Freedonia has having sole jurisdiction over any case arising from or relating to the agreement, with the law governing the agreement to be law of Smalldonia. After a few years, Freesmallco terminated the license agreement prematurely, and Smalldistrib sued Freesmallco in a Freedonian court for breach of contract. After obtaining a favorable judgment, Smalldistrib seeks to enforce the judgment in Smalldonia. Which of the following statements explains why Smalldistrib cannot rely on the Hague Convention to enforce its judgment?

I. The agreement between the parties does not relate to subject matter appropriate for the Hague Convention.
II. Smalldistrib is trying to enforce a judgment rather than the choice of court agreement.
III. The agreement is between two parties resident in Smalldonia.
IV. The choice of forum in the agreement has no reasonable relationship to the parties or agreement.

(a) I and II only
(b) I and III only
(c) II and III only
(d) II and IV only
(e) III and IV only

5. According to the reasoning of the Second Circuit's majority opinion in *Eli Lilly do Brasil v. Federal Express*, which of the following describes the presumption in favor of the state's law that tends to validate the alleged contract under federal common law choice-of-law principles?

(a) The presumption is only decisive if the state whose law would validate the agreement has the most significant relationship to the parties and agreement.
(b) The presumption is only decisive if the state whose law would validate the agreement is the domicile of one of the parties to the agreement.
(c) The presumption is decisive if the state whose law would validate the agreement has the most significant relationship to the parties and agreement, and that state is also the domicile of one parties to the agreement.
(d) The presumption is decisive if the law of a state with inferior interest in the agreement would validate the agreement, and the entire agrement might be invalidated by the application of the law of the state with a superior interest.
(e) The presumption is decisive if the law of a state with inferior interest in the agreement would validate the entire agreement, and any clause of the agrement might be invalidated by the application of the law of the state with a superior interest.

6. Your client is Zombie Technologies, Inc., a Ruritanian corporation that has a software development agreement with Chodorow PLC, a California tax and accounting firm. Under the agreement, Zombie agreed to design and publish Chodorow's cloud-based software in exchange for periodic milestone payments. When Chodorow ceased paying Zombie, Zombie sued Chodorow in a Ruritanian court for breach of contract, in compliance with the agreement's choice of forum clause designating Ruritanian courts as the exclusive forum for resolving dispute between the parties. Chodorow appealed to the highest Ruritanian court and lost, but it has still refused to pay the Ruritanian judgment. Chodorow has no assets for execution of the judgment in Ruritania. Ruritania is a party to the Hague Convention on Choice of Court Agreements. California adopted the Uniform Foreign-Country Money Judgments Recognition Act in 2007. If Zombie seeks to recognize the Ruritanian judgment in a California court, the most probable outcome is which of the following, based only on the facts given?

    (a) The judgment will not be recognized, because no U.S. state has a general policy of recognizing foreign court judgments.
    (b) The judgment will not be recognized, because the United States is obligated to enforce only foreign arbitral awards, not court judgments, under the New York Convention on the Recognition and Enforcement of Foreign Arbitral Awards, to which it is a party.
    (c) The judgment will be recognized, but only if the California court finds that comity weighs in favor of recognition.
    (d) The judgment will be recognized, because the Hague Convention requires not only the enforcement of choice of forum clauses in business agreements, but of foreign money judgments arising from such agreements.
    (e) The judgment will be recognized, but only if the California court determines that none of the exceptions in the Uniform Act applies on the facts of the case.

7. True or false?: All countries now recognize that, when a state government or its agency engages in *acta iure gestionis*, the state or agency does not benefit from sovereign immunity with respect to that act.

8. Which of the following is ***not*** an exception to sovereign immunity under the Foreign Sovereign Immunities Act?

    (a) The action is directed against an agency or instrumentality of the foreign state having a separate legal personality, and not the state itself.
    (b) The action is based upon a commercial activity by the foreign state in the United States.
    (c) The action is based upon a commercial activity by the foreign state

outside of the United States, but causing a direct effect in the United States.

(d) The action relates to property taken by the foreign state in violation of international law, and that property (or any property exchanged for that property) is present in the United States.

(e) The action is brought by a private party to enforce the arbitration clause of its agreement with the foreign state in the United States or any state party to the New York Convention on the Recognition and Enforcement of Foreign Arbitral Awards.

9. In which of the following scenarios would the Act of State doctrine present a valid defense to an action against a foreign sovereign, the Sultanate of Mohamia, in a U.S. court?

(a) Mohamia entered into an agreement with United Rail Co., a U.S. mass transit developer, to build a public light rail system in Mohamia. After United Rail began performing on the agreement by surveying the site in Mohamia and designing the system, the Mohamian government decided that the rail was not economical and breached the contract.

(b) The Mohamian secret service engaged in program of espionage against a U.S. company, American Wealth Finance LLC, by hacking into the company's U.S. servers and copying account information of the company's clients. Mohamia denies the act, but claims that several Mohamian dissidents who threaten the national security of Mohamia have accounts at American Wealth Finance.

(c) The Mohamian Intellectual Property Office has denied a U.S. inventor a patent on a new blockbuster pharmaceutical in violation of the WTO Agreement on Trade-Related Aspects of Intellectual Property Rights.

(d) Mohamia expropriated the manufacturing plant in Mohamia of a U.S. investor, Unron Corp., without paying adequate compensation. Unron sought and was denied compensation in Mohamian courts, and no further action by Mohamia has followed.

(e) The Mohamian Office of Tourism Promotion rented an office in a commercial property in New York City for tourism promotion activities. The Office has fallen three months behind in its rent, and the landlord, a New York partnership, seeks to recover the back rent and evict the tenant.

10. Which of the following statements about international litigation and international commercial arbitration is most accurate?

(a) A forum selection clause choosing a foreign court is more likely to be enforceable than a forum selection clause choosing international arbitration.

(b) The judgment of a municipal court is more likely to be enforceable in a foreign court than the award of a foreign arbitral tribunal.

(c) Unlike in arbitration, litigation before a court allows the parties to compel the joinder of a necessary nonparty to the relevant agreements.
(d) Unlike litigation, international arbitration ensures the parties can avoid costly litigation and judicial appeals.
(e) Unlike litigation, arbitration allows the parties to agree in advance upon dispute resolution in a country other than where the relevant agreement will be performed.

11. True or false?: In most countries, under the principle of metajurisdiction, courts will not rule on the jurisdiction of an arbitral tribunal if the tribunal has already held that it has jurisdiction over the pending dispute.

12. Smalldonia and Freedonia are parties to Convention on the Recognition and Enforcement of Foreign Arbitral Awards. Osterlich is not. Buyco recently entered into a commercial contract to purchase 50,000 widgets from a supplier, Sellco. The widgets are situated in Sellco's state and will be shipped directly to Buyco in Buyco's state. The contract includes an arbitration clause. After a dispute arose, the parties arbitrated and an award was rendered in favor of Sellco. In which of the following scenarios is the arbitration award enforceable under the NY Convention, absent any other facts?

    I. Buyco is based in Smalldonia. Sellco is based in Freedonia. The arbitration award was rendered in Osterlich. Sellco seeks recognition and enforcement in Osterlich.
    II. Buyco is based in Smalldonia. Sellco is based in Freedonia. The arbitration award was rendered in Freedonia. Sellco seeks recognition and enforcement in Smalldonia.
    III. Buyco is based in Smalldonia. Sellco is based in Osterlich. The arbitration award was rendered in Freedonia. Sellco seeks recognition and enforcement in Osterlich.
    IV. Buyco and Sellco are both based in Smalldonia. The arbitration award was rendered in Freedonia. Sellco seeks recognition and enforcement in Smalldonia.

(a) I and II only
(b) I and III only
(c) II and III only
(d) I and IV only
(e) II and IV only

13. As interpreted by the Second Circuit in *Bergesen v. Joseph Muller Corp.*, the U.S. implementing act for the NY Convention authorizes the

enforcement in U.S. courts of arbitral awards rendered in the United States if:

(a) The arbitration was conducted solely between foreign parties.
(b) The arbitration involved at least one foreign party.
(c) The arbitrator was not a U.S. national.
(d) The underlying contract envisioned performance outside the United States.
(e) The arbitration was conducted under a foreign law or involved parties resident outside the United States.

14. Under article 5 of the NY Convention, which of the following is ***not*** a valid ground for a court to refuse to recognize and enforce a foreign arbitral award?

(a) The award exceeded the arbitral tribunal's powers under the *compromis*.
(b) The claimant failed to exhaust local remedies before invoking the arbitration clause.
(c) The respondent did not receive proper notice of the initiation of arbitration.
(d) The arbitral tribunal refused to apply the procedural rules chosen by the parties in the *compromis*.
(e) The underlying agreement is invalid under the law governing that agreement.

15. The United States and Zembia have a bilateral investment treaty (BIT) identical to the U.S. Model BIT. Both the United States and Zembia are parties to the ICSID Convention.

Greenfields Infrastructure, Inc. is a Delaware corporation that designs, engineers, and manufactures transportation infrastructure such as roads, bridges, and facilities. Two years ago, Greenfields entered into a contract with a Zembian corporation, Zemways PLC, under which Greenfields would construct and operate toll roads and bridges between three growing cities in Zembia for a period of 10 years. Zemways is a corporation 51% owned by the Quilty Transportation Administration, an agency of the Zembian township of Quilty. The other 49% of Zemways stock is publicly traded.

Under the agreement, Zemways was to lease the land for the construction of the roads and bridges to Greenfields and obtain all necessary government permits for Greenfields, in exchange for a one-time payment to Zemways of $4 million. Greenfields would keep the revenue from the tolls for the term of the agreement, then turn over all property and operations to Zemways. After successfully constructing and operating the roads and bridges for 2 years, Zemways revoked the leases, effectively forcing Greenfields to abandon control over the roads and bridges. Greenfields immediately invoked ICSID arbitration against Zemways. Zemways deny the tribunal's jurisdiction. What is the most likely disposition of the jurisdictional dispute?

(a) Zemways will prevail, because it is not a foreign government.
(b) Zemways will prevail, because Greenfields failed to exhaust local remedies as required by the ICSID Convention.
(c) Zemways will prevail, because, although it is majority owned by a government entity, it is merely a municipal government and not the national government.
(d) Greenfields will prevail, because Zemways satisfies the definition of a foreign government as developed in the international investment jurisprudence.
(e) Greenfields will prevail, because Zemways expropriated a foreign investment in violation of the BIT's minimum standards of protection.

16. True or false?: Under the existing jurisprudence of the European Court of Human Rights, business organizations have a human right to property that may be asserted in case of an expropriation of their investments in Europe.

Multiple Choice Answers

1. d
2. True
3. b
4. b
5. e
6. e
7. False
8. a
9. c
10. c
11. False
12. e
13. e
14. b
15. d
16. True

Chapter 10

Extraterritorial Business Regulation

What You Will Learn in This Chapter

The previous chapter outlined the different forms of jurisdiction as part of the discussion about planning for possible litigation in international business. Prescriptive jurisdiction was described as having three primary bases under international law: territoriality, nationality, and effects in the territory. In the U.S. legal system, this schema provides a general guide to the limits of statutory jurisdiction. However, the extent to which a state's statutes apply beyond the state's borders is a matter for the legislature to decide. In the United States, Congress has the authority to define the reach of its statutes beyond U.S. territory, and it has sometimes exercised this authority.

When the jurisdictional scope of an act of Congress is unclear, as it frequently is, courts have the task of interpreting the statute. The subject matters of some statutes affecting business firms tend to cross national borders more than others. For example, cross-border intellectual property and competition law issues tend to arise regularly in international business, whereas such issues in environmental protection are less common.

In this chapter, you will become familiar with some of the most important substantive statutes affecting business beyond U.S. borders. You have already learned about some such statutes. Certain economic and trade sanctions, for example, apply to U.S. nationals and residents acting outside the United States, and others apply to non-U.S. companies owned or controlled by U.S. persons. But there are many others.

Regardless of the subject matter of any given statute, courts have developed doctrines to assist in interpreting the jurisdictional reach of acts of Congress. The variability of statutory language means that some statutes will be interpreted to apply outside of the state's national territory, and others will not. The doctrines guide the interpretation of the statutory language.

Specifically, in this chapter, you will learn:

- the general principles used by U.S. courts to determine whether a statute applies solely within the United States, or beyond its territory as well;

- the jurisdictional reach of the most important U.S. statutes regulating international business, including employment antidiscrimination laws, IP laws, antitrust laws, and securities regulation; and
- how other countries may differ in their approaches to extraterritorial legislation.

1 Basic U.S. Principles of Prescriptive Jurisdiction

Every country has its own rules about the application of its law outside of its territory. In this chapter, we will focus primarily on the U.S. approach for two reasons. First, as a U.S. lawyer, federal statutes are those most likely to affect the business of your clients. Second, the United States is more aggressive in applying its laws outside its territory than are most countries.

Whether a federal law applies outside of U.S. territory depends on whether the legislature has the power and intention to reach beyond U.S. borders in regulating extraterritorial conduct. The *Restatement (Fourth) of the Foreign Relations Law of the United States* describes the general rule in the United States, which is similar to the rules practiced by many other states:

> **§ 402. United States Practice with Respect to Jurisdiction to Prescribe**
>
> (1) Subject to the constitutional limits set forth in § 403,* the United States exercises jurisdiction to prescribe law with respect to:
>
> (a) persons; property, and conduct within its territory;
>
> (b) conduct that has a substantial effect within its territory;
>
> (c) the conduct, interests, status, and relations of its nationals and residents outside its territory;
>
> (d) certain conduct outside its territory that harms its nationals; * * *
>
> (2) In exercising jurisdiction to prescribe, the United States takes account of the legitimate interests of other nations as a matter of prescriptive comity. * * *

The Restatement does not explain the circumstances under which Congress has exercised its power to prescribe conduct beyond U.S. borders. This omission is intentional; Congress exercises jurisdiction beyond U.S. territory on a statute-by-statute basis. There is no universal rule teaching business firms when U.S. law reaches their conduct outside the United States. Each statute must be examined and interpreted individually.

When a statute applies outside of a state's territory, it is said to have **extraterritorial** application. As discussed in Chapter 5, both U.S. export controls and some economic and trade sanctions apply not only to U.S. nationals beyond U.S. borders, but to the transfer of partially U.S.-origin goods outside

---

*Restatement § 403 itself does not actually set forth any constitutional limits. It merely states that no government agency may exceed its constitutional authority.

the United States or the activities of foreign persons outside the United States if owned or controlled by a U.S. person. These statutes and regulations have extraterritorial application on their face. But the jurisdictional reach of many statutes is not so clear.

One of the most important cases setting the ground rules for how courts should interpret statutory jurisdiction arose in the context of antidiscrimination in employment law. Our discussion will therefore begin with this subject.

2 Extraterritoriality and U.S. Antidiscrimination Law

As a party to multilateral human rights treaties, prominently the International Covenant on Civil and Political Rights and the International Convention on the Elimination of All Forms of Racial Discrimination, the United States is obligated to protect all persons within its territory and subject to its jurisdiction from discrimination based on race, ethnicity, sex, national origin, religion, or other status. ICCPR arts. 2-3, 26; CERD arts. 2, 5-6. As interpreted by the United Nations Human Rights Committee and the Committee on the Elimination of Racial Discrimination, these obligations extend to protection from discrimination in private employment.

Figure 10.1. Extraterritorial laws, such as the Helms-Burton Act of 1996, may offend foreign sensibilities, as this Cuban cartoon illustrates.

The United States fulfills part of these obligations through federal and state law. At the federal level, **Title VII** of the **Civil Rights Act of 1964**, 42 U.S.C. §§ 2000e *et seq.*, prohibits discrimination or harassment based on sex, race, color, national origin, or religion. The **Age Discrimination in Employment Act** (**ADEA**), 29 U.S.C. §§ 621 *et seq.*, prohibits discrimination on the basis of age against individuals age 40 or older. The **Americans with Disabilities Act** (**ADA**), 42 U.S.C. §§ 12103-213, prohibits discrimination against disabled persons and requires employers to make reasonable accommodations for the disabled. In addition, many U.S. states have laws prohibiting various forms of discrimination and harassment in employment practices.

U.S. antidiscrimination laws apply to all employees of any company operating in, or formed under the law of, a U.S. state, regardless of the employee's nationality. However, these statutes previously did not specify the extent to which they apply outside of U.S. territory.

2.1 The General Presumption Against Extraterritoriality

In 1991, the U.S. Supreme Court interpreted Title VII to apply only within the United States and declined to hear a U.S. citizen's claim of racial and religious discrimination against his U.S. employer, because the location where he performed his employment duties was in a foreign country. *Equal Employment Opportunity Comm'n v. Arabian American Oil Co.*, 499 U.S. 244 (1991) ("*EEOC v. Aramco*"). According to the Court:

> It is a longstanding principle of American law "that legislation of Congress, unless a contrary intent appears, is meant to apply only within the territorial jurisdiction of the United States." This "canon of construction * * * is a valid approach whereby unexpressed congressional intent may be ascertained." It serves to protect against unintended clashes between our laws and those of other nations which could result in international discord.
>
> In applying this rule of construction, we look to see whether "language in the [relevant Act] gives any indication of a congressional purpose to extend its coverage beyond places over which the United States has sovereignty or has some measure of legislative control." We assume that Congress legislates against the backdrop of the presumption against extraterritoriality. Therefore, unless there is "the affirmative intention of the Congress clearly expressed," we must presume it "is primarily concerned with domestic conditions."

Id. at 248 (citations omitted).

The Court found that the broad language of Title VII could be interpreted equally as applying solely within the United States or to both domestic and foreign operations. Applying the presumption, it held that the ambiguity should be resolved in favor of an exclusively territorial application.

2.2 Statutory Extraterritoriality and Employment Discrimination

Congress quickly reacted by amending federal antidiscrimination in employment laws to apply extraterritorially with respect to U.S. citizens, thereby overruling *EEOC v. Aramco*. U.S. employment laws now define protected "employees" to include U.S. citizens employed by a U.S. employer wherever in the world the employees work or reside. The ADA is representative:

> (f) The term "employee" means an individual employed by an employer. With respect to employment in a foreign country, such term includes an individual who is a citizen of the United States.

42 U.S.C. § 12111(4). The ADEA and Title VII have similar language. Insofar as they exclude foreign employment from the obligation not to discriminate, the exclusion applies only to "an employer with respect to the employment of aliens outside of any [U.S.] State." 42 U.S.C. § 2000e-1.

Thus, it would be unlawful for a U.S. company to discriminate against U.S. citizens who work in their foreign branch offices based on the listed grounds of Title VII, the ADA, or the ADEA. Discrimination against non-U.S. citizens employed in foreign states is not prohibited by U.S. law. However, it may well be prohibited in the country in which the non-U.S. employees work. Many countries are parties to international human rights treaties forbidden discrimination on a wide variety of grounds.

The U.S. antidiscrimination laws do not apply solely to U.S. employers. It is also possible that, in some circumstances, the employees of a separate foreign subsidiary of a U.S. company could benefit from the protections of these laws. Each act provides that a U.S. employer that "controls a corporation whose place of incorporation is a foreign country" will be presumed responsible for the foreign subsidiary's violations of U.S. employment laws. The standard of "control" is defined in general terms in the acts. Title VII, for example, provides:

> (3) For purposes of this subsection, the determination of whether an employer controls a corporation shall be based on—
> (A) the interrelation of operations;
> (B) the common management;
> (C) the centralized control of labor relations; and
> (D) the common ownership or financial control,
> of the employer and the corporation.

42 U.S.C. § 2000e-1(c)(3). Title VII, like the other U.S. anti-discrimination laws, contains no prohibition on discrimination against non-U.S. citizens by independent foreign subsidiaries operating outside the United States that are *not* controlled by a U.S. employer.

The task of balancing these factors to determine whether a U.S. employer "controls" a foreign company is left initially to the **Equal Employment**

Opportunity Commission (**EEOC**). The EEOC is an independent federal agency created by Title VII, 42 U.S.C. § 2000e-4, and is composed of five commissioners and a General Counsel, all appointed by the President and Senate. The EEOC is charged with formulating regulations for, and enforcing, Title VII, the ADA, the ADEA, and other employee protection laws.

The effect of U.S. antidiscrimination statutes is to ensure that U.S. citizens working anywhere in the world for a U.S. company (or a foreign company controlled by a U.S. company) have the right to bring an action in the United States seeking redress for prohibited discrimination prohibited. If a U.S. citizen working for a U.S. company at a job site in Ruritania, for example, perceives that she has been the victim of discrimination, she may file a charge with the EEOC and sue in the United States. Similarly, if a U.S. citizen working for a Sylvanian company "controlled" by a U.S. company believes he has been denied reasonable accommodations for his disability, he may do the same.

The EEOC has drafted policy guidance for U.S. employers to assist in determining whether a foreign employer is "controlled by" a U.S. person:

EEOC NOTICE NO. 915.002 (Oct. 20, 1993)

1. Assessing the Nationality of Employers

An initial question to be addressed in investigating charges of overseas discrimination * * * is whether the entity that allegedly discriminated—or that controls the entity that allegedly discriminated—is an American employer.

Neither Section 109 nor its legislative history sets forth an explicit test for determining the nationality of employers. As an initial matter, however, investigators should look to a company's place of incorporation in ascertaining an employer's nationality. Where a respondent is incorporated in the United States, it will typically be deemed to be an American employer because an entity that chooses to enjoy the legal and other benefits of being incorporated here must also take on the concomitant obligations. In many cases, therefore, the nationality of an entity will be relatively easy to discern.

Nonetheless, it may sometimes be necessary to examine factors beyond (or in lieu of) the employer's place of incorporation. For example, other factors will have to be weighed to assess the nationality of those entities (such as law firms or accounting partnerships) that are "employers" or other covered entities within the meaning of Title VII or the ADA, but that are not incorporated companies. Moreover, where the discriminating entity is incorporated outside the United States but has numerous contacts here, investigators may need to review the totality of that company's contacts with the United States to make a nationality termination.

Potentially relevant factors for assessing an entity's nationality include, but are not limited to: (a) the company's principal place of business, i.e., the place where primary factories, offices, or other facilities are located; (b) the nationality of dominant shareholders and/or those holding voting control; and (c) the nationality and location of management, i.e., of the officers and directors of the company. In situations such as those described in the above paragraph, a company may be found to be American if these factors suggest a significant connection to the United States. The factors must be considered on a case-by-case basis, and no one factor is determinative; generally, the greater the number of factors that demonstrate an entity's connection to the United States, the more reasonable a conclusion that it is an American employer.

> **Example:** Paperworks, Inc., is a 2000-employee corporation that is incorporated in the island of Bakeria. Paperworks' corporate headquarters is located in New York, its primary factories are located in Oregon and California, the vast majority of its employees work in the United States, and its three principal shareholders are U.S. citizens. Paperworks also maintains distribution facilities in Europe, and Charging Party, an American citizen working for the Paperworks office in London, alleges that he was discharged from that office on the basis of his race. Based on its places of business and the identity of its dominant shareholders, the Commission will most likely find Paperworks to be an American corporation despite the fact that it is incorporated outside the United States. The Commission would then be able to assert jurisdiction over Charging Party's claim of discrimination in London.

2. Assessing "Control" by an American Employer

Even if an entity is not itself American, its discriminatory conduct overseas will be covered if it is "controlled" by an American employer. * * * Section 109 sets forth four factors to be considered in assessing whether such control exists. Those factors are: (a) the interrelation of operations; (b) the common management; (c) the centralized control of labor relations; and (d) the common ownership or financial control of the employer and the foreign corporation.

The factors identified in Section 109 are the same as those relied upon by the Commission for determining when two or more entities (whether foreign or domestic) may be treated as an integrated enterprise or a single employer. * * *

One case that discusses the integrated enterprise concept specifically in the context of a Title VII claim against a foreign subsidiary of an American parent is *Lavrov v. NCR Corp.*, 600 F. Supp. 923 (S.D. Ohio 1984). Relying on the four factors now incorporated into Section 109, the *Lavrov* court found that there was sufficient evidence of the possible interrelationship of the American parent and its foreign subsidiary to justify a trial on the question. The court first determined that the foreign entity, which was a wholly owned subsidiary of the American company, shared common ownership with it. The court treated as relevant evidence of the centralization of labor relations the facts that the American company instituted corporation-wide personnel policies; that certain personnel decisions with regard to individual employees required approval by the American company; and that the foreign subsidiary was not authorized to change any remuneration plans, benefits, or operating conditions without prior approval of its American parent. The court also pointed to the American company's appointment of management members of the foreign subsidiary's board, and to the foreign company's function to market products assigned by the American company, as factors relevant to assessing, respectively, the commonality of management and the interrelationship of operations of the two companies.

In discussing the evidence it found relevant, the *Lavrov* court also indicated that "'all four criteria [for assessing integrated status] need not be present in all cases'" and that "'the presence of any single factor in the Title VII context is not conclusive.'" 600 F. Supp. at 927. The determination of whether nominally separate entities are an integrated enterprise will depend on the facts of each case.

> **Example:** Charging Party (CP), an American citizen who is hearing impaired, alleges that he was discriminatorily terminated from his job in the country of Tangeria by Tangoods, a 200-person firm incorporated in Tangeria with offices only in that country. Tangoods was created by a 2000-employee American company, Amerigoods, to supervise international marketing of Amerigoods' products. Amerigoods owns 25% of the stock of Tangoods. Some of the members of Tangoods' board of directors are officers and/or board members of Amerigoods, but the two companies have distinct corporate forms, have entirely separate staffs, and perform all management and operational functions, e.g., payroll, hiring, and firing, independently. Amerigoods sets corporate policies, applicable to Tangoods, on such matters as acceptable employee behavior, employee sales quotas, amounts of annual and sick leave, salary scales, severance pay, and pension accrual and payout. Amerigoods representatives inspect the Tangoods facilities on numerous regularly scheduled visits each year, and dictate changes in marketing and sales strategy as necessary for continued sales of Amerigoods' products.
>
> Because it is incorporated and does business exclusively outside the United States, Tangoods is not itself an American employer. It may, however, be controlled by an American employer. Amerigoods is a partial owner of Tangoods. In addition, there is substantial interrelationship of operations between the two companies; Tangoods exists and performs services principally for the benefit of Amerigoods, and Amerigoods representatives monitor and modify Tangoods' operations to maintain sales. Although personnel operations are handled separately and there does not appear to be much overlap in managerial personnel, Amerigoods does set uniform corporate policies on some matters related to labor relations. There is also some overlap in board membership between the two companies. Under such circumstances, the Commission would consider Tangoods to be "controlled" by Amerigoods, and would assert jurisdiction over CP's charge challenging his termination.

Thus, if the alleged discrimination is perpetrated by an entity that is found to be American or to be controlled by an American employer, the Commission may assert jurisdiction over the charge and investigate the merits of the allegation. It is important to remember that this jurisdictional determination is to be made independently of any resolution of the merits of the underlying charge. * * *

2.3 The Foreign Laws Defense

Title VII, the ADA, and the ADEA also include a defense for employers whose compliance with U.S. employment laws would violate a foreign law. Title VII, for example, states:

> (b) Compliance with statute as violative of foreign law
> It shall not be unlawful * * * for an employer (or a corporation controlled by an employer) * * * to take any action otherwise prohibited by such section, with respect to an employee in a workplace in a foreign country if compliance with such section would cause such employer (or such corporation), such organization, such agency, or such committee to violate the law of the foreign country in which such workplace is located.

42 U.S.C. § 2000e-1(b). As with the question of "control," the determination of when a violation of U.S. employment laws is necessary to avoid violating a conflicting foreign law is a matter to be determined by the EEOC and courts.

The **foreign laws defense** is intended to solve the problem of conflicting U.S. and foreign laws regarding discrimination in employment. This may seem counterintuitive. After all, the human rights treaties mentioned earlier forbid discrimination based on sex, race, and other characteristics. The great majority of countries are parties to these (and other*) human rights treaties.

Unfortunately, not every state is in compliance with its international human rights obligations. For example, in Afghanistan, women are forbidden to work the same night hours as men and are barred from some industries. In Saudi Arabia, women are prohibited from working in the same workplace as men. In such cases, compliance with U.S. antidiscrimination law may cause the employer to run afoul of foreign employment law, and *vice versa*.

But when does the defense apply? Here, too, the EEOC has offered policy guidance:

*For example, the UN Convention on the Elimination of All Forms of Discrimination Against Women prohibits discrimination based on sex or gender; the International Covenant on Economic, Social and Cultural Rights prohibits discrimination based on a wide spectrum of grounds. Other multilateral treaties address discrimination directly as well, such as Article 5 of the Convention on the Rights of Persons with Disabilities. In addition, many states in Europe, the Americas, and Africa are parties to regional human rights treaties with strong prohibitions on discrimination. See generally Aaron X. Fellmeth, *Nondiscrimination as a Universal Human Right*, 34 YALE J. INT'L L. 588 (2009).

EEOC NOTICE NO. 915.002 (Oct. 20, 1993)

* * *

C. The "Foreign Laws Defense" of Section 109 of the Civil Rights Act of 1991

Section 109 makes clear that "it shall not be unlawful," under either Title VII or the ADA, for an employer to take otherwise prohibited action if compliance with either statute, with respect to an employee in a workplace in a foreign country, would cause an employer to violate the law of the foreign country in which the workplace is located.

Under this provision, a respondent must prove three elements to establish a foreign laws defense: that (1) the action is taken with respect to an employee in a workplace in a foreign country, where (2) compliance with Title VII or the ADA [and ADEA] would cause the respondent to violate the law of the foreign country, (3) in which the workplace is located. Each of the elements of the defense is discussed briefly below.
* * *

2. Violate the Law of the Foreign Country

a. Existence of a Law

An employer must next prove that compliance with Title VII or the ADA would "cause" it to "violate the law of the foreign country." Under this prong of the defense, a respondent must initially demonstrate that the source of authority on which it relies constitutes a foreign "law." * * * [T]he parameters of this element of the defense are uncertain.

The court in *Mahoney v. RFE/RL, Inc.*, 818 F. Supp. 1 (D.D.C. 1992), identified some such circumstances in a case involving the ADEA foreign laws defense. In *Mahoney*, the defendant, an American employer, terminated plaintiffs, U.S. citizens working in Germany, based on a union contract that expressly required mandatory retirement at age 65. Defendant first claimed that the union contract, and the German labor practices it incorporated, were German "laws" that would be violated were defendant forced to comply with the ADEA. The court rejected this argument, holding that the defendant's union contract, although "legally binding," was not "law" for purposes of the ADEA foreign laws defense; the mandatory retirement provision had not been mandated by the German government and did not have general applicability beyond the parties to the contract. Noting that "[t]he ADEA is a remedial statute and exceptions to it are to be construed narrowly," the court further held that foreign "[p]ractices and policies, even when embodied in contracts, are not 'laws'" for purposes of the defense.

The court also refused to treat as foreign "law" German court decisions enforcing the union contract. As noted by the court, the German court decisions

> did not hold that anything in *German* law compelled the decisions reached .... If overseas employers could avoid application of the ADEA simply by embedding an age-discriminatory provision in a contract, having a foreign court enforce the contract, and calling the court's decision "law," then the Act's extraterritorial provisions would be largely nullified, for employers could easily contract around the law.

Id. at 5. Although decided under the ADEA and applicable therefore to charges arising under that statute, the reasoning of *Mahoney* is equally applicable to analysis of the foreign laws defense under Title VII and the ADA (customs and preferences of host country do not justify gender discrimination against United States citizens).

b. "Cause" a Violation

Under the second prong of the foreign laws defense, an employer must also demonstrate that compliance with Title VII or the ADA would "cause" it to violate foreign law, i.e., that it is impossible to comply with both sets of requirements. Investigators should attempt to obtain copies of all documentary material that might be relevant in assessing the requirements of the foreign law, including the text of the law itself, and any available legislative history or case law interpreting it. In addition, investigators should consider the steps a respondent has taken or could take to avoid the conflict and to comply with Title VII or the ADA. *Compare Mahoney*, 818 F. Supp. at 5 (rejecting defendant's claim that it had done all it could to comply with the ADEA where it had not fully pursued possibility of changing union contract or of mediating mandatory retirement issue), *with* Commission Decision No. 85-10, CCH Employment Practices Guide ¶ 6851 (respondent not liable for refusing to hire woman for work overseas where it provided "authoritative" evidence that foreign law restricted employment of women and demonstrated that it had taken all possible steps to process her application despite foreign restrictions). The defense will be established only where compliance with Title VII or the ADA will inevitably lead to a violation of foreign law. * * *

> **Example:** A Casparian statute requires that, after the period of their pregnancy-related disability, new mothers be given six weeks paid leave for childcare purposes. In compliance with the law, R, a United States employer employing teachers of English in Caspar, provides its female employees with such paid leave. Charging Party, a male U.S. citizen employed by R in Caspar, challenges R's failure to provide him the six weeks' childcare leave when his wife gave birth to their first child. R asserts a foreign law defense based on the Casparian statute.
>
> R's foreign law defense would fail under the above facts. Title VII requires that childcare leave be granted, equally to male and female employees. Requiring R to meet this Title VII obligation would not, however, "cause" a violation of—or make it impossible for R to comply with—Casparian law. Although R is required by Casparian law to give paid childcare leave to female employees, Casparian law does not forbid R from offering such leave to male employees as well. R can meet the requirements of both Casparian law and of Title VII by offering paid childcare leave to new parents in its employ, without regard to their sex.

3. Where the Workplace is Located

The final element of a successful foreign laws defense is proof that the foreign laws involved are those of the country in which the charging party's workplace is (or, absent the discrimination, would be) located. The laws of the country in which an employer is headquartered or incorporated would not control for purposes of this element of the defense unless the charging party's workplace is also located in that country. * * *

3 Extraterritoriality and Competition Law

After *EEOC v. Aramco*, statutes with jurisdictional provisions phrased only in general and abstract terms would seem to have effect solely within U.S. territory. However, determining the jurisdictional scope of U.S. statutes is rarely so straightforward. One important test case for the presumption against extraterritoriality may be found in U.S. laws that protect competition in the marketplace, commonly known as antitrust law.

3.1 Jurisdictional Provisions of U.S. Antitrust Statutes

The oldest and most general U.S. antitrust law is the **Sherman Antitrust Act**. The Sherman Act forbids certain business arrangements that impair free competition in the marketplace. The actual provisions of the Sherman Act most frequently invoked are deceptively simple:

> **15 U.S.C. § 1. Trusts, etc., in restraint of trade illegal; penalty**
> Every contract, combination in the form of trust or otherwise, or conspiracy, in restraint of trade or commerce among the several States, or with foreign nations, is declared to be illegal. Every person who shall make any contract or engage in any combination or conspiracy hereby declared to be illegal shall be deemed guilty of a felony, and, on conviction thereof, shall be punished by fine not exceeding $100,000,000 if a corporation, or, if any other person, $1,000,000, or by imprisonment not exceeding 10 years, or by both said punishments, in the discretion of the court.
>
> **15 U.S.C. § 2. Monopolizing trade a felony; penalty**
> Every person who shall monopolize, or attempt to monopolize, or combine or conspire with any other person or persons, to monopolize any part of the trade or commerce among the several States, or with foreign nations, shall be deemed guilty of a felony, and, on conviction thereof, shall be punished by fine not exceeding $100,000,000 if a corporation, or, if any other person, $1,000,000, or by imprisonment not exceeding 10 years, or by both said punishments, in the discretion of the court.

Notice how Section 1 of the Sherman Act prohibits contracts and combinations in restraint, not only of U.S. domestic commerce, but of trade "with foreign nations" as well. Similarly, Section 2 prohibits attempts by any person to monopolize "any part of the trade or commerce * * * with foreign nations." A "person" is defined as follows:

> **15 U.S.C. § 7. "Person" or "persons" defined**
> The word "person", or "persons", wherever used in sections 1 to 7 of this title shall be deemed to include corporations and associations existing under or authorized by the laws of either the United States, the laws of any of the Territories, the laws of any State, or the laws of any foreign country.

Violations of the Sherman Act may be prosecuted as criminal offenses by the U.S. Department of Justice. Penalties for criminal violations of the Sherman Act include fines up to $100 million per violation and up to ten years imprisonment. The DoJ typically limits itself to prosecuting so-called *per se* violations of the Sherman Act. A ***per se* antitrust violation** is an act that is prohibited as a matter of law, subject to limited defenses, so that there is no need to prove actual anticompetitive effects on the market. Price fixing between competitors, for example, is a *per se* violation of the Sherman Act.

Antitrust violations may also trigger civil lawsuits by private persons injured by anticompetitive conduct. In a civil action, a plaintiff may recover treble damages and injunctive relief to prevent further violations of the Act. The jurisdictional reach of the Sherman Act is the same in both criminal and civil actions.

But what is that reach? A plain reading of the Act authorizes a criminal action against foreign corporations. Because the term "[e]very person" is all-inclusive and is not limited to "every U.S. citizen," a plain reading of the Act would authorize a criminal action against a foreign individual who engaged in prohibited behavior as well. Moreover, because sections 1 and 2 of the Act prohibit anticompetitive conduct in "trade or commerce . . . with foreign nations," it is possible to interpret the Act as reaching foreign conduct by foreign individuals that has no anticompetitive effect on U.S. markets.

3.2 Subject Matter Jurisdiction in Competition Law

A. Does the Conduct Affect U.S. Markets?

To foreclose such an interpretation, the Sherman Act was amended in 1982 by the addition of section 6a, commonly known as the **Foreign Trade Antitrust Improvements Act (FTAIA)**, 15 U.S.C. § 6a. The FTAIA was enacted to define the extraterritorial reach of the Sherman Act. Congress considered that the sole legitimate concern of antitrust law is the preservation of competition in the United States. Because Congress believed that certain kinds of foreign and export commerce would not injure U.S. competition, it exempted such conduct from antitrust scrutiny:

> **§ 6a. Conduct involving trade or commerce with foreign nations**
> Sections 1 to 7 of this title shall not apply to conduct involving trade or commerce (other than import trade or import commerce) with foreign nations unless—
> (1) such conduct has a direct, substantial, and reasonably foreseeable

effect—

(A) on trade or commerce which is not trade or commerce with foreign nations, or on import trade or import commerce with foreign nations; or

(B) on export trade or export commerce with foreign nations, of a person engaged in such trade or commerce in the United States; and

(2) such effect gives rise to a claim under the provisions of sections 1 to 7 of this title, other than this section.

If sections 1 to 7 of this title apply to such conduct only because of the operation of paragraph (1)(B), then sections 1 to 7 of this title shall apply to such conduct only for injury to export business in the United States.

Determining what kind of conduct has a "direct, substantial, and reasonably foreseeable effect" on U.S. domestic commerce or import trade, or on U.S. exporters, is not always easy. In the first place, unless foreign anticompetitive conduct is purposefully and effectively directed toward the United States, a policy decision must be made in drawing the line between the kinds of foreign

TRADE OR COMMERCE OTHER THAN . . . WHICH IS NOT . . .

The concept of "trade or commerce (other than import trade or import commerce) with foreign nations" that has an effect "on trade or commerce which is not trade or commerce with foreign nations, or on import trade or import commerce with foreign nations" may seem confusing. To understand how this might occur, consider an example.

Suppose two U.S. manufacturers, A Corp. and B Corp., are the world's largest suppliers of automotive tires. A and B agree to collude to fix prices on foreign sales of tires, but not on U.S. sales. This agreement restricts "trade or commerce (other than import trade or import commerce) with foreign nations," and so initially might seem exempt from U.S. antitrust scrutiny under the FTAIA.

Now further suppose that Z Auto Corp., a Zembian automobile manufacturer, purchases tires from A Corp. and incorporates them into its automobiles, which it then sells internationally, including many to the United States. Because the price fixing arrangement between A and B raises the price of a component of Z Auto's automobiles, and because this will inevitably raise the price of those automobiles sold on the U.S. market, U.S. purchasers of foreign automobiles will pay more for those automobiles than would occur in the absence of A and B's price fixing arrangement. This may well be a case of foreign anticompetitive conduct causing a "direct, substantial, and reasonably foreseeable effect" on import trade. This example illustrates how the international nature of much manufacturing can make seemingly foreign anticompetitive conduct have quite significant effects on U.S. markets.

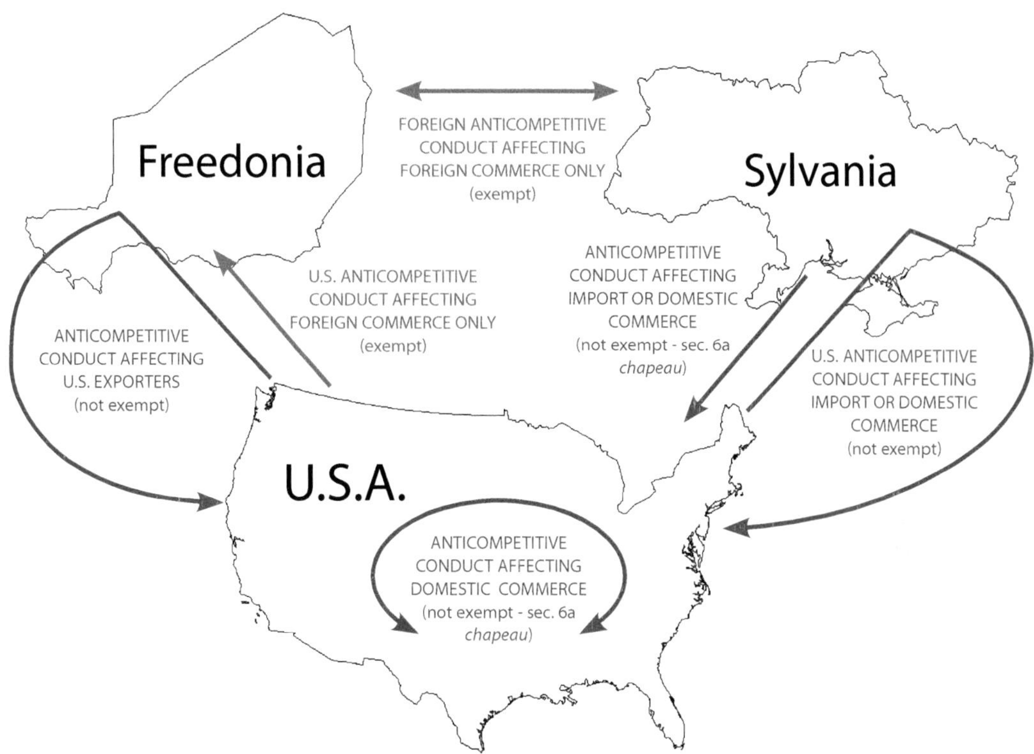

Figure 10.2. Schematic representation of anticompetitive conduct exempt from U.S. antitrust scrutiny under the FTAIA and other U.S. antitrust laws.

conduct the Sherman Act was intended to regulate and conduct beyond the scope of the Sherman Act. Moreover, the fact that foreign conduct does fall within the subject matter jurisdiction of the Sherman Act does not always mean that the court will exercise its jurisdiction.

B. International Comity

The concept of comity was introduced in Chapter 9, Part 3. A court will usually exercise its discretion to dismiss a case on comity grounds when, in its judgment, the interests of a foreign state in a case outweigh the interests of the United States. Comity is a principle of domestic law that has both judicial and legislative aspects. In the judicial context, a court might recognize and enforce the judgment of a foreign court if it considers the foreign judicial system impartial and fair both in general and in the case under consideration. In the legislative context, a court might use comity to interpret a U.S. statute not to reach conduct beyond U.S. borders under some circumstances.

The implications of comity are not always clear, however. The following case illustrates the difficulty of predicting how a court might apply a broad rule of comity in practice.

HARTFORD FIRE INSURANCE CO. v. CALIFORNIA

Supreme Court of the United States, 1993
509 U.S. 764

Justice SOUTER announced the judgment of the Court and delivered the opinion of the Court with respect to Parts I, II-A, III, and IV * * *.[2]

The Sherman Act makes every contract, combination, or conspiracy in unreasonable restraint of interstate or foreign commerce illegal. These consolidated cases present questions about the application of that Act to the insurance industry, both here and abroad. The plaintiffs (respondents here) allege that both domestic and foreign defendants (petitioners here) violated the Sherman Act by engaging in various conspiracies to affect the American insurance market. A group of * * * foreign defendants argues that the principle of international comity requires the District Court to refrain from exercising jurisdiction over certain claims against it. * * *

I

The two petitions before us stem from consolidated litigation comprising the complaints of 19 States and many private plaintiffs alleging that the defendants, members of the insurance industry, conspired in violation of § 1 of the Sherman Act to restrict the terms of coverage of commercial general liability (CGL) insurance[3] available in the United States. Because the cases come to us on motions to dismiss, we take the allegations of the complaints as true.

A

According to the complaints, the object of the conspiracies was to force certain primary insurers (insurers who sell insurance directly to consumers) to change the terms of their standard CGL insurance policies to conform with the policies the defendant insurers wanted to sell. * * *

* * * [P]rimary insurers themselves usually purchase insurance to cover a portion of the risk they assume from the consumer. This so-called "reinsurance" may serve at least two purposes, protecting the primary insurer from catastrophic loss, and allowing the primary insurer to sell more insurance than its own financial capacity might otherwise permit. Thus, "[t]he availability of reinsurance affects the ability and willingness of primary insurers to provide insurance to their customers." Insurers who sell reinsurance themselves often purchase insurance to cover part of the risk they assume

---

[2]Justice WHITE, Justice BLACKMUN, and Justice STEVENS join this opinion in its entirety, and THE CHIEF JUSTICE joins Parts I, II-A, III, and IV.

[3]CGL insurance provides "coverage for third party casualty damage claims against a purchaser of insurance (the 'insured')."

from the primary insurer; such "retrocessional reinsurance" does for reinsurers what reinsurance does for primary insurers. Many of the defendants here are reinsurers or reinsurance brokers, or play some other specialized role in the reinsurance business; defendant Reinsurance Association of America (RAA) is a trade association of domestic reinsurers.

B

* * * [T]he defendants began to take other steps to force a change in the terms of coverage of CGL insurance generally available, steps that, the plaintiffs allege, implemented a series of conspiracies in violation of § 1 of the Sherman Act. The plaintiffs recount these steps as a number of separate episodes corresponding to different claims for relief in their complaints; because it will become important to distinguish among these counts and the acts and defendants associated with them, we will note these correspondences.

The first four Claims for Relief in the California Complaint and the Second Claim for Relief in the Connecticut Complaint charge the four domestic primary insurer defendants and varying groups of domestic and foreign reinsurers, brokers, and associations with conspiracies to manipulate the ISO[4] CGL forms. * * *

The four primary insurer defendants (Hartford, Aetna, CIGNA, and Allstate) also encouraged key actors in the London reinsurance market, an important provider of reinsurance for North American risks, to withhold reinsurance for coverages written on the 1984 ISO CGL forms. As a consequence, many London-based underwriters, syndicates, brokers, and reinsurance companies informed ISO of their intention to withhold reinsurance on the 1984 forms, and at least some of them told ISO that they would withhold reinsurance until ISO incorporated all * * * desired changes into the ISO CGL forms.

* * * After ISO got regulatory approval of the 1986 forms in most [U.S.] States where approval was needed, it eliminated its support services for the 1973 CGL form, thus rendering it impossible for most ISO members to continue to use the form.

The Fifth Claim for Relief in the California Complaint, and the virtually identical Third Claim for Relief in the Connecticut Complaint, charge a conspiracy among a group of London reinsurers and brokers to coerce primary insurers in the United States to offer CGL coverage only on a claims-made basis. The reinsurers collectively refused to write new reinsurance contracts for, or to renew longstanding contracts with, "primary ... insurers unless they were prepared to switch from the occurrence to the claims-made form"; they also amended their reinsurance contracts to cover only claims made before a "sunset date," thus eliminating reinsurance for claims made on occurrence policies after that date. * * *

[The remaining three claims at issue on appeal allege various foreign and domestic conspiracies to violate the U.S. federal antitrust laws as well by manipulating the kinds of insurance that could be made available on the U.S. market, described below.]

---

[4]ISO refers to defendant Insurance Services Office, Inc., an association of some 1,400 U.S. property and casualty insurers, including the primary insurer defendants, that publishes standard insurance forms for use by the U.S. insurance industry. The ISO CGL is one such standard form.

C

Nineteen States and a number of private plaintiffs filed 36 complaints against the insurers involved in this course of events, charging that the conspiracies described above violated § 1 of the Sherman Act, 15 U.S.C. § 1. After the actions had been consolidated for litigation in the Northern District of California, the defendants moved to dismiss for failure to state a cause of action, or, in the alternative, for summary judgment. The District Court granted the motions to dismiss [on domestic jurisdictional grounds]. * * * The District Court also dismissed the three claims that named only certain London-based defendants, invoking international comity and applying the Ninth Circuit's decision in *Timberlane Lumber Co. v. Bank of America, N.T. & S.A.*, 549 F.2d 597 (1976).

The Court of Appeals reversed. * * * [A]s to the three claims brought solely against foreign defendants, the court applied its *Timberlane* analysis, but concluded that the principle of international comity was no bar to exercising Sherman Act jurisdiction.

We granted certiorari * * * to address the application of the Sherman Act to the foreign conduct at issue. * * *

III

Finally, we take up the question * * * whether certain claims against the London reinsurers should have been dismissed as improper applications of the Sherman Act to foreign conduct. The Fifth Claim for Relief in the California Complaint alleges a violation of § 1 of the Sherman Act by certain London reinsurers who conspired to coerce primary insurers in the United States to offer CGL coverage on a claims-made basis, thereby making "occurrence CGL coverage ... unavailable in the State of California for many risks." The Sixth Claim for Relief in the California Complaint alleges that the London reinsurers violated § 1 by a conspiracy to limit coverage of pollution risks in North America, thereby rendering "pollution liability coverage ... almost entirely unavailable for the vast majority of casualty insurance purchasers in the State of California." The Eighth Claim for Relief in the California Complaint alleges a further § 1 violation by the London reinsurers who, along with domestic retrocessional reinsurers, conspired to limit coverage of seepage, pollution, and property contamination risks in North America, thereby eliminating such coverage in the State of California.

At the outset, we note that the District Court undoubtedly had jurisdiction of these Sherman Act claims, as the London reinsurers apparently concede. Although the proposition was perhaps not always free from doubt, it is well established by now that the Sherman Act applies to foreign conduct that was meant to produce and did in fact produce some substantial effect in the United States. Such is the conduct alleged here: that the London reinsurers engaged in unlawful conspiracies to affect the market for insurance in the United States and that their conduct in fact produced substantial effect.[5]

---

[5]* * * The FTAIA was intended to exempt from the Sherman Act export transactions that did not injure the United States economy, and it is unclear how it might apply to the conduct alleged here. Also unclear is whether the Act's "direct, substantial, and reasonably foreseeable effect" standard amends existing law or merely codifies it. We need not address these questions here. Assuming that the FTAIA's standard affects this litigation, and assuming further that that standard differs from the prior law, the

According to the London reinsurers, the District Court should have declined to exercise such jurisdiction under the principle of international comity.[6] The Court of Appeals agreed that courts should look to that principle in deciding whether to exercise jurisdiction under the Sherman Act. This availed the London reinsurers nothing, however. To be sure, the Court of Appeals believed that "application of [American] antitrust laws to the London reinsurance market 'would lead to significant conflict with English law and policy,'" and that "[s]uch a conflict, unless outweighed by other factors, would by itself be reason to decline exercise of jurisdiction." But other factors, in the court's view, including the London reinsurers' express purpose to affect United States commerce and the substantial nature of the effect produced, outweighed the supposed conflict and required the exercise of jurisdiction in this litigation.

When it enacted the FTAIA, 96 Stat. 1246, 15 U.S.C. § 6a, Congress expressed no view on the question whether a court with Sherman Act jurisdiction should ever decline to exercise such jurisdiction on grounds of international comity. See H.R.Rep. No. 97-686, p. 13 (1982) ("If a court determines that the requirements for subject matter jurisdiction are met, [the FTAIA] would have no effect on the court['s] ability to employ notions of comity ... or otherwise to take account of the international character of the transaction") (citing *Timberlane*). We need not decide that question here, however, for even assuming that in a proper case a court may decline to exercise Sherman Act jurisdiction over foreign conduct (or, as Justice SCALIA would put it, may conclude by the employment of comity analysis in the first instance that there is no jurisdiction), international comity would not counsel against exercising jurisdiction in the circumstances alleged here.

The only substantial question in this litigation is whether "there is in fact a true conflict between domestic and foreign law." The London reinsurers contend that applying the Act to their conduct would conflict significantly with British law, and the British Government, appearing before us as *amicus curiae*, concurs. They assert that Parliament has established a comprehensive regulatory regime over the London reinsurance market and that the conduct alleged here was perfectly consistent with British law and policy. But this is not to state a conflict. "[T]he fact that conduct is lawful in the state in which it took place will not, of itself, bar application of the United States antitrust laws," even where the foreign state has a strong policy to permit or encourage such conduct. Restatement (Third) Foreign Relations Law § 415, Comment j. No conflict exists, for these purposes, "where a person subject to regulation by two states can comply with the laws of both." Restatement (Third) Foreign Relations Law § 403, Comment e. Since the London reinsurers do not argue that British law requires them to act in some fashion prohibited by the law of the United States or claim that their compliance with the laws of both countries is otherwise impossible, we see no conflict with British law. We have no need in this litigation to address other considerations

conduct alleged plainly meets its requirements.

[6]Justice SCALIA contends that comity concerns figure into the prior analysis whether jurisdiction exists under the Sherman Act. This contention is inconsistent with the general understanding that the Sherman Act covers foreign conduct producing a substantial intended effect in the United States, and that concerns of comity come into play, if at all, only after a court has determined that the acts complained of are subject to Sherman Act jurisdiction. In any event, the parties conceded jurisdiction at oral argument, and we see no need to address this contention here.

that might inform a decision to refrain from the exercise of jurisdiction on grounds of international comity.

IV

The judgment of the Court of Appeals is *affirmed in part* and *reversed in part*, and the cases are remanded for further proceedings consistent with this opinion. * * *

Notes and Questions

1. What limits, if any, does the majority opinion in *Hartford Fire v. California* put on the reach of U.S. antitrust laws to foreign conduct by foreign companies affecting the U.S. market? Suppose a group of foreign manufacturers fixed prices for their products on a worldwide basis. If some of those products were sold to consumers in the United States, should courts exercise their jurisdiction under U.S. antitrust laws to reach the foreign manufacturers? Under what conditions? Do the following factors matter?

- Whether the foreign manufacturers export directly to the United States, or only sell to independent foreign distributors who in turn resell to the United States?
- What portion of the group's sales go to the United States? What if U.S. sales account for only 25% of their worldwide sales? 10%? 1%?
- What portion of U.S. consumption of the goods are attributable to the group? What if the group supplies only 25% of the goods of that kind consumed on the U.S. market? 10%? 1%?
- Whether the foreign manufacturers were directing their activities toward Asia, and the effects on U.S. commerce were unintended and incidental?

Remember that we are dealing with two separate but related questions: first, whether a U.S. court may exercise jurisdiction over the foreign conduct and, second, whether U.S. antitrust legislation is intended to reach that conduct.

2. In dissent, Justice Scalia argued that, under public international law, principles of comity dictate that the Court should limit the reach of U.S. laws in deference to the interests in the case of other jurisdictions. But comity is a principle of domestic law, not international law. Moreover, even if it were otherwise, Congress' clear intent to extend prescriptive jurisdiction—even in violation of international law—must be enforced by the courts, and Congress' intent to do so was not in doubt in *Hartford Fire*.

Modern U.S. antitrust laws contain complex rules designed to reduce uncertainty about their application to foreign conduct. Cases like *Hartford Fire Insurance v. California* further reduce uncertainty by establishing a relatively clear rule on when comity will result in the dismissal of a case with an important international component. However, some uncertainty remains, and the antitrust jurisprudence has in many instances had to deal with apparently or actually conflicting U.S. and foreign competition policies and laws.

4 Extraterritoriality and Intellectual Property Law

Another field in which questions about the cross-border application of U.S. law frequently arise is intellectual property. As discussed in Chapter 3, intellectual property provides protection on a national basis only. Thus, the default rule is that the owner of a Freedonian patent on a product could not sue someone who makes or sells the patented product in Osterlich, either in a Freedonian court or an Osterlich court. The patent owner would need to own a Osterlich patent on the same product to complain of infringement.

However, there are cases in which courts will extend their jurisdiction to encompass foreign acts that infringe either domestic or foreign IP rights. Moreover, there are cases in which an infringement spans more than one state, and so it is difficult to pinpoint in which country the "infringement," if it *is* infringement, has occurred.

Before *EEOC v. Aramco*, the Supreme Court had decided several cases involving extraterritorial claims. However, the Court had not uniformly applied a strong presumption against extraterritoriality due to the nature or language of the statute under consideration. IP cases sometimes have posed a special challenge; being intangible, IP can cross national borders fluidly. For this reason, patent, copyright, and trademark infringement cases have often tested the reach of U.S. IP laws.

4.1 Extraterritorial Acts of Infringement

Most states are hesitant to sit in judgment of the validity of a patent or trademark granted in another state, even if the patent owner has an identical patent or trademark in the forum state. Except for two regional IP systems, no international treaty requires that a patent or trademark be enforceable anywhere other than the country in which it is granted.

This is partly a matter of comity and partly a matter of pragmatism. As discussed in the previous chapter, courts are reluctant to judge the validity of a foreign Act of State when exercising its sovereign authority within its own territory. Moreover, the state in the best position to enforce or invalidate an IP right effectively is the one that granted that right. It would be difficult and awkward for a U.S. court to try to prevent a Smalldonian private party from exercising its patent or trademark in Smalldonia.

A. Extraterritoriality and Patents

Consistent with the principle of territorial independence, U.S. courts have consistently interpreted the 1952 Patent Act not to apply abroad. Although some provisions of the Patent Act make foreign acts relevant to the question of infringement of a U.S. patent, a court will not apply U.S. law to determine whether a foreign patent is infringed.

The provisions of the Patent Act that make foreign conduct relevant to U.S. infringement claims mainly revolve around acts performed outside the United States that might circumvent the U.S. prohibition on infringement. For example, the Patent Act provides in section 271(f):

> (1) Whoever without authority supplies or causes to be supplied in or from the United States all or a substantial portion of the components of a patented invention, where such components are uncombined in whole or in part, in such manner as to actively induce the combination of such components outside of the United States in a manner that would infringe the patent if such combination occurred within the United States, shall be liable as an infringer.
>
> (2) Whoever without authority supplies or causes to be supplied in or from the United States any component of a patented invention that is especially made or especially adapted for use in the invention and not a staple article or commodity of commerce suitable for substantial noninfringing use, where such component is uncombined in whole or in part, knowing that such component is so made or adapted and intending that such component will be combined outside of the United States in a manner that would infringe the patent if such combination occurred within the United States, shall be liable as an infringer.

Why is section 271(f) of the Patent Act an anticircumvention provision? Section 271(a) of the Act makes it illegal to manufacture a patented invention in the United States and to sell it to a purchaser in a foreign country. If a U.S. person could simply make the components of the invention in the United States and ship them as a group to a foreign purchaser with instructions on how to assemble them into the completed patented invention, it would be easy to undermine some of the invention's economic benefit to the patent owner.

Another paragraph of section 271 prevents circumvention of process patents. Process patents are patents covering a series of steps for doing something. To infringe a process patent under Section 271(a), all steps of the process must be performed in the United States. For example, if the patent covers a process for manufacturing widgets, an accused infringer must perform all claimed manufacturing steps within U.S. territory to infringe the patent.

But what if a competitor performs the patented manufacturing process in a foreign country, and imports the resulting product into the United States? The Patent Act offers a legislative remedy for the patent owner.

> (g) Whoever without authority imports into the United States or offers to sell, sells, or uses within the United States a product which is made by a process patented in the United States shall be liable as an infringer, if the importation, offer to sell, sale, or use of the product occurs during the term of such process patent. * * * A product which is made by a patented process will, for purposes of this title, not be considered to be so made after—
>
> (1) it is materially changed by subsequent processes; or
>
> (2) it becomes a trivial and nonessential component of another product.

Why do you think Section 271(g) qualifies the prohibition with exceptions for material change or incorporation into another product?

POLICY ISSUE

Adjudicating infringement of a foreign patent

One reason most states refuse to adjudicate questions of foreign patent validity is that they have no way to nullify a patent granted and enforced in a foreign country. If a court in Greece found a U.S. patent invalid, U.S. courts would ignore the judgment and continue to enforce the patent unless a U.S. court itself invalidated the patent. That by itself doesn't explain why a court should refuse to hear a claim that a foreign patent is infringed by conduct in the forum state, however. So why would a Greek court refuse to entertain a claim that a company in Greece infringed a U.S. patent by building the patented device in Greece?

One answer is that a claim of infringement of any patent, domestic or foreign, almost always meets the defense that the patent is invalid or unenforceable. A foreign court will not be able to determine whether infringement has occurred without first judging the validity the patent. Even if the accused infringer does not argue that the patent is invalid, the court must still interpret the claims of the patent (i.e., define the scope of what the patent covers) to determine whether infringement has occurred. But there is no reason to believe the courts of the issuing state will agree with the way the forum court construes the patent claims. So the scope of the patent claims could be one thing in the forum state and another in the issuing state. This creates a potential conflict between decisions of the courts, and ultimately it is the issuing state that controls the continuing validity of the patent. The Act of State doctrine is relevant as well.

Is there some way to resolve this problem without denying the possibility of hearing infringement claims regarding patents issued in foreign countries? Or should courts always refuse to hear cases claiming the infringement of a foreign patent?

The issue of whether a U.S. court could hear a claim of infringement of a foreign patent has sometimes arisen. With rare exceptions, courts have rejected attempts to assert supplemental jurisdiction over claims of foreign patent infringement. See, e.g., *Mars Inc. v. Kabushiki-Kaisha Nippon Conlux,* 24 F.3d 1368 (Fed. Cir. 1994); *Voda v. Cordis Corp.*, 476 F.3d 887 (Fed. Cir. 2007).

In the EU, the general rule is similar. The Court of Justice of the European Union has held that courts of one EU member state may not adjudicate the validity of a patent granted in another EU member state. *Gesellschaft für Antriebstechnik mbH & Co. KG v. Lamellen und Kupplungsbau Beteiligungs KG,* Case No. C-4/03 (Eur. Ct. Just., July 13, 2006).

B. Trademark and Unfair Competition Law

The basic U.S. trademark and unfair competition law, the Lanham Trademarks Act, has less to say about extraterritoriality than the Patent Act. The Lanham Act defines infringement in Section 32 as follows:

> (1) Any person who shall, without the consent of the registrant—
>
> (a) use in commerce any reproduction, counterfeit, copy, or colorable imitation of a registered mark in connection with the sale, offering for sale, distribution, or advertising of any goods or services on or in connection with which such use is likely to cause confusion, or to cause mistake, or to deceive; or
>
> (b) reproduce, counterfeit, copy, or colorably imitate a registered mark and apply such reproduction, counterfeit, copy, or colorable imitation to labels, signs, prints, packages, wrappers, receptacles or advertisements intended to be used in commerce upon or in connection with the sale, offering for sale, distribution, or advertising of goods or services on or in connection with which such use is likely to cause confusion, or to cause mistake, or to deceive,
>
> shall be liable in a civil action by the registrant for the remedies hereinafter provided. Under subsection (b) hereof, the registrant shall not be entitled to recover profits or damages unless the acts have been committed with knowledge that such imitation is intended to be used to cause confusion, or to cause mistake, or to deceive.

15 U.S.C. § 1114(a). Notice how infringement is defined to include "use in commerce * * * in connection with the sale, offering for sale, distribution, or advertising of any goods or services" that is likely to cause confusion or deception. The Act does not clearly define the territorial reach of "commerce," it merely states that the word "commerce" means "all commerce which may lawfully be regulated by Congress." 15 U.S.C. § 1127.

What if someone applies a famous trademark registered in the United States to articles in a different country, where the mark is unregistered? Does U.S. law offer a remedy, or does it preserve the territorial independence of trademarks? After all, no law explicitly prevents Congress from regulating foreign commerce having no connection whatsoever with the United States. The following case addresses this question.

STEELE v. BULOVA WATCH CO., INC.

Supreme Court of the United States, 1952
344 U.S. 280

Mr. Justice CLARK delivered the opinion of the Court.

The issue is whether a United States District Court has jurisdiction to award relief to an American corporation against acts of trade-mark infringement and unfair competition consummated in a foreign country by a citizen and resident of the United States. Bulova Watch Company, Inc., a New York corporation, sued Steele, petitioner here, in the United States District Court for the Western District of Texas. The gist of its complaint charged that 'Bulova,' a trade-mark properly registered under the laws of the United States, had long designated the watches produced and nationally advertised and sold by the Bulova Watch Company; and that petitioner, a United States citizen residing in San Antonio, Texas, conducted a watch business in Mexico City where, without Bulova's authorization and with the purpose of deceiving the buying public, he stamped the name 'Bulova' on watches there assembled and sold. Basing its prayer on these asserted violations of the trade-mark laws of the United States, Bulova requested injunctive and monetary relief. Personally served with process in San Antonio, petitioner answered by challenging the court's jurisdiction over the subject matter of the suit and by interposing several defenses, including his due registration in Mexico of the mark 'Bulova' and the pendency of Mexican legal proceedings thereon, to the merits of Bulova's claim. The trial judge, having initially reserved disposition of the jurisdictional issue until a hearing on the merits, interrupted the presentation of evidence and dismissed the complaint 'with prejudice,' on the ground that the court lacked jurisdiction over the cause. This decision rested on the court's findings that petitioner had committed no illegal acts within the United States. With one judge dissenting, the Court of Appeals reversed; it held that the pleadings and evidence disclosed a cause of action within the reach of the Lanham Trade-Mark Act of 1946, 15 U.S.C. §§ 1051 *et seq*. The dissenting judge thought that 'since the conduct complained of substantially related solely to acts done and trade carried on under full authority of Mexican law, and were confined to and affected only that Nation's internal commerce, (the District Court) was without jurisdiction to enjoin such conduct.' We granted certiorari.

Petitioner concedes, as he must, that Congress in prescribing standards of conduct for American citizens may project the impact of its laws beyond the territorial boundaries of the United States. Resolution of the jurisdictional issue in this case therefore depends on construction of exercised congressional power, not the limitations upon that power itself. And since we do not pass on the merits of Bulova's claim, we need not now explore every facet of this complex and controversial Act.

The Lanham Act, on which Bulova posited its claims to relief, confers broad jurisdictional powers upon the courts of the United States. The statute's expressed intent is 'to regulate commerce within the control of Congress by making actionable the deceptive and misleading use of marks in such commerce; to protect registered marks used in such comme[r]ce from interference by State, or territorial legislation; to protect persons engaged in such commerce against unfair competition; to prevent fraud and deception in such commerce by the use of reproductions, copies, counterfeits, or colorable imitations of registered marks; and to provide rights and remedies stipulated by treaties and conventions respecting trade-marks, trade names, and unfair competition entered into between the United States and foreign nations.' § 45, 15 U.S.C. § 1127. To that end, § 32(1) holds liable in a civil action by a trade-mark registrant '[a]ny person who shall, in commerce,' infringe a registered trade-mark in a manner there detailed. 'Commerce' is defined as 'all commerce which may lawfully be regulated by Congress.' § 45, 15 U.S.C. § 1127. The district courts of the United States are granted jurisdiction over all actions 'arising under' the Act, § 39, 15 U.S.C. § 1121, and can award relief which may include injunctions, 'according to the principles of equity,' to prevent the violation of any registrant's rights. § 34, 15 U.S.C. § 1116.

The record reveals the following significant facts which for purposes of a dismissal must be taken as true: Bulova Watch Company, one of the largest watch manufacturers in the world, advertised and distributed 'Bulova' watches in the United States and foreign countries. Since 1929, its aural and visual advertising, in Spanish and English, has penetrated Mexico. Petitioner, long a resident of San Antonio, first entered the watch business there in 1922, and in 1926 learned of the trade-mark 'Bulova.' He subsequently transferred his business to Mexico City and, discovering that 'Bulova' had not been registered in Mexico, in 1933 procured the Mexican registration of that mark. Assembling Swiss watch movements and dials and cases imported from that country and the United States, petitioner in Mexico City stamped his watches with 'Bulova' and sold them as such. As a result of the distribution of spurious 'Bulovas,' Bulova Watch Company's Texas sales representative received numerous complaints from retail jewelers in the Mexican border area whose customers brought in for repair defective 'Bulovas' which upon inspection often turned out not to be products of that company. Moreover, subsequent to our grant of certiorari in this case the prolonged litigation in the courts of Mexico has come to an end. On October 6, 1952, the Supreme Court of Mexico rendered a judgment upholding an administrative ruling which had nullified petitioner's Mexican registration of 'Bulova.'

On the facts in the record we agree with the Court of Appeals that petitioner's activities, when viewed as a whole, fall within the jurisdictional scope of the Lanham Act. This Court has often stated that the legislation of Congress will not extend beyond the boundaries of the United States unless a contrary legislative intent appears. The question thus is 'whether Congress intended to make the law applicable' to the facts of this case. For 'the United States is not debarred by any rule of international law from governing the conduct of is own citizens upon the high seas or even in foreign countries when the rights of other nations or their nationals are not infringed. With respect to such an exercise of authority there is no question of international law, but solely of the purport of the municipal law which establishes the duty of the citizen in relation to his own government.' *Skiriotes v. State of Florida*, 1941, 313 U.S. 69, 73. As Mr. Justice Minton, then sitting on the Court of Appeals, applied the principle in a case involving unfair methods of competition: 'Congress has the power to prevent unfair trade practices in foreign commerce by citizens of the United States, although some of the acts are done outside the territorial limits of the United States.' *Branch v. Federal Trade Commission*, 7 Cir., 1944, 141 F.2d 31, 35. Nor has this Court in tracing the commerce scope of statutes differentiated between enforcement of legislative policy by the Government itself or by private litigants proceeding under a statutory right. The public policy subserved is the same in each case. In the light of the broad jurisdictional grant in the Lanham Act, we deem its scope to encompass petitioner's activities here. His operations and their effects were not confined within the territorial limits of a foreign nation. He bought component parts of his wares in the United States, and spurious 'Bulovas' filtered through the Mexican border into this country; his competing goods could well reflect adversely on Bulova Watch Company's trade reputation in markets cultivated by advertising here as well as abroad. Under similar factual circumstances, courts of the United States have awarded relief to registered trademark owners, even prior to the advent of the broadened commerce provisions of the Lanham Act. Even when most jealously read, that Act's sweeping reach into 'all commerce which may lawfully be regulated by Congress' does not constrict prior law or deprive courts of jurisdiction previously exercised. We do not deem material that petitioner affixed the mark 'Bulova' in Mexico City rather than here, or that his purchases in the United States when viewed in isolation do not violate any of our laws. They were essential steps in the course of business consummated abroad; acts in themselves legal lose that character when they become part of an unlawful scheme. '(I)n such a case it is not material that the source of the forbidden effects upon * * * commerce arises in one phase or another of that program.' *Mandeville Island Farms v. American Crystal Sugar Co.*, 1948, 334 U.S. 219, 237. In sum, we do not think that petitioner by so simple a device can evade the thrust of the laws of the United States in a privileged sanctuary beyond our borders.

American Banana Co. v. United Fruit Co., 1909, 213 U.S. 347, compels nothing to the contrary. This Court there upheld a Court of Appeals' affirmance of the trial court's dismissal of a private damage action predicated on alleged violations of the Sherman [Antitrust] Act, 15 U.S.C. §§ 1-7, 15 note. The complaint, in substance, charged United Fruit Company with monopolization of the banana import trade between Central America and the United States, and with the instigation of Costa Rican governmental authorities to seize plaintiff's plantation and produce in Panama. The Court of Appeals reasoned that plaintiff had shown no damage from the asserted monopoly and could not found liability on the seizure, a sovereign act of another nation. This Court agreed that a violation of American laws could not be grounded on a foreign nation's sovereign acts. Viewed in its context, the holding in that case was not meant to confer blanket immunity on trade practices which radiate unlawful consequences here, merely because they were initiated or consummated outside the territorial limits of the United States. Unlawful effects in this country, absent in the posture of the *Banana* case before us, are often decisive * * *. And, unlike the *Banana* case, whatever rights Mexico once conferred on petitioner its courts now have decided to take away.

Nor do we doubt the District Court's jurisdiction to award appropriate injunctive relief if warranted by the facts after trial. Mexico's courts have nullified the Mexican registration of 'Bulova'; there is thus no conflict which might afford petitioner a pretext that such relief would impugn foreign law. The question, therefore, whether a valid foreign registration would affect either the power to enjoin or the propriety of its exercise is not before us. Where, as here, there can be no interference with the sovereignty of another nation, the District Court in exercising its equity powers may command persons properly before it to cease or perform acts outside its territorial jurisdiction.

Affirmed.

Mr. Justice REED, with whom Mr. Justice DOUGLAS joins, dissenting.

The purpose of the Lanham Act is to prevent deceptive and misleading use of trade-marks. § 45, 15 U.S.C. § 1127. To further that purpose the Act makes liable in an action by the registered holder of the trade-mark 'any person who shall, in commerce,' infringe such trade-mark. § 32(1), 15 U.S.C. § 1114(1). 'Commerce' is defined as being 'all commerce which may lawfully be regulated by Congress.' § 45, 15 U.S.C. § 1127.

The Court's opinion bases jurisdiction on the Lanham Act. In the instant case the only alleged acts of infringement occurred in Mexico. The acts complained of were the stamping of the name 'Bulova' on watches and the subsequent sale of the watches. There were purchases of assembly material in this country by petitioners. Purchasers from petitioners in Mexico brought the assembled watches into the United States. Assuming that Congress has the power to control acts of our citizens throughout the world, the question presented is one of statutory construction: Whether Congress intended the Act to apply to the conduct here exposed.

'The canon of construction which teaches that legislation of Congress, unless a contrary intent appears, is meant to apply only within the territorial jurisdiction of the United States, is a valid approach whereby unexpressed congressional intent may be ascertained.' *Foley Bros., Inc. v. Filardo*, 336 U.S. 281, 285. Utilizing this approach, does such a contrary intent appear in the Lanham Act? If it does, it appears only in broad and general terms, i.e., 'to regulate commerce within the control of Congress * * *.' § 45, 15 U.S.C. § 1127. Language of such nonexplicit scope was considered by the Court in construing the Sherman Act in *American Banana Co. v. United Fruit Co.*, 213 U.S. 347, 357. 'Words having universal scope, such as 'every contract in restraint of trade,' 'every person who shall monopolize,' etc., will be taken, as a matter of course, to mean only everyone subject to such legislation, not all that the legislator subsequently may be able to catch.' The *American Banana Co.* case confined the Sherman Act in its 'operation and effect to the territorial limits over which the law-maker has general and legitimate power.' 213 U.S. at page 357. This was held to be true as to acts outside the United States, although the parties were all corporate citizens of the United States subject to process of the federal courts.

The generally phrased congressional intent in the Lanham Act is to be compared with the language of the Fair Labor Standards Act, 29 U.S.C. §§ 201 et seq., which we construed in *Vermilya-Brown Co. v. Connell*, 335 U.S. 377. There we held that by explicitly stating that the Act covered 'possessions' of the United States, Congress had intended that the Act was to be in effect in all 'possession' and was not to be applied merely in those areas under the territorial jurisdiction or sovereignty of the United States.

There are, of course, cases in which a statement of specific contrary intent will not be deemed so necessary. Where the case involves the construction of a criminal statute 'enacted because of the right of the government to defend itself against obstruction, or fraud * * * committed by its own citizens,' it is not necessary for Congress to make specific provisions that the law 'shall include the high seas and foreign countries'. This is also true when it is a question of the sovereign power of the United States to require the response of a nonresident citizen. A similar situation is met where a statute is applied to acts committed by citizens in areas subject to the laws of no sovereign.

In the instant case none of these exceptional considerations come into play. Petitioner's buying of unfinished watches in the United States is not an illegal commercial act. Nor can it be said that petitioners were engaging in illegal acts in commerce when the finished watches bearing the Mexican trade-mark were purchased from them and brought into the United States by such purchasers, all without collusion between petitioner and the purchaser. The stamping of the Bulova trade-mark, done in Mexico, is not an act 'within the control of Congress.' It should not be utilized as a basis for action against petitioner. The Lanham Act, like the Sherman Act, should be construed to apply only to acts done within the sovereignty of the United States. While we do not condone the piratic use of trade-marks, neither do we believe that Congress intended to make such use actionable irrespective of the place it occurred. Such extensions of power bring our legislation into conflict with the laws and practices of other nations, fully capable of punishing infractions of their own laws, and should require specific words to reach acts done within the territorial limits of other sovereignties.

Notes and Questions

1. The Court majority notes several times that the Supreme Court of Mexico eventually nullified Steele's Mexican registration of the BULOVA trademark. This point is irrelevant to infringement in Mexico. Not only did it occur after the events giving rise to the lawsuit; canceling the registration of a trademark does not make affixing that trademark to products tortious or illegal.

2. If Justice Reed's dissenting view had prevailed in this case, would Bulova Watch Company have had any remedy against anyone? What about the persons who imported the watches into the United States?

3. What is the basis for the majority opinion: the defendant's U.S. citizenship, the fact that his acts had some effects on U.S. commerce, both, or something else?

4. In *Aramco*, the Supreme Court distinguished *Steele* by pointing out that the Lanham Act defined "commerce" to mean "all commerce which may lawfully be regulated by Congress." 499 U.S. at 252. This is a very broad definition. In contrast, Title VII of the Civil Rights Act had no such definition. Is the Court's distinction convincing? Why or why not?

Consider the case of a Ruritanian company that owns a Ruritanian trademark. It accuses another Ruritanian company of infringing the trademark in Ruritania. Under the reasoning of *Steele*, does the Lanham Act govern the dispute? What makes it "unlawful" for Congress to regulate the Ruritanian infringement claim? Does this seem like a persuasive interpretation of the Lanham Act?

5. Assuming Congress has the power to regulate entirely foreign acts of

POLICY ISSUE
Protecting Famous Trademarks Across Borders

You might recall that TRIPS Agreement article 16(3) requires contracting parties to the WTO Agreements to refuse registration of any mark if it is likely to create confusion with a famous or well-known mark in the country, even though the famous mark has not yet been registered in that country.

The rationale is that it helps prevents free riding. Consider this scenario. A merchant in Zembia notice that a trademark in Freedonia is gaining international fame, but the Freedonian trademark owner has not yet registered the mark in Zembia. The Zembian merchant has a market incentive to register the trademark in Zembia, either take advantage of the trademark's growing global goodwill or to "squat" on it and force the Freedonian trademark owner to buy the Zembian trademark from it.

Consider *Steele v. Bulova Watch Co.* Would it be right to let Bulova suffer the consequences of having chosen not to register its mark in Mexico? Or should the owner of a famous trademark be expected to register the mark worldwide? Cases like *Steele* usually arise from the fact that the fame of the trademark owner's mark makes its goods desirable. Nobody sets up a foreign operation to counterfeit an unpopular trademark. The owner of a famous trademark is presumably more likely to be able to afford worldwide registration than the owner of a relatively unknown mark.

But is it sound policy to put the owners of famous marks to the trouble and expense of nearly 200 national registrations, even in insignificant markets for its products, merely to prevent someone in those countries from manufacturing knock-offs and selling them to customers from more lucrative markets? How could this problem be resolved without hyperextending U.S. jurisdiction?

infringement, would it be consistent with the reasoning of *EEOC v. Aramco* to assume that the Lanham Act's general language was intended to create a cause of action for infringement of a U.S. trademark everywhere in the world? Why or why not?

The majority decision in *Steele* did not clearly explain the circumstances under a U.S. court should consider commercial activities occurring outside the United States to fall within the subject matter jurisdiction of the Lanham Act. The next case sheds some light on how courts have interpreted and elaborated on the *Steele* opinion.

McBEE v. DELICA CO., LTD.

U.S. Court of Appeals, First Circuit, 2005
417 F.3d 107

LYNCH, Circuit Judge.

It has long been settled that the Lanham Act can, in appropriate cases, be applied extraterritorially. See *Steele v. Bulova Watch Co.*, 344 U.S. 280 (1952). This case, dismissed for lack of subject matter jurisdiction, requires us, as a matter of first impression for this circuit, to lay out a framework for determining when such extraterritorial use of the Lanham Act is proper.

In doing so, we choose not to adopt the formulations used by various other circuits. *See, e.g., Reebok Int'l, Ltd. v. Marnatech Enters.*, 970 F.2d 552, 554-57 (9th Cir.1992); *Vanity Fair Mills v. T. Eaton Co.*, 234 F.2d 633, 642-43 (2d Cir.1956). The best-known test, the *Vanity Fair* test, asks (1) whether the defendant is an American citizen, (2) whether the defendant's actions have a substantial effect on United States commerce, and (3) whether relief would create a conflict with foreign law. These three prongs are given an uncertain weight. * * *

Our framework asks first whether the defendant is an American citizen; that inquiry is different because a separate constitutional basis for jurisdiction exists for control of activities, even foreign activities, of an American citizen. Further, when the Lanham Act plaintiff seeks to enjoin sales in the United States, there is no question of extraterritorial application; the court has subject matter jurisdiction.

In order for a plaintiff to reach foreign activities of foreign defendants in American courts, however, we adopt a separate test. We hold that subject matter jurisdiction under the Lanham Act is proper only if the complained-of activities have a substantial effect on United States commerce, viewed in light of the purposes of the Lanham Act. If this "substantial effects" question is answered in the negative, then the court lacks jurisdiction over the defendant's extraterritorial acts; if it is answered in the affirmative, then the court possesses subject matter jurisdiction.

We reject the notion that a comity analysis is part of subject matter jurisdiction. Comity considerations, including potential conflicts with foreign trademark law, are properly treated as questions of whether a court should, in its discretion, decline to exercise subject matter jurisdiction that it already possesses. Our approach to each of these issues is in harmony with the analogous rules for extraterritorial application of the antitrust laws.

The plaintiff, Cecil McBee, an American citizen and resident, seeks to hold the defendant, Delica Co., Ltd. (Delica), responsible for its activities in Japan said to harm McBee's reputation in both Japan and the United States and for Delica's purported activities in the United States. McBee is a well-known American jazz musician; Delica is a Japanese corporation that adopted the name "Cecil McBee" for its adolescent female clothing line. McBee sued for false endorsement and dilution under the Lanham Act. The district court dismissed all of McBee's Lanham Act claims, concluding that it lacked subject matter jurisdiction.

We affirm, albeit on different reasoning. We conclude that the court lacked jurisdiction over McBee's claims seeking (1) an injunction in the United States barring access to Delica's Internet website, which is written in Japanese, and (2) damages for harm to McBee due to Delica's sales in Japan. McBee has made no showing that Delica's activities had a substantial effect on United States commerce. As to McBee's claim for (3) an injunction barring Delica from selling its goods in the United States, we hold that the district court had jurisdiction but conclude that this claim is without merit because the only sales Delica has made into the United States were induced by McBee for purposes of this litigation, and there is no showing that Delica plans on selling into the United States again.

I.

The relevant facts are basically undisputed. McBee, who lives in both Maine and New York, is a jazz bassist with a distinguished career spanning over forty-five years. He has performed in the United States and worldwide, has performed on over 200 albums, and has released six albums under his own name (including in Japan). He won a Grammy Award in 1989, was inducted into the Oklahoma Jazz Hall of Fame in 1991, and teaches at the New England Conservatory of Music in Boston. McBee has toured Japan several times, beginning in the early 1980s, and has performed in many major Japanese cities, including Tokyo. He continues to tour in Japan. McBee has never licensed or authorized the use of his name to anyone, except of course in direct connection with his musical performances, as for example on an album. In his own words, he has sought to "have [his] name associated only with musical excellence."

Delica is a Japanese clothing retailer. In 1984, Delica adopted the trade name "Cecil McBee" for a line of clothing and accessories primarily marketed to teen-aged girls. Delica holds a Japanese trademark for "Cecil McBee," in both Japanese and Roman or English characters, for a variety of product types. Delica owns and operates retail shops throughout Japan under the brand name "Cecil McBee"; these are the only stores where "Cecil McBee" products are sold. There are no "Cecil McBee" retail shops outside of Japan. Delica sold approximately $23 million worth of "Cecil McBee" goods in 1996 and experienced steady growth in sales in subsequent years; in 2002, Delica sold $112 million worth of "Cecil McBee" goods.

* * * It is undisputed that [Delica's distributor] has never shipped any "Cecil McBee" goods outside of Japan. As described later, Delica's policy generally is to decline orders from the United States.

Delica operates a website, http://www.cecilmcbee.net, which contains pictures and descriptions of "Cecil McBee" products, as well as locations and telephone numbers of retail stores selling those products. The website is created and hosted in Japan, and is written almost entirely in Japanese, using Japanese characters (although, like the style book, it contains some English words). The website contains news about the "Cecil McBee" line, including promotions. Customers can log onto the site to access their balance of bonus "points" earned for making past "Cecil McBee" purchases, as well as information about how to redeem those points for additional merchandise. However, the site does not allow purchases of "Cecil McBee" products to be made online. The website can be viewed from anywhere in the Internet-accessible world.

McBee produced evidence that, when searches on Internet search engines (such as Google) are performed for the phrase "Cecil McBee," Delica's website (www.cecilmcbee.net) generally comes up as one of the first few results, and occasionally comes up first, ahead of any of the various websites that describe the musical accomplishments of the plaintiff. Certain other websites associated with Delica's "Cecil McBee" product line also come up when such searches are performed; like www.cecilmcbee.net, it is evident from the search results page that these websites are written primarily in Japanese characters.

In 1995, plaintiff McBee became aware that Delica was using his name, without his authorization, for a line of clothing in Japan. * * * McBee petitioned the Japanese Patent Office to invalidate Delica's English-language trademark on "Cecil McBee." * * * [T]he Japanese Patent Office found for Delica * * *. McBee appealed that ruling to the Tokyo High Court and lost; the trademark reinstatement has become final.

In early 2002, Delica formulated a policy not to sell or ship "Cecil McBee" brand products to the United States and informed its managers throughout the company. Delica's admitted reason for this policy was to prevent McBee from being able to sue Delica in the United States. * * *

Further, there is virtually no evidence of "Cecil McBee" brand goods entering the United States after being sold by Delica in Japan. McBee stated in affidavit that "[f]riends, fellow musicians, fans, students, and others ... have reported seeing [his] name on clothing, shopping bags [and] merchandise (whether worn or carried by a young girl walking on the street in Boston or New York or elsewhere)...." But no further evidence or detail of these sightings in the United States was provided. McBee also provided evidence that Cecil McBee goods have occasionally been sold on eBay, an auction website that allows bids to be placed and items sold anywhere in the world. Most of the sellers were not located in the United States, and there is no evidence that any of the items were purchased by American buyers.

McBee states that he finds the use of his name by Delica "undignified, highly offensive and repugnant." He feels that he has been harmed by Delica's use of his name because people have reported to him that they have seen his name on Delica's products, either in the United States or in Japan, or on Delica's website, and have asked him if he endorsed those products. * * *

McBee produces little evidence relating to the frequency of such incidents, nor does he give many specific examples. * * * McBee told some of his students at the New England Conservatory of Music about his lawsuit against Delica, in order to help them understand the value of intellectual property law to a musician * * *. He feels that some of his students may have lost their focus during his classes because they are thinking about his connection to women's clothing. Further, his class enrollment has dropped "for one reason or another" and so his position as a professor at the Conservatory has been made more uncertain. * * *

II.

McBee's complaint, filed October 1, 2002, alleged trademark dilution and unfair competition claims under the Lanham Act, 15 U.S.C. § 1051 et seq., as well as various pendent Maine state law claims. McBee requested injunctive relief, damages, and attorney's fees. The core of McBee's Lanham Act claims is false endorsement: that the unlicensed use of his name has "made a misleading and false inference" that McBee endorses, approves, or sponsors Delica's product, and that inference has caused McBee harm. *See* 15 U.S.C. § 1125(a). * * *

The district court * * * [held] that it lacked subject matter jurisdiction over all of

Figure 10.3. The late Cecil McBee, jazz bassist and sometime plaintiff.
Credit: Oklahoma Music Archives

McBee's Lanham Act claims, including both those for injunctive relief and damages. The district court * * * applied essentially the test laid out by the Second Circuit in *Vanity Fair*. * * * [T]he court ordered McBee's Lanham Act claims dismissed for lack of subject matter jurisdiction without considering the effect of Delica's actions on United States commerce. With respect to this factor, however, the court noted that Delica's only sales into the United States "appear to have been made for purposes of this lawsuit alone." * * *

III.

A. *Framework for Assessing Extraterritorial Use of the Lanham Act*

By extraterritorial application of the Lanham Act, we mean application of the Act to activity (such as sales) of a defendant outside of the territorial boundaries of the United States. In addressing extraterritorial application of the Lanham Act, we face issues of Congressional intent to legislate extraterritorially, undergirded by issues of Congressional power to legislate extraterritorially. Usually in addressing questions of extraterritoriality, the Supreme Court has discussed Congressional intent, doing so by employing various presumptions designed to avoid unnecessary international conflict.

The parties characterize the extraterritoriality issue as, at least in part, one of subject matter jurisdiction under the Act, and it is often viewed that way.

The Supreme Court has long since made it clear that the Lanham Act could sometimes be used to reach extraterritorial conduct, but it has never laid down a precise test for when such reach would be appropriate. The circuit courts have established a variety of tests for determining when extraterritorial application of the Lanham Act is appropriate, treating different factual contexts as all subject to the same set of criteria. *See Vanity Fair Mills v. T. Eaton Co.*, 234 F.2d 633, 642 (2d Cir. 1956); *see also Nintendo of Am., Ltd., v. Aeropower Co.*, 34 F.3d 246, 250-51 (4th Cir. 1994) (adopting the *Vanity Fair* test, although requiring a "significant effect" rather than a "substantial effect" on United States commerce); *Reebok Int'l, Ltd. v. Marnatech Enters., Inc.*, 970 F.2d 552, 554-57 (9th Cir. 1992) (applying the jurisdictional "rule of reason" * * * : plaintiff must show (1) some effect on United States commerce, (2) an effect that is sufficiently great to be a cognizable injury to plaintiff under the Lanham Act, and (3) the interests and links to American commerce must be sufficiently strong in relation to those of other nations to justify, in terms of comity, an extraterritorial application of the act) * * *. This court has not previously addressed the question.

Steele found that there was Lanham Act jurisdiction over a defendant, selling watches in Mexico, who was a United States citizen and whose "operations and their effects were not confined within the territorial limits of a foreign nation." Defendant made no sales within the United States. The Court held that the Lanham Act conferred broad jurisdiction in that its purpose was to regulate "commerce within the control of

Congress." 15 U.S.C. § 1127. The Act prohibits the use of certain infringing marks "in commerce." 15 U.S.C. § 1114(1); *Id.* § 1125(a). Importantly, commerce is defined in the Act as "all commerce which may lawfully be regulated by Congress." *Id.* § 1127.

The *Steele* Court did not define the outer limits of Congressional power because it was clear that the facts presented a case within those limits. The *Steele* Court explicitly and implicitly relied on two different aspects of Congressional power to reach this conclusion. First, it explicitly relied on the power of Congress to regulate "the conduct of its own citizens," even extraterritorial conduct. This doctrine is based on an idea that Congressional power over American citizens is a matter of domestic law that raises no serious international concerns, even when the citizen is located abroad.

Second, *Steele* also implicitly appears to rely on Congressional power over foreign commerce, although the Foreign Commerce clause is not cited—the Court noted that the defendant's actions had an impact on the plaintiff's reputation, and thus on commerce within the United States. The *Steele* Court concluded that an American citizen could not evade the thrust of the laws of the United States by moving his operations to a "privileged sanctuary" beyond our borders.

For purposes of determining subject matter jurisdiction, we think certain distinctions are important at the outset. The reach of the Lanham Act depends on context; the nature of the analysis of the jurisdictional question may vary with that context. *Steele* addressed the pertinent Lanham Act jurisdictional analysis when an American citizen is the defendant. In such cases, the domestic effect of the international activities may be of lesser importance and a lesser showing of domestic effects may be all that is needed. We do not explore this further because our case does not involve an American citizen as the alleged infringer.

When the purported infringer is not an American citizen, and the alleged illegal activities occur outside the United States, then the analysis is different, and appears to rest solely on the foreign commerce power. Yet it is beyond much doubt that the Lanham Act can be applied against foreign corporations or individuals in appropriate cases; no court has ever suggested that the foreign citizenship of a defendant is always fatal. Some academics have criticized treating the Lanham Act differently from patent and copyright law, which generally are not applied extraterritorially. * * * The question becomes one of articulating a test for Lanham Act jurisdiction over foreign infringing activities by foreign defendants. * * *

In *Hartford Fire Ins. Co. v. California*, 509 U.S. 764 (1993), the Supreme Court addressed the issue of when a United States court could assert jurisdiction over Sherman Act claims brought against foreign defendants for a conspiracy that occurred abroad to raise reinsurance prices. It held that jurisdiction over foreign conduct existed under the antitrust laws if that conduct "was meant to produce and did in fact produce some substantial effect in the United States." The *Hartford Fire* Court also held that comity considerations, such as whether relief ordered by an American court would conflict with foreign law, were properly understood not as questions of whether a United States court possessed subject matter jurisdiction, but instead as issues of whether such a court should decline to exercise the jurisdiction that it possessed.

The framework stated in *Hartford Fire* guides our analysis of the Lanham Act jurisdictional question for foreign activities of foreign defendants. We hold that the Lanham Act grants subject matter jurisdiction over extraterritorial conduct by foreign defendants only where the conduct has a substantial effect on United States commerce. Absent a showing of such a substantial effect, at least as to foreign defendants, the court lacks jurisdiction over the Lanham Act claim. Congress has little reason to assert jurisdiction over foreign defendants who are engaging in activities that have no substantial effect on the United States, and courts, absent an express statement from Congress, have no good reason to go further in such situations.

The substantial effects test requires that there be evidence of impacts within the United States, and these impacts must be of a sufficient character and magnitude to give the United States a reasonably strong interest in the litigation. The "substantial effects" test must be applied in light of the core purposes of the Lanham Act, which are both to protect the ability of American consumers to avoid confusion and to help assure a trademark's owner that it will reap the financial and reputational rewards associated with having a desirable name or product. The goal of the jurisdictional test is to ensure that the United States has a sufficient interest in the litigation, as measured by the interests protected by the Lanham Act, to assert jurisdiction.

Of course, the *Vanity Fair* test includes a "substantial effects" inquiry as part of its three-part test. We differ from the *Vanity Fair* court in that we disaggregate the elements of its test: we first ask whether the defendant is an American citizen, and if he is not, then we use the substantial effects test as the sole touchstone to determine jurisdiction. If the substantial effects test is met, then the court should proceed, in appropriate cases, to consider comity. * * *

B. *Application of the Framework*

We apply the framework we have established to the facts of this case. * * * [H]ere all the relevant facts are undisputed and the district court did not find any facts. Our review is *de novo*, and the burden is on McBee to establish jurisdiction.

1. *Claim for Injunction Barring Delica's United States Sales*

McBee contends that his claim for an injunction against Delica's sales to consumers inside the United States does not constitute an extraterritorial application of the Lanham Act, and therefore the district court should have taken jurisdiction over this claim without pausing to consider whether there was a substantial effect on United States commerce. The factual predicate for this argument is the $2,500 of "Cecil McBee" brand goods that Delica sold to McBee's investigators in Maine; there is no evidence of any other sales made by Delica to United States consumers. McBee is correct that the court had subject matter jurisdiction over this claim.

There can be no doubt of Congress's power to enjoin sales of infringing goods into the United States, and as a matter of Congressional intent there can be no doubt that Congress intended to reach such sales via the Lanham Act. Courts have repeatedly distinguished between domestic acts of a foreign infringer and foreign acts of that foreign infringer; the extraterritoriality analysis to determine jurisdiction attaches only to the latter. Since sales in the United States are domestic acts, McBee need not satisfy the "substantial effect on United States commerce" test for this claim; jurisdiction exists because, under the ordinary domestic test, the $2,500 worth of goods sold by Delica to McBee's investigators in the United States were in United States commerce, at least insofar as some of those goods were shipped directly by Delica to the buyers in the United States. * * *

The district court thus had subject matter jurisdiction over McBee's claim for an injunction against Delica's sales of "Cecil McBee" goods in the United States.

Nonetheless, dismissal of the claim was appropriate for reasons stated later.

2. *Claim for Injunction Barring Access to Internet Website*

McBee next argues that his claim for an injunction against Delica's posting of its Internet website in a way that is visible to United States consumers also does not call for an extraterritorial application of the Lanham Act. Here McBee is incorrect: granting this relief would constitute an extraterritorial application of the Act, and thus subject matter jurisdiction would only be appropriate if McBee could show a substantial effect on United States commerce. McBee has not shown such a substantial effect from Delica's website.

We begin with McBee's argument that his website claim, like his claim for Delica's sales into the United States, is not an extraterritorial application of the Lanham Act. McBee does not seek to reach the website because it is a method, by Delica, for selling "Cecil McBee" goods into the United States. In such a case, if a court had jurisdiction to enjoin sales of goods within the United States, it might have jurisdiction to enjoin the website as well, or at least those parts of the website that are necessary to allow the sales to occur. Rather, the injury McBee complains about from the website is that its mere existence has caused him harm, because United States citizens can view the website and become confused about McBee's relationship with the Japanese clothing company. In particular, McBee argues that he has suffered harm from the fact that Delica's website often comes up on search engines ahead of fan sites about McBee's jazz career.

Delica's website, although hosted from Japan and written in Japanese, happens to be reachable from the United States just as it is reachable from other countries. That is the nature of the Internet. The website is hosted and managed overseas; its visibility within the United States is more in the nature of an effect, which occurs only when someone in the United States decides to visit the website. To hold that any website in a foreign language, wherever hosted, is automatically reachable under the Lanham Act so long as it is visible in the United States would be senseless. The United States often will have no real interest in hearing trademark lawsuits about websites that are written in a foreign language and hosted in other countries. McBee attempts to analogize the existence of Delica's website, which happens to be visible in any country, to the direct mail advertising that the *Vanity Fair* court considered to be domestic conduct and so held outside the scope of the extraterritoriality analysis. The analogy is poor for three reasons: first, the advertising in *Vanity Fair* was closely connected with mail-order sales; second, direct mail advertising is a far more targeted act than is the hosting of a website; and third, Delica's website, unlike the advertising in *Vanity Fair*, is in a foreign language. * * *

Something more is necessary, such as interactive features which allow the successful online ordering of the defendant's products. The mere existence of a website does not show that a defendant is directing its business activities towards every forum where the website is visible; as well, given the omnipresence of Internet websites today, allowing personal jurisdiction to be premised on such a contact alone would "eviscerate" the limits on a state's jurisdiction over out-of-state or foreign defendants. * * *

Our conclusion does not make it impossible for McBee to use the Lanham Act to attack a Japan-based website; it merely requires that McBee first establish that the website has a substantial effect on commerce in the United States before there is subject matter jurisdiction under the Lanham Act. * * * The substantial effects test * * * is not met here. * * *

3. *Claim for Damages for Delica's Japanese Sales*

McBee's claim for damages due to Delica's sales in Japan fares no better, because these sales as well have no substantial effect on commerce in the United States. McBee seeks damages for Delica's sales in Japan to Japanese consumers based on (a) tarnishing of McBee's image in the United States, and (b) loss of income in the United States due to loss of commercial opportunity as a jazz musician in Japan, stemming from the tarnishing of McBee's reputation there. The alleged tarnishing—both in the United States and Japan—is purportedly caused by the confusion of McBee's name with a brand selling (sometimes provocative) clothing to young teenage girls in Japan. McBee presents essentially no evidence that either type of tarnishing has occurred, much less that it has any substantial effect on United States commerce.

McBee's first argument, that *American* consumers are being confused and/or led to think less of McBee's name because of Delica's Japanese sales, cuts very close to the core purposes of the Lanham Act. * * * But no inference of dilution or other harm can be made in situations where American citizens are not exposed at all to the infringing product. The trouble with McBee's argument is that there is virtually no evidence that American consumers are actually seeing Delica's products. * * *

Beyond that, there is also nothing that indicates any harm to McBee's career in the United States due to Delica's product sales. McBee's argument that there has potentially been harm to McBee's career as a product endorser is most unlikely, especially given his own disinterest in performing such endorsements. Further, McBee's

Figure 10.4. The McBee in her bonnet. A Cecil McBee store in Nagano, Japan, in 2020. The Cecil McBee website is accessible worldwide, with menu choices in English. © 2020 by Aaron X. Fellmeth

statement that his teaching career may have been hindered by Delica is speculation.

McBee's second argument is that Delica's sales have confused Japanese consumers, hindering McBee's record sales and touring career in Japan. Evidence of economic harm to McBee in Japan due to confusion of Japanese consumers is less tightly tied to the interests that the Lanham Act intends to protect, since there is no United States interest in protecting *Japanese consumers*. American courts do, however, arguably have an interest in protecting American commerce by protecting *McBee from* lost income due to the tarnishing of his trademark in Japan. Courts have considered sales diverted from American companies in foreign countries in their analyses.

Assuming *arguendo* that evidence of harm to an American plaintiff's economic interests abroad, due to the tarnishing of his reputation there, might sometimes meet the substantial effects test, McBee has presented no evidence of such harm in this case. * * * McBee has not shown that Delica's Japanese sales have a substantial effect on United States commerce, and thus McBee's claim for damages based on those sales, as well as McBee's claim for an injunction against Delica's website, must be dismissed for lack of subject matter jurisdiction. We need not reach the issue of whether we should decline jurisdiction because of comity. * * *

IV.

The district court's decision ordering judgment for the defendant Delica is ***affirmed***. Costs are awarded to Delica.

Notes and Questions

1. In *Steele v. Bulova*, the U.S. citizenship of the defendant seems to have influenced the Court. In *McBee*, the defendant was not a U.S. company. The First Circuit based much of its decision on the absence of any substantial effect of the foreign defendant's activities on U.S. commerce. Both courts acknowledged that acts occurring in U.S. territory *would have* provided a basis for a claim under the Lanham Act. One might synthesize the holdings of these cases as follows: the Lanham Act prohibitions reach activities that satisfy at least one of the following conditions: (1) they occur in U.S. territory; (2) they are attributable to a U.S. citizen, at least if they have some effect on U.S. commerce; or (3) they have foreseeable and substantial effects on U.S. commerce.

If this characterization of the case decisions is accurate, is it also accurate to assert that U.S. courts interpret statutes with a presumption against extraterritorial application?

2. *McBee v. Delica Corp.* has a flip side. Imagine that a French corporation called "Frenentco" has sold its entertainment services under the name JOYEUX throughout Europe and has become widely known on both sides of the Atlantic due to its extensive marketing and advertising that has reached the United States and beyond. But Frenentco has not yet registered its mark in the United States, nor has it used the mark in U.S. commerce. Normally, the

JOYEUX mark would not be entitled to any protection in the United States until actually used here. However, a few courts have used state common law, especially unfair competition rules and the **famous marks doctrine**, also known as the **well-known marks doctrine**, to extend trademark protection to very well known marks not yet used locally but that have become famous.

For example, New York trial courts have sometimes held it to be unfair competition to open a restaurant in New York with the same name as well known European restaurants, even though the European restaurants never opened locations or otherwise did business in New York. See, e.g., *Maison Prunier v. Prunier's Restaurant & Café*, 288 N.Y.S. 529 (N.Y. Sup. Ct. 1936); *Vaudable v. Montmartre*, 193 N.Y.S.2d 332 (N.Y. Sup. Ct. 1959).

One federal appeals court has even held that, although the famous marks doctrine is nowhere found in the Lanham Act, it nonetheless applies under federal law:

> An absolute territoriality rule without a famous-mark exception would promote consumer confusion and fraud. Commerce crosses borders. In this nation of immigrants, so do people. Trademark is, at its core, about protecting against consumer confusion and "palming off." There can be no justification for using trademark law to fool immigrants into thinking that they are buying from the store they liked back home. * * *
>
> To determine whether the famous-mark exception to the territoriality rule applies, the district court must determine whether the mark satisfies the secondary meaning test. * * * But secondary meaning is not enough.
>
> In addition, where the mark has not before been used in the American market, the court must be satisfied, by a preponderance of the evidence, that a *substantial* percentage of consumers in the relevant American market is familiar with the foreign mark. The relevant American market is the geographic area where the defendant uses the alleged infringing mark.

Grupo Gigante SA de CV v. Dallo & Co., Inc., 391 F.3d 1088, 1098 (9th Cir. 2004). Other federal appellate courts have taken the opposite view, finding that no famous marks exception to the territoriality principle exists. See, e.g., *ITC Ltd. v. Punchgini, Inc.*, 482 F.3d 135 (2d Cir. 2007). Which approach seems most consistent with article 6*bis* of the Paris Convention and article 16(3) of the TRIPS Agreement?

C. Extraterritoriality and Copyrights

You will recall that, once a copyrightable work is fixed in a tangible medium, such as a book or stable computer memory, within the territory of a state party to the Berne Convention or TRIPs Agreement, the work benefits from automatic copyright protection. The same minimum standards of copyright protection apply to all Berne Convention parties and WTO members, but like other forms of IP, copyrights are granted by individual countries. There is no global copyright.

Territorial independence has important implications for copyright enforcement in an international business context. If someone in Ruritania reproduces without permission a protected work belonging to a copyright owner in Grand Fenwick, the Grand Fenwick owner can at least sue the alleged infringer in the courts of Ruritania. The state of infringement is sometimes called the ***forum loci delicti***, or "forum of the place of wrongdoing." The copyright is entitled to protection in both Ruritania and Grand Fenwick; the question is where the action to enforce the copyright may be brought, and the *forum loci delicti* is always a valid option. Of course, that will usually mean that the copyright owner must retain counsel and litigate in a distant forum. Enforcement is thus likely to be inconvenient and expensive. Most copyright owners would prefer, if possible, to sue the alleged infringer in the copyright owner's home state. But is it possible, if the Ruritanian and Grand Fenwick copyrights are legally separate?

Chapter 9 of this book introduced the concept of "effects jurisdiction." The courts of most countries will assume jurisdiction over alleged copyright infringement occurring abroad if the infringement had a direct, substantial, and reasonably foreseeable effect in the forum state, or if the actions of the alleged infringer were purposefully directed toward the forum state. For example, suppose a Smalldonian firm owns a copyright on a motion picture. The firm learns that a company in Freedonia has incorporated portions of the Smalldonian film into a new documentary film without authorization from the Smalldonian copyright owner. The Freedonian film is being sold only in Freedonia. Smalldonia and Freedonia are parties to the Berne Convention. The mere fact that the copyright owner lives in Smalldonia and is being deprived of revenue (in the form of royalties) by the infringement in Freedonia does not mean that Smalldonian courts will assume jurisdiction over an infringement claim against the Freedonian company. There must be something more than loss of foreign income, or else the Smalldonian copyright owner will be obligated to bring any action for relief in Freedonia.

Generally, if the infringer exports the infringing copies to the forum state, that would qualify as conduct purposefully directed toward that forum state. Countries vary in how much or little conduct of a foreign person within the territory of the forum state will qualify to give their courts jurisdiction over copyright infringement. Ambiguous cases are not difficult to imagine. For example, suppose a broadcasting company in California learned that someone in Freedonia was recording and rebroadcasting its copyrighted television shows throughout the continent without permission. Must suit be brought in Freedonia, or can it be initiated in any country in which the rebroadcast was received? The international nature of copyright protection adds a wrinkle to an analysis of how protection may be accomplished.

In the United States, the 1976 Copyright Act prohibits "anyone" to reproduce, distribute, or prepare derivative works based on a copyrighted work. 17

U.S.C. § 501. This prohibition lacks any express confinement to the territory of the United States, but the presumption against extraterritoriality discussed in *EEOC v. Aramco* would suggest that a territorial limitation is implicit in the general language. This is indeed how U.S. courts consistently interpret the Act's language. See, e.g., *Tire Engineering & Distribution, LLC v. Shandong Linglong Rubber Co.*, 682 F.3d 292, 306 (4th Cir. 2012) (per curiam) ("As a general matter, the Copyright Act is considered to have no extraterritorial reach.").

Nonetheless, U.S. courts have sometimes applied the Copyright Act to foreign acts of infringement. The following case deals with the question of whether a U.S. court may adjudicate a claim of infringement of a copyright to a work created in a foreign country, when the alleged infringement occurred in a foreign country as well.

LONDON FILM PRODUCTIONS LTD.
v.
INTERCONTINENTAL COMMUNICATIONS, INC.

U.S. District Court, Southern District of New York, 1984
580 F. Supp. 47

ROBERT L. CARTER, District Judge.

This case presents a novel question of law. Plaintiff, London Film Productions, Ltd. ("London"), a British corporation, has sued Intercontinental Communications, Inc. ("ICI"), a New York corporation based in New York City, for infringements of plaintiff's British copyright. The alleged infringements occurred in Chile and other South American countries. In bringing the case before this Court, plaintiff has invoked the Court's diversity jurisdiction. 28 U.S.C. § 1332(a)(2). Defendant has moved to dismiss plaintiff's complaint, arguing that the Court should abstain from exercising jurisdiction over this action.

Background

London produces feature motion pictures in Great Britain, which it then distributes throughout the world. ICI specializes in the licensing of motion pictures, produced by others, that it believes are in the public domain. London's copyright infringement claim is based mainly on license agreements between ICI and Dilatsa S.A., a buying agent for Chilean television stations. The agreements apparently granted the latter the right to distribute and exhibit certain of plaintiff's motion pictures on television in Chile. London also alleges that ICI has marketed several of its motion pictures in Venezuela, Peru, Ecuador, Costa Rica and Panama, as well as in Chile.

Plaintiff alleges that the films that are the subjects of the arrangements between Dilatsa S.A. and defendant are protected by copyright in Great Britain as well as in Chile and most other countries (but not in the United States) by virtue of the terms and provisions of the Berne Convention. The license agreements, it maintains, have unjustly enriched defendants and deprived plaintiff of the opportunity to market its motion pictures for television use.

Defendant questions this Court's jurisdiction because plaintiff has not alleged any acts of wrongdoing on defendant's part that constitute violations of United States law,[3] and, therefore, defendant claims that this Court lacks a vital interest in the suit. In addition, assuming jurisdiction, defendant argues that because the Court would have to construe "alien treaty rights," with which it has no familiarity, the suit would violate, in principle, the doctrine of *forum non conveniens*. In further support of this contention, defendant maintains that the law would not only be foreign, but complex, since plaintiff's claims would have to be determined with reference to each of the South American states in which the alleged copyright infringements occurred.

Determination

There seems to be no dispute that plaintiff has stated a valid cause of action under the copyright laws of a foreign country. Also clear is the fact that this Court has personal jurisdiction over defendant; in fact, there is no showing that defendant may be subject to personal jurisdiction in another forum. Under these circumstances, one authority on copyright law has presented an argument pursuant to which this Court has jurisdiction to hear the matter before it. It is based on the theory that copyright infringement constitutes a transitory cause of action, and hence may be adjudicated in the courts of a sovereign other than the one in which the cause of action arose. That theory appears sound in the absence of convincing objections by defendant to the contrary.

Although plaintiff has not alleged the violation of any laws of this country by defendant, this Court is not bereft of interest in this case. The Court has an obvious interest in securing compliance with this nation's laws by citizens of foreign nations who have dealings within this jurisdiction. A concern with the conduct of American citizens in foreign countries is merely the reciprocal of that interest. An unwillingness by this Court to hear a complaint against its own citizens with regard to a violation of foreign law will engender, it would seem, a similar unwillingness on the part of a foreign jurisdiction when the question arises concerning a violation of our laws by one of its citizens who has since left our jurisdiction. This Court's interest in adjudicating the controversy in this case may be indirect, but its importance is not thereby diminished.

Of course, not every violation of foreign law by a citizen of this country must be afforded a local tribunal, and defendants cite several cases in which, basically under general principles of comity, it would be inappropriate for this Court to exercise its jurisdiction. This is not one of those. The line of cases on which defendants rely can be distinguished on significant points. The Court in *Vanity Fair Mills, Inc. v. T. Eaton, Ltd.*, 234 F.2d 633 (2d Cir.), *cert. denied*, 352 U.S. 871 (1956), the principal case of those cited, found that the district court had not abused its discretion in declining to assume jurisdiction over a claim for acts of alleged trademark infringement and unfair competition arising in Canada under Canadian law. As defendant here has acknowledged, the complaint raised a "crucial issue" as to the validity of Canadian trademark law. This factor weighed heavily in the Court's decision.

---

[3]The films named, although formerly subject to United States copyrights, are no longer so subject.

> We do not think it the province of United States district courts to determine the validity of trademarks which officials of foreign countries have seen fit to grant. To do so would be to welcome conflicts with the administrative and judicial officers of the Dominion Canada.

Id. at 647. But as Nimmer has noted, "[i]n adjudicating an infringement action under a foreign copyright law there is ... no need to pass upon the validity of acts of foreign government officials," 3 Nimmer, *supra*, at § 1703, since foreign copyright laws, by and large, do not incorporate administrative formalities which must be satisfied to create or perfect a copyright.

The facts in this case confirm the logic of Nimmer's observation. The British films at issue here received copyright protection in Great Britain simply by virtue of publication there. Chile's adherence to the Berne Convention in 1970 automatically conferred copyright protection on these films in Chile. * * * Moreover, there is no danger that foreign courts will be forced to accept the inexpert determination of this Court, nor that this Court will create "an unseemly conflict with the judgment of another country." The litigation will determine only whether an American corporation has acted in violation of a foreign copyright, not whether such copyright exists, nor whether such copyright is valid.

With respect to defendant's *forum non conveniens* argument, it is true that this case will likely involve the construction of at least one, if not several foreign laws.[6] However, the need to apply foreign law is not in itself reason to dismiss or transfer the case. Moreover, there is no foreign forum in which defendant is the subject of personal jurisdiction, and an available forum is necessary to validate dismissal of an action on the ground of *forum non conveniens*, for if there is no alternative forum "the plaintiff might find himself with a valid claim but nowhere to assert it."

While this Court might dismiss this action subject to conditions that would assure the plaintiff of a fair hearing, neither plaintiff nor defendant has demonstrated the relative advantage in convenience that another forum, compared to this one, would provide. The selection of a South American country as an alternative forum, although it would afford greater expertise in applying relevant legal principles, would seem to involve considerable hardship and inconvenience for both parties. A British forum might similarly provide some advantages in the construction of relevant law, however, it would impose additional hardships upon defendant, and would raise questions, as would the South American forum, regarding enforceability of a resulting judgment. Where the balance does not tip strongly in favor of an alternative forum it is well-established that the plaintiff's choice of forum should not be disturbed.

For all of the above reasons, the Court finds it has jurisdiction over the instant case and defendant's motion to dismiss is denied, as is its motion to have the Court abstain from exercising its jurisdiction here. * * *

---

[6] Plaintiff has alleged infringements in Chile, Venezuela, Peru, Ecuador, Costa Rica and Panama. Since, under the Berne Convention, the applicable law is the copyright law of the state in which the infringement occurred, defendant seems correct in its assumption that the laws of several countries will be involved in the case.

Notes and Questions

1. What do you think the court was proposing to enforce in this case? A British copyright, a U.S. copyright, or a Chilean copyright? Does it matter?

2. Why do you think Intercontinental Communications (the defendant) sought to have the case dismissed if litigation in the alternative forums in South America were indeed less convenient than litigation in the United States?

3. In *Litecubes LLC v. Northern Light Products, Inc.*, 523 F.3d 1353 (Fed. Cir. 2008), the Federal Circuit noted that the Copyright Act was never intended to apply to a purely foreign act of infringement. Some sale or importation of the copyrighted work must occur in the United States. However, the court held that U.S. courts maintain subject matter jurisdiction even in the absence of evidence of an infringing act having occurred in the United States. In other words, the court held that entirely foreign acts of infringment fall within the court's subject matter jurisdiction, if the complaint pleads a relevant act in the United States. According to the court, "[t]here is no indication that Congress intended the extraterritorial limitations on the scope of the Copyright Act to limit the subject matter jurisdiction of the federal courts." *Id.* at 1369. In the absence of an infringing act in the United States, the court will normally find for the defendant. But that absence does not divest the court of subject matter jurisdiction. From what authority could courts derive such jurisdiction?

The ease with which copyrightable subject matter flows across borders makes transnational disputes fairly common. For example, in *Spanski Enterprises, Inc. v. Telewizja Polska, S.A.*, 883 F.3d 904 (D.C. Cir. 2018), the national public television broadcaster of Poland had allowed U.S. viewers to download from its Polish website a television program that was copyright-protected in the United States, without the permission of the U.S. copyright owner. The D.C. Circuit held that, even if the infringing act of allowing the downloads occurred in Poland, the broadcaster was nonetheless liable for infringement under the Copyright Act because U.S. consumers could view the content:

> The Copyright Act "focuses" * * * on policing infringement or, put another way, on protecting the exclusivity of the rights it guarantees. Here, although it was in Poland that TV Polska uploaded and digitally formatted the fifty-one episodes, the infringing performances—and consequent violation of [the U.S. copyright owner's] copyrights—occurred on the computer screens in the United States on which the episodes' "images" were "show[n]." Accordingly, because "the conduct relevant to the statute's focus occurred in the United States," this case "involves a permissible domestic application" of the Copyright Act, "even if other conduct occurred abroad."

Id. at 914 (citations omitted).

D. Other Approaches to Extraterritorial IP Infringement

Different countries take different approaches to the prescriptive jurisdiction of their IP laws. The global nature of the Internet in particular has convinced some states to assert jurisdiction over acts occurring outside their national borders because some effects of the act were felt within the state's territory. The following case illustrates this approach.

GOOGLE, INC. v. EQUUSTEK SOLUTIONS, INC.

Supreme Court of Canada
2017 [1] S.C.R. 824

Abella J.

1 The issue in this appeal is whether Google can be ordered, pending a trial, to globally de-index the websites of a company which, in breach of several court orders, is using those websites to unlawfully sell the intellectual property of another company. The answer turns on classic interlocutory injunction jurisprudence: is there a serious issue to be tried; would irreparable harm result if the injunction were not granted; and does the balance of convenience favour granting or refusing the injunction. Ultimately, the question is whether granting the injunction would be just and equitable in all the circumstances of the case.

BACKGROUND

2 Equustek Solutions Inc. is a small technology company in British Columbia. It manufactures networking devices that allow complex industrial equipment made by one manufacturer to communicate with complex industrial equipment made by another manufacturer.

3 The underlying action between Equustek and the Datalink defendants (Morgan Jack, Datalink Technology Gateways Inc., and Datalink Technologies Gateways LLC—"Datalink") was launched by Equustek on April 12, 2011. It claimed that Datalink, while acting as a distributor of Equustek's products, began to re-label one of the products and pass it off as its own. Datalink also acquired confidential information and trade secrets belonging to Equustek, using them to design and manufacture a competing product, the GW1000. Any orders for Equustek's product were filled with the GW1000. When Equustek discovered this in 2011, it terminated the distribution agreement it had with Datalink and demanded that Datalink delete all references to Equustek's products and trademarks on its websites.

4 The Datalink defendants filed statements of defence disputing Equustek's claims.

5 On September 23, 2011, Leask J. granted an injunction ordering Datalink to return to Equustek any source codes, board schematics, and any other documentation it

may have had in its possession that belonged to Equustek. The court also prohibited Datalink from referring to Equustek or any of Equustek's products on its websites. * * *

7 Datalink abandoned the proceedings and left the jurisdiction without producing any documents or complying with any of the orders. * * *

8 On July 26, 2012, Punnett J. granted [an] injunction freezing Datalink's worldwide assets, including its entire product inventory. He found that Datalink had incorporated "a myriad of shell corporations in different jurisdictions," continued to sell the impugned product, reduced prices to attract more customers, and was offering additional services that Equustek claimed disclosed more of its trade secrets. He concluded that Equustek would suffer irreparable harm if the injunction were not granted, and that, on the balance of convenience and due to a real risk of the dissipation of assets, it was just and equitable to grant the injunction against Datalink.

9 On August 3, 2012, Fenlon J. granted another interlocutory injunction prohibiting Datalink from dealing with broader classes of intellectual property, including "any use of whole categories of documents and information that lie at the heart of any business of a kind engaged in by both parties." She noted that Equustek's "earnings ha[d] fallen drastically since [Datalink] began [its] impugned activities" and concluded that "the effect of permitting [Datalink] to carry on [its] business [would] also cause irreparable harm to [Equustek]."

10 On September 26, 2012, Equustek brought an application to have Datalink and its principal, Morgan Jack, found in contempt. No one appeared on behalf of Datalink. Groves J. issued a warrant for Morgan Jack's arrest. It remains outstanding.

11 Despite the court orders prohibiting the sale of inventory and the use of Equustek's intellectual property, Datalink continues to carry on its business from an unknown location, selling its impugned product on its websites to customers all over the world.

12 Not knowing where Datalink or its suppliers were, and finding itself unable to have the websites removed by the websites' hosting companies, Equustek approached Google in September 2012 and requested that it de-index the Datalink websites. Google refused. Equustek then brought court proceedings seeking an order requiring Google to do so.

13 When it was served with the application materials, Google asked Equustek to obtain a court order prohibiting Datalink from carrying on business on the Internet. Google told Equustek it would comply with such an order by removing specific webpages. Pursuant to its internal policy, Google only voluntarily de-indexes individual webpages, not entire websites. Equustek agreed to try this approach.

14 On December 13, 2012, Equustek appeared in court with Google. An injunction was issued by Tindale J. ordering Datalink to "cease operating or carrying on business through any website." Between December 2012 and January 2013, Google advised Equustek that it had de-indexed 345 specific webpages associated with Datalink. It did not, however, de-index all of the Datalink websites.

15 Equustek soon discovered that de-indexing webpages but not entire websites was ineffective since Datalink simply moved the objectionable content to new pages within its websites, circumventing the court orders.

16 Google had limited the de-indexing to those searches that were conducted on google.ca. Google's search engine operates through dedicated websites all over the world. The Internet search services are free, but Google earns money by selling advertising space on the webpages that display search results. Internet users with Canadian Internet Protocol addresses are directed to "google.ca" when performing online searches. But users can also access different Google websites directed at other countries by using the specific Uniform Resource Locator, or URL, for those sites. That means that someone in Vancouver, for example, can access the Google search engine as though he or she were in another country simply by typing in that country's Google URL. Potential Canadian customers could, as a result, find Datalink's websites even if they were blocked on google.ca. Given that the majority of the sales of Datalink's GW1000 were to purchasers outside of Canada, Google's de-indexing did not have the necessary protective effect.

17 Equustek therefore sought an interlocutory injunction to enjoin Google from displaying any part of the Datalink websites on any of its search results worldwide. Fenlon J. granted the order. The operative part states:

> Within 14 days of the date of this order, Google Inc. is to cease indexing or referencing in search results on its internet search engines the [Datalink] websites ..., including all of the subpages and subdirectories of the listed websites, *until the conclusion of the trial of this action or further order of this court*. [Emphasis added]

18 Fenlon J. noted that Google controls between 70-75 percent of the global searches on the Internet and that Datalink's ability to sell its counterfeit product is, in large part, contingent on customers being able to locate its websites through the use of Google's search engine. Only by preventing potential customers from accessing the Datalink websites, could Equustek be protected. Otherwise, Datalink would be able to continue selling its product online and the damages Equustek would suffer would not be recoverable at the end of the lawsuit.

19 Fenlon J. concluded that this irreparable harm was being facilitated through Google's search engine; that Equustek had no alternative but to require Google to de-index the websites; that Google would not be inconvenienced; and that, for the order to be effective, the Datalink websites had to be prevented from being displayed on all of Google's search results, not just google.ca. As she said:

> On the record before me it appears that to be effective, even within Canada, Google must block search results on all of its websites. Furthermore, [Datalink's] sales originate primarily in other countries, so the Court's process cannot be protected unless the injunction ensures that searchers from any jurisdiction do not find [Datalink's] websites.

20 The Court of Appeal of British Columbia dismissed Google's appeal. Groberman

J.A. accepted Fenlon J.'s conclusion that she had *in personam* jurisdiction over Google and could therefore make an order with extraterritorial effect. He also agreed that courts of inherent jurisdiction could grant equitable relief against non-parties. Since ordering an interlocutory injunction against Google was the only practical way to prevent Datalink from flouting the court's several orders, and since there were no identifiable countervailing comity or freedom of expression concerns that would prevent such an order from being granted, he upheld the interlocutory injunction.

21 For the following reasons, I agree with Fenlon J. and Groberman J.A. that the test for granting an interlocutory injunction against Google has been met in this case.

ANALYSIS

22 The decision to grant an interlocutory injunction is a discretionary one and entitled to a high degree of deference. In this case, I see no reason to interfere.

23 Injunctions are equitable remedies. "The powers of courts with equitable jurisdiction to grant injunctions are, subject to any relevant statutory restrictions, unlimited." * * *

26 Google does not dispute that there is a serious claim. Nor does it dispute that Equustek is suffering irreparable harm as a result of Datalink's ongoing sale of the GW1000 through the Internet. And it acknowledges, as Fenlon J. found, that it inadvertently facilitates the harm through its search engine which leads purchasers directly to the Datalink websites.

27 Google argues, however, that the injunction issued against it is not necessary to prevent that irreparable harm, and that it is not effective in so doing. Moreover, it argues that as a non-party, it should be immune from the injunction. As for the balance of convenience, it challenges the propriety and necessity of the extraterritorial reach of such an order, and raises freedom of expression concerns that it says should have tipped the balance against granting the order. These arguments go both to whether the Supreme Court of British Columbia had jurisdiction to grant the injunction and whether, if it did, it was just and equitable to do so in this case.
* * *

36 Google's next argument is the impropriety of issuing an interlocutory injunction with extraterritorial effect. But this too contradicts the existing jurisprudence.

37 The British Columbia courts in these proceedings concluded that because Google carried on business in the province through its advertising and search operations, this was sufficient to establish the existence of *in personam* and territorial jurisdiction. Google does not challenge those findings. It challenges instead the global reach of the resulting order. Google suggests that if any injunction is to be granted, it should be limited to Canada (or google.ca) alone.

38 When a court has *in personam* jurisdiction, and where it is necessary to ensure the injunction's effectiveness, it can grant an injunction enjoining that person's conduct anywhere in the world.

39 Groberman J.A. pointed to the international support for this approach:

> I note that the courts of many other jurisdictions have found it necessary, in the context of orders against Internet abuses, to pronounce orders that have international effects. * * *

41 I agree. The problem in this case is occurring online and globally. The Internet has no borders—its natural habitat is global. The only way to ensure that the interlocutory injunction attained its objective was to have it apply where Google operates—globally. As Fenlon J. found, the majority of Datalink's sales take place outside Canada. If the injunction were restricted to Canada alone or to google.ca, as Google suggests it should have been, the remedy would be deprived of its intended ability to prevent irreparable harm. Purchasers outside Canada could easily continue purchasing from Datalink's websites, and Canadian purchasers could easily find Datalink's websites even if those websites were de-indexed on google.ca. Google would still be facilitating Datalink's breach of the court's order which had prohibited it from carrying on business on the Internet. There is no equity in ordering an interlocutory injunction which has no realistic prospect of preventing irreparable harm.

42 The interlocutory injunction in this case is necessary to prevent the irreparable harm that flows from Datalink carrying on business on the Internet, a business which would be commercially impossible without Google's facilitation. The order targets Datalink's websites—the list of which has been updated as Datalink has sought to thwart the injunction—and prevents them from being displayed where they do the most harm: on Google's global search results.

43 Nor does the injunction's worldwide effect tip the balance of convenience in Google's favour. The order does not require that Google take any steps around the world, it requires it to take steps only where its search engine is controlled. This is something Google has acknowledged it can do—and does—with relative ease. There is therefore no harm to Google which can be placed on its "inconvenience" scale arising from the global reach of the order.

44 Google's argument that a global injunction violates international comity because it is possible that the order could not have been obtained in a foreign jurisdiction, or that to comply with it would result in Google violating the laws of that jurisdiction is, with respect, theoretical. As Fenlon J. noted, "Google acknowledges that most countries will likely recognize intellectual property rights and view the selling of pirated products as a legal wrong." * * *

46 If Google has evidence that complying with such an injunction would require it to violate the laws of another jurisdiction, including interfering with freedom of expression, it is always free to apply to the British Columbia courts to vary the interlocutory order accordingly. To date, Google has made no such application.

47 In the absence of an evidentiary foundation, and given Google's right to seek a rectifying order, it hardly seems equitable to deny Equustek the extraterritorial scope it needs to make the remedy effective, or even to put the onus on it to demonstrate, country by country, where such an order is legally permissible. We are dealing with

the Internet after all, and the balance of convenience test has to take full account of its inevitable extraterritorial reach when injunctive relief is being sought against an entity like Google. * * *

53 This does not make Google liable for this harm. It does, however, make Google the determinative player in allowing the harm to occur. On balance, therefore, since the interlocutory injunction is the only effective way to mitigate the harm to Equustek pending the resolution of the underlying litigation, the only way, in fact, to preserve Equustek itself pending the resolution of the underlying litigation, and since any countervailing harm to Google is minimal to non-existent, the interlocutory injunction should be upheld.

54 I would dismiss the appeal with costs in this Court and in the Court of Appeal for British Columbia.

Notes and Questions

1. In dissent, Justices Côté and Rowe argued that the case called for judicial restraint on grounds, *inter alia*, that Google is a non-party to the litigation. The Canadian Supreme Court majority found that, when a Canadian court has personal jurisdiction, it also has the power to enjoin that person's conduct worldwide. In assessing whether to apply an injunction extraterritorially, should it matter that Google was not a party to the dispute and was not accused of infringing the plaintiff's IP? Why or why not?

2. In support of its argument for the necessity of a global injunction to prevent *foreign* purchasers from buying Datalink's products, the court states, if not for a global injunction, purchasers "outside Canada could easily continue purchasing from Datalink's websites." Recall from Chapter 3, Part 1.3, that intellectual property is fundamentally territorially independent. If Datalink is now located outside of Canada, as seems very probable, on what jurisdictional basis can Canada regulate Datalink's sales of products embodying Canadian patents, copyrights, trademarks, or trade secrets to persons outside of Canada?

To buttress its argument, the Court quotes Justice Fenlon's observation that most countries "likely recognize intellectual property rights and view the selling of pirated products as a legal wrong." What does the Court seem to mean by "pirated" in this context? If Equustek owns no IP in Smalldonia or Ruritania, and a Ruritanian company accesses a Ruritanian website to purchase products from a Smalldonian company, does Canada have prescriptive jurisdiction to prevent or impede the sale?

5 Extraterritoriality and Securities Regulation

Another form of business law that frequently raises transjurisdictional issues is securities regulation. Most states regulate the offering to the public of stock and bonds issued by business enterprises. Most countries have one or more **securities exchange markets** where securities are publicly bought and sold within the country. Every such market is regulated by the government of the country in which it is located. In the United Kingdom, an agency called the Financial Services Authority regulates public securities offerings. In Brazil, it is the *Comissão de Valores Mobiliários* (Securities Commission). In a few federal states, such as Canada, each province or territory has its own securities regulatory agency.

IOSCO

Most securities regulatory agencies participate in the **International Organization of Securities Commissions** (**IOSCO**), which coordinates and sets standards among securities regulatory agencies around the world. As of 2020, IOSCO regulates 115 securities markets, covering 95% of the securities exchanged worldwide.

5.1 U.S. General Securities Regulation

The United States has several securities exchanges; the best known and the largest are the **New York Stock Exchange** (**NYSE**) and the **National Association of Securities Dealers Automated Quotation System** (**NASDAQ**). Public securities exchanges in the United States such as NYSE and NASDAQ are regulated by the **Securities Exchange Commission** (**SEC**). The SEC is an independent federal agency whose stated mission is to protect investors; to maintain fair, orderly, and efficient markets; and to facilitate corporate capital formation.

U.S. SECURITIES AND EXCHANGE COMMISSION • MCMXXXIV •

The SEC is charged with interpreting federal securities laws; issuing and enforcing regulations to implement the federal statutes; overseeing the inspection of securities firms, brokers, and investment advisers; and overseeing private regulatory organizations in the securities, accounting, and auditing fields. It was created in response to the great stock market crash of 1929 to restore investor confidence in securities markets. It consists of five presidentially-appointed Commissioners with five-year terms.

The reason governments seek to regulate public offerings is complex. The typical missions of a governmental securities regulation agency are:

- to protect public investors from fraudulent stock offerings and covert manipulation of the stock market by monitoring the activities of publicly traded companies and their directors and officers, especially with respect to buying and selling of the stock of their own company;
- to protect the public from covert manipulation by other investors who

obtain private information about company performance from company personnel, stock traders, stock brokers, and others and use it to their own benefit before the information becomes publicly available, known as **insider trading**; and
- to facilitate informed investor decisions by collecting company information and making it available to current and potential investors.

There are several statutes administered by the SEC that regulate the offer, sale, and exchange of stocks. Of these, the most important for international business law purposes are:

- **Securities Act of 1933**. This act prohibits the sale or other offer to the public of most kinds of corporate stock unless the offering company has first registered with the SEC. It further prohibits certain defined fraudulent and deceptive practices relating to the sale of securities.

- **Securities Exchange Act of 1934** (**SEA**). The 1934 Act authorized the creation of the SEC and requires publicly-held corporations to report pertinent information to the SEC for release to the public. This information mostly regards its performance and value, as well as expected future events that might affect the company's prospects and value. The 1934 Act further expands on the list of deceptive or manipulative practices prohibited by the 1933 Act and imposes rules to increase the integrity and efficiency of stock exchanges.

These and related laws are codified in Title 15, Chapters 2A-2D of the U.S. Code. The SEC's regulations are found in 17 C.F.R. pts. 230 & 240. In addition, the SEC periodically releases various forms of guidance, including Commission decisions and reports.

5.2 U.S. Regulation of Foreign Securities Issuers

To what extent are foreign business firms that issue securities subject to regulation under these two statutes? This is far from being a hypothetical question. Hundreds of foreign corporations offer shares worth billions of dollars for sale on U.S. securities markets. Such sales are accomplished by means of **American Depository Receipts** (**ADRs**). ADRs are certificates issued by a U.S. bank on behalf of the foreign corporation and that represent one or more shares of the foreign corporation's stock. The owner of an ADR has the right to require the transfer to himself of the foreign stock certificate represented by the ADR, but the ADR itself suffices for most purposes.

The price of the ADR is usually determined by a ratio of foreign shares to ADR certificates multiplied by the exchange rate of dollars to the foreign issuer's securities. The sale of shares on the U.S. market through ADRs, whether offered privately or publicly, is regulated by the SEC. With some exceptions, normal U.S. regulations on disclosure of information to investors, insider trading, and other rules apply to foreign issuers just as they do to domestic issuers. See *Pinker v. Roche Holdings Ltd.*, 292 F.3d 361, 367 (3d Cir. 2002).

Aside from ADRs traded on the NYSE, the fact that a U.S. person purchases securities of a foreign company on a foreign market does not automatically subject the foreign securities issuer to U.S. law. Generally, a foreign issuer must either list its stock on a U.S. exchange or intentionally approach U.S. persons to solicit securities sales. But what about foreign purchasers of securities in foreign companies listed on U.S. securities exchanges? Do they benefit from the protections and remedies of U.S. securities regulation? In the following case, the Supreme Court answered that question by interpreting the securities laws as they existed at the time.

MORRISON v. NATIONAL AUSTRALIA BANK LTD.

Supreme Court of the United States, 2010
561 U.S. 247

Justice SCALIA delivered the opinion of the Court. * * *

I

Respondent National Australia Bank Limited (National) was, during the relevant time, the largest bank in Australia. Its Ordinary Shares—what in America would be called "common stock"—are traded on the Australian Stock Exchange Limited and on other foreign securities exchanges, but not on any exchange in the United States. There are listed on the New York Stock Exchange, however, National's American Depositary Receipts (ADRs), which represent the right to receive a specified number of National's Ordinary Shares.

The complaint alleges the following facts, which we accept as true. In February 1998, National bought respondent HomeSide Lending, Inc., a mortgage servicing company headquartered in Florida. HomeSide's business was to receive fees for servicing mortgages (essentially the administrative tasks associated with collecting mortgage payments). The rights to receive those fees, so-called mortgage-servicing rights, can provide a valuable income stream. How valuable each of the rights is depends, in part, on the likelihood that the mortgage to which it applies will be fully repaid before it is due, terminating the need for servicing. HomeSide calculated the present value of its mortgage-servicing rights by using valuation models designed to take this likelihood into account. It recorded the value of its assets, and the numbers appeared in National's financial statements.

From 1998 until 2001, National's annual reports and other public documents touted the success of HomeSide's business, and respondents Frank Cicutto (National's managing director and chief executive officer), Kevin Race (HomeSide's chief operating officer), and Hugh Harris (HomeSide's chief executive officer) did the same in public statements. But on July 5, 2001, National announced that it was writing down the value of HomeSide's assets by $450 million; and then again on September 3, by another $1.75 billion. The prices of both Ordinary Shares and ADRs slumped. After downplaying the July write-down, National explained the September writedown as the result of a failure to anticipate the lowering of prevailing interest rates (lower interest rates lead to more refinancings, i.e., more early repayments of mortgages), other mistaken assumptions in the financial models, and the loss of goodwill. According to the complaint, however, HomeSide, Race, Harris, and another HomeSide senior executive who is also a respondent here had manipulated HomeSide's financial models to make the rates of early repayment unrealistically low in order to cause the mortgage-servicing rights to appear more valuable than they really were. The complaint also alleges that National and Cicutto were aware of this deception by July 2000, but did nothing about it.

As relevant here, petitioners Russell Leslie Owen and Brian and Geraldine Silverlock, all Australians, purchased National's Ordinary Shares in 2000 and 2001, before the write-downs. They sued National, HomeSide, Cicutto, and the three HomeSide executives in the United States District Court for the Southern District of New York for alleged violations of §§ 10(b) and 20(a) of the Securities and Exchange Act of 1934, 15 U.S.C. §§ 78j(b) and 78t(a), and SEC Rule 10b-5, 17 CFR § 240.10b-5 (2009), promulgated pursuant to § 10(b). They sought to represent a class of foreign purchasers of National's Ordinary Shares during a specified period up to the September write-down.

Respondents moved to dismiss for lack of subject-matter jurisdiction under Federal Rule of Civil Procedure 12(b)(1) and for failure to state a claim under Rule 12(b)(6). The District Court granted the motion on the former ground, finding no jurisdiction because the acts in this country were, "at most, a link in the chain of an alleged overall securities fraud scheme that culminated abroad." The Court of Appeals for the Second Circuit affirmed on similar grounds. The acts performed in the United States did not "compris[e] the heart of the alleged fraud." We granted certiorari.

II

Before addressing the question presented, we must correct a threshold error in the Second Circuit's analysis. It considered the extraterritorial reach of § 10(b) to raise a question of subject-matter jurisdiction, wherefore it affirmed the District Court's dismissal under Rule 12(b)(1). In this regard it was following Circuit precedent. The Second Circuit is hardly alone in taking this position, see, *e.g.*, *In re CP Ships Ltd. Securities Litigation*, 578 F.3d 1306, 1313 (C.A.11 2009); *Continental Grain (Australia) Pty. Ltd. v. Pacific Oilseeds, Inc.*, 592 F.2d 409, 421 (C.A.8 1979).

But to ask what conduct § 10(b) reaches is to ask what conduct § 10(b) prohibits, which is a merits question. Subject-matter jurisdiction, by contrast, refers to a tribunal's "power to hear a case." It presents an issue quite separate from the question whether the allegations the plaintiff makes entitle him to relief. The District Court here had jurisdiction under 15 U.S.C. § 78aa[3] to adjudicate the question whether §10(b)

[3]Section 78aa provides:

"The district courts of the United States ... shall have exclusive jurisdiction of violations of [the Exchange Act] or the rules and regulations thereunder, and of all suits in equity and actions at law brought to enforce any liability or duty created by [the Exchange Act] or the rules and regulations applies to National's conduct.

* * * [W]e proceed to address whether petitioners' allegations state a claim.

III

A

It is a "longstanding principle of American law 'that legislation of Congress, unless a contrary intent appears, is meant to apply only within the territorial jurisdiction of the United States.'" *EEOC v. Arabian American Oil Co.*, 499 U.S. 244, 248 (1991) (*Aramco*) (quoting *Foley Bros., Inc. v. Filardo*, 336 U.S. 281, 285 (1949)). This principle represents a canon of construction, or a presumption about a statute's meaning, rather than a limit upon Congress's power to legislate. It rests on the perception that Congress ordinarily legislates with respect to domestic, not foreign matters. Thus, "unless there is the affirmative intention of the Congress clearly expressed" to give a statute extraterritorial effect, "we must presume it is primarily concerned with domestic conditions." *Aramco, supra*, at 248. The canon or presumption applies regardless of whether there is a risk of conflict between the American statute and a foreign law. When a statute gives no clear indication of an extraterritorial application, it has none.

Despite this principle of interpretation, long and often recited in our opinions, the Second Circuit believed that, because the Exchange Act is silent as to the extraterritorial application of § 10(b), it was left to the court to "discern" whether Congress would have wanted the statute to apply. This disregard of the presumption against extraterritoriality did not originate with the Court of Appeals panel in this case. It has been repeated over many decades by various courts of appeals in determining the application of the Exchange Act, and § 10(b) in particular, to fraudulent schemes that involve conduct and effects abroad. That has produced a collection of tests for divining what Congress would have wanted, complex in formulation and unpredictable in application.

As of 1967, district courts at least in the Southern District of New York had consistently concluded that, by reason of the presumption against extraterritoriality, § 10(b) did not apply when the stock transactions underlying the violation occurred abroad. * * * [The Court then explained that, in 1967, the Second Circuit applied U.S. securities laws to a sale in Canada of certain Canadian securities when the issuer also traded certain different securities on a U.S. stock exchange. Thenceforth, the Second Circuit did not apply the presumption against extraterritoriality, but instead asked whether it would be "reasonable" to apply U.S. securities laws in a given situation.]

The Second Circuit had thus established that application of § 10(b) could be premised upon either some effect on American securities markets or investors or significant conduct in the United States. It later formalized these two applications into (1) an "effects test," "whether the wrongful conduct had a substantial effect in the United States or upon United States citizens," and (2) a "conduct test," "whether the wrongful conduct occurred in the United States." *SEC v. Berger*, 322 F.3d 187, 192-193 (C.A.2 2003). These became the north star of the Second Circuit's § 10(b) jurisprudence, pointing the way to what Congress would have wished. Indeed, the Second Circuit declined to keep its two tests distinct on the ground that "an admixture or combination of the two often gives a better picture of whether there is sufficient United States involvement to justify the exercise of jurisdiction by an American court." The Second

---

thereunder."

Circuit never put forward a textual or even extratextual basis for these tests. As early as *Bersch* [*v. Drexel Firestone, Inc.*, 519 F.2d 974, 985 (2d Cir. 1975)], it confessed that "if we were asked to point to language in the statutes, or even in the legislative history, that compelled these conclusions, we would be unable to respond."

As they developed, these tests were not easy to administer. The conduct test was held to apply differently depending on whether the harmed investors were Americans or foreigners: When the alleged damages consisted of losses to American investors abroad, it was enough that acts "of material importance" performed in the United States "significantly contributed" to that result; whereas those acts must have "directly caused" the result when losses to foreigners abroad were at issue. And "merely preparatory activities in the United States" did not suffice "to trigger application of the securities laws for injury to foreigners located abroad." This required the court to distinguish between mere preparation and using the United States as a "base" for fraudulent activities in other countries. But merely satisfying the conduct test was sometimes insufficient without "some additional factor tipping the scales" in favor of the application of American law. District courts have noted the difficulty of applying such vague formulations. There is no more damning indictment of the "conduct" and "effects" tests than the Second Circuit's own declaration that "the presence or absence of any single factor which was considered significant in other cases ... is not necessarily dispositive in future cases." *IIT v. Cornfeld*, 619 F.2d 909, 918 (1980).

Other Circuits embraced the Second Circuit's approach, though not its precise application. Like the Second Circuit, they described their decisions regarding the extraterritorial application of § 10(b) as essentially resolving matters of policy. While applying the same fundamental methodology of balancing interests and arriving at what seemed the best policy, they produced a proliferation of vaguely related variations on the "conduct" and "effects" tests. As described in a leading Seventh Circuit opinion: "Although the circuits ... seem to agree that there are some transnational situations to which the antifraud provisions of the securities laws are applicable, agreement appears to end at that point."

* * * Commentators have criticized the unpredictable and inconsistent application of § 10(b) to transnational cases. * * *

The criticisms seem to us justified. The results of judicial-speculation-made-law—divining what Congress would have wanted if it had thought of the situation before the court—demonstrate the wisdom of the presumption against extraterritoriality. Rather than guess anew in each case, we apply the presumption in all cases, preserving a stable background against which Congress can legislate with predictable effects.

B

Rule 10b-5, the regulation under which petitioners have brought suit,[6] was

[6]Rule 10b-5 makes it unlawful:

"for any person, directly or indirectly, by the use of any means or instrumentality of interstate commerce, or of the mails or of any facility of any national securities exchange,

"(a) To employ any device, scheme, or artifice to defraud,

"(b) To make any untrue statement of a material fact or to omit to state a material fact necessary in order to make the statements made, in promulgated under § 10(b), and "does not extend beyond conduct encompassed by § 10(b)'s prohibition." *United States v. O'Hagan*, 521 U.S. 642, 651 (1997). Therefore, if § 10(b) is not extraterritorial, neither is Rule 10b-5.

On its face, § 10(b) contains nothing to suggest it applies abroad:

> "It shall be unlawful for any person, directly or indirectly, by the use of any means or instrumentality of interstate commerce or of the mails, or of any facility of any national securities exchange ... [t]o use or employ, in connection with the purchase or sale of any security registered on a national securities exchange or any security not so registered, ... any manipulative or deceptive device or contrivance in contravention of such rules and regulations as the [Securities Exchange] Commission may prescribe ... ." 15 U.S.C. § 78j(b).

Petitioners and the Solicitor General contend, however, that three things indicate that § 10(b) or the Exchange Act in general has at least some extraterritorial application.

First, they point to the definition of "interstate commerce," a term used in § 10(b), which includes "trade, commerce, transportation, or communication ... between any foreign country and any State." 15 U.S.C. § 78c(a)(17). But "we have repeatedly held that even statutes that contain broad language in their definitions of 'commerce' that expressly refer to '*foreign* commerce' do not apply abroad." *Aramco*, 499 U.S., at 251. The general reference to foreign commerce in the definition of "interstate commerce" does not defeat the presumption against extraterritoriality.

Petitioners and the Solicitor General next point out that Congress, in describing the purposes of the Exchange Act, observed that the "prices established and offered in such transactions are generally disseminated and quoted throughout the United States and foreign countries." 15 U.S.C. § 78b(2). The antecedent of "such transactions," however, is found in the first sentence of the section, which declares that "transactions in securities as commonly conducted upon securities exchanges and over-the-counter markets are affected with a national public interest." § 78b. Nothing suggests that this *national* public interest pertains to transactions conducted upon *foreign* exchanges and markets. The fleeting reference to the dissemination and quotation abroad of the prices of securities traded in domestic exchanges and markets cannot overcome the presumption against extraterritoriality.

Finally, there is § 30(b) of the Exchange Act, 15 U.S.C. § 78dd(b), which *does* mention the Act's extraterritorial application: "The provisions of [the Exchange Act] or of any rule or regulation thereunder shall not apply to any person insofar as he transacts a business in securities without the jurisdiction of the United States," unless he does so in violation of regulations promulgated by the Securities and Exchange Commission "to prevent ... evasion of [the Act]." (The parties have pointed us to no regulation

---

the light of the circumstances under which they were made, not misleading, or

"(c) To engage in any act, practice, or course of business which operates or would operate as a fraud or deceit upon any person,

in connection with the purchase or sale of any security." 17 CFR § 240.10b-5 (2009). * * *

promulgated pursuant to § 30(b).) The Solicitor General argues that "[this] exemption would have no function if the Act did not apply in the first instance to securities transactions that occur abroad."

We are not convinced. In the first place, it would be odd for Congress to indicate the extraterritorial application of the whole Exchange Act by means of a provision imposing a condition precedent to its application abroad. And if the whole Act applied abroad, why would the Commission's enabling regulations be limited to those preventing "evasion" of the Act, rather than all those preventing "violation"? The provision seems to us directed at actions abroad that might conceal a domestic violation, or might cause what would otherwise be a domestic violation to escape on a technicality. At most, the Solicitor General's proposed inference is possible; but possible interpretations of statutory language do not override the presumption against extraterritoriality. See *Aramco*, *supra*, at 253. * * *

In short, there is no affirmative indication in the Exchange Act that § 10(b) applies extraterritorially, and we therefore conclude that it does not.

IV

A

Petitioners argue that the conclusion that § 10(b) does not apply extraterritorially does not resolve this case. They contend that they seek no more than domestic application anyway, since Florida is where HomeSide and its senior executives engaged in the deceptive conduct of manipulating HomeSide's financial models; their complaint also alleged that Race and Hughes made misleading public statements there. This is less an answer to the presumption against extraterritorial application than it is an assertion—a quite valid assertion—that that presumption here (as often) is not self-evidently dispositive, but its application requires further analysis. For it is a rare case of prohibited extraterritorial application that lacks all contact with the territory of the United States.

But the presumption against extraterritorial application would be a craven watchdog indeed if it retreated to its kennel whenever *some* domestic activity is involved in the case. * * * In *Aramco*, for example, the Title VII plaintiff had been hired in Houston, and was an American citizen. The Court concluded, however, that neither that territorial event nor that relationship was the "focus" of congressional concern, but rather domestic employment.

Applying the same mode of analysis here, we think that the focus of the Exchange Act is not upon the place where the deception originated, but upon purchases and sales of securities in the United States. Section 10(b) does not punish deceptive conduct, but only deceptive conduct "in connection with the purchase or sale of any security registered on a national securities exchange or any security not so registered." 15 U.S.C. § 78j(b). * * * And it is in our view only transactions in securities listed on domestic exchanges, and domestic transactions in other securities, to which § 10(b) applies.

The primacy of the domestic exchange is suggested by the very prologue of the Exchange Act, which sets forth as its object "[t]o provide for the regulation of securities exchanges ... operating in interstate and foreign commerce and through the mails, to prevent inequitable and unfair practices on such exchanges ...." 48 Stat. 881. We know of no one who thought that the Act was intended to "regulat[e]" *foreign* securities exchanges—or indeed who even believed that under established principles of international law Congress had the power to do so. The Act's registration requirements apply only to securities listed on national securities exchanges. 15 U.S.C. § 78*l*(a).

With regard to securities *not* registered on domestic exchanges, the exclusive focus on *domestic* purchases and sales is strongly confirmed by § 30(a) and (b), discussed earlier. The former extends the normal scope of the Exchange Act's prohibitions to acts effecting, in violation of rules prescribed by the Commission, a "transaction" in a United States security "on an exchange not within or subject to the jurisdiction of the United States." § 78dd(a). And the latter specifies that the Act does not apply to "any person insofar as he transacts a business in securities without the jurisdiction of the United States," unless he does so in violation of regulations promulgated by the Commission "to prevent evasion [of the Act]." § 78dd(b). Under both provisions it is the foreign location of the transaction that establishes (or reflects the presumption of) the Act's inapplicability, absent regulations by the Commission.

The same focus on domestic transactions is evident in the Securities Act of 1933, enacted by the same Congress as the Exchange Act, and forming part of the same comprehensive regulation of securities trading. That legislation makes it unlawful to sell a security, through a prospectus or otherwise, making use of "any means or instruments of transportation or communication in interstate commerce or of the mails," unless a registration statement is in effect. 15 U.S.C. § 77e(a)(1). The Commission has interpreted that requirement "not to include ... sales that occur outside the United States." 17 CFR § 230.901 (2009).

Finally, we reject the notion that the Exchange Act reaches conduct in this country affecting exchanges or transactions abroad for the same reason that *Aramco* rejected overseas application of Title VII to all domestically concluded employment contracts or all employment contracts with American employers: The probability of incompatibility with the applicable laws of other countries is so obvious that if Congress intended such foreign application "it would have addressed the subject of conflicts with foreign laws and procedures." Like the United States, foreign countries regulate their domestic securities exchanges and securities transactions occurring within their territorial jurisdiction. And the regulation of other countries often differs from ours as to what constitutes fraud, what disclosures must be made, what damages are recoverable, what discovery is available in litigation, what individual actions may be joined in a single suit, what attorney's fees are recoverable, and many other matters. The Commonwealth of Australia, the United Kingdom of Great Britain and Northern Ireland, and the Republic of France have filed *amicus* briefs in this case. So have (separately or jointly) such international and foreign organizations as the International Chamber of Commerce, the Swiss Bankers Association, the Federation of German Industries, the French Business Confederation, the Institute of International Bankers, the European Banking Federation, the Australian Bankers' Association, and the Association Française des Entreprises Privées. They all complain of the interference with foreign securities regulation that application of § 10(b) abroad would produce, and urge the adoption of a clear test that will avoid that consequence. The transactional test we have adopted—whether the purchase or sale is made in the United States, or involves a security listed on a domestic exchange—meets that requirement.

B

The Solicitor General suggests a different test, which petitioners also endorse:

"[A] transnational securities fraud violates [§] 10(b) when the fraud involves significant conduct in the United States that is material to the fraud's success." Neither the Solicitor General nor petitioners provide any textual support for this test. The Solicitor General sets forth a number of purposes such a test would serve: achieving a high standard of business ethics in the securities industry, ensuring honest securities markets and thereby promoting investor confidence, and preventing the United States from becoming a "Barbary Coast" for malefactors perpetrating frauds in foreign markets. But it provides no textual support for the last of these purposes, or for the first two as applied to the foreign securities industry and securities markets abroad. It is our function to give the statute the effect its language suggests, however modest that may be; not to extend it to admirable purposes it might be used to achieve.

If, moreover, one is to be attracted by the desirable consequences of the "significant and material conduct" test, one should also be repulsed by its adverse consequences. While there is no reason to believe that the United States has become the Barbary Coast for those perpetrating frauds on foreign securities markets, some fear that it has become the Shangri-La of class-action litigation for lawyers representing those allegedly cheated in foreign securities markets. * * *

Section 10(b) reaches the use of a manipulative or deceptive device or contrivance only in connection with the purchase or sale of a security listed on an American stock exchange, and the purchase or sale of any other security in the United States. This case involves no securities listed on a domestic exchange, and all aspects of the purchases complained of by those petitioners who still have live claims occurred outside the United States. Petitioners have therefore failed to state a claim on which relief can be granted. We affirm the dismissal of petitioners' complaint on this ground.

It is so ordered.

Notes and Questions

1. The Court considers the question before it to be one of "merits" rather than subject matter jurisdiction (that is, "power" to hear the case). Does a federal court have the power to hear a case based on a claimed act that violates no federal statute? If so, on what legal basis? If not, how then can we distinguish subject matter jurisdiction from the question of whether the act violates the statute? Indeed, if the securities laws do not reach foreign fraud with respect to securities not listed on a U.S. exchange or traded in the United States, as the majority opinion holds, on what basis can U.S. courts assert subject matter jurisdiction over foreign fraud? In answering this question, it may help to revisit footnote 3 in the *Morrison* case.

Imagine a Zembian statute that provides: "Any act of *X* is a felony. The courts of Zembia shall have original jurisdiction over all acts of *X*." In Freedonia, a Freedonian national (Thierry) commits *X*. Thierry's commission of *X* has no effect in Zembia, but it does harm another Freedonian national, Vladimir. Due to Zembia's relaxed evidentiary requirements, Vladimir travels to Zembia and sues Thierry in a Zembian court. On what grounds should the court dismiss: its own lack of subject matter jurisdiction or because Thierry's act *X* does not violate the Zembian statute? What are the consequences of one or the other approach?

2. The majority opinion in *Morrison* held that, although SEA section 10(b) expressly applies to "foreign commerce," it was not intended to apply extraterritorially. What kinds of foreign commerce do not involve extraterritorial application of U.S. law? If you are having trouble imaging some examples, glance back at the options shown in Figure 10.1.

Congress reacted immediately to the Court's decision in *Morrison*. Under a 2010 amendment to the SEA, U.S. courts now have jurisdiction over any action brought by the SEC or Department of Justice if certain thresholds are satisfied:

> EXTRATERRITORIAL JURISDICTION.—The district courts of the United States and the United States courts of any Territory shall have jurisdiction of an action or proceeding brought or instituted by the Commission or the United States alleging a violation of [certain U.S. securities laws] involving—
> (1) conduct within the United States that constitutes significant steps in furtherance of the violation, even if the securities transaction occurs outside the United States and involves only foreign investors; or
> (2) conduct occurring outside the United States that has a foreseeable substantial effect within the United States.

15 U.S.C. §§ 77v(c), 78aa(b).

From this language, it is now clear that certain conduct within the United States, and certain conduct outside of the United States having a substantial effect within the United States, can subject a foreign securities issuer to penalties under U.S. securities laws. This jurisdiction applies even with respect to foreign investors who purchased the securities of the foreign issuer on a foreign market.

Will this statutory language resolve all future disputes about whether U.S. securities laws reach foreign conduct? Or will courts still need to interpret the statutes, and thereby supplement them with case law, notwithstanding the *Morrison* majority's condemnation of "judicial lawmaking?"

5.3 U.S. Securities Regulation of U.S. Issuers on Foreign Markets

As the majority in *Morrison* pointed out, every country that has security markets regulates them. For this reason, the SEC does not regulate the sale of securities by U.S. corporations to foreign investors outside of the United States. Its theory is that its primary mission is to protect U.S. investors and the integrity of U.S. securities markets, and foreign governments are capable of regulating their own securities markets. However, there are some nuances involving U.S. issuers acting on foreign markets.

Under **SEC Regulation S**, an offering of corporate shares outside the United States is generally exempt from U.S. registration and reporting requirements, only if no directed selling efforts are made in the United States by the issuer or its agents, and there is no substantial U.S. market interest in the securities. Regulation S is actually considerably more complex than this summary, but what is important is the general policy of exempting foreign securities issuers from U.S. regulation when the effect of their securities sales on the U.S. securities market is merely incidental and insubstantial.

One nuance is worth noting, however. To prevent the resale of securities to U.S. investors by foreign purchasers, securities abroad sold subject to the Regulation S exemption are considered **restricted securities**. Restricted securities are subject to resale limitations for one year after the foreign sale. See 17 C.F.R. §§ 230.901-905. This measure is designed to deter circumvention of the registration and reporting exemptions using foreign sales.

6 Summing Up Extraterritorial Jurisdiction

Chapter 9 of this book introduced the three most basic grounds of prescriptive jurisdiction: territoriality, nationality, and effects. The exercise of extraterritorial jurisdiction on any other basis is fairly rare in international practice. Yet, several chapters of this book discussed U.S. statutory schemes applying beyond U.S. jurisdiction, with at best a tenuous basis in any of the grounds.

In some cases, such as economic and trade sanctions, export regulations, and the Foreign Corrupt Practices Act, the statute regulates activities by non–U.S. nationals acting outside the United States having no direct, substantial, and reasonably foreseeable effect within the United States. A few other countries have adopted similar aggressively extraterritorial laws as well, although the practice remains the exception rather than the rule.

If a few U.S. statutes are explicit in their extraterritorial reach, the great majority of statutes affecting international business do not unequivocally specify the extent of their jurisdiction. In interpreting these laws, the U.S. Supreme Court has long applied a general presumption against extraterritoriality, subject to the specific language of the statute being interpreted. The Court has not always applied the presumption with perfect consistency, but the trend in its jurisprudence appears to be toward in its reliable application.

As illustrated in this chapter, Congress has at times exercised its legislative power to repudiate that presumption by amending the statute that the Court interpreted. But this is a prerogative that Congress does not often exercise. The Court's general approach, illustrated in *Morrison*, represents the norm in this country. In other countries, practices may vary.

Key Vocabulary

Age Discrimination in Employment Act (ADEA)
American Depository Receipt (ADR)
Americans with Disabilities Act (ADA)
Antitrust law / Competition law
Civil Rights Act of 1964, Title VII
Comity
Equal Employment Opportunity Commission (EEOC)
Extraterritoriality
Famous mark
Foreign laws defense
Foreign Trade Antitrust Improvements Act (FTAIA)
Forum loci delicti
Securities Exchange Commission (SEC)
SEC Regulation S
Securities Exchange Act of 1934 (SEA)
Sherman Antitrust Act

Practice Exercise

#1 Competition Law Jurisdiction over International Cartels

Your client is Xiaolung Pyrotechnics Co., a Taiwan manufacturer of fireworks. It has no facilities or subsidiaries in any country except Taiwan. It manufactures fireworks in Taiwan and sells them directly to independent wholesalers around the world. Xiaolung is engaged in intense global competition with only three serious competitors:

(1) Han Sparkle Co. (HSC), a Chinese company having no facilities or subsidiaries outside of China
(2) Dark Explosion, Inc. (DEI), a South Dakota corporation
(3) Pyrogyro Corp., a Kentucky partnership

Xiaolung has recently learned that DEI and Pyrogyro are coordinating prices in their sales to the European market. They are not setting a minimum price; on the contrary, they have agreed on a *maximum* price beyond which they will not sell their fireworks. Because DEI and Pyrogyro have lower shipping costs and better business contacts than Xiaolung, Xiaolung is being severely squeezed on the European market and having trouble keeping competitive prices.

Xiaolung is considering approaching HSC to form a similar export cartel to Europe and the United States. Xiaolung hopes that, by combining forces, HSC and Xiaolung can save on shipping costs and exercise more influence with wholesalers on the European and U.S. markets. Its plan is to agree with HSC to lower prices on the European market to match competition with the DEI-Pyro Gyro cartel, and to recover profits by raising prices on the U.S. market.

Before it engages in this step, however, it seeks legal advice from you on the risks and alternatives. Advise Xiaolung on the following questions it has posed to you:

(a) How is it possible that DEI and Pyrogyro are engaged in an export cartel without incurring criminal liability under U.S. antitrust law? Explain.

(b) Can Xiaolung bring a civil action against DEI and Pyrogyro for antitrust injury in a U.S. court?

(c) If Xiaolung and HSC form the contemplated cartel, will they be subject to U.S. antitrust law?

(d) Are there other competition law issues Xiaolung might be overlooking?

#2 Multifaceted Cross-Border IP Infringement

Puckerup, Inc. ("PI"), is a U.S. corporation that owns U.S. and Canadian patents on an exceptionally effective lip balm, as well as patents in both countries on the process of manufacturing the balm. PI also owns trademarks in both countries on the word FROGLIPS, registered for lip balm and other cosmetic products. It owns no patents or trademarks in any other country.

FROGLIPS is manufactured in the United States using a combination of ingredients, prominently featuring the unpatented compound Promelissin, a chemical that has no other known commercial uses except in the manufacture of FROGLIPS and for medical research.

The properties of FROGLIPS are so remarkable that it is beginning to attract worldwide attention. Although PI has not made any sales of the product outside of North America, it has begun to raise capital for marketing overseas with the help of the Export-Import Bank of the United States.

Buccaneer Manufacturing Corp. ("BMC") is a Ruritanian company wholly owned by its parent corporation, which in turn is incorporated and publicly traded in the Duchy of Grand Fenwick. PI has recently learned that a U.S. chemical manufacturer, Descu Idado Co. ("DIC"), has been selling Promelissin to BMC, knowing that BMC has no medical research operations.

Using this Promelissin, BMC performs PI's patented process in Ruritania to produce lip balm identical to PI's. It then labels the lip balm FROGLISP and sells it worldwide. BMC makes no direct sales into the United States or Canada, but PI has recently identified a Grand Fenwick wholesaler, A Wholesales Corp. ("AWC") that purchases FROGLISP from BMC and imports it into the

United States for sales to retailers, in direct competition with PI's FROGLIPS.

Finally, PI has also discovered that BMC maintains a website, www.froglisp.com, accessible worldwide in English, that makes direct bulk sales of FROGLISP anywhere in the world except the United States and Canada. BMC's servers are located in Ruritania. The website expressly states no sales will be made in those two countries. However, PI has reliable evidence that at least some U.S. and Canadian wholesalers have mistakenly visitedfroglisp.com in hopes of ordering supplies of FROGLIPS, become frustrated because the order was refused, and switched to selling competing brands of lip balm.

PI has turned to you for advice on how it might protect its patents and trademark. Advise PI about which companies and causes of action are available to it to protect its IP, what obstacles or challenges these claims are likely to face, and what are its chances of overcoming them. Note that, for trademark law purposes, the term FROGLISP will be considered confusing similar to PI's FROGLIPS mark.

Multiple Choice Questions

1. Fragwürdige Finazen AG (FFA) is a multinational enterprise headquartered in Grand Fenwick, with a large branch office in Pottsylvania and a wholly owned U.S. subsidiary corporation (FFUSA) in New York. FFUSA employs citizens of the United States and Grand Fenwick. FFA itself employs not only Grand Fenwick citizens, but some U.S. citizens in its Grand Fenwick headquarters.

   FFA's Pottsylvanian branch office also employs citizens of both the United States and Pottsylvania. When a U.S. citizen applies for work at FFA's headquarters, FFA consults the human resources director of FFUSA.

   FFA has been a major player in global finance for nearly a century, and it has inherited a reputation for machismo among its executives and mid-level managers. Recently, several female employees have accused FFA, its Pottsylvanian branch office, and FFUSA of sex discrimination and harassment. If brought today, which of the following cases would most probably fall within the subject matter jurisdiction of Title VII of the 1964 Civil Rights Act?

   (a) A U.S. citizen employed by FFA in Grand Fenwick claims sex discrimination in her denial of a promotion.
   (b) A Grand Fenwick citizen employed by FFUSA claims sexual harassment in the New York office.
   (c) A U.S. citizen who applied for work at FFA's Pottsylvania branch claims her application was rejected due to sex discrimination.
   (d) A U.S. citizen employed by FFA's Pottsylvania branch claims sexual harassment in the branch office.

(e) None of the above.

2. Your client, Quicklift Solutions, Inc. (QSI) is a Delaware corporation that provides helicopter services worldwide, including executive transportation; search and rescue; and security surveillance. One of the clients for which it provides security and search/rescue services is the government of the Islamic Republic of Mohamia. Every year during the Hajj, tens of thousands of devout Muslims travel through the arid Mohamian desert on pilgrimages to Mecca in Saudi Arabia. The extreme heat, long distances, and difficulty of finding water along the route make the pilgrimage perilous, and dozens of medical emergencies occur every year on the path.

   The Hajj route through Mohamia is considered a sacred path, and non-Muslims are unwelcome near it during the Hajj. Under its agreement with the Mohamian government, QSI must monitor the route and land its helicopters to assist anyone in medical distress. All of QSI's pilots are U.S. citizens, but QSI refuses to hire non-Muslims to fulfill the contract with Mohamia. Under which of the following conditions would QSI most probably be found to violate Title VII of the 1964 Civil Rights Act based on religious discrimination?

   I. Mohamian law provides that a non-Muslim setting foot on the sacred Hajj path will be executed by beheading.
   II. Mohamian law requires that any vehicle providing rescue assistance on the sacred Hajj path must have at least one Muslim on board. Although QSI's helicopters always have a crew of two (paramedic and pilot), QSI does not have enough Muslim paramedics to staff all helicopters.
   III. The Mohamian government required QSI to employ only non-Muslims under their air services agreement.

   (a) I only.
   (b) II only.
   (c) III only.
   (d) I and II only.
   (e) I, II, and III.

3. Which of the following kinds of commerce are exempt from the jurisdiction of the Sherman Antitrust Act, as amended by the Foreign Trade Antitrust Improvements Act?

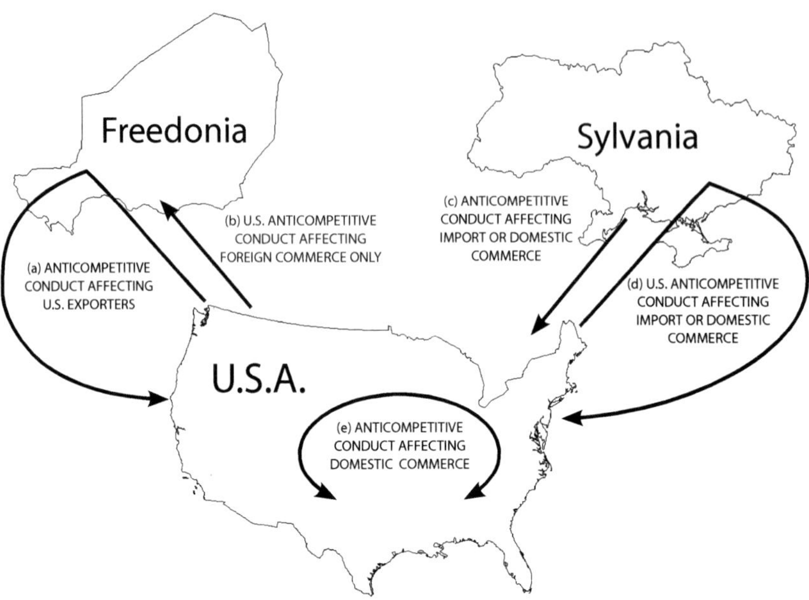

4. According to the reasoning of the Supreme Court in *Hartford Fire Insurance Co. v. California*, in which of the following scenarios should a district court consider international comity when evaluating the extraterritorial reach of the Sherman Act?

   (a) Defendants are located in Smalldonia. They coordinate commercial strategies to monopolize the Smalldonian market, but it has direct, substantial, and foreseeable anticompetitive effects in the United States. Smalldonia has no antitrust laws that prohibit the coordination.
   (b) Defendants are located in the United States. They coordinate their global commercial strategies with competitors in Osterlich in a manner that violates the Sherman Act in the United States, but which is completely acceptable under Osterlich law.
   (c) Defendants are located in Pottsylvania. They are required by Pottsylvanian law to coordinate their commercial strategies in Pottsylvania. Having already coordinated in their Pottsylvania business, defendants extend their strategy to the United States, with anticompetitive effects that violate the Sherman Act.
   (d) Defendants are located in Zembia. Zembian law requires the defendants to coordinate their global commercial strategies in a way that, if it occurred in the United States, would violate the Sherman Act. Their coordination has a direct and foreseeable anticompetitive effect on the U.S. market, but they choose to violate the Act rather than Zembian law.
   (e) A court should never consider comity in applying the Sherman Act.

5. Which kind of intellectual property has the U.S. Supreme Court held is entitled to extraterritorial protection under the applicable statute?

   (a) Patents
   (b) Copyrights
   (c) Trademarks
   (d) Trade secrets
   (e) None of the above.

6. In *McBee v. Delica*, the First Circuit formulated a new test for determining whether the Lanham Act reaches foreign conduct. Based on the court's reasoning, which of the following is most probably ***not*** an important factor in answering that question?

   (a) The accessibility of the defendant's website in the United States.
   (b) The nationality of the defendant.
   (c) Whether the defendant purposefully solicits business in the United States.
   (d) Evidence that consumers in the United States are actually exposed to the defendant's products or services.
   (e) Whether a court in the defendant's home state upheld the legality of the defendant's use of the trademark at issue.

7. Which of the following statements is consistent with the Supreme Court of Canada's opinion in *Google v. Equustek Solutions*?

   (a) If a Canadian court has subject matter jurisdiction over the violation of a Canadian statute, the court also has jurisdiction to enjoin conduct anywhere in the world, even if that conduct itself violates no Canadian statute.
   (b) Canadian courts have proper jurisdiction over conduct occurring on the Internet, no matter where the defendant is located, if the defendant's conduct causes an injury within Canada.
   (c) Canadian statutes are interpreted as having extraterritorial effect when a Canadian plaintiff is harmed by conduct on the Internet.
   (d) Because the Internet is global in nature, any person providing services over the Internet is subject to the jurisdiction of Canadian courts, as long as that person facilitates the violation of a Canadian statute.
   (e) A Canadian court need not consider comity in issuing an extraterritorial injunction to a provider of Internet services, because the global nature of the Internet gives every state an interest in regulating harmful online conduct.

8. True or false?: American depository receipts are a means by which foreign corporations can offer shares to foreign purchasers on a U.S. stock

exchange.

9. True or false?: A foreign corporation that offers shares for sale on a U.S. stock exchange is subject to regulation by the Securities Exchange Commission.

10. Which of the following is a holding of the U.S. Supreme Court in *Morrison v. National Australia Bank*?

    I. The presumption against extraterritoriality is overcome when a statute expressly regulates "foreign commerce."
    II. Even though a statute has no extraterritorial effect, a federal court retains jurisdiction to hear a case alleging its violation outside the United States.
    III. The 1934 Securities Exchange Act prohibits conduct within the United States that constitutes a significant step in furtherance of a violation involving securities transactions outside the United States.
    IV. The focus of the 1934 Securities Exchange Act is on purchases and sales of securities within the United States and not on deception originating within the United States.

(a) I and III only.
(b) I and IV only.
(c) II and III only.
(d) II and IV only.
(e) I, II, and III.

Multiple Choice Answers

1. b	4. d	7. a	10. d
2. e	5. c	8. True	
3. b	6. e	9. True	

Appendix

Table of Acronyms

Acronym	Stands for . . .	Chapter(s)
AAA	American Arbitration Association	9
ABC	atomic, biological, and chemical	5
ADA	Americans with Disabilities Act	10
ADD	antidumping duty	6
ADEA	Age Discrimination in Employment Act	10
ADR	alternative dispute resolution	9, 10
AECA	Arms Exports Control Act	5
ALJ	administrative law judge	3, 5
ASEAN	Association of Southeast Asian Nations	1
ATA	*Admission Temporaire*—Temporary Admission	5
BEA	Bureau of Economic Analysis	7
BIS	Bureau of Industry & Security	5
BIT	bilateral investment treaty	2, 9
BWC	Biological Weapons Convention	5
BXA	Bureau of Export Administration (antiquated)	5
CBP	U.S. Customs & Border Protection	3, 5, 7
CCL	Commerce Control List	5
CCPA	Court of Customs & Patent Appeals	5
CFIUS	Committee on Foreign Investment in the United States	7
CFR	Code of Federal Regulations	5
CIETAC	China International Economic & Trade Arbitration Commission	9
CIM	Uniform Rules Concerning the Contract of International Carriage of Goods by Rail	4
CISG	UN Convention on Contracts for the International Sale of Goods	4
CIT	Court of International Trade	5
CJ	commodity jurisdiction	5
CJEU	Court of Justice of the European Union	3
CMI	*Comité Maritime International*	4

Acronym	Stands for . . .	Chapter(s)
CMR	Convention on the Contract for the International Carriage of Goods by Road	4
COGSA	Carriage of Goods by Sea Act	4, 9
COTIF	Convention Concerning International Carriage by Rail	4
CROSS	Customs Rulings Online Search System	5
CSR	corporate social responsibility	7
CTM	Community Trade-Mark	3
CVD	countervailing duty	6
CWC	Chemical Weapons Convention	5
DDTC	Directorate of Defense Trade Controls	5
DFC	Development Finance Corporation	7
DHS	Department of Homeland Security	3, 5, 7
DoJ	Department of Justice	8
DoT	Department of Transportation	4
DSB	Dispute Settlement Body	2, 3, 6
DSU	Dispute Settlement Understanding	2, 3
EAA	Export Administration Act (antiquated)	5
EAEU	Eurasian Economic Union	1
EAR	Export Administration Regulations	5
EC	European Community	1
ECCN	Export Control Classification Number	5
ECHR	European Convention on Human Rights	9
ECJ	European Court of Justice	1
EEA	European Economic Area	5
EEOC	Equal Employment Opportunity Commission	10
EPC	European Patent Convention	3
EPO	European Patent Office	3
EU	European Union	*passim*
EWCP	Export Working Capital Program	4
FAA	Federal Arbitration Act	9
FARA	Foreign Agents Registration Act	1
FCL	full container load	4
FCN	friendship, commerce and navigation	2
FCPA	Foreign Corrupt Practices Act	8
FDI	foreign direct investment	2, 7, 8
FSIA	Foreign Sovereign Immunities Act	9
FTA	free trade agreement	*passim*
FTAIA	Foreign Trade Antitrust Improvements Act	10

Acronym	Stands for . . .	Chapter(s)
FTC	Free Trade Commission U.S. Federal Trade Commission	2 5, 7
FTSR	Foreign Trade Statistics Regulations	5
FTZ	Foreign Trade Zone / Free Trade Zone	5
FX	foreign exchange	4
GATS	General Agreement on Trade in Services	2
GATT	General Agreement on Tariffs and Trade	2, 5, 6
GRI	General Rule of Interpretation	5
GSP	Generalized System of Preferences	2, 5
HTS	Harmonized Tariff System / Harmonized Tariff Schedule	5
HTSUS	Harmonized Tariff Schedule of the United States	5
IAEA	International Atomic Energy Agency	5
ICC	International Chamber of Commerce	1, 4, 9
ICE	Immigration & Customs Enforcement	7
ICSID	International Centre for the Settlement of Investment Disputes	1, 2, 9
IEEPA	International Emergency Economic Powers Act	5, 7
IFC	International Finance Corporation	7
IGO	intergovernmental organization	1, 7, 8
IMF	International Monetary Fund	7
IOSCO	International Organization of Securities Commissions	10
IP	intellectual property	*passim*
IPEA	International Preliminary Examination Authority	3
IRC	Internal Revenue Code	5
IRS	Internal Revenue Service	5
ITAR	International Traffic in Arms Regulation	5
ITC	International Trade Commission	3, 5
JV	joint venture	2, 7, 9
L/C	letter of credit	4
LCA	Labor Conditions Application	7
LDA	Lobbying Disclosure Act	1
LLC	limited liability company	7
LLP	limited liability partnership	7
M&A	mergers and acquisitions	7
MAI	Multilateral Agreement on Investment	2
MERCOSUR	*Mercado Común del Sur* (Southern Common Market)	1
MFN	most favored nation	2, 3, 5
MIGA	Multilateral Investment Guarantee Agency	7
MNE	multilateral enterprise	*passim*

Acronym	Stands for . . .	Chapter(s)
MTCR	Missile Technology Control Regime	5
NAFTA	North American Free Trade Agreement	*passim*
NASDAQ	National Ass'n of Securities Dealers Automated Quotations	10
NGO	nongovernmental organization	1
NSG	Nuclear Suppliers Group	5
NYSE	New York Stock Exchange	10
OAC	U.S. Office of Antiboycott Compliance	5
OAPO	*Organisation Africaine de Propriété Intellectuelle*	3
OECD	Organization for Economic Cooperation and Development	2, 8
OFAC	Office of Foreign Assets Control	5
OHADA	Organization for the Harmonization of Business Laws in Africa	4
OHIM	EU Office for Harmonization in the Internal Market	3
OPEC	Organization of Petroleum Exporting Countries	9
OPIC	U.S. Overseas Private Investment Corporation	7
OUII	Office of Unfair Import Investigations	3
PCT	Patent Cooperation Treaty	3
PNTR	Permanent Normal Trade Relations	5, 6
PTO	Patent & Trademark Office	3
SBA	Small Business Administration	4, 7
SCM	Subsidies and Countervailing Measures Agreement	6
SDN	Specially Designated National	5
SEA	Securities Exchange Act of 1934	10
SEC	Securities Exchange Commission	8, 10
SED	Shipper's Export Declaration	5
SLA	service level agreement	4
SNAP-R	Simplified Network Application Process Redesign	5
TBT	technical barriers to trade	2
TIB	Temporary Import under Bond	5
TPP	Trans-Pacific Partnership	1
TRIMS	Trade-Related Investment Measures	2
TRIPS	Trade-Related Intellectual Property Rights	2, 3
TRQ	tariff-rate quota	2, 5, 6
TWEA	Trading with the Enemy Act	5
UCC	Uniform Commercial Code	4, 9
UCP	Uniform Customs & Practices for Documentary Credits	4
UFCMJRA	Uniform Foreign-Country Money Judgments Recognition Act	9
UN	United Nations	1
UNCAC	UN Convention Against Corruption	8

Acronym	Stands for . . .	Chapter(s)
UNCITRAL	UN Commission on International Trade Law	4, 9
USCIS	U.S. Customs & Immigration Service	7
USMCA	U.S.-Mexico-Canada Agreement	*passim*
USML	U.S. Munitions List	5
USTR	U.S. Trade Representative	1, 3, 6
VER	voluntary export restraint	6
WCO	World Customs Organization	5
WIPO	World Intellectual Property Organization	3
WMD	weapons of mass destruction	5
WTO	World Trade Organization	*passim*

"I knew it was time to simplify our organization when we started creating acronyms for our acronyms."

INDEX

B

C

I